k_{sL} Cost of equity of a levered firm

k_{sU} Cost of equity of an unlevered firm

M/B   Market to book ratio

MCC   Marginal cost of capital

n
(1) Number of periods or years
(2) Number of shares outstanding

NPV   Net present value

NWC   Net working capital

P
(1) Price of a share of stock
(2) Price per unit of output
(3) Probability of occurrence

P/E   Price/earnings ratio

PI   Profitability index

PV   Present value

PVIF   Present value interest factor for a lump sum

PVIFA   Present value interest factor for an annuity

Q   Unit sales

r
(1) Rate of return on new investment
(2) IRR of a project
(3) Correlation coefficient

ROA   Return on assets

ROE   Return on equity

RP   Risk premium

S
(1) Dollar sales
(2) Total market value of equity

SML   Security Market Line

Σ Summation sign (capital sigma)

σ Standard deviation (lower case sigma)

T   Tax rate

t   Time, when used as a subscript

TIE   Times-interest-earned ratio

V
(1) Value
(2) Variable cost per unit

V_L Total market value of a levered firm

V_U Total market value of an unlevered firm

WACC   Weighted average cost of capital = k_a

YTM   Yield to maturity

FINANCIAL MANAGEMENT

THEORY AND PRACTICE

Fifth Edition

FINANCIAL MANAGEMENT

THEORY AND PRACTICE

Fifth Edition

Eugene F. Brigham
University of Florida

Louis C. Gapenski
University of Florida

The Dryden Press
Chicago   New York   San Francisco   Philadelphia
Montreal   Toronto   London   Sydney   Tokyo

Acquisitions Editor: Ann Heath
Developmental Editor: Kathryn Jandeska/Judy Sarwark
Project Editor: Cate Rzasa
Design Director: Alan Wendt
Production Manager: Barb Bahnsen
Director of Editing, Design, and Production: Jane Perkins

Text and Cover Designer: Hunter Graphics, C. J. Petlick
Copy Editor: Karen Steib
Compositor: The Clarinda Company
Text Type: 10/12 ITC Garamond Book

Library of Congress Cataloging-in-Publication Data

Brigham, Eugene F., 1930–
  Financial management.

  Bibliography: p.
  Includes index.
  1. Corporations—Finance. I. Gapenski, Louis C.
II. Title.
HG4026.B669 1988   658.1′5   87-15616
ISBN 0-03-012543-X

Printed in the United States of America
789-039-98765432
Copyright © 1988 by The Dryden Press, a division of Holt, Rinehart and Winston, Inc.

Requests for permission to make copies of any part of the work should be mailed to: Permissions, Holt, Rinehart and Winston, Inc., 111 Fifth Avenue, New York, New York 10003.

Address orders:
111 Fifth Avenue
New York, NY 10003

Address editorial correspondence:
One Salt Creek Lane
Hinsdale, IL 60521

The Dryden Press
Holt, Rinehart and Winston
Saunders College Publishing

The Dryden Press Series in Finance

Preface

Financial management has changed significantly since 1984, when we last updated this text. The strong inflationary pressures that pushed interest rates to unprecedented heights have abated, at least for now, and the stock market has hit a new all-time high. However, all the financial markets have become increasingly volatile. Furthermore, distinctions among financial institutions are becoming increasingly blurred, and the rapid development of new markets and securities has continued. Academic researchers have also been busy developing new theory, business practitioners have made increasing use of financial theory, and feedback from the "real world" has led to modifications and improvements in academic financial theory. Finally, computers, especially personal computers, are being used with increasing effectiveness to analyze financial decisions, and this usage makes it more important than ever that finance students understand how to structure problems in a form suitable for quantitative analysis. To a large extent, these trends have dictated the revisions made in this edition.

The book begins with basic concepts, focusing on security markets and the valuation process, and then goes on to show how specific techniques and decision rules can be used to help maximize the value of a firm. This organization has three important advantages:

1. Explaining early in the book how financial markets operate, and how security prices are determined within these markets, lays the groundwork for explaining how financial management can affect the value of the firm. Also, this organization gives students an early exposure to discounted cash flow techniques, to valuation concepts, and to methods of risk analysis, which in turn permits us to use and reinforce these key concepts throughout the book.

2. Structuring the book around markets and valuation concepts provides a unifying theme that is missing in many texts. Some finance texts develop a series of topics in modular form, then attempt to integrate them in later chapters. The organization used in *Financial Management* gives students a better and more comprehensive understanding of how the topics interact with one another.

3. Students — even those who do not plan to major in finance — generally enjoy working with stock and bond valuation models, rates of return, and the like. Since people's ability to learn a subject is a function of their interest and motivation, and since *Financial Management* begins with a discussion of security prices and markets, the book's organization is sound from a pedagogic standpoint.

INTENDED MARKET AND USE

Financial Management is designed primarily for use as an introductory MBA text. However, it can be used as an undergraduate introductory text either with exceptionally good students or where the introductory course is taught over two terms. In the past, the book has also been used in the second corporate finance course, following the use of a lower-level book in the first course. *Financial Management* can still be used in this manner, but our more advanced book, *Intermediate Financial Management,* is generally preferable for the second corporate finance course.

There is too much material in the text to cover everything thoroughly in one term, and it is certainly not possible to go over everything in class. However, most students, and especially MBA students, can read on their own and understand reasonably well all but the most technical sections, so classroom coverage of everything is not necessary. In our introductory MBA course, we have taken two somewhat different approaches. At times, we have covered only the material in Chapters 1–15 plus Chapters 21 and 22, or 17 chapters in total. At other times, we have covered the entire text. Obviously, we cover things in greater depth when we assign less material, but in both situations, we expect students to learn much of the assigned materials by reading the book, and we concentrate on the more difficult concepts in class.

We have also made a special effort to make the text useful as a reference book. It is important that students have materials available for use in subsequent case courses and for on-the-job application after graduation. Based on reviewer comments, on a study of the leading casebooks, on our own experience in consulting assignments, on our work with executive development programs, and on discussions with numerous financial executives, we have tried to put into the book those materials that students will need to deal with most real-world financial decisions.

MAJOR CHANGES IN THE FIFTH EDITION

Based on student comments, on reviewers' suggestions, and on economic developments such as the recent change in tax laws, we have made a number of substantial changes in the fifth edition as summarized below:

Updates

We updated the entire book to reflect recent changes in tax laws, interest rates, financial markets, takeovers, and the like. The biggest update, by far, is in the tax area. This edition and all its ancillary materials incorporate fully the provisions of the Tax Reform Act of 1986, including (1) new personal and corporate rates, (2) elimination of the capital gains differential, (3) elimination of the investment tax credit, and (4) new depreciation rates. These changes have significant implications for dividend policy, capital structure policy, capital budgeting analysis, and lease analysis, and we have specifically addressed the impact of the new law in relevant chapters.

Size

Although we wanted the book to be useful as a reference source, the sheer bulk of the fourth edition intimidated many students. Thus, we have reduced the size of the book by more than 200 pages, primarily by streamlining some discussions and by eliminating certain technical materials not generally covered in most introductory courses, especially materials that are covered in advanced courses normally taken by finance majors. However, where we deleted material, we added references to journal articles and to other books, especially *Intermediate Financial Management.* Over the years, we added discussions of both interesting nuances and technical issues that are not of concern to most MBAs. To streamline the book, we deleted a number of these items, but we provided a reference to where they were covered in *Intermediate* for use by students who might be doing a special report on a given topic.

Introductory Examples

Each chapter begins with a real-world example that highlights the key issues in the chapter. These examples both motivate students to read the chapter and help them see where it is headed. The examples were updated to reflect current developments in finance.

Financial Calculators and Microcomputers

In the third edition, published in 1982, we took the traditional approach to time value of money — we used tables. In the fourth edition, we included footnotes to show how financial calculators could be used to solve most compound interest problems. Today, calculator costs have come down, and their power has gone up, to the point where a business student should purchase a financial calculator. Thus, in the fifth edition, we focus on calculator, rather than tabular, solutions. We still discuss the traditional approach, but primarily as an aid to understanding the mathematical concepts which underlie discounted cash flow analysis rather than as a way to actually solve problems.

Also, rapid advances in computer hardware and software are revolutionizing financial management. Powerful personal computers are now available to any business that can afford to hire a business student, and new software makes it easy to do things that were simply not feasible a few years ago. Today, a business that does not use microcomputers in its financial planning process is about as competitive as a student who tries to take a finance exam without a financial calculator. Therefore, wherever possible, we have included a discussion of how PCs are being used to help make better financial decisions. This orients students toward the kind of business environment they will face upon graduation.

Obviously, some students do not have access to a computer, so the text is written so that it can be covered without ever going near one. However, for those institutions whose students do have access to a PC and *Lotus 1-2-3®,* we have provided models for both selected end-of-chapter problems and for some cases, as discussed on the following pages.

Computer-Oriented Problems

Computer-oriented problems, along with models written in *Lotus 1-2-3*, were added to most chapters, and a diskette containing the models is available to adopting instructors. There are 35 of these problems, and they are identified by a diskette logo below the problem number. (For example, see Problem 2-5 on Page 52.) The computerized problems are designed to show students how computers and spreadsheet programs can assist in financial analyses, especially in the key areas of sensitivity and scenario analysis, which are used today in virtually all types of financial planning and decision processes. Essentially, very little knowledge of computers or of *Lotus 1-2-3* is required to use the models, but when students see how powerful these models can be, they are often motivated to learn more about *Lotus 1-2-3* and computer modeling in general. This is a great help — and rightly so — when students go into the job market.

Organization and Content

We made a number of changes in the organization and content of the book. The following are the most important ones:

1. Major works on asymmetric information and signaling theory have appeared in recent years. We have incorporated this material into relevant sections of the book, especially in the areas of capital structure and dividend policy.

2. Much current research is also being conducted on mergers, divestitures, and, more generally, the battle for corporate control. We have placed more emphasis on the research in this area, especially in the corporate restructuring chapter.

3. Our discussion of cash management has been updated to focus on current practices rather than decades-old academic models that have limited relevance to modern corporate decision making.

4. The bankruptcy material was condensed and placed as an appendix to the long-term debt chapter. In conjunction with this change, multiple discriminant analysis is now covered as an appendix to the financial analysis chapter.

5. International finance concepts have been integrated throughout the book in sections entitled "Multinational Finance."

6. The difference between accounting income and cash flows is now discussed earlier in the text (in Chapter 2) and given greater emphasis.

7. The concept of modified IRR (IRR*), which assumes reinvestment at the cost of capital out to a terminal date, was added to the discussion of capital budgeting decision rules.

8. Our coverage of risk analysis in capital budgeting was reformulated to emphasize the differences between a project's stand-alone, within-firm, and market risk.

9. The discussion of option pricing was expanded to include the binomial model.

10. Our coverage of working capital was condensed from four to three chapters.

11. Chapters 21 and 22 (Financial Statement Analysis and Financial Planning and Control) were modified to make it easier to cover them either late in the course, where they are used as a course capstone, or early in the course, where they can be used to introduce (or review) basic accounting concepts. The two orderings both work well, so instructors can choose the sequence which best fits their particular needs. We suggest covering Chapters 21 and 22 after Chapter 3 if cases that deal with financial analysis are to be used early in the course. Otherwise, students seem to get more out of this material toward the end of the course, when it can be used to tie earlier materials together.

ANCILLARY MATERIALS

The package of ancillary materials which accompanies *Financial Management* is perhaps the most complete available with any finance text. The following items are available free of charge to adopting instructors:

1. Instructor's Manual. A comprehensive, 400-page manual is available to instructors who adopt the book. The manual contains (1) a suggested course outline, (2) extensive lecture notes that focus on topics students find most difficult, (3) seven cases, one for each major section, with solutions, and (4) answers to all text questions and problems.

2. Transparencies. A set of transparency acetates, designed to highlight key materials in each chapter and keyed to the lecture notes in the *Instructor's Manual,* is available from The Dryden Press. In addition, the manual is designed to make it easy to xerox transparencies of end-of-chapter problem solutions.

3. Cases. The *Instructor's Manual* contains seven cases and solutions that can be used in the introductory MBA course. These cases are all modeled with *Lotus 1-2-3,* although they can be worked without a computer. They cover the following topics: (1) capital budgeting, (2) capital structure analysis, (3) bond refunding, (4) lease analysis, (5) cash budgeting, (6) financial analysis, and (7) financial forecasting.

4. Problem Diskette. This diskette contains the *Lotus 1-2-3* models that accompany selected end-of-chapter problems.

5. Case Diskette. This diskette contains the *1-2-3* models for the seven cases included in the *Instructor's Manual.*

6. Test Bank. A test bank with more than 600 class-tested questions and problems in objective format is available both in hardcopy form and on computer diskettes. The test bank questions are, in general, more challenging than those in most test banks, and they are well suited for exams. (Most other test banks are more suitable for quizzes than for midterm and final exams.)

A number of other items are available for purchase by students:

1. Study Guide. This supplement outlines the key sections of each chapter, gives some self-test questions for each chapter, and provides a set of solved problems similar to those in the test bank.

2. Casebooks. A tax update edition of *Cases in Managerial Finance,* Sixth Edition (Dryden Press, 1986), by Roy L. Crum and Eugene F. Brigham, is well suited for use with this text. In addition, a collection of Harvard-type cases by Diana Harrington, *Case Studies in Financial Decision Making,* also coordinated with this text, is available (Dryden Press, 1985). Note that both of these casebooks have *Lotus 1-2-3* models available which can be used in conjunction with the cases.

3. Readings Books. A new readings book, *Issues and Readings in Managerial Finance,* Third Edition (Dryden Press, 1987), edited by Ramon E. Johnson, provides an excellent mix of theoretical and practical articles which can be used to supplement the text.

4. Computer Books. A new Dryden book, *Finance With Lotus 1-2-3: Text, Cases, and Models,* by Eugene F. Brigham and Dana Aberwald, is available to teach students how to use *Lotus 1-2-3* and to explain how commonly encountered problems in financial management can be analyzed using this powerful software. For individuals or schools that do not have access to *Lotus 1-2-3,* a powerful new Lotus workalike, *Joe Spreadsheet,* by Goldstein Software Inc., is available from Dryden.

ACKNOWLEDGMENTS

We would like to thank the 33 professors who reviewed all or parts of the book and provided us with detailed comments and suggestions for the fifth edition: Les Barenbaum, William J. Bertin, Kirt Butler, Margaret Considine, John S. Cotner, Bernard C. Dill, Gregg Dimkoff, Richard B. Edelman, Dan French, Philip Glasgo, R. Stevenson Hawkey, Kendall P. Hill, John Houston, James F. Jackson, Duncan Kretovich, Martin Laurence, Judy Maese, Thomas E. McCue, Jamshid Mehran, David Nachman, Robert Niendorf, Kenneth Riener, Pietra Rivoli, Antonio Rodriguez, Ronald E. Shrieves, Jaye B. Smith, Edward Stendardi, Glen Strasburg, Ernest Swift, George Trivoli, George P. Tsetsekos, Edward R. Wolfe, and Dennis Zocco. A great many people helped with the book during its first four editions, and we would also like to thank them:

Michael Adler	Russ Boisjoly	Roy Crum
Ed Altman	Kenneth Boudreaux	Brent Dalrymple
Robert Angell	Donald Boyd	Fred Dellva
Vincent Apilado	Patricia Boyer	Mark Dorfman
Bob Aubey	Mary Broske	David Durst
Guilford Babcock	Bill Brueggeman	Edward Dyl
Peter Bacon	B. J. Campsey	A. Edwards
Thomas Bankston	Bob Carleson	John Ezzell
Charles Barngrover	Stephen Celec	Mike Ferri
William Beedles	Donald Chance	John Finnerty
Moshe Ben-Horim	S. K. Choudhury	James Garvin
Bill Beranek	Lal Chugh	Adam Gehr
Roger Bey	Phil Cooley	Walt Goulet
John Bildersee	David Crary	Edwin Grossnickle

John Groth
Manak Gupta
Donald Hakala
Robert Haugen
Robert Hehre
George Hettenhouse
Haws Heymann
Pearson Hunt
Kose John
Craig Johnson
Keith Johnson
Ramon Johnson
Ray Jones
Gus Kalogeras
Michael Keenan
Don Knight
Jarowslaw Komarynsky
Harold Krogh
Charles Kroncke
Larry Lang
P. Lange
Howard Lanser
Wayne Lee
John Lewis
Charles Linke
Jim Longstreet
Bob Magee
Phil Malone

Terry Martell
Andy McCollough
Larry Merville
James Millar
Carol Moerdyk
Bob Moore
Frederic Morrissey
Tim Nantell
Bill Nelson
Bob Nelson
Tim O'Brien
Dennis O'Connor
Jim Pappas
Rich Pettit
Dick Pettway
Hugo Phillips
John Pinkerton
Gerald Pogue
R. Potter
R. Powell
Chris Prestopino
Howard Puckett
Herbert Quigley
George Racette
Bob Radcliffe
Bill Rentz
Charles Rini
John Ritchie

E. N. Roussakis
Dexter Rowell
James Sachlis
Abdul Sadik
Mary Jane Scheuer
Carl Schweser
Sol Shalit
Ron Shrieves
Joe Sinkey
Don Sorenson
Kenneth Stanly
Don Stevens
Glen Strasburg
Al Sweetser
Philip Swensen
Ernest Swift
Gary Tallman
Craig Tapley
Russ Taussig
Mel Tysseland
Howard Van Auken
Pretorious Van den Dool
Pieter Vanderburg
Paul Vanderheiden
Jim Verbrugge
Tony Wingler
Don Woods

In addition, all or major parts of the book were reviewed by the following executives: James Dunn, GT&E; Larry Hastie, Bendix Corporation; Victor Leavengood, General Telephone of Florida; Archie Long, General Motors; and James Taggart, Tampa Electric Company.

Special thanks are due to David T. Brown, who coauthored the chapter on corporate restructuring; to Art Herrmann, who coauthored the bankruptcy appendix; to Dilip Shome, who coauthored the capital structure theory chapter; to Dana Aberwald and Mary Alice Hanebury, who worked on the *Lotus 1-2-3* problem and case models; to Edward R. Wolfe, who reviewed the end-of-chapter problems; and to Robert J. Porter, who reviewed the self-test problems. Kimberly McCollough worked through all the major parts of the book and ancillaries to help us remove errors, and Steve Ambrose, Bob Karp, and Carol Stanton typed and helped proof the various manuscripts. The Dryden Press staff, especially Barb Bahnsen, Ann Heath, Kathryn Jandeska, Mary Jarvis, Jane Perkins, Cate Rzasa, Judy Sarwark, Bill Schoof, Karen Steib, Betsy Webster, and Alan Wendt, helped greatly with all phases of the revision.

ERRORS IN THE TEXT

At this point in the preface, authors of most books say something like this: "We appreciate all the help we received from the people listed above, but any remaining errors are, of course, our own responsibility." And in many books there are plenty of remaining errors. Having experienced difficulties with errors ourselves, both as students and as instructors, we resolved to avoid this problem in *Financial Management*. As a result of the error detection procedures used, we are convinced that it is virtually free of mistakes.

Some of our colleagues suggested that if we are so confident about the book's accuracy, we should offer a reward to people who find errors. With this in mind, but primarily because we want to detect any remaining errors and correct them in subsequent printings, we hereby offer a reward of $7.50 per error (misspelled word, arithmetic mistake, and the like) to the first person who reports it to us. (Any error that has follow-through effects is counted as two errors only.) Two accounting students have set up a foolproof audit system to make sure we pay off. Accounting students tend to be skeptics!

CONCLUSION

Finance is, in a real sense, the cornerstone of the enterprise system, so good financial management is vitally important to the economic health of business firms, and hence to the nation and the world. Because of its importance, finance should be widely and thoroughly understood, but this is easier said than done. The field is relatively complex, and it is undergoing constant change in response to shifts in economic conditions. All of this makes finance stimulating and exciting, but also challenging and sometimes perplexing. We sincerely hope that *Financial Management* will meet its own challenge by contributing to a better understanding of the financial system.

Eugene F. Brigham
Louis C. Gapenski

Graduate School of Business Administration
University of Florida
Gainesville, Florida 32611

October 1987

Contents in Brief

Contents

FINANCIAL MANAGEMENT

THEORY AND PRACTICE

Fifth Edition

Foundations of
Financial Management

1

An Overview of Financial Management

In 1964 Eastern Airlines' stock sold for over $60 per share, while Delta's sold for $10. By 1986 Eastern had dropped below $4, while Delta was over $50. Delta's earnings and dividends had increased steadily over the years, while Eastern paid its last dividend in 1969 and suffered losses totaling over $500 million from 1980 through 1986. Further, Delta's employees had reasonably secure, well-paid positions, while Eastern had been laying off people and slashing the salaries of those who remained. Even Eastern's chairman, ex-astronaut Frank Borman, lost his job. Finally, with bankruptcy on the horizon, Eastern agreed to be taken over by Texas Air, the company that owns Continental Airlines and New York Air.

Although many factors combined to produce these divergent results, financial decisions exerted a major influence. Eastern had traditionally used a great deal of debt, while Delta had a policy of financing mostly with common equity. In 1986 Delta had about 44 percent debt versus Eastern's over 90 percent debt ratio. The dramatic increase in interest rates (for example, the prime business loan rate rose from 6 percent in the 1960s to 21 percent in the early 1980s) greatly increased Eastern's costs and lowered its profits, but it had only a minor effect on Delta. Further, when fuel price increases of over 1,000 percent made it imperative for the airlines to buy new, fuel-efficient planes, Delta was able to do so but Eastern was not. Finally, when the airlines were deregulated in the late 1970s, Delta was strong enough to expand into developing markets and to cut prices as necessary to attract business, but Eastern was not.

Similar stories could be told about hundreds of companies in scores of industries—autos, computers, insurance, banking, or you-name-it. One company does well while another goes under—and a major reason for the divergent results is a difference in some basic financial policy. In this chapter we outline the major types of financial decisions that must be made. Then, in the remainder of the book, we discuss how these decisions should be made.

Finance consists of three interrelated subareas: (1) *money and capital markets,* which deals with many of the topics covered in macroeconomics; (2) *investments,* which focuses on the decisions of individuals and financial institutions as they choose securities for their investment portfolios; and (3) *financial management,* or *corporate finance,* which involves decisions within the firm. Each of these areas interacts with the others, so good decisions in one area cannot be made without a knowledge of the other areas. In particular, a corporate financial manager must be knowledgeable about money and capital markets as well as about the way individual and institutional investors evaluate the firm's securities.

Financial management has undergone significant changes over the years. When it first emerged as a separate field of study in the early 1900s, the emphasis was on the legal aspects of mergers, consolidations, the formation of new firms, and the various types of securities issued by corporations. Industrialization was sweeping the country, and the critical problem firms faced was obtaining capital for expansion. The capital markets were relatively primitive, which made transfers of funds from individual savers to businesses difficult. Also, the earnings and asset values reported in accounting statements were unreliable, while stock trading by insiders and manipulators caused prices to fluctuate wildly, and this made investors reluctant to purchase stocks and bonds. As a result of these market conditions, finance in the early 1900s focused on legal issues relating to issuing and evaluating securities.

The emphasis remained on securities through the 1920s, but radical changes occurred during the depression of the 1930s, when an unprecedented number of business failures shifted the focus to bankruptcy and reorganization, to corporate liquidity, and to governmental regulation of securities markets. Finance was still a descriptive, legalistic subject, but the emphasis had shifted from expansion to survival.

During the 1940s and early 1950s, finance continued to be taught as a descriptive, institutional subject, viewed from the outside rather than from the standpoint of management. However, techniques designed to help firms maximize their profits and the prices of their stocks were beginning to receive attention.

The evolutionary pace toward rigorous analysis quickened during the late 1950s. Also, the major emphasis began to shift from the right-hand side of the balance sheet (liabilities and capital) to asset management. Computers were beginning to be used, and models were being developed to help manage inventories, cash, and accounts receivable, and to help decide upon fixed asset additions. Increasingly, the focus of finance shifted from the outsider's to the insider's point of view, as financial decisions within the firm were recognized as being the critical issue in corporate finance. Descriptive, institutional materials on capital markets and financing instruments were still studied, but within the context of corporate financial decisions.

The 1960s and 1970s witnessed a renewed interest in the liabilities and capital side of the balance sheet, with a focus (1) on the optimal way to finance a firm and (2) on the way in which individual investors make investment decisions, or *portfolio theory,* and its implications for corporate finance. Corporate financial management is designed to help general management take actions that will maximize the value of the firm and the wealth of its stockholders; therefore, the correctness of corporate financial decisions depends upon how investors react to them. *The relationship between investments and corporate finance was recognized in the 1960s and 1970s, and with this recognition came a merging of investments with corporate finance.*

Thus far in the 1980s four issues have received emphasis: (1) inflation, (2) deregulation of financial institutions, (3) the use of computers for analyzing financial decisions, and (4) differences in managers' and outside investors' knowledge of and expectations for the firm, and ways managers "signal" their expectations to investors. Inflation is being worked into the fabric of both financial theories and financial decision processes, and it has even led to the creation of new financial institutions and industries — for example, money market funds and interest rate futures markets. Older institutions have been forced into major structural changes, and it is getting harder and harder to tell a bank from a savings and loan, or an insurance company from a brokerage firm: Bank of America owns a stock brokerage firm; Merrill Lynch offers checking account services; and Sears, Roebuck is one of the largest U.S. financial institutions, owning such firms as Allstate Insurance, Coldwell Banker, a real estate brokerage operation, and Dean Witter, an investment banking firm. At the same time, technological developments in the computer hardware and telecommunications areas, and the availability of software packages that make otherwise very difficult numerical analyses relatively easy, are bringing about fundamental changes in the way managers manage. Data storage, transmittal, retrieval, and analysis techniques are reducing the "judgmental" aspects of management, as financial managers can often obtain accurate estimates of the effects of various courses of action.

INCREASING IMPORTANCE OF FINANCIAL MANAGEMENT

These evolutionary changes have greatly increased the importance of financial management. In earlier times the marketing manager would forecast sales, the engineering and production staffs would determine the assets necessary to meet these demands, and the financial manager's job was simply to raise the money needed to purchase the required plant, equipment, and inventories. This mode of operation is no longer prevalent. Decisions are now made in a much more coordinated manner, with the financial manager having direct responsibility for the control process.

Public Service of Indiana (PSI) can be used to illustrate this change. A few years ago, PSI's economic forecasters would project power demand on the basis of historical trends and give these forecasts to the engineers, who would then proceed to build the new plants necessary to meet the forecasted demand. The finance department simply had to raise the capital the engineers told them was needed. However, inflation, environmental regulations, and other factors combined to double or even triple plant construction costs, and this caused a corresponding increase in the need for new capital. At the same time, rising fuel costs caused dramatic increases in electricity prices, which lowered demand and made some of the new construction unnecessary. Thus, PSI found itself building a nuclear power plant that it did not need and whose output would cost far more than conventional power. Eventually, a $2.5 billion investment had to be written off, and the price of the company's stock declined from $35 in the late 1970s to a 1985 low of $6.88. As a result of this experience, PSI and other utilities now place far more emphasis on financial planning and control, and this has greatly increased the importance of the finance staff.

The direction in which business is moving, as well as the increasing importance of finance, was described in *Fortune*.[1] After pointing out that well over half of today's top executives majored in business administration versus about 25 percent a few years earlier, *Fortune* continued:

> Career patterns have followed the educational trends. Like scientific and technical schooling, nuts-and-bolts business experience seems to have become less important. The proportion of executives with their primary experience in production, operations, engineering, design, and research and development has fallen from a third of the total to just over a quarter. And the number of top officers with legal and financial backgrounds has increased more than enough to make up the difference. Lawyers and financial men now head two out of five corporations.
>
> It is fair to assume that the changes in training, and in the paths that led these men to the top, reflect the shifting priorities and needs of their corporations. In fact, the expanding size and complexity of corporate organizations, coupled with their continued expansion overseas, have greatly increased the importance of financial planning and controls. And the growth of government regulation and of obligations companies face under the law has heightened the need for legal advice. The engineer and the production man have become, in consequence, less important in management than the finance man and the lawyer.
>
> Today's chief executive officers have obviously perceived the shift in emphasis, and many of them wish they had personally been better prepared for it. Interestingly enough, a majority of them say they would have benefited from additional formal training, mainly in business administration, accounting, finance, and law.

These same trends are evident at lower levels within firms of all sizes, as well as in nonprofit and governmental organizations. Thus, it is becoming increasingly important for people in marketing, accounting, production, personnel, and other areas to understand finance in order to do a good job in their own fields. Marketing people, for instance, must understand how marketing decisions affect and are affected by funds availability, by inventory levels, by excess plant capacity, and so on. Similarly, accountants must understand how accounting data are used in corporate planning and are viewed by investors: The function of accounting is to

---

[1]Charles G. Burck, "A Group Profile of the Fortune 500 Chief Executive," *Fortune,* May 1976, 173.

provide quantitative financial information for use in making economic decisions, while the main functions of financial management are to plan for, acquire, and utilize funds in order to maximize the efficiency and value of the enterprise.[2]

There are financial implications in virtually all business decisions, and non-financial executives simply must know enough finance to work these implications into their own specialized analyses.[3]

ALTERNATIVE FORMS OF BUSINESS ORGANIZATION

There are three main forms of business organization: (1) the sole proprietorship, (2) the partnership, and (3) the corporation. In terms of numbers, about 80 percent of business firms are operated as sole proprietorships, while the remainder are divided equally between partnerships and corporations. By dollar value of sales, however, about 80 percent of business is conducted by corporations, about 13 percent by sole proprietorships, and about 7 percent by partnerships. Since most business is conducted by corporations, we shall concentrate on them in this book. However, it is important to understand the differences among the three forms, as well as their advantages and disadvantages.

Sole Proprietorship

A proprietorship is a business owned by one individual. Going into business as a single proprietor is very easy — one merely begins business operations. However, most cities require even the smallest establishments to be licensed, and occasionally state licenses are required as well.

The proprietorship has two important advantages for small businesses: (1) It is easily and inexpensively formed, since no formal charter for operations is required, and it is subject to few government regulations. (2) The business pays no corporate income taxes; however, as we shall see in Chapter 2, this is not always a net advantage, as all earnings of the firm, whether they are reinvested in the business or withdrawn, are subject to personal income taxes.

The proprietorship also has three important limitations: (1) it is difficult for a proprietorship to obtain large sums of capital; (2) the proprietor has unlimited personal liability for business debts and can lose assets beyond those invested in the company; and (3) the life of a business organized as a proprietorship is limited to the life of the individual who created it. For these three reasons, the individual proprietorship is restricted primarily to small business operations. *However, businesses are frequently started as proprietorships and then converted to corporations if and when their growth causes the disadvantages of the proprietorship form to outweigh its advantages.*

---

[2]American Institute of Certified Public Accountants, *Statement of the Accounting Principles Board #4* (New York: October 1970).

[3]It is an interesting fact that the course "Financial Analysis for Nonfinancial Executives" has the highest enrollment in most executive development programs.

Partnership

A partnership exists whenever two or more persons associate to conduct a business. Partnerships may operate under different degrees of formality, ranging from informal, oral understandings to formal agreements filed with the secretary of the state in which the partnership does business. The major advantage of a partnership is its low cost and ease of formation. The disadvantages are similar to those associated with proprietorships: (1) unlimited liability, (2) limited life of the organization, (3) difficulty of transferring ownership, and (4) difficulty of raising large amounts of capital. The tax treatment of a partnership is similar to that for proprietorships, and when compared to that of a corporation, this can be either an advantage or a disadvantage, depending on the situation; this point is illustrated in Chapter 2, where we discuss the federal tax system.

Regarding liability, the partners must all risk their personal assets, even those assets not invested in the business, for under partnership law each partner is liable for the business's debts. This means that if any partner is unable to meet his or her pro rata claim in the event the partnership goes bankrupt, the remaining partners must take over the unsatisfied claims, drawing on their personal assets if necessary.[4]

The first three disadvantages — unlimited liability, impermanence of the organization, and difficulty of transferring ownership — cause the fourth, the difficulty partnerships have in attracting substantial amounts of capital. This is no particular problem for a slow-growing business, but if a business's products really catch on, and it needs to raise large amounts of capital to expand and thus capitalize on its opportunities, the difficulty in attracting large amounts of capital becomes a real drawback. Thus, growth companies such as Hewlett-Packard and Apple Computer generally begin life as proprietorships or partnerships, but at some point they find it necessary to convert to corporations.

Corporation

A corporation is a legal entity, or "person," created by a state. It is separate and distinct from its owners and managers. This separateness gives the corporation three major advantages: (1) it has an *unlimited life* — it can continue after its original owners and managers are deceased; (2) it permits *easy transferability of ownership interest,* because ownership interests can be divided into shares of stock, which in turn can be transferred far more easily than can partnership interests; and (3) it permits *limited liability.* To illustrate the concept of limited liability, suppose you invested $10,000 in a partnership which then went bankrupt owing a considerable sum of money. Since the owners are liable for the debts of a partnership, you could be assessed for a share of these debts, and you could be

---

[4]However, it is possible to limit the liabilities of some of the partners by establishing a *limited partnership,* wherein certain partners are designated *general partners* and others *limited partners.* Limited partnerships are common in the area of real estate investment, but they do not work well with most types of businesses.

held liable for the entire debt if your partners could not pay their shares. Thus, an investor in a partnership is exposed to unlimited liability. On the other hand, if you invested $10,000 in the stock of a corporation which then went bankrupt, your potential loss on the investment would be limited to the $10,000 you had put up.[5] These three factors give corporations access to sources of capital unavailable to unincorporated businesses.

While the corporate form offers significant advantages over proprietorships and partnerships, it does have two primary disadvantages: (1) corporate earnings are subject to double taxation—first the earnings of the corporation are taxed and then any earnings paid out as dividends are taxed as income to the stockholders, and (2) setting up a corporation is more complex and time-consuming than setting up a proprietorship or a partnership. A proprietorship or a partnership can commence operations without much paperwork, but setting up a corporation requires that the incorporators prepare a charter and a set of bylaws. The *charter* includes the following information: (1) name of the proposed corporation, (2) types of activities it will pursue, (3) amount of capital stock, (4) number of directors, and (5) names and addresses of directors. The charter is filed with the secretary of the state in which the firm will be incorporated, and when it is approved, the corporation is officially in existence.[6]

The *bylaws* are a set of rules drawn up by the founders of the corporation to aid in governing the internal management of the company. Included are such points as (1) how directors are to be elected (all elected each year or, say, one-third each year for three-year terms); (2) whether the existing stockholders shall have the first right to buy any new shares the firm issues; (3) what provisions there are for management committees, such as an executive committee or a finance committee, and their duties; and (4) what procedures there are for changing the bylaws themselves, should conditions require it. Lawyers have standard forms for charters and bylaws in their word processors, and they can set up a corporation with very little effort. A small business can be incorporated for about $500—less if you find a hungry young lawyer fresh out of law school.

The value of any business other than a very small one will probably be maximized if it is organized as a corporation. The reasons are as follows:

1. Limited liability reduces risk to investors, and the lower the firm's risk, other things held constant, the higher its value.

2. A firm's value is dependent on its growth opportunities, which in turn are dependent on the firm's ability to attract capital. Since corporations can attract capital more easily than can unincorporated businesses, they have superior growth opportunities.

---

[5]In the case of small corporations, the limited liability feature does not always apply, because bankers and credit managers frequently require personal guarantees from the stockholders of small, weak businesses.

[6]Note that over 60 percent of U.S. corporations are chartered in Delaware, which has, over the years, provided a favorable legal environment for incorporation. It is not necessary for a firm to be headquartered, or even to conduct operations, in its state of incorporation.

3. The value of an asset also depends on its *liquidity,* which means the ease of selling the asset and converting it to cash. Since an investment in the stock of a corporation is much more liquid than a similar investment in a proprietorship or partnership, this too means that the corporate form of organization can enhance the value of a business.

4. Corporations are taxed differently than proprietorships and partnerships, and under certain conditions the tax laws favor corporations. This point is discussed in detail in Chapter 2.

As we will see later in the chapter, most firms are managed with value maximization in mind. Thus, most businesses are organized as corporations.

THE PLACE OF FINANCE IN A BUSINESS ORGANIZATION

Organization structures vary from firm to firm, but Figure 1-1 gives a fairly typical picture of the role of finance within a business. The chief financial officer — who has the title of vice president: finance — reports to the president. Key subordinates are the treasurer and the controller. The treasurer has direct responsibility for

Figure 1-1
Place of Finance in a Typical Business Organization

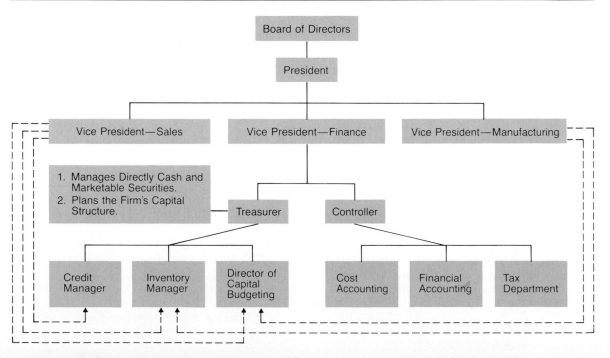

managing the firm's cash and marketable securities, for planning the financial structure, for selling stocks and bonds to raise capital, and for overseeing the corporate pension fund. Under the treasurer (but in some firms under the controller) are the credit manager, the inventory manager, and the director of capital budgeting (who analyzes decisions relating to investments in fixed assets). The controller is responsible for the activities of the accounting and tax departments.

THE GOALS OF THE FIRM

Decisions are not made in a vacuum, but, rather with some objective in mind. *Throughout this book we operate on the assumption that management's primary goal is stockholder wealth maximization, which translates into maximizing the price of the common stock.* Firms do, of course, have other objectives — managers, who make the actual decisions, are interested in their own personal satisfaction, in employees' welfare, and in the good of the community and society at large. Still, stock price maximization is the most important goal of most firms, and it is a reasonable operating objective upon which to build decision rules in a book such as this.

Social Responsibility

An issue that deserves consideration is social responsibility: Should businesses operate strictly in the stockholders' best interest, or are firms also partly responsible for the welfare of employees, customers, the communities in which they operate, and indeed society at large? In tackling this question, consider first those firms whose profits and rates of return on investment are close to normal, that is, close to the average for all firms. If some companies attempt to be social do-gooders, thereby increasing their costs over what they otherwise would have been, and if the other businesses in the industry do not follow suit, then the socially oriented firms will probably be forced by competition to abandon their efforts. Thus, any socially responsible acts that raise costs will be difficult, if not impossible, in industries subject to keen competition.

What about oligopolistic firms with profits above normal levels — can they not devote resources to social projects? Undoubtedly they can, for many large, successful firms do engage in community projects, in employee benefit programs, and the like, to a greater degree than appears to be called for by pure profit or wealth maximization goals.[7] Still, publicly owned firms are constrained in such actions by capital market factors. For example, suppose a saver who has funds to invest is considering two alternative firms. One firm devotes a substantial part of its resources to social actions, while the other concentrates on profits and stock prices. Most investors are likely to shun the socially oriented firm, thus putting it at a disadvantage in the capital market — after all, why should the stockholders of one

---

[7]Even firms such as these often find it necessary to justify such programs at stockholder meetings by stating that these programs contribute to long-run shareholder wealth maximization.

corporation subsidize society to a greater extent than those of other businesses? For this reason, even highly profitable firms (unless they are closely held rather than publicly owned) are generally constrained against taking unilateral cost-increasing social actions.

Does all this mean that firms should not exercise social responsibility? Not at all — it simply means that most cost-increasing actions may have to be put on a *mandatory* rather than a voluntary basis to insure that their burden will fall uniformly across all businesses. Thus, such social benefit programs as fair hiring practices, minority training, product safety, pollution abatement, and antitrust actions are most likely to be effective if realistic rules are established initially and then enforced by government agencies. Of course, it is critical that industry and government cooperate in establishing the rules of corporate behavior, that the costs as well as the benefits of such actions be accurately estimated and taken into account, and that firms follow the spirit as well as the letter of the law in their actions. In such a setting, the rules of the game become constraints. Throughout this book, we shall assume that managers are stock price maximizers who operate subject to a set of socially imposed constraints.

Stock Price Maximization and Social Welfare

If firms attempt to maximize stock prices, is this good or bad for society? In general, it is good. Aside from such illegal actions as attempting to form monopolies, violating safety codes, and failing to meet pollution control requirements — all of which are constrained by the government — *the same actions that maximize stock prices also benefit society.* First, stock price maximization requires efficient, low-cost operations that produce the desired quality and quantity of output at the lowest possible cost. Second, stock price maximization requires the development of products that consumers want and need, so the profit motive leads to new technology, new products, and new jobs. Finally, stock price maximization necessitates efficient and courteous service, adequate stocks of merchandise, and well-located business establishments, because these factors are all necessary to make sales, and sales are necessary for profits. *Therefore, the types of actions that help a firm increase the price of its stock are also directly beneficial to society at large.* This is why profit-motivated, free-enterprise economies have been so much more successful than socialistic and other types of economic systems. Since financial management plays a crucial role in the operation of successful firms, and since successful firms are absolutely necessary for a healthy, productive economy, it is easy to see why finance is important from a social standpoint.[8]

---

[8]People sometimes argue that firms, in their efforts to raise profits and stock prices, increase product prices and gouge the public. In a reasonably competitive economy, which we have, prices are constrained by competition and consumer resistance. If a firm raises its prices beyond reasonable levels, it will simply lose its market share. Even giant firms like General Motors lose business to the Japanese and Germans, as well as to Ford and Chrysler, if they do not set prices that merely cover production costs plus a "normal" profit. Of course, firms *want* to earn more, and they constantly try to cut costs, develop new products, and so on, and thereby earn above-normal profits. Yet, if they are successful and do earn above-normal profits, these very profits will attract competition and eventually drive prices down, so the main beneficiary is the consumer.

AGENCY RELATIONSHIPS

In a very important article, Michael Jensen and William Meckling defined an *agency relationship* as a contract under which one or more persons (the principals) hire another person (the agent) to perform some service on their behalf, and the principals delegate decision-making authority to the agent.[9] Within the financial management framework, agency relationships exist (1) between stockholders and managers and (2) between stockholders and bondholders (or creditors generally). These relationships are discussed in the following sections.

Stockholders Versus Managers

Jensen and Meckling contend that an agency problem arises whenever a manager owns less than 100 percent of the firm's common stock. If a firm is solely owned and managed by a single individual, that person will take action to increase his or her own welfare. If the owner-manager relinquishes a portion of his or her ownership by selling some of the firm's stock to outsiders, a potential conflict of interests arises. For example, the owner-manager may now decide (1) to lead a more relaxed life and not work as strenuously to maximize shareholder wealth, because less of this wealth will go to him or her, or (2) to consume more perquisites, because part of those costs will now fall on the outside stockholders.[10] This potential conflict between two parties, the principals (outside shareholders) and the agents (managers), is an important type of agency problem.

Another potential conflict between management and stockholders occurs when a *leveraged buyout* occurs. Here management itself (1) arranges a line of credit, (2) makes an offer, called a *tender offer,* to the stockholders to buy the stock not already owned by the management group, and (3) "takes the company private" after it buys the outstanding shares. Dozens of such buyouts of New York Stock Exchange listed companies have occurred recently, and a potential conflict clearly exists whenever one is contemplated. For example, the management of Cone Mills, the largest U.S. producer of denim, recently decided to make a leveraged buyout offer to the outside stockholders. It was in management's best interests to have the stock price minimized, not maximized, prior to the offer. Aware of this, Cone's management, like most who contemplate leveraged buyouts, obtained an outside opinion as to the value of the stock so as to head off lawsuits. Also, management's offer, like most, was contested by competing offers from other parties. In spite of competing offers, Cone Mills' managers were able to purchase the stock of the company for less than its true value. Thus, leveraged buyouts do constitute a type of agency problem between the stockholders and the managers of a firm.

To insure that the manager acts in the best interests of the outside shareholders, the firm must incur *agency costs,* which may take several forms: (1) expenditures to monitor managerial actions, (2) expenditures to structure the organization so

---

[9]See Michael C. Jensen and William H. Meckling, "Theory of the Firm: Managerial Behavior, Agency Costs, and Ownership Structure," *Journal of Financial Economics,* October 1976, 350–360. The discussion of agency theory which follows draws heavily from their work.

[10]*Perquisites* are executive fringe benefits such as luxurious offices, use of corporate planes and yachts, personal assistants, and so on.

that the possibility of undesirable managerial behavior will be limited, and (3) opportunity costs associated with lost profit opportunities because the organizational structure does not permit the manager to take actions on as timely a basis as would be possible if the manager were also the owner.

There are two extreme positions regarding how to solve the agency problem. First, if the manager were compensated only with shares of the firm's stock, then agency costs would be low because the manager would have less incentive to consume excessive leisure time or perquisites. However, it would be difficult to hire managers under these terms. At the opposite extreme, owners could monitor closely every managerial activity, but this solution would be extremely costly and inefficient. The optimal solution lies somewhere between the extremes, where executive compensation is tied to performance, but some monitoring is also done. Several mechanisms which tend to force managers to act in the shareholders' best interests are discussed next. These include (1) the threat of firing, (2) the threat of takeover, and (3) the proper structuring of managerial incentives.

The Threat of Firing

Until recently the probability of a large firm's management being ousted by its stockholders was so remote that it posed little threat. This situation existed because ownership of most firms was so widely distributed, and management's control over the proxy mechanism was so strong, that it was almost impossible for dissident stockholders to gain enough votes to overthrow the managers. However, stock ownership is being increasingly concentrated in the hands of large institutions rather than individuals, and the institutional money managers have the clout to exercise considerable influence over a firm's operations.

To illustrate, consider the case of GAF Corporation, a leading producer of building materials and industrial chemicals with 1987 sales of about $825 million. Its stock price had been as high as $41, but it went into a slide, and by the early 1980s it was selling below $8. At that point institutions began to buy heavily, and their ownership increased from 15 to 40 percent. Many bought shares with the expectation that GAF's chairman, Jesse Werner, would retire soon and the company would be broken up or taken over. This expectation was fueled by the fact that Mr. Werner, who had been chairman since 1964, announced that GAF would sell eight marginally profitable businesses representing about half its sales. Analysts figured that this would make the company cash-rich and a likely takeover candidate and that the price of its stock would rise — indeed, the stock price did more than double, from $7.75 to $16.38 in a year.

But Mr. Werner decided to keep his job. He obtained a new five-year contract and announced that the firm would reinvest internally most of the $212 million it had received from the sale of several unprofitable divisions. These actions caused GAF's stock price to drop back below $9. This in turn prompted Samuel Heyman, a Connecticut shopping center owner who held 4.2 percent of GAF's stock, to wage a *proxy fight,* in which dissident shareholders attempt to gain control by getting stockholders to vote a new management group into office. At the next annual meeting, Mr. Heyman received proxies representing about 60 percent of the shares, so he was able to oust Mr. Werner.

The victory for the dissidents was made possible because of support from large institutional holders. "We've got to outperform the market," explained one money manager. "Our clients have many money managers, and if we're performing poorly, the meter starts running. And pretty soon we'll be cut from the list." Another money manager said, "We simply can't afford to have much patience with poor management." So, whereas individual investors may be uninformed, lazy, or simply willing to "vote with their feet" by selling shares in companies whose performance is sub-par, institutional investors are more likely to work actively to oust an inefficient management. Recognizing this fact, people like Mr. Heyman are now more likely to "run against" a firmly entrenched management than would have been true some years ago.

The Threat of Takeover

Hostile takeovers (where management does not want the firm to be taken over) are most likely to occur when a firm's stock is undervalued relative to its potential as a result of poor managerial performance. In a hostile takeover, the managers of the acquired firm are generally fired, and any who are able to stay on lose the autonomy that they had prior to the acquisition. For example, San Francisco-based Wells Fargo recently acquired Crocker National, another large California bank. After the takeover, Wells Fargo fired 70 percent of Crocker's top executives. As stated in a press release, these executives, mostly senior vice presidents and above, "do not have a future" in the combined organization. Such action gets the attention of other managers and causes those managers to strive to maximize their firms' stock prices. In the words of one company president, "If you want to keep control, get your company's stock price as high as possible."

Actions to increase the firm's stock price and keep it from being a bargain are obviously good from the standpoint of the stockholders, but other tactics that managers can take to ward off a hostile takeover may not be. Two examples of questionable tactics are (1) taking poison pills and (2) paying greenmail. A *poison pill* is an action that a firm can take which practically kills it and thus makes it unattractive to potential suitors. Examples include Disney's decision to sell large blocks of its stock at low prices to "friendly" parties, Scott Industries' decision to make all of its debt immediately payable if its management changed, and Carleton Corporation's decision to give huge retirement bonuses, which would represent a large part of the company's wealth, to its managers if the firm were taken over (such payments are called "golden parachutes"). *Greenmail,* which is like blackmail, occurs when this sequence of events takes place: (1) A potential acquirer (firm or individual) buys a block of stock in a company, (2) the target company's management becomes frightened that the acquirer will make a tender offer and gain control of the company, and (3) to head off a possible takeover, management offers to pay greenmail, buying the stock of the potential raider at a price above the existing market price without offering the same deal to other stockholders. This siphons off part of the firm's value and makes it less valuable to other raiders. A good example of greenmail was Texaco's 1984 buy-back of 13 million shares of its stock from the Bass Brothers organization at a price of $50 at a time when the stock sold in the market at less than $40. As this book goes to press (summer

1987), the SEC and Congress are considering legislation to protect stockholders from poison pills, greenmail, and the like.

Structuring Managerial Incentives

Increasingly, firms are tying managers' compensation to the company's performance, and research suggests that this motivates managers to operate in a manner consistent with stock price maximization.[11] Such compensation plans, called *performance plans,* have become an accepted management tool. In the 1950s and 1960s, most of these plans involved stock options on the theory that allowing managers to purchase stock at a fixed price would provide an incentive for them to take actions which would maximize the stock's price. However, this type of managerial incentive lost favor in the 1970s because the options generally did not pay off. The whole stock market was relatively flat, and stock prices did not necessarily reflect companies' earnings growth. Incentive plans ought to be based on those factors over which managers have control, and since they cannot control the general stock market, stock option plans proved to have a weakness as an incentive device. Therefore, although 61 of the 100 largest U.S. firms used stock options as their sole incentive compensation in 1970, by 1986 not even one of the largest 100 companies relied exclusively on a stock option plan.

One important tool now is *performance shares,* which are shares of stock given to executives on the basis of performance as measured by earnings per share, return on assets, return on equity, and so on. For example, Honeywell uses growth in earnings per share as its primary performance measure. The firm has two overlapping four-year performance periods, beginning two years apart. At the start of each period, the participating executives are allocated a certain number of performance shares, say 10,000 shares for the president down to 1,000 shares for a lower-ranking manager. If the company achieves, say, a targeted 13 percent annual average growth in earnings per share, its managers will earn 100 percent of their shares. If the corporate performance is above the target, they can earn even more shares, up to a maximum of 130 percent, which requires a 16 percent growth rate. However, if growth is below 13 percent, they get less than 100 percent of the shares, and below a 9 percent growth rate, they get zero. Note that executives must continue with Honeywell through the performance period (four years) in order to receive the bonus shares.

Performance shares have a value even if the company's stock price does nothing because of a poor general stock market, whereas under similar conditions stock options could have no value even though managers had been successful in boosting earnings. Of course, the value of the shares received is dependent on market price performance, because 1,000 shares of Honeywell stock are a lot more valuable if the stock sells for $200 than if it sells for only $100.

---

[11]See Wilbur G. Lewellen, "Management and Ownership in the Large Firm," *Journal of Finance,* May 1969, 299–322. Lewellen concluded that managers seem to make decisions that are largely oriented toward stock price maximization, and economic events since his study was published suggest that the incentives for price maximization are even stronger today than they were during the period his data covered.

Other firms are using different measures for their performance shares, since there is mounting evidence that growth in earnings per share is not perfectly correlated with growth in a firm's stock price, and also because inflation has a large effect on earnings growth. For example, Sears, Roebuck & Company now bases its compensation package on the real (inflation-adjusted) return on equity, and Combustion Engineering, Inc., gives bonuses which depend on the spread between its cost of equity and its return on equity.

All performance plans — executive stock options, performance shares, profit-based bonuses, and so forth — are supposed to accomplish two purposes. First, they offer executives incentives to act on those factors under their control so as to maximize the stock price. Second, the existence of such performance plans helps companies attract and retain top-level executives. Well-designed plans can accomplish these goals.

Stockholders Versus Creditors

The second agency problem arises because of potential conflicts between stockholders and creditors. Creditors lend funds to the firm at rates that are based on (1) the riskiness of the firm's existing assets; (2) expectations concerning the riskiness of future asset additions; (3) the firm's existing capital structure, that is, the amount of debt financing it uses; and (4) expectations concerning future capital structure changes. These are the factors that determine the riskiness of the firm's cash flows and hence the safety of its debt issues. The creditors therefore set their required rates of return, and hence the cost of debt to the firm, on expectations regarding these factors.

Now suppose management, acting for the stockholders, causes the firm to take on new projects that have greater risks than were anticipated by the creditors. This increased risk will cause the required rate of return on the firm's debt to increase, which in turn will cause the value of the outstanding debt to fall.[12] If the riskier capital investments turn out to be successful, all of the benefits will go to the stockholders, because the creditors get only a fixed return, but if things go sour, the bondholders will share the losses. What we would have, from the stockholders' point of view, is a game of "heads I win, tails you lose," which is obviously not a good game from the creditors' standpoint. Similarly, if the firm increases its level of debt in an effort to boost profits, then the value of the old debt will decrease because the old debt's bankruptcy protection will be lessened by the issuance of the new debt. In both of these situations, stockholders would be expropriating wealth from the firm's creditors.

Should stockholders, through their managers/agents, try to expropriate wealth from the firm's creditors? In general, the answer is no. First, because such attempts have been made in the past, creditors today protect themselves against such stockholder actions through restrictions in credit agreements. Second, if creditors per-

---

[12]Basically, the higher the required rate of return on an outstanding bond, the lower its value. In Chapter 5 we will demonstrate this point.

ceive that the firm is trying to maximize shareholder wealth at the creditors' expense, they will either refuse to deal further with the firm or will require much higher than normal rates of return to compensate for the risks of such possible exploitation. Thus, firms which try to deal unfairly with creditors either lose access to the debt markets or are saddled with higher interest rates and consequently lower returns on equity, and generally with a decrease in the long-run value of the stock.

In view of these constraints, it follows that the goal of maximizing stockholder wealth is also consistent with fair play with creditors: Stockholder wealth depends on continued access to capital markets, and access depends on fair play and abiding by both the letter and the spirit of contracts and agreements. Therefore, the managers, as agents of both the creditors and the stockholders, must act in a manner which is fairly balanced between the interests of both classes of security holders. Similarly, because of other constraints and sanctions, management actions which would expropriate wealth from the firm's employees, customers, suppliers, or community will ultimately be to the detriment of stockholders. We conclude, then, that in our society the goal of stockholder wealth maximization requires the fair treatment of other groups.

MANAGERIAL ACTIONS TO MAXIMIZE STOCKHOLDER WEALTH

Assuming that a firm's management team does indeed seek to maximize the long-run value of its stock, what types of actions should it take? First, consider the question of stock prices versus profits: Will profit maximization also result in stock price maximization? In answering this question, we must analyze the matter of total corporate profits versus earnings per share (EPS).

For example, suppose Xerox had 100 million shares outstanding and earned $400 million, or $4 per share, and you owned 100 shares of the stock, so your share of the total profits was $400. Now suppose Xerox sold another 100 million shares and invested the funds received in assets which produced $100 million of income. Total income would rise to $500 million, but earnings per share would decline from $4 to $500/200 = $2.50. Now your share of the firm's earnings would be only $250, down from $400. You (and the other original stockholders) would have suffered an earnings dilution, even though total corporate profits had risen. Therefore, other things held constant, *if management is interested in the well-being of its current stockholders, it should concentrate on earnings per share rather than on total corporate profits.*

Will maximization of expected earnings per share always maximize stockholder welfare, or should other factors be considered? Think about the *timing of the earnings.* Suppose Xerox had one project that would cause earnings per share to rise by $0.20 per year for 5 years, or $1 in total, while another project would have no effect on earnings for 4 years but would increase earnings by $1.25 in the fifth year. Which project is better — in other words, is $0.20 per year for 5 years better than $1.25 in Year 5? The answer depends on which project adds the most to the value of the stock, which in turn depends on the time value of money to investors. Thus, timing is an important reason to concentrate on wealth as measured by the price of the stock rather than on earnings alone.

Still another issue relates to *risk*. Suppose one project is expected to increase earnings per share by $1, while another is expected to raise earnings by $1.20 per share. The first project is not very risky; if it is undertaken, earnings will almost certainly rise by about $1 per share. The other project is quite risky, so while our best guess is that earnings will rise by $1.20 per share, we must recognize the possibility that there may be no increase whatsoever. Depending on how averse stockholders are to risk, the first project may be preferable to the second.

The riskiness inherent in projected earnings per share (EPS) also depends on *how the firm is financed*. As we shall see, many firms go bankrupt every year, and the greater the use of debt, the greater the threat of bankruptcy. *Consequently, while the use of debt financing may increase expected EPS, debt also increases the riskiness of these projected earnings.*

Still another issue is the matter of paying dividends to stockholders versus retaining earnings and reinvesting them in the firm, thereby causing the earnings stream to grow over time. Stockholders like cash dividends, but they also like the growth in EPS that results from plowing earnings back into the business. The financial manager must decide how much of the current earnings should be paid out as dividends rather than retained and reinvested — this is called the *dividend policy decision*. The optimal dividend policy is the one that maximizes the firm's stock price.

We see, then, that the firm's stock price is dependent on the following factors:

1. Projected earnings per share.
2. Timing of the earnings stream.
3. Riskiness of these projected earnings.
4. Manner of financing the firm.
5. Dividend policy.

Every significant corporate decision should be analyzed in terms of its effect on these factors and hence on the price of the firm's stock. For example, suppose Exxon's coal division is considering opening a new mine. If this is done, will it increase expected EPS? How great is the danger that costs will exceed estimates, that prices and output will fall below projections, and that EPS will actually fall if the new mine is opened? Assuming things go as planned, how long will it take for the new mine to start showing a profit? How should the capital required to open the mine be raised, and if debt is used, how much will this increase Exxon's riskiness? Should Exxon reduce its current dividends and use the cash thus saved to finance the project, or should it maintain its dividends and finance the mine with external capital? Financial management is designed to help answer such questions as these, plus many more.

Figure 1-2
Summary of Major Factors Affecting Stock Prices

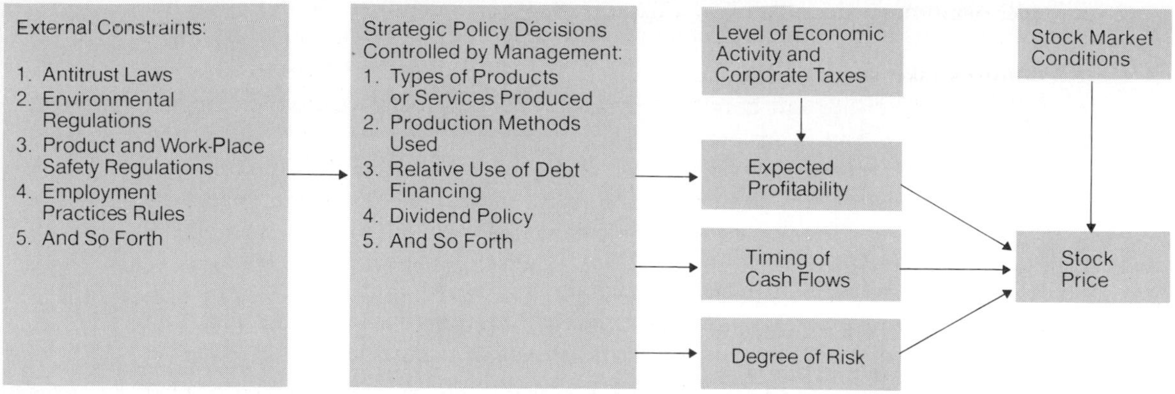

External Constraints:	Strategic Policy Decisions Controlled by Management:	Level of Economic Activity and Corporate Taxes	Stock Market Conditions
1. Antitrust Laws 2. Environmental Regulations 3. Product and Work-Place Safety Regulations 4. Employment Practices Rules 5. And So Forth	1. Types of Products or Services Produced 2. Production Methods Used 3. Relative Use of Debt Financing 4. Dividend Policy 5. And So Forth	Expected Profitability Timing of Cash Flows Degree of Risk	Stock Price

THE ECONOMIC ENVIRONMENT

Although the financial manager can take actions which affect the value of his or her firm's stock, there are additional factors which influence stock prices. Included are external constraints, the general level of economic activity, taxes, and conditions in the stock market. Figure 1-2 diagrams these general relationships. Working within the set of external constraints shown in the box at the extreme left, management makes a set of long-run strategic policy decisions which chart a future course for the firm. These policy decisions, along with the general level of economic activity and the level of corporate income taxes, influence the firm's expected profitability, the timing of its earnings, the eventual transfer of earnings to stockholders in the form of dividends, and the degree of uncertainty (or risk) inherent in projected earnings and dividends. Profitability, timing, and risk all affect the price of the firm's stock, but so does another factor, the state of the stock market as a whole, for all stock prices tend to move up and down together to some extent.

ORGANIZATION OF THE BOOK

Part I contains fundamental background materials and concepts upon which the book builds. Finance cannot be studied in a vacuum—financial decisions are profoundly influenced by the economic and social environment in which they are made. Our introduction to the economic/social side of this environment is contained in Chapters 1, 2, and 3.

Part II, consisting of Chapters 4 through 7, develops a set of valuation models which can be used to help see how different actions will affect the value of the firm's securities and the cost of its capital. The concepts and models developed here are used extensively throughout the remainder of the book.

Beginning with Part III, we move into the execution phase of the long-range strategic planning process, and in Chapters 8, 9, and 10 we consider the vital subject of long-term investment decisions, or capital budgeting. Since major capital expenditures take years to plan and execute, and since decisions in this area are generally not reversible and hence affect operations for many years, their impact on the value of the firm is profound.

Part IV, which contains Chapters 11, 12, and 13, sets forth the conceptual framework for an analysis of how the firm should raise the capital needed to finance its capital expenditures. Here we consider two fundamentally important issues — capital structure and dividend policy. Capital structure is, essentially, the firm's mix of debt and equity, while dividend policy relates to how much of its earnings the firm should retain and invest versus pay out to the stockholders as dividends.

Part V, which includes Chapters 14 through 17, focuses on the specific types of long-term capital available to the firm, and it addresses these three questions: What are the principal sources and forms of long-term capital? How are the terms on each type of security established? And how should the financial manager choose between the various types of long-term capital?

Part VI consists of Chapters 18, 19, and 20, which examine current, ongoing operations as opposed to long-term strategic decisions. From accounting, we know that assets which are expected to be converted to cash within a year, such as inventories and accounts receivable, are called *current assets,* and liabilities which must be paid off within a year are called *current liabilities.* The management of current assets and current liabilities is known as *working capital management,* and Part VI deals with this topic.

Parts I through VI focus on specific decisions which have a major impact on the firm's position and value. In the final three chapters, which form Part VII, we pull together these separate pieces and analyze the firm as a cohesive whole. In Chapter 21 we discuss the analysis of financial statements and show how it is used to determine the firm's current strengths and weaknesses, and then in Chapter 22 we look at the planning and control process. Finally, in Chapter 23 we examine corporate restructuring, the process by which firms make major changes in their basic structures.

It is worth noting that some instructors might choose to cover Chapters 21 and 22 early in the course, after Chapter 3, and use them to provide a framework for analysis rather than as a wrap-up. In our experience, both orderings work well, so each instructor can choose the one that best meets his or her own situation.

SUMMARY

This chapter has provided an overview of financial management. We began with a brief review of the evolution of finance as an academic discipline, tracing developments from 1900 to the present. We next examined the place of finance in the firm, and we saw that the financial manager has been playing an increasingly important role in the organization. We also considered the goals of financial management, and we concluded that *the key goal in most publicly owned firms is stock price maximization.*

However, there does exist the potential for conflicts of interest between stockholders and managers and between stockholders and creditors; these conflicts are called *agency problems.* There are a number of incentives for motivating managers to act in the best interest of stockholders, including (1) the threat of firing, (2) the threat of takeovers, and (3) properly structured managerial compensation packages. In a competitive economy, where managers serve at the pleasure of stockholders, stock price maximization must, in general, be the dominant goal.

The book's organization reflects this primary goal. First, we discuss the economic and social environment, after which we develop valuation models that can be used to show how corporate actions affect stock prices. Then, in the remainder of the book, we examine the actions that management can take to help maximize the price of the firm's stock.

MULTINATIONAL FINANCE

In theory, the models and analytical procedures developed throughout the text are valid for both domestic and multinational operations. However, problems uniquely associated with the international environment increase the complexity of financial management and often force managers to alter the way alternative courses of action are evaluated and compared. Five major factors complicate the situation and distinguish financial management as practiced by firms operating entirely in a single country in comparison to those that operate in several different countries:

1. Cash flows in various parts of a multinational corporate system are denominated in different currencies. Hence, a consideration of exchange rates and the effects of changing currency values must be included in all types of financial analyses.

2. Each country in which the firm operates will have its own unique political and economic institutions. Institutional differences among countries can cause significant problems when the corporation tries to coordinate and control the worldwide operations of its subsidiaries. For example, differences in tax laws among countries can cause a given economic transaction to have strikingly dissimilar after-tax consequences, depending on where it occurs. Similarly, differences in legal systems of host nations, such as the Common Law of Great Britain versus the French Civil Law, complicate matters ranging from the simple recording of a business transaction to the role played by the judiciary in resolving conflicts. Such differences can restrict the flexibility of multinational corporations to deploy resources as they wish, and even rule out procedures in one part of the company that are required in another part. These differences also make it difficult for executives trained under one system to control operations effectively in another.

3. Even within geographic regions that have long been considered relatively homogeneous, different countries have their own unique cultural heritages which shape their values and define the role of business in the society. Multinational corporations find that such matters as defining the appropriate goals of the firm, attitudes toward risk-taking, dealings with employees, the ability to curtail unprofitable operations, and so on, can vary dramatically from one country to the next.

4. Most traditional models in finance assume the existence of a competitive marketplace, in which the terms of competition are determined through the actions of participants. The government, through its power to establish basic ground rules, is only slightly involved in this process. Thus, the market provides both the primary barometer of success and an indicator of actions that need to be taken to remain competitive. This view of the process is reasonably correct for the United States and a few other major Western industrialized nations, but it does not accurately describe the situation in the majority of countries. Frequently, the terms under which companies compete, actions that must be taken or avoided, and the terms of trade on various transactions are determined not in the marketplace but by direct negotiation between the host government and the multinational corporation. This is essentially a political process, and it must be treated as such. Thus, many of our financial models must be recast to include political and other noneconomic facets of the decision.

5. The distinguishing characteristic of a nation state that differentiates it from a multinational corporation is that the nation state exercises sovereignty over people and property within its territory. Hence, a nation state can place constraints on the transfer of corporate resources and even expropriate, without compensation, the assets of the firm. This is a political risk, and it tends to be largely a given rather than a variable which can be changed by negotiation. Political risk varies from country to country, and it must be addressed explicitly in financial analyses.

These five factors complicate financial management within the multinational firm, and they clearly increase the business risk of the firms involved. However, the higher profitability associated with worldwide operations makes it worthwhile for firms to accept these risks, and to learn how to minimize or at least live with them.

Questions

1-1   Define each of the following terms:
   a. Profit maximization; stockholder wealth maximization
   b. Earnings per share; price per share
   c. Social responsibility
   d. Normal profits; normal rate of return
   e. Dividend policy
   f. Agency relationships; agency costs; performance shares
   g. Proxy fight; takeover; tender offer
   h. Leveraged buyout
   i. Poison pill; greenmail
   j. Proprietorship; partnership; corporation

1-2   Would the "normal" rate of return on investment be the same in all industries? Would "normal" rates of return change over time? Explain.

1-3   Should stockholder wealth maximization be thought of as a long-run or a short-run goal? For example, if one action would probably increase the firm's stock price from a current level of $20 to $25 in 6 months and then to $30 in 5 years, but another action would probably keep the stock at $20 for several years but then increase it to $40 in 5 years, which action would be better? Can you think of actual examples which might have these general tendencies? How could such situations affect the use of leveraged buyouts (LBOs)?

1-4   Drawing on your background in accounting, can you think of any accounting procedure differences which might make it difficult to establish the relative performance of different firms? How would this affect the agency problem and managerial compensation schemes?

1-5   Would the management of a firm in an oligopolistic or in a competitive industry be more likely to engage in what might be called "socially conscious" practices? Explain your reasoning.

1-6   What is the difference between stock price maximization and profit maximization? Would profit maximization lead to stock price maximization?

1-7   If you were running a large, publicly owned corporation, would you make decisions to maximize stockholder's welfare or your own interests? What are some actions stockholders could take to insure that your interests and theirs coincided? What are some other factors that might influence your actions?

1-8   The president of Continental Manufacturing Corporation made this statement in the company's annual report: "Continental's primary goal is to increase the value of the common stockholders' equity over time." Later on in the report, the following announcements were made:

  a. The company contributed $1 million to the symphony orchestra in the headquarters' city.

  b. The company is spending $300 million to open a new plant in South America. No revenues will be produced by the plant for 3 years, so earnings will be depressed during this period versus what they would have been had the decision been made not to open the new plant.

  c. The company is increasing its relative use of debt: Whereas assets were formerly financed with 40 percent debt and 60 percent equity, henceforth the financing mix will be 50–50.

  d. The company has been paying out only 30 percent of its earnings as dividends, retaining and reinvesting the remainder in the business. Henceforth, management will pay out 70 percent and retain only 30 percent.

  e. The company uses a great deal of electricity in its manufacturing operations, and it generates most of this power itself. Plans are to utilize nuclear fuel, rather than coal, to produce electricity in the future.

  Discuss how each of these factors might affect Continental's stock price.

1-9   What are the three principal forms of business organization? What are the advantages and disadvantages of each?

Selected Additional References

For a good summary of financial management, see

Pogue, Gerald A., and Kishore Lall, "Corporate Finance: An Overview," *Sloan Management Review,* Spring 1974, 19–38.

For alternative views on firms' goals and objectives, see the following articles:

Anthony, Robert N., "The Trouble with Profit Maximization," *Harvard Business Review,* November-December 1960, 126–134.

Donaldson, Gordon, "Financial Goals: Management versus Stockholders," *Harvard Business Review,* May-June 1963, 116–129.

Seitz, Neil, "Shareholder Goals, Firm Goals and Firm Financing Decisions," *Financial Management,* Autumn 1982, 20–26.

Treynor, Jack L., "The Financial Objective of the Widely Held Corporation," *Financial Analysts Journal,* March-April 1981, 68–71.

The following articles extend our discussion of agency relationships:

Barnea, Amir, Robert A. Haugen, and Lemma W. Senbet, "Market Imperfections, Agency Problems, and Capital Structure: A Review," *Financial Management,* Summer 1981, 7–22.

Hand, John H., William P. Lloyd, and Robert B. Rogow, "Agency Relationships in the Close Corporation," *Financial Management,* Spring 1982, 25–30.

For a general review of academic finance, together with an extensive bibliography of key research articles, see

Beranck, William, "Research Directions in Finance," *Quarterly Review of Economics and Business,* Spring 1981, 6–24.

Cooley, Philip L., and J. Louis Heck, "Significant Contributions to Finance Literature," *Financial Management,* Tenth Anniversary Issue, 1981, 23–33.

Weston, J. Fred, "Developments in Finance Theory," *Financial Management,* Tenth Anniversary Issue, 1981, 5–22.

For more information on managerial compensation, see

Cooley, Philip L., and Charles E. Edwards, "Ownership Effects on Managerial Salaries in Small Business," *Financial Management,* Winter 1982, 5–9.

Lambert, Richard A., and David F. Larcker, "Executive Compensation, Corporate Decision-Making, and Shareholder Wealth: A Review of the Evidence," *Midland Corporate Finance Journal,* Winter 1985, 6–22.

For additional insights into the optimal form of business, see

Maer, C. M., Jr., and R. A. Francis, "Whether to Incorporate," *Business Lawyer,* April 1967, 127–142.

2

Financial Statements, Taxes, and Cash Flows

A recent issue of the *Wall Street Journal* carried an advertisement by Fidelity Investments, the largest U.S. mutual fund company, promoting its Adjustable Rate Preferred Stock Portfolio. This particular fund, one of dozens offered by Fidelity, offered a current dividend yield of 6.6 percent, and the ad recommended it to corporate treasurers with temporary excess cash. Fidelity's other funds cater to individual investors, and they include funds targeted specifically for high tax rate or low rate investors, for people who need current cash income or those who want all of their investment income plowed back into the fund, for people who think companies in Europe (or Japan, or elsewhere) are likely to do better than those in the U.S., and on and on and on.

The same issue of the *Journal* reported that the yield on high-grade commercial paper, which is unsecured short-term debt issued by large corporations and which is also commonly used by financial managers as a temporary parking place for corporate cash, was 7.0 percent. The *Journal* also reported the yields on various common stocks, corporate bonds, government bonds, and a variety of other securities.

With such a wide variety of investments to choose from, how would a corporate treasurer — or an individual — decide where to place investable funds? The first step in the decision process is to estimate the potential returns, or yields, available on alternative securities. For example, assuming that Fidelity's 6.6 percent adjustable rate preferred stock mutual fund has similar risk and maturity characteristics to 7.0 percent commercial paper, which security should a corporate treasurer choose? Generally, the answer is, "The one with the higher yield." However, as we will see in this chapter, different types of securities may be taxed differently, and the relevant return for decision making is not the before-tax yield, but the after-tax yield. After you finish this chapter, you should know whether a treasurer with money to invest should choose the preferred stock or the commercial paper, and why.

Financial management cannot be studied in a vacuum — if the value of a firm is to be maximized, financial managers must understand the legal and economic environment in which financial decisions are made. This requires a consideration of the types of financial statements firms must provide to investors and the types of securities firms may issue. Further, the value of any asset, be it a financial asset such as a stock or a bond, or a real (physical) asset such as land, buildings, or equipment, depends on the usable cash flows it provides to its owner, and this means *after-tax* cash flows. Accordingly, this chapter presents some background information on financial statements, the major types of securities used by businesses, and the federal income tax system.[1]

FINANCIAL STATEMENTS AND SECURITIES

Any business must have *assets* if it is to operate, and in order to acquire assets, the firm must first raise *capital.* Capital comes in two basic forms, *debt* and *equity.* There are many different types of debt — long-term and short-term, interest-bearing and zero coupon, secured and unsecured, floating and fixed rate, and so on. Similarly, there are different types of equity. For example, the equity of a proprietorship is called *proprietor's interest* or *proprietor's net worth,* while for a partnership, the word *partner* is inserted in lieu of *proprietor.* For a corporation, equity is represented by both *preferred stock* and *common stockholders' equity.* Common equity, in turn, includes both *paid-in capital* and *retained earnings.*

Table 2-1 shows a simplified balance sheet for the L. F. Ambrose Company, a large manufacturer of commercial kitchen equipment for fast-food restaurants, as of December 31, 1987. Ambrose began life in 1957 as a proprietorship, then became a partnership, and finally converted to a corporation in 1965. Its 1987 sales were $401 million, and the $280 million of assets shown in Table 2-1 were necessary to support these sales. Ambrose and other companies obtain the bulk of the funds used to buy assets (1) by buying on credit from their suppliers (accounts payable); (2) by borrowing from banks, insurance companies, pension funds, and other institutions; (3) by selling preferred and common stock to investors; and (4) by "saving money" (retaining earnings) as reflected in the retained earnings account. (Recall from your accounting courses that a corporation saves whenever the company pays dividends which are less than its net income, and the savings that have accumulated since the company began are reported as retained earnings on its balance sheet.) Also, since wages and taxes are not paid on a daily basis, Ambrose obtains some "credit" from its labor force and from the government in the form of accrued wages and taxes.

The first claim against Ambrose's income and assets is by its creditors, whose claims are listed on the right-hand side of the balance sheet above preferred stock.

---

[1]This chapter contains essential information, but many business students will have been exposed to some or all of it in economics or accounting courses. Even if they have not, the material is both straightforward and descriptive. Therefore, some instructors may choose to have students cover Chapter 2 on their own rather than discuss it in class.

Table 2-1
L. F. Ambrose Company:
Balance Sheet as of December 31, 1987
(Millions of Dollars)

Assets		Liabilities and Equity	
Cash and marketable securities	$ 12.0	Accounts payable to suppliers	$ 23.8
Accounts receivable	50.3	Notes payable to banks	30.0
Inventories	91.6	Accrued wages and taxes	2.6
Prepaid expenses and other current assets	1.6	Other current liabilities	5.0
Total current assets	$155.5	Total current liabilities	$ 61.4
Gross fixed assets	149.7	Long-term bonds	107.0
Less depreciation	25.0	Preferred stock (112,000 shares)	11.2
Net fixed assets	$124.7	Common stockholders' equity:	
		Common stock (1,706,351 shares)	10.4
		Retained earnings	90.2
		Total common equity	$100.6
Total assets	$280.2	Total liabilities and equity	$280.2

However, the creditors' claims are limited to fixed amounts. For example, most of the long-term debt bears interest at a rate of 9 percent, so the bondholders in total get interest of 0.09 × $107 million = $9.63 million per year. If Ambrose did extremely well and had profits of, say, $80 million, the bondholders would still get only $9.63 million or $9.63/$80 − 0.12 = 12% of the income, even though they have supplied $107/$280.2 = 38.2% of the capital. However, if Ambrose lost money, the bondholders would nevertheless get their $9.63 million — assets would have to be sold, the cash would have to be used to pay the bond interest, and the value of the common equity would decline. Further, if the company's situation were so bad that it simply could not generate the cash needed to make the required payments to the bondholders and other creditors (if this occurs, the firm is said to have *defaulted* on its debt), then (1) the firm would be forced into bankruptcy, (2) the assets would be sold off (generally at much less than the values stated on the balance sheet), (3) the creditors would receive the proceeds from the bankruptcy liquidation, and (4) the common stock would be wiped out.[2]

The preferred stockholders stand next in line, after the creditors, for the firm's income and assets. Ambrose has 112,000 shares of preferred stock, each with a par

[2]The status of the different types of investors, and bankruptcy proceedings in general, are discussed in more detail in Appendix 15A. As a general rule, here is the order of priority of different claimants in the event of bankruptcy: (1) secured creditors' claims on the proceeds from the sale of the specific assets securing their loans, such as a building which secures a mortgage; (2) federal and state governments for accrued taxes; (3) employees for accrued wages and unfunded pension plan benefits; (4) unsecured creditors; (5) preferred stockholders; and (6) last in line, common stockholders. This priority system has a major effect on the riskiness and consequently on the rates of return on different classes of securities.

value of $100. This preferred pays a dividend of $8.125 per year, or 8.125 percent on its $100 par value. The preferred dividends must be paid before any dividends can be paid on the common, and in the event of bankruptcy, the preferred must be paid off in full before anything goes to the common stockholders.

After everyone else has been paid, the remaining income, often called *residual income,* belongs to the common stockholders. This income may be retained for reinvestment in the firm, or it may be paid out as dividends to the common stockholders. Firms such as Ambrose typically retain some earnings to support growth and pay the rest out as dividends. Ambrose has 1,706,351 shares of common stock outstanding. Investors actually paid about $6.09 on the average for these shares ($10,400,000/1,706,351 = $6.09), but the company has saved through retention of earnings $90,200,000/1,706,351 = $52.86 per share since it was incorporated in 1965. Therefore, stockholders on the average have a total investment of $6.09 + $52.86 = $58.95 per share in the company; this is the stock's *book value.*

Ambrose's debt and preferred stock is held primarily by its suppliers, by some banks, and by some other institutions including life insurance companies and pension funds. The debt is rarely if ever traded, since this particular set of investors tends to hold debt until it matures. Ambrose's common stock, on the other hand, is traded fairly actively. Individuals own about 65 percent of the stock, while institutions own the remaining 35 percent (these are typical percentages). In the fall of 1987, the stock traded in the general range of $80 to $90 per share, and it has ranged from a high of $95 to a low of $10 over the past 12 years. The price rises and falls depending (1) on how the company is doing at a given point in time, (2) on what is happening to other stock prices, and (3) most important, on how investors expect the company to do in the future. The *market value* (or price) does not depend directly on, and is usually different from, the book value. Book value, or the amount of equity per common share, is determined by accountants as the sum of assets valued at their original costs minus accumulated depreciation, less the borrowed capital and preferred stock, all divided by common shares outstanding, while market value is a function of the cash expected to flow to stockholders in the future. It is easy to imagine a situation where assets that were purchased years ago are worth far more today, and hence to see why market values can be far above (or below) book values.

Ambrose's income statement for 1987 is shown in Table 2-2. The firm had income available to common stockholders of $14.4 million, so Ambrose earned $8.44 per share of stock outstanding. Of this amount, Ambrose paid out $6 million, or $3.52 per share, in dividends, and it retained $8.4 million. When you studied income statements in accounting, the emphasis was on determining the net income of the firm. In finance, however, we focus on *cash flows.* The value of an asset (or a whole firm) is determined by the present value of the cash flow it generates. The firm's net income is important, but net cash flow is even more important, because it is cash that is paid out as dividends and used to purchase the assets required for growth.

As we discussed in Chapter 1, the goal of the firm should be to maximize the price of its stock. Since the value of any asset, including a share of stock, depends on the cash flows produced by the asset, managers should strive to maximize cash

---

Table 2-2
L. F. Ambrose Company:
Income Statement for the Year Ended December 31, 1987
(Millions of Dollars)

Sales	$401.0
Cost of goods sold (excluding depreciation)	280.7
Other operating expenses	79.6
Depreciation	4.9
Total operating costs	$365.2
Earnings before interest and taxes	$ 35.8
Interest expense	12.6
Earnings before taxes	$ 23.2
Taxes (34%)	7.9
Net income	$ 15.3
Preferred dividends	0.9
Income available to common stockholders	$ 14.4
Common dividends	6.0
Additions to retained earnings	$ 8.4
Net cash flow (Income available + Depreciation)	$ 19.3
Earnings per share (EPS)	$ 8.44
Dividends per share (DPS)	$ 3.52

---

flows available to investors over the long run. A business's cash flows are generally equal to cash from sales, minus cash operating costs, minus interest charges, and minus taxes. Depreciation is an operating cost, so the greater the depreciation charge, the lower the firm's profits. However, depreciation is not a cash expenditure — firms do not write checks to pay for depreciation, as they do for labor, materials, and taxes — and hence a firm's cash flow in any year can be found by adding its net income and depreciation expense. The greater the level of depreciation, other things held constant, the larger the firm's cash flows, because depreciation reduces taxable income, and hence taxes. In 1987, Ambrose had a net cash flow of $19.3 million, but $6.0 million of this was paid in dividends, so $13.3 million was left for asset additions, including replacement of worn-out plant and equipment. In the next two sections, we examine the U.S. tax system, including the way depreciation is calculated for tax purposes, and we show how the tax system affects cash flows and stock prices.

THE FEDERAL INCOME TAX SYSTEM

The value of any financial asset such as a share of stock, a bond, or a mortgage, and also the values of most real assets such as plants or even whole firms, depends on the stream of cash flows produced by the asset. Cash flows from an asset consist of *usable* income plus depreciation. Depreciation will be discussed later in this chapter, but usable income means income *after taxes*. Proprietorship and partnership income must be reported and taxed as personal income to the owners, but most corporations must first pay taxes on the corporation's own income, and then stockholders must pay additional taxes on all corporate after-tax income distributed as dividends. Therefore, both *personal* and *corporate* income taxes are important in the determination of the cash flows produced by assets.

In October of 1986, the President signed a sweeping new tax law that changed our tax system in several fundamental ways. We have incorporated the major provisions of the new tax law into this chapter and throughout the book. Most parts of the new tax law took effect in 1987, but to reduce adverse effects on individuals and corporations who had laid plans on the basis of the old law, parts of the new law will be phased in over a three-year transition period. During that period, certain provisions will be "blends" of the new and the old provisions. For example, the federal tax rate on the wealthiest individuals' income under the old law was 50 percent, and it will be 28 percent once the new law is fully implemented. However, the top rate for 1987 was set at 38.5 percent. To avoid unnecessary detail, we will, for the most part, focus on the tax system as it is scheduled to exist in 1988.

You should be aware of the fact that our tax laws are changed fairly often — indeed, a nontrivial change has occurred, on average, every 1½ years since 1913, when our federal income tax system began. Further, certain parts of our tax system are tied to the rate of inflation, so changes automatically occur each year, depending on the rate of inflation during the previous year. Therefore, while this chapter will give you a good knowledge of the basic nature of the tax system, you should consult current regulations as published by the Internal Revenue Service (and available in U.S. post offices) before you file your personal or business tax return!

Federal income tax rates for individuals go up to 33 percent, and when state and city income taxes are included, the marginal tax rate on an individual's income can exceed 40 percent. Business income is also taxed heavily. The income from partnerships and proprietorships is reported by the individual owners as personal income, and consequently is taxed at rates going up to 40 percent or more, while corporate profits are subject to marginal federal income tax rates of up to 39 percent, in addition to state income taxes. Because of the magnitude of the tax bite, taxes play an important role in many financial decisions.

Taxes are so complicated that university law schools offer master's degrees in taxation to practicing lawyers, many of whom also have CPA certification. In a field complicated enough to warrant such detailed study, we can cover only the highlights. This is really enough, though, because managers and investors should and do rely on tax specialists rather than trust their own limited knowledge. Still, it is necessary to know the basic elements of the tax system as a starting point for discussions with tax experts.

Individual Income Taxes

Individuals pay taxes on wages and salaries, on investment income (dividends, interest, and profits from the sale of securities), and on the profits of proprietorships and partnerships. Our tax rates are progressive to some extent, which means

Table 2-3
Individual Tax Rates for 1988

Single Individuals

If Your Taxable Income Is	You Pay This Amount on the Base of the Bracket	Plus This Percentage on the Excess over the Base	Average Tax Rate at Top of Bracket
Up to $17,850	$ 0	15%	15.0%
$17,850–$43,150	2,678	28	22.6
$43,150–$100,480	9,762	33	28.0
Over $100,480	28,680	28	28.0

Married Couples Filing Joint Returns

If Your Taxable Income Is	You Pay This Amount on the Base of the Bracket	Plus This Percentage on the Excess over the Base	Average Tax Rate at Top of Bracket
Up to $29,750	$ 0	15%	15.0%
$29,750–$71,900	4,462	28	22.6
$71,900–$171,090	16,264	33	28.0
Over $171,090	48,997	28	28.0

Notes:

a. The tax rates are for 1988 and beyond. However, the income ranges at which the 28 percent rate takes effect, and also the ranges for the surtax, are scheduled to be indexed with inflation beyond 1988, so they will change from those shown in the table.

b. Technically, a surtax of 5 percent is imposed on income in the range $43,150 to $100,480 for single individuals and in the range $71,900 to $171,090 for married couples. This surtax is designed to first eliminate the effects of the 15 percent rate on the initial increments of income, and then to eliminate the benefits of the personal exemption. The surtax ceases when the personal exemption has been fully offset, and hence the dollar amount at which the marginal rate drops back to 28 percent depends on the number of exemptions claimed. The amounts shown above assume one exemption for a single individual and two exemptions for a married couple. Different tables, similar to the one we present but with different numbers of exemptions, are available from the Internal Revenue Service.

that the higher the income, the larger the percentage paid in taxes.[3] Table 2-3 gives the tax rates for single individuals and married couples filing joint returns under the rate schedules for 1988. Here are the highlights of the table:

1. Taxable income is defined as gross income less a set of exemptions and deductions which are spelled out in the instructions to the tax forms individuals must file. In 1987, each taxpayer received an exemption of $1,900 for each dependent, including the taxpayer, which reduces taxable income. This exemption will rise to

---

[3]Prior to the 1986 Tax Code revisions, individual rates were more steeply progressive, going from 11 percent to 50 percent, but higher-income taxpayers were able to use a variety of tax shelters that lowered effective tax rates substantially. Indeed, many people had incomes in the millions of dollars yet were able to completely avoid taxes. The 1986 changes eliminated most tax shelters. Also, the revisions increased dramatically the rates on capital gains, most of which are earned by wealthy individuals. Therefore, in reality, the new law did not lower the progressivity of our tax system.

$1,950 in 1988, and to $2,000 in 1989, and thereafter it will be indexed to rise with inflation. However, high income taxpayers must pay a surtax which takes away the benefits of personal exemptions. Also, certain expenses such as mortgage interest paid, state and local income taxes paid, and charitable contributions can be deducted and thus used to reduce taxable income.

2. The marginal tax rate is defined as the tax on the last unit of income. Marginal rates begin at 15 percent, rise to 28 and then to 33 percent, and finally fall back to 28 percent. The average tax rate on all taxable income rises from zero to 28 percent.

3. One can calculate average tax rates from the data in the table. For example, if Carol Stanton, a single individual, had a taxable income of $30,000, then her tax bill would be $2,678 + ($30,000 − $17,850) (0.28) = $2,678 + $3,402 = $6,080. Her *average tax rate* would be $6,080/$30,000 = 20.3% versus a *marginal rate* of 28 percent. If Carol received a raise of $1,000, bringing her income to $31,000, she would have to pay $280 of it as taxes, so her after-tax raise would be $720.

4. As indicated in the footnotes to the table, current legislation provides for tax brackets to be indexed to inflation to avoid the *bracket creep* that occurred during the 1970s and which de facto raised tax rates substantially.[4]

Taxes on Dividend and Interest Income

Dividend and interest income received by individuals from corporate securities is added to other income and thus is taxed at rates going up to 33 percent. Since corporations pay dividends out of earnings that have already been taxed, there is *double taxation* of corporate income.

It should be noted that under U.S. tax laws, interest on most state and local government bonds, called *municipals* or *"munis,"* is not subject to federal income taxes. Thus, investors get to keep all of the interest paid on most municipal bonds, but only a fraction of the interest paid on bonds issued by corporations or by the U.S. government. This means that a lower-yielding muni can provide the same after-tax return as a higher-yielding corporate bond. For example, a taxpayer in the 33 percent marginal tax bracket who could buy a muni that yielded 9 percent

---

[4]For example, if you were single and had a taxable income of $17,850, your tax bill would be $2,678. Now suppose inflation caused prices to double and your income, being tied to a cost of living index, rose to $35,700. Because our tax rates are progressive, if tax brackets were not indexed, your taxes would jump to $7,676. Your after-tax income would thus increase from $15,172 to $28,024, but, since prices had doubled, your real income would *decline* from $15,172 to $14,012 (calculated as one-half of $28,024). You would be in a higher tax bracket, so you would be paying a higher percentage of your real income in taxes. If this happened to everyone, and if Congress failed to change tax rates sufficiently, then real disposable incomes would decline because the federal government would be taking a larger share of the national product. This was called the federal government's "inflation dividend." However, since tax brackets are indexed, if your income doubled due to inflation, your tax bill would double, but your after-tax real income would remain constant at $15,172. Bracket creep was a serious problem during the 1970s and early 1980s, but indexing — if it stays in the law — will put an end to it.

would have to receive a before-tax yield of 13.43 percent on a corporate or U.S. Treasury bond to have the same after-tax income:

$$\text{Equivalent pre-tax yield on taxable bond} = \frac{\text{Yield on muni}}{1 - \text{Marginal tax rate}}$$

$$= \frac{9\%}{1 - 0.33} = 13.43\%.$$

This exemption from federal taxes stems from the separation of federal and state powers, and its primary purpose is to help state and local governments borrow at lower rates than would otherwise be available to them.

Capital Gains Versus Ordinary Income

Assets such as stocks, bonds, and real estate are defined as *capital assets.* If you buy a capital asset and later sell it for more than your purchase price, the profit is defined as a capital gain; if you suffer a loss, it is called a capital loss. An asset sold within 6 months of the time it was purchased produces a *short-term gain or loss,* while one held for more than 6 months produces a *long-term gain or loss.* Thus, if you buy 100 shares of GE stock for $70 per share and sell it for $80, you make a capital gain of 100 × $10, or $1,000. However, if you sell the stock for $60, you will have a $1,000 capital loss. If you hold the stock for more than 6 months, the gain or loss is long-term; otherwise, it is short-term. If you sell the stock for exactly $70, you make neither a gain nor a loss; you simply get your $7,000 back and no tax liability is due.

From 1921 through 1986, long-term capital gains were taxed at substantially lower rates than ordinary income. For example, in 1986 long-term capital gains were taxed at only 40 percent of the tax rate on ordinary income. However, the tax law changes which took effect in 1987 eliminated this differential, and all capital gains income (both long-term and short-term) is now taxed as if it were ordinary income.

There was a great deal of controversy over the elimination of the preferential rate for capital gains. It was argued that lower tax rates on capital gains (1) stimulated the flow of venture capital to new, start-up businesses (which generally provide capital gains as opposed to dividend income) and (2) caused companies to retain and reinvest a high percentage of their earnings in order to provide their stockholders with capital gains as opposed to highly taxed dividend income. Thus, elimination of the favorable rates on capital gains might retard corporate investment and hence economic growth. The proponents of preferential capital gains tax rates lost the argument in 1986, but they did succeed in keeping in the law all the language dealing with capital gains, which will make it easy to reinstate the differential if economic conditions suggest that the differential is indeed needed to encourage growth. Therefore, you should not be surprised if the capital gains differential is reinstated in the future.

When capital gains were taxed at favorable rates, this had implications for dividend policy (it favored lower payouts and hence higher earnings retention), and it also favored stock investments over debt investments, because part of the income from stock normally comes from capital gains. Thus, one can anticipate changes in corporate dividend and capital structure policy as a result of the elimination of the differential.

Corporate Income Taxes

The corporate tax structure, shown in Table 2-4, is relatively simple. To illustrate, if a firm had $90,000 of taxable income, its tax bill would be

$$\text{Taxes} = \$13,750 + 0.34(\$90,000 - \$75,000)$$
$$= \$13,750 + \$5,100$$
$$= \$18,850,$$

and its average tax rate would be $18,850/$90,000 = 20.9\%$. Note that for all income over $335,000, one can disregard the surtax and simply calculate the corporate tax rate as 34 percent of all taxable income. Thus, the corporate tax is progressive up to $335,000 of income, but it is constant thereafter.[5]

Table 2-4
Corporate Tax Rates

If a Corporation's Taxable Income Is	It Pays This Amount on the Base of the Bracket	Plus This Percentage on the Excess over the Base	Average Tax Rate at Top of Bracket
Up to $50,000	$ 0	15%	15.0%
$50,000–$75,000	7,500	25	18.3
$75,000–$100,000	13,750	34	22.3
$100,000–$335,000	22,250	39	34.0
Over $335,000	113,900	34	34.0

Notes:
a. The rates shown here are for 1988 and beyond.

b. For income in the range of $100,000 to $335,000, a surtax of 5 percent is added to the base rate of 34 percent. This surtax, which eliminates the effects of the lower rates on income below $75,000, results in a marginal tax rate of 39 percent for income in the $100,000 to $335,000 range.

---

[5]Prior to 1987, many large, profitable corporations paid zero income taxes. The reasons this happened were (1) expenses, especially depreciation, are defined differently for calculating taxable income than for reporting earnings to stockholders, so some companies reported positive profits to stockholders but losses — hence no taxes — to the Internal Revenue Service (this is discussed later in the chapter), and (2) some companies that did have tax liabilities used various tax credits, including the investment tax credit (also discussed later in the chapter) to offset taxes that would otherwise have been payable. This situation will be drastically curtailed in the future.

Interest and Dividend Income Received by a Corporation

Interest income received by a corporation is taxed as ordinary income at regular corporate tax rates. However, 80 percent of the dividends received by one corporation from another is excluded from taxable income, while the remaining 20 percent is taxed at the ordinary tax rate. Thus, a corporation earning over $335,000 and paying a 34 percent marginal tax rate would pay only $(0.2)(0.34) = 0.068 = 6.8\%$ of its dividend income as taxes, so its effective tax rate on dividends received would be 6.8 percent. If this firm had $10,000 in pre-tax dividend income, its after-tax dividend income would be

$$
\begin{aligned}
\text{After-tax income} &= \text{Before-tax income} - \text{Taxes} \\
&= \text{Before-tax income} - (\text{Before-tax income})(\text{Effective tax rate}) \\
&= \text{Before-tax income}\,(1 - \text{Effective tax rate}) \\
&= \$10,000(1 - 0.068) = \$10,000(0.932) = \$9,320.
\end{aligned}
$$

If the corporation passes its own after-tax income on to its stockholders as dividends, the income is ultimately subjected to *triple taxation:* (1) The original corporation is first taxed, (2) the second corporation is then taxed on the dividends it received, and (3) the individuals who receive the final dividends are taxed again. This multiple taxation is the reason for the 80 percent exclusion on intercorporate dividends.

Notice that if a corporation has surplus funds which can be invested in marketable securities, the tax factor favors investment in stocks, which pay dividends, rather than in bonds, which pay interest. For example, suppose IBM had $100,000 to invest, and it could buy commercial paper (a type of debt security) that paid interest of $7,000 per year or preferred stock that paid dividends of $6,600. IBM is in the 34 percent tax bracket, so its tax on the interest, if it bought commercial paper, would be $0.34(\$7,000) = \$2,380$ and its after-tax income would be $4,620, or 4.62 percent. If it bought preferred stock, its tax would be $0.34[(0.2)(\$6,600)] = \$449$ and its after-tax income would be $6,151, or 6.151 percent. Other factors might lead IBM to invest in commercial paper, but the tax factor certainly favors stock investments when the investor is a corporation.[6]

Interest and Dividends Paid by a Corporation

A firm's operations can be financed with either debt or equity capital. If it uses debt, it must pay interest on this debt, while if it uses equity, it will pay dividends to the equity investors (stockholders). The interest paid by a corporation is de-

---

[6]Note that this illustration answers the question posed at the beginning of the chapter. When tax consequences are considered, the yield on the preferred stock, 6.151 percent, is higher than the 4.620 percent yield on the commercial paper. Note also that corporations are restricted in their use of borrowed funds to purchase another firm's preferred or common stock. Without such restrictions, firms could engage in *tax arbitrage,* whereby the interest on borrowed funds would reduce taxable income on a dollar-for-dollar basis, but taxable income would be increased by only $0.20 per dollar of dividend income. Thus, current tax laws reduce the 80 percent dividend exclusion in proportion to the amount of borrowed funds used to purchase the stock.

Table 2-5
Cash Flows to Investors under Bond and Stock Financing

	Use Bonds	Use Stock
Income before taxes and interest	$2,000,000	$2,000,000
Interest	2,000,000	0
Taxable income	$ 0	$2,000,000
Federal-plus-state taxes (40%)	0	800,000
After-tax income	$ 0	$1,200,000
Income to investors	$2,000,000	$1,200,000
Advantage to bonds	$ 800,000	

ducted from its operating income to obtain its taxable income, but dividends paid are not deductible. Therefore, a firm needs $1 of pre-tax income to pay $1 of interest, but if it is in the 40 percent federal-plus-state tax bracket, it needs

$$\frac{\$1}{1 - \text{Tax rate}} = \frac{\$1}{0.60} = \$1.6667$$

of pre-tax income to pay $1 of dividends.

To illustrate, Table 2-5 shows the situation for a firm whose assets produce $2 million of income before taxes. If the firm were financed entirely by bonds, and if the firm made interest payments of $2 million, then its taxable income would be zero, taxes would be zero, and its investors would receive the entire $2 million. (The term *investors* includes both stockholders and bondholders.) On the other hand, if the firm had no debt and was therefore financed only by stock, then all of the $2 million of operating income would be taxable income, the tax would be $2,000,000(0.40) = $800,000, and investors would receive only $1.2 million versus $2 million under debt financing.

Of course, it is generally not possible to finance exclusively with debt capital, and the risk of doing so would offset the benefits of the higher expected income. Still, the fact that interest is a tax deductible expense has a profound effect on the way businesses are financed — our tax system favors debt financing over equity financing. This point is discussed in more detail in Chapters 11 and 12.

Corporate Capital Gains
Before the 1986 Tax Code revision, corporate long-term capital gains were taxed at rates lower than ordinary income, just as with individuals. However, under current law, corporations' capital gains are taxed at the same rates as their operating income.

Corporate Loss Carry-Back and Carry-Forward

Ordinary corporate operating losses can be carried back to each of the preceding 3 years or carried forward for the following 15 years and used to offset taxable income in those years. For example, an operating loss in 1987 could be carried back and used to reduce taxable income in 1984, 1985, and 1986, or forward and used in 1988, 1989, and so on to the year 2002. The loss must be applied first to the earliest year, then to the next earliest year, and so on until losses have been used up or the 15-year carry-forward limit has been reached.

To illustrate, suppose Sunbelt Services, Inc., had a $1 million *pre-tax* profit (taxable income) in 1984, 1985, and 1986, but it then had a bad year in 1987 and lost $6 million. Sunbelt would use the carry-back feature to recompute taxes for 1984, using $1 million of the $6 million 1987 operating losses to reduce the 1984 pre-tax profit to zero. This would permit the company to recover the amount of taxes paid in 1984, so Sunbelt would receive a refund in 1988 of its 1984 taxes because of the loss experienced in 1987. Since $5 million of unrecovered losses would still be available, Sunbelt would repeat this procedure for 1985 and 1986. Thus, in 1988 it would receive a refund for taxes paid on $3 million of income from 1984 through 1986. Sunbelt would still have $3 million of unrecovered losses which it could carry forward and use annually, subject to the 15-year limit. The purpose of carry-back and carry-forward provisions is, of course, to avoid penalizing corporations whose incomes fluctuate significantly from year to year.

Improper Accumulation to Avoid Payment of Dividends

Corporations could refrain from paying dividends to enable their stockholders to avoid personal income taxes on dividends. To prevent this, the Tax Code contains an improper accumulation provision which states that earnings accumulated by a corporation are subject to penalty rates *if the purpose of the accumulation is to enable stockholders to avoid the personal income tax.* A cumulative total of $250,000 (the balance sheet item "retained earnings") is by law exempted from the improper accumulation tax. This is a benefit primarily to small corporations.

Note, however, that the improper accumulation penalty applies only if the retained earnings in excess of $250,000 are *shown to be unnecessary to meet the reasonable needs of the business.* A great many companies do indeed have legitimate reasons for retaining more than $250,000 of earnings. For example, earnings may be retained and used to pay off debt, to finance growth, or to provide the corporation with a cushion against possible cash drains caused by losses. How much a firm should properly accumulate for uncertain contingencies is a matter of judgment. We shall consider this matter again in Chapter 13, which deals with corporate dividend policy.

Consolidated Corporate Tax Returns

If a corporation owns 80 percent or more of another corporation's stock, it can aggregate income and file one consolidated tax return; thus, the losses of one company can be used to offset the profits of another. (Similarly, one division's losses can be used to offset another division's profits.) No business ever wants to incur losses (you can go broke losing $1 to save 34¢ in taxes), but tax offsets do make it more feasible for large, multidivisional corporations to undertake risky new ventures or ventures that will suffer losses during a developmental period.

S Corporation Tax Status

Subchapter S of the Internal Revenue Code allows small businesses, known as *S corporations,* to enjoy the limited-liability benefits of the corporate form of organization yet obtain the benefits of being taxed as a partnership. To qualify for S corporation status, a corporation must meet the legal definition of a small business, must be a domestic corporation, and must be owned by no more than 35 individuals.[7]

Owners of S corporations are taxed as if they were partners in a partnership. This tax treatment is especially beneficial in the early stages of a firm's development, when it is both making heavy investments in fixed assets and incurring start-up costs, which lead to operating losses. Many firms anticipate having one or more unprofitable years in their early lives while they are developing new products or trying to gain footholds in new markets. If such a firm was a partnership, the business's losses would be used to offset the owners' other income. *S corporation status allows the corporation to pass on those benefits as if the firm were a partnership, with the shareholders receiving the benefits on a pro rata basis in accordance with their fractional ownership of the firm's equity.*

If the firm is profitable during a year in which S corporation status has been elected, the earnings are added to the individual owners' ordinary incomes. Likewise, if an S corporation has an unprofitable year, the losses reduce the owners' ordinary incomes. This feature of Subchapter S tax treatment can be either an advantage or a disadvantage. If the corporation has income in excess of $75,000, then Subchapter S allows the firm (1) to be taxed at a maximum rate of 33 (or 28) percent versus 39 (or 34) percent, and also (2) to avoid double taxation if the earnings are to be paid out as dividends. On the other hand, if the firm is very small, and if the owners wish to retain all earnings in the firm to finance continued growth, then S corporation status may be a disadvantage. On balance, though, the new tax law has led most qualifying corporations to file for S corporation status.

DEPRECIATION

Suppose a firm buys a milling machine for $100,000 and uses it for 5 years, after which it is scrapped. The cost of the goods produced by the machine must include a charge for the machine, and this charge is called *depreciation.* Deprecia-

---

[7]The full set of conditions that must be met to qualify for S corporation status is spelled out in the Tax Code. Note too that these provisions are subject to change by Congress, so it is important to consult the current version of the Tax Code.

tion reduces profits as calculated by the accountants, so the higher a firm's depreciation charges, the lower its reported net income. However, depreciation is not a cash charge, so higher depreciation levels do not reduce cash flows. Indeed, higher depreciation levels *increase* cash flows, because the greater its depreciation, the lower the firm's tax bill.

Companies generally calculate depreciation one way when figuring taxes and another way when reporting income to investors. Most use the *straight line* method for stockholder reporting (or "book" purposes), but they use the fastest rate permitted by law for tax purposes. Under the straight line method for book purposes, one normally takes the cost of the asset, subtracts its estimated salvage value, and divides the net amount by the asset's economic life. For an asset with a 5-year life, a cost of $100,000, and a zero salvage value, the annual straight line depreciation charge is $100,000/5 = $20,000.

For tax purposes, Congress changes the permissible tax depreciation methods from time to time. Prior to 1954, the straight line method was required for tax purposes, but in 1954 *accelerated* methods (double declining balance and sum-of-years'-digits) were permitted. Then, in 1981, the old accelerated methods were replaced by a simpler procedure known as the *Accelerated Cost Recovery System (ACRS, which is pronounced "acres").* The ACRS system was changed again in 1986 as a part of the Tax Reform Act. (Note that the ACRS system contained in the 1986 Act is called "modified ACRS, or MACRS," to distinguish it from the original 1981 ACRS. We will not make this distinction in our discussion.)

Tax Depreciation Life

For tax purposes, the cost of an asset is expensed over its depreciable life. Historically, an asset's depreciable life was determined by its estimated useful economic life — it was intended that an asset would be fully depreciated at approximately the same time that it reached the end of its useful economic life. However, ACRS totally abandoned that practice — it set simple guidelines which created several classes of assets, each with a more-or-less arbitrarily prescribed life called a *recovery period* or *class life,* and these ACRS class lives bear only a rough relationship to expected economic lives.

A major effect of the ACRS system has been to shorten the depreciable lives of assets, thus giving businesses larger tax deductions and thereby increasing cash flows available for reinvestment. Table 2-6 describes what types of property fit into the different class life groups, while Table 2-7 sets forth the ACRS recovery allowances (depreciation rates) for the various classes of investment property. Consider Table 2-6 first. The first column gives the ACRS class life, while the second column describes the types of assets which fall into each category.

ACRS specifies two depreciation methods: straight line and accelerated. With the straight line method, a uniform annual depreciation charge is allowed — the annual depreciation charge is equal to the cost of the asset divided by the years of the asset's class life. However, the ACRS accelerated recovery allowances always equal or exceed the straight line rates. Therefore, a firm will always obtain a faster

Table 2-6
Major Classes and Asset Lives for ACRS under the Tax Reform Act of 1986

Class	Type of Property
3-year	Computers and equipment used in research.
5-year	Automobiles, tractor units, light-duty trucks, computers, and certain special manufacturing tools.
7-year	Most industrial equipment, office furniture, and fixtures.
10-year	Certain longer-lived types of equipment.
27.5-year	Residential rental real property such as apartment buildings.
31.5-year	All nonresidential real property, including commercial and industrial buildings.

Table 2-7
Recovery Allowance Percentages for Personal Property under the Tax Reform Act of 1986

Ownership Year	Class of Investment 3-Year	5-Year	7-Year	10-Year
1	33%	20%	14%	10%
2	45	32	25	18
3	15	19	17	14
4	7	12	13	12
5		11	9	9
6		6	9	7
7			9	7
8			4	7
9				7
10				6
11				3
	100%	100%	100%	100%

Notes:

a. We developed these recovery allowance percentages based on the 200 percent declining balance method prescribed in the 1986 Tax Act with a switch to straight line depreciation at some point in the asset's life. For example, consider the 5-year recovery allowance percentages. The straight line percentage would be 20 percent per year, so the 200 percent declining balance multiplier is $2.0(20\%) = 40\%$. However, the half-year convention applies, so the ACRS percentage for Year 1 is 20 percent. For Year 2, there is 80 percent of the depreciable basis remaining to be depreciated, so the recovery allowance percentage is $0.40(80\%) = 32\%$. In Year 3, $20\% + 32\% = 52\%$ of the depreciation has been taken, leaving 48%, so the percentage is $0.4(48\%) \approx 19\%$, while in Year 4, the percentage is $0.4(29\%) \approx 12\%$. After 4 years, straight line depreciation exceeds the declining balance depreciation, so a switch is made to straight line (this is permitted under the law). However, the half-year convention must also be applied at the end of the class life, and hence the remaining 17 percent of depreciation must be taken (amortized) over 1.5 years. Thus, the percentage in Year 5 is $17\%/1.5 \approx 11\%$, and in Year 6, $17\% - 11\% = 6\%$. We rounded to the nearest whole number.

b. Residential rental property (apartments) is depreciated over a 27.5-year life, while commercial and industrial structures are depreciated over 31.5 years. In both cases, straight line depreciation must be used, and the depreciation allowance for the first year is based, pro rata, on the month the asset was placed in service, with the remainder of the first year's depreciation being taken in the 28th or 32nd year.

depreciation write-off if it uses the ACRS accelerated recovery allowances than if it uses straight line, when an option exists.[8]

Computing ACRS Depreciation

The 1986 Act did not include tables of ACRS recovery allowances, but rather prescribed the procedures to be followed to calculate the depreciation expense in each year. We used these procedures to calculate the recovery allowance percentages shown in Table 2-7. The yearly recovery allowance, or depreciation expense, is determined by multiplying the asset's *depreciable basis* by the applicable recovery allowance percentage. Calculations are discussed below.

Half-Year Convention

Under the 1986 Act, the assumption is made that the property is placed in service in the middle of the first year. Thus, for 3-year class life property, the recovery period begins in the middle of the year the asset is placed in service and ends three years later. The effect of the mid-year convention is to extend the depreciation allowances one more year, so that 3-year class life property is depreciated over 4 years, 5-year property is depreciated over 6 years, and so on. This convention is incorporated into the Table 2-7 recovery allowance percentages.[9]

Depreciable Basis

The depreciable basis is a critical element of ACRS, because each year's allowance (depreciation expense) depends jointly on the asset's depreciable basis and on its ACRS class life. The depreciable basis under ACRS is *not* adjusted for salvage value, which is the estimated market value of the asset at the end of its useful life, whether the accelerated or the straight line method is used.

Investment Tax Credit

An investment tax credit (ITC) provides for a direct reduction of taxes, and its purpose is to stimulate business investment. ITCs were first introduced during the Kennedy administration, in 1961, and they have subsequently been put in and

---

[8]ACRS permits firms to use optional straight line depreciation rather than the accelerated recovery allowances in the 10-year and under classes. (Straight line is mandatory in the 27.5- and 31.5-year classes.) Note that salvage value is ignored when calculating depreciation for tax purposes. Also note that, as a benefit to very small companies, the Tax Code permits companies to *expense,* which is equivalent to depreciating over one year, up to $10,000 of equipment. (This is called *Section 179 expensing.*) Thus, if a company bought one asset worth up to $10,000, it could write the asset off in the year it was acquired. We shall disregard this provision throughout the book.

[9]The half-year convention also applies if the straight line option is used, with half of one year's depreciation being taken in the first year, a full year's depreciation in each of the remaining years of the asset's class life, and the remaining half-year's depreciation in the year following the end of the class life. However, for all classes of property, if a firm places 40 percent of its new assets into service in the fourth quarter, then the half-year convention cannot be used. In this case, depreciation is allowed for one-half of the quarter the asset is placed in service, with full depreciation for subsequent quarters. All of this may sound complicated and confusing, but it really is not. Further, you should recognize that virtually all companies have a computerized depreciation system, into which each asset's depreciation pattern is programmed at the time of its acquisition, and the computer aggregates the depreciation allowance for each asset when the accountants close the books and prepare the financial statements and tax returns.

taken out of the tax system depending on how Congress feels about the need to stimulate business investment versus the need for federal revenues. Immediately prior to the 1986 Tax Reform Act, ITCs applied to depreciable personal property with a life of 3 or more years, and the credit amounted to 6 percent for short-lived assets and 10 percent for longer-lived assets. The credit was determined by multiplying the cost of the asset by the applicable percentage. However, ITCs were eliminated by the 1986 tax revision. Nevertheless, you should be aware of what ITCs are, because there is a good chance that they will be reinstated at some future date if Congress deems that they are needed to stimulate investment.

Sale of a Depreciable Asset

If a depreciable asset is sold, then the sale price (actual salvage value) minus the then-existing book value, which reflects the depreciation taken up to the sale, is added to operating income and taxed at the firm's marginal rate.

ACRS Illustration

Assume that Sunbelt Services buys a $100,000 computer which falls into the ACRS 5-year class life and is placed into service on March 15, 1987. Further, Sunbelt paid an additional $20,000 for delivery and installation. Salvage value is not considered, so the computer's depreciable basis is $120,000. (Delivery and installation charges are capitalized and depreciated rather than expensed in the year incurred.) Each year's recovery allowance (tax depreciation expense) is determined by multiplying the depreciable basis by the applicable recovery allowance percentage. Thus, the depreciation expense for 1987 is $0.20(\$120,000) = \$24,000$ and it is $0.32(\$120,000) = \$38,400$ for 1988. Similarly, the depreciation expense is $22,800 for 1989, $14,400 for 1990, $13,200 for 1991, and $7,200 for 1992. The total depreciation expense over the 6-year recovery period is $120,000, which is equal to the depreciable basis of the machine.

CASH FLOW VERSUS ACCOUNTING INCOME

As noted earlier, management's primary goal is normally stock price maximization. As we shall see in Chapters 4 and 5, a stock's value is based on the *present value of the cash flows* investors expect it to provide in the future. Although any individual investor could sell the stock and receive cash for it, the cash flow provided by the stock itself is its future dividend stream, and the expected dividend stream provides the fundamental basis for the stock's value.

Dividends are paid in cash, so a company's ability to pay dividends depends on its cash flows. Cash flows are generally correlated with accounting profits (or net income as calculated on the income statement)—companies with relatively high accounting profits generally have relatively high cash flows—but the relationship is not precise. Therefore, investors are concerned about cash flow projections as well as profit projections.

It should be noted that firms can be thought of as having two separate but related bases of value—*existing assets,* which provide profits and cash flows, and *growth opportunities,* which represent opportunities to make new investments which will increase future profits and cash flows. Further, the ability to take advantage of growth opportunities often depends on the availability of the cash needed to buy new assets, and the cash flow from existing assets is often the primary source of the funds needed for profitable new investments. This is another reason why both investors and managers are concerned with cash flows as well as profits.

For our purposes, it is useful to divide cash flows into two classes: (1) *operating cash flows* and (2) *other cash flows.* Operating cash flows are those that arise from normal operations, and they are, in essence, the difference between sales revenues and cash expenses, including taxes paid. Other cash flows arise from the issuance of stock, from borrowing, or from the sale of fixed assets, as illustrated by CBS's recent sale of Dryden Press (the company that published this book) and its other textbook operations to Harcourt, Brace, Jovanovich for $550 million. Our focus in this chapter is on operating cash flows.

Operating cash flows can differ from accounting profits (or net income) for two primary reasons:

1. All the taxes reported on the income statement may not have to be paid during the current year, or, under other circumstances, the actual cash payments for taxes may exceed the tax figure deducted from pre-tax income to calculate reported net income.

2. Sales may be on credit, and hence not represent cash, and some of the expenses (or costs) deducted from sales to determine profits may not be cash costs. Most importantly, depreciation is not a cash cost.

Thus, operating cash flows could be larger or smaller than accounting profits during any given year. We consider the cash flow implications of credit sales in a later chapter, but the effect of the major noncash expense, depreciation, is discussed in the next section.

EFFECTS OF DEPRECIATION METHODS ON TAXES, NET INCOME, AND CASH FLOWS

As we just discussed, net income and cash flows are rarely, if ever, the same. We also noted that taxes paid can differ from reported taxes, and this too can affect cash flows. We explore that point in this section, and in the process we show how a firm's choice of depreciation methods affects both its cash flows and its accounting profits.

Tax Purposes Versus Reporting Purposes

All firms are required to use either the ACRS accelerated method or the optional straight line method when depreciating their assets for tax purposes, and most firms choose ACRS because it provides a faster write-off. Depreciation is a tax-deductible expense, so larger depreciation write-offs decrease current tax liabilities, and it is better to pay taxes later rather than sooner because you have the use

of the money in the meantime.[10] However, larger depreciation expenses also reduce firms' reported net income.

Generally accepted accounting principles, which specify the accounting methods a firm may use to determine its income as reported to its stockholders, state
that a firm should depreciate its assets for reporting purposes using the method
which most accurately reflects the decline in the value of its assets over time. For
most firms, this method is straight line depreciation. A few firms use ACRS (accelerated) depreciation for both tax and reporting purposes, but it is far more common for firms to use the ACRS method for calculating taxes and then use straight
line for reporting income to investors.

Effects of Depreciation on Taxes and Net Income

Table 2-8 shows the pre-tax income, taxes, and net income for a firm which has
sales of $100 million a year, costs which are equal to 50 percent of sales, and a
single asset which has a cost of $100 million. This asset has a 10-year economic
life, and it will have a zero salvage value at the end of the 10 years. Section I of
the table shows the calculation of actual taxes owed using the ACRS method; Section II shows the calculation of taxes and net income using the straight line
method for reporting purposes; and Section III (on page 48) shows the income
statements the company would report to investors if it used ACRS accelerated
depreciation for both tax and reporting purposes.[11]

Note that in Year 1 the firm reports to the Internal Revenue Service $20 million
in depreciation and $30 million of taxable income, and it pays $10.2 million in
taxes. If it uses ACRS accelerated depreciation for stockholder reporting, as shown
in Section III, it reports net income of $19.8 million. However, if it uses straight
line depreciation for stockholder reporting, as shown in Section II, it reports $10
million in depreciation, $10.2 + $3.4 = $13.6 million in taxes, and a net income
of $26.40 million, even though its actual tax bill is only $10.2 million. The difference of $13.6 − $10.2 = $3.4 million in reported versus paid taxes is shown on
the income statement as *deferred taxes* — that is, the firm has been able to defer
paying these taxes until a later date because it used an accelerated depreciation
method for calculating taxable income.

You can see from Section III that net income and EPS fluctuate for several years
if the firm uses ACRS for both tax and reporting purposes, whereas the numbers
reported to stockholders using straight line depreciation are stable over the entire
period as seen from Section II. Thus, firms that use deferred tax accounting as in

---

[10]If you think that your firm's tax rates are likely to rise in the future, either because its income will
grow and push it into a higher tax bracket or because Congress may increase corporate tax rates, then
it may be better to "save" depreciation by using the straight line method.

[11]We do not show it, but if the straight line method had been used for both reporting and tax purposes,
pre-tax income would have been $40 million each year (disregarding the half-year convention), so
taxes would have been 0.34 × $40 = $13.6 million each year, or 10 × $13.6 = $136 million in total.
This is exactly the same total as when the ACRS accelerated method is used for tax purposes, but the
timing of the tax payments is quite different.

Section II are said to be *normalizing,* where "normalize" means "stabilize." To the extent that investors (1) give weight to reported accounting profits and (2) prefer stable earnings to fluctuating earnings, there is an advantage to using straight line depreciation for reporting purposes.

Table 2-8
Effects of Depreciation on Taxes and Profits

1. The firm has a single asset which has a cost of $100 million, a 10-year economic life, and a zero salvage value. Revenues are $100 million per year over the 10 years, and costs other than depreciation are $50 million per year. The firm's tax rate is 34 percent, and it has 10 million shares of stock outstanding.
2. Straight line depreciation charges are $100,000,000/10 = $10,000,000 per year (ignoring the half-year convention). The asset has a 5-year tax life, so it can, under ACRS, be depreciated at these rates (in millions of dollars):

Year	ACRS Rate	Depreciation
1	0.20	$ 20.00
2	0.32	32.00
3	0.19	19.00
4	0.12	12.00
5	0.11	11.00
6	0.06	6.00
		$100.00

3. We show below (1) how the tax liability is calculated and (2) how income is reported to investors (in millions of dollars):

I. Tax Calculations

	Year 1	2	3	4	5	6	7...10[a]
Sales	$100.00	$100.00	$100.00	$100.00	$100.00	$100.00	$100.00
Costs	50.00	50.00	50.00	50.00	50.00	50.00	50.00
Depreciation (D)	20.00	32.00	19.00	12.00	11.00	6.00	0.00
Pre-tax income	$ 30.00	$ 18.00	$ 31.00	$ 38.00	$ 39.00	$ 44.00	$ 50.00
Taxes payable at 34% (T)	$ 10.20	$ 6.12	$ 10.54	$ 12.92	$ 13.26	$ 14.96	$ 17.00

II. Income Statements Reported to Stockholders Using Straight Line Depreciation with Deferred Taxes for Reporting Purposes (Normalizing)

	Year 1	2	3	4	5	6	7...10[a]
Sales	$100.00	$100.00	$100.00	$100.00	$100.00	$100.00	$100.00
Costs	50.00	50.00	50.00	50.00	50.00	50.00	50.00
Depreciation (D)	10.00	10.00	10.00	10.00	10.00	10.00	10.00
Pre-tax income	$ 40.00	$ 40.00	$ 40.00	$ 40.00	$ 40.00	$40.00	$ 40.00
Taxes paid (from Section I above)	10.20	6.12	10.54	12.92	13.26	14.96	17.00
Deferred taxes (D.T.)[b]	3.40	7.48	3.06	0.68	0.34	(1.36)	(3.40)
Net income after taxes (NI)	$ 26.40	$ 26.40	$ 26.40	$ 26.40	$ 26.40	$ 26.40	$ 26.40
Earnings per share	$ 2.64	$ 2.64	$ 2.64	$ 2.64	$ 2.64	$ 2.64	$ 2.64

continued

Table 2-8
Continued

III. Income Statements Reported to Stockholders Using ACRS (Accelerated) Depreciation for Both Book and Tax Purposes

	Year						
	1	2	3	4	5	6	7...10[a]
Sales	$100.00	$100.00	$100.00	$100.00	$100.00	$100.00	$100.00
Costs	50.00	50.00	50.00	50.00	50.00	50.00	50.00
Depreciation (D)	20.00	32.00	19.00	12.00	11.00	6.00	0.00
Pre-tax income	$ 30.00	$ 18.00	$ 31.00	$ 38.00	$ 39.00	$ 44.00	$ 50.00
Taxes payable at 34% $(T)^c$	10.20	6.12	10.54	12.92	13.26	14.96	17.00
Net income after taxes (NI)	$ 19.80	$ 11.88	$ 20.46	$ 25.08	$ 25.74	$ 29.04	$ 33.00
Earnings per share	$ 1.98	$ 1.19	$ 2.05	$ 2.51	$ 2.57	$ 2.90	$ 3.30

[a]The income statements are the same for Years 7 through 10.

[b]D.T. = (Pre-tax income) (Tax rate) − Taxes paid from Part I = ($40) (0.34) − $10.2 = $3.4 in Year 1. Deferred taxes represent tax savings that result from the use of ACRS depreciation in one year but which will have to be paid in some subsequent year when tax depreciation is low (or zero). Accounting rules require most firms that use straight line depreciation for reporting purposes to report deferred taxes.

[c]Taxes reported are identical to taxes paid as shown in Section I.

Notice that if we had set up Table 2-8 so that the normalizing firm had Year 1 costs of $80 million rather than $50 million, then its taxable income, hence taxes paid, would have been zero, yet it would still report a profit to stockholders. GE, Boeing, and a number of other very successful companies have in recent years been in exactly this situation — they reported high profits, yet they did not pay any federal income taxes. This situation helped create the political climate that led to the Tax Reform Act of 1986 which, among other things, imposes something called the *alternative minimum tax (AMT)* on such firms. The AMT is too complicated to cover in this text, but, basically, it insures that any company that reports profits to stockholders will pay at least some tax.

Effects of Depreciation on Cash Flows

The cash flows which accrue to our Table 2-8 firm are calculated in Table 2-9. In general, cash flows are equal to net income plus noncash expenses. Notice that the cash flows, which in this case are equal to net income plus depreciation plus deferred taxes, are the same regardless of the depreciation method used for reporting purposes; that is, regardless of whether the firm normalizes or not. This result always occurs. Thus, we can see that the depreciation method used for reporting purposes has no effect on the actual cash flows which accrue to a firm from its assets, even though depreciation methods do affect reported accounting profits.

Table 2-9
Effects of Depreciation on Cash Flows

I. ACRS (Accelerated Depreciation) Used for Stockholder Reporting (Do Not Normalize)

	Year						
	1	2	3	4	5	6	7...10[a]
Net income after taxes	$19.80	$11.88	$20.46	$25.08	$25.74	$29.04	$33.00
Depreciation	20.00	32.00	19.00	12.00	11.00	6.00	0
Deferred taxes	0	0	0	0	0	0	0
Cash flow[b]	$39.80	$43.88	$39.46	$37.08	$36.74	$35.04	$33.00

II. Straight Line Depreciation Used for Stockholder Reporting (Normalize)

	Year						
	1	2	3	4	5	6	7...10[a]
Net income after taxes	$26.40	$26.40	$26.40	$26.40	$26.40	$26.40	$26.40
Depreciation	10.00	10.00	10.00	10.00	10.00	10.00	10.00
Deferred taxes	3.40	7.48	3.06	0.68	0.34	(1.36)	(3.40)
Cash flow[b]	$39.80	$43.88	$39.46	$37.08	$36.74	$35.04	$33.00

[a]Cash flows do not change in Years 7 through 10.

[b]Cash flow = Net income + Depreciation + Deferred taxes.

Effects of Depreciation on the Balance Sheet

The cumulative deferred taxes for each year are reported on the balance sheet under an account titled "deferred taxes." Deferred taxes constitute a liability — in effect, they represent a loan from the federal government. Our normalizing company in Table 2-8, Part II, would show deferred taxes on its End-of-Year 1 balance sheet of $3.40 million. The amount shown at the end of Year 2 would be $3.40 + $7.48 = $10.88 million, and the account would peak at $14.96 million at the end of Year 5. Then, in Year 6, the account would be reduced by $1.36 million, and in Years 7–10, the account would be reduced by $3.40 million per year. Finally, the account would show a zero balance at the end of Year 10.

SUMMARY

This chapter has presented some background information on financial statements, business securities, income taxes, and cash flows. The capital raised to acquire business assets consists of *debt* and *equity.* The debtholders, or creditors, have first claim against the earnings and assets of the business, but these claims are limited to fixed amounts. The common equity holders are the owners of the business; thus, they have claims against all remaining earnings and assets.

The value of any asset is dependent on the effective income it produces for its owners. *Effective income* means *after-tax income.* Since corporate income is taxed at federal tax rates going up to 39 percent, and since personal income is subjected to additional federal tax rates of up to 33 percent, the tax consequences of various decisions have a most important impact on a firm's value. It is not necessary to memorize everything about taxes—indeed, this would be impossible. However, you should know the basic differences between corporate and personal taxes, that interest is a tax deduction to the payer of the interest, how tax depreciation is determined, and so on. These matters will come up throughout the book as we examine various types of financial decisions.

Our tax laws recognize that fixed assets depreciate over time, and the annual depreciation expense is a tax deduction. The current depreciation system is called the *Accelerated Cost Recovery System (ACRS)*. In Chapter 9, where we discuss cash flow estimation for capital budgeting purposes, tax depreciation rules have a major impact on the profitability of capital investments.

We also pointed out the difference between accounting profits and cash flows. Both concepts are important. Reported profits give investors an idea about how profitable the company was during some past period, and hence how well it might be expected to do in the future, while operating cash flows give both investors and managers an idea of how much cash the business is generating and thus has available for distribution to its owners or for reinvestment in profitable new projects.

Questions

2-1   Define each of the following terms:
a. Retained earnings

b. Common equity

c. Progressive tax

d. Marginal and average tax rates

e. Bracket creep

f. Capital gain or loss

g. Tax loss carry-back and carry-forward

h. Improper accumulation

i. ACRS depreciation; half-year convention; depreciable basis

j. Investment tax credit (ITC)

k. S corporation

l. Cash flow; operating cash flow; accounting profit

2-2   Suppose you owned 100 shares of General Motors stock, and the company earned $6 per share during the last reporting period. Suppose further that GM could either pay all its earnings out as dividends (in which case you would receive $600) or retain the earnings in the business, buy more assets, and cause the price of the stock to go up by $6 per share (in which case the value of your stock would rise by $600).
a. How would the tax laws influence what you, as a typical stockholder, would want the company to do?

b. Would your choice be influenced by how much other income you had? Why might the desires of a 45-year-old doctor differ with respect to corporate dividend policy from those of a pension fund manager or a retiree living on a small income?

   c. How might the corporation's decision with regard to dividend policy influence the price of its stock?

2-3   What does *double taxation of corporate income* mean?

2-4   If you were starting a business, what tax considerations might cause you to prefer to set it up as a proprietorship or a partnership rather than as a corporation?

2-5   Explain how the federal income tax structure affects the choice of financing (use of debt versus equity) of U.S. business firms.

2-6   How can the federal government influence the level of business investment by adjusting the ITC? By changing depreciation procedures?

2-7   For someone planning to start a new business, is the average or the marginal tax rate more relevant?

Problems

(Note: By the time this book is published, Congress may have changed rates and/or other provisions of current tax law—as noted in the chapter, such changes occur fairly often. Also, note that many of the provisions of the 1986 Tax Act are phased in over varying lengths of time. You should work all problems on the assumption that all aspects of the Act have been fully implemented and that the tax rates and other provisions as set forth in the text are still current.)

2-1   **(Corporate tax liability)** The Rentz Corporation had a 1988 income of $140,000 from operations after all operating costs but before (1) interest charges of $10,000, (2) dividends received of $20,000, (3) dividends paid of $25,000, and (4) income taxes. What is the firm's income tax liability and after-tax income?

2-2   **(Corporate tax liability)** The Garvin Corporation had $200,000 of taxable income from operations in 1988.

   a. What is the company's federal income tax bill for the year?

   b. Assume Garvin receives an additional $20,000 of interest income from some bonds it owns. What is the tax on this interest income?

   c. Now assume that Garvin does not receive the interest income but does receive an additional $20,000 as dividends on some stock it owns. What is the tax on this dividend income?

2-3   **(Loss carry-back, carry-forward)** The Phillips Metals Company has made $200,000 before taxes during each of the last 15 years, and it expects to make $200,000 a year before taxes in the future. However, this year (1988) the firm incurred a loss of $1,200,000. Phillips will claim a tax credit at the time it files its 1988 income tax return, and it will receive a check from the U.S. Treasury. Show how it calculates this credit, and then indicate the firm's tax liability for each of the next 5 years. Assume a 30 percent tax rate on *all* income to ease the calculations.

2-4   **(Loss carry-back, carry-forward)** The projected taxable income of the Bey Corporation, formed in 1988, is indicated below. (Losses are shown in parentheses.)

Year	Taxable Income
1988	($ 80,000)
1989	60,000
1990	50,000
1991	70,000
1992	(120,000)

What is the corporate tax liability for each year?

2-5 **(Form of organization)** Ernie Swift has operated his small repair shop as a sole proprietorship for several years, but projected changes in his business's income have led him to consider incorporating.

Swift is married and has two children. His family's only income, an annual salary of $40,000, is from operating the business. (The business actually earns more than $40,000, but Ernie reinvests the additional earnings in the business.) He itemizes deductions, and he is able to deduct $6,100. These deductions, combined with his four personal exemptions for $4 \times \$1,950 = \$7,800$, give him a taxable income of $40,000 − $6,100 − $7,800. (Assume the personal exemption remains at $1,950.) Of course, his actual taxable income, if he does not incorporate, would be higher by the amount of reinvested income. Swift estimates that his business earnings before salary and taxes for the period 1988 to 1990 will be:

Year	Earnings before Salary and Taxes
1988	$50,000
1989	70,000
1990	90,000

   a. What would his total taxes (corporate plus personal) be in each year under
     1. A corporate form of organization? (1988 tax = $5,415.)
     2. A proprietorship? (1988 tax = $6,241.)

   b. Should Swift incorporate? Discuss.
   (Do Parts c and d only if you are using the computerized diskette.)

   c. Suppose Swift decides to pay out (a) 50 percent or (b) 100 percent of the after-salary corporate income in each year as dividends. Would such dividend policy changes affect his decision about whether or not to incorporate?

   d. Suppose business improves, and actual earnings before salary and taxes in each year are twice the original estimate. However, Swift will continue to receive a salary of $40,000 and to reinvest additional earnings in the business. (No dividends would be paid.) Which form of business organization would allow him to pay the smallest amount of total income tax over the three years?

2-6 **(Personal taxes)** June Raymond has this situation for the year 1988: salary of $60,000; dividend income of $10,000; interest on IBM bonds of $5,000; interest on state of Florida municipal bonds of $10,000; proceeds of $22,000 from the sale of IBM stock purchased in 1982 at a cost of $9,000; and proceeds of $22,000 from the November 1988 sale of IBM stock purchased in October 1988 at a cost of $21,000. June gets one exemption ($1,950), and she has allowable itemized deductions of $5,000; these amounts will be deducted from her gross income to determine her taxable income.

    a. What is June's tax liability for 1988?

    b. What are her marginal and average tax rates?

    c. If she had some money to invest and was offered a choice of either Florida bonds with a yield of 9 percent or more IBM bonds with a yield of 11 percent, which should she choose, and why?

    d. At what marginal tax rate would June be indifferent in her choice between the Florida and IBM bonds?

2-7 (Depreciation) The Boyd Corporation will commence operations on January 1, 1988. Here are some data on the company: Sales revenues in 1988 are projected at $1,000,000; labor and materials costs are $700,000; on January 1, the company will purchase $100,000 of equipment which will have a 5-year ACRS class life; Boyd will receive $10,000 of dividends on some stock the company owns and $10,000 of interest on some bonds it owns. Also, on January 1 the company will issue $500,000 of long-term bonds which will carry an interest rate of 12 percent, and Boyd will pay its shareholders a dividend of $40,000 during 1988.

    a. What is the depreciation expense in each future year on the 5-year class life equipment?

    b. What is Boyd's 1988 tax liability?

    c. Suppose the firm had forecasted higher costs and lower revenues for the first few years of its operations, so when you developed the income statement, you found a loss and hence no taxes. Would this mean the company would lose the benefits of the loss? How would you recommend that it handle the situation? Assume for purposes of this question that losses were projected for 5 years, and after the 5-year start-up period, substantial profits were expected.

2-8 (Depreciation and cash flows) Broske Systems Incorporated (BSI) will commence operations on January 1, 1988. It expects to have sales of $200,000 in 1988, $250,000 in 1989, and $350,000 in 1990. Mary Broske, the founder, also forecasts that operating expenses will total 60 percent of sales in each year over this period and that BSI will have interest expenses of $10,000 in 1988, $12,500 in 1989, and $17,500 in 1990. BSI will make an investment of $100,000 on January 1, 1988, in fixed assets. Since they are used in research, the assets will be depreciated over a 3-year class life using ACRS.

    a. What is the depreciation expense in each future year on the 3-year class life equipment?

    b. What is BSI's tax liability in each year?

    c. What is BSI's cash flow in each year?

Selected Additional References

The following articles provide additional information on the effect of corporate taxes on business behavior:

Angell, Robert J., and Tony Wingler, "A Note on Expensing Versus Depreciating under the Accelerated Cost Recovery System," *Financial Management,* Winter 1982, 34–35.

Comiskey, Eugene E., and James R. Hasselback, "Analyzing the Profit and Tax Relationship," *Financial Management,* Winter 1973, 57–62.

McCarty, Daniel E., and William R. McDaniel, "A Note on Expensing Versus Depreciating under the Accelerated Cost Recovery System: Comment," *Financial Management,* Summer 1983, 37–39.

For a good reference guide to tax issues, see

Federal Tax Course (Englewood Cliffs, N. J.: Prentice-Hall, published annually).

3

Financial Markets, Institutions, and Interest Rates

Prosperity and calamity have strolled hand in hand down Wall Street in recent years. The securities industry has reaped huge profits and hence added greatly to its capital base, but it also suffered one of the most potentially damaging scandals in decades. In late 1986, Ivan Boesky, America's most flamboyant arbitrageur, admitted to illegal insider trading and agreed to pay a fine of $50 million and to return another $50 million in illegal profits to any company or investor who can demonstrate that it lost money from Boesky's moves. (Arbitrageurs, or "arbs," are speculators who buy and sell stocks that are potential takeover targets, and illegal insider trading involves someone who has been entrusted with nonpublic information and then uses that information for personal gain.) Boesky later implicated some senior executives from several leading investment banking firms, and these firms now face severe legal and credibility problems. Moreover, there has been a cry for more governmental regulation, which could hamper the investment industry's operations.

Amid all this uncertainty, one thing is clear — the giant investment banks that dominate the Street will survive and continue to grow, and they will also branch out into new activities. One of the newest wrinkles is "merchant banking," which involves direct money participation in takeover deals. For example, First Boston agreed to lend Campeau Corporation $1.8 billion to help finance its 1986 acquisition of Allied Stores. Indeed, over the past few years the giant houses like Merrill Lynch and First Boston have sunk 10 to 20 percent of their capital into such investments.

Financial markets and institutions are changing rapidly, and it is obvious that financial managers must keep abreast of these changes, for these markets and institutions affect the value of the firm's stock.

A knowledge of the environment in which financial managers operate is critical to an understanding of financial management. In this chapter, we examine the markets where capital is raised, securities are traded, and stock prices are established, and we also discuss the institutions which facilitate security transactions. In the process, we shall see both how money costs are determined and explore the principal factors that determine the level of interest rates in the economy.

THE FINANCIAL MARKETS

Business firms, as well as individuals and government units, often need to raise capital. For example, suppose Pacific Gas & Electric Company forecasts an increase in the demand for electricity in Northern California, and the company decides to build a new power plant. PG&E almost certainly will not have the $2 billion or so necessary to pay for the plant, so the company will have to raise this capital in the markets. Or suppose Mr. Jones, the proprietor of a Dallas hardware store, decides to expand into appliances. Where will he get the money to buy the initial inventory of TV sets, washers, and freezers? Similarly, if the Smith family wants to buy a home that costs $100,000, but they have only $20,000 in savings, how can they raise the additional $80,000? Or if the City of Boston wants to borrow $20 million to finance a new sewer plant, and the federal government needs $150 billion or so to cover the projected 1988 deficit, they too need sources for raising this capital.

On the other hand, some individuals and firms have incomes which are greater than their current expenditures, so they have savings available to invest. For example, Edgar Rice has an income of $36,000, but his expenses are only $30,000, and in 1987 General Electric had accumulated about $3 billion of excess cash which it could make available for investment.

People and organizations wanting to borrow money are brought together with those having surplus funds in the *financial markets*. Note that "markets" is plural — there are a great many different financial markets, each one consisting of many institutions, in a developed economy such as ours. Each market deals with a somewhat different type of security, serves a different set of customers, or operates in a different part of the country. Here are some of the major types of markets:

1. *Physical asset markets* and *financial asset markets* must be distinguished. *Physical asset markets* (also called "tangible" or "real" asset markets) deal with wheat, autos, real estate, computers, machinery, and so on. *Financial markets* deal with stocks, bonds, notes, mortgages, and other *claims on real assets.*

2. *Spot markets* and *futures markets* are terms that refer to whether the assets are being bought or sold for "on the spot" delivery (literally, within a few days) or for delivery at some future date, such as six months or a year in the future. The futures markets (which could include the options markets) are growing in importance, but we shall not discuss them until much later in the text.

3. *Money markets* are defined as the markets for debt securities with maturities of less than one year. The New York money market is the world's largest, and it is dominated by the major U.S. banks, although branches of foreign banks are also active there. London, Tokyo, and Paris are other major money market centers.

4. *Capital markets* are defined as the markets for long-term debt and corporate stocks. The New York Stock Exchange, which handles the stocks of the largest corporations, is a prime example of a capital market.

5. *Mortgage markets* deal with loans on residential, commercial, and industrial real estate, and on farmland.

6. *Consumer credit markets* involve loans on autos and appliances, as well as loans for education, vacations, and so on.

7. *World, national, regional,* and *local markets* also exist. Thus, depending on an organization's size and scope of operations, it may be able to borrow all around the world, or it may be confined to a strictly local, even neighborhood, market.

8. *Primary markets* are the markets in which newly issued securities are bought and sold for the first time. If IBM were to sell a new issue of common stock to raise capital, this would be a primary market transaction.

9. *Secondary markets* are markets in which existing, outstanding securities are bought and sold. Thus, if John Mitchell decided to buy 1,000 shares of GM stock, the purchase would occur in the secondary market. The New York Stock Exchange is a secondary market, since it deals in "used" as opposed to newly issued stocks and bonds. Secondary markets also exist for mortgages, certain types of loans, and other financial assets.

Other classifications could be made, but this breakdown is sufficient to show that there are many types of financial markets.

A healthy economy is vitally dependent on efficient transfers of funds from people who are net savers to firms and individuals who need capital — that is, the economy depends on *efficient financial markets.* Without efficient transfers, the economy simply could not function: Pacific Gas & Electric could not raise capital, so San Francisco's citizens would have no electricity, the Smith family would not have adequate housing; Edgar Rice would have no place to invest his savings; and so on. Obviously, the level of employment and productivity, and hence our standard of living, would be much lower, so it is absolutely essential that our financial markets function efficiently — not only quickly, but also at a low cost.[1]

FINANCIAL INSTITUTIONS

Transfers of capital between savers and those who need capital take place in the three different ways diagrammed in Figure 3-1:

1. *Direct transfers* of money and securities as shown in the top section occur when a business sells its stocks or bonds directly to savers, without going through any type of intermediary.

---

[1]When organizations such as the United Nations design plans to aid developing nations, just as much attention must be paid to the establishment of cost-efficient financial markets as to electrical power, transportation, communications, and other "infrastructure" systems. Economic efficiency is simply impossible without a good system for allocating capital within the economy.

Figure 3-1
Diagram of the Capital Formation Process

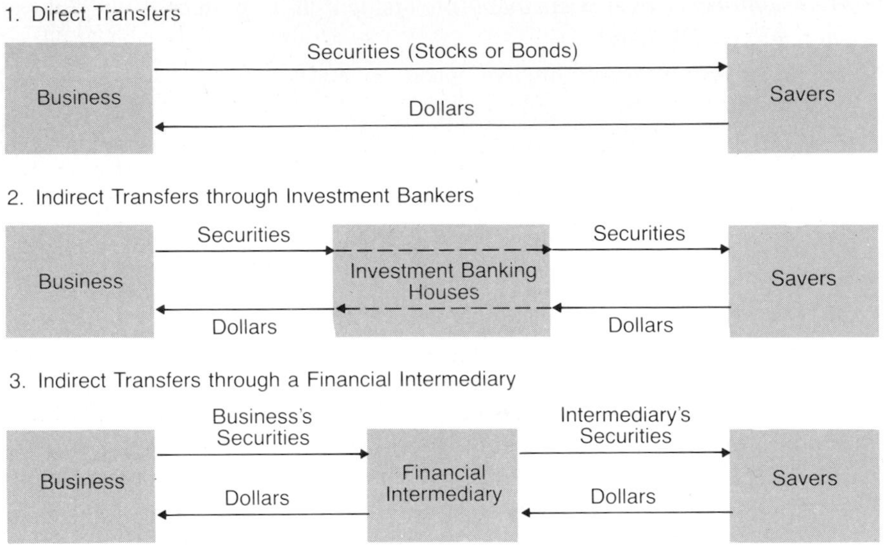

---

1. Direct Transfers

Business	Securities (Stocks or Bonds) →	Savers
	← Dollars	

2. Indirect Transfers through Investment Bankers

Business	Securities →	Investment Banking Houses	Securities →	Savers
	← Dollars		← Dollars	

3. Indirect Transfers through a Financial Intermediary

Business	Business's Securities →	Financial Intermediary	Intermediary's Securities →	Savers
	← Dollars		← Dollars	

---

2. As shown in the middle section, transfers may also go through an *investment banking house* such as Merrill Lynch, which serves as a middleman and facilitates the issuance of securities. The company sells its stocks or bonds to the investment bank, which in turns sells them to ultimate savers. The business's securities and the savers' money merely "pass through" the investment banking house.

3. Transfers can also be made through a *financial intermediary*, such as a bank or mutual fund, which obtains funds from savers and then issues its own securities in exchange. For example, a saver might give dollars to a bank, receiving from it a certificate of deposit, and then the bank might lend the money to a small business in the form of a mortgage loan. Thus, intermediaries literally create new forms of capital — in this case, certificates of deposit, which are more liquid than mortgages — and this increases general market efficiency.

For simplicity, we assumed that the entity which needs capital is a business, and specifically a corporation, although it is easy to visualize the demander of capital as a potential home purchaser, a government unit, and so on.

Direct transfers of funds from savers to businesses are possible and do occur on occasion, but it is generally more efficient for a business to obtain the services of an *investment bank*. Merrill Lynch, Salomon Brothers, and E. F. Hutton are examples of financial service corporations which offer investment banking services. Such organizations (1) help corporations design securities with the features that will be most attractive to investors, (2) buy these securities from the corporation, and (3) then resell them to savers in the primary markets. Thus, investment bankers typically operate as middlemen in the process of transferring capital from savers to businesses.

As noted above, the financial intermediaries shown in the third section of Figure 3-1 do more than simply transfer money and securities between firms and savers —they literally create new financial products. Since the intermediaries are generally large, they gain economies of scale in analyzing the creditworthiness of potential borrowers, in processing and collecting loans, and in pooling risks and thus helping individual savers diversify, which means not "putting all their financial eggs in one basket." Further, a system of specialized intermediaries can enable savings to do more than just draw interest—for example, people can put money into banks and get both interest income and a convenient way of making payments (checking), put money into life insurance companies and get both interest income and protection for their beneficiaries, and so on.

In the United States and other developed nations, a large set of specialized and highly efficient financial intermediaries has evolved. The situation is, however, changing rapidly, and different types of institutions are performing services that were formerly reserved for others, causing institutional distinctions to become blurred. Still, there is a degree of institutional identity, and here are the major classes of intermediaries:

1. *Commercial banks*, which are the traditional "department stores" of finance, serve a wide variety of savers and those with needs for funds. Historically, the commercial banks have been the major institutions for handling checking accounts and through which the Federal Reserve System expanded or contracted the money supply. Today, however, some of the other institutions discussed below also provide checking services and significantly influence the effective money supply. Conversely, commercial banks now provide an ever widening range of services, including stock brokerage services and insurance.

2. *Savings and loan associations (S&Ls),* which have traditionally served individual savers and residential and commercial mortgage borrowers, take the funds of many small savers and then lend this money to home buyers and other types of borrowers. The savers are provided a degree of liquidity that would be absent if they bought the mortgages or other securities directly, so perhaps the most significant economic function of the S&Ls is to "create liquidity" which would otherwise be lacking. Also, the S&Ls have more expertise in analyzing credit, setting up loans, and making collections than individual savers could possibly have, so they reduce the cost and increase the feasibility of making real estate loans. Finally, the S&Ls hold large, diversified portfolios of loans and other assets and thus spread risks in a manner that would be impossible if small savers were making mortgage loans directly. Because of these factors, savers benefit by being able to invest their savings in more liquid, better managed, and less risky accounts, while borrowers benefit by being able to obtain more capital, and at lower costs, than would otherwise be possible.

3. *Mutual savings banks*, which are similar to S&Ls, operate primarily in the northeastern states, accept savings largely from individuals, and lend mainly on a long-term basis to home buyers and consumers.

4. *Credit unions* are cooperative associations whose members have a common bond, such as being employees of the same firm. Members' savings are loaned only to other members, generally for auto purchases, home improvements, and the like. Credit unions are often the cheapest source of funds available to the individual borrower.

5. *Pension funds* are retirement plans funded by corporations or government agencies for their workers and administered primarily by the trust departments of commercial banks or by life insurance companies. Pension funds invest mainly in bonds, stocks, mortgages, and real estate.

6. *Life insurance companies* take savings in the form of annual premiums, then invest these funds in stocks, bonds, real estate, and mortgages, and finally make payments to the beneficiaries of the insured parties. In recent years life insurance companies have also offered a variety of tax-deferred savings plans designed to provide benefits to the participants when they retire.

7. *Mutual funds* are corporations which accept dollars from savers and then use these dollars to buy stocks, bonds, or other financial instruments issued by businesses or government units. These organizations pool funds and thus reduce risks by diversification. They also gain economies of scale, which lower the costs of analyzing securities, managing portfolios, and buying and selling securities. Different funds are designed to meet the objectives of different types of savers. Hence, there are bond funds for those who desire safety; stock funds for savers who are willing to accept significant risks in the hope of higher returns; and still other funds that are used as interest-bearing checking accounts (the money market funds). There are literally hundreds of different mutual funds with dozens of different goals and purposes.

Financial institutions have historically been heavily regulated, with the major purpose of this regulation being to insure the safety of the institutions and thus to protect depositors. However, these regulations—which have taken the form of prohibitions on nationwide branch banking, restrictions on the types of assets the institutions can buy, ceilings on the interest rates they can pay, and limitations on the types of services they can provide—have tended to impede the free flow of capital from surplus to deficit areas, and this has hurt the efficiency of our capital markets. Recognizing this fact, Congress has authorized some major changes, and more will be coming along.

The end result of the ongoing regulatory changes is a blurring of the distinctions among the different types of institutions. Indeed, the trend in the United States today is toward huge financial service corporations, which own banks, S&Ls, investment banking houses, insurance companies, pension plan operations, and mutual funds, and which have branches across the country and even around the world. Sears, Roebuck is, interestingly, one of the largest—if not *the* largest—financial service corporation. It owns Allstate Insurance, Dean Witter (a leading brokerage and investment banking firm), Coldwell Banker (the largest real estate brokerage firm), a huge credit card business, and a host of other related businesses. Other financial service corporations, most of which started in one area and have now diversified to cover a broad financial spectrum, include Transamerica, Merrill Lynch, American Express, Citicorp, and Prudential.

THE STOCK MARKET

As noted earlier, secondary markets are the markets in which outstanding, previously issued securities are traded. By far the most active market — and the most important one to financial managers — is the *stock market*, for it is here that the prices of firms' stocks are established. Since the primary goal of financial management is to contribute to the maximization of a firm's stock price, a knowledge of the market in which this price is established is essential for anyone involved in managing a business.

The Stock Exchanges

There are two basic types of stock markets — the *organized exchanges*, which include the New York Stock Exchange (NYSE), the American Stock Exchange (AMEX), and several regional exchanges, and the less formal *over-the-counter market*. Since the organized exchanges have actual physical market locations and are easier to describe and understand, we shall consider them first.

The organized security exchanges are tangible, physical entities. Each of the larger ones occupies its own building, has specifically designated members, and has an elected governing body — its board of governors. Members are said to have "seats" on the exchange, although everybody stands up. These seats, which are bought and sold, represent the right to trade on the exchange. In 1979 seats on the NYSE sold for as little as $40,000, but in May 1987, they hit an all-time high price of $1.1 million.

Most of the larger investment banking houses operate *brokerage departments* which own seats on the exchanges and designate one or more of their officers as members. The exchanges are open on all normal working days, with the members meeting in a large room equipped with telephones and other electronic equipment that enable each member to communicate with his or her firm's offices throughout the country.

Like other markets, security exchanges facilitate communication between buyers and sellers. For example, Merrill Lynch (the largest brokerage firm) might receive an order in its Atlanta office from a customer who wants to buy 100 shares of General Motors stock. Simultaneously, E. F. Hutton's Denver office might receive an order from a customer wishing to sell 100 shares of GM. Each broker communicates by wire with the firm's representative on the NYSE. Other brokers throughout the country are also communicating with their own exchange members. The exchange members with *sell orders* offer the shares for sale, and these are bid for by the members with *buy orders*. Thus, the exchanges operate as *auction markets*.[2]

The Over-the-Counter Market

In contrast to the organized security exchanges, the over-the-counter market is a nebulous, intangible organization. An explanation of the term "over-the-counter" will help clarify exactly what this market is. The exchanges operate as auction markets — buy and sell orders come in more or less simultaneously, and exchange members match these orders. But if a stock is traded less frequently, perhaps because it is the stock of a new or a small firm, few buy and sell orders come in, and matching them within a reasonable length of time would be difficult. To avoid this problem, some brokerage firms maintain an inventory of such stocks; they buy when individual investors wish to sell and sell when investors want to buy. At one time the inventory of securities was kept in a safe, and the stocks, when bought and sold, were literally passed over the counter.

Today, the over-the-counter market is defined as all facilities that provide for any security transactions not conducted on the organized exchanges. These facilities consist of (1) the relatively few *dealers* who hold inventories of over-the-counter securities and who are said to "make a market" in these securities, (2) the thousands of brokers who act as *agents* in bringing these dealers together with investors, and (3) the computers, terminals, and electronic networks that facilitate communications between dealers and brokers. The dealers who make a market in a particular stock continuously post a price at which they are willing to buy the stock (the *bid price*) and a price at which they will sell shares (the *asked price*).

---

[2]The NYSE is actually a modified auction market, wherein people (through their brokers) bid for stocks. Originally — a hundred or so years ago — brokers would literally shout, "I have 100 shares of Union Pacific for sale; how much am I offered?" and then sell to the highest bidder. If a broker had a buy order, he or she would shout, "I want to buy 100 shares of Union Pacific; who'll sell at the best price?" The same general situation still exists, although the exchanges now have members known as *specialists* who facilitate the trading process by keeping an inventory of shares of the stocks in which they specialize. If a buy order comes in at a time when no sell order arrives, the specialist will sell off some inventory. Similarly, if a sell order comes in, the specialist will buy and add to inventory. The specialist sets a *bid price* (the price the specialist will pay for the stock) and an *asked price* (the price at which shares will be sold out of inventory). The bid and asked prices are set at levels designed to keep the inventory in balance. If many buy orders start coming in because of favorable developments, or sell orders because of unfavorable events, the specialist will raise or lower prices to keep supply and demand in balance. Bid prices are somewhat lower than asked prices, with the difference, or *spread*, representing the specialist's profit margin.

It should also be noted that special facilities are available to help institutional investors such as mutual funds or pension funds sell large blocks of stock without depressing their prices. In essence, brokerage houses which cater to institutional clients will purchase blocks (defined as 10,000 or more shares) and then resell the stock to other institutions or individuals. Also, when a firm has a major announcement which is likely to cause its stock price to change sharply, it will ask the exchanges to halt trading in its stock until the announcement has been made and digested by investors. Thus, when Texaco announced that it planned to acquire Getty Oil, trading was halted for one day in both Texaco and Getty stock.

These prices, which are adjusted as supply and demand conditions change, can be read off computer screens all across the country. The spread between bid and asked prices represents the dealer's markup, or profit.

Brokers and dealers who make up the over-the-counter market are members of a self-regulating body known as the *National Association of Security Dealers (NASD)*, which licenses brokers and oversees trading practices. The computerized trading network used by NASD is known as the *NASD Automated Quotation System (NASDAQ),* and the *Wall Street Journal* and other newspapers contain information on NASDAQ transactions. In terms of number of issues, the majority of stocks are traded over-the-counter. However, because the stocks of larger companies arc listed on the exchanges, it is estimated that two-thirds of the dollar volume of stock trading takes place on the exchanges.

Some Trends in Security Trading Procedures.

From the NYSE's inception in the 1800s until the 1970s, the vast majority of all stock trading occurred on the Exchange and was conducted by member firms. The NYSE established a set of minimum brokerage commission rates, and no member firm could charge a commission lower than the set rate—this was a monopoly, pure and simple. However, on May 1, 1975, the Securities and Exchange Commission (SEC), with strong prodding from the Antitrust Division of the Justice Department, forced the NYSE to abandon its fixed commissions. Commission rates declined dramatically, falling in some cases as much as 80 percent from former levels. These changes were a boon to the investing public, but not to the brokerage industry. A number of "full service" brokerage houses went bankrupt, and others were forced to merge with stronger firms. Many Wall Street experts predict that, once the dust settles, the number of brokerage houses will have declined from literally thousands in the 1960s to a much smaller number of large, strong, nationwide companies, all of which are units of diversified financial service corporations. On the other hand, deregulation has spawned a number of small "discount brokers," some of which are affiliated with commercial banks or with savings and loans.

THE COST OF MONEY

Capital in a free economy is allocated through the price system. *The interest rate is the price paid to borrow capital, while in the case of equity capital, investors' returns come in the form of dividends and capital gains.* The factors which affect the supply of and the demand for investment capital, and hence the cost of money, are discussed in this section.

The two most fundamental factors affecting the cost of money are (1) production opportunities and (2) time preferences for consumption. To see how these factors operate, visualize an isolated island community where the people live on fish. They have a stock of fishing gear which permits them to survive reasonably well, but they would like to have more fish. Now suppose Mr. Crusoe had a bright idea for a new type of fishnet that would enable him to double his daily catch. However, it would take him a year to perfect his design, to build his net, and to learn how to use it efficiently, and Mr. Crusoe would probably starve before he could put his new net into operation. Therefore, he might suggest to Ms. Robinson, Mr. Friday, and several others that if they would give him one fish each day for a year, he would return two fish a day during all of the next year. If someone accepted the offer, then the fish which Ms. Robinson or one of the others gave to Mr. Crusoe would constitute *savings*; these savings would be *invested* in the fishnet; and the extra fish the net produced would constitute a *return on the investment*.

Obviously, the more productive Mr. Crusoe thought the new fishnet would be, the higher would be his expected return on the investment and the more he could offer to pay Ms. Robinson, Mr. Friday, or other potential investors for their savings. In this example we assume that Mr. Crusoe thought he would be able to pay, and thus he offered, a 100 percent rate of return — he offered to give back two fish for every one he received. He might have tried to attract savings for less — for example, he might have decided to offer only 1.5 fish next year for every one he received this year, which would represent a 50 percent rate of return to Ms. Robinson and the other potential savers.

How attractive Mr. Crusoe's offer would appear to potential savers would depend in large part on their *time preferences for consumption*. For example, Ms. Robinson might be thinking of retirement, and she might be willing to trade fish today for fish in the future on a one-for-one basis. On the other hand, Mr. Friday might have a wife and several young children and need his current fish, so he might be unwilling to "lend" a fish today for anything less than three fish next year. Mr. Friday would be said to have a high time preference for consumption, and Ms. Robinson a low time preference. Note also that if the whole population were living right at the subsistence level, then time preferences for current consumption would necessarily be high, aggregate savings would be low, interest rates would be high, and capital formation would be difficult.

In a more complex society there are many businesses like Mr. Crusoe's, many goods other than fish, and many savers like Ms. Robinson and Mr. Friday. Further, people use money as a medium of exchange rather than barter with fish. *Still, the interest rate paid to savers depends in a basic way (1) on the rate of return producers expect to earn on invested capital and (2) on consumers'/savers' time preferences for current versus future consumption.* Producers' expected returns on their business investments set an upper limit on how much they can pay for savings, while consumers' time preferences for consumption establish how much consumption they are willing to defer and hence how much they will save at different levels of interest offered by producers.[3]

---

[3]The term "producers" is really too narrow. A better word might be "borrowers," which would include corporations, home purchasers, people borrowing to go to college, or even people borrowing to buy autos or to pay for vacations. Also, the wealth of its society influences people's ability to save and hence their time preferences for current versus future consumption.

INTEREST RATE LEVELS

Capital is allocated among firms by interest rates: Firms with the most profitable investment opportunities are willing and able to pay the most for capital, so they tend to attract it away from inefficient firms or from those whose products are not in demand. Of course, our economy is not completely free in the sense of being influenced only by market forces. Thus, the federal government has agencies which help individuals or groups as stipulated by Congress obtain credit on favorable terms. Among those eligible for this kind of assistance are small businesses, certain minorities, firms willing to build plants in areas with high unemployment, and so on. Still, most capital in the U.S. economy is allocated through the price system.

Figure 3-2 shows how supply and demand interact to determine interest rates in two capital markets. Markets A and B represent two of the many capital markets in existence. The going interest rate, k, is 10 percent for the low-risk securities in Market A. Borrowers whose credit is strong enough to qualify for this market can obtain funds at a cost of 10 percent, and investors who want to put their money to work at low risk can obtain a 10 percent return. Riskier borrowers must obtain higher-cost funds in Market B. Investors who are more willing to take risks invest with the expectation of receiving a 12 percent return but also with the realization that they might receive much less.

If the demand for funds in a market declines, as it typically does during a business recession, the demand curve will shift to the left (or down) as shown by Curve D_2 in Market A. The market-clearing, or equilibrium, interest rate in this example will decline to 8 percent. You can also visualize what would happen if

Figure 3-2
Interest Rates as a Function of the Supply and Demand for Funds

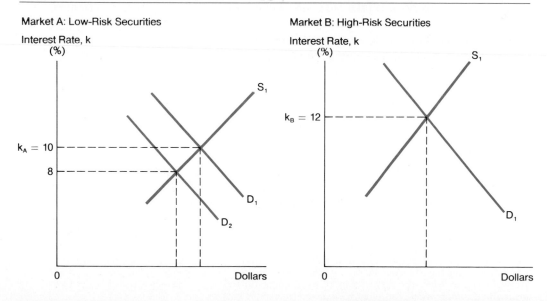

the Federal Reserve tightened credit: The supply curve, S_1, would shift to the left, and this would raise interest rates and lower the current level of borrowing in the economy.

Capital markets are interdependent. For example, assuming that Markets A and B were in equilibrium before the demand shift to D_2 in Market A, then investors were willing to accept the higher risk in Market B in exchange for a *risk premium* of 12% − 10% = 2%. After the shift to D_2, the risk premium would initially increase to 12% − 8% = 4%. In all likelihood, this much larger premium would induce some of the lenders in Market A to shift to Market B; this, in turn, would cause the supply curve in Market A to shift to the left (or up) and that in Market B to shift to the right. This transfer of capital between markets would raise the interest rate in Market A and lower it in Market B, thus bringing the risk premium back closer to the original level, 2 percent.

There are many, many capital markets in the United States. U.S. firms also invest and raise capital throughout the world, while foreigners both borrow and lend capital in the United States. There are markets in the United States for real estate loans; farm loans; business loans; federal, state, and local government loans; and consumer loans. Within each category, there are regional markets as well as different types of submarkets. For example, in real estate there are separate markets for first and second mortgages and for loans on owner-occupied homes, apartments, office buildings, shopping centers, vacant land, and so on. Within the business sector, there are dozens of types of debt and also several sharply differentiated markets for common stocks.

There is a price for each type of capital, and these prices change over time as shifts occur in supply and demand conditions. Figure 3-3 shows how long- and short-term interest rates to business borrowers have varied since the 1950s. Notice that short-term interest rates generally rise during booms and then fall during recessions. (The shaded areas of the chart indicate recessions.) When the economy is expanding, firms need capital, and this demand for capital pushes rates up. Also, inflationary pressures are strongest during business booms, so at such times the Federal Reserve tends to tighten the money supply, which also exerts an upward pressure on rates. Conditions are reversed during recessions — slack business reduces the demand for credit, the Fed increases the money supply, and the result is a drop in interest rates. In addition, inflationary pressures are normally weakest during recessions, and this too helps keep interest rates down.

These tendencies do not hold exactly — the period after 1984 is a case in point. The price of oil decreased dramatically in 1985 and 1986, reducing inflationary pressures on other prices and lowering fears of serious, long-term inflation. Earlier, inflation fears had pushed interest rates to record levels. Thus, from 1983 to 1987, declining concerns about inflation more than offset the normal tendency of interest rates to rise during good economic times, and the net result was lower interest rates.[4]

---

[4]Short-term rates are responsive to current economic conditions, while long-term rates primarily reflect long-run expectations for inflation. As a result, short-term rates are sometimes above and sometimes below long-term rates. The relationship between long-term and short-term rates is called the *term structure of interest rates*. This topic is discussed later in the chapter.

Figure 3-3
Long- and Short-Term Interest Rates, 1953–1987

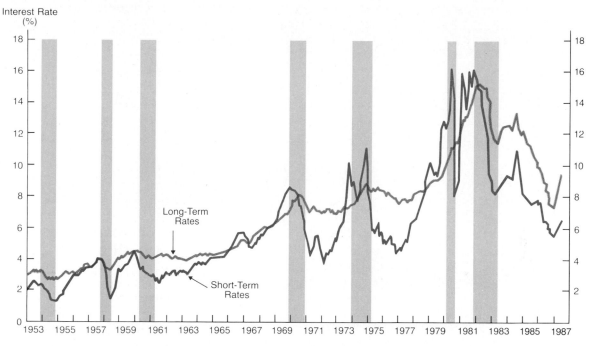

Notes:

a. The shaded areas designate business recessions.

b. Short-term rates are measured by four- to six-month loans to very large, strong corporations, and long-term rates by AAA corporate bonds.

Source: *Federal Reserve Bulletin.*

The relationship between inflation and long-term interest rates is highlighted in Figure 3-4, which plots rates of inflation along with long-term interest rates. Prior to 1965, when the average rate of inflation was about 1.0 percent, interest rates on AAA-rated bonds generally ranged from 4 to 5 percent. As the war in Vietnam accelerated in the mid-1960s, the rate of inflation increased and interest rates began to rise. The rate of inflation dropped after 1970, and so did long-term interest rates. However, the 1973 Arab oil embargo was followed by a quadrupling of oil prices in 1974, which caused a spurt in the price level, which in turn drove interest rates to new record highs in 1974 and 1975. Inflationary pressures eased in late 1975 and 1976 but then rose again after 1976. In 1980 inflation rates hit the highest level on record, and fears of continued double-digit inflation pushed interest rates up to historic highs. From 1981 through 1986, the inflation rate dropped steadily, and in 1986 inflation was only 1.1 percent, the lowest in 25 years. At first, investors' fears of a renewal of double-digit inflation kept long-term interest rates

Figure 3-4
Relationship between Annual Inflation Rates and Long-Term Interest Rates, 1953–1987

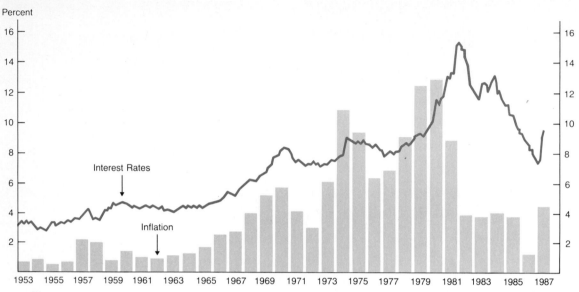

Notes:
a. Interest rates are those on AAA long-term corporate bonds.
b. Inflation is measured as the annual rate of change in the Consumer Price Index (CPI).
Source: *Federal Reserve Bulletin*.

at relatively high levels, but as confidence built that inflation was under control, long-term rates declined. In 1987, prices began to rise again, and renewed fears of inflation pushed interest rates up. Currently (1987), most observers expect prices to increase at a rate of about 4 to 5 percent per year on out into the future, but this expectation could change suddenly and sharply.

THE DETERMINANTS OF MARKET INTEREST RATES

In general, the nominal interest rate on a debt security, k, is composed of a pure rate of interest, k*, plus several premiums which reflect expected inflation, the riskiness of the security, and the security's marketability (or liquidity). This relationship can be expressed as follows:

$$k = k^* + IP + DRP + LP + MRP.$$

Here

$$k = \text{stated, or nominal, rate of interest.}^5$$

$$k^* = \text{pure, or real, rate of interest; pronounced "k-star."}$$

$$IP = \text{inflation premium.}$$

$$DRP = \text{default risk premium.}$$

$$LP = \text{liquidity, or marketability, premium.}$$

$$MRP = \text{maturity risk premium.}$$

We discuss these components, whose sum makes up the stated, or nominal, rate, in the following sections.

The Pure Rate of Interest

The *pure rate of interest, k**, is defined as the interest rate that would exist on a riskless security if no inflation were expected. The pure rate is also called the *real, risk-free rate*, and it may be thought of as the rate of interest on short-term U.S. Treasury securities (which are riskless) in an inflation-free world. The pure rate is not static — it changes over time depending on economic conditions, especially (1) the rate of return corporations and other borrowers can expect to earn on productive assets and (2) people's time preferences for current versus future consumption. Borrowers' expected returns on real asset investment set an upper limit on how much they can afford to pay for borrowed funds, while savers' time preferences for consumption establish how much consumption they are willing to defer and hence the amount of funds they will lend at different levels of interest. It is difficult to measure k* precisely, but most experts think that in the United States it has fluctuated in the range of 2 to 4 percent in recent years.

Inflation Premium

Inflation has a major impact on interest rates because it can erode the purchasing power of the dollar and lower the real rate of return on investments. To illustrate its effects, suppose you saved up $1,000 and invested it in a Treasury bond which matures in 1 year and which pays 5 percent interest. At the end of the year you would receive $1,050 — your original $1,000 plus $50 of interest. Now suppose the rate of inflation during the year was 10 percent, and it affected all items

---

[5]The term *nominal* as it is used here means the *stated* rate as opposed to the *real* rate, which is adjusted for inflation. If you bought a 10-year Treasury bond in March 1987, the stated, or nominal, rate would be about 8 percent, but if inflation averages 4.5 percent over the next 10 years, the real rate would be about 8% − 4.5% = 3.5%. In Chapter 4 we will use the term nominal in yet another way: to distinguish between stated rates and effective annual rates when compounding occurs more frequently than once a year.

equally. If beer had cost $1 per bottle at the beginning of the year, it would cost $1.10 at the end. Therefore, your $1,000 would have bought $1,000/$1 = 1,000 bottles at the beginning of the year but only $1,050/$1.10 = 955 bottles at the end. Thus, in *real terms*, you would be worse off — you would have received $50 of interest, but it would not have been sufficient to offset inflation. You would have been better off having bought and held 1,000 bottles of beer (or some other storable asset such as land, timber, apartment buildings, wheat, or gold) than having bought bonds.

Investors are well aware of all this, so when they lend money they add an *inflation premium (IP)* equal to the expected inflation rate over the life of the security to the rate they would have been willing to accept in the absence of inflation. For a short-term, default-free U.S. Treasury bill, the actual interest rate charged, $k_{\text{T-bill}}$, would be the pure rate, k^*, plus the inflation premium (IP):

$$k_{\text{T-bill}} = k^* + \text{IP}.$$

Therefore, if the pure rate of interest were $k^* = 3\%$, and if inflation were expected to be 4 percent (and hence IP = 4%) over the next year, then the rate of interest on 1-year T-bills would be 7 percent. On June 2, 1987, the expected 1-year inflation rate was about 4.5 percent and the yield on 1-year T-bills was 7.4 percent, which implies that the pure rate on that date was 2.9 percent.

It is important to note that the rate of inflation built into interest rates is the *rate of inflation expected in the future*, not the rate experienced in the past. Thus, the latest reported figures might show an annual inflation rate of 3 percent, but that is for a past period, and if people on the average expect a 6 percent inflation rate in the future, then 6 percent would be built into the current rate of interest. Note also that the inflation rate reflected in the interest rate on any security is the *average rate of inflation expected over the security's life*. Thus, the inflation rate built into a 1-year bond is the expected inflation rate for the next year, but the inflation rate built into a 30-year bond is the average rate of inflation expected over the next 30 years.[6]

Expectations for future inflation are closely related to, although not perfectly correlated with, rates experienced in the recent past. Therefore, if the inflation rate reported for the past few months increased, people would tend to raise their expectations for future inflation, and this change in expectations would cause an increase in interest rates.

---

[6]To be theoretically precise, we should use a *geometric average*. Also, note that since millions of investors are active in the market, it is impossible to determine exactly the consensus expected inflation rate. However, survey data are available which give us a reasonably good idea of what investors expect over the next few years. For example, in 1980 the University of Michigan's Survey Research Center reported that people expected inflation over the next year to be 11.9 percent and that the average rate of inflation expected over the next 5 to 10 years was 10.5 percent. However, the economy cooled in 1981 and 1982, and, as Figure 3-4 showed, actual inflation dropped sharply after 1980, which resulted in gradual reductions in the *expected future* inflation rate. In 1987, as we write this, the expected future inflation rate is about 5 percent. As inflationary expectations change, so does the market rate of interest.

Default Risk Premium

The risk that a borrower will *default* on a loan, which means that the borrower does not pay the interest or pay off the principal, also affects the market interest rate on a security: the greater the default risk, the higher the interest rate lenders must charge. Treasury securities have no default risk, and hence they carry the lowest interest rates on taxable securities in the United States. For corporate bonds, the higher the bond's rating, the lower its default risk, and, consequently, the lower its interest rate.[7] Here are some representative interest rates on long-term bonds during two months in 1987:

	February	June
U.S. Treasury	7.8%	8.6%
AAA	8.7	9.5
AA	9.2	9.8
A	9.5	10.1
BBB	10.1	10.6

The difference between the interest rate on a T-bond and that on a corporate bond *with similar maturity, liquidity, and other features* is defined as the *default risk premium (DRP)*. Therefore, if the bonds listed above were otherwise similar, the default risk premium in February would be DRP = 8.7% − 7.8% = 0.9 percentage points for AAA corporate bonds, 1.4 percentage points for AA, 1.7 percentage points for A corporate bonds, and 2.3 percentage points for BBB. Default risk premiums vary somewhat over time, but the February 1987 figures are representative of levels in recent years.

Liquidity (or Marketability) Premium

A *liquid asset* is one that can be sold (at a "fair" price) and thus converted to spendable cash on short notice. Active markets, which provide liquidity, exist for government bonds, for the stocks and bonds of the larger corporations, and for the securities of certain financial intermediaries. If a security is *not* liquid, investors will add a *liquidity premium (LP)* when they establish the market interest rate on the security. It is very difficult to measure liquidity premiums, but a differential of at least one and probably two percentage points exists between the least liquid and the most liquid financial assets of similar default risk and maturity.

Maturity Risk Premium

U.S. Treasury securities are free of default risk in the sense that one can be virtually certain that the federal government will pay interest on its bonds and also pay them off when they mature. Therefore, the default risk premium on Treasury se-

---

[7]Bond ratings, and bonds' riskiness in general, will be discussed in Chapter 15. For now, merely note that bonds rated AAA are judged to have less default risk than bonds rated AA, AA bonds are less risky than A bonds, and so on.

curities is essentially zero. Further, active markets exist for Treasury securities, so their liquidity premiums are also close to zero. Thus, as a first approximation, the rate of interest on a Treasury bond should be equal to the pure rate, k*, plus the inflation premium, IP. However, an adjustment is needed. The prices of long-term bonds decline whenever interest rates rise, and since interest rates can and do rise, all long-term bonds, even Treasury bonds, have an element of risk called *interest rate risk*. As a general rule, the bonds of any organization, from the U.S. government to USX Corporation (formerly US Steel), have more interest rate risk as the maturity of the bond increases.[8] Therefore, a *maturity risk premium (MRP)*, which is higher the longer the years to maturity, must be included in the required interest rate.

The effect of maturity risk premiums is to raise interest rates on long-term bonds relative to those on short-term bonds. This premium, like the others, is extremely difficult to measure, but (1) it seems to vary over time, rising when interest rates are more volatile and uncertain and falling when they are more stable, and (2) in recent years, the maturity risk premium on 30-year T-bonds appears to have generally been in the range of one to two percentage points.[9]

We should mention that while long-term bonds are exposed to interest rate risk, short-term bonds are exposed to *reinvestment rate risk*. When short-term bonds mature and the funds are reinvested, or "rolled over," a decline in interest rates would require reinvestment at a lower rate and, hence, a decline in interest income. To illustrate, suppose you had $100,000, invested it in 1-year T-bonds, and lived on the income. In 1981, short-term rates were about 15 percent, so your income would have been about $15,000. However, your income would have declined to about $9,000 by 1983, and to only $5,500 by 1987. Had you invested your money in long-term bonds, your income (but not the value of your principal) would have been stable. Thus, although the principal is preserved, the interest income provided by short-term bonds varies from year to year, depending on reinvestment rates.

THE TERM STRUCTURE OF INTEREST RATES

A study of Figure 3-3 above reveals that at certain times, such as 1986, short-term interest rates are lower than long-term rates, while at other times, such as 1979 and 1980, short rates are above long rates. The relationship between long and short rates is known as the *term structure of interest rates,* and it is important to corporate treasurers, who must decide whether to borrow by issuing long- or

---

[8]For example, if you had bought a 30-year Treasury bond for $1,000 in 1972, when the long-term interest rate was 7 percent, and held it until 1981, when long-term T-bond rates were about 14.5 percent, the value of your bond would have declined to about $513. That would represent a loss of almost half your money, and it demonstrates that long-term bonds, even U.S. Treasury bonds, are far from riskless. Had you invested in short-term bills in 1972 and subsequently reinvested your principal each time the bills matured, you would have still had $1,000 in 1981. This point will be discussed in detail in Chapter 5.

[9]The MRP has averaged 1.7 percentage points over the last 61 years. See *Stocks, Bonds, Bills, and Inflation 1987 Yearbook* (Chicago: Ibbotson Associates, 1987).

short-term debt. The term structure is also important to investors, who must decide whether to buy long- or short-term bonds. Thus, it is important that you understand (1) how long- and short-term rates are related to each other and (2) what causes shifts in their relative positions.

To begin, we can look up in a source such as the *Wall Street Journal* or the *Federal Reserve Bulletin* the interest rates on bonds of various maturities at a given point in time. For example, Figure 3-5 presents interest rates for Treasury issues of different maturities on two dates. The set of data for a given date, when plotted on a graph such as that in Figure 3-5, is defined as the *yield curve* for that date. Thus, a yield curve is a graphic representation of the term structure of interest

Figure 3-5
U.S. Treasury Bond Interest Rates on Different Dates

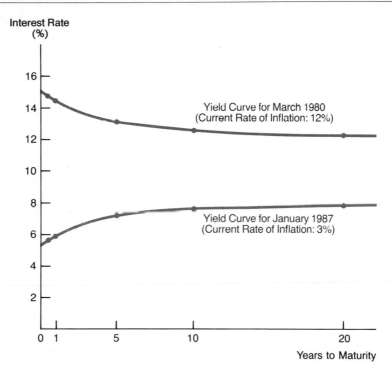

Term to Maturity	Interest Rate	
	March 1980	January 1987
6 months	15.0%	5.8%
1 year	14.0	6.0
5 years	13.5	6.8
10 years	12.8	7.1
20 years	12.5	7.6

Note: The curves are smoothed, so the points are not plotted exactly.

rates at a particular point in time. The yield curve changes both in position and in shape over time as interest rates rise and fall. In March of 1980, all rates were relatively high, and short-term rates were higher than long-term rates, so the yield curve on that date was high up on the graph and was *downward sloping*. However, in January of 1987, all rates had fallen, and short-term rates were lower than long-term rates, so the yield curve at that time was both lower on the graph and *upward sloping*. Had we drawn the yield curve during January of 1982, it would have been essentially horizontal, for long-term and short-term bonds on that date had about the same rate of interest. (See Figure 3-3.)

Figure 3-5 shows yield curves for U.S. Treasury securities, but we could have constructed curves for corporate bonds — for example, we could have developed yield curves for IBM, General Motors, Eastern Air Lines, or any other company that borrows money over a range of maturities. Had we constructed such curves and plotted them on Figure 3-5, the corporate yield curves would have been above those for Treasury securities on the same date because of the addition of default risk premiums, but they would have had the same general shape as the Treasury curves. Also, the more risky the corporation, the higher its yield curve; thus, Eastern, which was on the verge of bankruptcy prior to its being acquired by Texas Air in 1987, would have had a yield curve significantly higher than that of IBM, which is an extremely strong company.

In a stable economy such as we had in the 1950s and early 1960s, when (1) inflation fluctuated in the 1 to 3 percent range, (2) the expected future rate of inflation was about equal to the current rate, and (3) the Federal Reserve did not actively intervene in the markets, all interest rates were relatively low, and the yield curve generally had a slight upward slope to reflect maturity effects. People often define such an upward-sloping yield curve as being a *normal yield curve*, and a yield curve which slopes downward as being an *inverted*, or *abnormal, yield curve*. Thus, in Figure 3-5, the yield curve for March 1980 was inverted, but that for January 1987 was normal. We shall see in the next section why an upward slope is considered "normal."

Term Structure Theories

Several theories have been used to explain the shape of the yield curve. The three major ones are (1) the market segmentation theory, (2) the liquidity preference theory, and (3) the expectations theory.

Market Segmentation Theory

Briefly, the *market segmentation theory* states that each lender and each borrower has a preferred maturity. For example, a person borrowing to buy a long-term asset like a house, or an electric utility company borrowing to build a power plant, would want a long-term loan. However, a retailer borrowing in September to build its inventory for Christmas would prefer a short-term loan. Similar differences exist among savers, and a person saving up to take a vacation next summer would want to lend in the short-term market, but someone saving for retirement 20 years hence should probably buy long-term securities.

The thrust of the market segmentation theory is that the slope of the yield curve depends on relative supply/demand conditions in the long-term and short-term markets. Thus, according to this theory, the yield curve could at any given time be either upward sloping or downward sloping: An upward-sloping curve would occur when there was a large supply of funds relative to demand in the short-term market but a relative shortage of funds in the long-term market, while a downward-sloping curve would indicate relatively strong demand in the short-term market compared to that in the long-term market.

Liquidity Preference Theory

The *liquidity preference theory* states that long-term bonds normally yield more than short-term bonds for two reasons: (1) Investors generally prefer to hold short-term securities, because such securities are more liquid in the sense that they can be converted to cash with little danger of loss of principal. Investors will, therefore, insist on higher yields on long-term securities. (2) At the same time, borrowers react in exactly the opposite way — borrowers generally dislike short-term debt because such debt exposes them to the risk of having to repay the debt under adverse conditions. Accordingly, borrowers are willing to pay a higher rate, other things held constant, for long-term funds than for short-term funds. Taken together, these two sets of preferences — and hence the liquidity preference theory — imply that under normal conditions the maturity risk premium is positive and increases with maturity, and hence that the yield curve should be upward sloping.

Expectations Theory

The *expectations theory* states that the yield curve depends on expectations about future inflation rates. Specifically, k_t, the nominal interest rate on a U.S. Treasury bond that matures in t years, is assumed to be determined as follows:

$$k_t = k^* + IP_t.$$

Here k^* is the real, default-free interest rate (pure rate), IP_t is an inflation premium which is equal to the average rate of inflation over the t years before the bond matures, and the maturity risk premium (MRP) is assumed to be zero.

To illustrate, suppose that in late December 1987 the pure rate of interest was $k^* = 3\%$, and the expected inflation rates for each of the next 3 years were as follows:[10]

	Expected Annual (1-Year) Inflation Rate	Expected Average Inflation Rate over the Indicated Period
1988	4%	4%/1 = 4.0%
1989	6%	(4% + 6%)/2 = 5.0%
1990	8%	(4% + 6% + 8%)/3 = 6.0%

---

[10]Technically, we should be using geometric averages rather than arithmetic averages, but the differences are not material in this example. For a discussion of this point, see Robert C. Radcliffe, *Investment: Concepts, Analysis, and Strategy,* 2nd ed. (Glenview, Ill.: Scott, Foresman, 1987), Chapter 6.

Given these expectations, the following pattern of interest rates should exist:

	Real Rate (k*)		Inflation Premium, Which Is Equal to the Expected Average Inflation Rate (IP$_t$)		Treasury Bond Rate (k$_{T-bond}$)
1-year bond	3%	+	4.0%	=	7.0%
2-year bond	3%	+	5.0%	=	8.0%
3-year bond	3%	+	6.0%	=	9.0%

Had the pattern of expected inflation rates been reversed, with inflation expected to fall from 8 percent to 6 percent and then to 4 percent, the following situation would have existed:

	Real Rate		Average Inflation Rate		Treasury Bond Rate
1-year bond	3%	+	8.0%	=	11.0%
2-year bond	3%	+	7.0%	=	10.0%
3-year bond	3%	+	6.0%	=	9.0%

If these rates were plotted as yield curves, then as you can see from the above tables, according to the expectations theory, whenever the annual rate of inflation is expected to decline, the yield curve must be downward sloping, while it must be upward sloping if inflation is expected to increase.

Various tests of the three theories have been conducted, and these tests indicate that all of the theories have some validity. Thus, the shape of the yield curve at any given time is affected (1) by supply-demand conditions in long- and short-term markets, (2) by liquidity preferences, and (3) by expectations about future inflation. One factor may dominate at one time, another at another time, but they all affect the structure of interest rates.

OTHER FACTORS THAT INFLUENCE INTEREST RATE LEVELS

In addition to inflationary expectations, liquidity preferences, and normal supply-demand fluctuations, other factors also influence the general level of interest rates and the shape of the yield curve. The three most important ones are (1) Federal Reserve policy, (2) the level of the federal budget deficit, and (3) the level of business activity.

Federal Reserve Policy

As you probably learned in your economics courses, (1) the money supply has a major effect on both the level of economic activity and the rate of inflation, and (2) in the United States the Federal Reserve System controls the money supply. If the Fed wants to stimulate the economy, it increases growth in the money supply. The initial effect of such action is to cause interest rates to decline, but the action may also lead to an increase in the expected rate of inflation, which in turn could push interest rates up. The reverse holds if the Fed tightens the money supply.

To illustrate, in 1981 inflation was quite high, so the Fed tightened up the money supply. The Fed deals primarily in the short-term end of the market, so this tightening had the direct effect of pushing short-term interest rates up sharply. At the same time, the very fact that the Fed was taking strong action to reduce inflation led to a decline in expectations for long-run inflation, which led to a drop in long-term bond yields. Short-term rates decreased shortly thereafter.

During periods when the Fed is actively intervening in the markets, the yield curve will be distorted. Short-term rates will be temporarily "too high" if the Fed is tightening credit or "too low" if it is easing credit. Long-term rates are not affected as much by Fed intervention, except to the extent that such intervention affects expectations for long-term inflation.

Federal Deficits

If the federal government spends more than it takes in from tax revenues, it runs a deficit, and that deficit must be covered either by borrowing or by "printing money." If the government finances the deficit by borrowing, this added demand for funds pushes up interest rates. If it prints money, that increases expectations for future inflation, which also drives up interest rates. Thus, the larger the federal deficit, other things held constant, the higher the level of interest rates. Whether long- or short-term rates are affected more depends on how the deficit is financed, so we cannot state, in general, how deficits will affect the slope of the yield curve.

Business Cycles

Figure 3-3, presented earlier, can be examined to see how business conditions influence interest rates. Here are the key points revealed by the graph:

1. Because inflation has generally been increasing since 1953, the general tendency has been toward higher interest rates.

2. Until 1966, short-term rates were almost always below long-term rates. Thus, in those years the yield curve was almost always "normal" in the sense that it was upward sloping, as the liquidity preference theory suggests it should be if inflation rates are stable.

3. The shaded areas in the graph represent recessions. During such times the demand for money falls, and, at the same time, the Federal Reserve tends to increase the money supply in an effort to stimulate the economy. As a result, there is a tendency for interest rates to decline during recessions.

4. During recessions short-term rates experience sharper declines than long-term rates. This occurs because (1) the Fed operates mainly in the short-term sector and hence its intervention has a major effect here and (2) long-term rates reflect the average expected inflation rate over the next 20 to 30 years, and this expectation generally does not change much just because the current rate of inflation is low as a result of a recession.

INTEREST RATE LEVELS AND STOCK PRICES

Interest rates have two effects on corporate profits: (1) Interest is a cost, so the higher the rate of interest, the lower are corporate profits, other things held constant, and (2) interest rates affect the level of economic activity, and corporate profits are affected by economic activity. Interest rates obviously affect stock prices because of their effects on profits but, perhaps even more important, they have an effect due to competition in the marketplace between stocks and bonds. If interest rates rise sharply, investors can get a higher return on their money in the bond market, and these high bond yields induce them to sell stocks and to transfer funds to the bond market. Such transfers in response to rising interest rates depress stock prices. Of course, the reverse occurs if interest rates decline. Indeed, the bull market of 1985–1987, when the Dow Jones Industrial Index rose by about 1,000 points, was due almost entirely to the sharp drop in long-term interest rates.

The experience of Commonwealth Edison, the electric utility serving the Chicago area, can be used to illustrate the effects of interest rates on stock prices. In 1984 Commonwealth's stock sold for $21 per share, and since the company paid a $3 dividend, the dividend yield was $3/$21 = 14.3%. Commonwealth's bonds at that time also yielded about 14.3 percent, so if someone had $100,000 and invested it in either the stock or the bonds, his or her annual income would have been about $14,300. (They might also have expected the dividend and the stock price to grow over time, providing some capital gains, but that point is not relevant to this example.)

By early 1987, all interest rates were much lower, and Commonwealth's bonds were yielding only 9 percent. If the stock still yielded 14.3 percent, investors could switch $100,000 out of the bonds and into the stock, and in the process increase their annual income from $9,000 to $14,300. Many people did exactly that — as bond yields dropped, orders poured in for the stock, and its price was bid up. In January 1987, Commonwealth's stock sold for $35, up over 65 percent from the 1984 level, and the dividend yield (8.6%) was very close to the bond yield (9.0%).

INTEREST RATES AND BUSINESS DECISIONS

The yield curve for January 1987, shown earlier in Figure 3-5, indicates how much the U.S. government had to pay at that time to borrow money for 1 year, 5 years, 10 years, and so on. A business borrower would have had to pay somewhat more, but assume for the moment that we are back in January 1987 and that the yield curve at that time also applies to your company. Now suppose your company has decided (1) to build a new plant with a 20-year life which will cost $1 million and (2) to raise the $1 million by selling an issue of debt (or borrowing) rather than by selling stock. If you borrowed in January 1987 on a short-term basis—say, for one year—your interest cost for that year would be only 6.0 percent, or $60,000, while if you used long-term (20-year) financing, your cost would be 7.6 percent, or $76,000. Therefore, at first glance it would seem that you should have used short-term debt.

However, this might prove to be a horrible mistake. If you use short-term debt, you will have to renew your loan every year, and the rate charged on each new loan will reflect the then-existing short-term rate. Interest rates could return to their March 1980 levels, so by 1989 you could be paying 14 percent, or $140,000, per year. These high interest payments would cut into and perhaps eliminate your profits. Your reduced profitability could easily increase your firm's risk to the point where your bond rating would be lowered, causing lenders to increase the risk premium built into the interest rate they charge you, which in turn would force you to pay even higher rates. These very high interest rates would further reduce your profitability, worry lenders even more, and make them still more reluctant to renew your loan. If your lenders refused to renew the loan and demanded payments, as they have every right to do, you would have trouble raising the cash. If you had to make price cuts to convert inventories to cash, you might incur heavy operating losses, or even bankruptcy.

On the other hand, if you used long-term financing in January 1987, your interest costs would remain constant at $76,000 per year, so an increase in interest rates in the economy would not hurt you. You might even be able to buy up some of your bankrupted competitors at bargain prices—bankruptcies increase dramatically when interest rates rise, primarily because many firms do use short-term debt.

Does all this suggest that firms should always avoid short-term debt? Not necessarily. If inflationary expectations decrease further over the next few years, then so will interest rates. If you had borrowed on a long-term basis for 7.6 percent in January 1987, then your company would be at a major disadvantage if its debt were locked in at 7.6 percent while its competitors (who used short-term debt and thus rode interest rates down in subsequent years) had a borrowing cost of only 4 or 5 percent. On the other hand, large federal deficits might drive inflation and interest rates up to new record levels. In that case, you would wish you had borrowed on a long-term basis in 1987.

Financing decisions would be easy if we could develop accurate forecasts of future interest rates. Unfortunately, predicting future interest rates with consistent accuracy is somewhere between difficult and impossible—people who make a living by selling interest rate forecasts say it is difficult, but many others say it is impossible.

Even if it is difficult to predict future interest rates, it is easy to predict that interest rates will *fluctuate*—they always have, and they always will. This being the case, sound financial policy calls for using a mix of long- and short-term debt, as well as equity, in such a manner that the firm can survive in most interest rate environments. Further, the optimal financial policy depends in an important way on the nature of the firm's assets — the easier it is to sell off assets and thus to pay off debts, the more feasible it is to use large amounts of short-term debt. This makes it more feasible to finance current assets than fixed assets with short-term debt. We will return to this issue later in the book, when we discuss working capital management.

SUMMARY

In this chapter we discussed the nature of financial markets, the types of institutions that operate in these markets, how interest rates are determined, and some of the ways in which interest rates affect business decisions.

The *pure interest rate, k*,* is determined (1) by the *returns on investment available to producers* and (2) by *savers' time preferences* for current consumption as opposed to saving for future consumption. To establish the nominal interest rate for a given security, k, we must add to the pure rate an *inflation premium (IP)* which reflects expected inflation over the life of the security, a *default risk premium (DRP)* which reflects the default risk inherent in the security, a *liquidity premium (LP),* and a *maturity risk premium (MRP):*

$$k = k^* + IP + DRP + LP + MRP.$$

If the pure interest rate and the four premiums were constant over time, then interest rates in the economy would be stable. However, both the pure rate and the various premiums — especially the premium for expected inflation — do change over time, causing changes in market interest rates. Also, random events such as Federal Reserve intervention to increase or decrease the money supply and international currency flows can lead to random fluctuations in market rates. With so many forces at work, it is extremely difficult to predict future interest rates.

The *term structure* of interest rates, or the *yield curve,* describes the relationship between long- and short-term interest rates. When inflation is expected to continue at the current rate, the yield curve tends to slope upward because of the maturity risk premium; such a curve is called "normal." However, if current inflation is high, but future inflation is expected to be lower, then the yield curve will be "abnormal" or "inverted," and it will slope down. This latter situation existed often during the high inflation era of the late 1970s and early 1980s.

Interest rate levels have a profound effect on stock prices. Higher interest rates produce (1) a depressing effect on the economy, which hurts corporate profits, (2) higher interest expenses, which also lower corporate income, and (3) more competition from the bond market. All of these factors tend to depress stock prices.

Finally, interest rate levels have a significant influence on corporate financial policy. Since interest rate levels are difficult if not impossible to predict, sound financial policy calls for using a mix of short- and long-term debt and for positioning the firm to survive in any future interest rate environment.

Questions

3-1 Define each of the following terms:

    a. Money market; capital market

    b. Primary market; secondary market

    c. Investment banker; financial service corporation

    d. Financial intermediary

    e. Mutual fund; money market fund

    f. Organized security exchanges; over-the-counter market

    g. Production opportunities; time preferences for consumption

    h. Pure rate of interest (k^*); real risk-free rate of interest

    i. Inflation premium (IP)

    j. Default risk premium (DRP)

    k. Liquidity; liquid asset; liquidity premium (LP)

    l. Interest rate risk; maturity risk premium (MRP)

    m. Reinvestment rate risk

    n. Term structure of interest rates; yield curve

    o. "Normal" yield curve; inverted yield curve

3-2 What are financial intermediaries, and what economic functions do they perform?

3-3 Suppose interest rates on residential mortgages of equal risk were 8 percent in California and 10 percent in New York. Could this differential persist? What forces might tend to equalize rates? Would differentials in borrowing costs for businesses of equal risk located in California and New York be more or less likely to exist than differentials in residential mortgage rates? Would differentials in the cost of money for New York and California firms be more likely to exist if the firms being compared were very large or if they were very small? What are the implications of all this for the pressure now being put on Congress to permit banks to engage in nationwide branching?

3-4 What would happen to the standard of living in the United States if people lost faith in the safety of our financial institutions? Why?

3-5 How does a cost-efficient capital market help to reduce the prices of goods and services?

3-6 Which fluctuate more, long-term or short-term interest rates? Why?

3-7 Suppose you feel that the economy is just entering a recession. Your firm must raise capital immediately, and debt will be used. Should you borrow on a long-term or a short-term basis?

3-8 Suppose the population of Area A is relatively young while that of Area B is relatively old, but everything else about the two areas is equal.

    a. Would interest rates likely be the same or different in the two areas? Explain.

    b. Would a trend toward nationwide branching by banks and S&Ls, and the development of nationwide diversified financial corporations, affect your answer to Part a?

3-9 Suppose a new process was developed which could be used to make oil out of seawater. The equipment required was quite expensive but it would, in time, lead to very low prices for gasoline, electricity, and other types of energy. What effect would this have on interest rates?

3-10 Suppose a new and much more liberal Congress and administration were elected, and their first order of business was to take away the independence of the Federal Reserve System and to force the Fed to expand greatly the money supply. What effect would this have

   a. On the level and slope of the yield curve immediately after the announcement?

   b. On the level and slope of the yield curve that would probably exist two or three years in the future?

3-11 It is a fact that the federal government (1) encouraged the development of the S&L industry; (2) virtually forced the industry to make long-term, fixed interest rate mortgages; and (3) also forced the S&Ls to obtain most of their capital as deposits that were withdrawable on demand.

   a. Would S&Ls be better off in a world with a "normal" or an inverted yield curve?

   b. If federal actions such as deficit spending and expansion of the money supply produced a sharp increase in inflation, why might a federal "bailout" of the S&L industry be necessary?

3-12 Suppose interest rates on Treasury bonds rose from 10 to 15 percent. Other things held constant, what do you think would happen to the price of an average company's common stock?

Self-Test Problem

ST-1 (Inflation rates) Assume that it is now January 1, 1988. The rate of inflation is expected to be 4 percent throughout 1988. However, increased government deficits and renewed vigor in the economy are then expected to push inflation rates higher. Investors expect the inflation rate to be 5 percent in 1989, 6 percent in 1990, and 7 percent in 1991. The pure rate, k^*, is currently 3 percent. Assume that no maturity risk premiums are required on bonds with 5 years or less to maturity. The current interest rate on 5-year T-bonds is 9 percent.

   a. What is the expected arithmetic average inflation rate over the next 4 years?

   b. What should be the prevailing interest rate on 4-year T-bonds?

   c. What is the implied expected inflation rate in 1992, or Year 5?

Problems

3-1 (Yield curves) Suppose you and most other investors expect the rate of inflation to be 8 percent next year, to fall to 6 percent during the following year, and then to run at a rate of 4 percent thereafter. Assume that the pure rate, k^*, is 2 percent and that maturity risk premiums on Treasury securities rise from zero on very short-term bonds (those that mature in a few days) by 0.2 percentage points for each year to maturity up to a limit of 1.0 percentage points on 5-year or longer-term T-bonds.

   a. Calculate the interest rate on 1-, 2-, 3-, 4-, 5-, 10-, and 20-year Treasury securities, and plot the yield curve.

   b. Now suppose IBM, an AAA-rated company, had bonds with the same maturities as the Treasury bonds. As an approximation, plot an IBM yield curve on the same graph with the Treasury bond yield curve. (Hint: Think about the default risk premium on IBM's long-term versus its short-term bonds.)

c. Now plot the approximate yield curve of a firm such as LTV Corporation, which has serious financial problems.

3-2 **(Yield curves)** The following yields on U.S. Treasury securities were taken from the *Wall Street Journal* of January 29, 1987:

Term	Rate
6 months	5.6%
1 year	5.9
2 years	6.2
3 years	6.4
4 years	6.6
5 years	6.7
10 years	7.1
20 years	7.6
30 years	7.7

Plot a yield curve based on these data. (Note: If you looked the data up in the *Journal*, you would find that some of the bonds — for example, the 3 percent issue which matures in February 1995 — will show very low yields. These are "flower bonds," which are generally owned by older people and are associated with funerals because they can be turned in and used at par value to pay estate taxes. Thus, flower bonds always sell at close to par and have a yield which is close to the coupon yield, irrespective of the "going rate of interest." Also, the yields quoted in the *Journal* are not for the same point in time for all bonds, so random variations will appear. An interest rate series that is purged of flower bonds and random variations, and hence provides a better picture of the true yield curve, is known as the "constant maturity series"; this series can be obtained from the *Federal Reserve Bulletin.*)

3-3 **(Expected rate of interest)** Suppose the annual yield on a 2-year bond is 10.5 percent while that on a 1-year bond of comparable risk is 9 percent. Using the expectations theory, forecast the interest rate on a 1-year bond during the second year.

3-4 **(Expected rate of interest)** Assume that the real rate is 3 percent and that the maturity risk premium is zero. If the nominal rate of interest on 1-year bonds is 11 percent and that on 2-year bonds is 13 percent, what inflation rate is expected during Year 2? What is the 1-year interest rate that is expected for Year 2? Comment on why the average rate over the 2-year period differs from the 1-year rate expected for Year 2.

3-5 **(Inflation and interest rates)** In late 1980 the U.S. Commerce Department released new figures which showed that inflation was running at an annual rate of close to 15 percent. However, many investors expected the new Reagan administration to be more effective in controlling inflation than the Carter administration had been. At the time the prime rate of interest was 21 percent, a record high. However, many observers felt that the extremely high interest rates and generally tight credit, which were brought on by the Federal Reserve System's attempts to curb the inflation rate, would shortly bring about a recession, which in turn would lead to a decline in the inflation rate and also in the rate of interest. Assume that at the beginning of 1981 the expected rate of inflation for 1981 was 12 percent; for 1982, 10 percent; for 1983, 8 percent; and for 1984 and thereafter, 6 percent.

a. What was the average expected inflation rate over the 5-year period 1981–1985?

b. What average *nominal* interest rate would, over the 5-year period, be expected to produce a 2 percent real rate of return?

c. Assuming a pure rate of 2 percent and a maturity risk premium which starts at 0.1 percent and increases by 0.1 percent each year, estimate the interest rate in January 1981 on bonds that mature in 1, 2, 5, 10, and 20 years, and draw a yield curve based on these data.

d. Describe the general economic conditions that could be expected to produce an upward-sloping curve.

e. If the consensus view of investors in early 1981 had been that the expected rate of inflation for every future year was 10 percent — that is, $I_t = I_{t+1} = 10\%$ for $t = 1$ to ∞ — what do you think the yield curve would have looked like? Consider all the factors that are likely to affect the curve. Does your answer here make you question the yield curve you drew in Part c?

Solution to Self-Test Problem

ST-1

a. Average inflation rate $= (4\% + 5\% + 6\% + 7\%)/4 = 22\%/4 = 5.5\% = IP$.

b. $k_{\text{T-bond}} = k^* + IP + MRP = 3.0\% + 5.5\% + 0\% = 8.5\%$.

c. If the 5-year T-bond rate is 9 percent, then the inflation rate is expected to average approximately $9\% - 3\% = 6\%$ over the next 5 years. Thus, the Year 5 implied inflation rate is 8.0 percent:

$$6\% = (4\% + 5\% + 6\% + 7\% + IP_5)/5$$

$$30\% = 22\% + IP_5$$

$$IP_5 = 8\%.$$

Selected Additional References

Two of the most widely used textbooks on interest rates and financial markets are

Robinson, Ronald I., and Dwayne Wrightsman, *Financial Markets: The Accumulation and Allocation of Wealth* (New York: McGraw-Hill, 1980).

Van Horne, James C., *Financial Market Rates and Flows* (Englewood Cliffs, N. J.: Prentice-Hall, 1984).

For current empirical data and a forecast of monetary conditions, see the most recent edition of this annual publication:

Salomon Brothers, *Supply and Demand for Credit* (New York).

The classic works on term structure theories include the following:

Culbertson, John M., "The Term Structure of Interest Rates," *Quarterly Journal of Economics,* November 1957, 489–504.

Fisher, Irving, "Appreciation and Interest," *Publications of the American Economic Association,* August 1896, 23–29 and 91–92.

Hicks, J. R., *Value and Capital* (London: Oxford University Press, 1946).

Lutz, F. A., "The Structure of Interest Rates," *Quarterly Journal of Economics,* November 1940, 36–63.

Modigliani, Franco, and Richard Sutch, "Innovations in Interest Rate Policy," *American Economic Review,* May 1966, 178–197.

For additional information on financial institutions, see

Campbell, Tim S., *Financial Institutions, Markets, and Economic Activity* (New York: McGraw-Hill, 1982).

Gup, Benton E., *The Management of Financial Institutions* (Boston: Houghton Mifflin, 1984).

Kaufman, George G., *The U.S. Financial System: Money, Markets, and Institutions* (Englewood Cliffs, N. J.: Prentice-Hall, 1983).

Kidwell, David S., and Richard L. Peterson, *Financial Institutions, Markets, and Money* (Hinsdale, Ill.: Dryden Press, 1987).

Mishkin, Frederic S., *Money, Banking, and Financial Markets* (Boston: Little, Brown, 1986).

Valuation and the Cost of Capital

4

Discounted Cash Flow Analysis

AT&T's pension fund managers were recently offered the opportunity to buy Bank of America (B of A) bonds which cost $680.58 per bond, will pay *zero* interest during their lifetime, but will pay $1,000 when they mature after five years, in 1992. At the same time, AT&T's fund managers were offered "regular" B of A bonds which cost $1,000, pay interest of $87.50 per year, and then will return the $1,000 purchase price at maturity in 1992. Which is a better buy, the zero coupon bonds or the "regular" bonds?

A father, concerned about the rapidly rising cost of a college education, is planning a savings program to put his daughter through college. She is 13 years old, plans to enroll at the university 5 years from now, and should take 4 years to complete her education. Currently, the cost per year (for everything — food, clothing, tuition, books, transportation, and so forth) is $9,000, but a 10 percent inflation rate in these costs is forecasted. The daughter recently received $15,000 from her grandfather's estate; this money is invested in a bank account which pays 8 percent interest, compounded annually. In addition to the $15,000, how much will the father have to save each year between now and the time his daughter starts college in order to put her through school?

Suppose that in January 1988, General Motors' engineers informed top management that they had just made a breakthrough which would permit them to produce an electric auto capable of operating at an energy cost of about 3 cents per mile versus an energy cost of about 5 cents for a comparable gasoline-powered car. If GM were to produce the electric car, the company should be able to regain its market share previously lost to the Japanese. However, the investment required to complete development of the new batteries, design the new car, and tool up for production would amount to $5 billion per year for 5 years, starting immediately. Cash flows from the $25 billion investment should amount to $3 billion per year for 15 years, starting 5 years from now, or $45 billion in total. Assuming these cost and cash flow estimates are correct (and they are obviously subject to more forecasting errors than if GM simply bought $25 billion of Treasury bonds), should management give the go-ahead for full-scale electric car production?

These are a few of the many different kinds of questions that can only be answered after an analysis based on the concepts set forth in this chapter.

In Chapter 1 we saw that the primary goal of management is to maximize the value of a firm's stock. We also saw that stock values depend, in part, on the timing of the cash flows investors expect to receive — a dollar expected soon is worth more than a dollar expected in the distant future. Therefore, it is essential that a financial manager have a clear understanding of discounted cash flow analysis and its impact on the value of the firm. These concepts are extended and made more precise in this chapter, where we show how the timing of cash flows affects asset values and rates of return.

The principles of discounted cash flow analysis as developed here also have many other applications, ranging from setting up schedules for paying off loans to making decisions about whether to acquire new equipment — *in fact, of all the techniques used in finance, none is more important than discounted cash flow (DCF) analysis.* Since this concept is used throughout the remainder of the book, it is vital that you understand the material in this chapter thoroughly before going on to other topics.[1]

FUTURE VALUE

A dollar in hand today is worth more than a dollar to be received next year because, if you had it now, you could invest it, earn interest, and end up next year with more than one dollar. To illustrate the process of finding future values, or *compounding,* suppose you had $100 which you deposited in a bank savings account that paid 5 percent interest compounded annually. How much would you have at the end of 1 year? Let us define terms as follows:

PV = $100 = present value of your account, or the beginning amount.

k = 5% = interest rate the bank pays you. Expressed as a decimal, k = 0.05. On financial calculators, the symbol i is frequently used rather than k.

I = dollars of interest you earn during the year = PV(k).

---

[1]This chapter is written on the assumption that students have financial calculators: In today's world, it is mandatory that a student obtains a financial calculator and learns how to use it, for calculators — and not clumsy, rounded, and incomplete tables — are used exclusively in well-run, efficient businesses.

Even though financial calculators are efficient, they do pose a danger: People sometimes learn how to use them in a "cookbook" fashion without understanding the logical processes that underlie DCF analysis, and then, when confronted with a new type of problem, they cannot figure out how to set it up. Therefore, you are urged not only to get a good calculator and to learn how to use it but also to work through the illustrative problems "the long way" to insure that you understand the concepts involved.

FV_n = future value, or ending amount, of your account at the end of n years. Whereas PV is the value now, at the *present* time, FV_n is the value n years into the future, after compound interest has been earned. Note also that FV_0 is the future value *zero* years into the future, which is the *present,* so FV_0 = PV.

n = number of years, or, more generally, periods, involved in the transaction.

In our example, n = 1, so FV_n = FV_1, calculated as follows:

$$FV_1 = PV + I = PV + PV(k) = PV(1 + k). \qquad (4\text{-}1)$$

In words, the future value, FV, at the end of 1 period is the present value times 1 plus the interest rate.

We can now use Equation 4-1 to find how much your $100 will be worth at the end of 1 year at a 5 percent interest rate:

$$FV_1 = \$100(1 + 0.05) = \$100(1.05) = \$105.$$

Your account will earn $5 of interest (I = $5), so you will have $105 at the end of the year.

Now suppose you leave your funds on deposit for 5 years; how much will you have at the end of the fifth year? The answer is $127.63; this value is worked out in Table 4-1. Notice the following points: (1) You start with $100, earn $5 of interest during the first year, and end the year with $105 in your account. (2) You start the second year with $105, earn $5.25 on this now larger amount, and end the second year with $110.25. Your second-year earnings, $5.25, were higher because you earned interest on the first year's interest. (3) This process continues, and since in each year the beginning balance is higher, your interest income increases. (4) The total interest earned, $27.63, is reflected in the ending balance, $127.63.

Table 4-1
Compound Interest Calculations

Year	Amount at Beginning of Year, PV	×	(1 + k)	=	Amount at End of Year, FV_n	Interest Earned, PV(k)
1	$100.00		1.05		$105.00	$ 5.00
2	105.00		1.05		110.25	5.25
3	110.25		1.05		115.76	5.51
4	115.76		1.05		121.55	5.79
5	121.55		1.05		127.63	6.08
						$27.63

Notice that the Table 4-1 value for FV_2, the value of the account at the end of Year 2, is equal to

$$FV_2 = FV_1(1 + k) = PV(1 + k)(1 + k) = PV(1 + k)^2$$
$$= \$105.00(1.05) = \$100(1.05)(1.05) = \$100(1.05)^2$$
$$= \$100(1.1025) = \$110.25.$$

Continuing, we see that FV_3, the balance after Year 3, is

$$FV_3 = FV_2(1 + k) = PV(1 + k)^3$$
$$= \$110.25(1.05) = \$100(1.05)^3 = \$100(1.1576) = \$115.76.$$

In general, FV_n, the future value at the end of n years, is found as follows:

$$FV_n = PV(1 + k)^n. \tag{4-2}$$

Applying Equation 4-2 to our 5-year, 5 percent case, we obtain

$$FV_5 = \$100(1.05)^5$$
$$= \$100(1.2763) = \$127.63,$$

which is the same as the value worked out in Table 4-1.

We can solve future value problems in three ways:

1. Use a regular calculator. One method is to simply use your calculator, either multiplying $(1 + k)$ by itself $n - 1$ times or using the exponential function to raise $(1 + k)$ to the *nth* power. In our example, you would enter $1 + k = 1.05$ and multiply it by itself four times, or else enter 1.05, then enter 5, and then press the y^x (or exponential) function key. In either case, you would get the factor $(1.05)^5 = 1.2763$, which you would then multiply by \$100 to get the final answer, \$127.63.

2. Use compound interest tables. The term *future value interest factor for k,n* $(FVIF_{k,n})$ is defined to equal $(1 + k)^n$, and tables have been constructed for values of $(1 + k)^n$ for wide ranges of k and n. The table in the lower left section of Figure 4-1 is illustrative, and a more complete table, with more years and more interest rates, is given in Table A-3 in Appendix A at the end of the book.[2] Therefore, Equation 4-2 can be written as $FV_n = PV(FVIF_{k,n})$. It is necessary only to go to an appropriate interest factor table (the data below Figure 4-1 or Appendix A-3) to find the proper interest factor. For example, the correct interest factor for our 5-year, 5 percent illustration can be found by looking down the period column to 5 and then across this row to the 5 percent column to find the interest factor, 1.2763. Then, using this interest factor, we find the value of \$100 after 5 years to

---

[2]Notice that we have used the word *period* rather than *year* in Figure 4-1. As we shall see later in the chapter, compounding can occur over periods of time other than one year. Thus, while compounding is often on an annual basis, it can be quarterly, semiannually, monthly, or for any other period.

Figure 4-1
Relationship between Interest Rates, Time, and Interest Factors

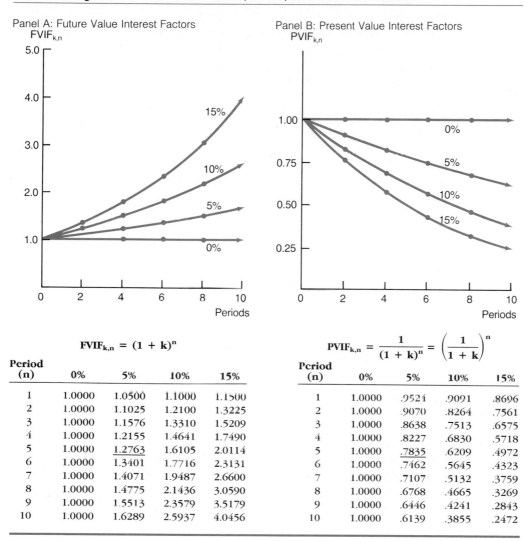

Panel A: Future Value Interest Factors
FVIF$_{k,n}$

Panel B: Present Value Interest Factors
PVIF$_{k,n}$

$$\text{FVIF}_{k,n} = (1 + k)^n$$

$$\text{PVIF}_{k,n} = \frac{1}{(1 + k)^n} = \left(\frac{1}{1 + k}\right)^n$$

Period (n)	0%	5%	10%	15%
1	1.0000	1.0500	1.1000	1.1500
2	1.0000	1.1025	1.2100	1.3225
3	1.0000	1.1576	1.3310	1.5209
4	1.0000	1.2155	1.4641	1.7490
5	1.0000	1.2763	1.6105	2.0114
6	1.0000	1.3401	1.7716	2.3131
7	1.0000	1.4071	1.9487	2.6600
8	1.0000	1.4775	2.1436	3.0590
9	1.0000	1.5513	2.3579	3.5179
10	1.0000	1.6289	2.5937	4.0456

Period (n)	0%	5%	10%	15%
1	1.0000	.9524	.9091	.8696
2	1.0000	.9070	.8264	.7561
3	1.0000	.8638	.7513	.6575
4	1.0000	.8227	.6830	.5718
5	1.0000	.7835	.6209	.4972
6	1.0000	.7462	.5645	.4323
7	1.0000	.7107	.5132	.3759
8	1.0000	.6768	.4665	.3269
9	1.0000	.6446	.4241	.2843
10	1.0000	.6139	.3855	.2472

be FV$_5$ = PV(FVIF$_{5\%,5 \text{ years}}$) = \$100(1.2763) = \$127.63, which is identical to the value obtained by the long method in Table 4-1.

The curves in Figure 4-1 plot the data shown below the graphs, and Panel A shows how \$1 (or any other sum) grows over time at various rates of interest. The higher the rate of interest, the faster the rate of growth. The interest rate is, in fact, a growth rate; if a sum is deposited and earns 5 percent, then the funds on deposit grow at the rate of 5 percent per period. Note also that these formulas can be applied to anything that is growing — sales, population, earnings per share, or what have you. If you ever need to figure the growth rate of anything, the formulas in this chapter can be used.

Note also that tables such as A-3 can be developed for fractional interest rates, such as $5\frac{1}{4}$ percent, and for fractional periods, such as $5\frac{5}{12}$ years. However, the finer the gradations, the more extensive the tables that are needed, and it is hard to imagine a "ready made" table that would contain the FVIF for 8.372 percent over 6 years and 250 days, or $6 + (250/365) = 6.6849$ years. Thus, the tables are of limited use in solving complex, real world problems.

3. Use a financial calculator. Financial calculators have been programmed to solve most future value problems. In effect, the calculators first generate the $FVIF_{k,n}$ factors for any specified values of k and n, and then multiply the computed factor by the PV to produce the FV. In our illustrative problem, you simply enter PV = $100, k = i = 5%, and n = 5, press the FV key, and the answer, $127.63 (rounded to two decimal places) will appear. (The FV will appear with a minus sign on some calculators. The logic here is that you put in the initial amount (the PV) and take out the ending amount (the FV), so one is an inflow and the other is an outflow, and the reverse signs remind you of that. At this point, though, you can ignore the minus sign.)

The most efficient way to solve most problems is to use a financial calculator. Therefore, you should get one and learn how to use it. However, you ought to understand how the tables are developed and used, and you should also understand the logic and the math that underlie all this. Otherwise, you simply will not understand stock and bond valuation, lease analysis, capital budgeting, and other critically important topics.

PRESENT VALUE

Suppose you are offered the alternative of receiving either $127.63 at the end of 5 years or X dollars today. There is no question that the $127.63 will be paid in full (perhaps the payer is the U.S. government). Having no current need for the money, you would deposit the X dollars in a bank account that pays 5 percent interest. (Five percent is defined to be your *opportunity cost,* or the rate of interest you could earn on alternative investments of equal risk.) What value of X would make you indifferent in your choice between X dollars today and the promise of $127.63 five years hence?

From Table 4-1 we saw that the initial amount of $100 growing at 5 percent a year will be worth $127.63 at the end of 5 years. Thus, you should be indifferent to the choice between $100 today and $127.63 at the end of 5 years. The $100 is defined as the *present value,* or *PV,* of $127.63 due in 5 years when the opportunity cost rate is 5 percent. Therefore, if X is anything less than $100, you should prefer the promise of $127.63 in 5 years to X dollars today; if X is greater than $100, you should prefer X.

In general, the present value of a sum due n years in the future is the amount which, if it were on hand today, would grow to equal the future sum when invested at the opportunity cost rate. Since $100 would grow to $127.63 in 5 years at a 5 percent interest rate, $100 is defined to be the present value of $127.63 due 5 years in the future when the appropriate interest rate is 5 percent.

Finding present values — or *discounting,* as it is commonly called — is simply the reverse of compounding, and Equation 4-2 can be transformed into a present value formula:

$$FV_n = PV(1 + k)^n, \tag{4-2}$$

which, when solved for PV, gives Equation 4-3 in three forms:

$$PV = \frac{FV_n}{(1 + k)^n} = FV_n(1 + k)^{-n} = FV_n \left[\frac{1}{(1 + k)} \right]^n. \tag{4-3}$$

Tables have been constructed for $[1/(1 + k)]^n$ for various values of k and n; the tabular data in Panel B of Figure 4-1 is an example. (For a more complete table, see Table A-1 in Appendix A at the end of the book.) For our illustrative case, look down the 5 percent column to the fifth row. The figure shown there, 0.7835, is the *present value interest factor (PVIF$_{k,n}$)* used to determine the present value of $127.63 payable in 5 years, discounted at 5 percent:

$$PV = FV_5(PVIF_{5\%,5 \text{ years}})$$
$$= \$127.63(0.7835) = \$100.$$

Again, you can also use a regular calculator to find the PVIF and a financial calculator to find the PV of $100. With a financial calculator, just enter n = 5, k = i = 5, and FV = 127.63, and then press the PV button to find PV = $100 (on some calculators, − $100).

Panel B of Figure 4-1 shows graphically how the current, or present, value of a sum to be received at some future date decreases (1) as the payment date is extended further into the future and (2) as the interest (or discount) rate increases. If relatively high discount rates apply, funds due in the future are worth very little today, and even at relatively low discount rates, the present values of funds due in the distant future are quite small. For example, $1 due in 10 years is worth about 61 cents today if the discount rate is 5 percent, but it is worth only 25 cents at a 15 percent discount rate. Similarly, $1 due in 5 years at 10 percent is worth 62 cents today, but at the same discount rate $1 due in 10 years is worth only 39 cents today. At a 15 percent discount rate, $1 due in 50 years is worth only $0.0009, or 9/10,000 of $1, today.

FUTURE VALUE VERSUS PRESENT VALUE

Notice that Equation 4-2, the basic equation for compounding, was developed from the logical sequence set forth in Table 4-1; the equation merely presents in mathematical form the steps outlined in the table. The present value interest factor (PVIF$_{k,n}$) in Equation 4-3, the basic equation for discounting (or finding present values) was found as the *reciprocal* of the future value interest factor ($FVIF_{k,n}$) for the same k,n combination:

$$PVIF_{k,n} = \frac{1}{FVIF_{k,n}}.$$

For example, since the *future value* interest factor for 5 percent over 5 years is seen in Figure 4-1 to be 1.2763, the *present value* interest factor for 5 percent over 5 years must be the reciprocal of 1.2763:

$$PVIF_{5\%,5 \text{ years}} = \frac{1}{1.2763} = 0.7835.$$

The $PVIF_{k,n}$ found in this manner does, of course, correspond with that shown in Figure 4-1.

The reciprocal nature of the relationship between present value and future value permits us to find present values in two ways — by multiplying or by dividing. Thus, the present value of $1,000 due in 5 years and discounted at 5 percent may be found as

$$PV = FV_n(PVIF_{k,n}) = FV_5\left[\frac{1}{(1 + k)}\right]^5 = \$1,000(0.7835) = \$783.50,$$

or as

$$PV = \frac{FV_n}{FVIF_{k,n}} = \frac{FV_5}{(1 + k)^5} = \frac{\$1,000}{1.2763} = \$783.50.$$

To conclude this comparison of present and future values, look again at Panels A and B in Figure 4-1. Notice that the vertical intercept is at 1.0 in each case, but future value interest factors rise while present value interest factors decline.[3]

FUTURE VALUE OF AN ANNUITY

An *annuity* is defined as a series of payments of an equal, or constant, amount of money at fixed intervals for a specified number of periods. Payments are given the symbol PMT, and if they occur at the end of each period, as they typically do, then we have an *ordinary annuity,* sometimes called a *deferred annuity.* If payments are made at the beginning of each period, then we have an *annuity due.* Since ordinary annuities are far more common in finance, when the word *annuity* is used in this book, you may assume that payments are received at the end of each period unless otherwise indicated.

---

[3]Notice that Panel B is not a mirror image of Panel A. The curves in Panel A approach ∞ as n increases; in Panel B the curves approach zero, not −∞.

Figure 4-2
Time Line for an Ordinary Annuity:
Future Value with k = 5%

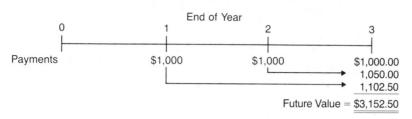

Future Value = $3,152.50

Ordinary Annuities

A promise to pay $1,000 a year for 3 years is a 3-year annuity, and if each payment is made at the end of the year, it is an *ordinary (deferred) annuity*. If you were to receive such an annuity and were to deposit each annual payment in a savings account paying 5 percent interest, how much would you have at the end of 3 years? The answer is shown graphically as a *time line* in Figure 4-2. The first payment is made at the end of Year 1, the second at the end of Year 2, and the third at the end of Year 3. Thus, the first payment is compounded over a 2-year period; the second payment is compounded for 1 year; and the last payment is not compounded at all. When the future values of each of the payments are summed, their total is the future value of the annuity. In the example, this total is $3,152.50.

Expressed algebraically, with FVA_n defined as the future value of an annuity over n periods, PMT as the periodic payment, and $FVIFA_{k,n}$ as the future value interest factor for an annuity, the formula is[4]

$$FVA_n = PMT(1 + k)^{n-1} + PMT(1 + k)^{n-2} + \ldots + PMT(1 + k)^1 + PMT(1 + k)^0$$

$$= PMT[(1 + k)^{n-1} + (1 + k)^{n-2} + \ldots + (1 + k)^1 + (1 + k)^0]$$

$$= PMT \sum_{t=1}^{n} (1 + k)^{n-t} \tag{4-4}$$

$$= PMT(FVIFA_{k,n}) = \text{future value of an annuity.}$$

---

[4]The third step in the equation is simply a shorthand expression in which sigma (Σ) signifies "sum up," or add the values of n factors. If $t = 1$, then $(1 + k)^{n-t} = (1 + k)^{n-1}$; if $t = 2$, then $(1 + k)^{n-t} = (1 + k)^{n-2}$; and so on until $t = n$, the last year the annuity provides any returns. The symbol

$$\sum_{t=1}^{n}$$

simply says, "Go through the following process: First, let $t = 1$ and find the first factor; then let $t = 2$ and find the second factor; then continue until each individual factor up to $t = n$ has been found, and then add these individual factors to find the total value of the annuity factor."

Table 4-2
Future Value of an Annuity of $1 per Period for n Periods

$$FVIFA_{k,n} = \sum_{t=1}^{n} (1 + k)^{n-t} = \frac{(1 + k)^n - 1}{k}$$

Number of Periods (n)	1%	2%	3%	4%	5%	6%	7%	8%	9%	10%
1	1.0000	1.0000	1.0000	1.0000	1.0000	1.0000	1.0000	1.0000	1.0000	1.0000
2	2.0100	2.0200	2.0300	2.0400	2.0500	2.0600	2.0700	2.0800	2.0900	2.1000
3	3.0301	3.0604	3.0909	3.1216	3.1525	3.1836	3.2149	3.2464	3.2781	3.3100
4	4.0604	4.1216	4.1836	4.2465	4.3101	4.3746	4.4399	4.5061	4.5731	4.6410
5	5.1010	5.2040	5.3091	5.4163	5.5256	5.6371	5.7507	5.8666	5.9847	6.1051
6	6.1520	6.3081	6.4684	6.6330	6.8019	6.9753	7.1533	7.3359	7.5233	7.7156
7	7.2135	7.4343	7.6625	7.8983	8.1420	8.3938	8.6540	8.9228	9.2004	9.4872
8	8.2857	8.5830	8.8923	9.2141	9.5491	9.8975	10.2598	10.6366	11.0285	11.4359
9	9.3685	9.7546	10.1591	10.5828	11.0266	11.4913	11.9780	12.4876	13.0210	13.5795
10	10.4622	10.9497	11.4639	12.0061	12.5779	13.1808	13.8164	14.4866	15.1929	15.9374

The expression in parentheses, $FVIFA_{k,n}$, has been calculated for various combinations of k and n. An illustrative set of these annuity interest factors is given in Table 4-2.[5] (A more complete set of $FVIFA_{k,n}$ factors is given in Table A-4 in Appendix A.) To find the answer to the 3-year, $1,000 annuity problem, simply refer to Table 4-2, look down the 5 percent column to the row of the third period, and multiply the factor 3.1525 by $1,000. The answer is the same as the one derived by the long method illustrated in Figure 4-2:

$$FVA_n = PMT(FVIFA_{k,n})$$
$$FVA_3 = \$1,000(FVIFA_{5\%,3 \text{ years}})$$
$$= \$1,000(3.1525) = \$3,152.50.$$

You could, with a financial calculator, find FVA_n directly. Just enter n = 3, k = i = 5, and PMT = 1,000, and then press the FV button to get the answer, FVA_3 = $3,152.50 (on some calculators, − $3,152.50). The calculator is, in effect, first calculating FVIFA and then multiplying it by PMT = $1,000. Financial calculators also handle fractional years and fractional interest rates with no trouble.

Notice that for all positive interest rates, the $FVIFA_{k,n}$ for the future value of an annuity is always equal to or greater than the number of periods the annuity runs.

---

[5]The equation given at the top of Table 4-2 recognizes that an FVIFA factor is the sum of a geometric progression. Notice that it is easy to use the equation to develop annuity factors; this is especially useful if you need the FVIFA for some interest rate not given in the tables, for example, 6.5 percent. The equation is also useful for finding factors for fractional periods — for example, 2.5 years — but one needs a calculator with an exponential function for this.

Note also that the entry for each period n in Table 4-2 is equal to 1.0 plus the sum of the entries in the lower left section of Figure 4-1 up to and including Period n − 1; for example, the entry for Period 3 under the 5 percent column in Table 4-2 is equal to $1.000 + 1.0500 + 1.1025 = 3.1525$.

Annuity Due

Had the three $1,000 payments in the previous example each been made at the beginning of the year, the annuity would have been an *annuity due.* In terms of Figure 4-2, each payment would have been shifted to the left, so there would have been a $1,000 under Period 0 and a zero under Period 3; thus, each payment would be compounded for one extra year.

We can modify Equation 4-4 to handle annuities due as follows:

$$FVA_n(\text{Annuity due}) = PMT(FVIFA_{k,n})(1 + k). \tag{4-4a}$$

Each payment is compounded for one extra year, and multiplying $PMT(FVIFA_{k,n})$ by $(1 + k)$ takes care of this extra compounding. Applying Equation 4-4a to the previous example, we obtain

$$FVA_n(\text{Anuity due}) = \$1,000(3.1525)(1.05) = \$3,310.13$$

versus $3,152.50 for the ordinary annuity. Since its payments come earlier, the annuity due is more valuable.

Annuity due problems can also be solved with a financial calculator, most of which have a switch or key marked "Due" or "Beginning" that permits you to convert from ordinary annuities to annuities due. Be careful, though: People (including us) sometimes change the setting to work an annuity due problem, then forget to switch the calculator back and consequently get wrong answers to subsequent ordinary annuity problems. Also, be sure to clear the calculator's financial registers prior to beginning a new calculation—failing to clear these registers can produce incorrect answers.

PRESENT VALUE OF AN ANNUITY

Suppose you were offered the following alternatives: (1) a 3-year annuity with payments of $1,000 at the end of each year or (2) a lump sum payment today. You have no need for the money during the next 3 years, so if you accepted the annuity, you would simply deposit the payments in a savings account that pays 5 percent interest. Similarly, the lump sum payment would be deposited in an account paying 5 percent, compounded annually. How large must the lump sum payment be to make it equivalent to the annuity?

The time line shown in Figure 4-3 will help explain the problem. The present value of the first payment is $PMT[1/(1 + k)]$, the second is $PMT[1/(1 + k)]^2$, and so on. Defining the present value of an annuity of n periods as PVA_n, and $PVIFA_{k,n}$

Figure 4-3
Time Line for an Ordinary Annuity:
Present Value with k = 5%

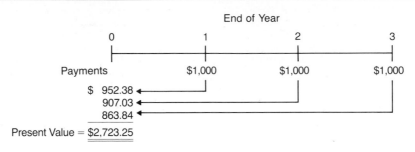

as the present value interest factor for the annuity, we may write the following equation in its several equivalent forms:

$$\text{PVA}_n = \text{PMT}\left(\frac{1}{1 + k}\right)^1 + \text{PMT}\left(\frac{1}{1 + k}\right)^2 + \ldots + \text{PMT}\left(\frac{1}{1 + k}\right)^n$$

$$= \text{PMT}\left[\left(\frac{1}{1 + k}\right)^1 + \left(\frac{1}{1 + k}\right)^2 + \ldots + \left(\frac{1}{1 + k}\right)^n\right] \qquad (4\text{-}5)$$

$$= \text{PMT} \sum_{t=1}^{n}\left(\frac{1}{1 + k}\right)^t = \text{PMT}(\text{PVIFA}_{k,n}).$$

Again, tables have been worked out for $\text{PVIFA}_{k,n}$. Table 4-3 is illustrative, and a more complete listing is found in Table A-2 in Appendix A. From Table 4-3, the $\text{PVIFA}_{k,n}$ for a 3-year, 5 percent annuity is found to be 2.7232. Multiplying this factor by the $1,000 annual payment gives $2,723.20, the present value of the annuity. This value is identical to the long-method answer shown in Figure 4-3 except for a rounding error. (The tables are only carried to four decimal places — the true $\text{PVIFA}_{k,n}$ is 2.723248029⋯.)

$$\text{PVA}_n = \text{PMT}(\text{PVIFA}_{k,n})$$
$$\text{PVA}_3 = \$1,000(\text{PVIFA}_{5\%,3 \text{ years}})$$
$$= \$1,000(2.7232) = \$2,723.20.$$

Again, this problem can be solved directly with a financial calculator. Just enter n = 3, k = i = 5, and PMT = 1,000, and then press the PV button to find PVA_n = $2,723.25 (on some calculators, − $2,723.25).

Notice that the entry for each value of n in Table 4-3 is equal to the sum of the entries in the lower right section of Figure 4-1 up to and including Period n. For

Table 4-3
Present Value of an Annuity of $1 per Period for n Periods

$$PVIFA_{k,n} = \sum_{t=1}^{n} \frac{1}{(1 + k)^t} = \frac{1 - \dfrac{1}{(1 + k)^n}}{k} = \frac{1}{k} - \frac{1}{k(1 + k)^n}$$

Number of Periods (n)	1%	2%	3%	4%	5%	6%	7%	8%	9%	10%
1	0.9901	0.9804	0.9709	0.9615	0.9524	0.9434	0.9346	0.9259	0.9174	0.9091
2	1.9704	1.9416	1.9135	1.8861	1.8594	1.8334	1.8080	1.7833	1.7591	1.7355
3	2.9410	2.8839	2.8286	2.7751	2.7232	2.6730	2.6243	2.5771	2.5313	2.4869
4	3.9020	3.8077	3.7171	3.6299	3.5460	3.4651	3.3872	3.3121	3.2397	3.1699
5	4.8534	4.7135	4.5797	4.4518	4.3295	4.2124	4.1002	3.9927	3.8897	3.7908
6	5.7955	5.6014	5.4172	5.2421	5.0757	4.9173	4.7665	4.6229	4.4859	4.3553
7	6.7282	6.4720	6.2303	6.0021	5.7864	5.5824	5.3893	5.2064	5.0330	4.8684
8	7.6517	7.3255	7.0197	6.7327	6.4632	6.2098	5.9713	5.7466	5.5348	5.3349
9	8.5660	8.1622	7.7861	7.4353	7.1078	6.8017	6.5152	6.2469	5.9952	5.7590
10	9.4713	8.9826	8.5302	8.1109	7.7217	7.3601	7.0236	6.7101	6.4177	6.1446

example, the PVIFA for 5 percent, 3 periods, as shown in Table 4-3 could have been calculated by summing values from Figure 4-1:

$$0.9524 + 0.9070 + 0.8638 = 2.7232.$$

Notice also that for all positive interest rates, $PVIFA_{k,n}$ for the *present value* of an annuity is always equal to or less than the number of periods the annuity runs, whereas $FVIFA_{k,n}$ for the *future value* of an annuity is equal to or greater than the number of periods.

Present Value of an Annuity Due

Had the payments in the preceding example occurred at the beginning of each year, the annuity would have been an *annuity due*. In terms of Figure 4-3, each payment would have been shifted to the left, so $1,000 would have appeared under Year 0 and a zero would have appeared under Year 3. Each payment occurs one period earlier, so it has a higher PV. To account for these shifts, we modify Equation 4-5 as follows to find the present value of an annuity due:

$$PVA_n(\text{Annuity due}) = PMT(PVIFA_{k,n})(1 + k). \qquad \textbf{(4-5a)}$$

Our illustrative 5 percent, 3-year annuity, with payments made at the beginning of each year, thus has a present value of $2,859.36 versus a value of $2,723.20 on an ordinary annuity basis:

$$PVA_3 = \$1,000(2.7232)(1.05)$$
$$= \$2,723.20(1.05) = \$2,859.36.$$

Since each payment comes earlier, the annuity due is worth more than the ordinary annuity.

PERPETUITIES

Most annuities call for payments to be made over some definite period of time — for example, \$1,000 per year for 3 years. However, some annuities go on indefinitely; here the payments constitute an *infinite series,* and the series is defined as a *perpetuity.* The present value of a perpetuity is found by applying Equation 4-6:[6]

$$PV(\text{perpetuity}) = \frac{\text{Payment}}{\text{Discount rate}} = \frac{PMT}{k}. \qquad (4\text{-}6)$$

Perpetuities can be illustrated by some British securities. After the Napoleonic Wars in 1815, the British government sold a huge bond issue and used the proceeds to pay off many smaller issues that had been floated in prior years to pay for the wars. Since the purpose of the new bonds was to consolidate past debts, the bonds were called consols. Suppose each consol promised to pay \$90 interest per year in perpetuity. (Actually, interest was stated in pounds.) What would each bond be worth if the going rate of interest, or the discount rate, were 8 percent? The answer is \$1,125:

$$PV = \frac{PMT}{k} = \frac{\$90}{0.08} = \$1,125.$$

Suppose interest rates rose to 12 percent; what would that do to the consol's value? The increase in interest rates lowers the value of the consol to \$750:

$$PV = \frac{\$90}{0.12} = \$750.$$

If k fell to 4 percent, the consol's value would rise to \$2,250.

We see, then, that the value of a perpetuity changes dramatically when interest rates change. Perpetuities are discussed further in Chapter 5, where procedures for finding the values of stocks and bonds are analyzed.

---

[6]The derivation of Equation 4-6 is given in Appendix 3A of Eugene F. Brigham and Louis C. Gapenski, *Intermediate Financial Management,* 2nd ed. (Hinsdale, Ill.: Dryden Press, 1987).

UNEVEN PAYMENT STREAMS

The definition of an annuity includes the words *constant amount*—in other words, annuities involve situations in which cash flows are *identical* in every period. Although some financial decisions do involve constant cash flows, many important decisions are concerned with uneven flows of cash—for example, common stocks are typically expected to pay an increasing series of dividends over time, and capital budgeting projects do not normally provide constant cash flows. Consequently, it is necessary to expand our analysis to deal with uneven payment streams.

The PV of an uneven stream of future cash flows is found as the sum of the PVs of the individual components of the stream. For example, suppose we are trying to find the PV of the stream of payments shown in Figure 4-4, discounted at 6 percent. As shown in the lower part of the figure, we multiply each payment by the appropriate $PVIF_{k,n}$ (taken from Appendix Table A-1) and then sum these products to obtain the PV of the stream, $1,413.24. The figure also provides a time line of the cash flow stream.

Figure 4-4
**Time Line for an Uneven Cash Flow Stream:
Present Value with k = 6%**

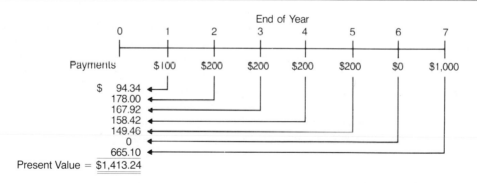

Year	Payment	×	$PVIF_{6\%,n}$	=	PV of Individual Payments
1	$ 100		0.9434		$ 94.34
2	200		0.8900		178.00
3	200		0.8396		167.92
4	200		0.7921		158.42
5	200		0.7473		149.46
6	0		0.7050		0
7	1,000		0.6651		665.10
				PV = Sum =	$1,413.24

The PV of the payments shown in Figure 4-4 for Years 2 through 5 can also be found by using the annuity equation. This alternative solution process involves the following steps:

Step 1. Find the PV of $100 due in Year 1:

$$\$100(0.9434) = \$94.34.$$

Step 2. Recognize that a $200 annuity will be received during Years 2 through 5. Thus, we could determine the value of a 4-year annuity and then, recognizing that this value occurs at Year 1, discount the annuity PV back 1 year to Year 0:

$$\text{PV of the annuity} = \$200(\text{PVIFA}_{6\%,4 \text{ years}})$$
$$= \$200(3.4651) = \$693.02,$$

and hence the present (Year 0) value of the annuity component of the uneven stream is

$$\$693.02(\text{PVIF}_{6\%,1 \text{ year}}) = \$693.02(0.9434) = \$653.80.$$

Step 3. Find the PV of the $1,000 due in Year 7:

$$\$1,000(0.6651) = \$665.10.$$

Step 4. Sum the components:

$$\$94.34 + \$653.80 + \$665.10 = \$1,413.24.$$

Either the Figure 4-4 method or the method utilizing the annuity formula can be used to solve problems of this type. However, the alternative annuity solution is much easier if the annuity component runs for many years. For example, the alternative solution would be clearly superior for finding the PV of a stream consisting of $100 in Year 1, $200 in Years 2 through 29, and $1,000 in Year 30.

Problems involving the present value of unequal cash flows can be solved quite easily with most financial calculators. With these calculators, you first enter the individual cash flows and the interest rate, and then you press the NPV button to obtain the solution. This feature is not found on some less expensive financial calculators, but most do include it.

The future value of an uneven payment stream, often called the *terminal value (TV)*, is found in a manner similar to finding the present value, except that the cash flows are compounded forward to the end of the stream.

DETERMINING INTEREST RATES

We can use the basic equations that were developed earlier in the chapter to determine the interest rates implicit in financial contracts.

Example 1. A bank offers to lend you $1,000 if you sign a note to pay $1,610.50 at the end of 5 years. What rate of interest would the bank be charging you?

1. Recognize that $1,000 is the PV of $1,610.50 due in 5 years:

$$\text{PV} = \$1,000 = \$1,610.50(\text{PVIF}_{k,5 \text{ years}}).$$

2. Solve for $\text{PVIF}_{k,5 \text{ years}}$:

$$\text{PVIF}_{k,5 \text{ years}} = \$1,000/\$1,610.50 = 0.6209.$$

3. Now turn to the lower right panel of Figure 4-1 (or Table A-1). Look across the row for Period 5 until you find the value 0.6209. It is in the 10 percent column, so you would be paying a 10 percent rate of interest if you were to take out the loan.

Financial calculators are especially useful for finding interest rates in problems such as this. Merely enter PV = 1,000, n = 5, and FV = 1,610.5, and then press the k = i button to obtain the interest rate. The calculator blinks a few times, and 10.00 percent appears. Your calculator may require that the FV be entered as a negative in recognition of the fact that the PV is an inflow and the FV is an outflow. If you get an error message, try entering FV = $-1,610.5$.

Example 2. A bank offers to lend you $25,000 to buy a home. You must sign a mortgage calling for payments of $2,545.16 at the end of each of the next 25 years. What interest rate is the bank offering you?

1. Recognize that $25,000 is the PV of a 25-year, $2,545.16 annuity:

$$\text{PV} = \$25,000 = \$2,545.16(\text{PVIFA}_{k,25 \text{ years}}).$$

2. Solve for $\text{PVIFA}_{k,25 \text{ years}}$:

$$\text{PVIFA}_{k,25 \text{ years}} = \$25,000/\$2,545.16 = 9.8226.$$

3. Turn to Table A-2. Looking across the row for 25 periods, you will find 9.8226 under the column for 9 percent. Therefore, the rate of interest on this mortgage loan is 9 percent.

To solve this problem with a financial calculator, enter PV = 25,000, n = 25, and PMT = 2,545.16 (or $-2,545.16$), and then press the k = i button to find the interest rate of 9 percent.

Consider also the situation in which the mortgage calls for annual payments of $2,400. Then $\text{PVIFA}_{k,n} = \$25,000/\$2,400 = 10.4167$. In Table A-2, this value lies between the $\text{PVIFA}_{k,n}$ for 8 and 9 percent, but it is closer to 8 percent. The approximate rate for the mortgage could be found by "linear interpolation," a cumbersome process discussed in algebra texts, but today we would use a financial calculator and find the interest rate merely by pressing the i button. The rate in this example is 8.2887 percent.

While the tables can be used to find the interest rate implicit in single payments and annuities, it is more difficult to find the interest rate implicit in an uneven series of payments. One can use a trial-and-error procedure or a financial calculator with an IRR function (IRRs are discussed in Chapter 8). We will defer further discussion of this problem for now, but we will take it up later in our discussion of bond values and again in the capital budgeting chapters.

SEMIANNUAL AND OTHER COMPOUNDING PERIODS

In all of our examples thus far, we have assumed that returns are received once a year, or annually. Suppose, however, that you put your $1,000 in a bank which advertises that it pays 6 percent compounded *semiannually*. How much will you have at the end of 1 year? Semiannual compounding means that interest is actually paid each 6 months. The procedures for semiannual compounding are illustrated in the calculations in Table 4-4. Here the annual interest rate is divided by 2, but twice as many compounding periods are used because interest is paid twice a year. Comparing the amount on hand at the end of the second 6-month period, $1,060.90, with what would have been on hand under annual compounding, $1,060, we see that semiannual compounding is better from your standpoint as a saver. This result occurs because you earn *interest on interest* more frequently. Semiannual compounding is handled easily with a financial calculator. We merely set i = 3, n = 2, and PV = 1,000, and then press the FV button to get the solution FV = $1,060.90.

Throughout the economy, different compounding periods are used for different types of investments. For example, bank accounts generally pay interest monthly or daily; most bonds pay interest semiannually; stocks pay dividends quarterly; and many loans pay interest annually. Thus, if we are to compare securities with different compounding periods, we need to put them on a common basis. This need has led to the development of the terms *nominal,* or *stated, interest rate* versus the *effective annual rate.*[7] The nominal, or stated, interest rate is the quoted rate; thus, in our example, the nominal rate is 6 percent. The nominal interest rate is often called the *annual percentage rate (APR)* when it is reported by banks and other lending institutions.[8] The effective annual rate *is the rate that would have pro-*

Table 4-4
Future Value Calculations with Semiannual Compounding

Period	Amount at Beginning of Period, PV	×	(1 + k/2)	=	Amount at End of Period, FV_n	Interest Earned, PV(k/2)
1	$1,000.00		(1.03)		$1,030.00	$30.00
2	1,030.00		(1.03)		1,060.90	30.90
						$60.90

---

[7]The term *nominal* as it is used here has a different meaning from the way it was used in Chapter 3. There, nominal interest rates meant market rates as opposed to real (inflation-adjusted) rates. In this chapter, the term "nominal rate" means the stated rate as opposed to the effective annual rate, which considers the effects of compounding more frequently than once a year.

[8]The nominal interest rate, or the APR, is the rate reported by banks. Although this is a widespread practice and apparently meets the minimum requirements of the "truth in lending" laws, it is somewhat deceptive because the true effective interest rate, which ought to be reported to borrowers, exceeds the nominal rate except when annual compounding is used.

duced the final compound value, $1,060.90, under annual rather than semi-annual compounding. In this case, the effective annual rate is 6.09 percent, found by solving for k in the following equation:

$$\$1,000(1 + k) = \$1,060.90$$

$$k = \frac{\$1,060.90}{\$1,000} - 1 = 0.0609 = 6.09\%.$$

Thus, if one bank offers 6 percent with semiannual compounding while another offers 6.09 percent with annual compounding, they are both paying the same effective annual rate of interest.

In general, we can determine the effective annual rate, given the nominal rate and the frequency of compounding, by solving Equation 4-7:

$$\text{Effective annual rate} = \left(1 + \frac{k_{Nom}}{m}\right)^m - 1.0. \qquad (4\text{-}7)$$

Here k_{Nom} is the nominal, or stated, interest rate, and m is the number of compounding periods per year. For example, to find the effective annual rate if the nominal rate is 6 percent and semiannual compounding is used, we make the following calculation:

$$\text{Effective annual rate} = \left(1 + \frac{0.06}{2}\right)^2 - 1.0 = (1.03)^2 - 1.0$$

$$= 1.0609 - 1.0 = 0.0609 = 6.09\%.$$

The points made about semiannual compounding can be generalized as follows. When compounding periods are more frequent than once a year, we use a modified version of Equation 4-2 to find the future value of a lump sum:

$$\text{Annual compounding: } FV_n = PV(1 + k)^n. \qquad (4\text{-}2)$$

$$\text{More frequent compounding: } FV_n = PV\left(1 + \frac{k_{Nom}}{m}\right)^{mn}. \qquad (4\text{-}2a)$$

Here m is the number of times per year compounding occurs, and n is the number of years. When banks compute daily interest, the value of m is set at 365 and Equation 4-2a is applied.[9]

To illustrate the effects of compounding more frequently than annually, consider the interest rate on credit cards. In January 1987, most interest rates had

---

[9]For example, the future value of $1 invested at 10 percent for 1 year under daily compounding is $1.1052:

$$FV_n = \$1\left(1 + \frac{0.10}{365}\right)^{365(1)} = \$1(1.1052) = \$1.1052.$$

declined sharply from earlier levels. For example, yields on 30-year Treasury bonds were 7.7 percent, down from 14 percent in 1981. However, credit card rates (the rate of interest charged to credit card users who do not pay within the no-interest period) were generally unchanged from earlier levels. Most states set maximum rates for credit card rates, and most banks charged the allowed limit, which ranged from 12 to 21 percent but averaged 19 percent nationwide.

Certain members of Congress raised this question: Why haven't credit card rates dropped along with other rates? Is there some conspiracy among bankers to keep these rates up, thus helping bank profits but exploiting those consumers who borrow on credit cards? As expected, the bankers replied that both administrative costs and bad debt losses are high on credit card loans, and that the rates charged are completely justified. The interesting thing to note for our purposes, though, is that the stated rates on bank card loans are lower than the true rates. For example, if a bank charges 1½ percent per month, it will state that it is charging an annual percentage rate (APR) of 1½% × 12 = 18%. Actually, though, the correct rate is the effective annual rate, 19.6%:

$$\text{Effective annual rate} = \left(1 + \frac{0.18}{12}\right)^{12} - 1.0 = (1.015)^{12} - 1.0 = 0.196 = 19.6\%.$$

Whether or not those rates are really justified is a moot question, but it surely pays to pay credit card charges within the interest-free period!

The interest factor tables can be used when compounding occurs more than once a year. Simply divide the nominal, or stated, interest rate by the number of times compounding occurs, and multiply the years by the number of compounding periods per year. For example, to find the amount to which $1,000 will grow after 5 years if semiannual compounding is applied to a stated 8 percent interest rate, divide 8 percent by 2 and multiply the 5 years by 2. Then look in Table A-3 under the 4 percent column and in the row for Period 10. You will find an interest factor of 1.4802. Multiplying this by the initial $1,000 gives a value of $1,480.20, the amount to which $1,000 will grow in 5 years at 8 percent, compounded semiannually. This compares with $1,469.30 for annual compounding.

The tables are terribly limited when dealing with non-annual compounding — for example, we would need values for 2¼ percent to get factors for 9 percent with quarterly compounding. However, any compounding period can be handled easily with a financial calculator. Thus, to work our illustrative problem, simply press in i = k_{Nom}/m = 4, n = m × n = 10, and then proceed as before.

The same procedures are applied in all the cases covered — compounding, discounting, single payments, and annuities. To illustrate semiannual discounting in finding the present value of an annuity, consider the case described in the section "Present Value of an Annuity": $1,000 a year for 3 years, discounted at 5 percent. With annual discounting, the interest factor is 2.7232 and the present value of the annuity is $2,723.20 (or $2,723.25 with a financial calculator). Now assume that the annuity consisted of 6 semiannual payments of $500. With a financial calculator, enter PMT = 500, n = 6, i = 5/2 = 2.5, and then press the PV key. The answer 2,754.06 (or −2,754.06) will appear. The payments come a little more rapidly—the first $500 is paid after only six months (similarly with other payments), so the annuity is a little more valuable if payments are received semiannually rather than annually.

CONTINUOUS COMPOUNDING AND DISCOUNTING

Equation 4-2a was developed to allow for any number of discrete compounding periods per year; we illustrate some variations in this section. For example, if PV = $100, k = 10%, and n = 5, we obtain the following future values at the end of 5 years for the listed compounding periods:

$$\text{Annual: } FV_5 = \$100\left(1.0 + \frac{0.10}{1}\right)^{1(5)} = \$100(1.10)^5 = \$161.05.$$

$$\text{Semiannual: } FV_5 = \$100\left(1.0 + \frac{0.10}{2}\right)^{2(5)} = \$100(1.05)^{10} = \$162.89.$$

$$\text{Monthly: } FV_5 = \$100\left(1.0 + \frac{0.10}{12}\right)^{12(5)} = \$100(1.0083)^{60} = \$164.53.$$

$$\text{Daily: } FV_5 = \$100\left(1.0 + \frac{0.10}{365}\right)^{365(5)} = \$164.86.$$

$$\text{Hourly: } FV_5 = \$100\left(1.0 + \frac{0.10}{8,760}\right)^{365(24)(5)} = \$164.87.$$

We could keep going, compounding every minute, every second, every 1/1,000th of a second, and so on. At the limit, we could compound every instant, or *continuously*. The equation for continuous compounding is

$$FV_n = PVe^{kn}, \tag{4-8}$$

where e is approximately equal to 2.7183.[10] If $100 is invested for 5 years at 10 percent compounded continuously, then FV_5 is computed as follows:

$$\text{Continuous: } FV_5 = \$100\left[e^{0.10(5)}\right] = \$100(2.7183)^{0.5}$$
$$= \$164.87.$$

Equation 4-8 can be transformed into Equation 4-9 and used to determine present values under continuous discounting:

$$PV = \frac{FV_n}{e^{kn}} = FV_n e^{-kn}. \tag{4-9}$$

---

[10]Scientific or financial calculators with antilogarithm, or e^x, functions can be used to evaluate Equation 4-8.

Thus, if $1,649 is due in 10 years, and if the appropriate *continuous* discount rate, k, is 5 percent, then the present value of this future payment is

$$\text{PV} = \$1{,}649\left[\frac{1}{(2.7183)^{0.5}}\right] = \frac{\$1{,}649}{1.649} = \$1{,}000.$$

Effective Annual Percentage Rate

Equation 4-10 can be used to determine the effective annual percentage rate under continuous compounding:

$$\text{Effective annual rate} = e^k - 1.0. \tag{4-10}$$

Thus, if the nominal rate is 10 percent, compounded continuously, the effective annual rate is 10.52 percent:

$$
\begin{aligned}
\text{Effective annual rate} &= e^{0.10} - 1.0 \\
&= (2.7183)^{0.10} - 1.0 \\
&= 1.1052 - 1.0 \\
&= 0.1052 = 10.52\%.
\end{aligned}
$$

Annuities

The principles of continuous compounding can also be applied to annuities. If the annuity cash flows occur at discrete intervals, but the interest rate is compounded continuously, then we merely determine the effective annual rate as above and apply the standard annuity valuation techniques developed earlier in this chapter.

For example, assume that you were offered a $1,000 ordinary annuity for 3 years, and your opportunity cost is 10 percent compounded continuously. First, as above, we find the effective annual rate to be 10.52 percent. Then we find the present value of the annuity by entering i = 10.52, n = 3, and PMT = 1,000 in a financial calculator and then pressing the PV key. The solution is $2,464.26.

AMORTIZED LOANS

One of the most important applications of compound interest involves loans that are to be paid off in installments over time. Examples include automobile loans, home mortgage loans, and most business debt other than very short-term loans. If a loan is to be repaid in equal periodic amounts (monthly, quarterly, or annually), it is said to be an *amortized loan*.[11]

To illustrate, suppose a firm borrows $1,000 to be repaid in 3 equal payments at the end of each of the next 3 years. The lender is to receive 6 percent interest

---

[11]The word *amortized* comes from the Latin *mors*, meaning "death," so an amortized loan is one that is "killed off" over time.

on the loan balance that is outstanding at each point in time. The first task is to determine the amount the firm must repay each year, or the annual payment. To find this amount, recognize that the $1,000 represents the present value of an annuity of PMT dollars per year for 3 years, discounted at 6 percent:

$$\text{PV of annuity} = \frac{\text{PMT}}{(1 + k)^1} + \frac{\text{PMT}}{(1 + k)^2} + \frac{\text{PMT}}{(1 + k)^3}$$

$$\$1,000 = \frac{\text{PMT}}{(1.06)} + \frac{\text{PMT}}{(1.06)^2} + \frac{\text{PMT}}{(1.06)^3}$$

$$= \text{PMT}\left[\frac{1}{1.06} + \frac{1}{(1.06)^2} + \frac{1}{(1.06)^3}\right]$$

$$= \text{PMT}(\text{PVIFA}_{6\%, 3 \text{ years}}).$$

The PVIFA is 2.6730, so

$$\$1,000 = \text{PMT}(2.6730).$$

Solving for PMT, we obtain

$$\text{PMT} = \$1,000/2.6730 = \$374.11.$$

If the firm pays the lender $374.11 at the end of each of the next 3 years, the percentage cost to the borrower, and the rate of return to the lender, will be 6 percent.

The payment can also be found using a financial calculator. Merely enter $n = 3$, $i = 6$, and PV $= 1,000$, and then press PMT. The solution, PMT $= \$374.11$ (or -374.11) will appear. Each payment consists partly of interest and partly of a repayment of principal. This breakdown is given in the amortization schedule shown in Table 4-5. The interest component is largest in the first year and declines as the outstanding balance of the loan goes down. For tax purposes, the borrower

---

Table 4-5
Loan Amortization Schedule

Year	Beginning Amount (1)	Payment (2)	Interest[a] (3)	Repayment of Principal[b] (4)	Remaining Balance (5)
1	$1,000.00	$ 374.11	$ 60.00	$ 314.11	$685.89
2	685.89	374.11	41.15	332.96	352.93
3	352.93	374.11	21.18	352.93	0.00
		$1,122.33	$122.33	$1,000.00	

[a]Interest is calculated by multiplying the loan balance at the beginning of the year by the interest rate. Therefore, interest in Year 1 is $1,000(0.06) = $60; in Year 2 it is $685.89(0.06) = $41.15; and in Year 3 it is $352.93(0.06) = $21.18.

[b]Repayment of principal is equal to the payment of $374.11 minus the interest charge for each year.

reports as a deductible cost each year the interest payments in Column 3, while the lender reports these same amounts as taxable income.

SUMMARY

Financial decisions often involve situations in which someone pays money at one point in time and receives money at some later time. Dollars that are paid or received at two different points in time are different, and this difference must be recognized when analyzing financial decisions and transactions. All of this is called *discounted cash flow (DCF) analysis,* and Chapter 4 presented the basics of DCF analysis.

Several basic equations are used in DCF analysis:

Future value:
(single payment)

$$FV_n = PV(1 + k)^n = PV(FVIF_{k,n}).$$

Present value:
(single payment)

$$PV = FV_n\left[\frac{1}{1 + k}\right]^n = FV_n(1 + k)^{-n}$$

$$= FV_n(PVIF_{k,n}).$$

Future value:
(annuity)

$$FVA_n = PMT \sum_{t=1}^{n} (1 + k)^{n-t}$$

$$= PMT\left[\frac{(1 + k)^n - 1}{k}\right]$$

$$= PMT(FVIFA_{k,n}).$$

Present value:
(annuity)

$$PVA_n = PMT \sum_{t=1}^{n} \left(\frac{1}{1 + k}\right)^t$$

$$= PMT\left[\frac{1 - \frac{1}{(1 + k)^n}}{k}\right]$$

$$= PMT(PVIFA_{k,n}).$$

Present value:
(perpetuity)

$$PV = \frac{PMT}{k}.$$

These equations can also be applied to find the present or future value of an uneven cash flow stream, and to find interest rates in situations where the other values are given but the value of k is unknown. To find the interest rate, one simply inserts the known values into a financial calculator and then presses the i button to solve for the interest rate.

The chapter also covered situations in which compounding occurs more frequently than once a year, for example, semiannually or quarterly. Here the stated, or nominal, interest rate, k_{Nom}, is divided by m, the number of compounding periods per year; the exponent used is m × n; and the equations given above are used with these modified values. Note that the *effective annual rate* is somewhat greater than k_{Nom} when compounding is more frequent than annual. *Continuous compounding* is a special case in which interest on interest is earned continuously, and special equations were presented to handle this situation.

The concepts covered in this chapter will be used throughout the remainder of the book. In Chapter 5 we apply DCF concepts to the process of valuing stocks and bonds; there we will see that the market prices of these securities are established by determining the present values of the cash flows they are expected to provide. Then, in Chapter 6, we examine the determinants of a stock's required rate of return (which is used to discount its expected future cash flows in order to find its present value). In later chapters, the same basic concepts are applied to corporate decisions involving both expenditures on capital assets and the types of capital that should be used to pay for assets.

Questions

4-1 Define each of the following terms:

a. PV; k; I; FV_n; n; PVA_n; FVA_n

b. $FVIF_{k,n}$; $PVIF_{k,n}$; $FVIFA_{k,n}$; $PVIFA_{k,n}$

c. Opportunity cost (k)

d. Annuity; lump sum payment; uneven payment stream

e. Ordinary (deferred) annuity; annuity due

f. Perpetuity; consol

g. Financial calculator versus "regular" calculator

h. Compounding; discounting

i. Annual, semiannual, quarterly, monthly, daily, and continuous compounding

j. Effective annual rate; nominal (stated) interest rate; APR

k. Amortization schedule; principal component versus interest component of a payment

4-2 Is it true that for all positive interest rates the following conditions hold: $FVIF_{k,n} \geq 1.0$; $PVIF_{k,n} \leq 1.0$; $FVIFA_{k,n} \geq$ number of periods the annuity lasts; and $PVIFA_{k,n} \leq$ number of periods the annuity lasts?

4-3 An *annuity* is defined as a series of payments of a fixed amount for a specific number of periods. Thus, $100 a year for 10 years is an annuity, but $100 in Year 1, $200 in Year 2, and $400 in Years 3 through 10 do *not* constitute an annuity. However, the second series *contains* an annuity. Is this statement true or false?

4-4 If a firm's earnings per share grew from $1 to $2 over a 10-year period, the *total growth* would be 100 percent but the *annual growth rate* would be *less than* 10 percent. Why is this so?

4-5 Would you rather have a savings account that pays 5 percent interest compounded semiannually or one that pays 5 percent interest compounded daily? Explain.

4-6 To find the present value of an uneven series of payments, you can use the $PVIF_{k,n}$ tables; the $PVIFA_{k,n}$ tables can never be of use, even if some of the payments constitute an annuity (for example, $100 each for Years 3, 4, 5, and 6), because the entire series is not an annuity. Is this statement true or false?

4-7   The present value of a perpetuity is equal to the payment on the annuity, PMT, divided by the discount rate, k: PV = PMT/k. What is the future value of a perpetuity of PMT dollars per year? (Hint: The answer is infinity, but explain why.)

Self-Test Problems

ST-1 (Future value) Assume that it is now January 1, 1988. On January 1, 1989, you will deposit $1,000 into a savings account paying an 8 percent nominal interest rate.

    a. If the bank compounds interest annually, how much will you have in your account on January 1, 1992?

    b. What would your January 1, 1992, balance be if the bank used quarterly compounding rather than annual compounding?

    c. Suppose you deposited the $1,000 in 4 payments of $250 each on January 1 of 1989, 1990, 1991, and 1992. How much would you have in your account on January 1, 1992, based on 8 percent annual compounding?

    d. Suppose you deposited 4 equal payments in your account on January 1 of 1989, 1990, 1991, and 1992. How large would each of your payments have to be with annual compounding for you to obtain the same ending balance you calculated in Part a?

ST-2 (Discounted cash flow analysis) Assume that it is now January 1, 1988, and you will need $1,000 on January 1, 1992. Your bank compounds interest at an 8 percent rate annually.

    a. How much must you deposit on January 1, 1989, to have a balance of $1,000 on January 1, 1992?

    b. If you want to make equal payments on each January 1 from 1989 through 1992 to accumulate the $1,000, how large must each of the 4 payments be?

    c. If your father were to offer either to make the payments calculated in Part b ($221.92) or to give you a lump sum of $750 on January 1, 1989, which would you choose?

    d. If you have only $750 on January 1, 1989, what interest rate, compounded annually, would you have to earn to have the necessary $1,000 on January 1, 1992?

    e. Suppose you can deposit only $186.29 each January 1 from 1989 through 1992, but you still need $1,000 on January 1, 1992. What interest rate, with annual compounding, must you seek out to achieve your goal?

    f. To help you reach your $1,000 goal, your father offers to give you $400 on January 1, 1989. You will get a part-time job and make 6 additional payments of equal amounts each 6 months thereafter. If all of this money is deposited in a bank which pays 8 percent, compounded semiannually, how large must your payments be?

    g. What is the effective annual rate being paid by the bank in Part f?

    h. "Reinvestment rate risk" was defined in Chapter 3 to be the risk that maturing securities will have to be reinvested at a lower rate of interest than they were previously earning. Is there a reinvestment rate risk implied in the preceding analysis? If so, how might this risk be eliminated?

ST-3 (Effective annual rates) Bank A pays 8 percent interest, compounded quarterly, on its money market account. The managers of Bank B want its money market account to equal Bank A's effective annual rate, but interest is to be compounded on a monthly basis. What nominal, or stated, rate must Bank B set?

Problems

4-1 **(Present and future values for different periods)** Find the following values *without using tables,* and then work the problems with tables to check your answers. Then use a financial calculator as a further check on your answers. Disregard rounding errors.
- a. An initial $300 compounded for 1 year at 8 percent.
- b. An initial $300 compounded for 2 years at 8 percent.
- c. The present value of $300 due in 1 year at a discount rate of 8 percent.
- d. The present value of $300 due in 2 years at a discount rate of 8 percent.

4-2 **(Present and future values for different interest rates)** Use the tables to find the following values. Check your work with a financial calculator.
- a. An initial $300 compounded for 10 years at 8 percent.
- b. An initial $300 compounded for 10 years at 16 percent.
- c. The present value of $300 due in 10 years at an 8 percent discount rate.
- d. The present value of $1,323.42 due in 10 years at a 16 percent discount rate. Give a verbal definition of the term "present value," and illustrate it with data from this problem. As a part of your answer, explain why present values are dependent upon interest rates.

4-3 **(Time for a lump sum to double)** To the closest year, how long will it take $200 to double if it is deposited and earns the following rates? (Note: This problem cannot be solved with some financial calculators. For example, if you enter 200, − 400, and 7 in a HP-12C, and then press the n key, you will get 11 years as the answer for part a. The correct answer is 10.2448, which rounds to 10, but the calculator rounds up. You should look up FVIF = $400/$200 = 2 in the tables for a, b, and c, but figure out d.)
- a. 7 percent.
- b. 9 percent.
- c. 12 percent.
- d. 100 percent.

4-4 **(Future value of an annuity)** Find the *future value* of the following annuities. The first payment in these annuities is made at the *end* of Year 1—that is, they are *ordinary* annuities.
- a. $200 per year for 10 years at 10 percent.
- b. $100 per year for 5 years at 5 percent.
- c. $200 per year for 5 years at 0 percent.
- d. Now rework Parts a, b, and c assuming that payments are made at the *beginning* of each year, that is, they are *annuities due*.

4-5 **(Present value of an annuity)** Find the *present value* of the following *ordinary* annuities:
- a. $200 per year for 10 years at 10 percent.
- b. $100 per year for 5 years at 5 percent.
- c. $200 per year for 5 years at 0 percent.
- d. Now rework Parts a, b, and c assuming that payments are made at the *beginning* of each year, that is, they are *annuities due*.

4-6   (Uneven cash flow stream)
a. Find the present values of the following cash flow streams. The appropriate discount rate is 10 percent.

Year	Cash Stream A	Cash Stream B
1	$100	$300
2	400	400
3	400	400
4	400	400
5	300	100

b. What is the value of each cash flow stream at a 0 percent discount rate?

4-7   (Uneven cash flow stream) Find the present value of the following cash flow stream, discounted at 5 percent: Year 1, $100; Year 2, $400; Years 3 through 20, $300.

4-8   (Present value comparison) Which amount is worth more at 10 percent: $1,000 in hand today or $2,000 due after 8 years?

4-9   (Growth rates) The Ezzell Company's 1987 sales were $6 million. Sales were $3 million 5 years earlier (in 1982).
a. To the nearest percentage point, at what rate have sales been growing?
b. Suppose someone calculated the sales growth in Part a as follows: "Sales doubled in 5 years. This represents a growth of 100 percent in 5 years, so, dividing 100 percent by 5, we find the growth rate to be 20 percent per year." Explain what is wrong with this calculation.

4-10   (Effective rate of interest) Find the interest rates, or rates of return, on each of the following:
a. You borrow $400 and promise to pay back $420 at the end of 1 year.
b. You lend $400 and receive a promise of $420 at the end of 1 year.
c. You borrow $40,000 and promise to pay back $65,156 at the end of 10 years.
d. You borrow $4,000 and promise to make payments of $1,028.36 per year for 5 years.

4-11   (Expected rate of return) The Beedles Company buys a machine for $20,000 and expects a return of $4,770.42 per year for the next 10 years. What is the expected rate of return on the machine? (Note: As we will see in Chapter 8, we are finding the internal rate of return (IRR) of the project.)

4-12   (Expected rate of return) Trivoli Forest Products invests $1 million to clear a tract of land and to set out some young pine trees. The trees will mature in 10 years, at which time the firm plans to sell the forest at an expected price of $3 million. What is the firm's expected rate of return?

4-13   (Effective rate of interest) Your broker offers to sell you a note for $11,300 that will pay $2,000 per year for 10 years. If you buy the note, what rate of interest will you be earning?

4-14   (Effective rate of interest) A mortgage company offers to lend you $50,000; the loan calls for payments of $5,477.36 per year for 20 years. What interest rate is the mortgage company charging you?

4-15 (Required lump sum payment) In order to complete your last year in business school and then go through law school, you will need $8,000 per year for 4 years, starting next year (that is, you will need to withdraw $8,000 one year from today). Your rich uncle offers to put you through school, and he will deposit in a bank time deposit paying 8 percent interest a sum of money that is sufficient to provide the four payments of $8,000 each. His deposit will be made today.

    a. How large must the deposit be?

    b. How much will be in the account immediately after you make the first withdrawal? After the last withdrawal?

4-16 (Repaying a loan) While Helen Burgess was a student at the University of North Carolina, she borrowed $5,000 in student loans at an annual interest rate of 9 percent. If Helen repays $900 a year, how long to the nearest year will it take her to repay the loan?

4-17 (Reaching a financial goal) If you deposit $1,500 a year in an account which pays 12 percent interest compounded annually, how long will it take you to accumulate a balance of $10,000? (Note that some calculators automatically round up to the nearest whole period. For example, if the solution to a problem is 3.2 periods, the answer will be displayed as 4 periods. These calculators show the correct number of payments — you cannot make 3.2 payments — but fail to indicate that the final payment would be smaller than the previous payments. You should be aware of that potential discrepancy when working this problem.)

4-18 (Future value for various compounding periods) Find the amount to which $200 will grow under each of the following conditions:

    a. 12 percent compounded annually for 5 years.

    b. 12 percent compounded semiannually for 5 years.

    c. 12 percent compounded quarterly for 5 years.

    d. 12 percent compounded monthly for 1 year.

4-19 (Present value for various compounding periods) Find the present values of $200 due in the future under each of the following conditions:

    a. 12 percent nominal rate, semiannual compounding, discounted back 5 years.

    b. 12 percent nominal rate, quarterly compounding, discounted back 5 years.

    c. 12 percent nominal rate, monthly compounding, discounted back 1 year.

4-20 (Annuity value for various compounding periods) Find the indicated value of the following regular annuities:

    a. FV of $200 each 6 months for 5 years at a nominal rate of 12 percent, compounded semiannually.

    b. PV of $200 each 3 months for 5 years at a nominal rate of 12 percent, compounded quarterly.

4-21 (Effective versus nominal interest rates) The Denver National Bank pays 9 percent interest, compounded annually, on time deposits. The Boulder City Bank pays 8 percent interest, compounded quarterly.

    a. In which bank would you prefer to deposit your money?

    b. Could your choice of banks be influenced by the fact that you might want to withdraw your funds during the year as opposed to the end of the year? In answering this question, assume that funds must be left on deposit during the entire compounding period in order for you to receive any interest.

4-22 (Present value of a perpetuity) What is the present value of a perpetuity of $100 per year if the appropriate discount rate is 5 percent? If interest rates in general were to double, and the appropriate discount rate rose to 10 percent, what would happen to the present value of the perpetuity?

4-23 (Amortization schedule)

a. Set up an amortization schedule for a $20,000 loan to be repaid in equal install-ments at the end of each of the next 3 years. The interest rate is 10 percent.
(Do Parts b through d only if you are using the computerized diskette.)

b. Set up an amortization schedule for a $40,000 loan to be repaid in equal install-ments at the end of each of the next 3 years. The interest rate is 10 percent.

c. Set up an amortization schedule for a $100,000 loan to be repaid in equal in-stallments at the end of each of the next 3 years. The interest rate is 9 percent.

d. Redo Parts b and c using a 20-year amortization schedule.

4-24 (Effective rates of return) AT&T's pension fund managers recently had to choose between two investments. Their choices were (1) a bond which costs $680.58 today, pays nothing during its life, and then pays $1,000 after 5 years or (2) a bond which costs $1,000 today, pays $87.50 in interest at the end of each of the next 4 years, and pays $1,087.50 interest and principal at the end of Year 5. (Note: This investment decision, along with those presented in the next two problems, was highlighted in the introduction to this chapter.) Now that you are familiar with discounted cash flow techniques, see if you can reach the right decisions.

a. Which alternative is expected to provide the higher rate of return?

b. Assume that the market interest rate dropped to 6 percent immediately after the bonds were purchased and that rates remained at that level for the next 5 years. (1) What would be the immediate gain or loss on the two bonds? (2) If AT&T holds the bonds until they mature, what annual rates of return would it realize on the two bond alternatives over the 5-year holding period?

4-25 (Required annuity payments) A father is planning a savings program to put his daughter through college. His daughter is now 13 years old. She plans to enroll at the university in 5 years, and it should take her 4 years to complete her education. Cur-rently, the cost per year (for everything — food, clothing, tuition, books, transportation, and so forth) is $9,000, but a 10 percent inflation rate in these costs is forecasted. The daughter recently received $15,000 from her grandfather's estate; this money, which is invested in a bank account paying 8 percent interest compounded annually, will be used to help meet the costs of the daughter's education. The rest of the costs will be met by money the father will deposit in the savings account. He will make equal de-posits to the account in each year from now until and including the year his daughter starts college. These deposits will also earn 8 percent interest.

a. If the first deposit is made today, how large must each deposit be in order to put the daughter through college?
(Do Parts b and c only if you are using the computerized diskette.)

b. How large must each deposit be if the interest rate is 6 percent?

c. How large must each deposit be if the interest rate is expected to remain at 8 percent for 2 years and then to fall to 6 percent?

4-26 (Present value of an annuity) Suppose that in January 1988, General Motors' engi-neers informed top management that they had just made a breakthrough which would permit them to produce an electric auto capable of operating at an energy cost of about 3 cents per mile versus an energy cost of about 5 cents for a comparable gasoline-powered car. If GM produces the electric car, it should be able to regain the market share it previously lost to the Japanese. However, the investment required to complete development of the new batteries, to design the new car, and to tool up for production would amount to $5 billion per year for 5 years, starting immediately. Cash inflows from the $25 billion investment should amount to $3 billion per year for 15 years, or $45 billion total, starting 5 years from now. If the electric car project is not undertaken, GM will invest the $25 billion in investments which earn 10 percent, compounded annually.

    a. Based on these cost and cash inflow estimates, should management give the go-ahead for full-scale electric car production?

    (Do Part b only if you are using the computerized diskette.)

    b. Suppose inflation is expected to average 5 percent per year over the 19-year forecast period. Therefore, all forecasted cash inflows and outflows will increase by 5 percent a year. Based on these cash flows, should GM produce the electric car?

Solutions to Self-Test Problems

ST-1   a.

1/1/88	1/1/89	1/1/90	1/1/91	1/1/92

$1,000

$1,000 is being compounded for 3 years, so your balance on January 1, 1992, is $1,259.71:

$$FV = PV(1 + k)^n = \$1,000(1 + 0.08)^3 = \$1,259.71.$$

b. The effective annual rate for 8 percent, compounded quarterly, is

$$\text{Effective annual rate} = \left(1 + \frac{0.08}{4}\right)^4 - 1.0$$
$$= (1.02)^4 - 1.0 = 0.0824 = 8.24\%.$$

Therefore, FV = $1,000(1.0824)^3 = $1,000(1.2681) = $1,268.10. Alternatively, use FVIF for 2%, 3 × 4 = 12 periods:

$$FV = \$1,000(FVIF_{2\%,12 \text{ periods}}) = \$1,000(1.2682) = \$1,268.20.$$

The future value found by calculator is $1,268.24. (Note that since the interest factors are carried to only four decimal places, rounding errors occur. Rounding errors also occur between calculator and tabular solutions.)

c.

1/1/88	1/1/89	1/1/90	1/1/91	1/1/92
	$250	$250	$250	$250

As you work this problem, keep in mind that the tables assume that payments are made at the end of each period. Therefore, you may solve this problem by finding the future value of an annuity of $250 for 4 years at 8 percent:

$$\text{PMT}(\text{FVIFA}_{k,n}) = \$250(4.5061) = \$1,126.53.$$

d. $FV = \$1,259.71; k = 8\%; n = 4; PMT = ?$

$$\text{PMT}(\text{FVIFA}_{8\%,4 \text{ years}}) = FV$$

$$\text{PMT}(4.5061) = \$1,259.71$$

$$\text{PMT} = \$1,259.71/4.5061 = \$279.56.$$

Therefore, you would have to make 4 payments of $279.56 each to have a balance of $1,259.71 on January 1, 1992.

ST-2   a. Set up a time line like those above, and note that your deposit will grow for 3 years at 8 percent. The fact that it is now January 1, 1988, is irrelevant. The deposit on January 1, 1989, is the PV, and $1,000 = FV. Here is the solution:

$FV = \$1,000; n = 3; k = 8\%; PMT = ?$

$$PV = FV(\text{PVIF}_{8\%,3 \text{ years}})$$

$$= \$1,000(0.7938) = \$793.80$$

$$= \text{Initial deposit to accumulate } \$1,000.$$

(Calculator solution = $793.83.)

b. Here we are dealing with a 4-year annuity whose first payment occurs one year from today, on 1/1/89, and whose future value must equal $1,000. You should set up a time line to help visualize the situation. Here is the solution:

$FV = \$1,000; n = 4; k = 8\%; PMT = ?$

$$FV = \text{PMT}(\text{FVIFA}_{8\%,4 \text{ years}})$$

$$\text{PMT} = \frac{FV}{(\text{FVIFA}_{8\%,4 \text{ years}})}$$

$$= \frac{\$1,000}{4.5061}$$

$$= \$221.92 = \text{Payment necessary to accumulate } \$1,000.$$

c. This problem can be approached in several ways. Perhaps the simplest is to ask this question: "If I received $750 on 1/1/89 and deposited it to earn 8 percent, would I have the required $1,000 on 1/1/92?" The answer is no:

$$\$750(1.08)(1.08)(1.08) = \$944.78.$$

This indicates that you should let your father make the payments rather than accept the lump sum $750.

You could also compare the $750 with the PV of the payments:

$\text{PMT} = \$221.92; k = 8\%; n = 4; PV = ?$

$$\text{PMT}(\text{PVIFA}_{8\%,4 \text{ years}}) = PV$$

$$\$221.92(3.3121) = \$735.02 = \text{PV of the required payments.}$$

This is less than the $750 lump sum offer, so your initial reaction might be to accept the lump sum of $750. However, this would be a mistake. As we saw above, if you were to deposit the $750 on January 1, 1989, at an 8 percent interest rate, to be withdrawn 6n January 1, 1992, interest would be compounded for only 3 years, from January 1, 1989, to December 31, 1991, and the future value would be only

$$PV(FVIF_{8\%,3 \text{ years}}) = \$750(1.2597) = \$944.78.$$

The problem is that when you found the $735.02 PV of the annuity, you were finding the value of the annuity *today,* on January 1, 1988. You were comparing $735.02 today with the lump sum $750 one year from now. This is, of course, invalid. What you should have done was take the $735.02, recognize that this is the PV of an annuity as of January 1, 1988, multiply $735.02 by 1.08 to get $793.82, and compare $793.82 with the lump sum of $750. You would then take your father's offer to make the payments rather than take the lump sum on January 1, 1988.

d. PV = $750; FV = $1,000; n = 3; k = ?

$$PV(FVIF_{k,3 \text{ years}}) = FV$$

$$FVIF_{k,3 \text{ years}} = \frac{FV}{PV}$$

$$= \frac{\$1,000}{\$750} = 1.333.$$

Use the Future Value of $1 table (Table A-3 at the end of the book) for 3 periods to find the interest rate corresponding to an FVIF of 1.3333. Look across the Period 3 row of the table until you come to 1.3333. The closest value is 1.3310, in the 10 percent column. Therefore, you would require an interest rate of approximately 10 percent to achieve your $1,000 goal. The exact rate required, found with a financial calculator, is 10.0642 percent.

e. FV = $1,000; PMT = $186.29; n = 4; k = ?

$$PMT(FVIFA_{k,4 \text{ years}}) = FV$$

$$\$186.29(FVIFA_{k,4 \text{ years}}) = \$1,000$$

$$FVIFA_{k,4 \text{ years}} = \frac{\$1,000}{\$186.29} = 5.3680.$$

Using Table A-4 at the end of the book, we find that 5.3680 corresponds to a 20 percent interest rate. You might be able to find a borrower willing to offer you a 20 percent interest rate, but there would be some risk involved — he or she might not actually pay you your $1,000!
(Calculator solution = 19.9997%.)

f.

1/1/88	1/1/89	1/1/90	1/1/91	1/1/92
$400	? ?	? ?	? ?	?

Find the future value of the original $400 deposit:

$$FV = PV(FVIF_{4\%,6}) = \$400(1.2653) = \$506.12.$$

This means that on January 1, 1992, you need an additional sum of $493.88:

$$\$1,000.00 - \$506.12 = \$493.88.$$

This will be accumulated by making 6 equal payments which earn 8 percent compounded semiannually, or 4 percent each 6 months:

$$FV = \$493.88; n = 6; k = 4\%; PMT = ?$$

$$PMT(FVIFA_{4\%,6}) = FV$$

$$PMT = \frac{FV}{(FVIFA_{4\%,6})}$$

$$= \frac{\$493.88}{6.6330} = \$74.46.$$

g. Effective annual rate $= \left(1 + \dfrac{k_{Nom}}{m}\right)^m - 1.0$

$$= \left(1 + \frac{0.08}{2}\right)^2 - 1 = (1.04)^2 - 1$$

$$= 1.0816 - 1 = 0.0816 = 8.16\%.$$

h. There is a reinvestment rate risk here, because we assumed that funds will earn an 8 percent return in the bank. In fact, if interest rates in the economy fall, the bank will lower its deposit rate, because it will be earning less when it lends out the funds you deposited with it. If you buy certificates of deposit (CDs) that mature on the date you need the money (1/1/92), you will avoid the reinvestment risk, but that will work only where you are making the deposit today. Other ways of reducing reinvestment rate risk will be discussed later in the text.

ST-3 Bank A's effective annual rate is 8.24 percent:

$$\text{Effective annual rate} = \left(1 + \frac{0.08}{4}\right)^4 - 1.0$$

$$= (1.02)^4 - 1 = 1.0824 - 1$$

$$= 0.082432 \approx 8.24\%.$$

Now Bank B must have the same effective annual rate:

$$\left(1 + \frac{k}{12}\right)^{12} - 1.0 = 0.082432$$

$$\left(1 + \frac{k}{12}\right)^{12} = 1.082432$$

$$1 + \frac{k}{12} = (1.082432)^{1/12}$$

$$1 + \frac{k}{12} = 1.0066227$$

$$\frac{k}{12} = 0.0066227$$

$$k = 0.0794724 \approx 7.95\%.$$

Selected Additional References

For a more complete discussion of the mathematics of finance, see

Cissell, Robert, Helen Cissell, and David C. Flaspohler, *Mathematics of Finance* (Boston: Houghton Mifflin, 1978).

To learn more about using financial calculators, see the owner's handbook which came with your calculator. For example, see

Hewlett-Packard, HP-12C, *Owner's Manual and Problem Solving Guide,* 1983.

5
Valuation Models

In the fall of 1979, IBM raised $1 billion of new capital by selling bonds to the public. The issue was in two parts: A $500 million, 7-year issue which paid 9½ percent interest and matured in 1986, and a $500 million, 25-year issue which pays 9⅜ percent interest and matures in 2004. In each case, the individual bonds had a par value of $1,000 and were sold initially at that price. In 1981, after a sharp increase in interest rates, the IBM 9½s of 1986 were selling for $800, and the 9⅜s of 2004 were selling for $645. In 1986, however, the holders of the 9½s were paid $1,000 per bond, and the 9⅜s were selling for $1,042.50. Thus, in the first 2 years, investors who sold out lost 20 percent on the 7-year bonds and over 35 percent on the 25-year bonds of a AAA, super blue chip company, but if they held on, they later recouped those losses and, in fact, made a capital gain on the longer term issue. How should IBM's financial executives use such information as they make their financial plans for 1988 and beyond? How should investors, both individual savers and institutional investors such as pension plan managers, use this type of information as they plan to put their money to work?

At the time of its 1979 bond issue, IBM's stock was selling for about $70 per share, and it had fluctuated narrowly around that price since 1968. IBM's earnings per share from 1968 to 1979 had grown from $1.54 to $5.16, or at a rate of 11.6 percent per year. Its dividend, which in 1979 was $3.44, had been growing even faster than its earnings, and most security analysts projected a continuation of these growth trends. Although IBM sold bonds rather than common stock to raise the $1 billion, selling stock was an alternative. How might IBM's managers have used the information on its stock price, earnings, and dividends to help reach the decision to finance with bonds rather than with stock? How could investors who were interested in IBM have used the information when deciding whether to buy new IBM bonds or to buy IBM stock on the New York Stock Exchange? What, if anything, could IBM's financial executives have done to increase the stock price and get it to move up and away from the $70 level at which it had been stuck for 11 years?

After studying Chapter 5, you will be in a better position to answer questions such as these, and others.

In Chapter 1 we noted that financial managers should work to maximize the value of their firms. Then, in Chapter 4, we examined discounted cash flow concepts, which are used by managers and investors to establish the worth of any asset whose value is derived from future cash flows; such assets include real estate, factories, machinery, oil wells, coal mines, farmland, stocks, and bonds. In this chapter we use discounted cash flow techniques to explain how financial managers and investors go about establishing the values of stocks and bonds. This material is obviously important to investors and potential investors, and equally important to corporate financial managers. *Indeed, since all important corporate decisions should be analyzed in terms of how they will affect the price of the firm's stock, it is essential that managers know how stock prices are determined.*

BOND VALUES

Corporations raise capital in two primary forms — debt and common equity. Our first task in this chapter is to examine the valuation process for bonds, the primary type of long-term debt.

A *bond* is a long-term promissory note issued by a business or governmental unit. For example, on January 2, 1988, the Senbet Electronics Company borrowed $50 million by selling 50,000 individual bonds for $1,000 each. Senbet received $50 million, and it promised to pay the lenders annual interest on the bonds and to repay the $50 million on a specified date. The lenders were willing to give Senbet $50 million for this promise, so the value of the bond issue was $50 million. But how did the investors decide that the issue was worth $50 million? As a first step in explaining how the values of this and other bonds are determined, we need to define some of the terms associated with these securities.

1. Par value. The *par value* is the stated face value of the bond; it is usually set at $1,000, although multiples of $1,000 (for example, $5,000) are used on occasion. The par value generally represents the amount of money the firm borrows and promises to repay at some future date.

2. Maturity date. Bonds generally have a specified *maturity date* on which the par value is to be repaid. Senbet's bonds, which were issued on January 2, 1988, will mature on January 1, 2003; thus, they had a 15-year maturity at the time they were issued. Most bonds have *original maturities* (the maturity at the time the bond is issued) of from 10 to 40 years, but any maturity is legally permissible. Of course, the maturity of a bond declines each year after it has been issued. Thus, Senbet's bonds had a 15-year original maturity, but in 1989 they will have a 14-year maturity, and so on.

3. Call provisions. Some bonds have a provision whereby the issuer may pay them off prior to maturity. This feature is known as a *call provision,* and it is discussed in detail in Chapter 15. If a bond is callable, and if interest rates in the economy decline, then the company can sell a new issue of low-interest-rate bonds and use the proceeds to retire the old, high-interest-rate issue, just as a homeowner can refinance a home mortgage.

4. Coupon interest rate. The bond requires the issuer to pay a specified number of dollars of interest each year (or, more generally, each six months). When this *coupon payment,* as it is called, is divided by the par value, the result is the *coupon interest rate.* For example, Senbet's bonds have a $1,000 par value, and they pay $150 in interest each year. The bond's coupon interest is $150, so its coupon interest rate is $150/$1,000 = 15%. The $150 is the yearly "rent" on the $1,000 loan. This payment, which is fixed at the time the bond is issued, remains in force, by contract, during the life of the bond. Incidentally, some time ago, most bonds literally had a number of small (½-by-2-inch), dated coupons attached to them, and on the interest payment date, the owner would clip off the coupon for that date and mail it to the company's paying agent, who then mailed back a check for the interest. A 30-year, semiannual bond started with 60 coupons, while a 5-year annual payment bond would start with only 5 coupons. Today, however, most bonds are *registered* — no coupons are involved, and interest checks are mailed automatically on the payment date to the bonds' registered owners. Even so, we continue to use the terms "coupon" and "coupon interest rate," even for registered bonds.

5. New issues versus outstanding bonds. As we shall see, a bond's market price is determined primarily by its coupon interest payment — the higher the coupon, other things held constant, the higher the market price of the bond. At the time a bond is issued, the coupon is generally set at a level that will force the market price of the bond to equal its par value. If a lower coupon were set, investors simply would not be willing to pay $1,000 for the bond, while if a higher coupon were set, investors would clamor for the bond and bid its price up over $1,000. Investment bankers can judge quite precisely the coupon rate that will cause a bond to sell at its $1,000 par value.

A bond that has just been issued is known as a *new issue.* (The *Wall Street Journal* classifies a bond as a new issue for about two weeks after it has first been issued.) Once the bond has been on the market for awhile, it is classified as an *outstanding bond,* also called a *seasoned issue.* As we shall see below, newly issued bonds do generally sell very close to par. However, the prices of outstanding bonds vary widely from par: Their coupon interest payments are constant, but when economic conditions change, a bond with a $150 coupon that sold at par when it was issued will sell for more or less than $1,000 thereafter.

The Basic Bond Valuation Model[1]

As we noted above, bonds call for the payment of a specified amount of interest for a stated number of years, and then for the repayment of the par value on the

---

[1] In finance the term *model* refers to an equation or set of equations designed to show how one or more variables affect some other variable. Thus, a bond valuation model shows the mathematical relationship between a bond's price and the set of variables that determine the price.

bond's maturity date. Thus, a bond represents an annuity plus a lump sum, and its value is found as the present value of this payment stream.

The following equation is used to find a bond's value:[2]

$$\text{Value} = V = \sum_{t=1}^{n} I\left(\frac{1}{1 + k_d}\right)^t + M\left(\frac{1}{1 + k_d}\right)^n \tag{5-1}$$

$$= I(\text{PVIFA}_{k_d,n}) + M(\text{PVIF}_{k_d,n}).$$

Here

I = dollars of interest paid each year = coupon interest rate × par value.

M = par value, or maturity value, which is typically $1,000.

k_d = appropriate rate of interest on the bond.[3]

n = number of years until the bond matures; n declines each year after the bond is issued, so a bond that had a maturity of 30 years when it was issued (original maturity = 30 years) becomes a 29-year bond a year later, then a 28-year bond, and so on.

We can use Equation 5-1 to find the value of Senbet's bonds when they were issued, assuming that the appropriate rate of interest was k_d = 15%. Simply substitute $150 for I, $1,000 for M, and the values of PVIFA and PVIF at 15 percent, 15 periods, as found in Tables A-2 and A-1 at the end of the book:

$$V = \$150(5.8474) + \$1,000(0.1229)$$

$$= \$877.11 + \$122.90$$

$$= \$1,000.01 \approx \$1,000 \text{ when } k_d = 15\%.$$

Figure 5-1 shows the same result on a time line.

You can also find the value of these bonds with many financial calculators. Enter n = 15, PMT = 150, FV = 1,000, and k_d = i = 15, and then press the PV key. The answer, $1,000 (or − $1,000), will appear.

If k_d remained constant at 15 percent, what would the value of the bond be 1 year after it was issued? We can find this value using Equation 5-1, but now the term to maturity is only 14 years — that is, n = 14. V remains at $1,000:

$$V = \$150(5.7245) + \$1,000(0.1413)$$

$$= \$999.98 \approx \$1,000.$$

---

[2]Actually, since most bonds pay interest semiannually, not annually, it is necessary for us to modify our valuation equation slightly. The modification is discussed later in the chapter. Also, we should note that some bonds issued in recent years either pay no interest during their lives ("zero coupon bonds") or else pay very low coupon rates. Such bonds are sold at a discount below par, and hence they are called *original issue discount (OID) bonds.* The "interest" earned on zero coupon bonds comes at the end, when the company pays off at par ($1,000) a bond which was purchased for, say, $321.97. The discount of $1,000 − $321.97 = $678.03 substitutes for interest. Original issue discount bonds are discussed at greater length in Chapter 15.

[3]The appropriate interest rate on debt securities was discussed in Chapter 3. The bond's riskiness and years to maturity, as well as supply and demand conditions in the capital markets, all have an influence.

Figure 5-1
Time Line for Senbet Electronics Bonds

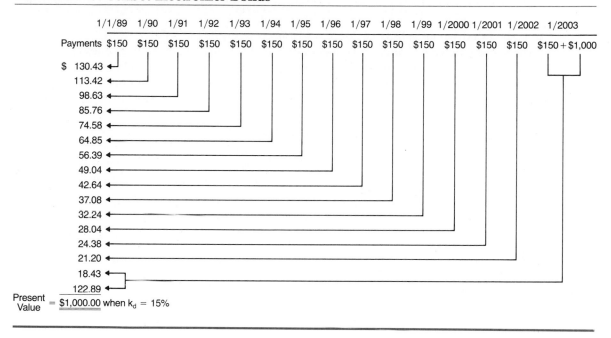

With a financial calculator, just replace n = 15 with n = 14, press the PV button, and you will get the same answer. The value of the bond will remain at $1,000 as long as the appropriate interest rate for it remains constant at 15 percent.[4]

Now suppose interest rates in the economy fell after the Senbet bonds were issued, and as a result k_d *decreased* from 15 to 10 percent. Both the coupon interest payments and the maturity value would remain constant, but now 10 percent values for PVIF and PVIFA would have to be used in Equation 5-1, or entered in your calculator. The value of the bond at the end of the first year would be $1,368.31:

---

[4]The bond prices quoted by brokers are calculated as described. However, if you bought a bond between interest payment dates, you would have to pay the basic price plus accrued interest. Thus, if you purchased a Senbet Electronics bond 6 months after it was issued, your broker would send you an invoice stating that you must pay $1,000 as the basic price of the bond plus $75 interest, representing one-half the annual interest of $150. The seller of the bond would receive $1,075. If you bought the bond the day before its interest payment date, you would pay $1,000 + (364/365)($150) = $1,149.59. Of course, you would receive an interest payment of $150 at the end of the next day. See Self-Test Problem 1 for a detailed discussion of bond quotations between interest payment dates.

Note also that throughout the chapter we assume that the bond is being evaluated immediately after an interest payment date. The better financial calculators have a built-in calendar which permits the calculation of exact values between interest payment dates.

$$V = \$150(\text{PVIFA}_{10\%,14 \text{ years}}) + \$1,000(\text{PVIF}_{10\%,14 \text{ years}})$$
$$= \$150(7.3667) + \$1,000(0.2633)$$
$$= \$1,105.01 + \$263.30 = \$1,368.31.$$

Thus, the bond would sell above, or at a *premium* over, its par value.

The arithmetic of the bond price increase should be clear, but what is the logic behind it? The reason for the increase is simple. The fact that k_d has fallen to 10 percent means that if you had $1,000 to invest, you could buy new bonds like Senbet's (every day some 10 to 12 companies sell new bonds), except that they would pay only $100 of interest each year rather than $150. Naturally, you would prefer $150 to $100, so you would be willing to pay more than $1,000 for Senbet bonds to obtain its higher coupons. All investors would recognize these facts, and, as a result, the Senbet bonds would be bid up in price to $1,368.31, at which point they would provide the same rate of return to a potential investor as the new bonds, 10 percent.

Assuming that interest rates remain constant at 10 percent for the next 14 years, what would happen to the value of a Senbet bond? It would fall gradually from $1,368.31 at present to $1,000 at maturity, when Senbet Electronics must redeem each bond for $1,000. This point can be illustrated by calculating the value of the bond 1 year later, when it has 13 years remaining to maturity:

$$V = \$150(\text{PVIFA}_{10\%,13 \text{ years}}) + \$1,000(\text{PVIF}_{10\%,13 \text{ years}})$$
$$= \$150(7.1034) + \$1,000(0.2897) = \$1,355.21.$$

Thus, the value of the bond will have fallen from $1,368.31 to $1,355.21, or by $13.10. If you were to calculate the value of the bond at other future dates, the price would continue to fall as the maturity date approached.

Notice also that if you purchased the bond at a price of $1,368.31 and then sold it 1 year later with k_d still at 10 percent, you would have a capital loss of $13.10, or a total return of $150.00 − $13.10 = $136.90. Your percentage rate of return would consist of an *interest yield* (also called the *current yield*) plus a *capital gains yield,* calculated as follows:

$$\text{Interest, or current, yield} = \$150/\$1,368.31 = 0.1096 = 10.96\%$$
$$\text{Capital gains yield} = -\$13.10/\$1,368.31 = -0.0096 = \underline{-0.96\%}$$
$$\text{Total rate of return, or yield} = \$136.90/\$1,368.31 = 0.1001 \approx \underline{\underline{10.00\%}}$$

Had interest rates risen from 15 to 20 percent during the first year after issue rather than fallen, the value of Senbet's bonds would have declined to $769.49:

$$V = \$150(\text{PVIFA}_{20\%,14 \text{ years}}) + \$1,000(\text{PVIF}_{20\%,14 \text{ years}})$$
$$= \$150(4.6106) + \$1,000(0.0779)$$
$$= \$691.59 + \$77.90 = \$769.49.$$

In this case, the bond would sell at a *discount* of $230.51 below its par value. The discount can be calculated as

$$\text{Discount} = \text{Price} - \text{Par value} = \$769.49 - \$1,000.00 = -\$230.51.$$

The total expected future return on the bond would again consist of a current yield and a capital gains yield, and the latter would be *positive*. The total return would be 20 percent.

The discount or premium on a bond may also be calculated as follows:

$$\begin{matrix} \text{Discount or} \\ \text{premium} \end{matrix} = \left[\begin{matrix} \text{Interest payment} \\ \text{on the old bond} \end{matrix} - \begin{matrix} \text{Interest payment} \\ \text{on a new bond} \end{matrix} \right] (\text{PVIFA}_{k_d,n}),$$

where n = years to maturity on the old bond and k_d = current rate of interest on a new bond. For example, if interest rates had risen to 20 percent 1 year after the Senbet bonds were issued, the discount on them would have been calculated as follows:

$$\text{Discount} = (\$150 - \$200)(4.6106) = -\$230.53.$$

(The minus sign indicates discount.) This value agrees, except for rounding, with the $-\$230.51$ value calculated above, and from these calculations we see that the discount is equal to the present value of the interest payment one sacrifices to buy a low-coupon old bond rather than a high-coupon new bond. The longer the bond has left to maturity, the greater the sacrifice, and hence the greater the discount.

Figure 5-2 graphs the values of the bond over time assuming that interest rates in the economy (1) rise to 20 percent and remain constant at that level, (2) remain constant at 15 percent, or (3) fall to 10 percent and then remain constant at that level. Of course, if interest rates do *not* remain constant, then the price of the bond will fluctuate. However, regardless of what future interest rates do, the bond's price will approach $1,000 as it nears the maturity date (barring bankruptcy, in which case the bond's value might drop to zero).

Figure 5-2 illustrates the following key points:

1. Whenever the going rate of interest, k_d, is *equal to* the coupon rate, a bond will sell at its par value.

2. Whenever the going rate of interest is *less than* the coupon rate, a bond will sell above its par value. Such a bond is called a *premium bond*.

3. Whenever the going rate of interest is *greater than* the coupon rate, a bond will sell below its par value. Such a bond is called a *discount bond*.

4. Thus, an *increase* in interest rates will cause the price of an outstanding bond to *fall*, while a *decrease* in rates will cause it to *rise*.

5. The market value of a bond will always approach its par value as its maturity date approaches, provided the firm does not go bankrupt.

These points are very important, for they show that bondholders may suffer capital losses or make capital gains depending on whether interest rates rise or fall — and, as we saw in Chapter 3, interest rates do indeed change over time.

Figure 5-2
Time Path of the Value of a 15% Coupon, $1,000 Par Value Bond
When Interest Rates Are 10%, 15%, and 20%

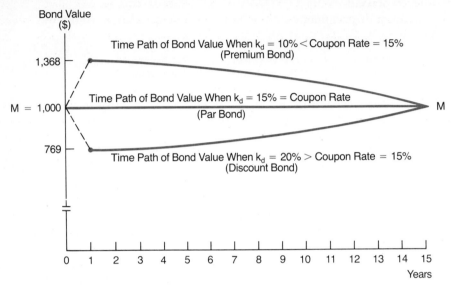

Note: The curves for 10% and 20% have a slight bow.

Finding the Interest Rate on a Bond: Yield to Maturity

Suppose you were offered a 14-year, 15 percent coupon, $1,000 par value bond at a price of $1,368.31. What rate of interest would you earn on your investment if you bought the bond and held it to maturity? This rate is defined as the bond's *yield to maturity (YTM),* and it is the interest rate discussed by bond traders when they talk about rates of return. To find the yield to maturity, you could solve Equation 5-1 for k_d:

$$V = \$1,368.31 = \frac{\$150}{(1 + k_d)^1} + \frac{\$150}{(1 + k_d)^2} + \cdots + \frac{\$150}{(1 + k_d)^{14}} + \frac{\$1,000}{(1 + k_d)^{14}}$$

$$= \$150(PVIFA_{k_d,14}) + \$1,000(PVIF_{k_d,14}).$$

We can substitute values for PVIFA and PVIF until we find a pair that "works" and forces this equality:

$$\$1,368.31 = \$150(PVIFA_{k_d,14}) + \$1,000(PVIF_{k_d,14}).$$

What would be a good interest rate to use as a starting point? First, we know that since the bond is selling at a premium over its par value ($1,368.31 versus $1,000), the bond's yield to maturity must be *below* its 15 percent coupon rate.

Therefore, we might try a rate of 12 percent. Substituting factors for 12 percent, we obtain

$$\$150(6.6282) + \$1,000(0.2046) = \$1,198.83 \neq \$1,368.31.$$

Our calculated bond value, $1,198.83, is *below* the actual market price, so the YTM is *not* 12 percent. To raise the calculated value, we must *lower* the interest rate used to discount the cash flows. Inserting interest factors for 10 percent, we obtain

$$V = \$150(7.3667) + \$1,000(0.2633)$$
$$= \$1,105.01 + \$263.30 = \$1,368.31.$$

This calculated value is equal to the market price of the bond; thus, 10 percent is the bond's yield to maturity: k_d = YTM = 10.0%.[5]

As you might guess, by far the easiest way to find a bond's YTM is with a financial calculator. In our example, enter n = 14, PMT = 150, FV = 1,000, and PV = 1,368.31 (−1,368.31 on some calculators). Now press the i button. The calculator will blink for several seconds, and then the answer, 10 percent, will appear.

The yield to maturity is identical to the total rate of return as discussed in the preceding section. The YTM for a bond that sells at par consists entirely of an interest yield, but if the bond sells at a price other than its par value, the YTM consists of the interest yield plus a positive or negative capital gains yield. Note also that a bond's yield to maturity changes whenever interest rates in the economy change — and this is almost daily. If you purchase a bond and hold it until it matures, you will receive the YTM that existed on the purchase date, but the bond's calculated YTM will change frequently between the purchase date and the maturity date.

Yield to Call

If you bought a bond that was callable and the company called it, you would not have the option of holding it until it matured, so the yield to maturity would not be applicable. For example, if Senbet Electronics' 15 percent coupon bonds were callable, and if interest rates fell from 15 percent to 10 percent, then the company

---

[5]A few years ago, bond traders all had specialized tables called *bond tables* that gave yields on bonds of different maturities selling at different premiums and discounts. Because calculators are so much more efficient (and accurate), bond tables are rarely used any more.

Also, note that R. J. Rodriguez recently developed a formula that can be used to find the *approximate* YTM on a bond:

$$k_d = YTM \approx \frac{I + (M - V)/n}{(M + 2V)/3}. \qquad \Rightarrow APX. \ NOT \ ON \ TESTS$$

The numerator gives the average total return (coupon plus capital gain or loss) over the life of the bond, while the denominator is the average price of the bond. In our example, I = $150, M = $1,000, V = $1,368.31, and n = 14, so

$$k_d \approx \frac{\$150 + (\$1,000 - \$1,368.31)/14}{(\$1,000 + \$2,736.62)/3} = 0.0993 = 9.93\%.$$

The exact value is 10 percent, so Rodriguez's formula provides a close approximation.

could call in the 15 percent bonds, replace them with 10 percent bonds, and save $150 − $100 = $50 interest per bond per year. This is beneficial to the company, but not to bondholders.

If current interest rates are well below an outstanding bond's coupon rate, then a callable bond is likely to be called, and investors should estimate the expected rate of return on the bond as the *yield to call (YTC)* rather than as the yield to maturity. To calculate the YTC, solve this equation for k_d:

$$\text{Price of bond} = \sum_{t=1}^{N} \frac{I}{(1 + k_d)^t} + \frac{\text{Call price}}{(1 + k_d)^N.}$$

Here N is the number of years until the company can call the bond; *call price* is the price the company must pay in order to call the bond (it often begins at par value plus one year's interest and then declines over time); and the solution value for k_d is the YTC. In the balance of the chapter, we assume that bonds are not callable unless otherwise noted, but some of the end-of-chapter problems deal with yield-to-call. The company's decision to call or not call a bond is discussed in Appendix 15B.

Call provisions can have a profound effect on a bond's value. Consider the following example. In 1984, the Duval County (Florida) Housing Authority sold some 30-year, zero coupon bonds (zeros) to yield 11.5 percent tax-exempt interest. The price of the bonds was $38.17 — an investor would pay $38.17, and, 30 years later, he or she would get back $1,000. The money the housing authority received was made available to low-income home buyers; these home buyers were able to get mortgage money for about 11.5 percent versus about 14.5 percent, which was the going mortgage loan rate at the time.

A provision in the bonds stated that if the Housing Authority received cash from home buyers who were paying off their loans, then that cash could be used to call and pay off the zeros, with the call price being set at $38.17(1.115)^N$, where N is the number of years since the bonds were issued. However, since the rate home buyers were paying in 1984 was so far below the going mortgage rate (11.5 percent versus 14.5 percent), few investors thought homeowners would want to pay off their mortgages, and hence the call provision in the zeros was ignored.

In 1986, interest rates dropped sharply, and the rate on tax-exempt bonds fell from 11.5 to 8 percent. The Duval zeros' price shot up from $38.17 to $89.55, where they yielded 9 percent. (Enter n = 28, PV = 89.55 or −89.55, and FV = 1,000, and then press the k = i key to obtain the yield, 8.999 ≈ 9 percent.) The 9 percent tax-exempt interest looked high in comparison to the 8 percent return on new municipal bonds with the same degree of risk, so some University of Florida professors bought heavily. That turned out to be a big mistake. Mortgage rates had dropped to 10 percent, so homebuyers whose mortgages cost 11.5 percent started refunding (that is, paying off their old mortgages and replacing them with lower-interest ones). Duval County began receiving cash, so it started calling the bonds at the price of $38.17(1.115)^2 = 47.45. Thus, people who had bought hundreds of these bonds at a price of $89.55 per bond a few months earlier ended up with $47.45 per bond. They learned an expensive lesson about the implications of call provisions!

Bond Values with Semiannual Compounding

Although some bonds do pay interest annually, most actually pay interest semi-annually. To evaluate semiannual payment bonds, we must modify the bond valuation model (Equation 5-1) as follows:

1. Divide the annual coupon interest payment by 2 to determine the amount of interest paid each 6 months.

2. Multiply the years to maturity, n, by 2 to determine the number of semiannual periods.

3. Divide the annual interest rate, k_d, by 2 to determine the semiannual interest rate.

By making these changes, we arrive at the following equation for finding the value of a bond that pays interest semiannually:

$$V = \sum_{t=1}^{2n} \frac{I}{2}\left(\frac{1}{1 + k_d/2}\right)^t + M\left(\frac{1}{1 + k_d/2}\right)^{2n}$$

$$= \frac{I}{2}(PVIFA_{k_d/2,2n}) + M(PVIF_{k_d/2,2n}).$$

(5-1a)

To illustrate, assume now that Senbet Electronics' bonds pay $75 interest each 6 months rather than $150 at the end of each year. Thus, each interest payment is only half as large, but there are twice as many of them. When the going rate of interest is 10 percent, the value of this 15-year bond is found as follows:

$$V = \$75(PVIFA_{5\%,30 \text{ periods}}) + \$1,000(PVIF_{5\%,30 \text{ periods}})$$

$$= \$75(15.3725) + \$1,000(0.2314)$$

$$= \$1,152.94 + \$231.40 = \$1,384.34.$$

With a financial calculator, you would enter n = 30, k = i = 5, PMT = 75, FV = 1,000, and then press the PV key to obtain the bond's value, $1,384.31. The $1,384.31 value with semiannual interest payments is slightly larger than $1,380.30, the value when interest is paid annually. This higher value occurs because interest payments are received somewhat faster under semiannual compounding.

Students sometimes want to discount the maturity value at 10 percent over 15 years, rather than at 5 percent over 30 six-month periods. This is incorrect — logically, all cash flows in a given contract must be discounted on the same basis, semiannually in this instance. For consistency, bond traders *must* apply semiannual compounding to the maturity value, and they do.

Interest Rate Risk on a Bond

As we saw in Chapter 3, interest rates go up and down over time, and as rates change, the values of outstanding bonds also fluctuate. Suppose you bought some 15 percent Senbet bonds at a price of $1,000 and interest rates subsequently rose to 20 percent. As we saw earlier, the price of the bonds would fall to $769.49, so you would have a loss of \$230.51 per bond.[6] Interest rates can and do rise, and rising rates cause a loss of value for bondholders. Thus, people or firms who invest in bonds are exposed to risk from changing interest rates, or *interest rate risk.*

One's exposure to interest rate risk is higher on bonds with long maturities than on those maturing in the near future. This point can be demonstrated by showing how the value of a 1-year bond with a 15 percent annual payment coupon fluctuates with changes in k_d and then comparing these changes with those on a 14-year bond as calculated above. The 1-year bond's values at different interest rates are shown here:

Value at k_d = 10%:

$$V = \$150(PVIFA_{10\%,1 \text{ year}}) + \$1,000(PVIF_{10\%,1 \text{ year}})$$
$$= \$150(0.9091) + \$1,000(0.9091)$$
$$= \$136.37 + \$909.10 = \$1,045.47.$$

Value at k_d = 15%:

$$V = \$150(0.8696) + \$1,000(0.8696)$$
$$= \$130.44 + \$869.60 = \$1,000.04 \approx \$1,000.$$

Value at k_d = 20%:

$$V = \$150(0.8333) + \$1,000(0.8333)$$
$$= \$125.00 + \$833.30 = \$958.30.$$

You could get the first value with a financial calculator by entering n = 1, PMT = 150, FV = 1,000, and i = 10, and then pressing PV to get the bond's value, \$1,045.45. Now, with everything still in your calculator, enter i = 15 to override the old i = 10, and then press PV to find the bond's value at k_d = i = 15; it is \$1,000. Then enter i = 20 and press the PV key to find the last bond value, \$958.33.

The values of the 1-year and 14-year bonds at several current market interest rates are summarized and plotted in Figure 5-3. Notice how much more sensitive the price of the long-term bond is to changes in interest rates. At a 15 percent interest rate, both the long- and the short-term bonds are valued at \$1,000. When rates rise to 20 percent, the long-term bond falls to \$769.47, but the short-term bond falls only to \$958.33. A similar situation occurs when rates fall below 15 percent.

For bonds with similar coupons, this differential sensitivity to changes in interest rates always holds true — the longer the maturity of the bond, the greater

---

[6]You would have an *accounting* (and tax) loss only if you sold the bond; if you held it to maturity, you would not have such a loss. However, even if you did not sell, you would still have suffered a *real economic loss in an opportunity cost sense,* because you would have lost the opportunity to invest at 20 percent and would be stuck with a 15 percent bond in a 20 percent market. In finance we regard "paper losses" as being just as bad as realized accounting losses.

Figure 5-3
Value of Long- and Short-Term 15% Annual Coupon Rate Bonds at Different Market Interest Rates

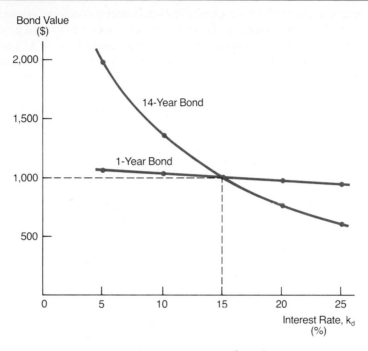

Current Market Interest Rate, k_d	Value of	
	1-Year Bond	14-Year Bond
5%	$1,095.24	$1,989.86
10	1,045.45	1,368.33
15	1,000.00	1,000.00
20	958.33	769.47
25	920.00	617.59

Note: Bond values calculated using a financial calculator.

its price changes in response to a given change in interest rates. Thus, even if the risk of default on two bonds is exactly the same, the one with the longer maturity is typically exposed to more risk from a rise in interest rates.

The logical explanation for this difference in interest rate risk is simple. Suppose you bought a 14-year bond that yielded 15 percent, or $150 a year. Now suppose interest rates on comparable-risk bonds rose to 20 percent. You would be stuck with only $150 of interest for the next 14 years. On the other hand, had you bought a 1-year bond, you would have a low return for only 1 year. At the end of the year, you would get your $1,000 back, and you could then reinvest it and receive 20 percent, or $200 per year, for the next 13 years. Thus, interest rate risk reflects the length of time one is committed to a given investment.[7]

Although a 1-year bond has less interest rate risk than a 14-year bond, the 1-year bond exposes the buyer to more *reinvestment rate risk.* Suppose you bought a 1-year bond that yielded 15 percent and then interest rates on comparable-risk bonds fell to 10 percent. After 1 year, when you got your $1,000 back, you would have to invest it at only 10 percent, so you would lose $150 − $100 = $50 in annual interest. Had you bought the 14-year bond, you would have continued to receive $150 in annual interest payments even if rates fell. Of course, if you intended to spend the $1,000 after 1 year, then investing in a 1-year bond would guarantee (ignoring bankruptcy) that you would get your $1,000 back (plus interest) after 1 year. The 14-year bond investment, on the other hand, if sold after 1 year, would return less than $1,000 if interest rates had risen.[8]

Bond Prices in Recent Years

We know from Chapter 3 that interest rates fluctuate, and we have just seen that the prices of outstanding bonds rise and fall inversely with changes in interest rates. Figure 5-4 shows what has happened to the price of a typical bond, Alabama Power's 8½ percent, 30-year bond which matures in 2001. When this bond was issued in 1971, it was worth $1,000, but at the 1981 interest rate peak, it sold for only $530. However, the recent drop in interest rates caused the price of the bond to rise, and by 1987 it was back over par, selling at a premium. The graph also shows that if interest rates remain at their 1987 level, the price of the bond will gradually fall, and it will sell for $1,000 (plus accrued interest) just before it matures in 2001.

Bond Markets

Corporate bonds are traded primarily in the over-the-counter market. Most bonds are owned by and traded among the large financial institutions (for example, life insurance companies, mutual funds, and pension funds, all of which deal in very large blocks of securities), and it is relatively easy for the over-the-counter bond dealers to arrange the transfer of large blocks of bonds among the relatively few holders of the bonds. It would be much more difficult to conduct similar operations in the stock market among the literally millions of large and small stockholders, so most stock trades occur on the exchanges.

---

[7]If a 10-year bond were plotted in Figure 5-3, its curve would lie between those of the 14-year bond and the 1-year bond. The curve of a 1-month bond would be almost horizontal, indicating that its price would change very little in response to an interest rate change, but a 50-year bond would have a very steep slope.

[8]Note that long-term bonds also have some reinvestment rate risk — to actually earn the YTM on a long-term bond, the coupon payments must be reinvested at the YTM rate. If interest rates fall, the coupon payments would be reinvested at less than the YTM, and hence the realized return would be less than the YTM. Note, though, that the reinvestment rate risk only applies to the coupon payments if you buy a long-term bond, but it applies to both interest and principal on the short-term bond.

Figure 5-4
Alabama Power 30-Year Bond: Value Over Time

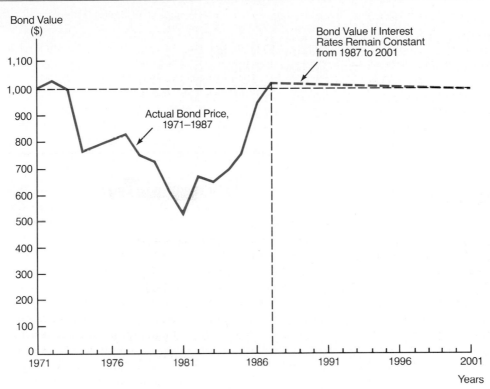

Note: The line from 1987 to 2001 appears linear, but it actually has a slight curve.

Information on bond trades in the over-the-counter market is not published, but a representative group of bonds is listed and traded in the bond section of the NYSE. Figure 5-5 gives a portion of the bond market page of the *Wall Street Journal* on trading for January 19, 1987. A total of 792 issues were traded on that date, but we show only the bonds of Alabama Power. Note that Alabama Power had 11 different bonds traded on January 19; the company actually had over 20 bond issues outstanding, but some of them did not trade on that date.

The Alabama Power and other bonds can have various denominations, but most have a par value of $1,000 — this is how much per bond the company borrowed and how much it must someday repay. However, since other denominations are possible, for trading and reporting purposes bonds are quoted as percentages of par. Looking at the second bond listed, which is the one we plotted in Figure 5-4, we see that there is an 8½ just after the company's name; this indicates that the bond is of the series which has an 8½ percent coupon rate, or $0.0850(\$1,000) = \$85.00$ of interest per year. The 01 which comes next indicates that this bond

Figure 5-5
NYSE Bond Market Transactions, January 19, 1987

Bonds	Cur Yld	Vol	High	Low	Close	Net Chg.
AlaP 9s2000	8.9	10	101⅜	101⅜	101⅜ +	¼
AlaP 8½s01	8.4	62	100⅝	100⅝	100⅝ +	½
AlaP 8⅞s03	8.8	18	101	100¾	100¾ +	⅛
AlaP 8¼s03	8.4	15	98¼	98	98 −	¼
AlaP 9¾s04	9.3	11	104½	104½	104½ −	⅛
AlaP 10⅞s05	10.2	15	106⅞	106⅞	106⅞	...
AlaP 10½s05	9.9	15	106¼	106¼	106¼ +	⅛
AlaP 8¾07	8.7	21	100½	100⅜	100½ +	⅛
AlaP 8⅝87	8.6	15	100½	100½	100½	...
AlaP 9¼07	9.0	10	102⅝	102¼	102¼ −	1¾
AlaP 12⅝10	11.7	109	108½	107⅝	107¾ −	¼

Source: The *Wall Street Journal,* January 20, 1987.

matures and must be repaid in the year 2001; it is not shown in the table, but this bond was issued in 1971, so it had a 30-year original maturity. The 8.4 in the fourth column is the bond's current yield, which is the annual interest payment divided by the closing price of the bond: Current yield = \$85/\$1006.25 = 8.4%. The 62 in the next column indicates that 62 of these bonds were traded on January 19, 1987. Since the prices shown are expressed as a percentage of par, the closing price of 100⅝ translates to \$1,006.25. Finally, the table shows that the closing price was up ½ percent, or \$5, from the previous day's close.

As we discussed earlier, interest rates vary over time, and companies generally set their coupon rates at levels which reflect the "going rate of interest" on the day a bond is issued. If the rates were set lower, investors simply would not buy the bonds at the \$1,000 par value, so the company would not get the money it needed. Thus, bonds generally sell at their par values when they are issued, but their prices fluctuate thereafter as interest rates in the economy change. All the bonds traded on a given day are listed in the newspaper, and hence in Figure 5-5, in the order of the dates on which they were originally issued, beginning with the earliest bond issued.

PREFERRED STOCK VALUATION

Preferred stock is a *hybrid* — it is similar to bonds in some respects and to common stock in others. Preferred dividends are similar to interest payments on bonds in that they are fixed in amount and generally must be paid before common stock dividends can be paid. However, like common dividends, preferred dividends can be omitted without bankrupting the firm if earnings are low. In addition, some preferred stock is similar to common stock in that it has no maturity date and is not callable; hence, such issues are never retired.

Most preferred stocks entitle their owners to regular, fixed dividend payments, and if the payments last forever, then the issue is a perpetuity whose value, as we discussed in Chapter 4, is found as follows:

$$V_{ps} = \frac{D_{ps}}{k_{ps}}.$$ **(5-2)**

V_{ps} is the value of the preferred stock, D_{ps} is the dividend, and k_{ps} is the required rate of return. (We will discuss required rates of return in Chapter 6.) Senbet has preferred stock outstanding which pays a perpetual dividend of $8.125 per year. If the required rate of return on this preferred stock is 10 percent, then its value is $81.25, found by solving Equation 5-2 as follows:

$$V_{ps} = \frac{\$8.125}{0.10} = \$81.25.$$

Preferred stocks which are not perpetual are valued by using the bond valuation model.

COMMON STOCK VALUATION

Common stock represents the ownership of a corporation, but to the typical investor, a share of common stock is simply a piece of paper distinguished by two features:

1. It entitles its owner to dividends, but only if the company has earnings out of which dividends can be paid and if management chooses to pay dividends rather than retain earnings. Note that whereas a bond contains a *promise* to pay interest, common stock provides no such promise (in an obligatory sense) to pay dividends — if you own a stock you may *expect* a dividend, but your expectations may not in fact be met. To illustrate, Long Island Lighting Company (Lilco) had paid dividends on its common stock for more than 50 years, and people expected these dividends to continue. However, when the company encountered severe problems in 1984, it stopped paying dividends. Note, though, that Lilco continued to pay interest on its bonds; if it had not, then it would have been declared bankrupt, and the bondholders could have taken over the company.

2. The second characteristic of common stock that is important to investors is the fact that it can be sold at some future date, hopefully at a price greater than the purchase price. If the stock is actually sold at a price above its purchase price, the investor will receive a *capital gain*. Generally, at the time people buy common stocks, they do expect to receive capital gains; otherwise, they would not buy the stocks. However, after the fact, one can end up with capital losses rather than capital gains. Lilco's stock price dropped from $17.50 in 1983 to $3.75 in 1984, so *expected* capital gains turned out to be *actual* capital losses.

Definitions of Terms Used in the Stock Valuation Models

Common stocks provide an expected future cash flow stream, and a stock's value is found in the same manner as the values of other financial assets, namely, as the present value of an expected future cash flow stream. The expected cash flows consist of two elements: (1) the dividends expected in each year and (2) the price investors expect to receive when they sell the stock. The final stock price includes the return of the original investment plus a capital gain (or minus a capital loss).

We saw in Chapter 1 that managers seek to maximize the value of their firms' stocks. Through their actions, managers affect the stream of income to investors and the riskiness of this stream. Managers need to know how alternative actions will affect stock prices. Therefore, at this point we develop some models to help show how the value of a share of stock is determined under several different sets of conditions. We begin by defining the following terms:

D_t = dividend the stockholder *expects* to receive at the end of Year t. D_0 is the most recent dividend, which has already been paid; D_1 is the next dividend expected, which will be paid at the end of this year; D_2 is the dividend expected at the end of 2 years; and so forth. D_1 represents the first cash flow a new purchaser of the stock will receive. Note that D_0, the dividend which has just been paid, is known with certainty. However, all future dividends are *expected* values, so the estimate of D_t may differ among investors.[9]

P_0 = *actual market price* of the stock today.

$\hat{P}_t$ = *expected price* of the stock at the end of each Year t (pronounced "P hat t"). $\hat{P}_0$ is the *intrinsic,* or *theoretical, value* of the stock today as seen by the particular investor doing the analysis; $\hat{P}_1$ is the price the investor expects at the end of 1 year; and so on. Note that $\hat{P}_0$ is the intrinsic value of the stock today based on one particular investor's estimate of the stock's expected dividend stream and perception of the stock's riskiness. Hence, whereas P_0 is established in the market and is a given for all investors, $\hat{P}_0$ could differ among investors depending on how optimistic or pessimistic they are regarding the company. The caret, or "hat," is used to indicate that $\hat{P}_t$ is an estimated value. $\hat{P}_0$, the investor's estimate of the intrinsic value today, could be above or below P_0, the current stock price, but an investor would buy the stock only if his or her $\hat{P}_0$ were equal to or greater than P_0.

Since there are many investors in the market, there can be many values for $\hat{P}_0$. However, we can think of an "average" or, really, "marginal," investor whose actions actually determine the market price. For this marginal investor, P_0 must equal $\hat{P}_0$; otherwise, a disequilibrium would exist, and buying and selling in the market would force P_0 to equal $\hat{P}_0$ for the marginal investor. We discuss this point further in Chapter 6.

g = *expected growth rate* in dividends as predicted by the investor. (If we assume that dividends are expected to grow at a constant rate, then g is also equal to the expected rate of growth in the stock's price.) Different investors may use different g's to evaluate a firm's stock, but the market price, P_0, is set on the basis of the g estimated by the marginal investor.

k_s = minimum acceptable, or *required, rate of return* on the stock, considering both its riskiness and the returns available on other investments. Again, P_0 is set on the basis of k_s as estimated by the marginal investor. The determinants of k_s will be discussed in detail in Chapter 6.

---

[9]Stocks generally pay dividends quarterly, so theoretically we should evaluate them on a quarterly basis. However, in stock valuation most analysts work on an annual basis because the data are generally not precise enough to warrant the refinement of a quarterly model. For additional information on the quarterly model, see Charles M. Linke and J. Kenton Zumwalt, "Estimation Biases in Discounted Cash Flow Analyses of Equity Capital Cost in Rate Regulation," *Financial Management,* Autumn 1984, 15–21.

$\hat{k}_s$ = *expected rate of return* which an investor who buys the stock actually expects to receive. $\hat{k}_s$ (pronounced "k hat s") could be above or below k_s, but one would buy the stock only if $\hat{k}_s$ were equal to or greater than k_s.

$\bar{k}_s$ = *actual,* or *realized,* after-the-fact *rate of return,* pronounced "k bar s." You may *expect* to obtain a return of $\hat{k}_s$ = 15 percent if you buy Exxon stock today, but, if the market goes down, you may end up next year with an actual, realized return that is much lower, perhaps even negative.

D_1/P_0 = expected *dividend yield* on the stock during the coming year. If the stock is expected to pay a dividend of $1 during the next 12 months, and if its current price is $10, then the expected dividend yield is $1/\$10 = 0.10 = 10\%$.

$\dfrac{\hat{P}_1 - P_0}{P_0}$ = expected *capital gains yield* on the stock during the coming year. If the stock sells for $10 today, and if it is expected to rise to $10.50 at the end of 1 year, then the expected capital gain is $\hat{P}_1 - P_0 = \$10.50 - \$10.00 = \$0.50$, and the expected capital gains yield is $\$0.50/\$10 = 0.05 = 5\%$.

Expected total return = expected dividend yield (D_1/P_0) plus expected capital gains yield $[(\hat{P}_1 - P_0)/P_0] = \hat{k}_s$ as defined above. In the previous example, the *expected total return* $= \hat{k}_s = 10\% + 5\% = 15\%$.

Expected Dividends as the Basis for Stock Values

In our discussion of bonds, we calculated the value of a bond as the present value of interest payments over the life of the bond plus the present value of the bond's maturity (or par) value:

$$V = \frac{I}{(1 + k_d)^1} + \frac{I}{(1 + k_d)^2} + \ldots + \frac{I}{(1 + k_d)^n} + \frac{M}{(1 + k_d)^n}.$$

Stock prices are likewise determined as the present value of a stream of cash flows, and the basic stock valuation equation is similar to the bond valuation equation. What are the cash flows that corporations provide to their stockholders? First, think of yourself as an investor who buys a stock with the intention of holding it (in the family) forever. In this case, all that you (and your heirs) will receive is a stream of dividends, and the value of the stock today is calculated as the present value of an infinite stream of dividends:

$$\text{Value of stock} = \hat{P}_0 = \text{PV of the expected future dividends}$$

$$= \frac{D_1}{(1 + k_s)^1} + \frac{D_2}{(1 + k_s)^2} + \ldots + \frac{D_\infty}{(1 + k_s)^\infty} \qquad (5\text{-}3)$$

$$= \sum_{t=1}^{\infty} \frac{D_t}{(1 + k_s)^t}.$$

What about the more typical case, where you expect to hold the stock for a finite period and then sell it—what will be the value of $\hat{P}_0$ in this case? For a company that is expected to remain in business (as opposed to a takeover candidate or a company you expect to be liquidated), *the value of the stock is again determined by Equation 5-3.* To see this, recognize that for any individual investor, expected cash flows consist of expected dividends plus the expected sale price of the stock. However, the sale price the current investor receives will be dependent upon the dividends some future investor expects. Therefore, for all present and future investors in total, expected cash flows must be based on expected future dividends. To put it another way, unless a firm is liquidated or sold to another concern, the cash flows it provides to its stockholders will consist only of a stream of dividends, so the value of a share of its stock must be equal to the present value of that expected dividend stream.

The general validity of Equation 5-3 can also be confirmed by asking this question: Suppose I buy a stock and expect to hold it for 1 year. I can expect dividends during the year plus the value $\hat{P}_1$ when I sell out at the end of the year. But what will determine the value of $\hat{P}_1$? It will be determined as the present value of the dividends during Year 2 plus the stock price at the end of that year, which in turn will be determined as the present value of another set of future dividends and an even more distant stock price. This process can be continued ad infinitum, and the ultimate result is Equation 5-3.[10]

Equation 5-3 is a generalized stock valuation model in the sense that the time pattern of D_t can be anything: D_t can be rising, falling, or constant, or it can even fluctuate randomly, and Equation 5-3 will still hold. Often, however, the projected stream of dividends follows a systematic pattern, in which case we can develop a simplified (that is, easier to evaluate) version of the stock valuation model expressed in Equation 5-3. In the following sections we consider the cases of zero growth, constant growth, and nonconstant growth.

Stock Values with Zero Growth

Suppose dividends are not expected to grow at all, but to remain constant. Here we have a *zero growth stock,* for which the dividends expected in future years are equal to some constant amount — that is, $D_1 = D_2 = D_3$ and so on. Therefore, we can drop the subscripts on D and rewrite Equation 5-3 as follows:

$$\hat{P}_0 = \frac{D}{(1 + k_s)^1} + \frac{D}{(1 + k_s)^2} + \ldots + \frac{D}{(1 + k_s)^n} + \ldots + \frac{D}{(1 + k_s)^\infty}. \quad \text{(5-3a)}$$

As we noted in Chapter 4 in connection with the British consol bond, and also in our discussion of preferred stocks, a security that is expected to pay a constant amount each year forever is defined as a perpetuity. Therefore, a zero growth stock may be thought of as a perpetuity. Although the stock is expected to provide a

---

[10]We should note that investors periodically lose sight of the long-run nature of stocks as investments and forget that in order to sell a stock at a profit, one must find a buyer who will pay the higher price. If you analyzed a stock's value in accordance with Equation 5-3, concluded that the stock's market price exceeded a reasonable value, and then bought the stock anyway, then you would be following the "bigger fool" theory of investment — you think you may be a fool to buy the stock at its excessive price, but you also think that when you get ready to sell it, you can find someone who is an even bigger fool. The bigger fool theory was widely followed in 1929, just before the Great Depression.

constant stream of dividends into the indefinite future, each dividend has a smaller present value than the preceding one, and as n gets very large, the present value of the individual future dividends approaches zero. To illustrate, suppose $D = \$1.82$ and $k_s = 16\% = 0.16$. We can rewrite Equation 5-3a as follows:

$$\hat{P}_0 = \frac{\$1.82}{(1.16)^1} + \frac{\$1.82}{(1.16)^2} + \frac{\$1.82}{(1.16)^3} + \ldots + \frac{\$1.82}{(1.16)^{50}} + \ldots + \frac{\$1.82}{(1.16)^{100}} + \ldots$$

$$= \$1.57 + \$1.35 + \$1.17 + \ldots + \$0.001 + \ldots + \$0.000001 + \ldots.$$

We can also show the perpetuity in graph form, as in Figure 5-6. The horizontal line shows the constant dividend stream, $D_t = \$1.82$, while the descending step function curve shows the present value of each future dividend. If we extended the analysis on out to infinity and then summed the present values of all the future dividends, the sum would be equal to the value of the stock.

As we saw in Chapter 4, and earlier in this chapter in our discussion of preferred stock valuation, the value of any perpetuity is simply the cash flow divided by the discount rate. Therefore, the value of a zero growth stock reduces to this formula:

$$\hat{P}_0 = \frac{D}{k_s}. \tag{5-4}$$

In our example, the value of the stock is $11.38:

$$\hat{P}_0 = \frac{\$1.82}{0.16} = \$11.38.$$

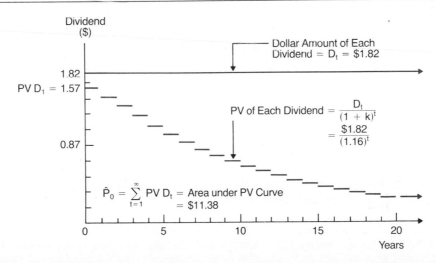

Figure 5-6
Present Values of Dividends of a Zero Growth Stock (Perpetuity)

Thus, if you extended Figure 5-6 on out forever and then added up the present value of each individual dividend, you would end up with the intrinsic value of the stock, $11.38.[11] The actual market value of the stock, P_0, could be greater than, less than, or equal to $11.38, depending on other investors' perceptions of the dividend pattern and the riskiness of the stock.

We could transpose the $\hat{P}_0$ and the k_s in Equation 5-4 and then solve for k_s to produce Equation 5-5:

$$\hat{k}_s = \frac{D}{P_0}. \qquad (5\text{-}5)$$

We could then look up the price of the stock and the latest dividend, P_0 and D, in the newspaper, and the value D/P_0 would be the rate of return we could expect to earn if we bought the stock. Since we are dealing with an *expected rate of return,* we put a "hat" on the k value. Thus, if we bought the stock at a price of $11.38 and expected to receive a constant dividend of $1.82, our expected rate of return would be

$$\hat{k}_s = \frac{\$1.82}{\$11.38} = 0.16 = 16\%.$$

Normal, or Constant, Growth

Although the zero growth model is applicable to some companies, the dividends on most common stocks are expected to increase each year. While expected growth rates vary from company to company, dividend growth in general is expected to continue in the foreseeable future at about the same rate as that of the nominal gross national product (real GNP plus inflation). On this basis, it is expected that an average, or "normal," dividend will grow at a rate of 6 to 8 percent a year. Thus, if a *normal, or constant, growth* company's last dividend, which has already been paid, was D_0, its dividend in any future Year t may be forecasted as $D_t = D_0(1 + g)^t$, where g is the constant expected rate of growth. For example, if Senbet Electronics just paid a dividend of $1.82 (that is, $D_0 = \$1.82$) and if investors expect a 10 percent growth rate, then the estimated dividend 1 year hence will be $D_1 = \$1.82(1.10) = \$2.00$; D_2 will be $2.20; and the estimated dividend 5 years hence will be

$$D_t = D_0(1 + g)^t = \$1.82(1.10)^5 = \$2.93.$$

Using this method of estimating future dividends, we can determine the current value, $\hat{P}_0$, using Equation 5-3 as set forth above—in other words, we find the expected future cash flow stream (the dividends), calculate the present value of each dividend payment, and then sum these present values to find the value of the

---

[11]If you think that having a stock pay dividends forever is unrealistic, then think of it as lasting only for 50 years. Here we would have an annuity of $1.82 per year for 50 years. The PV of a 50-year annuity would be $1.82(6.2463) = \$11.37$, which would differ by only a penny from that of the perpetuity. Thus, the dividends from Years 51 to infinity would not contribute much to the value of the stock.

stock. Thus, the intrinsic value of the stock is equal to the present value of its expected future dividends.

However, if g is constant, then Equation 5-3 may be simplified as follows:[12]

$$\hat{P}_0 = \frac{D_0(1 + g)}{k_s - g} = \frac{D_1}{k_s - g}. \qquad (5\text{-}6)$$

Inserting values into Equation 5-6, we find the value of our illustrative stock to be $33.33:

$$\hat{P}_0 = \frac{\$1.82(1.10)}{0.16 - 0.10} = \frac{\$2.00}{0.06} = \$33.33.$$

The *constant growth model* expressed in Equation 5-6 is often called the *Gordon Model,* after Myron J. Gordon, who did much to develop and popularize it.

Note that Equation 5-6 is sufficiently general to encompass the zero growth case described above: If growth is zero, this is simply a special case of constant growth, and Equation 5-6 is equal to Equation 5-4. Note also that a necessary condition for the derivation of Equation 5-6 is that k_s be greater than g. If the equation is used where k_s is not greater than g, the results will be meaningless.

The concept underlying the valuation process for a constant growth stock is graphed in Figure 5-7. Dividends are growing at the rate g = 10%, but since $k_s >$ g, the present value of each future dividend is declining. For example, the dividend in Year 1 is $D_1 = D_0(1 + g)^1 = \$1.82(1.10) = \$2.00$. However, the present value of this dividend, discounted at 16 percent, is $PV(D_1) = \$2.00/(\$1.16)^1 = \$2.00/1.16 = \$1.72$. The dividend expected in Year 2 grows to $\$2.00(1.10) = \$2.20$, but the present value of this dividend falls to $1.64. Continuing, $D_3 = \$2.42$ and $PV(D_3) = \$1.55$, and so on. Thus, the expected dividends are growing, but the present value of each successive dividend is declining.

If we summed the present value of each future dividend, this summation would be the value of the stock today, $\hat{P}_0$. As we have seen, when g is a constant, this summation is equal to $D_1/(k_s - g)$, as shown in Equation 5-6. Therefore, if we extended the lower step function curve in Figure 5-7 on out to infinity and then summed the present values of the future dividends, the summation would be identical to the value given by Equation 5-6, $33.33.

Growth in dividends occurs primarily as a result of growth in earnings per share (EPS). Earnings growth, in turn, results from a number of factors, including (1) inflation and (2) the reinvestment, or "plow-back," of earnings. Regarding inflation, if output (in units) is stable, and if both sales prices and input costs rise at the inflation rate, then EPS will also grow at the inflation rate. EPS will also grow as a result of the reinvestment of earnings. If the firm's earnings are not all paid out as dividends (that is, if some fraction of earnings is retained), then the dollars of investment behind each share will rise over time, and that should lead to growth in earnings and dividends.

---

[12]The derivation of Equation 5-6 is shown in Appendix 3A of Eugene F. Brigham and Louis C. Gapenski, *Intermediate Financial Management,* 2nd ed. (Hinsdale, Ill.: Dryden Press, 1987).

Figure 5-7
Present Values of Dividends of a Constant Growth Stock:
$D_0 = \$1.82$, $g = 10\%$, $k_s = 16\%$

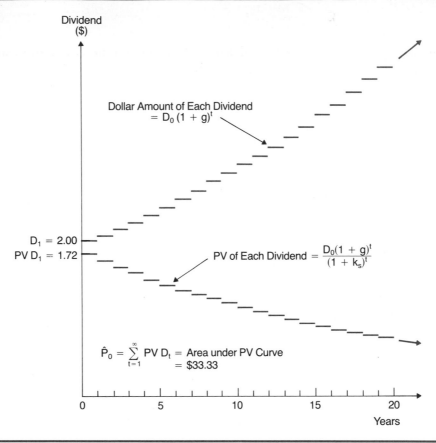

Expected Rate of Return on a Constant Growth Stock

We can solve Equation 5-6 for k_s, again using the hat to denote that we are dealing with an expected rate of return:[13]

$$\begin{array}{ccccc} \text{Expected rate} \\ \text{of return} \end{array} = \begin{array}{c} \text{Expected} \\ \text{dividend} \\ \text{yield} \end{array} + \begin{array}{c} \text{Expected growth, or} \\ \text{the capital} \\ \text{gains yield} \end{array}$$

$$\hat{k}_s = \frac{D_1}{P_0} + g. \tag{5-7}$$

---

[13]The k_s value in Equation 5-6 is a *required* rate of return, but when we transform to obtain Equation 5-7, we are finding an *expected* rate of return. Obviously, the transformation requires that $k_s = \hat{k}_s$. This equality holds if the stock market is in equilibrium, a condition discussed at length in Chapter 6.

Thus, if you buy a stock for a price P_0 = $33.33, and if you expect the stock to pay a dividend D_1 = $2.00 one year from now and to grow at a constant rate g = 10% in the future, then your expected rate of return is 16 percent:

$$\hat{k}_s = \frac{\$2.00}{\$33.33} + 10\% = 6\% + 10\% = 16\%.$$

In this form, we see that $\hat{k}_s$ is the *expected total return,* and that it consists of an *expected dividend yield,* D_1/P_0 = 6%, plus an *expected growth rate or capital gains yield,* g = 10%. In general, *for a constant growth stock,* these conditions will hold:

1. The dividend is expected to grow forever at a constant rate, g.

2. The stock price is expected to grow at this same rate.

3. The expected dividend yield is a constant.

4. The expected capital gains yield is also a constant, and it is equal to g.

5. The expected total rate of return, $\hat{k}_s$, is equal to the expected dividend yield plus the expected growth rate.

Nonconstant Growth

Firms typically go through life cycles. During the early part of their lives, growth is much faster than that of the economy as a whole; then growth matches that of the economy; and finally the firm's growth is slower than that of the economy.[14] Automobile manufacturers in the 1920s and computer software firms such as Lotus in the 1980s are examples of firms in the early part of the cycle, and these firms are called *supernormal growth* companies. Figure 5-8 illustrates such nonconstant growth and compares it with normal growth, zero growth, and negative growth.[15]

The dividends of the supernormal growth firm are expected to grow at a 30 percent rate for 3 years, after which the growth rate is expected to fall to 10 percent, the assumed average for the industry. The value of this firm, like any other, is the present value of its expected future dividends as determined by Equation 5-3. In the case where D_t is growing at a constant rate, we simplified Equation 5-3 to $\hat{P}_0 = D_1/(k_s - g)$. In the supernormal case, however, the expected growth rate is not a constant — it declines at the end of the period of supernormal growth.

[14]The concept of life cycles could be broadened to *product cycles,* which would include both small, start-up companies and large companies, such as IBM, which periodically introduce new products that typically give sales and earnings a boost. We should also mention *business cycles,* which alternately depress and boost sales and profits. The growth rate just after a major new product has been introduced, or as a firm emerges from the depths of a recession, is likely to be much higher than the "long-run average growth rate," which is the proper number for DCF analysis.

[15]A negative growth rate indicates a declining company. A mining company whose profits are falling because of a declining ore body is an example. Someone buying such a company would expect its earnings, and consequently its dividends and stock price, to decline each year, and this would lead to capital losses rather than capital gains. Obviously, a declining company's stock price will be low, and its dividend yield must be high enough to offset the expected capital loss and still produce a competitive total return. Students sometimes argue that they would not be willing to buy a stock whose price was expected to decline. However, if the annual dividends are large enough to *more than offset* the falling stock price, the stock could still provide a good return.

Figure 5-8
Illustrative Dividend Growth Rates

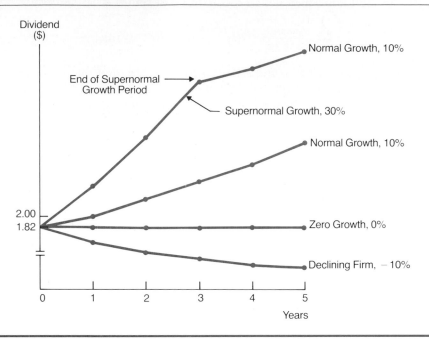

To find the value of such stock, or any nonconstant growth stock when the growth rate will eventually stabilize, we proceed in three steps:

1. Find the PV of the dividends during the period of nonconstant growth.

2. Find the price of the stock at the end of the nonconstant growth period, at which point it has become a constant growth stock, and then discount this price back to the present.

3. Add these two components to find the intrinsic value of the stock, $\hat{P}_0$.

To illustrate the process for valuing nonconstant growth stocks, suppose the following facts exist:

k_s = stockholders' required rate of return = 16%.

N = years of supernormal growth = 3.

g_s = rate of growth in both earnings and dividends during the supernormal growth period = 30%.

g_n = rate of growth after the supernormal period = 10%.

D_0 = last dividend the company paid = $1.82.

The valuation process is graphed in Figure 5-9 and explained in the steps set forth below:

Figure 5-9
Present Values of Dividends of a Supernormal Growth Stock

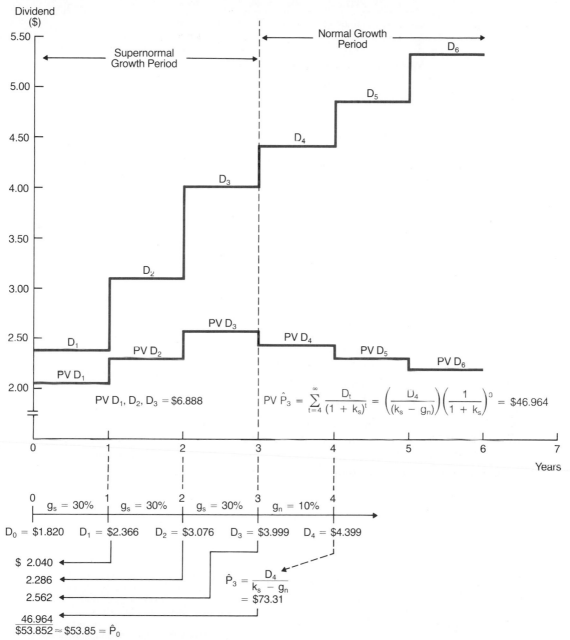

Notes:

a. Recognize that dividends are paid at the end of each year.

b. P_3, the stock price expected at the end of Year 3, is the sum of the PVs of dividends in Years 4 to infinity, and hence $\hat{P}_3 = D_4/(k_s - g_n)$.

Step 1. Find the PV of dividends paid (PV D_t) at the end of Years 1 to 3 using this procedure:

$$D_0 \ \times \ FVIF_{30\%,t} = \ D_t; \ \times \ PVIF_{16\%,t} = \ PV \ D_t$$

D_1:	\$1.82 ×	1.3000	= \$2.366 ×	0.8621	=	\$2.040
D_2:	1.82 ×	1.6900	= 3.076 ×	0.7432	=	2.286
D_3:	1.82 ×	2.1970	= 3.999 ×	0.6407	=	2.562

Sum of PVs of supernormal period dividends = \$6.888

Step 2. Find the PV of the dividends expected in Year 4 and thereafter. This requires that we (a) first find the expected value of the stock at the end of Year 3 and (b) then find the present value of the Year 3 stock price:

a.
$$\hat{P}_3 = \frac{D_4}{k_s - g_n} = \frac{D_0 (1 + g_s)^3 (1 + g_n)}{k_s - g_n} = \frac{D_3 (1 + g_n)}{0.16 - 0.10}$$

$$= \frac{\$3.999(1.10)}{0.06} = \frac{\$4.399}{0.06} = \$73.31.$$

b.
$$PV \ \hat{P}_3 = \$73.31(PVIF_{16\%,3 \text{ years}}) = \$73.31(0.6407) = \$46.96.$$

Step 3. Find $\hat{P}_0$, the value of the stock today:

$$\hat{P}_0 = \$6.89 + \$46.96 = \$53.85.$$

You would normally calculate the stream of dividends and their present values with a financial calculator rather than with FVIF and PVIF factors, but the steps would be the same.

Comparing Companies with Different Expected Growth Rates

It is useful to summarize our discussion of stock valuation models by comparing companies with the four growth situations graphed in Figure 5-8. There we have a zero growth company, one with a constant 10 percent expected growth rate, one whose earnings are expected to decline at the rate of 10 percent a year, and a supernormal growth company whose growth rate is nonconstant.

We can use the valuation equations developed above to determine the stock prices, dividend yields, capital gains yields, total expected returns, and price/earnings (P/E) ratios for the four companies; these are shown in Table 5-1.[16] We

---

[16]Price/earnings ratios relate a stock's price to its earnings per share (EPS). The higher the P/E ratio, the more investors are willing to pay for a dollar of the firm's current earnings. Other things held constant, investors will pay more for a dollar of current earnings of a rapidly growing firm than for one of a slow growth company; hence, rapid growth companies generally have high P/E ratios. The relationships between the P/E ratios, shown in the last column of Table 5-1, are similar to what one would intuitively expect — the higher the expected growth rate (all other things the same), the higher the P/E ratio.

We should note also that differences in P/E ratios among firms can also arise from differences in the required rates of return, k_s, which investors use in capitalizing the future dividend streams. If one company has a higher P/E ratio than another, this could be caused by a higher g, a lower k_s, or a combination of these two factors. We will discuss P/E ratios more in later chapters.

Table 5-1

Stock Prices, Dividend Yields, and Price/Earnings Ratios for 16 Percent Returns under Different Growth Assumptions

		Price	Current Dividend Yield (D_1/P_0)	Capital Gains Yield in Year 1 $[(\hat{P}_1 - P_0)/P_0]$	Total Expected Return	P/E Ratio[a]
Declining constant growth (−10%)	$\hat{P}_0 = \dfrac{D_1}{k_s - g} = \dfrac{\$1.64}{0.16 - (-0.10)}$ =	$ 6.31	26%	−10.0%	16%	1.85
Zero growth (0%)	$\hat{P}_0 = \dfrac{D}{k_s} = \dfrac{\$1.82}{0.16}$ =	11.38	16	0.0	16	3.34
Normal constant growth (10%)	$\hat{P}_0 = \dfrac{D_1}{k_s - g} = \dfrac{\$2.00}{0.16 - 0.10}$ =	33.33	6	10.0	16	9.77
Supernormal growth	$\hat{P}_0 = $ (See Steps 1-3 above) =	53.85	4.4	11.6[b]	16	15.79

[a]It was assumed at the beginning of this example that each company is earning $3.41 initially. This $3.41, divided into the various prices, gives the indicated P/E ratios.

We might also note that as the supernormal growth rate declines toward the normal rate (or as the time when this decline will occur becomes more imminent), the high P/E ratio must approach the normal P/E ratio—that is, the P/E of 15.79 will decline year by year and equal 9.77, that of the normal growth company, in the third year.

Note also that D_1 differs for each firm. It is calculated as follows:

$$D_1 = EPS_0 \, (1 + g) \, \text{(Fraction of earnings paid out)} = \$3.41(1 + g) \, (0.533).$$

For the declining firm, $D_1 = \$3.41(0.90)(0.533) = \$1.64.$

[b]With $k_s = 16\%$ and $D_1/P_0 = 4.4\%$, the capital gains yield must be $16.0\% - 4.4\% = 11.6\%$. We could calculate the expected price of the stock at the end of the year, $\hat{P}_1$, using the supernormal growth procedures, to confirm that the capital gains yield in Year 1 is indeed 11.6 percent, but this is not necessary.

assume that each firm had earnings per share (EPS) of $3.41 during the preceding reporting period (that is, $EPS_0 = \$3.41$) and paid out 53.3 percent of its reported earnings as dividends. Therefore, dividends per share last year, D_0, were $1.82 for each company, but the values of D_1 differ among the firms.

The value of each stock equals its market price, and the expected and required return is 16 percent on each; thus, $\hat{k}_s = k_s = 16\%$. For the declining firm, this return consists of a high current dividend yield, 26 percent, combined with a capital loss amounting to 10 percent a year. For the zero growth firm, there is neither a capital gain nor a capital loss expectation, so the 16 percent return must be obtained entirely from the dividend yield. The normal growth firm provides a 6 percent current dividend yield plus a 10 percent capital gains expectation. Finally, the supernormal growth firm has a low current dividend yield but a high capital gains expectation.

What is expected to happen to the prices of the four illustrative firms' stocks over time? Three of the four cases are straightforward: The zero growth firm's price is expected to be constant; the declining firm is expected to have a falling stock price; and the constant growth firm's stock price is expected to grow at a constant rate, 10 percent. We do not prove it here, but we could show that the supernormal firm's stock price growth rate starts at 11.6 percent per year but declines to 10 percent as the supernormal growth period ends.

Actual Stock Prices and Returns

Our discussion thus far has focused on *expected* stock prices and *expected* rates of return. Anyone who has ever invested in the stock market knows that there can be, and generally are, large differences between *expected* and *realized* prices and returns.

For example, on January 1, 1981, IBM's stock price was $67.875 per share. Its 1980 dividend, D_0, had been $3.44, and the consensus view among security analysts was that IBM would experience a growth rate of about 11 percent in the future. Thus, an average investor who bought IBM at $67.875 expected to earn a return of about 16.6 percent:

$$\hat{k}_s = \begin{array}{c} \text{Expected} \\ \text{dividend} \\ \text{yield} \end{array} + \begin{array}{c} \text{Expected growth rate,} \\ \text{or expected capital} \\ \text{gains yield} \end{array}$$

$$= \frac{D_0 (1 + g)}{P_0} + g$$

$$= \frac{\$3.44(1.11)}{\$67.875} + 11\%$$

$$= 5.6\% + 11.0\% = 16.6\%.$$

IBM's bonds at the time had a yield of about 13 percent.

In fact, things did not work out as expected. The economy in 1981 was weaker than had been predicted, so IBM's earnings did not grow as expected, and its dividend remained at $3.44. Further, interest rates soared during 1981, and capital was attracted out of the stock market and into the bond market to take advantage of the high interest rates. As a result of these two events, IBM's price declined, and it closed on December 31, 1981, at $56.875, down $11 for the year. Thus, on a beginning-of-the-year investment of $67.875, the actual return on IBM for 1981 was -11.1 percent:

$$\bar{k}_s = \begin{array}{c} \text{Actual} \\ \text{dividend} \\ \text{yield} \end{array} + \begin{array}{c} \text{Actual} \\ \text{capital gains} \\ \text{yield} \end{array}$$

$$= \frac{\$3.44}{\$67.875} + \frac{-\$11}{\$67.875}$$

$$= 5.1\% - 16.2\% = -11.1\%.$$

Most other stocks performed similarly to IBM in 1981.

However, the economy improved after 1981, and IBM's dividend and stock price improved apace. The total realized return on IBM in 1982 increased dramatically to 77 percent; in 1983 it was a strong 30 percent; it was only 5 percent in 1984; it was back up to 30 percent in 1985; but in 1986 the total return was a negative 19% even though the market as a whole was strong. On average, the realized return on IBM stock during this period has been about 19 percent, which is probably about the rate of return investors expected. However, in any one year, the realized return probably differed significantly from the return expected.

Panel A of Figure 5-10 shows how the price of an average share of stock has varied in recent years, and Panel B shows how total realized returns have behaved. The market has gone up in some years and down in others, and the stocks of individual companies have likewise gone up and down. We know from theory that expected returns as estimated by an average investor are always positive, but in some years, as Panel B shows, negative returns were realized. Of course, even in bad years some individual companies do well, so the "name of the game" in security analysis is to pick the winners. Also, financial managers attempt to take actions which will put their companies into the winners' column, but they do not always succeed. In subsequent chapters, we will examine the actions that managers can take to increase the odds of their firms' doing relatively well in the marketplace.

Stock Market Reporting

Figure 5-11, taken from the *Wall Street Journal,* shows a section of the stock market page which lists stocks on the NYSE. For each stock the *Journal* provides specific data on the trading that took place on the previous day, as well as other, more general, information. Similar information is available on stocks listed on the other exchanges and also on stocks traded over-the-counter.

Stocks are listed alphabetically, from AAR Industries to Zurn Industries; the data in Figure 5-11 were taken from the top of the listing. We will examine the data for Abbott Laboratories, AbtLb, shown about two-thirds of the way down the listing. The two columns on the left show the highest and lowest prices at which the stocks have sold during the past year; Abbott Labs has traded in the range from

Figure 5-10
New York Stock Exchange Prices and Total Returns, 1953–1986

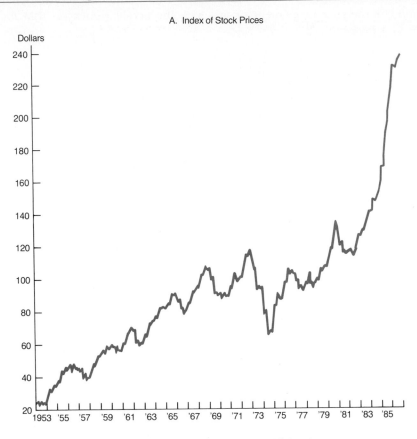

A. Index of Stock Prices

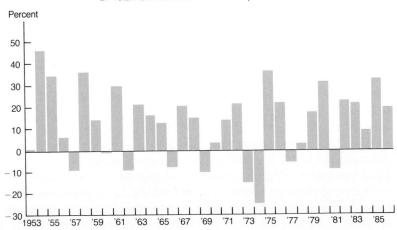

B. Total Returns: Dividend Yield + Capital Gain or Loss

Figure 5-11
Stock Market Transactions, January 19, 1987

52 Weeks High	Low	Stock	Div.	Yld %	P-E Ratio	Sales 100s	High	Low	Close	Net Chg.
		– A–A–A –								
27⅝	17	AAR s	.50	1.8	20	1335u	28	27	28	+ 1
30½	21¾	ADT	.92	3.2	...	132	29⅜	28¾	28⅞	– ½
36⅝	17½	AFG s	.12i	.3	10	1225	35	34	35	– ¼
34⅞	6¾	AGS		...	21	706	32⅞	31	32⅞	+ 1⅜
15	6¾	AMCA		...	...	19	7⅜	7¼	7⅜	+ ⅛
62⅛	43	AMR		...	14	9484	60½	57¼	60⅜	+ 2
27½	24	ANR pf	2.67	10.2	...	2	26¼	26¼	26¼	– ¾
16½	10	ARX	.71t	6.1	11	91	11¾	11⅜	11⅝	...
41½	28¾	ASA	2.00a	4.7	...	1614u	42⅛	41	42⅛	+ 2½
18⅜	9¾	AVX		2.2	...	1070	14⅞	14⅜	14⅞	+ ¼
32	26	AZP	2.72	8.7	9	2763	31¼	30⅞	31⅛	+ ⅛
55	31⅝	AbtLb s	.84	1.6	23	4317	52⅜	50⅝	52⅛	+ ⅝
32	25	AccoWd	.56	1.9	19	124	29⅜	29	29⅜	+ ½
14⅜	9	AcmeC	.40	3.5	...	261	11½	11⅛	11½	+ ⅜
9¼	6⅛	AcmeE	.32b	4.3	19	79	7⅜	7⅛	7⅜	+ ⅛
23⅞	17½	AdaEx	3.42e	16.0	...	177	21⅝	20⅞	21⅜	+ ⅛
16⅝	9¾	AdmM s		...	...	15	16	15¾	16	+ ⅛
20⅜	12⅛	AdvSys	.62t	3.3	15	268	19½	18⅞	18⅞	...
32⅞	12⅞	AMD		...	...	8827	18½	17½	18½	+ 1⅛

Source: The *Wall Street Journal*, January 20, 1987.

\$55 to \$31⅝ (or \$31.625) during the preceding 52 weeks. The amount just to the right of the company's abbreviated name is the dividend; Abbott Labs had a current indicated annual dividend rate of \$0.84 per share and a dividend yield (which is the dividend divided by the closing stock price) of 1.6 percent. Next comes the ratio of the stock's price to its last reported annual earnings (the P/E ratio), followed by the volume of trading for the day: 431,700 shares of Abbott Labs stock were traded on January 19, 1987. Following the volume come the high and the low prices for the day and then the closing price. On January 19, Abbott Labs traded as high as \$52⅜ and as low as \$50⅝, while the last trade was at \$52⅛. The last column gives the change from the closing price on the previous day. Abbott Labs was up ⅝, or \$0.625, so the previous close must have been \$51½, or \$51.50.

There are three other points to note in Figure 5-11: (1) An "s" following a stock's name, such as Abbott, indicates that the stock has recently been split. (2) The "pf" following the stock name on the ANR listing tell us that it is preferred rather than common stock. (3) The "u" preceding AAR's daily high indicates that the \$28 price is a new 52-week high. Note that the reported yearly high and low listing in the left columns does not include the current trading day.

SUMMARY

Corporate decisions should be analyzed in terms of how alternative courses of action are likely to affect the value of a firm. However, it is necessary to know how bond and stock prices in general are established before attempting to measure how a given decision will affect a specific firm's value. Accordingly, this chapter showed how bond and stock values are determined, as well as how investors go about estimating the rates of return they expect to receive if they purchase securities at the existing market prices. In all cases, security values were found to be *the present value of the security's expected future cash flows.* The cash flows from a bond consist of interest payments plus the bond's maturity value, while stocks' cash flows consist of a stream of dividends plus a sale price.

The following equation is used to find the value of an annual coupon bond:

$$V = \sum_{t=1}^{n} \frac{I}{(1 + k_d)^t} + \frac{M}{(1 + k_d)^n}$$

$$= I(PVIFA_{k_d,n}) + M(PVIF_{k_d,n}).$$

Here V is the value of the bond; I is the annual interest payment, or coupon; n is years to maturity; k_d is the appropriate interest rate; and M is the bond's maturity value, generally $1,000. This equation can also be solved for k_d, which is called the *yield to maturity (YTM).* If the bond pays interest semiannually, as most do, then you must divide I and k_d by 2 and multiply n by 2 before applying the formula.

Several different stock valuation formulas were developed, including the ones for zero growth and for constant growth:

$$\text{Zero growth: } \hat{P}_0 = \frac{D}{k_s}.$$

$$\text{Constant, or normal, growth: } \hat{P}_0 = \frac{D_1}{k_s - g}.$$

Here $\hat{P}_0$ is the intrinsic value of the stock; D is the expected constant dividend; D_1 is the dividend expected during the next year; k_s is the required rate of return on the stock; and g is the expected growth rate. In the second equation, g is a constant; if g is not a constant, then the nonconstant growth procedure must be used to find the stock's value.

We can express the equation for the *expected rate of return* on a constant growth stock as follows:

$$\hat{k}_s = \frac{D_1}{P_0} + g.$$

In this form we see that the total expected return, $\hat{k}_s$, consists of an *expected dividend yield* plus an *expected capital gains yield.* For constant growth stocks, the dividend and capital gains components of total yield are both expected to be constant over time. For supernormal growth stocks, the dividend yield should rise over time, while the capital gains component should decline, with the total yield remaining constant.

We saw that differences can and do exist between expected and actual returns in the stock and bond markets — only for short-term, riskless assets do expected and actual (or realized) returns equal each other.

Questions

5-1   Define each of the following terms:

    a. Bond

    b. Par value; maturity date; call provision

    c. Coupon payment; coupon interest rate

    d. Premium bond; discount bond

    e. Current yield (on a bond); yield to maturity (YTM); yield to call (YTC)

    f.   Interest rate risk; reinvestment rate risk

    g. Intrinsic value, $\hat{P}_0$; market price, P_0

    h. Required rate of return, k_s; expected rate of return, $\hat{k}_s$; actual, or realized, rate of return, $\bar{k}_s$

    i.   Capital gains yield; dividend yield; expected total return

    j.   Perpetuity; zero growth stock

    k. Normal, or constant, growth; nonconstant growth; supernormal growth

5-2   Two investors are evaluating AT&T's stock for possible purchase. They agree on the expected value of D_1 and also on the expected future dividend growth rate. Further, they agree on the riskiness of the stock. However, one investor normally holds stocks for 2 years, while the other normally holds stocks for 10 years. Based on the type of analysis done in this chapter, they should both be willing to pay the same price for AT&T's stock. True or false? Explain.

5-3   A bond that pays interest forever and has no maturity date is a perpetual bond. In what respect is a perpetual bond similar to a no-growth common stock and to a share of preferred stock?

5-4   Is it true that the following equation can be used to find the value of an n-year bond that pays interest once a year?

$$\text{Value} = \sum_{t=1}^{n} \frac{\text{Annual interest}}{(1 + k_d)^t} + \frac{\text{Par value}}{(1 + k_d)^n}.$$

5-5   "The values of outstanding bonds change whenever the going rate of interest changes. In general, short-term interest rates are more volatile than long-term interest rates. Therefore, short-term bond prices are more sensitive to interest rate changes than are long-term bond prices." Is this statement true or false? Explain.

5-6   The rate of return you would get if you bought a bond and held it to its maturity date is defined as the bond's yield to maturity. If interest rates in the economy rise after a bond has been issued, what will happen to its price and to its YTM? Does the length of time to maturity affect the extent to which a given change in interest rates will affect the bond price?

5-7   If you buy a *callable* bond and interest rates decline, will the value of your bond rise by as much as it would have if the bond had not been callable?

5-8   If you bought a share of common stock, you would typically expect to receive dividends plus capital gains. Would you expect the distribution between dividend yield and capital gains to be influenced by the firm's decision to pay more dividends rather than to retain and reinvest more of its earnings?

5-9   The next expected dividend, D_1, divided by the current price of a share of stock, P_0, is defined as the stock's expected dividend yield. What is the relationship between the dividend yield, the total yield, and the remaining years of supernormal growth for a supernormal growth firm?

5-10 Is it true that the following expression can be used to find the value of a constant growth stock?

$$\hat{P}_0 = \frac{D_0}{k_s + g}.$$

Self-Test Problems

ST-1 (Bond valuation) The Barenbaum Corporation issued a new series of bonds on January 1, 1967. The bonds were sold at par ($1,000), have a 12 percent coupon, and mature in 30 years, on December 31, 1996. Coupon payments are made semiannually (on June 30 and December 31).

    a. What was the YTM of Barenbaum's bonds on January 1, 1967?

    b. What was the price of the bond on January 1, 1972, 5 years later, assuming that the level of interest rates had fallen to 10 percent?

    c. Find the current yield and capital gains yield on the bond on January 1, 1972, given the price as determined in Part b.

    d. On July 1, 1987, Barenbaum's bonds sold for $896.64. What was the YTM at that date?

    e. What were the current yield and capital gains yield on July 1, 1987?

    f. Now assume that you purchased an outstanding Barenbaum bond on March 1, 1987, when the going rate of interest was 15.5 percent. How large a check must you have written to complete the transaction? This is a hard question!

ST-2 (Constant growth stock valuation) Adler Company's current stock price is $24, and its last dividend was $1.60. In view of Adler's strong financial position and its consequent low risk, its required rate of return is only 12 percent. If dividends are expected to grow at a constant rate, g, in the future, and if k_s is expected to remain at 12 percent, what is Adler's expected stock price 5 years from now?

ST-3 (Nonconstant growth stock valuation) Hettenhouse Computer Chips, Inc., is experiencing a period of rapid growth. Earnings and dividends are expected to grow at a rate of 18 percent during the next 2 years, at 15 percent in the third year, and then at a constant rate of 6 percent thereafter. The firm's last dividend was $1.15, and the required rate of return on the stock is 12 percent.

    a. Calculate the value of the stock today.

    b. Calculate $\hat{P}_1$ and $\hat{P}_2$.

    c. Calculate the dividend yield and capital gains yield for Years 1, 2, and 3.

Problems

5-1 (Bond valuation) The Sinkey Company has two bond issues outstanding. Both bonds pay $100 annual interest plus $1,000 at maturity. Bond L has a maturity of 15 years and Bond S a maturity of 1 year.

a. What will be the value of each of these bonds when the going rate of interest is (1) 6 percent, (2) 9 percent, and (3) 12 percent? Assume that there is only one more interest payment to be made on Bond S.

b. Why does the longer-term (15-year) bond fluctuate more when interest rates change than does the shorter-term bond (1-year)?

5-2 **(Yield to maturity)** The Lang Company's bonds have 4 years remaining to maturity. Interest is paid annually; the bonds have a $1,000 par value; and the coupon interest rate is 8 percent.

a. What is the yield to maturity at a current market price of (1) $825 or (2) $1,107?

b. Would you pay $825 for one of these bonds if you thought that the appropriate rate of interest was 10 percent; that is, if $k_d = 10\%$? Explain your answer.

5-3 **(Bond valuation)** Suppose Exxon sold an issue of bonds with a 10-year maturity, a $1,000 par value, a 12 percent coupon rate, and semiannual interest payments.

a. Two years after the bonds were issued, the going rate of interest on bonds such as these fell to 8 percent. At what price would the bonds sell?

b. Suppose that 2 years after the initial offering, the going interest rate had risen to 14 percent. At what price would the bonds sell?

c. Suppose the conditions in Part a existed — that is, interest rates fell to 8 percent 2 years after the issue date. Suppose further that the interest rate remained at 8 percent for the next 8 years. What would happen to the price of the Exxon bonds over time?

5-4 **(Perpetual bond valuation)** The bonds of the Powell Corporation are perpetuities with a 12 percent annual coupon and a par value of $1,000. Bonds of this type currently yield 10 percent.

a. What is the price of the Powell bonds?

b. Suppose interest rate levels rise to the point where such bonds now yield 15 percent? What would be the price of the Powell bonds?

c. At what price would the Powell bonds sell if the yield on these bonds were 12 percent?

d. How would your answers to Parts a, b, and c change if the bonds were not perpetuities but had a maturity of 20 years?

5-5 **(Perpetual bond yield to maturity)** The yield to maturity (YTM) is the rate of return earned on a bond that is held to maturity. What will be the yield to maturity of a perpetual bond with a $1,000 par value, a 9 percent coupon rate, and a current market price of (a) $700, (b) $900, (c) $1,000, and (d) $1,300? Assume interest is paid annually.

5-6 **(Constant growth stock valuation)** Your broker offers to sell you some shares of Dellva Company common stock that paid a dividend of $2 *last year*. You expect the dividend to grow at the rate of 5 percent per year for the next 3 years, and if you buy the stock you plan to hold it for 3 years and then sell it.

a. Find the expected dividend for each of the next 3 years; that is, calculate D_1, D_2, and D_3. Note that $D_0 = \$2$.

b. Given that the appropriate discount rate is 12 percent and that the first of these dividend payments will occur 1 year from now, find the present value of the dividend stream; that is, calculate the PV of D_1, D_2, and D_3, and then sum these PVs.

c. You expect the price of the stock 3 years from now to be $34.73; that is, you expct $\hat{P}_3$ to equal $34.73. Discounted at a 12 percent rate, what is the present value of this expected future stock price? In other words, calculate the PV of $34.73.

d. If you plan to buy the stock, hold it for 3 years, and then sell it for $34.73, what is the most you should pay for it?

e. Use Equation 5-6 to calculate the present value of this stock. Assume that g = 5%, and it is a constant.

f. Is the value of this stock dependent upon how long you plan to hold it? In other words, if your planned holding period were 2 years or 5 years rather than 3 years, would this affect the value of the stock today, $\hat{P}_0$?

5-7 **(Return on common stock)** You buy a share of Ferri Corporation stock for $35.33. You expect it to pay dividends of $1.06, $1.1236, and $1.1910 in Years 1, 2, and 3, respectively, and you expect to sell it at a price of $42.08 at the end of 3 years.

a. Calculate the growth rate in dividends.

b. Calculate the current dividend yield.

c. Assuming that the calculated growth rate is expected to continue, you can add the dividend yield to the expected growth rate to get the expected total rate of return. What is this stock's expected total rate of return?

5-8 **(Constant growth stock valuation)** Investors require a 20 percent rate of return on Potter Company's stock ($k_s = 20\%$).

a. What will be Potter's stock value if the previous dividend was $D_0 = 2 and if investors expect dividends to grow at a constant annual rate of (1) −5 percent, (2) 0 percent, (3) 5 percent, or (4) 15 percent?

b. Using data from Part a, what is the Gordon (constant growth) model value for the firm's stock if the required rate of return is 20 percent and the expected growth rate is (1) 20 percent or (2) 25 percent? Are these reasonable results? Explain.

c. Is it reasonable to expect that a constant growth stock would have $g > k_s$?

5-9 **(Stock price reporting)** Look up the prices of IBM's stock and bonds in the *Wall Street Journal* (or some other newspaper which provides this information).

a. What was the stock's price range over the last year?

b. What is IBM's current dividend? What is its dividend yield?

c. What change occurred in IBM's stock price since the previous day's close?

d. If IBM were to sell a new issue of $1,000 par value long-term bonds, approximately what coupon interest rate would it have to set on the bonds if it wanted to bring them out at par?

e. If you had $10,000 and wanted to invest it in IBM, what return would you expect to get if you bought the bonds and what return if you bought IBM's stock? (Hint: Think about capital gains when you answer the latter part of this question.)

5-10 **(Discount bond valuation)** In February 1956 the Los Angeles Airport authority issued a series of 3.4 percent, 30-year bonds. Interest rates rose substantially in the years following the issue, and as they did, the price of the bonds declined. In February 1969, 13 years later, the price of the bonds had dropped from $1,000 to $650. In answering the following questions, assume that the bond has annual interest payments.

a. Each bond originally sold at its $1,000 par value. What was the yield to maturity of these bonds at their time of issue?

b. Calculate the yield to maturity in February 1969.

c. Assume that interest rates stabilized at the 1969 level and stayed there for the remainder of the life of the bonds. What would have been their price in February 1981, when they had 5 years remaining to maturity?

d. What would the price of the bonds have been the day before they matured in 1986? (Disregard the last interest payment.)

e. In 1969 the Los Angeles Airport bonds were classified as "discount bonds." What happens to the price of a discount bond as it approaches maturity? Is there a "built-in capital gain" on such bonds?

f. The coupon interest payment divided by the market price of a bond is called the bond's *current yield.* Assuming the conditions in Part c, what would have been the current yield of a Los Angeles Airport bond (1) in February 1969 and (2) in February 1981? What would have been its capital gains yields and total yields (total yield equals yield to maturity) on those same two dates?

5-11 (Declining growth stock valuation) Wingler Mining Company's ore reserves are being depleted, so its sales are falling. Also, its pit is getting deeper each year, so its costs are rising. As a result, the company's earnings and dividends are declining at the constant rate of 10 percent per year. If $D_0 = \$6$ and $k_s = 15\%$, what is the value of Wingler Mining's stock?

5-12 (Supernormal growth stock valuation) It is now January 1, 1988. Nelson Electric, Inc., has just developed a solar panel capable of generating 200 percent more electricity than any solar panel currently on the market. As a result, Nelson is expected to experience a 20 percent annual growth rate for the next 5 years. By the end of 5 years, other firms will have developed comparable technology, and Nelson's growth rate will slow to 6 percent per year indefinitely. Stockholders require a return of 10 percent on Nelson's stock. The most recent annual dividend, D_0, which was paid yesterday, was $1.50 per share.

a. Calculate Nelson's expected dividends for 1988, 1989, 1990, 1991, and 1992.

b. Calculate the value of the stock today, $\hat{P}_0$. Proceed by finding the present value of the dividends expected at the end of 1988, 1989, 1990, 1991, and 1992 plus the present value of the stock price which should exist at the end of 1992. The year-end 1992 stock price can be found by using the constant growth equation. Notice that to find the December 31, 1992, price, you use the dividend expected in 1993, which is 6 percent greater than the 1992 dividend.

c. Calculate the current dividend yield, D_1/P_0, the capital gains yield expected in 1988, and the expected total return (dividend yield plus capital gains yield) for 1988. (Assume that $\hat{P}_0 = P_0$, and recognize that the capital gains yield is equal to the total return minus the dividend yield.) Also, calculate these same three yields for 1992.

d. How might an investor's tax situation affect his or her decision to purchase stocks of companies in the early stages of their lives, when they are growing rapidly, versus stocks of older, more mature firms? When does Nelson's stock become "mature" in this example?

(Do Parts e and f only if you are using the computerized diskette.)

e. Suppose your boss tells you that she believes that Nelson's annual growth rate will be only 15 percent over the next 5 years and that the firm's normal growth rate is only 5 percent. Calculate the expected dividends for the supernormal growth period and the value of the stock today under these assumptions.

f. Suppose your boss also tells you that she regards Nelson as being quite risky and that she believes the required rate of return is 13 percent, not 10 percent. Calculate the intrinsic value of Nelson's stock. Also, do the calculations with k_s values of 15 percent and 20 percent to see how k_s affects the stock's value.

5-13 (Supernormal growth stock valuation) Magee Motor Corporation has been growing at a rate of 25 percent per year in recent years. This same growth rate is expected to last for another 2 years.

a. If $D_0 = \$2$, $k_s = 14\%$, and $g_n = 6\%$, what is Magee's stock worth today? What are its current dividend yield and capital gains yield?

b. Now assume that the period of supernormal growth is 5 years rather than 2 years. How does this affect Magee's price, dividend yield, and capital gains yield? Answer in words only.

c. What will be the stock's dividend yield and capital gains yield the year after its period of supernormal growth ends? (Hint: These values will be the same regardless of whether you examine the case of 2 or 5 years of supernormal growth; the calculations are trivial.)

d. Of what interest to investors is the changing relationship between dividend yield and capital gains yield over time?

(Do Parts e and f only if you are using the computerized diskette.)

e. What will be Magee's stock price, dividend yield, and capital gains yield if the supernomal growth period is 5 years?

f. What will be the price, dividend yield, and capital gains yield if the required rate of return is 16 percent and the supernormal growth period is 2 years?

5-14 (Yield to call) It is now January 1, 1988, and you are considering the purchase of an outstanding Swift Corporation bond that was issued on January 1, 1986. Swift's bond has a 10.5 percent annual coupon and a 30-year original maturity (it matures on January 1, 2016). There was originally a 5-year call protection (until December 31, 1990), after which time the bond can be called at 110 (that is, at 110 percent of par, or $1,100). Interest rates have declined since the bond was issued, and the bond is now selling at 115.174 percent of par, or $1,151.74. You want to determine both the yield to maturity and the yield to call for this bond. (Note: The yield to call considers the impact of a call provision on the bond's probable yield. In the calculation, we assume that the bond will be outstanding until the call date, at which time it will be called. Thus, the investor will have received interest payments for the call-protected period and then will receive the call price—in this case, $1,100—on the call date.)

a. What is the yield to maturity in 1988 for Swift's bond? What is its yield to call?

b. If you bought this bond, which return do you think you would actually earn? Explain your reasoning.

c. Suppose the bond had sold at a discount. Would the yield to maturity or the yield to call have been more relevant?

(Do Parts d and e only if you are using the computerized diskette.)

d. Suppose the bond's price suddenly jumps to $1,250. What is the yield to maturity now, and what is the yield to call?

e. Suppose the price suddenly falls to $800; now what would the YTM and YTC be?

Solutions to Self-Test Problems

ST-1 a. Barenbaum's bonds were sold at par; therefore, the original YTM equaled the coupon rate of 12%.

b.
$$V = \sum_{t=1}^{50} \frac{\$120/2}{(1 + 0.10/2)^t} + \frac{\$1,000}{(1 + 0.10/2)^{50}}$$

$$= \$60(\text{PVIFA}_{5\%,50}) + \$1,000(\text{PVIF}_{5\%,50})$$

$$= \$60(18.2559) + \$1,000(0.0872)$$

$$= \$1,095.35 + \$87.20 = \$1,182.55.$$

c.
$$\text{Current yield} = \text{Annual coupon payment/Price}$$
$$= \$120/\$1,182.55 = 0.1015 = 10.15\%.$$

$$\text{Capital gains yield} = \text{Total yield} - \text{Current yield}$$
$$= 10\% - 10.15\% = -0.15\%.$$

Alternatively, $V_{1/1/73} = \$1,180.76$, and $(\$1,180.76 - \$1,182.55)/\$1,182.55 = -0.15\%$.

d.
$$\$896.64 = \sum_{t=1}^{19} \frac{\$60}{(1 + k_d/2)^t} + \frac{\$1,000}{(1 + k_d/2)^{19}}.$$

Use the approximate YTM formula to get a starting point:

$$\text{Approximate YTM} = \frac{I + (M - V)/n}{(M + 2V)/3}$$

$$= \frac{\$60 + (\$1,000 - \$896.64)/19}{(\$1,000 + \$1,793.28)/3} = 7.03\%.$$

Therefore, $k_d \approx 7.03(2) = 14.06\%$.
Try $k_d = 14\%$:

$$V = I(\text{PVIFA}_{7\%,19}) + M(\text{PVIF}_{7\%,19})$$
$$\$896.64 = \$60(10.3356) + \$1,000(0.2765)$$
$$= \$620.14 + \$276.50 = \$896.64.$$

Therefore, the YTM on July 1, 1987, was 14 percent.

e. Current yield = $\$120/\$896.64 = 13.38\%$.

$$\text{Capital gains yield} = 14\% - 13.38\% = 0.62\%.$$

f. The following time line illustrates the years to maturity of the bond:

Thus, on March 1, 1987, there were 19⅔ periods left before the bond matures. Bond traders actually use the following procedure to determine the price of the bond:

(1) Find the price of the bond on the next coupon date, July 1, 1987.

$$V_{7/1/87} = \$60(PVIFA_{7.75\%,19}) + \$1,000(PVIF_{7.75\%,19})$$
$$= \$60(9.7788) + \$1,000(0.2421)$$
$$= \$828.83.$$

Note that we could use a calculator to solve for $V_{7/1/87}$ or we could substitute k = 7.75% and n = 19 periods into the equations for PVIFA and PVIF:

$$PVIFA = \frac{1 - \dfrac{1}{(1 + k)^n}}{k} = \frac{1 - \dfrac{1}{(1 + 0.0775)^{19}}}{0.0775} = 9.7788.$$

$$PVIF = \frac{1}{(1 + k)^n} = \frac{1}{1 + 0.0775)^{19}} = 0.2421.$$

(2) Add the coupon, $60, to the bond price to get the total value, TV, of the bond on the next interest payment date: TV = $828.83 + $60.00 = $888.83.

(3) Discount this total value back to the purchase date:

$$\begin{array}{c}\text{Value at purchase date} \\ \text{(March 1, 1987)}\end{array} = \$888.83 \, (PVIF_{7.75\%,4/6})$$
$$= \$888.83(0.9515)$$
$$= \$845.72.$$

Here

$$PVIF_{7.75\%,2/3} = \frac{1}{(1 + 0.0775)^{2/3}} = \frac{1}{1.0510} = 0.9515.$$

(4) Therefore, you would have written a check for $845.72 to complete the transaction. Of this amount, $20 = (1/3)($60) would have represented accrued interest and $825.72 would have represented the bond's basic value. This breakdown would affect both your taxes and those of the seller.

ST-2 The first step is to solve for g, the unknown variable, in the constant growth equation. Since D_1 is unknown but D_0 is known, substitute $D_0(1 + g)$ as follows:

$$\hat{P}_0 = P_0 = \frac{D_1}{k_s - g} = \frac{D_0(1 + g)}{k_s - g}$$

$$\$24 = \frac{\$1.60(1 + g)}{0.12 - g}.$$

Solving for g, we find the growth rate to be 5 percent:

$$\$2.88 - \$24g = \$1.60 + \$1.60g$$
$$\$25.60g = \$1.28$$
$$g = 0.05 = 5\%.$$

The next step is to use the growth rate to project the stock price 5 years hence:

$$\hat{P}_5 = \frac{D_0(1 + g)^6}{k_s - g}$$

$$= \frac{\$1.60(1.05)^6}{0.12 - 0.05} = \$30.63.$$

(Alternatively, $\hat{P}_5 = \$24(1.05)^5 = \$30.63$.)

Therefore, Adler Company's expected stock price 5 years from now, $\hat{P}_5$, is $30.63.

ST-3   a. (1) Calculate the PV of the dividends paid during the supernormal growth period:

$$D_1 = \$1.1500(1.18) = \$1.3570.$$

$$D_2 = \$1.3570(1.18) = \$1.6013.$$

$$D_3 = \$1.6013(1.15) = \$1.8415.$$

PV D $= \$1.3570(0.8929) + \$1.6013(0.7972) + \$1.8415(0.7118)$

$= \$1.2117 + \$1.2766 + \$1.3108$

$= \$3.7991 \approx \$3.80.$

(2) Find the PV of Hettenhouse's stock price at the end of Year 3:

$$\hat{P}_3 = \frac{D_4}{k_s - g} = \frac{D_3(1 + g)}{k_s - g}$$

$$= \frac{\$1.8415(1.06)}{0.12 - 0.06} = \$32.53.$$

PV $\hat{P}_3 = \$32.53(0.7118) = \$23.15.$

(3) Sum the two components to find the value of the stock today:

$$\hat{P}_0 = \$3.80 + \$23.15 = \$26.95.$$

b. $\hat{P}_1 = \$1.6013(0.8929) + \$1.8415(0.7972) + \$32.53(0.7972)$

$= \$1.4298 + \$1.4680 + \$25.9329 = \$28.8307 \approx \$28.83.$

$\hat{P}_2 = \$1.8415(0.8929) + \$32.53(0.8929)$

$= \$1.6443 + \$29.0460 = \$30.6903 \approx \$30.69.$

c.

Year	Dividend Yield	+	Capital Gains Yield	=	Total Return
1	$\frac{\$1.3570}{\$26.95} = 5.04\%$		$\frac{\$28.83 - \$26.95}{\$26.95} = 6.98\%$		$\approx 12\%$
2	$\frac{\$1.6013}{\$28.83} = 5.55\%$		$\frac{\$30.69 - \$28.83}{\$28.83} = 6.45\%$		$\approx 12\%$
3	$\frac{\$1.8415}{\$30.69} = 6.00\%$		$\frac{\$32.53 - \$30.69}{\$30.69} = 6.00\%$		$\approx 12\%$

Selected Additional References

Many investments textbooks cover stock and bond valuation models in depth and detail. Here are some of the good recent ones:

Francis, Jack C., *Investments: Analysis and Management* (New York: McGraw-Hill, 1980).

Radcliffe, Robert C., *Investment: Concepts, Analysis, and Strategy* (Glenview, Ill.: Scott, Foresman, 1987).

Reilly, Frank K., *Investment Analysis and Portfolio Management* (Hinsdale, Ill.: Dryden, 1985).

Sharpe, William F., *Investments* (Englewood Cliffs, N.J.: Prentice-Hall, 1981).

The classic works on stock valuation models are:

Gordon, Myron J., and Eli Shapiro, "Capital Equipment Analysis: The Required Rate of Profit," *Management Science,* October 1956, 102–110.

Williams, John B., *The Theory of Investment Value* (Cambridge, Mass.: Harvard University Press, 1938).

6

Risk and Rates of Return

Common sense tells us that the required rate of return on an investment increases as the investment's riskiness increases. However, common sense does not tell us how to measure risk, and, indeed, the proper measurement of risk is rather subtle. To illustrate, consider these two examples:

1. Echo Bay Mines is a leading gold producer. Gold prices are volatile, and since Echo Bay's profits vary with the price of gold, its earnings and stock price also fluctuate widely from year to year. All this suggests that Echo Bay is relatively risky, and hence that the required rate of return on its stock, k_s, should be above returns on most other companies. However, this is not the case; the formula $\hat{k}_s = k_s = D_1/P_0 + g$ indicates that, with any reasonable value for growth, Echo Bay's k_s in 1987, and all other years, was quite low in relation to other companies. This, in turn, indicates that investors regard Echo Bay as being a low-risk company in spite of its unstable profits and dividends.

2. Such large, strong, and well-diversified companies as Du Pont and General Electric (GE) have more stable, predictable earnings and dividends than do the 1,600 or so smaller NYSE companies. This suggests that Du Pont, GE, and other giant companies have much less risk and, consequently, should have much lower required rates of return on their stocks than do smaller companies. However, this is not the case; a careful analysis indicates that Du Pont, GE, and other giant companies do not have materially lower required rates of return than many smaller, more volatile companies.

The reason for these somewhat counterintuitive facts has to do with diversification and its effects on risk. It so happens that Echo Bay's stock price rises with inflationary expectations, whereas other stocks tend to decline as inflation heats up. Therefore, holding Echo Bay's stock as part of a portfolio of "normal" stocks tends to stabilize returns on the entire portfolio. In the case of Du Pont and GE, it turns out that investors, by forming portfolios of the stocks of smaller companies, can and do diversify away much of the risk that would otherwise be inherent in small companies.

We also know that expectations for inflation, along with risk, have an impact on interest rates and required rates of return generally, and consequently on security prices. Inflationary expectations are worked into security prices in various ways. Sometimes the changes are slow and almost imperceptible, but sometimes they are quite rapid. For example, in January of 1987, Henry Kaufman, an economist and senior executive of Salomon Brothers (a major Wall Street investment banking firm), and probably the most listened-to interest rate forecaster in the United States, predicted that interest rates would decrease sharply. Kaufman's forecast caused the Dow Jones Industrial Average to rise by over 15 points within a few hours.

In this chapter, we take an in-depth look at how investment risk should be measured, and at how both risk and inflation affect security prices and rates of return.

In Chapter 5 we referred frequently to the terms *the appropriate interest rate on a bond, k_d,* and *the appropriate (or required) rate of return on a share of stock, k_s.* These rates, which investors use when establishing the values of bonds and stocks, depend primarily on the level of the riskless rate of interest, k_{RF}, and on the riskiness of the security in question. In this chapter we define the term *risk* as it relates to securities, examine procedures managers use for measuring risk, and discuss the relationships between risk, returns, and security prices. Financial managers use these concepts continuously as they plan actions which will shape their firms' futures.

DEFINING AND MEASURING RISK

Risk is defined in *Webster's* as "a hazard; a peril; exposure to loss or injury." Thus, risk refers to the chance that some unfavorable event will occur. If you engage in skydiving, you are taking a chance with your life — skydiving is risky. If you bet on the horses, you are risking your money. If you invest in speculative stocks (or, really, *any* stock), you are taking a risk in the hope of making an appreciable return.

To illustrate the riskiness of financial assets, suppose an investor buys $100,000 of short-term government bonds with a yield to maturity of 10 percent. In this case, the rate of return on the investment, 10 percent, can be estimated quite precisely, and the investment is defined as being risk-free. However, if the $100,000 were invested in the stock of a company just being organized to prospect for oil in the mid-Atlantic, then the investment's return could not be estimated precisely. One might analyze the situation and conclude that the *expected* rate of return, in a statistical sense, is 20 percent, but it should also be recognized that the *actual* rate of return could range from, say, +1,000 percent to −100 percent, and, because there is a significant danger of actually earning a return considerably less than the expected return, the stock would be described as being relatively risky.

Investment risk, then, is related to the probability of earning a return less than the expected return — the greater the chance of low or negative returns, the riskier the investment. However, we can define risk more precisely, and it is useful to do so.

Probability Distributions

An event's *probability* is defined as the chance that the event will occur. For example, a weather forecaster might state, "There is a 40 percent chance of rain today and a 60 percent chance that it will not rain." If all possible events, or outcomes, are listed, and if a probability is assigned to each event, then the listing is defined as a *probability distribution*. For our weather forecast, we could set up the following probability distribution:

Outcome (1)	Probability (2)
Rain	0.4 = 40%
No rain	0.6 = 60
	1.0 = 100%

The possible outcomes are listed in Column 1, while the probabilities of these outcomes, expressed both as decimals and as percentages, are given in Column 2. Notice that the probabilities must sum to 1.0, or 100 percent.

In Chapter 5 we defined the expected rate of return on a stock, $\hat{k}_s$, as the sum of the expected dividend yield plus the expected capital gain. We now examine the probability distribution concept as it relates to rates of return. To begin, consider the possible rates of return (dividend yield plus capital gain or loss) that you might earn next year on a $10,000 investment in the stock of either TeleCorp or Saveway Food Company. TeleCorp manufactures and distributes computers and equipment for the rapidly growing data transmission industry. Its sales are cyclical, so its profits rise and fall with the business cycle. Further, its market is extremely competitive, and some new company could develop better products which could literally bankrupt TeleCorp. Saveway, on the other hand, is a retail food chain which dominates its regional market, and hence it is not very vulnerable to competition. Further, people have to eat, so Saveway's sales and profits are not very vulnerable to downturns in the economy.

The rate of return probability distributions for the two companies are shown in Table 6-1. Here we see that there is a 30 percent chance of a boom, in which case both companies will have high earnings, pay high dividends, and enjoy capital gains; a 40 percent probability of a "normal" economy and moderate returns; and a 30 percent probability of a recession, which will mean low earnings and dividends and perhaps even capital losses. Notice, however, that TeleCorp's rate of return could vary far more widely than that of Saveway. There is a fairly high

Table 6-1
Probability Distributions for Telecorp and Saveway Foods

State of the Economy	Probability of This State Occurring	Rate of Return on Stock under This State	
		TeleCorp	Saveway
Boom	0.3	100%	20%
Normal	0.4	15	15
Recession	0.3	−70	10
	1.0		

probability that the value of the TeleCorp stock will drop significantly, resulting in a loss of 70 percent, while there is no chance of a loss on Saveway.[1]

EXPECTED RATE OF RETURN

If we multiply each possible outcome by its probability of occurrence and then sum these products, as in Table 6-2, we obtain a *weighted average* of outcomes. The weights are the probabilities, and the weighted average is defined as the *expected rate of return,* $\hat{k}$.[2] The expected rates of return for both Telecorp and Saveway are shown in Table 6-2 to be 15 percent. This type of table is known as a *payoff matrix.*

The expected rate of return calculation can also be expressed as an equation which does the same thing as the payoff matrix table:

$$\text{Expected rate of return} = \hat{k} = \sum_{i=1}^{n} P_i k_i. \tag{6-1}$$

---

[1] It is, of course, completely unrealistic to think that any stock has no chance of a loss. Only in hypothetical examples could this occur. To illustrate, the price of Commonwealth Edison's stock recently dropped from $27 to $21, a decline of 22 percent, in just one day. Don't tell a Commonwealth stockholder that the stock had no chance of a loss!

[2] In this section we discuss only returns on stocks; thus, the subscript s is unnecessary, so we use the symbol $\hat{k}$ rather than $\hat{k}_s$. Also, keep in mind that $\hat{k} = D_1/P_0 + g$ for a constant growth stock, and

$$\hat{k} = \frac{D_1}{P_0} + g = \sum_{i=1}^{n} P_i k_i,$$

where P_i is the probability of the ith outcome (return) and k_i is the ith outcome. Further, note that the uncertainty about $\hat{k}$, the expected *total* return, reflects uncertainty about the two return components, D_1/P_0 and g. There is more uncertainty regarding g than there is about the dividend yield. Thus, companies with high growth and low current dividend yields are often regarded as being riskier than low-growth companies. This point is discussed further in Chapter 13.

Table 6-2
Calculation of Expected Rate of Return: Payoff Matrix

State of the Economy (1)	Probability of This State Occurring (2)	TeleCorp		Saveway	
		Rate of Return if This State Occurs (3)	Product: (2) × (3) = (4)	Rate of Return if This State Occurs (5)	Product: (2) × (5) = (6)
Boom	0.3	100%	30%	20%	6%
Normal	0.4	15	6	15	6
Recession	0.3	−70	−21	10	3
	1.0		$\hat{k} = $ 15%		$\hat{k} = $ 15%

Here k_i is the ith possible outcome, P_i is the probability of the ith outcome, and n is the number of possible outcomes. Thus, $\hat{k}$ is a weighted average of the possible outcomes (the k_i values), with each outcome's weight being equal to its probability of occurrence. Using the data for TeleCorp, we obtain its expected rate of return as follows:

$$\hat{k} = P_1(k_1) + P_2(k_2) + P_3(k_3)$$
$$= 0.3(100\%) + 0.4(15\%) + 0.3(-70\%)$$
$$= 15\%.$$

Saveway's expected rate of return is also 15 percent:

$$\hat{k} = 0.3(20\%) + 0.4(15\%) + 0.3(10\%)$$
$$= 15\%.$$

We can graph the rates of return to obtain a picture of the variability of possible outcomes; this is shown in the bar charts in Figure 6-1. The height of each bar signifies the probability that a given outcome will occur. The range of probable returns for TeleCorp is from +100 to −70 percent, with an expected return of 15 percent. The expected return for Saveway is also 15 percent, but its range is much narrower.

Continuous Probability Distributions

Thus far, we have assumed that only three states of the economy can exist: recession, normal, and boom. Actually, of course, the state of the economy could range from a deep depression to a fantastic boom, and there are an unlimited number of possibilities in between. Suppose we had the time and patience to assign a proba-

Figure 6-1
Probability Distributions of TeleCorp's and Saveway's Rates of Return

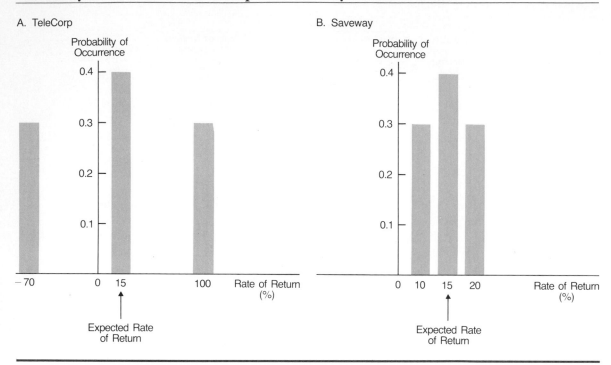

bility to each possible state of the economy (with the sum of the probabilities still equaling 1.0) and to assign a rate of return to each stock for each state of the economy. We would have a table similar to Table 6-2, except that it would have many more entries in each column. This table could be used to calculate expected rates of return as shown above, and the probabilities and outcomes could be approximated by continuous curves such as those presented in Figure 6-2. Here we have changed the assumptions so that there is essentially a zero probability that TeleCorp's return will be less than −70 percent or more than 100 percent, or that Saveway's return will be less than 10 percent or more than 20 percent, but virtually any return within these limits is possible.

The tighter, or more peaked, the probability distribution, the more likely it is that the actual outcome will be close to the expected value and, consequently, the less likely it is that the actual return will be far below the expected return. Thus, the tighter the probability distribution, the lower is the risk assigned to a stock. Since Saveway has a relatively tight probability distribution, its *actual return* is likely to be closer to its 15 percent *expected return* than is that of TeleCorp.

Figure 6-2
Continuous Probability Distributions of TeleCorp's and Saveway's Rates of Return

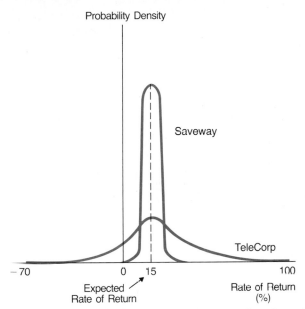

Note: The assumptions regarding the probabilities of various outcomes have been changed from those in Figure 6-1. The probability of obtaining exactly 15 percent was 40 percent in Figure 6-1; in Figure 6-2 it is *much smaller,* because here there are many possible outcomes instead of just three. With continuous distributions such as in Figure 6-2, it is more appropriate to ask what the probability is of obtaining at *least* some specified rate of return than to ask what the probability is of obtaining exactly that rate of return. This cumulative probability is equal to the area under the probability distribution curve to the right of the point of interest, or 1 minus the area under the curve up to the point of interest. This topic is covered in detail in statistics courses.

Measuring Risk: The Standard Deviation

Risk is a difficult concept to grasp, and a great deal of controversy has surrounded attempts to define and measure it. However, a common definition, and one that is satisfactory for many purposes, is stated in terms of probability distributions such as those presented in Figure 6-2: *The tighter the probability distribution of expected future returns, the smaller the total risk of a given investment.* According to this definition, Saveway is less risky than TeleCorp *because the chance of a return that is far below the expected level is smaller for Saveway than for TeleCorp.*

To be most useful, any measure of risk should have a definite value—we need a measure of the tightness of the probability distribution. One such measure is the *standard deviation,* the symbol for which is σ, pronounced "sigma." The smaller the standard deviation, the tighter the probability distribution and, accordingly, the

---

Table 6-3
Calculating TeleCorp's Standard Deviation

$k_i - \hat{k}$ (1)	$(k_i - \hat{k})^2$ (2)	$(k_i - \hat{k})^2 P_i$ (3)
$100 - 15 = 85$	$7,225$	$(7,225)(0.3) = 2,167.5$
$15 - 15 = 0$	0	$(0)(0.4) = 0$
$-70 - 15 = -85$	$7,225$	$(7,225)(0.3) = \underline{2,167.5}$
		Variance $= \sigma^2 = \underline{\underline{4,335.0}}$

Standard deviation $= \sigma = \sqrt{\sigma^2} = \sqrt{4,335} = 65.84\%$.

---

lower the total riskiness of the stock.[3] To calculate the standard deviation, we proceed as shown in Table 6-3, which is explained below:

1. Calculate the expected rate of return:

$$\text{Expected rate of return} = \hat{k} = \sum_{i=1}^{n} P_i k_i. \qquad (6\text{-}1)$$

For TeleCorp, we previously found $\hat{k} = 15\%$.

2. In Column 1 of the table, subtract the expected rate of return from each possible outcome to obtain a set of deviations about $\hat{k}$:

$$\text{Deviation}_i = k_i - \hat{k}.$$

3. In Columns 2 and 3 of the table, square each deviation, multiply the result by the probability of occurrence for its related outcome, and sum these products to obtain the *variance* of the probability distribution:

$$\text{Variance} = \sigma^2 = \sum_{i=1}^{n} (k_i - \hat{k})^2 P_i. \qquad (6\text{-}2)$$

Thus, the variance is an average of the squared deviations, weighted by the probability of each deviation's occurrence.

4. Now take the square root of the variance to obtain the standard deviation:

$$\text{Standard Deviation} = \sigma = \sqrt{\sum_{i=1}^{n} (k_i - \hat{k})^2 P_i}. \qquad (6\text{-}3)$$

---

[3]Since we define risk in terms of the chances of returns being less than expected, it would seem logical to measure risk in terms of the probability of returns below the expected return rather than by the entire distribution. Measures of below-expected returns, which are known as *semivariance measures,* have been developed, but they are difficult to analyze. Additionally, if the distribution is approximately symmetric, which is often the case for security returns, then the standard deviation is as good a risk measure as the semivariance.

Like the variance, the standard deviation is a weighted average of possible deviations from the expected value, so it gives you an idea of how far above or below the expected value the actual value is likely to be. TeleCorp's standard deviation is calculated in Table 6-3 to be 65.84 percent, and using these same procedures, we find Saveway's standard deviation to be 3.87 percent. Since TeleCorp's standard deviation is larger, it is the riskier stock according to this measure of risk.

If a probability distribution is normal, the *actual* return will be within ± 1 standard deviation of the *expected* return 68.26 percent of the time. Figure 6-3 illustrates this point, and it also shows the situation for $\pm 2\sigma$ and $\pm 3\sigma$. For TeleCorp, $\hat{k} = 15\%$ and $\sigma = 65.84\%$, while $\hat{k} = 15\%$ and $\sigma = 3.87\%$ for Saveway. Thus, there is a 68.26 percent probability that the actual return for TeleCorp will be in the range of 15 ± 65.84 percent, or from -50.84 to 80.84 percent. For Saveway, the 68.26 percent range is 15 ± 3.87 percent, or from 11.13 to 18.87 percent. With such a small σ, there is only a small probability that Saveway's return will be significantly less than expected, so the stock is not very risky. For the average firm listed on the New York Stock Exchange, σ has been close to 30 percent in recent years.[4]

Another useful measure of risk is the *coefficient of variation,* which is the standard deviation divided by the expected value. The coefficient of variation (CV) shows the risk per unit of return, and it provides a more meaningful basis for comparison when the expected returns on two alternatives are not the same. Since

---

[4]In this section we have described the procedure for finding the mean and standard deviation when the data are in the form of a known future probability distribution. If only sample returns over some past period are available, then the standard deviation of returns can be estimated using this formula:

$$\text{Estimated } \sigma = S = \sqrt{\frac{\sum_{t=1}^{n} (\bar{k}_t - \bar{k}_{Avg})^2}{n-1}} \tag{6-3a}$$

Here $\bar{k}_t$ denotes the past realized rate of return in Year t and $\bar{k}_{Avg}$ is the average annual return earned during the last n years. Here is an example:

Year	k_t
1985	15%
1986	-5
1987	20

$$\bar{k}_{Avg} = \frac{(15\% - 5\% + 20\%)}{3} = 10.0\%.$$

$$\text{Estimated } \sigma \text{ (or S)} = \sqrt{\frac{(15 - 10)^2 + (-5 - 10)^2 + (20 - 10)^2}{3 - 1}}$$

$$= \sqrt{\frac{350}{2}} = 13.2\%.$$

Often the historical σ is used as an estimate of the future σ. Much less often, and generally incorrectly, $\bar{k}_{Avg}$ for some past period is used as an estimate of $\hat{k}$, the expected future return. Past variability is likely to be repeated, so σ may be a good estimate of future risk, but it is much less reasonable to expect that the past *level* of return (which could have been as high as $+100\%$ or as low as -50%) is the best expectation of what investors think will happen in the future.

Figure 6-3
Probability Ranges for a Normal Distribution

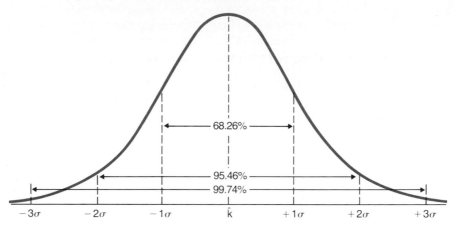

Notes:

a. The area under the normal curve equals 1.0, or 100 percent. *Thus, the areas under any pair of normal curves drawn on the same scale, whether they are peaked or flat, must be equal.*

b. Half of the area under a normal curve is to the left of the mean, indicating that there is a 50 percent probability that the actual outcome will be less than the mean and a 50 percent probability that it will be greater than the mean, or to the right of k̂.

c. Of the area under the curve, 68.26 percent is within ±1σ of the mean, indicating that the probability is 68.26 percent that the actual outcome will be within the range k̂ − 1σ to k̂ + 1σ.

d. Procedures exist for finding the probability of other earnings ranges. These procedures are covered in statistics courses.

e. For a normal distribution, the larger the value of σ, the greater the probability that the actual outcome will vary widely from, and hence perhaps be far below, the expected, or most likely, outcome. *Since the probability of having the actual result turn out to be far below the expected result is our definition of risk, and since σ measures this probability, we can use σ as a measure of risk.* This definition may not be a good one, however, if we are dealing with an asset held in a diversified portfolio. This point is covered later in the chapter.

Saveway and TeleCorp have the same expected return, the coefficient of variation is not particularly useful in this case — the firm with the larger standard deviation, TeleCorp, will necessarily have the larger coefficient of variation. In fact, the coefficient of variation for TeleCorp is 65.84%/15% = 4.39, and that for Saveway is 3.87%/15% = 0.26. Thus, TeleCorp is over 16 times more risky than Saveway on the basis of this criterion.

Now consider two other stocks, X and Y, which have different expected rates of return and different standard deviations. Stock X has a 30 percent expected rate of return and a standard deviation of 10 percent, while Stock Y has an expected return of 10 percent and a standard deviation of 5 percent. Is Stock X riskier since it has the larger standard deviation? If we calculate the coefficients of variation for these two stocks, we find that Stock X has a coefficient of variation of 10%/30% = 0.33, and Stock Y has a coefficient of variation of 5%/10% = 0.50. Thus, we see that Stock Y actually has more risk per unit of return than Stock X, in spite of the fact that X's standard deviation is larger. Therefore, by the coefficient of variation measure, Stock Y is riskier. Where substantial differences in expected returns occur, the coefficient of variation is a better risk measure than the standard deviation.

Risk Aversion and Required Returns

Suppose your father has worked hard and saved $1 million, which he now plans to invest. He can buy a 10 percent, 1-year U.S. Treasury note, and at the end of 1 year he will have a sure $1.1 million, his original investment plus $100,000 in interest. Alternatively, he can buy stock in R&D Enterprises. If R&D's research programs are successful, after one year his stock will increase in value to $2.2 million. However, if the research is a failure, the value of his stock will go to zero, and he will be penniless. He regards R&D's chances of success or failure as being 50-50, so the expected value of the stock investment one year hence is 0.5($0) + 0.5($2,200,000) = $1,100,000. Subtracting the $1 million cost of the stock leaves an expected profit of $100,000, or an expected (but risky) 10 percent rate of return:

$$\text{Expected rate of return} = \frac{\text{Expected investment value} - \text{Cost}}{\text{Cost}}$$

$$= \frac{\$1,100,000 - \$1,000,000}{\$1,000,000}$$

$$= \frac{\$100,000}{\$1,000,000} = 10\%.$$

Thus, he has a choice between a sure $100,000 profit (representing a 10 percent rate of return) on the Treasury note or a risky expected $100,000 profit (also representing a 10 percent expected rate of return) on the R&D Enterprises stock. Which one should he choose? *If he chooses the less risky investment, he is risk averse. Most investors are indeed risk averse, and certainly the average investor is risk averse, at least with regard to his or her "serious money." Since this is a well-documented fact, we shall assume risk aversion throughout the remainder of the book.*

What are the implications of risk aversion for security prices and rates of return? The answer is that, other things held constant, the higher a security's risk, (1) the lower its price and (2) the higher its required return. To see how this works, we can analyze the situation with Saveway and TeleCorp stocks. Suppose each stock now sells for $100 per share, and each has a 15 percent expected rate of return. Investors are averse to risk, so there would be a general preference for Saveway. People with money to invest would bid for Saveway rather than TeleCorp stock, and TeleCorp stockholders would start selling it and using the money to buy Saveway stock. The buying pressure would tend to drive up the price of Saveway stock, and the selling pressure would simultaneously cause TeleCorp's price to decline.

These price changes, in turn, would cause changes in the expected rates of return on the two securities. Suppose, for example, that the price of Saveway stock was bid up from $100 to $125, while the price of TeleCorp's stock declined from $100 to $75. Further, suppose this caused Saveway's expected return to fall to 10 percent, while TeleCorp's expected return rose to 20 percent. The difference in returns, 20% − 10% = 10%, is a *risk premium,* which represents the compensation investors require for assuming the additional risk of TeleCorp stock.

This example demonstrates a very important principle: *In a market dominated by risk-averse investors, riskier securities will have higher expected returns as estimated by the average investor than will less risky securities, for if this situation does not hold, then actions will occur in the market to force it to occur.* We will consider the question of *how much* higher the returns on risky securities must be later in the chapter, after we examine in more depth how risk should be measured.

PORTFOLIO RISK AND THE CAPITAL ASSET PRICING MODEL

In the preceding section we considered the riskiness of a stock held in isolation. Now we analyze the riskiness of stocks held in *portfolios.*[5] As we shall see, a stock held as part of a portfolio is less risky than the same stock held in isolation. This fact has been incorporated into a model for analyzing the relationship between risk and rates of return, the *Capital Asset Pricing Model (CAPM).* The CAPM is, as we shall see, an extremely important analytical tool in both financial management and investment analysis. In the following sections we discuss the elements of CAPM.[6]

Portfolio Risk and Return

Most financial assets are not held in isolation; rather, they are held as parts of portfolios. Banks, pension funds, insurance companies, mutual funds, and other financial institutions are required by law to hold diversified portfolios. Even individual investors — at least those whose security holdings constitute a significant part of their total wealth — generally hold stock portfolios, not the stock of only one firm. This being the case, from an investor's standpoint the fact that a particular stock goes up or down is not very important; *what is important is the return on his or her portfolio, and the portfolio's risk. Logically, then, the risk and return of an individual security should be analyzed in terms of how that security affects the risk and return of the portfolio in which it is held.*

---

[5]A *portfolio* is a collection of investment securities. If you owned some General Motors stock, some Exxon stock, and some IBM stock, you would be holding a three-stock portfolio. For reasons set forth in this section, the vast majority of all stocks are held as parts of portfolios.

[6]The CAPM is a relatively complex model, and we only present the basic conclusions in this text. For a more detailed discussion, see Eugene F. Brigham and Louis C. Gapenski, *Intermediate Financial Management,* Chapter 2.

Portfolio Returns

The *expected return on a portfolio, $\hat{k}_p$*, is simply the weighted average expected return of the individual stocks in the portfolio, with the weights being the fraction of the total portfolio invested in each stock:

$$\hat{k}_p = w_1\hat{k}_1 + w_2\hat{k}_2 + \ldots + w_n\hat{k}_n$$

$$= \sum_{i=1}^{n} w_i\hat{k}_i. \tag{6-4}$$

Here the $\hat{k}_i$'s are the expected returns on the individual stocks and the w_i's are the weights. There are n stocks in the portfolio. Note (1) that w_i is the proportion of the portfolio's dollar value invested in Stock i, that is, the value of the investment in Stock i divided by the total value of the portfolio, and (2) that the w_i's must sum to 1.0.

To illustrate, suppose that in March 1987, a security analyst estimated that the following returns could be attached to four leading computer software companies:

	Expected Return, $\hat{k}$
Lotus Development	14%
Microsoft	13%
Cullinet	15%
Computer Sciences	16%

If we formed a $100,000 portfolio, investing $25,000 in each stock, the expected portfolio return would be 14.5 percent:

$$\hat{k}_p = w_1\hat{k}_1 + w_2\hat{k}_2 + w_3\hat{k}_3 + w_4\hat{k}_4$$

$$= 0.25(14\%) + 0.25(13\%) + 0.25(15\%) + 0.25(16\%)$$

$$= 14.5\%.$$

Of course, after the fact and a year later, the *realized* rates of return on the individual stocks — the $\bar{k}_i$ values — will almost certainly be different from their expected values, so $\bar{k}_p$ will be different from $\hat{k}_p = 14.5\%$. For example, Lotus might double in price and provide a return of $+100\%$, while Cullinet might have a terrible year, fall sharply, and have a return of -75%. Note, though, that those two events would be somewhat offsetting, so the portfolio's return would still be close to its expected return, even though the individual stocks' returns were far from their expected returns.

Portfolio Risk

As we saw above, the expected return on a portfolio is a weighted average of the expected returns on the individual stocks in the portfolio. However, unlike returns, the riskiness of a portfolio, σ_p, is generally *not* a weighted average of the standard

Figure 6-4
Rate of Return Distributions for Two Perfectly Negatively Correlated Stocks (r = −1.0), and Portfolio WM

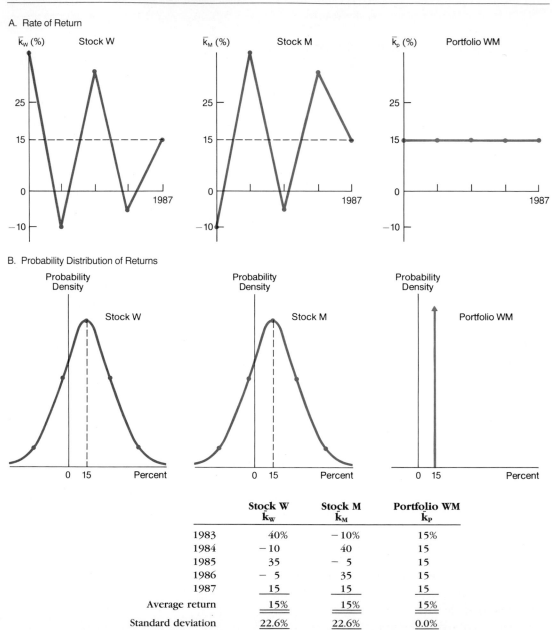

A. Rate of Return

B. Probability Distribution of Returns

	Stock W k_W	Stock M k_M	Portfolio WM k_P
1983	40%	−10%	15%
1984	−10	40	15
1985	35	−5	15
1986	−5	35	15
1987	15	15	15
Average return	15%	15%	15%
Standard deviation	22.6%	22.6%	0.0%

deviations of the individual securities in the portfolio — the portfolio's risk will be *smaller* than the weighted average of the stocks' σs, because variations in the individual stocks' returns will be offsetting to some degree. In fact, it may even be theoretically possible to combine two stocks which are individually quite risky as measured by their standard deviations and form a portfolio which is completely riskless, with $\sigma_p = 0$.

To illustrate, consider the situation in Figure 6-4. The bottom section gives data on rates of return both for Stocks W and M individually and for a portfolio invested 50 percent in each stock. Panel A plots the data in a time series format, and Panel B shows the probability distributions of returns, assuming the future is expected to be like the past. The two stocks would be quite risky if they were held in isolation, but when they are combined to form Portfolio WM, they are not risky at all. (Note: These stocks are called W and M because their returns graphs in Figure 6-4 resemble a W and an M.)

The reason Stocks W and M can be combined to form a riskless portfolio is that their returns move countercyclically to each other — when W's returns fall, those of M rise, and vice versa. The tendency of two variables to move together is called *correlation,* and the *correlation coefficient, r,* measures this tendency.[7] In statistical terms, we say that the returns on Stocks W and M are *perfectly negatively correlated,* with $r = -1.0$.

The opposite of perfect negative correlation, with $r = -1.0$, is *perfect positive correlation,* with $r = +1.0$. Returns on two perfectly positively correlated stocks would move up and down together, and a portfolio consisting of two such stocks would be just as risky as the individual stocks. This point is illustrated in Figure 6-5, where we see that the portfolio's standard deviation is equal to that of the individual stocks. Thus, diversification does nothing to reduce risk if the portfolio consists of perfectly positively correlated stocks.

Figures 6-4 and 6-5 demonstrate (1) that when stocks are perfectly negatively correlated ($r = -1.0$), all risk can be diversified away, but (2) that when stocks are perfectly positively correlated ($r = +1.0$), diversification does no good whatsoever in terms of reducing risk. In reality, most stocks are positively correlated, but not perfectly so. On average, the correlation coefficient for the returns on two randomly selected stocks would be about $+0.6$, and for most pairs of stocks, r would lie in the range of $+0.5$ to $+0.7$. *Under such conditions, combining stocks into portfolios reduces risk but does not eliminate it completely.* Figure 6-6 illustrates this point with two stocks whose correlation coefficient is $r = +0.65$. The portfolio's average return is 15.0 percent, which is exactly the same as the average return for each of the two stocks, but its standard deviation is 20.6 percent, which is less than the standard deviation of either stock. Thus, the portfolio's risk is *not* an average of the risks of its individual stocks — diversification has reduced, but not eliminated, risk.

---

[7]The *correlation coefficient, r,* can range from $+1.0$, denoting that the two variables move up and down in perfect synchronization, to -1.0, denoting that the variables always move in exactly opposite directions. A correlation coefficient of 0.0 indicates that the two variables are not related to each other — that is, changes in one variable are *independent* of changes in the other.

Figure 6-5
Rate of Return Distributions for Two Perfectly Positively Correlated Stocks (r = +1.0), and for Portfolio MM′

A. Rate of Return

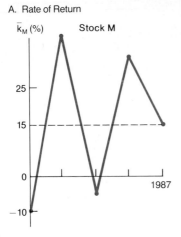
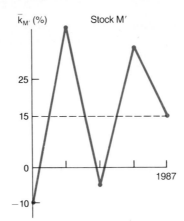
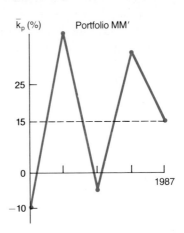

B. Probability Distribution of Returns

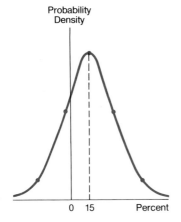
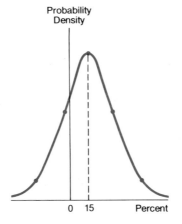
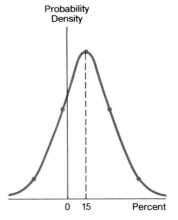

Year	Stock M $\bar{k}_M$	Stock M′ $\bar{k}_{M'}$	Portfolio MM′ $\bar{k}_P$
1983	−10%	−10%	−10%
1984	40	40	40
1985	−5	−5	−5
1986	35	35	35
1987	15	15	15
Average return	15%	15%	15%
Standard deviation	22.6%	22.6%	22.6%

Figure 6-6
**Rate of Return Distributions for Two Partially Correlated
Stocks (r = +0.65), and for Portfolio WY**

A. Rate of Return

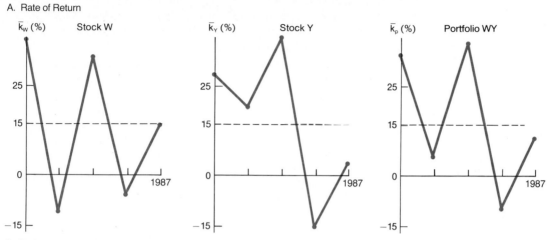

B. Probability Distribution of Returns

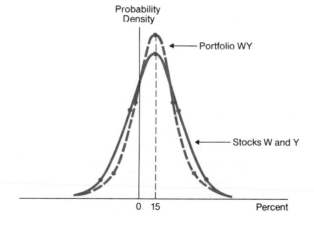

Year	Stock W k_W	Stock Y k_Y	Portfolio WY k_P
1983	40%	28%	34%
1984	−10	20	5
1985	35	41	38
1986	− 5	−17	−11
1987	15	3	9
Average return	15%	15%	15%
Standard deviation	22.6%	22.6%	20.6%

From these two-stock portfolio examples, we have seen that in one extreme case (r = −1.0) risk can be completely eliminated, while in the other extreme case (r = +1.0) diversification does no good whatever. In between these extremes, combining two stocks into a portfolio reduces, but does not eliminate, the riskiness inherent in the individual stocks.

What would happen if we included more than two stocks in the portfolio? *As a rule, the riskiness of a portfolio will be reduced as the number of stocks in the portfolio increases.* If we added enough partially correlated stocks, could we completely eliminate risk? In general, the answer is no, but the extent to which adding stocks to a portfolio reduces its risk depends on the *degree of correlation* among the stocks: The smaller the correlation coefficient, the lower the remaining risk in a large portfolio. If we could find a set of stocks whose correlation coefficients were zero or negative, all risk could be eliminated. *In the typical case, where the correlations among the individual stocks are positive but less than +1.0, some, but not all, risk can be eliminated.*

To illustrate, would you expect to find higher correlations between the returns on two companies in the same or in different industries? For example, would the correlation of returns on Ford and General Motors stocks be higher, or would the correlation coefficient be higher between Ford and IBM or between GM and IBM? Ford's and GM's returns have a correlation coefficient of about 0.9 with one another, but only about 0.6 with those of IBM. Thus, a 2-stock portfolio consisting of Ford and GM would be riskier than a 2-stock portfolio consisting of Ford or GM plus IBM, and to minimize risk, portfolios should be diversified across industries as well as within industries.

Company-Specific Risk Versus Market Risk

As noted earlier, it is very difficult, if not impossible, to find stocks whose expected returns are not positively correlated — most stocks tend to do well when the national economy is strong and badly when it is weak.[8] Thus, even very large portfolios end up with a significant amount of risk. For example, in Figure 5-10 in Chapter 5, we saw that actual realized returns varied quite a bit from year to year even on a portfolio which included all New York Stock Exchange (NYSE) stocks.

To see more precisely how portfolio size affects portfolio risk, consider Figure 6-7, which shows how portfolio risk is affected by forming larger and larger portfolios of randomly selected NYSE stocks. Standard deviations are plotted for an average 1-stock portfolio, an average 2-stock portfolio, and so on, up to a portfolio consisting of all 1,500-plus common stocks that were listed on the NYSE at the time the data were graphed. The graph illustrates that, in general, the riskiness of a portfolio consisting of average NYSE stocks tend to decline and to asymptotically approach a limit as the size of the portfolio increases. According to data accumulated in recent years, σ_1, the standard deviation of a one-stock portfolio (or an average stock) is approximately 28 percent. A portfolio consisting of all stocks, called the *market portfolio,* would have a standard deviation of about 15.1

---

[8]It is not too hard to find a few stocks that happened to rise because of a particular set of circumstances in the past while most other stocks were declining; it is much harder to find stocks that could logically be *expected* to go up in the future if other stocks were falling.

Figure 6-7
Effects of Portfolio Size on Portfolio Risk for Average Stocks

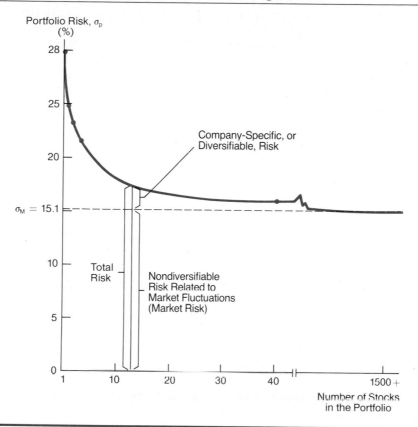

percent. The market portfolio's standard deviation is given the symbol σ_M, so $\sigma_M = 15.1\%$.

Thus, almost half of the riskiness inherent in an average individual stock can be eliminated if the stock is held in a reasonably well-diversified portfolio, one containing 40 or more stocks. Some risk always remains, however, so it is virtually impossible to diversify away the effects of broad stock market declines that drive down almost all stocks.

That part of the risk of a stock which can be eliminated is called *diversifiable,* or *company-specific, risk;* that part which cannot be eliminated is called *non-diversifiable,* or *market, risk.* The name is not especially important, but the fact that part of the riskiness of any individual stock can be eliminated is vitally important.[9]

---

[9]Market risk is sometimes called *systematic risk,* because it systematically affects all stocks, while company-specified risk is also known as *unsystematic risk.*

Company-specific risk is caused by such things as lawsuits, strikes, successful and unsuccessful marketing programs, winning and losing major contracts, and other events that are unique to a particular firm. Since these events are essentially random, their effects on a portfolio can be eliminated by diversification—bad events in one firm will be offset by good events in another. Market risk, on the other hand, stems from factors which affect all firms simultaneously, such as war, inflation, recessions, high interest rates, and extremes of optimism or pessimism. Since all stocks will tend to be affected by these factors, this type of risk cannot be eliminated by diversification.

We know that investors demand a premium for bearing risk—that is, the higher the riskiness of a security, the higher the expected return required to induce investors to buy (or to hold) it. But if investors are primarily concerned with *portfolio risk* rather than the risk of the individual securities in the portfolio, how should the riskiness of an individual stock be measured? The answer is this: *The relevant riskiness of an individual stock is its contribution to the riskiness of a well-diversified portfolio.* In other words, the riskiness of Lotus Development's stock to a doctor who has a portfolio of 40 stocks, or to a trust officer managing a 150-stock portfolio, is the contribution that the Lotus stock makes to the portfolio's riskiness. Lotus's stock might be quite risky if held by itself, but if most of its risk can be eliminated by diversification, then its relevant risk, which is its *contribution to the portfolio's risk,* may be small.

A simple example will help make this point clear. Suppose you can flip a coin once; if a head comes up, you win $10,000, but you lose $8,000 if a tail comes up. This is a good bet—the expected return is 0.5($10,000) + 0.5(−$8,000) = $1,000. However, it is a highly risky proposition, because you have a 50 percent chance of losing $8,000. Thus, you might well refuse to make the bet. Alternatively, suppose you were offered the chance to flip a coin 100 times, and you win $100 for each head but lose $80 for each tail. It is theoretically possible that you would flip all heads and win $10,000, and it is also possible that you would flip all tails and lose $8,000, but the chances are very high that you would actually flip about 50 heads and about 50 tails, and win a net of $1,000. Although each individual flip is a risky bet, collectively you have a very low-risk proposition because you have diversified away most of the risk by flipping 100 times. This is the idea behind holding portfolios of stocks rather than just one stock, except that with stocks all of the risk cannot be eliminated by diversification—those risks related to broad changes in the stock market will remain.

Are all stocks equally risky in the sense that adding them to a well-diversified portfolio would have the same effect on the portfolio's riskiness? The answer is no—different stocks will affect the portfolio differently, so different securities have different degrees of relevant risk. How can the relevant risk of an individual stock be measured? As we have seen, all risk except that related to broad market movements can, and presumably will, be diversified away. After all, why accept risk that can easily be eliminated? *The risk that remains after diversifying is market risk, or the risk that is inherent in the market, and it can be measured by the degree to which a given stock tends to move up and down with the market.*

The Concept of Beta

The tendency of a stock to move with the market is reflected in its *beta coefficient, b,* which is a measure of the stock's volatility relative to that of an average stock.

An *average-risk stock* is defined as one that tends to move up and down in step with the general market as measured by some index such as the Dow Jones Industrials, the S&P 500, or the New York Stock Exchange Index. Such a stock will, by definition, have a beta, b, of 1.0, which indicates that, in general, if the market moves up by 10 percent, the stock will also move up by 10 percent, while if the market falls by 10 percent, the stock will likewise fall by 10 percent. A portfolio of such b = 1.0 stocks will move up and down with the broad market averages, and it will be just as risky as the averages. If b = 0.5, the stock is only half as volatile as the market — it will rise and fall only half as much — and a portfolio of such stocks will be half as risky as a portfolio of b = 1.0 stocks. On the other hand, if b = 2.0, the stock is twice as volatile as an average stock, so a portfolio of such stocks will be twice as risky as an average portfolio.

Figure 6-8 shows betas in a graphic sense. Assume that in 1985 the "market," defined as a portfolio consisting of all stocks, had a total return (dividend yield plus capital gains yield) of 10 percent, and Stocks H, A, and L (for High, Average, and Low risk) also had returns of 10 percent. Now assume that in 1986 the market went up sharply and the return on the market portfolio was $\hat{k}_M$ = 20%. Returns on our three stocks also went up: H soared to 30 percent; A went up to 20 percent, the same as the market; and L went up only to 15 percent. Now suppose that the market dropped in 1987, and the market return was $\bar{k}_M$ = −10%. Our three stocks' returns also fell, H plunging to −30 percent, A falling to −10 percent, and L going down only to $\bar{k}_L$ = 0%. Thus, our three stocks all moved in the same direction as the market. However, H, the high-beta stock, was by far the most volatile; A was just as volatile as the market, and L was less volatile.

As we will see in the next section, betas are actually calculated by plotting lines such as those in Figure 6-8. The slopes of the lines show how much each stock moves in response to a movement in the general market, *and the slope coefficient is the beta coefficient.* Betas for literally thousands of companies are calculated and published by Merrill Lynch, Value Line, and numerous other organizations. The beta coefficients of some well-known companies are shown in Table 6-4. Most stocks have betas in the range of 0.50 to 1.50, and the average for all stocks is 1.0 by definition.[10]

If a higher-than-average-beta stock (one whose beta is greater than 1.0) is added to an average-beta (b = 1.0) portfolio, then the beta, and consequently the riskiness, of the portfolio will increase. Conversely, if a lower-than-average-beta stock (one whose beta is less than 1.0) is added to an average-risk portfolio, the portfolio's beta and risk will decline. *Thus, since a stock's beta measures its contri-*

---

[10]The betas we have been discussing are called *historical,* or *ex post, betas* because they are based strictly on historical, or past, data. Another type of beta, the *fundamental beta,* which is based partly on past actions and partly on expected future conditions not yet reflected in historical data, is also used. We will have more to say concerning different types of betas in Chapter 7.

Figure 6-8
Beta Graph

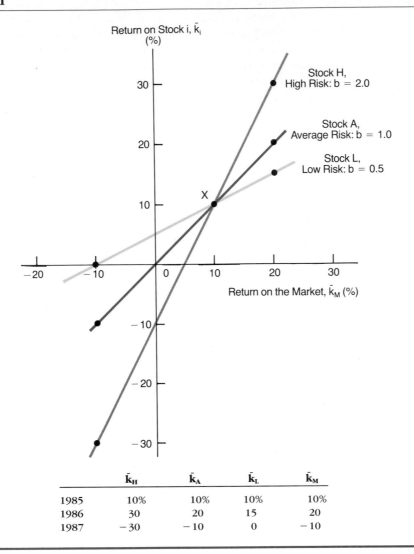

	$\bar{k}_H$	$\bar{k}_A$	$\bar{k}_L$	$\bar{k}_M$
1985	10%	10%	10%	10%
1986	30	20	15	20
1987	−30	−10	0	−10

bution to the riskiness of a portfolio, beta is the theoretically correct measure of the stock's riskiness.

We can summarize our analysis of the Capital Asset Pricing Model's logic to this point as follows:

1. A stock's risk consists of two components, market risk and company-specific risk.

2. Company-specific risk can be eliminated by holding a diversified portfolio, and most investors do indeed diversify, either directly or by purchasing mutual funds.

Table 6-4
Illustrative List of Beta Coefficients

Stock	Beta
Apple Computer	1.60
Union Pacific	1.43
Georgia-Pacific	1.36
Mattel	1.15
General Electric	1.09
Bristol Myers	1.00
General Motors	0.94
McDonald's	0.93
Proctor & Gamble	0.80
IBM	0.70
Anheuser-Busch	0.58
Pacific Gas & Electric	0.47

Source: Merrill Lynch, *Monthly Research Review,* January 1987.

We are left, then, with market risk, which is caused by general movements in the stock market and which reflects the fact that all stocks are affected by certain events such as war, recessions, and inflation. Market risk is the only relevant risk to a rational, diversified investor, because he or she has already eliminated company-specific risk.

3. Investors must be compensated for bearing risk — the greater the riskiness of a stock, the higher its required return. However, compensation is required only for risk which cannot be eliminated by diversification. If a risk premium existed for Stock X's diversifiable risk, then a well-diversified investor would buy it and bid up its price, and its final expected return would reflect only its nondiversifiable market risk.

4. The market risk of a stock is measured by its beta coefficient, which is an index of the stock's relative volatility. Some benchmark betas follow:

> $b = 0.5$: Stock is only half as volatile, or risky, as the average stock.
>
> $b = 1.0$: Stock is of average risk.
>
> $b = 2.0$: Stock is twice as risky as the average stock.

5. *Since a stock's beta coefficient determines how it affects the riskiness of a diversified portfolio, beta is the most relevant measure of a stock's risk.*

Calculating Beta Coefficients

The CAPM is an ex ante model, which means that all of the variables represent before-the-fact, expected values. In particular, the beta coefficient should reflect the expected volatility of a given stock versus the market during some future period. However, people generally calculate betas during some past period and then assume that the stocks' relative volatility will remain constant in the future.

Figure 6-9
Calculating Beta Coefficients

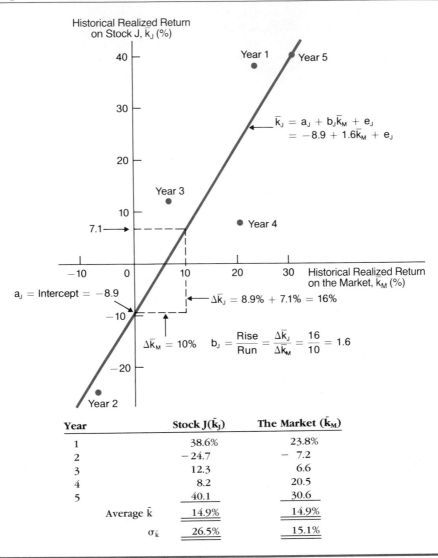

Year	Stock J($\bar{k}_J$)	The Market ($\bar{k}_M$)
1	38.6%	23.8%
2	−24.7	− 7.2
3	12.3	6.6
4	8.2	20.5
5	40.1	30.6
Average $\bar{k}$	14.9%	14.9%
$\sigma_{\bar{k}}$	26.5%	15.1%

To illustrate how betas are calculated, consider Figure 6-9. Assume that the data at the bottom of the figure show the historical realized returns for Stock J and for the market over the last five years. The data points were then plotted on the scatter diagram, and a regression line drawn. If all the data points fell on a straight line, as they did back in Figure 6-8, it would be easy to draw an accurate line. If they did not, then you could fit the line "by eye" as an approximation. Note that the regression line in Figure 6-9 is often called the stock's *characteristic line*.

Recall what the term regression line or regression equation means: The equation $Y = a + bX + e$ is the standard form of a simple linear regression. It states that the dependent variable, Y, is equal to a constant, a, plus b times X, where b is the slope coefficient (or parameter) and X is the "independent" variable, plus an error term, e. Thus, the rate of return on the stock during a given time period depends heavily on what happens to the general stock market, which is measured by $X = \bar{k}_M$.

Once the characteristic line has been drawn on a sheet of graph paper, we can estimate its intercept and slope, the a and b values in $Y = a + bX$. The intercept, a, is simply the point where the line cuts the vertical axis. The slope coefficient, b, can be estimated by the "rise over run" method, which involves calculating the amount by which $\bar{k}_J$ increases for a given increase in $\bar{k}_M$. For example, we observe (in Figure 6-9) that $\bar{k}_J$ increased from -8.9 to $+7.1$ percent (the rise) when $\bar{k}_M$ increased from 0 to 10.0 percent (the run). Thus, b, the beta coefficient, can be measured as follows:

$$b = \text{Beta} = \frac{\text{Rise}}{\text{Run}} = \frac{\Delta Y}{\Delta X} = \frac{7.1 - (-8.9)}{10.0 - 0.0} = \frac{16.0}{10.0} = 1.6.$$

Note that rise over run is a ratio, and it would be the same if measured using any two arbitrarily selected points on the line.

The characteristic line enables us to predict a rate of return for Stock J, given a value of $\bar{k}_M$. For example, if $\bar{k}_M = 15\%$, we would predict $\hat{k}_J = -8.9\% + 1.6(15\%) = 15.5\%$. The actual return would probably differ from the predicted return. This deviation is the error term, e_J, for the year, and it varies randomly from year to year depending on company-specific factors.

In actual practice, monthly rather than annual returns are generally used for $\bar{k}_J$ and $\bar{k}_M$, and five years of data are employed. Thus, there would be $5 \times 12 = 60$ dots on the scatter diagram. Also, in practice one would always use the least squares method for finding the regression coefficients a and b; the least squares procedure minimizes the squared values of the error terms, and it is discussed in statistics courses. Note also that the least squares value of beta can be obtained quite easily by computer or even with a financial calculator.

Portfolio Beta Coefficients

A portfolio consisting of low-beta securities will itself have a low beta, since the beta of any set of securities is a weighted average of the individual securities' betas:

$$b_p = \sum_{i=1}^{n} w_i b_i. \tag{6-5}$$

Here b_p is the beta of the portfolio, which reflects how volatile the portfolio is in relation to the market; w_i is the fraction of the portfolio invested in the *i*th stock; and b_i is the beta coefficient of the *i*th stock. For example, if an investor holds a $100,000 portfolio consisting of $10,000 invested in each of 10 stocks, and each of the stocks has a beta of 0.8, then the portfolio's beta will be $b_p = 0.8$. Thus, the portfolio will be less risky than the market, and it should experience relatively narrow price swings and have relatively small rate of return fluctuations.

Now suppose one of the existing stocks is sold and replaced by a stock with $b_i = 2.0$. This action will increase the riskiness of the portfolio from $b_{p1} = 0.8$ to $b_{p2} = 0.92$:

$$b_{p2} = \sum_{i=1}^{n} w_i b_i = 0.9(0.8) + 0.1(2.0)$$

$$= 0.92.$$

Had a stock with $b_i = 0.2$ been added, the portfolio beta would have declined from 0.8 to 0.74, so the riskiness of the portfolio would have declined.

THE RELATIONSHIP BETWEEN RISK AND RATES OF RETURN

In the preceding section we saw (1) that beta is the appropriate measure of a stock's relevant risk and (2) that beta can be estimated by the slope of the stock's characteristic (or regression) line. Now we must specify the relationship between risk and return — if beta rises by some specific amount, by how much must the stock's expected return increase to compensate for the increase in risk? To begin, let us define the following terms:

$\hat{k}_i$ = expected rate of return on the ith stock.

k_i = required rate of return on the ith stock. Note that if $\hat{k}_i$ is less than k_i, you would not purchase this stock, or you would sell it if you owned it. For the marginal (or "representative") investor in the market, $\hat{k}_i$ must equal k_i, or else a disequilibrium will exist.

k_{RF} = risk-free rate of return, generally measured by the rate of return on U.S. Treasury securities.

b_i = beta coefficient of the ith stock.

k_M = required rate of return on a portfolio consisting of all stocks, which is the market portfolio. k_M is also the required rate of return on an average ($b_A = 1.0$) stock.

$RP_M = (k_M - k_{RF})$ = market risk premium. This is the additional return over the risk-free rate required to compensate investors for assuming an "average" amount of risk. Average risk means $b_A = 1.0$.

$RP_i = (k_M - k_{RF})b_i$ = risk premium on the ith stock. The stock's risk premium is less than, equal to, or greater than the premium on an average stock depending on whether its beta is less than, equal to, or greater than 1.0. If $b_i = b_A = 1.0$, then $RP_i = RP_M$.

The market risk premium, RP_M, depends on the degree of aversion that investors in the aggregate have to risk.[11] Let us assume that at the current time, Treasury bonds yield $k_{RF} = 8\%$, and an average share of stock has a required return of $k_M = 12\%$. Therefore, the market risk premium is 4 percent:

$$RP_M = k_M - k_{RF} = 12\% - 8\% = 4\%.$$

It follows that if one stock were twice as risky as another, then its risk premiuim would be twice as high, and conversely, if its risk were only half as much, then its risk premium would be only half as large. Further, we can measure a stock's relative riskiness by its beta coefficient. Therefore, if we know the market risk premium, RP_M, and the stock's risk as measured by its beta coefficient, b_i, we can find its risk premium as the product $(RP_M)b_i$. For example, if $b_i = 0.5$ and $RP_M = 4\%$, then RP_i is 2 percent:

$$\text{Risk premium for Stock i} = RP_i = (RP_M)b_i \qquad (6\text{-}6)$$
$$= (4\%)0.5 = 2.0\%.$$

To summarize, given estimates of k_{RF}, k_M, and b_i, we can find the required rate of return on Stock i:

Security MKT Line

$$\boxed{k_i = k_{RF} + (k_M - k_{RF})b_i} = k_{RF} + (RP_M)b_i \qquad (6\text{-}7)$$
$$= 8\% + (12\% - 8\%)0.5 = 8\% + (4\%)0.5 = 10\%.$$

If some other stock, j, were more risky than Stock i and had $b_j = 2.0$, then its required rate of return would be 16 percent:

$$k_j = 8\% + (4\%)2.0 = 16\%.$$

An average stock, with $b = 1.0$, would have a required return of 12 percent, the same as the market return:

$$k_{Avg} = 8\% + (4\%)1.0 = 12\% = k_M.$$

Equation 6-7 is called the *Security Market Line (SML)* equation, and it is often expressed in graph form, as in Figure 6-10, which shows the SML when $k_{RF} = 8\%$ and $k_M = 12\%$. Note the following points:

1. Required rates of return are shown on the vertical axis, while risk as measured by beta is shown on the horizontal axis. This graph is quite different from the ones shown in Figures 6-8 and 6-9, where the returns on individual stocks are plotted on the vertical axis and returns on the market index are shown on the horizontal

---

[11]It should be noted that the risk premium of an average stock, $k_M - k_{RF}$, cannot be measured with great precision because it is impossible to obtain precise values for k_M. However, empirical studies suggest that where long-term U.S. Treasury bonds are used to measure k_{RF} and where k_M is the expected return on the S&P 400 Industrial Stocks, the market risk premium varies somewhat from year to year, and it has generally ranged from 3 to 6 percent during the last 20 years. We will discuss the estimation of the market risk premium in more detail in Chapter 7.

Figure 6-10
The Security Market Line (SML)

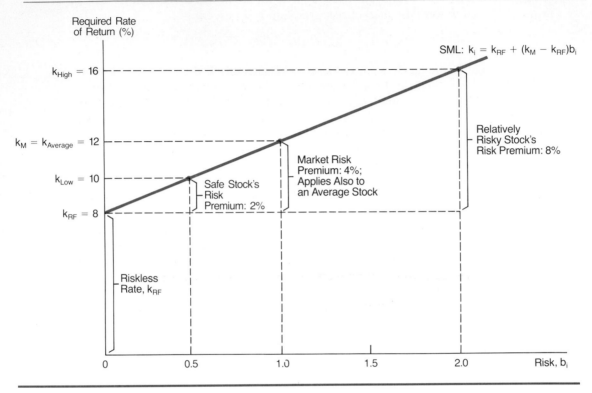

axis. The slopes of the characteristic lines in Figure 6-8 represent the three stocks' betas, and these three betas are then plotted on the horizontal axis in Figure 6-10.

2. Riskless securities have $b_i = 0$; therefore, k_{RF} appears as the vertical axis intercept in Figure 6-10.

3. The slope of the SML reflects the degree of risk aversion in the economy — the greater the average investor's aversion to risk, then (1) the steeper the slope of the line, (2) the greater the risk premium for any given stock, and (3) the higher the required rate of return on stocks.[12] These points are discussed further in a later section.

---

[12]Students sometimes confuse beta with the slope of the SML. This is a mistake. The slope of any line is equal to the "rise" divided by the "run," or $(Y_1 - Y_0)/(X_1 - X_0)$. If we let $Y = k$ and $X = $ beta, and go from the origin to $b = 1.0$, then we see that the slope is $(k_M - k_{RF})/(\text{beta}_M - \text{beta}_{RF}) = (12\% - 8\%)/(1 - 0) = 4\%$. Thus, the slope of the SML is equal to $(k_M - k_{RF})$, the market risk premium. In much of the finance literature, the SML equation is written as $k_i = k_{RF} + b_i(k_M - k_{RF})$, and in this form b_i looks like the slope coefficient and $(k_M - k_{RF})$ like the variable, whereas the reverse is actually true. To reduce confusion, we have written the second term as $(k_M - k_{RF})b_i$. In Figure 6-10, $k_i = 8\% + 4b_i$, so a unitary increase in beta (for example, from 1.0 to 2.0) would produce a 4 percentage point increase in k_i.

4. The values of k which we worked out for stocks with b = 0.5, b = 1.0, and b = 2.0 agree with the values shown on the graph for k_{Low}, k_{Avg}, and k_{High}.

Both the Security Market Line and a company's position on it change over time due to changes in interest rates, changes in investors' risk aversion, and changes in individual companies' betas. Such changes are discussed in the following sections.

The Impact of Inflation

As we saw in Chapter 3, interest amounts to "rent" on borrowed money, or the "price" of money; thus, k_{RF} is the price of money to a riskless borrower. As we also saw, the risk-free rate as measured by the rate on short-term Treasury securities consists of two elements: (1) a *real, or inflation-free, rate of return, k**, and (2) an *inflation premium, IP,* which is equal to the anticipated rate of inflation. Thus, $k_{RF} = k^* + IP$. The real rate on short-term government securities, which is also the pure rate of return, has historically ranged from 2 to 4 percent, with a mean of about 3 percent. Thus, if no inflation were expected, risk-free government bills would yield about 3 percent. However, as the expected rate of inflation increases, a premium must be added to the real rate of return to compensate investors for the loss of purchasing power that results from inflation. Therefore, the 8 percent k_{RF} shown in Figure 6-10 might be thought of as consisting of a 3 percent real rate of return plus a 5 percent inflation premium: $k_{RF} = k^* + IP = 3\% + 5\% = 8\%$.

If the expected rate of inflation rose to 7 percent, this would cause k_{RF} to rise to 10 percent. Such a change is shown in Figure 6-11. Notice that under the CAPM, the increase in k_{RF} also causes an *equal* increase in the rate of return on all risky assets, because the inflation premium is built into the required rate of return of both riskless and risky assets.[13] For example, the rate of return on an average stock, k_M, increases from 12 to 14 percent. Other risky securities' returns also rise by two percentage points.

Changes in Risk Aversion

The slope of the Security Market Line reflects the extent to which investors are averse to risk — the steeper the slope of the line, the greater the average investor's risk aversion. If investors were indifferent to risk, and if k_{RF} were 8 percent, then risky assets would also sell to provide an expected return of 8 percent — with no risk aversion, there would be no risk premium, so the SML would be horizontal. As risk aversion increases, so does the risk premium and, thus, the slope of the SML.

Figure 6-12 illustrates an increase in risk aversion. The market premium rises from 4 to 6 percent, and k_M rises from 12 to 14 percent. The returns on other risky assets also rise, with the impact of this shift in risk aversion being more pronounced on riskier securities. For example, the required return on a stock with

---

[13]Recall that the inflation premium for any asset is equal to the expected average rate of inflation over the life of the asset. Thus, in this analysis we must assume either that all securities plotted on the SML graph have the same life or else that the expected rate of future inflation is constant.

Figure 6-11
Shift in the SML Caused by an Increase in Expected Inflation

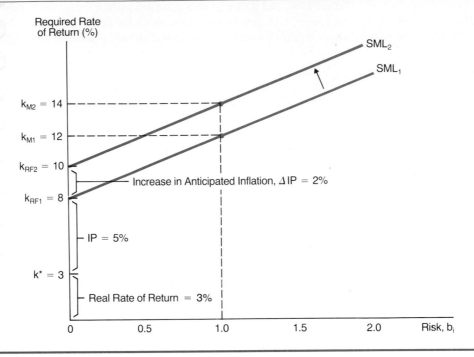

$b_i = 0.5$ increases by only one percentage point, from 10 to 11 percent, while that on a stock with $b_i = 1.5$ increases by three percentage points, from 14 to 17 percent.

Changes in a Stock's Beta Coefficient

As we shall see later in the book, a firm can affect its market, or beta, risk through changes in the composition of its assets and also through its use of debt financing. A company's beta can also change as a result of external factors such as increased competition in its industry, the expiration of basic patents, and the like. When such changes occur, the required rate of return also changes, and this will affect the price of the firm's stock. For example, consider the O'Brien Tile Company, a constant growth firm with $b = 1.0$, $D_1 = \$2.00$, and $g = 5\%$. Now suppose some action occurred that caused O'Brien's beta to increase from 1.0 to 1.5. If the conditions depicted in Figure 6-10 held, O'Brien's required rate of return would increase from

$$k_1 = k_{RF} + (k_M - k_{RF})b_i = 8\% + (12\% - 8\%)1.0 = 12\%$$

to

Figure 6-12

Shift in the SML Caused by Increased Risk Aversion

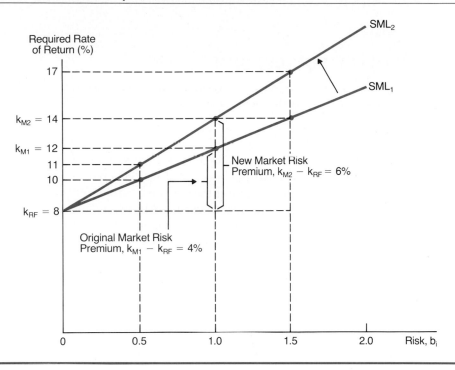

$$k_2 = 8\% + (12\% - 8\%)1.5 = 14\%.$$

This change in k would cause O'Brien's equilibrium stock price, assuming no change in its expected dividend and its expected growth rate, to fall from $28.57 to $22.22:[14]

$$\text{Old value: } \hat{P}_0 = \frac{D_1}{k_1 - g} = \frac{\$2.00}{0.12 - 0.05} = \$28.57.$$

$$\text{New value: } \hat{P}_0 = \frac{D_1}{k_2 - g} = \frac{\$2.00}{0.14 - 0.05} = \$22.22.$$

Notice that at its new equilibrium price of $22.22 O'Brien's new expected rate of return is exactly equal to its new 14 percent required rate of return:

$$\hat{k}_2 = D_1/P_0 + g = \$2/\$22.22 + 5\% = 14.0\%.$$
$$k_2 = k_{RF} + (k_M - k_{RF})b_i = 8\% + (12\% - 8\%)1.5 = 14.0\%.$$

---

[14]Companies do sometimes deliberately increase their risk, but only if the action that will raise risk will also raise the expected earnings and the expected growth rate. Trying to determine the effects of a given action on both risk and profitability is one of the financial manager's central tasks.

Since the expected rate of return is equal to the required return, $22.22 is O'Brien's new equilibrium stock price. If the expected and required returns were not equal, the stock price would adjust until equality had been established.

SECURITY MARKET EQUILIBRIUM

Suppose a "typical" or "representative" investor's required rate of return on Stock X, with $b_X = 2$, is 16 percent, determined as follows:

$$k_X = k_{RF} + (k_M - k_{RF})b_X = 8\% + (12\% - 8\%)2.0 = 16\%.$$

This 16 percent required return is shown as a dot on the SML in Figure 6-13.

Our typical investor will want to buy Stock X if its expected rate of return is more than 16 percent, will want to sell it if the expected rate of return is less than 16 percent, and will be indifferent, hence will hold but not buy or sell, if the expected rate of return is exactly 16 percent. Now suppose the investor's portfolio contains X, and our investor analyzes the stock's prospects and concludes that its earnings, dividends, and price can be expected to grow at a constant rate of 5 percent per year. The last dividend was $D_0 = \$2.8571$, so the next expected dividend is

$$D_1 = \$2.8571(1.05) = \$3.$$

Figure 6-13
Expected and Required Returns on Stock X

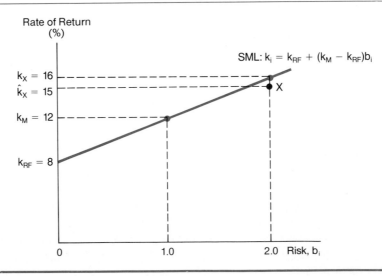

The investor observes that the present price of the stock, P_0, is $30. Should he or she purchase more of Stock X, sell the stock, or maintain the present position?

The investor can calculate Stock X's expected rate of return as follows:

$$\hat{k}_X = \frac{D_1}{P_0} + g = \frac{\$3}{\$30} + 5\% = 15\%.$$

This value is plotted on Figure 6-13 as Point X, which is below the SML. Since the expected rate of return is less than the required return, this "typical" investor will want to sell the stock, as will other holders. However, few people will want to buy at the $30 price, so present owners will be unable to find buyers unless they cut the price of the stock. Thus, the price will decline, and this decline will continue until the stock's price reaches $27.27, at which point the market for this security will be in *equilibrium* because its expected rate of return, 16 percent, will be equal to its required rate of return:

$$\hat{k}_X = \frac{\$3}{\$27.27} + 5\% = 16\% = k_X.$$

Had the stock initially sold for less than $27.27, say at $25, then events would have been reversed. Investors would have wanted to buy the stock, because its expected rate of return would have exceeded its required rate of return, and buy orders would have driven the stock's price up to $27.27.

To summarize, in equilibrium these two conditions must hold:

1. The expected rate of return as seen by the marginal investor must equal the required rate of return: $\hat{k}_i = k_i$.

2. The actual market price of the stock must equal its intrinsic value as estimated by the marginal investor: $P_0 = \hat{P}_0$.

Of course, some investors will believe that $\hat{k}_i > k_i$ and $\hat{P}_0 > P_0$, and hence they will invest most of their funds in the stock, while other investors will have an opposite view and will sell all of their shares. However, it is the marginal investor who establishes the actual market price, and for this investor, $\hat{k}_i = k_i$ and $P_0 = \hat{P}_0$, for if these conditions did not exist, trading would occur until they did exist.

Changes in Equilibrium Stock Prices

Stock prices are not constant—they undergo violent changes at times. Let us assume that Stock X is in equilibrium, selling at a price of $27.27 per share. If all expectations were exactly met, over the next year the price would gradually rise to $28.63, or by 5 percent. However, many different events could occur to cause a change in the equilibrium price of the stock. To illustrate, consider again the set of inputs used to develop Stock X's price of $27.27, along with a new set of assumed input variables:

	Variable Value	
	Original	New
Riskless rate, k_{RF}	8%	7%
Market risk premium, $k_M - k_{RF}$	4%	3%
Stock X's beta coefficient, b_X	2.0	1.0
Stock X's expected growth rate, g_X	5%	6%
D_0	$2.8571	$2.8571
Price of Stock X	$27.27	?

The first three variables influence k_X, which declines from 16 to 10 percent as a result of the new set of variables:

$$\text{Original } k_X = 8\% + (4\%)2.0 = 16\%.$$

$$\text{New } k_X = 7\% + (3\%)1.0 = 10\%.$$

Using these values, together with the new g value, we find that $\hat{P}_0$, and consequently P_0, rises from $27.27 to $75.71.[15]

$$\text{Original } \hat{P}_0 = \frac{\$2.8571(1.05)}{0.16 - 0.05} = \frac{\$3}{0.11} = \$27.27.$$

$$\text{New } \hat{P}_0 = \frac{\$2.8571(1.06)}{0.10 - 0.06} = \frac{\$3.0285}{0.04} = \$75.71.$$

At the new price, the expected and required rates of return will be equal:[16]

$$\hat{k}_X = \frac{\$3.0285}{\$75.71} + 6\% = 10\% = k_X.$$

Evidence suggests that stocks, and especially those of large, NYSE companies, adjust quite rapidly to disequilibrium situations. Consequently, equilibrium ordinarily exists for any given stock, and, in general, required and expected returns are equal. Stock prices certainly change, sometimes violently and rapidly, but this simply reflects changing conditions and expectations. There are, of course, times when a stock continues to react for several months to a favorable or unfavorable development, but this does not signify a long adjustment period; rather, it simply illustrates that as more new bits of information about the situation become available, the market adjusts to them. The ability of the market to adjust to new information is discussed in the next section.

---

[15]A price change of this magnitude is by no means rare. The prices of *many* stocks double or halve during a year. For example, during 1986 Reebok International increased in value by 153 percent; on the other hand, Western Union fell from 12⅜ to 4, a 68 percent loss.

[16]It should be obvious by now that actual realized rates of return are not necessarily equal to expected and required returns. Thus, an investor might have *expected* to receive a return of 15 percent if he or she had bought Western Union or Reebok International stock at the beginning of 1986, but, after the fact, the realized return on Reebok was far above 15 percent, while that on Western Union was far below.

The Efficient Markets Hypothesis

A body of theory called the *Efficient Markets Hypothesis (EMH)* holds (1) that stocks are always in equilibrium and (2) that it is impossible for an investor to consistently "beat the market." Essentially, those who believe in the EMH note that there are some 100,000 or so full-time, highly trained, professional analysts and traders operating in the market, while there are less than 3,000 major stocks. Therefore, if each analyst followed 30 stocks (which is about right, as analysts tend to specialize in the stocks of a specific industry), there would be 1,000 analysts following each stock. Further, these analysts work for organizations such as Citibank, Merrill Lynch, Prudential Insurance, and the like, which have billions of dollars available with which to take advantage of bargains. As a result of SEC disclosure requirements and electronic information networks, as new information about a stock becomes available, these 1,000 analysts all receive and evaluate it at approximately the same time, and their firms act on this information. Therefore, the price of the stock adjusts almost immediately to reflect the new developments.

Financial theorists generally define three forms, or levels, of market efficiency:

1. The *weak-form* of the EMH states that all information contained in past price movements is fully reflected in current market prices. Therefore, information about recent trends in a stock's price is of no use in selecting stock — the fact that a stock has risen for the past three days, for example, gives us no useful clues as to what it will do today or tomorrow. People who believe that weak-form efficiency exists also believe that "tape watchers" and "chartists" are wasting their time.[17]

2. The *semistrong-form* of the EMH states that current market prices reflect all *publicly available* information. If this is true, no abnormal returns can be gained by analyzing stocks.[18] Thus, if semistrong-form efficiency existed, it would do no good to pore over annual reports or other published data, because market prices would have adjusted to any good or bad news contained in such reports as soon as they came out. However, insiders (say, the presidents of companies) could, even under semistrong-form efficiency, still make abnormal returns on their own companies' stocks.

3. The *strong-form* EMH states that current market prices reflect all pertinent information, whether publicly available or privately held. If this form holds, then even insiders would find it impossible to earn abnormal returns in the stock market.[19]

---

[17]Tape watchers are people who watch the NYSE tape, while chartists plot past patterns of stock price movements. Both are called "technicians," and both believe that they can see if something is happening to the stock that will cause its price to move up or down in the near future.

[18]An abnormal return is one that exceeds the return justified by the riskiness of the investment, that is, a return that plots above the SML in a graph like Figure 6-13.

[19]Several cases of illegal insider trading made the headlines during 1986 and early 1987. These cases involved employees of several major investment banking houses and even an employee of the SEC. In the most famous case, Ivan Boesky admitted to making $50 million by purchasing the stock of firms he knew were about to merge. He and the others will go to jail and pay large fines as a result of trading on inside information, but they certainly helped disprove the strong-form EMH.

Many empirical studies have been conducted to test for the three forms of market efficiency. Most of these studies suggest that the stock market is indeed highly efficient in the weak-form and reasonably efficient in the semistrong-form, at least for the larger and more widely followed stocks. However, the strong-form EMH does not hold, so abnormal profits can be made by those who possess insider information.

What bearing does the EMH have on financial decisions? Since stock prices do reflect public information, most stocks do seem to be fairly valued. This does not mean that new information could not cause a stock's price to soar or to plummet, but it does mean that stocks, in general, are neither overvalued nor undervalued —they are fairly priced and in equilibrium. However, there are certainly situations where financial managers do have information not currently known to outsiders.

If the EMH is correct, then it would be a waste of time for most of us to look for stocks that are undervalued—if stock prices already reflect all available information, and hence are fairly priced, one could "beat the market" only by luck, and it would be difficult if not impossible for anyone to consistently outperform the market averages. Empirical tests generally indicate that the EMH is, in its weak and semistrong-forms, valid. People such as corporate officers who have insider information can do better than the averages, and individuals and organizations that are especially good at digging out information on small, new companies also seem to do consistently well. Also, some investors may be able to analyze and react more quickly than others to releases of new information, and these investors might have an advantage over others. However, the buy-sell actions of these investors quickly bring market prices into equilibrium. Therefore, it is generally safe to assume that $\hat{k} = k$, that $\hat{P}_0 = P_0$, and that stocks plot on the SML.

Market efficiency also has significant implications for managerial decisions, especially those pertaining to security issues, stock repurchases, and tender offers. Financial assets appear to be fairly valued, so decisions based on a stock's being undervalued or overvalued must be approached with caution. However, managers often have better information about their own companies than outsiders have, and this information can legally be used to the companies' (but not the managers' own) advantage.

PHYSICAL ASSETS VERSUS SECURITIES

In a book on financial management as opposed to investments, why do we spend so much time on the riskiness of securities? Why not focus on the riskiness of such business assets as plant and equipment? *The reason is that, for a management whose goal is stock price maximization, the overriding consideration is the riskiness of the firm's stock, and the relevant risk of any physical asset must be measured in terms of its effect on the stock's risk.* For example, suppose General Motors was considering a major investment in electric cars, and the sales and earnings of this proposed venture were highly uncertain. This would seem to be a very risky investment. However, suppose the returns of this particular operation were expected to be negatively correlated with returns on GM's other operations and with returns on GM's stockholders' other portfolio investments — perhaps because electric cars could be expected to sell best if gasoline prices rose sharply, an action which would pull down both sales of regular cars and corporate profits in general. In this case, most of the new plant's risk would not be relevant, because it would be offset in a diversification sense within GM's overall operations and also within stockholders' own portfolios. Thus, the riskiness of a corporate asset investment should be considered within the context of this question: What does the investment in a particular physical asset do to the riskiness of the firm's stock as viewed by its stockholders?

A WORD OF CAUTION

A word of caution about betas and the Capital Asset Pricing Model is in order. Although these concepts are logical, the entire theory rests upon a set of assumptions which are often violated in the "real world." Further, implementation of the CAPM requires us to specify *ex ante,* or expected, conditions, yet we have available only *ex post,* or past, data. Thus, the betas we calculate show how volatile a stock has been in the *past,* but conditions may change, and its *future volatility,* which is the item of real concern to investors, may be quite different from its past volatility. Although the CAPM represents a significant step forward in security pricing theory, it does have some potentially serious deficiencies when applied in practice, so estimates of k_i found through use of the SML may be subject to considerable error.[20]

ARBITRAGE PRICING THEORY[21]

The CAPM assumes that a stock's required return is based on just one factor — the general stock market. However, other factors such as relative sensitivity to inflation, to business cycles, to interest rates, and the like may also influence a stock's riskiness relative to those of other stocks. The *Arbitrage Pricing Theory (APT)* is designed to overcome this weakness. We should note at the outset that the APT is based on some complex mathematical and statistical theory which goes far beyond

---

[20]The concept of beta was discovered and developed by academicians and then seized upon and used by business practitioners. To some extent betas seem to have been oversold — the beauty of the concept has been overemphasized, and the difficulties with actually implementing the theory have not been pointed out sufficiently. In an important article, Anise Wallace ("Is Beta Dead?" *Institutional Investor,* July 1980, 23–30) reached this conclusion: "It took nearly a decade for money managers to learn to love beta. Now it looks as if they were sold a bill of goods — and the whole MPT [Modern Portfolio Theory] house of cards could come tumbling down." This judgment is, in the minds of most observers, far too harsh. The concept of beta reflects the way sophisticated investors should and do look at the risk inherent in a security. Problems arise when one attempts to measure *future* events on the basis of *past* data, but abandoning the CAPM because of these difficulties would be like throwing out the baby with the bath water!

[21]See Stephen A. Ross, "The Arbitrage Theory of Capital Asset Pricing," *Journal of Economic Theory,* December 1976, 341–360. This section is quite complex, but it may be omitted without loss of continuity.

the scope of this text. However, the APT model is widely discussed in the current academic literature, and it is being recommended in practitioner-oriented journals for such uses as measuring the cost of equity. Actual usage to date is extremely limited, but it may increase, so students of finance should at least have an intuitive idea of what APT is all about.

The CAPM assumes that equilibrium normally exists, and in equilibrium each stock's required and expected return is equal to the risk-free rate plus the market risk premium times the stock's beta coefficient:

$$\hat{k}_i = k_{RF} + (\hat{k}_M - k_{RF})b_i. \tag{6-7}$$

The stock's realized return, $\bar{k}_i$, will turn out to be

$$\bar{k}_i = \hat{k}_i + (\bar{k}_M - \hat{k}_M)b_i + e_i. \tag{6-8}$$

Thus, the realized return, $\bar{k}_i$, is equal to the expected return, $\hat{k}_i$, plus an increment or decrement, $(\bar{k}_M - \hat{k}_M)b_i$, which reflects both the market's deviation from its expected return and the stock's sensitivity to the market, plus a random error term, e_i.

The realized market return, $\bar{k}_M$, is in turn determined by a number of factors, including economic activity as measured by GNP, the strength of the world economy, the level of inflation, changes in tax laws, and so forth. Further, different groups of stocks are affected in different ways by these fundamental factors. Thus, rather than specifying the stock's returns as a function of just one factor (the return on the market), one could specify required and realized returns of individual stocks as a function of various fundamental economic factors. If this were done, we would transform the CAPM equation, 6-8, into 6-9:

$$\bar{k}_i = \hat{k}_i + (\bar{F}_1 - \hat{F}_1)b_{i1} + \ldots + (\bar{F}_j - \hat{F}_j)b_{ij} + e_i. \tag{6-9}$$

Here

$\bar{k}_i$ = realized rate of return on Stock i.

$\hat{k}_i$ = expected rate of return on Stock i.

b_{ij} = sensitivity of Stock i to economic Factor j.

$\bar{F}_j$ = realized value of economic Factor j.

$\hat{F}_j$ = expected value of Factor j.

e_i = effect of random, company-specific factors on the realized return of Stock i.

Equation 6-9 shows that the realized return on any stock is equal to the stock's expected return plus increments or decrements which depend on (1) changes in fundamental economic factors, (2) the sensitivity of the stock to these changes, b_{ij}, plus (3) a random term which reflects changes in those factors unique to the firm.

Certain stocks or groups of stocks are most sensitive to Factor 1, others to Factor 2, and so forth, and every portfolio's return depends on what happened to the different fundamental factors which affect it. Theoretically, we could construct a portfolio such that (1) the portfolio is riskless and (2) our net investment in it is zero. Such a portfolio would have to have a zero expected return, or else arbitrage operations would occur, which in turn would cause the prices of the underlying assets to change until the portfolio's expected return was zero. Using some complex mathematics, the APT equivalent of the CAPM's Security Market Line can be developed from Equation 6-9:[22]

$$\hat{k}_i = k_i = k_{RF} + (\lambda_1 - k_{RF})b_{i1} + \ldots + (\lambda_j - k_{RF})b_{ij}. \qquad \textbf{(6-10)}$$

Here λ_j is the required rate of return on a portfolio with 100 percent sensitivity to the jth economic factor ($b_j = 1.0$) and zero sensitivity to all other factors. Thus, for example, $(\lambda_2 - k_{RF})$ is the risk premium on a portfolio with $b_2 = 1.0$ and all other $b_j = 0.0$. Note that Equation 6-10 is identical in form to the SML, but it permits a stock's required return to be a function of multiple factors.

Many people believe the APT will eventually replace the CAPM as the primary theoretical model relating risks to returns. However, the APT has some serious drawbacks. Here are its main disadvantages:

1. The fundamental factors are not actually specified. People use a complex statistical procedure (factor analysis) to categorize stocks into groups whose returns (1) move up and down together but (2) are uncorrelated with returns movements in other stock groups. Presumably, the stocks in each group are affected by some "factor," but this factor cannot be identified with real precision.

2. The CAPM has been around a long time, and its implementation problems (for example, difficulties in measuring ex ante betas) are well known. The APT is new, and hence it has not been examined as closely, but when it is, the same kinds of implementation problems are likely to surface.

3. Finally, the CAPM is intuitively appealing, but the APT is not intuitively clear, and no one (to our knowledge) has figured out a way to explain it to practitioners. Until a clear explanation is forthcoming, the APT is not likely to be used to any extent by real-world decision makers.

SUMMARY

The primary goals of this chapter were (1) to show how risk is measured in financial analysis and (2) to explain how risk affects security prices and rates of return. We began by showing that risk is related to the variability of expected future returns. However, we soon saw that rational investors hold *portfolios of stocks*

---

[22]See Thomas E. Copeland and J. Fred Weston, *Financial Theory and Corporate Policy* (Reading, Mass.: Addison-Wesley, 1983).

and that such an investor is more concerned with the risk of his or her portfolios than with the risks of individual securities.

Next, we saw that the riskiness of a given stock can be split into two components — *market risk,* which is caused by changes in the broad stock market and which cannot be eliminated by diversification, and *company-specific risk,* which can be eliminated by holding a diversified portfolio. Since investors can and do diversify and thus eliminate company-specific risk, the *relevant risk* inherent in stocks is their market risk, which is measured by the *beta coefficient, b.*

Betas measure the tendency of stocks to move up and down with the market — a high-beta stock is more volatile than an average stock, while a low-beta stock is less volatile than average. An average stock has $b = 1.0$ by definition. Betas can be determined by graphing a stock's *characteristic line,* which is a plot of historical returns on the stock versus those on the market.

The required rate of return on a stock consists of the rate of return on risk-free securities, k_{RF}, plus a risk premium that depends on the stock's beta coefficient:

$$k_i = k_{RF} + (k_M - k_{RF})b_i.$$

This formula is called the *Security Market Line (SML) equation* or, sometimes, the *Capital Asset Pricing Model (CAPM) equation,* and it is of fundamental importance in finance. Note, though, that the CAPM is based on *investors' expectations* — for example, the beta and k_M used in the SML equation should be the values that an average investor expects in the future. Those expectations cannot be measured precisely, and because of that, CAPM estimates of required returns are subject to potentially large errors.

We also saw that stocks are typically in equilibrium, with their expected and required rates of return as seen by the marginal investor equal to one another. Further, we saw that the stock market is, in general, *efficient,* meaning that all public information is reflected in stocks' prices. However, even though stocks are generally in equilibrium, a number of things can happen to cause prices to change: the riskless rate can change because of changes in anticipated inflation; a stock's beta can change; or its expected growth rate can increase or decrease.

Finally, we briefly introduced another theoretical risk/return model, the *Arbitrage Pricing Theory (APT)* model. This model might someday replace the CAPM, but considerably more work will be required before it can hope to gain widespread acceptance among financial managers. In the remainder of this book, we will examine the ways in which a firm's management can influence its stock's riskiness, its expected growth rate, and hence its price.

MULTINATIONAL FINANCE

Chapter 6 implicitly focused on the risk and return of *domestic investments.* While the same concepts are involved when we move to the international scene, some important differences must also be observed. For example, someone who invests on a world-wide basis must be concerned with (1) sovereign risk and (2) exchange rate risk. *Sovereign risk* is the risk that the sovereign country in which the real assets backing an investment are located will take some action, such as nationalization without adequate compensation, that will decrease the value of the investment. Enron Corporation, a multibillion dollar U.S.-based energy company, experienced exactly this situation when Peru nationalized an Enron subsidiary in 1985, resulting in a sharp drop in Enron's stock price. Sovereign risk is diversifiable, but it is something that concerns both international investors and multinational corporations.

The second type of international risk, *exchange rate risk,* stems from the fact that different countries use different currencies, and the values of those currencies change over time. To illustrate, in February 1985, the exchange rate between yen and dollars was about 260:1, meaning that one dollar could buy 260 yen. By February 1987, two years later, the exchange rate had dropped to about 150:1. This change, defined as a *decline in the value of the dollar* because a dollar would now buy fewer yen, had a major effect on both U.S. and Japanese firms and investors. First, suppose a U.S. investor bought 100 shares of Toyota stock in February 1985 at a yen price of 1,000 per share, or 100,000 in total. That investment would have a dollar cost of 100,000/260 = $384.62. If the yen price of Toyota's stock had remained constant at 1,000, the decline in the value of the dollar would have caused the dollar value of the stock to rise from $384.62 to 100,000/150 = $666.67, a 73.3 percent increase in two years. Since the dollar also fell against most other major currencies, this same experience was repeated in other international capital markets, and, as a result, those U.S. investors who included foreign stocks in their portfolios benefited from this change in exchange rates. Indeed, mutual funds that emphasize foreign stocks had by far the best performances among mutual funds in 1986. Note, though, that the values of foreign stocks will decline if the dollar rises in the future, so these stocks are far from riskless.

One might think that due to the additional risks of international operations, U.S. firms that do business abroad would be viewed as being riskier than firms operating solely in the U.S. If this were true, international firms would have higher betas, hence higher required rates of return, than purely domestic firms. However, a recent study of multinational firms and otherwise equivalent purely domestic firms showed that the betas of multinational firms are actually lower and more stable than those of domestic firms.[1] The study also found that the rates of return on assets of firms engaged in international operations are more stable, and hence less risky, than returns for domestic firms.

The results of this study indicate that international diversification reduces the market risk of the firm. Market risk depends in large part on the stability of the economy of the country in which it operates. A multinational firm operates in many countries, and the economies of these countries are not perfectly correlated with each other or with the firm's home country economy. Hence, the effects of a poor economy in one country may be offset by a strong economy in its other

---

[1]Fatemi, Ali M., "Shareholder Benefits from Corporate International Diversification," *Journal of Finance,* December 1984, 1325–1344.

operating areas. As a result, multinational firms are exposed to less market risk than purely domestic firms. According to the CAPM, only market risk need be compensated with higher expected rates of return. Since firms operating in international markets appear to have less market risk than domestic firms, international firms should have lower betas, lower required rates of return, and hence lower costs of capital than comparable domestic firms.

Questions

6-1   Define the following terms, using graphs or equations to illustrate your answers wherever feasible:

    a. Risk; probability distribution

    b. *Expected* rate of return, $\hat{k}$

    c. Standard deviation, σ; variance, σ^2; coefficient of variation (cv)

    d. Risk aversion

    e. Risk premium, RP_i; market risk premium, RP_M

    f. Capital Asset Pricing Model (CAPM)

    g. Expected return on a portfolio, $\hat{k}_p$

    h. Correlation coefficient, r

    i. Market risk; company-specific risk; relevant risk

    j. Beta coefficient, b; average stock's beta, b_M

    k. Security Market Line (SML); SML equation

    l. Slope of SML as a measure of risk aversion

    m. Equilibrium

    n. Efficient Markets Hypothesis (EMH); forms of EMH

6-2   The continuous probability distribution of a less risky expected return is more peaked than that of a risky return. What shape would the continuous probability distribution have for (a) completely certain returns and (b) completely uncertain returns?

6-3   Security A has an expected rate of return of 6 percent, a standard deviation of expected returns of 30 percent, a correlation coefficient with the market of −0.25, and a beta coefficient of −0.5. Security B has an expected return of 11 percent, a standard deviation of returns of 10 percent, a correlation with the market of 0.75, and a beta coefficient of 0.5. Which security is more risky? Why?

6-4   Suppose you owned a portfolio consisting of $500,000 worth of long-term U.S. government bonds.

    a. Would your portfolio be riskless?

    b. Now suppose you hold a portfolio consisting of $500,000 worth of 30-day Treasury bills. Every 30 days your bills mature and you reinvest the principal ($500,000) in a new batch of bills. Assume that you live on the investment income from your portfolio and that you want to maintain a constant standard of living. Is your portfolio truly riskless?

    c. You should have concluded that both long-term and short-term portfolios of government securities have some element of risk. Can you think of any asset that would be completely riskless?

6-5   A life insurance policy is a financial asset. The premiums paid represent the investment's cost.

    a.   How would you calculate the expected return on a life insurance policy?

    b.   Suppose the owner of the life insurance policy has no other financial assets — the person's only other asset is "human capital," or lifetime earnings capacity. What is the correlation coefficient between returns on the insurance policy and returns on the policyholder's human capital?

    c.   Life insurance companies have to pay administrative costs and sales representatives' commissions; hence, the expected rate of return on insurance premiums is generally low or even negative. Use the portfolio concept to explain why people buy life insurance in spite of negative expected returns.

6-6   If investors' aversion to risk increased, would the risk premium on a high-beta stock increase more or less than that on a low-beta stock? Explain.

Self-Test Problem

ST-1 (Portfolio risk)   Stocks A and B have the following historical dividend and price data:

	Stock A		Stock B	
Year	Dividend	Year-End Price	Dividend	Year-End Price
1982	—	$12.25	—	$22.00
1983	$1.00	9.75	$2.40	18.50
1984	1.05	11.00	2.60	19.50
1985	1.15	13.75	2.85	25.25
1986	1.30	13.25	3.05	22.50
1987	1.50	15.50	3.25	24.00

    a.   Calculate the realized rate of return (or holding period return) for each stock in each year. Then assume that someone had held a portfolio consisting of 50 percent of A and 50 percent of B. (The portfolio is rebalanced every year so as to maintain these percentages.) What would the realized rate of return on the portfolio have been in each year from 1983 through 1987? What would the average returns have been for each stock and for the portfolio?

    b.   Now calculate the standard deviation of returns for each stock and for the portfolio.

    c.   On the basis of the extent to which the portfolio has a lower risk than the stocks held individually, would you guess that the correlation coefficient between returns on the two stocks is closer to 0.9 or to -0.9?

    d.   If you added more stocks at random to the portfolio, what is the most accurate statement of what would happen to σ_p?

       (1) σ_p would remain constant.

       (2) σ_p would decline to somewhere in the vicinity of 15 percent.

       (3) σ_p would decline to zero if enough stocks were included.

Problems

6-1   (Expected returns) Stocks A and B have the following probability distributions of expected future returns:

Probability	A	B
0.1	−25%	−40%
0.2	5	0
0.4	15	16
0.2	30	40
0.1	45	66

a. Calculate the expected rate of return, $\hat{k}$, for Stock B. ($\hat{k}_A = 15\%.$)

b. Calculate the standard deviation and coefficient of variation of expected returns for Stock A. (Those for Stock B are 27.0 percent and 1.59.) Is it possible that most investors might regard Stock B as being *less* risky than Stock A? Explain.

6-2   (Required rate of return) Suppose $k_{RF} = 10\%$, $k_M = 13\%$, and $b_A = 1.4$.

a. What is k_A, the required rate of return on Stock A?

b. Now suppose k_{RF} (1) increases to 11 percent or (2) decreases to 9 percent. The slope of the SML remains constant. How would this affect k_M and k_A?

c. Now assume k_{RF} remains at 10 percent but k_M (1) increases to 15 percent or (2) falls to 12 percent. The slope of the SML does not remain constant. How would these changes affect k_A?

6-3   (Expected returns) Suppose you were offered (1) $1 million or (2) a gamble where you would get $2 million if a head were flipped but zero if a tail came up.

a. What is the expected value of the gamble?

b. Would you take the sure $1 million or the gamble?

c. If you choose the sure $1 million, are you a risk averter or a risk seeker?

d. Suppose you actually take the sure $1 million. You can invest it in either a U.S. Treasury bond that will return $1,075,000 at the end of a year or a common stock that has a 50-50 chance of being either worthless or worth $2,300,000 at the end of the year.

(1) What is the expected dollar profit on the stock investment? (The expected profit on the T-bond investment is $75,000.)

(2) What is the expected rate of return on the stock investment? (The expected rate of return on the T-bond investment is 7.5 percent.)

(3) Would you invest in the bond or the stock?

(4) Just how large would the expected profit (or the expected rate of return) have to be on the stock investment to make *you* invest in the stock?

(5) How might your decision be affected if, rather than buying one stock for $1 million, you could construct a portfolio consisting of 100 stocks with $10,000 in each? Each of these stocks has the same return characteristics as the one stock, that is, a 50-50 chance of being worth either zero or $23,000 at year-end. Would the correlation between returns on these stocks matter?

6-4   (Equilibrium stock price) The risk-free rate of return, k_{RF}, is 10 percent; the required rate of return on the market, k_M, is 15 percent; and Moore Company's stock has a beta coefficient of 1.6.

a. If the dividend expected during the coming year, D_1, is $2.50, and if g = a constant 5%, at what price should Moore's stock sell?

b. Now suppose the Federal Reserve Board increases the money supply, causing the riskless rate to drop to 9 percent. What would this do to the price of the stock?

c. In addition to the change in Part b, suppose investors' risk aversion declines; this fact, combined with the decline in k_{RF}, causes k_M to fall to 13 percent. At what price would Moore's stock sell?

d. Now suppose Moore has a change in management. The new group institutes policies that increase the expected constant growth rate to 6 percent. Also, the new management stabilizes sales and profits and thus causes the beta coefficient to decline from 1.6 to 1.3. After all these changes, what is Moore's new equilibrium price? (Note: D_1 goes to $2.52.)

6-5 **(Beta coefficients)** Suppose Babcock Chemical Company's management conducts a study and concludes that if the firm expanded its consumer products division (which is less risky than its primary business, industrial chemicals), its beta would decline from 1.2 to 0.9. However, consumer products have a somewhat lower profit margin, and this would cause Babcock's constant growth rate in earnings and dividends to fall from 7 to 5 percent.

a. Should management make the change? Assume the following: $k_M = 12\%$; $k_{RF} = 9\%$; $D_0 = \$2$.

b. Assume all the facts as given above except the change in the beta coefficient. What would the beta have to equal to cause the expansion to be a good one? (Hint: Set $\hat{P}_0$ under the new policy equal to $\hat{P}_0$ under the old one, and find the new beta that will produce this equality.)

6-6 **(Expected rate of return)** The beta coefficient for Stock C is $b_C = 0.4$, while that for Stock D is $b_D = -0.5$. (Stock D's beta is negative, indicating that its rate of return rises whenever returns on most other stocks fall. There are very few negative beta stocks, although gold mining stocks are sometimes cited as an example.)

a. If the risk-free rate is 9 percent and the expected rate of return on an average stock is 13 percent, what are the required rates of return on Stocks C and D?

b. For Stock C, suppose the current price, P_0, is $25; the next expected dividend, D_1, is $1.50; and the stock's expected constant growth rate is 4 percent. Is the stock in equilibrium? Explain, and describe what will happen if the stock is not in equilibrium.

6-7 **(Security market line)** The Keenan Investment Fund has a total investment of $400 million in five stocks:

Stock	Investment	Stock's Beta Coefficient
A	$120 million	0.5
B	100 million	2.0
C	60 million	4.0
D	80 million	1.0
E	40 million	3.0

The beta coefficient for a fund such as Keenan Investment can be found as a weighted average of the fund's investments. The current risk-free rate is 7 percent, while the market return has the following estimated probability distribution for the next year:

Probability	Market Return
0.1	8%
0.2	10
0.4	12
0.2	14
0.1	16

a. What is the estimated equation for the Security Market Line (SML)? (Hint: Determine the expected market return and use this value for k_M.)

b. Compute the fund's required rate of return for the next year.

c. Suppose Keenan's management receives a proposal for a new stock. The investment needed to take a position in the stock is $50 million; it will have an expected return of 16 percent; and its estimated beta coefficient is 2.5. Should the new stock be purchased? At what expected rate of return should management be indifferent to purchasing the stock?

6-8   (Realized rates of return) Stocks A and B have the following historical dividend and price data:

Year	Stock A Dividend	Stock A Year-End Price	Stock B Dividend	Stock B Year-End Price
1982	—	$22.50	—	$43.75
1983	$2.00	16.00	$3.40	35.50
1984	2.20	17.00	3.65	38.75
1985	2.40	20.25	3.90	51.75
1986	2.60	17.25	4.05	44.50
1987	2.95	18.75	4.25	45.25

a. Calculate the realized rate of return (or holding period return) for each stock in each year. Then assume that someone had held a portfolio consisting of 50 percent of A and 50 percent of B (the portfolio was rebalanced at the end of each year). What would the realized rate of return on the portfolio have been in each year from 1983 through 1987? What would the average returns have been for each stock and for the portfolio?

b. Now calculate the standard deviation of returns for each stock and for the portfolio.

(Do Parts c through e only if you are using the computerized diskette.)

c. Add Stock C to the portfolio; C has the following historical dividend and price data:

	Stock C	
Year	Dividend	Year-End Price
1982	—	$23.40
1983	$1.85	23.90
1984	1.95	31.50
1985	2.05	27.20
1986	2.15	32.25
1987	2.25	26.00

Assume that the portfolio contains 33⅓ percent of A, 33⅓ percent of B, and 33⅓ percent of C. How does this affect the portfolio return and σ_p?

d. Make some other changes in the portfolio percentages, making sure the percentages sum to 100 percent. For example, put 100 percent in A; 25 percent in A, 25 percent in B, and 50 percent in C; and so forth. Explain why k_p and σ_p change.

e. Would you rather have a portfolio consisting of one-third of each stock or a portfolio with 50 percent A and 50 percent B? Explain.

6-9 **(Characteristic line and beta estimation)** You are given the following set of data:

	Historic Rates of Return	
Year	Stock X	NYSE
1	−14.0%	−26.5%
2	23.0	37.2
3	17.5	23.8
4	2.0	−7.2
5	8.1	6.6
6	19.4	20.5
7	18.2	30.6

a. Use a calculator with a linear regression function (or the computerized diskette) to determine Stock X's beta coefficient, or plot these data points on a scatter diagram, draw in the regression line, and then estimate the value of the beta coefficient.

b. Determine the arithmetic average rate of return for Stock X and the NYSE over the period given. Calculate the standard deviation of returns for both Stock X and the NYSE.

c. Assuming (1) that the situation during Years 1 to 7 is expected to hold true in the future (that is, $\hat{k}_X = \bar{k}_X$; $\hat{k}_M = \bar{k}_M$; and both σ_X and b_X in the future will equal their past values), and (2) that Stock X is in equilibrium (that is, it plots on the Security Market Line), what is the risk-free rate?

d. Plot the Security Market Line.

e. Suppose you hold a large, well-diversified portfolio and are considering adding to the portfolio either Stock X or another stock, Stock Y, that has the same beta as Stock X but a higher standard deviation of returns. Stocks X and Y have the same expected returns; that is, $\hat{k}_X = \hat{k}_Y = 10.6\%$. Which stock should you choose?

Solution to Self-Test Problem

ST-1   a. The realized return in each Period t is estimated as follows:

$$\bar{k}_t = \frac{D_t + P_t - P_{t-1}}{P_{t-1}}.$$

For example, the realized return for Stock A in 1983 was -12.24 percent:

$$\bar{k}_{1983} = \frac{D_{1983} + P_{1983} - P_{1982}}{P_{1982}}$$

$$= \frac{\$1.00 + \$9.75 - \$12.25}{\$12.25}$$

$$= -0.1224 = -12.24\%.$$

The table that follows shows the realized returns for each stock in each year, the averages for the five years, and the same data for the portfolio:

Year	Stock A's Return, $\bar{k}_A$	Stock B's Return, $\bar{k}_B$	Portfolio AB's Return, $\bar{k}_{AB}$
1983	-12.24%	-5.00%	-8.62%
1984	23.59	19.46	21.52
1985	35.45	44.10	39.78
1986	5.82	1.19	3.50
1987	28.30	21.11	24.71
$\bar{k}_{Avg}$	16.2%	16.2%	16.2%

b. The standard deviation of returns is estimated, using Equation 6-3a, as follows (see Footnote 4):

$$\text{Estimated } \sigma = S = \sqrt{\frac{\sum_{t=1}^{n} (\bar{k}_t - \bar{k}_{Avg})^2}{n - 1}}. \tag{6-3a}$$

For Stock A, the estimated standard deviation is 19.3 percent:

$$\sigma_A = \sqrt{\frac{(-12.24 - 16.2)^2 + (23.59 - 16.2)^2 + \ldots + (28.30 - 16.2)^2}{5 - 1}}$$

$$= \sqrt{\frac{1{,}488.15}{4}} = 19.3\%.$$

The standard deviation of returns for Stock B and for the portfolio are similarly determined, and they are shown here:

	Stock A	Stock B	Portfolio AB
Standard deviation	19.3%	19.3%	18.9%

c. Since the risk reduction from diversification is small (σ_{AB} falls only from 19.3 to 18.9 percent), the most likely value of the correlation coefficient is 0.9. If the correlation coefficient were -0.9, the risk reduction would be much larger. In fact, the correlation coefficient between Stocks A and B is 0.93.

d. If more randomly selected stocks were added to the portfolio; σ_p would decline to somewhere in the vicinity of 15 percent. σ_p would remain constant only if the correlation coefficient were $+1.0$, which is most unlikely. σ_p would decline to zero only if the correlation coefficient, r, were equal to zero and a large number of stocks were added to the portfolio, or if the proper proportions were held in a two-stock portfolio with r $= -1.0$.

Selected Additional References

Probably the best sources of additional information on probability distributions and single-asset risk measures are statistics textbooks. For example, see

McClave, James T., and P. George Benson, *Statistics for Business and Economics* (San Francisco: Dellen, 1982).

Mendenhall, William, Richard L. Schaeffer, and Dennis D. Wackerly, *Mathematical Statistics with Applications* (Boston: Duxbury, 1981).

Probably the best place to find an extension of portfolio theory concepts is one of the investments textbooks. These are some good recent ones:

Francis, Jack C., *Management of Investments* (New York: McGraw-Hill, 1983).

Levy, Haim, and Marshall Sarnat, *Portfolio and Investment Selection* (Englewood Cliffs, N. J.: Prentice-Hall, 1984).

Radcliffe, Robert C., *Investment: Concepts, Analysis, and Strategy* (Glenview, Ill.: Scott, Foresman, 1987).

Reilly, Frank K., *Investment Analysis and Portfolio Management* (Hinsdale, Ill.: Dryden, 1985).

Sharpe, William F., *Investments* (Englewood Cliffs, N. J.: Prentice-Hall, 1985).

For an excellent summary of portfolio theory and the CAPM, see

Modigliani, Franco, and Gerald A. Pogue, "An Introduction to Risk and Return: Concepts and Evidence, Part I," *Financial Analysts Journal,* March–April 1974, 68–80.

Modigliani, Franco, and Gerald A. Pogue, "An Introduction to Risk and Return: Concepts and Evidence, Part II," *Financial Analysts Journal,* May–June 1974, 69–86.

Those who want to start at the beginning in studying portfolio theory and the CAPM should see

Lintner, John, "Security Prices, Risk, and Maximal Gains from Diversification," *Journal of Finance,* December 1965, 587–616.

Markowitz, Harry M., "Portfolio Selection," *Journal of Finance,* March 1952, 77–91.

Mossin, Jan, "Security Pricing and Investment Criteria in Competitive Markets," *American Economic Review,* December 1969, 749–756.

Sharpe, William F., "Capital Asset Prices: A Theory of Market Equilibrium under Conditions of Risk," *Journal of Finance,* September 1964, 425–442.

Literally thousands of articles providing theoretical extensions and tests of the CAPM theory have appeared in finance journals. Some of the more important earlier papers are contained in a book compiled by Jensen:

Jensen, Michael C., ed., *Studies in the Theory of Capital Markets* (New York: Praeger, 1972).

However, the validity of the empirical tests has been questioned; see

Roll, Richard, "A Critique of the Asset Pricing Theory's Tests," *Journal of Financial Economics,* March 1977, 129–176.

Wallace, Anise, "Is Beta Dead?" *Institutional Investor,* July 1980, 23–30.

For a very readable discussion of Arbitrage Pricing Theory, see

Bower, Dorothy H., Richard S. Bower, and Dennis E. Logue, "A Primer on Arbitrage Pricing Theory," *Midland Corporate Finance Journal,* Fall 1984, 31–40.

Additional references concerning the use of the CAPM are given in Chapters 7 and 10.

7

The Cost of Capital

Shell Oil Company and the Newport News Shipbuilding and Drydock division of Tenneco, Inc., were recently involved in a lawsuit regarding two large tankers which Newport News had built for Shell at a cost of about $100 million. Shell paid in advance for the ships, and was to take delivery on a specified date. The contract stated that if the ships were not completed on time, Shell could sue for damages based on the cost of the capital which Shell had invested. Newport News did fail to complete the ships on time (they were about a year late), so Shell sued.

The theory behind the contract clause, and hence the lawsuit, was (1) that Shell was investing money, (2) that this money had a cost, (3) that Shell expected to earn a return on the ships which would cover the cost of the money invested, (4) that if Shell did not get the ships on time, then it could not start earning the cost of the capital it had invested, and (5) that Shell should then be entitled to recover its capital costs from Newport News. The principal issue in the suit was this: What was the cost of the approximately $100 million which Shell had invested in the tankers? That determination required an assessment of how Shell had actually raised the $100 million (it was raised partly as debt and partly as equity), and the cost of funds from each source. The techniques discussed in this chapter were used to help ascertain the proper amount of the damages, and exactly the same procedures are used by Shell and other companies for many other purposes.

A firm's cost of capital is critically important in finance for three reasons: (1) Maximizing value requires that the costs of all inputs, including capital, be minimized, and to minimize its cost of capital, a firm must be able to estimate it. (2) As we shall see in the next chapter, proper capital budgeting decisions require an estimate of the cost of capital. (3) Many other types of decisions, including those related to leasing, to bond refunding, and to working capital policy, also require estimates of the cost of capital.[1]

---

[1]Additionally, the cost of capital is vitally important in regulated industries, including electric, gas, telephone, and water companies. In essence, regulatory commissions first measure a utility's cost of capital, and then they set prices so that the company will just cover that cost. If the cost of capital estimate is too low, then the company will not be able to attract sufficient capital to meet long-run demands for its service, and the public will suffer. If the estimated cost of capital is too high, then customers will pay too much for service.

Although in theory a cost of capital estimate is easy to develop, in practice it is much more difficult. Our discussion in this chapter focuses on the actual estimation process, and we proceed in three steps: (1) We identify those capital components which should be included in the cost of capital, (2) we show how to determine the cost of each capital component, and (3) we then bring together the component costs to form a weighted average, or overall, cost of capital to the firm.

CAPITAL COMPONENTS AND COSTS

Capital, as we use the term, represents the funds used to finance the firm's assets and operations. The operations which produce sales and profits are not possible without the assets that are shown on the left side of the balance sheet, and those assets must be financed from the sources shown on the right side. Thus, capital constitutes the entire right-hand side of the balance sheet, including both short-term and long-term debt, preferred stock, and common equity.

Capital Components

Our ultimate goal is to estimate the firm's overall, or *weighted average, cost of capital (WACC),* and the first task is to decide which capital sources should be included. Since the WACC is used primarily in making long-term investment decisions (capital budgeting), our discussion will focus on the development of the cost of capital for this purpose. First, consider the firm's short-term, non-interest-bearing liabilities: accounts payable, accrued wages, and accrued taxes. All of these items arise from normal operations; if sales increase, then funds are spontaneously (automatically) generated from these sources. For example, if Macy's opens a new store, it will need new assets, including inventories, but as it orders and receives inventory, its accounts payable will automatically increase. Thus, an expansion spontaneously generates some of the capital needed to acquire the assets involved in the expansion. As we will see in Chapter 9, the dollar amount of the spontaneously generated liabilities associated with a given project is subtracted from the amount that would otherwise be required to finance the project. Then, the remainder is financed by nonspontaneous capital: interest-bearing debt, preferred stock, and common stock. *Since we are concerned with the cost of the nonspontaneous capital, accounts payable and accruals are not included when we calculate the weighted average cost of capital.*

We must also decide how to treat short-term debt (generally bank loans) which is not generated spontaneously. The answer depends on whether the firm deliberately uses short-term debt to finance long-term investments. If short-term debt is normally used as a temporary source of funds to finance cyclical or seasonal increases in assets, it should not be considered when the WACC is calculated. However, if the firm deliberately uses short-term debt as part of its permanent financing, then such debt should be included in the cost of capital calculation. As we will see in Chapter 18, the use of short-term debt to finance long-term assets is a highly risky procedure, and it is not common among well-managed firms. Therefore, in this chapter, we assume that interest-bearing, short-term debt is used to support temporary build-ups of current assets, and since our primary focus is on developing a cost of capital for use in capital budgeting, we therefore exclude short-term debt when we calculate the WACC unless otherwise noted. *Long-term debt, preferred stock, and common equity (including retained earnings) are the primary sources of capital for capital expansion, so they are the items normally included in the WACC calculation.*

Taxes

In developing the costs of the different capital components, the issue of taxes arises: Should we use a before- or an after-tax cost? In considering this question, remember that stockholders are concerned primarily with the cash flows that are available for their use, namely, those cash flows available to common shareholders after corporate taxes have been paid. Therefore, if management is to maximize stockholder well-being and thereby maximize the price of the stock, all cash flow and rate of return calculations must be done on an after-tax basis. *For this reason, the WACC must be developed on an after-tax basis, so we must consider corporate tax effects when we determine the cost of each relevant capital component.*

Historical Versus New (or Marginal) Costs

Another issue is this: Is the historical (or "embedded") cost of the capital that was raised in the past relevant, or should we focus exclusively on the cost of new funds? Embedded costs are important for some decisions. For example, the average cost of all the debt raised in the past and still outstanding is relevant to regulators who determine the allowed rate of return for a public utility. However, in financial management, the WACC is used primarily to make capital budgeting decisions, and these decisions hinge on the cost of *new* capital. *Thus, for purposes of this chapter, the relevant costs are not historical costs but, rather, the marginal costs of new funds to be raised during the planning period.*

COST OF DEBT

As discussed above, the relevant cost of debt is the after-tax cost of new debt. Although estimating this cost is relatively straightforward, a few problems do arise in practice. Most importantly, it is unlikely that the financial manager will know beforehand the exact types and amount of debt that will be used during the planning period — the type of debt actually used will depend on the specific assets to be financed and on capital market conditions as they develop over time. Even so, the financial manager does know what types of debt are typical for his or her firm. For example, McCue-Sachlis Computer Corporation, a full line computer manufacturer, typically uses short-term debt only to meet cyclical needs, and it uses 30-year bonds to raise long-term debt capital. Thus, for planning purposes, McCue-Sachlis' managers include only long-term debt in their WACC estimate, and they assume that this debt will consist of 30-year bonds.

Assume that it is January 1988. McCue-Sachlis' financial managers are developing the firm's WACC estimate for the 1988 planning year. How should they determine the component cost of debt? Most financial managers would begin by discussing current and prospective interest rates with their firms' investment bankers. Assume that McCue-Sachlis' investment bankers indicated that a new 30-year straight bond issue would require a 10 percent coupon rate, and that it would be offered to the public at a $1,000 par value. The *after-tax component cost of debt* is the interest rate on new debt, k_d, multiplied by $(1 - T)$, where T is the firm's marginal tax rate:

$$\text{After-tax component cost of debt} = k_d(1 - T). \qquad \textbf{(7-1)}$$

For example, if McCue-Sachlis is in the 40 percent federal-plus-state tax bracket, then its after-tax component cost of debt is 6.0%:

$$k_d(1 - T) = 10\%(0.60) = 6.0\%.$$

Note that the cost of debt is adjusted for taxes. The value of the firm's stock, which we want to maximize, depends on after-tax cash flows. Since interest is a tax-deductible expense, the federal government, in effect, pays part of the interest charges. Therefore, to put all component costs on a comparable basis, we reduce the cost of debt to take account of the preferential tax treatment of debt financing.[2]

COST OF PREFERRED STOCK

A number of firms, including McCue-Sachlis Computer Corporation, use preferred stock as part of their permanent financing mix. To determine this cost, we first note that preferred dividends, like common dividends, are not tax deductible. *Therefore, no tax adjustment is necessary when calculating the cost of preferred stock.* Second, most preferred is issued without a stated maturity date, although

---

[2]We should note some additional points regarding the tax adjustment. In our example, we used a marginal tax rate of 40 percent. Therefore, we were implicitly assuming that McCue-Sachlis' marginal tax rate over the next 30 years will remain at 40 percent. However, there are three potential problems with this assumption: (1) The value of the tax deduction depends on the taxable income for each year, and a change in taxable income might lead to a change in the marginal tax rate, and hence to a change in the after-tax cost of debt. (2) Tax losses can only be carried back for three years, and then they are carried forward. Therefore, several years of consecutive losses would mean that the benefits of tax deductibility could not be realized at the same time the interest is paid — instead, this benefit would be delayed until the firm becomes profitable, and this would raise the effective after-tax cost of debt. (3) Congress could, as it just did in 1986, raise or lower the applicable tax rate, which would also have an effect on the after-tax cost of debt. For all these reasons, we should recognize that firms cannot be certain of the true effects of tax deductibility, so the true cost of debt could be higher or lower than the calculated after-tax cost.

Also, note that we could include *flotation costs,* which are the costs of issuing the debt, in our calculations. However, flotation costs are typically small on debt issues — most debt is placed directly with banks, insurance companies, pension funds, and the like — and hence they do not materially affect a firm's cost of debt.

almost all preferred issued in recent years does have a call feature or some other provision which allows for early retirement. Finally, although it is not mandatory that preferred stock dividends be paid, firms do generally have every intention of meeting their preferred dividend payments, because if they do not (1) they cannot pay dividends on their common stock, (2) they will find it very difficult to raise additional funds in the capital markets, and (3) in some cases preferred stockholders have the right to take control of the firm.

With these points in mind, assume that McCue-Sachlis' investment bankers indicated that the firm could sell 9 percent perpetual preferred stock. If the stock had a par value of $100, then the annual dividend would be $9. Additionally, the investment bankers stated that the flotation costs would amount to 2.5 percent of the par value. Thus, the firm would net $97.50 from each share of preferred sold, and it would have an obligation to pay $9 of dividends per share per year. Thus, we calculate the component cost of preferred stock as follows:

$$\text{Component cost of preferred stock} = k_p = \frac{D_p}{P_n}. \tag{7-2}$$

Here D_p is the annual preferred dividend and P_n is the price the firm receives net of flotation costs. Applying Equation 7-2 to our example, we find McCue-Sachlis' cost of preferred stock to be 9.2 percent:[3]

$$k_p = \frac{D_p}{P_n} = \frac{\$9}{\$97.50} = 0.0923 \approx 9.2\%.$$

COST OF COMMON EQUITY

A firm can raise common equity capital in two ways: (1) by retaining earnings and (2) by issuing new common stock.[4] Thus, when we consider McCue-Sachlis' component cost of common equity, we are really considering the costs of two different types of common equity.

---

[3]We should note that firms have begun to issue variable, or floating rate, debt and preferred stock. Since future capital market rates are difficult, if not impossible, to predict, future interest payments and preferred dividends are normally estimated on the basis of current rates, and hence the expected costs of floating rate securities are the same as for fixed rate securities. However, the realized cost on a floating rate issue can be higher or lower than expected, depending on the actual rates over the life of the security, whereas the realized cost of a fixed rate security is known with relative certainty. Also, note that current tax laws do not permit either preferred or common stock flotation costs to be expensed against taxable income.

[4]The term "retained earnings" can be interpreted to mean the balance sheet item "Retained earnings," consisting of all the earnings retained in the business throughout the company's history, or it can mean the income statement item "Additions to retained earnings." The income statement definition is used in the present chapter. Retained earnings for our purpose here refers to that part of current earnings which is not paid out in dividends but, rather, is retained and reinvested in the business.

COST OF RETAINED EARNINGS

The costs of debt and preferred stock are based on the returns that investors require on these securities, and the cost of equity raised by retaining earnings can be defined similarly: *It is k_s, the rate of return stockholders require on the firm's common stock.*

The reason why we must assign a cost of capital to retained earnings involves the *opportunity cost principle.* The firm's net income after taxes literally belongs to its common stockholders. Bondholders are compensated by interest payments; preferred stockholders are compensated by preferred dividend payments; and the firm's remaining income belongs to its common stockholders and serves to "pay the rent" on stockholders' capital.

Management may either pay out earnings as dividends or retain earnings for reinvestment in the business. If part of the earnings is retained, an *opportunity cost* is incurred: stockholders could have received these earnings as dividends and then invested that money in stocks, bonds, real estate, and so on, and received a return on that investment. *Thus, the firm should earn on its retained earnings at least as much as its stockholders themselves could earn on alternative investments of equivalent risk.*

What rate of return can stockholders expect to earn on other investments of equivalent risk? The answer is k_s: they can get a return of k_s in the market by buying more of the same firm's stock or the stock of a similar firm. Therefore, if the firm cannot invest retained earnings and earn at least k_s, then it should pay these earnings to its stockholders so that they can invest the money themselves in assets that do provide this return.[5]

Whereas debt and preferred stocks are contractual obligations which have easily determined costs, it is not at all easy to measure k_s. Three methods are used in practice: (1) the Capital Asset Pricing Model (CAPM), (2) the Discounted Cash Flow (DCF) model, and (3) the bond yield plus risk premium approach. These methods should not be regarded as mutually exclusive, for none of them dominates the others, and all are subject to error when used in practice. When faced with the task of estimating a company's cost of equity, we generally use all three, but then we choose among them on the basis of how valid we judge the data used for each method in the specific case at hand.

THE CAPM APPROACH

As we saw in Chapter 6, the Capital Asset Pricing Model can be used to estimate the required rate of return on a firm's common stock. Under the CAPM, we assume that common stockholders are concerned only with market risk. Thus, the risk

---

[5]Alternatively, the firm can repurchase its own shares on the open market and earn a return of k_s, so again we see that k_s represents the opportunity cost of retained earnings. See Eugene F. Brigham and Louis C. Gapenski, *Intermediate Financial Management,* 2nd ed., "The Effects of Personal Taxes," 137–139, for a discussion of this point.

premium that investors demand is assumed to be based solely on (1) the stock's beta coefficient and (2) the market risk premium as set forth in the Security Market Line (SML) equation:

$$k_s = k_{RF} + (k_M - k_{RF})b_i.$$

Given an estimate of (1) the risk-free rate, k_{RF}; (2) the beta of the firm's stock, b_i; and (3) the required rate of return on the market, k_M, we can estimate the required return on the firm's stock, k_s. This required return can then be used as the cost of retained earnings.

Estimating the Risk-Free Rate

The starting point in the CAPM method is k_{RF}, the risk-free rate. There is really no such thing as a riskless asset — treasury securities are essentially free of default risk, but long-term T-bonds are subject to capital losses if interest rates rise, and a portfolio invested in short-term T-bills will provide a volatile earnings stream because the rate paid on T-bills varies over time. Since we cannot in practice find a truly riskless rate upon which to base the CAPM, what rate should we use? Our preference — and this preference is shared by most practitioners — is to use the rate on long-term Treasury bonds. Our reasons follow:

1. Capital market rates include a pure rate (generally thought to vary from 2 to 4 percent) plus a premium for expected inflation, which reflects the inflation rate expected over the life of the asset, be it 30 days or 30 years. The rate of inflation is likely to be relatively high during booms and low during recessions. Therefore, during booms T-bill rates tend to be high to reflect the high current inflation rate, but these rates are generally low during recessions. T-bond rates, on the other hand, reflect expected inflation rates over a long period, and hence they are far less volatile than T-bill rates.

2. Common stocks are long-term securities, and although a particular stockholder may not have a long investment horizon, most stockholders do invest on a long-term basis. Therefore, it seems more reasonable to think that stock returns embody long-term inflation expectations similar to those embodied in bonds rather than short-term inflation expectations as in bills. For this reason, the cost of equity should be more highly correlated with T-bond rates than with T-bill rates.

3. Treasury bill rates are subject to more random disturbances than are Treasury bond rates. For example, bills are used by the Federal Reserve System to control the money supply, and bills are also used by foreign governments, firms, and individuals as a temporary safe-house for money. Thus, if the Fed decides to stimulate the economy, it drives down the bill rate, and the same thing happens if trouble erupts somewhere in the world and money flows into the United States seeking a temporary haven.

4. We have seen the CAPM used with T-bills to estimate a particular firm's cost of equity at different points in time. When T-bill rates were low, as in 1977 and 1978, the CAPM cost of equity estimate was about 11 percent. When T-bill rates shot up in 1979 and 1980, the CAPM estimate more than doubled, to 23 percent. The company's bond yields, meanwhile, only rose from 9 to 14 percent. Neither we nor the company's management believed that the cost of equity rose by 12 full percentage points while the cost of long-term debt was rising by only 5 percentage points. CAPM estimates based on T-bond yields produced much more reasonable results.[6]

In view of the preceding discussion, it is our view that common equity costs are more logically related to Treasury bond rates than to T-bill rates. This leads us to favor T-bonds as the base rate, or k_{RF}, in a CAPM cost of equity analysis.[7] T-bond rates can be found in the *Wall Street Journal* or the *Federal Reserve Bulletin*. Generally, we use the yield on a 20-year T-bond as the proxy for the risk-free rate. Assuming that this rate were 8.2 percent in January 1988, we would use this as our estimate for k_{RF} in a January 1988 CAPM cost of equity estimate.

Estimating the Market Risk Premium

Financial services companies such as Merrill Lynch publish, on a regular basis, a forecast based on DCF methodology for the expected rate of return on the market, $\hat{k}_M$. For example, Merrill Lynch puts out such a forecast in its bimonthly publication *Quantitative Analysis*. One can subtract the current T-bond rate from such a market forecast to obtain an estimate of the current market risk premium, RP_M. To illustrate, assume that Merrill Lynch's reported expected return on the market in January 1988 were 14.0 percent. The T-bond rate, as mentioned earlier, is assumed to be 8.2 percent. Thus, Merrill Lynch's implied market risk premium over T-bonds would be 5.8 percentage points.[8]

---

[6]All of this can be illustrated by a true but not-very-funny story. A particular state public utility commission hired a professor who used T-bill rates as the base rate in his CAPM analysis to estimate the cost of capital for the state's utilities. Each utility's cost of capital in turn was built into its electric, gas, or telephone rates. Therefore, the lower the cost of capital, the lower were customers' bills, and the lower the bills, the less political heat the commission faced. This particular commission was very politically sensitive — so much so that one of its staff members admitted privately that the commission had selected its cost of capital expert on the basis of who could produce the lowest number.

The commission hired the professor in 1978, when T-bill rates were very low, as were his CAPM cost of equity estimates, because they were based on the T-bill rate. But the rate cases did not come up until 1979, and by then, the bill rate had gone through the roof. As a result, the professor's cost of equity estimates were even higher than the companies were asking permission to earn! At that point, the commission rejected the CAPM approach and sent the professor home. We have not heard much about him lately, but with short-term rates now below long-term rates, he may attempt a comeback.

[7]Astute students will note that the T-bond rate is not a true risk-free rate because long-term bond rates contain a maturity risk premium which compensates investors for interest rate risk. However, this premium is very difficult to measure at any point in time, and its impact on stocks and bonds is probably similar. We are willing, therefore, to accept the T-bond rate as a proxy for k_{RF}, especially since there is no better alternative.

[8]An alternative to "expected" risk premiums such as Merrill Lynch's are "historical" risk premiums, which are measured as the difference between past realized returns on stocks and bonds. The best known source of historical risk premiums is Ibbotson Associates, *Stocks, Bonds, Bills, and Inflation*, published annually. The 1987 Edition reports a 7.4 percent historical risk premium for stocks over long-term Treasury bonds.

Two potential problems arise when we use data from organizations such as Merrill Lynch. First, what we really want is *investors'* expectations, and not those of security analysts. However, this is probably not a major problem, since several studies have proved beyond much doubt that investors, on average, form their own expectations on the basis of professional analysts' forecasts. The second problem is that there are many professional forecasters besides Merrill Lynch, and, at any given time, their forecasts of future market returns are generally somewhat different. This suggests that it would be more appropriate to obtain a number of forecasts of $\hat{k}_M$, and then to use the average value to estimate RP_M for use in the CAPM. However, we have followed the forecasts of several of the larger organizations over a period of several years, and we have rarely found them to differ by more than ± 0.3 percentage points from one another. Therefore, for present purposes, the Merrill Lynch values of $\hat{k}_M = k_M = 14.0\%$ and $RP_M = 5.8$ percentage points are assumed to represent a "reasonable" proxy for the expectations of an average investor.

Estimating Beta

The last parameter needed for a CAPM cost of equity estimate is the beta coefficient. Recall from Chapter 6 that a stock's beta is a measure of its volatility relative to that of an average stock, and that betas are generally estimated from the stock's characteristic line, found by running a linear regression between past returns on the stock in question and past returns on a market index. We will define betas developed in this manner as *historical betas.*

Note, however, that historical betas show how risky a stock was *in the past,* whereas investors are interested in *future* risk. It may be that a given company was regarded as being quite safe in the past, but that things have changed, and its future risk is judged to be higher than its past risk, or vice versa. AT&T is a good example. Historically, AT&T was among the bluest of the blue chips, but investors today recognize that the Bell System was recently broken up, and that the surviving AT&T now faces far more competition than it ever faced in the past. Chrysler, on the other hand, was practically bankrupt a few years ago, but it now appears to be quite healthy. Therefore, one would think that Chrysler's risk had declined while AT&T's had increased.

Now consider the use of beta as a measure of a company's risk. If we use its historical beta in a CAPM framework to measure a firm's cost of equity, we are implicitly assuming that its future risk is the same as its past risk. This would be a troublesome assumption for a company like Chrysler or AT&T. But what about most companies in most years: As a general rule, is future risk sufficiently similar to past risk to warrant the use of historical betas in a CAPM framework? For individual firms, past risk is often *not* a good predictor of future risk, and historical betas of individual firms are not very stable.

Since historical betas are not very good predictors of future risk, researchers have sought ways to improve them. This has led to the development of two additional types of betas: (1) *adjusted historical betas* and (2) *fundamental betas.* Adjusted betas grew largely out of the work of Marshall E. Blume, who showed that true betas tend to move toward 1.0 over time.[9] One begins with a firm's pure historical beta, makes an adjustment for the expected future movement toward 1.0, and produces an adjusted beta which will, on average, be a better predictor of the future beta than would the unadjusted historical beta. The adjustment process involves some complex statistics, so we shall not cover it here.

Other researchers have extended the adjustment process to include such fundamental risk variables as financial leverage, sales volatility, and the like. The end product here is a *fundamental beta*.[10] These betas are constantly adjusted to reflect changes in a firm's operations and capital structure, whereas with historical betas (including adjusted ones) such changes might not be reflected until several years after the company's "true" beta had changed.

Adjusted historical betas are obviously heavily dependent on unadjusted betas, and so are fundamental betas as they are actually calculated. Therefore, the plain old historical beta, calculated as the slope of the characteristic line, is important even if one goes on to develop a more exotic version. With this in mind, it should be noted that several different sets of data can be used to calculate historical betas, and the different data produce different results.

Where does this leave financial managers regarding the proper beta? They must "pay their money and take their choice." Some managers will calculate their own betas, using whichever procedure seems most appropriate under the circumstances. Others will use betas calculated by organizations such as Merrill Lynch or Value Line, perhaps using one service or perhaps averaging the betas of several services. The choice is a matter of judgment and data availability, for there is no "right" beta. With luck, the betas derived from different sources will, for a given company, be close together. If they are not, then our confidence in the CAPM cost of capital estimate will be diminished.

Illustration of the CAPM Approach

We are now in a position to estimate McCue-Sachlis' cost of equity from retained earnings by the CAPM method. We use as the risk-free rate the assumed T-bond rate in January 1988, which is 8.2 percent, and Merrill Lynch's assumed estimate of the expected return on the market, $\hat{k}_M = k_M = 14.0\%$. Thus, we can write the SML equation for January 1988 as follows:

$$k_t = k_{RF} + (k_M - k_{RF})b_i$$
$$= 8.2\% + (14.0\% - 8.2\%)b_i$$
$$= 8.2\% + (5.8\%)b_i.$$

---

[9]See Marshall E. Blume, "Betas and Their Regression Tendencies," *Journal of Finance,* June 1973, 785–796.

[10]See Barr Rosenberg and James Guy, "Beta and Investment Fundamentals," *Financial Analysts' Journal,* May–June 1976, 60–72. Rosenberg, a professor at the University of California at Berkeley, set up a company which calculates fundamental betas by a proprietary procedure and then sells them to institutional investors.

Therefore, if we know a company's beta, we can insert it into the SML equation and estimate the company's cost of retained earnings, k_s. For example, we have obtained two estimates of McCue-Sachlis' beta: One service reported an adjusted beta of 1.03, and the other estimated an unadjusted beta of 1.16. Using the adjusted beta, we obtained 14.2%:

$$k_{M-S} = 8.2\% + (5.8\%)1.03 = 14.17\% \approx 14.2\%.$$

Using the unadjusted beta, we obtain an estimate of 14.9 percent. Therefore, on the basis of this CAPM analysis, McCue-Sachlis Computer's cost of retained earnings falls in the range of 14.2 to 14.9 percent.

Rather than picking single values, we could have developed high and low estimates for both the risk-free rate and the market risk premium. Then, by combining all of the low estimators and all of the high estimators, we could have estimated the extreme low and high values of the cost of retained earnings. Obviously, this expected range would have been greater than 14.2 to 14.9 percent.

THE DCF APPROACH

The second major procedure for estimating the cost of retained earnings is the Discounted Cash Flow (DCF) approach. We know that the intrinsic value of a stock is the present value of its expected dividend stream, $\hat{P}_0$:

$$\hat{P}_0 = \frac{D_1}{(1 + k_s)^1} + \frac{D_2}{(1 + k_s)^2} + \frac{D_3}{(1 + k_s)^3} + \ldots + \frac{D_\infty}{(1 + k_s)^\infty}.$$

Also, we know that we can recast this equation, given the market price of the stock, P_0, and solve for $\hat{k}_s$, the implied expected return:

$$P_0 = \frac{D_1}{(1 + \hat{k}_s)^1} + \frac{D_2}{(1 + \hat{k}_s)^2} + \frac{D_3}{(1 + \hat{k}_s)^3} + \ldots + \frac{D_\infty}{(1 + \hat{k}_s)^\infty}.$$

Finally, we know that in equilibrium, $\hat{k}_s = k_s$, so if a stock is in equilibrium, as it generally is, then an estimate of the expected rate of return also provides us with an estimate of the required rate of return.

If a stock is expected to grow at a constant rate, we can use the Gordon model to estimate k_s:[11]

$$k_s = \hat{k}_s = \frac{D_1}{P_0} + g.$$

Here P_0 is read from the *Wall Street Journal,* and next year's annual dividend, D_1, can be estimated relatively easily. It is less easy to estimate g, the growth rate expected by the marginal investor, but there are several ways to estimate growth rates. We examine three of them.

---

[11] If the stock is not expected to grow at a constant rate, then we must solve for k_s in the nonconstant growth model as developed in Chapter 5.

Historical Growth Rates

First, if earnings and dividend growth rates have been relatively stable in the past, and if investors expect these trends to continue, then the past realized growth rate may be used as an estimate of the expected future growth rate. To illustrate, McCue-Sachlis' earnings and dividends have grown at a 7.0 percent rate over the last 10 years. If this trend is expected to continue, then 7.0 percent would be a reasonable estimate for the dividend growth rate.

Retention Growth

Another method for estimating the growth rate is to use Equation 7-3:

$$g = b(r). \qquad\qquad (7\text{-}3)$$

Here, b is the fraction of its earnings that a firm is expected to retain, and r is the expected future return on equity.[12] Equation 7-3 produces a constant growth rate, and when we use it we are, by implication, making four important assumptions: (1) that we expect the retention ratio, b, to remain constant; (2) that we expect the return on equity on new investment, r, to equal the firm's current ROE, which implies that we expect the return on equity to remain constant; (3) that the firm is not expected to issue new common stock, or, if it does, that this new stock will be sold at a price equal to its book value; and (4) that future projects are expected to have the same degree of risk as the firm's existing assets.

McCue-Sachlis has had an average return on equity of about 15 percent over the past 10 years. In addition, its dividend payout ratio has averaged 0.48 over the past 10 years, so its retention rate, b, has averaged $1.0 - 0.48 = 0.52$. Using Equation 7-3, we estimate g to be 7.8 percent:

$$g = 0.52(15\%) = 7.8\%.$$

Analysts' Forecasts

Security analysts make and then publish forecasts of growth rates for most of the larger publicly owned companies. For example, *Value Line* contains such forecasts on about 1,700 companies, and all of the larger brokerage houses have similar forecasts. Further, several organizations compile all published growth rate forecasts on a regular basis, and make these forecasts available for a fee. The Institutional Brokers' Estimate Service (IBES) is one example.

---

[12]Since there are more terms for which symbols are needed than there are letters in the alphabet, some letters are used to denote several different things. This is one of those instances, and *b* is standard notation for both the beta coefficient and the retention rate. Note also that the retention rate is the complement of the payout rate, that is, Retention rate = $(1 -$ Payout ratio$)$. Finally, note that return on equity (ROE) is equal to net income divided by beginning-of-year total shareholders' equity.

Analysts virtually always begin by examining historical growth rates, and they also calculate g = br, using forecasts based on their knowledge of the company and its industry. Normally, these analysts are people with advanced degrees, years of experience following one industry and the companies in it. Further, their six figure salaries depend upon their credibility, which in turn depends on their ability to forecast future earnings and dividends. In fact, analysts are not able to forecast with real precision, but their forecasts are generally the best available, and since investors rely on analysts' forecasts, those forecasts reflect investors' views regarding g. Assume that you were able to obtain some analysts' forecasts of g for McCue-Sachlis, and that those forecasts ranged from 6 to 9 percent, with an average of 7.4 percent.

Illustration of the DCF Approach

We obtained dividend growth rate estimates of 7.0 percent from the historical growth rate and 7.8 percent using the retention growth model, and the average of the analysts' forecasts was 7.4 percent. Therefore, if we forecasted McCue-Sachlis' next annual dividend to be $2.40, and if we determined that its current stock price is $32, then its dividend yield would be $D_1/P_0 = \$2.40/\$32 = 0.075$ or 7.5%, and its DCF cost of retained earnings would be in the range of 14.5 to 15.3 percent:

$$\text{Lower End: } \hat{k}_{M\text{-}S} = k_{M\text{-}S} = 7.5\% + 7.0\% = 14.5\%.$$

$$\text{Upper end: } \hat{k}_{M\text{-}S} = k_{M\text{-}S} = 7.5\% + 7.8\% = 15.3\%.$$

This is reasonably close to the 14.2 to 14.9 percent estimate obtained by the CAPM method.

BOND YIELD PLUS RISK PREMIUM APPROACH

The last commonly used method for estimating the required rate of return on retained earnings calls for adding an assumed risk premium to the company's own bond yield:

$$k_s = \text{Bond yield} + \text{Risk premium}.$$

A corporate treasurer can easily look up his or her own firm's bond yield if the bond is publicly traded, or ask an investment banker for k_d if the bonds are not traded. The real problem is estimating the appropriate risk premium.

There are two common methods of estimating current risk premiums: a survey approach and a DCF-based approach. An example of the survey approach is the work of Charles Benore, a security analyst with Paine Webber. Benore has for several years conducted an annual survey of a large number of institutional investors, asking them what premium above the return on a company's bonds would make them indifferent to the choice of investing in the stock or the bonds. Over the years, Benore found that on average investors require a premium of 3 to 5 percentage points on stock over the company's bond yield, with a mean value of 3.6 percentage points. This mean could be used as an estimate of the risk premium. Benore's survey analyzes only public utility companies, but the approach is applicable to any company or industry. Note, though, that Benore has, in some recent years, reported average risk premiums as high as 6 percent, and in other years he found values closer to 3 percent. Generally, the larger premiums were found when interest rates were relatively low, and vice versa.

The second method for estimating risk premiums is based on the DCF model. To illustrate, we assumed earlier that in January 1988 Merrill Lynch, using the DCF approach, estimated that the expected rate of return on the market, as measured by the S&P 500, is 14.0 percent. Now, let's assume that the *Federal Reserve Bulletin* reported that the yield on an average corporate long-term bond is 10.5 percent. Using these data, we would estimate the risk premium of an average stock over an average bond to be $14.0 - 10.5 = 3.5$ percentage points. However, one should recognize that the figure of 3.5 percentage points is not precise; we would, ourselves, conclude that the risk premium of an average company's stock over its own bonds, in January 1988, was somewhere between 2.5 and 4.5 percentage points.

We can apply the bond yield plus risk premium approach to estimate the required rate of return on retained earnings for McCue-Sachlis. The company has some very well-received, high-quality products, and a loyal customer base. It also has a very strong balance sheet. Accordingly, its bonds are rated double A, which is quite good. Therefore, although the *Federal Reserve Bulletin* reported that an average corporate bond yielded 10.5 percent in January 1988, McCue-Sachlis' less-risky-than-average bonds yielded about 10.0 percent. (Our studies indicate that the average NYSE company's bonds are rated A.) Assuming that every company's required equity return exceeds its cost of debt by the risk premium estimated previously, we would determine McCue-Sachlis' high and low cost of retained earnings estimates as follows:

$$\text{Low: } k_{M-S} = 10.0\% + 2.5\% = 12.5\%.$$

$$\text{High: } k_{M-S} = 10.0\% + 4.5\% = 14.5\%.$$

Had McCue-Sachlis had a lower bond rating, its cost of debt and consequently its estimated cost of equity would have been higher.

Note again, however, that risk premiums have not been stable over time, so this procedure provides only a ball-park estimate of the cost of equity.

COMPARISON OF THE CAPM, DCF, AND RISK PREMIUM METHODS

We have discussed three methods for estimating the required rate of return on retained earnings — CAPM, DCF, and bond yield plus risk premium. Table 7-1 summarizes the results for McCue-Sachlis Computer Corporation. We see that the es-

Table 7-1
Estimated Required Rates of Return for McCue-Sachlis Computer Corporation

	Estimate	
Method	**Low**	**High**
CAPM	14.2%	14.9%
DCF	14.5	15.3
Bond yield plus risk premium	12.5	14.5
Average	13.7%	14.9%
Overall average	14.3%	

timates range from 12.5 to 15.3 percent, that the average highs and average lows produce a range of 13.7 to 14.9 percent, and that the overall average is 14.3 percent. Based on our judgment of the "quality" of the various methods, we decided to use 14.3 percent as the estimate of McCue-Sachlis' cost of retained earnings. Whenever the methods produce varied estimates, the financial manager must use his or her judgment as to the relative merits of each method, and then choose the estimate which seems most reasonable under the circumstances.

COST OF NEWLY ISSUED COMMON EQUITY

The cost of retained earnings as estimated in the preceding section is appropriate when retained earnings are being used to finance expansion. However, if the firm is expanding so rapidly that its retained earnings have been exhausted, then it must raise equity by selling newly issued common stock, and common equity has a higher cost than retained earnings. Specifically, the sale of new common equity involves significant flotation costs, which includes possible market pressure on the price of the stock, which raises the cost of equity. Flotation costs reduce the net usable dollars produced by a new stock issue, and this in turn increases the cost of the funds. We took account of flotation costs in our estimation of the cost of preferred stock, and the same general approach can be used with common equity.

When the firm sells new common stock, it nets $P_0(1 - F)$, where F is the percentage flotation cost expressed in decimal form. Note that F consists of issuance expenses such as printing costs and investment banker commissions, as well as any negative effects on the price of the stock which result from an increase in the supply of stock outstanding and from "signals" which investors may be given when a company announces that it plans to issue more common stock. These topics will be discussed in detail in Chapters 11 and 15, but for now just accept the facts (1) that direct costs must be incurred to issue stock and (2) that the announcement of a new stock offering typically causes the price of the stock to go down, at least until after the new stock has been sold. We designate the total effects (direct costs plus price decline), expressed as a percentage of the preannouncement price, as F.

If the firm is in a constant growth situation, the Gordon model, adjusted for flotation costs, can be used:

$$\text{Net proceeds} = P_0(1 - F) = \frac{D_1}{\hat{k}_e - g}. \qquad (7\text{-}4)$$

Here $\hat{k}_e = k_e$ is the cost of equity raised by selling new stock, and F is the percentage flotation cost. Solving Equation 7-4 for $\hat{k}_e$ produces this expression:

$$\hat{k}_e = \frac{D_1}{P_0(1 - F)} + g. \qquad (7\text{-}4a)$$

This procedure recognizes that the purchaser of a share of newly issued stock will expect the same dividend stream as the holder of an old share, but the company will, because of flotation expenses, receive less money from the sale of the new share, $P_0(1 - F)$, than the value of the old share, P_0. Therefore, the money raised from the sale of new stock will have to "work harder" to produce the earnings needed to provide the same dividend stream. As a result, $k_e > k_s$.

Note also that we could rewrite Equation 7-4a as follows:

$$\hat{k}_e = \frac{D_1/P_0}{(1 - F)} + g = \frac{\text{Dividend yield}}{(1 - F)} + g. \qquad (7\text{-}4b)$$

Equations 7-4a and 7-4b are equivalent, and either can be used, depending on the form of the available data.

To find McCue-Sachlis' cost of new equity, assuming that total flotation costs are 15 percent, we use Equation 7-4a as follows:

$$k_e = \hat{k}_e = \frac{D_1}{P_0(1 - F)} + g$$

$$= \frac{\$2.40}{\$32(1 - 0.15)} + 7.0\%$$

$$= \frac{\$2.40}{\$27.20} + 7.0\%$$

$$= 8.8\% + 7.0\% = 15.8\%.$$

Here we used input values of $P_0 = \$32$, $D_1 = \$2.40$, $F = 15\%$, and $g = 7.0\%$.

Thus, the DCF estimate for k_e is 15.8% when $g = 7.0\%$, while the DCF estimate for k_s, which we found earlier, was 14.5% when $g = 7.0\%$. Thus, the addition of flotation costs increased the cost of equity by 15.8% − 14.5% = 1.3 percentage points.

Notice that only one method (DCF) is commonly used to estimate the flotation cost adjustment, whereas three methods are used to estimate k_s. The flotation cost adjustment is then added to the final estimate of the cost of retained earnings. For McCue-Sachlis, the final estimate of the cost of retained earnings was 14.3 percent. Thus, the company's cost of new common equity is estimated to be 14.3% + 1.3% = 15.6%.

WEIGHTED AVERAGE COST OF CAPITAL

Thus far, we have discussed how to determine the costs of the various capital components. Now we must combine them to form a *weighed average cost of capital, WACC* $= k_a$. As we shall see in Chapters 11 and 12, each firm has in mind a target capital structure, defined as that mix of debt, preferred, and common equity which causes its stock price to be maximized. Further, when the firm raises new capital, it generally tries to keep the actual capital structure reasonably close to the target. Here is the general formula for the weighted average cost of capital:

$$\text{WACC} = k_a = w_d k_d (1 - T) + w_p k_p + w_s(k_s \text{ or } k_c). \tag{7-5}$$

Here w_d, w_p, and w_s are the weights used for debt, preferred stock, and common stock, respectively. The cost of the debt component of the WACC is $k_d(1 - T)$, the cost of the preferred component is k_p, and the common equity cost used in the calculation will be either the cost of retained earnings, k_s, or the cost of new common stock, k_c.

One point should be made immediately: k_a *is the weighted average cost of each new dollar of capital used at the margin* — it is not the average cost of all the dollars the firm has raised in the past, nor is it the average cost of all the dollars the firm will raise during the current year. We are primarily interested in obtaining a cost of capital for use in capital budgeting, and for such purposes, a *marginal cost* is required.[13] That means, conceptually, that we must estimate the cost of each dollar the firm raises during the year. Each of those dollars will consist of some debt, some preferred, and some common equity, and the equity will be either retained earnings or new common stock.

To illustrate, suppose McCue-Sachlis Computer has a target capital structure calling for 30 percent debt, 10 percent preferred stock, and 60 percent common equity. As we estimated earlier, the company's before-tax cost of debt, k_d, is 10.0 percent; its cost of preferred stock, k_p, is 9.2 percent; its cost of common equity from retained earnings, k_s, is 14.3 percent; its cost of equity from new common stock sales, k_c, is 15.6 percent. Further, the company's marginal tax rate is 40 percent. Therefore, McCue-Sachlis' after-tax, or component, cost of debt $= k_d(1 - T) = 10.0\%(0.6) = 6.0\%$.

Now suppose the firm needs to raise $100. In order to keep its capital structure on target, it must obtain $30 as debt, $10 as preferred, and $60 as common equity. (Common equity can come either from retained earnings or from the sale of new stock.) The weighted average cost of the $100, assuming the equity portion is from retained earnings, is calculated as follows, using Equation 7-5:

$$\begin{aligned}
\text{WACC} = k_a &= w_d k_d (1 - T) + w_p k_p + w_s k_s \\
&= 0.3(10.0\%)(0.6) + 0.1(9.2\%) + 0.6(14.3\%) \\
&= 11.3\%.
\end{aligned}$$

---

[13]The only use we can think of for the average cost of all the capital a firm has raised, as opposed to the marginal cost of capital, is in public utility ratemaking, where utility commissions are supposed to set rates such that customers pay for all costs of service, including the cost of the capital that was used to buy the assets that are used to provide service.

Every dollar of new capital that McCue-Sachlis obtains consists of 30 cents of debt with an after-tax cost of 6.0 percent, 10 cents of preferred with a cost of 9.2 percent, and 60 cents of common equity with a cost of 14.3 percent. The average cost of each new dollar is 11.3 percent.

The weights could be based either on the accounting values shown on the firm's balance sheet (book values) or on the market values of the different securities. Theoretically, the weights should be based on market values, but if a firm's book value weights are reasonably close to its market value weights, book value weights can be used as a proxy for market value weights. This point is discussed further in Chapters 11 and 12, but in the remainder of Chapter 7 we shall assume that the firm's market values are approximately equal to its book values, and on this basis we can use book value capital structure weights.

The Marginal Cost of Capital (MCC) Schedule

Since McCue-Sachlis' optimal capital structure calls for 30 percent debt, 10 percent preferred, and 60 percent equity, each new (or marginal) dollar will be raised as 30 cents of debt, 10 cents of preferred, and 60 cents of common equity. Otherwise, the capital structure would not stay on target. As long as the firm's debt has an after-tax cost of 6.0 percent, its preferred has a cost of 9.2 percent, and its common equity has a cost of 14.3 percent, then its weighted average cost of capital will be 11.3 percent. Thus, each new dollar will be raised as 30 cents of debt, 10 cents of preferred, and 60 cents of equity, and each new (or marginal) dollar will have a weighted average cost of 11.3 percent.

The graph shown in Figure 7-1 is defined as McCue-Sachlis' *marginal cost of capital (MCC) schedule.* Here the dots represent dollars raised. Since each dollar of new capital has a cost of 11.3 percent, the MCC schedule for McCue-Sachlis is constant at 11.3 percent under the assumptions we have used thus far.[14]

Breaks, or Jumps, in the MCC Schedule

Could McCue-Sachlis raise an unlimited amount of new capital at the 11.3 percent cost? The answer is *no.* As companies raise larger and larger sums during a given time period, the costs of both the debt and the equity components begin to rise, and as this occurs, the weighted average cost of new dollars also rises. Thus, just as corporations cannot hire unlimited numbers of workers at a constant wage, neither can they raise unlimited amounts of capital at a constant cost. At some point, the cost of each new dollar will increase above 11.3 percent.

Where will this point occur? As a first step to determining the point of increasing costs, recognize that all of McCue-Sachlis' existing capital was raised in the past, and all of it is invested in assets which are used in operations. Now suppose

---

[14]The MCC schedule in Figure 7-1 would be higher if the company used any capital structure other than 30 percent debt, 10 percent preferred, and 60 percent equity. This point will be developed in Chapters 11 and 12, but as a general rule, a different MCC schedule would exist for every possible capital structure, and the optimal structure is the one that produces the lowest MCC schedule.

Figure 7-1
Marginal Cost of Capital (MCC) Schedule Using Retained Earnings

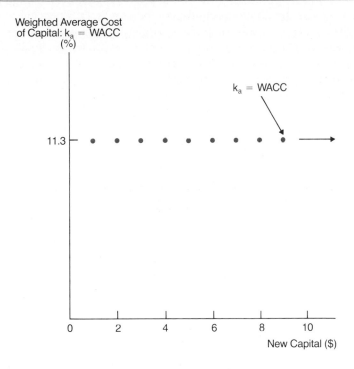

the capital budget calls for net expenditures of $1 million during 1988. This new (or marginal) capital will presumably be raised so as to maintain the 30/10/60 debt/preferred/common equity relationship. Therefore, the company will obtain $300,000 of debt, $100,000 of preferred, and $600,000 of common equity.[15] The new common equity could come from two sources: (1) that part of this year's profits which management decides to retain in the business rather than use for dividends (but not from earnings retained in the past, because those dollars will have already been invested) or (2) the sale of new common stock.

The debt will have an interest rate of 10.0 percent, or an after-tax cost of 6.0 percent. The preferred stock will have a cost of 9.2 percent. The cost of common equity will be k_s if the equity is obtained by retained earnings, but it will be k_e if

---

[15]In reality, the company might raise the entire $1 million by issuing new debt, or perhaps by issuing new common equity. By issuing large blocks of securities, there are savings on flotation costs. However, over the long haul the firm will stick to its target capital structure. Thus, any financing deviation in one year will be offset by opposite financing deviations in future years. The cost of capital remains a function of the target capital structure regardless of year-to-year financing decisions.

the company must sell new common stock. Consider first the case where the new equity comes from retained earnings. As we have seen, the company's cost of retained earnings is 14.3 percent, and its weighted average cost of capital when using retained earnings as the common equity component is 11.3 percent.

Now consider the case in which the company expands so rapidly that its retained earnings for the year are not sufficient to meet its needs for new equity, forcing it to sell new common stock. Since we previously estimated the cost of new equity, k_e, to be 15.6 percent, the WACC using new common stock is

$$\text{WACC} = k_a = w_d k_d (1 - T) + w_p k_p + w_s k_e$$
$$= 0.3(10.0\%)(0.6) + 0.1(9.2\%) + 0.6(15.6\%)$$
$$= 12.1\%.$$

We see that the WACC is 11.3 percent so long as retained earnings are used, but it jumps to 12.1 percent as soon as the firm exhausts its retained earnings and is forced to sell new common stock.[16]

How much new capital can McCue-Sachlis raise before it exhausts its retained earnings and is forced to sell new common stock? Assume that the company expects to have total earnings of $20 million for the year, and that it has a policy of paying out about 48 percent of its earnings as dividends. Thus, its *payout ratio,* which is the proportion of net income paid out as dividends, is 0.48. (The *retention ratio,* which is the proportion of net income retained within the firm, is 0.52. Note that the retention ratio is 1.0 minus the payout ratio.) Therefore, the addition to retained earnings will be 0.52($20,000,000) = $10,400,000 during the year. How much *total financing,* debt and preferred plus this $10.4 million of retained earnings, can be done before the retained earnings are exhausted and the firm is forced to sell new common stock? In effect, we are seeking some amount of capital, X, which is defined as a *break point* and which represents the total financing that can be done before McCue-Sachlis is forced to sell new common stock. We know that 60 percent of X will be the new retained earnings, while 40 percent will be debt plus preferred. We also know that retained earnings will amount to $10.4 million. Therefore,

$$0.6X = \text{Retained earnings} = \$10,400,000.$$

Solving for X, which is the *retained earnings break point,* we obtain

$$\text{Break point} = X = \frac{\text{Retained earnings}}{\text{Equity fraction}} = \frac{\$10,400,000}{0.6} = \$17,333,333.$$

Thus, the company can raise a total of $17,333,333, consisting of $10,400,000 of retained earnings and $17,333,333 − $10,400,000 = $6,9333,333 of new debt

---

[16]At relatively low growth rates, McCue-Sachlis' new assets could be financed by debt, preferred, and retained earnings, and its WACC would be 11.3 percent. However, if the growth rate were rapid enough to require the company to sell new common stock, then its WACC would rise to 12.1 percent.

and preferred stock supported by these new retained earnings, without altering its capital structure:

New debt supported by retained earnings	$ 5,200,000	30%
Preferred stock supported by retained earnings	1,733,333	10
Retained earnings	10,400,000	60
Total expansion supported by retained earnings (that is, break point for retained earnings)	$17,333,333	100%

Figure 7-2 graphs McCue-Sachlis' expanded marginal cost of capital schedule. Each dollar has a weighted average cost of 11.3 percent until the company has raised a total of $17,333,333. This $17,333,333 will consist of $5,200,000 of new debt with an after-tax cost of 6.0 percent, $1,733,333 of preferred stock with a cost of 9.2 percent, and $10,400,000 of retained earnings with a cost of 14.3 percent. However, if the firm raises $17,333,334, the last dollar will contain 60 cents of equity *obtained by selling new common equity at a cost of 15.6 percent,* so WACC = k_a rises from 11.3 to 12.1 percent.

Figure 7-2
Marginal Cost of Capital Schedule Using Both Retained Earnings and New Common Equity

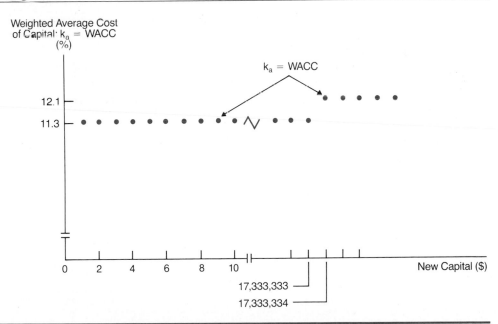

The MCC Schedule Beyond the Retained Earnings Break Point

There is a jump, or break, in McCue-Sachlis' MCC schedule at $17,333,333 of new capital. Could there be other breaks in the schedule? Yes, there could be. The cost of capital could also rise due to increases in the cost of debt or the cost of preferred stock, or as a result of further increases in F as the firm issues more and more common stock. Some people have argued that the costs of capital components other than common stock should not rise. Their argument is that as long as the capital structure does not change, and presuming that the firm uses new capital to invest in profitable projects with the same degree of risk as its existing projects, investors should be willing to invest additional capital at the same rate. However, this argument assumes an infinitely elastic demand for a firm's securities. For many firms, the demand curve of investors for its securities seems to be downward sloping, so the more securities sold during a given period, the lower the price received for the securities and the higher the required rate of return. In this situation, the more new financing required, the higher the firm's WACC.

We believe that firms do face increasing MCC schedules such as the one shown in Figure 7-3. Here we have identified a specific retained earnings break point, but because of estimation difficulties, we have not attempted to identify precisely any additional break points. However, we have (1) shown the MCC schedule to be upward sloping, reflecting a positive relationship between capital raised and capital

Figure 7-3
**Marginal Cost of Capital Schedule Using Retained Earnings,
New Common Stock, and Higher-Cost Debt**

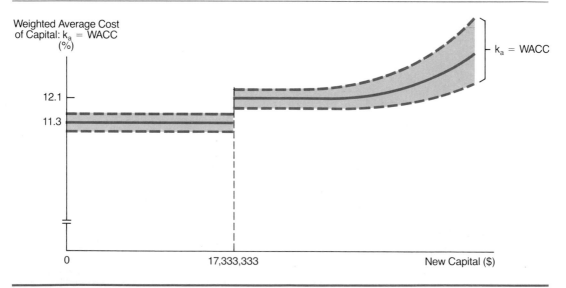

costs, and (2) indicated our inability to measure these costs precisely by using a band of costs rather than a line. Note that this band exists even at the first dollar of capital raised—our component costs are only estimates, these estimates become more uncertain as the firm requires more and more capital, and thus the band widens as new capital raised increases. In Chapter 10 we will use the MCC schedule to help determine a firm's optimal level of new investment.

THE COST OF DEPRECIATION-GENERATED FUNDS

The very first increment of internal funds used to finance investments in new assets, or the capital budget, is depreciation-generated funds. Further, in their statements of sources and uses of funds, corporations generally show depreciation charges to be one of the most important, if not the most important, source of funds.[17] Of course, depreciation is an allowance for the annual reduction in value of a firm's fixed assets. Thus, for an ongoing firm, depreciation-generated funds must be used to replace worn-out and obsolete assets.

For capital budgeting purposes, should depreciation be considered "free" capital, should it be ignored completely, or should a charge be assessed against it? *A charge should indeed be assessed against depreciation-generated funds, and the cost used should be the weighted average cost of capital before outside equity is used.* The reasoning here is that the firm could, if it so desired, distribute the depreciation-generated funds to its stockholders and creditors, the parties who financed the assets in the first place, so these funds definitely have an opportunity cost. For example, suppose McCue-Sachlis has $10 million of depreciation-generated funds available. Its WACC is 11.3 percent when retained earnings provide the common equity component and 12.1 percent when new common stock is used.

Now suppose no projects were available, not even projects which replace worn out equipment, that return 11.3 percent or more. The company obviously should

---

[17]Depreciation is a noncash charge. To illustrate, suppose a company reports the following income statement:

Sales	$100
Costs: Operating expenses	60
Depreciation	20
Taxable income	$ 20
Taxes (40%)	8
Net income	$ 12

If sales are all collected during the year, and if all costs except depreciation are paid in cash during the year, then cash flow from operations available for dividends or reinvestment will be $32:

$$\text{Cash flow} = \text{Net income} + \text{Depreciation} = \$12 + \$20 = \$32.$$

This point was discussed in Chapter 2, and it will be covered in greater depth in Chapter 9.

not raise any new capital, and it should not even retain any earnings for internal investment, because stockholders would be better off receiving the earnings as dividends and investing them themselves, or having the company repurchase its stock. Going on, the firm should not even invest its depreciation-generated $10 million. If it did keep and invest this money, it would receive a return of less than 11.3 percent. If it distributed the $10 million to its investors, with $6 million going to common stockholders and $4 million to bondholders and preferred stockholders, which would maintain the target capital structure, then the common stockholders could buy the stock of companies with similar risk and earn the 14.3 percent return that they required on McCue-Sachlis' stock. (Such a distribution would, under certain conditions, be a return of capital, and hence not taxable. If the distribution were taxable, then the company could repurchase its shares rather than make a direct distribution to stockholders. Note that in many recent years, U.S. companies have repurchased more old shares than they have issued new shares.) *The conclusion from all this is that depreciation-generated funds have a cost which is equal to the WACC before external equity is used.* This cost is based on the opportunity cost to existing investors rather than the required rate of return of new investors, but opportunity costs are just as real as other costs.

Depreciation affects the MCC schedule, and in a very significant way. The WACC increases when retained earnings are exhausted and the firm must begin to use new equity financing — for McCue-Sachlis, we saw that this would occur when $17,333,333 of new capital is raised. However, if depreciation is considered to be a source of funds available for capital budgeting purposes, as it should be, then the retention-based marginal cost of capital of 11.3 percent would be extended out by the amount of the depreciation. Therefore, the WACC would be 11.3 percent until $10,000,000 + $17,333,333 = $27,333,333 of capital has been raised (depreciation and retained earnings plus some external debt and preferred stock). After $27.3 million, the WACC would increase from 11.3 to 12.1 percent.

What difference does all this make, and should we be concerned with a cost of capital schedule that includes or excludes depreciation? If we were concerned only with the effects of net increases in assets, then the schedule without depreciation would be appropriate. However, we are normally concerned with gross capital expenditures — replacement as well as expansion investments — so the schedule that includes depeciation is the relevant one.

SUMMARY

This chapter focused on the estimation of a firm's weighted average cost of capital (WACC). We first discussed the relevant components and costs. If a capital component is part of the firm's permanent financing mix, then its cost should be included in the WACC. The relevant cost of each component is the after-tax cost of new money.

We saw that it is relatively easy to estimate the costs of debt and preferred stock — generally, market data from a firm's existing debt and preferred stock issues can be used to estimate these costs. Estimating the cost of equity is much more difficult, but these three approaches can be used: *CAPM, Discounted Cash Flow (DCF),* and *bond yield plus risk premium*. Each of these methods requires parameters which are themselves difficult to estimate, so the cost of equity, although generally expressed as a single number, is really better described as a range of values. We normally use all three techniques, and then average the results, when we estimate the cost of equity.

The next task is to combine the component costs to form a weighted average cost of capital, WACC. The weights used to develop WACC should be based on the firm's target capital structure.

Capital typically has a higher cost if the firm expands beyond certain limits, so its *marginal cost of capital (MCC) schedule* turns up beyond some point. In this chapter, we noted that the firm's cost of capital increases when it exhausts its retained earnings and must begin to issue new common stock. Further, beyond that point the cost of capital continues to rise as more and more new capital is raised.

Finally, we discussed the implications of depreciation. We concluded (1) that depreciation has an opportunity cost which is equal to the weighted average cost of capital based on retained earnings (rather than external equity), and (2) that the MCC schedule should be shifted out, or to the right, in Figure 7-3, by the amount of depreciation estimated for the year.

Questions

7-1   Define each of the following terms:

    a. Weighted average cost of capital, WACC = k_a

    b. After-tax cost of debt, $k_d(1 - T)$

    c. Cost of preferred stock, k_p

    d. Cost of retained earnings, k_s

    e. Historical beta; adjusted beta; fundamental beta

    f. Cost of new common equity, k_e

    g. Flotation cost, F

    h. Target capital structure

    i. MCC schedule; break, or jump, in the MCC schedule; break point

    j. Cost of depreciation-generated funds

7-2   In what sense is the WACC an average cost? A marginal cost?

7-3   How would each of the following affect a firm's cost of debt, $k_d(1 - T)$; its cost of equity, k_s; and its average cost of capital, WACC = k_a? Indicate by a plus (+), a minus (−), or a zero (0) if the factor would raise, lower, or have an indeterminate effect on the item in question. Assume other things are held constant. Be prepared to justify your answer, but recognize that several of the parts probably have no single correct answer; these questions are designed to stimulate thought and discussion.

		Effect on	
	$k_d(1 - T)$	k_s	WACC
a.	The corporate tax rate is lowered.	_____	_____	_____
b.	The Federal Reserve tightens credit.	_____	_____	_____
c.	The firm uses more debt.	_____	_____	_____
d.	The dividend payout ratio is increased.	_____	_____	_____
e.	The firm doubles the amount of capital it raises during the year.	_____	_____	_____
f.	The firm expands into a risky new area.	_____	_____	_____
g.	The firm merges with another firm whose earnings are countercyclical to those of the first firm and to the stock market.	_____	_____	_____
h.	The stock market falls drastically, and our firm's stock price falls along with the rest.	_____	_____	_____
i.	Investors become more risk averse.	_____	_____	_____
j.	The firm is an electric utility with a large investment in nuclear plants. Several states propose a ban on nuclear power generation.	_____	_____	_____

Self-Test Problem

ST-1 (MCC schedule) Lee Communications, Inc. (LCI), has the following capital structure, which it considers to be optimal:

Debt	25%
Preferred stock	15
Common stock	60
Total capital	100%

LCI's net income expected this year is $17,142.86; its established dividend payout ratio is 30 percent; its tax rate is 40 percent; and investors expect earnings and dividends to grow at a constant rate of 9 percent in the future. LCI paid a dividend of $3.60 per share last year (D_0), and its stock currently sells at a price of $60 per share. Treasury bonds yield 11 percent; an average stock has a 14 percent expected rate of return; and LCI's beta is 1.51. These terms would apply to new security offerings:

Common: New common stock would have a flotation cost of 10 percent.

Preferred: New preferred could be sold to the public at a price of $100 per share, with a dividend of $11. Flotation costs of $5 per share would be incurred.

Debt: Debt could be sold at an interest rate of 12 percent.

a. Find the component costs of debt, preferred stock, retained earnings, and new common stock.

b. How much new capital can be raised before LCI must sell new equity? (In other words, find the retained earnings break point.)

c. What is the WACC when LCI meets its equity requirement with retained earnings? With new common stock?

d. Construct a graph showing LCI's MCC schedule.

Problems

7-1 **(Component cost of debt)** Calculate the after-tax cost of debt under each of the following conditions:

a. Interest rate, 10 percent; tax rate, 0 percent.

b. Interest rate, 10 percent; tax rate, 40 percent.

c. Interest rate, 10 percent; tax rate, 60 percent.

7-2 **(Cost of retained earnings)** Knight Company's last dividend per share was $1; that is, $D_0 = \$1$. The stock sells for $20 per share. The expected growth rate is a constant 5 percent. Calculate Knight's cost of retained earnings using the DCF method.

7-3 **(WACC estimation)** On January 1, the total market value of the Beranek Company was $60 million. During the year, the company plans to raise and invest $30 million in net new projects. The firm's present market value capital structure, shown below, is considered to be optimal. Assume that there is no short-term debt.

Debt	$30,000,000
Common equity	30,000,000
Total capital	$60,000,000

New bonds will have an 8 percent coupon rate, and they will be sold at par. Common stock, currently selling at $30 a share, can be sold to net the company $27 a share. Stockholders' required rate of return is estimated to be 12 percent, consisting of a dividend yield of 4 percent and an expected constant growth rate of 8 percent. (The next expected dividend is $1.20, so $1.20/\$30 = 4\%$.) Retained earnings for the year are estimated to be $3 million. The marginal corporate tax rate is 40 percent.

a. To maintain the present capital structure, how much of the new investment must be financed by common equity?

b. How much of the new common equity funds needed must be generated internally? Externally?

c. Calculate the cost of each of the common equity components.

d. At what level of capital expenditures will Beranek's WACC increase?

e. Calculate Beranek's WACC using (1) the cost of retained earnings, and (2) the cost of new equity.

7-4 **(WACC estimation)** The following tabulation gives earnings per share figures for Campsey Manufacturing during the preceding 10 years. The firm's common stock, 140,000 shares outstanding, is now selling for $50 a share, and the expected dividend for the current year (1988) is 50 percent of EPS for the year. Investors expect past trends to continue, so g may be based on the historical earnings growth rate.

Year	EPS
1978	$2.00
1979	2.16
1980	2.33
1981	2.52
1982	2.72
1983	2.94
1984	3.18
1985	3.43
1986	3.70
1987	4.00

The current interest rate on new debt is 8 percent. The firm's marginal federal-plus-state tax rate is 40 percent. The firm's market value capital structure, considered to be optimal, is as follows:

Debt	$ 3,000,000
Common equity	7,000,000
Total capital	$10,000,000

a. Calculate Campsey's after-tax cost of new debt and of common equity, assuming new equity comes only from retained earnings. Calculate the cost of equity assuming constant growth; that is, $\hat{k}_s = D_1/P_0 + g = k_s$.

b. Find the firm's WACC, assuming no common stock is sold.

c. How much can be spent for net new capital investments before external equity must be sold?

d. What is the WACC beyond the retained earnings break point if new common stock can be sold to the public at $50 a share to net the firm $45 a share?

7-5 **(Market value capital structure)** Suppose the Tapley Company has this *book value* balance sheet:

Current assets	$30,000,000	Current liabilities	$10,000,000
Fixed assets	50,000,000	Long-term debt	30,000,000
		Common equity:	
		Common stock (1 million shares)	1,000,000
		Retained earnings	39,000,000
Total assets	$80,000,000	Total claims	$80,000,000

The current liabilities consist entirely of notes payable to banks, and the interest rate on this debt is 10 percent, the same as the rate on new bank loans. The long-term debt consists of 30,000 bonds, each of which has a par value of $1,000, carries a coupon interest rate of 6 percent, and matures in 20 years. The going rate of interest on new long-term debt, k_d, is 10 percent, and this is the present yield-to-maturity on the bonds.

The common stock sells at a price of $60 per share. Calculate Tapley's market value capital structure.

7-6   **(Cost of equity)** The Malone Tractor Company's EPS in 1987 was $2.00. EPS in 1982 was $1.3612. The company pays out 40 percent of its earnings as dividends, and the stock currently sells for $21.60. The company expects earnings of $10 million in 1988. Its optimal market value debt/assets ratio is 60 percent, and the firm has no preferred stock outstanding.

   a. Calculate Malone's growth rate in earnings.

   b. Calculate the firm's dividend per share expected in 1988. Assume that the growth rate calculated in Part a will continue.

   c. What is Malone's cost of retained earnings, k_s?

   d. What amount of retained earnings is expected in 1988?

   e. At what amount of total financing will Malone's cost of equity increase?

   f. The sale of new stock would net the company $18.36 per share. What is Malone's percentage flotation cost, F? What is the cost of new common stock, k_e?

7-7   **(Cost of equity estimation methods)** You have just estimated the cost of equity for Freeway Shipping Company using all three estimation techniques. The results are summarized in the following table:

Method	k_s Estimate
CAPM	12.1%
DCF	14.0
Bond yield plus risk premium	15.4

The inconsistency of the results are worrisome, but you must still develop your equity cost estimate. What factors might you consider as you attempt to place confidence in the above estimates?

7-8   **(Integrative problem)** A summary of the balance sheet of Travellers Inn, Inc. (TII), a company which was formed by merging a number of regional motel chains and which hopes to rival Holiday Inn on the national scene, is shown in the table:

Travellers Inn
December 31, 1987
(Millions of Dollars)

Cash	$ 10	Accounts payable		$ 10
Accounts receivable	20	Accruals		10
Inventories	20	Short-term debt		5
Current assets	$ 50	Current liabilities		$ 25
Net fixed assets	50	Long-term debt		30
		Preferred stock		5
		Common equity:		
		Common stock	$10	
		Retained earnings	30	
		Total common equity		40
Total assets	$100	Total claims		$100

These facts are also given for TII:

(1) Short-term debt consists of bank loans which currently cost 10 percent, with interest payable quarterly. These loans are used to finance receivables and inventories on a seasonal basis, so in the off-season, bank loans are zero.

(2) The long-term debt consists of 20-year, semiannual payment mortgage bonds with a coupon rate of 8 percent. Currently, these bonds provide a yield to investors of $k_d = 12\%$. If new bonds were sold, they would yield investors 12 percent, but a flotation cost of 5 percent would be required to sell new bonds.

(3) TII's perpetual preferred stock has a $100 par value, pays a quarterly dividend of $2, and has a yield to investors of 11 percent. New preferred would have to provide the same yield to investors, and the company would incur a 5 percent flotation cost to sell it.

(4) The company has 4 million shares of common stock outstanding. $P_0 = \$20$, but the stock has recently traded in a range of $17 to $23. $D_0 = \$1$ and $EPS_0 = \$2$. ROE based on average equity was 24 percent in 1987, but management expects to increase this return on equity to 30 percent; however, security analysts are not aware of management's optimism in this regard.

(5) Betas, as reported by security analysts, range from 1.3 to 1.7; the T-bond rate is 10 percent; and k_M is estimated by various brokerage houses to be in the range of 14.5 to 15.5 percent. Brokerage house reports forecast growth rates in the range of 10 to 15 percent over the foreseeable future. However, some analysts do not explicitly forecast growth rates, but they indicate to their clients that they expect TII's historic trends as shown in the table to continue.

(6) At a recent conference, TII's financial vice president polled some pension fund investment managers on the minimum rate of return they would have to expect on TII's common to make them willing to buy the common rather than TII bonds, when the bonds yielded 12 percent. The responses suggested a risk premium over TII bonds of 4 to 6 percent.

(7) TII is in the 40 percent federal-plus-state tax bracket. Its dominant stockholders are in the 28 percent bracket.

(8) New common stock would have a 10 percent flotation cost.

(9) TII's principal investment banker, Henry, Kaufman & Company, predicts a decline in interest rates, with k_d falling to 10 percent and the T-bond rate to 8 percent, although Henry, Kaufman & Company acknowledges that an increase in the expected inflation rate could lead to an increase rather than a decrease in rates.

(10) Here is the historical record of EPS and DPS:

Year	EPS[a]	DPS[a]	Year	EPS[a]	DPS[a]
1973	$0.09	$0.00	1981	$0.78	$0.00
1974	−0.20	0.00	1982	0.80	0.00
1975	0.40	0.00	1983	1.20	0.20
1976	0.52	0.00	1984	0.95	0.40
1977	0.10	0.00	1985	1.30	0.60
1978	0.57	0.00	1986	1.60	0.80
1979	0.61	0.00	1987	2.00	1.00
1980	0.70	0.00			

[a]Adjusted for a 2:1 stock split in 1977, a 3:1 split in 1985, and 10 percent stock dividends in 1974 and 1982.

Assume that you are a recently hired financial analyst, and your boss, the treasurer, has asked you to estimate the company's WACC for both retained earnings and new common stock sales. Your cost of capital figures at each level should be appropriate for use in evaluating projects which are in the same risk class as the firm's average assets now on the books.

Solution to Self-Test Problem

ST-1   a. *Cost of debt:*

$$k_d(1 - T) = 12\%(1 - 0.40) = 12\%(0.60) = 7.20\%.$$

Cost of preferred stock:

$$k_p = \frac{D}{P_n} = \frac{\$11}{\$100 - \$5} = \frac{\$11}{\$95} = 11.58\%.$$

Cost of retained earnings (using DCF method):

$$k_s = \frac{D_1}{P_0} + g = \frac{D_0(1 + g)}{P_0} + g$$

$$- \frac{\$3.60(1.09)}{\$60} + 0.09$$

$$= 0.0654 + 0.09 = 0.1554 = 15.54\%.$$

Cost of retained earnings (using CAPM method):

$$k_s = k_{RF} + (k_M - k_{RF})b_i$$

$$= 11\% + (14\% - 11\%)1.51$$

$$= 15.53\%.$$

Cost of new common stock:

$$k_e = \frac{D_1}{P_0(1.0 - F)} + g = \frac{\$3.924}{\$60(0.9)} + 9\% = 16.27\%.$$

b. LCI's forecasted retained earnings are $17,142.86(1 - 0.30) = \$12,000$. Thus, the retained earnings break point, BP_{RE}, is $20,000:

$$BP_{RE} = \frac{RE}{\text{Equity fraction}} = \frac{\$12,000}{0.60} = \$20,000.$$

c. *WACC using retained earnings:*

$$WACC_1 = k_a = w_d k_d(1 - T) + w_p k_p + w_s k_s$$

$$= 0.25(7.25\%) + 0.15(11.58\%) + 0.60(15.54\%)$$

$$= 1.80\% + 1.74\% + 9.32\% = 12.86\%.$$

WACC using new common stock:

$$\text{WACC}_2 = k_a = 1.80\% + 1.74\% + 0.60(16.27\%) = 13.30\%.$$

d. See the following graph:

MCC Schedule for LCI

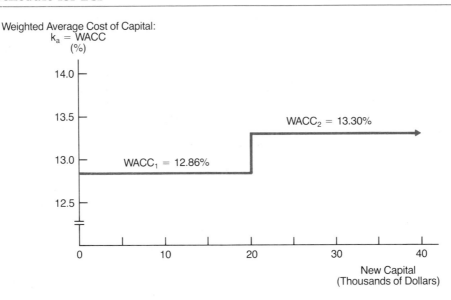

Selected Additional References and Cases

The following articles provide some valuable insights into the CAPM approach to estimating the cost of equity:

Beaver, William H., Paul Kettler, and Myron Scholes, "The Association between Market Determined and Accounting Determined Risk Measures," *Accounting Review,* October 1970, 654–682.

Bowman, Robert G., "The Theoretical Relationship between Systematic Risk and Financial (Accounting) Variables," *Journal of Finance,* June 1979, 617–630.

Chen, Carl R., "Time-Series Analysis of Beta Stationarity and Its Determinants: A Case of Public Utilities," *Financial Management,* Autumn 1982, 64–70.

Cooley, Philip L., "A Review of the Use of Beta in Regulatory Proceedings," *Financial Management,* Winter 1981, 75–81.

Harrington, Diana R., "Whose Beta Is Best?," *Financial Analysts Journal,* July–August 1983, 67–73.

Rosenberg, Barr, and Andrew Rudd, "The Corporate Uses of Beta," *Issues in Corporate Finance* (New York: Stern Stewart Putnam & Macklis, 1983).

The weighted average cost of capital as described in this chapter is widely used in both industry and academic circles. It has been criticized on several counts, but to date it has withstood the challenges. See the following articles:

Arditti, Fred D., and Haim Levy, "The Weighted Average Cost of Capital as a Cutoff Rate: A Critical Examination of the Classical Textbook Weighted Average," *Financial Management,* Fall 1977, 24–34.

Beranek, William, "The Weighted Average Cost of Capital and Shareholder Wealth Maximization," *Journal of Financial and Quantitative Analysis,* March 1977, 17–32.

Boudreaux, Kenneth J., and Hugh W. Long; John R. Ezzell and R. Burr Porter; Moshe Ben Horim; and Alan C. Shapiro, "The Weighted Average Cost of Capital: A Discussion," *Financial Management,* Summer 1979, 7–23.

Reilly, Raymond R., and William E. Wacker, "On the Weighted Average Cost of Capital," *Journal of Financial and Quantitative Analysis,* January 1973, 123–126.

Some other works that are relevant include the following:

Alberts, W. W., and Stephen H. Archer, "Some Evidence on the Effect of Company Size on the Cost of Equity Capital," *Journal of Financial and Quantitative Analysis,* March 1973, 229–242.

Chen, Andrew, "Recent Developments in the Cost of Debt Capital," *Journal of Finance,* June 1978, 863–883.

Myers, Stewart C., "Interactions of Corporate Financing and Investments Decisions — Implications for Capital Budgeting," *Journal of Finance,* March 1974, 1–25.

Nantell, Timothy J., and C. Robert Carlson, "The Cost of Capital as a Weighted Average," *Journal of Finance,* December 1975, 1343–1355.

For some insights into the cost of capital techniques used by major firms, see

Gitman, Lawrence J., and Vincent A. Mercurio, "Cost of Capital Techniques Used by Major U.S. Firms: Survey and Analysis of Fortune's 1000," *Financial Management,* Winter 1982, 21–29.

The following cases focus on the estimation of a firm's cost of capital:

"American Telephone & Telegraph," which illustrates the estimation of AT&T's cost of capital in the summer of 1983. Harrington, Diana, *Case Studies in Financial Decision Making* (Hinsdale, Ill.: Dryden, 1985).

"Communications Satellite Corporation," which examines the problems in estimating equity costs when new technology is involved. Available from HBS Case Services, Cambridge, Mass.

Part

III

Capital Budgeting

8

The Basics of Capital Budgeting

Businesses invest hundreds of billions of dollars in fixed assets each year. By their very nature, such investments affect a firm's fortunes for many years. A good decision can boost earnings sharply and increase dramatically the price of a firm's stock. A bad decision can lead to bankruptcy.

A classic example of a bad capital budgeting decision which could have easily been avoided involved Lockheed's production of the L-1011 Tri-Star commercial aircraft. When Lockheed made the final decision to go forward with Tri-Star production, it estimated the breakeven volume at about 200 planes. The company had orders for about 180 planes, and it was sure of getting at least 20 more orders. Consequently, it decided to commit $1 billion and to commence production.

However, Lockheed's analysis was flawed — it failed to account properly for the cost of the capital tied up in the project. Had its analysts appraised the project correctly, they would have found that the breakeven point was far above 200 planes — so far above that the Tri-Star program was almost certainly doomed to fail. This mistake contributed to a decline in Lockheed's stock from $73 per share to $3. Had Lockheed's managers read Chapter 8 and heeded its advice, at least some of that loss might have been avoided.

In previous chapters we have seen (1) how investors value corporate securities and (2) how firms estimate their costs of capital based on investors' required rates of return. Now we turn to investment decisions involving fixed assets, called *capital budgeting*. The term *capital* refers to fixed assets used in production, while a *budget* is a plan which details projected inflows and outflows during some future period. Thus, the *capital budget* outlines the planned expenditures on fixed assets, and *capital budgeting* is the whole process of analyzing projects and deciding whether they should be included in the capital budget. This process is of fundamental importance to the success or failure of the firm, for its fixed asset investment decisions chart the course of a company for many years into the future, and, more than anything else, *determine* its future.

Our treatment of capital budgeting is divided into three parts. First, Chapter 8 gives an overview and explains the basic techniques used in capital budgeting analysis. Then, in Chapter 9, we go on to consider how cash flows are estimated. Finally, in Chapter 10, we discuss how risk is brought into the analysis, and we also explain how the overall capital budget is established.

PROJECT PROPOSALS AND CLASSIFICATIONS

The same general concepts are involved in both capital budgeting and security analysis. However, whereas a set of stocks and bonds exists in the securities market, and investors select a portfolio from this set, *capital budgeting projects are created by the firm.* For example, a sales representative may report that customers are asking for a particular product that the company does not now produce. The sales manager then discusses the idea with the marketing research group to determine the size of the market for the proposed product. If it appears likely that a significant market does exist, cost accountants and engineers will be asked to estimate production costs. If it appears that the product can be produced and sold to yield a sufficient profit, then the project will be undertaken.

A firm's growth and development, even its ability to remain competitive and to survive, depend upon a constant flow of ideas for new products and ways to make existing products better and/or at a lower cost. Accordingly, a well-managed firm will go to great lengths to develop good capital budgeting proposals. For example, the executive vice-president of one very successful corporation indicated that his company takes the following steps to generate projects:

> Our R&D department is constantly searching for new products and also for ways to improve existing products. In addition, our executive committee, which consists of senior executives in marketing, production, and finance, identifies the products and markets in which our company will compete, and the committee sets long-run targets for each division. These targets, which are formalized in the corporation's strategic business plan, provide a general guide to the operating executives who must meet them. These executives then seek new products, set expansion plans for existing products, and look for ways to reduce production and distribution costs. Since bonuses and promotions are based in large part on each unit's ability to meet or exceed its targets, these economic incentives encourage our operating executives to seek out profitable investment opportunities.
>
> While our senior executives are judged and rewarded on the basis of how well their units perform, people further down the line are given bonuses for specific suggestions, including ideas that lead to profitable investments. Additionally, a percentage of our corporate profit is set aside for distribution to nonexecutive employees. Our objective is to encourage employees at all levels to keep on the lookout for good ideas, including those that lead to capital investments.

If a firm has capable and imaginative executives and employees, and if its incentive system is working properly, many ideas for capital investment will be advanced. Since some ideas will be good ones while others will not, procedures must be established for screening projects.

Analyzing capital expenditure proposals is not a costless operation—benefits can be gained from a careful analysis, but such an investigation does have a cost. For certain types of projects, a relatively detailed analysis may be warranted; for others, cost/benefit studies suggest that simpler procedures should be used. Accordingly, firms generally classify projects into the following categories and analyze those in each category somewhat differently:

1. Replacement: maintenance of business. Category 1 consists of expenditures necessary to replace worn-out or damaged equipment used to produce profitable products. These projects are necessary if the firm is to continue in its current businesses. The only issues here are (1) should we continue to produce these products or services, and (2) should we continue to use our existing plant and equipment? Usually, the answers are "yes," so maintenance decisions are normally made without going through an elaborate decision process.

2. Replacement: cost reduction. This group includes expenditures to replace serviceable but obsolete equipment. The purpose of these expenditures is to lower the costs of labor, materials, or other items such as electricity. These decisions are somewhat more discretionary, so a more detailed analysis is generally required to support the expenditure.

3. Expansion of existing products or markets. Expenditures to increase output of existing products, or to expand outlets or distribution facilities in markets now being served, are included here. These decisions are more complex, because they require an explicit consideration of future demand in the firm's product markets. Mistakes are more likely, so still more detailed analysis is required, and the final decision is made at a higher level within the firm.

4. Expansion into new products or markets. These are expenditures necessary to produce a new product, or to expand into a geographic area not currently being served. These projects involve strategic decisions that could change the fundamental nature of the business, and they normally require the expenditure of very large sums of money over long periods. Invariably, a very detailed analysis is required, and final decisions on new product or market decisions are generally made by the board of directors.

5. Safety and/or environmental projects. Expenditures necessary to comply with government orders, labor agreements, or insurance policy terms fall into this category. These expenditures are often called *mandatory investments,* or *nonrevenue-producing projects.* How they are handled depends on their size, with small ones being treated much like the Category 1 projects described above.

6. Other. This catch-all includes office buildings, parking lots, executive aircraft, and so on. How they are handled also depends on their size.

In general, relatively simple calculations and only a few supporting documents are required for replacement decisions, especially maintenance-type investments in profitable plants. More detailed analysis is required for cost reduction replacements, for expansion of existing product lines, and especially for investments in new products or areas. Also, within each category, projects are broken down by their dollar costs: The larger the required investment, the more detailed is the analysis and the higher is the level of the officer who must authorize the expenditure. Thus, while a plant manager may be authorized to approve maintenance expenditures up to $10,000 on the basis of a relatively unsophisticated analysis, the full board of directors may have to approve decisions which involve either amounts over $1 million or expansions into new products or markets, and a very detailed, refined analysis will be required to support these decisions.

SIMILARITIES BETWEEN CAPITAL BUDGETING AND SECURITY VALUATION

Conceptually, the capital budgeting process involves exactly the same six steps that are used in security analysis as described in Chapters 5 and 6:

1. First, the cost of the project must be determined. This is similar to finding the price that must be paid for a stock or bond.

2. Next, management estimates the expected cash flows from the project, including the value of the asset at a specified terminal date. This is similar to estimating the future dividend or interest payment stream on a stock or bond.

3. Third, the riskiness of the projected cash flows must be estimated. To do this, management needs information about the probability distributions of the cash flows.

4. Then, given the riskiness of the projected cash flows and the general level of money costs in the economy as reflected in the riskless rate, k_{RF}, the firm determines the appropriate discount rate, or cost of capital, at which the project's cash flows are to be discounted. This is equivalent to finding the required rate of return on a stock, as we did in Chapter 6.

5. Next, the expected cash flows are put on a present value basis to obtain an estimate of the asset's value to the firm. This is equivalent to finding the present value of expected future dividends.

6. Finally, the present value of the expected cash inflows is compared with the required outlay, or cost, of the project; if the asset's present value exceeds its cost, the project should be accepted. Otherwise, the project should be rejected.

If an individual investor identifies and invests in a stock or bond whose market price is less than its true value, then the value of the investor's portfolio will increase. Similarly, if a firm identifies (or creates) an investment opportunity with a present value greater than its cost, the value of the firm will increase. This increase in firm value from capital budgeting will be reflected in the growth factor, g, that we discussed in Chapters 5 and 6. Thus, there is a very direct link between capital budgeting and stock values: The more effective the firm's capital budgeting procedures, the higher will be its growth rate, and hence the higher the price of its stock.

CAPITAL BUDGETING DECISION RULES

Five major methods are used to rank projects and to decide whether or not they should be accepted for inclusion in the capital budget: (1) payback, (2) net present value (NPV), (3) regular internal rate of return (IRR), (4) modified internal rate of return (IRR*), and (5) profitability index (PI). We first explain how each ranking criterion is calculated, and then we evaluate how well each performs in terms of identifying those projects which will maximize the firm's stock price.[1]

Table 8-1
Cash Flows for Projects S and L

Year (t)	Expected After-Tax Net Cash Flow, CF_t	
	Project S	Project L
0	($1,000)[a]	($1,000)[a]
1	500	100
2	400	300
3	300	400
4	100	600

[a]Represents the net investment outlay, or initial cost. The parentheses indicate a negative number, or cash outflow.

We use the cash flow data shown in Table 8-1 for Projects S and L to illustrate each method, and throughout this chapter we assume that the projects are equally risky. Note that the cash flows, CF_t, are expected values, and that they have been adjusted to include depreciation, salvage values, and tax effects. Also, since many projects require an investment in both fixed assets and working capital, the investment outlays shown as CF_0 include any necessary changes in net working capital.[2]

---

[1]Various types of "accounting rates of return" are occasionally used in project evaluation, but all of these methods have serious flaws, and hence we omit them from this text. See Eugene F. Brigham and Louis C. Gapenski, *Intermediate Financial Management,* 2nd ed., Chapter 7, for a discussion.

[2]The most difficult part of the capital budgeting process is the estimation of the relevant cash flows. For simplicity, the net cash flows are treated as a given in this chapter, which allows us to focus on our main idea of concern, the capital budgeting decision rules. However, in Chapter 9 we will discuss cash flow estimation in detail. Also, note that *working capital* is defined as the firm's current assets, and that *net working capital* is current assets minus current liabilities.

Finally, we assume that all cash flows occur at the end of the designated year. Incidentally, the S stands for *short* and the L for *long:* Project S is a short-term project in the sense that its cash inflows tend to come in sooner than L's.

Payback Period

The *payback period,* defined as the expected number of years required to recover the original investment, was the first formal method used to evaluate capital budgeting projects. When applied to Projects S and L, the payback period is $2\frac{1}{3}$ years for S and $3\frac{1}{3}$ years for L:[3]

$$\text{Payback}_S: 2\frac{1}{3} \text{ years.}$$

$$\text{Payback}_L: 3\frac{1}{3} \text{ years.}$$

If the firm required a payback of three years or less, Project S would be accepted, but Project L would be rejected. If the projects were *mutually exclusive,* S would be ranked over L because S has the shorter payback.[4]

Some firms use a variant of the regular payback, the *discounted payback period,* which is similar to the regular payback period except that the expected cash flows are discounted by the project's cost of capital.[5] Thus, the discounted payback period is defined as the number of years required to recover the investment from

---

[3]The easiest way to calculate the payback period is to accumulate the project's net cash flows and see when they sum to zero. For example, the annual and cumulative net cash flows of Project S are shown below:

Year (t)	S's Net Cash Flows Annual	S's Net Cash Flows Cumulative
0	($1,000)	($1,000)
1	500	(500)
2	400	(100)
3	300	200
4	100	300

Thus, the investment is recovered by the end of Year 3. Assuming that cash flows occur evenly during the year, the recovery actually occurs one-third of the way into Year 3: $100 remains to be recovered at the end of Year 2, and since Year 3 produces $300 in net cash flow, the payback period for Project S is $2\frac{1}{3}$ years.

[4]*Mutually exclusive* means that if one project is taken on, the other must be rejected. For example, the installation of a conveyor-belt system in a warehouse and the purchase of a fleet of forklift trucks for the same warehouse would be mutually exclusive projects — accepting one implies rejection of the other. *Independent* projects are projects whose cash flows are independent of one another.

[5]The project's cost of capital reflects (1) the marginal cost of capital to the firm and (2) the differential risk between the firm's existing projects and the project being evaluated. This concept will be discussed in detail in Chapter 10.

Table 8-2
Discounted Cash Flows for Projects S and L

| Year (t) | Discounted Net Cash Flows | | | |
| | Project S | | Project L | |
	Annual	Cumulative	Annual	Cumulative
0	($1,000)	($1,000)	($1,000)	($1,000)
1	455	(545)	91	(909)
2	331	(214)	248	(661)
3	225	11	301	(360)
4	68	79	410	50

discounted net cash flows. Table 8-2 contains the discounted net cash flows for Projects S and L, assuming a 10 percent cost of capital. To construct Table 8-2, each cash inflow in Table 8-1 is divided by $(1 + k)^t = (1.10)^t$, where t is the year in which the cash flow occurs and k is the project's cost of capital. After 3 years, Project S will have generated $1,011 in discounted cash inflows. Since the cost is $1,000, the discounted payback is just under 3 years, or, to be precise, $2 + ($214/$225) = 2.95$ years. Project L's discounted payback is 3.88 years. Thus,

$$\text{Discounted payback}_S: 2.0 + 214/225 = 2.95 \text{ years.}$$

$$\text{Discounted payback}_L: 3.0 + 360/410 = 3.88 \text{ years.}$$

For Projects S and L, the rankings are the same regardless of which payback method is used; that is, Project S is preferred to Project L, and Project S would still be selected if the firm were to require a payback of three years or less. However, it is possible for the regular and the discounted paybacks to produce conflicting rankings.

Note that the payback is a type of "breakeven" calculation in the sense that if cash flows come in at the expected rate until the payback year, then the project will break even in an accounting sense. However, the regular payback does not take account of the cost of capital — the cost of the debt and equity used to undertake the project is not reflected in the cash flows or the calculation. The discounted payback does take account of capital costs — it shows the breakeven year after covering debt and equity costs. However, as we shall see, both payback methods have serious deficiencies, especially the fact that they take no account of any cash flows beyond the payback year. Therefore, other procedures are more likely to lead to correct project selections.

It should be noted, however, that the payback period does provide information on how long funds will be tied up in a project. Thus, the shorter the payback period, other things held constant, the greater the project's liquidity. Also, cash flows expected in the distant future are generally regarded as being riskier than near-term cash flows. Therefore, the payback is often used as a rough measure of both the liquidity and the riskiness of a project.

Net Present Value (NPV)

As the flaws in the payback method were recognized, people began to search for methods to improve the effectiveness of project evaluations. One such method is the *net present value (NPV)* method. To implement this approach, one proceeds as follows:

1. Find the present value of each cash flow, including both inflows and outflows, discounted at the project's cost of capital.

2. Sum these discounted cash flows; this sum is defined as the project's NPV.

3. If the NPV is positive, the project should be accepted; if the NPV is negative, it should be rejected; and if two projects are mutually exclusive, the one with the higher positive NPV should be chosen.

The NPV can be expressed as follows:

$$\text{NPV} = \sum_{t=0}^{n} \frac{CF_t}{(1 + k)^t} = \sum_{t=0}^{n} CF_t(PVIF_{k,t}). \tag{8-1}$$

Here CF_t is the expected net cash flow in Period t, and k is the project's cost of capital.[6] Cash outflows (expenditures on the project, such as the cost of buying equipment or building factories) are treated as *negative* cash flows. In evaluating Projects S and L, only CF_0 is negative, but for many large projects such as the Alaska Pipeline, an electric generating plant, or IBM's new Sierra series of computers, outflows occur for several years before operations begin and cash flows turn positive. Also, note that Equation 8-1 is quite general, so inflows and outflows could occur on any basis, say quarterly or monthly, and t could represent quarters or months rather than years.

At a 10 percent cost of capital, the NPV of Project S is $78.82:

$$\begin{aligned}
\text{NPV}_S &= \frac{-\$1,000}{(1.10)^0} + \frac{\$500}{(1.10)^1} + \frac{\$400}{(1.10)^2} + \frac{\$300}{(1.10)^3} + \frac{\$100}{(1.10)^4} \\
&= -\$1,000 + \$454.55 + \$330.58 + \$225.39 + \$68.30 \\
&= \$78.82.
\end{aligned}$$

By a similar process, we find $\text{NPV}_L = \$49.18$. On this basis, both projects should be accepted if they are independent, but S should be the one chosen if they are mutually exclusive. (Note: With many financial calculators, you input the five cash flows, enter i = 10, and press the NPV key to find the net present value.)

Rationale for the NPV Method

The rationale for the NPV method is straightforward. The value of a firm is the sum of the values of its parts. If a firm takes on a zero-NPV project, the wealth of the current stockholders is unchanged — the firm becomes larger by the amount of investment, but the value of its stock remains constant. However, if the firm takes

---

[6]In Equation 8-1, we assume that the project's cost of capital, k, is constant across all periods. For a discussion of nonconstant capital costs, see Eugene F. Brigham and Louis C. Gapenski, *Intermediate Financial Management*, 2nd ed., Chapter 7.

on a project with a positive NPV, the position of the current stockholders is improved. In our example, current stockholders' wealth would increase by $78.82 if the firm takes on Project S, but by only $49.18 if it takes on Project L. Thus, it is easy to see why S is preferred to L, and it is also easy to see the logic of the NPV approach.[7]

Internal Rate of Return (IRR)

In Chapter 5, we presented procedures for finding the yield to maturity, or rate of return, on a bond — if you invest in the bond and hold it to maturity, you will earn the YTM on the money you invested. Exactly the same concepts are employed in capital budgeting when the IRR method is used. *The IRR is defined as that discount rate, r, which equates the present value of a project's expected cash inflows to the present value of the project's expected costs:*

$$\text{PV inflows} = \text{PV investment costs.}$$

This is equivalent to

$$\sum_{t=0}^{n} \frac{CF_t}{(1 + r)^t} = 0,$$
(8-2)

which can also be written as

$$\sum_{t=0}^{n} CF_t(PVIF_{r,t}) = 0.$$

For our Project S, here is the set-up:

$$\frac{-\$1,000}{(1 + r)^0} + \frac{\$500}{(1 + r)^1} + \frac{\$400}{(1 + r)^2} + \frac{\$300}{(1 + r)^3} + \frac{\$100}{(1 + r)^4} = 0,$$

or

$$-\$1,000 + \$500(PVIF_{r,1}) + \$400(PVIF_{r,2}) + \$300(PVIF_{r,3}) + \$100(PVIF_{r,4}) = 0.$$

Here we know the value of each CF_t, but we do not know the value of r. Thus, we have an equation with one unknown, and we can solve for the value of r. *The solution value of r is defined as the IRR.*

---

[7]This description of the process is somewhat oversimplified. Both analysts and investors anticipate that firms will identify and accept positive NPV projects, and stock prices reflect these expectations. Thus, stock prices react to announcements of new capital projects only to the extent that such projects were not already expected. In this sense, we may think of a firm's value as consisting of two parts: (1) the value of its existing assets and (2) the value of its "growth opportunities," or projects with positive NPVs. AT&T is a good example of this: the company has the world's largest long-distance network plus telephone manufacturing facilities, both of which provide earnings and cash flows, and it has Bell Labs, which has the *potential* for coming up with new products in the computer/telecommunication area that could be extremely profitable. Security analysts (and investors) thus analyze AT&T as a company with a set of cash-producing assets plus a set of growth opportunities that will materialize if and only if it can come up with positive NPV projects through its capital budgeting process.

Notice that the internal rate of return formula, Equation 8-2, is simply the NPV formula, Equation 8-1, solved for the particular discount rate that forces the NPV to equal zero. Thus, the same basic equation is used for both methods, but in the NPV method the discount rate, k, is specified and the NPV is found, whereas in the IRR method the NPV is specified to equal zero and the value of r = IRR that forces this equality is determined.

Equation 8-2 can be solved in several ways:

1. Trial-and-error. Substitute in different values for r until you find the value of r that forces the NPV to equal zero. This would be an extremely tedious and inefficient process.

2. Newton's method or similar procedures. One can select values of r in a systematic manner such that the equation quickly converges on zero. Newton's method for solving polynomial equations, which is discussed in math books, is one such procedure, and it is often used in calculators and computers to solve IRR problems quickly and efficiently. We explain the basis of Newton's method later in this chapter.

3. Financial calculators/computers. Better financial calculators and computer spreadsheet packages such as *Lotus 1-2-3* have IRR functions which solve Equation 8-2 rapidly. (Very rapidly with a computer, and after several seconds with a calculator.) Simply input the cash flows, and the computer or calcultor uses Newton's method or a similar algorithm to find the IRR.

Since internal rates of return can be calculated very easily with financial calculators and/or computers, most firms have now computerized their capital budgeting processes and automatically generate IRRs, NPVs, and paybacks for all projects. (See Problem 8-2 at the end of this chapter.) Thus, businesses have no difficulty whatever with the mechanical side of capital budgeting, and a serious business student should have a financial calculator capable of finding IRRs. All IRRs reported hereafter in this and the following chapters were obtained by using a financial calculator (or a PC). By keying in the cash flows and then pressing the IRR button, we find that Project S has $IRR_S = 14.5\%$, while $IRR_L = 11.8\%$. If both projects have a cost of capital of 10 percent, the internal rate of return rule indicates that if the projects are independent, both should be accepted — they both are expected to earn more than the cost of the capital needed to finance them. If they are mutually exclusive, S ranks higher and should be accepted, while L should be rejected. If the cost of capital is more than 14.5 percent, both projects should be rejected.

Rationale for the IRR Method

Why is the particular discount rate that equates a project's cost with the present value of its receipts (the IRR) so special? To answer this question, let us first assume that our illustrative firm obtains the $1,000 needed to take on Project S by borrowing from a bank at an interest rate of 14.5 percent. Since the internal rate of return was calculated to be 14.5 percent, the same as the cost of the bank loan, the firm can invest in the project, use the cash flows generated by the investment

Table 8-3
Analysis of Project S's IRR as a Loan Rate

Beginning Loan Balance (1)	Cash Flow (2)	Interest on the Loan at 14.5% $0.145 \times (1) = (3)$	Repayment of Principal $(2) - (3) = (4)$	Ending Loan Balance $(1) - (4) = (5)$
$1,000.00	$500	$145.00	$355.00	$645.00
645.00	400	93.53	306.47	338.53
338.53	300	49.09	250.91	87.62
87.62	100	12.70	87.30	0.32

to pay off the principal and interest on the loan, and come out exactly even on the transaction. This point is demonstrated in Table 8-3, which shows that Project S provides cash flows that are just sufficient to pay 14.5 percent interest on the unpaid balance of the bank loan, retire the loan over the life of the project, and end up with a balance that differs from zero only by a rounding error of 32 cents.

If the internal rate of return exceeds the cost of the funds used to finance a project, a surplus remains after paying for the capital, and this surplus accrues to the firm's stockholders. Therefore, taking on a project whose IRR exceeds its cost of capital increases the value of the firm's stock. On the other hand, if the internal rate of return is less than the cost of capital, then taking on the project imposes a cost on existing stockholders. It is this "breakeven" characteristic that makes the IRR useful in evaluating capital projects.[8]

Profitability Index

Another method used to evaluate projects is the *profitability index (PI)*, or the *benefit/cost ratio,* as it is sometimes called:

$$PI = \frac{PV \text{ benefits}}{PV \text{ costs}} = \frac{\sum_{t=0}^{n} \dfrac{CIF_t}{(1 + k)^t}}{\sum_{t=0}^{n} \dfrac{COF_t}{(1 + k)^t}} = \frac{\sum_{t=0}^{n} CIF_t (PVIF_{k,t})}{\sum_{t=0}^{n} COF_t (PVIF_{k,t})}. \tag{8-3}$$

Here, CIF_t represents the expected cash inflows, or benefits, and COF_t represents the expected cash outflows, or costs. The PI shows the *relative* profitability of any project, or the present value of benefits per dollar of costs. The PI for Project S, based on a 10 percent cost of capital, is 1.079:

$$PI_S = \frac{\$1,078.82}{\$1,000} = 1.079.$$

---

[8]This example illustrates the logic of the IRR method, but for technical correctness, the capital used to finance the project should be assumed to come from both debt and equity, and not from debt alone.

Similarly, $PI_L = 1.049$. A project is acceptable if its PI is greater than 1.0, and the higher the PI, the higher is the project's ranking. Therefore, both S and L would be accepted by the PI criterion if they were independent, and S would be ranked ahead of L if they were mutually exclusive.

Mathematically, the NPV, the IRR, and the PI methods must always lead to the same accept/reject decisions for independent projects: If a project's NPV is positive, then (1) its IRR must exceed k and (2) its PI must be greater than 1.0. However, NPV, IRR, and PI can give conflicting rankings for mutually exclusive projects. This point will be discussed in more detail later in the chapter.

EVALUATION OF THE DECISION RULES

We have presented four possible capital budgeting rules, all of which are used to a greater or lesser extent in practice, and we shall discuss a fifth method later in the chapter. However, the methods can lead to different capital budgeting decisions, so we need to answer this question: Which method is best, where "best" is defined as the method that selects the set of projects which maximizes the firm's value and hence its shareholders' wealth. If more than one method does this, then the best method would be the one that is easiest to use in practice.

There are three properties which must be exhibited by a selection method if it is to lead to consistently correct capital budgeting decisions:

1. The method must consider all cash flows throughout the entire life of a project.

2. The method must consider the time value of money; that is, it must reflect the fact that dollars which come in sooner are more valuable than distant dollars.

3. When the method is used to select from a set of mutually exclusive projects, it must choose that project which maximizes the firm's stock price.

How do the various methods stand in regard to the required properties? Both the regular and the discounted paybacks violate Property 1 — they do not consider all cash flows. Additionally, the undiscounted payback also violates Property 2. The NPV, IRR, and PI methods all satisfy Properties 1 and 2, and all three lead to identical (and correct) accept/reject decisions for independent projects. However, only the NPV method satisfies Property 3 under all conditions: There are certain conditions under which the IRR and the PI methods fail to identify correctly that project, within a set of mutually exclusive projects, which maximizes the firm's stock price. This point is explored in depth in the following sections.

COMPARISON OF THE NPV AND IRR METHODS

We have noted that the NPV method exhibits all the desired decision rule properties and, as such, is the best method for evaluating projects. Because the NPV method is better than IRR and PI, we were tempted to explain NPV only, to state that it should be used as the acceptance criterion, and to go on to the next topic.

However, the IRR and PI methods are familiar to many corporate executives, and they are widely entrenched in industry. Indeed, surveys continually show that business executives prefer the IRR method to the NPV approach, apparently because they think in terms of rates of return rather than dollars of NPV. Therefore, it is important that finance students thoroughly understand the IRR and PI methods and be prepared to explain why, at times, a project with a lower IRR or PI may be preferable to one with a higher IRR or PI.

NPV Profiles

A graph which relates a project's NPV to the discount rate used to calculate the NPV is defined as the project's *net present value profile;* profiles for Projects L and S are shown in Figure 8-1. To construct the profiles, we first note that at a zero discount rate, the NPV is simply the sum of the undiscounted cash flows of the project; thus, at a zero discount rate $NPV_S = \$300$, and $NPV_L = \$400$. These values are plotted as the vertical axis intercepts in Figure 8-1. Next, we calculate the projects' NPVs at three discount rates, say 5, 10, and 15 percent, and plot these values. The four points plotted on our graphs are shown at the bottom of the figure.

Recall that the IRR is defined as the discount rate at which a project's NPV equals zero. Therefore, *the point where its net present value profile crosses the horizontal axis indicates a project's internal rate of return.* Since we calculated IRR_S and IRR_L in an earlier section, we have two other points which we can use in plotting the projects' NPV profiles.

When we connect the plot points, we have the net present value profiles.[9] NPV profiles are useful in project analysis, and we will use them often in the remainder of the chapter.

NPV Rankings Depend on the Discount Rate

We saw in Figure 8-1 that the NPV profiles of both Project L and Project S decline as the discount rate increases. However, notice in the figure that Project L has the higher NPV at low discount rates, but NPV_S exceeds NPV_L if the discount rate is above 7.2 percent. Notice also that Project L's NPV is "more sensitive" to changes in the discount rate than is NPV_S; that is, Project L's net present value profile has

---

[9]Notice that the NPV profiles are curved — they are *not* straight lines. Also, the NPVs approach the $t = 0$ cash flow (the cost of the project) as the discount rate increases without limit. The reason is that, at an infinitely high discount rate, the PV of the inflows would be zero, so $NPV = CF_0$, which in our example is $-\$1,000$. We should also note that under certain conditions the NPV profiles can cross the horizontal axis several times, or never cross it. This point is discussed later in the chapter.

Figure 8-1 can also be used to explain the logic of Newton's Method for calculating IRRs. Under that method, we first pick an arbitrary discount rate, say $r = 0\%$, and calculate the NPV. Then calculate the NPV at a very slightly higher r, say $r = 0.0001\%$. Then (using geometry) find the line that connects those two NPVs, which is essentially the line tangent to the NPV profile at $r = 0$. Then extend the tangent line to the X-axis, and observe the r value where the tangent line intersects the X-axis. Use that r to find a third NPV, and use the new $r + 0.0001\%$ to find a fourth NPV, and repeat the process. Very quickly (in 3 or 4 trials), you will be at the value of r where $NPV = 0$.

Figure 8-1
Net Present Value Profiles:
NPVs of Projects S and L at Different Discount Rates

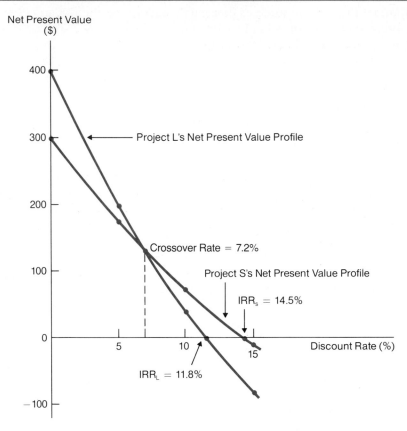

Discount Rate	NPV$_S$	NPV$_L$
0%	$300.00	$400.00
5	180.42	206.50
10	78.80	49.15
15	(8.33)	(80.13)

the steeper slope, indicating that a change in k has a larger effect on NPV$_L$ than on NPV$_S$.

To see why L has the greater sensitivity, recall first that the cash flows from S are received faster than those from L; in a payback sense, S is a short-term project, while L is a long-term project. Next, recall the equation for the NPV:

$$NPV = \frac{CF_0}{(1+k)^0} + \frac{CF_1}{(1+k)^1} + \frac{CF_2}{(1+k)^2} + \frac{CF_3}{(1+k)^3} + \frac{CF_4}{(1+k)^4}.$$

Now notice that the denominators of the terms in this equation increase as k and t increase, and the increase is exponential, so the effect of a higher k is more pronounced if t is larger. To understand this point more clearly, consider the following data:

PV of a $100 cash flow due in 1 year, discounted at 5%	$95.24
PV of a $100 cash flow due in 1 year, discounted at 10%	$90.91
Percentage decline in PV resulting from doubling k when t = 1	− 4.5%
PV of a $100 cash flow due in 10 years, discounted at 5%	$61.39
PV of a $100 cash flow due in 10 years, discounted at 10%	$38.55
Percentage decline in PV resulting from doubling k when t = 10	− 37.2%

A doubling of the discount rate causes only a slight decline in the PV of a Year 1 cash flow, but the same increase in the discount rate causes the PV of a Year 10 cash flow to fall by 37 percent. Thus, if a project has most of its cash flows coming in the early years, its NPV will not be lowered very much by a discount rate increase, but a project whose cash flows come later will be severely penalized by high discount rates. Accordingly, Project L, which has most of its cash flows in the later years, is hurt badly when the discount rate is high, while Project S, which has relatively rapid cash flows, is less affected by rising discount rates.

Independent Projects

If two projects are *independent,* then the NPV and IRR criteria always lead to the same accept/reject decision. if NPV says accept, IRR also says accept. To see why this is so, look back at Figure 8-1 and focus on Project L. Notice (1) that the IRR criterion for acceptance is that the project's cost of capital is less than (or to the left of) the IRR, and (2) that whenever the project's cost of capital is less than the IRR, its NPV is positive. Thus, for any cost of capital less than 11.8 percent, Project L is acceptable by both the NPV and the IRR criteria, while both methods reject the project if the cost of capital is greater than 11.8 percent. Project S — and all other independent projects under consideration — could be analyzed similarly, and it will always turn out that if the project's IRR is greater than k, then its NPV is also greater than 0. Thus, if a project is acceptable by the IRR criterion, then it must also be acceptable by the NPV criterion.

Mutually Exclusive Projects

Now assume that Projects S and L are *mutually exclusive,* rather than independent. That is, we can choose either Project S or Project L, or we can reject both, but we cannot accept both projects. Notice in Figure 8-1 that, as long as the cost of capital is *greater than* the crossover rate of 7.2 percent, then (1) NPV_S is greater than NPV_L and (2) IRR_S is also greater than IRR_L. Therefore, if k is greater than the crossover rate of 7.2 percent, then the two methods must lead to the selection of the same project. However, if the cost of capital is *less than* the crossover rate, the NPV method ranks Project L higher, but the IRR method indicates that Project S is better. Thus, a conflict exists: NPV says choose mutually exclusive L, while IRR says take S. Which answer is correct? Logic suggests that the NPV method is best, since it selects that project which adds the most to shareholder wealth.

Conditions Required for Conflict

There are two basic conditions which cause NPV profiles to cross, and thus which lead to potential conflicts between NPV and IRR: (1) the *projects differ in size (or scale),* meaning that the cost of one project is larger than that of the other, or (2) they differ in the *time patterns of cash flows,* meaning that the cash flows of one project come in relatively early vis-à-vis the cash flows of the other project, as occurred with Projects L and S.[10]

When either size or timing differences occur, the firm will have different amounts of funds to invest in the various years, depending on which of the two mutually exclusive projects it chooses. For example, if one project costs more than the other, then the firm will have additional funds to invest at t = 0 if it selects the smaller project. Similarly, for projects of equal size, the one with the larger early cash inflows provides more funds for reinvestment in the early years. Given this situation, the rate of return at which differential cash flows can be invested becomes quite important.

THE REINVESTMENT RATE (OPPORTUNITY COST) ASSUMPTION

Conflicts between mutually exclusive projects arise as a result of scale- or timing-induced cash flow differentials. Therefore, the critical issue in resolving conflicts between mutually exclusive projects is this: Of what benefit is it to have cash flows earlier rather than later? The answer depends on what the firm can do with the additional funds, or the *opportunity cost rate* at which the firm can invest differential early years' cash flows. *The use of the NPV method implicitly assumes that the opportunity cost rate at which cash flows generated by a project can be reinvested is the cost of capital, whereas use of the IRR method implies that the firm*

---

[10]Of course, it is possible for mutually exclusive projects to differ with respect to both scale and timing. Also, if mutually exclusive projects have different lives (as opposed to different cash flow patterns over a common life), this introduces further complications, and for meaningful comparisons, some mutually exclusive projects must be evaluated over a common life. This point is discussed in Chapter 9. For a number of specific examples of size and timing conflicts, see Eugene F. Brigham and Louis C. Gapenski, *Intermediate Financial Management,* 2nd ed., Chapter 7, and also see Problems 8-3 and 8-4 at the end of this chapter.

has the opportunity to reinvest at the IRR. These assumptions are inherent in the mathematics of the discounting process.[11] Thus, the NPV method evaluates cash flows at the cost of capital, while the IRR method evaluates cash flows at the project's IRR. The cash flows may actually be withdrawn as dividends by the stockholders and spent on beer and pizza, but the assumption of a reinvestment opportunity is still implicit in IRR and NPV calculations.

Which is the better assumption, reinvestment at the cost of capital or reinvestment of each project's cash flows at that project's IRR? We can answer the question as follows:

1. Assume that the firm's cost of capital is 10 percent. Management can obtain all the funds it wants at this rate so long as it invests in projects whose risk is similar to that of its existing assets. This condition is expected to hold in the future.

2. The capital budgeting process calls for all potential projects to be evaluated at k = 10%. All projects with NPV > 0 are accepted. Plenty of capital is available at a 10 percent cost to finance these projects, both now and in the future.

3. As cash flows come in from past investments, what will be done with them? These cash flows can either (a) be paid back to the equity and debt investors who supplied the capital and who, on average, require a 10 percent rate of return, or (b) be used as a substitute for outside capital that costs 10 percent. Thus, since the cash flows are expected to either yield investors or save the firm 10 percent, this is their opportunity cost reinvestment rate.

4. The IRR method implicitly assumes that funds are reinvested at the internal rate of return itself. However, given (a) ready access to capital markets and (b) a constant expected future cost of capital, the appropriate reinvestment rate is the opportunity cost of capital, or 10 percent. Therefore, even if the firm takes on projects in the future whose IRRs average some high rate, say 30 percent, this is not the reinvestment rate — those projects could always be financed with new external capital costing 10 percent, so cash flows from past projects have an opportunity cost reinvestment rate which is only equal to the cost of capital.

---

[11]In both the NPV and IRR formulas, cash flows are discounted back to the present. Note, though, that the discounting process implicitly assumes that the opportunity exists to reinvest cash flows at whatever discount rate, k, is being used. For example, when you found the NPV of Project S to be $78.82, you were implicitly assuming that cash flows could be reinvested at the cost of capital, 10 percent, and when you found $IRR_S = 14.5\%$, you were assuming that cash flows could be reinvested to earn 14.5 percent. To see why this is so, recall the definition of present value as given in Chapter 4:

The present value of a sum due in n years is the amount which, if it were on hand today and were invested at the rate k, would grow to equal the future amount:

$$FV_n = PV(1 + k)^n$$

$$PV = \frac{FV_n}{(1 + k)^n}$$

There is simply no way to think about future values without thinking about the rate at which cash flows can be reinvested, and there is no way to define present values except in terms of future values. Therefore, both present values and future values depend upon the rate at which cash flows can be reinvested.

5. Note also that the use of the IRR method assumes that the cash flows from each project will be reinvested at the project's own IRR. Thus, if a firm is considering 1,000 different projects, use of the IRR method implicitly assumes that 1,000 different reinvestment rates exist. Following the arguments just set forth, it would seem illogical to argue that 1,000 different opportunity cost rates exist.

As a result of all this, we simply must come to the conclusion that *the correct reinvestment rate assumption is the cost of capital, which is implicit in the NPV method.* This, in turn, leads us to prefer the NPV method, at least for firms willing and able to obtain capital at a cost reasonably close to their current cost of capital. In Chapter 10, when we discuss capital rationing, we will see that under certain conditions the NPV rule may be questionable, but for most firms at most times, NPV is without a doubt conceptually better than IRR.

We should reiterate that, when projects are independent, the NPV and IRR methods both lead to exactly the same accept/reject decision. However, *when evaluating mutually exclusive projects, the NPV method is better.* We should also note that there is one other situation in which the IRR approach may not be usable — this is when evaluating "nonnormal" projects. A *normal* capital project is one that has one or more cash outflows (costs) followed by a series of cash inflows. If, however, a project calls for a large cash outflow either sometime during or at the end of its life, then it is defined as a *nonnormal* project. Nonnormal projects can present unique difficulties when evaluated by the IRR method. The most common problem encountered when evaluating nonnormal projects is multiple IRRs, which we discuss later in the chapter.

MODIFIED INTERNAL RATE OF RETURN (IRR*)

In spite of a strong academic preference for the NPV, surveys indicate that business executives prefer the IRR over the NPV by a margin of 3 to 1. Apparently, managers find it intuitively more appealing to analyze investments in terms of percentage rates of return than dollars of NPV. Given this fact, can we devise a percentage evaluator that is better than the regular IRR? The answer is yes — we can modify the IRR and make it a better indicator of relative profitability, and hence better for use in capital budgeting. The new measure is called the *modified IRR, or IRR*,* and it is defined as follows:

$$\text{PV costs} = \text{PV terminal value}$$

$$\sum_{t=0}^{n} \frac{COF_t}{(1+k)^t} = \frac{\sum_{t=0}^{n} CIF_t(1+k)^{n-t}}{(1+IRR^*)^n} \tag{8-2a}$$

$$\text{PV costs} = \frac{TV}{(1+IRR^*)^n}.$$

Here COF refers to cash outflows, or the cost of the project, and CIF refers to cash inflows. The left term is simply the PV of the investment outlays when discounted at the cost of capital, and the numerator of the right term is the future value of the inflows, assuming that the cash inflows are reinvested at the cost of capital. The compounded sum in the numerator is also called the *terminal value,* or *TV.* The discount rate that forces the PV of the costs to equal the PV of the TV is defined as IRR*.

If the investment costs are all incurred at t = 0, and if the first operating inflow occurs at t = 1, as is true for our illustrative Projects S and L, then this equation may be used:

$$\text{Cost} = \frac{TV}{(1 + IRR^*)^n} = \frac{\sum_{t=1}^{n} CIF_t(1 + k)^{n-t}}{(1 + IRR^*)^n}. \qquad \text{(8-2b)}$$

We can illustrate the calculation with Project S:

$$\$1,000 = \frac{\$500(1.10)^{4-1} + \$400(1.10)^{4-2} + \$300(1.10)^{4-3} + \$100(1.10)^{4-4}}{(1 + IRR^*)^4}$$

$$= \frac{\$665.50 + \$484.00 + \$330.00 + \$100.00}{(1 + IRR^*)^4} = \frac{\$1,579.50}{(1 + IRR^*)^4}.$$

Using a financial calculator, enter PV = 1,000, FV = 1,579.5 (or −1,579.5), and n = 4, and press the i button to find IRR*$_S$ = 12.1%. Similarly, we find IRR*$_L$ = 11.3%.

The modified IRR has a significant advantage over the regular IRR. IRR* assumes that cash flows from all projects are reinvested at the cost of capital, while the regular IRR assumes that the cash flows from each project are reinvested at the project's own IRR. Since reinvestment at k is generally more correct, the modified IRR is a better indicator of a project's true profitability.

Is IRR* as good as NPV for selecting among competing (mutually exclusive) projects? If the two projects are of equal size, then NPV and IRR* will always lead to the same project selection decision. Thus, for any projects like our Projects S and L, if NPV$_S$ > NPV$_L$, then IRR*$_S$ > IRR*$_L$ and the kinds of conflicts we encountered between NPV and the regular IRR will not occur. However, if the projects differ in scale (or size), then conflicts can still occur—if we were comparing a large project with a small mutually exclusive one, then we might find NPV$_L$ > NPV$_S$, but IRR*$_S$ > IRR*$_L$.

Our conclusion is that the modified IRR is superior to the regular IRR as an indicator of a project's "true" rate of return, or "expected long-term rate of return," but the NPV method is still better for choosing among competing projects that differ in scale, because it provides a better indicator of how much the projects increase the value of the firm.

We can close this section by asking this question: "Which would most firms prefer, a 30 percent return on a $10 million investment or a 100 percent return on a $1 investment?" Most would prefer the large project with the lower return. NPV would lead to that choice, but both IRR or IRR* would select the smaller project.

COMPARISON OF THE NPV AND PI METHODS

The PI method, where PI = PV cash inflows/PV investment cost, measures the present value of benefits per dollar of investment, whereas the NPV measures the total dollars of net present value. These two methods can lead to conflicts when used to evaluate mutually exclusive projects. To illustrate, suppose a firm is comparing Project L (for large), which requires a $5 million investment and returns $6 million after 1 year, with Project S (for small), which requires an outlay of $100,00 and returns $130,000 at the end of 1 year. Both projects have average risk and hence will be evaluated at the firm's 10 percent cost of capital. Here are the projects' NPVs and PIs:

$$\text{NPV}_L = -\$5,000,000 + \$6,000,000/1.10 = \$454,545.$$

$$\text{NPV}_S = -\$100,000 + \$130,000/1.10 = \$18,182.$$

$$\text{PI}_L = (\$6,000,000/1.10)/\$5,000,000 = 1.09.$$

$$\text{PI}_S = (\$130,000/1.10)/\$100,000 = 1.18.$$

Thus, the NPV method indicates that we should accept Project L because $\text{NPV}_L > \text{NPV}_S$, but the PI method indicates that Project S is preferable, because $\text{PI}_S > \text{PI}_L$.

Given this conflict, which project should be accepted? Remembering that shareholders' wealth increases by the NPV of a project, it is clear that Project L contributes most to shareholder wealth, so L should be selected over S. Thus, for a firm that seeks to maximize stockholders' wealth, the NPV method is better. Of course, if the projects were independent, both would be chosen, since both projects have positive NPVs and hence positive PIs.

In general, the NPV method leads to better decisions than does the PI method. However, the PI may be useful when capital rationing exists. We explore this topic in Appendix 10A.

PRESENT VALUE OF FUTURE COSTS

Often, firms make decisions on mutually exclusive projects on the basis of the present value of future costs rather than on the basis of the projects' NPVs. For example, Du Pont recently evaluated several different methods for disposing of wastes at one of its processing plants. The choice of disposal system would have no effect on either the prices or the quantity of products produced by the plant — these would be set in the competitive marketplace. Therefore, the revenue stream would be the same regardless of which waste disposal process was selected, so revenues can be disregarded in this capital budgeting decision.

Since the revenue stream would be the same, Du Pont could make the decision on the basis of expected future costs alone, choosing the process that would do the job for the lowest cost. Table 8-4 contains the expected net costs for the best two processes over their 5-year expected lives. Process A requires a lower expenditure on capital equipment than B, but A is more labor intensive. Therefore, A's Year 0 cost is relatively low, but its operating costs are relatively high.

Table 8-4
Production Costs for Processes A and B

| | | Expected Net Cost | |
Year		Process A	Process B
0		($50,000)	($100,000)
1		(22,000)	(10,000)
2		(22,000)	(10,000)
3		(22,000)	(10,000)
4		(22,000)	(10,000)
5		(22,000)	(10,000)
PV(12%)		($129,305)	($136,048)

Du Pont's analysts regarded both processes as having about as much risk as an average project, and thus they used the firm's overall cost of capital, 12 percent, to discount the flows of each project. As shown in Table 8-4, Process A has a lower present value of future costs, so it was chosen. We will have more to say about discounting costs (or outflows) in Chapter 10, where we discuss risk adjustments.

MULTIPLE IRRs

A fairly common problem occurs when one uses the regular IRR method. In solving Equation 8-2,

$$\sum_{t=0}^{n} \frac{CF_t}{(1 + r)^t} = 0, \tag{8-2}$$

it is possible to obtain more than one positive value of r, which means there are multiple IRRs. Notice that Equation 8-2 is a polynomial of degree n, so it has n different roots, or solutions. All roots except one are either negative or imaginary numbers when investments are normal (one or more negative outflows followed by positive cash inflows), so in the normal case, only one positive value of r appears. However, the possibility of multiple real roots, and hence multiple IRRs, arises when the project is nonnormal (negative net cash flows occur after the project has gone into operation).

To illustrate this problem, suppose a firm is considering the expenditure of $1.6 million to develop a strip mine. The mine will produce a cash flow of $10 million at the end of Year 1. Then, at the end of Year 2, $10 million must be expended to restore the land to its original condition. Therefore, the project's expected net cash flows are as follows (in millions of dollars):

| | Expected Net Cash Flow | |
Year 0	End of Year 1	End of Year 2
− $1.6	+ $10	− $10

Figure 8-2
NPV Profile for Project M

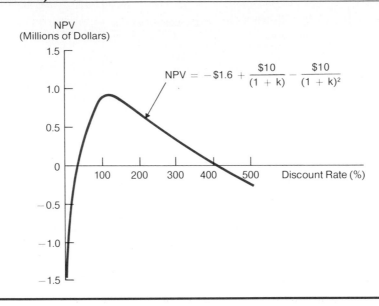

These values can be substituted into Equation 8-2:

$$\frac{-\$1.6 \text{ million}}{(1 + r)^0} + \frac{\$10 \text{ million}}{(1 + r)^1} + \frac{-\$10 \text{ million}}{(1 + r)^2} = 0.$$

When solved, we find that NPV = 0 when r = 25% and also when r = 400%.[12] Therefore, the IRR of the investment is both 25 and 400 percent. This relationship is depicted graphically in Figure 8-2.[13] Note that no dilemma would arise if either the NPV method or the IRR* method were used; we would simply find NPV or IRR* and use them to evaluate the project. If Project M's cost of capital is 10 percent, then its NPV is − $0.77 million and the project should be rejected. Also,

---

[12]If you attempted to find the IRR of this project with most financial calculators, you would get an error message: this message always occurs if a project has more than one IRR. We actually found our project's IRRs using *Lotus 1-2-3* to calculate NPVs at a number of different values for k and then plotting the NPV profile. The intersections with the X-axis gave a good idea of the IRR values. Then we could either use trial and error or the *Lotus 1-2-3* IRR function to find the exact value of k which forces the equation to zero.

[13]Does Figure 8-2 suggest that the firm should try to *raise* its cost of capital to about 100 percent in order to maximize the NPV of the project? Certainly not. Logically, the firm should seek to *minimize* its cost of capital; this will cause the price of its stock to be maximized. Actions taken to raise the cost of capital might make this particular project look good, but those actions would be terribly harmful to the firm's more numerous normal projects. Only if the firm's cost of capital is high, in spite of efforts to keep it down, will the illustrative project have a positive NPV.

IRR* is -20.9 percent, and since it is less than the cost of capital, the IRR* method also indicates that the project should be rejected.

The author encountered a good example of problems caused by multiple internal rates of return when a major California bank *borrowed* funds from an insurance company and then used these funds (plus an initial investment of its own) to buy a number of jet engines, which it then leased to a major airline. The bank expected to receive positive net cash flows (lease payments plus tax savings minus interest on the insurance company loan) for a number of years, then several large negative cash flows as it repaid the insurance company loan, and, finally, a large inflow from the sale of the engines when the lease expired.[14]

The bank discovered two IRRs and wondered which was correct. It could not ignore the IRR and use the NPV method, since the lease was already on the books, and the bank's senior loan committee, as well as Federal Reserve bank examiners, wanted to know the return on the lease. We recommended that the bank use IRR*, discounting its cash outflows back to the initial decision point at the bank's cost of funds, and compounding its cash inflows forward to the end of the lease's life at that same rate, and then finding IRR* as the discount rate which equated the PV of the costs with the PV of the TV of the inflows. This procedure satisfied both the loan committee and the bank examiners.[15]

The examples just presented illustrate one problem, multiple IRRs, that can arise when the IRR criterion is used with a project that has nonnormal cash flows. Use of the IRR method on nonnormal cash flow projects could produce other problems, such as no IRR or an IRR which leads to an incorrect accept/reject decision. In all such cases, the NPV criterion could be easily applied, and this method leads to conceptually correct capital budgeting decisions. Also, note that IRR* avoids many of the regular IRR's problems.

THE POST-AUDIT

An important aspect of the capital budgeting process is the *post-audit*, which involves (1) comparing actual results with those predicted by the project's sponsors and (2) explaining why any differences occurred. For example, many firms require that the operating divisions send a monthly report for the first six months after a project goes into operation, and a quarterly report thereafter until the project's results are up to expectations. From then on, reports on the project are handled like those of other operations.

The post-audit has several purposes, including the following:

1. Improve forecasts. When decision makers systematically compare their projections to actual outcomes, there is a tendency for estimates to improve. Conscious or unconscious biases are observed and eliminated; new forecasting meth-

---

[14]The situation described here is a *leveraged lease*. See Chapter 16 for more on leveraged leases.

[15]For additional insights into the multiple root problem, see William H. Jean, "On Multiple Rates of Return," *Journal of Finance*, March 1968, 187–192.

ods are sought as the need for them becomes apparent; and people simply tend to do everything better, including forecasting, if they know that their actions are being monitored.

2. Improve operations. Businesses are run by people, and people can perform at higher or lower levels of efficiency. When a divisional team has made a forecast about a new installation, its members are, in a sense, putting their reputations on the line. If costs are above predicted levels, sales below expectations, and so on, then executives in production, sales, and other areas will strive to improve operations and to bring results into line with forecasts. In a discussion related to this point, an IBM executive made this statement: "You academicians worry only about making good decisions. In business, we also worry about making decisions good."

The post-audit is not a simple process. There are a number of factors that can cause complications. First, we must recognize that each element of the cash flow forecast is subject to uncertainty, so a percentage of all projects undertaken by any reasonably venturesome firm will necessarily go awry. This fact must be considered when appraising the performances of the operating executives who submit capital expenditure requests. Second, projects sometimes fail to meet expectations for reasons beyond the control of the operating executives and for reasons that no one could realistically be expected to anticipate. For example, the decline in oil prices in the mid-1980s adversely affected many energy-related projects, as well as real estate projects in Texas and other oil-producing areas. Third, it is often difficult to separate the operating results of one investment from those of a larger system. For example, while some projects stand alone and permit ready identification of costs and revenues, the actual cost savings that result from a new computer system may be very hard to measure. Fourth, if the post-audit process is not used with care, executives may be reluctant to suggest potentially profitable but risky projects. And fifth, the executives who were actually responsible for a given decision may have moved on by the time the results of long-term investments are known.

Because of these difficulties, some firms tend to play down the importance of the post-audit. However, observations of both businesses and governmental units suggest that the best-run and most successful organizations are the ones that put the greatest stress on post-audits. Accordingly, we regard the post-audit as being one of the most important elements in a good capital budgeting system.

SUMMARY

Capital budgeting is similar in principle to security valuation—future cash flows are estimated, risks are appraised and reflected in a project's cost of capital discount rate, all cash flows are put on a present value basis, and if a project's *net present value (NPV)* is positive, it is accepted. Alternatively, if a project's *internal rate of return (IRR or IRR*)* is greater than its cost of capital, it is accepted. Because of differing reinvestment rate assumptions, the NPV and IRR methods can lead to conflicts when evaluating *mutually exclusive* projects. When conflicts exist, they should, in general, be resolved in favor of the project with the higher NPV.

In outline form, the capital budgeting process centers around the following steps:

1. The expected future cash flows from a project are estimated. This involves estimating (a) the investment outlay required for the project and (b) the cash inflows over the project's projected life. Cash flow estimation is the most important, yet the most difficult, step in the capital budgeting process. It will be discussed in detail in the next chapter.

2. The riskiness inherent in the project is appraised. This important subject is taken up in Chapter 10.

3. The next step is to rank projects by their NPVs or IRRs, accepting those with NPV > 0 or IRR > the cost of capital. Conflicts between NPV and IRR rankings should be resolved in favor of the NPV. Some firms also calculate projects' *payback periods, profitability indices (PIs),* and *modified internal rates of return (IRR*).* The payback provides an indication of a project's risk and liquidity, because it shows how long the original capital will be "at risk." Therefore, firms often calculate projects' NPVs, IRRs, PIs, and IRR*s as measures of profitability, and their paybacks as risk/liquidity indicators.

Although this chapter has presented the basic elements of the capital budgeting process, there are many other aspects of this crucial topic. Some of the more important ones are discussed in the following two chapters.

Questions

8-1   Define each of the following terms:
   a. The capital budget
   b. Regular payback; discounted payback
   c. DCF techniques; net present value (NPV)
   d. Internal rate of return (IRR)
   e. Modified internal rate of return (IRR*)
   f. Profitability index (PI)
   g. NPV profile; crossover rate
   h. Independent projects; mutually exclusive projects
   i. Project cost of capital, or discount rate
   j. Post-audit
   k. Reinvestment rate assumption

8-2   How is a project classification scheme (for example, replacement, expansion into new markets, and so forth) used in the capital budgeting process?

8-3   Explain why the NPV of a relatively long-term project, defined as one where a high percentage of its cash flows is expected in the distant future, is more sensitive to changes in the cost of capital than is the NPV of a short-term project.

8-4   Explain why, if two mutually exclusive projects are being compared, the short-term project might have the higher ranking under the NPV criterion if the cost of capital is high, but the long-term project might be deemed better if the cost of capital is low. Would changes in the cost of capital ever cause a change in the IRR ranking of two such projects?

8-5   For independent projects, is it true that if PI > 1.0, then NPV > 0 and IRR > k? Prove it.

8-6   In what sense is a reinvestment rate assumption embodied in the NPV, IRR, and IRR* methods? What is the implicitly assumed reinvestment rate of each method?

Self-Test Problem

ST-1 (Project analysis) You are a financial analyst for Porter Electronics Company. The director of capital budgeting has asked you to analyze two proposed capital investments, Projects X and Y. Each project has a cost of $10,000, and the cost of capital for both projects is 12 percent. The projects' expected net cash flows are as follows:

	Expected Net Cash Flow	
Year	Project X	Project Y
0	($10,000)	($10,000)
1	6,500	3,500
2	3,000	3,500
3	3,000	3,500
4	1,000	3,500

    a. Calculate each project's payback, net present value (NPV), internal rate of return (IRR), modified internal rate of return (IRR*), and profitability index (PI).

    b. Which project, or projects, should be accepted if they are independent?

    c. Which project should be accepted if they are mutually exclusive?

    d. How might a change in the cost of capital produce a conflict between the NPV and IRR rankings of these two projects? At what values of k would this conflict exist? (Hint: Plot the NPV profiles.)

    e. Why does the conflict exist?

Problems

8-1   (Capital budgeting methods) Project S has a cost of $10,000 and is expected to produce benefits (cash flows) of $3,000 per year for five years. Project L costs $25,000 and is expected to produce cash flows of $7,400 per year for five years. Calculate the two projects' NPVs, IRRs, IRR*s, and PIs, assuming a cost of capital of 12 percent. Which project would be selected, assuming they are mutually exclusive, using each ranking method? Which should actually be selected?

8-2   (NPV and IRR analysis) Rivoli Products Company is considering two mutually exclusive investments. The projects' expected net cash flows are as follows:

	Expected Net Cash Flow	
Year	Project A	Project B
0	($300)	($405)
1	(387)	134
2	(193)	134
3	(100)	134
4	600	134
5	600	134
6	850	134
7	(180)	0

a. Construct NPV profiles for Projects A and B.

b. What is each project's IRR?

c. If you were told that each project's cost of capital is 10 percent, which project should be selected? If the cost of capital were 17 percent, what would the proper choice be?

d. What is each project's IRR* at a cost of capital of 10 percent? At k = 17%?

e. What is the crossover rate, and what is its significance?

(Do Parts f and g only if you are using the computerized diskette.)

f. Rivoli's management is confident of the projects' cash flows in Years 0 to 6 but is uncertain as to what the Year 7 cash flows will be for the two projects. Under a worst case scenario, Project A's Year 7 cash flow will be − $300 and B's will be − $150, while under a best case scenario, the cash flows will be − $70 and + $120 for Projects A and B, respectively. Answer Parts b through d using these new cash flows. Which project should be selected under each scenario?

g. Put the Year 7 cash flows back to − $180 for A and zero for B. Now change the cost of capital and observe what happens to NPV at k = 0%, 5%, 20%, and 400% (input as 4.0).

8-3   (Timing differences) The Jackson Exploration Company is considering two mutually exclusive plans for extracting oil on property for which it has mineral rights. Both plans call for the expenditure of $10,000,000 to drill development wells. Under Plan A, all the oil will be extracted in one year, producing a cash flow at t = 1 of $12,000,000, while under Plan B, cash flows will be $1,750,000 per year for 20 years.

a. What are the annual incremental cash flows that will be available to Jackson Exploration if it undertakes Plan B rather than Plan A? (Hint: Subtract Plan A's flows from B's.)

b. If Jackson Exploration accepts Plan A, then invests the extra cash generated at the end of Year 1, what rate of return (reinvestment rate) would cause the cash flows from reinvestment to equal the cash flows from Plan B?

c. Suppose a company has a cost of capital of 10 percent. Is it logical to assume that it would take on all available independent projects (of average risk) with returns greater than 10 percent? Further, if all available projects with returns greater than 10 percent have been taken, would this mean that cash flows from past investments would have an opportunity cost of only 10 percent, because all the firm could do with these cash flows would be to replace money that has a cost of 10 percent? Finally, does this imply that the cost of capital is the correct rate to assume for the reinvestment of a project's cash flows?

d. Construct NPV profiles for Plans A and B, identify each project's IRR, and indicate the crossover rate of return.

8-4   **(Scale differences)** The Maese Publishing Company is considering two mutually exclusive expansion plans. Plan A calls for the expenditure of $50 million on a large-scale, integrated plant which will provide an expected cash flow stream of $8 million per year for 20 years. Plan B calls for the expenditure of $15 million to build a somewhat less efficient, more labor intensive plant which has an expected cash flow stream of $3.4 million per year for 20 years. Maese's cost of capital is 10 percent.

a. Calculate each project's NPV and IRR.

b. Set up a Project Δ by showing the cash flows that will exist if Maese goes with the large plant rather than the smaller plant. What are the NPV and the IRR for this Project Δ?

c. Graph the NPV profiles for Plan A, Plan B, and Project Δ.

d. Give a logical explanation, based on reinvestment rates and opportunity costs, as to why the NPV method is better than the IRR method when the firm's cost of capital is constant at some value such as 10 percent.

8-5   **(Multiple rates of return)** The Stenardi Uranium Company is deciding whether or not it should open a strip mine, the net cost of which is $4.4 million. Net cash inflows are expected to be $27.7 million, all coming at the end of Year 1. The land must be returned to its natural state at a cost of $25 million, payable at the end of Year 2.

a. Plot the project's NPV profile.

b. Should the project be accepted if k = 8%? If k = 14%? Explain your reasoning.

c. Can you think of some other capital budgeting situations where negative cash flows during or at the end of the project's life might lead to multiple IRRs?

8-6   **(Multiple rates of return)** The Wolfe Development Company (WDC) has many excellent investment opportunities, but it has insufficient cash to undertake them all. Now WDC is offered the chance to borrow $2 million from the Pacific City Retirement Fund at 10 percent, the loan to be repaid at the end of one year. Also, a "consulting fee" of $700,000 will be paid to Pacific City's mayor at the end of one year for helping to arrange the credit. Of the $2 million received, $1 million will be used immediately to buy an old city-owned hotel and to convert it to a gambling casino. The other $1 million will be invested in other lucrative WDC projects that otherwise would have to be foregone because of a lack of capital. For two years, all cash generated by the casino will be plowed back into the casino project. At the end of the two years, the casino will be sold for $2 million.

Assuming that (1) the deal has been worked out in the sunshine and is completely legal and (2) cash from other WDC Company operations will be available to make the required payments at the end of Year 1, under what rate of return conditions should WDC accept the offer? Disregard taxes.

8-7   **(Present value of costs)** The Zocco Coffee Company is evaluating the within-plant distribution system for its new roasting, grinding, and packing plant. The two alternatives are (1) a conveyor system with a high initial cost, but low annual operating costs, and (2) several forklift trucks, which cost less, but have considerably higher operating costs. The decision to construct the plant has already been made, and the choice here will have no effect on the overall revenues of the project. The cost of capital for the plant is 8 percent, and the projects' expected net costs are listed in the table:

	Expected Net Cost	
Year	Conveyor	Forklift
0	($500,000)	($200,000)
1	(120,000)	(160,000)
2	(120,000)	(160,000)
3	(120,000)	(160,000)
4	(120,000)	(160,000)
5	(20,000)	(160,000)

a. What is the IRR of each alternative?

b. What is the present value of costs of each alternative? Which method should be chosen?

Solution to Self-Test Problem

ST-1   a. *Payback:*

To determine the payback, construct the cumulative cash flows for each project:

	Cumulative Cash Flow	
Year	Project X	Project Y
0	($10,000)	($10,000)
1	(3,500)	(6,500)
2	(500)	(3,000)
3	2,500	500
4	3,500	4,000

$$\text{Payback}_X = 2 + \frac{\$500}{\$3,000} = 2.17 \text{ years.}$$

$$\text{Payback}_Y = 2 + \frac{\$3,000}{\$3,500} = 2.86 \text{ years.}$$

Net Present Value (NPV):

$$NPV_X = -\$10,000 + \frac{\$6,500}{(1.12)^1} + \frac{\$3,000}{(1.12)^2} + \frac{\$3,000}{(1.12)^3} + \frac{\$1,000}{(1.12)^4}$$

$$= \$966.01.$$

$$NPV_Y = -\$10,000 + \frac{\$3,500}{(1.12)^1} + \frac{\$3,500}{(1.12)^2} + \frac{\$3,500}{(1.12)^3} + \frac{\$3,500}{(1.12)^4}$$

$$= \$630.72.$$

Internal Rate of Return (IRR):
To solve for each project's IRR, find the discount rates which equate each NPV to zero:

$$IRR_X = 18.0\%.$$

$$IRR_Y = 15.0\%.$$

Modified Internal Rate of Return (IRR*):
To obtain each project's IRR*, begin by finding each project's terminal value (TV) of cash inflows:

$$TV_X = \$6,500(1.12)^3 + \$3,000(1.12)^2$$
$$+ 3,000(1.12)^1 + \$1,000 = \$17,255.23.$$

$$TV_Y = \$3,500(1.12)^3 + \$3,500(1.12)^2$$
$$+ \$3,500(1.12)^1 + \$3,500 = \$16,727.65.$$

Now, each project's IRR* is that discount rate which equates the PV of the TV to each project's cost, \$10,000:

$$IRR^*_X = 14.61\%.$$

$$IRR^*_Y = 13.73\%.$$

Profitability Index (PI):

$$PI_X = \frac{PV \text{ benefits}}{PV \text{ costs}} = \frac{\$10,966.01}{\$10,000} = 1.10.$$

$$PI_Y = \frac{\$10,630.72}{\$10,000} = 1.06.$$

b. The following table summarizes the project rankings by each method:

	Project Which Ranks Higher
Payback	X
NPV	X
IRR	X
IRR*	X
PI	X

Note that all methods rank Project X over Project Y. Additionally, both projects are acceptable under the NPV, IRR, IRR*, and PI criteria. Thus, both projects should be accepted if they are independent.

c. Choose the project with the higher NPV at k = 12%, or Project X. Note that both projects have 4-year lives — if Project X and Project Y had different lives and were repeatable, a different procedure would be required. This point is discussed in Chapter 9.

NPV Profiles for Projects X and Y

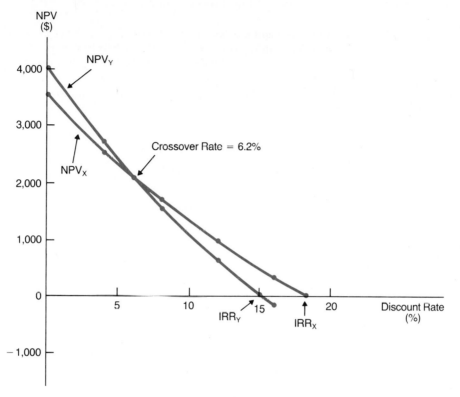

Discount Rate	NPV$_X$	NPV$_Y$
0%	$3,500	$4,000
4	2,546	2,705
8	1,707	1,592
12	966	630
16	307	(206)

d. To determine the effects of changing the cost of capital, plot the NPV profiles of each project. The crossover rate occurs at about 6-7 percent. To find this rate exactly, create a Project Δ, which is the difference in cash flows between Projects X and Y:

Year	Project X − Project Y = Project Δ Net Cash Flow
0	$ 0
1	3,000
2	(500)
3	(500)
4	(2,500)

Then find the IRR of Project Δ:

$$IRR_\Delta = \text{Crossover rate} = 6.2\%.$$

Thus, if the firm's cost of capital is less than 6.2 percent, a conflict exists since $NPV_Y > NPV_X$, but $IRR_X > IRR_Y$. Note, however, that when $k = 5.0\%$, $IRR^*_X = 10.64\%$ and $IRR^*_Y = 10.83\%$, and hence the modified IRR ranks the projects correctly, even to the left of the crossover point.

e. The basic cause of conflict is differing reinvestment rate assumptions between NPV and IRR. The conflict occurs in this situation because the projects differ in their cash flow timing.

Selected Additional References

For an in-depth treatment of capital budgeting techniques, see

Bierman, Harold, Jr., and Seymour Smidt, *The Capital Budgeting Decision* (New York: Macmillan, 1984).

Grant, Eugene L., William G. Ireson, and Richard S. Leavenworth, *Principles of Engineering Economy* (New York: Ronald, 1976).

Levy, Haim, and Marshall Sarnat, *Capital Investment and Financial Decisions* (Englewood Cliffs, N.J.: Prentice-Hall, 1982).

Osteryoung, Jerome S., *Capital Budgeting: Long-Term Asset Selection* (Columbus, Ohio: Grid, 1979).

For a discussion of strategic considerations in capital budgeting, see

Crum, Roy L., and Frans G. J. Derkinderen, eds., *Readings in Strategies for Corporate Investments* (New York: Pitman, 1981).

Shapiro, Alan C., "Corporate Strategy and the Capital Budgeting Decision," *Midland Corporate Finance Journal,* Spring 1985, 22–36.

The following articles present interesting comparisons of four different approaches to finding NPV:

Brick, Ivan E., and Daniel G. Weaver, "A Comparison of Capital Budgeting Techniques in Identifying Profitable Investments," *Financial Management,* Winter 1984, 29–39.

Greenfield, Robert L., Maury R. Randall, and John C. Woods, "Financial Leverage and Use of the Net Present Value Investment Criterion," *Financial Management,* Autumn 1983, 40–44.

Four articles related directly to the topics in Chapter 8 are

Bacon, Peter W., "The Evaluation of Mutually Exclusive Investments," *Financial Management,* Summer 1977, 55–58.

Kim, Suk H., and Edward J. Farragher, "Current Capital Budgeting Practices," *Management Accounting,* June 1981, 26–30.

Lewellen, Wilbur G., Howard P. Lanser, and John J. McConnell, "Payback Substitutes for Discounted Cash Flow," *Financial Management,* Summer 1973, 17–23.

Mukherjee, Tarun K., "Capital Budgeting Surveys: The Past and the Future," *Review of Business and Economic Research,* Spring, 1987, 37–56.

Additional capital budgeting references are provided in Chapters 9 and 10.

9

Cash Flow Estimation and Other Topics in Capital Budgeting

In 1984 Federal Express Corporation unveiled its ZapMail electronic delivery service. The concept went like this: ZapMail customers would lease a state-of-the-art facsimile machine that is capable of transmitting documents via a special satellite communications network established for this purpose. Then, in just seconds, a customer in Atlanta, for example, could transmit a document to another customer, say in Boise. ZapMail was intended to replace overnight air delivery as the best way to ship important documents to far-flung locations.

Federal invested more than $300 million in ZapMail, and it expected to earn a high return on this investment. However, potential customers were turned off by the costs involved—initially $35, but eventually lowered to $25, for up to 10 pages—so the system never generated the expected revenues. At the same time, software and hardware problems caused costs to exceed estimates. As a result, ZapMail had operating losses of $132 million on revenues of only $33 million for the 1986 fiscal year, and the project was terminated.

Federal Express performed a careful, sophisticated capital budgeting analysis, using all the right techniques, yet the ZapMail project was a failure. Revenues were projected too high, and costs too low, so cash flows failed to meet the forecasted levels. This example demonstrates a basic truth—if cash flow estimates are not reasonably accurate, then any analytical technique, no matter how sophisticated, can lead to poor decisions, and hence to losses and depressed stock prices.

The basic principles of capital budgeting were covered in Chapter 8. Now we examine some additional issues, including (1) cash flow estimation, (2) replacement decisions, (3) mutually exclusive projects with unequal lives, (4) abandonment value, and (5) effects of inflation on capital budgeting analysis.

CASH FLOW ESTIMATION

The most important, but also the most difficult, step in the analysis of a capital project is estimating its cash flows — the investment outlays and the annual net cash inflows after the project goes into operation. Many variables are involved in cash flow forecasting, and many individuals and departments participate in the process. For example, the forecasts of unit sales and sales prices are normally made by the marketing department, based on its knowledge of price elasticity, advertising effects, the state of the economy, competitors' reactions, and trends in consumers' tastes. Similarly, the capital outlays associated with a new product are generally obtained from the engineering and product development staffs, while operating costs are estimated by cost accountants, production experts, personnel specialists, purchasing agents, and so forth.

It is difficult to make accurate forecasts of the costs and revenues associated with a large, complex project, so forecast errors can be quite large. For example, when several major oil companies decided to build the Alaska Pipeline, the original cost forecasts were in the neighborhood of $700 million, but the final cost was closer to $7 billion. Similar, or even worse, miscalculations are common in forecasts of product design costs, such as the costs to develop a new personal computer. Further, as difficult as plant and equipment costs are to estimate, sales revenues and operating costs over the life of the project are generally even more uncertain. For example, when AT&T developed the Picturephone, it envisaged large sales in both the residential and business markets, yet it turned out that virtually no one was willing to pay the price required to cover the project's costs. Because of its financial strength, AT&T was able to absorb losses on the project with no problem, but the Picturephone venture could have forced a weaker firm into bankruptcy.

The financial staff's role in the forecasting process includes (1) coordinating the efforts of the other departments, such as engineering and marketing, (2) ensuring that everyone involved with the forecast uses a consistent set of economic assumptions, and (3) making sure that no biases are inherent in the forecasts. This last point is extremely important, because division managers often become emotionally involved with pet projects and/or develop empire-building complexes, leading to cash flow forecasting biases which make bad projects look good — on paper. The AT&T Picturephone project is an example of this problem.

Note also that unbiased point estimates of the key variables are not sufficient — as we shall see in the next chapter, data on probability distributions or other indications of the likely range of errors are also essential.

It is almost impossible to overstate the difficulties one can encounter in cash flow forecasts. It is also difficult to overstate the importance of these forecasts. However, if the principles discussed in the next several sections are observed, this will help to minimize forecast errors.

IDENTIFYING THE RELEVANT CASH FLOWS

Cash flows for a project are defined as the differences in cash flows for each period if the project is undertaken versus if it is not undertaken:

$$\text{Project } CF_t = \underset{\text{with project}}{CF_t \text{ for corporation}} - \underset{\text{without project}}{CF_t \text{ for corporation}}. \qquad (9\text{-}1)$$

Defined this way, we see that project cash flows are *incremental cash flows*. In this section, we discuss how to measure the incremental cash flows attributable to a project.

Cash Flow Versus Accounting Income

Accounting income statements are in some respects a mix of apples and oranges. For example, accountants deduct labor costs, which are cash outflows, from revenues, which may or may not be entirely cash (some sales may be on credit). At the same time, accountants do not deduct capital outlays, which are cash outflows, but they do deduct depreciation expenses, which are not cash outflows. In capital budgeting, it is critical that we base decisions strictly on cash flows, the actual dollars that flow into and out of the company during each time period.

As noted above, the relevant cash flows for capital budgeting purposes are the incremental cash flows attributable to a project. It is possible to construct a firm's pro forma cash flow statements with and without a project for each year of the project's life, and then to measure the annual project cash flows as the differences in cash flows between the two sets of statements. When this is done, the following formula results:

$$CF_t = [(R_{1t} - R_{0t}) - (OC_{1t} - OC_{0t}) - (D_{1t} - D_{0t})](1 - T) + (D_{1t} - D_{0t}). \qquad (9\text{-}2)$$

Here CF_t is the project's net operating cash flow in Period t; R_1 is the corporation's revenue if the project is undertaken while R_0 is the sales revenue if it is not accepted; OC_1 and OC_0 are the operating costs with and without the project; and D_1 and D_0 are the respective depreciation charges.[1]

To illustrate, suppose a firm is considering a new project that has a cost of $1 million and a 10-year life. If the project is undertaken, the cash flow statement in the left column below is expected to result, while if the project is not undertaken, the middle column is projected. The third column shows the changes resulting from the project, so the project's projected net operating cash flow is $298,000 per year for 10 years:

---

[1]Note that we are concentrating solely on operating cash flows. Financing flows (interest expense) are not included in a project's cash flows because financing costs are incorporated in the firm's WACC. When we use the WACC as a discount rate to obtain a project's NPV, we automatically account for capital costs.

	With Project	Without Project	Change
Sales (R)	$1,600,000	$1,000,000	$600,000
Operating costs (OC)	600,000	400,000	200,000
Depreciation (D)	200,000	100,000	100,000
Pre-tax income	$ 800,000	$ 500,000	$300,000
Taxes (34%)	272,000	170,000	120,000
Net income (NI)	$ 528,000	$ 330,000	$198,000
CF (NI + D)	$ 728,000	$ 430,000	$298,000

Equation 9-2 would show exactly the same incremental cash flow, $298,000.

As we will see later in the chapter, there are times when a new project affects the sales and costs associated with the firm's original assets, and in such cases it is essential to think in terms of either Equation 9-2 or comparative cash flow statements as shown above. However, new projects often do not affect the firm's existing cash flows, and in such cases we can use a short-cut cash flow formula:

$$CF_t = [R_t - OC_t - D_t](1 - T) + D_t. \tag{9-3}$$

Here R, OC, and D represent the sales, operating costs, and depreciation of the project itself, and T is the firm's marginal tax rate. To illustrate, suppose a project has a cost of $1 million, will increase sales by $600,000 per year for 10 years, will have operating costs of $200,000 per year, and will be depreciated by the straight line method toward a zero salvage value over 10 years. If the firm's marginal tax rate is 34 percent, then Equation 9-3 may be solved as follows:

$$CF_t = [\,\$600,000 - \$200,000 - \$100,000](0.66) + \$100,000 = \$298,000.$$

Going through some algebra, we can transform Equation 9-3 into

$$CF_t = (R_t - OC_t)(1 - T) + TD_t. \tag{9-3a}$$

Equation 9-3a states that the net operating cash flow, CF_t, consists of two terms: (1) sales revenues minus cash operating costs, reduced by taxes, and (2) a depreciation cash flow equal to the amount of depreciation taken during the period times the tax rate. In this form, we see that depreciation affects cash flows because it reduces taxes, and the higher the firm's tax rate, the greater the benefits from depreciation. Equations 9-3 and 9-3a are equivalent methods for calculating cash flows, and either can be used in capital budgeting analysis.

Timing of Cash Flows

In financial analysis, we must be careful to account properly for the timing of cash flows. Accounting income statements are for periods such as years or months, so they do not reflect exactly when, during the period, revenues or expenses occur. Because of the time value of money, capital budgeting cash flows should in theory be analyzed exactly as they occur. Of course, there must be a compromise between accuracy and simplicity. A time line with daily cash flows would in theory provide the most accuracy, but daily cash flow estimates would be costly to construct, unwieldy to use, and probably no more accurate than annual cash flow estimates because we simply cannot forecast well enough to warrant this degree of detail. Therefore, in most cases, we simply assume that all cash flows occur at the end of every year. However, for some projects, it may be useful to assume that cash flows occur at midyear, or even to forecast quarterly or monthly cash flows.

Incremental Cash Flows

As noted previously, in capital budgeting our concern is with those cash flows that result directly from the project, or the project's incremental cash flows. Three special problems can occur when estimating incremental cash flows; they are discussed next.

1. Sunk costs. Sunk costs are not incremental costs, so they should not be included in the analysis. A *sunk cost* refers to an outlay that has already occurred (or been committed), so it is an outlay that is not affected by the accept/reject decision under consideration. Suppose, for example, that in 1988 Southwest BankCorp was evaluating the establishment of a branch office in a newly developed section of Albuquerque. To help perform the analysis, Southwest had, back in 1987, hired a consulting firm to perform a site analysis at a cost of $100,000, and this $100,000 was expensed for tax purposes in 1987. Is this 1987 expenditure a relevant cost with respect to the 1988 capital budgeting decision? The answer is no. The $100,000 is a sunk cost; Southwest cannot recover it regardless of whether or not the new branch is built. It often turns out that a particular project looks bad (i.e., has a negative NPV, or an IRR less than the cost of capital) when all the associated costs, including sunk costs, are considered. However, on an incremental basis, the project may be a good one, because the incremental cash flows are large enough to produce a positive NPV on the incremental investment. Thus, the correct treatment of sunk costs is critical to a proper capital budgeting analysis.[2]

2. Opportunity costs. The second potential problem relates to *opportunity costs:* All relevant opportunity costs must be included in a correct capital budgeting analysis. For example, suppose Southwest BankCorp already owns a piece of land that is suitable for the branch location. When evaluating the prospective branch, should the cost of the land be disregarded because no additional cash outlay would be required? The answer is "no," because there is an opportunity cost inherent in the use of the property. For example, suppose the land could be sold to net $150,000 after commissions and taxes. Use of the site for the branch

---

[2]For an excellent example of the improper treatment of sunk costs by a major corporation, see U. E. Reinhardt, "Break-Even Analysis for Lockheed's TriStar: An Application of Financial Theory," *Journal of Finance,* September 1973, 821–838.

would require foregoing this inflow, so the $150,000 must be charged as an opportunity cost against the project. Note, though, that the proper land cost in this example would be the $150,000 market-determined value, irrespective of whether Southwest had paid $50,000, or $500,000 for the property when it was acquired.

3. Effects on other parts of the firm (externalities). The third potential problem involves the effects of the project on other parts of the firm. For example, suppose some of the customers Southwest projects will use the new branch are already banking with Southwest's downtown office. The loans and deposits, and hence profits, generated by these customers would not be new to the bank, but, rather, they would represent a transfer from the main office to the branch. Thus, the net revenues produced by these customers should not be treated as incremental income in the capital budgeting analysis. On the other hand, having a suburban branch might actually attract new customers to the downtown office, because some potential customers would like to be able to make transactions both from home and from work. In this case, the additional revenues projected to flow to the downtown office should be attributed to the branch.

Although often difficult to determine, "externalities" such as these must be considered. They should, if possible, be quantified, or at least noted, so the final decision maker will be aware of their existence.

TAX EFFECTS

Taxes can have a major impact on cash flows, and in many cases tax effects can make or break a project. Therefore, it is critical that taxes be dealt with correctly in capital budgeting decisions. However, as financial analysts, we encounter two problems: (1) the tax laws are extremely complex, and (2) these laws are subject to interpretation and to change. The financial staff can get assistance from the firm's accountants and tax lawyers, but even so, it is necessary for financial analysts to have a working knowledge of the current tax laws and their effects on cash flows. Corporate taxes, including the tax implications of fixed asset investments, were discussed in Chapter 2.

SALVAGE VALUE

In Chapter 2 we noted that salvage value has no effect on the depreciable basis, and hence on the depreciation expense taken under ACRS. Still, when performing a cash flow analysis, we must estimate the market value of the asset at the end of the project's economic life, as this is an expected cash inflow, but any difference between the asset's salvage value and its book value is treated as ordinary income and is taxed at the firm's marginal tax rate. Since the ACRS class life is normally less than the economic life of the asset, the book value will usually be less (often zero) than actual market value when the asset is retired, in which case taxes must be paid on the difference.[3] If your understanding of corporate taxes is hazy, it would be a good idea to review Chapter 2 before you go on with this chapter.

INVESTMENT IN NET WORKING CAPITAL

Normally, additional inventories are required to support a new operation, and the new sales will also produce additional accounts receivable. Thus, both inventories and receivables will increase as a result of capital budgeting decisions, so the "investment outlay" of a new project must include the associated current assets as well as the fixed assets involved. However, accounts payable and accruals will also increase spontaneously as a result of the expansion, and this will reduce the need to raise capital to finance the project. The difference between the projected increase in current assets and that in current liabilities is defined as a *change in net working capital*. The change associated with a project is normally positive, so some additional investment, over and above the cost of the fixed assets, is required.[4] (In the unlikely event that the change in net working capital is negative, then the project would be generating an initial cash inflow from the change in net working capital.)

Net working capital changes may occur over several periods, so the increase (or decrease) could be reflected in cash flows for several periods. However, once the operation has stabilized, working capital will also stabilize at the new level, and beyond this time no changes will occur until the project is terminated. At the end of the project's life, the firm's total working capital requirements should revert to prior levels, so it will receive an end-of-project cash inflow equal to the net investment in working capital. This point is illustrated in the next section.

AN EXAMPLE OF CASH FLOW ESTIMATION

Up to this point, we have discussed several important aspects of cash flow analysis, but we have not seen how they relate to one another and affect the capital budgeting decision. In this section, we illustrate all this by examining a capital budgeting decision that faces Hawkey-Weigle Corporation (HWC), a San Francisco-based technology company. HWC's research and development department has been applying its expertise in microprocessor technology to develop a small computer specifically designed to control home appliances. Once programmed, the computer would automatically control the heating and air conditioning systems,

---

[3]In this case, the tax depreciation charges exceed "true" depreciation, and the excess depreciation is "recaptured." Since depreciation reduces ordinary income, its recapture is treated as ordinary income.

[4]Actually, the entire change in net working capital does not require additional investment, because some of the increase in receivables represents profits, and hence do not require financing. However, profit margins are normally just a few percentage points, so ignoring this factor does not lead to serious errors. This topic is discussed further in Chapter 19.

security system, hot water heater, and even small appliances such as a coffee maker. By increasing the energy efficiency of a home, the appliance control computer can save on costs and hence pay for itself. This effort has now reached the stage where a decision on whether or not to go forward with production must be made.

HWC's marketing department plans to target sales of the appliance control computer to the owners of larger homes — the computer is cost effective only on homes with 2,000 or more square feet of heated/air conditioned space. The marketing vice-president believes that annual sales would be 25,000 units if the appliance control computers were priced at $2,200 each. The engineering department has estimated that the firm would need a new manufacturing plant; this plant could be built and made ready for production in 2 years, once the "go" decision is made. The plant would require a 25-acre site, and HWC currently has an option to purchase a suitable tract of land for $1.2 million. Building construction would begin in early 1989 and would continue through 1990. The building, which would fall into the ACRS 31.5-year class, would cost an estimated $8 million, and a $4 million payment would be due to the contractor on December 31, 1989, and the remaining $4 million would be payable on December 31, 1990.

The necessary manufacturing equipment would be installed late in 1990 and would be paid for on December 31, 1990. The equipment, which would fall into the ACRS 7-year class, would have a cost of $9.5 million, including transportation, plus another $500,000 for installation.

The project would also require an initial investment in net working capital equal to 12 percent of the estimated sales in the first year. The initial working capital investment would be made on December 31, 1990, and on December 31 of each following year, net working capital would be increased by an amount equal to 12 percent of any sales increase expected during the coming year. The project's estimated economic life is 6 years. At that time, the land is expected to have a market value of $1.7 million, the building a value of $1.0 million, and the equipment a value of $2 million. The production department has estimated that variable manufacturing costs would total 65 percent of dollar sales, and that fixed overhead costs, excluding depreciation, would be $8 million for the first year of operations. Sales prices and fixed overhead costs, other than depreciation, are projected to increase with inflation, which is expected to average 6 percent per year over the 6-year life of the project.

HWC's marginal federal-plus-state tax rate is 40 percent; its weighted average cost of capital is 11.5 percent; and the company's policy, for capital budgeting purposes, is to assume that cash flows occur at the end of each year. Since the plant would begin operations on January 1, 1991, the first operating cash flows would thus occur on December 31, 1991.

As one of the company's financial analysts, you have been assigned the task of supervising the capital budgeting analysis. For now, you may assume that the project has the same risk as the firm's current average project, and hence use the corporate WACC, 11.5 percent, for this project. Later on, we will examine additional information concerning the riskiness of the project, but at this point assume that the project is of average risk.

Analysis of the Cash Flows

The first step in the analysis is to summarize the investment outlays required for the project; this is done in Table 9-1. Note that the land cannot be depreciated, and hence we show its depreciable basis to be $0. Also, since the project will require an increase in net working capital during 1990, this is shown as an investment outlay for that year.

Table 9-1
Investment Outlays, 1988–1990

Fixed Assets	1988	1989	1990	Total Costs, 1988–1990	Depreciable Basis
Land	$1,200,000	$ 0	$ 0	$ 1,200,000	$ 0
Building	0	4,000,000	4,000,000	8,000,000	8,000,000
Equipment	0	0	10,000,000	10,000,000	10,000,000
Total fixed assets	$1,200,000	$4,000,000	$14,000,000	$19,200,000	
Net working capital[a]	0	0	6,600,000	6,600,000	
Total investment	$1,200,000	$4,000,000	$20,600,000	$25,800,000	

[a]12 percent of first year's sales, or 0.12($55,000,000) = $6,600,000.

Having estimated the capital requirements, we must now estimate the cash flows that will occur once production begins; these are set forth in Table 9-2. The operating cash flow estimates are based on information provided by Hawkey-Weigle's various departments. Note that the sales price and fixed costs are projected to increase each year by the 6 percent inflation rate, and since variable costs are 65 percent of sales, they too will rise by 6 percent each year. The changes in net working capital (NWC) represent the additional investments required to support sales increases (12 percent of the next year's sales increase, which in this case results only from inflation) during 1991–1995, and the recovery of the cumulative net working capital investment in 1996. The depreciation amounts were obtained by multiplying the depreciable basis by the ACRS recovery allowance rates set forth in Footnote c to Table 9-2.

The analysis also requires an estimation of the cash flows generated by salvage values; Table 9-3 summarizes this analysis. First, we compare the projected 1996 market values against the 1996 book values. The land cannot be depreciated, and it has an estimated 1996 salvage value greater than the initial purchase price. Thus, Hawkey-Weigle would have to pay taxes on the profit. The building has an estimated salvage value less than the book value — it will be sold at a loss for tax purposes. The loss will reduce taxable income and thus generate a tax savings; in effect, the company has been depreciating the building too slowly, so it would write off the loss against ordinary income. On the other hand, the equipment will

Table 9-2
Net Cash Flows, 1991–1996

	1991	1992
Unit sales	25,000	25,000
Sale price[a]	$ 2,200	$ 2,332
Net sales[a]	$55,000,000	$58,300,000
Variable costs[b]	35,750,000	37,895,000
Fixed costs (overhead)[a]	8,000,000	8,480,000
Depreciation (building)[c]	120,000	240,000
Depreciation (equipment)[c]	2,000,000	3,200,000
Earnings before taxes	$ 9,130,000	$ 8,485,000
Taxes (40%)	3,652,000	3,394,000
Projected net operating income	$ 5,478,000	$ 5,091,000
Add back noncash expenses[d]	2,120,000	3,440,000
Cash flow from operations[e]	$ 7,598,000	$ 8,531,000
Investment in NWC[f]	(396,000)	(420,000)
Net salvage value[g]		
Total projected cash flows	$ 7,202,000	$ 8,111,000

[a]1991 estimate increased by the assumed 6 percent inflation rate.

[b]65 percent of net sales.

[c]ACRS depreciation rates (see Chapter 2) were estimated as follows:

Year	1	2	3	4	5	6
Building	1.5%	3%	3%	3%	3%	3%
Equipment	20	32	19	12	11	6

These percentages are multiplied by the depreciable basis to get the depreciation expense for each year. Note that the allowances have been rounded for ease of computation.

be sold for more than book value, so the company would have to pay ordinary taxes on the $2 million profit. In all cases, the book value is the depreciable basis less accumulated depreciation, and the total cash flow from salvage is merely the sum of the land, building, and equipment components.

Making the Decision

To summarize the data and get it ready for evaluation, it is useful to combine all of the net cash flows on a time line such as the one shown in Table 9-4. The table also shows the payback period, IRR, IRR*, and NPV (at the 11.5 percent cost of capital). The project appears to be acceptable using the NPV, IRR, or IRR* methods, and it would also be acceptable if HWC required a payback of six years or less. Note, however, that the analysis thus far has been based on the assumption that the project has the same degree of risk as the company's average project. If

Table 9-2
Net Cash Flows, 1991–1996 *Continued*

1993	1994	1995	1996
25,000	25,000	25,000	25,000
$ 2,472	$ 2,620	$ 2,777	$ 2,944
$61,800,000	$65,500,000	$69,425,000	$73,600,000
40,170,000	42,575,000	45,126,250	47,840,000
8,988,800	9,528,128	10,099,816	10,705,805
240,000	240,000	240,000	240,000
1,900,000	1,200,000	1,100,000	600,000
$10,501,200	$11,956,872	$12,858,934	$14,214,195
4,200,480	4,782,749	5,143,574	5,685,678
$ 6,300,720	$ 7,174,123	$ 7,715,360	$ 8,528,517
2,140,000	1,440,000	1,340,000	840,000
$ 8,440,720	$ 8,614,123	$ 9,055,360	$ 9,368,517
(444,000)	(471,000)	(501,000)	8,832,000
			5,972,000
$ 7,996,720	$ 8,143,123	$ 8,554,360	$24,172,517

[d]In this case, depreciation on building and equipment.

[e]Net operating income plus noncash expenses.

[f]12 percent of next year's increase in sales. For example, 1992 sales are $3.3 million over 1991 sales, so the addition to NWC in 1991 required to support 1992 sales is $(0.12)($3,300,000) = $396,000$. The cumulative working capital investment is recovered when the project ends in 1996.

[g]See Table 9-3 for the net salvage value calculation.

the project is riskier than an average project, then it would be necessary to increase the cost of capital, which in turn might cause the NPV to become negative and the IRR to fall below k. In Chapter 10, we will extend the evaluation of this project to include the necessary risk analysis.

At this point, before going on to take risk into account, it is useful to sit back and take a hard look at the estimated cash flows and the resulting return. Sometimes things look better than they really are. For example, suppose the project has a relatively long life and an IRR or IRR* which is significantly above the firm's cost of capital, as this project has. The very fact that the project is so profitable might attract other firms into the market, and new entry might cause the actual cash flows to fall far below those originally estimated. Thus, the financial analyst should view long-term, high-profitability projects with at least some skepticism, for only if the firm has some basic cost or marketing advantage over other firms can above-normal rates of return be sustained over time. In this case, management does not

Table 9-3
Net Salvage Values, 1996

	Land	Building	Equipment
Salvage (ending market) value	$1,700,000	$1,000,000	$ 2,000,000
Initial cost	1,200,000	8,000,000	10,000,000
Depreciable basis (1990)	0	8,000,000	10,000,000
Book value (1996)[a]	1,200,000	6,680,000	0
Capital gains income	$ 500,000	$ 0	$ 0
Ordinary income (loss)[b]	0	(5,680,000)	2,000,000
Taxes[c]	$ 200,000	($2,272,000)	$ 800,000
Net salvage value (Salvage value − Taxes)	$1,500,000	$3,272,000	$ 1,200,000

Total cash flow from salvage value = $1,500,000 + $3,272,000 + $1,200,000 = $5,972,000.

[a]Book value for the building in 1996 equals depreciable basis minus accumulated ACRS depreciation of $1,320,000. The accumulated depreciation on the equipment is $10,000,000. See Table 9-2.

[b]Building: $1,000,000 market value − $6,680,000 book value = $5,680,000 depreciation shortfall, which is treated as an operating expense in 1996.

Equipment: $2,000,000 market value − $0 book value = $2,000,000 depreciation recapture, which is treated as ordinary income in 1996.

[c]Since capital gains are now taxed at the ordinary income rate, all taxes are based on Hawkey-Weigle's 40 percent marginal federal-plus-state rate. The table is set up to differentiate ordinary income from capital gains because Congress may reinstate differential tax rates on those two income sources.

think that competitors will be able to develop and produce a competing computer within the next 8 years. Additionally, even though IRR and IRR* are relatively high, we shall see in Chapter 10 that the project is also relatively risky, and a 25.1 percent (or 17.9 percent) return on a risky project is not likely to cause a competitor to embark on a crash program.

Table 9-4
Time Line of Consolidated End-of-Year Net Cash Flows, 1988–1996

1988	1989	1990	1991	1992
($1,200,000)	($4,000,000)	($20,600,000)	$7,202,000	$8,111,000

Payback period: 5.3 years from first outflow.
IRR: 25.1% versus a 11.5% cost of capital.
IRR*: 17.9% versus an 11.5% cost of capital.
NPV: $12,075,384.

REPLACEMENT ANALYSIS

Hawkey-Weigle's appliance control computer project was used to show how an expansion project is analyzed. All companies, including this one, also make *replacement decisions,* and the analysis relating to replacements is somewhat different from that for expansion projects because the cash flows from the old asset must be considered. Replacement analysis is illustrated with another HWC example, this time from the company's research and development division.

A lathe for trimming molded plastics was purchased 10 years ago at a cost of $7,500. The machine had an expected life of 15 years at the time it was purchased, and management originally estimated, and still believes, that the salvage value will be zero at the end of the 15-year life. The machine is being depreciated on a straight line basis; therefore, its annual depreciation charge is $500, and its present book value is $2,500.[5]

The R&D manager reports that a new special purpose machine can be purchased for $12,000 (including freight and installation) which, over its 5-year life, will reduce labor and raw materials usage sufficiently to cut operating costs from $7,000 to $4,000. This reduction in costs will cause before-tax profits to rise by $7,000 − $4,000 = $3,000 per year.

It is estimated that the new machine can be sold for $2,000 at the end of 5 years; this is its estimated salvage value. The old machine's actual current market value is $1,000, which is below its $2,500 book value. If the new machine were acquired, the old lathe would be sold to another company rather than exchanged for the new machine. The company's marginal federal-plus-state tax rate is 40 percent, and the replacement project is of average risk. Net working capital requirements will also increase by $1,000 at the time of replacement. By an IRS ruling, the new machine falls into the 3-year ACRS class, and the cost of capital is 11.5 percent. Should the replacement be made?

---

[5]This machine was purchased prior to the Economic Recovery Tax Act of 1981, so the Accelerated Cost Recovery System was not in place at the time. The company chose to depreciate the lathe on a straight line basis.

Table 9-4
Time Line of Consolidated End-of-Year Net Cash Flows, 1988–1996 *Continued*

1993	1994	1995	1996
$7,996,720	$8,143,123	$8,554,360	$24,172,517

Table 9-5
Replacement Analysis Worksheet

I. Net Cash Flow at the Time the Investment Is Made			t = 0			
1. Cost of new equipment			($12,000)			
2. Market value of old equipment			1,000			
3. Tax effect of sale of old equipment			600			
4. Increase in net working capital			(1,000)			
5. Total net investment			($11,400)			

	Year:	0	1	2	3	4	5
II. Operating Inflows over the Project's Life							
6. After-tax decrease in costs			$1,800	$1,800	$1,800	$1,800	$1,800
7. Depreciation on new machine			$3,960	$5,400	$1,800	$ 840	$ 0
8. Depreciation on old machine			500	500	500	500	500
9. Change in depreciation			$3,460	$4,900	$1,300	$ 340	($ 500)
10. Tax savings from depreciation			1,384	1,960	520	136	(200)
11. Net operating cash flows (6+10)			$3,184	$3,760	$2,320	$1,936	$1,600
III. Terminal Year Cash Flows							
12. Estimated salvage value of new machine							$2,000
13. Tax on salvage value							(800)
14. Return of net working capital							1,000
15. Total termination cash flows							$2,200
IV. Net Cash Flows							
16. Total net cash flows		($11,400)	$3,184	$3,760	$2,320	$1,936	$3,800

V. Results

Payback period: 4.1 years.
IRR: 10.1% versus an 11.5% cost of capital.
IRR*: 10.7% versus an 11.5% cost of capital.
NPV: − $388.77

Table 9-5 shows the worksheet format the company uses to analyze replacement projects. A line-by-line description of the table follows.

Line 1. The top section of the table, Lines 1 through 5, sets forth the cash flows which occur at (approximately) t = 0, the time the investment is made. Line 1 shows the purchase price of the new machine, including any installation and freight charges.

Line 2. Here we show the price received from the sale of old equipment.

Line 3. Since the old equipment would be sold at less than book value, this creates a loss which reduces the firm's taxable income, and hence its next quarterly income tax payment. The tax saving is equal to (Loss)(T) = ($1,500)(0.40) = $600, where T is the marginal corporate tax rate. The Tax Code defines this loss as an operating loss, because it reflects the fact that inadequate depreciation was taken on the old asset. If there had been a profit on the sale (that is, if the sales price had exceeded book value), Line 3 would have shown taxes *paid,* a cash outflow. In the actual case, the equipment would be sold at a loss, so no taxes would be paid, and the company would realize a tax savings of $600.[6]

Line 4. The investment in additional net working capital (new current asset requirements less increases in accounts payable and accruals) is shown here. This investment will be recovered at the end of the project's life (see Line 14). No taxes are involved.

Line 5. Here we show the total net cash outflow at the time the replacement is made. The company writes a check for $12,000 to pay for the machine, and another $1,000 is invested in net working capital. However, these outlays are partially offset by the sale of the old equipment.

Line 6. Section II of the table shows the *incremental operating cash flows,* or benefits, that are expected if the replacement is made. The cash flows for each year are based on Equation 9-2 as set forth earlier in the chapter. The first of these benefits is the reduction in operating costs shown on Line 6, which (1) increases cash flows because operating costs are reduced by $3,000, but (2) reduced costs also mean higher taxable income, and hence higher income taxes. Therefore, the after-tax benefit is $3,000(1 − T) = $3,000(1 − 0.40) = $3,000(0.60) = $1,800. Note that had the replacement resulted in an increase in sales in addition to the reduction in costs (if the new machine had been both larger and more efficient), then this amount would also be reported on Line 6 (or a separate line could be added). Finally, note that the $3,000 cost savings is constant over Years 1–5; had the annual savings been expected to change over time, this fact would have to be built into the analysis.

Line 7. The depreciable basis of the new machine, $12,000, is multiplied by the appropriate ACRS recovery allowance for 3-year class property to obtain the depreciation figures shown on Line 7. Note that if you summed Line 7, the total would be $12,000, the depreciable basis.

Line 8. Line 8 shows the $500 straight line depreciation on the old machine.

Line 9. The depreciation expense on the old machine as shown on Line 8 can no longer be taken if the replacement is made, but the new machine's depreciation will be available. Therefore, the $500 depreciation on the old machine is subtracted from that on the new machine to show the net change in annual depreciation. The change is positive in Years 1–4, but negative in Year 5. The Year 5 negative net change in annual depreciation signifies that the purchase of the replacement machine results in a *decrease* in depreciation expense in that year.

Line 10. The net change in depreciation results in a tax savings (or cost) which is equal to the change in depreciation multiplied by the tax rate: Depreciation

---

[6]If the old asset were being exchanged for the new asset, rather than being sold to a third party, the tax consequences would be different. In an exchange of similar assets, no gain or loss is recognized. If the market value of the old asset is greater than its book value, the depreciable basis of the new asset is decreased by the excess amount. Conversely, if the market value of the old asset is less than its book value, the depreciable basis is increased by the shortfall.

savings = T(Change in depreciation) = 0.40($3,460) = $1,384 for Year 1. Note that the relevant cash flow is the tax saving on the *net change* in depreciation, rather than on only the depreciation on the new equipment. Capital budgeting decisions are based on *incremental* cash flows, and since we lose $500 of depreciation if we replace the old machine, that fact must be taken into account.

Line 11. Here we show the net operating cash flows over the project's 5-year life. These flows are found by adding the after-tax cost decrease to the depreciation tax savings, or Line 6 + Line 10.

Line 12. Part III shows the cash flows associated with the termination of the project. To begin, Line 12 shows the estimated salvage value of the new machine at the end of its 5-year life, $2,000.[7]

Line 13. Since the book value of the new machine at the end of Year 5 is zero, the company will have to pay taxes of $2,000(0.4) = $800.

Line 14. An investment of $1,000 in net working capital was shown as an outflow at t = 0. This investment, like the new machine's salvage value, will be recovered when the project is terminated at the end of Year 5. Accounts receivable will be collected, inventories will be drawn down and not replaced, and the result is an inflow of $1,000 at t = 5.

Line 15. Here we show the total cash flows resulting from terminating the project.

Line 16. Part IV shows, on Line 16, the total net cash flows in a form suitable for capital budgeting evaluation.

Part V of the table, "Results," shows the replacement project's payback, IRR, IRR*, and NPV. The project is assumed to be of similar risk to the old project, and the old project is assumed to be about as risky as the company's average project. Therefore, an 11.5 percent project cost of capital is appropriate. At this cost of capital, the project is not acceptable, and hence the old lathe should not be replaced.

EVALUATING PROJECTS WITH UNEQUAL LIVES

Note that a replacement decision involves two mutually exclusive projects: retain the old asset or buy a new one. To simplify matters, in our replacement example we assumed that the new machine had a life equal to the remaining life of the old machine. If, however, we were choosing between two mutually exclusive alternatives with significantly different lives, an adjustment would be necessary. We now discuss two procedures — (1) the replacement chain method and (2) the equivalent annual annuity method — to both illustrate the problem and to deal with it.

---

[7]In this analysis, the salvage value of the old machine is zero. However, if the old machine could be sold at the end of five years, then replacing the old machine now would eliminate this cash flow. Thus, the after-tax salvage value of the old machine would represent an opportunity cost to the firm, and it would be included as a Year 5 cash outflow in the terminal cash flow section of the worksheet.

Table 9-6
Expected Net Cash Flows for Projects C and F

Year	Project C	Project F
0	($40,000)	($20,000)
1	8,000	7,000
2	14,000	13,000
3	13,000	12,000
4	12,000	—
5	11,000	—
6	10,000	—
NPV at 11.5%	$7,165	$5,391

Suppose Hawkey-Weigle is planning to modernize its production facilities, and as a part of the process, it is considering either a conveyor system (Project C) or a forklift truck (Project F) for moving materials from the parts department to the main assembly line. Table 9-6 shows both the expected net cash flows and the NPV for each of these mutually exclusive alternatives. We see that Project C, when discounted at an 11.5 percent cost of capital, has the higher NPV and hence appears to be the better project.

Replacement Chain (Common Life) Approach

Although the analysis in Table 9-6 suggests that Project C should be selected, this analysis is incomplete, and the decision to choose Project C is actually incorrect. If we choose Project F, we will have the opportunity to make a similar investment after 3 years, and if cost and revenue conditions continue at the Table 9-6 levels, this second investment will also be profitable. However, if we choose Project C, we will not have this second investment opportunity. Therefore, to make a proper comparison of Projects C and F, we must find the NPV of Project F over a 6-year period and then compare this extended NPV with the NPV of Project C over the same 6 years.

The NPV for Project C, as calculated in Table 9-6, is already over a 6-year life. For Project F, however, we must take three additional steps: (1) determine the NPV of a second Project F three years hence, (2) discount this NPV back to the present, and (3) sum these two component NPVs:

1. If we make the assumption that Project F's cost and annual cash inflows will not change if the project were repeated in 3 years, and that Hawkey-Weigle's cost of capital will remain at 11.5 percent, then Project F's second-stage NPV would remain the same as its first-stage NPV, $5,391. However, the second NPV would not accrue for 3 years, and hence it would represent a present value at $t = 3$.

2. The present value (at $t = 0$) of the replicated Project F is determined by discounting the second NPV (at $t = 3$) back 3 years at 11.5 percent: $5,391/$(1.115)^3 = \$3,889$.

3. The "true" NPV of Project F is $5,391 + $3,889 = $9,280. This is the value which should be compared with the NPV of Project C, $7,165. Since the "true" NPV of Project F is greater than the NPV of Project C, Project F should be selected.

Equivalent Annual Annuity Approach

Although the preceding example illustrates why an extended analysis is necessary if we are comparing mutually exclusive projects with different lives, the arithmetic is generally more complex in practice. For example, one project might have an 8-year life versus an 11-year life for the other. This would require an analysis over 88 years, the lowest common denominator of the two lives. In such a situation, it is often simpler to use a second procedure, the equivalent annual annuity method (EAA), which involves three steps:

1. Find each project's NPV over its initial life. In the previous example, we found $NPV_C = \$7,165$ and $NPV_F = \$5,391$.

2. Find the annuity cash flow that has the same present value as each project's NPV. For example, for Project C, enter 7,165 as the PV, $k = i = 11.5$, and $n = 6$ in your calculator and solve for PMT. The answer is $1,718. This cash flow stream, when discounted back 6 years at 11.5 percent, has a present value equal to Project C's original NPV, $7,165. The value $1,718 is called the project's *equivalent annual annuity (EAA)*. The EAA for Project F was found similarly to be $2,225. Thus, Project C has an NPV which is equivalent to an annuity of $1,718 per year for 6 years, while Project F's NPV is equivalent to an annuity of $2,225 for 3 years.

3. Assuming that continuous replacements can and will be made each time a project's life ends, these EAAs will continue on out to infinity; that is, they will constitute perpetuities. Recognizing that the value of a perpetuity is V = Annual receipt/k, we can find the net present values of the infinite EAAs of Projects C and F as follows:

$$\text{Infinite horizon } NPV_C = \$1,718/0.115 = \$14,939.$$
$$\text{Infinite horizon } NPV_F = \$2,225/0.115 = \$19,348.$$

In effect, the EAA method assumes that each project will, if taken on, be replaced each time it wears out, and will provide cash flows equivalent to the calculated annuity value. The PV of this infinite annuity is then the infinite horizon NPV for the project. Since the infinite horizon NPV of F exceeds that of C, Project F should be accepted. Therefore, the EAA method leads to the same decision rule as the simple chain method — accept Project F.

The EAA method is generally easier to apply than the replacement chain method. However, the chain method is often easier to explain to decision makers, and it does not require the assumption of an infinite time horizon. Still, the two methods always lead to the same decision if consistent assumptions are used. Also, note that Step 3 of the EAA method is not really necessary — we could have stopped after Step 2, because the project with the higher EAA will always have the higher NPV over any common life.

When should we worry about unequal life analysis? As a general rule, the unequal life issue (1) does not arise for independent projects but (2) can arise if mutually exclusive projects with significantly different lives are being evaluated. However, even for mutually exclusive projects, it is not always appropriate to extend the analysis to a common life. This should only be done if there is a high probability that the projects will actually be replicated beyond their initial lives.

We should note several potentially serious weaknesses inherent in this type of unequal life analysis: (1) If inflation is expected, then replacement equipment will have a higher price, and both sales prices and operating costs will probably change, and thus the static conditions built into the analysis would be invalid. (2) Replacements that occur down the road would probably employ new technology, which in turn might change the cash flows. This factor is not built into either replacement chain analysis or the EAA approach. (3) It is difficult enough to estimate the lives of most projects, so estimating the lives of a series of projects is often just a speculation.

In view of these problems, no experienced financial analyst would be too concerned about comparing mutually exclusive projects with lives of, say, 8 years and 10 years. Given all the uncertainties in the estimation process, such projects could, for all practical purposes, be assumed to have the same life. Still, it is important for you to recognize that a problem does exist if mutually exclusive projects have substantially different lives. When we encounter such problems in practice, we build expected inflation and/or possible efficiency gains directly into the cash flow estimates, and then use the replacement chain approach (but not the equivalent annual annuity method). The cash flow estimation is more complicated, but the concepts involved are exactly the same as in our example.

ABANDONMENT VALUE

Customarily, projects are analyzed as though the firm will definitely operate each project over its assumed useful life. However, this may not be the best course of action — it may be best to abandon a project prior to its potential life, and this possibility can materially affect the project's calculated NPV and IRR.[8] The situation in Table 9-7 can be used to illustrate the abandonment value concept and its effects on capital budgeting. The abandonment values are equivalent to salvage values, except that they have been estimated for each year of Project A's life.

Using an assumed cost of capital of 10 percent, the expected NPV over the 3-year estimated life is $- \$117$:

$$NPV = -\$4{,}800 + \$2{,}000/(1.10)^1 + \$1{,}875/(1.10)^2 + \$1{,}750/(1.10)^3$$
$$= -\$117.$$

---

[8]See Alexander A. Robichek and James C. Van Horne, "Abandonment Value and Capital Budgeting," *Journal of Finance*, December 1967, 577–589.

Table 9-7

Investment, Net Operating, and Abandonment Cash Flows for Project A

Year (t)	Initial Investment and Operating Cash Flow	Abandonment Value in Year t
0	($4,800)	$4,800
1	2,000	3,000
2	1,875	1,900
3	1,750	0

Thus, Project A would not be accepted if we considered the single alternative of a 3-year life with a zero salvage (abandonment) value. However, what would its NPV be if the project were abandoned after 2 years? In this case, we would receive operating cash flows in Years 1 and 2, plus the abandonment value at the end of Year 2, and the NPV would be $138:

$$NPV = -\$4,800 + \$2,000/(1.10)^1 + \$1,875/(1.10)^2 + \$1,900/(1.10)^2$$
$$= \$138.$$

Thus, Project A becomes acceptable if we plan to operate it for 2 years and then dispose of it. To complete the analysis, we note that if the project were abandoned after 1 year, its NPV would be $-\$255$. Thus, the optimal life for this project is 2 years.

Abandonment value should be considered in the capital budgeting process because, as our example illustrates, there are cases in which recognition of abandonment can make an otherwise unacceptable project acceptable. Indeed, this type of analysis is required to determine a project's economic life. For Project A, the *economic life* is actually two years rather than the three-year *physical life,* with the economic life being defined as that project life which maximizes the project's NPV and thus maximizes shareholder wealth.

Two very different types of abandonment occur: (1) sale by the original user of a still-valuable asset to some other party who can obtain greater cash flows from the asset and (2) abandoning an asset because the project is losing money. The first type situation can be illustrated by Pan Am's sale of its Pacific Division to United Airlines. United is a more efficient company, and it badly needed a link to the rapidly developing Asian nations. Thus, these assets were simply worth more to United than to Pan Am.

The second type of abandonment — closing down money-losing operations — can cut losses and thus greatly reduce the riskiness of a project. This aspect of abandonment, which is illustrated by the Federal Express example given at the beginning of the chapter, is discussed in Chapter 10. The main point for you to understand now is that the cash flows from a project can be materially different if it is abandoned (or sold off) at some point rather than operated to the end of its initially projected life, and if abandonment possibilities are not considered when in fact they exist, then the cash flows from the project may be badly misspecified.

ADJUSTING FOR INFLATION

Inflation is a fact of life in the United States and most other nations, so it must be considered in any sound capital budgeting analysis.[9] To see how inflation enters the picture, suppose an investor makes a loan of $100 for one year at a rate of 5 percent. At the end of the year, the investor would have $100(1.05)' = $105. However, if prices rose by 6 percent during the year, the ending $105 would have a purchasing power, in terms of beginning-of-year values, of only $105/1.06 = $99. Thus, the investor would have lost about 1 percent of his or her original purchasing power, in spite of having earned a 5 percent rate of return.

As we discussed in Chapter 3, investors recognize this problem, so they incorporate expectations about inflation into their required rates of return. For example, suppose investors seek a *real rate of return,* k_r, of 8 percent on an investment with a given degree of risk. Suppose, further, they anticipate that the annual rate of inflation, i, will be 6 percent. Then, in order to end up with an 8 percent real rate of return, the *nominal rate of return,* k_n, must be a value such that

$$1 + k_n = (1 + k_r)(1 + i), \qquad (9\text{-}4)$$

or

$$\begin{aligned} k_n &= (1 + k_r)(1 + i) - 1 \\ &= 1 + k_r + i + k_r i - 1 \\ &= k_r + i + k_r i. \end{aligned} \qquad (9\text{-}4a)$$

In words, the nominal interest rate, k_n, must be equal to the real rate, k_r, plus the expected inflation rate, i, plus a cross-product term, $k_r i$. In our example,

$$\begin{aligned} k_n &= 0.08 + 0.06 + (0.08)(0.06) \\ &= 0.08 + 0.06 + 0.0048 \\ &= 0.1448 = 14.48\%. \end{aligned}$$

Thus, if the investor earns a nominal return of 14.48 percent on a $100 investment, the ending value, in real terms, will be

$$\frac{\$100(1.1448)}{1.06} = \frac{\$114.48}{1.06} = \$108,$$

---

[9]For a formal discussion of this subject, see James C. Van Horne, "A Note on Biases in Capital Budgeting Introduced by Inflation," *Journal of Financial and Quantitative Analysis,* January 1971, 653–658; Philip L. Cooley, Rodney L. Roenfeldt, and It-Keong Chew, "Capital Budgeting Procedures under Inflation," *Financial Management,* Winter 1975, 18–27; and "Cooley, Roenfeldt, and Chew vs. M. C. Findlay and A. W. Frankle," *Financial Management,* Autumn 1976, 83–90.

producing the required 8 percent real rate of return. This example demonstrates the fact that Equation 9-4a produces the desired result.[10]

The Cost of Capital under Inflation

Note that *in the absence of inflation,* (1) the real rate, k_r, and the nominal rate, k_n, are equal, and (2) so are the real and nominal expected net cash flows — RCF_t and NCF_t, respectively. Therefore, a project's NPV may be calculated using either of these two equations:

$$\text{NPV (no inflation)} = \sum_{t=0}^{n} \frac{RCF_t}{(1 + k_r)^t} \tag{9-5a}$$

$$= \sum_{t=0}^{n} \frac{NCF_t}{(1 + k_n)^{t\cdot}} \tag{9-5b}$$

Now suppose the expected rate of inflation is positive, and *we expect both sales prices and all costs, including depreciation, to rise at the same rate i.* Further, this same inflation rate, i, is built into the market cost of capital. In this event, the nominal cash flow, NCF_t, will increase annually at the rate i percent, producing this situation:

$$NCF_t = RCF_t(1 + i)^t. \tag{9-6}$$

For example, if we expected a net operating cash flow of $100 in Year 5 in the absence of inflation, then with a 5 percent rate of inflation, $NCF_5 = \$100(1.05)^5 = \$127.63$.

Now if net operating cash flows increase at the rate i percent per year, and if this same inflation factor is built into the firm's cost of capital, then we can substitute Equation 9-4 into the denominator and Equation 9-6 into the numerator of Equation 9-5a to produce this expression for the inflation-adjusted NPV:

$$\text{NPV (with inflation)} = \sum_{t=0}^{n} \frac{RCF_t(1 + i)^t}{(1 + k_r)^t(1 + i)^{t\cdot}}. \tag{9-5c}$$

Since the $(1 + i)^t$ terms in the numerator and denominator cancel, Equation 9-5c reduces to our early expression, Equation 9-5a:

$$\text{NPV} = \sum_{t=0}^{n} \frac{RCF_t}{(1 + k_r)^{t\cdot}}.$$

---

[10]Notice that if the cross-product term in Equation 9-4a, $k_r i$, is disregarded as it often is because it is typically small, we are left with this equation for nominal interest rates:

$$k_n = k_r + i.$$

This is the well-known "Fisher Equation," named after the great economist Irving Fisher, who studied the relationship between inflation and the cost of capital in the early 20th century.

Thus, whenever all costs and sales prices, and hence annual cash flows, are expected to rise at the same inflation rate that investors have built into the cost of capital, then the inflation-adjusted NPV determined using Equation 9-5c is identical to the inflation-free NPV found using Equation 9-5a.

Firms occasionally use base year, or constant, dollars throughout the analysis — say 1988 dollars if the analysis is done in 1988 — along with a cost of capital as determined in the market place. This is wrong: *If the cost of capital includes an inflation premium, as it typically does, but the cash flows are all stated in constant dollars, then the calculated NPV will be downward biased.* You can see this by examining Equation 9-5c. The denominator reflects inflation, but the $(1 + i)^t$ term will be absent from the numerator, and this will produce a downward bias in NPV. Thus, if sales prices and all costs were expected to rise at the same rate, and if that rate is also built into the cost of capital, then we can obtain an unbiased NPV estimate using (1) constant dollar cash flows discounted at the real cost of capital (Equation 9-5a) or (2) nominal cash flows discounted at the nominal, or market, cost of capital (Equation 9-5c). However, as we discuss in the next section, this situation does not hold in practice.

Adjusting for Nonneutral Inflation

With nonneutral inflation (which means a situation where input costs, output prices, and/or the cost of capital are each subject to different inflation rates), it is necessary to develop nominal cash flows, NCF_t, which specifically account for inflation. This is what we did earlier in our Hawkey-Weigle Corporation example as summarized in Table 9-4. There we assumed that sales prices, variable costs, and fixed overhead costs would all increase at a rate of 6 percent per year, but that depreciation charges would not be affected by inflation. Of course, we could have assumed different rates of inflation for sales prices, for variable costs, and for fixed overheads, and yet another inflation rate might be built into the cost of capital. For example, Hawkey-Weigle might have long-term labor contracts which cause wage rates to rise with the Consumer Price Index (CPI), but its raw materials might be purchased under a fixed price contract, with the net result that variable costs are expected to rise by a smaller percentage than sales prices. In any event, one should build inflation into the capital budgeting analysis, with the specific adjustment reflecting as accurately as possible the most likely set of circumstances.[11]

Our conclusions about inflation may be summarized as follows. First, inflation is critically important, for it can and does have major effects on businesses. Therefore, it must be recognized and dealt with. Second, the most effective way of dealing with inflation is to build it into each cash flow element, using the best available information on how each element will be affected. Third, since we cannot estimate future inflation rates with precision, errors are bound to be made. Thus, inflation adds to the uncertainty, or riskiness, of capital budgeting as well as to its complex-

---

[11]See Problem 9-9 for a specific example of how inflation affects capital budgeting analyses. Also note that in practice, inflation is always nonneutral — depreciation is not affected by inflation since it is based solely on the cost of the asset and is not adjusted for price changes in future years.

ity. Fortunately, computers and spreadsheet models are available to help with inflation analysis.

SUMMARY

This chapter has dealt with five issues in capital budgeting: cash flow estimation, replacement decisions, unequal life analyses, abandonment value, and inflation adjustments.

The most important, yet most difficult, step in capital budgeting analysis is *cash flow estimation*. The key is to consider only *incremental* after-tax cash flows. *Replacement analysis* is conceptually similar to new project analysis, except that replacement cash flow estimation requires consideration of the fact that the old asset could continue to generate additional cash flows. Further, if the replacement asset has a life different from the remaining life of the old asset, it may be necessary to adjust to a common life. This adjustment can be made either by the *replacement chain method* or by the *equivalent annual annuity method*. Adjusting for unequal lives may be necessary for analyzing any set of mutually exclusive projects when (1) different lives are involved and (2) the projects are expected to continue beyond the assets' initial lives.

If a project does not have a clearly defined economic life, part of the project evaluation is the determination of the project's optimal life. One method for accomplishing this is to estimate the project's *abandonment values*, and then to use these to find that life which maximizes the project's NPV.

Inflation exists in the United States and most other countries, and it must be dealt with in capital budgeting analysis. If inflation is ignored, then (1) the cash flows in the numerator of the NPV equation are not adjusted for expected inflation, but (2) an adjustment is automatically (and generally unconsciously) made in the denominator, because market forces build inflation into the cost of capital. Thus, the net result is to create a downward bias in the calculated NPV. The best way of correcting for this bias is to build inflation directly into the estimated cash flows.

Questions

9-1   Define each of the following terms:

    a. Cash flow; accounting income

    b. Incremental cash flow; sunk cost; opportunity cost

    c. Net working capital changes

    d. Salvage value

    e. Replacement decision

    f. Replacement chain

    g. Equivalent annual annuity

    h. Abandonment value

    i. Real rate of return, k_r, versus nominal rate of return, k_n

9-2   Operating cash flows rather than accounting profits are listed in Table 9-2. What is the basis for this emphasis on cash flows as opposed to net income?

9-3   Why is it true, in general, that a failure to adjust expected cash flows for expected inflation biases the calculated NPV downward?

9-4   Suppose a firm is considering two mutually exclusive projects. One has a life of 4 years and the other a life of 10 years. Would the failure to employ some type of replacement chain analysis bias an NPV analysis against one of the projects? Explain.

9-5   Look at Table 9-5 and answer these questions:

a. Why is the salvage value shown on Line 12 reduced for taxes on Line 13?

b. Why is depreciation on the old machine deducted on Line 8 to get Line 9?

c. What would happen if the new machine permitted a *reduction* in net working capital?

d. Why are the cost savings on Line 6 reduced by multiplying the before-tax figure by $(1 - T)$, whereas the change in depreciation figure on Line 9 is multiplied by T?

Self-Test Problems

ST-1 (New project analysis) You have been asked by the president of Ellis Construction Company, headquartered in Toledo, to evaluate the proposed acquisition of a new earthmover. The mover's basic price is $50,000, and it would cost another $10,000 to modify it for special use by Ellis Construction. Assume that the mover falls into the ACRS 3-year class. It would be sold after 3 years for $20,000, and it would require an increase in net working capital (spare parts inventory) of $2,000. The earthmover would have no effect on revenues, but it is expected to save Ellis $20,000 per year in before-tax operating costs, mainly labor. Ellis' marginal federal-plus-state tax rate is 40 percent.

a. What is the net cost of the earthmover? (That is, what are the Year 0 cash flows?)

b. What are the operating cash flows in Years 1, 2, and 3?

c. What are the additional (nonoperating) cash flows in Year 3?

d. If the project's cost of capital is 10 percent, should the earthmover be purchased?

ST-2 (Replacement project analysis) The Merville Toy Corporation currently uses an injection molding machine that was purchased 2 years ago. This machine is being depreciated on a straight line basis toward a $500 salvage value, and it has 6 years of remaining life. Its current book value is $2,600, and it can be sold for $3,000 at this time. Thus, the annual depreciation expense is ($2,600 − $500)/6 = $350 per year.

Merville is offered a replacement machine which has a cost of $8,000, an estimated useful life of 6 years, and an estimated salvage value of $800. This machine falls into the ACRS 5-year class, and under current law it does not qualify for an investment tax credit. The replacement machine would permit an output expansion, so sales would rise by $1,000 per year; even so, the new machine's much greater efficiency would still cause operating expenses to decline by $1,500 per year. The new machine would require that inventories be increased by $2,000, but accounts payable would simultaneously increase by $500.

Merville's marginal federal-plus-state tax rate is 40 percent, and its cost of capital is 15 percent. Should it replace the old machine?

Problems

9-1   (Depreciation effects) Ronald Clay, great grandson of the founder of Clay Tile Products and current president of the company, believes in simple, conservative accounting. In keeping with his philosophy, he has decreed that the company shall use alternative straight line depreciation, based on the ACRS class lives, for all newly acquired assets. Your boss, the financial vice president and the only non-family officer, has asked you to develop an exhibit which shows how much this policy costs the company in terms of market value. Mr. Clay is interested in increasing the value of the firm's stock because he fears a family stockholder revolt which might remove him from office. For your exhibit, assume that the company spends $50 million each year on new capital projects, that the projects have on average a 10-year class life, that the company has a 10 percent cost of debt, and that its tax rate is 34 percent. (Hint: Show how much the NPV of projects in an average year would increase if Clay used the standard ACRS recovery allowances.)

9-2   (New project analysis) You have been asked by the president of your company to evaluate the proposed acquisition of a new spectrometer for the firm's R&D department. The equipment's basic price is $70,000, and it would cost another $15,000 to modify it for special use by your firm. The spectrometer, which falls into the ACRS 3-year class, would be sold after 3 years for $30,000. Use of the equipment would require an increase in net working capital (spare parts inventory) of $4,000. The spectrometer would have no effect on revenues, but it is expected to save the firm $25,000 per year in before-tax operating costs, mainly labor. The firm's marginal federal-plus-state tax rate is 40 percent.

    a. What is the net cost of the spectrometer? (That is, what is the Year 0 net cash flow?)

    b. What are the net operating cash flows in Years 1, 2, and 3?

    c. What is the additional (nonoperating) cash flow in Year 3?

    d. If the project's cost of capital is 10 percent, should the spectrometer be purchased?

9-3   (New project analysis) The Angell Company is evaluating the proposed acquisition of a new milling machine. The machine's base price is $180,000, and it would cost another $25,000 to modify it for special use by your firm. The machine falls into the ACRS 3-year class, and it would be sold after 3 years for $80,000. The machine would require an increase in net working capital (inventory) of $7,500. The machine would have no effect on revenues, but it is expected to save the firm $75,000 per year in before-tax operating costs, mainly labor. Angell's marginal tax rate is 34 percent.

    a. What is the net cost of the machine for capital budgeting purposes? (That is, what is the Year 0 net cash flow?)

    b. What are the operating cash flows in Years 1, 2, and 3?

    c. What is the additional (nonoperating) cash flow in Year 3?

    d. If the project's cost of capital is 10 percent, should the machine be purchased? *(Do Parts e, f, g, and h only if you are using the computerized diskette.)*

    e. Determine the NPV if the cost of capital were (1) to rise to 12 percent or (2) to fall to 8 percent.

    f. There is some uncertainty about the salvage value. It could be as low as $50,000 or as high as $90,000. What would the NPV be at those two salvage value levels? (Assume k = 10 percent.) Should this uncertainty affect the decision to invest? What salvage value (to the nearest thousand) would make you indifferent to the project?

    g. Return to the original salvage value of $80,000. What would be the project's NPV if the corporate tax rate were increased to 46 percent?

    h. Return the tax rate to 34 percent. Now assume that the manufacturer of the machine calls you with bad news: The base price of the machine has increased to $200,000. What does this do to the project's NPV? At what cost (to the nearest hundred) would Angell be indifferent to the project?

9-4 **(Replacement analysis)** The Diamond Equipment Company purchased a machine 5 years ago at a cost of $100,000. It had an expected life of 10 years at the time of purchase and an expected salvage value of $10,000 at the end of the 10 years. It is being depreciated by using the straight line method toward a salvage value of $10,000, or by $9,000 per year.

    A new machine can be purchased for $150,000, including installation costs. Over its 5-year life, it will reduce cash operating expenses by $50,000 per year. Sales are not expected to change. At the end of its useful life, the machine is estimated to be worthless. ACRS depreciation will be used, and it will be depreciated over its 3-year class life rather than its 5-year economic life.

    The old machine can be sold today for $65,000. The firm's tax rate is 34 percent. The appropriate discount rate is 15 percent.

    a. If the new machine is purchased, what is the amount of the initial cash flow at Year 0?

    b. What incremental operating cash flows will occur at the end of Years 1–5 as a result of replacing the old machine?

    c. What incremental nonoperating cash flow will occur at the end of Year 5 if the new machine is purchased?

    d. What is the NPV of this project? Should Diamond replace the old machine?

9-5 **(Replacement analysis)** The Orange Fizz Company is contemplating the replacement of one of its bottling machines with a newer and more efficient one. The old machine has a book value of $500,000 and a remaining useful life of 5 years. The firm does not expect to realize any return from scrapping the old machine in 5 years, but it can sell it now to another firm in the industry for $200,000. The old machine is being depreciated toward a zero salvage value, or by $100,000 per year, using the straight line method.

    The new machine has a purchase price of $1.2 million, an estimated useful life and ACRS class life of 5 years, and an estimated salvage value of $175,000. It is expected to economize on electric power usage, labor, and repair costs, and also to reduce the number of defective bottles. In total, an annual savings of $275,000 will be realized if it is installed. The company is in the 40 percent federal-plus-state tax bracket, and it has a 10 percent cost of capital.

    a. What is the initial cash outlay required for the new machine?

    b. Calculate the annual depreciation allowances for both machines, and compute the change in the annual depreciation expense if the replacement is made.

    c. What are the operating cash flows in Years 1 to 5?

    d. What is the cash flow from the salvage value in Year 5?

   e. Should the firm purchase the new machine? Support your answer.

   f. In general, how would each of the following factors affect the investment decision, and how should each be treated?
     (1) The expected life of the existing machine decreases.
     (2) The cost of capital is not constant but is increasing.

(Do Parts g, h, and i only if you are using the computerized diskette.)

   g. The firm may be able to purchase an alternative new bottling machine from another supplier. Its purchase price would be $1,050,000, and its salvage value would be $250,000. This machine has a lower annual operating savings of $210,000. Should the firm purchase this machine?

   h. If the salvage value on the alternative new machine were $200,000 rather than $250,000, how would this affect the decision?

   i. With everything as in Part h, assume that the cost of capital declined from 10 percent to 8 percent. How would this affect the decision?

9-6 **(Unequal lives)** Toddler Clothes, Inc., is considering the replacement of its old, fully depreciated knitting machine. Two new models are available: Machine 190-3, which has a cost of $190,000, a 3-year expected life, and after-tax cash flows (labor savings and depreciation) of $87,000 per year; and Machine 360-6, which has a cost of $360,000, a 6-year life, and after-tax cash flows of $98,300 per year. Knitting machine prices are not expected to rise, because inflation will be offset by cheaper components (microprocessors) used in the machines. Assume that Toddler's cost of capital is 14 percent.

   a. Should the firm replace its old knitting machine, and, if so, which new machine should it use?

   b. Suppose the firm's basic patents will expire in 9 years, and the company expects to go out of business at that time. Assume further that the firm depreciates its assets using the straight line method, that its marginal federal-plus-state tax rate is 40 percent, and that the used machines can be sold at their book values. Under these circumstances, should the company replace the old machine and, if so, which new model should the company purchase?

9-7 **(Abandonment value)** The Motown Milk Company recently purchased a new delivery truck. The new truck cost $22,500, and it is expected to generate net after-tax operating cash flows, including depreciation, of $6,250 per year. The truck has a 5-year expected life. The expected abandonment values (in this case, salvage values after tax adjustments) for the truck are given below. The company's cost of capital is 10 percent.

Year	Annual Operating Cash Flow	Abandonment Value
0	($22,500)	$22,500
1	6,250	17,500
2	6,250	14,000
3	6,250	11,000
4	6,250	5,000
5	6,250	0

   a. Should Motown operate the truck until the end of its 5-year life, or, if not, what is its optimal economic life?

b. Would the introduction of abandonment values, in addition to operating cash flows, ever *reduce* the expected NPV and/or the IRR of a project?

9-8 **(Inflation adjustments)** The Roth Company is considering an average risk investment in a mineral water spring project that has a cost of $150,000. The project will produce 1,000 cases of mineral water per year indefinitely. The current sales price is $138 per case, and the current cost per case (all variable) is $105. Roth is taxed at a rate of 34 percent. Both prices and costs are expected to rise at a rate of 6 percent per year. Roth uses only equity, and it has a cost of capital of 15 percent. Assume that cash flows consist only of after-tax profits, since the spring has an indefinite life and will not be depreciated.

    a. Should Roth accept the project? (Hint: The project is a perpetuity, so you must use the formula for a perpetuity to find the NPV.)

    b. If total costs consisted of a fixed cost of $10,000 per year and variable costs of $95 per unit, and if only the variable costs were expected to increase with inflation, would this make the project better or worse? Continue with the assumption that the sales price will rise with inflation.

9-9 **(Inflation adjustments)** The Aronson Company is evaluating an average-risk capital project having both a 3-year economic and ACRS class life. The net investment outlay at Time 0 is $18,800. The expected end-of-year cash flows, expressed in Time 0 dollars, are listed below: (Ignore salvage value and Year 4 depreciation.)

	Year 1	Year 2	Year 3
Revenues	$30,000	$30,000	$30,000
Variable costs	15,000	15,000	15,000
Fixed costs	6,500	6,500	6,500
Depreciation	6,204	8,460	2,820

The firm has a marginal federal-plus-state tax rate of 40 percent. Aronson's current cost of debt is 12 percent, and its cost of equity is 16 percent. These costs include an estimated inflation premium of 6 percent. The firm's target capital structure is 50 percent debt and 50 percent equity.

    a. What is Aronson's nominal WACC? Its real WACC?

    b. What are the project's relevant real cash flows? What discount rate should be utilized when calculating a project's NPV based upon real cash flows? Why?

    c. What is the NPV for this project? Should this project be accepted? What might have occurred if you had used the *nominal* WACC with *real* cash flows?

    d. Now assume that all revenues and costs, except depreciation, are expected to increase at the inflation rate of 6 percent. What are the project's nominal cash flows and NPV based on these flows? Why is this NPV different from the NPV calculated in Part c?

(Do Part e only if you are using the computerized diskette.)

    e. Assume that the firm's management anticipates a rate of inflation resulting in a 6 percent inflation premium for Year 1 through Year 3. Based upon this assumption, the firm accepts the project. However, suppose the firm actually experiences nonneutral inflation such that revenues increase by only 6 percent, while variable and fixed costs increase by 7.5 percent. What are the actual after-tax cash flows in this case? What effect would the acceptance of the project coupled with unanticipated nonneutral inflation have had upon the value of the firm?

f. If a company, in its capital budgeting process, bases its cash flows on sales prices and unit costs as of the time it analyzes the project, (1) would this tend to produce systematic errors in its capital budgeting evaluations, (2) would any such error be more serious for long-term or short-term projects, and (3) if you do think that systematic errors are likely to occur, how could they be corrected?

Solutions to Self-Test Problems

ST-1   a. *Estimated investment requirements:*

Price	($50,000)
Modification	(10,000)
Change in net working capital	(2,000)
Total investment	($62,000)

b. *Operating cash flows:*

	Year 1	Year 2	Year 3
1. After-tax cost savings	$12,000	$12,000	$12,000
2. Depreciation*	19,800	27,000	9,000
3. Depreciation tax savings**	7,920	10,800	3,600
Net cash flow (1 + 3)	$19,920	$22,800	$15,600

*Depreciable basis = $60,000; the ACRS percentage allowances are 0.33, 0.45, and 0.15 in Years 1, 2, and 3, respectively; hence depreciation in Year 1 = 0.33($60,000) = $19,800, and so on.

**Depreciation tax savings = T(Depreciation) = 0.4($19,800) = $7,920 in Year 1, and so on.

c. *End of project cash flows:*

Salvage value	$20,000
Tax on salvage value*	(6,320)
Net working capital recovery	2,000
	$15,680

*Sale price	$20,000
Less book value	4,200
Taxable income	$15,800
Tax at 40%	6,320

Note that Book value = Depreciable basis − Accumulated depreciation = $60,000 − $55,800 = $4,200.

d. *Project NPV:*

$$NPV = -\$62,000 + \frac{\$19,920}{(1.10)^1} + \frac{\$22,800}{(1.10)^2} + \frac{\$31,280}{(1.10)^3}$$

$$= -\$1,547.$$

Since the earthmover has a negative NPV, it should not be purchased.

ST-2 *First determine the net cash flow at t = 0:*

Purchase price	($8,000)
Sale of old machine	3,000
Tax on sale of old machine	(160)*
Change in net working capital	(1,500)**
Total investment	($6,660)

*The market value is $3,000 − $2,600 = $400 above the book value. Thus, there is a $400 recapture of depreciation, and Merville would have to pay 0.40($400) = $160 in taxes.

**The change in net working capital is a $2,000 increase in current assets less a $500 increase in current liabilities, which totals a $1,500 increase in net working capital.

Now, examine the operating cash inflows:

Sales increase	$1,000
Cost decrease	1,500
Pre-tax operating revenue increase	$2,500

After-tax operating revenue increase:

$$\$2,500(1 - T) = \$2,500(0.60) = \$1,500.$$

Depreciation:

Year	1	2	3	4	5	6
New*	$1,600	$2,560	$1,520	$ 960	$ 880	$ 480
Old	350	350	350	350	350	350
Change	$1,250	$2,210	$1,170	$ 610	$ 530	$ 130
Depreciation tax savings**	$ 500	$ 884	$ 468	$ 244	$ 212	$ 52

*Depreciable basis = $8,000. Depreciation expense in each year equals depreciable basis times the ACRS percentage allowance of 0.20, 0.32, 0.19, 0.12, 0.11, and 0.06 in Years 1–6, respectively.

**Depreciation tax-savings = T(Δ Depreciation) = 0.4(Δ Depreciation).

Now recognize that at the end of Year 6 Merville would recover its net working capital investment of $1,500, and it would also receive $800 from the sale of the replacement machine. However, since the machine is fully depreciated, the firm must pay 0.40($800) = $320 in taxes on the sale. Note also that by undertaking the replacement now, the firm foregoes the right to sell the old machine for $500 in Year 6; thus, this $500 in Year 6 must be considered as an opportunity cost in that year. There is no tax effect here since the $500 salvage value would equal the old machine's Year 6 book value.

Finally, place all the cash flows on a time-line:

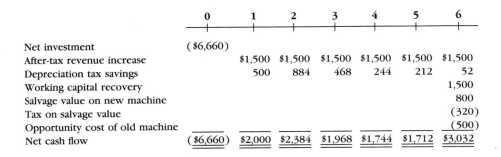

	0	1	2	3	4	5	6
Net investment	($6,660)						
After-tax revenue increase		$1,500	$1,500	$1,500	$1,500	$1,500	$1,500
Depreciation tax savings		500	884	468	244	212	52
Working capital recovery							1,500
Salvage value on new machine							800
Tax on salvage value							(320)
Opportunity cost of old machine							(500)
Net cash flow	($6,660)	$2,000	$2,384	$1,968	$1,744	$1,712	$3,032

The net present value of this incremental cash flow stream, when discounted at 15 percent, is $1,335. Thus, the replacement should be made.

Selected Additional References and Cases

Several articles have been written regarding the implications of the Accelerated Cost Recovery System (ACRS). Among them are the following:

Angell, Robert J., and Tony R. Wingler, "A Note on Expensing Versus Depreciating Under the Accelerated Cost Recovery System," *Financial Management,* Winter 1982, 34–35.

McCarty, Daniel E., and William R. McDaniel, "A Note on Expensing Versus Depreciating Under the Accelerated Cost Recovery System: Comment," *Financial Management,* Summer 1983, 37–39.

For further information on replacement analysis, as well as other aspects of capital budgeting, see the texts by Bierman and Smidt, by Grant, Ireson, and Leavengood, and by Levy and Sarnat referenced in Chapter 8.

Three additional papers on the impact of inflation on capital budgeting are the following:

Bailey, Andrew D., and Daniel L. Jensen, "General Price Level Adjustments in the Capital Budgeting Decision," *Financial Management,* Spring 1977, 26–32.

Mehta, Dileep R., Michael D. Curley, and Hung-Gay Fung, "Inflation, Cost of Capital, and Capital Budgeting Procedures," *Financial Management,* Winter 1984, 48–54.

Rappaport, Alfred, and Robert A. Taggart, Jr., "Evaluation of Capital Expenditure Proposals Under Inflation," *Financial Management,* Spring 1982, 5–13.

For additional insights into unequal life analysis, see

Emery, Gary W., "Some Guidelines for Evaluating Capital Investment Alternatives with Unequal Lives," *Financial Management,* Spring 1982, 15–19.

For an interesting discussion on cash flow estimation biases, see

Statman, Meir, and Tyzoon T. Tyebjee, "Optimistic Capital Budgeting Forecasts: An Experiment," *Financial Management,* Autumn 1985, 27–33.

For information on alternative NPV formulations, see

Brick, Ivan E., and Daniel G. Weaver, "A Comparison of Capital Budgeting Techniques in Identifying Profitable Investments," *Financial Management,* Winter 1984, 29–39.

The Crum-Brigham casebook contains the following cases which focus on Chapter 8 and 9 material:

Case 12, "Granville Pump Company," which focuses on the replacement decision.

Case 13, "Sugar Lake Refining and Processing Company," which illustrates the difference between accounting income and economic cash flow.

Case 14, "Narwhal Sports Industries, Inc.," which emphasizes the determination of relevant costs.

Case 17, "Composite Technologies Corporation," which illustrates the need to use replacement chains when alternatives with unequal lives are being compared.

The Harrington casebook contains the following relevant cases:

"Ing. C. Olivetti & Co. S.p.A.," which describes alternative plant investments.

"R. G. Barry Corporation," which focuses on the introduction of a new product.

"Massalin Particulares," which illustrates capital budgeting in an inflationary environment.

10

Risk Analysis and the Optimal Capital Budget

Capital budgeting is, in theory, a relatively straightforward, mechanical exercise — we simply estimate the cost of a project and its expected future cash flows, find the PV of the cash flows, and, if this PV exceeds the project's cost, accept it. This is fine if we have an accurate estimate of the project's cost and its future cash flows. However, if our cost and cash flow estimates are wrong, what initially looked like a good project can turn out to be a disaster.

To illustrate, Long Island Lighting Company (LILCO) decided to build the Shoreham nuclear power plant in the 1970s. At the time, the demand for electricity was growing at a rate of 7 percent per year, so it looked as though LILCO would have to double its generating capacity every 10 years to meet the electrical needs of its area. Thus, LILCO began the construction of Shoreham at a forecasted cost of $500 million.

The project turned out to be a fiasco. First, growth in the demand for power began to fall shortly after Shoreham was started, but LILCO failed to make adequate adjustments to its demand forecast. Second, the cost of building the plant had been drastically underestimated — by 1987, construction costs were estimated at about $6 billion versus the originally forecasted $0.5 billion, an 1,100 percent error!

With lower revenues and a higher initial cost, Shoreham's projected positive NPV turned out to be a huge negative one. As this book goes to press, the future of Shoreham is uncertain — the final cost of the plant is uncertain, as is demand for its output. LILCO is no longer able to pay dividends, and if the plant is abandoned and LILCO is forced to write it off, the company will be bankrupt. Its stockholders have already lost millions, as have its bondholders, and the company's top executives have lost their jobs. LILCO's customers have also suffered, as they must pay close to the highest rates in the nation for electricity, largely as a result of the Shoreham project.

About the same time LILCO decided to build Shoreham, Florida Power Corporation (FPC) was also studying the feasibility of a new nuclear plant. Several University of Florida finance professors met with the FPC planners and discussed with them the topics contained in this chapter as applied to their capital budgeting decision. FPC rejected nuclear and built a coal generating plant, and today its financial position is as good as LILCO's is bad. If you learn the lessons of this chapter, it will help you make good decisions like that of FPC and avoid LILCO-type disasters.

Risk analysis is important in all financial decisions, especially those relating to capital budgeting. As we saw in Chapter 6, the higher an investment's risk, the higher its required rate of return. This is equally true when the investor is a corporation and the investment is a capital project, and in this chapter we discuss procedures (1) for measuring the riskiness of potential capital projects, (2) for incorporating this information into the capital budgeting decision, and (3) for determining a firm's optimal capital budget.

INTRODUCTION TO RISK ASSESSMENT

Three separate and distinct types of project risk can be measured: (1) *market,* or *beta, risk,* which measures project risk from the standpoint of an investor who holds a highly diversified portfolio, (2) *within-firm total risk,* which looks at the effects a project has on the company's total risk, without considering the effects of the stockholders' own personal diversification, and (3) the project's own *stand-alone total risk,* or its risk disregarding the fact that it is but one asset within the firm's portfolio of assets and also the fact that the firm in question is but one stock in most investors' stock portfolios. As we shall see, a particular project might have highly uncertain returns, yet taking it on might not have much effect on the firm's risk or that of its owners because of portfolio effects.

A project's stand-alone risk is measured by the variability of the project's expected returns; its within-firm risk is measured by its impact on the firm's earnings variability; and its market risk is measured by its effect on the firm's beta coefficient. Taking on a project with a high degree of either stand-alone or within-firm risk will not necessarily affect the firm's beta to any great extent. However, if the project has highly uncertain returns, and if those returns are highly correlated with those of the firm's other assets and most other assets in the economy, then the project will have a high degree of all three types of risk. For example, suppose General Motors decides to undertake a major expansion to build solar-powered autos. GM is not sure how its technology will work on a mass production basis, so there are great risks in the venture — its stand-alone risk is high. Now suppose management also estimates that the project will have a higher probability of success if the economy is strong, for then people will have money to spend on the new autos. This means that the project will tend to do well if GM's other divisions are also doing well, and to do badly if other divisions do badly. In this case, the project will also have high within-firm risk. Finally, since GM's prospects are highly correlated with those of most other firms, the project's beta coefficient will be high, and it will be risky by all three measures.

Market risk is important because of its direct impact on stock price. Within-firm risk, often called *corporate risk,* is also important for three primary reasons:

1. Undiversified stockholders, including the owners of small businesses, are more concerned about corporate risk than about market risk.

2. Many financial theorists argue that investors, even those who are well diversified, consider factors other than market risk when setting required returns. Empirical studies of the determinants of required rates of return generally find both market and corporate risk to be important.

3. The firm's stability is important to its managers, workers, customers, suppliers, and creditors, and also to the community in which it operates. Firms that are in serious danger of bankruptcy, or even of suffering low profits and reduced output, have difficulty attracting and retaining good managers and workers. Also, both suppliers and customers are reluctant to depend on weak firms, and such firms have difficulty borrowing money except at high interest rates. These factors will tend to reduce risky firms' profitability, and hence the prices of their stocks.

For these reasons, corporate risk is also important, even to well-diversified stockholders.

TECHNIQUES FOR MEASURING STAND-ALONE RISK

What about a project's stand-alone risk — is it of any importance to anyone? In theory, this type of risk should be of little or no concern. However, it is of great importance, for these reasons:

1. It is much easier to estimate a project's stand-alone risk than its within-firm risk, and far, far easier to measure its stand-alone risk than its market risk.

2. In the vast majority of cases, all three types of risk are highly correlated — if the general economy does well, then so will the firm, and if the firm does well, then so will most of its projects. Thus, stand-alone risk is generally a good proxy for hard-to-measure market risk.

3. Therefore, if management wants a reasonably accurate assessment of a project's riskiness, it probably ought to spend considerable effort on ascertaining the riskiness of the project's own cash flows; that is, on its stand-alone risk.

The starting point for analyzing a project's stand-alone risk involves determining the uncertainty inherent in the project's cash flows. This analysis can be handled in a number of ways, ranging from informal judgments to complex economic and statistical analyses involving large-scale computer models. To illustrate what is involved, let's refer back to Hawkey-Weigle Corporation's appliance control computer project that we discussed in Chapter 9. Most of the individual cash flows in Tables 9-1, 9-2, and 9-3, which produced the expected net cash flows for the project as set forth in Table 9-4, are subject to uncertainty. For example, sales for

1991 were projected at 25,000 units to be sold at a net price of $2,200 per unit, or $55 million in total. However, unit sales would almost certainly be somewhat higher or lower than 25,000, and the sales price would probably be different from $2,200 per unit. In effect, the sales quantity and price estimates are really expected values taken from probability distributions, as are many of the other values listed in Tables 9-1 through 9-3. The distributions could be relatively "tight," reflecting small standard deviations and low risk, or they could be "flat," denoting a great deal of uncertainty about the variable in question and hence a high degree of stand-alone risk.

The nature of the individual cash flow distributions and their correlations with one another determine the nature of the NPV distribution, and thus the project's stand-alone risk. In the next section, we discuss four techniques for assessing a project's stand-alone risk: (1) sensitivity analysis, (2) scenario analysis, (3) Monte Carlo simulation, and (4) decision tree analysis.

Sensitivity Analysis

Intuitively, we know that many of the variables which determine a project's cash flows are based on some type of probability distribution rather than known with certainty. We also know that if a key input variable such as units sold changes, so will the project's NPV. *Sensitivity analysis is a technique which indicates exactly how much the NPV will change in response to a given change in an input variable, other things held constant.*

Sensitivity analysis begins with a *base case* situation developed using the expected input values. To illustrate, consider the data given in Table 9-2 in Chapter 9, where projected income statements for Hawkey-Weigle's computer project are shown. The values for unit sales, sales price, fixed costs, and variable costs are the *expected,* or *base case,* values, and the resulting $12,075,384 NPV shown in Table 9-4 is called the *base case NPV.* Now we ask a series of "what if" questions: "What if unit sales falls 20 percent below the expected level?" "What if the sales price per unit falls?" "What if variable costs are 70 percent of dollar sales rather than the expected 65 percent?" *Sensitivity analysis is designed to provide the decision maker with answers to questions such as these.*

In a sensitivity analysis, we change each variable by specific percentages above and below the expected value, holding other things constant, then calculate new NPVs, and finally plot the derived NPVs against the variable that was changed. Figure 10-1 shows the computer project's sensitivity graphs for three of the key input variables. The table below the graphs gives the NPVs that were used to construct the graphs. The slopes of the lines in the graphs show how sensitive NPV is to changes in each of the inputs: the steeper the slope, the more sensitive the NPV is to a change in the variable. Here we see that the project's NPV is very sensitive to changes in variable costs, fairly sensitive to changes in sales volume, and relatively insensitive to changes in the cost of capital.

If we were comparing two projects, the one with the steeper sensitivity lines would be regarded as riskier because a relatively small error in estimating a variable such as the variable cost per unit would produce a large error in the project's

---

Figure 10-1
Sensitivity Analysis (Thousands of Dollars)

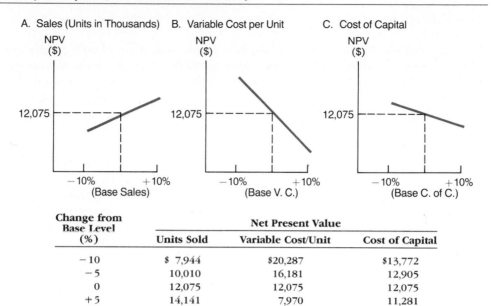

Change from Base Level (%)	Net Present Value		
	Units Sold	**Variable Cost/Unit**	**Cost of Capital**
− 10	$ 7,944	$20,287	$13,772
− 5	10,010	16,181	12,905
0	12,075	12,075	12,075
+ 5	14,141	7,970	11,281
+ 10	16,207	3,864	10,521

Note: This analysis was performed using *Lotus 1-2-3*, so the values are slightly different than those that would be obtained using interest factor tables due to rounding differences.

---

projected NPV. Thus, sensitivity analysis can provide useful insights into the riskiness of a project.

Before we move on, note these two additional points about sensitivity analysis. First, spreadsheet computer models are ideally suited for performing sensitivity analysis, because such models automatically recalculate NPV when an input value is changed. We used a *Lotus 1-2-3* model to conduct the analyses represented in Figure 10-1, both the tabular data and the graphs. Second, we could have plotted all of the sensitivity lines on one graph; this would have facilitated direct comparisons of the sensitivities among different input variables.

Scenario Analysis

Although sensitivity analysis is probably the most widely used risk analysis technique, it does have limitations. Consider, for example, a proposed coal mine whose NPV is highly sensitive to changes in output, variable costs, and sales prices. However, if a utility company has contracted to buy a fixed amount of coal at a fixed price per ton, plus inflation adjustments, then the mining venture may be quite safe in spite of its steep sensitivity lines. *In general, a project's stand-alone risk depends on both (1) the sensitivity of its NPV to changes in key variables and (2) the range of likely values of these variables as reflected in their probability distributions.* Because sensitivity analysis considers only the first factor, it is incomplete.

A risk analysis technique that considers both the sensitivity of NPV to changes in key variables and also the range of likely variable values is *scenario analysis.* Here, the financial analyst asks operating managers to pick a "bad" set of circumstances (low unit sales, low sales price, high variable cost per unit, high construction cost, and so on) and a "good" set. The NPVs under the "bad" and "good" conditions are then calculated and compared to the expected, or base case, NPV.

As an example, let us return to the appliance control computer project. Assume that Hawkey-Weigle's managers are fairly confident of their estimates of all the project's cash flow variables except price and unit sales. Further, suppose they regard a drop in unit sales below 15,000, or a rise above 35,000 units, as being extremely unlikely. Similarly, they expect the sales price as set in the marketplace to fall within the range of $1,700 to $2,700. Thus, 15,000 units at a price of $1,700 defines the lower bound, or the worst case scenario, while 35,000 units at a price of $2,700 defines the upper bound, or the best case scenario. Remember that the expected, or base case, values are 25,000 units and a price of $2,200. Also, note that the indicated sales prices are for 1991, with future years' prices expected to rise because of inflation.

To carry out the scenario analysis, we use the worst case variable values to obtain the worst case NPV and the best case variable values to obtain the best case NPV.[1] We actually performed the analysis using our *Lotus* model, and Table 10-1 summarizes the results of our analysis. We see that the base case forecasts a positive NPV; the worst case produces a negative NPV; and the best case results in a very large positive NPV. We can use the results of the scenario analysis to determine the expected NPV, standard deviation of NPV, and coefficient of variation. To begin, we need an estimate of the probabilities of occurrence of the three scenarios. Suppose management estimates that there is a 25 percent probability of the worst case occurring, a 50 percent probability of the base case, and a 25 percent probability of the best case. Of course, it is *very difficult* to estimate scenario probabilities accurately.

Now we have a discrete probability distribution of returns just like those we dealt with in Chapter 6, except that the returns are measured in dollars (NPV) rather than in percentages (rate of return). The expected NPV (in thousands of dollars) is

$$0.25(-\$10,079) + 0.50(\$12,075) + 0.25(\$41,752) = \$13,956.$$

---

[1] We could have included worst and best case values for fixed and variable costs, the inflation rate, salvage values, and so on. For illustrative purposes, we limited the changes to only two variables. Also, note that we are treating sales price and quantity as independent variables; that is, a low sales price could occur when unit sales were low, and a high sales price could be coupled with high unit sales, or vice versa. As we discuss in the next section, it is relatively easy to vary these assumptions if the facts of the situation suggest a different set of conditions.

Table 10-1
Scenario Analysis

Scenario	Probability of Outcome	Sales Volume (Units)	Sales Price	NPV (Thousands)
Worst case	0.25	15,000	$1,700	($10,079)
Base case	0.50	25,000	2,200	12,075
Best case	0.25	35,000	2,700	41,752
			Expected NPV =	$13,956
			σ_{NPV} =	$18,421

Note: Variables other than unit sales and sales prices were set at their expected values.

Note that the expected NPV is *not* the same as the base case NPV, $12,075 (in thousands). This is because the two uncertain variables, sales volume and sales price, are multiplied together to get dollar sales, and this process causes the NPV distribution to be skewed to the right. (A big number times another big number produces a very big number, which in turn causes the average, or expected value, to be increased.) The standard deviation of NPV is $18,421 (in thousands of dollars):[2]

$$\sigma_{NPV} = [0.25(-\$10,079 - \$13,956)^2 + 0.50(\$12,075 - \$13,956)^2$$
$$+ 0.25(\$41,752 - \$13,956)^2]^{1/2} = \$18,421.$$

---

[2]If we had a probability distribution for the net cash flow for each year of a project's life, then we could calculate the expected net cash flow for each year, CF_t, and the variance of that cash flow, σ_t^2. We could then calculate the expected NPV as

$$E(NPV) = \sum_{t=0}^{n} \frac{CF_t}{(1 + k)^t}. \tag{10-1}$$

If the net cash flow distributions across time were normal and were not correlated with one another (intertemporally independent), then the standard deviation of the NPV would be calculated as follows:

$$\text{Independent cash flow case: } \sigma_{NPV} = \left[\sum_{t=0}^{n} \frac{\sigma_t^2}{(1 + k)^{2t}} \right]^{1/2}. \tag{10-2}$$

If the net cash flow distributions from one year to the next were normal and were completely dependent on one another (intertemporally dependent) such that the correlation coefficient between them is 1.0, then σ_{NPV} is calculated as

$$\text{Dependent cash flow case: } \sigma_{NPV} = \sum_{t=0}^{n} \frac{\sigma_t}{(1 + k)^t}. \tag{10-3}$$

See Frederick S. Hillier, "The Derivation of Probabilistic Information for the Evaluation of Risky Investments," *Managerial Science*, April 1963, 443–457. Although Hillier's approach to finding projects' standard deviations is relatively simple, it is rarely used in practice because (1) many project cash flow distributions are not normal and (2) most project cash flow distributions over time are neither totally independent nor perfectly positively correlated. Still, Hillier's model does show that if a project's cash flows are independent across time (that is, fluctuate randomly from year to year), this indicates a less risky situation than if cash flows are dependent, because for a given set of σ_t, Equation 10-2 produces a lower σ_{NPV} than Equation 10-3.

Finally, the project's coefficient of variation is 1.3:

$$CV_{NPV} = \frac{\sigma_{NPV}}{E(NPV)} = \frac{\$18,421}{\$13,956} = 1.3.$$

The project's coefficient of variation can be compared with the coefficient of variation of Hawkey-Weigle's "average" project to get an idea of the relative corporate riskiness of the appliance control computer project. Hawkey-Weigle's existing projects have an aggregate coefficient of variation of about 1.0. Thus, on the basis of this stand-alone total risk measure, Hawkey-Weigle's managers would conclude that the appliance computer project is riskier than the firm's "average" project.

Scenario analysis provides useful information about a project's stand-alone risk. However, it is limited in that it only considers a few discrete outcomes (NPVs) for the project, although there are in reality an infinite number of possibilities. In the next section, we describe a more rigorous method of assessing a project's stand-alone risk.

Monte Carlo Simulation

Monte Carlo simulation, so named because this type of analysis grew out of work on the mathematics of casino gambling, ties together sensitivities and input variable probability distributions.[3] However, simulation requires a relatively powerful computer, coupled with an efficient financial planning software package, while scenario analysis can be done using a PC with a spreadsheet program, or even with a calculator.

The first step in a computer simulation is to specify the probability distribution of each uncertain cash flow variable. Once this has been done, the simulation proceeds as follows:

1. The computer chooses at random a value for each uncertain variable based on its specified probability distribution. For example, a value for unit sales would be chosen.

2. The value selected for each uncertain variable, along with values for fixed factors such as the tax rate and depreciation charges, are then used by the model to determine the net cash flows for each year, and these cash flows are then used to determine the project's NPV.

3. Steps 1 and 2 are repeated many times, say 500, resulting in 500 NPVs which make up a probability distribution.

We used the *Interactive Financial Planning System (IFPS)* to conduct a simulation analysis on the appliance control computer project. The results are summarized in Table 10-2, and the resulting NPV probability distribution is plotted in

---

[3]The use of simulation analysis in capital budgeting was first reported by David B. Hertz, "Risk Analysis in Capital Investments," *Harvard Business Review,* January–February 1964, 95–106. Usually, continuous distributions are used in simulations.

Table 10-2
Summary of Simulation Results

	Probability of NPV or IRR Being Greater than the Indicated Value: (Thousands of Dollars)								
	0.90	**0.80**	**0.70**	**0.60**	**0.50**	**0.40**	**0.30**	**0.20**	**0.10**
NPV	($8,397)	($2,917)	$2,562	$8,041	$13,521	$19,796	$26,072	$32,347	$38,622
IRR	0.090	0.129	0.161	0.189	0.214	0.231	0.252	0.273	0.309

NPV Sample Statistics (Thousands of Dollars)		
Mean	**Standard Deviation**	**Skewness Coefficient**
$13,779	$10,124	0.1

Figure 10-2. There is a 90 percent probability that NPV will exceed − $8,397,000 and IRR will exceed 9 percent. Thus, there is a 10 percent probability of NPV < − $8,397,000 and IRR < 9%. There is about a 25 percent chance that the project would have a negative NPV. Also, note that the simulation output includes the NPV's expected value (mean) and standard deviation. Thus, the project's coeffi-

Figure 10-2
NPV Probability Distribution (Millions of Dollars)

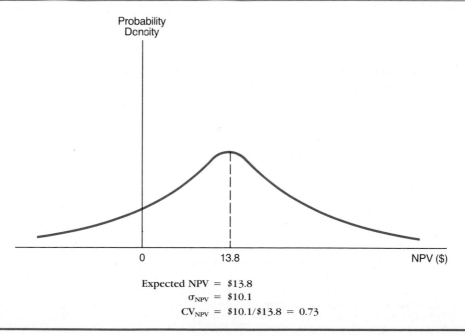

Expected NPV = $13.8
σ_{NPV} = $10.1
CV_{NPV} = $10.1/$13.8 = 0.73

cient of variation of NPV can be calculated, and the project's stand-alone risk can be estimated in the same way as we did in our discussion of scenario analysis.[4]

Limitations of Scenario and Simulation Analysis

In spite of its obvious appeal, simulation analysis has not been widely used in industry. One of the major problems is specifying the correlations among the uncertain cash flow variables. Mechanically, it is easy to incorporate any type of correlation among variables into a simulation analysis; for example, *IFPS* permits us to specify both intervariable and intertemporal correlations. However, it is *not* easy to specify what the correlations should be. Indeed, people who have tried to obtain such relationships from the operating managers who must estimate them have eloquently emphasized the difficulties involved. Clearly, the problem is not insurmountable, as simulation is used in business. Still, it is important not to underestimate the difficulty of obtaining valid estimates of probability distributions and correlations among the variables.[5]

Another problem with both scenario and simulation analyses is that even when the analysis has been completed, no clear-cut decision rule emerges. We end up with an expected NPV and a distribution about this expected value, which we can use to judge the project's stand-alone risk. However, the analysis provides no mechanism to indicate whether a project's profitability as measured by the expected NPV is sufficient to compensate for its risk as measured by σ_{NPV} or CV_{NPV}.

Finally, scenario and simulation analyses ignore the effects of diversification, both among projects within the firm and by investors in their personal investment portfolios. Thus, an individual project may have highly uncertain returns when evaluated on a "stand-alone" basis, but if those returns are not correlated with the returns on the firm's other assets, then the project may not be very risky in terms of either within-firm or market risk. Indeed, if the project's returns are negatively correlated with the returns on the firm's other assets, then it may decrease the firm's corporate risk, and the larger its σ_{NPV}, the more it will reduce the firm's overall risk. Similarly, if a project's returns are not positively correlated with the

---

[4]Note that the standard deviation of NPV in the simulation is much smaller than the standard deviation we obtained in the scenario analysis. In the scenario analysis, we assumed that the low unit sales figure would be coupled with the low sales price for the worst case, and high values for each for the best case. That is, we assumed that these variables were *dependent* on one another, so high unit sales would mean high price, and vice versa. Thus, we ended up with only 3 NPVs, and a 25 percent probability of the worst case occurring.

In the simulation, we assumed that unit sales and price are *independent* of one another. Thus, in the simulation a high unit sales could be picked, and in the same run the computer could choose a low sales price. When the two variables are independent, the probability of a very low unit sales coupled with a very low sales price is remote. Further, in a simulation there are many possible values for each uncertain variable, while in a scenario analysis there is a discrete number (3 in our example). These two differences led to a lower standard deviation in the simulation analysis.

[5]For an interesting discussion of the pros and cons of simulation analysis, see Wilbur G. Lewellen and Michael S. Long, "Simulation Versus Single-Value Estimates in Capital Expenditure Analysis," *Decision Sciences,* October 1972, 19–33. For more insight into the difficulties involved in estimating probability distributions and correlations in practice, see K. Larry Hastie, "One Businessman's View of Capital Budgeting," *Financial Management,* Winter 1974, 36–43. Hastie was treasurer of Bendix Corporation.

stock market, then even a project with highly variable returns might not be regarded as risky by well-diversified stockholders, who are normally more concerned with market risk than with total risk.

Decision Tree Analysis

Up to this point, we have focused primarily on techniques for estimating a project's stand-alone riskiness. Although this is an integral part of capital budgeting, managers are much more concerned about *reducing* risk than they are about *measuring* it. Often, project expenditures are not made at one point in time, but, rather, are made over a period of years, which gives managers the opportunity to reevaluate decisions and either invest additional funds or cancel (abandon) the project. Projects that require capital outlays over several years are often evaluated using a *decision tree*.

For example, suppose General Robotics Corporation is considering the production of industrial robots for the television manufacturing industry. The net investment for this project will be broken down into three stages, as set forth in Figure 10-3.

Stage 1. At t − 0, conduct a $500,000 study of the market potential for robot use in television assembly lines.

Stage 2. If it appears that a sizable market for television assembly robots does exist, then at t = 1 spend $1,000,000 to design and fabricate several prototype robots.

Figure 10-3
General Robotics Corporation Decision Tree (Thousands of Dollars)

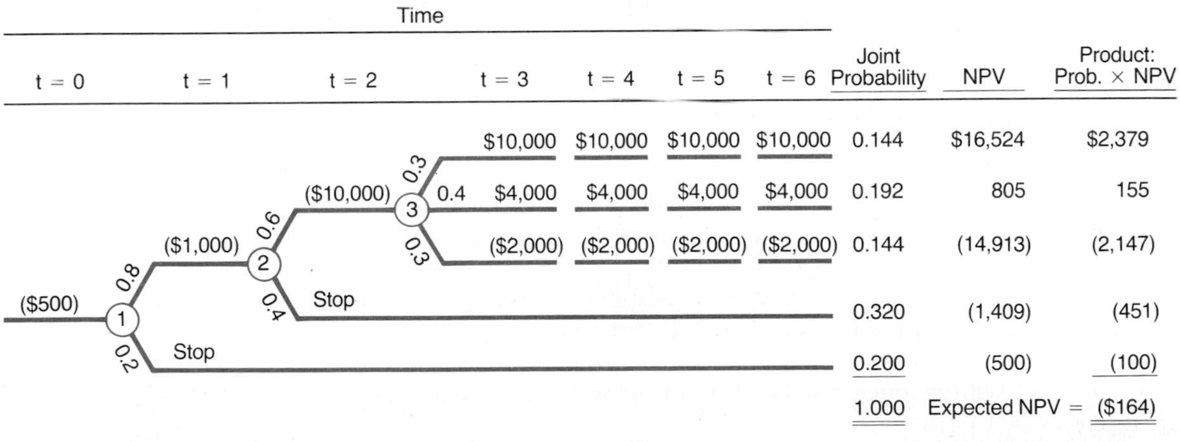

t = 0	t = 1	t = 2	t = 3	t = 4	t = 5	t = 6	Joint Probability	NPV	Product: Prob. × NPV
			$10,000	$10,000	$10,000	$10,000	0.144	$16,524	$2,379
		($10,000)	$4,000	$4,000	$4,000	$4,000	0.192	805	155
	($1,000)		($2,000)	($2,000)	($2,000)	($2,000)	0.144	(14,913)	(2,147)
		Stop					0.320	(1,409)	(451)
($500)	Stop						0.200	(500)	(100)
							1.000	Expected NPV =	($164)

These robots would then be evaluated by television industry engineers, and their reactions would determine whether General Robotics would proceed with the project.

Stage 3. If reaction to the prototype robots is good, then at t = 2 build a production plant at a net cost of $10,000,000. If this stage were reached, managers estimate that the project would generate net cash flows over the following 4 years which depend on how well the final product was received by TV manufacturers.

A decision tree such as the one in Figure 10-3 is often used to analyze such multistage, or sequential, decisions. Here, we assume that one year goes by between decisions. Each circle represents a decision point, or stage. The dollar value to the left of each decision point represents the net investment required to reach that decision point, and the cash flows shown under t = 3 to t = 6 represent the cash inflows if the project is pushed on to completion. Each diagonal line represents a branch of the decision tree, and each branch has an estimated probability. For example, if General Robotics decides to "go" with the project at Decision Point 1, it will have to spend $500,000 on a marketing study. Management estimates that there is a probability of 0.8 that the study will produce favorable results, leading to the decision to move on to Stage 2, and a 0.2 probability that the marketing study will produce negative results, indicating that the project should be canceled after Stage 1. If the project is stopped here, the cost to the company will be $500,000 for the initial marketing study, and it will be a loss.

If the marketing study is undertaken, and if it does yield positive results, then General Robotics will spend $1,000,000 on the prototype robot and thus go on to Decision Point 2. Management estimates (before even making the initial $500,000 investment) that there is a 60 percent probability that the television engineers will find the robot useful and a 40 percent probability that they will not like it. These are conditional probabilities; that is, they are conditioned upon reaching Decision Point 2.

If the engineers accept the robot, General Robotics will then spend the final $10,000,000 to build the plant and go into production, while if the engineers do not like the prototype, the project will be dropped. If General Robotics does go into production, the operating cash flows over the project's 4-year life will depend on how well the market receives the final product. There is a 30 percent chance that reception will be quite good and net cash flows will be $10,000,000 per year, a 40 percent probability of $4,000,000 each year, and a 30 percent chance of a $2,000,000 negative cash flow per year. These cash inflows are shown under Years 3 through 6. Also, note that General Robotics could elect to terminate or abandon the project even after it goes into operation.

The joint probabilities shown in Figure 10-3 give the probability of occurrence of each final outcome. Each joint probability is obtained by multiplying together all probabilities on a particular branch. For example, the probability that the company will, if Stage 1 is undertaken, move through Stages 2 and 3, and that a strong demand will produce $10,000,000 of inflows over 4 years, is $(0.8)(0.6)(0.3) = 0.144 = 14.4\%$.

The NPV of each final outcome is also given in Figure 10-3. The company has a cost of capital of 10 percent, and management assumes initially that all projects have average risk. The NPV of the top (most favorable) outcome is about $16,524 (in thousands of dollars):

$$\text{NPV} = -\$500 - \frac{\$1,000}{(1.10)^1} - \frac{\$10,000}{(1.10)^2} + \frac{\$10,000}{(1.10)^3} + \frac{\$10,000}{(1.10)^4} + \frac{\$10,000}{(1.10)^5} + \frac{\$10,000}{(1.10)^6}$$

$$= \$16,524.$$

Other NPVs were calculated similarly.

The last column in Figure 10-3 gives the product of the NPV for each branch times the joint probability of that branch, and the sum of the NPV products is the expected NPV of the project. Based on the expectations set forth in Figure 10-3 and a cost of capital of 10 percent, the expected NPV is − $164,000.

Since the expected NPV is negative, it would appear that General Robotics should reject the project, but that conclusion is not necessarily correct. First, recall that management assumed that the project is of average risk, and hence used the unadjusted cost of capital to evaluate it. However, the company should now consider whether this project is more, less, or as risky as an average project. The expected NPV is a negative $164,000, and the standard deviation of that NPV is $8,493,000, so the coefficient of variation is quite large. This suggests that the project is highly risky in terms of stand-alone risk. Note also that there is a 0.144 + 0.320 + 0.200 = 0.664 probability of incurring a loss. Based on all this, the project appears to be unacceptable. However, there is another consideration — the project can be abandoned, and this option could have a considerable impact on the analysis. We discuss this point in the next section.

THE IMPACT OF ABANDONMENT ON NPV AND PROJECT RISK

In Chapter 9 we introduced the concept of abandonment value. We now illustrate how the possibility of abandonment can affect a project's risk as well as its expected NPV. Suppose General Robotics is not contractually bound to continue the project once operations have begun. Thus, if sales are poor and cash flows amount to only − $2,000 during the first year of operations, and a similar cash flow situation is expected for the remainder of the project's life, the project can be abandoned at the beginning of Year 4 rather than continue to suffer losses over the next 3 years. (In this case, low first year cash flows signify that the product is not well received in the market, and hence that future sales will be poor. In other cases, the cash flows could vary from year to year depending on economic conditions, in which case low first year sales and cash flows might be followed by high cash flows in subsequent years.)

The ability to abandon the project changes the branch of the decision tree in Figure 10-3 that contains the series of $2,000 losses. It now looks like this:

	Joint Probability	NPV	Product: Prob. × NPV
	0.144	(11,176)	(1,609)

Changing this branch to reflect the abandonment alternative causes the NPV for the branch to be less negative, and this increases the project's expected NPV to about $374,000 and lowers its standard deviation to $7,633,000. Thus, abandonment considerations changed the project's NPV from negative to positive, and also lowered its stand-alone risk as measured by either the standard deviation or the coefficient of variation.

Here are some additional points to note concerning decision tree analysis and abandonment:

1. Managers can reduce project risk if they can structure the decision process to include several decision points rather than just one. To illustrate, if General Robotics made a total commitment at t = 0, signing contracts that would in effect require completion of the project, it might save some money and accelerate the project, but in doing so it would substantially increase the project's riskiness.

2. Once production begins, if the firm can shut down or spin off the operation, this could dramatically reduce its risk. Indeed, firms do this frequently. To illustrate, in 1982 Woolworth liquidated every one of its 336 Woolco discount stores in the United States. These stores had been operating at a loss, and Woolworth abandoned the entire division, selling off the stores piecemeal. In another example, General Motors recently sold several of its plants which produce parts required in its autos. These plants were sold to non-union companies, and hence the buyers were able to produce the parts using low-cost labor. GM ended up getting the parts at a lower cost than when they were produced in GM-owned plants. Similar spin-offs have occurred in many industries, including the airlines, where a non-union carrier such as Texas Air can buy a high-cost, unionized carrier such as Eastern, paint the planes and operate them with non-union crews, and turn a negative cash flow situation into a positive one. Such possibilities must be considered when major capital budgeting decisions are being made.

3. Finally, note that capital budgeting is a dynamic process. Virtually all inputs to a capital budgeting decision change over time, and firms must periodically review both their capital expenditure plans and their on-going projects. In the General Robotics example, conditions might change between Decision Points 1 and 2, and if so, this new information should be used to develop revised probability and cash flow estimates.

A dramatic example of both good and bad decisions in this area is nuclear power plant construction. When the demand for electric power dropped sharply, and construction costs rose in the aftermath of the TMI accident, some utilities reexamined their nuclear plant construction plans and decided to cancel plants. This required write-offs amounting to millions of dollars. Other companies decided to keep building, and ended up losing literally billions of dollars.

The key concept to remember is that decisions can often be structured with multiple decision points; if so, and if the company has the willpower to admit it when a project is not likely to work out as initially planned, then risks can be reduced and expected cash flows can be increased.

MARKET RISK

The types of risk analysis discussed thus far provide insights into a project's stand-alone risk. However, as we noted, these methods do not take account of portfolio risk, and they are subjective rather than objective in the sense that they do not specify which projects should be accepted and which rejected. In this section, we discuss how the CAPM might be used to help overcome those shortcomings. Of course, the CAPM has shortcomings of its own, but it can provide some useful insights into capital budgeting risk analysis.

To begin, recall that the Security Market Line expresses the risk/return relationship as follows:

$$k_s = k_{RF} + (k_M - k_{RF})b_i.$$

For example, if General Robotic's beta $= 1.2$, $k_{RF} = 8\%$, and $k_M = 13\%$, then General's cost of equity is 14 percent:

$$k_s = 8\% + (13\% - 8\%)1.2$$
$$= 8\% + (5\%)1.2 = 14.0\%.$$

Further, if General's cost of debt is 10 percent, its marginal federal-plus-state tax rate is 40 percent, and its target capital structure calls for 50 percent debt and 50 percent common equity, then its WACC is 10 percent:

$$WACC = k_a = w_dk_d(1 - T) + w_sk_s$$
$$= 0.5(10\%)(0.60) + 0.5(14\%)$$
$$= 3.0\% + 7.0\% = 10.0\%.$$

This suggests that investors would be willing to give General money to invest in average-risk projects if the company could earn 10 percent or more on this money. In this case, the term "average risk" means projects which have *market* risk— which is the risk that concerns the investors who supply capital to the company —similar to that of the firm's existing assets.

Now recall that a firm is a portfolio of assets, and its beta as established in the market is an average of its assets' betas. Therefore, if taking on a particular project will cause a change in General's 1.2 beta coefficient, then taking on the project will also cause a change in the company's cost of equity. For example, a new project might have a beta of 2.0, so taking it on would cause the overall corporate beta to rise, and it will end up somewhere between the original beta of 1.2 and the new project's beta of 2.0. The new corporate beta will depend on the relative size of the investment in the new project versus the company's investment in other assets. If 80 percent of General's total funds would be in other assets with an average beta of 1.2, and 20 percent in the new project with a beta of 2.0, then the new corporate beta would be 1.36, up from 1.2:

$$\text{New } b = 0.8(1.2) + 0.2(2.0) = 1.36.$$

This increase in General's market risk would cause the stock price to decline *unless the increased beta were offset by a higher expected overall rate of return.* Specifically, taking on the new project would cause the required rate of return on equity to rise to 14.8 percent,

$$k_s = 8\% + (5\%)1.36 = 14.8\%,$$

and the overall corporate cost of capital would rise to 10.4 percent:

$$\text{WACC} = k_a = 0.5(10\%)(0.60) + 0.5(14.8\%) = 10.4\%.$$

Therefore, to keep the new project from lowering the value of the firm, General's expected overall rate of return would have to rise from 10.0 to 10.4 percent.

If investments in General's original assets must earn 10.0 percent, how much must the new project earn in order for the new overall rate of return to equal 10.4 percent? We know that if it completes the new project, General would have 80 percent of its assets invested in other assets earning 10.0 percent, that 20 percent of its assets would be in the new project earning X percent, and that the average required rate of return would be 10.4 percent. Therefore,

$$0.8(10.0\%) + 0.2X = 10.4\%$$
$$0.2X = 10.4\% - 8.0\%$$
$$X = 2.4\%/0.2 = 12.0\%.$$

Therefore, the new project must have an overall expected return of 12.0 percent if the corporation is to expect to earn its new cost of capital.

In summary, if General takes on the new project, its corporate beta would rise from 1.2 to 1.36; its cost of equity would increase from 14.0 to 14.8 percent; its weighted average cost of capital would rise from 10.0 to 10.4 percent; and the new project would have to earn at least 12.0 percent for General to earn its overall cost of capital.

This line of reasoning leads to the conclusion that if the beta coefficient for each project, b_i, could be determined, then an individual project's weighted average cost of capital, $\text{WACC}_i = k_{ai}$, could be found as follows:

1. Find Project i's required rate of return on equity, k_{si}:

$$k_{si} = k_{RF} + (k_M - k_{RF})b_i.$$

2. Use k_{si} to find the project's overall required rate of return, $k_{ai} = \text{WACC}_i$:

$$\text{WACC}_i = k_{ai} = w_d k_d (1 - T) + w_s k_{si}.$$

Applying these two steps to General's new project gives this result:

$$k_{si} = 8\% + (5\%)2.0 = 18.0\%,$$

and

$$\text{WACC}_i = k_{ai} = 0.5(10\%)(0.60) + 0.5(18.0\%) = 12.0\%.$$

We see that the required rate of return on the new project is the same using this "short-cut" method as it was when we developed the project's cost of capital by solving for X in the equation $10.4\% = 0.8(10\%) + 0.2X$. Note, however, that both solutions disregard any effects of the new project on either the firm's capital structure or its cost of debt; implicitly, we assumed that the cost of the debt used to support the new project, and the financing mix, would be the same as for the firm's existing assets.

TECHNIQUES FOR MEASURING MARKET RISK

In Chapter 7, when we discussed the estimation of firms' betas, we indicated that it is difficult to estimate "true future betas" for common stocks. The estimation of *project* betas is even more difficult and more fraught with uncertainty, primarily because individual operating assets pay no dividends and have no quoted market prices, and hence we cannot calculate historical betas for use in the analysis. However, two approaches have been used for estimating the betas of individual assets: (1) the pure play method and (2) the accounting beta method.

The Pure Play Method

In the *pure play method,* the company tries to find one or more nonintegrated, single product companies in the same line of business as the project being evaluated.[6] For example, suppose General could find several existing single-product firms that were in the same line of business as the new project being evaluated. Further, suppose General believes that its new project would be subject to the same risks as those of the other firms. It could then determine the betas of these firms by the regular regression process, average them, and use this average as a proxy for the project's beta.[7]

---

[6]One important article on this subject is Russell J. Fuller and Halbert S. Kerr, "Estimating the Divisional Cost of Capital: An Analysis of the Pure-Play Technique," *Journal of Finance,* December 1981, 997–1009. Fuller and Kerr used the method to estimate divisional betas and then tested the results empirically. They concluded that the pure play method is a valid technique for estimating the betas of major sub-parts of a firm.

[7]Our discussion here is somewhat simplified. The proxy betas reflect each proxy firm's capital structure. If the proxy firm's capital structure is different from the financing mix that the evaluating firm would use, then the proxy beta must be adjusted to account for this difference. We will discuss a procedure for making this adjustment in Chapter 12.

The pure play approach is often difficult to implement because it is difficult to find pure play proxy firms. However, there are times when the method is feasible. For example, when IBM was considering going into personal computers, it was able to get data on Apple Computer and several other essentially pure play personal computer companies. Similarly, Pillsbury can employ this technique when it is considering capital budgeting decisions in its Burger King, Godfather's Pizza, Steak and Ale, and Bennigan's divisions. However, it is impossible to employ the technique when considering an asset such as a lathe.

The Accounting Beta Method

As previously noted, it is generally not possible to find single-product, publicly traded firms suitable for the pure play approach. When this is the case, companies sometimes use the *accounting beta method.* As you know, betas are normally found by regressing the returns on a particular company's stock against returns on a stock market index. However, one could run a time series regression of the company's basic earning power (EBIT/Total assets) against the average basic earning power for a large sample of stocks such as the NYSE or the S&P 500. Such data are readily available from Standard & Poor's Compustat tapes. Betas determined in this way, using accounting data rather than stock market data, are called *accounting betas.*

Historical accounting betas can be calculated for all types of companies (publicly owned or privately held), for divisions, or even for certain types of large projects. But how good are accounting betas as proxies for market betas? Many studies have addressed this issue.[8] Although the results vary, most studies do support the conclusion that firms with high accounting betas tend to have high market betas, whereas firms with low accounting betas tend to have low market betas. However, the correlations are generally only in the 0.5 to 0.6 range, so accounting-determined betas provide only rough approximations for market-determined betas, systematic risk, and consequently the cost of capital.

Note that the accounting beta technique can also be used to estimate different divisions' within-firm risk. Here the firm's overall accounting rate of return would be used as the benchmark in lieu of the S&P's rate of return, and the results would reflect the degree of correlation between different divisions. If a company is interested in how a project (or a division) affects the stability of the corporation's earnings, this technique is useful.

PROBLEMS WITH PROJECT RISK ASSESSMENT

We have discussed the three types of risk normally considered in capital budgeting analyses — stand-alone risk, within-firm risk, and market risk — and we have discussed ways of assessing each. However, two important questions remain: (1) Is it

---

[8]The original work on this subject was William H. Beaver and James Manegold, "The Association between Market-Determined Measures of Systematic Risk: Some Further Evidence," *Journal of Financial and Quantitative Analysis,* June 1975, 231–284. That study, and many subsequent ones, are summarized in George Foster, *Financial Statement Analysis* (Englewood Cliffs, N. J.: Prentice-Hall, 1986).

correct for a firm to be concerned with stand-alone and within-firm risk in its capital budgeting decisions, and (2) what do we do when the stand-alone and/or within-firm assessments and the market risk assessment lead to different conclusions?

These questions do not have easy answers. From a theoretical standpoint, well-diversified investors should be concerned only with market risk, managers should be concerned only with stock price maximization, and these two factors should lead to the conclusion that market, or beta, risk ought to be given virtually all the weight in capital budgeting decisions. However, if investors are not well diversified, if the CAPM does not really operate as theory says it should, or if measurement problems keep us from implementing the CAPM approach in capital budgeting, then it might be appropriate to give stand-alone and within-firm risk more weight than financial theorists would suggest. Note also that the CAPM ignores financial distress costs, even though such costs can be significant, and that the probability of financial distress depends on a firm's total risk, not on its beta risk. Therefore, one could easily conclude that even well-diversified investors should want a firm's management to give at least some consideration to a project's within-firm risk rather than concentrating entirely on market risk.

Although it would be desirable to reconcile these problems and to measure project risk on some absolute scale, the best we can do in practice is to determine project risk in a somewhat nebulous, relative sense. For example, we can generally say, with a fair degree of confidence, that a particular project has more or less stand-alone risk than the firm's average project. Then, assuming that stand-alone and within-firm, or corporate, risk are highly correlated (which is typical), a project's stand-alone risk is a good measure of its corporate risk. Finally, assuming that market risk and corporate risk are highly correlated (as studies suggest), a project with more corporate risk than average will also have more market risk, and vice versa for projects with low corporate risk.[9]

INCORPORATING PROJECT RISK AND CAPITAL STRUCTURE INTO CAPITAL BUDGETING DECISIONS

Thus far, we have seen that capital budgeting can affect a firm's market risk, its corporate risk, or both. We have also seen that it is exceedingly difficult to quantify either type of risk. In other words, it may be possible to reach the general conclusion that one project is riskier than another (in either the market or the corporate sense), but it is difficult to develop a really good *measure* of project risk. Further, this lack of precision in measuring project risk makes it difficult to incorporate differential risk into capital budgeting decisions.

There are two methods for incorporating project risk into the capital budgeting decision process. In the *certainty equivalent* method, the expected cash flows in each year are adjusted to reflect project risk — cash flows with above-average risk

---

[9]For example, see M. Chapman Findlay III, Arthur E. Gooding, and Wallace Q. Weaver, Jr., "On the Relevant Risk for Determining Capital Expenditure Hurdle Rates," *Financial Management,* Winter 1976, 9–16.

are scaled down, and the riskier the flows, the lower their certainty equivalent values.[10] However, the certainty equivalent method is difficult to implement in practice, and hence we will focus on the *risk-adjusted discount rate* method. Here, differential project risk is dealt with by changing the discount rate — average risk projects are discounted at the firm's WACC, above-average risk projects are discounted at a higher cost of capital, and below-average risk projects are discounted at a rate below the firm's WACC. Unfortunately, since risk cannot be measured precisely, there is no good way of specifying exactly *how much* higher or lower these discount rates should be — given the present state of the art, risk adjustments are necessarily judgmental and somewhat arbitrary.

Capital structure must also be taken into account if a firm finances different assets in different ways. For example, one division might have a lot of real estate, which is well suited as collateral for loans, whereas some other division might have most of its capital tied up in special purpose machinery, which is not good collateral. As a result, the division with the real estate might have a higher *debt capacity* than the machinery division, and hence an optimal capital structure which contains a higher percentage of debt. In this case, the division with more real estate contributes more to the overall debt capacity of the firm, and management might calculate its WACC using a higher debt ratio than for the other division.[11]

Although the process is not exact, many companies use a two-step procedure to develop risk-adjusted discount rates for use in capital budgeting: (1) *Divisional costs of capital* are established for each of the major operating divisions on the basis of each division's estimated riskiness and capital structure. (2) Within each division, all projects are classified into three categories — high risk, average risk, and low risk — and then each division uses its basic divisional WACC as the discount rate for average-risk projects, reduces the divisional WACC by one or two percentage points when evaluating low-risk projects, and raises the WACC by several percentage points for high-risk projects. For example, if a division's basic WACC is estimated to be 10 percent, then a 12 percent discount rate might be used for a high-risk project and a 9 percent rate for a low-risk project. Average-risk projects, which constitute about 80 percent of most capital budgets, would be evaluated at the 10 percent divisional cost of capital. This procedure is far from precise, but it does at least recognize that different divisions have different characteristics, and hence different costs of capital, and it also acknowledges differential project riskiness within divisions.

RISKY CASH OUTFLOWS

In Chapter 9 we stated that some projects are evaluated on the basis of minimizing the present value of future costs rather than on the basis of the projects' NPVs. This is done because (1) it is often impossible to allocate revenues to a particular

---

[10]For further discussion of the certainty equivalent method, and a comparison of the certainty equivalent and risk-adjusted discount rate methods, see Eugene F. Brigham and Louis C. Gapenski, *Intermediate Financial Management,* Chapter 9.

[11]We will say much more about optimal capital structure and debt capacity in Chapters 11 and 12.

project that must be undertaken if the firm is to continue in operation (such as a pollution control project), and (2) it is appropriate to focus on comparative costs when two projects will produce exactly the same revenues. For example, suppose Duke Power must build a new generating plant to provide electricity in North and South Carolina. Several alternative types of plants are available, but they have different initial costs, different lives, and different operating costs (mainly fuel). There is no question about building some type of plant, because Duke Power's franchise agreement with the state requires it to supply power to consumers in the region. In this case, the decision will be based on the *minimization of the PV of expected future costs.*

Some projects also have large cash outflows which occur at the end of the projects' lives. For example, in 1987 Toronto Development Company (TDC) was offered the opportunity to use a large city-owned warehouse along the lake, to refurbish it, and to lease space to others for a period of 10 years. During the 10 years, TDC would receive large cash inflows. However, at the end of the 10-year period, TDC would be required to raze the building and to develop the site as a park, at a cost estimated at $5 million. However, the cost could be much higher or lower, depending on conditions at the time.

In the case of both Duke Power's generating plant and TDC's warehouse-to-park project, risk adjustments must be made to future cash *outflows* (rather than inflows), and *the risk adjustment for a risky cash outflow is the exact opposite of that for an inflow.*

Consider again the Duke Power example. Suppose Duke is choosing between a coal-fired plant and a nuclear plant. The coal plant has a lower initial cost but a much higher annual operating cost. Also, the coal plant has a zero expected salvage value — removal costs are expected to equal the scrap value of the plant — while the cost of disassembling and disposing of the radioactive nuclear plant will be quite high, and very uncertain. Further, nuclear plants are less reliable than coal plants, and, hence, costly shut-downs and mid-life repairs may be necessary. There is also more uncertainty about nuclear plants' construction costs, in-service timing, and service lives. For all these reasons, there is good reason to regard the nuclear plant as being riskier than the coal plant.

Both nuclear and coal plants generally take a number of years to build, and they have expected lives of about 30 years. However, for simplicity, we shall assume that both plants have a 1-year construction period and a 5-year operating life. Further, we shall disregard inflation, and we also assume that the two plants have an equal capacity and that the electricity produced by both plants would be sold at the same price per unit.

Table 10-3 gives the projected costs associated with the two power plants: the investment costs at Year 0, and the operating costs plus nuclear decommissioning cost in Years 1 to 5. We assume that Duke Power's overall WACC, before it announces plans for a new generating plant, is 10 percent. If this discount rate were used to find the PV of future costs, we see from Table 10-3 that the plants would be judged equal. However, if Duke recognizes that the nuclear plant is more risky, and it therefore evaluates this project with a 12 percent cost of capital, then the nuclear plant's PV of future costs declines to $2,973 million, while at a still higher

Table 10-3
Expected Costs:
Coal Versus Nuclear Power Plants
(Millions of Dollars)

Year	Coal Plant	Nuclear Plant
0	($1,500)	($2,500)
1	(400)	(10)
2	(400)	(10)
3	(400)	(10)
4	(400)	(10)
5	(400)	(10) + (770) = (780)
PV of costs at: 10%	($3,016)	($3,016)
12%	n.a.	(2,973)
15%	n.a.	(2,916)

Correct analysis: PV_{Coal} (at 10%) = ($3,016).

$PV_{Nuclear}$ (at 7%) = ($3,090).
Therefore, build the coal plant.

rate of 15 percent, the nuclear plant's costs drop to only $2,916 million. Thus, the riskier the nuclear plant is judged to be, the better it looks!

The two alternative investments have the same expected revenue stream, and, at a 10 percent cost of capital, the same PV of future costs, and hence the same calculated NPV. Now we want to reflect the nuclear plant's higher risk, so we raise its discount rate, and that makes the nuclear plant look better. Something is obviously wrong. If we want to penalize a cash outflow for higher-than-average risk, then that outflow must have a *higher* present value, not a *lower* value. *Therefore, a cash outflow that has higher-than-average risk must be evaluated with a lower-than-average cost of capital.*

Recognizing this situation, Duke Power might discount the nuclear plant's costs at a 7 percent rate versus a 10 percent rate for the coal plant. In that case, the coal plant, with a PV cost of $3,016 million versus $3,090 million for the nuclear plant, would be chosen. This example illustrates both the problem that a negative outflow can cause and an approach for dealing with the problem.[12]

[12]The negative outflow problem could arise in a conventional NPV analysis as well as a PV of future costs analysis. For example, in the Toronto Development Company illustration, if the cash outflow at the end of the project's life was judged to be more risky than the cash inflows during the project's life, and if the outflow was discounted at a high risk-adjusted discount rate, then this would incorrectly bias the evaluation toward acceptance of the project. For more on the effects of negative cash flows, see Wilbur G. Lewellen, "Some Observations on Risk-Adjusted Discount Rates," *Journal of Finance,* September 1977, 1331–1337; and a comment on that paper by Stephen E. Celec and Richard H. Pettway, plus a reply by Lewellen, in the September 1979 issue of the *Journal,* 1061–1066.

THE OPTIMAL CAPITAL BUDGET

In Chapter 7, we developed the concept of the weighted average cost of capital (WACC). Then, in Chapters 8 and 9, and up to this point in Chapter 10, we have discussed how the cost of capital is used in project evaluations. However, capital budgeting and the cost of capital are actually interrelated — we cannot determine the cost of capital until we determine the size of the capital budget, and we cannot determine the size of the capital budget until we determine the cost of capital. Therefore, as we show in the next sections, *the cost of capital and the capital budget must be determined simultaneously.* Niendorf-Stewart-Lang, Inc., a Midwestern grocery wholesaler, is used to illustrate the concepts involved.

The Investment Opportunity Schedule (IOS)

Consider first Figure 10-4, which gives some information on Niendorf's potential capital projects for next year. The tabular data show each project's cash flows, IRR, and payback. The graph is defined as the firm's *investment opportunity schedule (IOS),* which is a plot of each project's IRR, in descending order, versus the dollars of new capital required to finance it (or the cash flow at t = 0). For example, Project B has an IRR of 38.5 percent, shown on the vertical axis, and a cost of $100,000, shown on the horizontal axis.[13] Notice also that Projects A and B are mutually exclusive. Thus, Niendorf has two possible IOS schedules: the one defined by the solid line, which contains Project B plus C, D, E, and F, and the one defined by the dotted line, which contains Project A plus C, D, E, and F. Beyond $600,000, the two IOS schedules are identical. Thus, the two alternative schedules differ only in that one contains B and has C ranked second while the other contains A, in which case C ranks first because $IRR_C > IRR_A$. For now, we assume that all six projects have the same risk as Niendorf's "average" project.

The Marginal Cost of Capital (MCC) Schedule

In Chapter 7, we discussed the concept of the weighted average cost of capital (WACC). However, the exact value of the WACC depends on the amount of new capital raised — the WACC will, at some point, rise if more and more capital is raised during a given year. This increase occurs because (1) flotation costs (including any "signaling" costs and supply/demand imbalance costs associated with stock issues) cause the cost of new equity to be higher than the cost of retained earnings, and (2) higher rates of return on debt, preferred stock, and common stock may be required to induce additional investors to supply capital to the firm.

Suppose Niendorf's cost of retained earnings is 15.0 percent, while its cost of new common stock is 16.8 percent. The company's target capital structure calls

[13]Do not be concerned at this point by the fact that we use IRR in this analysis rather than IRR* or NPV. The fact is, we cannot calculate either IRR* or NPV until we know k, and we are using this analysis to develop a first-approximation estimate of k. Later on, we could switch to IRR* or NPV, but such a switch is not necessary for this type of analysis.

Figure 10-4
Niendorf-Stewart-Lang, Inc.: IOS Schedules

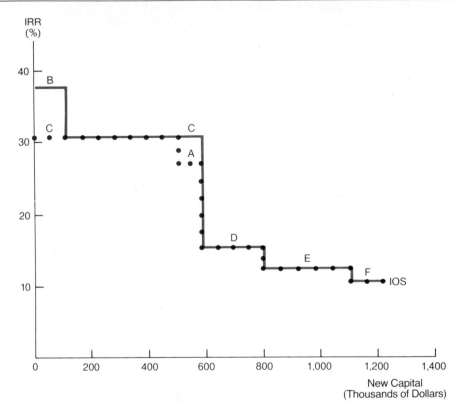

			Potential Capital Projects			
Year	A[a]	B[a]	C	D	E	F
0	($100,000)	($100,000)	($500,000)	($200,000)	($300,000)	($100,000)
1	10,000	90,000	190,000	52,800	98,800	58,781
2	70,000	60,000	190,000	52,800	98,800	58,781
3	100,000	10,000	190,000	52,800	98,800	—
4	—	—	190,000	52,800	98,800	—
5	—	—	190,000	52,800	—	—
6	—	—	190,000	52,800	—	—
IRR	27.0%	38.5%	30.2%	15.2%	12.0%	11.5%
Payback	2.2	1.2	2.6	3.8	3.0	1.7

[a]Projects A and B are mutually exclusive.

for 40 percent debt and 60 percent common equity; its marginal federal-plus-state tax rate is 40 percent, and its before-tax cost of debt is 10 percent. Thus, Niendorf's WACC using retained earnings as the common equity component is 11.4 percent:

$$WACC_1 = k_a = w_d(k_d)(1 - T) + w_sk_s$$
$$= 0.4(10\%)(0.6) + 0.6(15\%) = 11.4\%.$$

Niendorf is forecasting $420,000 of retained earnings for the planning period, and hence the firm's retained earnings break point is $700,000:

$$\text{Break point} = \$420,000/0.6 = \$700,000.$$

After $700,000 of new capital is raised, Niendorf's WACC increases to 12.5 percent:

$$WACC_2 = k_a = 0.4(10\%)(0.6) + 0.6(16.8\%) \approx 12.5\%.$$

Figure 10-5 graphs Niendorf's *marginal cost of capital (MCC) schedule*. Each dollar has a weighted average cost of 11.4 percent until the company has raised a total of $700,000. This $700,000 will consist of $280,000 of new debt with an after-tax cost of 6 percent, and $420,000 of retained earnings with a cost of 15 percent. However, if the company raises $700,001 or more, each additional dollar will contain 60 cents of equity obtained by selling new common stock, so k_a = WACC rises from 11.4 to 12.5 percent.

Figure 10-5
Niendorf-Stewart-Lang, Inc.: Marginal Cost of Capital Schedule Using Both Retained Earnings and New Common Equity

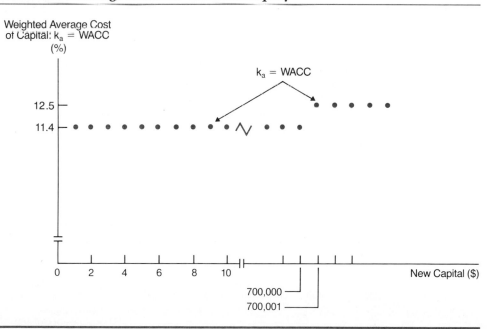

Combining the MCC and IOS Schedules

Now that we have estimated the MCC schedule, we can use it to determine the base discount rate for the capital budgeting process, *that is, we can use the MCC schedule to find the cost of capital for use in determining an average-risk project's net present value.* To do this, we combine the IOS and MCC schedules on the same graph, as in Figure 10-6, and then analyze this consolidated figure.

Finding the Marginal Cost of Capital

Just how far down its IOS curve should Niendorf go? That is, which of the firm's available projects should it accept? *First, Niendorf should accept all independent projects that have rates of return in excess of the cost of the capital that will be used to finance them, and it should reject all others.* Projects E and F should be rejected, because they would have to be financed with capital that has a cost of 12.5 percent, and at that cost of capital, we know that these projects must have negative NPVs since their IRRs are below their costs of capital. Therefore, Nien-

Figure 10-6
Niendorf-Stewart-Lang, Inc.: Combined IOS and MCC Schedules

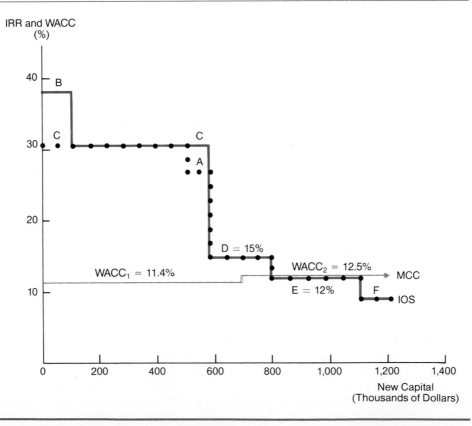

dorf's capital budget should consist of either A or B, plus C and D, and the firm should thus raise and invest a total $800,000.

The preceding analysis, as summarized in Figure 10-6, reveals a very important point: The cost of capital used in the capital budgeting process is actually determined at the intersection of the IOS and MCC schedules. This cost is called the firm's *marginal cost of capital (MCC),* and if it is used, then the firm will make correct accept/reject decisions, and its level of financing and investment will be optimal. If it uses any other rate for average risk projects, its capital budget will not be optimal.

If Niendorf had fewer good investment opportunities, then its IOS schedule would be shifted to the left, possibly causing the intersection to occur at the $WACC_1 = 11.4\%$ portion of the MCC curve. Then, Niendorf's MCC would be 11.4 percent, and average risk projects would be evaluated at that rate. Conversely, if the firm had more and better investment opportunities, its IOS would be shifted to the right, and if the shift is very far to the right, then Niendorf might have to raise its MCC above 12.5 percent because its higher capital requirements could lead to further increases in capital costs. Thus, we see that the discount rate used for evaluating average risk projects is influenced by the set of projects that is available. We have, of course, abstracted from differential project riskiness in this section, because we assumed that all of Niendorf's projects are equally risky.

Choosing between Mutually Exclusive Projects

We have not, at this point, actually determined Niendorf's optimal capital budget. We know that it should total $800,000, and that Projects C and D should be included, but we do not know which of the mutually exclusive projects, A or B, should be made part of the final budget. How can we choose between A and B? We know that in general the final set of projects should be the one which has the highest total NPV, as this set will increase the value of the firm by the largest amount. We also know that Projects C and D should be included in the final set, so their contributions to the total NPV will be the same regardless of whether we choose Project A or Project B. This narrows our analysis to the NPVs of A and B. The project with the higher NPV should be chosen.

Notice that Figure 10-4 contained the projects' paybacks and IRRs, but no NPVs. We were not able to determine the NPVs at that point, because we did not know Niendorf's marginal cost of capital. Now, in Figure 10-6, we see that the last dollar raised will cost 12.5 percent, so Niendorf's marginal cost of capital is 12.5 percent. Therefore, assuming the projects are equally risky, we can use a 12.5 percent discount rate to find $NPV_A = \$34,431$ and $NPV_B = \$34,431$. Thus, in our example, Niendorf should be indifferent between the two mutually exclusive projects, according to the NPV criterion. To break the tie, assume for the sake of argument that Project B is selected because of its faster payback and higher IRR.[14]

---

[14]For a more detailed discussion of the points covered in this section, see Eugene F. Brigham and Louis C. Gapenski, *Intermediate Financial Management,* 2nd ed., Chapter 10. Also, note that if the MCC schedule cuts through a project, and if that project must be accepted in total or else rejected, then we can calculate the average cost of the capital that will be used to finance the project (some at the higher WACC and some at the lower WACC) and compare that average WACC to the project's IRR.

CAPITAL RATIONING

Under ordinary circumstances, capital budgeting is, in essence, an application of this classic economic principle: A firm should expand to the point where its marginal return is just equal to its marginal cost. However, under some circumstances, a firm may deviate from this principle and place an absolute limit on the size of its capital budget. This is called capital rationing, and we discuss this topic in Appendix 10A.

ESTABLISHING THE OPTIMAL CAPITAL BUDGET IN PRACTICE

The procedures set forth above are conceptually correct, and it is important that you understand the logic of this process. However, Niendorf-Stewart-Lang (and most other companies) actually uses a more judgmental, less quantitative process for establishing its final capital budget:

Step 1

The financial vice president obtains a reasonably good fix on the firm's IOS schedule from the director of capital budgeting, and a reasonably good estimate of the MCC schedule from the treasurer. These two schedules are then combined, as in Figure 10-6, to get a reasonably good approximation of the corporation's marginal cost of capital (the cost of capital at the intersection of the IOS and MCC schedules).

Step 2

The corporate MCC is scaled up or down by each division to reflect the division's capital structure and risk characteristics. Niendorf, for example, assigns a factor of 0.9 to its stable, low-risk canned vegetables division but a factor of 1.1 to its more risky gourmet frozen foods group. Therefore, if the corporate MCC is determined to be 12.5 percent, the cost for the canned vegetables division is $0.9(12.5\%) = 11.25\%$, while that for the gourmet frozen foods division is $1.1(12.5\%) = 13.75\%$.

Step 3

Each project within each division is classified into one of three groups — high-risk, average-risk, and low-risk — and the same 0.9 and 1.1 factors are used to adjust the divisional MCCs. For example, a low-risk project in the canned vegetables division would have a cost of capital of $0.9(11.25\%) = 10.13\%$ if the corporate cost of capital were 12.5 percent, while a high-risk project in the gourmet frozen foods division would have a cost of $1.1(13.75\%) = 15.13\%$.

Step 4

Each project's NPV is then determined, using its risk-adjusted project cost of capital. The optimal capital budget consists of all independent projects with positive risk-adjusted NPVs plus those mutually exclusive projects with the highest positive risk-adjusted NPVs.

These steps implicitly assume that the projects taken on have, on average, about the same risk characteristics and consequently the same average cost of capital as the firm's existing assets. If this is not true, then the corporate MCC determined in Step 1 will not be correct, and it will have to be adjusted. However, given all the measurement errors and uncertainties inherent in the entire cost of capital/capital budgeting process, it would be most unrealistic to push the adjustment process very far.

All of this may seem quite arbitrary, and we agree. Nevertheless, the procedure does force the firm to think carefully about each division's relative risk, about the risk of each project within the divisions, and about the relationship between the total amount of capital raised and the cost of that capital. Further, the procedure forces the firm to adjust its capital budget to reflect capital market conditions — if the cost of debt and equity rises, this fact will be reflected in the cost of capital used to evaluate projects, and projects that would be marginally acceptable when capital costs were low would (correctly) be ruled unacceptable when capital costs were high.

SUMMARY

Our analysis of risk has focused on three important issues: (1) the variability of a project's cash flows, and consequently its riskiness on a stand-alone basis, (2) its effect on the variability of the firm's cash flows (within-firm or corporate risk), and (3) the effect of a given project on the firm's beta coefficient (market risk). *Market risk* should, in theory, have the greatest effect on the value of the stock. *Corporate risk* affects the firm's financial strength, and this, in turn, influences its ability to use debt, to maintain smooth operations over time, and to avoid crises that might consume management's energy and disrupt employees, customers, suppliers, and community.

There are several analytical techniques available to help measure a project's stand-alone risk. Among these are (1) *sensitivity analysis,* (2) *scenario analysis,* (3) *Monte Carlo simulation,* and (4) *decision tree analysis.* However, the final decision regarding a project's risk is always judgmental. The major difficulty in determining a project's market risk is to establish the project's *beta coefficient.* The beta of an asset such as a truck or a machine is generally meaningless, but betas can be established for divisions that are large enough to be operated as independent firms. In practice, market risk is generally estimated for entire divisions and then used to establish divisional costs of capital. There are two approaches to measuring market risk: (1) the *pure play method* and (2) the *accounting beta method.*

Both the measurement of risk and its incorporation into capital budgeting decisions involve judgment. It is possible to use quantitative techniques such as simulation and decision trees as an aid to judgment, but in the final analysis, the assessment of risk in capital budgeting will always remain a judgmental process.

The chapter also explained how *MCC* and *IOS schedules* can be used to help determine the optimal capital budget. We use the *break point concept* to develop a step-function MCC schedule, which we then combine with the IOS schedule to determine the firm's *marginal cost of capital (MCC),* which is then used to determine the optimal capital budget.

We noted, however, that most firms actually use a judgmental four-step process for establishing the optimal capital budget: (1) The treasurer develops an estimate of the firm's marginal cost of capital, say 12.5 percent. (2) The corporate MCC is scaled up or down by each division to reflect the division's capital structure and risk characteristics. (3) Each project within each division is classified as high-risk, average-risk, or low-risk, and the divisional cost of capital is then adjusted up or down. (4) Those independent projects with positive risk-adjusted NPVs are then included in the firm's final capital budget.

MULTINATIONAL FINANCE

Although the same basic capital budgeting principles apply to both foreign and domestic operations, there are three crucial differences: (1) Cash flow estimation is generally more complex for overseas investments. (2) Foreign cash flows are in foreign currencies, so exchange rate risk fluctuations add to the riskiness of overseas investments. (3) The possibility of deliberate government acts that truncate or divert cash flows adds another risk element to foreign investments. In this section, we briefly discuss multinational capital budgeting.

The first issue to be addressed in foreign project analysis is defining the relevant cash flows: Is the relevant flow the net cash generated by the foreign subsidiary, or is it the incremental cash flows that will be sent back to the U.S. parent? As long as there are no restrictions on the repatriation of cash flows, these two cash flow streams will be the same. However, if there are local withholding taxes on dividends, restrictions on the return of capital, or other blockages of international cash flows, both the timing and magnitude of the cash flows back to the parent will be different from the operating cash flows of the project. The parent corporation cannot use cash flows blocked in a foreign country to pay current dividends to its shareholders, nor does it have the flexibility to reinvest the capital in its other subsidiaries. Hence, from the perspective of the parent organization, *the relevant capital budgeting cash flows are the financial cash flows that are expected to be repatriated to the parent.*

The foreign currency cash flows to be repatriated must be converted into U.S. dollar values by translating them at expected future exchange rates. Sensitivity or simulation analyses should be conducted to ascertain the effects of exchange rate variations, and, based on these analyses, an *exchange rate risk premium* should be added to the cost of capital to reflect the exchange rate risk inherent in the investment. Note that exchange rate risk may be reduced by hedging with currency futures, and the costs of such hedging can be built into the project's cash flows. However, it is not always possible to hedge cash flows expected in the distant future, and unless the foreign operation uses a currency which is actively traded on the exchange markets, it may not be possible to hedge even short-run cash flows.

Sovereignty risk also differentiates international investment decisions from domestic capital budgeting. Sovereignty refers to the supreme and independent political authority of a nation state to do as it pleases within its own borders. Since foreign subsidiaries are physically located within the jurisdiction of a host country, they are subject to rules and regulations established by local government authorities, no matter how arbitrary or apparently unfair such requirements may be. Sovereignty risk includes both the possibility of expropriation or nationalization without adequate compensation, and of unanticipated restrictions on cash flows to the parent company, such as tighter controls on repatriation of dividends or higher taxes. The risk of expropriation of U.S. assets abroad is small in traditionally friendly and stable countries such as the United Kingdom or Switzerland. However, in Eastern Bloc countries, and in most developing nations in Latin America, Africa, and the Far East, the risk may be substantial. Past expropriations include those of ITT and Anaconda Copper in Chile, Gulf Oil in Bolivia, Occidental Petroleum in Libya, Enron Corporation in Peru, and many companies in both Cuba and Iran.

Generally, sovereignty risk premiums are not added to the cost of capital to adjust for sovereignty risk. If management has a serious concern that a given country might expropriate foreign assets, it simply will not make significant investments in that country. Expropriation is viewed as a catastrophic or ruinous event, and managers have been shown to be extraordinarily risk averse in the presence of ruinous loss possibilities. However, companies can take steps to reduce the potential loss from expropriation in three major ways: (1) by financing the subsidiary with local sources of capital, (2) by structuring operations so that the subsidiary has value only as a part of the integrated corporate system, and (3) by obtaining insurance against economic losses from expropriation from a source such as the Overseas Private Investment Corporation (OPIC). In the latter case, insurance premiums would have to be added to the project's cost.

Questions

10-1 Define each of the following terms:
   a. Stand-alone risk versus within-firm risk versus market risk
   b. Corporate risk
   c. Sensitivity analysis
   d. Simulation analysis
   e. Scenario analysis
   f. Coefficient of variation versus standard deviation
   g. Project beta versus corporate beta
   h. Accounting beta versus stock market beta
   i. Pure play method of estimating divisional betas
   j. Decision tree analysis
   k. Corporate diversification versus stockholder diversification
   l. Risk-adjusted discount rate; project cost of capital
   m. IOS schedule; intersection of the IOS and MCC schedules

10-2 Differentiate between (a) simulation analysis, (b) optimistic-pessimistic-most likely analysis, and (c) sensitivity analysis. If AT&T were considering two investments, one calling for the expenditure of $100 million to develop a satellite communications system and the other involving the expenditure of $5,000 for a new truck, on which one would the company be more likely to use simulation?

10-3 Distinguish between beta risk, within-firm (or corporate) risk, and stand-alone risk for a project being considered for inclusion in the capital budget. Which type do you feel should be given the greatest weight in capital budgeting decisions?

10-4 Suppose Lima Locomotive Company, which has a high beta and also a great deal of corporate risk, merged with Homestake Mining, which has a low beta but relatively high corporate risk. What would the merger do to the cost of capital in the consolidated company's locomotive division and its gold mining division?

10-5 Suppose a firm estimates its MCC and IOS schedules for the coming year and finds that they intersect at the point 10%, $10 million. What cost of capital should be used to evaluate average-risk projects, high-risk projects, and low-risk projects?

10-6 The MCC and IOS schedules can be thought of as "bands" rather than as lines to show that they are not known with certainty but, rather, are merely estimates of the true MCC and IOS schedules.

   a. Do you think that the bands would be wider for the MCC or for the IOS schedule? In answering this question, visualize each point on the MCC and IOS schedules as being the expected value of a probability distribution.

   b. For the IOS schedule, would the band, or confidence interval, associated with each project be identical? If not, what would this imply, and how might it affect the firm's capital budgeting analysis?

Self-Test Problems

ST-1 **(Corporate risk analysis)** The staff of O'Connor Manufacturing has estimated the following net cash flows and probabilities for a new manufacturing process:

	Net Cash Flow		
Year	P = 0.2	P = 0.6	P = 0.2
0	($100,000)	($100,000)	($100,000)
1	20,000	30,000	40,000
2	20,000	30,000	40,000
3	20,000	30,000	40,000
4	20,000	30,000	40,000
5	20,000	30,000	40,000
5*	0	20,000	30,000

Line 0 is the cost of the process, Lines 1-5 are operating cash flows, and Line 5* contains the estimated salvage values. O'Connor's cost of capital for an average risk project is 10 percent.

   a. Assume that the project has average risk. Find the project's base case NPV. (Hint: Use expected values for the net cash flow in each year.)

   b. Find the best case and worst case NPVs. What is the probability of occurrence of the worst case if the cash flows are perfectly dependent (perfectly positively correlated) over time? If they are independent over time?

c. Assume that all the cash flows are perfectly positively correlated; that is, there are only three possible cash flow streams over time: (1) the worst case, (2) the most likely case, and (3) the best case, with probabilities of 0.2, 0.6, and 0.2, respectively. These cases are represented by each of the columns in the table. Find the expected NPV, its standard deviation, and its coefficient of variation.

d. The coefficient of variation of O'Connor's average project is in the range 0.8 to 1.0. If the coefficient of variation of a project being evaluated is greater than 1.0, 2 percentage points are added to the firm's MCC. Similarly, if the coefficient of variation is less than 0.8, 1 percentage point is deducted from the MCC. What is the project's cost of capital? Should O'Connor accept or reject the project?

ST-2 (Optimal capital budget) Grossnickle Enterprises has the following capital structure, which it considers to be optimal under the present and forecasted conditions:

Debt	30%
Common equity	70
Total capital	100%

For the coming year, management expects to realize net earnings of $105,000. The past dividend policy of paying out 50 percent of earnings will continue. Present commitments from its banker will allow Grossnickle to borrow at a rate of 8 percent.

The company's federal-plus-state tax rate is 40 percent; the current market price of its stock is $50 per share; its *last* dividend was $1.85 per share; and its expected constant growth rate is 8 percent. External equity (new common) can be sold at a flotation cost of 15 percent.

The firm has the following investment opportunities for the next period:

Project	Cost	IRR
A	$50,000	12%
B	15,000	11
C	20,000	10
D	50,000	9

Management asks you to help them determine what projects (if any) should be undertaken. You proceed with this analysis by following these steps:

a. Calculate the WACC using both retained earnings and new common stock.

b. Graph the IOS and MCC schedules.

c. Which projects should Grossnickle accept?

d. What implicit assumptions about project risk are embodied in this problem? If you learned that Projects A and B were of above-average risk, yet Grossnickle chose the projects which you indicated in Part c, how would this affect the situation?

e. The problem stated that Grossnickle pays out 50 percent of its earnings as dividends. How would the analysis change if the payout ratio were changed to 0 percent? To 100 percent?

Problems

10-1 (Risky cash outflows) Cal State Utilities is deciding if it should build an oil or a coal generating plant. Its MCC is 8 percent for low-risk projects, 10 percent for projects of average risk, and 12 percent for high-risk projects. Management believes that an oil plant is of average risk, but that a coal plant is of high risk due to the problem of acid rain. The cash *outflows* required to construct each plant are listed below. The revenues, fuel costs, and other operating costs are expected to be the same under both plans:

	Construction Costs (Thousands of Dollars)	
Year	Coal Plant	Oil Plant
0	($ 100)	($ 400)
1	(500)	(1,000)
2	(1,500)	(1,000)
3	(1,500)	(1,000)
4	(1,500)	(1,500)
5	(1,000)	(1,000)
6	(500)	(200)

Which type of plant should be constructed?

10-2 (Sequential decisions) The Horgan Yacht Company (HYC), a prominent sailboat builder in Florida, may design a new 30-foot sailboat based on the "winged" keels being used on the 12-meter yachts that race for the America's Cup.

First, HYC would have to invest $10,000 at $t = 0$ for the design and model tank testing of the new boat. HYC's managers believe that there is a 60 percent probability that this phase will be successful and the project will continue. If Stage 1 is not successful, the project will be abandoned with zero salvage value.

The next stage, if undertaken, would consist of making the molds and producing two prototype boats. This would cost $500,000 at $t = 1$. If the boats test well, HYC would go into production. If they do not, the molds and prototypes could be sold for $100,000. The managers estimate that the probability is 80 percent that the boats will pass testing, and that Stage 3 will be undertaken.

Stage 3 consists of changing over one current production line to produce the new design. This would cost $1,000,000 at $t = 2$. If the economy is strong at this point, the net value of sales would be $3,000,000, while if the economy is weak, the net value would be $1,500,000. Both net values occur at $t = 3$, and each state of the economy has a probability of 0.5. HYC's marginal cost of capital is 12 percent.

   a. Assume that this project has average risk. Construct a decision tree and determine the project's expected NPV.

   b. Find the project's standard deviation of NPV and coefficient of variation (CV) of NPV. If HYC's average project had a CV of between 1.0 and 2.0, would this project be of high, low, or average corporate risk?

10-3 (Divisional market risk adjustments) SureGrip Rubber Company has two divisions: (1) the tire division, which manufactures tires for new autos; and (2) the recap division, which manufactures recapping materials that are sold to independent tire recapping shops throughout the United States. Since auto manufacturing fluctuates with the general economy, the tire division's earnings contribution to SureGrip's stock price is highly correlated with returns on most other stocks. If the tire division were operated as a separate company, its beta coefficient would be about 1.60. The sales and profits of the recap division, on the other hand, tend to be counter-cyclical, since recap sales boom when people cannot afford to buy new tires. The recap division's beta is estimated to be 0.40. Approximately 75 percent of SureGrip's corporate assets are invested in the tire division and 25 percent are in the recap division.

Currently, the rate of interest on Treasury securities is 10 percent, and the expected rate of return on an average share of stock is 15 percent. SureGrip uses only common equity capital, and hence it has no debt outstanding.

   a. What is the required rate of return on SureGrip's stock?

   b. What discount rate should be used to evaluate capital budgeting projects? Explain your answer fully, and in the process, illustrate your answer with a project which costs $100,000, has a 10-year life, and provides expected after-tax net cash flows of $20,000 per year.

10-4 (Scenario and sensitivity analysis) Your firm, Agrico, is considering the purchase of a tractor which will have a net cost of $30,000, will increase pre-tax operating cash flows exclusive of depreciation effects by $10,000 per year, and will be depreciated on a straight line basis to zero over 5 years at the rate of $6,000 per year, beginning the first year. (Annual cash flows will be $10,000, reduced by taxes, plus the tax savings that result from $6,000 of depreciation.) The board of directors, however, is having a heated debate as to whether the tractor will actually last 5 years. Specifically, Charles Cornwell insists that he knows of some that have lasted only 4 years. Jim Adams agrees with Cornwell, but he argues that most tractors do give 5 years of service. Jane Wright, on the other hand, says she has seen some last as long as 8 years.

   a. Given this discussion, the board asks you to prepare a scenario analysis to ascertain the importance of the uncertainty about the tractor's life. Assume a 40 percent marginal federal-plus-state tax rate, a zero salvage value, and a marginal cost of capital of 10 percent. (Hint: Here straight-line depreciation is based on the ACRS class life of the tractor and is not affected by the actual life. Also, ignore the half-year convention for this problem.)

   (Do Parts b and c only if you are using the computerized diskette.)

   b. The board would also like to know how changes in the cost of capital affect the analysis. Assume that the machine's life is 5 years, and analyze the effects of a change in the cost of capital to 8 percent or to 12 percent. Is the project very sensitive to changes in the cost of capital?

   c. The board would like to determine the sensitivity of the project's NPV to changes in certain variables. First, they would like to examine the effect of changes in pre-tax operating revenues upon NPV. Calculate the project's NPV at plus 10, 20, and 30 percent of the estimated $10,000 pre-tax revenues, as well as minus 10, 20, and 30 percent of this figure. (Hold all other variables constant.) Second, calculate the effect upon NPV of various project lives. (Hint: Hold all other variables constant, and try lives ranging from 1 to 10 years.) Finally, examine NPV while changing the cost of capital. (Once again, hold all other variables constant at their original levels.) Plot a separate sensitivity diagram for each variable examined above.

10-5 (Simulation) Hospital Supplies Corporation (HSC) manufactures medical products for hospitals, clinics, and nursing homes. HSC may introduce a new type of X-ray scanner designed to identify certain types of cancers in their early stages. There are a number of uncertainties about the proposed project, but the following data are believed to be reasonably accurate.

	Probability	Value	Random Numbers
Developmental	0.3	$2,000,000	00–29
costs	0.4	4,000,000	30–69
	0.3	6,000,000	70–99
Project life	0.2	3 years	00–19
	0.6	8 years	20–79
	0.2	13 years	80–99
Sales in units	0.2	100	00–19
	0.6	200	20–79
	0.2	300	80–99
Sales price	0.1	$13,000	00–09
	0.8	13,500	10–89
	0.1	14,000	90–99
Cost per unit	0.3	$5,000	00–29
(excluding developmental	0.4	6,000	30–69
costs)	0.3	7,000	70–99

HSC uses a cost of capital of 15 percent to analyze average-risk projects, 12 percent for low-risk projects, and 18 percent for high-risk projects. These risk adjustments reflect primarily the uncertainty about each project's NPV and IRR as measured by the coefficients of variation of NPV and IRR. HSC is in the 40 percent federal-plus-state income tax bracket.

a. What is the expected IRR for the X-ray scanner project? Base your answer on the expected values of the variables. Also, assume the after-tax "profits" figure you develop is equal to annual cash flows. All facilities are leased, so depreciation may be disregarded. Can you determine the value of σ_{IRR} short of actual simulation or a fairly complex statistical analysis?

b. Assume that HSC uses a 15 percent cost of capital for this project. What is the project's NPV? Could you estimate σ_{NPV} without either simulation or a complex statistical analysis?

c. Show the process by which a computer would perform a simulation analysis for this project. Use the random numbers 44, 17, 16, 58, 1; 79, 83, 86; and 19, 62, 6 to illustrate the process with the first computer run. Actually calculate the first-run NPV and IRR. Assume that the cash flows for each year are independent of cash flows for other years. Also, assume that the computer operates as follows: (1) A developmental cost and a project life are estimated for the first run. (2) Next, sales volume, sales price, and cost per unit are estimated and used to derive a cash flow for the first year. (3) Then, the next three random numbers are used to estimate sales volume, sales price, and cost per unit for the second year, and hence the cash flow for the second year. (4) Cash flows for other years are developed similarly, on out to the first run's estimated life. (5) With the developmental cost and the cash flow stream established, NPV and IRR for the first run are derived and stored in the computer's memory. (6) The process is repeated to generate perhaps 500 other NPVs and IRRs. (7) Frequency distributions for NPV and IRR are plotted by the computer, and the distributions' means and standard deviations are calculated.

d. Does it seem a little strange to conduct a risk analysis such as the one here *after* having already established a cost of capital for use in the analysis? What might be done to improve this situation?

e. In this problem, we assumed that the probability distributions were all independent of one another. It would have been possible to use conditional probabilities where, for example, the probability distribution for cost per unit would vary from trial to trial, depending on the unit sales for the trial. Also, it would be possible to construct a simulation model such that the sales distribution in Year t would depend on the sales level attained in Year t − 1. Had these modifications been made in this problem, do you think the standard deviation of the NPV distribution would have been larger (riskier) or smaller (less risky) than where complete independence is assumed?

f. Name two *major* difficulties not mentioned above that occur in the kind of analysis discussed in this problem.

10-6 (Simple optimal capital budget) The Singleton Corporation's present capital structure, which is also its target capital structure, calls for 50 percent debt and 50 percent common equity. The firm has only one potential project, an expansion program with a 10.2 percent IRR and a cost of $20 million but which is completely divisible; that is, Singleton can invest any amount up to $20 million. The firm expects to retain $3 million of earnings next year. It can raise up to $5 million in new debt at a before-tax cost of 8 percent, and all debt after the first $5 million will have a cost of 10 percent. The cost of retained earnings is 12 percent and Singleton can sell any amount of new common stock desired at a constant cost of new equity of 15 percent. The firm's marginal federal-plus-state tax rate is 40 percent. What is Singleton's optimal capital budget?

10-7 (Optimal capital budget) The management of Florida Phosphate Industries (FPI) is planning next year's capital budget. FPI projects its net income at $10,500, and its payout ratio is 40 percent. The company's earnings and dividends are growing at a constant rate of 5 percent; the last dividend, D_0, was $0.90; and the current stock price is $8.59. FPI's new debt will cost 14 percent. If FPI issues new common stock, flotation costs will be 20 percent. FPI is at its optimal capital structure, which is 40 percent debt and 60 percent equity, and the firm's marginal tax rate is 40 percent. FPI has the following independent, indivisible, and equally risky investment opportunities:

Project	Cost	IRR
A	$15,000	17%
B	20,000	14
C	15,000	16
D	12,000	15

What is FPI's optimal capital budget?

10-8 (Risk-adjusted optimal capital budget) Refer to Problem 10-7. Management neglected to incorporate project risk differentials into the analysis. FPI's policy is to add 2 percentage points to the cost of capital of those projects significantly more risky than average and to subtract 2 percentage points from the cost of capital of those which are substantially less risky than average. Management judges Project A to be of high risk, Projects C and D to be of average risk, and Project B to be of low risk. No projects are divisible. What is the optimal capital budget after adjustment for project risk?

Solutions to Self-Test Problems

ST-1   a. First, find the expected cash flows:

Year	Expected Cash Flow			
0	$0.2(-\$100,000) + 0.6(-\$100,000) + 0.2(-\$100,000)$			$= (\$100,000)$
1	$0.2(\$20,000)$	$+ 0.6(\$30,000)$	$+ 0.2(\$40,000)$	$= \$30,000$
2				$\$30,000$
3				$\$30,000$
4				$\$30,000$
5				$\$30,000$
5*	$0.2(\$0)$	$+ 0.6(\$20,000)$	$+ 0.2(\$30,000)$	$= \$18,000$

Next, determine the NPV based on the expected cash flows:

$$NPV = -\$100,000 + \frac{\$30,000}{(1.10)^1} + \frac{\$30,000}{(1.10)^2} + \frac{\$30,000}{(1.10)^3}$$
$$+ \frac{\$30,000}{(1.10)^4} + \frac{\$30,000 + \$18,000}{(1.10)^5} = \$24,900.$$

b. For the worst case, the cash flow values from the left-most cash flow column are used to calculate NPV:

$$NPV = -\$100,000 + \frac{\$20,000}{(1.10)^1} + \frac{\$20,000}{(1.10)^2} + \frac{\$20,000}{(1.10)^3}$$
$$+ \frac{\$20,000}{(1.10)^4} + \frac{\$20,000 + \$0}{(1.10)^5} = -\$24,184.$$

Similarly, for the best case, use the values from the right-most column. Here the NPV is $70,259.

If the cash flows are perfectly dependent, then the low cash flow in the first year would mean a low cash flow in every year. Thus, the probability of the worst case occurring is the probability of getting the $20,000 net cash flow in Year 1, or 20 percent. If the cash flows are independent, then the cash flow in each year could be low, high, or average, and the probability of getting all low cash flows would be $0.2(0.2)(0.2)(0.2)(0.2) = 0.2^5 = 0.00032$.

c. Under these conditions, the NPV distribution is

P	NPV
0.2	($24,184)
0.6	26,142
0.2	70,259

Thus, the expected NPV is $0.2(-\$24,184) + 0.6(\$26,142) + 0.2(\$70,259) = \$24,900$. Note that, as is generally the case, the expected NPV is the same as the base case NPV found in Part a. The standard deviation is $29,904:

$$\sigma^2{}_{NPV} = 0.2(-\$24{,}184 - \$24{,}900)^2 + 0.6(\$26{,}142 - \$24{,}900)^2$$
$$+ 0.2(\$70{,}259 - \$24{,}900)^2$$
$$= \$894{,}261{,}126.$$

$$\sigma_{NPV} = \sqrt{\$894{,}261{,}126} = \$29{,}904.$$

The coefficient of variation, CV, is $\$29{,}904/\$24{,}900 = 1.20$.

d. Since the project's coefficient of variation is 1.20, the project is riskier than average, and hence the project's risk-adjusted cost of capital is $10\% + 2\% = 12\%$. Now the project should be evaluated by finding the NPV of the base case as in Part a, but using a 12 percent discount rate. The risk-adjusted NPV is $\$18{,}357$, and thus the project should be accepted.

ST-2   a. *Cost using retained earnings:*

$$WACC_1 = 0.3(8\%)(0.6) + 0.7(12.0\%^*) = 9.84\%.$$

Cost using new common stock:

$$WACC_2 = 0.3(8\%)(0.6) + 0.7(12.7\%^{**}) = 10.33\%.$$

*Cost of retained earnings:

$$k_s = \frac{D_1}{P_0} + g = \frac{(\$1.85)(1.08)}{(\$50)} + 0.08 = 12.0\%.$$

**Cost of external equity:

$$k_e = \frac{D_1}{P_0(1 - F)} + g = \frac{(\$1.85)(1.08)}{(\$50)(0.85)} + 0.08 - 12.7\%.$$

Break point:

$$\text{Break point} = \frac{\$52{,}500}{0.7} = \$75{,}000.$$

b. The MCC and IOS schedules are shown on the next page.

c. From this graph, we conclude that Grossnickle should definitely undertake Projects A and B, assuming that these projects have about "average risk" in relation to the rest of the firm. Now, to evaluate Project C, recognize that one-half of its capital would cost 9.84 percent, while the other half would cost 10.33 percent. Thus, the cost of the capital required for Project C is 10.09 percent:

$$0.5(9.84\%) + 0.5(10.33\%) = 10.09\%.$$

Since the cost is greater than Project C's return of 10 percent, Grossnickle should not accept Project C.

d. The solution implicitly assumes (1) that all of the projects are equally risky and (2) that these projects are as risky as the firm's existing assets. If the accepted

MCC and IOS Schedules for Grossnickle

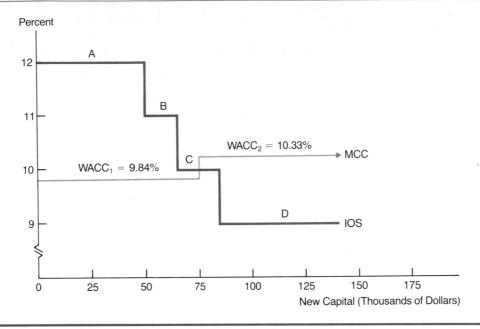

projects (A and B) were of above average risk, this could raise the company's overall risk, and hence its cost of capital. Taking on these projects could result in a decline in the company's value.

e. If the payout ratio were lowered to zero, this would shift the break point to the right, from $75,000 to $150,000. As the problem is set up, this would make Project C acceptable. If the payout were changed to 100 percent, there would be no retained earnings, and hence no break point, and the optimal capital budget would still consist of Projects A and B. This assumes that the change in payout would not affect k_s or k_d; as we shall see in Chapter 13, this assumption may not be correct.

Selected Additional References and Cases

The literature on risk analysis in capital budgeting is vast; here is a small but useful selection of additional references that bear directly on the topics covered in this chapter:

Ang, James S., and Wilbur G. Lewellen, "Risk Adjustment in Capital Investment Project Evaluations," *Financial Management,* Summer 1982, 5–14.

Bower, Richard S., and Jeffrey M. Jenks, "Divisional Screening Rates," *Financial Management,* Autumn 1975, 42–49.

Fama, Eugene F., "Risk-Adjusted Discount Rates and Capital Budgeting under Uncertainty," *Journal of Financial Economics,* August 1977, 3–24.

Gehr, Adam K., Jr., "Risk-Adjusted Capital Budgeting Using Arbitrage," *Financial Management,* Winter 1981, 14–19.

Gup, Benton E., and S. W. Norwood III, "Divisional Cost of Capital: A Practical Approach," *Financial Management,* Spring 1982, 20–24.

Lessard, Donald R., and Richard S. Bower, "An Operational Approach to Risk Screening," *Journal of Finance,* May 1973, 321–338.

Myers, Stewart C., and Samuel M. Turnbull, "Capital Budgeting and the Capital Asset Pricing Model: Good News and Bad News," *Journal of Finance,* May 1977, 321–333.

Robichek, Alexander A., "Interpreting the Results of Risk Analysis," *Journal of Finance,* December 1975, 1384–1386.

The Crum-Brigham casebook contains the following cases which are suitable for use at this point:

Case 15, "Egret Printing & Publishing Company," which illustrates alternative expansion paths.

Case 16, "Lotis Electronics," which focuses on sequential investment strategies.

Case 18, "Wayland Control & Instrument Corporation," which illustrates project evaluation under uncertainty.

Case 32, "Sub Contractor," which illustrates many of the techniques used in marginal cost of capital calculation.

Case 33, "Osborne Abrasives Manufacturing Corporation," which illustrates divisional hurdle rates.

The Harrington casebook contains the following applicable cases:

"Interchemical Consumer Products Division," which focuses on simulation analysis.

"Alaska Interstate," which illustrates a variety of ways to measure the riskiness of a conglomerate's subsidiaries.

"The Jacobs Division," which focuses on the riskiness of mutually exclusive alternatives.

10A
Capital Rationing

As we discussed in Chapter 10, under ordinary circumstances a firm should expand to the point where its marginal return is just equal to its marginal cost. A simplified view of the concept is shown in Figure 10A-1. Here we assume that the firm has five equally risky and independent investment opportunities which would cost a total of $23 million. Its cost of capital is assumed to be constant at 10 percent, implying that the firm can raise all the money it wants at a cost of 10 percent. Under these conditions, the firm would accept Projects V, W, and X, since they all have IRRs greater than the cost of capital, and hence NPVs greater than zero. It would reject Y and Z because they have IRRs less than k, indicating negative NPVs. This decision would maximize the value of the firm and the wealth of its stockholders.

Firms ordinarily operate in the manner depicted in the graph — they accept all independent projects having positive NPVs, reject those with negative NPVs, and choose between mutually exclusive investments on the basis of the higher NPV. However, some firms set an absolute limit on the size of their capital budgets such

Figure 10A-1
The Typical Capital Budgeting Situation

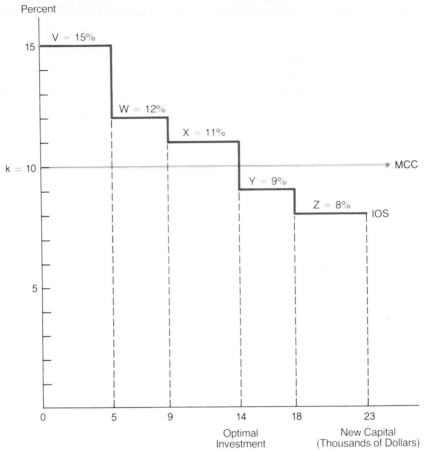

Note: If IRR > 10%, NPV is positive. Therefore, Projects V, W, and X have NPV > 0, while Y and Z have NPV < 0.

that the size of the budget is less than the level of investment called for by the NPV (or IRR) criterion. This is called *capital rationing,* and it is the topic of this appendix.

Reasons for Capital Rationing

The principal reason for capital rationing is that some firms are reluctant to engage in external financing (either borrowing or selling stock). One management, recalling the plight of firms with substantial amounts of debt during recent credit crunches, may simply refuse to use debt. Another management, which has no objection to selling debt, may not want to sell equity capital for fear of losing some measure of voting control. Still others may refuse to use any form of outside financing, considering safety and control to be more important than additional profits. These are all cases of capital rationing, and they result in limiting the rate of expansion to a slower pace than would be dictated by "purely rational wealth-maximizing behavior."

We should make three points here. First, a decision to hold back on expansion is not necessarily irrational. If the owners/managers of a privately held firm have what they consider to be plenty of income and wealth, then it might be quite rational for them to "trim their sails," relax, and concentrate on enjoying what they have already earned rather than on earning still more. Such behavior would not, however, be appropriate for a publicly owned firm.

Second, it is not correct to interpret as capital rationing a situation where the firm is willing to sell additional securities at the going market price but finds that it cannot because the market simply will not absorb more of its issues. Rather, such a situation indicates that the weighted average cost of capital is rising. If more acceptable investments are indicated than can be financed, then the marginal cost of capital being used is too low and should be raised.

Third, firms sometimes set a limit on capital expenditures, not because of a shortage of funds, but because of limitations on other resources, especially managerial talent. A firm might, for example, feel that its personnel development program is sufficient to handle an expansion of no more than 10 percent a year, and then set a limit on the capital budget to insure that expansion is held to that rate. This is not capital rationing—rather, it involves a downward reevaluation of project returns if growth exceeds some limit; that is, expected rates of return are, after some point, a decreasing function of the level of expenditures.

Project Selection under Capital Rationing

How should projects be selected under conditions of true capital rationing? First, note that if a firm truly rations capital, its value is not being maximized: If management were maximizing, then they would move to the point where the marginal project's NPV was zero, and capital rationing as defined would not exist. So, if a firm uses capital rationing, it has ruled out value maximization. The firm may, however, want to maximize value *subject to the constraint that the capital ceiling not be exceeded.* Constrained maximization behavior will, in general, result in a lower value than following unconstrained maximization, but some type of constrained maximization may produce reasonably satisfactory results. *Linear programming* is one method of constrained maximization that has been applied to capital rationing. Much work has been done in this area, and linear programming may, in the future, be widely applied in capital budgeting.[1]

---

[1]For further information on mathematical programming solutions to capital rationing, and for a review and analysis of the literature on this issue, see H. Martin Weingarten, "Capital Rationing: n Authors in Search of a Plot," *Journal of Finance,* December 1977, 1403–1431; and Stephen P. Bradley and Sherwood C. Frey, Jr., "Equivalent Mathematical Programming Models of Pure Capital Rationing," *Journal of Financial and Quantitative Analysis,* June 1978, 345–361.

If the firm does face capital rationing, and if the constraint cannot be lifted, what can the financial manager do? The objective should be to select projects, subject to the capital rationing constraint, such that the sum of the projects' NPVs is maximized. Linear programming can be used, or if there are not too many projects involved, the financial manager can simply enumerate all the sets of projects that meet the budget constraint and then select the set with the largest total NPV.

The complexities involved in a capital rationing situation are indicated in Table 10A-1. Here we assume that the firm is considering a total of eight potential projects; all are independent and have average risk. The firm has a 10 percent cost of capital, but management has decided to limit capital expenditures during the year to the amount of money that can be generated internally, $500,000. In the table, the projects are listed in the order of their NPVs, but their IRRs and profitability indices (PIs) are also shown.

Table 10A-1
Illustration of Capital Rationing

Project Number	Project Cost, or Outlay, at t = 0	Project Life (Years)	Cash Flow per Year	NPV at the 10% Cost of Capital	IRR	Profitability Index
1	$400,000	20	$58,600	$98,894	13.5%	1.25
2	250,000	10	55,000	87,951	17.7	1.35
3	100,000	8	24,000	28,038	17.3	1.28
4	75,000	15	12,000	16,273	13.7	1.22
5	75,000	6	18,000	3,395	11.5	1.05
6	50,000	5	14,000	3,071	12.4	1.06
7	250,000	10	41,000	1,927	10.2	1.01
8	250,000	3	99,000	(3,802)	9.1	0.98

If it is to maximize the value of the firm, management must choose the set of projects with the greatest total NPV, subject to the constraint that total expenditures must not exceed $500,000. With only eight projects in total, we can try all different combinations and, by "brute force," determine the set which maximizes NPV. This set is optimal:

Project	Cost	NPV
2	$250,000	$87,951
3	100,000	28,038
4	75,000	16,273
5	75,000	3,395
	$500,000	$135,657

This analysis seems simple enough, but there are three factors which complicate it greatly in realistic situations:

1. Number of projects. In the example, we have only eight projects, so it is easy to simply list all the combinations whose costs do not exceed $500,000 and then see which combination provides the greatest total NPV. For a large firm with thousands of projects, this would be a tedious process, although computer programs are available to solve such problems. However, the other problems listed below are more serious.

2. Project risk. In our example, we assumed that the eight projects are equally risky, and hence have the same cost of capital. If this were not the case, and if the number of projects were so large as to preclude hand analysis, then it would be difficult, if not impossible, to reach an optimal solution, because the computer programs currently available cannot deal efficiently with projects having differential risks.

3. Multiple time constraints. Our example also assumed a single-time-period capital constraint. Yet, realistically, when capital rationing is practiced the constraints usually extend for several years. However, the funds available in future years depend on cash throw-offs from investments made in earlier years. Thus, the constraint in Year 2 depends on the investments made in Year 1, and so on. For example, we might have investment funds of $500,000 per year available from external sources for 1988 through 1992 plus the cash flows from investments made in previous years. To solve this type of multiperiod problem, we need information on both investment opportunities and funds availability in future years, and not just on the situation in the current year. Also, the NPV we seek to maximize is the sum of the present values of the NPVs in each year over the time horizon being analyzed, say 1988 to 1992. In such a situation, we might even choose Project 8 in Table 10A-1, in spite of its negative NPV, because it has rapid cash throw-offs. In fact, if excellent investment opportunities are expected to be available in 1989, 1990, and 1991, taking Project 8 might be part of the best long-run strategy.

A Better Approach to Capital Rationing

Our main conclusion thus far about capital rationing — which means deliberately foregoing projects with positive NPVs — is that practicing it is irrational for any firm which seeks to maximize its stockholders' wealth. Also, while mathematical programming methods are available to help solve the simpler cases of capital rationing so that management can make the best of a bad situation, programming methods are really not capable of dealing with all the complexities encountered in the real world.

Fortunately, there is a better method for handling the types of situations that give rise to capital rationing. Usually, capital rationing occurs when the firm believes that it will encounter severe problems if it attempts to raise capital beyond some specified amount. For example, the interest rate it would have to pay would rise sharply if it attempted to increase its existing lines of credit. Such situations can be rationally handled by increasing the firm's WACC as the amount of capital raised increases. In effect, in terms of Figure 10A-1, the MCC schedule would begin to rise beyond some amount of capital, resulting in a higher MCC, and this higher MCC should be used as the discount rate when determining a project's NPV.

Capital Structure and Dividend Policy

11

Capital Structure Theory

At the end of 1983, AT&T and its subsidiaries had $148 billion of assets. These assets were financed with $84 billion of debt and $64 billion of common and preferred equity. Thus, from a total financing perspective, AT&T had a debt-to-assets ratio of $84/$148 = 57%. This ratio was high in comparison with most other companies, and it reflected primarily the earnings stability that had been associated with regulation.

However, on January 1, 1984, AT&T was forced to divest its local operating subsidiaries. They took with them $100 billion of assets, leaving the "new" AT&T with $48 billion. One key issue in the breakup was this — how much of the consolidated debt, and how much equity, should be transferred to the newly spun-off operating companies, and how much debt and equity should AT&T keep? In other words, how should the debt be allocated, and what capital structures should the various entities have after the breakup? This issue was addressed in the court, where it was noted that the Bell operating companies will continue to be regulated monopolies (to a large extent) whereas the surviving AT&T (to a large extent) will no longer be operated in a regulatory environment but must compete against such information services giants as IBM, MCI, and GTE. In the debate, questions such as these were raised: Why do firms use debt financing at all, and why do different firms use different proportions of debt? Further, should AT&T and its subsidiaries' use of debt change as a result of the change in their economic environment from a regulated monopoly to one in which they face different degrees of competition?

The materials covered in Chapters 11 and 12 are useful in addressing the issues posed by the AT&T breakup. Financial theorists have grappled with these questions for years, and many theories have been proposed to explain why firms use debt financing. We begin our discussion of financing mix by examining capital structure theory as it has developed in recent years. Then, in Chapter 12, we discuss the ways in which firms actually go about setting their optimal capital structure in view of the data limitations which make strict application of the theoretical rules impossible.

This chapter was coauthored with Dilip K. Shome of Virginia Polytechnic Institute and State University.   369

One of the most perplexing issues facing financial managers is the relationship between capital structure and firm value. Several theories of capital structure have been proposed, and we will discuss them in some detail. We begin by presenting some key terms and equations. Then, we briefly discuss three early (pre-1958) theories: the net income (NI) approach, the net operating income (NOI) approach, and the traditional approach. Next, we consider the classic 1958 Modigliani and Miller (MM) analysis, which marked the beginning of "modern capital structure theory." We then go on to expand the basic MM analysis to include the effects of corporate and personal taxes, financial distress, and agency costs. Finally, we present the asymmetric information (or signaling) theory, an alternative capital structure hypothesis which has recently been proposed and which is in many respects consistent with the capital structures one actually observes in practice.

Our conclusions are as follows: (1) There does exist an optimal capital structure, or at least an optimal range of structures, for every firm. (2) However, financial theory is not powerful enough at this point to enable us to locate a firm's optimal structure with any degree of precision. (3) Still, financial theory does help us identify the key factors which influence the value-maximizing structure, so an understanding of the material in this chapter will aid a firm that is choosing its target capital structure.

KEY TERMS AND EQUATIONS

Several theories have been set forth regarding how *leverage,* or the use of debt, affects the value of a firm and its cost of capital. These theories address two basic questions: Can a firm increase the wealth of its stockholders by replacing some of its equity with debt, and, if so, exactly how much debt should the firm use? As we explore these two questions, we will utilize several valuation equations; the key terms used in these equations are as follows:

S = market value of the firm's common stock (price per share times number of shares outstanding). We will solve for S.

D = market value of its debt. For simplicity, we shall ignore preferred stock and assume that the firm uses only one class of debt, which is a perpetuity. (Assuming perpetual debt simplifies the analysis.) For illustrative purposes, assume that $D = \$4,000,000$.

$V = D + S$ = total market value of the firm.

$EBIT$ = earnings before interest and taxes, also called net operating income (NOI). Again, for simplicity we shall assume that the expected value of EBIT is a constant over time. Realized EBIT could rise or fall, but the best estimate for the EBIT in any future year is the same as that for any other year. Assume that EBIT = $900,000.

k_d = interest rate on the firm's single class of perpetual debt. Assume that $k_d = 7.5\%$.

k_s = cost of equity, or required rate of return on the firm's common stock. Assume *initially* that $k_s = 10\%$.

k_a = weighted average cost of capital.

T = corporate tax rate. Assume that T = 40%.

We assume that the firm is in a zero-growth situation; that is, EBIT is expected to remain constant, and all earnings are paid out as dividends. Therefore, the total market value of its common stock, S, is a perpetuity whose value is found as follows:

$$S = \frac{\text{Dividends}}{k_s} = \frac{\text{Net income}}{k_s} = \frac{(\text{EBIT} - k_d D)(1 - T)}{k_s}. \qquad \textbf{(11-1)}$$

Under our assumptions,

$$S = \frac{[\$900{,}000 - 0.075(\$4{,}000{,}000)](0.6)}{0.10} = \frac{\$360{,}000}{0.10} = \$3{,}600{,}000.$$

Equation 11-1 is merely the value of a perpetuity, with the numerator being the net income available to common stockholders, which we assume is all paid out as dividends, while the denominator is the cost of common equity. We shall use Equation 11-1 to show how changes in the amount of debt financing would affect the value of the firm's stock under the different capital structure theories. Also, note that we can solve Equation 11-1 for k_s, the cost of equity:

$$k_s = \frac{(\text{EBIT} - k_d D)(1 - T)}{S}. \qquad \textbf{(11-1a)}$$

In our example,

$$k_s = \frac{\$360{,}000}{\$3{,}600{,}000} = 0.10 = 10\%,$$

which illustrates numerically that Equations 11-1 and 11-1a are equivalent. We will use this form of the equation when we discuss the effects of leverage on the cost of equity.

Another basic required equation is that for the weighted average cost of capital as developed in Chapter 7:

$$k_a = \text{WACC} = w_d k_d (1 - T) + w_s k_s = \left(\frac{D}{V}\right) k_d (1 - T) + \left(\frac{S}{V}\right) k_s. \qquad \textbf{(11-2)}$$

In our example, V = D + S = $4 million + $3.6 million = $7.6 million, so

$$\text{WACC} = (\$4/\$7.6)(7.5\%)(0.6) + (\$3.6/\$7.6)(10\%)$$

$$= \quad 0.5263(4.5\%) \quad + \quad 0.4737(10\%)$$

$$= 7.1053\%.$$

We will use Equation 11-2 to examine how changes in the debt ratio affect the firm's weighted average cost of capital.

A third basic equation is that for the total market value of the firm, V. Note that we found V above by first using Equation 11-1 to find the value of the equity and then adding the value of the debt: V = S + D. However, another expression for the value of the firm is required in our analysis:[1]

$$V = \frac{EBIT(1 - T)}{k_a} \tag{11-3}$$

$$= \frac{\$900,000(0.60)}{0.071053} = \$7,600,000.$$

Equation 11-3 shows that V can be found as the value of a perpetuity which capitalizes the constant after-tax operating income, EBIT(1 − T), at the firm's WACC, k_a. Note that Equation 11-1 capitalizes the earnings available to common stockholders, and Equation 11-3 capitalizes after-tax operating cash flows, which must service both debtholders and stockholders. Note also that we could solve Equation 11-3 for k_a to obtain an alternative expression for the WACC:

$$k_a = WACC = \frac{EBIT(1 - T)}{V} \tag{11-3a}$$

$$= \frac{\$900,000(0.60)}{\$7,600,000} = 7.1053\%.$$

We will use Equations 11-1, 11-1a, 11-2, 11-3, and 11-3a to examine the way changes in capital structure affect the firm's value and cost of capital under the different capital structure theories. This is our next task.

---

[1]Equation 11-3 is derived as follows:
Step 1. Solve Equation 11-2 for V:

$$V = \frac{(D)k_d(1 - T) + (S)k_s}{k_a}.$$

Step 2. Substitute Equation 11-1 for S in the Step 1 equation:

$$V = \frac{(D)k_d(1 - T) + \left[\frac{(EBIT - k_dD)(1 - T)}{k_s} \right]k_s}{k_a}.$$

Step 3. Cancel the k_s values in the numerator and then modify the equation to produce this expression:

$$V = \frac{k_dD(1 - T) + EBIT(1 - T) - k_dD(1 - T)}{k_a}.$$

Step 4. Cancel the $k_dD(1 - T)$ terms, producing this important new equation:

$$V = \frac{EBIT(1 - T)}{k_a}. \tag{11-3}$$

EARLY THEORIES OF CAPITAL STRUCTURE

One of the earliest formal works on the theory of capital structure was David Durand's 1952 study, which identified the three positions that had been taken by writers up to that time:[2] (1) the net income (NI) approach, (2) the net operating income (NOI) approach, and (3) a middle-ground position Durand called the traditional approach. The differences among the three approaches result solely from differing assumptions about how investors establish the value of a firm's debt and equity. To simplify things, we examine the three approaches under the assumption of zero taxes.

The Net Income (NI) Approach

The *NI approach* assumes (1) that investors capitalize, or value, the firm's net income at a constant rate (k_s = constant) and (2) that firms can raise all the debt they want at a constant rate (k_d = constant). With both k_s and k_d constant, as the firm uses more and more debt, the weighted average cost of capital, k_a, as given by Equation 11-2, declines, because debt is cheaper than equity. Further, if k_a declines as debt is increased, then, because of the Equation 11-3 relationship, the firm's value must increase as its use of debt increases.

The situation as viewed under the NI approach is shown on the left side of Figure 11-1: As the firm moves from zero toward 100 percent debt, its weighted average cost of capital decreases continuously, and its value increases continuously. Thus, if the NI assumptions are correct, firms should use (almost) 100 percent debt in order to maximize value.

The Net Operating Income (NOI) Approach

The *NOI approach*, graphed in the middle section of Figure 11-1, assumes that investors have an entirely different reaction to corporate debt. Specifically, the NOI approach assumes that investors value NOI (or EBIT) at a constant rate (WACC = constant). As in the NI approach, NOI advocates assume that k_d is a constant. Notice (1) that a constant WACC results in a constant value for the firm regardless of its use of debt (this follows when Equation 11-3 is applied), and (2) that a constant WACC, along with a constant k_d, implies that k_s increases with leverage (Equation 11-2), and hence that stockholders regard the use of leverage as increasing the riskiness of the equity cash flows. If the NOI assumptions are true, then

---

[2]See David Durand, "Costs of Debt and Equity Funds for Business: Trends and Problems of Measurement," *Conference on Research in Business Finance* (New York: National Bureau of Economic Research, 1952). Although Durand's work is dated, we include it in the text to provide historical perspective.

Figure 11-1
Effects of Leverage:
NI, NOI, and Traditional Approaches

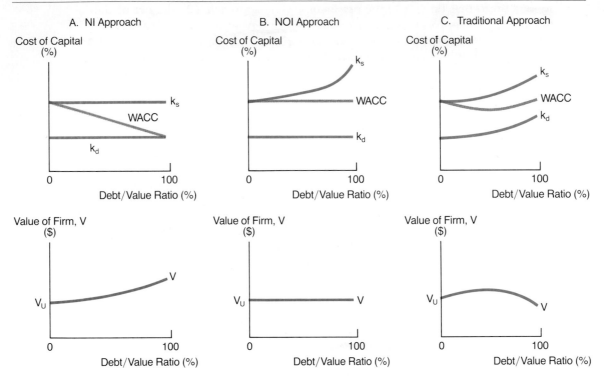

Notes: a. Under the NI approach, the plot of value versus D/V is slightly bowed. A plot of value versus dollars of debt would be linear.

   b. The graphs do not extend all the way to a 100 percent debt/value ratio because at that point the creditors become the equity holders. See Footnote 6 for a discussion.

capital structure decisions will be unimportant — one capital structure is as good as any other.[3]

The Traditional Approach

Most academicians and practitioners at the time of Durand's work took a middle-of-the-road approach, somewhere between NI and NOI, which Durand called the *traditional approach.* The graphs on the right side of Figure 11-1 illustrate the

---

[3]The NI and NOI theories, as they were originally set forth, assumed away corporate income taxes. However, Durand did examine the two approaches including corporate income taxes, and he found that under the NOI approach, the firm's value does increase with leverage due to the tax deductibility of interest. Note, though, that the firm's value under the NI approach increases at a faster rate. Thus, in a world with corporate taxes, both approaches would indicate that the optimal capital structure calls for virtually 100 percent debt.

traditionalists' view, which suggested that up to some "moderate" amount of leverage, risk does not increase noticeably on either the debt or the equity, so k_d and k_s are both relatively constant out to some point. However, beyond this threshold debt ratio, both debt and equity costs begin to rise sharply, and these increases more than offset the advantages of cheaper debt. The result is (1) a U-shaped weighted average cost of capital curve and (2) a value of the firm which first rises, then hits a peak, and finally declines as the debt ratio increases. Thus, according to the traditionalists, there is some capital structure with less than 100 percent debt which maximizes the value of the firm.

Whereas the NI and NOI theories as set forth by Durand are mathematically precise, the traditional approach was more judgmental in nature. Moreover, a review of the literature of the time offers little in the way of an explanation for the assumed shape of the traditional curves; they were drawn on the basis of judgment rather than statistical evidence. We will return to a discussion of the traditional view later in the chapter, but first we must examine the Modigliani-Miller models and their extensions.

THE MODIGLIANI-MILLER MODELS

The three capital structure theories presented above were based on assertions about investor behavior rather than on either a carefully constructed formal proof or formal statistical studies. In what has been called the most influential financial research ever published, Franco Modigliani and Merton H. Miller (MM) addressed the capital structure issue in a rigorous, scientific fashion, and they set off a chain of research that continues to this day.[4]

Assumptions

To begin, MM made the following assumptions, some of which were later relaxed:

1. Firms' business risk can be measured (by σ_{EBIT}), and firms with the same degree of business risk are said to be in a *homogeneous risk class*.

2. All present and prospective investors have identical estimates of each firm's future EBIT; that is, investors have *homogeneous expectations* about expected future corporate earnings and the riskiness of these earnings. This assumption is comparable to our use of a "representative investor" in earlier chapters when we discussed the DCF model and market equilibrium ($\hat{k}_s = k_s$).

---

[4]See Franco Modigliani and Merton H. Miller, "The Cost of Capital, Corporation Finance and the Theory of Investment," *American Economic Review,* June 1958, 261–297; "The Cost of Capital, Corporation Finance and the Theory of Investment: Reply," *American Economic Review,* September 1958, 655–669; "Taxes and the Cost of Capital: A Correction," *American Economic Review,* June 1963, 433–443; and "Reply," *American Economic Review,* June 1965, 524–527. In a 1979 survey of Financial Management Association members, the original MM article was judged to have had the greatest impact on the field of finance of any work ever published. See Philip L. Cooley and J. Louis Heck, "Significant Contributions to Finance Literature," *Financial Management,* Tenth Anniversary Issue 1981, 23–33.

3. Stocks and bonds are traded in *perfect capital markets.* This assumption implies, among other things, (1) that there are no brokerage costs and (2) that investors (both individuals and institutions) can borrow at the same rate as corporations.

4. The debt of firms and individuals is riskless, so the interest rate on debt is the risk-free rate. Further, this situation holds regardless of how much debt a firm (or an individual) issues.

5. All cash flows are perpetuities; that is, the firm is a zero-growth firm with an "expectationally constant" EBIT, and its bonds are perpetuities. "Expectationally constant" means that the best guess as to the EBIT for any future year is the same as for any other year, but investors know that the realized level could be different from the expected level in any year.

MM without Corporate Taxes

MM first performed their analysis under the assumption that there are no corporate income taxes. On the basis of the preceding assumptions, and in the absence of corporate taxes, MM stated and algebraically proved two propositions:[5]

Proposition I
The value of any firm is established by capitalizing its expected net operating income (NOI = EBIT) at a constant rate which is appropriate for the firm's risk class:

$$V_L = V_U = \frac{\text{EBIT}}{\text{WACC}} = \frac{\text{EBIT}}{k_{sU}}. \tag{11-4}$$

Here the subscripts L and U designate levered and unlevered firms in a given risk class, and the constant rate, k_{sU} = WACC, is the required rate of return for an unlevered, or all-equity, firm.

Since V as established by the Proposition I equation is a constant, *then under the MM theory, the value of the firm is independent of its leverage.* This also implies that the weighted average cost of capital to any firm, leveraged or not, is (1) completely independent of its capital structure and (2) equal to the cost of equity to an unlevered firm in the same risk class. *Thus, MM's Proposition I is identical to the NOI hypothesis as expressed in Figure 11-1.*

Proposition II
The cost of equity to a levered firm is equal to (1) the cost of equity to an unlevered firm in the same risk class plus (2) a risk premium whose size depends on both the differential between the costs of equity and debt to an unlevered firm and the amount of leverage used:

$$k_{sL} = k_{sU} + \text{Risk premium} = k_{sU} + (k_{sU} - k_d)(D/S). \tag{11-5}$$

---

[5]MM actually developed three propositions. See Eugene F. Brigham and Louis C. Gapenski, *Intermediate Financial Management,* 2nd ed., Chapter 5, for a discussion of the third one.

Proposition II states that as the firm's use of debt increases, its cost of equity also rises, and in a mathematically precise manner.

Taken together, the two MM propositions imply that the inclusion of more debt in the capital structure will not increase the value of the firm, because the benefits of cheaper debt will be exactly offset by an increase in the cost of equity. *Thus, MM theory states that in a world without taxes, both the value of a firm and its cost of capital are unaffected by its capital structure.*

Proof of the MM Propositions without Corporate Taxes

Proof of Proposition I

MM used an *arbitrage proof* to support their propositions. They showed that, under their assumptions, if two companies differed only (1) in the way they are financed and (2) in their total market values, then investors would sell shares of the overvalued firm, buy those of the undervalued firm, and continue this process until the companies had exactly the same market value. To illustrate, assume that two firms, Firm L (for levered) and Firm U (for unlevered), are identical in all important respects except financial structure. Firm L has $4,000,000 of 7.5 percent debt, while Firm U uses only equity. Both firms have EBIT = $900,000, and σ_{EBIT} is the same for both firms, so they are in the same business risk class.

In the initial situation, before any arbitrage occurs, assume that both firms have the same equity capitalization rate: $k_{sU} = k_{sL} = 10\%$. Under this condition, according to Equation 11-1, the following situation would exist:

Firm U:

$$\text{Value of Firm U's stock} = S_U = \frac{EBIT}{k_{sU}} \quad \frac{k_dD}{} \quad \frac{\$900,000 - \$0}{0.10} = \$9,000,000.$$

$$\text{Total market value of Firm U} = V_U = D_U + S_U = \$0 + \$9,000,000 = \$9,000,000.$$

Firm L:

$$\text{Value of Firm L's stock} = S_L = \frac{EBIT - k_dD}{k_{sL}}$$

$$= \frac{\$900,000 - 0.075(\$4,000,000)}{0.10} = \$6,000,000.$$

$$\text{Total market value of Firm L} = V_L = D_L + S_L = \$4,000,000 + \$6,000,000 = \$10,000,000.$$

Thus, before arbitrage, and assuming that $k_{sU} = k_{sL}$, the value of the levered company, Firm L, exceeds that of unlevered Firm U.

MM argue that this is a disequilibrium situation which cannot persist. To see why, suppose you owned 10 percent of L's stock, so the market value of your investment was $600,000. According to MM, you could increase your total investment income without increasing your exposure to risk. To do so, you would (1) sell your stock in L for $600,000, (2) borrow an amount equal to 10 percent of L's debt ($400,000), and then (3) buy 10 percent of U's stock for $900,000. Notice that you would receive $1 million from the sale of your 10 percent of L's stock plus your borrowing, and you would be spending only $900,000 on U's stock, so you would have an extra $100,000, which MM assumed you would invest in riskless debt to yield 7.5 percent, or $7,500 annually.

Now consider your income position:

Old Income:	10% of L's $600,000 equity income		$60,000
New Income:	10% of U's $900,000 equity income	$90,000	
	Less 7.5% interest on $400,000 loan	(30,000)	$60,000
	Plus 7.5% interest on extra $100,000		7,500
	Net investment income		$67,500

Thus, your net investment income from common stock would be exactly the same as before, $60,000, but you would have $100,000 left over for investment in riskless debt, which would increase your income by $7,500. Therefore, the total return on your $600,000 net worth would rise. Further, your risk (according to MM) would be the same as before; you would have simply substituted $400,000 of "homemade" leverage for your 10 percent share of Firm L's $4 million of corporate leverage, and hence neither your "effective" debt nor your risk would have changed. Thus, you would have increased your income without raising your risk, which is obviously a desirable thing to do.

MM argue that this arbitrage process would actually occur, with sales of L's stock driving its price down, and purchases of U's stock driving its price up, until the market values of the two firms were equal. Until this equality was established, you and others would switch from one stock to the other, so the profit motive would force the equality to be reached. When equilibrium was established, the values of Firms L and U, and their weighted average costs of capital, would be equal, but k_{sL} would be greater than k_{sU}. Thus, according to Modigliani and Miller, V and WACC must be independent of capital structure under equilibrium conditions.

Proof of Proposition II

The proof of Proposition II is relatively straightforward. See Eugene F. Brigham and Louis C. Gapenski, *Intermediate Financial Management,* 2nd ed., Appendix 5A. Note that this appendix also contains the proofs of MM's propositions with corporate taxes, which we discuss next.

MM with Corporate Taxes

MM's original work, published in 1958, assumed a zero corporate tax rate. In 1963, they published a second article which included corporate tax effects. With corporate income taxes, they concluded that leverage will increase a firm's value, because interest on debt is a tax deductible expense, and hence more of a leveraged firm's operating income flows through to investors. The MM propositions when corporations are subject to income taxes follow.

Proposition I

The value of a levered firm is equal to (1) the value of an unlevered firm in the same risk class plus (2) the gain from leverage, which is the value of the tax savings and which equals the corporate tax rate times the amount of debt the firm uses:

$$V_L = V_U + TD. \tag{11-4a}$$

The important point here is that when corporate taxes are introduced, the value of the levered firm exceeds that of the unlevered firm by the amount TD. Note also that the differential increases as the use of debt increases, so a firm's value is maximized at virtually 100 percent debt financing. (Note: The value of the unlevered firm is found by using Equation 11-3, with WACC $-$ k_{sU}.)

Proposition II

The cost of equity to a levered firm is equal to (1) the cost of equity to an unlevered firm in the same risk class plus (2) a risk premium whose size depends on the differential between the costs of equity and debt to an unlevered firm, the amount of financial leverage, and the corporate tax rate:

$$k_{sL} = k_{sU} + (k_{sU} - k_d)(1 - T)(D/S). \tag{11-5a}$$

Notice that Equation 11-5a is identical to the corresponding without-tax equation, 11-5, except for the term $(1 - T)$ in 11-5a. Since $(1 - T)$ is less than 1.0, the imposition of corporate taxes causes the cost of equity to rise at a slower rate than it did in the absence of taxes. It is this characteristic that produces the Proposition I result, namely, an increasing value as leverage increases.

Illustration of the MM Model with Corporate Taxes

To illustrate the MM model with corporate taxes, assume that the following data and conditions hold for Mid-State Water Company, an old, established firm that supplies water to business and residential customers in several low-growth midwestern metropolitan areas.

1. Mid-State currently has no debt; it is an all-equity company.
2. Expected EBIT = $4,000,000. EBIT is not expected to increase over time, so Mid-State is in a no-growth situation.
3. Mid-State has a 40 percent federal-plus-state tax rate, so T = 40%.
4. Mid-State pays out all of its income as dividends.

5. If Mid-State begins to use debt, it can borrow at a rate $k_d = 8\%$. This borrowing rate is constant, and it is independent of the amount of debt used. Any money raised by selling debt would be used to retire common stock, so Mid-State's assets would remain constant.

6. The risk of Mid-State's assets, and thus its EBIT, is such that its shareholders require a rate of return, k_{sU}, of 12 percent if no debt is used.

When Mid-State has zero debt, Equation 11-3 can be used to find its value, $20 million:

$$V_U = \frac{\text{EBIT}(1 - T)}{k_{sU}} = \frac{\$4 \text{ million}(0.6)}{0.12} = \$20.0 \text{ million.}$$

With $10 million of debt, we see by Proposition I (Equation 11-4a) that total market value rises to $24 million:

$$V_L = V_U + TD = \$20 \text{ million} + 0.4(\$10 \text{ million}) = \$24 \text{ million.}$$

Therefore, the value of Mid-State's stock must be $14 million:

$$S = V - D = \$24 \text{ million} - \$10 \text{ million} = \$14 \text{ million.}$$

We can also find Mid-State's cost of equity, k_{sL}, and its weighted average cost of capital, k_a, at a debt level of $10 million. First, we use Equation 11-5a, Proposition II, to find k_{sL}, the leveraged cost of equity:

$$k_{sL} = k_{sU} + (k_{sU} - k_d)(1 - T)(D/S)$$
$$= 12\% + (12\% - 8\%)(0.6)(\$10 \text{ million}/\$14 \text{ million})$$
$$= 12\% + 1.71\% = 13.71\%.$$

Now we can find the company's weighted average cost of capital, $\text{WACC} = k_a$:

$$\text{WACC} = k_a = (D/V)(k_d)(1 - T) + (S/V)k_s$$
$$= (\$10/\$24)(8\%)(0.6) + (\$14/\$24)(13.71\%) = 10\%.$$

Alternatively, we could find the WACC by using Equation 11-3a as follows:

$$\text{WACC} = \frac{\text{EBIT}(1 - T)}{V} = \frac{\$4 \text{ million}(0.6)}{\$24 \text{ million}} = 0.10 = 10\%.$$

Mid-State's value and cost of capital based on the MM model at various debt levels are shown in Figure 11-2. Here we see that in an MM world with corporate

Figure 11-2
Effects of Leverage:
MM with Taxes (Millions of Dollars)

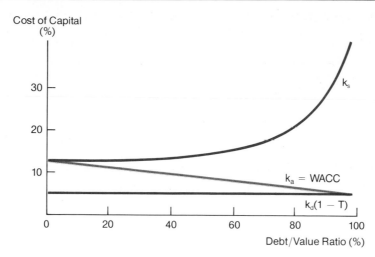

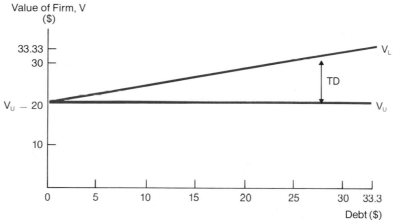

D (1)	V (2)	S (3)	D/V (4)	k_d (5)	k_s (6)	k_a = WACC (7)
$ 0	$20.00	$20.00	0.00%	8.0%	12.00%	12.00%
5	22.00	17.00	22.73	8.0	12.71	10.91
10	24.00	14.00	41.67	8.0	13.71	10.00
15	26.00	11.00	57.69	8.0	15.27	9.23
20	28.00	8.00	71.43	8.0	18.00	8.57
25	30.00	5.00	83.33	8.0	24.00	8.00
30	32.00	2.00	93.75	8.0	48.00	7.50
33.33[a]	33.33	0.00	100.00	12.0	—	12.00

[a]The case of 100 percent debt is the theoretically limiting case. See Footnote 6 for a discussion.

taxes, financial leverage does matter: the value of the firm is maximized, and its cost of capital is minimized, if it uses virtually 100 percent debt financing.[6]

THE MILLER MODEL

Although MM included *corporate* taxes in the second version of their model, they did not extend the model to analyze the effects of *personal* taxes. However, in his 1976 presidential address to the American Finance Association, Merton Miller did introduce a model designed to show how leverage affects firms' values when both personal and corporate taxes are taken into account.[7] To explain Miller's model, let us begin by defining T_c as the corporate tax rate, T_s as the personal tax rate on income from stocks, and T_d as the personal tax rate on income from debt. Note that stock returns come partly as dividends and partly as capital gains, so T_s is a weighted average of the effective tax rates on dividends and capital gains, while essentially all debt income comes from interest, which is effectively taxed at an investor's top rate.

With personal taxes included, *and under the same set of assumptions used in the earlier MM models,* the value of an unlevered firm is found as follows:

$$V_U = \frac{EBIT(1 - T_c)(1 - T_s)}{k_{sU}}. \tag{11-6}$$

The $(1 - T_s)$ term adjusts for personal taxes. Therefore, the numerator shows how much of the firm's operating income is left after the unlevered firm itself pays corporate income taxes and its investors subsequently pay personal taxes on their equity income. Since the introduction of personal taxes lowers the usable income to investors, personal taxes reduce the value of the unlevered firm, other things held constant.

---

[6]In the limiting case, where the firm used 100 percent debt financing, the bondholders would own the entire company, and hence they would have to bear all the business risk. (Up until this point, MM assume that the stockholders bear all the risk.) If the bondholders bear all the risk, then the capitalization rate on the debt should be equal to the equity capitalization rate at zero debt, $k_d = k_{sU} = 12\%$.

The income stream to the stockholders in the all-equity case was $\$4,000,000(1 - T) = \$2,400,000$, and the value of the firm was

$$V_U = \frac{\$2,400,000}{0.12} = \$20,000,000.$$

With all debt, the entire $\$4,000,000$ of EBIT would be used to pay interest charges. k_d would be 12%, so $0.12(\text{Debt}) = \$4,000,000$. Taxes would be zero, and investors (bondholders) would get the entire $\$4,000,000$ of operating income; they would not have to share it with the government. Thus, at 100 percent debt, the value of the firm would be

$$V_L = \frac{\$4,000,000}{0.12} = \$33,333,333 = D.$$

There is, of course, a transition problem in all this—MM assume that $k_d = 8\%$ regardless of how much debt the firm has until debt reaches 100 percent, at which point k_d jumps to 12 percent, the cost of equity. As we shall see later in the chapter, k_d realistically rises as the use of financial leverage increases.

[7]See Merton H. Miller, "Debt and Taxes," *Journal of Finance,* May 1977, 261–275.

Miller's results can be obtained as follows. To begin, we first partition the levered firm's annual cash flows, CF_L, into those going to the stockholders and those going to the bondholders, considering both corporate and personal taxes:

$$CF_L = \text{Net CF to stockholders} + \text{Net CF to bondholders}$$
$$= (EBIT - I)(1 - T_c)(1 - T_s) + I(1 - T_d). \tag{11-7}$$

Here I is the annual interest payment. Equation 11-7 can be rearranged as follows:

$$CF_L = EBIT(1 - T_c)(1 - T_s) - I(1 - T_c)(1 - T_s) + I(1 - T_d). \tag{11-7a}$$

The first term in Equation 11-7a is identical to the after-tax cash flow of an all-equity firm as shown in Equation 11-6, and its present value is found by discounting the perpetual cash flow by k_{sU}. The second and third terms, which reflect leverage, result from the cash flows associated with interest payments. These two cash flows are assumed to have a risk equal to that of the basic interest payment stream, and hence their present values are obtained by discounting at the cost of debt, k_d. (Remember, these are all perpetual cash flows, so the basic perpetuity valuation model, $V = CF/k$, applies.) Combining the present values of the three terms, we obtain this value for the levered firm:

$$V_L = \frac{EBIT(1 - T_c)(1 - T_s)}{k_{sU}} - \frac{I(1 - T_c)(1 - T_s)}{k_d} + \frac{I(1 - T_d)}{k_d}. \tag{11-8}$$

The first term in Equation 11-8 is identical to V_U as set forth in Equation 11-6, and we can consolidate the second two terms as follows:

$$V_L = V_U + \left[1 - \frac{(1 - T_c)(1 - T_s)}{(1 - T_d)} \right] \frac{I(1 - T_d)}{k_d}. \tag{11-8a}$$

Now recognize that the after-tax perpetual interest payment divided by the required rate of return on debt, $I(1 - T_d)/k_d$, equals the market value of the debt, D. Substituting D into the preceding equation, we obtain this very important expression:

$$V_L = V_U + \left[1 - \frac{(1 - T_c)(1 - T_s)}{(1 - T_d)} \right] D. \tag{11-9}$$

Equation 11-9 is the Miller model for the value of a levered firm in a world with both corporate and personal taxes.

The Miller model has several important implications:

1. The term in brackets,

$$\left[1 - \frac{(1 - T_c)(1 - T_s)}{(1 - T_d)} \right],$$

multiplied by D, represents the gain from leverage. The bracketed term replaces the factor $T = T_c$ in the earlier MM model with corporate taxes, $V_L = V_U + TD$.

2. If we ignore all taxes, that is, if $T_c = T_s = T_d = 0$, then the bracketed term reduces to zero, so Equation 11-9 is the same as the original MM model without corporate taxes, $V_L = V_U$.

3. If we ignore personal taxes, that is, if $T_s = T_d = 0$, then the bracketed term reduces to $[1 - (1 - T_c)] = T_c$, so Equation 11-9 is the same as the MM model with corporate taxes, $V_L = V_U + TD$.

4. If the effective personal tax rates on stock and bond incomes were equal, that is, if $T_s = T_d$, then $(1 - T_s)$ and $(1 - T_d)$ would cancel, and the bracketed term would again reduce to T_c.

5. Note that if $(1 - T_c)(1 - T_s) = (1 - T_d)$, then the bracketed term would go to zero, and the value of using leverage would also be zero. This implies that the tax advantage of debt to the firm would be exactly offset by the personal tax advantage of equity. Under this condition, capital structure would have no effect on a firm's value or its cost of capital, and hence we would be back to MM's original zero-tax theory.

6. Because taxes on capital gains are deferred, the effective tax rate on stock income is normally less than the effective tax rate on bond income. This being the case, what would the Miller model predict as the gain from leverage? To answer this question, assume that the tax rate on corporate income is $T_c = 34\%$, the effective rate on bond income is $T_d = 28\%$, and the effective rate on stock income is $T_s = 20\%$.[8] Using these values in the Miller model, we find that a levered firm's value increases over that of an unlevered firm by 27 percent of the market value of corporate debt:

$$\text{Gain from leverage} = \left[1 - \frac{(1 - T_c)(1 - T_s)}{(1 - T_d)} \right] D$$

$$= \left[1 - \frac{(1 - 0.34)(1 - 0.20)}{(1 - 0.28)} \right] D$$

$$= [1 - 0.73]D = 0.27(D).$$

Note that the MM model with corporate taxes would indicate a gain from leverage of $T_c(D) = 0.34D$, or 34 percent of the amount of corporate debt. Thus, with these assumed tax rates, adding personal taxes to the model lowers the value of corporate debt financing. In general, whenever the effective tax rate on stock income is less than the effective rate on bond income, the Miller model produces a lower gain from leverage than is produced by the MM model.

In his paper, Miller argued that firms in the aggregate would issue a mix of debt and equity securities such that the before-tax yields on corporate securities

---

[8]Note that, in a follow-on article, Miller and Scholes describe how investors could, theoretically, shelter or delay income from stock to the point where the effective personal tax rate on such income is essentially zero. See Merton H. Miller and Myron S. Scholes, "Dividends and Taxes," *Journal of Financial Economics,* December 1978, 333–364. However, the 1986 changes in the tax law eliminated most of the shelters Miller and Scholes discussed.

and the personal tax rates of the investors who bought these securities would adjust until an equilibrium was reached. At the equilibrium, $(1 - T_d)$ would equal $(1 - T_c)(1 - T_s)$, and hence, as we noted in Point 5 above, the tax advantage of debt to the firm would be exactly offset by personal taxation, and capital structure would have no effect on a firm's value or its cost of capital. Thus, according to Miller, the results obtained from the original Modigliani-Miller zero-tax model are correct!

Others have extended and tested Miller's 1977 analysis. Generally, these extensions disagree with Miller's conclusion that there is no advantage to the use of corporate debt. In the United States, even though the differential rate on dividends and capital gains was eliminated by the new tax law, the effective tax rate on stock income is probably less than the effective tax rate on bond income due to the deferral of taxes on capital gains. Thus, it appears that $(1 - T_c)(1 - T_s)$ is less than $(1 - T_d)$, and there is an advantage to the use of corporate debt. However, Miller's work does show that personal taxes offset some of the benefits of corporate debt, and hence that the tax advantages of corporate debt are less than were implied by the earlier MM model that considered only corporate taxes.

As we note in the next section, there are a number of problems with both the MM and the Miller models, so one should not put much trust in results such as those in our examples.

Criticisms of the MM and Miller Theories

The conclusions of each of the various capital structure theories follow logically from their initial assumptions: If their assumptions are correct, then their conclusions must be reached. However, both academicians and financial executives have voiced concern over the validity of the MM and Miller theories because of the fact that virtually no firms follow their recommendations. Both the MM model with corporate taxes and the Miller model with "reasonable" tax rates lead to the conclusion that firms should use 100 percent debt. That situation is not observed in practice except by firms such as Frontier Airlines whose equity was eroded by operating losses. People who disagree with the MM and Miller theories and their suggestions for financial policy generally attack them on the grounds that their assumptions do not reflect actual market conditions. Some of the main objections are listed next:

1. Both MM and Miller assume that personal and corporate leverage are perfect substitutes. However, an individual investing in a levered firm has less loss exposure, which means a more *limited liability,* than if he or she used "homemade" leverage. For example, in our earlier illustration of the MM arbitrage argument, it should be noted that only the $600,000 our investor had in Firm L would be lost if that firm went bankrupt. However, if the investor engaged in arbitrage transactions and employed "homemade" leverage to invest in Firm U, then he or she could lose $900,000—the original $600,000 investment plus the $400,000 loan less the $100,000 investment in riskless bonds. This much higher personal risk exposure would tend to restrain investors from engaging in arbitrage, and that could cause the equilibrium values of V_L, V_U, k_{sL}, and k_{sU} to be different from those specified by the equations. Restrictions on institutional investors, who dominate capital markets today, may also retard the arbitrage process, because most institutional investors cannot legally borrow to buy stocks, and hence they are prohibited from engaging in homemade leverage.

2. Brokerage costs were assumed away by MM and Miller, making the switch from L to U costless. However, brokerage and other transactions costs do exist, and they too impede the arbitrage process.

3. MM initially assumed that corporations and investors can borrow at the risk-free rate. Although risky debt has been introduced into the analysis by others, to reach the MM and Miller conclusions it is still necessary to assume that both corporations and investors can borrow at the same rate. Although major institutional investors probably can borrow at the corporate rate, many institutions are not allowed to borrow to buy securities. Further, most individual investors probably must borrow at higher rates than those paid by large corporations.

4. In his article, Miller concluded that an equilibrium would be reached, but to reach his equilibrium the tax benefit from corporate debt (1) must be the same for all firms, and (2) must be constant for an individual firm regardless of the amount of leverage used. However, we know that the tax benefit varies from firm to firm: Highly profitable companies gain the maximum tax benefit from leverage, while the benefits to firms that are struggling are much smaller. Further, some firms make greater use of tax shields such as high depreciation and pension plan contributions (or have operating losses), and these shields and losses reduce the tax savings value of interest payments.[9] It also appears simplistic to assume that the expected tax shield is unaffected by the amount of debt financing used. Higher leverage increases the probability that the firm cannot effectively use the full tax shield in the future, because higher leverage increases the probability of future unprofitability and consequently lower tax rates. All things considered, it appears likely that the corporate tax shield is more valuable to some firms than to others.

5. MM and Miller assume that there are no costs associated with financial distress. Further, they ignore agency costs. These topics are discussed in the next section.

FINANCIAL DISTRESS AND AGENCY COSTS

Some of the assumptions inherent in the MM and Miller models can be relaxed, and when this is done, the basic conclusions remain unchanged.[10] However, as we discuss next, when financial distress and agency costs are added, the results are altered significantly.

---

[9]For a discussion of the impact of tax shields other than debt financing, see Harry DeAngelo and Ronald W. Masulis, "Optimal Capital Structure under Corporate and Personal Taxation," *Journal of Financial Economics,* March 1980, 3–30.

[10]For example, see Robert A. Haugen and James L. Pappas, "Equilibrium in the Pricing of Capital Assets, Risk-Bearing Debt Instruments, and the Question of Optimal Capital Structure," *Journal of Financial and Quantitative Analysis,* June 1971, 943–954; Joseph Stiglitz, "A Re-Examination of the Modigliani-Miller Theorem," *American Economic Review,* December 1969, 784–793; and Mark E. Rubenstein, "A Mean-Variance Synthesis of Corporate Financial Theory," *Journal of Finance,* March 1973, 167–181.

Costs of Financial Distress

A number of firms experience financial distress each year, and some of them are forced into bankruptcy. When financial distress, including but not restricted to bankruptcy, occurs, several things can happen:

1. Arguments between claimants often delay the liquidation of assets, thus leading to physical deterioration and/or obsolescence of inventories and fixed assets. Bankruptcy cases can take many years to settle, and during this time machinery rusts, buildings are vandalized, inventories become obsolete, and the like.

2. Lawyer's fees, court costs, and administrative expenses can absorb a large part of the firm's value. Together, the costs of physical deterioration plus legal fees and expenses are called the *direct costs* of bankruptcy.

3. Managers and other employees generally lose their jobs when a firm fails. Knowing this, the management of a firm that is in financial distress may take actions which keep it alive in the short run but which also reduce its long-run value. For example, the firm may defer maintenance of machinery, sell off valuable assets at bargain prices to raise cash, or cut costs so much that the quality of its products is impaired and the firm's long-run market position is eroded.

4. Both customers and suppliers of companies that are experiencing financial difficulties are aware of the problems that can arise, and they often take "evasive action" that further damages the troubled firm. For example, Frontier Airlines, as it struggled to avoid bankruptcy in 1986, was having trouble making sales because potential customers were worried about buying a seat for a future flight and then have the company shut down before they could take the trip. Some potential customers were also worried that the company might cut back on maintenance expenditures, and its suppliers were reluctant to grant normal credit terms, or to gear up to supply Frontier with parts and other materials on a long-term basis. Further, Frontier was having great difficulty obtaining capital. Finally, Frontier had trouble attracting and retaining the highest quality workers, as most workers with a choice preferred employment with a more stable airline to one that could go bankrupt any day. Eventually, Frontier did go bankrupt, and thousands of employees lost their jobs.

Nonoptimal managerial actions associated with financial distress, as well as the costs imposed by customers, suppliers, and capital providers, are called the *indirect costs* of financial distress. Of course, these costs may be incurred by a firm in financial distress even if it does not go into bankruptcy: Bankruptcy is just one point on the continuum of financial distress.

All things considered, the direct and indirect costs associated with financial distress are high.[11] Further, financial distress occurs only if a firm has debts — debt-free firms do not experience financial distress. *Therefore, the greater the use of debt financing, and the larger the fixed interest charges, the greater the probabil-*

---

[11]See Edward I. Altman, "A Further Empirical Investigation of the Bankruptcy Cost Question," *Journal of Finance,* September 1984, 1067–1089. On the basis of a sample of bankrupt companies, Altman found that bankruptcy costs often exceeded 20 percent of firm value.

Table 11-1
Expected Cost of Financial Distress

		Amount of Debt			
	$0	$5 Million	$10 Million	$20 Million	$30 Million
Probability of financial distress	0.0	0.05	0.15	0.50	0.95
PV of expected costs of financial distress ($5 million times the indicated probability)	$0	$250,000	$750,000	$2,500,000	$4,750,000

ity that a decline in earnings will lead to financial distress and, hence, the higher the probability that the costs of financial distress will be incurred.

An increase in the probability of financial distress lowers the current value of a firm and raises its cost of capital. To see why, suppose we estimate that Mid-State Water will incur financial distress costs of $7 million if it fails at some future date, and that the *present value* of this possible future cost is $5 million. Further, the probability of financial distress increases with leverage, causing the expected present value cost of financial distress to rise from zero at zero debt to $4.75 million at $30 million of debt as shown in Table 11-1.

These expected costs of financial distress must be subtracted from the values we previously calculated in the lower section of Figure 11-2 to find the firm's value at various amounts of leverage: They would reduce the values of V and S in Columns 2 and 3 and, as a result, would raise k_s and k_a = WACC in Columns 6 and 7. For example, at $20 million of debt, we would obtain the values in Table 11-2.[12] These changes would, of course, then have carry-through effects on the graphs in Figure 11-2 — most important, they would (1) reduce the decline of the WACC line and (2) reduce the slope of the V_L line.

The effects of financial distress are also felt by a firm's bondholders. Firms experiencing financial distress have a higher probability of defaulting on debt payments, and hence the expectation of financial distress influences bond investors' required rates of return: The higher the probability of financial distress, the higher the required yield on debt. Thus, as firms use more and more debt financing, and hence increase the probability of distress, the value of k_d also increases, causing several elements in Figure 11-2 to change.

---

[12]To find k_s and WACC in Table 11-2, apply Equations 11-1a and 11-2, respectively:

$$k_s = \frac{(EBIT - K_dD)(1 - T)}{S} = \frac{[\$4 - 0.08(\$20)](1 - 0.4)}{\$5.5} = 26.18\%.$$

$$k_a = WACC = (D/V)(k_d)(1 - T) + (S/V)(k_s)$$
$$= (20/25.5)(8\%)(0.6) + (5.5/25.5)(26.18\%)$$
$$= 3.76\% + 5.65\% = 9.41\%.$$

Table 11-2
Effects of Financial Distress (Millions of Dollars)

	Figure 11-2 Values at D = \$20 Million with Financial Distress Effects Ignored: Pure MM	**Figure 11-2 Values at D = \$20 Million with Financial Distress Effects Considered: Modified MM**
V	\$28.00	\$28.00 − \$2.5 = \$25.5
S	\$8.00	\$8.00 − \$2.5 = \$5.5
k_s	18.00%	26.18%
k_a = WACC	8.57%	9.41%

Agency Costs

We introduced the concept of agency costs in Chapter 1. One type of agency cost is associated with the use of debt, and it involves the relationship between a firm's stockholders and its bondholders. In the absence of any restrictions, a firm's management would be tempted to take actions that would benefit stockholders at the expense of bondholders. For example, if Mid-State Water were to sell only a small amount of debt, then this debt would have relatively little risk, and hence a high bond rating and a low interest rate. Yet, having sold the low-risk debt, Mid-State could then issue more debt secured by the same assets as the original debt. This would raise the risks faced by *all bondholders,* cause k_d to rise, and consequently cause the original bondholders to suffer capital losses. Similarly, suppose that after issuing a substantial amount of debt, Mid-State decided to restructure its assets, selling off assets with low business risk and acquiring assets that were more risky but that also had higher expected rates of return. If things worked out well, the stockholders would benefit. If things went sour, most of the loss in a highly leveraged firm would fall on the bondholders. In other words, the stockholders would be playing a game of "heads, I win; tails, you lose" with the bondholders.

Because of the possibility that stockholders might try to take advantage of bondholders in these and other ways, bonds are protected by restrictive covenants. These covenants hamper the corporation's legitimate operations to some extent. Further, the company must be monitored to insure that the covenants are being obeyed, and the costs of monitoring are passed on to the stockholders in the form of higher debt costs. The costs of lost efficiency plus monitoring are what we mean here by the term *agency costs,* and the existence of these costs increases the cost of debt to the firm and thus reduces the advantage of using leverage.[13]

---

[13]Jensen and Meckling point out that there are also agency costs between outside equity holders and management. See "Theory of the Firm: Managerial Behavior, Agency Costs, and Ownership Structure," *Journal of Financial Economics,* October 1976, 305–360. Their study further suggests that (1) bondholder agency costs increase as the debt ratio increases, but (2) outside stockholder agency costs move in reverse fashion, falling with increased use of debt.

Firm Value and the Cost of Capital with Financial Distress and Agency Costs

If the MM model with corporate taxes were correct, a firm's value would rise continuously as it moved from zero debt toward 100 percent debt — the equation $V_L = V_U + TD$ shows that TD, and hence V_L, is maximized if D is at a maximum. Recall that the rising component of value, TD, results directly from the tax shelter provided by interest on the debt. However, the following factors, which were ignored by MM, could cause V_L to decline with increases in debt: (1) the present value of costs associated with potential future financial distress and (2) the present value of agency costs. Therefore, MM's relationship between a firm's value and its use of leverage should look like this:

$$V_L = V_U + TD - \begin{pmatrix} \text{PV of} \\ \text{expected} \\ \text{financial} \\ \text{distress costs} \end{pmatrix} - \begin{pmatrix} \text{PV of} \\ \text{agency} \\ \text{costs} \end{pmatrix}. \qquad \textbf{(11-10)}$$

The relationship expressed in Equation 11-10 is graphed in Figure 11-3. The tax shelter effect totally dominates until the amount of debt reaches Point A. After Point A, financial distress and agency costs become increasingly important, offsetting some of the tax advantages. At Point B, the marginal tax shelter benefits of

Figure 11-3
Net Effects of Leverage on the Value of the Firm

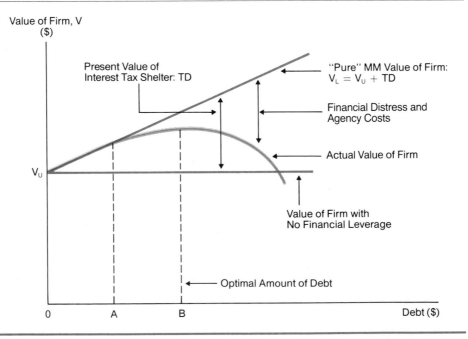

additional debt are exactly offset by the disadvantages of debt, and beyond Point B, the disadvantages outweigh the tax benefits.

Equation 11-9, the Miller model, could also be modified to reflect financial distress and agency costs. The equation would be identical to Equation 11-10, except that the gain from leverage term, TD, would reflect the addition of personal taxes. In either the pure MM or Miller models, the gain from leverage can at least be roughly estimated, but the value reduction resulting from potential financial distress and agency costs is almost entirely subjective. We know that these costs must increase as leverage rises, but we simply do not know the specific functional relationship.

REVIEW OF THE TRADEOFF MODELS

Both the MM with corporate taxes and the Miller models as modified to reflect financial distress and agency costs can be described as *tradeoff* models. That is, the optimal capital structure is found by balancing the tax shield benefits of leverage against the financial distress and agency costs of leverage, and hence the costs and benefits are "traded off" against one another.

Implications of the Models

The tradeoff models are not capable of specifying precise optimal capital structures, but they do lead to three qualitative statements about financing behavior:

1. Risky firms, as measured by the variability of expected returns on the firm's assets, ought to borrow less, other things equal. The greater this variability, the greater the probability of financial distress at any level of debt, and hence the greater the expected costs of distress. Thus, firms with lower business risk can borrow more before the expected costs of distress offset the tax advantages of borrowing.

2. Firms that employ tangible assets such as real estate and standard production machinery should borrow more than firms whose value is derived either from intangible assets such as patents and goodwill or from growth opportunities. The costs of financial distress depend not only on the probability of incurring distress but also on what happens if distress occurs. Specialized assets, intangible assets, and growth opportunities are more likely to lose value if financial distress occurs than are standardized, tangible assets.

3. Firms that are currently paying taxes at the highest rate, and that are likely to continue to do so in the future, should carry more debt than firms with current and/or prospectively lower tax rates. High corporate tax rates produce greater benefits from debt financing, and hence high-rate firms can carry more debt, other factors held constant, before the tax shield is offset by financial distress and agency costs.

According to the tradeoff models, each firm should set a target capital structure which balances the costs and benefits of leverage, because such a structure will maximize its value. We would expect to find actual target structures that are consistent with the three points just raised. Further, we would generally expect to find that firms within an industry have similar capital structures, because such firms have roughly the same business risk, types of assets, and profitability.

The Empirical Evidence

The tradeoff models have intuitive appeal because they lead to the conclusion that both no debt and all debt are bad, while a "moderate" debt level is good. However, we must ask ourselves whether these models explain actual behavior. If they do not, then we must search for other explanations or else assume that managers, and hence investors, are acting irrationally, an assumption that we are unwilling to make.

The tradeoff models do have a degree of empirical support.[14] For example, firms that have tangible assets in place tend to borrow more heavily than firms whose value stems from intangibles and/or growth opportunities. However, there is other empirical evidence which indicates that the tradeoff models are not entirely valid. First, several studies have examined models of financing behavior to see if firms' financing decisions reflect adjustment toward a target capital structure. These studies provide some evidence that this occurs, but the explanatory power of the models is very low, suggesting that tradeoff models capture only a small part of actual behavior. Second, no study has clearly demonstrated that a firm's tax rate has a predictable, material effect on its capital structure. In fact, firms used debt financing long before corporate income taxes even existed. Finally, actual debt ratios tend to vary widely across apparently similar firms, whereas the tradeoff models suggest that debt usage should be relatively constant within industries.

All in all, the empirical support for the tradeoff models is not strong, which suggests that other factors not incorporated into these models are also at work. In other words, the tradeoff models do not tell the full story.

ASYMMETRIC INFORMATION THEORY

In the early 1960s, Professor Gordon Donaldson of Harvard University conducted an extensive survey of how corporations actually establish their capital structures.[15] Here is a summary of his findings:

1. Firms prefer to finance with internally generated funds, that is, retained earnings and depreciation.

---

[14]For examples of the empirical research in this area, see Robert Taggart, "A Model of Corporate Financing Decisions," *Journal of Finance,* December 1977, 1467–1484; and Paul Marsh, "The Choice Between Equity and Debt: An Empirical Study," *Journal of Finance,* March 1982, 121–144.

[15]Gordon Donaldson, *Corporate Debt Capacity: A Study of Corporate Debt Policy and the Determination of Corporate Debt Capacity* (Boston: Harvard Graduate School of Business Administration, 1961).

2. Firms set their target dividend payout ratios based on (1) their expected future investment opportunities and (2) their expected future cash flows. The target payout ratio is set at a level such that, under normal conditions, retained earnings plus depreciation will meet capital expenditure requirements.

3. Dividends are "sticky" in the short run — firms are reluctant to make major changes in their dividend payments, and they are especially reluctant to cut the dividend. Thus, in any given year, depending on realized cash flows and actual investment opportunities, a firm may or may not have sufficient internally generated funds to cover its capital expenditures.

4. If the firm has more retained earnings than are needed for expansion purposes, then it will invest in marketable securities or else use the funds to retire debt. If it has insufficient retained earnings to finance non-postponable new projects, then it will first draw down its marketable securities portfolio. If still more funds are needed, then the firm will go to the external capital markets, first issuing debt, then convertible bonds, and then common stock only as a last resort. *Thus, Donaldson observed a "pecking order" of financing, not the balanced approach that is called for under the tradeoff theories.*

Professor Stewart Myers noted the inconsistency between Donaldson's findings and the MM/Miller theories, and that led him to propose a new theory.[16] First, Myers noted that Donaldson's pecking order findings led away from rather than toward a well-defined capital structure. Equity is raised in two forms, and one, retained earnings, is at the top of the pecking order, while the other, new common stock, is at the bottom.

Next, Myers noted that the tradeoff theories assume that all market participants have homogeneous expectations, which implies (1) that all participants have the same information set and (2) that any changes in operating income are purely random as opposed to anticipated by some parties. Myers had the insight to see that if the assumption of homogeneous expectations is relaxed, and if asymmetric (or different) information by different groups of market participants is admitted, Donaldson's results could be explained in a logical manner. Myers' work resulted in what is now called the *asymmetric information theory of capital structure.*

The basis for the theory, as articulated by Myers, rests on the existence of asymmetric information. To illustrate, assume that a firm has 10,000 common shares outstanding which have a current price of $19 per share, so the market value of its equity is $190,000. However, its managers have better information about the firm's prospects than stockholders, and the managers believe that the actual share value based on existing assets is $21, giving the equity a total "true" market value of $210,000. Such information asymmetry could easily exist, for managers often know more about their firms' prospects than do current and potential investors.[17]

---

[16]Stewart C. Myers, "The Capital Structure Puzzle," *Journal of Finance,* July 1984, 575–592. It is interesting to note that, like the Miller model, Myers' paper was presented as a presidential address to the American Finance Association.

[17]This assumption is contrary to the strong-form efficient markets hypothesis (EMH) presented in Chapter 6, but few observers — including people who believe ardently in weak and semistrong efficiency — are willing to accept strong-form efficiency.

Suppose further that the firm now identifies a new project which requires external financing of $100,000 and which has an estimated net present value (NPV) of $5,000. (Remember that a project's NPV is a residual value over its costs, and that this residual accrues to the shareholders.) This project is unanticipated by the firm's investors, and hence its $5,000 NPV has not been incorporated into the firm's $190,000 equity market value. Should the firm accept the project?

To begin, assume that the firm plans to sell new equity to raise the $100,000 to finance the project. Several possibilities are set forth below.

1. Symmetric information. First, as a point of departure, consider the situation in which all investors *do* have the same information as management regarding existing asset values. Under these conditions, the stock would be selling at $21 per share, for a total market value of $210,000, and the firm would have to sell $100,000/$21 = 4,762 new shares to finance the project. Acceptance of the project would result in a new stock price of $21.34:

$$\text{New stock price} = \frac{\text{Original market value} + \text{New money raised} + \text{NPV}}{\text{Original shares} + \text{New shares}}$$

$$= \frac{\$210,000 + \$100,000 + \$5,000}{10,000 + 4,762} = \$21.34.$$

Clearly, both old and new shareholders would benefit if the project were accepted.

2. Asymmetric information prior to stock issue. Consider now the situation in which our firm's management can in no way inform investors about the stock's "true" value. Perhaps it is necessary to hold back such information to maintain a competitive edge, or perhaps SEC regulations cause management to refrain from "touting" the stock price prior to the new issue (if things did not work out as expected, new shareholders might sue the managers who had provided the rosy forecast). In this situation, the stock would sell for $19 per share, the current value of the equity would be $190,000, and new stock would fetch only $19 per share, so the company would have to sell $100,000/$19 = 5,263 shares in order to raise the required $100,000. If this were done, this new price would result if the project were accepted *and then the asymmetric information regarding the value of the current equity was removed:*

$$\text{New stock price} = \frac{\text{New market value} + \text{New money raised} + \text{NPV}}{\text{Original shares} + \text{New shares}}$$

$$= \frac{\$210,000 + \$100,000 + \$5,000}{10,000 + 5,263} = \$20.64.$$

Under this condition, the project should not be undertaken, for if the project were not accepted, and hence new shares not sold, then the price of the stock would rise to $21 when the information asymmetry was removed. The sale of new stock at $19 per share would lead to a $0.36 loss to the firm's existing shareholders and to a $1.64 gain to the new shareholders.

3. A more profitable project. Suppose now the project had an NPV of $20,000, and other conditions were unchanged. Now the firm's stock price would rise to $21.62 after the asymmetric information was removed if it undertook the project:

$$\text{New stock price} = \frac{\$210,000 + \$100,000 + \$20,000}{10,000 + 5,263} = \$21.62.$$

Under these conditions, the firm should take on the project. Note, though, that most of the positive NPV will go to the new stockholders, who will pay $19 per share and thus enjoy a capital gain of $2.62 versus a gain of only $0.62 for the original stockholders.

4. Dark clouds on the horizon. Now suppose an entirely different situation faced the firm. Stockholders think the firm is worth $19 per share, but the firm's managers think (1) that investors are entirely too optimistic about the firm's growth opportunities, (2) that investors have not properly recognized proposed legislation which will require large, nonearning investments in pollution control equipment, and (3) that investors do not fully anticipate the need for new R&D expenditures which will be required to keep the firm's products competitive. If and when all of these bad events materialize, profit margins will be under pressure, cash flows will be down, and the company will not be able to carry safely its present level of debt. Moreover, the stock price will fall sharply, and it will be extremely difficult to raise the capital that will be necessary to assure the firm's survival.

Faced with these conditions, management might well conclude that the "true" value of the firm's stock is only $17 per share, and further decide to sell a new issue of 10,000 shares at the current price of $19, raising $190,000 and using the funds to retire debt or to support this year's capital budget. This action would increase the "true" value of the stock from $17 to $18·

$$\text{New "true" value} = \frac{\text{Old "true" equity value} + \text{New money}}{\text{Original shares} + \text{New shares}}$$

$$= \frac{\$170,000 + \$190,000}{10,000 + 10,000} - \$18.00.$$

Current stockholders will, if and when management's expectations come true, suffer a loss, but the sale of new stock would reduce that loss. (Note: Management would have to word the prospectus for the new issue carefully, pointing out the potential problems. However, virtually all prospectuses are filled with cautionary language, so investors cannot tell from them what management really expects.)

5. Finance the original $5,000 NPV project with debt. If the firm used debt to finance the original $100,000 project, *and then the information asymmetry was removed,* the new stock price would be $21.50:

$$\text{New stock price} = \frac{\text{New market value} + \text{NPV}}{\text{Original shares}}$$

$$= \frac{\$210,000 + \$5,000}{10,000} = \$21.50.$$

Thus, if debt financing were used, all of the "true" value of the firm's existing assets plus the residual value of the new project would accrue to the old shareholders. If stock financing were used, we saw that the value of the original stock would end up at $20.64 rather than $21, the true value without the new investment.

What does all this suggest about corporate financial policy? First, in a world where asymmetric information exists, corporations should issue new shares only if they have extraordinarily profitable investments that cannot be postponed or financed by debt, or if management thinks the shares are overvalued. Good, but not great, projects should be financed internally or with debt. Second, investors recognize all this, and they tend to mark down a company's share price when it announces plans to issue new shares, because chances are that the announcement is signaling bad news, not good news. Third, the financing pecking order that Donaldson observed is rational when asymmetric information exists — it pays to retain a large fraction of earnings, and to keep the equity ratio up and the debt ratio down, so as to maintain some "reserve borrowing capacity" which can be used to support the capital budget if and when an unusually large volume of positive NPV projects come along, or if problems arise which require outside capital.[18]

OUR VIEW OF CAPITAL STRUCTURE THEORY

START

The great contribution of the tradeoff models of MM, Miller, and their followers is that these models identified and quantified the benefits and costs of using debt — the tax effects, financial distress costs, and so on. Prior to these models, no capital structure theory existed, and we had no systematic way of analyzing the effects of debt financing.

The tradeoff view is summarized graphically in Figure 11-4. The top graph shows the relationships between the debt ratio and the costs of debt, equity, and the WACC. Both k_s and $k_d(1 - T_c)$ rise steadily with increases in leverage, but the rate of increase accelerates at higher debt levels, reflecting agency costs and the increased probability of financial distress and its attendant costs. The WACC first declines, then hits a minimum at D/V*, and then begins to rise. It is interesting to note that Figure 11-4 looks very much like the graphs on the right side of Figure 11-1, which represent the traditional position prior to MM's work. Although the traditionalists did not state very clearly why they believed the graphs took their assumed shapes, we can use the tradeoff models, with the effects of financial distress and agency costs included, to help with this explanation. Also, note that the general shapes of the curves apply regardless of whether we are using the MM with corporate taxes model, the Miller model, or a variant of these models.

Unfortunately, it is extremely difficult for financial managers to actually quantify the costs and benefits of debt financing to their firms, and hence it is virtually impossible to pinpoint D/V*, the capital structure that truly maximizes the firm's

---

[18]Flotation costs also play a role in capital structure theory. In general, flotation costs are smaller on debt issues than on equity issues, and this provides an additional rationale for using debt rather than outside equity. We will discuss this issue in more detail in Chapter 15.

Figure 11-4
**Effects of Leverage:
The Tradeoff View**

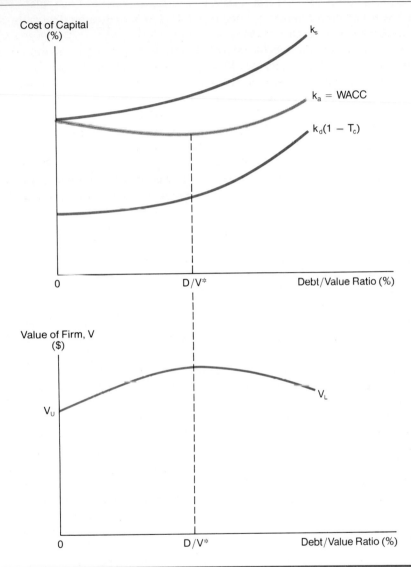

value. Most experts believe such a structure exists for every firm, but that it changes substantially over time as the nature of the firm and the capital markets change. Most experts also believe that, as shown in Figure 11-4, the relationship between firm value and leverage is relatively flat, and hence that relatively large deviations from the optimum can occur without materially affecting a firm's value or its weighted average cost of capital.

Now consider the asymmetric information theory. Because of asymmetric information, investors know less about a firm's prospects than do its managers. Further, managers try to maximize value for current stockholders, not new ones, so if the firm has excellent prospects, management will not want to issue new shares, but if things look bleak, then a new stock offering may be sold. Therefore, investors take a stock offering to be a signal of bad news, and as a result stock prices tend to decline when new issues are announced. Because of this, new equity financing is especially expensive, and this fact must be incorporated into the capital structure decision. Its effect is to motivate firms to maintain a reserve borrowing capacity, for with such a reserve, future investment opportunities can be financed by debt when internal funds are insufficient.

By combining the two theories, we obtain this possible explanation for firms' behavior: (1) Debt financing provides benefits because of the tax deductibility of interest. Hence, firms should have some debt in their capital structures. (2) However, financial distress and agency costs place limits on debt usage—beyond some point, these costs offset the tax advantage of debt. (3) Finally, because of asymmetric information, firms maintain a borrowing capacity reserve in order to take advantage of good investment opportunities or to avoid having to issue stock in troubled times and at distressed prices.

Of course, all this sounds reasonable, but how should financial decisions be made in practice? The answer is rather fuzzy, and many factors must be considered when actually choosing a capital structure. This topic will be covered in the next chapter.

SUMMARY

This chapter presented the major elements of the theory of capital structure. We saw that three early theories—*net income* (*NI*), *net operating income* (*NOI*), and *traditional*—were advanced to explain the relationship between leverage and the firm's value and cost of capital. However, these theories were more speculations than true theories. Then, in 1958, Franco Modigliani and Merton H. Miller (MM) startled the financial community by proposing, and proving, that under a certain set of assumptions capital structure is irrelevant. This was MM's famous zero tax article. But firms do pay taxes, and MM went on to expand their model to include corporate taxes. Here, capital structure is relevant, and firms maximize value by using almost 100 percent debt financing.

Finally, Miller went one step further and added personal taxes to the model. The interpretation of the *Miller model* is somewhat controversial, but most professionals believe that the addition of personal taxes reduces, but does not eliminate, the value of debt financing. Miller's model still prescribes that firms should use virtually all debt financing. However, both the MM and Miller analyses ignored financial distress and agency costs. The addition of these costs results in a *tradeoff framework*. Here the costs and benefits of debt financing are balanced against one another, resulting in an optimal capital structure that falls somewhere between zero debt and 100 percent debt.

An alternative theory, called the *asymmetric information theory,* was recently proposed by Stewart Myers. This theory, which is based on managers having better information than investors, postulates that there is a preferred order of financing: first retained earnings, then debt, and then new common stock only as a last resort. Firms finance according to this "pecking order," and hence observed capital structures reflect the cumulative need for external financing over time.

We believe that there is some benefit to debt financing, and further that firms probably try to maintain a borrowing reserve. Thus, firms use debt based on their tax rates, asset structures, and inherent riskiness, but they also try to maintain the ability to issue new debt if it becomes necessary to raise external capital. Note, though, that establishing a target capital structure in practice is more a matter of informed judgment than of quantitative analysis. In the next chapter, we discuss the many factors that influence this important corporate decision.

Questions

11-1 Define each of the following terms:
  a. Leverage
  b. Net income (NI) theory
  c. Net operating income (NOI) theory
  d. Traditional theory
  e. MM Proposition I without corporate taxes; with corporate taxes
  f. MM Proposition II without corporate taxes; with corporate taxes
  g. Miller model
  h. Financial distress costs; agency costs
  i. Tradeoff theory
  j. Asymmetric information theory

11-2 Explain why agency costs would probably be more of a problem for a large, publicly owned firm that uses both debt and equity capital than for a small, unleveraged, owner-managed firm.

11-3 Use Equation 11-3 to explain why the capital structure which maximizes a firm's value must also minimize its weighted average cost of capital.

11-4 The stock of Gentech Company is currently selling at its low for the year, but management feels that the stock price is only temporarily depressed because of investor pessimism. The firm's capital budget this year is so large that the use of new outside equity is contemplated. However, management does not want to sell new stock at the current low price and is therefore considering a temporary departure from the firm's "optimal" capital structure by borrowing the funds it would otherwise have raised in the equity markets. Does this seem to be a wise move? Does this action conform to any of the theories presented in the chapter?

11-5 Explain, in words, how MM use the arbitrage process to prove the validity of Proposition I. Also, list the major MM assumptions and explain why each of these assumptions is necessary in the arbitrage proof.

11-6 A utility company is supposed to be allowed to charge prices high enough to cover all costs, including its cost of capital. Public service commissions are supposed to take actions to stimulate companies to operate as efficiently as possible in order to keep costs, and hence prices, as low as possible. Several years ago, AT&T's debt ratio was about 33 percent. Some people (Myron J. Gordon in particular) argued that a higher debt ratio would lower AT&T's cost of capital and permit it to charge lower rates for telephone service. Gordon thought an optimal debt ratio for AT&T was about 50 percent. Do the theories presented in the chapter support or refute Gordon's position?

Self-Test Problem

ST-1 (MM with financial distress costs) Nadir, Inc., is an unlevered firm, and it has constant expected operating earnings (EBIT) of $2 million per year. Nadir's tax rate is 40 percent, and its market value is $V = S = \$12$ million. Management is considering the use of some debt financing. (Debt would be issued and used to buy back stock, so the size of the firm would remain constant.) Since interest expense is tax deductible, the value of the firm would tend to increase as debt is added to the capital structure, but there would be an offset in the form of a rising risk of financial distress. The firm's analysts have estimated, as an approximation, that the present value of any future financial distress costs is $8 million, and that the probability of distress would increase with leverage according to the following schedule:

Value of Debt	Probability of Financial Distress
$ 2,500,000	0.00%
5,000,000	1.25
7,500,000	2.50
10,000,000	6.25
12,500,000	12.50
15,000,000	31.25
20,000,000	75.00

a. What is Nadir's cost of equity and average cost of capital at this time?

b. According to the "pure" MM after-tax valuation model, what is the optimal level of debt?

c. What is the optimal capital structure when financial distress costs are included?

d. Plot the value of the firm, with and without distress costs, as a function of the level of debt.

Problems

11-1 (MM without taxes) Companies U and L are identical in every respect except that U is unlevered while L has $10 million of 5 percent bonds outstanding. Assume (1) that all of the MM assumptions are met, (2) that there are no corporate or personal taxes, (3) that EBIT is $2 million, and (4) that the cost of equity to Company U is 10 percent.

    a. What value would MM estimate for each firm?

    b. What is k_s for Firm U? For Firm L?

    c. Find S_L, and then show that $S_L + D = V_L = \$20$ million.

    d. What is k_a = WACC for Firm U? For Firm L?

    e. Suppose $V_U = \$20$ million and $V_L = \$22$ million. According to MM, do these values represent an equilibrium? If not, explain the process by which equilibrium will be restored.

11-2 (MM with corporate taxes) Refer to Problem 11-1. Assume that all the facts hold, except that firms are subject to a 40 percent federal-plus-state corporate tax rate.

    a. What value would MM now estimate for each firm? (Use Proposition I.)

    b. What is k_s for Firm U? Firm L?

    c. Find S_L, and then show that $S_L + D = V_L$ results in the same value as obtained in Part a.

    d. What is k_a = WACC for Firm U? For Firm L?

11-3 (Miller model) Refer to Problems 11-1 and 11-2. Assume that all facts hold, except that both corporate and personal taxes apply. Assume that both firms must pay a federal-plus-state corporate tax rate of $T_c = 40\%$, and that investors in both firms face a tax rate of $T_d = 28\%$ on debt income and $T_s = 20\%$, on average, on stock income.

    a. What is the value of the unlevered firm, V_U? (Note that V_U is now reduced by the tax on stock income, and hence $V_U \neq \$12$ million as in Problem 11-2a.)

    b. What is the value of V_L?

    c. What is the gain from leverage in this situation? Compare this with the gain from leverage in Problem 11-2.

    d. Set $T_c = T_s = T_d = 0$. What is the value of the levered firm? The gain from leverage?

    e. Now suppose $T_s = T_d = 0$. What are the value of the levered firm and the gain from leverage?

    f. Assume that $T_d = 28\%$, $T_s = 28\%$, and $T_c = 40\%$. Now what are the value of the levered firm and the gain from leverage?

11-4 (MM with and without taxes) Far East Unlimited (FEU) is just about to commence operations as an international trading company. The firm will have book assets of $10 million, and it expects to earn a 16 percent return on these assets before taxes. However, because of certain tax arrangements with foreign governments, FEU will not pay any taxes, that is, its tax rate will be zero. Management is trying to decide how to raise the required $10 million. It is known that the capitalization rate for an all-equity firm in this business is 11 percent, that is, $k_{sU} = 11\%$. Further, FEU can borrow at a rate $k_d = 6\%$. Assume that the MM assumptions apply.

    a. According to MM, what will be the value of FEU if it uses no debt and it uses $6 million of 6 percent debt?

    b. What are the values of k_a = WACC and k_s at debt levels of D = $0, D = $6 million, and D = $10 million? What effect does leverage have on firm value? Why?

c. Assume the initial facts of the problem (k_d = 6%, EBIT = $1.6 million, k_{sU} = 11%), but now assume that a 40 percent federal-plus-state corporate tax rate exists. Find the new market values for FEU with zero debt and with $6 million of debt, using the MM formulas.

d. What are the values of k_a = WACC and k_s at debt levels of D = $0, D = $6 million, and D = $10 million, assuming a 40 percent corporate tax rate? Plot the relationships between the value of the firm and the debt ratio, and between capital costs and the debt ratio.

e. What is the maximum dollar amount of debt financing that can be used? What is the value of the firm at this debt level? What is the cost of this debt?

f. How would each of the following factors tend to change the values you plotted in your graph?
   (1) The interest rate on debt increases as the debt ratio rises.
   (2) At higher levels of debt, the probability of financial distress rises.

11-5 (Agency costs) Until recently, the Dorfman Company carried a triple-A bond rating and was strong in every respect. However, a series of problems has afflicted the firm: It is currently in severe financial distress, and its ability to make future payments on outstanding debt is questionable. If the firm were forced into bankruptcy at this time, the common stockholders would almost certainly be wiped out. Although Dorfman has limited financial resources, its cash flows (primarily from depreciation) are sufficient to support one of two mutually exclusive investments, each costing $150 million and having a 10-year expected life. These projects have the same market (or systematic) risk, but different total risk as measured by the variance of returns. Each project has the following after-tax cash flows for 10 years:

| | **Annual Cash Inflows** | |
Probability	Project A	Project B
0.5	$30,000,000	$10,000,000
0.5	35,000,000	50,000,000

Assume that both projects have the same market risk as the firm's "average" project. Dorfman's weighted average cost of capital is 15 percent.

a. What is the expected annual cash inflow from each project?

b. Which project has the greater total risk?

c. Which project would you choose if you were a Dorfman stockholder? Why?

d. What project would the bondholders prefer to see management select? Why?

e. If the choices conflict, what "protection" do the bondholders have against the firm's making a decision that is contrary to their interests?

f. Who bears the cost of this "protection"? How is this cost related to leverage and the optimal capital structure?

11-6 (MM with financial distress costs) Concord, Inc., currently has no debt. An in-house research group has just been assigned the job of determining whether the firm should change its capital structure. Because of the importance of the decision, management has also hired the investment banking firm of Stanley Morgan & Company to conduct a parallel analysis of the situation. Mr. Smith, the in-house analyst, who is well versed in modern finance theory, has decided to carry out the analysis using the MM framework. Mr. Jones, the Stanley Morgan consultant, who has a good knowledge of capital market conditions and is confident of his ability to predict the firm's debt and equity costs at various levels of debt, has decided to estimate the optimal capital structure as that structure which minimizes the firm's weighted average cost of capital. The following data are relevant to both analyses:

$$\text{EBIT} = \$4 \text{ million per year, in perpetuity.}$$
$$\text{Federal-plus-state tax rate} = 40\%.$$
$$\text{Dividend payout ratio} = 100\%.$$
$$\text{Current required rate of return on equity} = 12\%.$$

The cost of capital schedule predicted by Mr. Jones follows:

	At a Debt Level of (Millions of Dollars)						
	$0	$2	$4	$6	$8	$10	$12	$14
Interest rate (%)	—	8.0	8.3	9.0	10.0	11.0	13.0	16.0
Cost of equity (%)	12.0	12.25	12.75	13.0	13.15	13.4	14.65	17.0

Mr. Smith estimated the present value of financial distress costs at $8 million. Additionally, he estimated the following probabilities of financial distress:

	At a Debt Level of (Millions of Dollars)						
	$0	$2	$4	$6	$8	$10	$12	$14
Probability of financial distress	0	0	0.05	0.07	0.10	0.17	0.47	0.90

   a. What level of debt would Mr. Jones and Mr. Smith recommend as optimal?

   b. Comment on the similarities and differences in their recommendations.

11-7 (MM with financial distress costs) The Wallace Corporation is an unlevered firm, and it has constant expected operating earnings (EBIT) of $2 million per year. Wallace's federal-plus-state tax rate is 40 percent, its cost of equity is 10 percent, and its market value is $V = S = \$12$ million. Management is considering the use of debt. (Debt would be issued and used to buy back stock, so the size of the firm would remain constant.) Since interest expense is tax deductible, the value of the firm would tend to increase as debt is added to the capital structure, but there would be an offset in the form of rising risk of financial distress. The firm's analysts have estimated, as an approximation, that the present value of any future financial distress costs is $8 million, and that the probability of distress would increase with leverage according to the following schedule:

Value of Debt	Probability of Distress
$ 0	0.0%
2,500,000	2.5
5,000,000	5.0
7,500,000	10.0
10,000,000	25.0
12,500,000	50.0
15,000,000	75.0

a. According to the "pure" MM with corporate taxes model, what is the optimal level of debt? (Consider only those debt values listed above.)

b. What is the optimal capital structure when financial distress costs are included? *(Do Parts c, d, e, and f only if you are using the computerized diskette.)*

c. Plot the value of the firm, with and without distress costs, as a function of the level of debt.

d. Assume that the firm's unlevered cost of equity is 8 percent. What is the firm's optimal capital structure now? (From this point on, include distress costs in all your analyses.)

e. Return to the base case k_{sU} of 10 percent. Now assume that the firm's tax rate increases to 60 percent. What effect does this change have on the firm's optimal capital structure?

f. Return to the base case tax rate of 40 percent. Assume that the estimated present value of financial distress costs is only $5 million. Now what is the firm's optimal capital structure?

Solution to Self-Test Problem

ST-1   a. Value of unlevered firm, $V_U = EBIT(1 - T)/k_{sU}$:

$$\$12 = \$2(1 - 0.4)/k_{sU}$$

$$\$12 = \$1.2/k_{sU}$$

$$k_{sU} = \$1.2/\$12 = 10.0\%.$$

Therefore, $k_{sU} = k_a = 10.0\%$.

b. Value of levered firm according to MM model with taxes:

$$V_L = V_U + TD.$$

As shown in the following table, value increases continuously with debt, and the optimal capital structure consists of 100 percent debt. Note: The table is not necessary to answer this question, but the data (in millions of dollars) are necessary for Part c of this problem.

Debt, D	V_U	TD	$V_L = V_U + TD$
$ 0	$12.0	$ 0	$12.0
2.5	12.0	1.0	13.0
5.0	12.0	2.0	14.0

Debt, D	V_U	TD	$V_L = V_U + TD$
$ 7.5	$12.0	$3.0	$15.0
10.0	12.0	4.0	16.0
12.5	12.0	5.0	17.0
15.0	12.0	6.0	18.0
20.0	12.0	8.0	20.0

c. With financial distress costs included in the analysis, the value of the levered firm, V_B, is

$$V_B = V_U + TD - PC,$$

where

$$V_U + TD = \text{value according to MM after-tax model.}$$
$$P = \text{probability of financial distress.}$$
$$C = \text{present value of distress costs.}$$

D	$V_U + TD$	P	$PC = (P)\$8$	$V_B = V_U + TD - PC$
$ 0	$12.0	0	$ 0	$12.0
2.5	13.0	0	0	13.0
5.0	14.0	0.0125	0.10	13.9
7.5	15.0	0.0250	0.20	14.8
10.0	16.0	0.0625	0.50	15.5
12.5	17.0	0.1250	1.00	16.0
15.0	18.0	0.3125	2.50	15.5
20.0	20.0	0.7500	6.00	14.0

Optimal debt level: D = $12.5 million.
Maximum value of firm: V = $16.0 million.
Optimal debt/value ratio: D/V = $12.5/$16 = 78%.

d. Value of firm versus value of debt (millions of dollars):

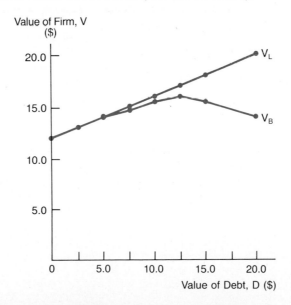

Selected Additional References

The body of literature on capital structure — and the number of potential references — is huge. Therefore, only a sampling can be given here. For an extensive review of the recent literature, as well as a detailed bibliography, see

Beranek, William, "Research Directions in Finance," *Quarterly Review of Business and Economics,* Spring 1981, 6–24.

The major theoretical works on capital structure theory are discussed in an integrated framework in

Fama, Eugene F., and Merton H. Miller, *The Theory of Finance* (New York: Holt, Rinehart and Winston, 1972).

In addition to Miller's work, the effect of personal taxes on capital structure decisions has been addressed by

Gordon, Myron J., and Lawrence I. Gould, "The Cost of Equity Capital with Personal Income Taxes and Flotation Costs," *Journal of Finance,* September 1978, 1201–1212.

Some other references of note include the following:

Conine, Thomas E., Jr., "Debt Capacity and the Capital Budgeting Decision: Comment," *Financial Management,* Spring 1980, 20–22.

Ferri, Michael, and Wesley H. Jones, "Determinants of Financial Structure: A New Methodological Approach," *Journal of Finance,* June 1979, 631–644.

Flath, David, and Charles R. Knoeber, "Taxes, Failure Costs, and Optimal Industry Capital Structure," *Journal of Finance,* March 1980, 89–117.

Lee, Wayne Y., and Henry H. Barker, "Bankruptcy Costs and the Firm's Optimal Debt Capacity: A Positive Theory of Capital Structure," *Southern Economic Journal,* April 1977, 1453–1465.

Martin, John D., and David F. Scott, "Debt Capacity and the Capital Budgeting Decision: A Revisitation," *Financial Management,* Spring 1980, 23–26.

Schneller, Meir I., "Taxes and the Optimal Capital Structure of the Firm," *Journal of Finance,* March 1980, 119–127.

Taggart, Robert A., Jr., "Taxes and Corporate Capital Structure in an Incomplete Market," *Journal of Finance,* June 1980, 645–659.

There has been considerable discussion in the literature concerning a financial leverage clientele effect. Many theorists postulate that firms with low leverage are favored by high-tax bracket investors and vice versa. Two recent articles on this subject are

Harris, John M., Jr., Rodney L. Roenfeldt, and Philip L. Cooley, "Evidence of Financial Leverage Clienteles," *Journal of Finance,* September 1983, 1125–1132.

Kim, E. Han, "Miller's Equilibrium, Shareholder Leverage Clienteles, and Optimal Capital Leverage," *Journal of Finance,* May 1982, 301–319.

For a very readable discussion of the many issues involved in capital structure theory, see

"A Discussion of Corporate Capital Structure," *Midland Corporate Finance Journal,* Fall 1985, 19–48.

12
Capital Structure Policy

Harcourt Brace Jovanovich (HBJ) is a NYSE listed company engaged in insurance, entertainment (Sea World and other theme parks), and textbook publishing. In late 1986, HBJ paid $500 million for CBS's textbook operations, which included Dryden Press, publisher of this textbook. Then, in March 1987, HBJ offered $220 million for Harper & Row, another major publisher. The CBS purchase was paid for with debt, and this raised HBJ's debt ratio from an already fairly high 46 percent to a quite high 65 percent. If the Harper & Row acquisition goes through, and if it is also financed with debt, HBJ's debt ratio will rise to about 75 percent.

As a result of the sharp increase in HBJ's debt ratio, and in anticipation of still more debt-financed acquisitions, Moody's (the bond rating agency) announced that it was reviewing the company's situation for a possible downgrading. At the same time, Value Line and other stock rating organizations were looking at the risk of HBJ's equity, so it too may be downgraded. Without a doubt, the riskiness, and hence the component costs, of HBJ's debt and equity have risen as a result of its increased use of debt.

Why do you suppose HBJ decided to increase its debt ratio? Why didn't it issue stock, or a mix of stock and debt, to pay for its acquisitions? The answer is that HBJ's management, based on the type of analysis described in this chapter, concluded (1) that the company could safely carry the additional debt and (2) that an increase in the debt ratio would lead to an increase in the value of the stock. At any rate, a study of this chapter will give you the knowledge necessary to make good capital structure decisions.

In Chapter 11, we saw that the tax benefit/financial distress tradeoff models imply that each firm has an optimal, or value-maximizing, capital structure which exactly balances the costs and the benefits of debt financing. Also, we saw that the existence of asymmetric information could influence a firm's capital structure decisions. However, because of measurement problems, we noted that it is virtually impossible to pinpoint a firm's value-maximizing capital structure. Still, it is possible to identify the factors that influence capital structure, and then to establish a *target capital structure.* This target may actually be set as a range, and it will change over time as conditions vary, but at any given moment, a firm's management should have a specific capital structure in mind, and financing decisions over time should be consistent with this target. If the actual debt ratio is below the prescribed ratio, expansion capital should normally be raised by issuing debt, while stock should be sold if the debt ratio is above the target level.

Some factors which affect the optimal capital structure are related to the firm's industry; other factors are unique to the individual firm. Empirical evidence shows that definite industry patterns exist, and this and other evidence reinforces our conclusion that an optimal capital structure does exist for each firm. However, the evidence also reinforces our conclusion that establishing the proper target structure is an imprecise process at best, and one that involves a combination of quantitative analysis and informed judgment.

BUSINESS AND FINANCIAL RISK: TOTAL RISK PERSPECTIVE

In Chapter 6, when we examined risk from the viewpoint of the individual investor, we distinguished between *market risk,* which is measured by the firm's beta coefficient, and *total risk,* which includes both market risk and an element of risk which can be eliminated by diversification. Now we introduce two new dimensions of risk: (1) *business risk,* or the riskiness of the firm's assets if it used no debt, and (2) *financial risk,* which is the additional risk placed on the common stockholder as a result of the firm's decision to use debt.[1] Conceptually, the firm has a certain amount of risk inherent in its operations: this is its business risk. Part of this business risk is company-specific and can be eliminated by diversification, while the remaining business risk is market risk. If the firm uses debt, then it in effect partitions its business risk and concentrates most of it on one class of investors — the common stockholders. However, the common stockholders are compensated for their higher risk by a higher expected return.

Business Risk

Business risk is defined as the uncertainty inherent in projections of future *operating income,* or *earnings before interest and taxes (EBIT),* and it is the single most important determinant of a firm's capital structure. Figure 12-1 gives some clues about Porter Electronics Company's business risk. The top graph shows the trend in EBIT from 1977 through 1987, and it gives both security analysts and Porter's management an idea of the degree to which EBIT has varied in the past and might vary in the future. Note that Porter is growing, and the relevant variation of EBIT is the dispersion about its trend line. The bottom graph shows the begin-

---

[1]Using preferred stock also adds to financial risk. To simplify matters somewhat, we shall consider only debt and common equity in this chapter.

Figure 12-1
**Porter Electronics Company: Trend in EBIT, 1977–1987,
and Subjective Probability Distribution of EBIT, 1987**

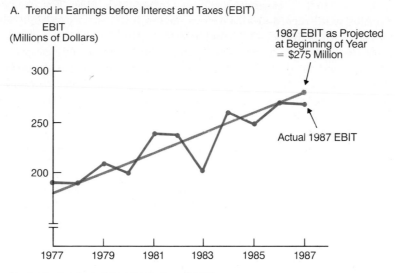

A. Trend in Earnings before Interest and Taxes (EBIT)

EBIT
(Millions of Dollars)

1987 EBIT as Projected
at Beginning of Year
= $275 Million

Actual 1987 EBIT

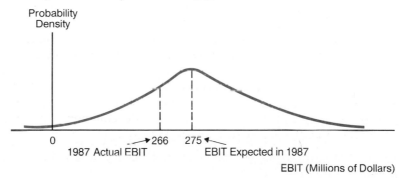

B. Subjective Probability Distribution of EBIT

Probability
Density

0

266
1987 Actual EBIT

275
EBIT Expected in 1987

EBIT (Millions of Dollars)

ning-of-year subjectively estimated probability distribution of Porter's EBIT for
1987 based on the trend line in the top section of Figure 12-1. As the graphs
indicate, actual EBIT in 1987 was only $266 million, compared to an expected
value of $275 million.

Porter's past fluctuations in EBIT were caused by many factors — booms and
recessions in the national economy, successful new products introduced by Porter
and its competitors, labor strikes, price controls, a fire in Porter's major plant, and
so on. Similar events will doubtless occur in the future, and when they do, the
realized EBIT will be higher or lower than the projected level. Further, there is
always the possibility that a long-term disaster might strike, permanently depress-

ing the company's earning power. For example, a competitor might introduce a new product that would permanently lower Porter's earnings. This uncertainty regarding Porter's future operating income is defined as its *basic business risk.*

Business risk varies not only from industry to industry, but also among firms in a given industry. Further, business risk can change over time. For example, the electric utilities were regarded for years as having little business risk. However, a combination of events in the 1970s and 1980s altered the utilities' situation, producing sharp declines in their operating income and greatly increasing their business risk. Now, food processors and grocery retailers are frequently given as examples of industries with low business risk, while cyclical manufacturing industries such as steel are regarded as having especially high business risk. Also, smaller companies, and those that are dependent on a single product, generally have a high degree of business risk.[2]

Business risk depends on a number of factors; the more important ones are listed below:

1. **Demand variability.** The more stable the demand for a firm's products, other things held constant, the lower its business risk.

2. **Sales price variability.** Firms whose products are sold in highly volatile markets are exposed to more business risk than similar firms whose output prices are more stable.

3. **Input cost variability.** Firms whose input costs are highly uncertain are exposed to a high degree of business risk.

4. **Ability to adjust output prices for changes in input costs.** Some firms are better able to raise their own output prices when input costs rise than are others. The greater the ability to adjust output prices to reflect cost conditions, the lower the degree of business risk, other things held constant.

5. **Exposure to product liability suits.** If a company's products could cause harm to users, then its business risk will be increased. Drug companies provide an example of this type of risk.

6. **The extent to which costs are fixed: operating leverage.** If a high percentage of a firm's costs are fixed, and hence do not decline when demand falls off, then it is exposed to a relatively high degree of business risk. This factor is called *operating leverage,* and it is discussed at length in the next section.

Each of these factors is determined partly by the firm's industry characteristics, but each of them is also controllable to some extent. For example, most firms can, through their marketing policies, take actions to stabilize both unit sales and sales prices. However, this stabilization may require firms to spend a great deal on advertising and/or price concessions in order to get commitments from their customers to purchase fixed quantities at fixed prices in the future. Similarly, firms such

---

[2]We have avoided any discussion of market versus company-specific risk in this section. We note now (1) that any action which increases business risk in the total risk sense will generally also increase a firm's beta coefficient, and (2) that a part of business risk will generally be company-specific, and hence subject to elimination by diversification by stockholders. This point is discussed at some length in the next major section.

as Porter Electronics can reduce the volatility of future input costs by negotiating long-term labor and materials supply contracts, but they may have to agree to pay prices above the current spot price level to obtain these contracts.[3]

Operating Leverage

As we have noted, business risk depends in part on the extent to which a firm builds fixed costs into its operations — if fixed costs are high, even a small decline in sales can lead to a large decline in EBIT, so, other things held constant, the higher a firm's fixed costs, the greater is its business risk. Higher fixed costs are generally associated with more highly automated, capital intensive firms and industries. Also, businesses that employ highly skilled workers who must be retained and paid even during recessions have relatively high fixed costs.

If a high percentage of a firm's total costs are fixed, then the firm is said to have a high degree of *operating leverage.* In physics, leverage implies the use of a lever to raise a heavy object with a small force. In politics, if people have leverage, their smallest word or action can accomplish a lot. *In business terminology, a high degree of operating leverage, other factors held constant, implies that a relatively small change in sales results in a large change in operating income.*

Figure 12-2 illustrates the concept of operating leverage by comparing the results that a new firm would achieve if it used different degrees of operating leverage. Plan A calls for a relatively small amount of fixed charges, $20,000. Here the firm would not have much automated equipment, so its depreciation, maintenance, property taxes, and so on would be low, but the total operating costs line has a relatively steep slope, indicating that variable costs per unit are higher than they would be if the firm used more operating leverage. Plan B calls for a higher level of fixed costs, $60,000. Here the firm uses automated equipment (with which one operator can turn out a few or many units at the same labor cost) to a much larger extent. The breakeven point is higher under Plan B: Breakeven occurs at 60,000 units under Plan B versus only 40,000 units under Plan A.

We can calculate the breakeven quantity by recognizing that breakeven occurs when EBIT = 0:

$$\text{EBIT} = 0 = PQ - VQ - F. \tag{12-1}$$

Here P is average sales price per unit of output, Q is units of output, V is variable cost per unit, and F is fixed operating costs.[4] We can solve Equation 12-1 for the breakeven quantity, Q_{BE}:

$$Q_{BE} = \frac{F}{P - V}. \tag{12-1a}$$

---

[3]For example, in 1986 utilities could buy coal in the spot market for about $30 per ton. Under a 5-year contract, coal cost about $50 per ton. Clearly, the price for reducing uncertainty was high!

[4]This definition of breakeven does not include fixed financial costs. If there are fixed financial costs, the firm will suffer an accounting loss at the operating breakeven point. Thus, Equation 12-1 defines the *operating* breakeven level of sales. We will introduce financial costs shortly.

Figure 12-2
Illustration of Operating Leverage

Plan A

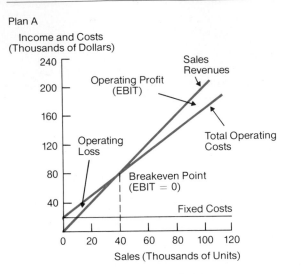

Plan B

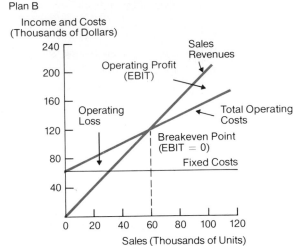

		Plan A					Plan B		
Probability	Units Sold, Q	Sales	Operating Costs	Operating Profit (EBIT)	Probability	Units Sold, Q	Sales	Operating Costs	Operating Profit (EBIT)
0.03	0	$ 0	$ 20,000	($20,000)	0.03	0	$ 0	$ 60,000	($ 60,000)
0.07	40,000	80,000	80,000	0	0.07	40,000	80,000	100,000	(20,000)
0.15	60,000	120,000	110,000	10,000	0.15	60,000	120,000	120,000	0
0.50	110,000	220,000	185,000	35,000	0.50	110,000	220,000	170,000	50,000
0.15	160,000	320,000	260,000	60,000	0.15	160,000	320,000	220,000	100,000
0.07	180,000	360,000	290,000	70,000	0.07	180,000	360,000	240,000	120,000
0.03	220,000	440,000	350,000	90,000	0.03	220,000	440,000	280,000	160,000

Selling price = $2.00
Fixed costs = $20,000
Variable costs = $1.50 per unit

Selling price = $2.00
Fixed costs = $60,000
Variable costs = $1.00 per unit

Expected EBIT $35,000
σ_{EBIT} $23,249

Expected EBIT $50,000
σ_{EBIT} $46,497

Thus, for Plan A,

$$Q_{BE} = \frac{\$20,000}{\$2.00 - \$1.50} = 40,000 \text{ units,}$$

and for Plan B,

$$Q_{BE} = \frac{\$60,000}{\$2.00 - \$1.00} = 60,000 \text{ units.}$$

How does operating leverage affect business risk? *Other things held constant, the higher a firm's operating leverage, the higher is its business risk.* This point is demonstrated in Figure 12-3, where we show how probability distributions for EBIT under Plans A and B are developed.

Figure 12-3
Analysis of Business Risk

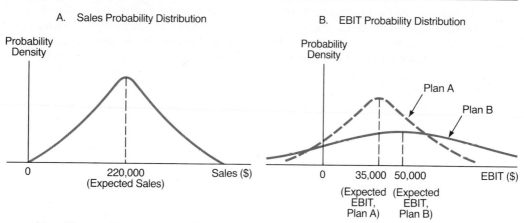

A.   Sales Probability Distribution

B.   EBIT Probability Distribution

Note: We are using continuous distributions to approximate the discrete distributions contained in Figure 12-2. Using data from Figure 12-2, we calculate $\sigma_{Sales} = \$92,995$.

The left-hand section of Figure 12-3 graphs the probability distribution of sales that was presented in tabular form in Figure 12-2. The sales probability distribution depends on how demand for the product varies, and not on whether the product is manufactured by Plan A or by Plan B. Therefore, the same sales probability distribution applies to both production plans; this distribution has expected sales of $220,000, and it ranges from zero to about $450,000, with $\sigma_{Sales} = \$92,995$.

We use the sales probability distribution, together with the operating costs at each sales level, to develop graphs of the EBIT probability distributions under Plans A and B. These are shown in the right-hand section of Figure 12-3. Plan B has a higher expected EBIT, but this plan also entails a much higher probability of large losses. Clearly, Plan B, the one with more fixed costs and a higher degree of operating leverage, is riskier. *In general, holding other factors constant, the higher the degree of operating leverage, the greater the business risk as measured by standard deviation of expected EBIT.*

To what extent can firms control their operating leverage? To a large extent, operating leverage is determined by technology. Electric utilities, telephone companies, airlines, steel mills, and chemical companies simply *must* have heavy investments in fixed assets; this results in high fixed costs and operating leverage. Grocery stores, on the other hand, generally have significantly lower fixed costs, and hence lower operating leverage. Still, although industry factors do exert a major influence, all firms do have some control over their operating leverage. For example, an electric utility can expand its generating capacity by building either a nuclear reactor or a coal-fired plant. The nuclear generator would require a larger investment, and hence higher fixed costs, but its variable operating costs would be relatively low. The coal plant, on the other hand, would require a smaller investment and would have lower fixed costs, but the variable costs (for coal) would be high. Thus, by its capital budgeting decisions, a utility (or any other company) can influence its operating leverage, and hence its basic business risk.

The concept of operating leverage was, in fact, originally developed for use in capital budgeting. Mutually exclusive projects which involve alternative methods for producing a given product often have different degrees of operating leverage, and hence different breakeven points and different degrees of risk. Porter Electronics and many other companies regularly undertake a type of breakeven analysis (the sensitivity analysis discussed in Chapter 10) for each proposed project as a part of their regular capital budgeting process. Still, once a corporation's operating leverage has been established, this factor influences its capital structure decisions. This point is covered next.

Financial Risk

Financial risk is the additional risk placed on the common stockholders as a result of the decision to use debt and/or preferred stock financing. Conceptually, the firm has a certain amount of risk inherent in its operations — this is its business risk, which is defined as the uncertainty inherent in projections of future EBIT. If a firm uses debt and preferred stock (financial leverage), this concentrates its business risk on the common stockholders. To illustrate, suppose 10 people decide to form a corporation to manufacture steel roof trusses. There is a certain amount of business risk in the operation. If the firm is capitalized only with common equity, and if each person buys 10 percent of the stock, then each investor shares equally in the business risk. However, suppose the firm is capitalized with 50 percent debt and 50 percent equity, with five of the investors putting up their capital as debt and the other five putting up their money as equity. In this case, those investors who put up the equity will have to bear all of the business risk, so the common stock will be twice as risky as it would have been had the firm been financed only with equity. Thus, the use of debt, or *financial leverage,* concentrates the firm's business risk on its stockholders.

To illustrate the concentration of business risk, consider a new firm which expects an EBIT of $4 million, requires assets of $20 million, and has a zero tax rate. To begin the analysis, divide the $4 million expected EBIT by the $20 million of assets to obtain the expected return on assets, which in this case is ROA = $4/$20 = 0.20 = 20%.[5] If the company used no debt, then these conditions would exist:

1. Its assets would be equal to its equity.
2. Its return on equity (ROE) would be equal to its return on assets (ROA).
3. Its equity would be exactly as risky as its assets.

Now suppose the firm decides to change its capital structure by issuing $10 million of debt at k_d = 15%, substituting these funds for $10 million of equity. Its ex-

---

[5]We assume a zero tax rate to simplify the illustration. However, the same conclusions would be reached had we used a positive tax rate. Also note that ROA is generally defined as Net income/Total assets, but an unlevered firm with a zero tax rate has EBIT = Net income, and hence ROA = EBIT/ Total assets.

pected return on equity (which would now be only $10 million) would rise from 20 to 25 percent:

Expected EBIT (unchanged)	$4,000,000
Interest (15% on $10 million of debt)	1,500,000
Income available to common (zero taxes)	$2,500,000
Expected ROE = $2,500,000/$10,000,000 =	25%

Thus, the use of debt would "leverage up" the expected ROE from 20 percent to 25 percent.

Financial leverage increases risk as well as expected return to the equity investors. For example, suppose EBIT actually turned out to be $2 million rather than the expected $4 million, so ROA turned out to be 10 percent rather than 20 percent. If the firm used no debt, then ROE would decline from 20 percent to 10 percent. However, with debt financing, ROE would fall from 25 to only 5 percent:

	ROA = 10%	
	Zero Debt	**$10 Million of Debt**
Actual EBIT	$2,000,000	$2,000,000
Interest (15%)	0	1,500,000
Income available to common (zero taxes)	$2,000,000	$ 500,000
Actual ROE: $2,000,000/$20,000,000 =	10%	
$500,000/$10,000,000 =		5%
Expected ROE =	20%	25%

A more complete analysis of the effects of leverage on this firm's ROE is illustrated in Figure 12-4. The two lines in the top graph show the level of ROE that would exist at different levels of ROA under the two different capital structures. The lines were plotted from data developed as described previously, and they show that the greater the use of financial leverage, the more sensitive ROE is to changes in the return on assets.[6]

---

[6]If still more debt — say $15 million — were used, the ROE line would be even steeper, while if $5 million of debt were used, the new line would be between the two lines now shown in Figure 12-4. The lines would all intersect at the point where ROE = ROA = 15%, showing that if ROA = k_d, then leverage has no effect on ROE. Note also that the vertical axis intercept reflects the fixed interest cost that must be borne by the stockholders; that is, at the intercept, the ROA is zero, but interest must be paid, and this interest must come out of the stockholders' share of the business, and hence it produces an accounting loss and a 15 percent negative return to stockholders. The stockholders' loss would be greater or smaller if the firm used a greater or lesser amount of debt. For example, if the firm uses only $5 million of debt, then the stockholders would have a 7.5 percent negative return if ROA were zero.

Note also that we have assumed away taxes. If taxes were introduced, the effect would be to lower the ROE. For example, if the tax rate were 50 percent, then the ROE for any ROA would be half the level currently shown in Figure 12-4, and the ROE lines in the top panel of the figure would shift downward so that the lines intersected at ROA = 15%, ROE = 7.5%.

Figure 12-4
Effects of Financial Leverage on ROE

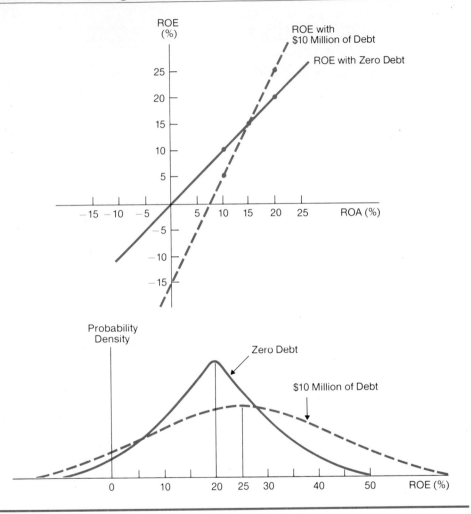

The lower panel of Figure 12-4 shows the effects of leverage on the firm's ROE probability distribution. With zero debt, the company would have an expected ROE of 20 percent, the same as its expected ROA, and a relatively tight distribution. With $10 million of debt, the expected ROE would be 25 percent, but the ROE distribution would be much flatter, indicating a larger standard deviation of returns (σ_{ROE}) and a more risky situation for the equity investors.

Our conclusions from this analysis may be stated as follows:

1. The use of debt generally increases the expected ROE; this situation occurs whenever the expected return on assets exceeds the cost of debt.

2. σ_{ROA} is a measure of business risk, and σ_{ROE} is a measure of the risk borne by stockholders. $\sigma_{ROE} = \sigma_{ROA}$ if the firm does not use any debt, or financial leverage. However, if the firm does use debt, then $\sigma_{ROE} > \sigma_{ROA}$ because business risk is being concentrated on the stockholders.

3. The difference between σ_{ROA}, the risk that stockholders would bear if no financial leverage were used, and σ_{ROE}, the risk stockholders actually face, is a measure of the risk-increasing effects of financial leverage:

$$\text{Risk from financial leverage} = \sigma_{ROE} - \sigma_{ROA}.$$

BUSINESS AND FINANCIAL RISK: MARKET RISK PERSPECTIVE

Thus far, our discussion of business and financial risk has focused on total risk. We have used σ_{ROA} as the measure of business risk and σ_{ROE} as the measure of the total risk borne by the stockholders. Thus, in the total risk sense, $\sigma_{ROE} - \sigma_{ROA}$ is a measure of financial risk. Now we shift our focus from total risk to *market,* or *beta, risk.*

In an important article, Robert Hamada combined the CAPM with the MM after-tax model to obtain this expression for k_{sL}, the cost of equity to a leveraged firm:[7]

$$k_{sL} = \frac{\text{Risk-free}}{\text{rate}} + \frac{\text{Business risk}}{\text{premium}} + \frac{\text{Financial risk}}{\text{premium}} \qquad (12\text{-}2)$$

$$= k_{RF} + (k_M - k_{RF})b_U + (k_M - k_{RF})b_U(1 - T)(D/S).$$

Here b_U is the beta coefficient the firm would have if it used no financial leverage, and the other terms are as defined in Chapters 6 and 11. In effect, Equation 12-2 partitions the required rate of return to a leveraged firm into three components: k_{RF}, the risk-free rate, which compensates shareholders for the time value of money; a premium for business risk as reflected by the term $(k_M - k_{RF})b_U$; and a premium for financial risk as reflected by the third term, $(k_M - k_{RF})b_U(1 - T)$ (D/S). If a firm has no financial leverage (D = \$0), then the financial risk premium term would be zero, the third term would drop out, and equity investors would be compensated only for business risk.

As we saw in the last chapter, the MM model with corporate taxes does not hold exactly, and we also know that the CAPM does not fully describe investor behavior. Therefore, Equation 12-2 must be regarded as an approximation. Nevertheless, Equation 12-2 can provide financial managers with some useful insights. As an illustration, assume that Firm U, an unlevered company with $b_U = 1.5$ and \$100,000 of equity (S = \$100,000) is considering replacing \$20,000 of equity with debt. If $k_{RF} = 10\%$, $k_M = 15\%$, and $T = 34\%$, then Firm U's current unlevered required rate of return on equity would be 17.5 percent:

---

[7]See Robert S. Hamada, "Portfolio Analysis, Market Equilibrium, and Corporation Finance," *Journal of Finance,* March 1969, 13–31.

$$k_{sU} = 10\% + (15\% - 10\%)1.5$$
$$= 10\% + 7.5\% = 17.5\%.$$

This shows that the business risk premium is 7.5 percentage points. If the firm were to add $20,000 of debt to its capital structure, then its new value, according to MM, would be $V_L = V_U + TD = \$100,000 + 0.34(\$20,000) = \$106,800$, and its k_s, using Equation 12-2, would rise to 18.64 percent:

$$k_{sL} = 10\% + (15\% - 10\%)1.5 + (15\% - 10\%)1.5(1 - 0.34)(\$20,000/\$86,800)$$
$$= 10\% + 7.5\% + 1.14\% = 18.64\%.$$

Thus, adding $20,000 of debt to the capital structure would result in a financial risk premium on the stock equal to 1.14 percentage points, which would be added to the business risk premium of 7.5 percentage points.

   Hamada also showed that Equation 12-2 can be used to analyze the effect of a firm's financial leverage on its beta. We know that under the CAPM, the SML can be used to determine a firm's required rate of return on equity:

$$\text{SML: } k_{sL} = k_{RF} + (k_M - k_{RF})b_L.$$

Now, by equating the SML equation with Equation 12-2, we obtain:

$$k_{RF} + (k_M - k_{RF})b_L = k_{RF} + (k_M - k_{RF})b_U + (k_M - k_{RF})b_U(1 - T)(D/S)$$
$$(k_M - k_{RF})b_L = (k_M - k_{RF})b_U + (k_M - k_{RF})b_U(1 - T)(D/S)$$
$$b_L = b_U + b_U(1 - T)(D/S), \tag{12-3}$$

or

$$b_L = b_U[1 + (1 - T)(D/S)]. \tag{12-3a}$$

Thus, under the MM and CAPM assumptions, the beta of a levered firm is equal to the beta the firm would have if it used zero debt, adjusted upward by a factor that depends on (1) the corporate tax rate and (2) the amount of financial leverage employed. Therefore, the firm's relevant (or market) risk, which is measured by b_L, depends on both the firm's business risk as reflected in b_U and financial risk as reflected in the leverage ratio, D/S.

   To continue our illustration, if Firm U were to replace $20,000 of equity with debt, its beta would increase to 1.728 according to Equation 12-3a:

$$b_L = b_U[1 + (1 - T)(D/S)]$$
$$= 1.5[1 + (1 - 0.34)(20,000/\$86,800)]$$
$$= 1.5(1.152) = 1.728.$$

We can confirm the Equation 12-2 value of $k_{sL} = 18.64\%$ by using $b_L = 1.728$ in the SML:

$$k_{sL} = k_{RF} + (k_M - k_{RF})b_L$$
$$= 10\% + (15\% - 10\%)1.728 = 18.64\%.$$

These relationships can be used to help estimate a company's or division's cost of equity. In both instances, we proceed by obtaining betas for similar publicly traded firms and then "lever them up or down" to make them consistent with our own firm's (or division's) capital structure and tax rate. The result is an estimate of our firm's (or division's) beta, given (1) its business risk as measured by the betas of other firms in the same industry and (2) its financial risk as measured by its own capital structure and tax rate.

ESTIMATING THE TARGET CAPITAL STRUCTURE: A SIMPLIFIED EXAMPLE

We saw in Chapter 11 that the tax benefit/financial distress tradeoff theory leads to the conclusion that each firm has an optimal capital structure, one which maximizes its value and minimizes its weighted average cost of capital. In this section, we present an illustration which demonstrates many of the points that we discussed in Chapter 11.

Nachman-Smith Software, Inc.

Nachman-Smith Software (NSS) was founded in 1980 to develop and market a new type of operating system for personal computers. The basic program was written and patented by Dave Nachman and Steve Smith, the firm's founders. Nachman and Smith own a majority of the stock, although a significant portion is held by institutional investors. The company has no debt. NSS's key financial data are shown in Table 12-1. Assets are carried at a book value of $1 million; hence, the common equity also has a balance sheet value of $1 million. However, these balance sheet figures are not very meaningful because (1) the asset figures do not include any value for patents and (2) the fixed assets were purchased several years ago at lower than today's prices.

Nachman and Smith plan to retire shortly, and they are planning to sell a major part of their interest in the company to the public, using the proceeds of the sale to diversify their personal portfolios. As a part of the planning process, the question of capital structure has arisen. Should the firm continue its policy of using no debt, or should it recapitalize? And if it does decide to substitute debt for equity, how far should it go? As in all such decisions, the correct answer is that *it should choose that capital structure which maximizes the value of the company*. If the company's total market value is maximized, so will be the price of its stock, and its cost of capital will simultaneously be minimized.

To simplify the analysis, we assume that the long-run demand for NSS's products is not expected to grow; hence, its EBIT is expected to continue at $4 million. (However, future sales may turn out to be different from the expected level, so realized EBIT may be more or less than the expected $4 million.) Also, since the company has no need for new capital, all of its income will be paid out as dividends.

Now assume that NSS's financial manager consults with investment bankers and learns that debt can be sold, but the more debt used, the riskier the debt and the

---

Table 12-1
Data on Nachman-Smith Software, Inc.

Balance Sheet as of December 31, 1987

Current assets	$ 500,000	Debt	$	0
Net fixed assets	500,000	Common equity (1.0 million shares outstanding)		1,000,000
Total assets	$1,000,000	Total claims		$ 1,000,000

Income Statement for 1987

Sales		$20,000,000
Fixed operating costs	$ 4,000,000	
Variable operating costs	12,000,000	16,000,000
Earnings before interest and taxes (EBIT)		$ 4,000,000
Interest		0
Taxable income		$ 4,000,000
Taxes (40% federal-plus-state)		1,600,000
Net income		$ 2,400,000

Other Data

1. Earnings per share = EPS = $2,400,000/1,000,000 shares = $2.40.
2. Dividends per share = DPS = $2,400,000/1,000,000 shares = $2.40. Thus, the company has a 100 percent payout ratio.
3. Book value per share = $1,000,000/1,000,000 shares = $1.
4. Market price per share = P_0 = $20. Thus, the stock sells at 20 times its book value.
5. Price/earnings ratio = P/E = $20/2.40 = 8.33 times.
6. Dividend yield = DPS/P_0 = $2.40/$20 = 12%.

---

higher the interest rate, k_d. Also, the bankers state that the more debt NSS uses, the greater the riskiness of its stock, and hence the higher its required rate of return on equity, k_s. Estimates of k_d, beta, and k_s at different debt levels are given in Figure 12-5, along with a graph of the relationship between k_s and debt.

Given the data in Table 12-1 along with those in Figure 12-5, we can determine NSS's total market value, V, at different capital structures, and we can then use this information to establish the company's stock price as a function of its capital structure. These equations, which were developed in Chapter 11, are used in the analysis:[8]

$$V = D + S. \tag{12-4}$$

$$S = \frac{\text{Net income after taxes}}{k_s} = \frac{(\text{EBIT} - k_dD)(1 - T)}{k_s}. \tag{12-5}$$

---

[8]Note that Equations 12-4 through 12-7 do not stem from a particular capital structure theory — they do not require acceptance of MM, Miller, or any other theory. Rather, they are definitions and basic DCF valuation equations for perpetual cash flows.

Figure 12-5
NSS's Cost of Debt, Cost of Equity, and Beta

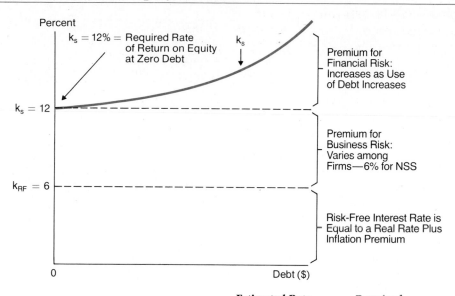

Amount Borrowed[a] (1)	Interest Rate on All Debt, k_d (2)	Estimated Beta Coefficient of Stock, b (3)	Required Rate of Return on Stock, k_s[b] (4)
$ 0	—	1.50	12.0%
2,000,000	8.0%	1.55	12.2
4,000,000	8.3	1.65	12.6
6,000,000	9.0	1.80	13.2
8,000,000	10.0	2.00	14.0
10,000,000	12.0	2.30	15.2
12,000,000	15.0	2.70	16.8
14,000,000	18.0	3.25	19.0

[a]NSS is unable to borrow more than $14 million because of limitations on interest coverage in its corporate charter.

[b]We assume that $k_{RF} = 6\%$ and $k_M = 10\%$. Therefore, at zero debt, $k_s = 6\% + (10\% - 6\%)1.5 = 12\%$. Other values of k_s are calculated similarly.

$$P_0 = \frac{DPS}{k_s} = \frac{EPS}{k_s}. \tag{12-6}$$

$$k_a = (D/V)(k_d)(1 - T) + (S/V)(k_s). \tag{12-7}$$

We first substitute values for k_d, D, and k_s into Equation 12-5 to obtain values for S, the market value of common equity, at each level of debt, D, and we then sum S and D to find the total value of the firm. Table 12-2 and Figure 12-6, which plots selected data from the table, were developed by this process. The values shown in Columns 1, 2, and 3 of the table were taken from Figure 12-5, while those in

Table 12-2
NSS's Value, Stock Price, and Cost of Capital at Different Debt Levels

Value of Debt, D (in Millions) (1)	k_d (2)	k_s (3)	Value of Stock, S (in Millions) (4)	Value of Firm, V (in Millions) (1) + (4) = (5)	Stock Price, P_0 (6)	D/V (7)	k_a = WACC (8)
$ 0.0	—	12.0%	$20.000	$20.000	$20.00	0.0%	12.0%
2.0	8.0%	12.2	18.885	20.885	20.89	9.6	11.5
4.0	8.3	12.6	17.467	21.467	21.47	18.6	11.2
6.0	**9.0**	**13.2**	**15.727**	**21.727**	**21.73**	**27.6**	**11.0**
8.0	10.0	14.0	13.714	21.714	21.71	36.8	11.1
10.0	12.0	15.2	11.053	21.053	21.05	47.5	11.4
12.0	15.0	16.8	7.857	19.857	19.86	60.4	12.1
14.0	18.0	19.0	3.160	17.160	17.16	81.6	12.3

Notes:

a. The data in Columns 1 through 3 were taken from Figure 12-5.

b. The values for S in Column 4 were found by use of Equation 12-5:

$$S = \frac{\text{Net income}}{k_s} = \frac{(\text{EBIT} - k_dD)(1 - T)}{k_s}.$$

For example, at D = $0,

$$S = \frac{(\$4.0 - 0)(0.6)}{0.12} = \frac{\$2.4}{0.12} = \$20.0 \text{ million,}$$

and at D = $6.0,

$$S = \frac{[\$4.0 - 0.09(\$6.0)](0.6)}{0.132} = \frac{\$2.076}{0.132} = \$15.727 \text{ million.}$$

c. The values for V in Column 5 were obtained as the sum of D + S. For example, at D = $6.0, V = $6.0 + $15.727 = $21.727 million.

d. The stock prices shown in Column 6 are equal to the value of the firm as shown in Column 5 divided by the original number of shares outstanding, which in this case is 1 million. The logic behind this procedure is explained in the text.

e. Column 7 is found by dividing Column 1 by Column 5. For example, at D = $6.0, D/V = $6/$21.727 = 27.6%.

f. Column 8 is found by use of Equation 12-7. For example, at D = $6.0, k_a = WACC = 11.0%:

$$k_a = (D/V)(k_d)(1 - T) + (S/V)(k_s)$$

$$= (0.276)(9\%)(0.6) + (0.724)(13.2\%) = 11.0\%.$$

Figure 12-6
Relationship between NSS's Capital Structure, Cost of Capital, and Stock Price

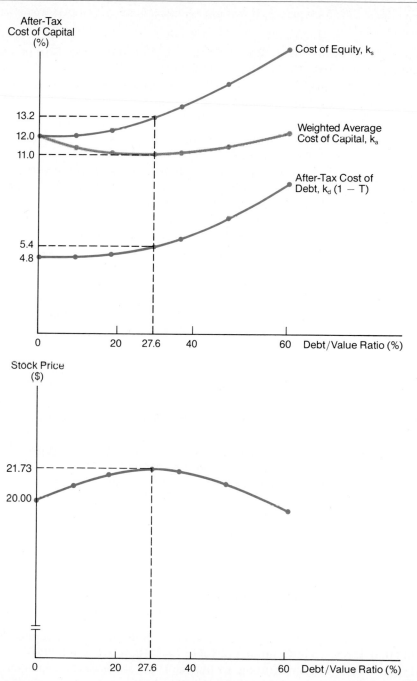

Column 4 were obtained by solving Equation 12-5 at different debt levels. The values for the firm given in Column 5 were obtained by summing Columns 1 and 4, D + S = V.

To see how the stock prices shown in Column 6 were developed, visualize this series of events:

1. Initially, NSS has no debt. The firm's value is $20 million, or $20 for each of its 1 million shares. (See the top line of Table 12-2.)

2. Management announces a decision to change the capital structure; legally, the firm *must* make an explicit announcement or run the risk of having stockholders sue the directors.

3. The values shown in Columns 1 through 5 of Table 12-2 are estimated as described previously. The major institutional investors, and the large brokerage companies which advise individual investors, have analysts just as capable of making these estimates as the firm's management. These analysts would start making their own estimates as soon as NSS announced the planned change in leverage, and they would presumably reach the same conclusions as the NSS analysts. (Indeed, for a company whose management did not have 51 percent ownership, analysts might do the analysis on their own, before any announcement, and then start buying stock with a takeover and forced restructuring in mind.)

4. NSS's stockholders initially own the entire company. (There are not yet any bondholders.) They see, or are told by their advisor-analysts, that very shortly the value of the enterprise will rise from $20 million to some higher amount, presumably the maximum attainable, or $21,727,000. Thus, they anticipate that the value of the firm will increase by $1,727,000.

5. This additional $1,727,000 will accrue to the firm's current stockholders. Since there are 1 million shares of stock, each share will rise in value by $1.73, or from $20 to $21.73.

6. This price increase will occur *before* the transaction is completed. Suppose, for example, that the stock price remained at $20 after the announcement of the recapitalization plan. Shrewd investors would immediately recognize that the stock's price will soon go up to $21.73, and they would place orders to buy at any price below $21.73. This buying pressure would quickly run the price up to $21.73, at which point it would remain constant. Thus, $21.73 is the *equilibrium stock price* for NSS once the decision to recapitalize has been announced.

7. The firm sells $6 million of bonds at an interest rate of 9 percent. This money is used to buy stock at the market price, which is now $21.73, so 276,116 shares are repurchased:

$$\text{Shares repurchased} = \frac{\$6,000,000}{\$21.73} = 276,116.$$

8. The value of the stock after the 276,116 shares have been repurchased is $15,727,000, as shown in Column 4 of Table 12-2. There are 1,000,000 − 276,116 = 723,884 shares still outstanding, so the value per share of the remaining stock is

$$\text{Value per share} = \frac{\$15,727,000}{723,884} = \$21.73.$$

This confirms our earlier calculation of the equilibrium stock price.

9. The same process was used to find stock prices at other capital structures; these prices are given in Column 6 of Table 12-2 and plotted in the lower graph of Figure 12-6. *Since the maximum price occurs when NSS uses $6 million of debt, its optimal capital structure calls for $6 million of debt.* Note that $6 million of debt corresponds to a firm value of $21.727 million. Thus, the optimal market value capital structure, D/V*, is $6/$21.727 = 27.6%.

10. In this example, we assume that EBIT would decline from $4 million to $3.52 million if the firm's debt rose to $14 million. The reason for the decline is that, at this very high level of debt, managers and employees would be worried about the firm's failing and about losing their jobs; suppliers would not sell to the firm on normal credit terms; orders would be lost because of customers' fears that the company might go bankrupt and thus be unable to deliver; and so on. EBIT is independent of financial leverage at "reasonable" debt levels, but at extreme degrees of leverage, EBIT is adversely affected.

11. Quite obviously, the situation in the real world is much more complex, and less exact, than this example suggests. Most important, different investors will have different estimates for EBIT and k_s, and hence will form different expectations about the equilibrium stock price. This means that NSS might have to pay more than $21.73 to repurchase its shares, or perhaps that the shares could be bought at a lower price. These changes would cause the optimal amount of debt to be somewhat higher or lower than $6 million. Still, $6 million represents our best estimate as to the optimal debt level; hence, it is the level we should use as our target capital structure.

12. The WACC for the various levels of debt is shown in Column 8 of Table 12-2. It can be seen that the minimum cost of capital, 11.0 percent, corresponds to the level of debt at which the value of the firm and its stock price are maximized, $6.0 million.

The stock price and cost of capital relationships developed in Table 12-2 are graphed in Figure 12-6. Here we see that NSS's stock price is maximized, and its weighted average cost of capital is minimized, at the same D/V ratio, 27.6 percent.

Extensions of the Example

In the preceding section, we examined the effects of debt on its stock price if NSS went from zero debt to some positive level of debt. Now we will examine the general effects of a change from one debt level to some other level, using this equation:

$$P_1 = \frac{\text{Ending value of firm } - \text{ Beginning value of debt}}{\text{Beginning number of shares}}. \qquad \text{(12-8)}$$

Note that the beginning value of debt could be zero, so Equation 12-8 is general in the sense that it could apply to any analysis, zero initial debt or not. In this section, we explain the logic of Equation 12-8, and we illustrate it with three different cases.

Example 1

Suppose we wish to determine what would happen to NSS's stock price if it went from zero debt to $4 million of debt. This requires us to find V_1 and P_1 with $4 million of debt:

$$V_1 = D_1 + S_1 = D_1 + \frac{(EBIT - k_dD)(1 - T)}{k_s}$$

$$= \$4,000,000 + \frac{(\$4,000,000 - \$332,000)(0.6)}{0.126}$$

$$= \$4,000,000 + \$17,466,667 = \$21,466,667.$$

$$P_1 = \frac{Ending\ value - Beginning\ debt}{Beginning\ shares} = \frac{\$21,466,667 - \$0}{1,000,000}$$

$$= \$21.47,\ versus\ P_0 = \$20\ with\ zero\ debt.$$

As explained previously, this stock price would exist *as soon as investors learned of the recapitalization plans, before the plans were actually carried out.* Stockholders would recognize that the company will have a value of $21,466,667 very shortly, and this value will belong entirely to them because they will receive the $4,000,000 brought in by the sale of bonds as payment for shares repurchased. Note also that management must inform all stockholders of the planned recapitalization. If you were a stockholder, you would certainly not be willing to sell your stock back to the company at $20 per share if you expected to see the stock price rise to $21.47. You and the other stockholders would insist on receiving as much if you sold your stock back to the company as you would end up with if you chose not to sell it.[9]

Once the plan had been carried out, the shares outstanding would decline from 1,000,000 to 813,694:

$$New\ shares = Old\ shares - Shares\ repurchased$$

$$n_1 = n_0 - Shares\ repurchased$$

---

[9]Indeed, if you and other stockholders were silly enough to sell at $20 per share, then the $4 million of debt could be used to buy and retire even more shares, so the remaining shares would be worth even more than $21.47. In fact, the stock would, under these conditions, be worth $21.83:

$$P_1 = \frac{S_1}{n_1} = \frac{\$17,466,667}{1,000,000 - (\$4,000,000/\$20)} = \$21.83.$$

Of course, you might be afraid that the recapitalization plan would fall through, so you might be willing to sell out for slightly less than $21.47, say for $21, figuring that $21 in the hand is better than $21.47 in the bush.

$$= n_0 - \frac{\text{Incremental debt}}{\text{Price per share}}$$

$$= 1{,}000{,}000 - \frac{\$4{,}000{,}000}{\$21.47}$$

$$= 1{,}000{,}000 - 186{,}306$$

$$= 813{,}694 \text{ shares after repurchase.}$$

Check on stock price:

$$P_1 = \frac{\text{New value of equity}}{\text{New shares outstanding}} = \frac{S_1}{n_1} = \frac{\$17.466{,}667}{813{,}694} = \$21.47.$$

Had we made similar calculations, but used $6 million of debt, the resulting stock price would have been $21.73 as shown in Table 12-2.

Example 2

Now assume that NSS actually made the move to $4 million of debt, and management is now considering another increase in leverage. What would happen to NSS's stock price if it increased its leverage from $4 million to $6 million of debt? Assume that its old debt must be retired if new debt is issued, so the entire $6 million of debt will have a cost of 9 percent (from Figure 12-5). Now the analysis will begin with these initial values:

$$\text{Initial debt value} = D_0 = \$4{,}000{,}000.$$
$$\text{Initial stock value} = S_0 = \$17{,}466{,}667.$$
$$\text{Initial total value} = V_0 = \$21{,}466{,}667.$$
$$\text{Initial stock price} = P_0 = \$21.47.$$
$$\text{Initial number of shares} = n_0 = 813{,}694.$$

The new equilibrium total value will be

$$V_1 = D_1 + S_1$$

$$= \$6{,}000{,}000 + \frac{(\$4{,}000{,}000 - \$540{,}000)(0.6)}{0.132}$$

$$= \$6{,}000{,}000 + \$15{,}727{,}272 = \$21{,}727{,}272,$$

and the new equilibrium stock price will be

$$P_1 = \frac{V_1 - D_0}{n_0} = \frac{\$21{,}727{,}272 - \$4{,}000{,}000}{813{,}694}$$

$$= \frac{\$17{,}727{,}272}{813{,}694} = \$21.79.$$

Thus, NSS could increase the value of its stock from $21.47 to $21.79 by increasing its leverage from $4 million to $6 million.[10] This second round of debt financing would increase the stockholders' gain by ($21.79 − $21.47)813,694 = $260,382.

Example 3

Now assume that NSS again plans to increase its leverage from $4 million to $6 million, but that the old debt need not be retired. Here, the $4 million in old debt would remain in force, carrying a coupon rate of 8.3 percent. As before, assume that the new debt issue of $2 million would have a cost of 9 percent. Assuming the same initial values as in Example 2, the new equilibrium values are calculated as follows:

1.
$$S_1 = \frac{\left[EBIT - \binom{\text{Cost of}}{\text{old debt}}\binom{\text{Amount of}}{\text{old debt}} - \binom{\text{Cost of}}{\text{new debt}}\binom{\text{Amount of}}{\text{new debt}} \right](1 - T)}{k_s}$$

$$= \frac{[\$4,000,000 - (0.083)(\$4,000,000) - (0.09)(\$2,000,000)](0.6)}{0.132}$$

$$= \frac{(\$3,488,000)(0.6)}{0.132} = \$15,854,545.$$

2. The old debt has a book value of $4,000,000. However, because more debt is to be issued, the risk of the old debt will rise, and consequently its market value will fall to $3,688,889:

$$D_0' = \frac{0.083(\$4,000,000)}{0.09} = \$3,688.889.$$

3. The loss suffered by the old bondholders is $311,111:

$$D_0 - D_0' = \$4,000,000 - \$3,688,889 = \$311,111.$$

4. The new value of the firm will be

$$V_1 = D_1 + S_1 = D_0' + \text{New debt} + S_1$$

$$= \$3,688,889 + \$2,000,000 + \$15,854,545$$

$$= \$21,543,434.$$

5. The new equilibrium stock price will be

$$P_1 = \frac{\$21,543,434 - \$3,688,889}{813,694} = \$21.943$$

---

[10]Notice the slight difference in equilibrium stock prices at $6 million of debt: $21.73 in the first example versus $21.79 now. This difference demonstrates two points: (1) If NSS could move to its optimal capital structure in stages, it could repurchase shares at a lower average price than the equilibrium price of $21.73, and (2) if it could buy back shares at a lower price, its final price would be higher because more shares could be repurchased for a given expenditure (debt raised), and hence fewer shares would be outstanding in the end.

6. The stockholders will have an aggregate gain calculated as follows:

$$\text{Stockholders' gain} = (P_1 - P_0)n_0$$
$$= (\$21.943 - \$21.467)(813,694)$$
$$= \$387,318.$$

7. Of the stockholders' $387,318 gain, $311,111 will have "come out of the hides of the old bondholders," while $76,207 will have come as a "true gain from leverage" as a result of tax savings net of costs associated with financial distress:

$$\text{True gain from leverage} = V_1 - V_0$$
$$= \$21,543,434 - \$21,466,667$$
$$= \$76,767.$$

(There are rounding errors in these calculations.)

Thus, NSS could increase the value of its stock from $21.47 to $21.94 by increasing its leverage from $4 million to $6 million, if it did not have to refund its initial lower-cost debt. Of course, this gain to stockholders would come mostly at the expense of the old bondholders. The addition of $2 million of new debt would increase the riskiness of all the firm's securities. The stockholders would be compensated, as would the new bondholders, but the old bondholders would still be receiving coupon payments of only 8.3 percent, even though the new debt increased the riskiness of NSS's bonds to the point where $k_d = 9\%$.[11] Therefore, the value of the old debt would fall, and there would be a transfer of wealth from the old bondholders to NSS's stockholders. Because of the possibility of such events, bond indentures generally limit the amount of debt a firm can issue; this point is discussed in Chapter 15.

The Effect of Financial Leverage on EPS

Thus far we have focused on the impact of leverage on a firm's total value and its stock price. Before we leave the NSS illustration, we should also take a look at how leverage affects earnings per share (EPS); this is done in Table 12-3. The top third of the table gives operating income data. It begins by recognizing that NSS's future EBIT is not known with certainty. Expected EBIT is $4 million, but the realized EBIT could be less than or greater than $4 million. To simplify matters, we have

---

[11]The $2 million of additional debt might actually have a cost somewhat below 9 percent. This is because retention of the old debt at 8.3 percent would result in lower total interest payments at the new debt level than if the entire $6 million of debt had cost 9 percent. Given equal business risk, the lower interest payments would lower the probability of financial distress, and thus lower the riskiness of the new debt. Additionally, lower distress risk would mean that equity holders might have a required return somewhat less than the 13.2 percent indicated in Table 12-2. However, these gains all come at the expense of the existing bondholders — the addition of new debt makes the old debt more risky, yet the old debtholders will not be compensated for the additional risk. Our analysis does not include these effects; they would, of course, be extremely hard to measure with any degree of confidence.

Table 12-3
NSS's EPS at Different Amounts of Debt
(Millions of Dollars Except per Share Figures)

Operating Income (EBIT)			
Probability of indicated sales	0.2	0.6	0.2
Sales	$10.00	$20.00	$30.00
Fixed costs	4.00	4.00	4.00
Variable costs (60% of sales)	6.00	12.00	18.00
Total costs (except interest)	$10.00	$16.00	$22.00
Earnings before interest and taxes (EBIT)	$ 0.00	$ 4.00	$ 8.00
EPS with Zero Debt			
Less interest	$ 0.00	$ 0.00	$ 0.00
Earnings before taxes	$ 0.00	$ 4.00	$ 8.00
Less taxes (40%)	0.00	1.60	3.20
Net income	$ 0.00	$ 2.40	$ 4.80
Earnings per share on 1 million shares (EPS)	$ 0.00	$ 2.40	$ 4.80
Expected EPS		$ 2.40	
Standard deviation of EPS[a]		$ 1.52	
Coefficient of variation of EPS[a]		0.63	
EPS with $10 Million of Debt			
Less interest (0.12 × $10,000,000)	$ 1.20	$ 1.20	$ 1.20
Earnings before taxes	($ 1.20)	$ 2.80	$ 6.80
Less taxes (40%)[b]	(0.48)	1.12	2.72
Net income	($ 0.72)	$ 1.68	$ 4.08
Earnings per share on 524,940 shares (EPS)[c]	($ 1.37)	$ 3.20	$ 7.77
Expected EPS		$ 3.20	
Standard deviation of EPS[a]		$ 2.90	
Coefficient of variation of EPS[a]		0.91	

[a]Procedures for calculating the standard deviation and the coefficient of variation were discussed in Chapter 6.

[b]Assumes tax credit on losses. If credits were not available, expected EPS would be lower, and risk higher, at high debt levels.

[c]Shares outstanding is determined as follows:

$$\text{Shares} = \text{Original shares} - \frac{\text{Debt}}{\text{Stock price}} = 1,000,000 - \frac{\text{Debt}}{\text{Stock price}},$$

where the stock price is taken from Table 12-2, Column 6. With $10 million of debt, P = $21.05. After the recapitalization, 524,940 shares will remain outstanding:

$$\text{Shares} = 1,000,000 - \frac{\$10,000,000}{\$21.05} = 524,940.$$

EPS figures can also be calculated using this formula:

$$\text{EPS} = \frac{(\text{EBIT} - k_d D)(1 - T)}{\text{Original shares} - \text{Debt/Price}}.$$

For example, at D = $10 million,

$$\text{EPS} = \frac{[\$4,000,000 - (0.12)(10,000,000)](0.6)}{1,000,000 - \$10,000,000/\$21.05} = \frac{\$1,680,000}{524,940} = \$3.20.$$

assumed a discrete distribution of sales, and hence EBIT, with only three possible outcomes. Notice that here EBIT is assumed not to depend on financial leverage.[12]

The middle third of Table 12-3 shows the situation that would exist if NSS continues to use no debt. Net income after taxes is divided by the 1 million shares outstanding to calculate EPS. If sales were as low as $10 million, EPS would be zero, but EPS would rise to $4.80 at sales of $30 million.

The EPS at each sales level is next multiplied by the probability of that sales level to obtain the expected EPS, which is $2.40 if NSS uses no debt. We also calculate the standard deviation of EPS and its coefficient of variation to get an idea of the firm's total risk at a zero debt ratio: $\sigma_{EPS} = \$1.52$, and $CV_{EPS} = 0.63$.

The lower third of Table 12-3 shows the financial results that would occur if the company decided to use $10 million of debt. The interest rate on the debt, 12 percent, is taken from Figure 12-5. With $10 million of 12 percent debt outstanding, the company's interest expense is $1.2 million per year. This is a fixed cost, and it is deducted from EBIT as calculated in the top section. Next, taxes are taken out, and we work on down to the EPS figures that would result at each sales level. With $10 million of debt, EPS would be $-\$1.37$ if sales were as low as $10 million; it would rise to $3.20 if sales were $20 million; and it would soar to $7.77 if sales were as high as $30 million.

Continuous approximations of the EPS distributions under the two financial structures are graphed in Figure 12-7. Although expected EPS is much higher if the firm uses financial leverage, the graph makes it clear that the risk of low or even negative EPS is also higher if debt is used. Figure 12-7 shows clearly that using leverage involves a risk/return tradeoff — higher leverage increases expected earnings per share, but using more leverage also increases the firm's risk. It is this increasing risk that causes k_s and k_d to increase at higher amounts of financial leverage.

The relationship between expected EPS and financial leverage is plotted in the top section of Figure 12-8. Here we see that expected EPS first rises as the use of debt increases — interest charges rise, but a smaller number of shares outstanding as debt is substituted for equity still causes EPS to increase. However, EPS peaks when $12 million of debt is used. Beyond this amount, interest rates rise rapidly, and EBIT begins to fall, so EPS is depressed in spite of the falling number of shares outstanding.

Does the same amount of debt maximize both price and EPS? The answer is *no.* As we can see from the lower graph in Figure 12-8, NSS's stock price is maximized with $6 million of debt, while expected EPS is maximized by using $12 million of debt. *Since management is primarily interested in maximizing the value of the stock, the optimal capital structure calls for the use of $6 million of debt.*

---

[12]As we discussed earlier, capital structure does affect EBIT at very high debt levels. For example, we assumed that NSS's EBIT would fall from $4 million to $3.52 million if the level of debt rose to $14 million. However, debt in Table 12-3 is limited to $10 million, so the "excessive leverage effect on EBIT" is not present in this particular example.

Figure 12-7
Probability Distribution of EPS for NSS with
Different Amounts of Financial Leverage

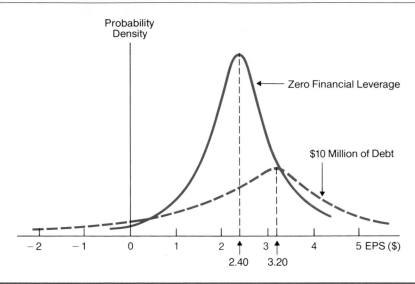

Problems with the NSS Analysis

The Nachman-Smith Software example illustrates the effects of leverage on the firm's value, stock price, earnings per share, and debt value. However, the example was obviously simplified to facilitate the discussion, and we cannot overemphasize the difficulties that are encountered when one attempts to use this type of analysis in practice. First, the capitalization rates (k_d and especially k_s) are very difficult to estimate. The cost of debt at different debt levels can generally be estimated with some degree of confidence, but cost of equity estimates must be viewed as very rough approximations.[13]

Second, the mathematics of the valuation process make the outcomes very sensitive to the input estimates. Thus, fairly small errors in the estimates of k_d, k_s, and EBIT can lead to large errors in estimated EPS and stock price.

Third, our example was restricted to the case of a no-growth firm. In view of the input requirements to model even a simple no-growth situation, and the still

---

[13]The statistical relationship between k_s and financial leverage has been studied extensively by using both cross-sectional and time series data. In the cross-sectional studies, a sample of firms is analyzed, with multiple regression techniques used in an attempt to "hold constant" all factors other than financial leverage that might influence k_s. The general conclusion of the cross-sectional studies is that k_s rises as leverage increases, but statistical problems preclude us from specifying the functional relationship with much confidence.

In the time series studies, a single firm's k_s is analyzed over time in an attempt to see how k_s changes in response to changes in its debt ratio. Here again, "other factors" do not remain constant, so it is impossible to specify exactly how k_s is affected by financial leverage.

Figure 12-8
Relationship between NSS's Expected EPS and Stock Price

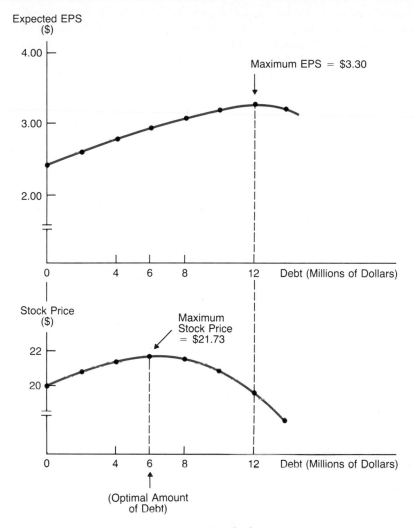

Debt	Expected EPS	Standard Deviation of EPS	Coefficient of Variation	Stock Price
$ 0	$2.40[a]	$1.52[a]	0.63[a]	$20.00
2,000,000	2.55	1.68	0.66	20.89
4,000,000	2.70	1.87	0.69	21.47
6,000,000	2.87	2.09	0.73	21.73
8,000,000	3.04	2.40	0.80	21.71
10,000,000	3.20[a]	2.90[a]	0.91[a]	21.05
12,000,000	3.30	3.83	1.16	19.86
14,000,000	3.26	5.20	1.60	17.16

[a]These values are taken from Table 12-3. Values at other debt levels were calculated similarly. Stock prices are from Table 12-2.

greater requirements for the growth model, it is unrealistic to think that a precise optimal capital structure can really be identified.

Finally, many firms are not publicly owned, and that causes still more difficulties. If a privately held firm's owner never plans to have his or her firm go public, then potential market value data are irrelevant. However, an analysis based on market values for a privately owned firm is very useful if the owner is interested in knowing how the firm's market value would be affected by leverage should the decision be made to go public.

SOME CONSIDERATIONS IN THE CAPITAL STRUCTURE DECISION

Since no one can determine the precise optimal capital structure, managers must apply judgment along with quantitative analysis when making capital structure decisions. The judgmental analysis involves several different factors, and in one situation a particular factor might have great importance, while the same factor might be relatively unimportant in another situation. This section discusses some of the more important judgmental issues that should be taken into account.

Long-Run Viability

Managers of large firms, especially those providing vital services such as electricity or telephone service, have a responsibility to provide *continuous* service, so they should refrain from using leverage to the point where the firm's long-run viability is threatened. Long-run viability may conflict with short-run stock price maximization and cost of capital minimization.[14]

Managerial Conservatism

Well-diversified investors have eliminated most, if not all, of the diversifiable risk from their portfolios. Therefore, the typical investor can tolerate some chance of financial distress, because a loss on one stock would probably be offset by random gains on other stocks in his or her portfolio. However, managers generally view potential distress with more concern — they are typically not well diversified, and their careers, thus the present value of their expected earnings, can be seriously affected by the onset of financial distress. Thus, it is not difficult to imagine that managers might be more "conservative" in their use of leverage than the average stockholder would desire. If this is true, then managers would set somewhat lower target capital structures than the ones which maximize the expected stock prices.

---

[14]Recognizing this fact, most public service commissions require utilities to obtain their approval before issuing long-term securities, and Congress has empowered the SEC to supervise the capital structures of public utility holding companies. However, in addition to concern over the firms' safety, which suggests low debt ratios, both managers and regulators recognize a need to keep all costs as low as possible, including the cost of capital. Since a firm's capital structure affects its cost of capital, regulatory commissions and utility managers try to select capital structures that minimize utilities' cost of capital, subject to the constraint that a firm's ability to finance its operations is not endangered.

The managers of a publicly owned firm would never admit this, for unless they owned voting control, they would quickly be removed from office. However, in view of the uncertainties about what constitutes the value-maximizing structure, management could always say that the target capital structure employed is, in its judgment, the value-maximizing structure, and it would be difficult to prove otherwise.[15]

Lender and Rating Agency Attitudes

Regardless of a manager's own analysis of the proper leverage for his or her firm, there is no question but that lenders' and rating agencies' attitudes are frequently important determinants of financial structures. In the majority of cases, the corporation discusses its financial structure with lenders and rating agencies, and gives much weight to their advice. Also, if a particular firm's management is so confident of the future that it seeks to use leverage beyond the norms for its industry, its lenders may be unwilling to accept such debt increases, or may do so only at a high price.

One of the primary measures of the risk of financial distress used by lenders and rating agencies is the ability of a firm to pay its fixed financing costs. Accordingly, managements give considerable weight to such ratios as the *times-interest-earned (TIE) ratio,* which is defined as EBIT divided by total interest charges. The lower this ratio, the higher is the probability that a firm will encounter financial distress.

Table 12-4 shows how NSS's expected TIE ratio declines as its use of debt increases. When only $2 million of debt is used, the expected TIE is a high 25 times, but the interest coverage ratio declines rapidly as debt rises. Note, however, that

Table 12-4
NSS's Expected Times-Interest-Earned Ratio at Different Amounts of Debt

Amount of Debt (in Millions)	Expected TIE[a]
$ 0	Undefined
2	25.0
4	12.1
6	7.4
8	5.0
10	3.3
12	2.2

[a]TIE = EBIT/Interest. Example: TIE = $4,000,000/$1,200,000 = 3.3 at $10 milliion of debt. Data are from Table 12-1 and Figure 12-5.

[15]It is, of course, possible for a particular manager to be less conservative than his or her firm's average stockholder. However, this condition is less likely to occur than is excessive managerial conservatism, which is just another manifestation of the agency problem. If excessive conservatism exists, then managers, as agents of the stockholders, are not acting in the best interests of their principals.

these coverages are expected values — the actual TIE will be higher if sales exceed the expected $20 million level, but lower if sales fall below $20 million.

The variability of the TIE ratio is highlighted by Figure 12-9, which shows the probability distributions of the ratio at $8 million and $12 million of debt. The expected TIE is much higher if only $8 million of debt is used. Even more important, with less debt there is a much lower probability of a TIE of less than 1.0, the level at which the firm is not earning enough to meet its required interest payment and thus becomes seriously exposed to the threat of bankruptcy.

Another ratio that is often used by lenders and rating agencies is the *fixed charge coverage (FCC) ratio*. This is a more precise measure than the TIE ratio because it recognizes that there are fixed charges other than interest payments which could lead to financial distress. The FCC ratio is defined as follows:

$$FCC = \frac{EBIT + Lease\ payments}{Interest + \left(\begin{array}{c} Lease \\ payments \end{array}\right) + \left(\dfrac{Sinking\ fund\ payments}{1 - T}\right)}.$$

Note that this definition "grosses up" the sinking fund payments in recognition of the fact that these payments must be made with after-tax dollars (net income), because sinking fund payments are not tax deductible.

If NSS had $1 million of lease payments and $1 million of sinking fund payments, its FCC ratio at a debt level of $10 million would be 1.3:

$$FCC = \frac{\$4,000,000 + \$1,000,000}{\$1,200,000 + \$1,000,000 + \dfrac{\$1,000,000}{0.6}}$$

$$= \frac{\$5,000,000}{\$3,866,667} = 1.3.$$

Thus, the coverage of total fixed charges is considerably less than the 3.3 times-interest-earned coverage at the $10 million debt level.

Reserve Borrowing Capacity

When we discussed the information asymmetry theory in Chapter 11, we noted that firms should attempt to maintain an ability to issue debt at all times. For example, suppose Firm Y had just successfully completed an R&D program, and its internal projections showed much higher earnings in the foreseeable future. However, the new earnings are not yet anticipated by investors, and hence are not reflected in the price of its stock. Firm Y would not want to issue stock — it would prefer to finance with debt until the higher earnings materialize and are reflected in the stock price, at which time it could sell an issue of common stock, retire the debt, and return to its target capital structure. Similarly, if the financial manager felt that interest rates were temporarily low, but were likely to rise fairly soon, he or she would want to be able to issue long-term bonds and thus "lock in" the favorable rates. To build up a reserve borrowing capacity, firms generally use less

Figure 12-9
Probability Distributions of Times-Interest-Earned Ratio for NSS with Different Capital Structures

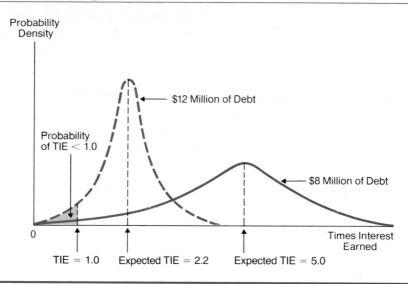

debt than the MM-type analysis would suggest under "normal" conditions, and hence present a stronger financial picture than they otherwise would. This is not suboptimal from a long-run standpoint, although it might appear so if viewed strictly on a short-run basis.

Note too that firms' debt contracts often specify that no new debt can be issued unless certain ratios exceed minimum levels. Very frequently, the TIE ratio is required to exceed 2 or 2.5 times as a condition for the issuance of additional debt. With this in mind, look at Figure 12-9 and note that if NSS used $12 million of debt, its TIE would be less than 2.0 almost half the time, whereas the probability of a coverage less than 2.0 would be quite small if it used only $8 million of debt.

Control

The effect that its choice of securities has on a management's control position may also influence its capital structure decision. If a firm's management just barely has majority control (just over 50 percent of the stock), but is not in a position to buy any more stock, debt may be the choice for new financings. On the other hand, a management group that is not concerned about voting control may decide to use equity rather than debt if the firm's financial situation is so weak that the use of debt might subject the company to serious risk of default. If the firm gets into serious difficulties, the creditors (through covenants in the debt agreements) would assume control and perhaps force a management change. This has happened to Chrysler, International Harvester (now Navistar International), Braniff, Continental Illinois Bank, and a number of other companies in recent years. However, if too little debt is used, management runs the risk of a takeover, where some other company or management group persuades stockholders to turn over control to the new group, which may boost earnings and stock prices by using financial leverage. This recently happened to Lenox, the china company. Control considerations do not necessarily suggest the use of either debt or equity, but if management is at all insecure, the effects of capital structure on control will surely be taken into account.

Additional Considerations

In addition to those factors just listed, the following considerations, which were discussed in Chapter 11, are also relevant to the capital structure decision:

Asset Structure
Firms whose assets are suitable as security for loans tend to use debt rather heavily. Thus, real estate companies tend to be highly leveraged, but companies involved in technological research employ relatively little debt.

Growth Rate
Other factors the same, faster growing firms must rely more heavily on external capital—slow growth can be financed with retained earnings, but rapid growth generally requires the use of external funds. As postulated in the information asymmetry theory, firms first turn to debt financing to meet external funding needs. Further, the flotation costs involved in selling common stock exceed those incurred when selling debt. Thus, rapidly growing firms tend to use somewhat more debt than do slower-growth companies.

Profitability
One often observes that firms with very high rates of return on investment use relatively little debt. This behavior is consistent with the information asymmetry theory, and the practical reason seems to be that highly profitable firms such as IBM, 3M, and Kodak simply do not need to do much debt financing—their high rates of return enable them to do most of their financing with retained earnings.

Taxes
Interest is a deductible expense, while dividends are not deductible; hence, the higher a firm's corporate tax rate, the greater is the advantage of using corporate debt.

AN APPROACH TO SETTING THE TARGET CAPITAL STRUCTURE

Thus far in Chapters 11 and 12, we have discussed (1) several theories of capital structure, (2) a method of analysis based on these theories (including a discussion of the very severe problems one encounters with such an application of the theory), and (3) a myriad of factors which influence the capital structure decisions of most firms. In this section, we describe a pragmatic approach to setting the target capital structure. Our approach requires judgmental assumptions, but it also allows managers to see how alternative capital structures would affect future returns on equity, EPS, coverage, and external financing requirements under a variety of assumptions.

The starting point for the analysis is a *Lotus 1-2-3* forecasting model set up to test the effects of capital structure changes. Here is a brief description of the model and how it has been used.[16] Basically, the model generates forecasted data based on historical, or base year, data plus additional inputs supplied by the financial manager. Each data item can be fixed, or it can be allowed to vary from year to year. The required additional data, all of which represent either expectations or policy variables, include the following:

1. Annual growth rates in unit sales
2. Annual inflation rates
3. Corporate tax rate
4. Variable costs as a percentage of sales
5. Fixed costs
6. Interest rate on already outstanding (or embedded) debt
7. Marginal cost of common equity
8. Marginal cost of debt
9. Capital structure ratios
10. Dividend growth rate
11. Long-term dividend payout ratio

The model uses the input data to forecast balance sheets and income statements for some specified number of years. Further, the model calculates and displays selected other information such as external financing requirements, ROE, EPS, DPS, times interest earned, stock price, and WACC on an annual basis.

The financial manager begins by entering base year values and data on expected unit sales growth rates, expected inflation rates, and so on. This input is used by the model to forecast operating income and asset requirements which, in general, will be independent of the financing decision. Next, the financial manager must consider the financing mix. Our model takes as inputs both the debt/equity mix and the debt maturity mix, which is the proportion of short-term versus long-term debt. Further, the manager must estimate the effects of the capital structure on the component costs, and then must enter those cost rates. In general, a higher debt ratio will increase the costs of all components. With all inputs entered, the model then completes the forecasted financial statements and generates projected stock prices.

---

[16]One such model is described in Chapter 12 of Paul D. Cretien, Susan E. Ball, and Eugene F. Brigham, *Financial Management with Lotus 1-2-3* (Dryden Press, 1986). That model has been used in a number of consulting assignments, including work for New York Telephone, New England Telephone, and Consolidated Edison.

The model's output can then be reviewed and analyzed. Since we are focusing on the capital structure decision, we pay particular attention to the forecasted EPS, WACC, coverage, and external funding requirements, as well as to the projected stock price. Finally, the model is used to analyze alternative scenarios. This analysis takes two forms: (1) changing the financing inputs to get some idea of how the financing mix affects the key outputs, and (2) changing the operating inputs to see how the basic business risk of the firm affects the key outputs under various financing strategies.

The model can generate the output associated with various scenarios quite easily, but it remains up to the financial manager to assign input values, to interpret the output, and finally to set the target capital structure. The final decision is based on all the factors we have discussed in Chapters 11 and 12, and the decision-maker must judge which factors are most relevant to his or her firm. Reaching a decision is not easy, but a capital structure forecasting model such as the one we use at least permits an analysis of the effects of alternative courses of action.

It should be noted that while capital structure decisions affect the prices of companies' stocks, those effects are relatively small in comparison to the effects of operating decisions. A company's ability to identify (or create) market opportunities, and to produce and sell products efficiently, are the primary determinants of its success. Its financial structure can facilitate or hamper operations, but the best of financial plans cannot overcome deficiencies in the operations area. These statements are supported by empirical studies, which generally find a weak statistical relationship between capital structure and stock prices. The statements are also supported by runs of our computer model, which show stock prices to be affected significantly by changes in unit sales, sales prices, fixed costs, and variable costs, but affected much less by changes in capital structure. This last point can also be seen from the NSS example discussed above. Refer again to Table 12-2. Nachman-Smith Software's stock price is maximized at a D/V ratio of 27.6 percent. However, at a much lower D/V of 18.6 percent, the firm's stock price drops only from $21.73 or $21.47, or by a slight 1.2 percent, while if D/V rises to 36.8 percent, NSS's stock price hardly drops at all. Thus, NSS could set its target D/V ratio anywhere in the range of 18 to 37 percent and still come very close to maximizing its stock price. That is a typical situation.

VARIATIONS IN CAPITAL STRUCTURES AMONG FIRMS

As might be expected, wide variations in the use of financial leverage occur both among industries and among the individual firms within industries. Table 12-5 illustrates differences for selected industries, ranked in descending order of common equity ratios as shown in Column 5.[17]

---

[17]Information on capital structures and financial strength is available from a multitude of sources. We used the *Compustat* data tapes to develop Table 12-5, but other published sources include *The Value Line Investment Survey, Robert Morris Associates Annual Studies,* and *Dun & Bradstreet Key Business Ratios.*

Table 12-5
Capital Structure Percentages, 1986:
Selected Industries Ranked by Common Equity Ratios

Industry	Short-Term Debt (1)	Long-Term Debt (2)	Total Debt (3)	Preferred Stock (4)	Common Equity (5)	Times-Interest-Earned Ratio (6)
Drugs	8.5%	10.6%	19.1%	0.1%	80.8%	10.3×
Automotive	4.3	17.5	21.8	1.9	76.3	7.0
Electronics	9.1	16.5	25.6	1.1	73.3	6.2
Retailing	20.3	31.0	51.3	1.3	47.4	2.9
Utilities (electric, gas, and telephone)	2.6	46.5	49.1	6.4	44.5	2.9
Steel	3.4	54.0	57.4	3.9	38.7	0.7
Composite (average of all industries, not just those listed above)	21.0%	32.0%	53.0%	2.5%	44.5%	2.2×

Note: These ratios are based on accounting (or book) values. Stated on a market value basis, the equity percentages would rise because most stocks sell at prices that are much higher than their book values.

Source: *Compustat* Data Tape, 1987.

The drug, automotive, and electronics companies do not use much debt; these companies have generally been quite profitable, and hence able to finance through retained earnings, and the uncertainties inherent in industries that are oriented toward research and subject to huge product liability suits render the heavy use of leverage unwise. Retailers, steel, and utility companies, on the other hand, use debt relatively heavily, but for different reasons. Retailers use short-term debt to finance inventories, and long-term debt secured by mortgages on their stores. The steel companies have been losing money in recent years, and these losses have eroded their equity positions and also made it difficult for them to sell new common stock. Therefore, the steel companies have been forced to borrow (at relatively high interest rates) to modernize their plants, and the result is a high debt ratio and an average coverage of less than 1.0. The utilities have traditionally used large amounts of debt — their fixed assets make good security for mortgage bonds, and their relatively stable sales make it safe for them to carry more debt than would be true for firms with more business risk.

Particular attention should be given to the times-interest-earned ratio. This ratio is a function of (1) financial leverage and (2) profitability. Generally, the least-levered industries, such as the drug companies, have the highest coverage ratios, while industries such as steel, which had profit problems in 1986, have low ratios.

Wide variations in capital structures also exist among firms within given industries — for example, although the average common equity ratio in 1986 for the drug industry was 80.8 percent, Warner-Lambert's equity ratio was only 62.8 percent, but Bristol-Myers' ratio was near 90 percent. Thus, factors unique to individual firms, including managerial attitudes, do play an important role in setting target capital structures.

BOOK WEIGHTS VERSUS MARKET WEIGHTS

In Chapter 7, we calculated the weighted average cost of capital with market value rather than book value weights. Further, in our discussions of capital structure in Chapters 11 and 12 we continued to focus on market value, not book value. However, survey data indicate that financial managers generally focus on book value structures. Thus, there seems to be a conflict between academic theory and business practice. Here are some thoughts on this issue:

1. If stocks and bonds do not sell exactly at book value — and they almost never do — then it is impossible for a growing firm to establish and maintain at constant levels a target book value and a target market value capital structure. The firm could maintain its book value target or its market value target, but not both. To illustrate, assume that a company has, at book value, $50 million of debt and $50 million of equity, for a total book value of $100 million. However, its stock sells at twice book. Here is the capital structure situation, with dollars in millions:

	Book Value		**Market Value**	
Debt	$ 50	50%	$ 50	33%
Equity	50	50	100	67
Total	$100	100%	$150	100%

Now suppose the company needs to raise an additional $50 million. If it sells $25 million of debt and $25 million of common stock, it will add these amounts to its balance sheet, so its book value capital structure will remain constant. However, adding $25 million to both debt and equity will cause its market value capital structure to change. On the other hand, if it raises $16.7 million as debt and $33.3 million as equity, its market value capital structure will remain constant, but its book value structure will change. Thus, it can maintain either its book value or its market value capital structure, but not both.

2. Book values, as reported on balance sheets, reflect the historical cost of assets. At times, historical costs have little to do with assets' current earning power, with the actual value of these assets, or with their ability to produce cash flows which can be used to service debt. Market values would, almost always, better reflect earning power, cash generation, and debt service ability.

3. As we have repeatedly noted throughout this chapter and the last one, we want to find that capital structure which maximizes the firm's stock price. Since this optimum is defined in terms of market values, it can only be determined by an analysis of the market value capital structure.

4. Now suppose a firm found its optimal market value structure, but then financed so as to maintain a constant book value structure. This would lead to a departure from value maximization. Therefore, if a firm is growing, it must finance so as to hold constant its market value structure. That will, as we saw above, lead to a change in the book value structure.

5. Since the firm should finance so as to hold its market value structure constant, the weighted average cost of capital, k_a, should be found using market value weights.

6. Business executives prefer stability and predictability to volatility and uncertainty. Book values are far more predictable than market values. Further, a financial manager can set a target book value capital structure and then attain it, right on the money. It would be virtually impossible to maintain a target market value structure because bond and stock prices fluctuate. This is one reason why executives focus on book value structures rather than the more logical market value structures. Also, many financial executives have accounting backgrounds, and accountants tend to focus on accounting numbers. However, as financial executives gain a knowledge of financial (as opposed to accounting) theory, the focus seems to be shifting toward market values.

7. For purposes of developing the weighted average cost of capital, we strongly recommend the use of market value weights. However, if a company does focus on a book value capital structure, and does seek to maintain that structure, then it will finance in accordance with book value weights, and in that case its weighted average cost of capital should be based on book weights.

8. Some executives have argued against the use of market value weights on the grounds that as stock prices change, so would capital structure weights, with the result being a volatile cost of capital. This argument is incorrect. The cost of capital should be based on *target* weights, and not the actual capital structure, and there is no reason to think that a target market value structure would be any less stable than a target book value structure.

What can we conclude from all this? We are absolutely convinced that the procedures we recommend are correct — namely, firms should focus on market value capital structures and base their cost of capital calculations on market value weights. Because market values do change, it would be impossible to keep the capital structure on target at all times, but this fact in no way detracts from the validity of market value targets.

SUMMARY

In this chapter, we saw how firms actually establish target capital structures. We began by defining (1) *business risk,* which is the riskiness of the firm if it uses no debt, and (2) *financial risk,* which is the additional risk placed on the common stockholders as a result of debt financing. Business risk and financial risk can be viewed from either a total risk or market risk standpoint; we examined both, using the Hamada equation to bring in market risk.

We next examined the effects of financial leverage on stock prices, earnings per share, and the cost of capital. Our analysis suggests that an *optimal capital structure* — one which simultaneously maximizes the firm's total market value and stock price while minimizing its average cost of capital — exists for each firm. However, as a practical matter we cannot estimate this structure with precision. Accordingly, financial executives generally treat the optimal capital structure as a range — for example, 40 to 50 percent debt — rather than as a precise point, such as 45 percent debt. Also, we saw that financial executives analyze the effects of different capital structures on expected earnings per share and interest coverage ratios, and they also tend to consider such factors as business risk, asset structure, effects on control, and so on. Finally, the optimal capital structure should be thought of in market value rather than book value terms, even though managers often seem to pay more attention to book than to market values. In the final analysis, the final target capital structure is more judgmentally than rigorously determined.

MULTINATIONAL FINANCE

Significant differences have been observed in the capital structures of U.S. corporations versus their German and Japanese counterparts. For example, in 1984 the Organization for Economic Cooperation and Development (OECD) reported that, on average, Japanese firms use 85 percent debt-to-total assets (in book value terms), German firms use 63 percent, and U.S. firms use 37 percent. Of course, different countries use somewhat different accounting conventions with regard (1) to reporting assets on a historical versus a replacement cost basis, (2) to the treatment of leased assets, (3) to pension plan funding, and (4) to capitalizing versus expensing R&D costs, and these differences make comparisons difficult. Still, even after adjusting for accounting differences, we find that Japanese and German firms use considerably more financial leverage than U.S. companies.

Why do international differences in financial leverage exist? Since taxes are thought to be a major reason for using debt, the effects of differential tax structures in the three countries have been examined. The interest on corporate debt is deductible in each country, and individuals must pay taxes on dividends and interest received. However, capital gains are not taxed in either Germany or Japan. The conclusions from this analysis are as follows: (1) From a tax standpoint, corporations should be equally inclined to use debt in all three countries. (2) Since capital gains are not taxed in Germany or Japan, but they are taxed in the United States, and since capital gains are associated more with stocks than with bonds, investors in Germany and Japan should show a preference for stocks vis-à-vis U.S. investors. (3) Investor preferences should lead to relatively low equity capital costs in Germany and Japan, and this, in turn, should cause German and Japanese firms to use more equity capital than their U.S. counterparts. Of course, this is exactly the opposite of the actual capital structures, so differential tax laws certainly do not explain the observed capital structure differences.

If tax systems cannot explain differential capital structures, what else might explain the observed differences? Another possibility is differences in bankruptcy costs. In Chapter 11 we saw that actual bankruptcy, and even the threat of potential bankruptcy, imposes a costly burden on firms with large amounts of debt. Note, though, that bankruptcy costs are dependent on the *probability* of bankruptcy — only if the probability of bankruptcy is high will bankruptcy costs be high. Now recall our discussion of *agency costs* in Chapter 1. There we saw that agency costs arise from two agency relationships: (1) the relationship between shareholders and managers and (2) the relationship between bondholders and shareholders. In the United States, equity agency costs are comparatively low — corporations produce quarterly reports, pay quarterly dividends, and must comply with relatively stringent audit requirements. These conditions are less prevalent in the other countries. Conversely, debt agency costs are probably lower in Germany and Japan than in the United States. In these countries, the bulk of corporate debt consists of bank loans as opposed to publicly issued bonds, but, more important, the banks are closely linked to their debtor corporations. German and Japanese banks often (1) hold major equity positions in their debtor corporations, (2) vote the shares of individual shareholders for whom banks hold shares in trust, and (3) have bank officers sit on the boards of debtor corporations. Given these close relationships, the bank creditors are much more directly involved with the debtor firms' affairs, and as a result they are also more accommodating in the event of financial distress than U.S. bondholders would be. This, in turn, suggests that a given amount of debt brings with it a lower threat of bankruptcy for a German or a Japanese firm than for a U.S. firm with the same amount of business risk. Thus, an analysis of both bankruptcy and equity agency costs leads to the conclusion that U.S. firms ought to have more equity and less debt than firms in Japan and Germany.

We cannot state that one financial system is better or worse than another in the sense of making the firms in one country more efficient than those in another. However, as U.S. firms become increasingly involved in worldwide operations, they must become increasingly aware of worldwide conditions, and they must be prepared to adapt to conditions in the various countries in which they operate.

Questions

12-1 Define each of the following terms:

    a. Capital structure; optimal capital structure; target capital structure

    b. Business risk; financial risk

    c. Operating leverage; financial leverage

    d. Breakeven point

    e. Tax shelter; tax shelter benefit; financial distress costs

    f. Book weights; market value weights

    g. Reserve borrowing capacity

12-2 What term refers to the uncertainty inherent in projections of future operating income?

12-3 Firms with relatively high nonfinancial fixed costs are said to have a high degree of what?

12-4 "One type of leverage affects both EBIT and EPS. The other type affects only EPS." Explain what the statement means.

12-5 What is the relationship between market (or beta) risk and leverage?

12-6 Why is the following statement true? "Other things being the same, firms with relatively stable sales are able to carry relatively high debt ratios."

12-7 Why do public utility companies usually have capital structures that are different from those of retail firms?

12-8 Some economists believe that swings in business cycles will not be as wide in the future as they have been in the past. Assuming that they are correct, what effect might this added stability have on the types of financing used by firms in the United States? Would your answer be true for all firms?

12-9 Why is EBIT generally considered to be independent of financial leverage? Why might EBIT actually be influenced by financial leverage at high debt levels?

12-10 If a firm with no debt could buy back and retire its stock at the initial price, would its final stock price be higher than that resulting from the procedure outlined in the chapter? Would it be fair for a firm to buy back its stock without telling stockholders that stock was being repurchased?

12-11 How might increasingly volatile inflation rates, interest rates, and bond prices affect the optimal capital structure for corporations?

12-12 If a firm went from zero debt to successively higher levels of debt, why would you expect its stock price to first rise, then hit a peak, and then begin to decline?

12-13 Why is the debt level that maximizes a firm's expected EPS generally higher than the debt level that maximizes its stock price?

Self-Test Problems

ST-1 (Operating leverage and breakeven) Boston Scientific, Inc., produces satellite earth stations which sell for $100,000 each. Boston's fixed costs, F, are $2 million; 50 earth stations are produced and sold each year; profits total $500,000; and Boston's assets (all equity financed) are $5 million. Boston estimates that it can change its production process, adding $4 million to investment and $500,000 to fixed operating costs. This change will (1) reduce variable costs per unit by $10,000 and (2) increase output by 20 units, but (3) the sales price on all units will have to be lowered to $95,000 to permit sales of the additional output. Boston has tax loss carry-forwards that cause its tax rate to be zero, and its cost of capital is 15 percent. Boston uses no debt.

    a. Should Boston make the change?

    b. Would Boston's operating leverage increase or decrease if it made the change? What about its breakeven point?

    c. Would the new situation expose Boston to more or less business risk than the old one?

ST-2 (Optimal capital structure) Suppose, some years later, Boston Scientific found itself in this situation: (1) EBIT = $4 million; (2) tax rate, T = 35%; (3) value of debt, D = $2 million; (4) k_d = 10%; (5) k_s = 15%; and (6) shares of stock outstanding, n = 600,000. Boston's market is stable, and it expects no growth, so all earnings are paid out as dividends. The debt consists of perpetual bonds.

a. What is the total market value of Boston's stock, S, its price per share, P_0, and the firm's total market value, V?

b. What is Boston's weighted average cost of capital, k_a?

c. Boston can increase its debt by $8 million, to a total of $10 million, using the new debt to buy back and retire some of its shares. Its interest rate on all debt will be 12 percent (it will have to call and refund the old debt), and its cost of equity will rise from 15 to 17 percent. EBIT will remain constant. Should Boston change its capital structure?

d. If Boston did not have to refund the $2 million of old debt, how would this have affected things? Assume the new and the old debt are equally risky, with $k_d = 12\%$, but the coupon rate on the old debt is 10 percent.

e. What is Boston's TIE ratio under the original conditions and under the conditions in Part c?

Problems

12-1 (Business and financial risk: total) Here are the estimated ROE distributions for Firms A, B, and C:

	Probability				
	0.1	**0.2**	**0.4**	**0.2**	**0.1**
Firm A: ROE_A	0.0%	5.0%	10.0%	15.0%	20.0%
Firm B: ROE_B	(2.0)	5.0	12.0	19.0	26.0
Firm C: ROE_C	(5.0)	5.0	15.0	25.0	35.0

a. Calculate the expected value and standard deviation for Firm C's ROE. $ROE_A = 10.0\%$, $\sigma_A = 6.3\%$; $ROE_B = 12.0\%$, $\sigma_B = 7.7\%$.

b. Discuss the relative riskiness of the three firms' returns. (Assume that these distributions are expected to remain constant over time.)

c. Now suppose all three firms have the same standard deviation of basic earning power (EBIT/Total assets), $\sigma_A = \sigma_B = \sigma_C = 6.3\%$. What can we tell about the financial risk of each firm?

12-2 (Business and financial risk: market) Air Tampa has just been incorporated, and its new board of directors is currently grappling with the question of optimal capital structure. The company plans to offer commuter air services between Tampa and smaller surrounding cities. Jaxair has been around for a few years, and it has about the same basic business risk as Air Tampa would have. Jaxair's market-determined beta is 1.8, and it has a current market value debt ratio (total debt/total assets) of 50 percent and a federal-plus-state tax rate of 40 percent. Air Tampa expects only to be marginally profitable at start up, and hence its tax rate would only be 25 percent. Air Tampa's owners expect that the total book and market value of the firm's stock, if it uses zero debt, would be $10 million.

a. Estimate the beta of an unlevered firm in the commuter airline business based on Jaxair's market-determined beta. (Hint: Jaxair's market-determined beta is a levered beta. Use Equation 12-3a and solve for b_U.)

b. Now assume that k_{RF} = 10% and k_M = 15%. Find the required rate of return on equity for an unlevered commuter airline. What is the business risk premium for this industry?

c. Air Tampa is considering three capital structures: (1) $2 million debt, (2) $4 million debt, and (3) $6 million debt. Estimate Air Tampa's k_s for these debt levels. What is the financial risk premium at each level?

d. Calculate Air Tampa's k_s and financial risk premium at $6 million debt assuming its federal-plus-state tax rate is now 40 percent. Compare this with your corresponding answer to Part c. (Hint: The increase in the tax rate causes V_U to drop to $8 million.)

12-3 (Capital structure analysis) The following data reflect the current financial conditions of Davis Corporation:

Value of debt (book = market)	$1,000,000
Market value of equity	$5,257,143
Sales, last 12 months	$12,000,000
Variable operating costs (50% of sales)	$6,000,000
Fixed operating costs	$5,000,000
Tax rate, T (federal-plus-state)	40%

At the current level of debt, the cost of debt, k_d, is 8 percent and the cost of equity, k_s, is 10.5 percent. Management questions whether or not the capital structure is optimal, so the financial vice president has been asked to consider the possibility of issuing $1 million of additional debt and using the proceeds to repurchase stock. It is estimated that if the leverage were increased by raising the level of debt to $2 million, the interest rate on new debt would rise to 9 percent and k_s would rise to 11.5 percent. The old 8 percent debt is senior to the new debt, and it would remain outstanding, continue to yield 8 percent, and have a market value of $1 million. Davis is a zero-growth firm, with all of its earnings paid out as dividends.

a. Should Davis increase its debt to $2 million?

b. If the firm decided to increase its level of debt to $3 million, its cost of the additional $2 million of debt would be 12 percent and k_s would rise to 15 percent. The original 8 percent of debt would again remain outstanding, and its market value would remain at $1 million. What level of debt should the firm choose: $1 million, $2 million, or $3 million?

c. The market price of Davis Corporation's stock was originally $20 per share. Calculate the new equilibrium stock prices at debt levels of $2 million and $3 million.

d. Calculate the firm's earnings per share if it uses debt of $1 million, $2 million, and $3 million. Assume that the firm pays out all of its earnings as dividends. If you find that EPS increases with more debt, does this mean that the firm should choose to increase its debt to $3 million, or possibly higher?

e. What would happen to the value of the old bonds if Davis uses more leverage and the old bonds are not senior to the new bonds?

12-4 (Capital structure analysis) ABC, Inc., has no debt outstanding, and its financial position is given by the following data:

Assets (book = market)	$3,000,000
EBIT	$500,000
Cost of equity, k_s	10%
Stock price, P_0	$15
Shares outstanding, n	200,000
Tax rate, T (federal-plus-state)	40%

The firm is considering selling bonds and simultaneously repurchasing some of its stock. If it uses $900,000 of debt, its cost of equity, k_s, will increase to 11 percent to reflect the increased risk. Bonds can be sold at a cost, k_d, of 7 percent. ABC is a no-growth firm. Hence, all its earnings are paid out as dividends, and earnings are expectationally constant over time.

a. What effect would this use of leverage have on the value of the firm?

b. What would be the price of ABC's stock?

c. What happens to the firm's earnings per share after the recapitalization?

d. The $500,000 EBIT given above is actually the expected value from the following probability distribution:

Probability	EBIT
0.10	($ 100,000)
0.20	200,000
0.40	500,000
0.20	800,000
0.10	1,100,000

What is the probability distribution of EPS with zero debt and with $900,000 of debt? Which EPS distribution is riskier?

e. Determine the probability distributions of times interest earned for each debt level. What is the probability of not covering the interest payment at the $900,000 debt level?

12-5 **(Capital structure analysis)** Stead Printing, Inc., has a total market value of $100 million, consisting of 1 million shares selling for $50 per share and $50 million of 10 percent perpetual bonds now selling at par. The company's EBIT is $13.24 million, and its tax rate is 15 percent. Stead can change its capital structure by either increasing its debt to $70 million or decreasing it to $30 million. If it decides to *increase* its use of leverage, it must call its old bonds and issue new ones with a 12 percent coupon. If it decides to *decrease* its leverage, it will call in its old bonds and replace them with new 8 percent coupon bonds. The company will sell or repurchase stock at the new equilibrium price to complete the capital structure change.

Stead pays out all earnings as dividends; hence, its stock is a zero growth stock. If it increases leverage, k_s will be 16 percent. If it decreases leverage, k_s will be 13 percent.

a. What is the cost of equity to Stead at present?

b. Should the firm change its capital structure?

c. Suppose the tax rate is changed to 34 percent. This would lower after-tax income and also cause a decline in the price of the stock and the total value of the equity, other things held constant. Calculate the new stock price (at $50 million of debt).

d. Continue the scenario of Part c, but now re-examine the question of the optimal amount of debt. Does the tax rate change affect your decision about the optimal use of financial leverage?

e. Go back to Part b; that is, assume T = 15%. How would your analysis of the capital structure change be modified if the firm's presently outstanding debt could not be called, and it did not have to be replaced; that is, if the $50 million of 10 percent debt continued even if the company issued new 12 percent bonds?

f. Suppose these probabilities for EBIT exist: P[EBIT = $5 million] = 0.2; P[EBIT = $15 million] = 0.6; and P[EBIT = $25 million] = 0.2. Under the assumptions of Part e, what is (1) expected EPS and σ_{EPS}, and (2) expected TIE and σ_{TIE}, assuming an increase in book value of debt to $70 million?

12-6 **(Pro forma analysis)** The C.S. Grant Company is currently all-equity financed, but the firm is considering a change to 50 percent debt financing. The debt would cost 12 percent, and would be used to repurchase shares currently selling at $25 per share. Grant now has 40,000 shares outstanding and $1,000,000 in total assets. Its pro forma income statement for 1988, assuming zero debt usage, is as follows:

Sales	$900,000
Operating costs	750,000
EBIT	$150,000
Taxes (40%)	60,000
Net income	$ 90,000

a. What is the expected EPS for 1988 using zero debt? At a debt level of $500,000?

b. Assume that operating costs remain at 83.33 percent of sales over a wide range of sales levels. Further, the 1988 pro forma income statement is based on expected sales of $900,000, but the actual sales distribution is as follows:

Probability	Sales
0.10	$ 500,000
0.15	700,000
0.50	900,000
0.15	1,100,000
0.10	1,300,000

Find the EPS at each sales level for both zero debt and 50 percent debt financing.

c. Make a plot of EPS versus sales level for both financing alternatives. Place the plots on the same set of axes. Interpret this graph.

(Do Parts d and e only if you are using the computerized diskette.)

d. At a zero debt level, Grant's expected ROE = $90,000/$1,000,000 = 9.0%, while at $500,000 of debt, expected ROE = $54,000/$500,000 = 10.8%. Determine the firm's ROE at each debt level for every possible sales level. Plot the two ROE distributions.

e. Now, assume that the $500,000 debt financing would cost 15 percent. Repeat the Part d analysis. Is there a significant difference? Why?

12-7 (Subjective analysis) You have been hired as a financial consultant by two firms, Alpha Industries (Firm A) and Zed Corporation (Firm Z). Firm A is in the fast-growing microcomputer retail sales industry, while Firm Z manufactures office equipment such as pencil sharpeners, staplers, and tape dispensers. Your task is to recommend the optimal capital structure for the two firms. Discuss the factors that would influence your decision, and specifically how each of these factors apply to each firm. Here are some additional points about the two firms:

(1) Firm A generally leases its stores, while Firm Z purchases its plants.

(2) Firm A's stock is widely held, while the family of Firm Z's founder holds 40 percent of its stock.

(3) Firm Z has a significant amount of accelerated depreciation expense each year, while Firm A has almost none.

(4) Firm A has demonstrated high growth and profitability over the last few years. On the other hand, Firm Z's growth has averaged a modest 5 percent per year, and its profit margins and ROEs have been unspectacular.

Solutions to Self-Test Problems

ST-1   a. (1) Determine the variable cost per unit at present, V:

$$\text{Profit} = PQ - VQ - F$$
$$\$500,000 = (\$100,000)(50) - V(50) - \$2,000,000$$
$$50V = \$2,500,000$$
$$V = \$50,000.$$

(2) Determine the new profit level if the change is made:

$$\text{New Profit} = PQ - VQ - F$$
$$= \$95,000(70) - (\$50,000 - \$10,000)(70) - \$2,500,000$$
$$= \$1,350,000.$$

(3) Determine the incremental profit:

$$\text{Incremental profit} = \$1,350,000 - \$500,000 = \$850,000.$$

(4) Estimate the approximate rate of return on the new investment:

$$\text{Return} = \frac{\Delta\text{Profit}}{\Delta\text{Investment}} = \frac{\$850,000}{\$4,000,000} = 21.25\%.$$

Since the return exceeds the 15 percent cost of capital, this analysis suggests that Boston should go ahead with the change.

b. If we measure operating leverage by the ratio of fixed costs to total costs (fixed costs plus total variable costs) at the expected output, then the change would increase operating leverage:

$$\text{Old: } \frac{F}{F + VQ} = \frac{\$2,000,000}{\$2,000,000 + \$2,500,000} = 44.44\%.$$

$$\text{New: } \frac{\$2,500,000}{\$2,500,000 + \$2,800,000} = 47.17\%.$$

The change would also increase the breakeven point:

$$\text{Breakeven, old: } Q_{BE} = \frac{F}{P - V} = \frac{\$2,000,000}{\$100,000 - \$50,000} = 40 \text{ units.}$$

$$\text{Breakeven, new: } Q_{BE} = \frac{\$2,500,000}{\$95,000 - \$40,000} = 45.45 \text{ units.}$$

c. It is impossible to state unequivocally whether the new situation would have more or less business risk than the old one. We would need information on both the sales probability distribution and the uncertainty about variable input costs in order to make this determination. However, since a higher breakeven point, other things held constant, is more risky, the change in breakeven points — and also the higher percentage of fixed cost — suggests that the new situation is more risky.

ST-2   a.

$$S = \frac{(EBIT - k_d D)(1 - T)}{k_s}$$

$$= \frac{[\$4,000,000 - 0.10(\$2,000,000)](0.65)}{0.15} = \$16,466,667.$$

$$P_0 = S/n = \frac{\$16,466,667}{600,000} = \$27.44.$$

$$V = D + S = \$2,000,000 + \$16,466,667 = \$18,466,667.$$

b.

$$k_a = (D/V)(k_d)(1 - T) + (S/V)(k_s)$$

$$= \left(\frac{\$2,000,000}{\$18,466,667}\right)(10\%)(0.65) + \left(\frac{\$16,466,667}{\$18,466,667}\right)(15\%)$$

$$= 14.08\%.$$

c. Under the new capital structure,

$$S = \frac{[\$4,000,000 - 0.12(\$10,000,000)](0.65)}{0.17} = \$10,705,882.$$

$$V = \$10,000,000 + \$10,705,882 = \$20,705,882.$$

The new value of the firm will thus be $20,705,882. This value belongs to the *present* stockholders and bondholders, so we may calculate the new equilibrium price of the stock, P_1:

$$P_1 = \frac{V_1 - D_0}{n_0} = \frac{\$20,705,882 - \$2,000,000}{600,000} = \$31.18.$$

$$\text{Check: Shares repurchased} = \frac{\text{New debt}}{P_1} = \frac{\$8,000,000}{\$31.18} = 256,575.$$

$$P_1 = \frac{S_1}{n_1} = \frac{\$10,705,882}{600,000 - 256,575} \approx \$31.18.$$

$$k_a = \left(\frac{\$10,000,000}{\$20,705,882}\right)(12\%)(0.65) + \left(\frac{\$10,705,882}{\$20,705,882}\right)(17\%) = 12.56\%.$$

Thus, the proposed capital structure change would increase the value of the firm and the price of the stock (from $27.44 to $31.18), and lower the cost of capital. Therefore, Boston should increase its use of financial leverage. Of course, it is possible that some amount of debt other than $10 million would result in an even higher value, but we do not have enough information to make this determination.

d. Offhand, we would expect the value of the equity and the price of the stock to rise. We would also expect the value of the old debt to decline. Here is the situation:

$$S = \frac{(\text{EBIT} - I_{Old} - I_{New})(1 - T)}{k_s}$$

$$= \frac{[\$4,000,000 - 0.10(\$2,000,000) - 0.12(\$8,000,000)](0.65)}{0.17}$$

$$= \$10,858,824.$$

$$\begin{aligned}
\text{Value of debt} &= \text{Old debt} + \text{New debt} \\
&= \$200,000/0.12 + \$8,000,000 = \$9,666,667.
\end{aligned}$$

$$\begin{aligned}
V &= D + S \\
&= \$9,666,667 + \$10,858,824 \\
&= \$20,525,491.
\end{aligned}$$

$$\begin{aligned}
P_1 &= \frac{\text{New total value} - \text{New value of old debt}}{\text{Old shares outstanding}} \\
&= \frac{\$20,525,491 - (\$200,000/0.12)}{600,000} = \$31.43.
\end{aligned}$$

In this case, the old stockholders gain from the use of increased leverage, and they also extract a further gain from the old bondholders. This illustrates why bond indentures place restrictions on the sale of future debt issues.

e.
$$\text{TIE} = \frac{\text{EBIT}}{\text{I}}.$$

$$\text{Original TIE} = \frac{\$4,000,000}{\$200,000} = 20 \text{ times.}$$

$$\text{New TIE} = \frac{\$4,000,000}{\$1,200,000} = 3.33 \text{ times.}$$

Selected Additional References and Cases

Chapter 11 provided references on the theory of capital structure; the references listed here are oriented more toward applications than theory.

Donaldson's work on the setting of debt targets is old but still relevant:

Donaldson, Gordon, "New Framework for Corporate Debt Capacity," *Harvard Business Review,* March–April 1962, 117–131.

———, "Strategy for Financial Emergencies," *Harvard Business Review,* November–December 1969, 67–79.

Definitive references on the empirical relationship between capital structure and (1) the cost of debt, (2) the cost of equity, (3) earnings, and (4) the price of a firm's stock are virtually nonexistent — statistical problems make the precise estimation of these relationships extraordinarily difficult, if not impossible. One good way to get a feel for the issues involved is to obtain a set of the cost of capital testimonies filed in a major utility rate case — such testimony is available from state public utility commissions, the Federal Communications Commission, the Federal Energy Regulatory Commission, and utility companies themselves. For an academic discussion of the issues, see

Caks, John, "Corporate Debt Decisions: A New Analytical Framework," *Journal of Finance,* December 1978, 1297–1315.

Gordon, Myron J., *The Cost of Capital to a Public Utility* (East Lansing, Mich.: Division of Research, Graduate School of Business Administration, Michigan State University, 1974).

Hamada, Robert S., "The Effect of the Firm's Capital Structure on the Systematic Risk of Common Stocks," *Journal of Finance,* May 1972, 435–452.

Masulis, Ronald W., "The Impact of Capital Structure Change on Firm Value: Some Estimates," *Journal of Finance,* March 1983, 107–126.

Shalit, Sol S., "On the Mathematics of Financial Leverage," *Financial Management,* Spring 1975, 57–66.

Shiller, Robert J., and Franco Modigliani, "Coupon and Tax Effects on New and Seasoned Bond Yields and the Measurement of the Cost of Debt Capital," *Journal of Financial Economics,* September 1979, 297–318.

To learn more about the link between market risk and operating and financial leverage, see

Gahlon, James M., and James A. Gentry, "On the Relationship between Systematic Risk and the Degrees of Operating and Financial Leverage," *Financial Management,* Summer 1982, 15–23.

See the following three articles for additional insights into the relationship between industry characteristics and financial leverage:

Bowen, Robert M., Lane A. Daley, and Charles C. Huber, Jr., "Evidence on the Existence and Determinants of Inter-Industry Differences in Leverage," *Financial Management,* Winter 1982, 10–20.

Long, Michael, and Ileen Malitz, "The Investment-Financing Nexus: Some Empirical Evidence," *Midland Corporate Finance Journal,* Fall 1985, 53–59.

Scott, David F., Jr., and John D. Martin, "Industry Influence on Financial Structure," *Financial Management,* Spring 1975, 67–73.

For a more thorough discussion of the international implications of capital structure, see

Rutterford, Janette, "An International Perspective on the Capital Structure Puzzle," *Midland Corporate Finance Journal,* Fall 1985, 60–72.

The following cases contain many of the concepts we present in Chapters 11 and 12:

Crum, Roy L., and Eugene F. Brigham, *Cases in Managerial Finance* (Hinsdale, Ill.: Dryden, 1987):

Case 29, "Floral Fancy Plant Company," which shows the effect of leverage on EPS and stock price.

Case 30, "Elektra Aerospace Corporation," which illustrates how operating and financial leverage interact to affect a firm's value.

Case 31, "Sanitary Solutions," which concentrates on the effect of financial leverage on a firm's value and WACC.

Harrington, Diana, *Cases in Financial Decision Making* (Hinsdale, Ill.: Dryden, 1985):

"Marriott," which illustrates several ways to measure debt capacity when determining the optimal capital structure.

13
Dividend Policy

On February 13, 1987, when its stock was selling for close to $100 per share, General Electric announced that it was considering a 2-for-1 stock split. Also, the company announced that it was considering boosting its dividend by 4.8 percent. The dividend increase would follow an 8.6 percent increase that took effect only three months earlier. GE's last stock split, also a 2-for-1 distribution, occurred in June 1983, when its shares were trading at $102. The 1987 split would be the company's sixth since 1892. In the past, GE has split the stock when the shares traded at $100 or more.

Analysts expected the split announcement, but they expressed surprise at the planned dividend increase. Although GE has raised its dividend in each of the past 11 years, the company has recently timed its dividend increases so that all four quarterly payouts during a calendar year are equal. Martin A. Sankey, an analyst with First Boston, said "This latest increase comes out of cycle. GE executives appear to like what is happening to earnings, so they are sharing the wealth with stockholders." Indeed, John F. Welch, GE's chairman and chief executive officer, stated "The potential dividend boost reflects our confidence in both the short- and long-range prospects for the company."

What factors prompted GE to split its shares and raise its dividend? What impact does a firm's dividend policy and/or stock splits have on the value of its stock? When GE announced the dividend increase and split, its share price rose by $5.375 to $103.50, but analysts debated whether the increase was due to the split, the dividend increase, or the fact that the company's actions signaled to investors that earnings were likely to increase sharply in the future. Thus, there are questions about the effects of dividend policy on value, and hence about the optimal dividend policy for a firm. However, in this chapter we do provide some clues, and after reading it you can form your own opinions about dividend policy and its effects.

Dividend policy involves the decision to pay out earnings versus retaining them for reinvestment in the firm. An examination of the constant growth stock price model, $\hat{P}_0 = D_1/(k_s - g)$, indicates that a policy of paying out more cash dividends, which raises D_1, will tend to increase the price of the stock. However, if

457

cash dividends are increased, then less money will be available for reinvestment; this will reduce the expected growth rate, which in turn will depress the price of the stock. Thus, a change in dividends has two opposing effects, and *the optimal dividend policy strikes the balance that investors in the aggregate want between current dividends and future growth, thereby maximizing the price of a firm's stock.*

A firm that pays out some of its earnings as dividends is limiting its retained earnings, and hence the asset expansion it can finance with relatively cheap internal equity. Further expansion is possible, of course, but it will have to be supported either by the sale of more expensive new common stock or with debt. Thus, for any given rate of asset expansion, decisions on dividend policy also imply decisions on new stock issues or on capital structure. In this chapter, we examine the factors which the financial manager should consider when setting the firm's dividend policy.

DIVIDEND POLICY THEORIES

Many factors influence dividend policy, including the number of good investment opportunities available to the firm, the availability and cost of alternative sources of capital, stockholders' preferences for current versus future income, and the signals dividend actions give to investors regarding management's expectations about future operations. Our major goal in this chapter is to show how these and other factors interact to influence a firm's optimal dividend policy. We begin by examining three theories of dividend policy: (1) The dividend irrelevance theory, (2) the "bird-in-the-hand" theory, and (3) the tax differential theory.

Dividend Irrelevance

In the first important theoretical work on dividend policy, Merton Miller and Franco Modigliani (MM) argued that dividend policy has no effect on either the price of a firm's stock or its cost of capital—MM stated that dividend policy is *irrelevant.*[1] They reasoned that the value of the firm is determined by its basic earnings power and its risk class, and therefore that the firm's value depends on its asset investment policy rather than on how earnings are split between dividends and retained earnings. MM demonstrated, under a particular set of assumptions, that if a firm pays higher dividends, then it must sell more stock to new investors, and that the share of the value of the company given up to new investors is exactly equal to the dividends paid out. For example, if IBM's capital budget calls for the expenditure of $1 billion in 1988, and if the company expects $1 billion of earn-

---

[1]See Merton H. Miller and Franco Modigliani, "Dividend Policy, Growth, and the Valuation of Shares," *Journal of Business,* October 1961, 411–433. For a summary of their proof, see Eugene F. Brigham and Louis C. Gapenski, *Intermediate Financial Management,* 2nd ed., Appendix 11A.

ings, then (1) it could pay all of its earnings out as dividends and finance the capital budget by selling $1 billion of new stock, (2) it could retain the entire $1 billion of earnings, sell no new stock, and provide stockholders with a capital gain of $1 billion, or (3) it could pick a payout anywhere between 0 to 100 percent and thus provide stockholders with a total of $1 billion in dividends and capital gains.

MM proved their proposition theoretically, but only under these five assumptions: (1) There are no personal or corporate income taxes. (2) There are no stock flotation or transaction costs. (3) Dividend policy has no effect on the firm's cost of equity. (4) The firm's capital investment policy is independent of its dividend policy. (5) Investors and managers have the same set of information (symmetric information) regarding future investment opportunities.

The MM assumptions are very strong, and they obviously do not hold precisely. Firms and investors do pay income taxes, firms do incur flotation costs, investors do incur transactions costs, both taxes and transactions costs could cause k_s to be affected by dividend policy, and managers often have better information than outside investors. Thus, the MM conclusions on dividend irrelevancy may not be valid under real world conditions. Therefore, since their article appeared in 1961, other theories have been put forth.

"Bird-in-the-Hand" Theory

One critical assumption inherent in MM's dividend irrelevance theory is that dividend policy does not affect investors' required rates of return on equity, k_s. This issue has been hotly debated in academic circles. Myron Gordon and John Lintner, on the one hand, argued that k_s increases as the dividend payout is reduced, because investors can be more sure of receiving dividend payments than the income from capital gains which should result from retaining earnings.[2] They say, in effect, that investors value a dollar of expected dividends more highly than a dollar of expected capital gains because the dividend yield component, D_1/P_0, is less risky than the g component in the total expected return equation, $\hat{k}_s = D_1/P_0 + g$.

On the other hand, MM argued that investors are indifferent between D_1/P_0 and g, and hence that k_s is not affected by dividend policy. MM call the Gordon-Lintner argument "the bird-in-the-hand fallacy" because, in MM's view, many if not most investors are going to reinvest their dividends in the same or similar firms anyway, and, in any event, the riskiness of the firm's cash flows to investors in the long run is determined only by the riskiness of its asset cash flows, not by its dividend payout policy.[3]

---

[2]See Myron J. Gordon, "Optimal Investment and Financing Policy," *Journal of Finance,* May 1963, 264–272; and John Lintner, "Dividends, Earnings, Leverage, Stock Prices, and the Supply of Capital to Corporations," *Review of Economics and Statistics,* August 1962, 243–269.

[3]Academicians other than MM have also rebutted the "bird-in-the-hand" theory. For example, see Michael Brennan, "A Note on Dividend Irrelevance and the Gordon Valuation Model," *Journal of Finance,* December 1971, 1115–1121.

Tax Differential Theory

In Chapter 2, where we discussed U.S. tax laws, we pointed out that up until 1986, only 40 percent of long-term capital gains were taxed. Thus, an investor in the 50 percent marginal tax bracket paid a 50 percent tax rate on his or her dividend income, but only $(0.4)(0.5) = 20\%$ on long-term capital gains. Further, by not selling stock, the investor could defer realization of the capital gains and hence payment of the tax, and since a dollar paid in the future is less valuable than a dollar paid today, the deferral feature provides yet another advantage to capital gains. Under current tax laws, capital gains and dividend income are taxed at the same statutory rate, but the deferral feature still exists.

To illustrate, suppose an individual investor in the 28 percent tax bracket is considering the purchase of two stocks: Stock G, which is a growth stock with a 10 percent capital gains yield and a 5 percent dividend yield, and Stock Y, which is a yield stock with a 5 percent capital gains yield and a 10 percent dividend yield. Both stocks sell for $10, have the same risk, and are constant growth stocks, and hence $\hat{k}_G = \hat{k}_Y =$ Dividend yield + Capital gains yield = 15% on a before-tax basis. Table 13-1 shows the expected after-tax rates of return on Stocks G and Y for selected holding periods. For all holding periods except one year, the after-tax yield on Stock G is greater than the after-tax yield on Stock Y. Further, the after-tax yield differential increases as the holding period increases. Stock G has the higher after-tax yield because a larger percentage of its return comes from capital gains, and these taxes are deferred until the end of the holding period. Of course, under the old tax laws, when capital gains were taxed at a lower rate as well as deferred, the yield differentials were even more pronounced.

Table 13-1
After-Tax Rates of Return: Stock G and Stock Y

Stock	Holding Period in Years					
	1	2	3	4	5	∞
G	10.80%	10.94%	11.07%	11.20%	11.32%	13.60%
Y	10.80	10.87	10.94	11.00	11.07	12.20
Yield Differential	0.00	0.07	0.13	0.20	0.25	1.40

Note: The after-tax rates of return in Table 13-1 were calculated as follows: (1) Determine the after-tax dollar dividend for each year during the holding period; (2) calculate the after-tax capital gain and the end-of-holding-period cash flow; and (3) calculate the IRR of the resulting cash flow stream, which is the expected after-tax rate of return. For example, Stock G's after-tax rate of return for a two-year holding period was found in this way: (1) Stock G sells for $10 and has a 5 percent dividend yield. Thus, $D_1 = \$10(0.05) = \$0.50$ and $D_2 = D_1(1 + g) = \$0.50(1.10) = \$0.55$. T = 28% and hence $(1 - T) = 0.72$, so the after-tax dividend stream is $D_{1AT} = \$0.50(0.72) = \$0.36$ and $D_{2AT} = \$0.55(0.72) = \$0.396$. (2) $\hat{P}_{2AT} = P_0(1 + g)^2 = \$10(1.10)^2 = \$12.10$. Thus, the Year 2 capital gain is $\$12.10 - \$10.00 = \$2.10$, the tax is $\$2.10(0.28) = \$0.588$, and the after-tax proceeds from the sale are $\$12.10 - \$0.588 = \$11.512$. (3) The after-tax cash flows are $CF_0 = -\$10.00$, $CF_1 = \$0.36$, and $CF_2 = \$0.396 + \$11.512 = \$11.908$. The IRR of this stream, which is Stock G's expected after-tax rate of return, is 10.94 percent.

Tax-paying investors with long holding periods would recognize that Stock G offers a higher after-tax return than Stock Y, and hence would bid up the price of G relative to Y. Thus, Stock G's price might rise to $10.25, while Stock Y's might fall to $9.75. The end result would be a higher before-tax yield on Stock Y than on Stock G, but equal after-tax returns to the marginal investor. If investors in the aggregate behave in this way, the result would be higher pre-tax rates of return on high dividend yield stocks than on low dividend yield stocks.

TESTS OF DIVIDEND THEORIES

In the preceding section, we presented three theories of dividend policy:

1. MM argued that dividend policy is irrelevant; that is, dividend policy does not affect a firm's value or its cost of capital. Thus, according to MM, there is no optimal dividend policy — one dividend policy is as good as any other.

2. Gordon and Lintner disagreed with MM, arguing that dividends are less risky than capital gains, so a firm should set a high dividend payout ratio and offer a high dividend yield in order to minimize its cost of capital. MM disagreed, and they called this the "bird-in-the-hand fallacy."

3. A third group, whose position is the reverse of Gordon-Lintner, stated that since dividends are effectively taxed at higher rates than capital gains, investors require higher rates of return on stocks with high dividend yields. According to this theory, a firm should pay a low (or zero) dividend in order to minimize its cost of capital and maximize its value.

These three theories offer contradictory advice to corporate managers. MM say dividend policy doesn't matter, Gordon-Lintner say set a high payout, and the tax differential advocates say set a low payout. Which theory should we believe?

Two primary types of empirical tests have been conducted in an attempt to determine the true relationship between dividend policy and required returns. In theory, one could take a sample of companies which have different dividend policies, and hence different dividend yield and growth rate components, and plot them in graphs such as those shown in Figure 13-1.[4] Here we show three possible results. Only one result could actually exist, but we show three possibilities on one graph. If the plot resembled the center line in the graph, then, for the sample of firms, $\hat{k}_s = k_s = D_1/P_0 + g = $ a constant 13.3% for all dividend policies — both the X and Y axes have an intercept of 13.3 percent. In this case, the equilibrium total return would be a constant whether it comes entirely as a dividend yield (the Y-axis intercept), entirely as expected capital gains (the X-axis intercept), or as any combination of the two. The line has a slope of -1.0, and if the test actually resulted in this line, then it would support the MM irrelevance hypothesis.

---

[4]The earliest such test was Eugene F. Brigham and Myron J. Gordon, "Leverage, Dividend Policy, and the Cost of Capital," *Journal of Finance,* March 1968, 85–104. In work done in conjunction with writing this chapter, we reexamined the issue and reached the conclusions reported herein.

Figure 13-1
Alternative Views of the Effects of Dividend Policy

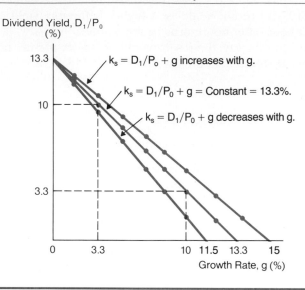

If the plot looked like the upper line in Figure 13-1, with a slope less negative (less steep) than -1.0 (say -0.8), then the test would support the Gordon-Lintner "bird-in-the-hand" hypothesis. Here investors would require a larger total return if the company provided a larger capital gains component, g, than dividend yield, D_1/P_0. An all-dividend stock would have $k_s = 13.3\%$, while a stock which provides only capital gains would have $k_s = 15.0\%$. Thus, more than 1 percent of additional g is required to offset a 1 percent reduction in the lower-risk dividend yield.

Finally, if the tax differential theory were correct, the plot would resemble the lower line in Figure 13-1, with a slope more negative (steeper) than -1.0 (say -1.2). Here the deferral of capital gains taxes causes investors to favor capital gains over dividends. In this situation, an all-dividend stock might have $k_s = 13.3\%$, while a similar stock whose returns all come as capital gains might have $k_s = 11.5\%$. Thus, less than 1 percent of additional g would be required to offset a 1 percent reduction in dividend yield.

In fact, when such tests have been conducted with reasonably good data, the slope of the regression line is found to be about -1.0. This seems to refute both Gordon-Lintner and tax differential advocates, and to support MM. However, statistical problems prevent us from saying that these tests *prove* that MM are right and that dividend policy does not affect k_s. The two statistical problems are these: (1) For a valid statistical test, things other than dividend policy must be held constant;

that is, the sample companies must differ only in their dividend policies. (2) We must be able to measure with a high degree of accuracy the expected growth rates for the sample firms.[5] Neither of these two conditions actually holds: We cannot find a set of publicly owned firms that differ only in their dividend policies, nor can we obtain precise estimates of the growth rates which the marginal investor expects. Therefore, we cannot determine with much precision what effect, if any, dividend policy has on the cost of equity. Our conclusion is that this particular type of test is not capable of solving the dividend policy riddle.

Researchers have also studied the dividend yield effect from a CAPM perspective. They hypothesized that required returns are a function of both market risk, as measured by beta, and dividend yield. If so, then a stock's required return, k_i, could be expressed as follows:

$$k_i = k_{RF} + (k_M - k_{RF})b_i + (D_i - D_M)\lambda_i. \tag{13-1}$$

Here, D_i is the dividend yield of Stock i, D_M is the dividend yield of an average stock, and λ_i is the dividend impact coefficient. Researchers have tested Equation 13-1 by regressing historic values of k_{RF}, k_M, D_i, and D_M against historic values of k_i. If the coefficient of λ_i turns out to be zero, dividend yield would not appear to affect required returns and MM would be supported. If λ_i were positive, then investors would appear to require a higher return on stocks with high dividend yields, as the tax differential theory predicts. If λ_i were negative, this would support Gordon-Lintner.

The results of this line of research have been mixed. Litzenberger and Ramaswamy showed, using NYSE data from 1936 through 1977, that stocks with high dividend yields did have higher total yields than did stocks with low dividend yields, after adjusting for market risk.[6] Their study indicates that investors' required rates of return increased about 0.24 percentage points for every percentage point increase in dividend yield. However, other studies have reached contradictory conclusions; namely, that the λ_i term is zero and consequently that dividend yield has no effect on required returns.[7] (Of course, when these studies were conducted, capital gains and dividend income were taxed at different rates.) The major problem with all of these studies is that they used historical earned rates of return as proxies for expected future returns, and with such a poor proxy, the tests are almost bound to have mixed results. Thus, these CAPM empirical tests, like the pure DCF-based tests, have not led to definitive conclusions as to which dividend theory is most correct. The issue is still unresolved.

---

[5] Also, the expected future growth rate must be constant, or we must measure g as an average of expected future growth rates. This complicates the problem of estimating the correct growth for use in the empirical tests.

[6] See Robert H. Litzenberger and Krishna Ramaswamy, "The Effect of Personal Taxes and Dividends on Capital Asset Prices," *Journal of Financial Economics,* June 1979, 163–196.

[7] For example, see Fischer Black and Myron Scholes, "The Effects of Dividend Yield and Dividend Policy on Common Stock Prices and Returns," *Journal of Financial Economics,* May 1974, 1–22.

OTHER DIVIDEND POLICY ISSUES

Before we discuss dividend policy in practice, we need to examine two other theoretical issues that could affect our views toward the three theories presented earlier. These issues are (1) the information content, or signaling, hypothesis, and (2) the clientele effect.

Information Content, or Signaling, Hypothesis

The MM dividend irrelevance theory assumes, among other things, that everyone — investors and managers alike — has an identical opinion about the firm's future operations and hence about its expected future earnings and dividend stream. In reality, however, investors have conflicting opinions regarding both the level of future dividend payments and the degree of uncertainty inherent in those payments, and managers often have better information about future prospects than public stockholders.

It has been observed that an increase in the dividend is often accompanied by an increase in the price of the stock, while a dividend cut generally leads to a stock price decline. This could suggest that investors, in the aggregate, prefer dividends to capital gains. However, MM argued differently. They noted the well-established fact that corporations are always reluctant to cut dividends, and hence do not raise dividends unless they anticipate equal or higher earnings in the future. Thus, MM argued that a higher-than-normal dividend increase is a "signal" to investors that the firm's management forecasts good future earnings.[8] Conversely, a dividend reduction, or a smaller-than-normal increase, is a signal that management is forecasting poor earnings in the future. Thus, MM claim that investors' reactions to changes in dividend policy do not necessarily show that investors prefer dividends to retained earnings. Rather, the fact that price changes follow dividend actions simply indicates to MM that there is an important *information,* or *signaling, content* in dividend announcements.

Like most other aspects of dividend policy, empirical studies on this topic have been inconclusive. There clearly is some information content in dividend announcements. However, it is difficult to tell whether stock price changes that follow increases or decreases in dividends reflect only signaling effects or both signaling and dividend preference effects, because these increases or decreases typically include both a change in the percentage payout ratio and a change in the dollars of dividends paid.

---

[8]Stephen Ross has suggested that managers can use capital structure as well as dividends to give signals concerning firms' future prospects. For example, a firm with good earnings prospects can carry more debt than a similar firm with poor earnings prospects. This theory, called "incentive-signaling," rests on the premise that signals based on cash-based variables (either debt interest or dividends) cannot be mimicked by unsuccessful firms because such firms do not have the future cash-generating power to maintain the announced interest or dividend payment. Thus, investors are more likely to believe a glowing verbal report when it is accompanied by a dividend increase or a debt-financed expansion program. See Stephen A. Ross, "The Determination of Financial Structure: The Incentive-Signaling Approach," *The Bell Journal of Economics,* Spring 1977, 23–40.

Clientele Effect

Different groups, or *clienteles,* of stockholders prefer different dividend payout policies. For example, some stockholders such as retired individuals and university endowment funds prefer current income, so they would want the firm to pay out a higher percentage of its earnings. Such investors are often in a low or even zero tax bracket, so taxes are of no concern. On the other hand, stockholders in their peak earning years prefer reinvestment, because they have no need for current investment income and would simply reinvest any dividends received, after first paying income taxes on the dividend income.

If the firm retains and reinvests income, rather than paying dividends, those stockholders who need current income would be disadvantaged. They would receive capital gains, but they would be forced to go to the trouble and expense of selling off some of their shares to obtain cash. Also, some institutional investors (or trustees for individuals) may be precluded from selling stock and then "spending capital." The other group, the stockholders who are saving rather than spending dividends, would favor the low dividend policy, for the more the firm pays out in dividends, the more these stockholders will have to pay in current taxes and the more trouble and expense they will have to go through to reinvest their after-tax dividends. Thus, investors who desire current investment income should own shares in high dividend payout firms, while investors with no need for current investment income should own shares in low dividend payout firms.

To the extent that stockholders can shift their investments among firms, a firm can set the specific policy that seems appropriate to its management and then let stockholders who do not like this policy sell to other investors who do. However, switching may be inefficient because of (1) brokerage costs, (2) the likelihood that stockholders who are selling will have to pay capital gains taxes (the "lock-in effect"), and (3) a possible shortage of investors in the aggregate who like the firm's newly adopted dividend policy. Thus, management might be reluctant to change its dividend policy, because such changes might cause current shareholders to sell their stock, forcing the stock price down. Such a price decline might be temporary, but it might also be permanent—if few investors were attracted by the new dividend policy, then the stock price would remain depressed. Of course, it is possible that the new policy would attract an even larger clientele than the firm had previously, and if so, the stock price would rise.

Evidence from several studies suggests that there is in fact a clientele effect.[9] However, MM and others have argued that one clientele is as good as any other, so the existence of a clientele effect does not imply that one dividend policy is better than any other dividend policy. Still, neither MM nor anyone else has offered proof that the aggregate makeup of investors permits firms to disregard clientele effects. This issue, like most others in the dividend arena, is still up in the air.

---

[9]For example, see R. Richardson Pettit, "Taxes, Transactions Costs and the Clientele Effect of Dividends," *The Journal of Financial Economics,* December 1977, 419–436.

DIVIDEND POLICY IN PRACTICE

We noted above that there are three conflicting theories as to what type of dividend policy firms *should* follow. We also noted that empirical tests do not answer the question of which theory is correct. In this section, we present four alternative dividend payment policies that firms actually *do* follow. As a part of this discussion, we discuss a number of factors which are not generally discussed by the theorists but which do influence dividend policy in practice.

Residual Dividend Policy

In practice, dividend policy is influenced by both investment opportunities and the availability of funds to finance those opportunities. This fact has led to the development of the *residual dividend policy,* under which a firm follows these four steps when deciding its payout ratio: (1) It determines the optimal capital budget; (2) it determines the amount of equity needed to finance that budget; (3) it uses retained earnings to supply this equity to the extent possible; and (4) it pays dividends only if more earnings are available than are needed to support the optimal capital budget. The word *residual* implies "left over," and the residual policy implies that dividends are paid out of "leftover" earnings.

We saw in Chapter 7 that the cost of retained earnings is an *opportunity cost* which reflects rates of return available to equity investors. If a firm's stockholders could buy other stocks of equal risk and obtain a 12 percent dividend-plus-capital-gains yield, then 12 percent is the firm's cost of retained earnings. The cost of new outside equity raised by selling common stock is higher because of the costs of floating the issue, including both underwriting costs and any downward price pressure resulting from "negative signals" investors might get from the announcement of a stock offering.

Also, most firms have a target capital structure that calls for at least some debt, so new financing is done partly with debt and partly with equity. As long as the firm finances with the optimal mix, using the proper amounts of debt and equity, and provided it uses only internally generated equity (retained earnings), its marginal cost of each new dollar of capital will be minimized. Internally generated equity is available for financing a certain amount of new investment, but beyond that amount, the firm must turn to more expensive new common stock. At the point where new stock must be sold, the cost of equity, and consequently the weighted average cost of capital (k_a = WACC), rises.

These concepts, which were developed in Chapters 7 and 10, are illustrated in Figure 13-2 with data from the Dallas Oil Company (DOC). DOC has a WACC of 10 percent as long as retained earnings are available, but its MCC schedule begins to rise at the point where new stock must be sold. DOC has $60 million of earnings and a 40 percent optimal debt ratio. Provided it does not pay cash dividends, DOC can make net investments (investments in addition to asset replacements financed from depreciation) of $100 million, consisting of $60 million from retained earnings plus $40 million of new debt supported by the retained earnings, at a 10 percent cost of capital. Therefore, its WACC is constant at 10 percent up

Figure 13-2
Dallas Oil Company:
Marginal Cost of Capital Schedule

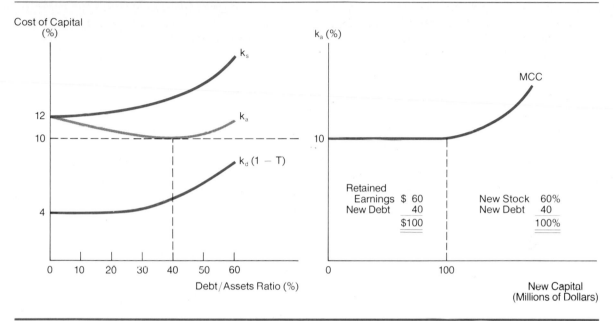

to $100 million of capital. Beyond $100 million, the WACC rises as the firm begins to use more expensive new common stock.

Of course, if DOC does not retain all of its earnings, its WACC will begin to rise before $100 million. For example, if DOC retained only $30 million, then its WACC would begin to rise at $30 million retained earnings + $20 million debt = $50 million.

Now suppose DOC's director of capital budgeting constructs several investment opportunity schedules and plots them on a graph. The investment opportunity schedules for three different years — a good year (IOS$_G$), a normal year (IOS$_N$), and a bad year (IOS$_B$) — are shown in Figure 13-3. DOC can invest the most money, and at the highest rates of return, when the investment opportunities are as given by IOS$_G$.

In Figure 13-4, we combine these investment opportunity schedules with the cost of capital schedule. The point where the relevant IOS curve cuts the MCC curve defines the firm's marginal cost of capital and its optimal level of new investment. When investment opportunities are relatively bad (IOS$_B$), the optimal level of investment is $40 million; when opportunities are normal (IOS$_N$), $70 million should be invested; and when opportunities are relatively good (IOS$_G$), DOC should make new investments in the amount of $150 million.

Figure 13-3
Dallas Oil Company:
Investment Opportunity (or IRR) Schedules

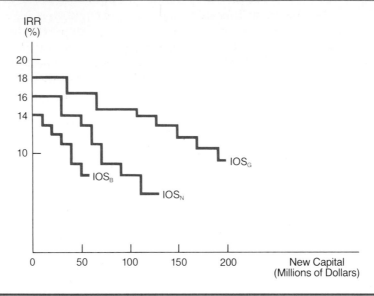

Figure 13-4
Dallas Oil Company:
Combined IOS and MCC Schedules

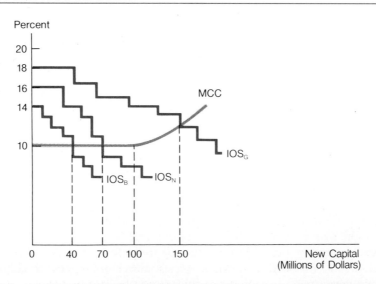

If IOS_G is the appropriate schedule, the company should raise and invest $150 million. DOC has $60 million in earnings and a 40 percent target debt ratio. Thus, it can finance $100 million, consisting of $60 million of retained earnings plus $40 million of new debt, at an average cost of 10 percent if it retains all of its earnings. The remaining $50 million will include external equity and thus have a higher cost. If DOC pays out part of its earnings in dividends, it will have to begin to use costly new common stock earlier than need be, so its MCC schedule will rise earlier than it otherwise would. *This suggests that under the conditions of IOS_G, DOC should retain all of its earnings. According to the residual policy, DOC's payout ratio should be zero if IOS_G applies.*

Under the conditions of IOS_N, however, DOC should invest only $70 million. How should this investment be financed? First, notice that if DOC retained all of its earnings, $60 million, it would need to sell only $10 million of new debt. However, if DOC retained $60 million and sold only $10 million of new debt, it would move away from its target capital structure. To stay on target, DOC must finance 60 percent of the required $70 million by equity — retained earnings — and 40 percent by debt; this means DOC must retain $42 million and sell $28 million of new debt. If DOC retains only $42 million of its $60 million total earnings, it must distribute the residual, $18 million, to its stockholders. Thus, its optimal payout ratio under IOS_N is $18/$60 = 30\%$.

Under the conditions of IOS_B, DOC should invest only $40 million. Because it has $60 million in earnings, it could finance the entire $40 million out of retained earnings and still have $20 million available for dividends. Should this be done? Under our assumptions, this would not be a good decision, because DOC would move away from its optimal capital structure. To stay at the 40 percent target debt/assets ratio, DOC must retain $24 million of earnings and sell $16 million of debt. When the $24 million of retained earnings is subtracted from the $60 million total earnings, DOC is left with a residual of $36 million, the amount that should be paid out in dividends. Thus, the payout ratio as prescribed by the residual policy is $36/$60 = 60 percent.

If either the IOS schedule or the earnings level varies from year to year, strict adherence to the residual dividend policy would result in dividend variability — one year, when investment opportunities are good, the firm would declare zero dividends, whereas the next year the same firm, with poor investment opportunities, might declare a large dividend. Similarly, fluctuating profits would lead to variable dividends, even if investment opportunities were stable over time. As we will see shortly, such fluctuations could lead to an increase in k_s. As a result, few if any firms follow the residual theory exactly. However, as we also discuss, many firms do use the residual theory concept to help establish a long-run target payout ratio.

Constant or Steadily Increasing Dividends

In the past, many firms set a specific annual dollar dividend per share and then maintained it, increasing the annual dividend only if it seemed clear that future earnings would be sufficient to allow the new dividend to be maintained. A corollary of that policy was this rule: *Try to avoid ever having to reduce the annual dividend.*

More recently, inflation has tended to push up earnings, so most firms that would otherwise have followed the stable dividend payment policy have switched over to what is called the "stable growth rate" policy. Here the firm sets a target growth rate for dividends, say 6 percent per year, and strives to increase dividends by this amount each year. Obviously, earnings must be growing at a reasonably steady rate for this to be feasible.

Both a stable payment policy and a stable growth rate policy, using data for Morris Pharmaceuticals, Inc., over a 38-year period, are illustrated in Figure 13-5. Initially, in 1950, earnings were $2 a share and dividends were $1 a share, so the payout ratio was 50 percent. During most of the 1950s, earnings fluctuated, but no clear trend was evident, so the dividend was kept at the $1 level. However, by the early 1960s, earnings had increased above earlier levels, causing the payout ratio to drop below 50 percent. Further, management believed the new earnings would be sustained, so the company raised the dividend in three steps to $1.50 to re-establish the 50 percent payout. During 1965 a strike caused earnings to fall below the regular dividend. Expecting the earnings decline to be temporary, management

Figure 13-5
Morris Pharmaceuticals, Inc.:
Dividends and Earnings over Time

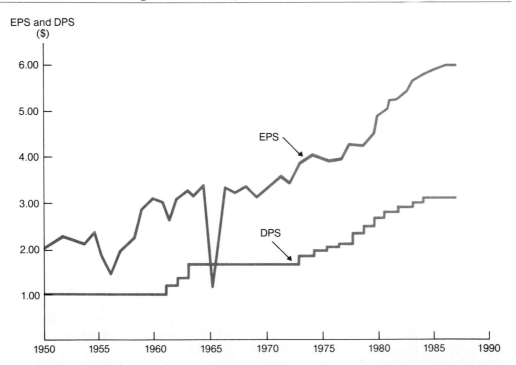

maintained the $1.50 dividend. Earnings fluctuated on a fairly high plateau from 1966 through 1973, during which time dividends remained constant.

Due in large part to inflation, earnings grew rather steadily during the 1970s and early 1980s, and investors came to expect most successful companies to increase dividends at a rate which, they hoped, would offset inflation. Therefore, after 1973 management adopted the policy of increasing the dividend annually. Inflation, and hence Morris' earnings growth, began to subside in the mid-1980s, and, in 1985, management made the decision to revert back to a constant dividend policy, with dividend increases occurring only after earnings gains.

There are several logical reasons for following a stable, predictable dividend policy. First, given the existence of the information content (or signaling) hypothesis, a fluctuating payment policy might lead to greater uncertainty, a higher k_s, and consequently a lower stock price than would exist under a stable policy. Second, stockholders who use dividends for current consumption want to be able to count on receiving dividends on a regular basis, so irregular dividends might lower demand for the stock and cause its price to decline. Therefore, even though the optimal payout prescribed by the residual policy might vary somewhat from year to year, a mix of actions such as delaying some investment projects, departing from the target capital structure during a particular year, or even selling common stock would be preferable to cutting the dividend or reducing the growth rate investors expect.

Constant Payout Ratio

A very few firms follow a policy of always paying out a constant percentage of earnings. Earnings will surely fluctuate, so following this policy necessarily means that the dollar amount of dividends will fluctuate. For reasons discussed in the preceding section, this policy is not likely to maximize a firm's stock price. Before its bankruptcy, Penn Central Railroad did follow the policy of paying out one-half its earnings: "A dollar for the stockholders and a dollar for the company," as one director put it. Logic like this could drive any company to bankruptcy!

Note, though, that many companies do have *target payout ratios* that are based on the residual theory. For example, Morris Pharmaceuticals has, over the period 1950–1987, paid out an average of about 50 percent of its earnings, even though the payout ratio is not constant on a year-to-year basis. The 50 percent long-run target payout is based on investment opportunities and capital availability as determined in a residual analysis study.

Low Regular Dividend plus Extras

A policy of paying a low regular dividend plus a year-end extra in good years is another commonly encountered policy. It gives the firm flexibility, yet investors can count on receiving at least a minimum dividend. Therefore, if a firm's earnings and cash flows are quite volatile, this policy may well be its best choice. The directors can set a relatively low regular dividend — low enough so that this dividend can be maintained even in low-profit years or in years when a considerable amount of retained earnings is needed — and then supplement it with an extra dividend in years when excess funds are available. General Motors, whose earnings fluctuate widely from year to year, has long followed such a policy, declaring the extra dividend toward the end of the year, when its profits and investment requirements are known. Eastman Kodak Company has also followed this policy. Recently, Kodak declared an extra $0.25 per share dividend along with its regular $0.55 quarterly dividend.

Payment Procedures

Dividends are normally paid quarterly. For example, Consolidated Insurance Company (CIC) paid dividends of $3.00, $0.75 each quarter, during 1987. In common financial language, we say that CIC's *regular quarterly dividend* is $0.75 or that its *regular annual dividend* is $3.00. The actual payment procedure is as follows:

1. Declaration date. CIC's directors meet each quarter and declare the regular dividend. On the basis of their August 14, 1987 meeting the directors issued the following statement: "On August 14, 1987, the directors of CIC met and declared the regular quarterly dividend of 75 cents per share, payable to holders of record on September 15, payment to be made on October 2, 1987."

2. Holder-of-record date. At the close of business on the *holder-of-record date,* September 15, the company closes its stock transfer books and makes up a list of the shareholders as of that date. If CIC is notified of the sale and transfer of some stock before 5 p.m. on September 15, the new owner receives the dividend. However, if notification is received on or after September 16, the previous owner of the stock gets the dividend check.

3. Ex-dividend date. Suppose Jean Buyer buys 100 shares of CIC stock from John Seller on September 11. Will the company be notified of the transfer in time to list Buyer as the new owner and thus pay the dividend to her? To avoid conflict, the stock brokerage business has set up a convention of declaring that the right to the dividend remains with the stock until the close of business four *business days* prior to the holder-of-record date; on the fourth day before the record date, the right to the dividend no longer goes with the shares. The date when the right to the dividend leaves the stock is called the *ex-dividend date.* In this case, the ex-dividend date is six days prior to September 15, or September 9, because September 12 and 13, 1987 are nonbusiness days:

	September 8
Ex-dividend date:	September 9
	September 10
	September 11
	September 14
Holder-of-record date:	September 15

Therefore, if Buyer is to receive the dividend, she must buy the stock by September 8. If she buys it on September 9 or later, Seller will receive the dividend.

The CIC dividend amounts to $0.75, so the ex-dividend date is important. Barring fluctuations in the stock market, we would normally expect the price of a stock to drop by approximately the amount of the dividend on the ex-dividend date. Thus, if CIC closed at $30¾ on September 8, it would probably open at about $30 on September 9.[10]

4. Payment date. The company actually mails the checks to the holders of record on October 2, the payment date.

Dividend Reinvestment Plans

During the 1970s, most large companies instituted *dividend reinvestment plans,* or *DRPs,* whereby stockholders can automatically reinvest their dividends in the stock of the paying corporation.[11] Today it is estimated that about 1,000 companies offer DRPs and, although participation rates vary considerably, on average about 25 percent of the firms' shareholders are enrolled. There are two types of DRPs: (1) plans which involve only "old stock" that is already outstanding, and (2) plans which involve newly issued stock. In either case, the stockholder must pay income taxes on the amount of the dividends, even though stock rather than cash is received.

Under both types of DRP, the stockholder elects either to continue receiving dividend checks or to use the dividends to buy more stock in the corporation. Under the "old stock" type of plan, if the stockholder elects reinvestment, a bank, acting as trustee, takes the total funds available for reinvestment (less a fee), purchases the corporation's stock on the open market, and allocates the shares purchased to the participating stockholders' accounts on a pro rata basis. The transactions costs of buying shares (brokerage costs) are low because of volume purchases, so these plans benefit small stockholders who do not need cash dividends for current consumption.

---

[10]Tax effects actually cause the price decline, on average, to be less than the full amount of the dividend. Suppose you were an investor in the 50 percent federal-plus-state tax bracket. If you bought CIC's stock on September 8, you would receive the dividend but then have to pay half of it out in taxes. Thus, you would want to wait until September 9 to buy the stock, if you thought you could get it for $0.75 per share less. Your reaction, and that of others, would influence stock prices around dividend payment dates. Here is what would happen:

1. Other things held constant, a stock's price should rise during the quarter, with the daily price increase (for CIC) equal to $0.75/90 = $0.0083. Therefore, if it started at $30 just after its last ex-dividend date, it would rise to $30.75 on September 8.

2. In the absence of taxes, the stock's price would fall to $30 on September 9, and it would then start moving up again as the next dividend accrual period began. Thus, over time, if everything else were held constant, the stock's price would follow a sawtooth pattern, with the depth of each tooth being $0.75.

3. Because of taxes, the stock's price will not rise by the full amount of the dividend, or fall by the full dividend amount when it goes ex dividend.

4. The amount of the rise and subsequent fall depends on the marginal investor's marginal tax rate. See Edwin J. Elton and Martin J. Gruber, "Marginal Stockholder Tax Rates and the Clientele Effect," *Review of Economics and Statistics,* February 1970, 68−74, for an interesting discussion of these topics.

[11]See Richard H. Pettway and R. Phil Malone, "Automatic Dividend Reinvestment Plans," *Financial Management,* Winter 1973, 11−18, for an excellent discussion of the subject.

The "new stock" type of DRP provides for dividends to be invested in newly issued stock; hence, these plans raise new capital for the firm. AT&T, Xerox, Union Carbide, and many other companies have had such plans in effect in recent years, using them to raise substantial amounts of new equity capital. No fees are charged to stockholders, and many companies offer stock at a discount of 5 percent below the actual market price. The companies absorb these costs as a trade-off against flotation costs that would be incurred if stock were sold through investment bankers rather than through the dividend reinvestment plans. Discussions with corporate treasurers suggest that many other companies are seriously considering establishing or switching to new-stock DRPs.[12]

SUMMARY OF FACTORS THAT INFLUENCE DIVIDEND POLICY

In earlier sections, we described the major theories of how dividend policy affects the value of a firm, and we discussed four alternative payment policies. Firms choose a particular policy based on managements' beliefs concerning the dividend theories, plus a host of other factors. All of the factors which are taken into account may be grouped into four broad categories: (1) constraints on dividend payments, (2) investment opportunities, (3) availability and cost of alternative sources of capital, and (4) effects of dividend policy on k_s. Each of these categories has several subparts. They are all discussed in the following paragraphs.

Constraints

1. Bond indentures. Debt contracts often restrict dividend payments to earnings generated after the loan was granted. Also, debt contracts frequently stipulate that no dividends can be paid unless the current ratio, the times-interest-earned ratio, and other safety ratios exceed stated minimums.

2. Preferred stock restrictions. Typically, common dividends cannot be paid if the company has omitted (passed) its preferred dividend. The preferred arrearages must be satisfied before common dividends can be resumed.

3. Impairment of capital rule. Dividend payments cannot exceed the balance sheet item "retained earnings." This legal restriction, known as the "impairment of

---

[12]One interesting aspect of DRPs is that they are forcing corporations to reexamine their basic dividend policies. A high participation rate in a DPR suggests that stockholders might be better off if the firm simply reduced cash dividends to save stockholders some personal income taxes. Quite a few firms are surveying their stockholders to learn more about their preferences and to find out how they would react to a change in dividend policy. A more rational approach to basic dividend policy decisions may emerge from this research.

Note that companies use or stop the use of new-stock DRPs depending on their need for equity capital. Thus, both Union Carbide and AT&T recently stopped offering a new-stock DRP with a 5 percent discount because their needs for equity capital declined, but Xerox began such a plan in 1986.

capital rule," is designed to protect creditors. (*Liquidating dividends* can be paid out of capital, but they must be indicated as such and must not reduce capital below limits stated in the firm's debt contracts.)

4. Availability of cash. Cash dividends can only be paid with cash. Thus, a shortage of cash in the bank can restrict dividend payments. However, unused borrowing capacity can offset this factor.

5. Penalty tax on improperly accumulated earnings. To prevent wealthy individuals from using corporations to avoid personal taxes, the Tax Code provides for a special surtax on improperly accumulated income. Thus, if the IRS can demonstrate that the dividend payout ratio is being deliberately held down to help stockholders avoid personal taxes, heavy penalties will be imposed on the firm. However, as a practical matter, the penalty has been applied only to privately owned firms.

Investment Opportunities

1. Location of the IOS schedule. If the relevant IOS schedule in Figure 13-4 is far to the right, this will tend to produce a low payout ratio, and conversely if the IOS is far to the left.

2. Possibility of accelerating or delaying projects. The ability to accelerate or postpone projects will permit a firm to set and then maintain a high payout. If projects could not be delayed, then prudence would dictate a lower payout to avoid a possible later forced dividend reduction.

Alternative Sources of Capital

1. Cost of issuing new stock. If a firm needs to finance a given level of investment, it can obtain equity by retaining earnings or by issuing new common stock. If flotation costs and downward price pressure are high, k_e will be well above k_s, making it much better to finance through retention than through sale of new common stock. On the other hand, if these costs are low, dividend policy will be less important. Flotation and downward pressure costs differ among firms. For example, these costs are generally higher for small than for large firms. Hence, the importance of equity issuance costs, and consequently the degree of flexibility in setting a dividend policy, varies among firms.

2. Control. If management is concerned about maintaining control, it may be reluctant to sell new stock, and hence may retain more earnings than it otherwise would. This factor is especially important for small, closely held firms.

3. Capital structure flexibility. As we have seen, if stock issuance costs are low, a high payout ratio is more feasible, because additional equity can be raised whenever necessary by selling new stock. A similar situation holds for debt policy. If the firm can adjust its debt ratio without seriously affecting its cost of capital, then it can maintain a constant dollar dividend or constant growth rate by using a variable debt ratio. The shape of the average cost of capital curve (left panel in Figure 13-2) determines the practical extent to which the debt ratio can be varied. If the average cost of capital curve is relatively flat over a wide range, then capital structure policy is less critical than it would be if the curve had a "V" shape with a distinct minimum, and consequently a relatively flat cost of capital curve makes it easier to pay out a high percentage of earnings and still follow a constant dollar dividend or constant growth rate dividend policy.

Effects of Dividend Policy on k_s

The effects of dividend policy on k_s may be considered in terms of these four factors: (1) deferral of capital gains taxes, (2) stockholders' desire for current versus future income, (3) perceived riskiness of dividends versus capital gains, and (4) the information content of dividends (signaling). Since we discussed each of these factors in detail earlier, we need only note here that the importance of each factor's effect on k_s varies from firm to firm, depending on the makeup of its stockholders. Management certainly ought to take its own stockholders' views into account when it sets its dividend policy.

AN APPROACH TO SETTING DIVIDEND POLICY

In many ways our discussion of dividend policy parallels our discussion of optimal capital structure: We have both presented the relevant theories and listed the key factors thought to influence dividend policy, but we have not come up with any hard-and-fast rules to follow when establishing a payout policy. It should be apparent from our discussion that dividend policy decisions are truly exercises in informed judgment, and not decisions that can be based on a precise mathematical model.

In general, firms set dividend policies within the framework of their overall financial plans. Thus, a firm's key strategic decisions — those related to capital budgeting, to capital structure, and to dividend policy — are interrelated. A decision in one area impacts decisions in the other two, and hence these decisions, in practice, must be made simultaneously. The primary tool used to assist decision makers is the firm's financial plan, which often consists of a short-term plan, usually for one year, and a long-term plan, usually covering five years.

A key element in these plans are the financial forecasts, which are usually developed by a financial planning model similar to the one we described in Chapter 12 in connection with setting the target capital structure. In such a model, the firm's investment opportunities, capital structure, and dividend policy (payout ratio) can all be changed, and managers can assess the impact of such changes on external financing requirements, on ROE, on EPS, and so on. In general, the driving force of the model is the firm's planned capital expenditures. Once its capital budget has been established (at least on a first approximation basis), the financial manager can then focus on capital structure and dividend policy decisions. The target capital structure is chosen to minimize the firm's WACC as we discussed in the previous chapter, and a dividend policy is established consistent with the investment and capital structure decisions.

An established firm typically sets its dividend policy in this way: (1) A long-run (5-year) target payout range is determined such that the firm can meet its equity financing requirement with retained earnings. Because of flotation costs and negative signaling effects, firms do not want to issue new common equity unless such action is absolutely necessary. (2) An actual dollar dividend per share is selected so that there is an extremely low probability that the dividend, once set, will have to be lowered, or worse yet, omitted. Further, the initial dividend will generally be set low enough so that it can be raised by some amount (say 6 percent) each year under normal operating conditions.

Of course, these decisions are being made in the planning process, so there exists a considerable amount of uncertainty concerning future investment opportunities and cash flows. Variances from forecasted data will mean that the required retention ratio will be higher or lower than forecast, and hence earnings available for dividends will fluctuate from the predicted values. The degree of this uncertainty must be considered when setting dividend policy. If there is a great deal of uncertainty in the forecasts of cash inflows and required cash outflows, then the firm will be conservative and set a relatively low initial dollar dividend, for this will minimize the probability that the firm will have to either reduce the dividend or sell new common stock.

STOCK REPURCHASES

As an alternative to paying cash dividends, a firm may distribute income to stockholders by *repurchasing its own stock*, and stock that has been repurchased by a firm is called *treasury stock*. If some of the outstanding stock is repurchased and held as treasury stock, fewer shares will remain outstanding. Assuming the repurchase does not adversely affect the firm's earnings, the earnings per share on the remaining shares will increase, resulting in a higher market price per share, which means that capital gains will have been substituted for dividends.

Companies have been repurchasing their stock in record amounts in recent years. For example, in 1985 Phillips Petroleum repurchased about 81 million shares of common stock having a total value of over $4.1 billion, the largest repurchase on record, and in 1986, IBM repurchased about 16 million shares valued at $2.1 billion. Other billion dollar repurchases in 1986 were made by Union Carbide, Goodyear, SmithKline, Ameritech, GM, and Federated Department Stores.

Most of these very large repurchase programs were part of a general corporate restructuring, wherein certain major assets, such as whole divisions or subsidiaries, were sold off, or where the debt ratio was increased substantially. Asset sales and the issuance of new debt both bring in additional capital, and this capital can then be distributed to stockholders through a major, one-time stock repurchase. A repurchase that is part of a corporate restructuring is quite different from a "regular" repurchase, where the repurchase is merely a substitute for cash dividends as a method for distributing corporate income to shareholders.

The effects of a "regular" repurchase can be illustrated with data on American Development Corporation (ADC). The company expects to earn $4.4 million in 1988, and 50 percent of this amount, or $2.2 million, has been allocated for distribution to common shareholders. There are 1,100,000 shares outstanding, and the market price is $20 a share. ADC could use the $2.2 million to repurchase 100,000 of its shares through a tender offer for $22 a share, or it could pay a cash dividend of $2 a share.[13]

The effect of the repurchase on the EPS and market price per share of the remaining stock can be determined in the following way:

1. $\text{Current EPS} = \dfrac{\text{Total earnings}}{\text{Number of shares}} = \dfrac{\$4.4 \text{ million}}{1.1 \text{ million}} = \$4 \text{ per share.}$

2. $\text{Current P/E ratio} = \dfrac{\$20}{\$4} = 5\times, \text{ assumed to remain constant.}$

3. $\dfrac{\text{EPS after repurchase}}{\text{of 100,000 shares}} = \dfrac{\$4.4 \text{ million}}{1 \text{ million}} = \$4.40 \text{ per share.}$

4. $\begin{aligned}\text{Expected market price} \\ \text{after repurchase}\end{aligned} = (\text{P/E})(\text{EPS}) = (5)(\$4.40)$

$$= \$22 \text{ per share.}$$

5. Expected capital gains per remaining share $= \$22 - \$20 = \$2.00.$

It should be noticed from this example that investors would receive benefits of $2 per share in any case, either in the form of a $2 cash dividend or a $2 increase in the stock price. This result occurs because we assumed (1) that shares could be repurchased at exactly $22 a share and (2) that the P/E ratio would remain constant. If shares could be bought for less than $22, the repurchase would be even better for *remaining* stockholders, but the reverse would hold if ADC paid more than $22 a share. Furthermore, the P/E ratio might change as a result of the repurchase, rising if investors viewed the repurchase favorably and falling if they viewed it unfavorably. Some factors that might affect P/E ratios are considered next.

---

[13]Stock repurchases are commonly made in three ways. First, a publicly owned firm can simply buy its own stock through a broker on the open market. Second, it can issue a *tender,* under which it permits stockholders to send in (that is, "tender") their shares to the firm in exchange for a specified price per share. When tender offers are made, the firm generally indicates that it will buy up a specified number of shares within a particular time period (usually about two weeks); if more shares are tendered than the company wishes to purchase, then purchases are made on a pro rata basis. Finally, the firm can purchase a block of shares from one or more large holders on a negotiated basis. If a negotiated purchase is employed, care should be taken to insure that these stockholders do not receive preferential treatment not available to other stockholders.

Advantages of Repurchases from the Stockholder's Viewpoint

1. Repurchase announcements may be viewed as positive signals by investors because the repurchase could be motivated by management's belief that the firm's shares are undervalued. For example, Teledyne, a $3 billion conglomerate, earns about $400 million per year, yet it has not paid a cash dividend in over 20 years. Profits are, however, used to repurchase stock and thus to stimulate growth. Teledyne's stock rose from $4 in 1975 to $355 in 1986, so the company is clearly doing something right!

2. The stockholder has a choice — to sell or not to sell. On the other hand, one must accept a dividend payment and pay the tax. Thus, Teledyne stockholders who want cash can sell some of their shares, and those who do not need cash can simply retain their stock and defer their tax liabilities.

3. A qualitative advantage advanced by market practitioners is that repurchase can often remove a large block of stock which is overhanging the market and keeping the price per share down.

Advantages of Repurchases from Management's Viewpoint

1. As noted earlier, dividends are "sticky" in the short run because managements are reluctant to raise dividends if the new dividend cannot be maintained in the future — because of signaling effects, managements dislike cutting cash dividends. Hence, if the excess cash flow is thought to be only *temporary,* management may prefer to make the distribution in the form of a share repurchase rather than to declare a cash dividend which they believe cannot be maintained.

2. Repurchased stock can be used for acquisitions or released when stock options are exercised, when convertibles are converted, or when warrants are exercised. Discussions with financial managers indicate that they often like to use repurchased stock rather than newly issued stock for these purposes so as to avoid dilution of per share earnings. To illustrate the first two points, in March 1986 Rockwell International, a major manufacturer of aerospace, automotive, and electronic products, announced a $500 million stock repurchase program that reduced its common shares outstanding by about 8 percent. This buyback was financed from earnings from B1-B bomber sales, a source which will not continue indefinitely. Further, some analysts speculated that the repurchased stock will eventually be used to acquire another firm.

3. Repurchases are the only practical alternative when management has decided to undertake a major restructuring such as a large asset sale, a substantial increase in the debt ratio, or a combination of the two. For example, at one time American Standard (a major plumbing supply company) had virtually no long-term debt outstanding. The company decided that its optimal capital structure called for the use of considerably more debt, but even if it had financed only with debt, it would have taken years to get the debt ratio up to the new target. What should the company do? It decided to sell long-term debt and to use the proceeds to repurchase its common stock, thus producing an instantaneous change in its capital structure.

4. Treasury stock can be resold in the open market if the firm needs additional funds.[14]

Disadvantages of Repurchases from the Stockholder's Viewpoint

1. The price of the stock might benefit more from cash dividends than from repurchases, because cash dividends are generally thought to be relatively dependable, but repurchases are not. Further, if a firm announces a regular, dependable repurchase program, the improper accumulation tax would become more of a threat. Although Teledyne has apparently had no problems in this regard, Teledyne's repurchases are irregular, which makes a difference.

2. The *selling* stockholders may not be fully aware of all the implications of a repurchase, or they may not have all the pertinent information about the corporation's present and future activities. However, firms generally announce a repurchase program before embarking on it to avoid potential lawsuits from selling stockholders.

3. The corporation may pay too high a price for the repurchased stock, to the disadvantage of remaining stockholders. If the shares are inactively traded, and if the firm seeks to acquire a relatively large amount of its own stock, the price may be bid above its equilibrium price. If so, the price will fall after the firm ceases its repurchase operations.

Disadvantages of Repurchases from Management's Viewpoint

1. Some people have argued that firms which repurchase substantial amounts of stock often have poorer growth rates and fewer good investment opportunities than firms which do not engage in repurchases. If the announcement of a repurchase program is taken as a signal that the firm has especially unfavorable growth opportunities, then there could be an adverse impact on the price of its stock. However, if the firm really does have a shortage of good investment opportunities, then it would probably be better for management to distribute funds to investors, who could then redeploy the funds elsewhere in the market. There is, in our view, little empirical support for the position that stockholders dislike repurchases.[15]

---

[14]Another interesting use of stock repurchases was St. Joe Minerals' strategy of repurchasing its own stock to thwart an attempted takeover. Seagram Company was attempting to acquire a controlling interest in St. Joe through a tender offer of $45 a share. St. Joe's management countered with a tender offer of its own for seven million shares at $60 per share, to be financed by the sale of several divisions plus borrowings. Similarly, Texaco recently bought back over $1 billion of its stock from the Bass brothers of Texas, who were rumored to be planning a takeover of Texaco. Texaco paid the Bass brothers a premium of about 40 percent over the market price. Some Texaco stockholders sued management, arguing that Texaco's management was giving away corporate assets in order to preserve their own jobs. This type of payment is called "greenmail."

[15]In fact, there is some evidence that the stocks of companies which repurchased large quantities of their common stock in the 10 years from 1974 through 1983 had above-average stock price appreciation. See "Beating the Market By Buying Back Stock," *Fortune*, April 29, 1985, 42–48.

2. Repurchases might involve some risk from a legal standpoint. If the Internal Revenue Service could establish that the repurchases were primarily for the avoidance of taxes on dividends, then penalties could be imposed on the firm under the improper accumulation of earnings provision of the Tax Code. Such actions have been brought against privately held companies, but we know of no case involving a publicly owned firm, even though some firms have retired over one-half of their outstanding stock.

3. The SEC could raise questions if it appears that the firm may be manipulating the price of its shares. This factor, in particular, keeps firms from doing much repurchasing if they plan offerings of other types of securities in the near future, or if they contemplate merger negotiations where their stock would be exchanged for that of the acquired company.

Conclusions on Stock Repurchases

When all the pros and cons on stock repurchases are totaled, where do we stand? Our conclusions may be summarized as follows:

1. Repurchases on a regular, systematic, dependable basis may not be feasible because of uncertainties both about the tax treatment of such a program and about such factors as the market price of the shares, how many shares would be tendered, and so forth.

2. However, repurchases do offer investors tax deferral advantages over dividends, so this procedure should be given careful consideration on the basis of the firm's unique situation.

3. Repurchases can be especially valuable to a firm that is restructuring and consequently wants to significantly increase its debt ratio within a short period or else to dispose of cash generated from the sale of assets.

STOCK DIVIDENDS AND STOCK SPLITS

Stock dividends and stock splits are related to the firm's cash dividend policy. The rationale for stock dividends and splits can best be explained through an example; we will use the Nashville Company, a large multimedia entertainment company specializing in country and western music, in our illustrations.

Nashville's markets are expanding, and as the company continues to grow and to retain earnings, its book value per share should also grow. More important, its earnings per share and market price per share should also rise. The company began its life with only a few thousand shares outstanding. After some years of growth, each share had a very high EPS and DPS. When a "normal" P/E ratio was applied to the stock, the derived market price was so high that few people could afford to buy a "round lot" of 100 shares. This limited the demand for the stock, thus keeping the total market value of the firm below what it would have been if more shares, at lower prices, were outstanding. To correct this situation, Nashville "split its stock" as described next.

Stock Splits

Although there is little empirical evidence to support the contention, there is nevertheless a widespread belief in financial circles that an *optimal price range* exists for stocks. "Optimal" means that if the price is in this range, the price/earnings ratio, and hence the value of the firm, will be maximized. Many observers, including Nashville's management, believe that the best range for most New York Stock Exchange stocks is from $20 to $80 per share. Companies whose shares are owned largely by institutions tend to move toward the high end of the range, while those owned largely by individuals, such as the public utilities, generally operate in the lower end of the range. Companies with average institutional ownership, like Nashville Company, cluster in the $30 to $50 range. Accordingly, if the price of Nashville's stock rose to $80, management would probably declare a two-for-one stock split, thus doubling the number of shares outstanding, halving the earnings and dividends per share, and thereby lowering the price of the stock. Each stockholder would have more shares, but each share would be worth less. If the post-split price were $40, Nashville's stockholders would be exactly as well off as they were before the split. If the price of the stock were to stabilize above $40, stockholders would be better off. Stock splits can be of any size. For example, the stock could be split two-for-one, three-for-one, 1.5-for-one, or in any other way.[16]

Stock splits can also be used to increase the "float," or the number of shares held by outsiders. For example, Care Corporation, a nursing home operator, recently declared a 4-for-1 split, in large part because about 60 percent of the company's 500,000 shares outstanding were controlled by insiders and relatives, leaving only 200,000 shares for trading by others. The split increased the float to 800,000 which, according to the firm's management, increased the trading activity in the stock. Note, though, that academic studies have suggested that stock splits actually lower trading volume when measured on a proportional basis, primarily because brokerage commissions are increased.[17]

Stock Dividends

Stock dividends are similar to stock splits in that they divide the pie into smaller slices without affecting the fundamental position of the current stockholders. On a 5 percent stock dividend, the holder of 100 shares would receive an additional five shares (without cost); on a 20 percent stock dividend, the same holder would receive 20 new shares; and so on. Again, the total number of shares is increased, so earnings, dividends, and price per share all decline.

---

[16]*Reverse splits,* which reduce the shares outstanding, can even be used. For example, a company whose stock sells for $5 might employ a one-for-five reverse split, exchanging one new share for five old shares and raising the value of the shares to about $25, which is within the "acceptable" range. LTV Corporation did this after several years of losses had driven its stock price down below the optimal range.

[17]Commissions are generally higher on trades of, say, 75 shares at $10 per share than on a trade of 10 shares at $75 a share, even though the dollar value of the trades is the same. For a further discussion of the effects of stock splits on market liquidity, see Thomas E. Copeland, "Liquidity Changes Following Stock Splits," *Journal of Finance,* March 1979, 115–141.

Table 13-2
Nashville Company:
Stockholders' Equity Accounts, Pro Forma 12/31/88

1. *Before a stock split or a stock dividend*

Common stock (6 million shares authorized, 5 million outstanding, $1 par)	$ 5,000,000
Additional paid-in capital	10,000,000
Retained earnings	155,000,000
Total common stockholders' equity	$170,000,000

2. *After a two-for-one stock split*

Common stock (12 million shares authorized, 10 million outstanding, $0.50 par)	$ 5,000,000
Additional paid-in capital	10,000,000
Retained earnings	155,000,000
Total common stockholders' equity	$170,000,000

3. *After a 20 percent stock dividend*

Common stock (6 million shares authorized, 6 million outstanding, $1 par)[a]	$ 6,000,000
Additional paid-in capital[b]	89,000,000
Retained earnings[b]	75,000,000
Total common stockholders' equity	$170,000,000

[a]Shares outstanding are increased by 20 percent, from 5 million to 6 million.

[b]A transfer equal to the market value of the new shares is made from the retained earnings account to the additional paid-in capital and common stock accounts: Transfer = (1 million shares)($80) = $80 million. Of this $80 million, (1 million shares)($1 par) = $1 million goes to common stock and $79 million to paid-in capital.

If a firm wants to reduce the price of its stock, should a stock split or a stock dividend be used? Stock splits are generally used after a sharp price run-up, when a large price reduction is sought. Stock dividends are frequently used on a regular annual basis to keep the stock price more or less constrained. For example, if a firm's earnings and dividends are growing at about 10 percent per year, the price would tend to go up at about that same rate, and the price would soon be outside the desired trading range. For this company, a 10 percent annual stock dividend would maintain the stock price within the optimal trading range.

Although the economic effects of stock splits and stock dividends are virtually identical, accountants treat them somewhat differently. On a two-for-one split, the shares outstanding are doubled, and the stock's par value is halved. This treatment is shown in Table 13-2, Section 2, for Nashville Company, using a pro forma 1988 balance sheet.

With a stock dividend, the par value is not reduced, but an accounting entry is made transferring capital from the retained earnings account to the common stock and paid-in capital accounts. The transfer from retained earnings is calculated as follows:

$$\begin{pmatrix} \text{Dollars} \\ \text{transferred from} \\ \text{retained} \\ \text{earnings} \end{pmatrix} = \begin{pmatrix} \text{Number} \\ \text{of shares} \\ \text{outstanding} \end{pmatrix} \begin{pmatrix} \text{Percentage} \\ \text{of the} \\ \text{stock dividend} \end{pmatrix} \begin{pmatrix} \text{Market} \\ \text{price of} \\ \text{the stock} \end{pmatrix}.$$

For example, if Nashville, which had 5 million shares outstanding selling at $80 each, declared a 20 percent stock dividend, the transfer would be

$$\text{Dollars transferred} = (5 \text{ million})(0.2)(\$80) = \$80,000,000.$$

As shown in Section 3 of Table 13-2, $1 million of this $80 million transfer would be added to the common stock account and $79 million to the additional paid-in capital account. The retained earnings account would be reduced from $155 to $75 million.[18]

Price Effects

If a company splits its stock or declares a stock dividend, will this action increase the market value of its stock? Several empirical studies have sought to answer this question, and in general here are their findings:[19]

1. On average, the price of a company's stock rises shortly after it announces a stock split or dividend.

2. However, these price increases appear to be more the result of the fact that investors take stock splits/dividends as signals of higher earnings and dividends than of a desire for stock dividends/splits per se. Since only those companies whose managements think things look good tend to use stock splits/dividends, the announcement of a stock split is taken as a signal that earnings and cash dividends are likely to rise. Thus, the price increases that are associated with stock splits/dividends may be the result of signals of favorable prospects for earnings and dividends, not a desire for stock splits/dividends per se.

3. It has been observed that if a company announces a stock split or dividend, its price will tend to rise. However, if during the next few months it does not announce earnings and dividends above the levels expected before the split/stock dividend, then its stock price will drop back to the earlier level.

4. As we noted earlier, brokerage commissions are higher in percentage terms on lower priced stocks. This means that it is more expensive to trade low-priced than

---

[18]Note that Nashville could not pay a stock dividend that exceeded 38.75 percent; a stock dividend of that percentage would exhaust the retained earnings. Thus, a firm's ability to declare stock dividends is constrained by the amount of its retained earnings. Of course, if Nashville had wanted to pay a 50 percent stock dividend, it could just switch to a 1.5-for-1 stock split and accomplish the same objective.

[19]See Eugene F. Fama, Lawrence Fisher, Michael C. Jensen, and Richard Roll, "The Adjustment of Stock Prices to New Information," *International Economic Review,* February 1969, 1–21; Mark S. Grinblatt, Ronald M. Masulis, and Sheridan Titman, "The Valuation Effects of Stock Splits and Stock Dividends," *Journal of Financial Economics,* December 1984, 461–490; C. Austin Barker, "Evaluation of Stock Dividends," *Harvard Business Review,* July–August 1958, 99–114; and Copeland op. cit.

high-priced stocks, and this in turn means that stock splits reduce the liquidity of a company's shares. This particular piece of evidence suggests that stock splits/ dividends are actually harmful.

What do we conclude from all this? From a pure economic standpoint, stock dividends and splits are just additional pieces of paper. However, they do provide management with a relatively low-cost way of signaling that the firm's prospects look good. Further, we should note that since no large, publicly owned stocks sell at prices above several hundred dollars, we simply do not know what the effect would be if IBM, Xerox, Hewlett-Packard, and other highly successful firms had never split their stock and consequently sold at prices in the thousands or even tens of thousands of dollars. All in all, it probably makes sense to employ stock dividends/splits when a firm's prospects are favorable, especially if the price of its stock has gone beyond the normal trading range.

SUMMARY

Dividend policy reflects the firm's decision to pay out earnings versus retaining them for reinvestment in the firm. Any change in dividend policy has both favorable and unfavorable effects on the price of the firm's stock: Higher dividends mean higher near-term cash flows to investors, which is good, but lower future growth, which is bad. The optimal dividend policy balances these opposing forces and maximizes the price of the stock.

We first identified three dividend theories: (1) *dividend irrelevance,* (2) *"bird-in-the-hand",* and (3) *tax differential.* We then described a number of factors that affect dividend policy, including the following: *legal constraints* such as bond indenture provisions, the firm's *investment opportunities,* the *availability and cost of funds from other sources* (new stock and debt), *stockholders' desire for current income,* and the *information effect* of dividend changes. Because of the large number of factors that influence dividend policy, and also because the relative importance of these factors changes over time and across companies, it is impossible to develop a precise, generalized model for use in establishing dividend policy.

The *residual dividend policy* is used by most firms to set a long-run target payout, but most firms set their actual dividends either (1) as a *stable or continuously increasing dollar dividend* per share or (2) as a *low regular dividend plus extras* that depends on annual earnings. Also, we noted that many firms today are using *dividend reinvestment plans* to help stockholders reinvest dividends at minimal brokerage costs.

We also discussed *stock repurchases,* both as an element in corporate restructuring programs and also as an alternative to cash dividends. Repurchases have certain advantages — especially tax deferral — over dividends, but repurchases also have disadvantages. The volume of repurchase activity has been quite high in recent years, and barring adverse changes in our tax laws, this activity should continue or even increase.

Stock splits and *stock dividends* were also discussed. Our conclusion was that these actions may be beneficial if the firm's stock price is quite high, but otherwise they have little effect on the value of the firm.

Questions

13-1 Define each of the following terms:

a. Optimal dividend policy

b. Dividend irrelevance theory

c. "Bird-in-the-hand" theory

d. Tax differential theory

e. Residual dividend policy

f. Constraints on dividend policy

g. Clientele effect

h. Information content of dividends; signaling

i. Extra dividend

j. Ex-dividend date

k. Dividend reinvestment plans (each of two types)

l. Stock split; stock dividend

m. Stock repurchase

13-2 As an investor, would you rather invest in a firm that has a policy of maintaining (a) a constant payout ratio, (b) a constant dollar dividend per share, (c) a target dividend growth rate, or (d) a constant regular quarterly dividend plus a year-end extra when earnings are sufficiently high or corporate investment needs are sufficiently low? Explain your answer, stating how these policies would affect your k_s.

13-3 How would each of the following changes probably affect aggregate (that is, the average for all corporations) payout ratios? Explain your answers.

a. An increase in the personal income tax rate. The corporate tax rate.

b. A liberalization in depreciation for federal income tax purposes, that is, faster tax writeoffs.

c. A rise in interest rates.

d. An increase in corporate profits.

e. A decline in investment opportunities.

f. Reinstatement of a differential (lower) capital gains tax rate.

13-4 Discuss the pros and cons of having the directors formally announce what a firm's dividend policy will be in the future.

13-5 Most firms would like to have their stock selling at a high P/E ratio and also have an extensive public ownership (many different shareholders). Explain how stock dividends or stock splits may help achieve these goals.

13-6 What is the difference between a stock dividend and a stock split? As a stockholder, would you prefer to see your company declare a 100 percent stock dividend or a two-for-one split? Assume that either action is feasible.

13-7 "The cost of retained earnings is less than the cost of new outside equity capital. Consequently, it is totally irrational for a firm to sell a new issue of stock and to pay dividends during the same year." Discuss this statement.

13-8 Would it ever be rational for a firm to borrow money in order to pay dividends? Explain.

13-9 Union representatives have presented arguments similar to the following: "Corporations such as General Motors retain about one-half their profits for financing needs. If they financed by selling stock instead of by retaining earnings, they could raise wages substantially and still earn enough to pay the same dividend to their shareholders. Therefore, their profits are too high." Evaluate this statement.

13-10 "Executive salaries have been shown to be more closely correlated to the size of the firm than to its profitability. If a firm's board of directors is controlled by management instead of by outside directors, this might result in the firm's retaining more earnings than can be justified from the stockholders' point of view." Discuss the statement, being sure (a) to use Figure 13-4 in your answer and (b) to explain the implied relationship between dividend policy and stock prices.

Problems

13-1 **(Dividend theories)** Modigliani and Miller, on the one hand, and Gordon and Lintner, on the other, have expressed strong views regarding the effect of dividend policy on a firm's cost of capital and value.
   a. In essence, what are the MM and the GL views regarding the effect of dividend policy on cost of capital and value? Illustrate your answer with a graph.
   b. How does the tax differential model differ from the views of MM and GL?
   c. According to the text, which position (MM, GL, or tax differential) has received statistical confirmation from empirical tests?
   d. How could MM use the information content, or signaling, hypothesis to counter their opponents' arguments? If you were debating MM, how would you counter them?
   e. How could MM use the clientele effect concept to counter their opponents' arguments? If you were debating MM, how would you counter them?

13-2 **(Residual dividend policy)** One position expressed in the literature is that firms should set their dividends as a residual, after using income to support new investment.
   a. Explain what a residual dividend policy implies, illustrating your answer with a graph showing how different conditions could lead to different dividend payout ratios.
   b. Could the residual dividend policy be consistent with (1) a constant dividend growth rate policy, (2) a constant payout policy, and/or (3) a low-regular-plus-extras policy? Explain.
   c. In Chapters 11 and 12, we considered the relationship between capital structure and the cost of capital. If the k_a = WACC versus debt ratio plot were shaped like a sharp V, would this have a different implication for the importance of setting dividends according to the residual policy than if the ratio relationship were shaped like a shallow bowl (or a U)?
   d. Companies A and B both have IOS schedules which intersect their MCC schedules at a point which, under the residual policy, calls for a 20 percent payout. In both cases, a 20 percent payout would require a cut in the annual dividend from $2 to $1. One company cut its dividend and accepted all projects, while the other did not cut its dividend and accepted less than the optimal number

of projects. One company had a relatively steep IOS curve, while the other had a relatively flat IOS. Explain which company had the steep, and which the flat, IOS.

13-3 (Stock dividends and splits) More NYSE companies had stock dividends and stock splits during 1983 and 1984 than ever before. What events in these years could have made stock splits and dividends so popular? Explain the rationale that a financial vice president might give the board of directors to support a stock split/dividend recommendation.

13-4 (Residual dividend policy) Bankston Manufacturing Corporation (BMC) has an all-equity capital structure which includes no preferred stock. It has 200,000 shares of $2 par value common stock outstanding.

When BMC's founder, who was also its research director and most successful inventor, died unexpectedly in 1988, BMC was left suddenly and permanently with materially lower growth expectations and relatively few attractive new investment opportunities. Unfortunately, there was no way to replace the founder's contributions to the firm. Previously, BMC had found it necessary to plow back most of its earnings to finance growth, which has been averaging 12 percent per year. Future growth at a 5 percent rate is considered realistic, but that level would call for an increase in the dividend payout. Further, it now appears that new investment projects with at least the 14 percent rate of return required by BMC's stockholders ($k_s = 14\%$) would amount to only $800,000 for 1988 in comparison to a projected $2,000,000 of net income after taxes. If the existing 20 percent dividend payout were continued, retained earnings would be $1.6 million in 1988, but as noted, investments which yield the 14 percent cost of capital amount to only $800,000.

The one encouraging thing is that the high earnings from existing assets are expected to continue and net income of $2 million is still expected for 1988. Given the dramatically changed circumstances, BMC's management is reviewing the firm's dividend policy.

    a. Assuming that the acceptable 1988 investment projects would be financed entirely by earnings retained during the year, calculate DPS in 1988 assuming BMC uses the residual payment policy.

    b. What payout ratio does this imply for 1988?

    c. If the increased payout ratio is maintained for the foreseeable future, what should be the present intrinsic value of the common stock? How does this compare with the price that should have prevailed under the assumptions existing just prior to the news about the death of the founder? If the two values of $\hat{P}_0$ are different, comment on why.

    d. What are the implications of continuing the 20 percent payout? Assume that if this payout is maintained then the average rate of return on the retained earnings will be 7.5 percent and the new growth rate will be

$$g = (1.0 - \text{Payout ratio})(\text{ROE})$$
$$= (1.0 - 0.2)(7.5\%) = (0.8)(7.5\%) = 6.0\%.$$

13-5 (Stock dividends) The board of directors of Strasburg Corporation declared a 4 percent stock dividend and a cash dividend of $0.40 per share in December 1987. The cash dividend will be paid on old shares *plus* shares received in the stock dividend. Construct a pro forma balance sheet that shows the effect of these actions; use one new balance sheet that incorporates both actions. The stock is selling for $25 per share.

A condensed version of Strasburg's balance sheet as of December 31, 1987, before the dividends, follows (in millions of dollars):

Cash	$ 50	Debt	$1,000
Other assets	1,950	Common stock (60 million shares authorized, 50 million shares outstanding, $1 par)	50
		Paid-in capital	200
		Retained earnings	750
Total assets	$2,000	Total claims	$2,000

13-6 (Dividend policy and capital structure) The Tennessee Bourbon Company (TBC) has for many years enjoyed a moderate but stable growth in sales and earnings. However, bourbon consumption has been falling recently, primarily because of an increasing use of lighter alcoholic beverages such as vodka and wines. Anticipating further declines in sales for the future, TBC's management hopes eventually to move almost entirely out of the liquor business and into a newly developed, diversified product line in growth-oriented industries. The company is especially interested in the prospects for pollution-control devices, because its research department has already done much work in this area. Right now the company estimates that an investment of $24 million is necessary to purchase new facilities and to begin operations on these products, but the investment could be earning a return of about 18 percent within a short time. The only other available investment opportunity totals $9.6 million, is expected to return about 11.2 percent, and is indivisible, that is, it must be accepted in its entirety or else be rejected.

The company is expected to pay a $2.00 dividend on its 7 million outstanding shares, the same as its dividend last year. The directors might, however, change the dividend if there are good reasons for doing so. Net income for the year is expected to be $22.5 million; the common stock is currently selling for $45; the firm's target debt ratio (debt/assets ratio) is 45 percent; and its tax rate is 34 percent. The costs of various forms of financing are listed below:

New bonds: $k_d = 11\%$. This is a before-tax rate.

New common stock sold at $45 per share will net $41.

Required rate of return on retained earnings: $k_s = 14\%$.

a. Calculate TBC's expected payout ratio, the break point where its MCC schedule rises, and its marginal cost of capital above and below the point of exhaustion of retained earnings at the current payout. (Hint: k_s is given, and D_1/P_0 can be found. Then, knowing k_s and D_1/P_0, and assuming constant growth, g can be determined.)

b. How large should TBC's capital budget be for the year?

c. What is an appropriate dividend policy for the firm? How should the capital budget be financed?

d. How might risk factors influence TBC's cost of capital, capital structure, and dividend policy?

e. What assumptions, if any, do your answers to the above make about investors' preferences for dividends versus capital gains, that is, their preferences regarding the D_1/P_0 and g components of k_s?

(Do Part f only if you are using the computerized diskette.).

f. Assume that TBC's management is considering a change in its capital structure to include more debt, and thus it would like to analyze the effects of an increase in the debt ratio to 60 percent. However, the treasurer believes that such a move would cause lenders to increase the required rate of return on new bonds to 12 percent and k_s would rise to 14.5 percent. How would this change affect the optimal capital budget? If k_s rose to 16 percent, would the low-return project be acceptable? Would the project selection be affected if the dividend were reduced to $1.25 from $2.00, still assuming k_s = 16 percent?

13-7 **(Stock repurchases)** Goldware, Inc., has earnings this year of $16.5 million, 50 percent of which is required to take advantage of the firm's excellent investment opportunities. The firm has 2,062,500 shares outstanding, selling currently at $32 per share. Greg Beaumont, a major stockholder (187,500 shares), has expressed displeasure with a great deal of managerial policy. Management has approached him about selling his holdings back to the firm, and he has expressed a willingness to do this at a price of $32 a share. Assuming that the market uses a constant P/E ratio of 4 in valuing the stock, should the firm buy Beaumont's shares? Assume that dividends will not be paid on Beaumont's shares if they are repurchased. (Hint: Calculate the ex-dividend price of the stock with and without the repurchase, and add to these values the dividends received to determine the remaining shareholders' value per share.)

Selected Additional References and Cases

Dividend policy has been studied extensively by academicians. The first major academic work, and still a classic that we recommend highly, is Lintner's analysis of the way corporations actually set their dividend payment policies:

Lintner, John, "Distribution of Incomes of Corporations among Dividends, Retained Earnings, and Taxes," *American Economic Review,* May 1956, 97–113.

The effects of dividend policy on stock prices and capital costs have been examined by many researchers. The classic theoretical argument that dividend policy is important, and that stockholders like dividends, was set forth by Gordon, while Miller and Modigliani (MM) developed the notion that dividend policy is not important. Many researchers have extended both Gordon's and MM's theoretical arguments, and have attempted to test the effects of dividend policy in a variety of ways. Although statistical problems have precluded definitive conclusions, the following articles, among others, have helped to clarify the issues:

Brennan, Michael, "Taxes, Market Valuation, and Corporate Financial Policy," *National Tax Journal,* Spring 1975, 417–427.

Hayes, Linda S., "Fresh Evidence That Dividends Don't Matter," *Fortune,* May 4, 1981, 351–354.

Lewellen, Wilbur G., Kenneth L. Stanley, Ronald C. Lease, and Gary G. Schlarbaum, "Some Direct Evidence on the Dividend Clientele Phenomenon," *Journal of Finance,* December 1978, 1385–1399.

Mukherjee, Tarun, and Larry M. Austin, "An Empirical Investigation of Small Bank Stock Valuation and Dividend Policy," *Financial Management,* Spring 1980, 27–31.

On stock dividends and stock splits, see

Baker, H. Kent, and Patricia L. Gallagher, "Management's View of Stock Splits," *Financial Management,* Summer 1980, 73–77.

Copeland, Thomas E., "Liquidity Changes Following Stock Splits," *Journal of Finance,* March 1979, 115–141.

On repurchases, see

Finnerty, Joseph E., "Corporate Stock Issue and Repurchase," *Financial Management,* Autumn 1975, 62–71.

Stewart, Samuel S., Jr., "Should a Corporation Repurchase Its Own Stock?" *Journal of Finance,* June 1976, 911–921.

Woolridge, J. Randall, and Donald R. Chambers, "Reverse Splits and Shareholder Wealth," *Financial Management,* Autumn 1983, 5–15.

For a survey of managers' views on dividend policy, see

Baker, H. Kent, Gail E. Farrelly, and Richard B. Edelman, "A Survey of Management Views on Dividend Policy," *Financial Management,* Autumn 1985, 78–84.

Other pertinent articles include

Brealey, Richard A., "Does Dividend Policy Matter?" *Midland Corporate Finance Journal,* Spring 1983, 17–25.

Woolridge, J. Randall, and Chinmoy Gosh, "Dividend Cuts: Do They Always Signal Bad News?" *Midland Corporate Finance Journal,* Summer 1985, 20–32.

The following cases from the Crum-Brigham casebook focus on the issues contained in this chapter:

Case 34, "Hansen Mineral Resources," which emphasizes the effect of dividend policy on stock prices.

Case 35, "Warner Body Works," which deals with virtually all the aspects of dividend policy.

The Harrington casebook contains the following applicable case:

"New Hampshire Savings Bank Corporation," which illustrates the traditional arguments set forth as the board of directors attempt to establish the company's dividend policy.

Part

V

Long-Term Financing Decisions

14

Common Stock, Preferred Stock, and the Investment Banking Process

The July 21, 1986 issue of *Fortune* contained a cover story titled "Inside the Deal that Made Bill Gates $350,000,000." The story presented a rare inside view of the five months of negotiation that culminated in Microsoft Corporation's going public.

Microsoft, a Seattle-based software maker for personal computers best known for developing the disk operating system (DOS) for IBM's PC line, was co-founded in 1975 by William H. Gates III, a Harvard dropout. By 1984, its archcompetitors, Lotus Development and Ashton-Tate, along with numerous other microcomputer software companies, had already gone public. But Microsoft remained privately held. Unlike its competitors, Microsoft was not dominated by venture capitalists eager to harvest some of their gains. Further, the business gushed cash, and the firm needed no outside money to expand. Most important, however, was Bill Gates' attitude towards selling stock to the public. "The whole process looks like a pain," he said, "and an ongoing pain once you're public. People get confused because the stock price doesn't reflect your financial performance. And to have a stock trader call up the chief executive and ask him questions is uneconomic — the ball bearings shouldn't be asking the driver about the grease."

But a public offering was just a matter of time. To attract the best managers and programmers, Gates had been selling them shares, and it was estimated that over 500 people would own shares by 1987, enough to require SEC registration. Once registered, the stock in effect would have a public market, but one so narrow that trading would be difficult. Since it would have to register anyway, Microsoft decided it might as well sell enough shares to enough investors to create a liquid market.

On March 13, 1986, Microsoft sold 2,300,000 shares of new stock, and existing shareholders (including Bill Gates) sold an additional 600,000 shares, at a price of $21 per share. At 9:35 a.m. Microsoft's stock traded publicly on the over-the-counter market for the first time at a price of $25.75. By the end of the first day of trading, some 2.5 million shares had changed hands, and Microsoft's stock price stood at $27.75. Microsoft and its original shareholders raised $61 million. Bill Gates got only $1.6 million for the shares he sold, but going public established a market value of $350 million on the 45 percent stake he retained. Gates, at 30, was made one of the 100 richest Americans by the deal.

Initial public offerings, or IPOs, do not always work out as well as Microsoft's. Success or failure in the equity markets is a function of many factors. We discuss the primary ones in this chapter.

In Part III we examined the analysis financial managers employ when making decisions regarding the investment in long-term (or fixed) assets, and in Part IV we discussed capital structure and dividend decisions. With this background, we now turn our attention to specific types of long-term capital. Any decision to acquire new assets necessitates the raising of new capital, and, generally, long-term assets are financed with long-term capital. In this chapter, we consider in some detail the decisions financial managers must make regarding stock financings. As a part of this analysis, we also examine in detail the procedures used to raise new long-term capital, or the investment banking process.

BALANCE SHEET ACCOUNTS AND DEFINITIONS

Legal and accounting terminology is vital to both investors and financial managers if they are to avoid misinterpretations and possibly costly mistakes. Therefore, we begin our analysis of common stock with a discussion of accounting and legal issues. Consider first Table 14-1, which shows the common equity section of American Chemical Company's balance sheet. American's owners, its stockholders, have authorized management to issue a total of 30 million shares, and management has thus far actually issued (or sold) 25 million shares. Each share has a *par value* of $1; this is the minimum amount for which new shares can be issued.[1]

---

[1]A stock's par value is an arbitrary figure that indicates the minimum amount of money stockholders have put up, or must put up in the event of bankruptcy. Actually, the firm could legally sell new shares at below par, but any purchaser would be liable for the difference between the issue price and the par value in the event the company went bankrupt. Thus, if American sold an investor 10,000 shares at 40 cents per share, for $4,000, then the investor would have to put up an additional $6,000 if the company later went bankrupt. This contingent liability effectively precludes the sale of new common stock at prices below par.

Also, we should point out that firms are not required to establish a par value for their stock. Thus, American could have elected to use "no par" stock, in which case the common stock and additional paid-in capital accounts could have been consolidated under one account called *common stock,* which would show a 1987 balance of $75 million.

Table 14-1
American Chemical Company:
Stockholders' Equity Accounts as of December 31, 1987

Common stock (30 million shares authorized, 25 million shares outstanding, $1 par)	$ 25,000,000
Additional paid-in capital	50,000,000
Retained earnings	375,000,000
Total common stockholders' equity (or common net worth)	$450,000,000

$$\text{Book value per share} = \frac{\text{Total common stockholders' equity}}{\text{Shares outstanding}} = \frac{\$450,000,000}{25,000,000} = \$18.$$

American Chemical is an old company — it was established back in 1912. Its initial equity capital consisted of 3,000 shares sold at the $1 par value, so on its first balance sheet the total stockholders' equity was $3,000. The initial paid-in capital and retained earnings accounts showed zero balances. Over the years American has retained some of its earnings, and the firm has issued new stock to raise capital from time to time. During 1987 American earned $60 million, paid $50 million in dividends, and retained $10 million. The $10 million was added to the $365 million accumulated *retained earnings* shown on the year-end 1986 balance sheet to produce the $375 million retained earnings at year-end 1987. Thus, since its inception in 1912, American has retained, or plowed back, a total of $375 million. This is money that belongs to the stockholders and that they could have received in the form of dividends. Instead, the stockholders chose to let management reinvest the $375 million in the business.

Now consider the $50 million additional *paid-in capital*. This account shows the difference between the stock's par value and what new stockholders paid when they bought newly issued shares. As we noted, American was formed in 1912 with 3,000 shares issued at the $1 par value; thus, the first balance sheet showed a zero balance for additional paid-in capital. By 1920 the company had demonstrated its profitability and was earning 50 cents per share. Further, it had built up the retained earnings account to a total of $6,000, so the total stockholders' equity was $3,000 of par value plus $6,000 of retained earnings = $9,000, and the *book value per share* was $9,000/3,000 shares = $3. American had also borrowed heavily, and, even though it had retained most of its earnings, the company's debt ratio had risen to an unacceptable level, precluding further use of debt without an infusion of equity.

The company had profitable investment opportunities, so in order to take advantage of them, management decided to issue another 2,000 shares of stock. The market price at the time was $4 per share, which was eight times the 50 cents earnings per share (the price/earnings ratio was 8×). This $4 market value per share was well in excess of the $1 par value and also higher than the $3 book value per share, demonstrating that par value, book value, and market value are not necessarily equal. Had the company lost money since its inception, it would have had negative retained earnings, the book value would have been below par, and the market price might well have been below book.

Table 14-2
Effects of 1920 Stock Sale on American Chemical's Equity Accounts

	Before Sale of Stock	
Common stock (3,000 shares outstanding, $1 par)		$ 3,000
Additional paid-in capital		0
Retained earnings		6,000
Total stockholders' equity		$ 9,000
Book value per share = $9,000/3,000 =		$3.00
	After Sale of Stock	
Common stock (5,000 shares outstanding, $1 par)		$ 5,000
Additional paid-in capital ($4 − $1) × 2,000 shares		6,000
Retained earnings		6,000
Total stockholders' equity		$17,000
Book value per share = $17,000/5,000 =		$3.40

Table 14-2 shows how the 1920 stock sale affected American's common equity accounts. A total of 2,000 new shares were sold to investors at the market price of $4 per share. Each share brought in $4, of which $1 represented the par value and $3 represented the excess of the sale price above par. Since 2,000 shares were involved, a total of $2,000 was added to common stock, and $6,000 was entered in additional paid-in capital. Notice also that book value per share rose from $3 to $3.40; whenever stock is sold at a price above book, the book value increases, and vice versa if stock is sold below book.[2]

Similar transactions have taken place down through the years to produce the current situation, as shown earlier in Table 14-1.[3]

LEGAL RIGHTS AND PRIVILEGES OF COMMON STOCKHOLDERS

The common stockholders are the owners of a corporation, and as such they have certain rights and privileges. The most important of these rights are discussed in this section.

---

[2]The effects of stock sales on book value are not important for industrial firms, but they are *very* important for utility companies, whose allowable earnings per share are in effect determined by regulators as a percentage of book value. Thus, if a utility's stock is selling below book and the company sells stock to raise new equity, this will dilute the book value per share of its existing stockholders and drive down their allowable earnings per share, which in turn will drive down the market price. Most U.S. electric utilities' stocks sold below book value during the late 1970s and early 1980s. The firms needed to raise large amounts of capital, including equity, since they had to keep their capital structures in balance. This meant selling stock at prices below book, which tended to depress the market value of the stock still further.

[3]Stock dividends, stock splits, and stock repurchases (the reverse of stock issues) also affect the capital accounts. These topics were discussed in Chapter 13.

Control of the Firm

The stockholders have the right to elect the firm's directors, who in turn elect the officers who will manage the business. In a small firm, the major stockholder typically assumes the positions of president and chairman of the board of directors. In a large, publicly owned firm, the managers typically have some stock, but their personal holdings are insufficient to exercise voting control. Thus, the managements of most publicly owned firms can be removed by the stockholders if they decide a management team is not effective.

Various state and federal laws stipulate how stockholder control is to be exercised. First, corporations must hold an election of directors periodically, usually once a year, with the vote taken at the annual meeting. Frequently, one-third of the directors are elected each year for a three-year term. Each share of stock has one vote; thus, the owner of 1,000 shares has 1,000 votes. Stockholders can appear at the annual meeting and vote in person, but typically they transfer their right to vote to a second party by means of an instrument known as a *proxy*. Management always solicits stockholders' proxies and usually gets them. However, if earnings are poor and stockholders are dissatisfied, an outside group may solicit the proxies in an effort to overthrow management and take over control of the business. This is known as a *proxy fight*.

The question of control has become a central issue in finance in recent years. The frequency of proxy fights has increased, as have attempts by one corporation to take over another by purchasing a majority of the outstanding stock. This latter action, which is called a *takeover*, is discussed in detail in Chapter 23. Some well-known examples of recent takeover battles include General Electric's acquisition of RCA, Chevron's acquisition of Gulf Oil, and CBS's successful defense against a takeover attempt by Ted Turner. (Subsequently, though, CBS's management lost control to another group headed by Larry Tisch.)

Managers who do not have majority control (over 50 percent) of their firms' stocks are very much concerned about proxy fights and takeovers, and many of them are attempting to get stockholder approval for changes in their corporate charters that would make takeovers more difficult. For example, a number of companies tried in 1987 to get their stockholders to agree (1) to elect only one-third of the directors each year (rather than electing all directors each year) and (2) to require 75 percent of the stockholders (rather than 50 percent) to approve a merger. Other takeover prevention tactics are discussed in Chapter 23. Managements seeking such changes generally cite a fear that the firm will be picked up at a bargain price, but it often appears that managers' concern over their own positions is an even more important consideration.

The Preemptive Right

Common stockholders often have the right, called the *preemptive right,* to purchase any new shares sold by the firm. In some states the preemptive right is automatically included in every corporate charter; in others it is necessary to specifically insert it into the charter.

The purpose of the preemptive right is twofold. First, it protects the power of control of present stockholders. If it were not for this safeguard, the management of a corporation under criticism from stockholders could prevent stockholders from removing it from office by issuing a large number of additional shares and purchasing these shares itself. Management would thereby secure control of the corporation and frustrate the will of the current stockholders.

The second, and by far the more important, reason for the preemptive right is that it protects stockholders against a dilution of value. For example, suppose 1,000 shares of common stock, each with a price of $100, were outstanding, making the total market value of the firm $100,000. If an additional 1,000 shares were sold at $50 a share, or for $50,000, this would raise the total market value of the firm to $150,000. When the total market value is divided by the new total shares outstanding, a value of $75 a share is obtained. The old stockholders thus lose $25 per share, and the new stockholders have an instant profit of $25 per share. Thus, selling common stock at a price below the market value would dilute its price and would transfer wealth from the present stockholders to those who purchase the new shares. The preemptive right prevents such occurrences.[4]

TYPES OF COMMON STOCK

Although most firms have only one type of common stock, in some instances *classified stock* is used to meet the special needs of the company. Generally, when special classifications of stock are used, one type is designated *Class A,* another *Class B,* and so on. Small, new companies seeking to obtain funds from outside sources frequently use different types of common stock. For example, when Genetic Concepts, Inc., went public in 1985, its Class A stock was sold to the public, paid a dividend, but had no voting rights for five years. Its Class B stock was retained by the organizers of the company and had full voting rights for five years, but the legal terms stated that dividends would not be paid on the Class B stock until the company had established its earning power by building up retained earnings to a designated level. Because of the use of classified stock, the public was able to take a position in a conservatively financed growth company without sacrificing income, while the founders retained absolute control during the crucial early stages of the firm's development. At the same time, outside investors were protected against excessive withdrawals of funds by the original owners. As is often the case in such situations, the Class B stock was also called *founders' shares.*

Note that "Class A," "Class B," and so on, have no standard meanings. Most firms have no classified shares, but a firm that does could designate its Class B shares as founders' shares and its Class A shares as those sold to the public, while another could reverse these designations. Still other firms could use the A and B designations for entirely different purposes.

---

[4]For a discussion of the procedures for issuing stock to existing stockholders, called a "rights offering," see Eugene F. Brigham and Louis C. Gapenski, *Intermediate Financial Management,* 2nd ed., Chapter 12.

General Motors recently introduced yet another type of common stock. When GM acquired Hughes Aircraft for $5 billion in 1985, it paid in part with a new Class H common, GMH, which had limited voting rights and whose dividends were tied in part to the performance of Hughes as it operated as a GM subsidiary. The reasons for the new stock are reported to be these: (1) GM wanted to limit voting privileges on the new stock because of management's concern about a possible takeover and (2) Hughes employees wanted to participate more directly in Hughes' own performance than would have been possible through regular GM stock.

GM's deal posed a problem for the NYSE, which had a rule against listing any company's common stock if the company had any nonvoting common stock outstanding. GM made it clear that it was willing to delist if the Exchange did not change its rules. The NYSE concluded that such arrangements as GM had made were logical and were likely to be made by other companies in the future, so it changed its rules to accommodate GM.

EVALUATION OF COMMON STOCK AS A SOURCE OF FUNDS

Thus far this chapter has covered the main characteristics of common stock. Now we will appraise stock financing both from the viewpoint of the corporation and from a social perspective.

From the Corporation's Viewpoint

Advantages

There are several advantages to the corporation associated with common stock financing:

1. Common stock does not obligate the firm to make fixed payments to investors. If the company generates earnings and has no pressing internal needs for them, it can pay common stock dividends. Had it used debt, it would have incurred a legal obligation to pay interest on it, regardless of its operating conditions, its cash flows, and so on.

2. Common stock carries no fixed maturity date—it never has to be "repaid" as would a debt issue.

3. Common stock provides a cushion against losses from the creditors' viewpoint, so the sale of common stock increases the creditworthiness of the firm. This, in turn, raises its bond rating, lowers its cost of debt, and increases its future ability to use debt.

4. If a company's prospects look bright, then common stock can often be sold on better terms than debt. Stock appeals to certain groups of investors because (a) it typically carries a higher expected total return (dividends plus capital gains) than does preferred stock or debt and (b) since stock represents the ownership of the firm, it provides the investor with a better hedge against unanticipated inflation than does preferred stock or bonds. Ordinarily, common stock increases in value when real asset values rise during inflationary periods.[5]

5. When a company is having operating problems, it often needs new funds to overcome its problems. However, investors are reluctant to supply capital to a troubled company, and if they do, they generally require some type of security. From a practical standpoint, this means that a firm which is experiencing problems can often obtain new capital only by issuing debt, which is safer from the investor's standpoint. Corporate treasurers are well aware of this, so they often opt to finance with common stock so as to maintain a *reserve borrowing capacity* — indeed, surveys have indicated that maintenance of an adequate reserve of borrowing capacity is a major consideration in most financing decisions.

Disadvantages

Disadvantages to a company which issues common stock include the following:

1. The sale of common stock extends voting rights, and perhaps even control, to new stockholders. For this reason, additional equity financing is often avoided by managers who are concerned about maintaining control. The use of classified shares such as those GM issued can, however, mitigate this problem.

2. Common stock gives new owners the right to share in the income of the firm — if profits soar, the new stockholders get to share in this bonanza, while if debt had been used, new investors would have received only a fixed return, no matter how profitable the company.[6]

3. As we shall see, the costs of underwriting and distributing common stock are usually higher than those associated with underwriting and distributing preferred stock or debt. Flotation costs in the sale of common stock are characteristically higher because (a) the costs of investigating an equity security investment are higher than those for a comparable debt security and (b) stocks are riskier than debt, meaning that investors must diversify their equity holdings, which in turn means that a given dollar amount of new stock must be sold to a larger number of purchasers than the same amount of debt.

4. As we saw in Chapters 11 and 12, if a firm has more equity than is called for in its optimal capital structure, its weighted average cost of capital will be higher than necessary. Therefore, a firm would not want to sell stock to the point where its equity ratio exceeded the optimal level.

---

[5]During the inflation of the last decade, the lags of product price increases behind increases in input costs depressed corporate earnings and increased the uncertainty of earnings growth, causing stock prices to fall. Thus, stocks were not a good hedge against inflation during the 1960s and 1970s. However, many analysts think that this period was unique and that in the future stocks will be a better inflation hedge than bonds. Indeed, the latter situation has prevailed during the 1980s — stocks have outperformed bonds and have more than offset the effects of inflation.

[6]This point has given rise to an interesting new theory: "If a firm sells a large issue of bonds, this is a signal that management expects the company to earn high profits on investments financed by the new capital, and it does not wish to share these profits with new stockholders. On the other hand, if the firm issues stock, this is a signal that its prospects are not so bright." This issue was discussed earlier, in Chapters 11 and 12.

5. Under current tax laws, common stock dividends are not deductible as an expense for calculating the corporation's taxable income, but bond interest is deductible. As we saw in Chapter 7, the impact of this factor is reflected in the relative cost of equity vis-à-vis debt.

From a Social Viewpoint

From a social viewpoint, common stock is a desirable form of financing because it renders companies less vulnerable to the consequences of declines in sales and earnings. Common stock financing involves no fixed charges, the payment of which might force a faltering firm into reorganization or bankruptcy. From the standpoint of the economy as a whole, if too many firms used too much debt, business fluctuations would be amplified, and minor recessions could turn into major ones. During 1987, when many mergers and management buyouts financed heavily with debt were occurring and raising the aggregate debt ratio (the average debt ratio of all firms), Federal Reserve Chairman Volcker and other authorities voiced concern over the situation, and congressional leaders debated the wisdom of social controls over corporations' use of debt. Like most important issues, this one is debatable, and the debate centers around who can better determine "appropriate" capital structures, corporations' managers or government officials.[7]

THE MARKET FOR COMMON STOCK

Some companies are so small that their common stocks are not actively traded — they are owned by only a few people, usually the companies' managers. Such firms are said to be *privately owned,* or *closely held, corporations,* and their stock is said to be *closely held stock.* On the other hand, the stocks of most larger companies are owned by a large number of investors, most of whom are not active in management. Such companies are said to be *publicly owned corporations,* and their stock is said to be *publicly held stock.*

As we saw in Chapter 3, the stocks of smaller publicly owned firms are not listed on an exchange; they trade in the *over-the-counter (OTC) market,* and the companies and their stocks are said to be *unlisted.* However, larger publicly owned companies generally apply for listing on an *organized security exchange,* and they and their stocks are said to be *listed.* As a general rule, companies are first listed on a regional exchange such as the Pacific Coast or Midwest, then they move up to the American Stock Exchange (AMEX), and, finally, if they grow large enough, they are listed on the "Big Board," the New York Stock Exchange (NYSE). About 7,000 stocks are traded in the OTC market, but in terms of market value of both outstanding shares and daily transactions, the NYSE is most important, having about 60 percent of the business.

---

[7]When business executives hear someone say, "I'm from Washington and I'm here to help you," they generally cringe, and often with good reason.

Institutional investors such as pension trusts, insurance companies, and mutual funds own about 35 percent of all common stocks. However, the institutions buy and sell relatively actively, so they account for about 75 percent of all transactions. Thus, the institutional investors have a heavy influence on the price of individual stocks — in a real sense, they determine the prices of individual stocks and hence set the tone of the market.

Types of Stock Market Transactions

We can classify stock market transactions into three distinct categories:

1. Trading in the outstanding shares of established, publicly owned companies: the secondary market. American Chemical Company has 25 million shares of stock outstanding. If the owner of 100 shares sells his or her stock, the trade is said to have occurred in the *secondary market*. Thus, the market for outstanding shares, or *used shares,* is defined as the secondary market. The company receives no new money when sales occur in this market.

2. Additional shares sold by established, publicly owned companies: the primary market. If American Chemical decides to sell (or issue) an additional 1 million shares to raise new equity capital, this transaction is said to occur in the *primary market.*[8]

3. New public offerings by privately held firms: the primary market. In 1975 the Coors Brewing Company, which was owned by the Coors family at the time, decided to sell some stock to raise capital needed for a major expansion program.[9] This type of transaction is defined as *going public* — whenever stock in a closely held corporation is offered to the public for the first time, the company is said to be going public. The market for stock that has recently gone public is often called the *new issue market,* and the issue is called an *initial public offering (IPO).*

Firms can go public without raising any additional capital. For example, in its early days the Ford Motor Company was owned exclusively by the Ford family. When Henry Ford died, he left a substantial part of his stock to the Ford Foundation. When the Foundation later sold some of this stock to the general public, the Ford Motor Company went public, even though the company raised no capital in the transaction.

---

[8]Recall that American has 30 million shares authorized but only 25 million outstanding; thus, it has 5 million authorized but unissued shares. If it had no authorized but unissued shares, management could increase the authorized shares by obtaining stockholders' approval, which would generally be granted without any arguments.

[9]The stock Coors offered to the public was designated Class B, and it was nonvoting. The Coors family retained the founders' shares, called Class A stock, which carried full voting privileges. The company was large enough to obtain a NYSE listing, but at that time the exchange had a requirement that listed common stock have full voting rights, which precluded Coors from obtaining a NYSE listing. Now that GM has forced the Exchange to change its rules, Coors could presumably list its stock.

The Decision to Go Public

Most businesses begin life as proprietorships or partnerships, and the more successful ones, as they grow, find it desirable at some point to convert into corporations. Initially these new corporations' stocks are owned by the firms' officers, key employees, and/or a very few investors who are not actively involved in management. However, if growth continues, the companies may decide at some point to go public. The advantages and disadvantages of public ownership are discussed next.

Advantages of Going Public

1. Facilitates stockholder diversification. As a company grows and becomes more valuable, its founders often have most of their wealth tied up in the company. By selling some of their stock in a public offering, the founders can diversify their holdings and thereby reduce somewhat the riskiness of their personal portfolios.

2. Increases liquidity. The stock of a closely held firm is illiquid: no ready market exists for it. If one of the holders wants to sell some shares to raise cash, it is hard to find potential buyers, and even if a buyer is located, there is no established price at which to complete the transaction. These problems do not exist with publicly owned firms.

3. Makes it easier to raise new corporate cash. If a privately held company wants to raise cash by the sale of new stock, it must either go to its existing owners, who may neither have any money nor want to put any more eggs into this particular basket, or shop around for wealthy investors who are willing to make an investment in the company. However, it is usually difficult to get outsiders to put money into a closely held company, because if they do not have voting control (over 50 percent) of the stock, then the inside stockholders-managers can run roughshod over them. The insiders can pay or not pay dividends, pay themselves exorbitant salaries, have private deals with the company, and so on. For example, the president might buy a warehouse and lease it to the company at a high rental, get the use of a Rolls Royce, and enjoy all-the-frills travel to conventions. The insiders can even keep the outsiders from knowing the company's actual earnings or its real worth. There are not many positions more vulnerable than that of an outside stockholder in a closely held company, and for this reason it is hard for closely held companies to raise new equity capital. Going public, which brings with it disclosure and regulation by the Securities and Exchange Commission (SEC), greatly reduces these problems and thus makes people more willing to invest in the company.

4. Establishes a value for the firm. For a number of reasons, it is often useful to establish a firm's value in the marketplace. For one thing, when the owner of a privately owned business dies, state and federal inheritance tax appraisers must set a value on the company for estate tax purposes. Often, these appraisers set too high a value, which creates all sorts of problems. However, a company that is publicly owned has its value established, with little room for argument. Similarly, if a company wants to give incentive stock options to key employees, it is useful to know the exact value of those options; employees much prefer to own stock, or options on stock, that is publicly traded, because public trading increases liquidity. As noted at the outset of the chapter, this factor was important in Microsoft's decision to go public.

Disadvantages of Going Public

1. Cost of reporting. A publicly owned company must file quarterly and annual reports with the SEC and/or various state agencies. These reports can be costly, especially for very small firms.

2. Disclosure. Management may not like the idea of reporting operating data, because such data will then be available to competitors. Similarly, the owners of the company may not want people to know their net worth: Since publicly owned companies must disclose the number of shares owned by officers, directors, and major stockholders, it is easy enough for anyone to multiply shares held by price per share to estimate the net worth of insiders.

3. Self-dealings. The owners-managers of closely held companies have many opportunities for various types of questionable but legal self-dealings, including the payment of high salaries, nepotism, personal transactions with the business (such as a leasing arrangement), excellent retirement programs, and not-truly-necessary fringe benefits. Such self-dealings are much harder to arrange if a company is publicly owned — they must be disclosed, and the managers are also subject to stockholder suits.

4. Inactive market. If a firm is very small, and if its shares are not traded with much frequency, then its stock will not really be liquid, and the market price may not be representative of the stock's true value. Security analysts and stockbrokers simply will not follow the stock, because there will not be sufficient trading activity to generate enough sales commissions to cover the analysts' or brokers' costs of keeping up with it.

5. Control. Because of the dramatic increase in tender offers and proxy fights in the 1980s, the managers of publicly owned firms who do not have at least 50 percent of the stock must be concerned about maintaining control. Further, there is pressure on such managers to produce annual earnings gains, even when it would be in the shareholders' best long-term interests to adopt a strategy that might penalize short-run earnings but lead to higher earnings in future years. These factors have led a number of public companies to "go private" in "leveraged buyout" deals in which the managers borrow the money to buy out the nonmanagement stockholders.

Conclusions on Going Public

It should be obvious from this discussion that there are no hard and fast rules regarding whether or when a company should go public. This is an individual decision that should be made on the basis of the company's and its stockholders' own unique circumstances.

If a company does decide to go public, either by the sale of newly issued stock to raise new capital for the corporation or by the sale of stock by the current owners, one key issue is that of setting the price at which shares will be offered to the public. The company and its current owners want to set the price as high as possible — the higher the offering price, the smaller the fraction of the company the current owners will have to give up to obtain any specified amount of money. On the other hand, potential buyers will want the price set as low as possible. We will return to the establishment of the offering price later in the chapter, after we have described some other aspects of common stock financing.

The Decision to List the Stock

The decision to go public, as discussed above, is a truly significant milestone in a company's life — it leads to major changes in the relationship between the firm's managers and its owners. The decision to *list,* on the other hand, is not a major event. The company will have to file a few new reports with an exchange; it will have to abide by the rules of the exchange; and the stock's price will be quoted in the newspaper under a stock exchange rather than in the over-the-counter section. These are not very significant differences.

In order to have its stock listed, a company must apply to an exchange, pay a relatively small fee, and meet the exchange's minimum requirements. These requirements relate to the size of the company's net income as well as to the number of shares outstanding and in the hands of outsiders (as opposed to the number held by insiders, who generally do not trade their stock very actively). Also, the company must agree to disclose certain information to the exchange; this information is designed to help the exchange track trading patterns and thus try to prevent manipulation of the price of the stock.[10] The size qualifications increase as one moves from the regional exchanges to the AMEX and on to the NYSE.

Assuming a company qualifies, many people believe that listing is beneficial both to it and to its stockholders. Listed companies receive a certain amount of free advertising and publicity, and their status as a listed company enhances their prestige and reputation. This may have a beneficial effect on the sales of the firm's products, and it is probably advantageous in terms of lowering the required rate

---

[10]It is illegal for anyone to attempt to manipulate the price of a stock. Prior to the creation of the SEC in the 1930s, syndicates would buy and sell stock back and forth at rigged prices for the purpose of deceiving the public into thinking that a particular stock was worth more or less than its true value. The exchanges, with the encouragement and support of the SEC, utilize sophisticated computer programs to help spot any irregularities that suggest manipulation. They can identify the exact day and time of each trade, and the broker who executed it, and they can require the broker to disclose the name of the person for whom the trade was made. Such a system can obviously help identify manipulators. This same system also helps to identify illegal insider trading, as discussed in the next section.

of return on its common stock. Investors respond favorably to increased information, increased liquidity, and confidence that the quoted price is not being manipulated. By providing investors with these benefits in the form of listing their companies' stocks, financial managers may lower their firms' costs of capital and increase the value of their stocks.

Regulation of Securities Markets

Sales of new securities, and also operations in the secondary markets, are regulated by the *Securities and Exchange Commission (SEC)* and, to a lesser extent, by each of the 50 states. Here are the primary elements of SEC regulation.

1. The SEC has jurisdiction over all interstate offerings of new securities to the public in amounts of $1.5 million or more.

2. Newly issued securities must be registered with the SEC at least 20 days before they are publicly offered. The *registration statement* provides financial, legal, and technical information about the company. A *prospectus* summarizes this information for use in selling the securities. SEC lawyers and accountants analyze both the registration statement and the prospectus; if the information is inadequate or misleading, the SEC will delay or stop the public offering.

3. After the registration has become effective, new securities may be offered, but any sales solicitation must be accompanied by the prospectus. Preliminary, or *"red herring," prospectuses* may be distributed to potential buyers during the 20-day waiting period, but no sales may be finalized during this time. The "red herring" prospectus contains all the key information that will appear in the final prospectus except the price, which is generally set after the market closes the day before the new securities are actually offered to the public.

4. If the registration statement or prospectus contains misrepresentations or omissions of material facts, any purchaser who suffers a loss may sue for damages. Severe penalties may be imposed on the issuer or its officers, directors, accountants, engineers, appraisers, underwriters, and all others who participated in the preparation of the registration statement or prospectus.

5. The SEC also regulates all national securities exchanges, and companies whose securities are listed on an exchange must file annual reports similar to the registration statement with both the SEC and the exchange.

6. The SEC has control over corporate *insiders.* Officers, directors, and major stockholders must file monthly reports of changes in their holdings of the stock of the corporation. Any short-term profits from such transactions are payable to the corporation.

7. The SEC has the power to prohibit manipulation by such devices as pools (aggregations of funds used to affect prices artificially) or wash sales (sales between members of the same group to record artificial transaction prices).

8. The SEC has control over the form of the proxy and the way the company uses it to solicit votes.

Control over the flow of credit into security transactions is exercised by the Board of Governors of the Federal Reserve System. The Fed exercises this control through *margin requirements,* which specify the maximum percentage of the purchase price of a security that can be borrowed. If a great deal of margin borrowing has been going on, then a decline in stock prices can result in inadequate coverages; this forces the stockbrokers to issue *margin calls,* which in turn require investors either to put up more money or to have their margined stock sold to pay off their loans. Such forced sales further depress the stock market and can set off a downward spiral. The margin requirement has been 50 percent since 1974.

States also have some control over the issuance of new securities within their boundaries. This control is usually exercised by a "corporation commissioner" or someone with a similar title. State laws relating to security sales are called *blue sky laws,* because they were put into effect to keep unscrupulous promoters from selling securities that offered the "blue sky" but which actually had little or no asset backing.

The security industry itself realizes the importance of stable markets, sound brokerage firms, and the absence of stock manipulation. Therefore, the various exchanges work closely with the SEC to police transactions on the exchanges and to maintain the integrity and credibility of the system. Similarly, the *National Association of Securities Dealers (NASD)* cooperates with the SEC to police trading in the OTC market. These industry groups also cooperate with regulatory authorities to set net worth and other standards for securities firms, to develop insurance programs to protect the customers of brokerage houses, and the like.

In general, government regulation of securities trading, as well as industry self-regulation, is designed to insure that investors receive information that is as accurate as possible, that no one artificially manipulates the market price of a given stock, and that corporate insiders do not take advantage of their position to profit in their companies' stocks at the expense of other stockholders. Neither the SEC, the state regulators, nor the industry itself can prevent investors from making foolish decisions or from having "bad luck," but they can and do help investors obtain the best data possible for making sound investment decisions.

PREFERRED STOCK

Preferred stock is a *hybrid* — it is similar to bonds in some respects and to common stock in others. The hybrid nature of preferred stock becomes apparent when we try to classify it in relation to bonds and common stock. Like bonds, preferred stock has a par value. Preferred dividends are also similar to interest payments in that they are fixed in amount and generally must be paid before common stock dividends can be paid. However, if the preferred dividend is not earned, the directors can omit (or "pass") it without throwing the company into bankruptcy. So, while preferred stock has a fixed payment like bonds, a failure to make this payment will not lead to bankruptcy.

Accountants classify preferred stock as equity and generally list it in the equity portion of the balance sheet under the title "Preferred Stock" or "Preferred Equity." However, in financial analysis, preferred is sometimes treated as debt and sometimes as equity, depending on the type of analysis being made. If the analysis is being made by a common stockholder, then the key consideration is the fact that the preferred dividend is a fixed charge which must be paid ahead of common stock dividends, so the common stockholder will view preferred stock as being similar to debt. Suppose, however, that the analysis is being made by a bondholder studying the firm's vulnerability to failure due to a decline in sales and income. If the firm's income declines, the debtholders have a prior claim ahead of preferred stockholders to the available income, and if the firm fails, debtholders have a prior claim to assets when the firm is liquidated. Thus to the bondholder preferred stock is similar to common equity. From management's perspective, preferred lies between debt and common equity. Since the dividends on preferred stock are not a fixed charge in the sense that failure to pay them represents a default on an obligation, preferred stock is safer to use than debt. On the other hand, if the firm is highly successful, then the common stockholders will not have to share that success with the preferred stockholders, because preferred dividends are fixed. We see, then, that preferred stock has some of the characteristics of debt and some of the characteristics of common stock, and it is used in situations where conditions are such that neither debt nor common stock appear to be entirely appropriate.

Major Provisions of Preferred Stock Issues

Preferred stock has a number of features, the most important of which are covered in the following sections.

Priority in Assets and Earnings

Preferred stockholders have priority over common stockholders with regard to earnings and assets. Thus, dividends must be paid on preferred stock before they can be paid on the common stock, and in the event of bankruptcy, the claims of the preferred shareholders must be satisfied before the common stockholders receive anything. To reinforce these features, most corporate charters include coverage requirements similar to those contained in bond indentures. These restrictions limit the amount of preferred stock a company can use, and they also require that the balance sheet show a minimum level of retained earnings before common dividends are permitted.

Par Value

Unlike common stock, preferred stock always has a par value (or its equivalent under some other name), and this value is a meaningful quantity. First, the par value establishes the amount due the preferred stockholders in the event of liquidation. Second, the preferred dividend is frequently stated as a percentage of the par value. For example, J. I. Case's preferred stock has a par value of $100 and a stated dividend of 7 percent of par. The same results would, of course, be produced if the Case preferred stock simply called for an annual dividend of $7.

Cumulative Dividends

Most preferred stock provides for *cumulative dividends* — that is, all preferred dividends in arrears must be paid before common dividends can be paid. The cumulative feature is a protective device, for if the preferred stock dividends were not cumulative, a firm could avoid paying preferred and common stock dividends for, say, 10 years and thus plow back all of its earnings, then pay a huge common stock dividend but pay only the stipulated annual dividend to the preferred stockholders. Obviously, such an action could be used to effectively void the preferred position that the preferred stockholders have tried to obtain. The cumulative feature helps prevent such abuses. Note, however, that compounding is absent in most cumulative plans — in other words, the arrearages themselves earn no return. Also, many preferred issues have a limited cumulative feature — for example, arrearages might accumulate for only three years.

Convertibility

Approximately 40 percent of the preferred stock that has been issued in recent years is convertible into common stock. For example, each share of Enron's $10.50 Class J preferred stock can be converted into 3.413 shares of its common stock at the option of the preferred shareholders. (Convertibility is discussed in more detail in Chapter 17.)

Other Provisions

Some other provisions one occasionally encounters in preferred stocks include the following:

1. Voting rights. Preferred stockholders are generally given the right to vote for directors if the company has not paid the preferred dividend for a specified period, say, four, eight, or ten quarters. This feature motivates management to make every effort to pay preferred dividends.

2. Participating. A rare type of preferred stock is one that participates with the common stock in sharing the firm's earnings. The following sequence generally relates to participating preferred stocks: (a) the stated preferred dividend is paid, for example, $5 a share; (b) the common stock is then entitled to a dividend in an amount equal to the preferred dividend; (c) if the company wishes to increase the common dividend over the preferred dividend, say to $5.50, then the preferred dividend must likewise be raised to $5.50.

3. Sinking fund. In the past (before the mid-1970s), few preferred issues had sinking funds. Today, however, most newly issued preferred stocks have a sinking fund which calls for the purchase and retirement of a given percentage of the preferred stock each year. If the amount is 2 percent, which is used frequently, then the relevant preferred issue will have a maximum life of 50 years and an average life of 25 years.

4. Maturity. Before the mid-1970s, most preferred stock was perpetual — it had no maturity and never needed to be paid off. However, today most preferred has a sinking fund which effectively creates a maturity date.

5. Call provision. A call provision gives the issuing corporation the right to call in the preferred stock for redemption, as in the case of bonds. Call provisions generally state that the company must pay an amount greater than the par value of the preferred stock, the additional sum being defined as a *call premium.* For example, Trivoli Corporation's 12 percent, $100 par value preferred stock, issued in 1986, is noncallable for 10 years, but it may be called at a price of $112 after 1996.

Evaluation of Preferred Stock

There are both advantages and disadvantages to financing with preferred stock. These are discussed in the following sections.

Issuer's Viewpoint

By using preferred stock, a firm can fix its financial costs and thus keep more of the potential future profits for its existing set of common stockholders, yet avoid the danger of bankruptcy if earnings are too low to meet these fixed charges. Also, by selling preferred rather than common stock, the firm avoids sharing either control or earnings with new investors.

However, preferred does have a major disadvantage from the issuer's standpoint: It has a higher after-tax cost of capital than debt. The reason for this higher cost is taxes — preferred dividends are not deductible as a tax expense, whereas interest expense is deductible.[11] This makes the component cost of preferred stock much greater than that of bonds: the after-tax cost of debt is approximately two-thirds of the stated coupon rate for profitable firms, while the cost of preferred stock is the full percentage amount of the preferred dividend. Of course, the deductibility differential is most important for issuers that are in relatively high tax brackets — if a company pays little or no taxes because it is unprofitable or because it has a great deal of accelerated depreciation, then the deductibility of interest does not make much difference. Thus, the lower a company's tax bracket, the more likely it is to issue preferred stock.

Investor's Viewpoint

In designing securities, the financial manager must also consider the investor's point of view. It is sometimes asserted that preferred stock has so many disadvantages to both the issuer and the investor that it should never be issued. Nevertheless, preferred stock is issued in substantial amounts. It provides investors with a more steady and assured income than common stock, and it has a preference over common in the event of liquidation. In addition, 80 percent of the preferred dividends received by corporations are not taxable. For this reason, most preferred stock is owned by corporations.

The principal disadvantage of preferred stock from an investor's standpoint is that although preferred stockholders bear some of the ownership risk, their returns

---

[11]One would think that a given firm's preferred stock would carry a higher coupon rate than its bonds because of the preferred's greater risk from the holder's viewpoint. However, the fact that 80 percent of preferred dividends received by corporate owners is exempt from income taxes has made preferred stock very attractive to corporate investors. Therefore, most preferred stock is owned by corporations, and in recent years high-grade preferreds, on average, have sold on a lower-yield basis than high-grade bonds. As an example, Alabama Power recently sold a preferred issue yielding 11 percent to investors. On the day the preferred was issued, Alabama Power's bonds yielded 13 percent, or two percentage points more than the preferred. The tax treatment accounted for this differential; the *after-tax* yield to a corporate investor was greater on the preferred stock than on the bonds.

are limited. Other disadvantages are (1) that preferred stockholders have no legally enforceable right to dividends, even if a company earns a profit, and (2) that for individual as opposed to corporate investors, after-tax bond yields are generally higher than those of riskier preferred stock.[12]

Recent Trends

Since preferred dividends are not tax deductible, many companies have retired their preferred stocks and replaced them with debentures or subordinated debentures. However, as the following examples illustrate, preferred is still used to raise long-term capital when conditions are such that neither common stock nor long-term debt can be issued on reasonable terms, and consequently a hybrid such as preferred is useful.

1. Chrysler's issue of preferred stock with warrants in the late 1970s proved a successful means of raising capital in the face of adverse circumstances. Because of recent losses, Chrysler's common stock was depressed and very much out of favor — investors were so worried about the company's ability to survive that they were unwilling to make additional commitments without receiving some sort of senior position. Therefore, common stock was ruled out. Chrysler had already borrowed to the hilt, and it could not obtain any more debt without first building its equity base (and preferred was equity from the bondholders' viewpoint). Various incentives were offered to the brokers who handled the preferred issue, and a relatively high yield was set. As a result, the issue was so successful that its size was raised from $150 to $200 million during the underwriting. Chrysler got the money it needed, and that money helped the company regain profitability. Chrysler's common stock is currently at $57, up from about $5 when the preferred was issued. The preferred stock helped the company survive and achieve that gain in the common stock price.

2. Utility companies often use preferred stock to bolster the equity component of their capital structure. These companies are capital intensive and make heavy use of debt financing, but lenders and rating agencies require minimum equity ratios as a condition for further sales of bonds. Also, the utilities have made very heavy investments in fixed assets and thus have high depreciation, which has held down their effective tax rates and thus has lowered the tax disadvantage of preferred stock in relation to debt.

3. In recent years there has also been a pronounced movement toward convertible preferred, which is used primarily in connection with mergers. For example, in 1983, when Belco Petroleum was negotiating its acquisition by Enron, it was pointed out that if the buyout were for cash, Belco's stockholders (one of whom owned about 40 percent of the stock and thus could block the merger) would be

---

[12]Another disadvantage of owning preferred stock is the fact that companies often manage to avoid paying off all accumulated dividends when they emerge from a troubled, low-income period. Such companies frequently go through reorganization under the Bankruptcy Act, and preferred stockholders often do not fare well in these proceedings.

required to pay immediately substantial amounts of capital gains taxes. However, under our tax laws, if preferred stock were exchanged, this would constitute a tax-free exchange of securities. Thus, Belco's stockholders could obtain a fixed-income security and at the same time postpone the payment of taxes on their capital gains.

Enron actually offered a choice of straight or convertible preferred to Belco's stockholders. Those stockholders who were interested primarily in income could take the straight preferred, while those interested in capital gains could take the convertible preferred. After the exchange, both preferred issues traded on the NYSE; the straight preferred had a yield of 11 percent, while the convertible preferred yielded 7.5 percent. However, the convertibles had a chance of gains—indeed, by 1987 the Enron convertible preferred had risen from $100 to $165 per share due to an increase in the price of the common into which it could be converted. Meanwhile, the price of the nonconvertible preferred declined from $100 to $97 because of an increase in interest rates.

4. In 1984, Alabama Power sold a new type of security, *floating rate preferred stock.* Since this stock has a floating rate, its price stays relatively constant, making it suitable for liquidity portfolios (marketable securities held by corporations to provide funds either for planned expenditures or to meet emergencies). The combination of a floating rate, and hence a stable price, plus the 80 percent tax exemption for corporations, makes these preferreds quite attractive, and thus they enable Alabama Power and other firms to obtain capital at a low cost. Note, however, that floating rate preferred is riskier to the issuer than fixed rate preferred.

THE INVESTMENT BANKING PROCESS

The role of investment bankers was discussed in general terms in Chapter 3. There we saw (1) that the major investment banking houses are often divisions of large financial service corporations engaged in a wide range of activities and (2) that these bankers help firms issue new securities in the primary markets and also operate as brokers in the secondary markets. Sears, Roebuck is one of the largest financial services corporations; in addition to its insurance and credit card operations, it owns a large brokerage house and a major investment banking house. Similarly, Merrill Lynch has a brokerage department which operates thousands of offices and an investment banking department which helps companies issue securities. Of course, Merrill Lynch's and Sears' brokers also sell securities that have been issued through their investment banking departments. In this section we describe how securities are issued and explain the role of investment bankers in this process.

Stage I Decisions

The decision to issue securities is made in two stages. At Stage I, the firm itself makes some initial, preliminary decisions, including the following:

1. Dollars to be raised. How much new capital is needed?

2. Type of securities used. Should common, preferred, bonds, or hybrid securities, or a combination, be used? Further, if common stock is to be issued, should it be done as a rights offering or by a direct sale to the general public?

3. Competitive bid versus a negotiated deal. Should the company simply offer a block of its securities for sale to the highest bidder, or should it negotiate a deal with an investment banker? These two procedures are called *competitive bids* and *negotiated deals,* respectively. Only about 100 of the largest firms listed on the NYSE, whose securities are already well known to the investment banking community, are in a position to use the competitive bidding process. The investment banks must do a large amount of investigative work in order to bid on an issue unless they are already quite familiar with the firm, and such costs would be too high to make it worthwhile unless the banker were sure of getting the deal. Therefore, except for the very largest firms, offerings of stock or bonds are generally on a negotiated basis.

4. Selection of an investment banker. If the issue is to be negotiated, the firm must select an investment banker. This can be an important decision for a firm that is going public. On the other hand, an older firm that has already "been to market" will have an established relationship with an investment banker. However, it is easy to change bankers if the firm is dissatisfied. Different investment banking houses are better suited for different companies. The older, larger "establishment houses" such as Morgan Stanley deal mainly with companies such as AT&T, IBM, and Exxon. Other bankers such as Drexel Burnham Lambert handle more speculative issues. Some houses specialize in new issues, while others are not well suited to handle such issues because their brokerage clients are relatively conservative. (Investment banking firms sell new issues largely to their own regular brokerage customers, so the nature of these customers has a major effect on the ability of the house to do a good job for a corporate client.) Table 14-3 lists the ten largest investment bankers for 1986 as measured by the dollar amount of domestic corporate financing.

Table 14-3
Ten Largest Investment Bankers for 1986

	Total Amount Managed (In Billions of Dollars)
1. Salomon Brothers	$51.0
2. First Boston	44.1
3. Morgan Stanley	29.5
4. Drexel Burnham Lambert	30.6
5. Merrill Lynch	30.4
6. Goldman Sachs	31.8
7. Shearson Lehman	17.5
8. Kidder Peabody	10.2
9. Paine Webber	5.0
10. Bear, Stearns	4.1

Source: IDD Information Services.

Stage II Decisions

Stage II decisions, which are made jointly by the firm and its selected investment banker, include the following:

1. **Reevaluating the initial decisions.** The firm and its banker will reevaluate the initial decisions regarding the size of the issue and the type of securities to use. For example, the firm may have decided initially to raise $50 million by selling common stock, but the investment banker may convince management that it would be better off, in view of current market conditions, to limit the stock issue to $25 million and to raise the other $25 million as debt.

2. **Best efforts or underwritten issues.** The firm and its investment banker must decide whether the banker will work on a *best efforts* basis or will *underwrite* the issue. In a best efforts sale, the banker does not guarantee that the securities will be sold or that the company will get the cash it needs, only that it will put forth its best efforts to sell the issue. On an underwritten issue, the company does get a guarantee. Therefore, the banker bears significant risks in underwritten offerings. For example, on IBM's $1 billion bond sales in 1979, interest rates rose sharply, and bond prices fell, after the deal had been set but before the investment bankers could sell the bonds to ultimate purchasers. The bankers lost somewhere between $10 million and $20 million. Had the offering been on a best efforts basis, IBM would have been the loser. This well-known instance of risk-bearing by investment bankers is described in more detail later in the chapter.

Table 14-4
Issuance Costs for Underwritten, Nonrights Offerings
(Expressed as Percentage of Gross Proceeds)

Size of Issue (Millions of Dollars)	Bonds			Preferred Stock		
	Underwriting Commission	Other Expenses	Total Costs	Underwriting Commission	Other Expenses	Total Costs
Under 1.0	10.0%	4.0%	14.0%	—	—	—
1.0–1.9	8.0	3.0	11.0	—	—	—
2.0–4.9	4.0	2.2	6.2	—	—	—
5.0–9.9	2.4	0.8	3.2	1.9%	0.7%	2.6%
10.0–19.9	1.2	0.7	1.9	1.4	0.4	1.8
20.0–49.9	1.0	0.4	1.4	1.4	0.3	1.7
50.0 and over	0.9	0.2	1.1	1.4	0.2	1.6

Notes:

a. Small issues of preferred are rare, so no data on issues below $5 million are given.

b. Flotation costs tend to rise somewhat when interest rates are cyclically high, indicating that money is in relatively tight supply, and hence investment bankers will have a relatively hard time placing issues with permanent investors. Thus, the figures shown in Table 14-4 represent averages, as flotation costs actually vary somewhat over time.

c. Underpricing is shown as a separate cost component for initial public offerings because it has been measured and is reasonably predictable. Underpricing also exists for common stock offerings by companies that already have publicly traded stock, but the effects are unstable and difficult to measure; these effects are discussed later in the chapter.

3. Banker's compensation; other expenses. The investment banker's compensation must be negotiated. Also, the firm must estimate the other underwriting expenses it will incur in connection with the issue — lawyers' fees, accountants' costs, printing and engraving, and so on. Usually, the banker will buy the issue from the company at a discount below the price at which the securities are to be offered to the public, with this "spread" being set to cover the banker's costs and to provide a profit.

Table 14-4 gives an indication of the issuance costs associated with public issues of bonds, preferred stock, and common stock. As the table shows, costs as a percentage of the proceeds are higher for stocks than for bonds, and costs are higher for small than for large issues. The relationship between size of issue and flotation cost is due primarily to the existence of fixed costs — certain costs must be incurred regardless of the size of the issue, so the percentage flotation cost is quite high for small issues.

Also, it should be noted that when companies go public to raise new capital, the new shares are typically underpriced. Thus, the stock closes on the first day of trading at a price above the issue price. Underpricing represents a potentially large cost to existing shareholders, as shown in the initial public offerings section of Table 14-4. Further, the investment bankers frequently take part of their compensation in the form of options to buy stock in the firm. For example, Glasgo Technologies, Inc., went public with a $10 million issue in 1987 by selling 1 million shares at a price of $10 per share. Its investment bankers bought the stock from

Table 14-4

Issuance Costs for Underwritten, Nonrights Offerings (Expressed as Percentage of Gross Proceeds) *Continued*

Common Stock: Additional Shares			Common Stock: Initial Public Offerings			
Underwriting Commission	Other Expenses	Total Costs	Underwriting Commission	Other Expenses	Underpricing Costs	Total Costs
13.0%	9.0%	22.0%	9.8%	9.6%	12.3%	31.7%
11.0	5.9	16.9	9.8	9.6	12.3	31.7
8.6	3.8	12.4	9.4	6.6	6.9	22.9
6.3	1.9	8.1	8.0	4.3	5.5	17.8
5.1	0.9	6.0	7.2	2.1	7.0	16.3
4.1	0.5	4.6	7.2	2.1	7.0	16.3
3.3	0.2	3.5	7.2	2.1	7.0	16.3

Sources: Securities and Exchange Commission, *Cost of Flotation of Registered Equity Issues* (Washington, D.C.: U.S. Government Printing Office, December 1974); Pettway, Richard H., "A Note on the Flotation Costs of New Equity Capital Issues of Electric Companies," *Public Utilities Fortnightly,* March 18, 1982; Hansen, Robert, "Evaluating the Costs of a New Equity Issue," *Midland Corporate Finance Journal,* Spring 1986; Ritter, Jay R., "The Costs of Going Public," *Journal of Financial Economics,* Forthcoming; and informal surveys of common stock, preferred stock, and bond issues conducted by the authors.

the company at a price of $9.75 per share, so the direct underwriting fee was only 1,000,000($10.00 − $9.75) = $250,000, or 2.5 percent, but they also received a 5-year option to buy 200,000 shares at a price of $10 per share. If the stock should go up to $15 per share, which the bankers expected it to do, then the investment banking firm would make a $1 million profit, which would in effect be an additional underwriting fee.

4. Setting the offering price. If the company is already publicly owned, the offering price will be based upon the existing market price of the stock or the yield on the bonds. Typically, for common stock, the investment banker buys the securities at a prescribed number of points below the closing price on the last day of registration. For example, suppose that in October 1987, the stock of Microwave Telecommunications, Inc., (MTI) had a current price of $28.50 per share, and the stock had traded between $25 and $30 per share during the previous three months. Suppose further that MTI and its underwriter agreed that the investment banker would buy 10 million new shares at $1 per share below the closing price on the last day of registration. If the stock closed at $25 on the day the SEC released the issue, MTI would receive $24 per share. Typically, such agreements have an escape clause that provides for the contract to be voided if the price of the securities drops below some predetermined figure. In the illustrative case, this "upset" price might be set at $24 per share. Thus, if the closing price of the shares on the last day of registration had been $23.50, MTI would have had the option of withdrawing from the agreement.

The investment banker will have an easier job if the issue is priced relatively low, but the issuer of the securities naturally wants as high a price as possible. Some conflict of interest on price therefore arises between the investment banker and the issuer. If the issuer is financially sophisticated and makes comparisons with similar security issues, the investment banker will be forced to price close to the market.

As we discussed in Chapter 11, the announcement of a new stock offering by a mature firm is often taken as a negative signal — if the firm's prospects were very good, management would not want to issue new stock and thus share the rosy future with new stockholders, so the announcement of a new offering is taken as bad news. Consequently, the price will probably fall when the announcement is made, so the offering price will probably have to be set at a price substantially below the pre-announcement market price. Consider Figure 14-1, in which d_0 is the estimated pre-announcement market demand curve for MTI's stock and S_0 is the number of shares currently outstanding. Initially, there are 50 million shares outstanding, and the equilibrium price of the stock is $28.60 per share, determined as follows:

$$P_0 = \frac{D_1}{k_s - g} = \frac{\$2.00}{0.12 - 0.05} \approx \$28.60.$$

The values shown for D_1, k_s, and g are the *estimates of the marginal investor.* Investors who do not now own MTI's stock, on average, regard the stock as being more risky, and hence assign it a higher value for k_s, or perhaps they estimate the

Figure 14-1
Microwave Telecommunications, Inc.:
Estimated Common Stock Demand Curves

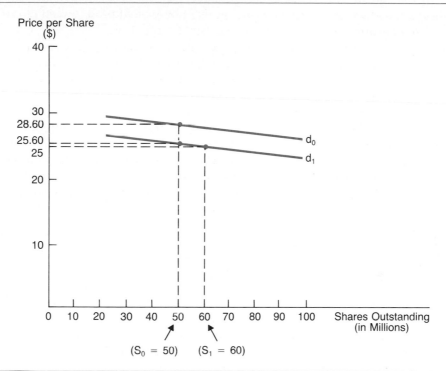

company's growth rate as being lower than do people who now own the stock, and so use $g < 5$ percent when calculating the stock's intrinsic value. Thus, people who do not now own the stock think the stock is worth less than $28.60.

When MTI announces that it is going to sell another 10 million shares, this is taken as a negative signal. Consequently, the demand curve for the stock drops from d_0 to d_1, and the price falls. The new equilibrium price, if 50 million shares were outstanding, and if the marginal investor now expects MTI's growth rate to be 4.2 percent, would be about $25.60:

$$P_0 = \frac{\$2.00}{0.12 - 0.042} \approx \$25.60.$$

However, if MTI is to sell another 10 million shares of stock, it will either have to attract investors who would not be willing to own the stock at the $25.60 per share price or else induce present stockholders to buy additional shares. There are two ways this can be accomplished: (1) by reducing the offering price of the stock or (2) by "promoting" or "advertising" the company and thus shifting the demand curve for its stock back to the right.[13] If the demand curve does not shift at all from d_1, we see from Figure 14-1 that the only way the 10 million additional shares could be sold would be by setting the offering price at about $25 per share. However, if the investment banker could promote the stock sufficiently to shift the demand curve back up to d_0, then the offering price could be set much closer to the pre-announcement equilibrium price of $28.60 per share.[14]

The extent to which the demand curve can be shifted depends primarily on two factors: (1) what investors think the company can do with the money brought in by the stock sale and (2) how effectively the brokers promote the issue. If investors can be convinced that the new money will be invested in highly profitable projects that will substantially raise earnings and the earnings growth rate, then the demand curve shift will occur, and the stock price might actually go above $28.60. Even if investors do not radically change their expectations about the company's fundamental factors, the fact that MTI's stock is brought to their attention may shift the demand curve. The extent to which this promotion campaign is successful in shifting the demand curve depends, of course, upon the effectiveness of the investment banking firm. Therefore, the effectiveness of different investment bankers, as perceived by MTI's financial manager, will be an important factor in the choice of an underwriter.

One final point is that *if pressure from the new shares and/or negative signaling effects drives down the price of the stock, all shares outstanding, not just the new shares, are affected.* Thus, if MTI's stock should fall from $28.60 to $25 per share as a result of the financing, and if the price should remain at that new level, then the company would incur a loss of $3.60 on each of the 50 million shares previously outstanding, or a total market value loss of $180 million. This loss, like underwriting expenses, is a flotation cost, and hence should be considered as a cost associated with the stock issue. However, if the company's prospects really were poorer than investors thought, then the price decline would have occurred sooner or later anyway. On the other hand, if the company's prospects are really not all that bad (the signal was incorrect), then over time MTI's demand curve will move back to d_0, or even above d_0, so the company would not suffer a permanent loss anywhere close to $180 million on an issue such as this one.

If the company is "going public," there will be no established price or demand curve, so the bankers will have to estimate the *equilibrium price* at which the

---

[13]It should be noted that investors can buy newly issued stock without paying normal brokerage commissions, and brokers are careful to point this out to potential purchasers. Thus, if an investor were to buy MTI's stock at $25.60 per share in the regular market, the commission would be about 1 percent, or 26 cents per share. If the stock were purchased in an underwriting, this commission would be avoided.

It should also be noted that for years many academicians argued that the demand curve for a firm's stock is either horizontal or has an extremely slight downward slope, and that signalling effects are minimal. Most corporate treasurers, on the other hand, have long felt that both effects exist for mature companies, and recent empirical studies confirm the treasurers' position. For example, see Andrei Shleifer, "Do Demand Curves for Stocks Slope Down?" *Journal of Finance,* July 1986, 579–590.

[14]Note that the supply curve is a vertical line, first at 50 million and then, after the new issue, at 60 million.

stock will sell after issue. Note that if the offering price is set below the true equilibrium price, the price will rise sharply after the issue, and the company and its selling stockholders will have given away too much stock to raise the required capital. If the offering price is set above the true equilibrium price, either the issue will fail or, if the bankers succeed in selling the stock to their investment clients, these clients will be unhappy when the stock subsequently falls to its equilibrium level. Therefore, it is important that the equilibrium price be closely approximated, although it is hard to estimate this price.

Selling Procedures

Once the company and its investment bankers have decided how much money to raise, the type of securities to issue, and the basis for pricing the issue, they will prepare and file an SEC registration statement and a "red herring" prospectus as described earlier in the chapter. It generally takes about 20 days for the issue to be approved by the SEC. The final price of the stock (or the interest rate on a bond issue) is set at the close of business the day the issue clears the SEC, and the securities are offered to the public the following day.

If the offering is an initial public offering (IPO) such as the Microsoft issue described at the beginning of the chapter, company executives will accompany members of the underwriting team on a "road show" that goes to all the major financial centers around the country. A hall will be rented, and a show will literally be put on. The company's executives will describe their products, sales, trends, various financial ratios, and other relevant data. The investment bankers present comparisons of the company's financial data against those of similar companies that are publicly traded. Sales representatives of the investment banker will have brought their larger clients to the meeting, and when it is over, at the cocktail party, they will try to get an expression of investors' interests in the issue. For example, Sales Rep A might get from Insurance Company B's equity portfolio manager a tentative agreement to buy 10,000 shares if they are offered at $25 per share, 5,000 shares if they are offered at $27.50, and none at all if they are priced at over $27.50. These expressions of interest are not firm commitments, but they are often close to it, as it is in both parties' interests to do future business, and the portfolio manager will not be given an allocation of future "hot new issues" if he or she reneges very often on tentative commitments to purchase shares.

Information from all the sales reps is entered into "the book," which today is a computer. The sales reps keep in touch with their clients, and as things change, the "book" is constantly updated. As the offering date approaches, the underwriter will typically have an excellent idea of how many shares can be sold at different prices, and thus the highest price that can be set and still market a given sized offering successfully. The day before the sale will actually take place, the number of shares offered, and the price, will be finalized and agreed to by the issuer and the investment banker.

Investors are not required to pay for the stock until ten days after they place their buy orders, but the investment bankers must pay the issuing firm within four days of the time the offering officially begins. Typically, the bankers sell the stock within a day or two after the offering begins, but on occasion they miscalculate, set the offering price too high, and are unable to move the issue. At still other times, the market declines during the offering period, forcing the bankers to reduce the price of the stock. In either instance, on an underwritten offering the firm receives the price that was agreed upon, and the bankers must absorb any losses that are incurred.

Most underwritten stock offerings include a *Green Shoe provision,* so called because it was first used in an offering by the Green Shoe Company. This provision gives the investment bankers the right to purchase up to, for example, 20 percent more stock than the planned offering. In other words, a Green Shoe provision is an over-allocation provision. The purpose of a Green Shoe is to reduce the underwriter's risk. With this provision included, an investment banker that has committed to the company to sell say 100,000 shares can have its sales reps promise their customers 120,000 shares. Then, if 20 percent of the customers back out of the deal, the banker will still sell the required 100,000 shares. Without this provision, the banker would be exposed to more risk and, consequently, would have to charge higher underwriting fees.

Because they are exposed to large potential losses, investment bankers typically do not handle the purchase and distribution of an issue singlehandedly unless it is a very small one. If the amount of money involved is large and the risk of price fluctuations substantial, investment bankers form *underwriting syndicates* in an effort to minimize the amount of risk each one carries. The banking house which sets up the deal is called the *lead,* or *managing, underwriter.*

In addition to the underwriting syndicate, on larger offerings still more investment bankers are included in a *selling group,* which handles the distribution of securities to individual investors. The selling group includes all members of the underwriting syndicate plus additional dealers who take relatively small participations (or shares of the total issue) from the syndicate members. Thus, the underwriters act as *wholesalers,* while members of the selling group act as *retailers.* The number of houses in a selling group depends partly on the size of the issue; for example, the one set up when Communications Satellite Corporation (Comsat) went public consisted of 385 members.

Shelf Registrations

The selling procedures described above, including the 20-day minimum waiting period between registration with the SEC and sale of the issue, apply to most security sales. However, it should be noted that large, well-known public companies which issue securities frequently may file a *master registration statement* with the SEC and then update it with a *short-form statement* just prior to each individual offering. In such a case, a company that decided at 10 a.m. to sell registered securities could have the sale completed before noon. This procedure is known as *shelf registration,* because in effect the company puts its new securities "on the shelf" and then sells them to investors when it feels the market is "right."

Maintenance of the Secondary Market

In the case of a large, established firm such as American Chemical, the investment banking firm's job is finished once it has disposed of the stock and turned the net proceeds over to the company. However, in the case of a company going public for the first time, the investment banker is under an obligation to maintain a market for the shares after the issue has been completed. Such stocks are typically traded in the over-the-counter market, and the lead underwriter generally agrees to "make a market" in the stock so as to keep it reasonably liquid. The company wants a good market to exist for its stock, as do the stockholders. Therefore, if the banking house wants to do business with the company in the future, to keep its own brokerage customers happy, and to have future referral business, it will hold an inventory and help to maintain an active secondary market in the stock.

IBM's INITIAL DEBT OFFERING

IBM's first public debt offering, in 1979, provides an informative case study of the nature of investment banking.[15] The offering, still the largest in U.S. corporate history, represented a combination of $500 million in 7-year notes and $500 million in 25-year debentures (unsecured long-term debt) for a total of $1 billion. IBM's customary investment banker had been Morgan Stanley & Co. However, for this offering IBM requested separate underwriting proposals from Morgan Stanley and from Salomon Brothers, another major investment banking house; these proposals were presented in September 1979. IBM's financial management was of the opinion that two managers would provide better execution of the sale and back it up with a larger amount of capital. John H. Gutfreund, Salomon Brothers' managing partner, is quoted as stating, "A major corporation is best served by two sets of eyes and ears." Robert H. B. Baldwin, president of Morgan Stanley, is said to have responded, "You need only one brain surgeon." Morgan Stanley dropped out, refusing to participate if it could not be sole manager, and Salomon Brothers and Merrill Lynch became co-managers, with an underwriting group totaling 227 members.

During the month of September, the prime rate was increased five times, reaching a level of 13.5 percent on September 28. A "pricing meeting" took place on Wednesday, October 3, 1979; at the time, rapidly rising yields were being experienced in the money markets. It was agreed that the prices on IBM's notes would be based on a yield of 7 basis points above Treasury notes and that prices for the IBM debentures would be based on a yield of 12 basis points above Treasury bonds.[16] This meant that IBM would have to pay 9.62 percent for the 7-year notes and 9.41 percent for the 25-year debentures. The underwriting spread, or commis-

---

[15]This summary is based on contemporary accounts in the financial press and in the article by Walter Guzzardi, Jr., "The Bomb IBM Dropped on Wall Street," *Fortune,* November 19, 1979, 52–56.

[16]One basis point is equal to one one-hundredth of 1 percent. Therefore, IBM's notes were priced to yield 0.07 percentage points more than Treasury notes.

sion, was set at ⅝ of 1 percent on the notes and ⅞ of 1 percent on the debentures. Since there were $500,000,000 of notes and an equal amount of debentures, the total underwriting fees were 0.00625 ($500,000,000) + 0.00875 ($500,000,000) = $7,500,000.

Only hours after the pricing meeting had ended and the securities' yields and prices had been fixed, the market yield for Treasury bonds moved up by 5 basis points. The IBM offering began the next day, Thursday, October 4. On that same day, the Treasury auctioned $2.5 billion of 4-year notes yielding 9.79 percent, which was higher than the 9.62 percent on the IBM 7-year notes. Naturally, the IBM securities did not sell at all well.

On Saturday, October 6, the Federal Reserve System announced an increase in its discount rate from 11 percent to 12 percent in an effort to combat the high rate of inflation that was developing. At the same time, a number of other credit-tightening policies, which Wall Street experts called "draconian" in their severity, were implemented. As a result of the Fed's actions, on Tuesday, October 9, the New York banks announced a full percentage point increase in the prime rate, to 14.5 percent. The next morning, the underwriting syndicate was disbanded. The prices of both the notes and the debentures fell by about 5 percent each, or $50 per $1,000 bond, with yields rising to 10.65 percent on the notes and to 10.09 percent on the debentures.

When the syndicate was disbanded, it was estimated that only $650 million of the $1 billion issue had been sold, earning syndicate members less than $5 million in underwriting fees. The $350 million remaining portion of the issue was sold after prices fell, and the investment bankers had an estimated loss of between $10 and $20 million. To put it mildly, the underwriters "took a bath."

A controversy arose over whether the IBM issue was priced "too tight." During the entire month preceding the actual offering, the prime rate and the discount rate had both been increasing, and the financial markets were chaotic during the week of October 3, when the pricing decision was made. Undoubtedly, the severe measures taken by the Federal Reserve System on Saturday, October 6, 1979, were being anticipated during the week. Whether the underwriters should have given themselves more cushion to avoid a subsequent price decline is a matter of judgment. From one standpoint, the price decline of $50 per $1,000 bond after the disbanding of the underwriting syndicate was relatively modest, given the sharply rising interest rates during the period and the Fed announcement on October 6. Differences in judgment on this matter are natural — and such differences are what make markets.

The IBM offering illustrates a number of basic characteristics of investment banking. First, the risks are real. Second, competition among investment bankers continues to be vigorous and tough. Third, a corporate issue of a well-managed, financially strong firm which is taking on debt for the first time, and in moderate quantity in relation to its total assets, will be rated high and priced close to Treasury issues. Fourth, turbulence in the financial markets during the period immediately preceding the offering makes the task of the underwriters extremely difficult: Great risk-taking and judgment are required when making decisions in the face of an extremely volatile financial environment. In sum, the episode illustrates the high drama, the considerable financial sophistication, and the continued great challenges that exist in the field of financial decision making.[17]

EMERGING TRENDS

Many new developments are taking place in the financial markets. Some have resulted from legislative changes, others arose from fundamental shifts in the nature of economic and financial relationships, and still others are due to technological developments in the computer and telecommunications areas.

One important set of changes was brought about by the Depository Institutions Deregulation and Monetary Control Act of 1980. The law directed the Federal Reserve to lower bank reserve requirements and to phase out deposit interest rate ceilings. It permitted depository institutions to offer interest-bearing checking accounts, it gave savings and loan associations expanded lending and investing powers, and it allowed commercial banks to offer money market funds and some brokerage services.

Competition has increased dramatically among the different types of financial institutions, as "financial service corporations," which encompass investment banking, brokerage operations, insurance, and commercial banking, are dominating the scene. Investment banking firms often earn more income in the form of interest on customer balances than in commissions, and additional new sources of income for those firms include credit card operations, money market funds, and counseling on corporate merger activity.

When the SEC ordered the end of fixed commission schedules on May 1, 1975, investment bankers were placed under severe financial pressure. To avoid financial disaster, numerous "mergers of necessity" took place, as is evident in the compound names of some of the surviving firms: Merrill Lynch White Weld Capital Markets Group, Blyth Eastman Paine Webber, and Dean Witter Reynolds, Inc. In addition to mergers within the investment banking and brokerage business, mergers between different types of financial institutions have taken place. Bache and Co., once the eighth largest investment banking firm, was taken over by Prudential Insurance; American Express acquired Shearson Loeb Rhoades, ranked the seventh largest investment banking firm in 1985; and Sears, Roebuck bought out Dean Witter. There is a very clear trend toward *financial service conglomerates*. At the same time, institutional investors, especially pension funds, are continuing to replace individuals on the buying side — about 75 percent of all stock transactions are among institutions, and competition for institutional business has changed the way both brokerage and investment banking houses operate.

---

[17]To close out the story, (1) at least some of the underwriters had hedged their IBM positions in the futures market, so they were protected against rising interest rates, and (2) Salomon Brothers, the lead underwriter, was at the time aggressively (and successfully) seeking to expand its operations — and that required taking some chances. Salomon's overall strategy has certainly worked well even if this one issue did not, for by 1984 Salomon surpassed Morgan Stanley as the world's leading underwriter; Salomon maintained its number one ranking in 1986, while Morgan Stanley dropped to third.

14-7 It is frequently stated that the primary purpose of the preemptive right is to allow individuals to maintain their proportionate share of the ownership and control of a corporation.

   a. How important do you suppose this consideration is for the average stockholder of a firm whose shares are traded on the New York or American Stock Exchanges?

   b. Is the preemptive right likely to be of more importance to stockholders of publicly owned or closely held firms? Explain.

   c. Is a firm likely to get a wider distribution of shares if it sells new stock through a preemptive rights offering to existing stockholders or directly to underwriters?

   d. Why would management be interested in getting a wider distribution of its shares?

Problems

14-1 **(Book value per share)** The Olson Music Company had the following balance sheet at the end of 1987.

Olson Music Company:
Balance Sheet as of
December 31, 1987

		Accounts payable	$ 48,000
		Notes payable	54,000
		Long-term debt	108,000
		Common stock (30,000 shares authorized, 20,000 shares outstanding)	270,000
		Retained earnings	225,000
Total assets	$705,000	Total liabilities and equity	$705,000

   a. What is the book value per share of Olson's common stock?

   b. Suppose the firm sold the remaining authorized shares and netted $22.50 per share from the sale. What would be the new book value per share?

14-2 **(Profit or loss on new stock issue)** Security Brokers, Inc., specializes in underwriting new issues by small firms. On a recent offering of Meran, Inc., the terms were as follows:

Price to public:	$5 per share
Number of shares:	3 million
Proceeds to Meran:	$14,000,000

The out-of-pocket expenses incurred by Security Brokers in the design and distribution of the issue were $300,000. What profit or loss would Security Brokers incur if the issue were sold to the public at an average price of

a. $5 per share?

b. $6 per share?

c. $4 per share?

14-3 (Underwriting and flotation expenses) The Kato Company, whose stock price is now $25, needs to raise $20 million in common stock. Underwriters have informed Kato's management that they must price the new issue to the public at $22 per share because of a downward-sloping demand curve. The underwriters' compensation will be 5 percent of the issue price, so Kato will net $20.90 per share. Kato will also incur expenses in the amount of $150,000.

How many shares must Kato sell to net $20 million after underwriting and flotation expenses?

14-4 (New stock issue) The Ewert Gem Company, a small jewelry manufacturer, has been successful and has enjoyed a good growth trend. Now Ewert is planning to go public with an issue of common stock, and it faces the problem of setting an appropriate price on the stock. The company and its investment bankers believe that the proper procedure is to select several similar firms with publicly traded common stock and to make relevant comparisons.

Several jewelry manufacturers are reasonably similar to Ewert with respect to product mix, asset composition, and debt/equity proportions. Of these companies, Groth Jewelers and Hill Fashions are most similar. When analyzing the following data, assume that 1982 and 1987 were reasonably "normal" years for all three companies — that is, these years were neither especially good nor especially bad in terms of sales, earnings, and dividends. At the time of the analysis, k_{RF} was 8 percent and k_M was 12 percent. Groth is listed on the AMEX and Hill on the NYSE, while Ewert will be traded in the OTC market.

	Groth	Hill	Ewert (Totals)
Earnings per share			
1987	$ 4.50	$ 7.50	$1,200,000
1982	3.00	5.50	816,000
Price per share			
1987	$36.00	$65.00	—
Dividends per share			
1987	$ 2.25	$ 3.75	$ 600,000
1982	1.50	2.75	420,000
Book value per share, 1987	$30.00	$55.00	$ 9 million
Market/book ratio, 1987	120%	118%	—
Total assets, 1987	$28 million	$ 82 million	$20 million
Total debt, 1987	$12 million	$ 30 million	$11 million
Sales, 1987	$41 million	$140 million	$37 million

a. Assume that Ewert has 100 shares of stock outstanding. Use this information to calculate earnings per share (EPS), dividends per share (DPS), and book value per share for Ewert. (Hint: Ewert's 1987 EPS = $12,000.)

b. Calculate earnings and dividend growth rates for the three companies. (Hint: Ewert's EPS g is 8%.)

   c. On the basis of your answer to Part a, do you think Ewert's stock would sell at a price in the same "ballpark" as that of Groth and Hill, that is, in the range of $25 to $100 per share?

   d. Assuming that Ewert's management can split the stock so that the 100 shares could be changed to 1,000 shares, 100,000 shares, or any other number, would such an action make sense in this case? Why?

   e. Now assume that Ewert did split its stock and has 400,000 shares. Calculate new values for EPS, DPS, and book value per share. (Hint: Ewert's new 1987 EPS is $3.00.)

   f. Return on equity (ROE) can be measured as EPS/book value per share or as total earnings/total equity. Calculate ROEs for the three companies for 1987. (Hint: Ewert's 1987 ROE = 13.3%.)

   g. Calculate dividend payout ratios for the three companies for both years. (Hint: Ewert's 1987 payout ratio is 50%.)

   h. Calculate debt/total assets ratios for the three companies for 1987. (Hint: Ewert's 1987 debt ratio is 55%.)

   i. Calculate the P/E ratios for Groth and Hill for 1987. Are these P/Es reasonable in view of relative growth, payout, and ROE data? If not, what other factors might explain them? (Hint: Groth's P/E = 8×.)

   j. Now determine a range of values for Ewert's stock price, with 400,000 shares outstanding, by applying Groth's and Hill's P/E ratios, price/dividends ratios, and price/book value ratios to your data for Ewert. For example, one possible price for Ewert's stock is (P/E Groth)(EPS Ewert) = 8($3) = $24 per share. Similar calculations would produce a range of prices based on both Groth and Hill data. (Hint: Our range was $24 to $27.)

   k. Using the equation $k = D_1/P_0 + g$, find approximate k values for Groth and Hill. Then use these values in the constant growth stock price model to find a price for Ewert's stock. (Hint: We averaged the EPS and DPS g's for Ewert.)

   l. At what price do you think Ewert's shares should be offered to the public? You will want to select a price that will be low enough to induce investors to buy the stock but not so low that it will rise sharply immediately after it is issued. Think about relative growth rates, ROEs, dividend yields, and total returns $(k = D/P + g)$.

Selected Additional References and Cases

For a wealth of facts and figures on a major segment of the stock market, see New York Stock Exchange, *Fact Book* (New York: published annually).

For both a description of the stock markets and some further facts and figures, see the investment textbooks referenced in Chapter 5. For a discussion of the current state of investment banking and trends in the industry, see

Hayes, S. L., "The Transformation of Investment Banking," *Harvard Business Review,* January–February 1979, 153–170.

Rogowski, Robert, and Eric Sorensen, "The New Competitive Environment of Investment Banking: Transactional Finance and Concession Pricing of New Issues," *Midland Corporate Finance Journal,* Spring 1986, 64–71.

Other good references on specific aspects of equity financing include the following:

Block, Stanley, and Marjorie Stanley, "The Financial Characteristics and Price Movement Patterns of Companies Approaching the Unseasoned Securities Market in the Late 1970s," *Financial Management,* Winter 1980, 30–36.

Bowyer, John W., and Jess B. Yawitz, "Effect of New Equity Issues on Utility Stock Prices," *Public Utilities Fortnightly,* May 22, 1980, 25–28.

Fabozzi, Frank J., "Does Listing on the AMEX Increase the Value of Equity?" *Financial Management,* Spring 1981, 43–50.

Hansen, Robert S., and John M. Pinkerton, "Direct Equity Financing: A Resolution to a Paradox," *Journal of Finance,* June 1982, 651–665.

Logue, Dennis, and Robert A. Jarrow, "Negotiation versus Competitive Bidding in the Sale of Securities by Public Utilities," *Financial Management,* Autumn 1978, 31–39.

For more information on shelf registration, see

Bhagat, Sanjai, "The Evidence on Shelf Registration," *Midland Corporate Finance Journal,* Spring 1984, 6–12.

For an excellent discussion of the various procedures used to raise capital, see

Smith, Clifford W., Jr., "Raising Capital: Theory and Evidence," *Midland Corporate Finance Journal,* Spring 1986, 6–22. Also, Pages 72–76 of the Spring 1986 issue of the *Midland Corporate Finance Journal* contain a bibliography of recent articles pertaining to investment banking and capital acquisition.

For an additional discussion of adjustable rate preferred stock, see

Winger, Bernard J., et al., "Adjustable Rate Preferred Stock," *Financial Management,* Spring 1986, 48–57.

The following cases from the Crum-Brigham casebook focus on the issues contained in this chapter:

Case 20, "Helios Engineering," which emphasizes the investment banking process.

Case 22, "Grafton Timber Company," which illustrates the decision to go public.

The Harrington casebook contains the following applicable case:

"Hop-In Food Stores, Incorporated," which focuses on a firm's decision to go public.

15
Long-Term Debt

On any given day, corporations go to the markets for vast amounts of new debt capital, and they use many types and forms of securities. To illustrate, during one week in February 1987, the *Wall Street Journal* announced the following debt-related actions: (1) Bear Stearns Companies, a holding company involved in investment banking, securities trading, and brokerage services, issued $100 million of 10-year, 8⅛ percent senior notes. The notes, noncallable for 7 years, were priced at 99.825 (or 99.825 percent of face value) to yield 8.15 percent. (2) Sun Microsystems, Inc., a California-based maker of engineering computer work stations, sold at par $100 million of 5½ percent, 25-year debentures which are convertible into 25.25 common shares per $1,000 bond. (3) Cleveland Electric Illuminating Company sold $300 million of 9⅜ percent first mortgage bonds. Proceeds from the sale will be used to redeem $84 million of outstanding higher coupon bonds, to pay off short-term debt, and for general purposes. (4) Beverly Enterprises, a health care company, arranged a $400 million unsecured revolving credit agreement with a group of banks headed by Morgan Guaranty. At Beverly's option, the 3-year agreement can be converted to a 5-year, amortized term loan. (5) Union Carbide announced the $340 million sale and leaseback of its corporate headquarters in Danbury, Connecticut. The company received the $340 million from investors who bought the complex, and Carbide simultaneously executed a long-term lease for its continued use. (6) General Electric Credit Corporation borrowed $250 million using 7⅛ percent, 5-year Eurobonds. These bonds, which are denominated in dollars, were sold in Europe through Union Bank of Switzerland. (7) Moody's Investors Service announced that it had lowered its ratings on AT&T's $8 billion of outstanding debt and preferred stock from Aa3 to A1 because of AT&T's continuing difficulty in maintaining profits in its new, highly competitive environment. (8) Appalachian Power Company announced that it was calling for redemption $33 million of 14⅝ percent bonds with a 1992 maturity date and $15 million of 12⅞ bonds due in 2013.

Why did these companies use so many different types of debt? How are bond ratings determined, and how do they affect the cost of debt? How does a company decide when to call a bond, or, at the time of issue, whether or not to make the bond callable? These are some of the issues discussed in this chapter.

Different groups of investors prefer different types of securities, and investors' tastes change over time. Thus, astute financial managers offer a variety of securities, "packaging" their new security offerings at each point in time so as to attract the greatest possible number of potential investors and thereby holding their costs of capital to a minimum. In this chapter, we consider various types of long-term debt available to financial managers.

Long-term debt is often called *funded debt*. When a firm is said to be planning to "fund" its short-term debt, this means it is planning to replace short-term debt with securities of longer maturity. Funding does not imply that the financial manager places money with a trustee or other repository; it is simply part of the jargon of finance, and it means "that the manager replaces short-term debt with permanent capital." Pacific Gas & Electric Company (PG&E) provides a good example of funding. PG&E has a continuous construction program, and it typically uses short-term debt to finance construction expenditures. However, once short-term debt has built up to about $100 million, the company sells a stock or bond issue, uses the proceeds to pay off (or fund) its bank loans, and starts the cycle again. As we discussed in Chapter 14, the flotation costs of selling stocks or bonds make it quite expensive to issue small amounts of these securities. Therefore, the process used by PG&E and other companies is quite logical.

TRADITIONAL DEBT INSTRUMENTS

There are many types of long-term debt instruments: term loans, bonds, secured and unsecured notes, marketable and nonmarketable notes, and so on. In this section, we discuss briefly the traditional long-term debt instruments, after which we discuss some important features of debt contracts. Finally, we discuss recent innovations in long-term debt financing.

Term Loans

A *term loan* is a contract under which a borrower agrees to make a series of interest and principal payments on specific dates to the lender.[1] Term loans are usually negotiated directly between the borrowing firm and the lender — generally a bank, an insurance company, or a pension fund. Although term loans' maturities vary from 2 to 30 years, most are for periods in the 3-year to 15-year range.

Term loans have three major advantages over public offerings — *speed, flexibility,* and *low issuance costs.* Also, because they are negotiated directly between the lender and the borrower, formal documentation is minimized. The key provisions

---

[1]Most term loans are *amortized,* which means paid off in equal installments over the life of the loan. Amortization protects the lender against the possibility that the borrower will not make adequate provisions for the loan's retirement during the life of the loan. See Chapter 4 for a review of amortization. Also, if the interest and maturity payments required under a term loan agreement are not met on schedule, the borrowing firm is said to have *defaulted,* and it can then be forced into bankruptcy. See Appendix 15A for a discussion of bankruptcy.

of a term loan can be worked out much more quickly than can those for a public issue, and it is not necessary for the loans to go through the Securities and Exchange Commission registration process. A further advantage of term loans has to do with future flexibility: If a bond issue is held by many different bondholders, it is virtually impossible to obtain permission to alter the terms of the agreement, even though new economic conditions may make such changes desirable. With a term loan, the borrower can generally sit down with the lender and work out mutually agreeable modifications to the contract.

The interest rate on a term loan can either be fixed for the life of the loan or be variable. If a fixed rate is used, it will be close to the rate on bonds of equivalent maturity and risk. If the rate is variable, it will usually be set at a certain number of percentage points over the prime rate, the commercial paper rate, the T-bill rate, or the London Inter-Bank Offered Rate (LIBOR). Thus, when the index rate goes up or down, so does the rate on the outstanding balance of the term loan. Rates may be adjusted annually, semiannually, quarterly, monthly, or on some other basis, depending on what the contract specifies. In 1986, over 50 percent of the dollar amount of all term loans made by banks had floating rates, up from virtually zero in 1970. Banks obtain most of the funds they themselves lend by selling certificates of deposit, and since the CD rate rises along with other market rates, banks need to raise the rate they charge in order to meet their own interest costs. With the increased volatility of interest rates in recent years, banks and other lenders have become increasingly reluctant to make long-term, fixed rate loans.

Bonds

A *bond* is a long-term contract under which a borrower agrees to make payments of interest and principal on specific dates to the holder of the bond. While bonds have traditionally been issued with maturities of between 20 and 30 years, in the 1980s shorter maturities, such as 7 to 10 years, have been used to an increasing extent. Although bonds are similar to term loans, a bond issue is generally advertised, offered to the public, and actually sold to many different investors — indeed, thousands of individual and institutional investors may purchase bonds when a firm sells a bond issue, while there is generally only one lender in the case of a term loan.[2] With bonds the interest rate is generally fixed, although in recent years there has been an increase in the use of various types of floating rate bonds. There are a number of different types of bonds, the more important of which are discussed next.

Mortgage Bonds

Under a *mortgage bond,* the corporation pledges certain assets as security for the bond. To illustrate, in 1987 Snellings Corporation needed $10 million to purchase land and to build a major regional distribution center. Bonds in the amount of $4

---

[2]However, for very large term loans, 20 or more financial institutions may form a syndicate to grant the credit. Also, it should be noted that a bond issue can be sold to one lender (or to just a few); in this case, the issue is said to be "privately placed." Companies that place bonds privately do so for the same reasons that they use term loans — speed, flexibility, and low issuance costs.

million, secured by a mortgage on the property, were issued. (The remaining $6 million was financed with equity capital.) If Snellings defaults on the bonds, the bondholders can foreclose on the property and sell it to satisfy their claims.

If Snellings chose to, it could issue *second mortgage bonds* secured by the same $10 million plant. In the event of liquidation, the holders of these second mortgage bonds would have a claim against the property, but only after the first mortgage bondholders had been paid off in full. Thus, second mortgages are sometimes called *junior mortgages* because they are junior in priority to claims of *senior mortgages,* or *first mortgage bonds.*

All mortgage bonds are written subject to an *indenture*, whch is a legal document that spells out in detail the rights of both the bondholders and the corporation. The indentures of most major corporations were written 20, 30, 40, or more years ago. These indentures are generally "open ended," meaning that new bonds may be issued from time to time under the existing indenture. However, the amount of new bonds that can be issued is virtually always limited to a specified percentage of the firm's total "bondable property," which generally includes all plant and equipment.

An example is provided by Savannah Electric Company. Savannah Electric can issue first mortgage bonds totaling up to 60 percent of its fixed assets. If its fixed assets totaled $1 billion, and if it had $500 million of first mortgage bonds outstanding, then it could, by the property test, issue another $100 million of bonds (60% of $1 billion = $600 million).

Savannah Electric has at times been unable to issue any new first mortgage bonds because of another indenture provision: its times-interest-earned (TIE) ratio was below 2.5, the minimum coverage that it must maintain in order to sell new bonds. Thus, although Savannah Electric passed the property test, it failed the coverage test; hence, it could not issue first mortgage bonds, and it had to finance with junior securities. Since first mortgage bonds carry lower rates of interest than junior long-term debt, this restriction was a costly one.

Savannah Electric's neighbor, Georgia Power Company, has more flexibility under its indenture — its interest coverage requirement is only 2.0. In hearings before the Georgia Public Service Commission, it was suggested that Savannah Electric change its indenture coverage to 2.0 so that it could issue more first mortgage bonds. However, this is simply not possible — the holders of the outstanding bonds would have to approve the change, and it is inconceivable that they would vote for a change that would seriously weaken their position.

Debentures

A *debenture* is an unsecured bond, and as such it provides no lien against specific property as security for the obligation. Debenture holders are therefore general creditors whose claims are protected by property not otherwise pledged. In practice, the use of debentures depends both on the nature of the firm's assets and on its general credit strength. An extremely strong company such as IBM will tend to use debentures — it simply does not need to put up property as security for its debt. Debentures are also issued by companies in industries where it would not be practical to provide security through a mortgage on fixed assets. Examples of such industries are the large mail-order houses and commercial banks, which characteristically hold most of their assets in the form of inventory or loans, neither of which is satisfactory security for a mortgage bond.

Subordinated Debentures

The term *subordinate* means "below" or "inferior to," and in the event of bankruptcy subordinated debt has claims on assets only after senior debt has been paid off. *Subordinated debentures* may be subordinated either to designated notes payable — usually bank loans — or to all other debt. In the event of liquidation or reorganization, holders of subordinated debentures cannot be paid until all senior debt, as named in the debentures' indenture, has been paid. Precisely how subordination works, and how it strengthens the position of senior debtholders, is explained in Appendix 15A.

Other Types of Bonds

Several other types of bonds are used sufficiently often to warrant mention. First, *convertible bonds* are securities that are convertible into shares of common stock, at a fixed price, at the option of the bondholder. Basically, convertibles provide investors with a chance for capital gains in exchange for a lower coupon rate, while the issuing firm gets the advantage of that lower rate. Bonds issued with warrants are similar to convertibles. *Warrants* are options which permit the holder to buy stock for a stated price, thereby providing a capital gain if the price of the stock rises. Bonds that are issued with warrants, like convertibles, carry lower coupon rates than straight bonds. Warrants and convertibles are discussed in detail in Chapter 17.

Income bonds pay interest only when the interest is earned. Thus, these securities cannot bankrupt a company, but from an investor's standpoint they are riskier than "regular" bonds.

Another type of bond that has been discussed in the United States but not yet used here to any extent is the *indexed,* or *purchasing power, bond,* which is popular in Brazil, Israel, and a few other countries long plagued by high rates of inflation. The interest rate paid on these bonds is based on an inflation index such as the consumer price index, so the interest paid rises when the inflation rate rises, thus protecting the bondholders against inflation. In a similar vein, Mexico has used bonds whose interest rate is pegged to the price of oil to finance the development of its huge petroleum reserves; since oil prices and inflation are correlated, these bonds also protect investors against inflation. At the same time, Mexico's ability to pay interest depends on the price of oil, so it too is protected by this indexing scheme.[3] The British government has issued an indexed bond whose in-

---

[3]At this time (summer of 1987), Mexico is in serious economic trouble — it owes billions to international banks, and interest payments are siphoning off much of its capital. Most of Mexico's debt was *not* tied to the price of oil — it pays interest rates that are either fixed or that float based on the LIBOR rate. Oil prices were as high as $40 per barrel when the debt was issued; now oil sells for about $20 per barrel. Thus, Mexico's interest payments are either fixed or have fallen only slightly, yet its income, which comes primarily from oil exports, has fallen by about 70 percent. Had Mexico indexed all of its interest payments to oil prices, it would be in a vastly better financial condition today. It is ironic that the oil index bonds that originally appealed to investors as a protection against inflation have turned out to be bad for investors but good for the issuer, Mexico.

terest rate is set equal to the British inflation rate plus 3 percent. Thus, these bonds provide a real rate of return of 3 percent.

SPECIFIC DEBT CONTRACT FEATURES

A firm's managers are vitally concerned about (1) the effective cost of debt and (2) any restrictions or provisions which might limit the firm's future alternatives. In this section, we discuss features which could affect either the cost of the firm's debt or its future flexibility.

Bond Indentures

As noted above, an *indenture* is a legal document that spells out the rights of both the bondholders and the issuing corporation. A *trustee,* usually a bank officer, is assigned to represent the bondholders and to make sure that the terms of the indenture are carried out. The indenture may be several hundred pages in length, and it will include *restrictive covenants* that cover such points as the conditions under which the issuer can pay off the bonds prior to maturity, the level at which the issuer's times-interest-earned ratio must be maintained if the company is to sell additional bonds, and restrictions against the payment of dividends when earnings do not meet certain specifications. Overall, these covenants relate to the agency problem discussed in Chapter 1, and they are designed to insure, insofar as possible, that the firm does nothing to cause the quality of its bonds to deteriorate after they are issued.

The trustee is responsible both for trying to make sure the covenants are not violated and for taking appropriate action if they are. What constitutes "appropriate action" varies with the circumstances. It might be that to insist on immediate compliance would result in bankruptcy, which in turn might lead to large losses on the bonds. In such a case, the trustee might decide that the bondholders would be better served by giving the company a chance to work out its problems rather than forcing it into bankruptcy.

The Securities and Exchange Commission (1) approves indentures for publicly traded bonds and (2) makes sure that all indenture provisions are met before allowing a company to sell new securities to the public. Also, it should be noted that the indentures of most larger corporations were actually written back in the 1930s or 1940s and that many issues of new bonds, all covered by the same indenture, have been sold down through the years. The interest rates on the bonds, and perhaps also the maturities, will change from issue to issue, but bondholders' protection as spelled out in the indenture will be the same for all bonds of a given type.[4]

---

[4] A firm will have different indentures for each of the major types of bonds it issues, including its first mortgage bonds, its debentures, its convertibles, and so on.

Call Provisions

Most bonds contain a *call provision* which gives the issuing corporation the right to call the bonds for redemption. The call provision generally states that the company must pay the bondholder an amount greater than the par value for the bond when it is called. The additional sum, which is defined as a *call premium,* is typically set equal to one year's interest if the bond is called during the first year, with the premium declining at a constant rate of I/n each year thereafter, where $I =$ Annual interest and $n =$ Original maturity in years. For example, the call premium on a \$1,000 par value, 10-year, 10 percent bond would generally be \$100 if it were called during the first year, \$90 during the second year (calculated by reducing the \$100, or 10 percent, premium by one-tenth), and so on. However, as noted below, bonds are often not callable until several years — generally 5 or 10 — after they were issued.

Suppose a company sold bonds or preferred stock when interest rates were relatively high. Provided the issue is callable, the company could sell a new issue of low-yielding securities if and when interest rates drop. It could then use the proceeds to retire the high-rate issue and thus reduce its interest or preferred dividend expenses. This is called a *refunding operation.* Refunding operations are discussed in detail in Appendix 15B.

The call privilege is valuable to the firm but potentially detrimental to the investor, especially if the bond was issued in a period when interest rates were cyclically high. Accordingly, the interest rate on a new issue of callable bonds will exceed that on a new issue of noncallable bonds. For example, on March 12, 1987, Great Falls Timber Company sold a bond issue yielding 10.375 percent; these bonds were callable immediately. On the same day, Midwest Milling Company sold an issue of similar risk and maturity which yielded 10.0 percent; its bonds were noncallable for 10 years. (This is known as a *deferred call,* and the bonds are said to have *call protection.*) Investors were apparently willing to accept a 0.375 percent lower interest rate on Midwest's bonds for the assurance that the relatively high (by historic standards) rate of interest would be earned for at least 10 years. Great Falls, on the other hand, had to incur a 0.375 percent higher annual interest rate to obtain the option of calling the bonds in the event of a subsequent decline in interest rates.

Sinking Funds

A *sinking fund* is a provision that facilitates the orderly retirement of a bond issue (or, in some cases, an issue of preferred stock). Typically, the sinking fund provision requires the firm to retire a portion of the bond issue each year. On rare occasions the firm may be required to deposit money with a trustee, who invests the funds and then uses the accumulated sum to retire the bonds when they mature. Usually, though, the sinking fund is used to buy back a certain percentage of the issue each year. A failure to meet the sinking fund requirement causes the bond issue to be thrown into default, which may force the company into bankruptcy. Obviously, then, a sinking fund can constitute a dangerous cash drain on the firm.

In most cases, the firm is given the right to handle the sinking fund in either of two ways:

1. The company may call in for redemption (at par value) a certain percentage of the bonds each year — for example, it might be able to call 2 percent of the total original amount of the issue at a price of $1,000 per bond. The bonds are numbered serially, and those called for redemption are determined by a lottery administered by the trustee.

2. The company may buy the required amount of bonds on the open market.

Since the firm will choose the least-cost method, if interest rates have risen, causing bond prices to fall, it will elect to use the option of buying bonds in the open market at a discount; otherwise, it will call them. Note that a call for sinking fund purposes is quite different from a refunding call as discussed above. A sinking fund call requires no call premium; however, only a small percentage of the issue is normally callable in any one year.

Although sinking funds are designed to protect bondholders by insuring that an issue is retired in an orderly fashion, it must be recognized that sinking funds will at times work to the detriment of bondholders. For example, suppose the bond carries a 15 percent interest rate, but yields on similar bonds have fallen to 10 percent. A sinking fund call at par would require an investor to give up $150 of interest and reinvest in a bond that pays only $100 per year. This obviously disadvantages those bondholders whose bonds are called. On balance, however, securities that provide for a sinking fund are regarded as being safer than those without such a provision, so at the time they are issued they have lower coupon rates than otherwise similar bonds without sinking funds.

RECENT INNOVATIONS

In this section, we discuss three new types of long-term debt: (1) zero coupon bonds, (2) floating rate bonds, and (3) junk bonds.

Zero (or Very Low) Coupon Bonds

Some bonds pay no interest but are offered at a substantial discount below their par values and hence provide capital appreciation rather than current cash income. These securities are called *zero coupon bonds ("zeros"),* or *original issue discount bonds (OIDs).* Zeros were first used in a major way in 1981. In recent years IBM, Alcoa, J. C. Penney, ITT, Cities Service, GMAC, Martin-Marietta, and many other companies have used them to raise billions of dollars. Moreover, investment bankers have in effect created zero coupon Treasury bonds. To understand what zeros are, consider Penney's zeros, which were sold in 1981 for $332.41 per $1,000 bond and which mature after 8 years, in 1989, at which time holders will be paid $1,000. The annual interest rate which causes $332.41 to grow to $1,000 over 8 years is 14.76 percent. Penney received $332.41 per bond less underwriting expenses for the issue, but it will have to pay back $1,000 in 1989.

The advantages of the zeros to Penney include the following: (1) no cash outlays are required for either interest or principal until the bonds mature; (2) the bonds have a relatively low yield to maturity (Penney would have had to pay about 15.25 percent versus 14.76 percent had it issued regular coupon bonds at par); and (3) Penney receives an annual tax deduction equal to the yearly amortization of the discount, which means that the bonds provide a positive cash flow in the form of tax savings over their life. There are also two disadvantages to Penney: (1) If they were called, the bonds would have to be paid off at their $1,000 par value, and, since it is better to pay the $1,000 in 1989 than at some earlier date, the effect is that Penney cannot refund the issue if interest rates should fall. (2) Penney will have a very large nondeductible cash outlay coming up in 1989.

There are two principal advantages to investors in zero coupon bonds: (1) they generally have no danger of a call, and (2) they are guaranteed a "true" yield (14.76 percent in the Penney case) irrespective of what happens to interest rates — the holders of Penney's bonds do not have to worry about having to reinvest coupon payments at low rates if interest rates should fall, which would result in a realized yield to maturity of less than 14.76 percent. This second feature is extremely important to pension funds, life insurance companies, and other institutions which make actuarial contracts based on assumed reinvestment rates. For such investors, the risk of declining interest rates, and hence an inability to reinvest cash inflows at the assumed rate, is greater than the risk of an increase in rates and the accompanying fall in bond values. To illustrate, suppose Southeast Mutual Insurance Company signed a contract to pay $100,000 in 8 years in exchange for a lump sum premium of $33,241 today. The premium was based on the assumption that Southeast could invest the $33,241 at a return of 14.76 percent. If the $33,241 were invested in regular coupon bonds paying a 14.76 percent annual coupon rate, then the accumulated value 8 years hence would be equal to the required $100,000 only if all coupon payments could be reinvested at 14.76 percent over the next 8 years. If interest rates were to fall, then the accumulated amount would fall short of the required $100,000. Note, however, that if the $33,241 were invested in a zero coupon bond with a 14.76 percent yield, Southeast would end up with the required $100,000 irrespective of what happened to interest rates in the future. Thus, Southeast would have been "immunized" against a decline in interest rates.

To analyze a zero coupon bond and compare it with a regular coupon bond, a corporate treasurer (or pension fund administrator) must employ the valuation models developed in Chapter 5. Consider again Penney's bonds. At the time the bonds were issued, the corporate tax rate was $T = 46\%$. Penney would receive $332.41 per bond at $t = 0$. Also, it would have a tax deduction each year equal

---

[5]At the time the Penney bonds were issued, the Tax Code permitted straight line amortization of the discount as shown in our example. Subsequently, the Tax Code was changed to require the use of an amortization procedure which produces lower early-year deductions and hence a slightly higher effective cost to the company. Also, since most bonds pay interest on a semiannual basis, people often analyze zeros on a semiannual compounding basis to make the calculated yields comparable to those on regular coupon bonds. See Eugene F. Brigham and Louis C. Gapenski, *Intermediate Financial Management,* 2nd ed., Chapter 13.

to the $83.45 amortization of the discount: ($1,000 − $332.41)/8 = $83.45, and this deduction would save taxes each year in the amount of T(Deduction) = 0.46($83.45) = $38.39 per bond.[5] Penney would have to make a payment of $1,000 at t = 8. Thus, the after-tax cash flow time line is as follows:

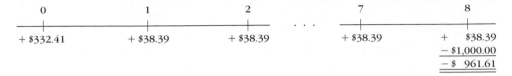

The IRR of this cash flow stream, which is the discount rate which solves the equation below, is Penney's after-tax cost of debt capital from the zero coupon bond, k_d:

$$\sum_{t=0}^{n} \frac{C_t}{(1 + k_d)^t} = 0$$

$$\frac{C_0}{(1 + k_d)^0} + \frac{C_1}{(1 + k_d)^1} + \cdots + \frac{C_n}{(1 + k_d)^n} = 0$$

$$\frac{\$332.41}{(1 + k_d)^0} + \frac{\$38.39}{(1 + k_d)^1} + \cdots + \frac{\$38.39}{(1 + k_d)^7} - \frac{\$961.61}{(1 + k_d)^8} = 0.$$

The solution value for k_d is 7.6 percent; this was Penney's after-tax cost of its zero coupon debt.[6]

If Penney had sold an annual payment coupon bond, it would have had to pay about 15.25 percent. Its after-tax interest payments would have been (Coupon) (1 − T) = ($152.50)(0.54) = $82.35, and its after-tax cost of debt would have been k_d in this equation:

$$\frac{\$1,000}{(1 + k_d)^0} - \frac{\$82.35}{(1 + k_d)^1} - \cdots - \frac{\$82.35}{(1 + k_d)^7} - \frac{\$1,082.35}{(1 + k_d)^8} = 0.$$

The solution value is k_d = 8.235 percent, so on an after-tax basis, the zero coupon bond had a lower cost to Penney than a regular coupon bond — 7.6 percent versus 8.235 percent. For a purchaser, of course, the reverse is true: A tax-exempt bond buyer would receive the yield to maturity, which is 14.76 percent, for the zero coupon bond and an expected 15.25 percent for the regular coupon bond. Purchasers apparently believed that call protection plus interest rate immunization were worth the 0.49 percentage point cost.

One might think that zeros would provide an advantage to investors in that the return would be reported as income in the year that the zeros mature, thus delay-

---

[6]Since interest is a deductible expense, the government in effect pays a portion of the interest on a bond, and hence the after-tax cost of debt is equal to the pre-tax cost times (1 − Tax rate). Thus, if Penney could sell regular coupon debt with a yield of 14.76 percent, its after-tax cost of that debt would be 14.76%(1 − T) = 14.76%(0.54) = 7.97% versus 7.6% on the zeros. The difference is caused by the fact that on the zeros, Penney gets to take tax deductions *before* it makes any payments, whereas on a coupon bond, deductions are taken in the year interest is paid. The new tax regulations that were issued after Penney sold its bonds eliminated that advantage of zeros.

ing the payment of taxes until that time. However, that is not the case under current U.S. tax regulations — the purchaser of a zero (or really, any original issue discount bond) must report as ordinary income each year the same amortization of discount that the company claims as a deduction. Thus, a company like Penney is required to keep a record of all the holders of its zeros and to report, on a Form 1099, the amortization of discount attributable to each bondholder each year. Had a regular coupon bond been used, the Form 1099 would have reported interest income, so the tax consequences to investors are the same for interest and discount amortization. Of course, if you receive interest, you have cash to pay the taxes, but if you buy a zero, you get a tax bill but no cash to pay it with. For that reason, most zeros are sold to pension funds and other tax exempt investors.

Also, note that not all original issue discount bonds (OIDs) have zero coupons. For example, K. Zumwalt Corporation sold an issue of 20-year bonds with a 5 percent coupon at a time when other bonds with similar ratings and maturities are yielding 10 percent. These bonds had a value of about $575:

$$\text{Value} = \sum_{t=1}^{20} \frac{\$50}{(1.10)^t} + \frac{\$1,000}{(1.10)^{20}} = \$574.32.$$

If an investor purchased these bonds at a price of $574.32, the yield to maturity would be 10 percent. The discount of $1,000 − $574.32 = $425.68 would be amortized over the bond's 20-year life, and it would be handled by both Zumwalt and the bondholders exactly as the discount on the zeros was handled.

Thus, zero coupon bonds are just one type of original issue discount bond — any nonconvertible bond whose coupon rate is set below the going market rate at the time of its issue will sell at a discount, and it will be classified (for tax and other purposes) as an OID.

Shortly after corporations began to issue zeros, investment bankers figured out a way to create zeros from U.S. Treasury bonds, which are issued only in coupon form. In 1982 Salomon Brothers bought $1 billion of 12 percent, 30-year Treasuries. Each bond had 60 coupons worth $60 each, which represented the interest payments due every 6 months. Salomon then in effect clipped the coupons and placed them in 60 piles; the last pile also contained the now "stripped" bond itself, which represented a promise of $1,000 in the year 2012. These 60 piles of U.S. Treasury promises were then placed with the trust department of a bank and used as collateral for 60 maturities of "zero coupon U.S. Treasury Trust Certificates," which are in essence zero coupon Treasury bonds. A pension fund that expected to need money in 1993 could buy an 11-year certificate backed by the interest the Treasury will pay in 1993. Treasury zeros are, of course, safer than corporate zeros, so they are very popular with pension fund managers.

Floating Rate Bonds

In the early 1980s, inflation pushed interest rates up to unprecedented levels, causing sharp declines in the prices of long-term bonds. Even some supposedly "risk-free" U.S. Treasury bonds lost fully half their value, and a similar situation occurred with corporate bonds, mortgages, and other fixed rate, long-term securities. The lenders who held the fixed rate debt were of course hurt very badly. Bankruptcies (or forced mergers to avoid bankruptcy) were commonplace in the banking and especially the savings and loan industries. Insurance company reserves also plummeted, causing those companies severe problems, including the bankruptcy of Baldwin-United, a $9 billion diversified insurance firm. As a result, many lenders became reluctant to lend money at fixed rates on a long-term basis, and they would do so only at high rates.

There is normally a *maturity risk premium* embodied in long-term interest rates — this is a risk premium designed to offset the risk of declining bond prices if interest rates rise. Prior to the 1970s, the maturity risk premium on 30-year bonds was about one percentage point, meaning that under "normal" conditions a firm might expect to pay about one percentage point more to borrow on a long-term than on a short-term basis. However, in the early 1980s, the maturity risk premium is estimated to have jumped to about three percentage points, which made long-term debt very expensive relative to short-term debt. Lenders were able and willing to lend on a short-term basis, but corporations were correctly reluctant to borrow short-term to finance long-term assets — such action is, as we will see in Chapter 18, extremely dangerous. Therefore, we had a situation in which lenders did not want to lend on a long-term basis, but corporations needed long-term money. The problem was solved by the introduction of *long-term, floating rate debt.*

A typical *floating rate bond* works as follows. The coupon rate is set for, say, the initial six-month period, after which it is adjusted every six months based on some market rate. For example, Gulf Oil sold a floating rate bond that was pegged at 35 basis points above the going rate on 30-year Treasury bonds. Other companies' issues have been tied to short-term rates. Many additional provisions have been included in floating rate issues; for example, some are convertible to fixed rate debt, while others have upper and lower limits on how high or low the yield can go.

Floating rate debt is advantageous to investors because the interest rate moves up if market rates rise, which (1) causes the market value of the debt to be stabilized and (2) provides lenders such as banks with more income to meet their own obligations (for example, a bank which owns floating rate bonds can use the interest it earns to pay interest on its own deposits). Moreover, floating rate debt is advantageous to corporations because by using it they can issue debt with a long maturity without committing themselves to paying an historically high rate of interest for the entire life of the loan. Of course, if interest rates increase after a floating rate note has been signed, then the borrower would have been better off issuing conventional, fixed rate debt.[7]

Junk Bonds

Another new type of bond is the *junk bond,* a high-risk, high-yield bond issued to finance a leveraged buyout, or merger, or to finance a troubled company. For example, when Ted Turner attempted to buy CBS, he planned to finance the acqui-

---

[7]For a general discussion of floating rate debt, see Kenneth R. Marks and Warren A. Law, "Hedging against Inflation with Floating-Rate Notes," *Harvard Business Review,* March-April 1980, 106–112.

sition by issuing junk bonds to CBS's stockholders in exchange for their shares. Similarly, Merrill Lynch helped Public Service of New Hampshire finance contruction of its troubled Seabrook nuclear plant with junk bonds, and People Express used junk bonds to finance its expansion program. In junk bond deals, the debt ratio is generally extremely high, so the bondholders must bear as much risk as stockholders normally would. The bonds' yields reflect this fact — Ted Turner's bonds would have carried a coupon rate of about 16 percent, and Merrill Lynch has reported that a coupon rate in the 25 to 30 percent range was required to sell the Public Service of New Hampshire bonds.

The emergence of junk bonds as an important type of debt is another example of how the investment banking industry adjusts to and facilitates new developments in capital markets. In the 1980s, mergers and takeovers increased dramatically. People like T. Boone Pickens and Ted Turner thought that certain old-line, established companies were run inefficiently and were financed too conservatively, and they wanted to take these companies over and restructure them. To help finance these takeovers, the investment banking firm of Drexel Burnham Lambert began an active campaign to persuade certain institutions to purchase high-yield bonds. Drexel developed expertise in putting together deals that would be attractive to the institutions yet feasible in the sense that cash flows would be sufficient to meet the required interest payments. The fact that interest on the bonds is tax deductible, combined with the much higher debt ratios of the restructured firms, also increased after-tax cash flows and helped make the deals feasible.

The development of junk bond financing has done as much as any single factor to reshape the U.S. financial scene. It led directly to the loss of independence of Gulf Oil and hundreds of other companies, and it led to major shake-ups in such companies as CBS, Union Carbide, and USX (formerly U.S. Steel). It also caused Drexel Burnham Lambert to leap from essentially nowhere in the 1970s to fourth place in the investment banking industry in 1986.

BOND RATINGS

Since the early 1900s, bonds have been assigned quality ratings that reflect their probability of going into default. The two major rating agencies are Moody's Investors Service (Moody's) and Standard & Poor's Corporation (S&P). These agencies' rating designations are shown in Table 15-1.[8] The triple and double A bonds are extremely safe. Single A and triple B bonds are strong enough to be called *investment grade bonds,* and they are the lowest-rated bonds that many banks and other institutional investors are permitted by law to hold. Double B and lower bonds are speculations, or junk bonds; they have a significant probability of going into default, and many financial institutions are prohibited from buying them.

---

[8]In the discussion to follow, reference to the S&P code is intended to imply the Moody code as well. Thus, for example, triple B bonds mean both BBB and Baa bonds; double B bonds, both BB and Ba bonds; and so on.

Table 15-1
Comparison of Bond Ratings

	High Quality		Investment Grade		Junk Bonds			
					Substandard		Speculative	
Moody's	Aaa	Aa	A	Baa	Ba	B	Caa	C
S&P	AAA	AA	A	BBB	BB	B	CCC	D

Note: Both Moody's and S&P use "modifiers" for bonds rated below triple A. S&P uses a plus and minus system; thus, A+ designates the strongest A-rated bonds and A− the weakest. Moody's uses a 1, 2, or 3 designation, with 1 denoting the strongest and 3 the weakest; thus, within the double A category, Aa1 is the best, Aa2 is average, and Aa3 is the weakest.

Bond Rating Criteria

Although the rating assignments are judgmental, they are based on both qualitative and quantitative factors, some of which are listed below:

1. Debt ratio.

2. Times-interest-earned ratio.

3. Fixed charge coverage ratio.

4. Current ratio.

5. Mortgage provisions: Is the bond secured by a mortgage? If it is, and if the property has a high value in relation to the amount of bonded debt, the bond's rating is enhanced.

6. Subordination provisions: Is the bond subordinated to other debt? If so, it will be rated at least one notch below the rating it would have if it were not subordinated. Conversely, a bond with other debt subordinated to it will have a somewhat higher rating.

7. Guarantee provisions: Some bonds are guaranteed by other firms. If a weak company's debt is guaranteed by a strong company (usually the weak company's parent), then the bond will be given the strong company's rating.

8. Sinking fund: Does the bond have a sinking fund to insure systematic repayment? This feature is a plus factor to the rating agencies.

9. Maturity: Other things the same, a bond with a shorter maturity will be judged less risky than a longer-term bond, and this will be reflected in the ratings.

10. Stability: Are the issuer's sales and earnings stable?

11. Regulation: Is the issuer regulated, and could an adverse regulatory climate cause the company's economic position to decline? Regulation is especially important for utilities, railroads, and telephone companies.

12. Antitrust and legal: Are any antitrust actions or lawsuits pending against the firm that could erode its position?

13. Overseas operations: What percentage of the firm's sales, assets, and profits are from overseas operations, and what is the political climate in the host countries?

14. Environmental factors: Is the firm likely to face heavy expenditures for pollution control equipment?

15. Pension liabilities: Does the firm have unfunded pension liabilities that could pose a future problem?

16. Labor unrest: Are there potential labor problems on the horizon that could weaken the firm's position? As this is written, the entire airline industry faces this problem, and it has caused ratings of airlines to be lowered.

17. Resource availability: Is the firm likely to face supply shortages that could force it to curtail operations?

18. Accounting policies: If a firm uses relatively conservative accounting policies, then its reported earnings will be of "higher quality" than if it uses less conservative procedures. Thus, conservative accounting policies are a plus factor in bond ratings.

Representatives of the rating agencies have consistently stated that no precise formula is used to set a firm's rating — all the factors listed, plus others, are taken into account, but not in a mathematically precise manner. Statistical studies have borne out this contention, for researchers who have tried to predict bond ratings on the basis of quantitative data have had only limited success, indicating that the agencies do indeed use a good deal of subjective judgment when establishing a firm's rating.[9]

Importance of Bond Ratings

Bond ratings are important both to firms and to investors. First, a bond's rating is an indicator of its default risk; hence, the rating has a direct, measurable influence on the bond's interest rate and the firm's cost of debt capital. Second, ratings have an effect on the availability of debt capital. Most bonds are purchased by institutional investors rather than individuals, and if an institutional investor buys BBB bonds and these bonds are subsequently downgraded to BB or lower, then (1) the institution's regulators will reprimand or perhaps impose restrictions on it if it continues to hold the bonds, but (2) since many other institutional investors will not be able to purchase them, the institution that owns down-graded bonds will probably not be able to sell them except at a sizable loss. Because of this fear of downgrading, many institutions restrict their bond portfolios to at least A, or even AA, and some even confine purchases to AAA bonds. Thus, the lower a firm's rating, the smaller the group of available purchasers for its new issues.

As a result of their higher risk and more restricted market, lower-grade bonds have higher required rates of return, k_d, than high-grade bonds. Figure 15-1 illus-

---

[9]See Ahmed Belkaoui, *Industrial Bonds and the Rating Process* (London: Quorum Books, 1983).

Figure 15-1
Yields on Selected Long-Term Bonds, 1953–1987

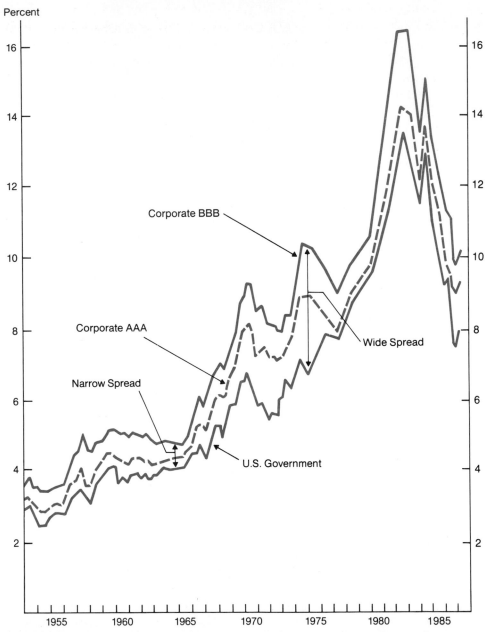

Sources: Federal Reserve Board, *Historical Chart Book,* 1983, and *Federal Reserve Bulletin,* various issues.

trates this point. In each of the years shown on the graph, U.S. government bonds have had the lowest yields, AAAs have been next, and BBB bonds have had the highest yields. The figure also shows that the gaps between yields on the three types of bonds vary over time, indicating that the cost differentials, or risk premiums, fluctuate from year to year. This point is highlighted in Figure 15-2, which gives the yields on the three types of bonds and the risk premiums for AAA and

Figure 15-2

Relationship between Bond Ratings and Bond Yields, 1963, 1975, and 1987

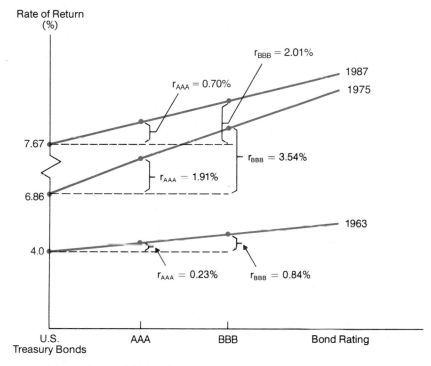

r_{AAA} = risk premium on AAA bonds
r_{BBB} = risk premium on BBB bonds

	Long-Term Government Bonds (Default-Free) (1)	AAA Corporate Bonds (2)	BBB Corporate Bonds (3)	Risk Premiums	
				AAA (4) = (2) − (1)	BBB (5) = (3) − (1)
June 1963	4.00%	4.23%	4.84%	0.23%	0.84%
June 1975	6.86	8.77	10.40	1.91	3.54
February 1987	7.67	8.37	9.68	0.70	2.01

Source: *Federal Reserve Bulletins.*

BBB bonds in June 1963, June 1975, and February 1987.[10] Note first that the riskless rate, or vertical axis intercept, rose almost 4 percentage points from 1963 to 1987, reflecting primarily the increase in realized and anticipated inflation. Second, the slope of the line also has increased since 1963, indicating an increase in investors' risk aversion; this increase was quite pronounced from 1963 to 1975, but it fell somewhat between 1975 and 1987.[11] Thus, the penalty for having a low credit rating varies over time. Occasionally, as in 1963, it is quite small, but at other times, as in 1975, it is very large. These slope differences reflect investors' risk aversion — in 1975 we were emerging from a severe recession caused by a quadrupling of oil prices in 1973–1974, and investors were afraid the economy would slip back into a slump. At such times people seek safety in bonds, Treasuries are in great demand, and the premium on low-quality over high-quality bonds increases.

Changes in Ratings

A change in a firm's bond rating will have a significant effect on its ability to borrow long-term capital as well as on the cost of that capital. Rating agencies review outstanding bonds on a periodic basis, occasionally upgrading or downgrading a bond as a result of its issuer's changed circumstances. For example, when Mobil Oil announced that it was planning to spin off its Montgomery Ward unit (Mobil had acquired Montgomery Ward in a diversification move back in the early 1970s), S&P immediately placed Ward on its *CreditWatch* list. (*CreditWatch* is a weekly publication that discusses developing situations that may lead to upgradings or downgradings.) The statement made in *CreditWatch* was that without Mobil's backing, Montgomery Ward's credit position might deteriorate to the point where

---

[10]The term *risk premium* ought to reflect only the difference in expected (and required) returns between two securities that results from differences in their risk. However, the differences between *yields to maturity* on different types of bonds consist of (1) a true risk premium; (2) a liquidity premium, which reflects the fact that U.S. Treasury bonds are more readily marketable than most corporate bonds; (3) a call premium, because most Treasury bonds are not callable while corporate bonds are; and (4) an expected loss differential, which reflects the probability of loss on the corporate bonds. As an example of the last point, suppose the yield to maturity on a BBB bond was 10 percent versus 7 percent on government bonds, but there was a 5 percent probability of total default loss on the corporate bond. In this case, the expected return on the BBB bond would be $0.95(10\%) + 0.05(0\%) = 9.5\%$, and the risk premium would be 2.5 percent, not the full 3.0 percentage point difference in "promised" yields to maturity. Because of all these points, the risk premiums given in Figure 15-2 overstate somewhat the true (but unmeasurable) risk premiums.

[11]The relationship graphed here is akin to the Security Market Line developed in Chapter 6, although bond ratings rather than beta coefficients are used to measure risk. A word about the scaling of the horizontal axis and about the placement of the points is in order. (1) We have shown a linear fit, although there is no theoretical reason to think that yields plotted against bond ratings are necessarily linear. (2) We have shown the interval on the horizontal axis between AAA and BBB to be equal to that between U.S. Government bonds and AAA, but this is an arbitrary scaling. (3) Finally, on an accurate, large-scale graph, it would be clear that the plotted points for the AAA and BBB bonds are not precisely on the straight lines shown in the graph; however, they are sufficiently close to warrant our analysis.

Attempts have been made to calculate beta coefficients for bonds and to plot bonds on the same SML that is used for common stocks. However, these results have not been successful — bonds do not plot on the same linear SML as stocks.

its first mortgage bonds would have to be lowered from BBB− to BB, and its debentures from BB+ to some lower rating. The final outcome will depend on Ward's condition when Mobil does spin it off. Similarly, in March 1987, when it was announced that Allegheny International had agreed to go private in a leveraged buyout, it was immediately placed on the *CreditWatch* list for possible raising or lowering. S&P indicated that Allegheny's ratings could be raised if the buyout results in improvements in debt servicing capabilities, but lowered if the plan doesn't address the company's near-term financial problems.

If a company announces a large new bond issue, a rating agency review generally will be triggered. If the firm's situation has recently deteriorated, but its bonds have not been reviewed and downgraded, then it may choose to use a term loan or short-term debt rather than finance through a public bond issue. This will perhaps postpone a rating agency review until the situation has improved. For example, Midwest Utilities delayed a bond issue in the spring of 1986, financing with short-term debt until a rate increase could be obtained to improve interest coverage ratios to acceptable levels. In 1987, after the rate increase was in effect and coverages had improved, the company sold bonds and used the proceeds to retire the short-term debt.

RATIONALE FOR USING DIFFERENT TYPES OF SECURITIES

Why are there so many different types of long-term securities? At least a partial answer to this question may be seen from Figure 15-3, which depicts the now familiar risk/return trade-off function drawn to show the risk and the expected after-personal-tax returns for the various securities of the Riener Company.[12] First, U.S. Treasury bills, representing the risk-free rate, are shown for reference. The lowest-risk long term securities offered by Riener are its floating rate notes; these securities are free of interest rate risk, but they are exposed to some risk of default. The first mortgage bonds are somewhat riskier than the notes (because the bonds are exposed to interest rate risk), and they sell at a somewhat higher required and expected after-tax return. The second mortgage bonds are even riskier, so they have a still higher expected return. Subordinated debentures, income bonds, and preferred stocks are all increasingly risky, and their expected returns increase accordingly. The firm's convertible preferred is riskier than its straight preferred, but less risky than its common stock. Riener's warrants, the riskiest security it issues, have the highest required return of any of its offerings. (Warrants and convertibles are discussed in Chapter 17.)

Why does Riener issue so many different classes of securities? Why does it not offer just one type of bond plus common stock? The answer lies in the fact that different investors have different risk/return trade-off preferences, so to appeal to the broadest possible market, Riener must offer securities that attract as many

[12]The yields in Figure 15-3 are shown on an after-tax basis to the recipient. If yields were on a before-personal-tax basis, those on preferred stocks would lie below those on bonds because of the tax treatment of preferreds. In essence, 80 percent of preferred dividends are tax exempt to corporations owning preferred shares, so a preferred stock with a 10 percent pre-tax yield will have a higher after-tax return to a corporation in the 34 percent tax bracket than will a bond with a 12 percent yield.

Figure 15-3
Riener Company:
Risk and Expected Returns on Different Classes of Securities

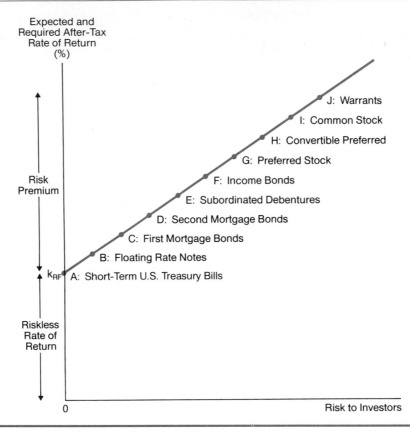

different types of investors as possible. Also, different securities are more popular and hence in demand at different points in time, and firms tend to issue whatever is popular at the time they need money. Used wisely, a policy of selling differentiated securities to take advantage of market conditions can lower a firm's overall cost of capital below what it would be if the firm issued only one class of debt, plus common stock.

FACTORS INFLUENCING LONG-TERM FINANCING DECISIONS

As we show in this section, many factors influence a firm's long-term financing decisions. The factors' relative importance varies among firms at any point in time and for any given firm over time, but any company planning to raise new long-term capital should consider each of these points.

Target Capital Structure

As we saw in Chapter 12, firms typically establish target capital structures, or target debt/equity mixes. One of the most important considerations in any financing decision is how the firm's actual capital structure compares to its target structure. Of course, few firms in any one year finance exactly in accordance with their target capital structures, primarily because exact adherence would increase their flotation costs: since smaller issues of new securities have proportionally larger flotation costs, firms tend to use debt one year and stock the next.

For example, Handyman Equipment, Inc., a Cleveland machine tool manufacturer, requires $20 million of new external capital in each of the next two years. Its target capital structure calls for 40 percent debt, so if Handyman were to raise debt each year, it would issue $8 million of new bonds each year. The flotation costs, based on data back in Table 14-4, would be 3.2 percent of each $8 million issue. To net $8 million, Handyman would have to sell $8,000,000/0.968 = $8,264,463 each year and thus pay $264,463 in flotation costs on each issue for a total of $528,926 in flotation costs over the two years. Alternatively, Handyman could elect to raise the total $16 million of debt in one year. The flotation cost for a $16 million issue would be about 1.9 percent, so the firm would float an issue for $16,000,000/0.981 = $16,309,888 and pay $309,888 in total flotation costs. By issuing debt only once, Handyman could cut its debt flotation costs by more than 40 percent. The same relationship would apply to sales of preferred stock and new common equity issues.

Note that making fewer but larger security offerings would cause Handyman's capital structure to fluctuate about its optimal level rather than stay right on target. However, as we saw in Chapter 12, small fluctuations about the optimal capital structure have little effect either on a firm's required returns on debt and equity or on its overall cost of capital. Also, investors would recognize that its actions were prudent and that the firm would save substantial amounts of flotation costs by financing in this manner. Therefore, while firms such as Handyman do tend to finance over the long haul in accordance with their target capital structures, flotation costs plus the other factors discussed in the following sections have a definite influence on the specific financing decisions in any given year.

Maturity Matching

Assume that Handyman decides to float a single $16 million nonconvertible bond issue with a sinking fund. It must next choose a maturity for the issue, taking into consideration the shape of the yield curve, management's own expectations about future interest rates, and the maturity of the assets being financed. In the case at hand, Handyman's capital projects over the next two years consist primarily of new, automated milling and stamping machinery for its Cleveland plant. This machinery has an expected economic life of 10 years (even though it falls into the ACRS 5-year class life). Should Handyman finance the debt portion of the capital raised for this equipment with 5-year, 10-year, 20-year, or 30-year debt, or with debt of some other maturity? *One approach is to match the maturity of the liabilities with the maturity of the assets being financed.*

Note that some of the new capital for the machinery will come from common stock, which is generally considered to be a perpetual security with an infinite maturity. Of course, common stock can always be repurchased on the open market or by a tender offer, so its effective maturity can be reduced significantly.

On the other hand, debt maturities are specified at the time of issue. If Handyman financed its capital budgets over the next two years with 10-year sinking fund bonds, it would be matching its asset and liability maturities. The cash flows resulting from the new machinery should be sufficient to make the interest and sinking fund payments on the issue, and the bonds would be retired as the machinery wore out. However, if Handyman used 1-year debt, it would have to pay off the loan with cash flows derived from assets other than the machinery in question. Of course, it could probably roll over the 1-year debt, but, if it did so and interest rates rose, then it would have to pay a higher rate. If Handyman subsequently experienced difficulties, its lenders might be hesitant to extend the loan, and the company might be unable to obtain new short-term debt at any reasonable rate. On the other hand, if it used 20-year or 30-year debt, Handyman would still be servicing the debt long after the assets that were purchased with it had been scrapped and had ceased to provide cash flows; this would worry the lenders.

For all these reasons, one commonly used financing strategy is to match debt maturities with asset maturities. In recognition of this fact, firms do consider maturity relationships, and this factor has a major influence on the type of debt securities used.

Interest Rate Levels and Forecasts

Financial managers also consider interest rate levels and forecasts, both absolute and relative, when making financing decisions. For example, long-term interest rates were high by historic standards in 1981 and 1982, so many managers were reluctant to issue long-term debt and thus lock in those costs for long periods. We already know that one solution to this problem is to use long-term debt with a call provision. Callability permits the company to refund the issue should interest rates drop, but there is a cost, because firms must pay more if they make their debt callable. Alternatively, firms may finance with short-term debt whenever long-term rates are historically high and then, assuming that interest rates subsequently fall, sell a long-term issue to replace the short-term debt. Of course, this strategy has its risks. If interest rates move even higher, firms will be forced to renew the debt at higher and higher short-term rates, or to replace the short-term debt with a long-term bond which will now cost even more than it would have when the original decision was made.

In early September of 1983, the interest rate on AAA corporate bonds was about 12.5 percent, up from 11.5 percent in April. Exxon's investment bankers advised the company to tap the Eurodollar bond market for relatively cheap fixed rate financing.[13] At the time, Exxon could have issued its bonds in London at 0.4 per-

---

[13]A *Eurodollar bond* is a bond sold outside of the United States but denominated in U.S. dollars. See the section entitled "Multinational Finance" at the end of this chapter for a discussion of Eurodollar bonds.

centage points *below* comparable-maturity Treasury bonds. However, one of Exxon's officers was quoted as saying, "I say so what. The absolute level of rates is too high. We would rather wait." The managers of Exxon, as well as those of many other companies, were betting that the next move in interest rates would be down. This belief was also openly expressed by executives of ITT, Ontario Hydro, and RCA, among others.

This example confirms that many firms base their financing decisions on expectations about future interest rates. In Exxon's case, the financial staff turned out to be correct. However, the success of such a strategy requires that interest rate forecasts be right more often than they are wrong — and it is very difficult to find someone with a long-term forecasting track record better than 50-50.

The Firm's Current and Forecasted Condition

If a firm's current financial condition is poor, its managers may be reluctant to issue new long-term debt because (1) a new bond issue would probably trigger a review by the rating agencies, and (2) long-term debt issued when a firm is in poor financial condition would probably cost more and be subject to more severe restrictive covenants than debt issued from strength. Thus, a firm that is in a weakened condition but is forecasting a better time in the future would be inclined to delay permanent financing of any type until things improved. Conversely, a firm that is strong now but whose forecasts indicate a potentially bad time in the period just ahead would be motivated to finance long-term now rather than to wait. These scenarios imply that the capital markets are inefficient in the sense that investors do not have as much information about the firm's future as does its financial manager. This situation is undoubtedly true at times.

The firm's earnings outlook, and the extent to which forecasted higher earnings per share are reflected in stock prices, also has an effect on the choice of securities. If a successful R&D program has just been concluded, and consequently management forecasts higher earnings than do most investors, then the firm would not want to issue common stock. It would use debt and then, once earnings had risen and pushed up the stock price, it would sell common stock to restore the capital structure to its target level.[14]

Restrictions in Existing Debt Contracts

Earlier we discussed the fact that Savannah Electric has at times been restricted from issuing new first mortgage bonds by its indenture coverage requirements. This is just one example of how indenture covenants can influence a firm's financing decision. Restrictions on the current ratio, the debt ratio, and so on, could also restrict a firm's ability to use different types of financing at a given time.

---

[14]Many of the factors discussed in this section imply an ability on the part of managers to forecast capital market conditions. Managers can generally forecast their own firms' internal conditions better than outside investors, but no one can consistently forecast interest rates and the general level of stock prices. Note also that financial managers can minimize the adverse effects of changes in capital costs through transactions in the *futures market*. For a discussion of the futures market, see Chapter 17.

Availability of Collateral

Generally, secured long-term debt will be less costly than unsecured debt. Thus, firms with large amounts of unencumbered fixed assets that have a ready resale value are likely to use a relatively large amount of debt, especially mortgage bonds. Additionally, each year's financing decision would be influenced by the amount of new qualified assets that are available as security for new bonds.

SUMMARY

This chapter has described the characteristics, advantages, and disadvantages of the major types of long-term debt securities. The key difference between *bonds* and *term loans* is the fact that term loans are sold directly by a corporate borrower to between 1 and 20 lenders, while bonds are generally sold to many public investors through investment bankers.

It is impossible to state as a generalization that long-term debt is the "best" method of financing at a particular time. Each type of security has advantages and disadvantages vis-à-vis the others, and the relative advantages of long-term debt vary over time and from company to company. There are many factors that influence a firm's long-term financing decisions, including (1) its target capital structure, (2) maturity matching, (3) current interest rate levels, (4) forecasts of future interest rates, (5) the firm's current and forecasted future condition, (6) restrictive covenants, and (7) the availability of collateral.

Two related issues are discussed in Appendixes 15A and 15B: bankruptcy and bond refundings. Bankruptcy is an important consideration both to companies that issue debt and to investors, for the sequence of events which occurs if a firm is unable to meet scheduled interest and maturity payments has a profound effect on all parties. Refunding, or paying off high interest rate debt with new, lower rate debt, is also an important consideration, especially today (1987), for many firms that previously issued long-term debt at rates of 18 percent or more now have an opportunity to refund this debt at a cost of 10 percent or less.

MULTINATIONAL FINANCE

Thus far, we have concentrated on the U.S. capital markets, where firms raise most of their long-term capital. However, many firms, both multinational and domestic, raise large sums of debt capital in the international markets. For example, in 1986 General Electric raised over $1 billion in the Eurobond market. These bonds were dollar denominated but issued in Europe to European holders of dollars. What was the big attraction that caused GE to look to Europe for its borrowing needs? As you might suspect, the answer is lower cost. To illustrate, one issue GE sold on April 30, 1986, cost the firm only 20 basis points more than the U.S. Treasury was paying on its bonds. Had it borrowed in the U.S. bond market, GE, a AAA-rated firm, would have paid at least 50 basis points over Treasury rates. In this section we briefly describe the international bond markets.

Any bond sold outside the country of the borrower is called an *international bond,* but it is necessary to distinguish further between two types of international bonds that are issued under sharply different institutional arrangements and which have different consequences from the perspectives of both borrowers and investors.

Foreign Bonds

Borrowers sometimes raise long-term debt capital in the domestic capital market of a foreign country. For instance, Bell Canada may need U.S. dollars to finance the operations of its subsidiaries located in the United States. If it decides to raise the needed capital in the domestic U.S. bond market, the bond would be underwritten by a syndicate of U.S. investment bankers, would be denominated in (that is, pay interest and principal in terms of) U.S. dollars, and would be sold to investors in the United States in accordance with SEC and applicable state regulations. Except for the foreign origin of the borrower — Canada — this bond would be indistinguishable from bonds issued by equivalent U.S. corporations. Since Bell Canada is a foreign corporation, though, this bond would be called a *foreign bond.* Therefore, a foreign bond is a bond that is (1) issued by a foreign borrower, (2) underwritten by a syndicate whose members all come from the country where the funds are raised, (3) denominated in the currency of that same country, and (4) sold entirely within that country.

Eurobonds

The second type of international bond is the *Eurobond,* which is internationally syndicated and is denominated in a currency *other than* that of the country in which it is sold. For example, when GE sold U.S. dollar denominated bonds in Europe, through investment bankers who operate worldwide, to people who paid for the bonds with dollars, that was a Eurobond issue. The institutional arrangements by which Eurobonds are brought to market are different from those for most other bond issues. To a corporation issuing a Eurobond, perhaps the most important feature of the process is the far lower level of required disclosure than would usually be found for bonds issued in domestic markets, particularly in the United States. Also, governments tend not to apply as strict a set of regulations to securities denominated in foreign currencies but sold in domestic markets to investors holding foreign currencies as they would for home-currency securities. This often leads to lower total transaction costs for the issue.

Investors like Eurobonds for several reasons. Generally, they are issued in bearer form rather than as registered bonds, so the names and nationalities of investors are not recorded. Individuals who desire anonymity, whether for privacy reasons or for less worthy motives such as tax evasion, find Eurobonds to their liking. Similarly, most governments do not withhold tax on interest payments associated with Eurobonds. If the investor requires an effective yield of 10 percent, a Eurobond that is exempt from tax withholding would need a coupon rate of 10 per-

(6) Treasury bills which yield 8.5 percent.

a. Does it appear that these securities are in equilibrium?

b. If these were your only choices, which would you recommend? Why?

Self-Test Problem

ST-1 (Sinking funds) The Vancouver Development Company has just issued a $100 million, 10-year, 12 percent bond. A sinking fund will retire the issue over its life. Sinking fund payments are of equal amounts and will be made *semiannually,* and the proceeds will be used to retire bonds as the payments are made. Assume that the bonds will be called at par for sinking fund purposes.

a. How large must each semiannual sinking fund payment be?

b. What will happen, under the conditions of the problem thus far, to the company's debt service requirements per year for this issue over time?

c. Now suppose Vancouver Development had set its sinking fund so that *equal annual amounts,* payable at the end of each year, were paid into a sinking fund trust held by a bank, with the proceeds being used to buy government bonds that pay 9 percent interest. The payments, plus accumulated interest, must total $100 million at the end of 10 years, and the proceeds will be used to retire the bonds at that time. How large must the annual sinking fund payment now be?

d. What are the annual cash requirements for covering bond service costs under the trusteeship arrangement described in Part c? (Note: Interest must be paid on Vancouver's outstanding bonds but not on bonds that have been retired.)

e. Now assume that Vancouver has the option of buying the bonds on the open market. What would have to happen to interest rates to cause the company to buy bonds on the open market rather than call them under the original sinking fund plan?

Problems

15-1 (Loan amortization) Suppose a firm is setting up an amortized term loan. What are the annual payments for a $10 million loan under the following terms:

a. 9 percent, 5 years?

b. 9 percent, 10 years?

c. 12 percent, 5 years?

d. 12 percent, 10 years?

15-2 (Amortization schedule) Set up an amortization schedule for a $1 million, 3-year, 10 percent loan.

15-3 (Yield to call) Five years ago Sorenson Company sold a 20-year bond issue with a 17 percent coupon rate and a 10 percent constant call premium. Today Sorenson called the bonds. The bonds originally were sold at their face value of $1,000. Compute the realized rate of return for investors who purchased the bonds when they were issued and will surrender them today in exchange for the call price.

15-4 (Perpetual bond analysis) In 1936 the Canadian government raised $55 million by issuing bonds at a 3 percent annual rate of interest. Unlike most bonds issued today, which have a specific maturity date, these bonds can remain outstanding forever; they are, in fact, perpetuities.

At the time of issue, the Canadian government stated in the bond indenture that cash redemption was possible at face value ($100) on or after September 1966; in other words, the bonds were callable at par after September 1966. Believing that the bonds would in fact be called, many investors purchased these bonds in 1965 with expectations of receiving $100 in 1966 for each perpetual bond they had. In 1965 the bonds sold for $55, but a rush of buyers drove the price to just below the $100 par value by 1966. Prices fell dramatically, however, when the Canadian government announced that these perpetual bonds were indeed perpetual and would not be paid off. A new, 30-year supply of coupons was sent to each bondholder.

The bonds' market price declined to $42 in December 1966. Because of their severe losses, hundreds of Canadian bondholders formed the Perpetual Bond Association to lobby for face value redemption of the bonds, claiming that the government had reneged on an implied promise to redeem the bonds. Government officials in Ottawa insisted that claims for face value payment were nonsense, for the bonds were and always had been clearly identified as perpetuals. One Ottawa official stated, "Our job is to protect the taxpayer. Why should we pay $55 million for less than $25 million worth of bonds?"

The issue heats up again every few years, and it recently resurfaced once more. Here are some questions relating to the Canadian issue that will test your understanding of bonds in general:

a. Would it make sense for a business firm to issue bonds such as the Canadian bonds described above? Would it matter whether the firm were a proprietorship or a corporation?

b. Suppose the U.S. government today sold $100 million each of these four types of bonds: 5-year bonds, 50-year bonds, "regular" perpetuities, and Canadian-type (callable) perpetuities. What do you think the relative order of interest rates would be? In other words, rank the bonds from the one with the lowest to the one with the highest rate of interest. Explain your answer.

c. (1) Suppose that because of pressure by the Perpetual Bond Association you believe that the Canadian government will redeem this particular perpetual bond issue in 5 years. Which course of action would be more advantageous to you if you owned the bonds: (a) sell your bonds today at $42, or (b) wait 5 years and have them redeemed? Assume that similar-risk bonds earn 8 percent today and that interest rates are expected to remain at this level for the next 5 years.

(2) If you had the opportunity to invest your money in bonds of similar risk, at what rate of return would you be indifferent to the choice of selling your perpetuals today or having them redeemed in 5 years — that is, what is the expected yield to maturity on the Canadian bonds?

d. Show mathematically the perpetuities' value if they yield 7.15 percent, pay $3 interest annually, and are considered "regular" perpetuities. Show what would happen to the price of bonds if the going interest rate fell to 2 percent.

e. Are the Canadian bonds more likely to be valued as "regular" perpetuities if the going rate of interest is above or below 3 percent? Why?

f. Do you think the Canadian government would have taken the same action with regard to retiring the bonds if the interest rate had fallen rather than risen after they were issued?

g. Do you think the Canadian government was "fair" or "unfair" in its actions? Give the pros and cons, and justify your reason for thinking that one outweighs the other. Would it matter if the bonds had been sold to "sophisticated" as opposed to "naive" purchasers?

15-5 (Zero coupon bond) Suppose Mid-State Insurance Company needs to raise $400 million, and its investment bankers have indicated that 10-year zero coupon bonds could be sold at a YTM of 12 percent while a 14 percent yield would be required on *annual* payment coupon bonds sold at par. Mid-State's tax rate is 34 percent. (Assume that the discount can be amortized by the issuer using the straight line method. This cannot be done under current tax laws, but assume it anyway.)

    a. How many $1,000 par value bonds would Mid-State have to sell under each plan?

    b. What would be the after-tax YTM on each type of bond (1) to a holder who is tax exempt and (2) to a taxpayer in the 50 percent federal-plus-state bracket?

    c. What would be the after-tax cost of each type of bond to Mid-State?

    d. Why would investors be willing to buy the zero coupon bonds?

    e. Why might Mid-State turn down the offer to issue zero coupon bonds?

(Do Part f only if you are using the computerized diskette.)

    f. Redo Parts a, b, and c assuming that the YTM on zero coupon bonds falls to 10 percent and that on annual coupon bonds falls to 12 percent. As in the previous analysis, the after-tax yield to investors on the annual coupon bond exceeds that of the zero coupon bond. Has the differential between the annual and zero coupon bond yields changed? Would investors be more willing to purchase the zero coupon bond under the original assumptions or under the new assumptions? If the before-tax YTM were 10 percent on each type of bond, what would the after-tax YTMs be to zero and to 50 percent taxpayers, what would the after-tax cost be to the company, and what type of investors would be likely to hold the zeros and what type the regular coupon bonds?

Solution to Self-Test Problem

ST-1   a. $100,000,000/10 = $10,000,000 per year, or $5 million each 6 months. Since the $5 million placed into the sinking fund will be used to retire bonds immediately, no interest will be earned on it.

    b. The debt service requirements will decline as follows (in millions of dollars):

Semiannual Payment Period (1)	Sinking Fund Payment (2)	Outstanding Bonds on Which Interest Is Paid (3)	Interest Payment[a] (4)	Total Bond Service (2) + (4) = (5)
1	$5	$100	$6.0	$11.0
2	5	95	5.7	10.7
3	5	90	5.4	10.4
.	.	.	.	.
.	.	.	.	.
.	.	.	.	.
20	5	5	0.3	5.3

[a]Interest is calculated as $(0.5)(0.12)($ Column 3$)$; for example: interest in Period 2 = $(0.5)(0.12)($\$95$) = 5.7.

The company's total annual cash bond service requirement will be $21.7 million for the first year. The requirement will decline by $0.12(\$10,000,000) = \$1,200,000$ per year for the remaining years.

c. Here we have a 10-year, 9 percent annuity whose future value is $100 million, and we are seeking the annual payment, PMT, in this equation:

$$\$100,000,000 = \sum_{t=1}^{10} PMT(1 + k)^t$$

$$= PMT(FVIFA_{9\%,10})$$

$$= PMT(15.193)$$

$$PMT = \$6,581,979 = \text{Sinking fund payment.}$$

The solution could also be obtained with a financial calculator: Input FV = 100,000,000, n = 10, and i = 9, and press the PMT key to obtain $6,582,009. The difference is due to rounding the FVIFA to 3 decimal places.

d. Annual debt service costs will be $\$100,000,000(0.12) + \$6,582,009 = \$18,582,009$.

e. If interest rates rose, causing the bonds' price to fall, the company would use open market purchases. This would reduce its debt service requirements.

Selected Additional References and Cases

The investment textbooks listed in the Chapter 5 references provide useful information on bonds, as well as the markets in which they are traded. In addition, the following articles offer useful insights:

Backer, Morton, and Martin L. Gosman, "The Use of Financial Ratios in Credit Downgrade Decisions," *Financial Management,* Spring 1980, 53–56.

Clark, John J., with Brenton W. Harries, "Some Recent Trends in Municipal and Corporate Securities Markets: An Interview with Brenton W. Harries, President of Standard & Poor's Corporation," *Financial Management,* Spring 1976, 9–17.

Ferri, Michael G., "An Empirical Examination of the Determinants of Bond Yield Spreads," *Financial Management,* Autumn 1978, 40–46.

Kalotay, Andrew J., "Sinking Funds and the Realized Cost of Debt," *Financial Management,* Spring 1982, 43–54.

———, "Innovations in Corporation Finance: Deep Discount Private Placements," *Financial Management,* Spring 1982, 55–57.

Pinches, George E., J. Clay Singleton, and Ali Jahankhani, "Fixed Coverage as a Determinant of Electric Utility Bond Ratings," *Financial Management,* Summer 1978, 45–55.

Smith, Clifford W., and J. B. Warner, "On Financial Contracting: An Analysis of Bond Covenants," *Journal of Financial Economics,* June 1979, 117–161.

Weinsten, Mark I., "The Seasoning Process of New Corporate Bond Issues," *Journal of Finance,* December 1978, 1343–1354.

Zwick, Burton, "Yields on Privately Placed Corporate Bonds," *Journal of Finance,* March 1980, 23–29.

References on bond refunding include the following:

Ang, James S., "The Two Faces of Bond Refunding," *Journal of Finance,* June 1975, 869–874.

———, "The Two Faces of Bond Refunding: Reply," *Journal of Finance,* March 1978, 354–356.

Dyl, Edward A., and Michael D. Joehnk, "Refunding Tax Exempt Bonds," *Financial Management,* Summer 1976, 59–66.

Emery, Douglas R., "Overlapping Interest in Bond Refunding: A Reconsideration," *Financial Management,* Summer 1978, 19–20.

Finnerty, John D., "Refunding High-Coupon Debt," *Midland Corporate Finance Journal,* Winter 1986, 59–74.

Harris, Robert S., "The Refunding of Discounted Debt: An Adjusted Present Value Analysis," *Financial Management,* Winter 1980, 7–12.

Kalotay, Andrew J., "On the Advanced Refunding of Discounted Debt," *Financial Management,* Summer 1978, 14–18.

———, "On the Structure and Valuation of Debt Refundings," *Financial Management,* Spring 1982, 41–42.

Kraus, Alan, "An Analysis of Call Provisions and the Corporate Refunding Decision," *Midland Corporate Finance Journal,* Spring 1983, 46–60.

Laber, Gene, "The Effect of Bond Refunding of Discounted Debt," *Financial Management,* June 1979, 795–799.

———, "Implications of Discount Rates and Financing Assumptions for Bond Refunding Decisions," *Financial Management,* Spring 1979, 7–12.

———, "Repurchases of Bonds through Tender Offers: Implications for Shareholder Wealth," *Financial Management,* Summer 1978, 7–13.

Livingston, Miles, "The Effect of Bond Refunding on Shareholder Wealth: Comment," *Journal of Finance,* June 1979, 801–804.

———, "Bond Refunding Reconsidered: Comment," *Journal of Finance,* March 1980, 191–196.

Mayor, Thomas H., and Kenneth G. McCoin, "Bond Refunding: One or Two Faces?" *Journal of Finance,* March 1978, 349–353.

Ofer, Ahron R., and Robert A. Taggart, Jr., "Bond Refunding Reconsidered: Reply," *Journal of Finance,* March 1980, 197–200.

Riener, Kenneth D., "Financial Structure Effects of Bond Refunding," *Financial Management,* Summer 1980, 18–23.

Yawitz, Jess B., and James A. Anderson, "The Effect of Bond Refunding on Shareholder Wealth," *Journal of Finance,* December 1977, 1738–1746.

———, "The Effect of Bond Refunding on Shareholder Wealth: Reply," *Journal of Finance,* June 1979, 805–809.

Zeise, Charles H., and Roger K. Taylor, "Advance Refunding: A Practitioner's Perspective," *Financial Management,* Summer 1977, 73–76.

For more information on Eurodollar bonds, see

Kidwell, David S., M. Wayne Marr, and G. Rodney Thompson, "Eurodollar Bonds: Alternative Financing for U.S. Companies," *Financial Management,* Winter 1985, 18–27; and the same authors' correction in the Spring 1986 issue of *Financial Management.*

The following Crum-Brigham cases focus on the topics covered in this chapter:

Case 19, "Seminole Gas and Electric," which illustrates the bond refunding decision.

Cases 23 and 24, "Environgard Corporation" and "Visual Imagery," which illustrate the stock versus bond decision.

The following Harrington cases are also relevant:

"Exxon Corporation," which describes three early 1980 debt/equity swaps.

"Treeline, Inc.," which illustrates the choice among various debt alternatives.

15A
Bankruptcy and Reorganization

In the event of bankruptcy, debtholders have a prior claim over the claims of both common and preferred stockholders to a firm's income, as well as to its assets. Further, different classes of debtholders are treated differently in the event of bankruptcy. Since bankruptcy is a fairly common occurrence, and since it affects both the bankrupt firm and its customers, suppliers, and creditors, it is important to know who gets what if a firm fails. These topics are discussed in this appendix.[1]

Federal Bankruptcy Laws

Bankruptcy actually begins when a firm is unable to meet scheduled payments on its debt, or when the firm's cash flow projections indicate that it will soon be unable to meet payments. As the bankruptcy proceedings go forward, these central issues arise:

1. Does the firm's inability to meet scheduled payments result from a temporary cash flow problem, or does it represent a permanent problem caused by asset values having fallen below debt obligations?

2. If the problem is a temporary one, then an agreement which stretches out payments may be worked out to give the firm time to recover and to satisfy everyone. However, if basic long-run asset values have truly declined, economic losses will have occurred. In this event, who should bear the losses?

3. Is the company "worth more dead than alive" — that is, would the business be more valuable if it were maintained and continued in operation or if it were liquidated and sold off in pieces?

4. Who should control the firm while it is being liquidated or rehabilitated? Should the existing management be left in control, or should a *trustee* be placed in charge of operations?

These are the primary issues that are addressed in the federal bankruptcy statutes.

Our bankruptcy laws were first enacted in 1898, modified substantially in 1938, changed again in 1978, and further fine-tuned in 1984. The 1978 Act, which provides the basic laws which govern bankruptcy today, was a major revision designed to streamline and expedite proceedings, and it consists of eight odd-numbered chapters, the even-numbered chapters of the earlier act having been deleted. Chapters 1, 3, and 5 of the 1978 Act contain general provisions applicable to the other chapters; Chapter 7 details the procedures to be followed when liquidating a firm;

This appendix was coauthored by Arthur L. Herrmann of the University of Hartford.

[1]Much of the current work in this area is based on writings by Edward I. Altman. For a summary of his work, and that of others, see Edward I. Altman, "Bankruptcy and Reorganization," in *Financial Handbook,* Edward I. Altman, ed. (New York: Wiley, 1986), Chapter 19.

Chapter 9 deals with financially distressed municipalities; Chapter 11 is the business reorganization chapter; Chapter 13 covers the adjustment of debts for "individuals with regular income"; and Chapter 15 sets up a system of trustees who help administer proceedings under the new law.

When you read in the paper that Manville Corporation or some other company has "filed for Chapter 11," this means that the company is bankrupt and is trying to reorganize under Chapter 11 of the Act. If a reorganization plan cannot be worked out, then the company will be liquidated as prescribed in Chapter 7 of the Act.

The 1978 Act is quite flexible, and it provides much scope for informal negotiations between a company and its creditors. Under this law, a case is opened by the filing of a petition with a federal district bankruptcy court. The petition may be either voluntary or involuntary — that is, it may be filed either by the firm's management or by its creditors. A committee of unsecured creditors is then appointed by the court to negotiate with management for a reorganization, which may include the *restructuring* of debt and other claims against the firm. (A "restructuring" could involve extending the maturity of debt, lowering the interest rate on it, reducing the principal amount owed, exchanging common or preferred stock for debt, or some combination of these actions.) A trustee may be appointed by the court if that is deemed to be in the best interests of the creditors and stockholders; otherwise, the existing management will retain control. Under Chapter 11, if no fair and feasible reorganization can be worked out, the firm will be liquidated under the procedures spelled out in Chapter 7.

Reorganization Procedures

When a business becomes insolvent, a decision must be made whether to dissolve the firm through *liquidation* or to keep it alive through *reorganization*. Fundamentally, this decision depends on a determination of the value of the firm if it is rehabilitated versus the value of its assets if they are sold off individually. The procedure that promises higher returns to the creditors and owners will be adopted. If the decision is made to reorganize the firm, the courts, and possibly the SEC, will be called upon to determine the *fairness* and the *feasibility* of the proposed reorganization plan.

Standard of Fairness
The basic doctrine of *fairness* states that claims must be recognized in the order of their legal and contractual priority. Carrying out this concept of fairness in a reorganization (as opposed to a liquidation) involves the following steps:

1. Future sales must be estimated.

2. Operating conditions must be analyzed so that the future earnings and cash flows can be predicted.

3. A capitalization (or discount) rate to be applied to these future cash flows must be determined.

4. This capitalization rate must then be applied to the estimated cash flows to obtain a present value figure, which is the indicated value for the reorganized company.

5. Provision for distribution of the restructured firm's securities to its claimants must be made.

Standard of Feasibility

The primary test of *feasibility* in a reorganization is whether the fixed charges after reorganization can be covered by cash flows. Adequate coverage generally requires an improvement in operating earnings, a reduction of fixed charges, or both. Among the actions that must generally be taken are the following:

1. Debt maturities are usually lengthened, interest rates may be scaled back, and some debt may be converted into equity.

2. When the quality of management has been substandard, a new team must be given control of the company.

3. If inventories have become obsolete or depleted, they must be replaced.

4. Sometimes the plant and equipment must be modernized before the firm can operate on a competitive basis.

Liquidation Procedures

If a company is too far gone to be reorganized, it must be liquidated. Liquidation should occur if a business is worth more dead than alive, or if the possibility of restoring it to financial health is so remote that the creditors would face a high risk of even greater losses if operations were continued.

Chapter 7 of the Bankruptcy Act is designed to do these three things: (1) provide safeguards against the withdrawal of assets by the owners of the bankrupt firm; (2) provide for an equitable distribution of the liquidation proceeds among the creditors; and (3) allow insolvent debtors to discharge all their obligations and to start over unhampered by a burden of prior debt.

The distribution of proceeds in a liquidation under Chapter 7 of the Bankruptcy Act is governed by the following priority of claims:

1. *Secured creditors, who are entitled to the proceeds of the sale of specific property pledged for a lien or a mortgage.* If the proceeds do not fully satisfy the secured creditors' claims, the remaining balance is treated as a general creditor claim. (See Item 9.)

2. *Trustee's costs to administer and operate the bankrupt firm.*

3. *Expenses incurred after an involuntary case has begun but before a trustee is appointed.*

4. *Wages due workers if earned within three months prior to the filing of the petition in bankruptcy.* The amount of wages is limited to $2,000 per person.

5. *Claims for unpaid contributions to employee benefit plans that were to be paid within six months prior to filing.* However, these claims, plus wages in Item 4, are not to exceed the $2,000 per wage earner limit.

6. *Unsecured claims for customer deposits, not to exceed a maximum of $900 per individual.*

7. *Taxes due to federal, state, county, and any other government agency.*

8. *Unfunded pension plan liabilities.* Unfunded pension plan liabilities have a claim above that of the general creditors for an amount up to 30 percent of the common and preferred equity; any remaining unfunded pension claims rank with the general creditors.[2]

9. *General, or unsecured, creditors.* Holders of trade credit, unsecured loans, the unsatisfied portion of secured loans, and debenture bonds are classified as *general creditors.* Holders of subordinated debt also fall into this category, but they must turn over required amounts to the holders of senior debt, as discussed later in this section.

10. *Preferred stockholders, who can receive an amount up to the par value of the issue.*

11. *Common stockholders, who receive any remaining funds.*

To illustrate how this priority system works, consider the balance sheet of Bronson, Incorporated, shown in Table 15A-1. The assets have a book value of $90 million. The claims are indicated on the right-hand side of the balance sheet. Note that the debentures are subordinate to the notes payable to banks. Bronson had filed for reorganization under Chapter 11, but since no fair and feasible reorganization could be arranged, the trustee is liquidating the firm under Chapter 7. Note also that the firm has $15 million of unfunded pension liabilities.

The assets as reported in the balance sheet in Table 15A-1 are greatly overstated; they are, in fact, worth about half of the $90 million at which they are carried. The following amounts are realized on liquidation:

Proceeds from sale of current assets	$41,950,000
Proceeds from sale of fixed assets	5,000,000
Total receipts	$46,950,000

---

[2]Under the federal statutes which regulate pension funds, corporations are required to estimate the amount of money needed to provide for the pensions which have been promised to their employees. This determination is made by professional actuaries, taking into account when employees will retire, how long they are likely to live, and the rate of return that can be earned on pension fund assets. If the assets currently in the pension fund are deemed sufficient to make all required payments, then the plan is said to be *fully funded.* If assets in the plan are less than the present value of expected future payments, then an *unfunded liability* exists. Under federal laws, companies are given up to 30 years to fund any unfunded liabilities. (Note that if a company were fully funded in 1986 but then agreed, in 1987, to double pension benefits, this would immediately create a large unfunded liability, and it would need time to make the adjustment. Otherwise, it would be difficult for companies to agree to increase pension benefits.)

Unfunded pension liabilities, including medical benefits to retirees, represent a time bomb ticking in the bowels of many companies. If a company has a relatively old labor force, and if it has promised them substantial retirement benefits but has not set aside assets in a funded pension fund to cover these benefits, then it could be in real trouble in the future. These unfunded pension benefits could drive the company into bankruptcy, at which point the pension plan would be subject to the bankruptcy laws.

Table 15A-1
Bronson, Inc.:
Balance Sheet at Liquidation
(Thousands of Dollars)

Current assets	$80,000	Accounts payable	$20,000
Net fixed assets	10,000	Notes payable (to bank)	10,000
		Accrued wages, 1,400 @ $500	700
		U.S. taxes	1,000
		State and local taxes	300
		Total current liabilities	$32,000
		First mortgage	$ 6,000
		Second mortgage	1,000
		Subordinated debentures[a]	8,000
		Total long-term debt	$15,000
		Preferred stock	$ 2,000
		Common stock	26,000
		Paid-in capital	4,000
		Retained earnings	11,000
		Total equity	$43,000
Total assets	$90,000	Total liabilities and equity	$90,000

[a]Subordinated to $10 million in notes payable to the bank.

Notes:
a. Unfunded pension liabilities are $15 million.
b. Bankruptcy fees and expenses total $6 million.

The order of priority of the claims is shown in Table 15A-2. The holders of the first mortgage bonds receive the $5 million in net proceeds from the sale of fixed assets, leaving $41.95 million available to the remaining creditors. Note that a $1 million unsatisfied claim of the first mortgage holders remains; this claim is added to that of the other general creditors. Next come the fees and expenses of administration, which are typically about 20 percent of gross proceeds; in this example, they are assumed to be $6 million. Next in priority are wages due workers, which total $700,000, taxes due, which amount to $1.3 million, and unfunded pension liabilities up to 30 percent of the common plus preferred equity, or $12.9 million. Thus far, the total of claims paid from the $46.95 million is $25.90 million, leaving $21.05 million for the general creditors.

The claims of the general creditors total $42.1 million. Since $21.05 million is available, claimants would initially be allocated 50 percent of their claims, as shown in Column 2, before the subordination adjustment. This adjustment requires that the subordinated debentures turn over to the notes payable all amounts received until the notes are satisfied. In this situation, the claim of the notes payable is $10 million, but only $5 million is available; the deficiency is therefore $5 million. After transfer of $4 million from the subordinated debentures, there remains a deficiency of $1 million on the notes; this amount will remain unsatisfied.

Note that 90 percent of the bank claim and 93 percent of the unfunded pension fund claims are satisfied, whereas a maximum of 50 percent of other unsecured

---

Table 15A-2
Bronson, Inc.:
Order of Priority of Claims

Distribution to Priority Claimants

1. Proceeds from sale of assets			$46,950,000
2. First mortgage, paid from sale of fixed assets		$5,000,000	
3. Fees and expenses of administration of bankruptcy		6,000,000	
4. Wages due workers earned within three months prior to filing of bankruptcy petition		700,000	
5. Taxes		1,300,000	
6. Unfunded pension liabilities		12,900,000[a]	25,900,000
7. Available to general creditors			$21,050,000

Distribution to General Creditors

	Claim[b] (1)	Application of 50 Percent[c] (2)	After Subordination Adjustment[d] (3)	Percentage of Original Claims Received[e] (4)
Unsatisfied portion of first mortgage	$ 1,000,000	$ 500,000	$ 500,000	92%
Unsatisfied portion of second mortgage	1,000,000	500,000	500,000	50
Notes payable	10,000,000	5,000,000	9,000,000	90
Accounts payable	20,000,000	10,000,000		
Subordinated debentures	8,000,000	4,000,000	0	0
Pension plan	2,100,000	1,050,000	1,050,000	93
	$42,100,000	$21,050,000	$21,050,000	

[a]Unfunded pension liabilities are $15,000,000, and the common and preferred equity total $43,000,000. Unfunded pension liabilities have a prior claim of up to 30 percent of the equity, or $12,900,000, with the remainder, $2,100,000, being treated as a general creditor claim.

[b]Column 1 is the claim of each class of general creditor. Total claims equal $42.1 million.

[c]From Line 7 in the upper section of the table, we see that $21.05 million is available for general creditors. This sum, divided by the $42.1 million of claims, indicates that general creditors will initially receive 50 percent of their claims; this is shown in Column 2.

[d]The debentures are subordinated to the notes payable, so $4 million is reallocated from debentures to notes payable in Column 3.

[e]Column 4 shows the results of dividing the amount in Column 3 by the original claim amount given in Column 1, except for the first mortgage, where the $5 million received from the sale of fixed assets is included, and the pension plan, where the $12.9 million is included.

---

claims will be satisfied. These figures illustrate the usefulness of the subordination provision to the security to which the subordination is made. Since no other funds remain, the claims of the holders of preferred and common stock are completely wiped out. Studies of bankruptcy liquidations reveal that unsecured creditors receive on the average about 15 cents on the dollar, while common stockholders generally receive nothing.

Informal Procedures

Both reorganization and liquidation can be accomplished without a formal bankruptcy court filing. In this section, we briefly discuss these informal procedures.

Informal Reorganization

In the case of a fundamentally sound company whose financial difficulties appear to be temporary, the creditors generally prefer to work directly with the company, helping it to recover and reestablish itself on a sound financial basis. Such voluntary plans usually require some type of restructuring of the firm's debt, which involves either postponing payment of debt obligations or reducing creditor claims, or both. These procedures are designed to keep the debtor in business and to avoid the court costs associated with formal bankruptcy. Although creditors may not obtain immediate payment, and they may even have to accept less than is owed them, they often recover more money, and sooner, than if formal bankruptcy is declared. Also, for both trade creditors and bankers, chances are good that a customer will be preserved.

We should point out that informal voluntary settlements are not reserved for small firms. International Harvester (now Navistar) avoided formal bankruptcy proceedings by getting its creditors to agree to restructure some $3.5 billion of debt. Likewise, Chrysler's creditors accepted both an extension of maturities and a reduction of accounts to help it through its bad years. Finally, prior to its acquisition by Texas Air, People Express was attempting to get its creditors to accept interest rates of about 9 percent versus coupon rates of up to 16 percent, and also to extend debt maturities by about 10 years.

Informal Liquidation

Assignment is an informal procedure for liquidating debts, and it usually yields creditors a larger amount than they would receive in a formal Chapter 7 liquidation. However, assignments are feasible only if the firm is small, and its affairs are not too complex. An assignment calls for title to the debtor's assets to be transferred to a third person, known as an *assignee* or *trustee.* The assignee is instructed to liquidate the assets through a private sale or a public auction, and then to distribute the proceeds among the creditors on a pro rata basis. The assignment does not automatically discharge the debtor's obligations. However, the debtor may have the assignee write on the check to each creditor the requisite legal language to make endorsement of the check acknowledgment of full settlement of the claim.

Assignment has some advantages over Chapter 7 liquidation, which involves more time, legal formality, and expense. The assignee has more flexibility in disposing of property than does a bankruptcy trustee. Action can be taken sooner, before the inventory becomes obsolete or the machinery rusts, and, since the assignee is often familiar with the channels of trade in the debtor's business, better results may be achieved. However, an assignment does not automatically result in a full and legal discharge of all the debtor's liabilities, nor does it protect the creditors against fraud.

Problems

15A-1 The Georgia Aluminum Company has the following balance sheet:

Current assets	$4,200	Accounts payable	$ 900
Fixed assets	2,250	Notes payable (to bank)	450
		Accrued taxes	150
		Accrued wages	150
		Total current liabilities	$1,650
		First mortgage bonds	750
		Second mortgage bonds	750
		Total mortgage bonds	$1,500
		Subordinated debentures	900
		Total debt	$4,050
		Preferred stock	300
		Common stock	2,100
Total assets	$6,450	Total liabilities and equity	$6,450

The debentures are subordinated only to the notes payable. Suppose Georgia Aluminum goes bankrupt and is liquidated, with $1,100 being received from the sale of the fixed assets, which were pledged as security for the first and second mortgage bonds, and $2,000 from the sale of current assets.

a. How much will each class of investors receive?

(Do Part b only if you are using the computerized diskette.)

b. How much would each class of investors receive if:
   (1) $800 were received from the sale of fixed assets and $1,300 from the sale of current assets?
   (2) $1,400 were received from the sale of fixed assets and $2,500 from the sale of current assets?

15A-2 A firm has the following balance sheet:

Current assets	$1,500,000	Bank debt	$ 300,000
Fixed assets	1,500,000	Trade credit	600,000
		Subordinated debentures	600,000
		Total debt	$1,500,000
		Common equity	1,500,000
Total assets	$3,000,000	Total liabilities and equity	$3,000,000

If the debentures are subordinated only to the bank debt and the firm goes bankrupt, how much will each class of investors receive under each of the following conditions?

a. A total of $2 million is received from sale of assets.

b. A total of $1.5 million is received from sale of assets.

(Do Parts c through e only if you are using the computerized diskette.)

c. A total of $1 million is received from sale of assets.

d. A total of $500,000 is received from sale of assets.

e. What is the significance of these findings for the banks, the trade creditors, the debenture holders, and the common stockholders?

15B
Refunding Operations

A great deal of long-term debt was sold during the early 1980s at interest rates going up to 18 percent or more, even for double A companies. Since the period of call protection on much of this debt is, or soon will be, ending, many companies are analyzing the pros and cons of bond refundings. Refunding decisions actually involve two separate questions: (1) Is it profitable to call an outstanding issue in the current period and replace it with a new issue, and (2) even if refunding is currently profitable, would the expected value of the firm be increased even more if the refunding were postponed to a later date? We consider both questions in this appendix.[1]

First, note that the decision to refund a security is analyzed in much the same way as a capital budgeting expenditure. The costs of refunding — the investment outlays — are (1) the call premium paid for the privilege of calling the old issue and (2) the flotation costs incurred in selling the new issue. The primary benefits, in a capital budgeting sense, are the interest payments that are saved each year. For example, if the interest expense on the old issue is $1,000,000 while that on the new issue is $700,000, the $300,000 reduction in interest savings constitutes an annual benefit.

The net present value method is used to analyze the advantages of refunding — discount the future interest savings back to the present, and then compare this discounted value with the cash outlays associated with the refunding. The firm should refund the bond if the present value of the savings exceeds the cost, that is, if the NPV of the refunding operation is positive.

In the discounting process, the after-tax cost of the new debt, k_d, should be used as the discount rate. The reason is that there is relatively little risk to the savings — cash flows in a refunding are known with relative certainty, which is quite unlike the situation with cash flows in most capital budgeting decisions.

---

[1]During the early 1980s, there was a flurry of work on the pros and cons of refunding bond issues that had fallen to deep discounts as a result of rising interest rates. At such times a company could go into the market, buy its debt at a low price, and retire it. The difference between the bonds' par value and the price the company paid would be reported as income, and taxes would have to be paid on it. The results of the research on the refunding of discount issues suggest that, in general, bonds should not be refunded after a rise in rates. See Robert S. Harris, "The Refunding of Discounted Debt: An Adjusted Present Value Analysis," *Financial Management,* Winter 1980, 7–12; and Andrew J. Kalotay, "On the Structure and Valuation of Debt Refundings," *Financial Management,* Spring, 1982, 41–42.

The easiest way to examine the refunding decision is through an example. Langley Publishing Company has outstanding a $60 million bond issue which has a 15 percent coupon interest rate and 20 years remaining to maturity. This issue, which was sold 5 years ago, had flotation costs of $3 million, which the firm has been amortizing on a straight line basis over the 25-year original life of the issue. The bond has a call provision which makes it possible for the company to retire the issue at this time by calling the bonds in at a 10 percent call premium. Investment bankers have assured the company that it could sell an additional $60 million to $70 million worth of new 20-year bonds at an interest rate of 12 percent. To insure that the funds required to pay off the old debt will be available, the new bonds would be sold one month before the old issue is called, so for one month, interest would have to be paid on both issues. Current short-term interest rates are 11 percent. Predictions are that long-term interest rates are unlikely to fall below 12 percent.[2] Flotation costs on a new refunding issue would amount to $2,650,000. Langley's marginal tax rate is 40 percent. Should the company refund the $60 million of 15 percent bonds?

The following steps outline the decision process; they are summarized in worksheet form in Table 15B-1.

Step 1
Determine the net investment required to refund the issue.

a. Call premium:

$$\text{Before tax: } 0.10(\$60,000,000) = \$6,000,000.$$
$$\text{After tax: } \$6,000,000(1 - T) = \$6,000,000(0.6)$$
$$= \$3,600,000.$$

Although Langley must expend $6 million on the call premium, this is a deductible expense in the year the call is made. Since the company is in the 40 percent tax bracket, it saves $2.4 million in taxes; therefore, the after-tax cost of the call is only $3.6 million. This amount is shown on Line 1 of Table 15B-1.

b. Flotation costs on the new issue:
Flotation costs on the new issue will be $2,650,000. For tax purposes, flotation costs must be amortized over the life of the new bond, or 20 years. Therefore, the annual tax deduction is

$$\frac{\$2,650,000}{20} = \$132,500.$$

Since Langley is in the 40 percent tax bracket, it has a tax savings of $132,500(0.4) = $53,000 a year for 20 years. This is an annuity of $53,000 for

---

[2]The firm's management has estimated that interest rates will probably remain at their present level of 12 percent or else rise; there is only a 25 percent probability that they will fall further.

20 years. In a refunding analysis, all cash flows should be discounted at the after-tax cost of new debt, in this case, $12\%(1 - T) = 12\%(0.6) = 7.2\%$. The present value of the tax savings, discounted at 7.2 percent, is \$552,859. Thus, the net after-tax cost of flotation for the new issue is

Gross flotation costs on new issue	\$2,650,000
PV of associated tax savings	(552,859)
Net after-tax flotation cost on new issue	\$2,097,141

The gross costs and tax savings are reflected on Lines 2 and 3 of Table 15B-1.

c. Flotation costs on the old issue:

The old issue has an unamortized flotation cost of $(20/25)(\$3,000,000) = \$2,400,000$ at this time. If the issue is retired, the unamortized flotation cost may be recognized immediately as an expense, thus creating an after-tax savings of $\$2,400,000(T) = \$960,000$. The firm will, however, no longer receive a tax deduction of \$120,000 a year for 20 years, which is equivalent to an after-tax benefit of \$48,000 a year. The present value of this tax savings, discounted over 20 years at 7.2 percent, is \$500,702. Thus, the net after-tax effect of the old flotation costs is a savings of \$459,298:

Tax savings from immediate write-off of old flotation costs	(\$960,000)
PV of tax savings on old flotation costs had refunding not occurred	500,702
Net after-tax savings on old flotation costs	(\$459,298)

These figures are reflected on Lines 4 and 5 of Table 15B-1.

Note that, because of the refunding, the flotation costs provide an immediate tax saving rather than annual savings over the next 20 years. Thus, the \$459,298 net savings simply reflects the difference between the present value of benefits received in the future without the refunding versus an immediate benefit if the refunding occurs.

d. Additional interest:

One month's "extra" interest on the old issue, after taxes, costs \$450,000:

$$(\text{Dollar amount})(1/12 \text{ of } 15\%)(1 - T) = \text{Interest cost}$$
$$(\$60,000,000)(0.0125)(0.6) = \$450,000.$$

However, the proceeds from the new issue can be invested in short-term securities for one month. Thus, \$60 million invested at a rate of 11 percent will return \$330,000 in after-tax interest:

$$(\$60,000,000)(1/12 \text{ of } 11\%)(1 - T) = \text{Interest earned}$$
$$(\$60,000,000)(0.009167)(0.6) = \$330,012 \approx \$330,000.$$

Table 15B-1
Worksheet for the Bond Refunding Decision

	Amount before Tax	Amount after Tax	Time Event Occurs	PV Factor at 7.2%	PV
Cost of Refunding: t = 0					
1. Call premium on old bond	$6,000,000	$3,600,000	0	1.0000	$3,600,000
2. Flotation costs on new issue	2,650,000	2,650,000	0	1.0000	2,650,000
3. Tax savings on new issue flotation cost amortization	(132,500)	(53,000)	1-20	10.4313	(552,859)
4. Immediate tax savings on old flotation cost expense	(2,400,000)	(960,000)	0	1.0000	(960,000)
5. Periodic tax benefits no longer received on old flotation costs	120,000	48,000	1-20	10.4313	500,702
6. Extra interest on old issue	750,000	450,000	0	1.0000	450,000
7. Interest on short-term investment	(550,000)	(330,000)	0	1.0000	(330,000)
8. Total after-tax investment (PV of investment)					$5,357,843
Interest Savings over the Life of the New Issue: t = 1 to 20					
9. Interest on old bond	$9,000,000	$5,400,000			
10. Interest on new bond	(7,200,000)	(4,320,000)			
11. Net savings of interest	$1,800,000	$1,080,000	1-20	10.4313	$11,265,804

Refunding NPV

12. NPV = PV of interest savings − PV of investment
    = $11,265,804 − $5,357,843
    = $5,907,961.

The net after-tax additional interest cost is thus $120,000:

Interest paid on old issue	$450,000
Interest earned on short-term securities	(330,000)
Net additional interest	$120,000

These figures are reflected on Lines 6 and 7 of Table 15B-1.

e. Total after-tax investment:

The total investment required to refund the bond issue, which will be financed by debt, is thus $5,357,843:[3]

---

[3]The investment outlay (in this case, $5,357,843) is usually obtained by increasing the amount of the new bond issue. In the example given, the new issue would be $65,357,843. However, the interest on the additional debt *should not* be deducted at Step 2, because the $5,357,843 itself will be deducted at Step 3. If additional interest on the $5,357,843 were deducted at Step 2, then interest would in effect be deducted twice. The situation here is exactly like that in regular capital budgeting decisions. Even though some debt may be used to finance a project, interest on that debt is not subtracted when developing the annual cash flows — rather, the annual cash flows are *discounted* by the project's cost of capital.

Call premium	$3,600,000
Flotation costs, new, net of tax savings	2,097,141
Flotation costs, old, net savings	(459,298)
Net additional interest	120,000
Total investment	$5,357,843

This total is shown on Line 8 of Table 15B-1.

Step 2

Calculate the PV of the annual interest savings.

a. Interest on the old issue, after tax:

The annual after-tax interest on the old issue is $5.4 million:

$$(\$60,000,000)(0.15)(0.6) = \$5,400,000.$$

This is shown on Line 9 of Table 15B-1.

b. Interest on the new issue, after tax:

The new issue has an annual after-tax cost of $4,320,000:

$$(\$60,000,000)(0.12)(0.6) = \$4,320,000.$$

This is shown on Line 10 as a negative saving.

c. Net annual savings:

Thus, the net annual after-tax savings is $1,080,000:

Interest on old bonds, after tax	$5,400,000
Interest on new bonds, after tax	(4,320,000)
Annual net savings	$1,080,000

This is shown on Line 11.

d. PV of annual savings:

The PV of $1,080,000 a year for 20 years is $11,265,804:

$$PV = \$1,080,000(PVIFA_{7.2\%,20})$$

$$= \$1,080,000(10.4313) = \$11,265,804.$$

This is also shown on Line 11.

Step 3

Determine the NPV of the refunding.

PV of annual savings	$11,265,804
Net investment	(5,357,843)
NPV from refunding	$ 5,907,961

Since the net present value of the refunding is positive, it would be profitable to refund the old bond issue.

Several other points should be noted. First, since the cash flows are based on differences between contractual obligations, their risk is the same as that of the underlying obligations. Therefore, the present values of the cash flows should be found by discounting at the firm's least risky rate — its after-tax cost of marginal debt. Second, since the refunding operation is advantageous to the firm, it must be disadvantageous to bondholders; they must give up their 15 percent bonds and reinvest in new ones yielding 12 percent. This points out the danger of the call provision to bondholders, and it also explains why bonds without a call feature command higher prices than callable bonds. Third, although it is not emphasized in the example, we assumed that the firm raises the investment required to undertake the refunding operation (the $5,357,843 shown on Line 8 of Table 15B-1) as debt. This should be feasible, since the refunding operation will improve the interest coverage ratio even though a larger amount of debt is outstanding.[4] Fourth, we set up our example in such a way that the new issue had the same maturity as the remaining life of the old one. Often the old bonds have only a relatively short time to maturity (say, 5 to 10 years), while the new bonds would have a much longer maturity (say, 25 to 30 years). In this situation, the analysis should include only cash flows up to the maturity of the old issue.[5] Fifth, refunding decisions are well suited for analysis with a computer spreadsheet such as *Lotus 1-2-3*. The spreadsheet is simple to set up, and once it is, it is easy to vary the assumptions, especially the assumption about the interest rate on the refunding issue, and to see how such changes affect the NPV. See Problem 15B-1 for an example.

One final point should be addressed: Although our analysis shows that the refunding would increase the value of the firm, would refunding *at this time* truly maximize the firm's expected value? Note that, if interest rates continue to fall, then the company might be better off waiting, for this could increase the NPV of the refunding operation even more. The mechanics of calculating the NPV of a refunding are easy, but the decision of *when* to refund is not a simple one at all, because it requires a forecast of future interest rates. Thus, the final decision on refunding now versus waiting for a possibly more favorable time is a judgmental decision.[6]

---

[4]See Ahron R. Ofer and Robert A. Taggart, Jr., "Bond Refunding: A Clarifying Analysis," *Journal of Finance,* March 1977, 21–30, for a discussion of how the method of financing the refunding affects the analysis. Ofer and Taggart prove that (1) if the refunding investment outlay is to be raised as debt, then the after-tax cost of debt is the proper discount rate, while (2) if these funds are to be raised as common equity, then the before-tax cost of debt is the proper rate. Since a profitable refunding will virtually always raise the firm's debt-carrying capacity (because total interest charges after the refunding will be lower than before it), it is more logical to use debt than either equity or a combination of debt and equity to finance the operation. Therefore, firms generally do use additional debt to finance refunding operations, and we therefore assume debt financing for the costs of refunding and discount at the after-tax cost of debt.

[5]It should also be noted that, to be exactly precise, the old bond in our example should have had a maturity of 20 years plus one month at the time the analysis was undertaken so that it would have a 20-year remaining maturity when it is actually refunded. This is really an immaterial detail.

[6]For more insight into the refund now versus refund later decision, see Eugene F. Brigham and Louis C. Gapenski, *Intermediate Financial Management,* 2nd ed., Chapter 13.

Problem

15B-1 Carleton Can Corporation (CCC) is considering whether to refund a $60 million, 16 percent coupon, 30-year bond issue that was sold 5 years ago. It is amortizing $3 million of flotation costs on the 16 percent bonds over the issue's 30-year life. CCC's investment bankers have indicated that the company could sell a new, 25-year issue at an interst rate of 13 percent in today's market. Neither they nor CCC's management sees much chance that interest rates will fall below 13 percent any time soon, but there is a chance that rates will increase.

A call premium of 16 percent would be required to retire the old bonds, and flotation costs on the new issue would amount to $3 million. CCC's marginal federal-plus-state tax rate is 40 percent. The new bonds would be issued one month before the old bonds were called, with the proceeds being invested in short-term government securities returning 10 percent annually during the interim period.

a. Perform a complete bond refunding analysis. What is the bond refunding's NPV?

b. What factors would influence CCC's decision to refund now rather than later? *(Do Part c only if you are using the computerized diskette.)*

c. (1) Determine the interest rate on new bonds at which CCC would be indifferent to refunding; that is, the interest rate at which the NPV of the refunding decision would be approximately zero. (Hint: You will need to perform the analysis using different rates of interest on new bonds until you find the one which causes the NPV to be zero.)

(2) Assume the corporate tax rate is lowered from 40 percent to 30 percent. How would this affect the refunding decision?

16
Lease Financing

General Electric Credit Corporation (GECC), the financing arm of GE, has total assets of about $25 billion and is involved in many financial services, ranging from leveraged buyouts to commercial real estate. GECC was originally set up to help finance the sale of GE's products, but recently its major business has been leasing big ticket items such as Boeing 747s and railway freight cars.

GECC's shift into general equipment leasing was motivated to a large extent by "safe-harbor" leasing — now largely repealed — which allowed unprofitable companies to sell tax losses and tax credits to profitable companies which could use these shelters. In GECC's case, these benefits amounted to hundreds of millions of dollars, and they reduced the parent GE's taxes to zero or to trivial amounts for several years.

However, the Tax Reform Act of 1986 will make it more difficult for GE to use GECC as a tax shelter, largely because the new law repeals the investment tax credit. Further, increased competition has reduced the profitability of straightforward leasing. "The investment bankers have commoditized the leasing business, often in the form of investor syndicates that can offer lower rates," said James H. Ozanne, GECC's senior vice-president.

In response to the tax law changes and increased competition, GECC is creating new types of leases. Instead of its traditional full-payout lease, which lasts for the useful life of the asset and which depends on tax benefits to make it work, GECC is now offering shorter-term leases at higher rates. In return for the higher rates, GECC assumes the risk for finding a use for the asset when the lease is up. Further, GECC is now offering additional services such as maintenance and asset management. Such services — as opposed to walkaway leasing — is a way "to replace what we've been making under old tax law," said Ozanne.

What are the various types of leases, and what are the costs and benefits involved? We address those issues in this chapter.

Firms generally own fixed assets and report them on their balance sheets, but it is the *use* of buildings and equipment that is important, not their ownership per se. One way of obtaining the use of facilities and equipment is to buy them, but an alternative is to lease them. Prior to the 1950s, leasing was generally associated with real estate — land and buildings. Today, however, it is possible to lease virtually any kind of fixed asset, and in 1986 about 20 percent of all new capital equipment acquired by businesses was financed through lease arrangements. It is estimated that $200 billion worth of capital equipment is currently being leased.

TYPES OF LEASES

Leasing takes several different forms, the four most important of which are (1) sale-and-leaseback arrangements, (2) operating leases, (3) straight financial, or capital, leases, and (4) combination leases.

Sale and Leaseback

Under a *sale-and-leaseback* arrangement, a firm that owns land, buildings, or equipment sells the property to another firm and simultaneously executes an agreement to lease the property back for a specified period under specific terms. The capital supplier could be an insurance company, a commercial bank, a specialized leasing company, the finance arm of an industrial firm, or an individual investor. The sale-and-leaseback plan is an alternative to a mortgage.

Note that the seller, or *lessee,* immediately receives the purchase price put up by the buyer, or *lessor.*[1] At the same time, the seller-lessee retains the use of the property. The parallel to borrowing is carried over to the lease payment schedule. Under a mortgage loan arrangement, the lender would normally receive a series of equal payments just sufficient to amortize the loan while providing a specified rate of return on the outstanding loan balance. Under a sale-and-leaseback arrangement, the lease payments are set up exactly the same way — the payments are just sufficient to return the full purchase price to the investor, plus a stated return on the lessor's investment.

Operating Leases

Operating leases, sometimes called *service leases,* provide for both *financing* and *maintenance.* IBM was one of the pioneers of the operating lease contract, and computers and office copying machines, together with automobiles and trucks, are the primary types of equipment involved in operating leases. Ordinarily, these leases require the lessor to maintain and service the leased equipment, and the cost of the maintenance is built into the lease payments.

Another important characteristic of operating leases is the fact that they are generally *not fully amortized.* In other words, the payments required under the lease contract are not sufficient to recover the full cost of the equipment. However, the lease contract is written for a period considerably less than the expected economic life of the leased equipment, and the lessor expects to recover all costs

---

[1]The term *lessee* is pronounced "less-ee," not "lease-ee," and *lessor* is pronounced "less-or."

either in subsequent renewal payments, by re-leasing the equipment to other lessees, or by sale of the equipment.

A final feature of operating leases is that they frequently contain a *cancellation clause* which gives the lessee the right to cancel the lease and to return the equipment before the expiration of the basic lease agreement. This is an important consideration to the lessee, for it means that the equipment can be returned if it is rendered obsolete by technological developments or if it is no longer needed because of a decline in the lessee's business.

Financial, or Capital, Leases

Financial leases, sometimes called *capital leases,* are differentiated from operating leases in that (1) they *do not* provide for maintenance service, (2) they *are not* cancellable, and (3) they *are* fully amortized (that is, the lessor receives rental payments equal to the full price of the leased equipment plus a return on investment). In a typical arrangement, the firm that will use the equipment (the lessee) selects the specific items it requires, and then it negotiates the price and delivery terms with the manufacturer. The user firm then arranges to have a leasing company (the lessor) buy the equipment from the manufacturer or the distributor. When the equipment is purchased, the user firm simultaneously executes an agreement to lease the equipment from the financial institution. The terms of the lease call for full amortization of the lessor's investment, plus a rate of return on the unamortized balance which is close to the percentage rate the lessee would have paid on a secured term loan. For example, if the lessee would have to pay 10 percent for a term loan, then a rate of about 10 percent would be built into the lease contract.

The lessee is generally given an option to renew the lease at a reduced rate upon expiration of the basic lease. However, the basic lease usually cannot be canceled unless the lessor is completely paid off. Also, the lessee generally pays the property taxes and insurance on the leased property. Since the lessor receives a return *after,* or *net of,* these payments, this type of lease is often called a "net, net" lease.

Financial leases are almost the same as sale-and-leaseback arrangements, the major difference being that the leased equipment is new and the lessor buys it from a manufacturer or a distributor instead of from the user-lessee. A sale and leaseback may, then, be thought of as a special type of financial lease. Both sale-and-leaseback arrangements and financial leases are analyzed in the same manner.

Combination Leases

As noted in the opening section of this chapter, GECC and many other lessors now offer leases under a wide variety of terms. Therefore, in practice, many leases do not fit exactly into the operating lease or financial lease category, but rather combine some features of each. Such leases are called *combination leases.* To illustrate, cancellation clauses are normally associated with operating leases, but most of today's financial leases also contain cancellation clauses. However, in financial leases these clauses generally include pre-payment provisions whereby the lessee must make penalty payments sufficient to enable the lessor to recover the unamortized investment cost of the leased property.

TAX EFFECTS

The full amount of the annual lease payment is a deductible expense for income tax purposes *provided the Internal Revenue Service agrees that a particular contract is a genuine lease and not simply an installment loan called a lease.* This makes it important that a lease contract be written in a form acceptable to the IRS. The IRS considers any agreement to be a sale if (1) the total lease payments are made over a relatively short period and are approximately equal to the cost of the property, (2) the lessee may continue to use the property over the remainder of its useful life for relatively nominal renewal payments, or (3) a purchase option at a favorable price is written into the lease contract.

The reason for the IRS's concern about these factors is that, without restrictions, a company could set up a "lease" transaction calling for very rapid payments, which would be tax deductions. The effect would be to depreciate the equipment over a much shorter period than its ACRS class life. For example, suppose a firm planned to acquire a $2 million computer which had a 3-year ACRS class life. The annual depreciation allowances would be $660,000 in Year 1, $900,000 in Year 2, $300,000 in Year 3, and $140,000 in Year 4. If the firm were in the 40 percent federal-plus-state tax bracket, the depreciation would provide a tax saving of $264,000 in Year 1, $360,000 in Year 2, $120,000 in Year 3, and $56,000 in Year 4, for a total savings of $800,000. At a 6 percent discount rate, the present value of these tax savings would be $757,441.

Now suppose the firm could acquire the computer through a 1-year lease arrangement with a leasing company for a payment of $2 million, with a one-dollar purchase option. If the $2,000,000 payment were treated as a lease payment, it would be fully deductible, and hence would provide a tax saving of $0.4($2,000,000) = $800,000 versus a present value of only $757,441 for the depreciation shelters. Thus, the lease payment and the depreciation would both provide the same total amount of tax savings (40% of $2 million, or $800,000), but the savings would come in faster, and hence have a higher present value, with the 1-year lease. Therefore, if just any type of contract could be called a lease and given tax treatment as a lease, then the timing of the tax shelters could be speeded up as compared with ownership depreciation tax shelters. This speedup would benefit companies, but it would be costly to the government. For this reason, the IRS has established the rules described above for defining a lease for tax purposes.

Even though leasing can be used only within limits to speed up the effective depreciation schedule, there are still times when very substantial tax benefits can be derived from a leasing arrangement. For example, if a firm like Tucson Electric has a very large construction program which has generated so many investment tax credits and so much accelerated depreciation that it has no current tax liabilities, then depreciation shelters are not very useful. In this case, a leasing company set up by a profitable company like GE can buy the equipment, receive the depreciation shelters, and then share these benefits with the lessee by charging lower lease payments. This point will be discussed in detail later in the chapter, but the point to be made now is that if firms are to obtain tax benefits from leasing, the lease contract must be written in a manner that will qualify it as a true lease under IRS guidelines. If there is any question about the legal status of the contract, the financial manager must be sure to have the firm's lawyers and accountants check the latest IRS regulations.[2]

EFFECTS ON THE BALANCE SHEET

Lease payments are shown as operating expenses on a firm's income statement, but under certain conditions, neither the leased assets nor the liabilities under the lease contract appear on the firm's balance sheet. For this reason, leasing is often called *off balance sheet* financing. This point is illustrated in Table 16-1 by the balance sheets of two hypothetical firms, B and L. Initially, the balance sheets of both firms are identical, and they both have debt ratios of 50 percent. Next, each firm decides to acquire a fixed asset costing $100. Firm B borrows $100 and buys the asset, so both an asset and a liability go on its balance sheet, and its debt ratio rises from 50 to 75 percent. Firm L leases the equipment. The lease may call for fixed charges as high or even higher than the loan, and the obligations assumed

Table 16-1
Balance Sheet Effects of Leasing

Before Asset Increase				After Asset Increase							
Firms B and L				Firm B, Which Borrows and Buys				Firm L, Which Leases			
Current assets	$ 50	Debt	$ 50	Current assets	$ 50	Debt	$150	Current assets	$ 50	Debt	$ 50
Fixed assets	50	Equity	50	Fixed assets	150	Equity	50	Fixed assets	50	Equity	50
	$100		$100		$200		$200		$100		$100

[2]Under the Economic Recovery Tax Act of 1981, Congress relaxed the normal IRS rules to permit *safe harbor leases,* which had virtually no IRS restrictions and which were explicitly designed to permit the transfer of the tax benefits under the 1981 Act from low-profit companies which could not use them to high-profit companies which could. The point of safe harbor leases was to provide incentives for capital investment to companies which had little or no tax liability — under safe harbor leasing, companies with a low tax liability could sell the benefit to companies in a high marginal tax bracket. In 1981 and 1982, literally billions of dollars were paid by such profitable firms as GE for the tax shelters of such unprofitable ones as Ford and Eastern Airlines. However, in 1983, Congress sharply curtailed the use of safe harbor leases.

under the lease may be equally or more dangerous from the standpoint of potential bankruptcy, but the firm's debt ratio remains at 50 percent.

To correct this problem, the Financial Accounting Standards Board issued FASB Statement 13, which requires that, for an unqualified audit report, firms that enter into certain financial (or capital) leases must restate their balance sheets to report the leased asset as a fixed asset and the present value of the future lease payments as a debt. This process is called *capitalizing the lease,* and its net effect is to cause Firms B and L to have similar balance sheets, both of which will, in essence, resemble the one shown for Firm B.[3]

The logic behind Statement 13 is as follows. If a firm signs a lease contract, its obligation to make lease payments is just as binding as if it had signed a loan agreement — the failure to make lease payments can bankrupt a firm just as fast as the failure to make principal and interest payments on a loan. Therefore, for all intents and purposes, a financial lease is identical to a loan.[4] This being the case, if a firm signs a lease agreement, this has the effect of raising its true debt ratio, and thus its true capital structure is changed. Therefore, if the firm had previously established a target capital structure, and if there is no reason to think that the optimal capital structure has changed, then using lease financing requires additional equity support exactly like debt financing.

If no disclosure of leases were made, then investors could be deceived into thinking that a firm which uses lease financing is in a stronger position than it really is. Thus, even before FASB Statement 13 was issued in 1976, firms were required to disclose the existence of long-term leases in footnotes to their financial statements. At that time, it was debated as to whether or not investors recognized fully the impact of leases and, in effect, would see that Firms B and L were in essentially the same financial position. Some people argued that leases were not fully recognized, even by sophisticated investors. If this were the case, then leasing could alter the capital structure decision in a really significant manner — a firm could increase its true leverage through a lease arrangement, and this procedure would have a smaller effect on its cost of conventional debt, k_d, and on its cost of equity, k_s, than if it had borrowed directly and reflected this fact on its balance sheet. These benefits of leasing would accrue to existing investors at the expense of new investors who would, in effect, be deceived by the fact that the firm's balance sheet did not reflect its true liability situation.

---

[3]FASB Statement 13, "Accounting for Leases," November 1976, spells out in detail the conditions under which the lease must be capitalized and the procedures for capitalizing it.

[4]There are, however, certain legal differences between loans and leases. In the event of liquidation in bankruptcy, a lessor is entitled to take possession of the leased asset, and if the value of the asset is less than the required payments under the lease, the lessor can enter a claim (as a general creditor) for one year's lease payments. In a reorganization, the lessor receives the asset plus three years' lease payments if needed to cover the value of the lease. The lender under a secured loan arrangement has a security interest in the asset, meaning that if it is sold, the lender will be given the proceeds, and the full unsatisfied portion of the lender's claim will be treated as a general creditor obligation. It is not possible to state, as a general rule, whether a supplier of capital is in a stronger position as a secured creditor or as a lessor. Usually, one position is regarded as being about as good as the other at the time the financial arrangements are being made.

The question of whether investors were truly deceived was debated but never resolved. Those who believed strongly in efficient markets thought that investors were not deceived and that footnotes were sufficient, while those who questioned market efficiency thought that leases should be capitalized. Statement 13 represents a compromise between these two positions, though one that is tilted heavily toward those who favor capitalization.

A lease is classified as a capital lease, and hence is capitalized and shown directly on the balance sheet, if one or more of the following conditions exist:

1. Under the terms of the lease, ownership of the property is effectively transferred from the lessor to the lessee.

2. The lessee can purchase the property at less than its true market value when the lease expires.

3. The lease runs for a period equal to or greater than 75 percent of the asset's life. Thus, if an asset has a 10-year life and the lease is written for 8 years, the lease must be capitalized.

4. The present value of the lease payments is equal to or greater than 90 percent of the initial value of the asset.[5]

These rules, together with strong footnote disclosure rules for operating leases, are sufficient to insure that no one will be fooled by lease financing; thus, leases are regarded as debt for capital structure purposes, and they have the same effects as debt on k_d and k_s. Therefore, leasing is not likely to permit a firm to use more financial leverage than could be obtained with conventional debt.

EVALUATION BY THE LESSEE

Leases are evaluated by both the lessee and the lessor. The lessee must determine whether leasing an asset is less costly than buying the asset, and the lessor must decide what the lease payments must be to produce a reasonable rate of return. This section focuses on the analysis by the lessee.

In the typical case, the events leading to a lease arrangement follow the sequence described next. We should note that a degree of uncertainty exists regarding the theoretically correct way to evaluate lease versus purchase decisions, and some very complex decision models have been developed to aid in the analysis. However, the simple analysis given here leads to the correct decision in all the cases we have ever encountered.

1. The firm decides to acquire a particular building or piece of equipment; this decision is based on regular capital budgeting procedures. The decision to acquire

---

[5]The discount rate used to calculate the present value of the lease payments must be the lower of (1) the rate used by the lessor to establish the lease payments (this rate is discussed later in the chapter) or (2) the rate of interest which the lessee would have to pay for new debt with a maturity equal to that of the lease.

the machine is not at issue in the typical lease analysis — that decision was made previously as part of the capital budgeting process. In a lease analysis, we are concerned simply with whether to obtain the use of the machine by lease or by purchase.

2. Once the firm has decided to acquire the asset, the next question is how to finance its acquisition. Well-run businesses do not have excess cash lying around, so capital to finance new assets must be obtained from some source.

3. Funds to purchase the asset could be obtained by borrowing, by retaining earnings, or by selling new equity. Alternatively, the asset could be leased. Because of the capitalizaton/disclosure provision for leases, leasing normally has the same capital structure effect as borrowing.

As indicated earlier, a lease is comparable to a loan in the sense that the firm is required to make a specified series of payments, and a failure to meet these payments could result in bankruptcy. Thus, the most appropriate comparison is the cost of lease financing versus the cost of debt financing.[6] The lease versus borrow-and-purchase analysis is illustrated with data on the Anderson Equipment Company. The following conditions are assumed:

1. Anderson plans to acquire an automated assembly line with a 5-year life at a cost of $10 million, delivered and installed.

2. Anderson can borrow the required $10 million on a 10 percent loan to be amortized over 5 years. Therefore, the loan will call for payments of $10,000,000/ $PVIFA_{10\%,5}$ = $2,637,974.81 per year. The exact payment was determined using a financial calculator, recognizing that $10 million is the present value of a 5-year, 10 percent ordinary annuity.

3. The equipment's estimated salvage value is $1,000,000. Thus, if Anderson buys the equipment, it would expect to receive $1,000,000 before taxes when the equipment is sold after 5 years' use. Note that in leasing, the asset's salvage value is generally called the *residual value.*

4. Anderson can lease the equipment for 5 years at a rental charge of $2,750,000, payable at the beginning of each year, but the lessor will own the equipment upon the expiration of the lease. (The lease payment schedule is established by the potential lessor, as described in the next major section, and Anderson can accept it, reject it, or negotiate.)

5. The lease contract stipulates that the lessor will maintain the equipment at no additional charge to Anderson. However if Anderson borrows and buys, it will have to bear the cost of maintenance, which will be performed by the equipment manufacturer at a fixed contract rate of $500,000 per year, payable at the beginning of each year.

---

[6]Note that the analysis should compare the cost of leasing to the cost of debt financing *regardless* of how the asset is actually financed. The asset may be purchased with surplus cash if not leased, but since leasing is a substitute for debt financing in an opportunity cost sense, the appropriate comparison would still be to debt financing.

6. The equipment falls in the ACRS 5-year class life, and Anderson's marginal federal-plus-state tax rate is 40 percent.

NPV Analysis

Table 16-2 shows the steps involved in an NPV lease analysis. Part I of the table is devoted to the costs of borrowing and buying. Here, Columns 2 through 5 give the loan amortization schedule; Column 6 shows the maintenance expense; and Column 7 gives depreciation charges. Tax-deductible expenses — interest, maintenance, and depreciation — are summed and shown in Column 8, while Column 9 gives the taxes saved due to these deductions. Column 10 summarizes the preceding columns, giving the annual net cash outflows that Anderson will incur if it borrows and buys the equipment. Further, if Anderson buys the equipment, it will net $840,000 after taxes from the sale of the equipment in Year 5. This amount is shown as an inflow (negative cash outflow) in Column 10.

Part II of Table 16-2 contains an analysis of the cost of leasing. The lease payments, shown in Column 11, are $2,750,000 per year; this rate, which includes maintenance, was established by the prospective lessor and offered to Anderson Equipment. If Anderson accepts the lease, the full amount will be a deductible expense, so the tax savings, shown in Column 12, is 0.40(Lease payment) = 0.40($2,750,000) = $1,100,000. Thus, the after-tax cost of the lease payment is Lease payment − Tax savings = $2,750,000 − $1,100,000 = $1,650,000. This amount is shown in Column 13, Years 0 through 4.

The next step is to compare the net cost of owning with the net cost of leasing. However, we must first put the annual cash flows of leasing and owning on a common basis. This requires converting them to present values, which brings up the question of the proper rate at which to discount the costs. In Chapter 6, we saw that the riskier the cash flows, the higher will be the discount rate used to find present values. This same principle was observed in our discussion of capital budgeting, and it also applies in lease analysis. Just how risky are the cash flows under consideration here? Most of them are relatively certain, at least when compared with the types of cash flow estimates that were developed in capital budgeting. For example, the loan payment schedule is set by contract, as is the lease payment schedule. The depreciation expenses are also established by law and are not subject to change, and the $500,000 annual maintenance cost is fixed by contract as well. The tax savings are somewhat uncertain, but they will be as projected so long as Anderson's marginal tax rate remains at 40 percent. The residual value is the least certain of the cash flows, but even here, Anderson's management is fairly confident because the estimated residual value distribution is relatively tight.

Since the cash flows under the lease and under the borrow-and-purchase alternatives are both relatively certain, they should be discounted at a relatively low rate. Most analysts recommend that the company's cost of debt be used, and this rate seems reasonable in our example. Further, since all the cash flows are on an after-tax basis, *the after-tax cost of debt, which is 6.0 percent, should be used.* Accordingly, we discount the cash outflows in Columns 10 and 13 using a rate of

Table 16-2
Anderson Equipment Company:
NPV Analysis
(Thousands of Dollars)

I. Cost of Owning (Borrowing and Buying)

		Loan Amortization Schedule					Tax Deductible Expenses:	Tax Savings:	Net Cash Outflow If Owned:
Year (1)	Total Payment (2)	Interest (3)	Principal (4)	Remaining Balance (5)	Maintenance Cost (6)	Depreciation (7)	(3) + (6) + (7) = (8)	0.40 × (8) = (9)	(2) + (6) − (9) = (10)
0					$500		$ 500	$ 200	$ 300
1	$ 2,638	$1,000	$ 1,638	$8,362	500	$2,000	3,500	1,400	1,738
2	2,638	836	1,802	6,560	500	3,200	4,536	1,814	1,324
3	2,638	656	1,982	4,578	500	1,900	3,056	1,222	1,916
4	2,638	458	2,180	2,398	500	1,200	2,158	863	2,275
5	2,638	240	2,398	0		1,100	1,340	536	2,102
5									(840)
	$13,190	$3,190	$10,000			$9,400			

PV cost of owning = $7,471

II. Cost of Leasing

Year (1)	Lease Payment (11)	Tax Savings: 0.40 × (11) = (12)	Net Cash Outflow If Leased: (11) − (12) = (13)
0	$2,750	$1,100	$1,650
1	2,750	1,100	1,650
2	2,750	1,100	1,650
3	2,750	1,100	1,650
4	2,750	1,100	1,650
5			

PV cost of leasing = $7,367

III. Cost Comparison

Net advantage to leasing (NAL) = PV cost of leasing − PV cost of owning = − $7,367 − (− $7,471) = $104.

Notes:

a. The net cash outflows are discounted at the lessee's after-tax cost of debt, 6.0 percent.

b. Two lines are shown in Part I for Year 5 in order to account for the residual value cash flow.

c. The ACRS depreciation allowances are 0.20, 0.32, 0.19, 0.12, and 0.11 in Years 1–5 respectively. Thus, the depreciation expense is 0.20($10,000) = $2,000 in Year 1, and so on.

d. The residual value is $1,000 while the book value is $600. Thus, Anderson would have to pay 0.4($1,000 − $600) = $160 in taxes, producing a net after-tax residual value of $1,000 − $160 = $840.

e. In practice, a lease analysis such as this would be done using an electronic spreadsheet such as Lotus 1-2-3.

6.0 percent. The resulting present values are $7,741,000 for the cost of owning and $7,367,000 for the cost of leasing. The financing method that produces the smaller present value of costs is the one that should be selected. We define the net advantage to leasing (NAL) as follows:

$$NAL = PV \text{ cost of leasing} - PV \text{ cost of borrowing and buying.}$$

Thus, the NAL for Anderson's lease is $-\$7,367,000 - (-\$7,741,000) = \$104,000$, so in this instance, it is to Anderson's advantage to lease.[7]

EVALUATION BY THE LESSOR

Thus far, we have considered leasing only from the lessee's viewpoint. It is also useful to analyze the transaction as the lessor sees it: Is the lease a good investment for the party who must put up the money? The lessor will generally be a specialized leasing company, a bank or bank affiliate, an individual or group of individuals, or a subsidiary of a manufacturer such as GECC, which is probably the largest leasing company in existence. Investment banking houses such as Merrill Lynch also set up and/or work with specialized leasing companies, where brokerage clients' money is made available to leasing customers in deals which permit the investors to share in the tax shelters provided by the lease.

Regardless of who the lessor is, any potential lessor needs to know the rate of return on the capital invested in the lease, and this information is also useful to the prospective lessee: Lease terms on large leases are generally negotiated, so the lessor and the lessee should know one another's position. The lessor's analysis

---

[7]The more complicated methods which exist for analyzing leasing generally focus on the issue of the discount rate that should be used to discount the cash flows. Conceptually, we could assign a separate discount rate to each individual cash flow component, then find the present values of each of the cash flow components, and finally sum these present values to determine the net advantage or disadvantage to leasing. This approach has been taken by Stewart C. Myers, David A. Dill, and Alberto J. Bautista (MDB) in "Valuation of Financial Lease Contracts," *Journal of Finance,* June 1976, 799–819, among others. MDB correctly note that procedures like the one presented in this chapter are valid only if (1) leases and loans are viewed by investors as being equivalent and (2) all cash flows are equally risky, and hence appropriately discounted at the same rate. The first assumption is valid today for virtually all financial leases, and even where it is not, no one knows how to adjust properly for any capital structure effects that leases might have. (MDB, and others, have presented an adjustment formula, but it is based on the assumption that the Modigliani-Miller leverage argument, with no financial distress costs, is correct. Since even MM do not regard the pure MM model as being correct, the MDB formula cannot be correct.) Regarding the second assumption, it is generally believed that all of the cash flows in Table 16-2 except the residual value are of about the same degree of risk, at least to the extent that we are able to evaluate risk. Therefore, the procedures used in Table 16-2 normally meet the MDB assumption; hence, the Table 16-2 analysis is usually correct.

Regarding the residual value, advocates of multiple discount rates often point out that the salvage value is more uncertain than are the other cash flows and thus recommend discounting it at a higher rate. However, there is no way of knowing precisely how much to increase the after-tax cost of debt to account for the increased riskiness of the salvage value cash flow. Further, in a CAPM sense, all cash flows could be equally risky even though individual items such as the salvage value might have more or less total variability than others.

For all these reasons, most analysts use only one discount rate — the after-tax cost of debt — to evaluate the cash flows in a lease analysis.

involves (1) determining the net cash outlay, which is usually the invoice price of the leased equipment less any lease payments made in advance; (2) determining the periodic cash inflows, which consist of the lease payments minus both income taxes and any lessor's maintenance expense; (3) estimating the after-tax residual value of the property when the lease expires; and (4) determining whether the rate of return on the lease exceeds the lessor's opportunity cost of capital or, equivalently, whether the NPV of the lease exceeds zero.

To illustrate the lessor's analysis, we assume the same facts as for the Anderson Equipment Company lease, as well as this situation: (1) The potential lessor is a wealthy individual whose current income is in the form of interest, and whose marginal federal-plus-state income tax rate, T, is 40 percent. (2) The investor can buy 5-year bonds that have a 9 percent yield to maturity, providing an after-tax yield of $(9\%)(1 - T) = (9\%)(0.6) = 5.4\%$. This is the after-tax return that the investor can obtain on alternative investments of similar risk. (3) The before-tax salvage (or residual) value is $1,000,000. Since the asset will be depreciated to a book value of $600,000 at the end of the 5-year lease, $400,000 of this $1 million will be taxable at the 40 percent rate because of the recapture of depreciation rule, so the lessor will receive $840,000 after taxes from the sale of the equipment after the lease expires.

NPV Analysis

The lease analysis from the investor's standpoint is developed in Table 16-3. Here we see that the lease as an investment has a net present value of $26,000. On a present value basis, the investor who invests in the lease rather than in the 9

Table 16-3
Lease Analysis from the Lessor's Viewpoint
(Thousands of Dollars)

Year (1)	Net Equipment Cost (2)	Lease Payment (3)	Maintenance Expense (4)	Depreciation (5)	Taxes: $[(3) - (4) - (5)]T = (6)$	After-Tax Salvage (Residual) Value (7)	Net Cash Flow: $(2) + (3) - (4) - (6) + (7) = (8)$
0	($10,000)	$ 2,750	500		$900		($8,650)
1		2,750	500	$2,000	100		2,150
2		2,750	500	3,200	(380)		2,630
3		2,750	500	1,900	140		2,110
4		2,750	500	1,200	420		1,830
5				1,100	(440)	$840	1,280
		$13,750	$2,500	$9,400	$740		

$$NPV = \sum_{t=0}^{5} \frac{NCF_t}{(1 + k)^t} = \$26 \text{ when } k = 5.4\%.$$

percent bonds (5.4 percent after taxes) is better off by this amount, indicating that the investor should be willing to write the lease. Since we saw earlier that the lease is also advantageous to Anderson Equipment Company, the transaction should be completed.

Leveraged Lease Analysis

Historically, only two parties have been involved in lease transactions — the lessor, who puts up the money, and the lessee. In recent years, however, a new type of lease, the *leveraged lease,* has come into widespread use. Under a leveraged lease, the lessor arranges to borrow part of the required funds, generally giving the lender a first mortgage on the plant or equipment being leased. The lessor still receives the tax shelter associated with accelerated depreciation. However, the lessor now has a riskier position, because the lessor's position is junior to that of the lender, who has a first mortgage on the plant or equipment.

Such leveraged leases, often with syndicates of wealthy individuals seeking tax shelters acting as owner-lessors, are an important part of the financial scene today. Incidentally, whether or not a lease is leveraged is not important to the lessee; from the lessee's standpoint, the method of analyzing a proposed lease is unaffected by whether or not the lessor borrows part of the required capital.

The example in Table 16-3 is not set up as a leveraged lease. However, it is easy enough to modify the analysis if the lessor borrows all or part of the required $10 million, making the transaction a leveraged lease. First, we would add a set of columns to Table 16-3 to show the financing cash flows. The interest component would represent another tax deduction, while the loan repayments would constitute additional cash outlays. The "initial cost" would be reduced by the amount of the loan. With these changes made, a new NPV could be calculated and used to evaluate whether or not the lease represents a good investment.

To illustrate, assume that the lessor can borrow $5 million of the $10 million net purchase price at a rate of 9 percent on a 5-year balloon loan. Table 16-4 contains the lessor's leveraged lease NPV analysis. The NPV of the leveraged lease investment based on the net cash flows shown in Column 4 is $26,000, which is the same as the $26,000 NPV for the unleveraged lease. Note, though, that the lessor has only spent $3.65 million on this lease. Therefore, the lessor could invest in 2.37 similar leveraged leases for the same $8.65 million investment required to finance a single unleveraged lease, producing a total net present value of $2.37($26,000) = $61,620.[8]

Typically, a leveraged lease provides the lessor with a higher expected NPV per dollar of invested capital than an unleveraged lease. However, the riskiness of such leases is also higher for the same reason that any leveraged investment is riskier. Since leveraged leases are a relatively new development, no standard methodology

---

[8]Note that in this situation leveraging had no impact on the lessor's per lease NPV. This is because the cost of leveraging (5.4 percent after taxes) equals the discount rate, and hence the leveraging cash flows are netted out on a present value basis.

Table 16-4
Leveraged Lease Analysis
(Thousands of Dollars)

Year (1)	Net Cash Flow from Table 16-3 (2)	Cash Flows from Leveraging[a] (3)	Net Cash Flow: (2) + (3) = (4)
0	($8,650)	$5,000	($3,650)
1	2,150	(270)	1,880
2	2,630	(270)	2,360
3	2,110	(270)	1,840
4	1,830	(270)	1,560
5	1,280	(5,270)	(3,990)

$$NPV = \sum_{t=0}^{5} \frac{NCF_t}{(1 + k)^t} = \$26 \text{ when } k = 5.4\%.$$

[a]The lessor borrows $5 million at t = 0 and repays it at t = 5. Interest expense, payable at the end of each year, is $0.09(\$5,000) = \$450$, but it is tax deductible, so the after-tax interest cash flow is $-\$450(1 - T) = -\$450(0.6) = -\$270$.

has been developed for analyzing them in a risk/return framework. However, sophisticated lessors are now developing simulations similar to those described in Chapter 10. Then, given the apparent riskiness of the lease investment, the lessor can decide whether the returns built into the contract are sufficient to compensate for the risk involved.

OTHER ISSUES IN LEASE ANALYSIS

The NPV method of analysis for both the lessee and the lessor were presented in the previous sections. However, some other issues warrant discussion.

Other Analytical Techniques

The NPV method is not the only analytical technique that can be used in lease analysis: A type of IRR analysis which leads to identical decisions can also be used by both the lessee and the lessor. See Eugene F. Brigham and Louis C. Gapenski, *Intermediate Financial Management,* 2nd ed., Chapter 14 for a discussion.

Feedback Effect on Capital Budgeting

In our example, we assumed that Anderson has already made a firm decision to acquire the new equipment, and thus the lease analysis was conducted solely to determine whether the equipment should be leased or purchased. However, if the cost of leasing is less than the cost of debt, it is possible for a project that was rejected in the regular capital budgeting process to become acceptable if it is financed through a lease. Again, this point is discussed in Chapter 14 of *Intermediate Financial Management.*

Estimated Residual Value

It is important to note that the lessor owns the property upon expiration of a lease, and hence the lessor has claim to the asset's salvage (or residual) value. Superficially, it would appear that if residual values are expected to be large, owning would have an advantage over leasing. However, this apparent advantage may not hold up. If expected residual values are large — as they may be under inflation for certain types of equipment and also if real property is involved — competition between leasing companies and other financial sources, as well as competition among leasing companies themselves, will force leasing rates down to the point where potential residual values are fully recognized in the lease contract. Thus, the existence of large residual values on equipment is not likely to result in materially higher costs for leasing.

Increased Credit Availability

As noted earlier, leasing is sometimes said to have an advantage for firms that are seeking the maximum degree of financial leverage. First, it is sometimes argued that firms can obtain more money, and for longer terms, under a lease arrangement than under a loan secured by a specific piece of equipment. Second, since some leases do not appear on the balance sheet, lease financing has been said to give the firm a stronger appearance in a *superficial* credit analysis and thus to permit the firm to use more leverage than would be possible if it did not lease.

There may be some truth to these claims for smaller firms. However, now that large firms are required to capitalize major leases and to report them on their balance sheets, this point is of questionable validity for any firm large enough to have audited financial statements.

Depreciation Tax Savings

If a firm is unprofitable, or if it is expanding so rapidly and generating so much depreciation expense that its taxable income is driven down to zero, then it may be worthwhile for it to enter a lease arrangement. Here the lessor (a bank, a leasing company, or a high-tax-bracket corporation or individual) will take the depreciation tax savings and give the lessee a corresponding reduction in lease charges. Railroads and airlines have been large users of leasing for this reason in recent years, as have unprofitable industrial companies such as U.S. Steel (now USX Corporation).

Computer Models

Lease analysis, like capital budgeting analysis, is particularly well suited for computer analysis; see Problems 16-2, 16-3, and 16-4. Both the lessee and lessor could create computer models for their analyses. Setting the analysis up on a computer is especially useful when negotiations are underway, and when investment banking houses such as Merrill Lynch are working out a leasing deal between a group of investors and a company, the analysis would always be computerized.

Leasing under the 1986 Tax Act

The 1986 Tax Act contained three provisions that reduce the potential advantages of leasing: (1) The investment tax credit (ITC) was eliminated. Prior to 1987, many leases were signed for the primary purpose of transferring ITCs from zero tax bracket corporations such as U.S. Steel to high bracket investors such as IBM. (2) Under the 1986 Act, depreciation rates were effectively lowered. Thus, the depreciation benefits associated with owning buildings and equipment were lowered. (3) Tax rates were lowered, generally from 46 percent to 34 percent for corporations, and from 50 percent to 28 percent for individuals. The first two factors lower the tax shelters that are available for transfer from low-bracket to high-bracket investors, while the third lowers the economic value of any such transfer (because the tax saving is equal to the deduction times the tax rate).

We used our lease analysis models to analyze a number of recent (1986) lease deals, but under the assumption the new tax laws were in effect. Invariably, the advantage of leasing fell sharply, often to the point where the lease deal would simply not be viable. This suggests that the volume of leasing will fall as a result of the new tax law. However, another feature of the new law — the Alternative Minimum Tax (AMT) on corporations — may stimulate leasing. As we noted in Chapter 2, corporations can use accelerated depreciation and other tax shelters to hold down their actual taxes paid, but then use straight line depreciation for stockholder reporting and hence report high profits. Thus, IBM, GE, and other profitable companies have reported high earnings yet paid little or no federal income taxes in recent years. The AMT, which is figured at approximately 20 percent of *reported* profits, is designed to force profitable companies to pay at least some taxes.

Many companies have forecasted that they will be exposed to heavy tax liabilities under the AMT, and they are looking for ways to reduce reported income. Leasing can be beneficial here — use a relatively short period for the lease, consequently have a high annual payment, and the result will be low reported profits and hence a low AMT liability. Note that in this case the lease payments would not necessarily have to qualify as a deductible expense for regular tax purposes — all that is needed is that they be used to hold down income as reported to stockholders.

We have not attempted to set up a model to deal with AMT considerations. However, people in the leasing industry are designing such models, and they expect to generate a substantial amount of new leasing business as a direct result of the AMT.

SUMMARY

This chapter discussed the four major types of leases: (1) *operating leases,* (2) *sale-and-leaseback plans,* (3) *financial leases,* and (4) *combination leases.* Operating leases generally provide both for the financing of an asset and for its maintenance, whereas both sale-and-leaseback plans and regular financial leases usually provide only financing and are alternatives to debt financing. Today, many leases contain features of both operating and financial leases.

Financial leases (and sale-and-leaseback plans) are evaluated by a cash flow analysis. We start with the assumption that an asset will be acquired, and that the acquisition will be financed either by debt or by a lease. Next, we develop the annual net cash outflows associated with each financing plan. Then we discount the two sets of outflows at the company's after-tax cost of debt. Finally, we choose the alternative with the lower present value of costs.

Leasing sometimes represents "off balance sheet" financing, which permits a firm to obtain more financial leverage if it leases than if it uses straight debt. This was formerly cited as a major reason for leasing. Today, however, taxes are the primary reason for the growth of financial leasing. Leasing permits depreciation tax savings to be transferred from the user of an asset to the supplier of capital, and if these parties are in different tax brackets, both can benefit from the lease arrangement. Also, under the Tax Reform Act of 1986, leasing allows some firms to lower taxes paid under the alternative minimum tax.

Questions

16-1 Define each of the following terms:
   a. Lessee; lessor
   b. Sale and leaseback; operating lease; financial lease; capital lease; leveraged lease
   c. "Off balance sheet" financing
   d. FASB #13
   e. Residual value
   f. Lease analysis
   g. Alternative minimum tax (AMT)

16-2 Distinguish between operating leases and financial leases. Would you be more likely to find an operating lease employed for a fleet of trucks or for a manufacturing plant?

16-3 Would you be more likely to find that lessees are in high or low income tax brackets as compared to lessors?

16-4 Commercial banks moved heavily into equipment leasing during the early 1970s, acting as lessors. One major reason for this invasion of the leasing industry was to gain the benefits of accelerated depreciation and the investment tax credit on leased equipment. During this same period, commercial banks were investing heavily in municipal securities, and they were also making loans to real estate investment trusts (REITs). In the mid 1970s, these REITs got into such serious difficulty that many banks suffered large losses on their REIT loans. Explain how its investments in municipal bonds and REITs could reduce a bank's willingness to act as a lessor.

16-5 One alleged advantage of leasing voiced in the past is that it kept liabilities off the balance sheet, thus making it possible for a firm to obtain more leverage than it otherwise could have. This raised the question of whether or not both the lease obligation and the asset involved should be capitalized and shown on the balance sheet. Discuss the pros and cons of capitalizing leases and related assets.

16-6 Suppose there were no IRS restrictions on what constituted a valid lease. Explain, in a manner that a legislator might understand, why some restrictions should be imposed. Illustrate your answer with numbers.

16-7 What are the advantages and disadvantages of leveraged leases from the standpoint of (a) the lessee, (b) the equity investor in the lease, and (c) the supplier of the debt capital?

16-8 Suppose Congress enacted new tax law changes that would (1) permit equipment to be depreciated over a shorter period, (2) lower corporate tax rates, and (3) reinstate the investment tax credit. Discuss how each of these potential changes would affect the relative volume of leasing versus conventional debt in the U.S. economy.

16-9 In our example, we assumed that the lease could not be cancelled. What effect would a cancellation clause have on the lessee's analysis? On the lessor's analysis?

Self-Test Problem

ST-1 (Lease versus buy) The Nachman Company has decided to acquire a new truck. One alternative is to lease the truck on a 4-year contract for a lease payment of $10,000 per year, with payments to be made at the *beginning* of each year. The lease would include maintenance. Alternatively, Nachman could purchase the truck outright for $40,000, financing the purchase by a bank loan for the net purchase price and amortizing the loan over a 4-year period at an interest rate of 10 percent per year. Under the borrow-to-purchase arrangement, Nachman would have to maintain the truck at a cost of $1,000 per year, payable at year-end. The truck falls into the ACRS 3-year class. It has a salvage value of $10,000, which is the expected market value after 4 years, when Nachman plans to replace the truck irrespective of whether it leases or buys. Nachman has a marginal federal-plus-state tax rate of 40 percent.

    a. What is Nachman's PV cost of leasing?

    b. What is Nachman's PV cost of owning? Should the truck be leased or purchased?

    c. The appropriate discount rate for use in the analysis is the firm's after-tax cost of debt. Why?

    d. The salvage value is the least certain cash flow in the analysis. How might Nachman incorporate differential riskiness on this cash flow into the analysis?

Problems

16-1 (Balance sheet effects) Two companies, Electroway and Lewis Corporation, began operations with identical balance sheets. A year later, both required additional manufacturing capacity at a cost of $50,000. Electroway obtained a 5-year, $50,000 loan at an 8 percent interest rate from its bank. Lewis, on the other hand, decided to lease the required $50,000 capacity for 5 years; an 8 percent return was built into the lease. The balance sheet for each company, before the asset increases, follows:

		Debt	$ 50,000
		Equity	100,000
Total assets	$150,000	Total claims	$150,000

    a. Show the balance sheets for both firms after the asset increase and calculate each firm's new debt ratio.

b. Show how Lewis's balance sheet would look immediately after the financing if it capitalized the lease.

c. Would the rate of return (1) on assets and (2) on equity be affected by the choice of financing? How?

16-2 (Lease versus buy) J. B. Smith Industries must install $1 million of new machinery in its Texas plant. It can obtain a bank loan for 100 percent of the required amount. Alternatively, a Texas investment banking firm which represents a group of investors believes that it can arrange for a lease financing plan. *Assume* that these facts apply:

(1) The equipment falls in the ACRS 3-year class.

(2) Estimated maintenance expenses are $50,000 per year.

(3) Smith's tax rate is 34 percent.

(4) If the money is borrowed, the bank loan will be at a rate of 14 percent, amortized in 3 equal installments at the end of each year.

(5) The tentative lease terms call for payments of $320,000 at the end of each year for 3 years.

(6) Under the proposed lease terms, the lessee must pay for insurance, property taxes, and maintenance.

(7) Smith must use the equipment if it is to continue in business, so it will almost certainly want to acquire the property at the end of the lease. If it does, then under the lease terms it can purchase the machinery at its fair market value at that time. The best estimate of this market value is the $200,000 residual value, but it could be much higher or lower under certain circumstances.

To assist management in making the proper lease-versus-buy decision, you are asked to answer the following questions:

a. Assuming that the lease can be arranged, should Smith lease or borrow and buy the equipment? Explain.

b. Consider the $200,000 estimated residual value. Is it appropriate to discount it at the same rate as the other cash flows? What about the other cash flows — are they all equally risky? (Hint: Riskier cash flows are normally discounted at higher rates, but when the cash flows are *costs* rather than *inflows,* the normal procedure must be reversed.)

(Do Parts c and d only if you are using the computerized diskette.)

c. Determine the lease payment at which Smith would be indifferent to buying or leasing; that is, the lease payment which equates the PV cost of leasing to that of buying. (Hint: Use trial-and-error.)

d. Using the $320,000 lease payment, what would be the effect if Smith's tax rate fell to zero?

16-3 (Lessor's analysis) The Cary Company has decided to acquire some new R&D equipment. One alternative is to lease the equipment on a 4-year contract for a lease payment of $11,500 per year, payments to be made at the *beginning* of each year. The lease, which would include maintenance, is being offered by LePage Credit Corporation, a local leasing company. LePage would purchase the equipment outright for $40,000, and would have to pay the local dealer $1,000 at the beginning of each year to provide maintenance service. The equipment falls into the ACRS 3-year class; and it has a residual value of $10,000, which is the expected market value after 4 years. The lessor's marginal state-plus-federal tax rate is 40 percent. The analysts at LePage compare the returns on potential leases with returns available on comparable maturity commercial loans which the firm also writes. Currently, LePage is charging 9 percent on 4-year commercial loans.

   a. What is the NPV on the lease investment?

   b. Should LePage write the lease? Why?
   (Do Parts c, d, e, g, and h only if you are using the computerized diskette.)

   c. Assume that interest rates rise, and LePage can now earn 14 percent (before taxes) on its commercial loans. How does this affect the lease analysis?

   d. What lease payment must LePage charge to be indifferent between writing the lease and loaning at 14 percent?

   e. Return to the original situation. Suppose there is a 25 percent chance that the residual value will be only $5,000, and another 25 percent probability that the residual value will be $15,000. There is a 50 percent probability that the residual value will be $10,000. What is LePage's best case and worst case NPVs? Suppose that the LePage analysts account for differential risk by increasing the residual value discount rate. What residual value discount rate forces NPV = $0 when the residual value is $10,000?

   f. Now suppose that LePage can leverage the lease. LePage could borrow up to $30,000 using the truck as collateral on a term loan at an 8 percent rate. Should LePage leverage the lease? Should LePage leverage the lease at 9 percent?

   g. Refer back to Part f. Suppose that the loan for $30,000 may only be obtained at a rate of 10 percent. What is the new NPV to the lessor of the leveraged lease? Should LePage leverage the lease under these circumstances? Why?

   h. If LePage were able to borrow only $15,000 for this project due to restrictive covenants contained in a previous loan agreement, would it be beneficial to leverage the lease at 8 percent? At 9 percent? At 10 percent?

16-4 (Lessee's analysis) As part of its overall plant modernization and cost reduction program, Southern Fabrics' management has decided to install a new automated weaving loom. In the capital budgeting analysis of this equipment, the IRR of the project was found to be 29 percent versus a project required return of 14 percent.

   The loom has an invoice price of $100,000, including delivery and installation charges. The funds needed could be borrowed from the bank through a 4-year amortized loan at a 15 percent interest rate, with payments to be made at the end of each year. In the event the loom is purchased, the manufacturer will contract to maintain and service it for a fee of $8,000 per year paid at the end of each year. The loom falls in the ACRS 5-year class, and Southern's marginal federal-plus-state tax rate is 40 percent.

   Brooks Automation, Inc., maker of the loom, has offered to lease the loom to Southern for $30,500 upon delivery and installation (at t = 0) plus 4 additional annual lease payments of $30,500 to be made at the end of Years 1 to 4. (Note that there are 5 lease payments in total.) The lease agreement includes maintenance and servicing. Actually, the loom has an expected life of 8 years, at which time its expected salvage value is zero; however, after 4 years, its market value is expected to equal its book value. Southern plans to build an entirely new plant in 4 years, so it has no interest in either leasing or owning the proposed loom for more than that period.

   a. Should the loom be leased or purchased?
   (Do the remainder of the problem only if you are using the computerized diskette.)

b. Southern's managers disagree on the appropriate discount rate to be used in the analysis. What effect would a discount rate change have on the lease-versus-purchase decision?

c. The salvage value is clearly the most uncertain cash flow in the analysis. What effect would a salvage value risk adjustment have on the analysis? (Assume that the appropriate salvage value pre-tax discount rate is 18 percent.)

d. The original analysis assumed that the firm would not need the loom after 4 years. Now assume that the firm will continue to use it after the lease expires. Thus, if it leased, Southern would have to buy the asset after 4 years at the then existing market value, which is assumed to equal the book value. What effect would this requirement have on the basic analysis?

e. Under the original lease terms, it was to Southern's advantage to purchase the loom. However, if you had analyzed the lease from the lessor's viewpoint, you would have found that it was more profitable for Brooks Automation to lease the machine than to sell it — in fact, the manager of Brooks has found that the company can lower the lease payment to $30,000 and still make more by leasing the machine than by selling it. With an annual lease payment of $30,000, should the loom be leased or bought?

f. Perform the lease analysis assuming that Southern's marginal tax rate is (1) 0 percent and (2) 50 percent. Assume a lease payment of $30,500 and a 15 percent pre-tax discount rate. What effect, if any, would the lessee's tax rate have on the lease-buy decision?

Solution to Self-Test Problem

ST-1 a. Cost of leasing:

Year	After-Tax Lease Payment	Present Value at 6%
0	$6,000	$6,000
1	6,000	5,660
2	6,000	5,340
3	6,000	5,038
	PV cost of leasing =	$22,038

b. Cost of owning:

In our solution, we will consider the $40,000 cost as a Year 0 outflow rather than include all the financing cash flows. The net effect is the same since the PV of the financing flows, when discounted at the after-tax cost of debt, is the cost of the asset.

Year (1)	Net Cost (2)	Depreciation (3)	Depreciation Tax Savings: 0.4(3) = (4)	After-Tax Maintenance Cost (5)	After-Tax Salvage Value (6)	Net Cash Flow: (2) − (4) + (5) − (6) = (7)	Present Value at 6% (8)
0	$40,000					$40,000	$40,000
1		$13,200	$ 5,280	$600		(4,680)	(4,415)
2		18,000	7,200	600		(6,600)	(5,874)
3		6,000	2,400	600		(1,800)	(1,511)
4		2,800	1,120	600	$6,000	(6,500)	(5,164)
		$40,000	$16,000			PV cost of owning =	$23,036

Since the present value of the cost of leasing is less than the present value of the cost of owning, the truck should be leased.

c. Use the cost of debt because most cash flows are fixed by contract and consequently are relatively certain; thus, lease cash flows have about the same risk as the firm's debt. Also, leasing is considered as a substitute for debt. Use an after-tax cost rate because the cash flows are stated net of taxes.

d. Nachman could increase the discount rate on the salvage value cash flow. Note that since Nachman plans to replace the truck after 4 years, the salvage value is treated as an inflow in the cost of owning analysis. This makes it reasonable to raise the discount rate for analysis purposes. However, had Nachman planned to continue using the truck, then we would have had to place the estimated salvage value as an additional Year 4 outflow in the leasing section, but without a tax adjustment. Then, higher risk would have been reflected in a *lower* discount rate. This is all very ad hoc, which is why we prefer to use one discount rate throughout the analysis.

Selected Additional References and Cases

For a description of lease analysis in practice, as well as a comprehensive bibliography of the leasing literature, see

O'Brien, Thomas J., and Bennie H. Nunnally, Jr., "A 1982 Survey of Corporate Leasing Analysis," *Financial Management,* Summer 1983, 30–36.

Many of the theoretical issues surrounding lease analysis are discussed in the following articles:

Hockman, Shalom, and Ramon Rabinovitch, "Financial Leasing under Inflation," *Financial Management,* Spring 1984, 17–26.

Levy, Haim, and Marshall Sarnat, "Leasing, Borrowing, and Financial Risk," *Financial Management,* Winter 1979, 47–54.

Lewellen, Wilbur G., Michael S. Long, and John J. McConnell, "Asset Leasing in Competitive Capital Markets," *Journal of Finance,* June 1976, 787–798.

Miller, Merton H., and Charles W. Upton, "Leasing, Buying and the Cost of Capital Services," *Journal of Finance,* June 1976, 761–786.

Schall, Lawrence D., "The Evaluation of Lease Financing Opportunities," *Midland Corporate Finance Journal,* Spring 1985, 48–65.

Leveraged lease analysis is discussed in these articles:

Athanasopoulos, Peter J., and Peter W. Bacon, "The Evaluation of Leveraged Leases," *Financial Management,* Spring 1980, 76–80.

Dyl, Edward A., and Stanley A. Martin, Jr., "Setting Terms for Leveraged Leases," *Financial Management,* Winter 1977, 20–27.

Grimlund, Richard A., and Robert Capettini, "A Note on the Evaluation of Leveraged Leases and Other Investments," *Financial Management,* Summer 1982, 68–72.

Perg, Wayne F., "Leveraged Leasing: The Problem of Changing Leverage," *Financial Management,* Autumn 1978, 47–51.

The Summer 1987 issue of Financial Management *contains articles by H. Martin Weingartner, Roger L. Cason, and Lawrence D. Schall which focus on the impact of asset life uncertainty on lease analysis.*

The Option Pricing Model (OPM) has recently been used in lease analysis by

Copeland, Thomas E., and J. Fred Weston, "A Note on the Evaluation of Cancellable Operating Leases," *Financial Management,* Summer 1982, 60–67.

Lee, Wayne Y., John D. Martin, and Andrew J. Senchack, "The Case for Using Options to Evaluate Salvage Values in Financial Leases," *Financial Management,* Autumn 1982, 33–41.

The Crum-Brigham casebook contains three cases which deal with lease analysis:

Case 25, "Biotech Services," which illustrates the standard lease-versus-purchase decision.

Case 26, "Sure Strike Tackle Company," which focuses on the analysis of sale-and-leaseback versus conventional mortgage financing.

Case 27, "Huysman Steel Corporation," which illustrates leveraged lease analysis and multiple IRRs.

ter, we shall see how a company can use warrants and convertibles to make its securities attractive to a broader range of investors, thereby increasing the potential supply of capital. We also introduce options and futures markets, and illustrate how these markets provide a method for locking in future financing costs.

OPTIONS

Both warrants and convertibles are types of option securities, and options themselves represent an important part of today's financial scene. Therefore, we begin the chapter by discussing both the rapidly growing option markets and option pricing theory. An *option* is a contract which gives its holder the right to buy (or sell) an asset at some predetermined price within a specified period of time. "Pure options" are instruments that (1) are created by outsiders (generally investment banking firms) rather than the firm, (2) are bought and sold primarily by investors (or speculators), and (3) are of greater importance to investors than to financial managers. However, financial managers should understand option theory, because such an understanding will help them structure warrant and convertible financings. Additionally, option theory provides some useful insights into many other facets of corporate finance.

Option Types and Markets

There are many types of options and option markets.[1] To illustrate how options work, suppose you owned 100 shares of IBM, which, on February 26, 1987, sold for $139.75 per share. You could give (or sell) to someone else the right to buy the 100 shares at any time during the next 2 months at a price of, say, $145 per share. The $145 is called the *striking,* or *exercise, price.* Such options exist, and they are traded on a number of exchanges, with the Chicago Board Options Exchange (CBOE) being the oldest and the largest. This type of option is defined as a *call option,* because the purchaser has a "call" on 100 shares of stock. The seller of an option is defined as the *writer.* An investor who "writes" call options against stock held in his or her portfolio is said to be selling *covered options.* Options sold without the stock to back them up are called *naked options.* When the exercise price exceeds the current stock price, the option is said to be *out-of-the-money.* When the exercise price is less than the current price of the underlying stock, the option is *in-the-money.*

You can also buy an option which gives you the right to *sell* a stock at a specified price within some future period — this is called a *put option.* For example, suppose you think IBM's stock price is likely to decline from its current level of $139.75 sometime during the next 2 months. For $450 you could buy a 2-month put option giving you the right to sell 100 shares (which you would not necessar-

---

[1]For an in-depth treatment of options, see Robert C. Radcliffe, *Investment Concepts, Analysis, and Strategy* (Glenview, Ill.: Scott, Foresman, 1987).

Table 17-1
February 26, 1987, Listed Option Quotations (CBOE)

NYSE Close	Strike Price	Calls — Last Quote			Puts — Last Quote		
		March	April	July	March	April	July
IBM							
139¾	135	6⅜	8¼	11¾	1⅜	2½	5
139¾	140	3¼	5¼	8½	3⅜	4½	7⅛
139¾	145	1⁹⁄₁₆	3⅛	6¼	6⅝	7½	9½
Chrysler							
46¾	50	½	1³⁄₁₆	2⅝	4	4⅜	5⅝
Sears							
51	50	2⅛	3⅛	4½	⅞	1½	2⅝

ily own) at a price of $140 per share ($140 is the striking price). If you bought a 100-share contract for $450 and then IBM's stock actually fell to $130, your put option would be worth ($140 − $130)(100) = $1,000. After subtracting the $450 you paid for the option, your net profit (before taxes and commissions) would be $550.

Table 17–1 contains an extract from the February 27, 1987 *Wall Street Journal* Listed Option Quotations Table. This extract, which focuses on IBM, Chrysler, and Sears options, reflects the trading which occurred on the previous day. On February 26, 1987, Sears' April (2-month), $50 call option sold on the CBOE for $3.125. Thus, for ($3.125)(100) = $312.50 you could buy an option that would give you the right to purchase 100 shares of Sears at a price of $50 per share at any time during the next 2 months.[2] If the stock price stayed below $50 during that period, you would lose your $312.50, but if it rose to $75, then your $312.50 investment would have grown to ($75 − $50)(100) = $2,500. That translates into a very healthy annual rate of return. Incidentally, if the stock price did go up, you would probably not actually exercise your option and buy the stock—you would sell the options, which would then have a value of at least $2,500 versus the $312.50 you paid, to another option buyer.

Options trading is one of the hottest financial activities in the United States today. In addition to options on individual stocks, options are now available on several stock indexes such as the NYSE Index and the S&P 100 Index. The leverage involved makes it possible for speculators with just a few dollars to make a fortune almost overnight. Also, investors with sizable portfolios can sell options against their stocks and earn the value of the option (less brokerage commissions), even

[2]Actually, the *exercise date,* which is the last date that the option can be exercised, is the third Friday of the exercise month. Thus, the April options actually expire on April 17, 1987, so they have a term somewhat less than two months. Also, note that option contracts are generally written in 100-share multiples.

if the stock's price remains constant. Further, options can be used to create hedges which protect the value of an individual stock or portfolio. We will discuss hedging strategies in more detail later in the chapter.[3]

Corporations such as Sears and IBM, on whose stocks options are written, have nothing to do with the options market. The corporations do not raise money in the options market, nor do they have any direct transactions in it, and option holders do not vote for corporate directors (unless they exercise their options to purchase the stock, which few actually do). There have been studies by the SEC and others as to whether options trading stabilizes or destabilizes the stock market, and whether this activity helps or hinders corporations seeking to raise new capital. The studies have not been conclusive, but options trading does seem to be here to stay, and many regard it as the most exciting game in town.

Call Option Valuation

An analysis of Table 17-1 provides some insights into call option valuation. First, we see that there are at least three factors which affect a call option's value: (1) For a given striking price, the higher the stock's market price, the higher will be the call option price. Thus, Chrysler's $50 April call option sells for $1.1875, whereas Sears' $50 April option sells for $3.125 because Sears' current stock price is $51 versus $46.75 for Chrysler. (2) For a given stock price, the higher the striking price, the lower will be the call option price. Thus, all of IBM's call options, regardless of exercise month, decline as the striking price increases. (3) The longer the option period, the higher will be the option price, because the longer the time before expiration, the greater chance that the stock price will climb substantially above the exercise price. Thus, for all of the striking prices, option prices increase as the expiration date is lengthened.

Theoretical Value Versus Option Price

How is the actual price of an option determined in the market? We shall, shortly, present a widely-used model (the Black-Scholes model) for pricing options, but first it is useful to establish some basic concepts. To begin, we define an option's *theoretical value* as follows:

---

[3]Illegal inside trading is very much in the news as we write this (Spring 1987). It should be noted that the recently caught insiders generally bought options rather than stock. For example, in May 1986, Burroughs made an offer of $75 per share for Sperry. At the time, Sperry common sold for $54.50, and its June option sold for $2.375. After the offer, the Sperry June option jumped in price to $20. Thus, someone who bought Sperry stock in April would have made a gain of $75/$54.5 − 1.0 = 37.6%. A Sperry option would have provided a return of $20/$2.375 − 1.0 = 742.1%. Thus, if someone had knowledge that Burroughs planned to make a $75 offer for Sperry, a given dollar investment in options would provide a much larger payoff than the stock. Note, though, that it is illegal to use insider information for personal gain, and the insider in our example would be taking advantage of the option seller. Insider trading, in addition to being unfair and essentially equivalent to stealing, hurts the economy: Investors lose confidence in the capital markets, raise their required returns because of an increased element of risk, raise the cost of capital, and thus reduce the level of investment.

$$\text{Theoretical value} = \frac{\text{Current price}}{\text{of the stock}} - \text{Striking price.}$$

For example, if a stock sells for $50, and its option has a striking price of $20, then the theoretical value is $30. The theoretical value can be thought of as the value of the option if it expired today. Note that the theoretical value of a call option can be negative, but realistically the minimum value of an out-of-the-money option is zero.

Now consider Figure 17-1, which presents some data on Space Technology, Incorporated, (STI) a company which recently went public and whose stock has fluctuated widely during its short history. The third column in the tabular data shows the theoretical values for STI's options when the stock was selling at different prices; the fourth column gives the actual market prices for the option; and the fifth column shows the premium of the actual option price over its theoretical value. At any stock price below $20, the theoretical value is zero; above $20, each $1 increase in the price of the stock brings with it a $1 increase in the option's theoretical value. Note, however, that the actual market price of the option lies above the theoretical value at each price of the common stock, but the premium declines as the price of the common stock increases. For example, when the common stock sold for $20 and the option had a zero theoretical value, its actual price, and the premium, was $9. Then, as the price of the stock rose, the *theoretical value* matched the increase dollar for dollar, but the *market price* of the option climbed less rapidly, and the premium declined. The premium was $9 when the stock sold for $20 a share, but it declined to $1 by the time the stock price had risen to $73 a share. Beyond this point the premium virtually disappeared.

Why does this pattern exist? Why should the option ever sell for more than its theoretical value, and why does the premium decline as the price of the stock increases? The answer lies in the speculative appeal of options — they enable someone to gain a high degree of personal leverage when buying securities. To illustrate, *suppose STI's options sold for exactly their theoretical value.* Now suppose you were thinking of investing in the company's common stock at a time when it was selling for $21 a share. If you bought a share and the price rose to $42, you would have made a 100 percent capital gain. However, had you bought the option at its theoretical value ($1 when the stock was selling for $21), your capital gain would have been $21 on a $1 investment, or 2,100 percent! At the same time, your total loss potential with the option would be only $1 versus a potential loss of $21 if you purchased the stock. The huge capital gains potential, combined with the loss limitation, is clearly worth something — the exact amount it is worth to investors is the amount of the premium.

But why does the premium decline as the price of the stock rises? Part of the answer is that both the leverage effect and the loss protection feature decline at high stock prices. For example, if you were thinking of buying STI stock when its price was $73 a share, the theoretical value of the option would be $53. If the stock price doubled to $146, the theoretical value of the option would go from $53 to $126. The percentage capital gain on the stock would still be 100 percent, but the percentage gain on the option would now be only 138 percent versus

---

Figure 17-1
Space Technology, Inc.:
Option Price and Theoretical Value

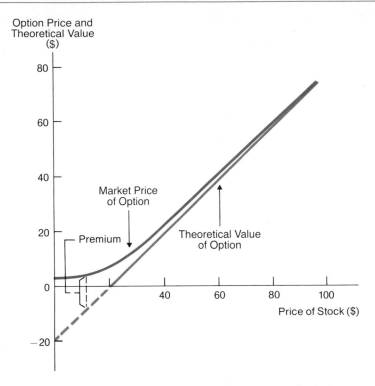

Price of Stock (1)	Striking Price (2)	Theoretical Value of Option (1) − (2) = (3)	Market Price of Option (4)	Premium (4) − (3) = (5)
$20.00	$20.00	$ 0.00	$ 9.00	$9.00
21.00	20.00	1.00	9.75	8.75
22.00	20.00	2.00	10.50	8.50
35.00	20.00	15.00	21.00	6.00
42.00	20.00	22.00	26.00	4.00
50.00	20.00	30.00	32.00	2.00
73.00	20.00	53.00	54.00	1.00
98.00	20.00	78.00	78.50	0.50

2,100 percent in the earlier case. Notice also that the potential loss on the option is much greater when the option is selling at high prices. These two factors, the declining leverage impact and the increasing danger of losses, help explain why the premium diminishes as the price of the common stock rises.

In addition to the stock price and the exercise price, the price of an option depends on three other factors: (1) the option's time to maturity, (2) the variability of the stock price, and (3) the risk-free rate. We will explain precisely how these factors affect option prices shortly, but for now, note these points:

1. The longer an option has to run, the greater is its value and the larger is its premium. If an option expires at 4 p.m. today, there is not much chance that the stock price will go way up, so the option must sell at close to its floor value, and its premium must be small. On the other hand, if the expiration date is a year away, the stock price could rise sharply, pulling the option's value up with it.

2. An option on an extremely volatile stock will be worth more than one on a very stable stock. If the stock price rarely moves, then there is a small chance of a large gain. However, if the stock price is highly volatile, the option could become very valuable. At the same time, losses on options are limited, so large declines in a stock's price do not have a corresponding bad effect on option holders. Therefore, the more volatile a stock, the higher is the value of its options.

Because of points (1) and (2), in a graph such as Figure 17-1, if everything else were constant, then the longer an option's life, the higher its market price line would be above the floor value line. Similarly, the more volatile the price of the underlying stock, the higher is the market price line. We will see precisely how these factors affect option values when we discuss the option pricing model.

INTRODUCTION TO OPTION PRICING

In the next section, we will discuss the option pricing model, but first we shall gain some insights into option pricing by examining a simple example. Assume that 1-year call options are available on Butler Company, a midwestern firm which owns 32 McDonald's franchises. Each option has an exercise price of $35, and Butler's stock is now selling for $40 a share. Now assume that at the expiration of the option 1 year hence, Butler's shares will be selling at one of only two possible prices, $30 or $50. Under these simple conditions, what is the value of the call option on Butler's stock?

To answer this question, we proceed as follows:

1. Examine the payoffs at maturity. At expiration, the stock price will be either $30 or $50, and the value of the option at expiration will depend on Butler's stock price. Thus, we have the following situation at expiration:

	Stock Price	Option Value	
Low	$30	$ 0	(option is worthless)
High	50	15	(theoretical value)
Range	$20	$15	

2. Create the same range of payoffs. Note that the range of payoffs as shown above is $20 for a stock investment (either a $30 or $50 payoff) and $15 for an option investment (either a $0 or $15 payoff). The ranges would be identical on the two investments if you could buy 0.75 shares of Butler's stock. In this situation, the payoff matrix would look like this:

	Stock Price	Value of 0.75 Shares	Option Value
Low	$30	$22.50	$ 0
High	50	37.50	15
Range	$20	$15.00	$15

3. Create a riskless hedge. You can now create a riskless portfolio by buying 0.75 shares of Butler's stock and selling 1 call option, which would result in this payoff matrix:

	Stock Price	Value of 0.75 Shares	+	Value of Call Option to You	=	Value of Portfolio
Low	$30	$22.50	+	$ 0	=	$22.50
High	50	37.50	+	(15)	=	22.50

If the stock price at expiration is $30, the stock investment returns $22.50, but the call is worthless and hence the buyer would not exercise his or her option. On the other hand, if the stock price is $50 at expiration, the value of the stock investment would be $37.50, but the holder of the call would exercise his or her option. Thus, you must provide one share at the exercise price, $35, which you must purchase at the market price of $50, and hence incur a $15 loss. In either case, your portfolio's return is $22.50 — you have created a riskless portfolio by buying the stock and writing (selling) a call option on that stock.

4. Valuing the call option. Your riskless portfolio will provide a certain $22.50 at option expiration in 1 year. If the risk-free rate is 8 percent, the value of the portfolio today is $22.50/1.08 = $20.83. Since Butler's stock is currently selling at $40 a share, creating the riskless portfolio would require a stock investment of 0.75($40) = $30. Since your total investment outlay to create the riskless portfolio must be equal to or less than $20.83, the present value of the portfolio, you must be able to sell the call option for at least $30 − $20.83 = $9.17. Assuming that competition exists in the options market, $9.17 will be the equilibrium price of the option.

Clearly, this example is unrealistic — Butler's stock price could be almost anything after 1 year, and you cannot purchase 0.75 shares of stock. But the example does illustrate that investors can in principle create riskless portfolios by buying stocks and selling call options, and the return on such portfolios should be the risk-free rate. If call options are not priced to reflect this condition, arbitrageurs will actively trade stocks and options until option prices do reflect such equilibrium conditions. In the next section, we discuss the Black-Scholes Option

Pricing Model, which is based on the general premise we developed here — the creation of a riskless portfolio — but which is much more applicable to real-world option pricing because it allows for a wide range of ending stock prices.

THE BLACK-SCHOLES OPTION PRICING MODEL (OPM)

The *Black-Scholes Option Pricing Model (OPM)* was developed in 1973, just as the rapid growth in options trading began.[4] This model, which has actually been programmed into the permanent memories of some hand-held calculators, is widely used by option traders. Our interest, however, lies in the insights that option theory provides in valuing all securities subject to contingent claims, including warrants, convertibles, and even the equity of a corporation.

In deriving their option pricing model, which calculates the value of a call option, Black and Scholes make the following assumptions:

1. The stock underlying the call option pays no dividends during the life of the option.

2. There are no transactions costs in buying or selling either the stock or the option.

3. The short-term, risk-free interest rate is a known constant during the life of the option.

4. Any purchaser of a security may borrow any fraction of the purchase price at the short-term, risk-free interest rate.

5. Short selling is permitted without penalty, and the short seller will receive immediately the full cash proceeds for a security sold short.[5]

6. Trading in all securities takes place in continuous time, and the stock price moves randomly in continuous time.[6]

---

[4]See Fischer Black and Myron Scholes, "The Pricing of Options and Corporate Liabilities," *Journal of Political Economy,* May/June 1973, 637–659.

[5]Suppose an investor (or speculator) does not now own any IBM stock. If the investor anticipates a rise in the stock price and consequently buys IBM stock, he or she is said to have *gone long* in IBM. On the other hand, if the investor thinks IBM's stock is likely to fall, he or she could *go short,* or *sell IBM short.* Since the short seller had no IBM stock, he or she would have to borrow the shares sold short from a broker. If the stock price falls, the short seller could, later on, buy shares on the open market and use them to pay back the broker. The short seller's profit, before commissions and taxes, would be the difference in the price received from the short sale and the price paid later to purchase the replacement stock.

[6]It is also assumed that the option can only be exercised on its expiration date, which is characteristic of a *European* option. *American* options can be exercised at any time up to and including the expiration date. However, it has been shown that for nondividend paying stocks, the market price of an American call option is always greater than the value it would have if it were exercised immediately. Hence, a rational investor would never exercise an American call option on a nondividend paying stock before it expired — the investor would sell the option on the open market. Therefore, the value of an American call option is the same as that of a European option. See Robert C. Merton, "The Theory of Rational Option Pricing," *Bell Journal of Economics and Management Science,* Spring 1973, 141–183.

The derivation of the Black-Scholes Option Pricing Model rests on the concept of the *riskless hedge.* By buying shares of a stock and simultaneously selling call options on that stock, an investor can create a risk-free investment position — gains on the stock will exactly offset losses on the option, and vice versa. This riskless hedged position must earn a rate of return equal to the risk-free rate; otherwise, an arbitrage opportunity would exist, and people trying to take advantage of this opportunity would drive the price of the option to the equilibrium level specified by the Black-Scholes model.

The Black-Scholes model consists of the following three equations:

$$V = P[N(d_1)] - Xe^{-k_{RF}t}[N(d_2)]. \tag{17-1}$$

$$d_1 = \frac{\ln(P/X) + [k_{RF} + (\sigma^2/2)]t}{\sigma\sqrt{t}} \tag{17-2}$$

$$d_2 = d_1 - \sigma\sqrt{t}. \tag{17-3}$$

Here

$$V = \text{current value of a call option with time t until expiration.}$$

$$P = \text{current price of the underlying stock.}$$

$N(d_1)$ and $N(d_2) =$ probability that a deviation less than d_1 or d_2 will occur in a standard normal distribution. Thus, $N(d_1)$ and $N(d_2)$ represent two different areas under a standard normal distribution function.

$$X = \text{exercise, or striking, price of the option.}$$

$$e = \text{exponential function} \approx 2.7183.$$

$$k_{RF} = \text{risk-free interest rate.}$$

$$t = \text{time until the option expires (the option period).}$$

$$\ln(P/X) = \text{natural logarithm of the ratio P/X.}$$

$$\sigma^2 = \text{variance of the rate of return on the stock.}$$

Note that the value of the option is a function of the variables we discussed earlier: (1) P, the stock's price; (2) t, the option's time to expiration; (3) X, the striking price; (4) σ^2, the price variance of the underlying stock; and (5) k_{RF}, the risk-free rate. We do not derive the Black-Scholes model — the derivation involves some extremely complicated mathematical statistics that go far beyond the scope of this text. However, it is not difficult to use the model, and, under the assumptions set forth above, any option price different from the one found by Equation 17-1 would provide the opportunity for arbitrage profits, which would, in turn, force the option price back to the value indicated by the model. As we noted earlier, the Black-Scholes model is widely used by traders, so actual option prices do conform reasonably well to values derived from the model.

In essence, the first term of Equation 17-1, $P[N(d_1)]$, can be thought as the present value of the expected terminal stock price, while the second term, $Xe^{-k_{RF}t}[N(d_2)]$, can be thought of as present value of the exercise price. However, rather than try to figure out exactly what the equations mean, it is more productive to work out some values and to see how changes in the inputs change the value of the option.

OPM Illustration

The current stock price, P, the exercise price, X, and the time to maturity, t, of the option can be obtained from a newspaper such as the *Wall Street Journal*. The risk-free rate, k_{RF}, used in the OPM is the yield on Treasury bills with a maturity date equal to the option expiration date. The stock price variance, σ^2, can be estimated by calculating the variance of the percentage change in daily stock prices for the past year, that is, the variance of $(P_t - P_{t-1})/P_t$ on a daily basis.

Assume that the following information has been obtained:

$$P = \$20.$$
$$X = \$20.$$
$$t = 3 \text{ months or } 0.25 \text{ years.}$$
$$k_{RF} = 12\% = 0.12.$$
$$\sigma^2 = 0.16.$$

Given this information, we can now use the OPM by solving Equations 17-1 through 17-3. Since d_1 and d_2 are required inputs for Equation 17-1, we solve Equations 17-2 and 17-3 first:

$$d_1 = \frac{\ln(\$20/\$20) + [0.12 + (0.16/2)](0.25)}{0.40(0.50)}$$

$$= \frac{0 + 0.05}{0.20} = 0.25.$$

$$d_2 = d_1 - 0.20 = 0.05.$$

Note that $N(d_1) = N(0.25)$ and $N(d_2) = N(0.05)$ represent areas under a standard normal distribution function. From Table A-5 at the end of the book, we see that the value $d_1 = 0.25$ implies a probability of $0.0987 + 0.5000 = 0.5987$, so $N(d_1) = 0.5987$. Similarly, $N(d_2) = 0.5199$. We can use those values to solve Equation 17-1:

$$V = \$20[N(d_1)] - \$20e^{-(0.12)(0.25)}[N(d_2)]$$
$$= \$20[N(0.25)] - \$20(0.9704)[N(0.05)]$$
$$= \$20(0.5987) - \$19.41(0.5199)$$
$$= \$11.97 - \$10.09 = \$1.88.$$

Thus, the value of the option, under the assumed conditions, is $1.88. Suppose the actual option price were $2.25. Arbitrageurs could simultaneously sell the option and buy the underlying stock, and earn a riskless profit. Such trading would occur until the price of the option was driven to $1.88. The reverse would occur if the

Table 17-2
Effects of OPM Factors on the Value of a Call Option

Case	P	X	t	k_{RF}	σ^2	V
Base case	$20	$20	0.25	12%	0.16	$1.88
Increase P by $5	**25**	20	0.25	12	0.16	5.81
Increase X by $5	20	**25**	0.25	12	0.16	0.39
Increase t to 6 months	20	20	**0.50**	12	0.16	2.81
Increase k_{RF} to 16%	20	20	0.25	**16**	0.16	1.99
Increase σ^2 to 0.25	20	20	0.25	12	**0.25**	2.27

option sold for less than $1.88. Thus, investors would be unwilling to pay more than $1.88 for the option, and they could not buy it for less.

To see how each of the five OPM factors affects the value of the option, V, consider Table 17-2. Here the top row shows the base case input values and the resulting option value, V = $1.88. These base case input values are those we used above to illustrate how to solve the OPM. In each of the subsequent rows, one factor is increased, while the values of the other four are held constant at their base case levels. The value of the call option is given in the last column. Now consider the effects of a change in each factor:

1. Current stock price. If the current stock price, P, increases from $20 to $25, the option value increases from $1.88 to $5.81. Thus, the value of the call increases as the stock price increases, but not by as much as the stock price increases ($3.93 versus $5.00). Note, though, that the percentage increase in the option value, ($5.81 − $1.88)/$1.88 = 209%, far exceeds the percentage increase in the stock price, ($25 − $20)/$20 = 25%.

2. Exercise price. If the exercise price, X, increases from $20 to $25, the value of the option declines. Again, though, the option value does not decrease in absolute amount by as much as the exercise price increases, but the percentage change in the option value, ($0.39 − $1.88)/$1.88 = −79%, exceeds the percentage change in the exercise price, ($25 − $20)/$20 = 25%.

3. Option period. As the time to expiration increases from t = 3 months (or 0.25 years) to t = 6 months (or 0.50 years), the value of the option also increases, from $1.88 to $2.81. This result should not be surprising. The value of the option depends on the chances for an increase in the price of the underlying stock. Obviously, the longer the option runs, the higher the stock price may go. Thus, other factors held constant, a 6-month option is worth more than a 3-month option.

4. Risk-free rate. The next factor is the risk-free rate, k_{RF}. As the risk-free rate increases from 12 to 16 percent, the call option value increases slightly, from $1.88 to $1.99. Equations 17-1, 17-2, and 17-3 suggest that the principal effect of an increase in k_{RF} is the reduction of the present value of the exercise price of the option, $Xe^{-k_{RF}t}$, and hence an increase in the current value of the call option.[7] The risk-free rate also plays a role in determining the values of the normal distribution functions $N(d_1)$ and $N(d_2)$, but this effect is of secondary importance. Indeed, option prices in general are not very sensitive to interest rate changes, at least not to changes within the ranges normally encountered.

5. Variance. As the variance increases from the base case level of 0.16 to 0.25, the value of the call option increases from $1.88 to $2.27. That is, if all other factors are held constant, the riskier the underlying security, the more valuable will be the call option. This result is logical. First, if you bought an option to buy a stock that sells at its exercise price, and if $\sigma^2 = 0$, then there would be a zero probability of the stock price going up, and hence a zero probability of making any money on the option. On the other hand, if you bought an option on a high-variance stock, there would be a fairly high probability of the stock price going way up, and hence of making a high profit on the option. Of course, the price of a high-variance stock could go way down, but as an option holder, your losses would be limited to the price paid to buy the option—only the right-hand side of the stock's probability distribution counts. All of this makes options on risky stocks more valuable than those on safer, low-variance stocks. Put another way, an increase in the price of the stock helps options holders more than a decrease hurts them; thus, the greater the variance, the greater is the value of the option.

This concludes our brief discussion of options and option pricing theory. The next two sections describe warrants and convertibles, the major types of option securities issued by firms.[8]

WARRANTS

A *warrant* is an option issued by a company which gives the warrant's owner the right to buy a stated number of shares of the company's stock at a specified price. Generally, warrants are distributed with debt, and they are used to induce investors to buy a firm's long-term debt at a lower interest rate than would otherwise be required. For example, when Infomatics Corporation, a rapidly growing high-tech company, wanted to sell $50 million of 20-year bonds in 1987, the company's investment banker informed the financial vice president that the bonds would be difficult to sell, and that an interest rate of 10 percent would be required. However, as an alternative, the banker suggested that investors might be willing to buy

---

[7] At this point, you may be wondering why the first term in Equation 17-1, $P[N(d_1)]$, is not discounted. In fact, it has been, because the current stock price, P, already represents the present value of the expected expiration date stock price; that is, P is a discounted value, and the discount rate used in the market to determine today's stock price includes the risk-free rate. Thus, Equation 17-1 can be thought of as the present value of the end-of-option-period spread between the stock price and the striking price, adjusted for the probability that the stock price will be higher than the striking price.

[8] Option pricing theory can also be used to gain insights into financial management decisions. See Eugene F. Brigham and Louis C. Gapenski, *Intermediate Financial Management,* 2nd ed., Appendix 15A.

the bonds with a coupon rate of only 8 percent if the company would offer 20 warrants with each $1,000 bond, each warrant entitling the holder to buy one share of common stock at a price of $22 per share. The stock was selling for $20 per share at the time, and the warrants would expire in 1997 if they had not been exercised previously.

Why would investors be willing to buy Infomatics' bonds at a yield of only 8 percent in a 10 percent market just because warrants were also offered as part of the package? Because the warrants are long-term options which have value as discussed in the previous section, and this value offsets the low interest rate on the bonds and makes the package of low-yield bonds plus warrants attractive to investors.

Initial Market Price of Bond with Warrants

The Infomatics bonds, if they had been issued as straight debt, would have carried a 10 percent interest rate. However, with warrants attached, the bonds were sold to yield 8 percent. Someone buying the bonds at their $1,000 initial offering price would thus be receiving a package consisting of an 8 percent, 20-year bond plus 20 warrants. Since the going interest rate on bonds as risky as those of Infomatics was 10 percent, we can find the straight-debt value of the bonds, assuming an annual coupon, as follows:

$$\text{Value} = \sum_{t=1}^{20} \frac{\$80}{(1.10)^t} + \frac{\$1,000}{(1.10)^{20}}$$

$$= \$681.09 + \$148.64 = \$829.73.$$

Thus, a person buying the bonds in the initial underwriting would pay $1,000 and receive in exchange a straight bond worth about $830 plus 20 warrants presumably worth about $1,000 − $830 = $170:

Price paid for bond with warrants	=	Straight-debt value of bond	+	Value of warrants
$1,000	=	$830	+	$170.

Since investors receive 20 warrants with each bond, each warrant has an implied value of $170/20 = $8.50.

The key issue in setting the terms of a bond-with-warrants offering is valuing the warrants. The straight-debt value of the bond can be estimated quite accurately. However, it is much more difficult to estimate the value of the warrants. Even the Black-Scholes OPM provides only a rough estimate because (1) its parameters are not easily estimated and (2) it assumes no dividends on the underlying stock, which is not generally a reasonable assumption for a long-term option. If, in setting the terms, the warrants are overvalued relative to their true market value, then it will be difficult to sell the issue at its par value. Conversely, if the warrants are undervalued, then investors who subscribe to the issue will receive a windfall profit since they can sell the warrants in the market for more than they implicitly paid for them. This windfall profit would come out of the pockets of Infomatics' current stockholders.

Use of Warrants in Financing

In the past, warrants were generally used by small, rapidly growing firms as "sweeteners" when they were selling either debt or preferred stock. Such firms are typically regarded by investors as being highly risky, and their bonds could be sold only if they were willing to pay extremely high rates of interest and also to accept very restrictive indenture provisions. To avoid this, firms such as Infomatics often offered warrants along with the bonds. However, several years ago, AT&T raised $1.57 billion by selling bonds with warrants. This was the largest financing of any type ever undertaken by a business firm, and it marked the first use ever of warrants by a large, strong corporation.[9]

Getting warrants along with bonds enables investors to share in the company's growth, if it does in fact grow and prosper; therefore, investors are willing to accept a lower bond interest rate and less restrictive indenture provisions. A bond with warrants has some characteristics of debt and some characteristics of equity. It is a hybrid security that provides the firm with an opportunity to expand its mix of securities and to appeal to a broader group of investors.

Virtually all warrants today are *detachable*. Thus, after a bond with attached warrants is sold, the warrants can be detached and traded separately from the bond. Further, when these warrants are exercised, the bond issue (with its low coupon rate) remains outstanding, so the warrants bring in additional funds to the firm while leaving its interest costs relatively low.

The exercise price is generally set at from 10 to 30 percent above the market price of the stock on the date the bond is issued. If the firm does grow and prosper, and if its stock price rises above the exercise price at which shares may be purchased, warrant holders could exercise their warrants and buy stock at the stated price. However, without some incentive, warrants would never be exercised prior to maturity — their value in the market would be greater than their floor, or exercise, value, and hence holders would sell rather than exercise. There are three conditions which encourage holders to exercise their warrants: (1) Warrant holders will surely exercise warrants and buy stock if the warrants are about to expire

---

[9]It is interesting to note that before the AT&T issue, the New York Stock Exchange's stated policy was that warrants could not be listed because they were "speculative" instruments rather than "investment" securities. When AT&T issued warrants, however, the Exchange changed its policy, agreeing to list warrants that met certain requirements. Many other warrants have since been listed.

It is also interesting to note that, prior to the sale, AT&T's treasury staff, working with Morgan Stanley analysts, estimated the value of the warrants as a part of the underwriting decision. The package was supposed to sell for a total price in the neighborhood of $1,000. The bond value could be determined accurately, so the trick was to estimate the equilibrium value of the warrant under different possible exercise prices and years to expiration, and then use that exercise price and life that caused Bond value + Warrant value ≈ $1,000. Using the option pricing model, the AT&T/Morgan Stanley analysts set terms which caused the warrant to sell on the open market at within $0.35 of the estimated price.

with the market price of the stock above the exercise price. (2) Warrant holders will tend to exercise voluntarily and buy stock if the company raises the dividend on the common stock by a sufficient amount. No dividend is earned on the warrant, so it provides no current income. However, if the common stock pays a high dividend, it provides an attractive dividend yield. This induces warrant holders to exercise their option to buy the stock. (3) Warrants sometimes have *stepped-up exercise prices,* which prod owners into exercising them. For example, the Williamson Scientific Company has warrants outstanding with an exercise price of $25 until December 31, 1990, at which time, the exercise price rises to $30. If the price of the common stock is over $25 just before December 31, 1990, many warrant holders will exercise their options before the stepped-up price takes effect.

Another desirable feature of warrants is that they generally bring in funds only if funds are needed. If the company grows, it will probably need new equity capital. At the same time, growth will cause the price of the stock to rise, the warrants to be exercised, and the firm to obtain additional cash. If the company is not successful and cannot profitably employ additional money, the price of its stock will probably not rise sufficiently to induce exercise of the warrants.

The Cost of Capital for Bonds with Warrants

When Infomatics issued its debt with warrants, the firm received $50 million, or $1,000 for each bond. Simultaneously, the company assumed an obligation to pay $80 interest for 20 years plus $1,000 at the end of 20 years. The cost of the money would have been 10 percent if no warrants had been attached, but each Infomatics bond had 20 warrants, each of which entitles its holder to buy one share of Infomatics stock for $22. A cost rate must be assigned to the warrants to determine the total cost of the issue. As we shall see, the total cost is well above 8 percent.

Assume that Infomatics' stock price, which is now $20, is expected to grow, and does grow, at 10 percent per year. When the warrants expire 10 years from now, the stock price will be $20(1.10)^{10} = 51.87. Assuming the warrants had not been exercised during the 10-year period, the company would then have to issue one share of stock worth $51.87 for each warrant exercised, and in return, Infomatics would receive the exercise price, $22. Thus, a purchaser of the bonds, if he or she holds the complete package, will make a profit in Year 10 of $51.87 − $22 = 29.87 for each common share issued. Since each bond has 20 warrants attached, investors would have a gain of $20($29.87) = 597.40 per bond at the end of Year 10. Here is a time line of the cash flow stream to an investor:

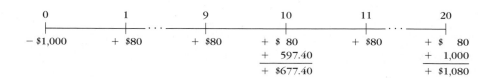

The IRR of this stream is 10.7 percent, which is the investor's overall rate of return on the issue. This return is 70 basis points higher than the return on straight debt, which reflects the fact that the issue is riskier to investors than a straight debt issue because some of the return is expected to come in the form of stock price appreciation, and that part of the return is riskier than interest and maturity payments.

The expected rate of return to investors is, of course, also the cost of the issue to the company — this was true of common stocks, straight bonds, and preferred stocks, and it is also true of bonds sold with warrants. In thinking about this, note that the investor's Year 10 gain of $597.40 does not just appear out of thin air — the company is giving the warrant holders the right to buy for $22 a share of stock with a market value of $51.87. That obviously dilutes the value of the stock, so Infomatics' original shareholders are incurring an opportunity cost which is exactly equal to the warrant holders' gain.

The cost of warrants can also be illustrated in terms of the effect on earnings per share (EPS). Suppose Infomatics had 1,000,000 common shares outstanding just prior to the expiration of the warrants. Further, assume that the company earns 13.5 percent on its market value equity, so earnings per share are $0.135($51.87) = 7, and total earnings are $1,000,000($7) = $7,000,000$. Now, if there were 100,000 warrants outstanding at expiration, exercise of these warrants would bring in $100,000($22) = $2,200,000$ of new equity funds, and the number of shares would increase by 100,000. Assuming that the earning power of the $2.2 million of new assets was also 13.5 percent, then $0.135($2,200,000) = $297,000$ of new earnings would be produced, making the new total earnings $7,000,000 + $297,000 = $7,297,000$. When that new total earnings figure is divided by the new total shares outstanding $(1,000,000 + 100,000 = 1,100,000)$, we get a new EPS of $6.63:

$$\text{New EPS} = \$7,297,000/1,100,000 = \$6.63.$$

Thus, exercise of the warrants results in a dilution of EPS from $7 to $6.63, or by $0.37. This $0.37 EPS dilution is a real cost, it is borne by Infomatics' original shareholders, and it must be worked in when calculating the cost of the bonds-with-warrants.

CONVERTIBLES

Convertible securities are bonds or preferred stocks which, under specified terms and conditions, can be exchanged for common stock at the option of the holder. Unlike the exercise of warrants, which brings in additional funds to the firm, conversion does not bring in additional capital: Debt (or preferred stock) is simply replaced on the balance sheet by common stock. Of course, the reduction of the debt or preferred stock will improve the financial strength of the company and make it easier to raise additional fixed charge capital, but that requires a separate action.

Conversion Ratio and Conversion Price

One of the most important provisions of a convertible security is the *conversion ratio, R,* defined as the number of shares of stock a bondholder will receive upon conversion. Related to the conversion ratio is the *conversion price, P_c,* which is the effective price the company will receive for the common stock when conversion occurs. The relationship between the conversion ratio and the conversion price can be illustrated by the Silicon Valley Software Company's convertible debentures, issued at their $1,000 par value in July of 1987. At any time prior to maturity on July 1, 2007, a debenture holder can exchange a bond for 20 shares of common stock; therefore, the conversion ratio, R, is 20. The bond has a par value of $1,000, so the holder would be relinquishing the right to receive $1,000 at maturity upon conversion. Dividing the $1,000 par value by the 20 shares received gives a conversion price of P_c = $50 a share:

$$\text{Conversion price} = P_c = \frac{\text{Par value of bond given up}}{\text{Shares received}}$$

$$= \frac{\$1,000}{R} = \frac{\$1,000}{20} = \$50.$$

Solving for R, we obtain the conversion ratio:

$$\text{Conversion ratio} = R = \frac{\$1,000}{P_c} = \frac{\$1,000}{\$50} = 20 \text{ shares.}$$

Once R is set, the value of P_c is established, and vice versa.

Like a warrant's exercise price, the conversion price is characteristically set at from 10 to 30 percent above the prevailing market price of the common stock at the time the convertible issue is sold. Exactly how the conversion price is established can best be understood after examining some of the reasons firms use convertibles.

Generally, the conversion price and conversion ratio are fixed for the life of the bond, although sometimes a stepped-up conversion price is used. For example, Breedon Industries' 1987 convertible debentures are convertible into 12.5 shares until 1997; into 11.76 shares from 1997 until 2002; and into 11.11 shares from 2002 until maturity in 2007. The conversion price thus starts at $80, rises to $85, and then goes to $90. Breedon's convertibles, like most, become callable after a 10-year call-protection period.

Another factor that may cause a change in the conversion price and ratio is a standard feature of almost all convertibles — the clause protecting the convertible against dilution from stock splits, stock dividends, and the sale of common stock at prices below the conversion price. The typical provision states that if common stock is sold at a price below the conversion price, then the conversion price must be lowered (and the conversion ratio raised) to the price at which the new stock was issued. Also, if the stock is split, or if a stock dividend is declared, the conversion price must be lowered by the percentage amount of the stock dividend or split. For example, if Breedon Industries had a two-for-one stock split during the first 10 years of its convertible's life, the conversion ratio would automatically be adjusted from 12.5 to 25, and the conversion price lowered from $80 to $40. If this protection were not contained in the contract, a company could completely thwart conversion by the use of stock splits and stock dividends. Warrants are similarly protected against dilution.

The standard protection against dilution from selling new stock at prices below the conversion price can, however, get a company into trouble. For example, assume that Breedon's stock was selling for $65 per share in 1987 at the time of the convertible issue. Further, suppose the market went sour, and Breedon's stock price dropped to $50 per share. A new common stock sale now would require lowering the conversion price on the convertible debentures from $80 to $50. That would raise the value of the convertibles and, in effect, transfer wealth from the shareholders to the convertible holders. Potential problems such as this must be kept in mind by firms considering the use of convertibles or bonds with warrants.

Convertible Bond Model

In the spring of 1987, Silicon Valley Software was evaluating the use of the convertible bond issue described earlier. The issue would consist of 20-year convertible bonds which would sell at a price of $1,000 per bond; this $1,000 would also be the bond's par (and maturity) value. The bonds would pay a 10 percent annual coupon interest rate, or $100 per year. Each bond would be convertible into 20 shares of stock, so the conversion price would be $1,000/20 = $50. The stock was expected to pay a dividend of $2.80 during the coming year, and it sold at $35 per share. Further, the stock price was expected to grow at a constant rate of 8 percent per year. Therefore, $k_s = \hat{k}_s = D_1/P_0 + g = \$2.80/\$35 + 8\% = 8\% + 8\% = 16\%$. If the bonds were not made convertible, they would have to offer a yield of 13 percent, given their riskiness and the yields on other bonds. The convertible bonds would not be callable for 10 years, after which they could be called at a price of $1,050, with this price declining by $5 per year thereafter. If, after 10 years, the conversion value exceeded the call price by at least 20 percent, management would probably call the bonds.

Figure 17-2 shows the expectations of both an average investor and the company:[10]

1. The horizontal line at M = $1,000 represents the par (and maturity) value. Also, $1,000 is the price at which the bond is initially offered to the public.

2. The bond is protected against call for 10 years. It is initially callable at a price of $1,050, and the call price declines thereafter by $5 per year. Thus, the call price is represented by the solid section of the line V_0M''.

---

[10]For a more complete discussion of how this model can be used to structure the terms of a convertible offering, see Eugene F. Brigham, "An Analysis of Convertible Debentures: Theory and Some Empirical Evidence," *Journal of Finance*, March 1966, 35–54; and M. Wayne Marr and G. Rodney Thompson, "The Pricing of New Convertible Bond Issues," *Financial Management*, Summer 1984, 31–37.

3. Since the convertible has a 10 percent coupon rate, and since the yield on a nonconvertible bond of similar risk was stated to be 13 percent, the "straight bond" value of the convertible, B_t, must be less than par. At the time of issue, assuming an annual coupon, B_0 is $789:

$$B_0 = \sum_{t=1}^{20} \frac{\$100}{(1.13)^t} + \frac{\$1,000}{(1.13)^{20}} = \$789.$$

Note, however, that the bond's straight debt value must be $1,000 just prior to maturity, so the bond's expected straight debt value rises over time. B_t follows the line B_0M'' in the graph.

4. The bond's initial conversion value, or the value of the stock the investor would receive if the bonds were converted at $t = 0$, is $700: The bond's conversion value is $P_t(R)$, so at $t = 0$, conversion value $= P_0(R) = \$35(20 \text{ shares}) = \$700$. Since the stock's price is expected to grow at an 8 percent rate, the conversion value of the bond should rise over time. For example, in Year 5 it should be $P_5(R) = \$35(1.08)^5(20) = \$1,029$. The expected conversion value over time is given by the line C_t in Figure 17-2.

5. The actual market price of the bond can never fall below the higher of its straight debt value or its conversion value. If the market price were below the straight bond value, those who wanted bonds would recognize the bargain and buy the convertible as a bond. If the market price were below the conversion value, people would buy the convertibles, turn them in for stock, and sell the stock at a profit. Therefore, the higher of the bond value and conversion value curves in the graph represents a *floor price* for the bond. In Figure 17-2, the floor price is represented by the thicker shaded line B_0XC_t.

6. In fact, the bond's market value will typically exceed its floor value. It will exceed the straight bond value because the option to convert is worth something — a 10 percent bond with conversion possibilities is worth more than a 10 percent bond without this option. The actual price will also exceed the conversion value because holding the convertible is safer than holding the common stock — the stock can fall to zero, but the convertible bond cannot fall below its straight bond value.[11] We cannot say exactly where the market value line will lie, but it will typically be above the floor set by the straight bond and conversion value lines.

7. At some point, the market value line will hit the conversion value line. This convergence will occur for two reasons. First, the stock should pay higher and higher dividends as the years go by, but the interest payments on the convertible are fixed. For example, Silicon's convertibles would pay $100 in interest annually, while the dividends on the 20 shares received upon conversion would initially be

---

[11]Note, though, that the bond value line B_0M'' would fall later on if interest rates rose in the economy, or if the company's credit risk deteriorated and consequently its k_d rose.

20($2.80) = $56. However, at an 8 percent growth rate, the dividends after 10 years would be up to $120.90, while the interest would still be $100. Thus, at some point, rising dividends could be expected to push against the fixed interest payments, causing investors to convert voluntarily. Second, once the bond becomes callable, its market value cannot get very far above the higher of the conversion value and the call price without exposing investors to the danger of a call. For example, suppose that 10 years after issue (when the bonds were callable), the market value of the bonds was $1,600, the conversion value was $1,500, and the call price was $1,050. If the company called the bonds the day after you bought 10 bonds for $16,000, you would be forced to convert into stock worth only $15,000, so you would suffer a loss of $100 per bond, or $1,000, in one day. Recognizing this danger, you and other investors would simply not pay much of a premium over the higher of the call price or the conversion value once the bond becomes callable. Therefore, in Figure 17-2, we assume that the market value line hits the conversion value line in Year 10, when the bond becomes callable.

Figure 17-2
Model of a Convertible Bond

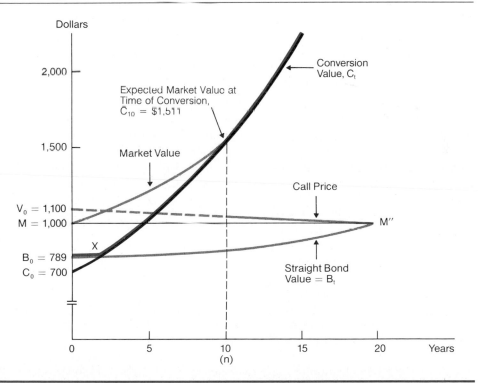

8. We can let n represent the year when investors expect conversion to occur, either voluntarily because of rising dividends or because the company calls the convertibles to strengthen its balance sheet by substituting equity for debt. In our example, we assume that $n = 10$, the first call date. Had the company used a lower initial conversion value, or a lower expected growth rate for the stock, such that C_{10} was less than V_{10}, n would have been greater than 10, the first call date.

9. An investor can find the expected rate of return on the convertible bond, k_c, by solving for k_c in the following equation:

$$\text{Price paid for bond} = \$1,000 = \sum_{t=1}^{n} \frac{\$100}{(1 + k_c)^t} + \frac{\text{Expected market value at time of conversion}}{(1 + k_c)^n}.$$

Since $n = 10$, the expected market value at Year 10 is $\$35(1.08)^{10}(20) = \$1,511$. We can substitute this value into the above equation and solve for k_c, the expected return on the convertible:

$$\$1,000 = \sum_{t=1}^{10} \frac{\$100}{(1 + k_c)^t} + \frac{\$1,511}{(1 + k_c)^{10}}.$$

The solution value of k_c is 12.8 percent.

10. The return on a convertible is expected to come partly from interest income and partly from capital gains; in this case, the total return is 12.8 percent, with 10 percent representing interest income and 2.8 percent representing the expected capital gain. The interest component is relatively assured, while the capital gain component is more risky. On a new straight bond, all of the return is in the form of interest. Therefore, a convertible's expected yield is more risky than is that of a straight bond, so k_c should be larger than the cost of straight debt, k_d. Thus, it would seem that the expected rate of return on Silicon's convertibles, k_c, should lie between its cost of straight debt, $k_d = 13\%$, and its cost of common stock, $k_s = 16\%$.

Investment bankers use the type of model described here, plus a knowledge of the market, to set the terms on convertibles (the conversion ratio and the coupon interest rate) such that the security will just "clear the market" at its $1,000 offering price. In this example, the required conditions do not seem to hold — the calculated rate of return on the convertible is only 12.8 percent, which is less, rather than more, than the 13 percent cost of straight debt. Therefore, it would appear that the terms on the bond must be made more attractive to investors. Silicon Valley Software would have to increase the coupon interest rate to a level above 10 percent, raise the conversion ratio above 20 (and thereby lower the conversion price from $50 to a level closer to the current $35 market price of the stock), or use a combination of these two such that the expected rate of return on the convertible ends up between 13 and 16 percent.

Use of Convertibles in Financing

Convertibles have two important advantages from the issuer's standpoint. (1) Convertibles, like bonds with warrants, offer a company the chance to sell debt with lower interest rates and less restrictive covenants in exchange for a chance to participate in the company's success if it does well. (2) Convertibles provide a way to sell common stock at prices higher than those currently prevailing. Many companies actually want to sell common stock, and not debt, but feel that the price of their stock is temporarily depressed. Management may know, for example, that earnings are depressed because of start-up costs associated with a new project, but they expect earnings to rise sharply during the next year or so, pulling the price of the stock up with them. Such management might think that if it sold stock now, it would be giving up more shares than necessary to raise a given amount of money. However, if it set the conversion price 20 to 30 percent above the present market price of the stock, then 20 to 30 percent fewer shares would be given up when the bonds were converted than would be required if stock were sold directly at the current time. Notice, however, that management is counting on the stock's price to rise above the conversion price to make the bonds attractive in conversion. If earnings do not rise and pull the stock price up, and hence conversion does not occur, then the company will be saddled with debt in the face of low earnings, which could be disastrous.

How can the company be sure that conversion will occur if the price of the stock rises above the conversion price? Typically, convertibles contain a call provision that enables the issuing firm to force bondholders to convert. Suppose the conversion price is $50, the conversion ratio is 20, the market price of the common stock has risen to $60, and the call price on the convertible bond is $1,050. If the company calls the bond, bondholders can either convert into common stock with a market value of 20($60) = $1,200 or allow the company to redeem the bond for $1,050. Naturally, bondholders prefer $1,200 to $1,050, so conversion occurs. The call provision therefore gives the company a way to force conversion, provided the market price of the stock is greater than the conversion price. Note, however, that most convertibles have a fairly long period of call protection — 10 years is the general rule. Therefore, if the company wants to be able to force conversion fairly early, then it will have to set a short call protection period. This will, in turn, require that it set a higher coupon rate or a lower conversion price.

From the standpoint of the issuer, convertibles have three important disadvantages. (1) Although the use of a convertible security does give the issuer the opportunity to sell common stock at a price higher than the price at which it could be sold currently, if the common stock greatly increases in price, the issuing firm would probably find that it would have been better off if it had used straight debt in spite of its higher cost and then later sold common stock and refunded the debt. (2) If the company truly wants to raise equity capital, and if the price of the stock does not rise sufficiently after the bond is issued, then the company will be stuck with debt. This debt will, however, have a low interest rate. (3) Convertibles typically have a low coupon interest rate, and the advantage of this low-cost debt will be lost when conversion occurs.

REPORTING EARNINGS WHEN WARRANTS OR CONVERTIBLES ARE OUTSTANDING

If warrants or convertibles are outstanding, a firm could theoretically report earnings per share in one of three ways:

1. *Simple EPS,* where earnings available to common stockholders are divided by the average number of shares actually outstanding during the period.

2. *Primary EPS,* where earnings available are divided by the average number of shares that would have been outstanding if warrants and convertibles "likely to be converted in the near future" had actually been exercised or converted. Earnings are pro formed by "backing out" the interest on the convertibles. Accountants have a formula which basically compares the conversion or exercise price with the actual market value of the stock to determine the likelihood of conversion when deciding on the need to use this adjustment procedure.

3. *Fully diluted EPS,* which is similar to primary EPS except that *all* warrants and convertibles are assumed to be exercised or converted, regardless of the likelihood of exercise or conversion.

Simple EPS is virtually never reported by firms which have warrants or convertibles likely to be exercised or converted — the SEC requires that primary and fully diluted earnings be shown. For firms with large amounts of option securities outstanding, there can be a substantial difference between the primary and fully diluted EPS figures. The purpose of the provision is, of course, to give investors a more accurate picture of the firm's true profit position.

FUTURES

Recent years have been characterized by record capital markets volatility. To illustrate, in June 1982, AA bonds were yielding 15.3 percent, while the same bonds yielded only 8.9 percent in May 1986. Further, it is not unusual for long-term rates to move by over 100 basis points within a 2- or 3-month period; for example, AA rates fell from 10.4 percent in February 1986 to 8.9 percent in May 1986. At the same time, the level of stock prices was bouncing around like a rubber ball. All this instability in the capital markets has made corporate financing much more difficult than it was in the 1950s, 1960s, and 1970s.

Although the evidence strongly indicates that managers can forecast their own firms' internal conditions better than outside investors, no one has been able to make consistently accurate forecasts of either interest rates or the general level of stock prices. If one believes that it is impossible to forecast future capital costs, then the major concern should be to minimize the adverse effects of changes in capital costs from today's "spot" costs. This can be done through transactions in the *futures markets.*[12]

---

[12]Our discussion of futures is necessarily limited in scope. For a more detailed description of futures and their use in financial management, see Robert W. Kolb, *Understanding Futures Markets* (Glenview, Ill.: Scott, Foresman, 1985).

Futures Markets and Contracts

Most financial and real asset transactions occur in what is known as the *spot*, or *cash, market*. Here, the asset is delivered immediately (or within a few days). *Futures*, or *futures contracts*, on the other hand, call for the purchase or sale of a financial or real asset at some future date, but at a price which is fixed today.

In 1987, futures contracts were available on more than 30 real and financial assets traded on 14 U.S. exchanges, the largest of which are the Chicago Board of Trade (CBT) and the Chicago Mercantile Exchange (CME). Futures contracts are divided into two classes, *commodity futures* and *financial futures*. Commodity futures, which cover various grains and oilseeds, livestock and meats, foods and fibers, metals, and wood, were first traded in the United States in the middle 1800s. Financial futures, which were first traded in 1975, include Treasury bills, Treasury notes and bonds, certificates of deposit, Eurodollar deposits, foreign currencies, and stock indexes.

To illustrate how futures contracts work, consider the CBT's contract on Treasury bonds. The basic contract is for $100,000 of a hypothetical 8 percent coupon, semiannual payment, Treasury bond with approximately 20 years to maturity. Table 17-3 shows an extract from the Treasury bond futures prices which appeared in a recent edition of the *Wall Street Journal*.

The first column gives the delivery month; the next three give the opening, high, and low prices on that contract for that day. The opening price for the June future, 100-20, means 100 and 20/32, or 100.625 percent of par. Column 5 gives the settlement price, which is typically the price at the close of trading. Column 6 reports the change in the settlement price from the preceding day—the June contract dropped by 13/32, or 0.4063 percent. Column 7 gives the yield on the 8 percent bonds at the settlement price, while Column 8 reports the change in the settlement yield from the previous trading day. Finally, Column 9 shows the "open interest," which is the number of contracts outstanding.

To illustrate, we focus on the Treasury bonds for December delivery. The settlement price on May 6 was 98-30, or 98 and 30/32 percent of the $100,000 contract value. Thus, the futures price closed at 98.9375 percent, or at 0.989375($100,000) = $98,937.50. The contract price declined by 10/32 of 1

Table 17-3
Futures Prices on May 6

Treasury Bonds (CBT) — $100,000; pts. 32nds of 100%

(1)	Open (2)	High (3)	Low (4)	Settle (5)	Change (6)	Yield Settle (7)	Yield Change (8)	Open Interest (9)
June	100-20	101-11	100-07	100-16	−13	7.950	+.041	188,460
Sept.	99-25	100-18	99-16	99-24	−11	8.025	+.034	42,622
Dec.	99-00	99-24	98-24	98-30	−10	8.108	+.032	5,207

percent of $100,000, or by $312.50, from the previous day. The settlement yield on the contract was 8.108 percent, and the yield increased by 0.032 percentage points from the previous day. Finally, there were 5,207 contracts outstanding on the December futures, representing a total value of about $520 million. Thus, on May 6, futures contracts for December delivery (7-month futures) of this hypothetical bond sold for $98,937.50 for 100 bonds with a par value of $100,000, which translates to a yield to maturity of about 8.1 percent.[13] This yield reflects investors' beliefs in May about the interest rate level which will prevail in December. The spot yield on T-bonds on May 6 was about 7.9 percent, so the marginal participant in the futures market was predicting a 20 basis point increase in yields over the next 7 months.

Suppose now that three months later, on August 6, interest rates in the futures market had fallen from the May levels, say from 8.1 to 7.5 percent. Falling interest rates mean rising bond prices, so the December contract would now be worth about $105,138. Thus, the contract's value would have increased by $105,138 − $98,938 = $6,200 as a result of the increase in interest rates.

When futures contracts are purchased, the purchaser does not have to put up the full amount of the purchase price; rather, the purchaser is required to post an initial *margin,* which for CBT Treasury bond contracts is $3,000 per $100,000 contract. However, investors are required to maintain a certain value in the margin account, called a *maintenance margin.* If the value of the contract declines, then the owner may be required to add additional funds to the margin account. The value of the contract is checked at the end of every working day, and margin account adjustments are made at that time. If an investor purchased the T-bond contract in May and then sold it in August, he or she would have made a profit of $6,200 on a $3,000 investment, or a return of over 200 percent in only three months. It is clear, therefore, that futures contracts offer a considerable amount of leverage. Of course, if interest rates had risen, then the value of the contract would have declined, and the investor could easily have lost his or her $3,000, or more.

Commodity futures contracts are often settled by the actual delivery of the commodity — for example, a wheat farmer might sell in April a futures contract for 5,000 bushels of wheat for October delivery, and then deliver 5,000 bushels of wheat to satisfy the contract. The purchaser of the contract might be General Mills. The price would have been established in April, so the farmer would know how much he would get for his wheat, and General Mills would know its cost for flour. Financial futures, on the other hand, are virtually never settled by delivery of the securities involved. Rather, the transaction is completed by reversing the trade,

---

[13]The yield is calculated by solving for k_d in the following equation:

$$\$989.375 = \sum_{t=1}^{40} \frac{\$40}{(1 + k_d/2)^t} + \frac{\$1,000}{(1 + k_d/2)^{40}}.$$

Recall that the hypothetical bond is assumed to be on a semiannual payment basis with an 8 percent coupon and a 20-year maturity.

which amounts to selling the contract back to the original seller.[14] The actual gains and losses on the contract are realized when the futures contract is closed.

Futures Versus Options

Futures contracts and options are similar to one another — so similar that people often confuse the two. Therefore, it is useful to compare the two instruments.

A *futures contract* is a definite agreement on the part of one party to buy something on a specific date and at a specific price, and the other party agrees to sell on the same terms. No matter how low or how high the price goes, the two parties must settle the contract at the agreed-upon price. An *option,* on the other hand, merely gives someone the right to buy (a call option) or sell (a put option), but the holder of the option does not have to complete the transaction.

Note also that options exist (1) for individual stocks and (2) for "bundles" of stocks such as those in the S&P or Value Line index, whereas futures are used (1) for commodities, (2) for debt securities, and (3) for stock indexes. The two types of instruments can be used for the same purposes. One is not necessarily better or worse than another — they are simply different.

Hedging

Futures markets are used for both speculation and hedging. Speculation involves betting on future price movements, and futures are used because the leverage inherent in the contract enhances expected returns. Hedging, on the other hand, is done by a firm or individual engaged in a business where a price change could adversely affect profits. Of course, one party to a futures contract could be a speculator, the other a hedger. Thus, to the extent that they broaden the market and make hedging possible, speculators decrease the risk exposure of others in the economy. There are two basic types of hedges: (1) *long hedges,* in which futures contracts are bought in anticipation of (or to guard against) price increases, and (2) *short hedges,* where a firm or individual sells futures contracts to guard against price declines. Recall that rising interest rates lower bond prices, and thus the value of bond futures contracts. Therefore, if a firm or individual needs to guard against an *increase* in interest rates, a futures contract that makes money if rates rise should be used. That means selling, or going short, on the futures contract. To illustrate, assume that Carson Foods plans to issue $10,000,000 of 20-year bonds in September 1987 to finance a capital expenditure program. The bonds would cost 10 percent if they were issued today, May 6, and at that rate, the project

---

[14]The buyers and sellers of financial futures contracts do not actually trade with one another, even though a contract cannot be bought without a seller, and vice versa. Each trader's contractual obligation is with the futures exchange. This feature helps to guarantee the fiscal integrity of the trade. Incidentally, commodities futures traded on the exchanges are settled in the same way as financial futures, but in the case of commodities, much of the contracting is done off the exchange, between farmers and processors, and in these cases actual deliveries occur.

being financed has a positive NPV. However, Carson's financial manager fears that interest rates may rise over the next four months, and that, when the issue is actually sold, it will have a cost substantially above 10 percent, which would make the project a bad investment. Carson can protect itself against such a rise in rates by hedging in the futures market.

In this situation, Carson would be hurt by an increase in interest rates, and hence the company would use a short hedge. It would choose a futures contract on the security most similar to the company's underlying security, long-term bonds. In this case, Carson would probably choose to hedge with Treasury bond futures. Since it has $10,000,000 in underlying securities, Carson would sell $10,000,000/$100,000 = 100 Treasury bond contracts for delivery in September. In doing so, it would have to put up 100($3,000) = $300,000 in margin money as well as pay brokerage commissions. We can see from Table 17-3 that each September contract has a value of 99 and 24/32 percent, so the total value of the 100 contracts is 0.9975($100,000)(100) = $9,975,000. Now suppose the interest rate on Carson's debt rises by 100 basis points, to 11 percent, over the next 4 months. Carson's own 10 percent coupon bonds would bring only about $920 per bond, because investors now require an 11 percent return. Thus, Carson would lose $80 per bond times 10,000 bonds, or $800,000, as a result of delaying the financing. However, the increase in interest rates has also brought about a change in the value of Carson's short position in the futures market. Since interest rates have increased, the futures contract value will fall, and if the interest rate on the futures contract also increased by a full percentage point, from 8.025 to 9.025 percent, the contract value would fall to $9,059,000. Carson would then close its position in the futures market by repurchasing for $9,059,000 the contracts which it sold short for $9,975,000, giving it a profit of $916,000, less commissions.

Thus, Carson has, if we ignore commissions and the opportunity cost of the margin money, offset the loss on the bond issue. In fact, Carson more than offset the loss, pocketing an additional $116,000 in our example. If futures contracts existed on Carson's own debt, then the firm could construct a *perfect hedge,* in which gains on the futures contract would exactly offset losses due to rising interest rates. In reality, it is virtually impossible to construct perfect hedges, because in most cases the underlying asset is not identical to the futures asset. Of course, if in our example interest rates had fallen, Carson would have lost on its futures position. However, this loss would have been offset by the fact that the company could now sell its bonds at a lower yield.

Similarly, if Carson had been planning an equity offering, and if its stock tended to move fairly closely with one of the stock indexes on which futures are written, it could have hedged against falling stock prices by selling short the index future. Alternatively, if options on Carson Foods were traded in the option market, then options, rather than futures, could be used to hedge against falling stock prices. The futures and option markets permit flexibility in the timing of financial transactions, because the firm can be protected, at least partially, against changes that occur between the present and the time when a particular transaction will be completed.

There is, however, a cost for this protection, and it is the commissions plus the opportunity cost of the margin money. Whether or not the protection is worth the cost is a matter of judgment, and it depends on management's risk aversion as well as the company's strength and ability to assume the risk of changing interest rates and stock prices. Clearly, many firms believe that hedging is worthwhile. Trammell Crow, a large Texas real estate developer, recently used T-bill futures to lock in interest costs on floating rate construction loans, while Dart & Kraft recently used Eurodollar futures to protect its marketable securities portfolio. Merrill Lynch, Salomon Brothers, and the other investment banking houses hedge in the futures and options markets to protect themselves when they are engaged in major underwritings. Similarly, commercial banks engage in hedging activities to protect their bond portfolios against interest rate increases.

SUMMARY

Both bonds with *warrants* and *convertibles* are forms of options used to finance business firms. The use of such securities is encouraged by an economic environment in which either recessions or booms can occur. The senior position of the fixed charge portion of those securities protects against recessions, while the option feature offers the opportunity for participation in rising stock markets.

The conversion of convertible securities does not provide additional funds to the company, but the exercise of warrants does bring in additional capital. In the past, larger and stronger firms tended to favor convertibles over bonds with warrants, so most warrants were issued by smaller, weaker concerns. However, AT&T's use of warrants in its $1.57 billion financing caused other large firms to reexamine their positions on warrants, and warrants have come into increasing use in recent years.

Partly because of investors' interest in warrants and convertibles, a new market in pure options was developed during the 1970s. Option contracts are created by investors, not by the firms whose securities are involved in option contracts. The corporations themselves do not raise capital from the sale of these options and, in fact, they have no direct involvement with this market. The *Black-Scholes Option Pricing Model (OPM)* can be used to estimate the value of a call option, and financial managers can use it when setting the terms on warrant and convertible issues.

Financial futures markets first appeared in the mid-1970s, although commodity futures have been traded since the 1850s. Futures permit firms to create hedge positions and thus protect themselves against the damage done by rising or falling interest rates or stock prices. Futures markets are now used routinely by insurance companies and pension funds, and we expect that more and more nonfinancial firms will be using them in the future.

Questions

17-1 Define each of the following terms:

a. Option; call option; put option

b. Striking price; exercise price; variance

c. Warrant; detachable warrant

d. Theoretical value

e. Stepped-up price

f. Convertible security

g. Conversion ratio; conversion price; conversion value

h. "Sweetener"

i. Simple EPS; primary EPS; fully diluted EPS

j. Futures; hedging

17-2 Why do options typically sell at prices higher than their theoretical values?

17-3 What effect does the trend in stock prices (subsequent to issue) have on a firm's ability to raise funds through (a) convertibles and (b) warrants?

17-4 If a firm expects to have additional financial requirements in the future, would you recommend that it use convertibles or bonds with warrants? What factors would influence your decision?

17-5 How does a firm's dividend policy affect each of the following?

a. The value of its long-term warrants.

b. The likelihood that its convertible bonds will be converted.

c. The likelihood that its warrants will be exercised.

17-6 Evaluate the following statement: "Issuing convertible securities represents a means by which a firm can sell common stock at a price above the existing market."

17-7 Why do corporations often sell convertibles on a rights basis?

17-8 Suppose a company simultaneously issues $50 million of convertible bonds with a coupon rate of 10 percent and $50 million of straight bonds with a coupon rate of 14 percent. Both bonds have the same maturity. Does the fact that the convertible issue has the lower coupon rate suggest that it is less risky than the straight bond? Is its cost of capital lower on the convertible than on the straight bond? Explain.

Problems

17-1 **(Black-Scholes OPM)** Cotner Software Corporation (CSC) options are actively traded on one of the regional exchanges. CSC's current stock price is $10, with a 0.16 instantaneous variance of returns. The current 6-month risk-free rate is 12 percent.

a. What is the value of CSC's 6-month option with an exercise price of $10 according to the Black-Scholes model?

b. What would be the effect on the option price if CSC redeployed its assets and thereby reduced its variance of returns to 0.09?

(Do Parts c and d only if you are using the computerized diskette.)

c. Assume that CSC returns to its initial asset structure; that is, its stock return variance is 0.16. Now assume that CSC's current stock price is $15. What effect does the stock price increase have on the option value?

    d. Return to base case (Part a) values. Now assume that the striking price is $15. What is the new option value?

17-2 (Warrants) Goode Industries, Inc., has warrants outstanding that permit the holders to purchase one share of stock per warrant at a price of $25.

    a. Calculate the theoretical value of Goode's warrants if the common sells at each of the following prices: (1) $20, (2) $25, (3) $30, (4) $100.

    b. At what approximate price do you think the warrants would actually sell under each condition indicated above? What premium is implied in your price? Your answer is a guess, but your prices and premiums should bear reasonable relationships to one another.

    c. How would each of the following factors affect your estimates of the warrants' prices and premiums in Part b?
      (1) The life of the warrant.
      (2) Expected variability (σ_p) in the stock's price.
      (3) The expected growth rate in the stock's EPS.
      (4) The company announces a change in dividend policy: Whereas it formerly paid no dividends, henceforth it will pay out *all* earnings as dividends.

    d. Assume Goode's stock now sells for $20 per share. The company wants to sell some 20-year, annual interest, $1,000 par value bonds. Each bond will have attached 50 warrants, each exercisable into one share of stock at an exercise price of $25. The firm's straight bonds yield 12 percent. Regardless of your answer to Part b above, assume that each warrant will have a market value of $3 when the stock sells at $20. What coupon interest rate, and dollar coupon, must the company set on the bonds-with-warrants if they are to clear the market? Round to the nearest dollar or percentage point.

17-3 (Convertible premiums) The Tsetsekos Company was planning to finance an expansion in the summer of 1987. The principal executives of the company were agreed that an industrial company such as theirs should finance growth by means of common stock rather than by debt. However, they felt that the price of the company's common stock did not reflect its true worth, so they decided to sell a convertible security. They considered a convertible debenture but feared the burden of fixed interest charges if the common stock did not rise in price to make conversion attractive. They decided on an issue of convertible preferred stock, which would pay a dividend of $2.10 per share.

    The common stock was selling for $42 a share at the time. Management projected earnings for 1987 at $3 a share and expected a future growth rate of 10 percent a year in 1988 and beyond. It was agreed by the investment bankers and the management that the common stock would sell at 14 times earnings, the current price/earnings ratio.

    a. What conversion price should be set by the issuer? The conversion ratio will be 1.0; that is, each share of convertible preferred can be converted into one share of common. Therefore, the convertible's par value (and also the issue price) will be equal to the conversion price, which in turn will be determined as a percentage over the current market price of the common. Your answer will be a guess, but make it a reasonable one.

    b. Should the preferred stock include a call provision? Why?

17-4 (Convertible bond analysis) In June 1976, U.S. Steel (now USX Corporation) sold $400 million of convertible bonds, the largest issue on record. The bonds had a 25-year maturity, a 5¾ percent coupon rate, and were sold at their $1,000 par value. The conversion price was set at $62.75 against a current price of $55 per share of common. The bonds were subordinated debentures, and they were given an A rating; straight nonconvertible debentures of the same quality yielded about 8¾ percent at the time.

    a. Calculate the premium on the bonds, that is, the percentage excess of the conversion price over the current stock price.

    b. What is U.S. Steel's annual interest savings on the convertible issue versus a straight debt issue?

    c. Look up U.S. Steel's current stock price in the paper. On the basis of this price, do you think it likely that the bonds would have been converted? (Calculate the value of the stock one would receive by converting a bond.)

    d. The bonds originally sold for $1,000. If interest rates on A-rated bonds had remained constant at 8¾ percent, what do you think would have happened to the price of the convertible bonds?

    e. Now suppose the price of U.S. Steel's common stock had fallen from $55 on the day the bonds were issued to $20 at present. (At the time this problem was written, that is exactly what had happened.) Suppose also that the rate of interest had fallen from 8¾ to 5¾ percent. (This had not happened when the problem was being written — the interest rate on A-rated bonds was about 9 percent.) Under these conditions, what do you think would have happened to the price of the bonds?

    f. Set up a graphic model to illustrate how investors valued the U.S. Steel convertibles in 1976. How well were these expectations realized?

17-5 (Warrant/convertible decisions) The Houston Carpet Company has grown rapidly during the past 5 years. Recently its commercial bank urged the company to consider increasing permanent financing. Its bank loan under a line of credit has risen to $250,000, carrying an 8 percent interest rate. Houston has been 30 to 60 days late in paying trade creditors.

    Discussions with an investment banker have resulted in the decision to raise $500,000 at this time. Investment bankers have assured the firm that the following alternatives are feasible (flotation costs will be ignored):

- *Alternative 1:* Sell common stock at $8.

- *Alternative 2:* Sell convertible bonds at an 8 percent coupon, convertible into 100 shares of common stock for each $1,000 bond (that is, the conversion price is $10 per share).

- *Alternative 3:* Sell debentures at an 8 percent coupon, each $1,000 bond carrying 100 warrants to buy common stock at $10.

John L. Houston, the president, owns 80 percent of the common stock and wishes to maintain control of the company. One hundred thousand shares are outstanding. The following are extracts of Houston's latest financial statements:

Balance Sheet

		Current liabilities	$400,000
		Common stock, par $1	100,000
		Retained earnings	50,000
Total assets	$550,000	Total claims	$550,000

Income Statement

Sales	$1,100,000
All costs except interest	990,000
EBIT	$ 110,000
Interest	20,000
EBT	$ 90,000
Taxes (40%)	36,000
Net income	$ 54,000
Shares outstanding	100,000
Earnings per share	$0.54
Price/earnings ratio	15.83×
Market price of stock	$8.55

a. Show the new balance sheet under each alternative. For Alternatives 2 and 3, show the balance sheet after conversion of the bonds or exercise of the warrants. Assume that one-half of the funds raised will be used to pay off the bank loan and one-half to increase total assets.

b. Show Mr. Houston's control position under each alternative, assuming that he does not purchase additional shares.

c. What is the effect on earnings per share of each alternative, if it is assumed that profits before interest and taxes will be 20 percent of total assets?

d. What will be the debt ratio under each alternative?

e. Which of the three alternatives would you recommend to Houston, and why?

17-6 **(Convertible bond model)** Niendorf Incorporated needs to raise $25 million to construct production facilities for a new model diskette drive. The firm's straight nonconvertible debentures currently yield 14 percent. Its stock sells for $30 per share; the last dividend was $2; and the expected growth rate is a constant 9 percent. Investment bankers have tentatively proposed that the firm raise the $25 million by issuing convertible debentures. These convertibles would have a $1,000 par value, carry a coupon rate of 10 percent, have a 20-year maturity, and be convertible into 20 shares of stock. The bonds would be noncallable for 5 years, after which they would be callable at a price of $1,075; this call price would decline by $5 per year in Year 6 and each year thereafter. Management has called convertibles in the past (and presumably it will call them again in the future), once they were eligible for call, when the bonds' conversion value was about 20 percent above the bonds' par value (not their call price).

a. Draw an accurate graph similar to Figure 17-2 representing the expectations set forth above. (Assume an annual coupon.)

b. What is the expected rate of return on the proposed convertible issue?

c. Do you think that these bonds could be successfully offered to the public at par? That is, does $1,000 seem to be an equilibrium price in view of the stated terms? If not, suggest the type of change that would have to be made to cause the bonds to trade at $1,000 in the secondary market, assuming no change in capital market conditions.

d. Suppose the projects outlined here work out on schedule for 2 years, but then the firm begins to experience extremely strong competition from Japanese firms. As a result, Niendorf's expected growth rate drops from 9 percent to zero. Assume that the dividend at the time of the drop is $2.38. The company's credit strength is not impaired, and its value of k_s is also unchanged. What would happen (1) to stock price and (2) to the convertible bond's price? Be as precise as you can.

17-7 **(Futures)** Refer back to Table 17-3. It is now May 6. The Hill Company plans to negotiate a $100,000 semiannual interest loan in December. However, its managers are concerned about rising interest rates, and plan to use the futures market to hedge against this possibility. Discussions with their lenders indicate that the loan rate would be 10 percent if the loan were negotiated today.

a. Suppose the company planned to use T-bond futures for the hedge. Would the firm buy or sell futures contracts? How many contracts would be involved?

b. Assume that interest rates on all securities increased by 2 percentage points from May to December. What impact would the rate rise have on the value of Hill's loan? On its futures position? Overall?

c. Did the firm create a perfect hedge? Why not?

d. Now assume that interest rates dropped by 2 percentage points. What impact does the hedge now have on the pending financing transaction? Does this imply that firms should not hedge future financings?

Selected Additional References and Cases

The investment texts listed in Chapter 6 provide extended discussions of options, warrants, convertibles, and futures.

The original Black-Scholes article tested the OPM to see how well predicted prices conformed to market values. For additional empirical tests, see

Galai, Dan, "Tests of Market Efficiency of the Chicago Board Options Exchange," *Journal of Business,* April 1977, 167–197.

Gultekin, N. Bulent, Richard J. Rogalski, and Seha M. Tinic, "Option Pricing Model Estimates: Some Empirical Results," *Financial Management,* Spring 1982, 58–69.

MacBeth, James D., and Larry J. Merville, "An Empirical Examination of the Black-Scholes Call Option Pricing Model," *Journal of Finance,* December 1979, 1173–1186.

Quite a bit of work has also been done on warrant pricing. Two of the more prominent articles are

Galai, Dan, and Mier I. Schneller, "The Pricing of Warrants and the Value of the Firm," *Journal of Finance,* December 1978, 1333–1342.

Schwartz, Eduardo S., "The Valuation of Warrants: Implementing a New Approach," *Journal of Financial Economics,* January 1977, 79–93.

For more insights into convertible pricing and use, see

Alexander, Gordon J., and Roger D. Stover, "Pricing in the New Issue Convertible Debt Market," *Financial Management,* Fall 1977, 35–39.

Alexander, Gordon J., Roger D. Stover, and D. B. Kuhnau, "Market Timing Strategies in Convertible Debt Financing," *Journal of Finance,* March 1979, 143–155.

Brennan, Michael, "The Case for Convertibles," *Issues in Corporate Finance* (New York: Stern Stewart Putnam & Macklis, 1983), 102–111.

Ingersoll, Jonathan E., "A Contingent Claims Valuation of Convertible Securities," *Journal of Financial Economics,* May 1977, 289–322.

————, "An Examination of Corporate Call Policies on Convertible Securities," *Journal of Finance,* May 1977, 463–478.

For additional insights into the use of financial futures for hedging, see

Bacon, Peter W., and Richard Williams, "Interest Rate Futures Trading: A New Tool for the Financial Manager," *Financial Management,* Spring 1976, 32–38.

McCabe, George M., and Charles T. Franckle, "The Effectiveness of Rolling the Hedge Forward in the Treasury Bill Futures Market," *Financial Management,* Summer 1983, 21–29.

The following cases cover issues presented in this chapter:

Case 28, "Biolog Development Corporation," in the Crum-Brigham casebook, which illustrates convertible bond valuation.

"FLX, Incorporated," in the Harrington casebook, which focuses on the retirement of convertible subordinated debentures which are selling below par.

VI

Working Capital Management

18

Working Capital Policy and Financing

A recent issue of *Fortune* magazine contained a 10-page Merrill Lynch advertising supplement titled "Running Your Own Business Successfully." It stated that four financial issues are of particular importance to businesses: (1) managing working capital, (2) financing capital equipment, (3) providing retirement benefits, and (4) maintaining appropriate insurance protection. It is significant that working capital management was first on the list of key financial issues.

To help businesses manage their working capital, Merrill Lynch provides a service called the "Working Capital Management Account, or WCMA." The WCMA account consolidates a firm's cash management, short-term investments, short-term financing, and disbursements into a single management system. This account can automatically (1) use cash inflows to reduce any outstanding loans, (2) sweep excess cash inflows (after loans have been paid off) into an interest-bearing account, (3) transfer cash from the interest-bearing accounts to a checking account to cover disbursement checks presented for payment, and (4) provide a short-term loan, if needed, from a pre-arranged line of credit.

The advertisement also contains this statement: "Managing working capital requires a great deal of precision. A company should have enough working capital to operate smoothly, but it should also avoid wasting valuable resources. Although the task of working capital management is complex, the tools needed to handle this task are available to the successful business owner."

How much of each type of working capital should a firm have, and how should working capital be financed? This chapter addresses these questions.

Working capital policy and management involves decisions relating to current assets, including decisions about financing them. Since about half of the typical firm's capital is invested in current assets, working capital policy is important to the firm and its shareholders. In fact, about 60 percent of a typical financial manager's time is devoted to short-term decision making, and many finance students' first assignment on the job will involve working capital management. For all these reasons, working capital is a vitally important topic. Chapter 18 provides an overview of working capital policy and financing, while Chapters 19 and 20 focus on accounts receivable, inventories, cash, and marketable securities.

WORKING CAPITAL TERMINOLOGY

It is useful to begin by defining some basic definitions and concepts:

1. *Working capital,* sometimes called *gross working capital,* simply means current assets.

2. *Net working capital* is defined as current assets minus current liabilities.

3. One key working capital ratio is the *current ratio,* which is computed by dividing current assets by current liabilities. This ratio measures a firm's liquidity, or its ability to meet current obligations.

4. The *quick ratio,* or *acid test,* which also measures liquidity, is current assets less inventories, divided by current liabilities. The quick ratio removes inventories from current assets because they are the least liquid of current assets. It is thus an "acid test" of a company's ability to meet its current obligations.

5. *Working capital policy* refers to basic policy decisions regarding (1) target levels for each category of current assets and (2) how current assets will be financed.

6. *Working capital management* involves the administration, within the policy guidelines, of current assets and current liabilities.

We must be careful to distinguish between (1) those current liabilities which are specifically used to finance current assets and (2) those which represent either current maturities of long-term debt or financing associated with a construction program which will, after the project is completed, be funded with the proceeds of a long-term security issue.

Table 18-1 contains the December 31, 1987, and projected June 30, 1988, balance sheets of Ewert Printing Company, a manufacturer of greeting cards. Note that, according to the definitions given, Ewert's December 31 working capital is $200,000, and its net working capital is $200,000 − $150,000 = $50,000. Also, Ewert's year-end current ratio is 1.33, and its quick ratio is 0.67. However, the total current liabilities of $150,000 includes the current portion of long-term debt, which is $40,000. This account is unaffected by changes in working capital policy, since it is a function of past long-term financing decisions. Thus, even though we define long-term debt coming due during the next 12 months as a current liability, it is not a working capital decision variable. Similarly, if Ewert were building a new factory and financing this construction with short-term loans which were to be converted to a mortgage bond when the building was completed, the construction loans would be segregated out with regard to working capital management.

Table 18-1
Ewert Printing Company:
Balance Sheets as of December 31, 1987, and June 30, 1988
(Thousands of Dollars)

	12/31/87	6/30/88		12/31/87	6/30/88
Cash	$ 20	$ 20	Accounts payable	$ 30	$ 50
Accounts receivable	80	20	Accrued wages	15	10
Inventories	100	200	Accrued taxes	15	10
			Notes payable	50	80
			Current portion of long-term debt	40	40
Current assets	$200	$240	Current liabilities	$150	$190
Fixed assets	500	500	Long-term debt	150	140
			Stockholders equity	400	410
Total assets	$700	$740	Total liabilities and equity	$700	$740

THE REQUIREMENT FOR EXTERNAL
WORKING CAPITAL FINANCING

The manufacture of greeting cards is a seasonal business. In June of each year, Ewert begins producing Christmas cards for sale in the July-November period, and by December 31, it has sold most of its Christmas and New Year cards, so its inventories are relatively low. However, most of its buyers purchase on credit, so the year-end receivables are at a seasonal high. Now look at Ewert's projected balance sheet for June 30, 1988. Here we see that Ewert's June inventories will be relatively high ($200,000 versus $100,000 the previous December), as will accounts payable ($50,000 versus $30,000), but receivables are projected to be relatively low ($20,000 versus $80,000).

Now consider what happens to Ewert's current assets and current liabilities over the period from December 1987 to June 1988. Current assets increase from $200,000 to $240,000, so the firm must raise $40,000 — increases on the left side of the balance sheet must be financed by increases on the right-hand side. However, note that the higher volume of materials purchases and labor expenditures associated with increased production to build inventories will cause payables and accruals to increase *spontaneously,* on net, by $10,000: from $30,000 + $15,000 + $15,000 = $60,000 to $50,000 + $10,000 + $10,000 = $70,000. This leaves a $30,000 projected working capital financing requirement, which we assume will be obtained from the bank as a short-term loan. Therefore, on June 30, 1988, we show notes payble of $80,000, up from $50,000 on December 31, 1987.

These fluctuations for Ewert resulted from seasonal factors. Similar fluctuations in working capital requirements, and hence in financing needs, can occur over business cycles — typically, financing needs contract during recessions and expand during booms. In the next two sections, we examine (1) the working capital cash flow cycle and (2) alternative policies for establishing the level of current assets and methods of financing these assets.

THE WORKING CAPITAL CASH FLOW CYCLE

The concept of the *cash flow cycle* is important in working capital management. This cycle can be described for a typical manufacturing firm as follows. (1) The firm orders and then receives the raw materials it needs to produce the goods it expects to sell. Since firms usually purchase their raw materials on credit, this transaction creates an account payable. (2) Labor is used to convert the raw materials into finished goods. To the extent that wages are not fully paid at the time the work is done, accrued wages build up. (3) The finished goods are sold, usually on credit, which creates receivables. No cash has been received yet. (4) At some point during the cycle, accounts payable and accruals must be paid. This usually occurs before the receivables have been collected, and at that point, a net cash drain which requires financing occurs. (5) The working capital cash flow cycle is completed when the firm's receivables have been collected. At that point, the firm is ready to repeat the cycle and/or pay off the loans that were used to finance it.

Verlyn Richards and Eugene Laughlin developed a useful approach to analyzing the working capital cash flow cycle.[1] Their approach centers on relating operating events to cash flows, and it is called the *cash conversion cycle model.* Here are some terms used in the model:

1. *Inventory conversion period,* which is the average length of time required to first convert raw materials into finished goods and then to sell these goods. It might take, on average, 50 days from receipt of raw materials to manufacture and then sell the finished product.

2. *Receivables conversion period,* which is the average length of time required to convert the firm's receivables into cash, that is, to collect cash following a sale. That might take another 40 days.

3. *Payables deferral period,* which is the length of time between the purchase of raw materials and the cash payment for them. That would be 30 days if the firm buys on 30-day terms and pays on time.

4. *Cash conversion cycle,* which is the length of time between actual cash expenditures on productive resources (raw materials and labor) and actual cash receipts from the sale of products, that is, from the day labor and/or suppliers are paid to the day receivables are collected.

---

[1]See Verlyn D. Richards and Eugene J. Laughlin, "A Cash Conversion Cycle Approach to Liquidity Analysis," *Financial Management,* Spring 1980, 32–38.

Figure 18-1
The Cash Conversion Cycle

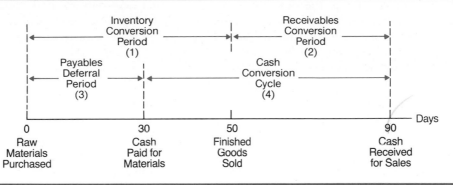

These concepts are diagrammed in Figure 18-1. Each component is given a number, and the cash conversion cycle can be expressed by this equation:

$$\begin{array}{ccccc} \text{Inventory} & & \text{Receivables} & & \text{Payables} & & \text{Cash} \\ \text{conversion} & + & \text{conversion} & - & \text{deferral} & = & \text{conversion} \\ \text{period} & & \text{period} & & \text{period} & & \text{cycle} \\ (1) & & (2) & & (3) & & (4) \end{array}.$$

For our illustrative firm, it takes an average of 50 days to convert raw materials to inventory and to sell the goods, and 40 more days to collect on receivables. However, 30 days normally lapse between receipt of goods and payment of the associated account payable, so the cash conversion cycle is 60 days:

$$50 \text{ days} + 40 \text{ days} - 30 \text{ days} = 60 \text{ days}.$$

Given these data, the firm knows when it receives an order that it will have to finance the costs of processing the order for a 60-day period. The firm's goal should be to shorten the cash conversion cycle as much as possible without hurting operations. This would improve profits, because the longer the cash conversion cycle, the greater the need for external financing, and such financing has a cost.

The cash conversion cycle can be shortened (1) by reducing the inventory conversion period, that is, by processing and selling goods more quickly, (2) by reducing the receivables conversion period, that is, by speeding up collections, or (3) by lengthening the payables deferral period, that is, by slowing down its own payments. To the extent that these actions can be taken *without increasing costs or depressing sales,* they should be carried out. You should keep the cash conversion cycle in mind as we go through both the remainder of this chapter and the other working capital chapters.

WORKING CAPITAL INVESTMENT AND FINANCING POLICIES

We should mention at the outset that working capital decisions are conceptually similar to long-term decisions such as those relating to capital structure and capital budgeting in that they are made within a risk/return trade-off framework. However, financial theorists have not been totally successful in applying the goal of shareholder wealth maximization to working capital decisions in the sense of showing how a specific working capital decision affects stock values. Thus, there is no strong theoretical foundation which provides direction to financial managers.

Working capital policy involves two basic questions: (1) What is the appropriate level for current assets, both in total and by specific accounts? (2) How should current assets be financed?

Alternative Current Asset Investment Policies

Figure 18-2 shows three alternative policies regarding the total amount of current assets carried. Under each policy, a different amount of working capital is carried to support a given level of sales. The line with the steepest slope represents a "liberal" policy, where relatively large amounts of cash, marketable securities, and inventories are carried, and sales are stimulated by the use of a credit policy that provides liberal financing to customers and a corresponding high level of receivables. Conversely, with the "tight" policy, the holdings of cash, securities, inventories, and receivables are minimized. The moderate policy is between the two extremes.

Under conditions of certainty — when sales, costs, lead times, payment periods, and so on, are known for sure — all firms would hold only minimal levels of current assets. Any larger amounts would increase the need for external funding without a corresponding increase in profits, while any smaller holdings would involve late payments to labor and suppliers, lost sales and production inefficiencies because of inventory shortages, and lost sales due to an overly restrictive credit policy.

However, the picture changes when uncertainty is introduced. Here the firm requires some minimum amount of cash and inventories based on expected payments, expected sales, expected order lead times, and so on, plus additional amounts, or *safety stocks,* which enable it to deal with ex post departures from the expected values. Similarly, accounts receivable levels are determined by credit terms, and the tougher the credit terms, the lower the receivables for any given level of sales. With a tight working capital policy, the firm would hold minimal levels of safety stocks for cash and inventories, and it would have a tight credit policy even though this meant running the risk of a decline in sales. A tight working capital policy often provides the highest expected return on investment because the amount of investment is held to the bare minimum, but it entails the greatest risk, while the converse is true under a liberal policy. The moderate policy falls in between the two extremes in terms of expected risk and return.

Figure 18-2
Alternative Current Asset Investment Policies
(Millions of Dollars)

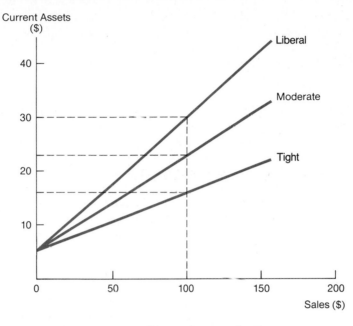

Policy	Current Assets to Support Sales of $100
Liberal	$30
Moderate	23
Tight	16

Note: The sales/current assets relationship is shown here as being linear. This is often not the case.

Corporate policy with regard to the level of current assets is never set all by itself — it is always established in conjunction with the firm's working capital financing policy, which we consider next.

Alternative Financing Policies

Most businesses experience seasonal and/or cyclical fluctuations. For example, construction firms have peaks in the spring and summer, retailers peak around Christmas, and the manufacturers who supply both construction companies and retailers follow similar patterns. Similarly, virtually all businesses must build up working capital when the economy is strong, but they then sell off inventories and have net reductions of receivables when the economy slacks off. Still, it is apparent that current assets rarely drop to zero, and this realization has led to the development of the idea of *permanent current assets.* Applying this idea to Ewert Printing, Table 18-1 suggests that, at this stage in its life, the company's total assets fluctuate between $700,000 and $740,000. Thus, Ewert has $700,000 in permanent assets, composed of $500,000 of fixed assets and $200,000 in permanent current assets, plus *seasonal,* or *temporary, current assets* which fluctuate from zero to a maximum of $40,000. The manner in which the permanent and temporary current assets are financed defines the firm's *working capital financing policy.*

Maturity Matching

One policy is to match asset and liability maturities as shown in Panel A of Figure 18-3. This strategy minimizes the risk that the firm will be unable to pay off its maturing obligations. To illustrate, suppose Ewert borrows on a 1-year basis and uses the funds obtained to build and equip a plant. Cash flows from the plant (profits plus depreciation) would almost never be sufficient to pay off the loan at the end of only one year, so the loan must be renewed. If for some reason the lender refuses to renew the loan, then Ewert would have problems. Had the plant been financed with long-term debt, however, the required loan payments would have been better matched with cash flows from profits and depreciation, and the problem of renewal would not have arisen.

At the limit, a firm could attempt to match exactly the maturity structure of its assets and liabilities. Inventory expected to be sold in 30 days could be financed with a 30-day bank loan; a machine expected to last for 5 years could be financed by a 5-year loan; a 20-year building could be financed by a 20-year mortgage bond; and so forth. Actually, of course, uncertainty about the lives of assets prevents this exact maturity matching. For example, Ewert might finance inventories with a 30-day loan, expecting to sell the inventories and to use the cash generated to retire the loan. But if sales were slow, the cash would not be forthcoming, and the use of short-term credit could end up causing a problem. Still, if Ewert makes an attempt to match asset and liability maturities, we would define this as a moderate working capital financing policy.

Aggressive Approach

Panel B of Figure 18-3 illustrates the situation for an aggressive firm which finances all of its fixed assets with long-term capital but part of its permanent current assets with short-term credit. A look back at Table 18-1 will show that Ewert actually follows this strategy. Assuming that the $40,000 current portion of long-term debt will be refinanced with new long-term debt, Ewert has $500,000 in fixed assets and $590,000 of long-term capital, leaving only $90,000 of long-term capital to finance $200,000 in permanent current assets. Additionally, Ewert has a minimum of $60,000 of "costless" short-term credit consisting of payables and accruals. Thus, Ewert uses $50,000 of short-term notes payable to help finance its permanent level of current assets.

Returning to Figure 18-3, the dashed line in Panel B could have been drawn *below* the line designating fixed assets, indicating that all of the current assets and part of the fixed assets were financed with short-term credit; this would be a highly

Figure 18-3
Alternative Current Asset Financing Policies

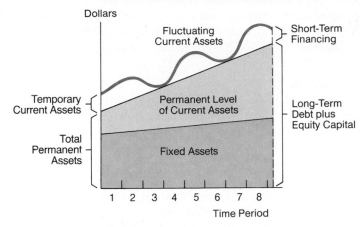

A. Moderate Approach (Maturity Matching)

Dollars

Fluctuating Current Assets

Short-Term Financing

Temporary Current Assets

Permanent Level of Current Assets

Long-Term Debt plus Equity Capital

Total Permanent Assets

Fixed Assets

1 2 3 4 5 6 7 8

Time Period

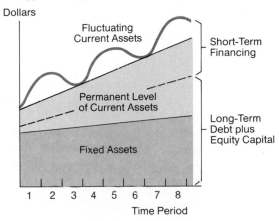

B. Aggressive Approach

Dollars

Fluctuating Current Assets

Short-Term Financing

Permanent Level of Current Assets

Long-Term Debt plus Equity Capital

Fixed Assets

1 2 3 4 5 6 7 8

Time Period

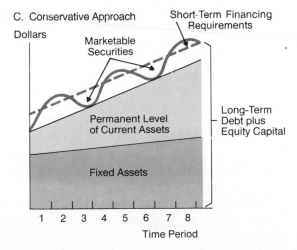

C. Conservative Approach

Short-Term Financing Requirements

Dollars

Marketable Securities

Permanent Level of Current Assets

Long-Term Debt plus Equity Capital

Fixed Assets

1 2 3 4 5 6 7 8

Time Period

aggressive, extremely nonconservative position, and the firm would be very much subject to dangers from rising interest rates as well as to loan renewal problems. However, short-term debt is often cheaper than long-term debt, and some firms are willing to sacrifice safety for the chance of higher profits.

Conservative Approach

As shown in Panel C of Figure 18-3, the dashed line could also be drawn *above* the line designating permanent current assets, indicating that permanent capital is being used to finance all permanent asset requirements and also to meet some or all of the seasonal demands. In the situation depicted in our graph, the firm uses a small amount of short-term credit to meet its peak requirements, but it also meets a part of its seasonal needs by "storing liquidity" in the form of marketable securities during the off-season. The humps above the dashed line represent short-term financing; the troughs below the dashed line represent short-term security holdings. Panel C represents a very safe, conservative working capital financing policy.

ADVANTAGES AND DISADVANTAGES OF SHORT-TERM CREDIT

The three possible financing policies described above were distinguished by the relative amounts of short-term debt used under each policy. The aggressive policy called for the greatest use of short-term debt, while the conservative policy called for the least. Maturity matching fell in between. Although using short-term credit is generally riskier for the borrower than using long-term credit, short-term credit does have some significant advantages. The pros and cons of short-term financing are considered in this section.

Speed

A short-term loan can be obtained much faster than long-term credit. Lenders will insist on a more thorough financial examination before extending long-term credit, and the loan agreement will have to be spelled out in considerable detail because a lot can happen during the life of a 10- to 20-year loan. Therefore, if funds are needed in a hurry, the firm should look to the short-term markets.

Flexibility

If its needs for funds are seasonal or cyclical, a firm may not want to commit itself to long-term debt for three reasons: (1) Flotation costs are generally high when raising long-term debt but trivial for short-term credit. (2) While long-term debt can be repaid early, provided the loan agreement includes a prepayment provision, prepayment penalties can be expensive. Accordingly, if a firm thinks its need for funds may diminish in the near future, it should choose short-term debt for the flexibility it provides. (3) Long-term loan agreements always contain provisions, or covenants, which constrain the firm's future actions. Short-term credit agreements are generally much less onerous in this regard.

Cost of Long-Term Versus Short-Term Debt

The yield curve is normally upward sloping, indicating that generally interest rates are lower on short-term than on long-term debt. Thus, under normal conditions, interest expense at the time the funds are obtained will be lower if the firm borrows on a short-term rather than a long-term basis.

Risk of Long-Term Versus Short-Term Debt

Even though short-term debt is often less expensive than long-term debt, short-term credit subjects the firm to more risk than does long-term financing. This occurs for two reasons: (1) If a firm borrows on a long-term basis, its interest costs will be relatively stable over time, but if it uses short-term credit, its interest expense will fluctuate widely, at times going quite high. For example, the short-term rate banks charge large corporations more than tripled from the late 1970s to the early 1980s, rising from 6.25 to 21 percent. Many firms that had borrowed heavily on a short-term basis simply could not meet their rising interest costs, and as a result bankruptcies hit record levels in the early 1980s. (2) If a firm borrows heavily on a short-term basis, it may find itself unable to repay this debt, and it may be in such a weak financial position that the lender will not extend the loan; this too could force the firm into bankruptcy. Braniff Airlines, which failed during the credit crunch of 1982, is an example.

Another good example of the riskiness of short-term debt is provided by Transamerica Corporation, a major financial services company. Transamerica's chairman, Mr. Beckett, described how his company was moving to reduce its dependency on short-term loans whose costs vary with short-term interest rates. According to Mr. Beckett, Transamerica had reduced its variable-rate (short-term) loans by about $450 million over the past two years. "We aren't going to go through the enormous increase in debt expense again that had such a serious impact (on earnings)," he said. The company's earnings fell sharply because money rates rose to record highs. "We were almost entirely in variable-rate debt," he said, but currently "about 65 percent is fixed rate and 35 percent variable. We've come a long way, and we'll keep plugging away at it." Transamerica's earnings were badly depressed by the increase in short-term rates, but companies such as Braniff were even less fortunate — they simply could not pay the rising interest charges, and this forced them into bankruptcy.

SOURCES OF SHORT-TERM FINANCING

Statements about the flexibility, cost, and riskiness of short-term versus long-term debt depend, to a large extent, on the type of short-term credit that is actually used. There are numerous sources of short-term funds, and in the following sections we describe four major types: (1) accruals, (2) accounts payable (trade credit), (3) bank loans, and (4) commercial paper.

ACCRUALS

Firms generally pay employees on a weekly, biweekly, or monthly basis, so the balance sheet will typically show some accrued wages. Similarly, the firm's own estimated income taxes, social security and income taxes withheld from employee payrolls, and sales taxes the firm collects are generally paid on a weekly, monthly, or quarterly basis, so the balance sheet will typically show some accrued taxes along with accrued wages.

Accruals increase automatically as a firm's operations expand. Further, this type of debt is "free" in the sense that no explicit interest is paid on funds raised through accruals. However, a firm cannot ordinarily control its accruals. Payrolls and the timing of wage payments are set by economic forces and industry custom, while tax payment dates are established by law. Thus, firms use all the accruals they can, but they have little control over the levels of these accounts.

ACCOUNTS PAYABLE, OR TRADE CREDIT

Firms generally make purchases from other firms on credit, recording the debt as an *account payable.* Accounts payable, or *trade credit,* is the largest single category of short-term debt, representing about 40 percent of the current liabilities of the average nonfinancial corporation. The percentage is somewhat larger for smaller firms: Because small companies often do not qualify for financing from other sources, they rely especially heavily on trade credit.[2]

Trade credit is a spontaneous source of financing in the sense that it arises from ordinary business transactions. For example, suppose a firm makes average purchases of $2,000 a day on terms of net 30, meaning that it must pay for goods 30 days after the invoice date. On average, it will owe 30 times $2,000, or $60,000, to its suppliers. If its sales, and consequently its purchases, were to double, then its accounts payable would also double, to $120,000. Simply by growing, the firm would have spontaneously generated an additional $60,000 of financing. Similarly, if the terms under which it bought were extended from 30 to 40 days, its accounts payable would expand from $60,000 to $80,000. Thus, lengthening the credit period, as well as expanding sales and purchases, generates additional financing.

---

[2]In a credit sale, the seller records the transaction as a receivable; the buyer, as a payable. We will examine accounts receivable as an asset investment in Chapter 19. Our focus in this chapter is on accounts payable, a liability item. We might also note that if a firm's accounts payable exceed its receivables, it is said to be *receiving net trade credit,* whereas if its receivables exceed its payables, it is *extending net trade credit.* Smaller firms frequently receive net credit; larger firms generally extend it.

The Cost of Trade Credit

Firms that sell on credit have a *credit policy* that includes certain *terms of credit.* For example, Microchip Electronics sells on terms of 2/10, net 30, meaning that a 2 percent discount is given if payment is made within 10 days of the invoice date, with the full invoice amount being due and payable within 30 days if the discount is not taken.

Suppose Personal Computer Company (PCC) buys an average of $12 million of electronic components from Microchip each year, less a 2 percent discount, for net purchases of $11,760,000/360 = $32,666.67 per day. For simplicity, suppose Microchip is PCC's only supplier. If PCC takes the discount, paying at the end of the tenth day, its payables will average (10)($32,666.67) = $326,667; PCC will, on average, be receiving $326,667 of credit from its only supplier, Microchip Electronics.

Now suppose PCC decides *not* to take the discount; what will happen? First, PCC will begin paying invoices after 30 days, so its accounts payable will increase to 30($32,666.67) = $980,000.[3] Microchip will now be supplying PCC with an *additional* $653,333 of credit. PCC could use this additional credit to pay off bank loans, to expand inventories, to increase fixed assets, to build up its cash account, or even to increase its own accounts receivable.

Personal's new credit from Microchip has a cost — PCC is foregoing a 2 percent discount on its $12 million of purchases, so its costs will rise by $240,000 per year. Dividing this $240,000 by the additional credit, we find the implicit cost of the added trade credit as follows:

$$\text{Approximate percentage cost} = \frac{\$240,000}{\$653,333} = 36.7\%.$$

Assuming that PCC can borrow from its bank (or from other sources) at an interest rate less than 36.7 percent, it should not expand its payables by foregoing discounts.

The following equation can be used to calculate the approximate percentage cost, on an annual basis, of not taking discounts:

$$\begin{array}{c}\text{Approximate}\\ \text{percentage}\\ \text{cost}\end{array} = \frac{\text{Discount percent}}{100 - \begin{array}{c}\text{Discount}\\ \text{percent}\end{array}} \times \frac{360}{\begin{array}{c}\text{Days credit is}\\ \text{outstanding}\end{array} - \begin{array}{c}\text{Discount}\\ \text{period}\end{array}}. \qquad \textbf{(18-1)}$$

The numerator of the first term, discount percent, is the cost per dollar of credit, while the denominator in this term (100 − Discount percent) represents the

---

[3]A question arises here: Should accounts payable reflect gross purchases or purchases net of discounts? Although generally accepted accounting practices permit either treatment on the grounds that the difference is not material, most accountants prefer to record both inventories and payables net of discounts, and then to report the higher payments that result from not taking discounts as an additional expense, called "discounts lost." *Thus, we show accounts payable net of discounts even if the company does not expect to take the discount.*

funds made available by not taking the discount. The second term shows how many times each year this cost is incurred. To illustrate the equation, the approximate cost of not taking a discount when the terms are 2/10, net 30, is computed as follows:

$$\text{Approximate percentage cost} = \frac{2}{98} \times \frac{360}{20} = 0.0204(18)$$
$$= 0.367 = 36.7\%.$$

In effective annual interest terms, the rate is even higher. The discount amounts to interest, and with terms of 2/10, net 30, the firm gains use of the funds for $30 - 10 = 20$ days, so there are $360/20 = 18$ "interest periods" per year. The first term in Equation 18-1, (Discount percent)/(100 − Discount percent) = 0.02/0.98 = 0.0204, is the periodic interest rate. This rate is paid 18 times each year, so the effective annual rate cost of trade credit is

$$\text{Effective annual rate} = (1.0204)^{18} - 1.0 = 1.438 - 1.0 = 43.8\%.$$

Thus, the 36.7 percent approximate cost calculated with Equation 18-1 understates the true cost of trade credit.

Notice, however, that the cost of trade credit can be reduced by paying late. Thus, if PCC could get away with paying in 60 days rather than in the specified 30, then the effective credit period would become $60 - 10 = 50$ days, and the approximate cost would drop from 36.7 percent to $(2/98)(360/50) = 14.7\%$. The effective annual rate would drop from 43.8 to 15.7 percent:

$$\text{Effective annual rate} = (1.0204)^{7.2} - 1.0 = 1.157 - 1.0 = 15.7\%.$$

In periods of excess capacity, firms may be able to get away with late payments, but they will also suffer a variety of problems associated with "stretching" accounts payable and being branded a "slow payer" account. These problems are discussed later in the chapter.

The cost of the additional trade credit that results from not taking discounts can be worked out for other purchase terms. Some illustrative costs are shown below:

Credit Terms	Cost of Additional Credit if Cash Discount Not Taken	
	Approximate Cost	Effective Cost
1/10, net 20	36%	44%
1/10, net 30	18	20
2/10, net 20	73	107
3/15, net 45	37	44

As these figures show, the cost of not taking discounts can be substantial. Incidentally, throughout the chapter, we assume that payments are made either on the *last day* for taking discounts or on the *last day* of the credit period, unless otherwise noted. It would be foolish to pay, say, on the fifth day or on the twentieth day if the credit terms were 2/10, net 30.

Effects of Trade Credit on the Financial Statements

A firm's policy with regard to taking or not taking discounts can have a significant effect on its financial statements. To illustrate, let us assume that PCC is just beginning its operations. On the first day, it makes net purchases of $32,666.67. This amount is recorded on its balance sheet under accounts payable.[4] The second day it buys another $32,666.67. The first day's purchases are not yet paid for, so at the end of the second day, accounts payable total $65,333.34. Accounts payable increase by another $32,666.67 on the third day, for a total of $98,000, and after 10 days, accounts payable are up to $326,667.

If PCC takes discounts, then on the 11th day it will have to pay for the $32,666.67 of purchases made on the 1st day, which will reduce accounts payable. However, it will buy another $32,666.67, which will increase payables. Thus, after the 10th day of operations, PCC's balance sheet will level off, showing a balance of $326,667 in accounts payable, assuming that the company pays on the 10th day in order to take discounts.

Now suppose PCC decides not to take discounts. In this case, on the 11th day, it will add another $32,666.67 to payables, but it will not pay for the purchases made on the 1st day. Thus, the balance sheet figure for accounts payable will rise to 11($32,666.67) = $359,333.37. This buildup will continue through the 30th day, at which point payables will total 30($32,666.67) = $980,000. On the 31st day, PCC will buy another $32,667 of goods, which will increase accounts payable, but it will also pay for the purchases made the 1st day, which will reduce payables. Thus, the balance sheet item accounts payable will stabilize at $980,000 after 30 days, assuming PCC does not take discounts.

Table 18-2, Part I, shows PCC's balance sheet, after it reaches a steady state, under the two trade credit policies. Total assets are unchanged by this policy decision, and we also assume that the accruals and common equity accounts are unchanged. The differences show up in accounts payable and notes payable; when PCC elects to take discounts and thus gives up some of the trade credit it otherwise could have obtained, it will have to raise $653,333 from some other source. It could have sold more common stock, or it could have used long-term bonds, but it chose to use bank credit, which has a 10 percent cost and is reflected in the notes payable account.

Part II of Table 18-2 shows PCC's income statement under the two policies. If the company does not take discounts, then its interest expense will be zero, but it will have a $240,000 expense for discounts lost. On the other hand, if it does take discounts, it will incur an interest expense of $65,333, but it will avoid the cost of discounts lost. Since discounts lost exceed the interest expense, the take-discounts policy results in the higher net income and, thus, in a higher stock price.

---

[4]Inventories also increase by $32,666.67, but we are not now concerned with inventories.

Table 18-2
PCC's Financial Statements with Different Trade Credit Policies

---

I. Balance Sheets

	Take Discounts: Borrow from Bank	Do Not Take Discounts; Use Maximum Trade Credit
Cash	$ 500,000	$ 500,000
Receivables	1,000,000	1,000,000
Inventories	2,000,000	2,000,000
Fixed assets	2,980,000	2,980,000
Total assets	$ 6,480,000	$ 6,480,000
Accounts payable	$ 326,667	$ 980,000
Notes payable	653,333	0
Accruals	500,000	500,000
Common equity	5,000,000	5,000,000
Total claims	$ 6,480,000	$ 6,480,000

II. Income Statements

	Take Discounts: Borrow from Bank	Do Not Take Discounts; Use Maximum Trade Credit
Sales	$15,000,000	$15,000,000
Less: Purchases	11,760,000	11,760,000
Labor	2,000,000	2,000,000
Interest	65,333	0
Discounts lost	0	240,000
Net income before tax	$ 1,174,667	$ 1,000,000
Tax (40%)	469,867	400,000
Net income	$ 704,800	$ 600,000

Components of Trade Credit: Free Versus Costly

On the basis of the preceding discussion, trade credit can be divided into two components: (1) *free trade credit,* which involves credit received during the discount period and which for PCC amounts to 10 days' net purchases, or $326,667, and (2) *costly trade credit,* which involves credit in excess of the free credit, and whose cost is an implicit one based on the foregone discounts.[5] PCC could obtain $653,333, or 20 days' net purchases, of non-free trade credit at a cost of approximately 37 percent. *Financial managers should always use the free component, but they should use the costly component only after analyzing the cost of this capital to make sure that it is less than the cost of funds which could be obtained from other sources.* Under the terms of trade found in most industries, the

---

[5]There is some question as to whether any credit is really "free," because the supplier will have a cost of carrying receivables which must be passed on to the customer in the form of higher prices. Still, where suppliers sell on standard terms such as 2/10, net 30, and where the base price cannot be negotiated downward for early payment, then for all intents and purposes, the 10 days of trade credit are indeed "free."

costly component will involve a relatively high percentage cost, so stronger firms will avoid using it.

We noted earlier that firms sometimes can and do deviate from the stated credit terms, thus altering the percentage cost figures cited above. For example, a California manufacturing firm that buys on terms of 2/10, net 30, makes a practice of paying in 15 days (rather than 10), but it still takes discounts. Its treasurer simply waits until 15 days after receipt of the goods to pay, and then writes a check for the invoiced amount less the 2 percent discount. The company's suppliers want its business, so they tolerate this practice. Similarly, a Wisconsin firm that also buys on terms of 2/10, net 30, does not take discounts, but it pays in 60 rather than in 30 days, thus "stretching" its trade credit. As we saw earlier, both practices reduce the cost of trade credit. Neither of these firms is "loved" by its suppliers, and neither could continue these practices in times when suppliers were operating at full capacity and had order backlogs, but these practices can and do reduce the costs of trade credit during times when suppliers have excess capacity.

SHORT-TERM BANK LOANS

Commercial banks, whose loans generally appear on firms' balance sheets under the notes payable account, are second in importance to trade credit as a source of short-term financing.[6] The banks' influence is actually greater than appears from the dollar amounts they lend, because banks provide *nonspontaneous* funds. As a firm's financing needs increase, it requests its bank to provide the additional funds. If the request is denied, the firm may be forced to abandon attractive growth opportunities.

Bank Loan Features

Some features of bank loans are discussed in the following paragraphs.

Maturity
Although banks do make longer-term loans, *the bulk of their lending is on a short-term basis* — about two-thirds of all bank loans mature in a year or less. Bank loans to businesses are frequently written as 90-day notes, so the loan must be repaid or renewed at the end of 90 days. Of course, if a borrower's financial position has deteriorated, the bank may well refuse to renew the loan. This can mean serious trouble for the borrower.

Promissory Note
When a bank loan is approved, the agreement is executed by signing a *promissory note.* The note specifies (1) the amount borrowed; (2) the percentage interest rate; (3) the repayment schedule, which can involve either a lump sum or a series

---

[6]Although commercial banks remain the primary source of short-term loans, other sources are available. For example, in 1987 General Electric Credit Corporation (GECC) had over $2 billion in commercial loans outstanding. Firms such as GECC, which was initially established to finance consumers' purchases of GE's durable goods, often find business loans to be more profitable than consumer loans.

of installments; (4) any collateral that might have to be put up as security for the loan; and (5) any other terms and conditions to which the bank and the borrower may have agreed. When the note is signed, the bank credits the borrower's checking account with the amount of the loan, while on the borrower's balance sheet, both cash and notes payable increase.

Compensating Balances

Banks typically require that a regular borrower maintain an average demand deposit (checking account) balance equal to from 10 to 20 percent of the face amount of the loan. This is called a *compensating balance,* and such balances raise the effective interest rate on the loans. For example, if a firm needs $80,000 to pay off outstanding obligations, but if it must maintain a 20 percent compensating balance, then it must borrow $100,000 to obtain a usable $80,000. If the stated interest rate is 8 percent, the effective cost is actually 10 percent: $8,000 interest divided by $80,000 of usable funds equals 10 percent.[7]

Line of Credit

A *line of credit* is a formal or informal understanding between the bank and the borrower indicating the maximum credit the bank will extend to the borrower. For example, on December 31 a bank loan officer may indicate to a financial manager that the bank regards the firm as being "good" for up to $80,000 during the forthcoming year. If on January 10 the financial manager signs a promissory note for $15,000 for 90 days, this would be called "taking down" $15,000 of the total line of credit. This amount would be credited to the firm's checking account at the bank, and before repayment of the $15,000, the firm could borrow additional amounts up to a total of $80,000 outstanding at any one time.

Revolving Credit Agreement

A *revolving credit agreement* is a formal line of credit often used by large firms. To illustrate, in 1986 Bankston Petroleum Company negotiated a revolving credit agreement for $100 million with a group of banks. The banks were formally committed for 4 years to lend Bankston up to $100 million if the funds were needed. Bankston, in turn, paid a commitment fee of one-quarter of 1 percent on the unused balance of the commitment to compensate the banks for making the commitment. Thus, if Bankston did not take down any of the $100 million commitment during a year, it would still be required to pay a $250,000 fee. If it borrowed $50 million, the unused portion of the line of credit would fall to $50 million, and the fee would fall to $125,000. Of course, interest also had to be paid on the money Bankston actually borrowed. As a general rule, the rate of interest on "revolvers"

---

[7]Note, however, that the compensating balance may be set as a minimum monthly *average,* and if the firm would maintain this average anyway, the compensating balance requirement would not raise the effective interest rate. Also, note that these *loan* compensating balances are added to any compensating balances that the firm's bank may require for *services performed,* such as clearing checks.

is pegged to the prime rate, so the cost of the loan varies over time as interest rates change.[8] Bankston's rate was set at prime plus 0.5 percentage points.

Note that a revolving credit agreement is very similar to a line of credit. However, there is an important distinguishing feature: The bank has a *legal obligation* to honor a revolving credit agreement, and it receives a commitment fee. Neither the legal obligation nor the fee exist under a less formal line of credit.

The Cost of Bank Loans

The cost of bank loans varies for different types of borrowers at a given point in time, and for all borrowers over time. Interest rates are higher for riskier borrowers, and rates are also higher on smaller loans because of the fixed costs involved in making and servicing loans. If a firm can qualify as a "prime risk" because of its size and financial strength, it can borrow at the *prime rate,* which has traditionally been the lowest rate banks charge. Rates on other loans tend to be scaled up from the prime rate.

Bank rates vary widely over time depending on economic conditions and Federal Reserve policy. When the economy is weak, then (1) loan demand is usually slack, and (2) the Fed also makes plenty of money available to the system. As a result, rates on all types of loans are relatively low. Conversely, when the economy is booming, loan demand is typically strong and the Fed restricts the money supply; the result is high interest rates. As an indication of the kinds of fluctuations that can occur, the prime rate during 1980 rose from 11 percent in August to 21 percent in December. Interest rates on other bank loans also vary, but generally they are kept in phase with the prime rate.

Interest rates on bank loans are calculated in three ways: as *simple interest,* as *discount interest,* and as *add on interest.* These three methods are explained next.

Regular, or Simple, Interest
Simple interest forms the basis for comparison of all loan rates. In a *simple interest* loan, the borrower receives the face value of the loan and repays the principal and interest at maturity. For example, in a simple interest loan of $10,000 at 12 percent

---

[8]Each bank sets its own prime rate, but, because of competitive forces, most banks' prime rates are identical. Further, most banks follow the rate set by the large New York City banks, and they, in turn, generally follow the rate set by Citibank, the U.S.'s largest. Citibank had a policy of setting the prime rate each week at 1¼ to 1½ percentage points above the average rate on large certificates of deposit (CDs) during the three weeks immediately preceding. CD rates represent the "price" of money in the open market, and they rise and fall with the supply and demand of money, so CD rates are "market-clearing" rates. By tying the prime rate to CD rates, the banking system insured that the prime rate would also be a market-clearing rate.

However, in recent years the prime rate has been held relatively constant even during periods when open market rates fluctuated. Also, in recent years many banks have been lending to the very strongest companies at rates below the prime rate. As we discuss later in this chapter, larger firms have ready access to the commercial paper market, and if banks want to do a significant volume of business with these larger companies, they must match or at least come close to the commercial paper rate. As competition in financial markets increases, as it has been doing because of the deregulation of banks and other financial institutions, "administered" rates such as the prime rate must give way to flexible, negotiated rates based on market forces.

for one year, the borrower receives the $10,000 upon approval of the loan and pays back the $10,000 principal plus $10,000(0.12) = $1,200 in interest at maturity (one year later). The 12 percent is the stated, or nominal, rate. On this 1-year loan, the effective annual rate is also 12 percent:

$$\text{Effective rate}_{\text{Simple}} = \frac{\text{Interest}}{\text{Amount received}} = \frac{\$1,200}{\$10,000} = 12\%.$$

On a simple interest loan of one year or more, the nominal rate equals the effective rate. However, if the loan had a term of less than one year, say 90 days, then the effective rate would be calculated as follows:

$$\text{Effective rate}_{\text{Simple}} = \left(1 + \frac{k_{\text{Nom}}}{m}\right)^m - 1.0$$
$$= (1 + 0.12/4)^4 - 1.0 = 12.55\%.$$

Here k_{Nom} is the nominal, or stated, rate and m is the number of loan periods per year, or $360/90 = 4$. The bank gets the interest sooner than under a 1-year loan, and hence the effective rate is higher.

Discount Interest

In a *discount interest* loan, the bank deducts the interest in advance (*discounts the loan*). Thus, the borrower receives less than the face value of the loan. On a 1-year, $10,000 loan with a 12 percent (nominal) rate, discount basis, the interest (discount) is $10,000(0.12) = $1,200, so the borrower obtains the use of only $10,000 - $1,200 = $8,800. The effective rate is 13.64 percent versus 12 percent on a 1-year simple interest loan:[9]

$$\text{Effective rate}_{\text{Discount}} = \frac{\text{Interest}}{\text{Amount received}}$$
$$= \frac{\text{Interest}}{\text{Face value} - \text{Interest}}$$
$$= \frac{\$1,200}{\$10,000 - \$1,200} = 13.64\%.$$

An alternative procedure for finding the effective annual rate on a discount interest loan is

---

[9]Note that if the borrowing firm actually requires $10,000 of cash, it must borrow $11,363.64:

$$\text{Face value} = \frac{\text{Funds required}}{1.0 - \text{Nominal rate (fraction)}}$$
$$= \frac{\$10,000}{1.0 - 0.12} = \frac{\$10,000}{0.88} = \$11,363.64.$$

Now, the borrower will receive $11,363.64 - 0.12($11,363.64) = $10,000. Increasing the face value of the loan does not change the effective rate of 13.64 percent on the $10,000 of usable funds.

$$\text{Effective rate}_{\text{Discount}} = \frac{\text{Nominal rate (\%)}}{1.0 - \text{Nominal rate (fraction)}}$$

$$= \frac{12\%}{1.0 - 0.12} = \frac{12\%}{0.88} = 13.64\%.$$

If the discount loan is for a period of less than one year, its effective annual rate is found as follows:

$$\text{Effective rate}_{\text{Discount}} = \left(1.0 + \frac{\text{Interest}}{\text{Face value} - \text{Interest}}\right)^m - 1.0.$$

For example, if we borrow $10,000 face value at a nominal rate of 12 percent, discount interest, for 3 months, then m = 12/3 = 4, and the interest payment is $(0.12/4)($10,000) = 300, so

$$\text{Effective rate}_{\text{Discount}} = \left(1.0 + \frac{\$300}{\$10,000 - \$300}\right)^4 - 1.0$$

$$= 0.1296 = 12.96\%.$$

Thus, discount interest imposes less of a penalty on shorter-term than on longer-term loans.

Installment Loans: Add-On Interest

Lenders typically charge *add-on interest* on automobile and other types of small installment loans. The term "add-on" means that the interest is calculated based on the nominal rate and then added to the amount received to obtain the loan's face value. To illustrate, suppose you borrow $10,000 on an add-on basis at a nominal rate of 12 percent to buy a car, with the loan to be repaid in 12 monthly installments. At a 12 percent nominal rate, you will pay a total interest charge of $1,200. However, since the loan is paid off in monthly installments, you have the use of the full $10,000 for only the first month, and the amount actually advanced by the lender declines until, during the last month, only $\frac{1}{12}$ of the original loan will still be outstanding. Thus, you are paying $1,200 for the use of only about half the loan's face amount, as the average outstanding balance of the loan is only about $5,000. Therefore, we can approximate the effective rate as follows:

$$\text{Approximate effective rate}_{\text{Add-on}} = \frac{\text{Interest}}{(\text{Amount received})/2}$$

$$= \frac{\$1,200}{\$10,000/2} = 24.0\%.$$

To determine the precise effective rate under add-on, we proceed as follows:

1. The total amount to be repaid is $10,000 of principal, plus $1,200 of interest, or $11,200.

2. The monthly payment is $11,200/12 = $933.33.

3. The bank is, in effect, buying a 12-period annuity of $933.33 for $10,000, so $10,000 is the present value of the annuity. Expressed in equation form,

$$PV = \$10,000 = \sum_{t=1}^{12} \$933.33 \left(\frac{1}{1 + k_d}\right)^t.$$

4. This equation can be solved for k_d, which is the rate per month, using a financial calculator. Here $k_d = 1.788\% = 0.01788$.

5. The annual effective rate is found as follows:[10]

$$
\begin{aligned}
\text{Effective rate}_{\text{Add-on}} &= (1 + k_d)^{12} - 1.0 \\
&= (1.01788)^{12} - 1.0 \\
&= 1.2370 - 1.0 = 23.7\%.
\end{aligned}
$$

Simple Interest with Compensating Balances

Compensating balances tend to raise the effective rate on a loan. To illustrate this, suppose a firm needs $10,000 to pay for some equipment that it recently purchased. A bank offers to lend the company money for one year at a 12 percent simple rate, but the company must maintain a *compensating balance (CB)* equal to 20 percent of the loan amount. If the firm did not take the loan, it would keep no deposits with the bank. What is the effective annual rate on the loan?

First, note that if the firm requires $10,000, it must, assuming it does not have current cash to use as the compensating balance, borrow $12,500:

$$\text{Face value} = \frac{\text{Funds required}}{1.0 - \text{CB (fraction)}} = \frac{\$10,000}{1.0 - 0.20} = \$12,500.$$

The interest paid at the end of the year will be $12,500(0.12) = \$1,500$, but the firm will only get the use of $10,000. Therefore, the effective annual rate is 15 percent:

$$
\begin{aligned}
\text{Effective rate}_{\text{Simple/CB}} &= \frac{\text{Interest}}{\text{Amount received}} \\
&= \frac{\$1,500}{\$10,000} = 15\%.
\end{aligned}
$$

An alternative formulation is

$$
\begin{aligned}
\text{Effective rate}_{\text{Simple/CB}} &= \frac{\text{Nominal rate (\%)}}{1.0 - \text{CB (fraction)}} \\
&= \frac{12\%}{1.0 - 0.2} = 15\%.
\end{aligned}
$$

---

[10]Note that if an installment loan is paid off ahead of schedule, additional complications arise. For a discussion of this point, see Dick Bonker, "The Rule of 78," *Journal of Finance,* June 1976, 877–888.

Discount Interest with Compensating Balances

The analysis can be extended to the case where compensating balances are required and the loan is on a discount basis. In this situation, if a firm required $10,000 for one year and a 20 percent compensating balance (CB) is required on a 12 percent discount loan, it must borrow $14,705.88:

$$\text{Face value} = \frac{\text{Funds required}}{1.0 - \text{Nominal rate (fraction)} - \text{CB (fraction)}}$$

$$= \frac{\$10,000}{1.0 - 0.12 - 0.2} = \$10,000/0.68 = \$14,705.88.$$

The firm would record this $14,705.88 as a note payable offset by these asset accounts: (Note that a small rounding error occurs.)

To cash account	$10,000.00
Prepaid interest (12% of $14,705.88)	1,764.71
Compensating balance (20% of $14,705.88)	2,941.18
	$14,705.89

Now the effective annual rate is 17.65 percent:

$$\text{Effective rate}_{\text{Discount/CB}} = \frac{\text{Nominal rate}}{1.0 - \text{Nominal rate (fraction)} - \text{CB (fraction)}}$$

$$= \frac{12\%}{1.0 - 0.12 - 0.2} = 12\%/0.68 = 17.65\%.$$

In our example, compensating balances and discount interest combined to push the effective rate of interest up from 12 to 17.65 percent. Note, however, that in our analysis we assumed that the compensating balance requirement forced the firm to increase its bank deposits. Had the company had transactions balances which could be used to supply all or part of the compensating balances, the effective annual rate would have been less than 17.65 percent. Also, if the firm earns interest on its bank deposits, including the compensating balance, then the effective annual rate would be decreased.

Choosing a Bank

Individuals whose only contact with their bank is through the use of its checking services generally choose a bank for the convenience of its location and the competitive cost of its services. However, a business that borrows from banks must look at other criteria, and a potential borrower seeking banking relations should recognize that important differences exist among banks. Some of these differences are considered next.

Willingness to Assume Risks

Banks have different basic policies toward risk. Some banks are inclined to follow relatively conservative lending practices, while others engage in what are properly termed "creative banking practices." These policies reflect partly the personalities of officers of the bank and partly the characteristics of the bank's deposit liabilities. Thus, a bank with fluctuating deposit liabilities in a static community will tend to be a conservative lender, while a bank whose deposits are growing with little interruption may follow "liberal" credit policies. A large bank with broad diversification over geographic regions or across industries can obtain the benefit of combining and averaging risks. Thus, marginal credit risks that might be unacceptable to a small bank or to a specialized unit bank can be pooled by a branch banking system to reduce the overall risk of a group of marginal accounts.

Advice and Counsel

Some bank loan officers are active in providing counsel and in stimulating development loans to firms in their early and formative years. Certain banks have specialized departments which make loans to firms expected to grow and thus to become more important customers. The personnel of these departments can provide valuable counseling to customers: The bankers' experience with other firms in growth situations may enable them to spot, and then to warn their customers about, developing problems.

Loyalty to Customers

Banks differ in the extent to which they will support the activities of the borrower in bad times. This characteristic is referred to as the degree of *loyalty* of the bank. Some banks may put great pressure on a business to liquidate its loans when the firm's outlook becomes clouded, whereas others will stand by the firm and work diligently to help it get back on its feet. An especially dramatic illustration of this point was Bank of America's bail-out of Memorex Corporation. The bank could have forced Memorex into bankruptcy, but instead it loaned the company additional capital and helped it survive a bad period. Memorex's stock price subsequently rose on the New York Stock Exchange from $1.50 to $68, so Bank of America's help was indeed substantial.

Specialization

Banks differ greatly in their degrees of loan specialization. Larger banks have separate departments that specialize in different kinds of loans—for example, real estate loans, farm loans, and commercial loans. Within these broad categories, there may be a specialization by line of business, such as steel, machinery, cattle, or textiles. The strengths of banks are also likely to reflect the nature of the business and the economic environment in which they operate. For example, Texas banks have become specialists in lending to oil companies, while many midwestern banks are agricultural specialists. A sound firm can obtain more creative cooperation and more active support by going to the bank that has the greatest experience and familiarity with its particular type of business. The financial manager should therefore choose a bank with care. A bank that is excellent for one firm may be unsatisfactory for another.

Maximum Loan Size

The size of a bank can be an important factor. Since the maximum loan a bank can make to any one customer is limited to 15 percent of the bank's capital accounts (capital stock plus retained earnings), it is generally not appropriate for large firms to develop borrowing relationships with small banks.

Other Services

Banks also provide lockbox systems (see Chapter 20), assist with electronic funds transfers, help firms obtain foreign exchange, and the like, and such services should be taken into account in selecting a bank. Also, if the firm is a small business whose manager owns most of its stock, the bank's willingness and ability to provide trust and estate services should also be considered.

COMMERCIAL PAPER

Commercial paper is a type of unsecured promissory note issued by large, strong firms, and it is sold primarily to other business firms, to insurance companies, to pension funds, to money market mutual funds, and to banks. Although the amount of commercial paper outstanding is smaller than bank loans outstanding, this form of financing has grown rapidly in recent years. At the end of January 1987, there was approximately $300 billion of commercial paper outstanding, versus about $500 billion of bank loans to businesses.

Maturity and Cost

Maturities of commercial paper generally vary from one to nine months, with an average of about five months.[11] The rates on commercial paper fluctuate with supply and demand conditions — they are determined in the marketplace, varying daily as conditions change. Recently, commercial paper rates have generally ranged from $1\frac{3}{4}$ to $2\frac{1}{2}$ percentage points below the stated prime rate, and about $\frac{1}{2}$ of a percentage point above the T-bill rate. For example, on a recent day the average rate on 3-month commercial paper was 7.6 percent, the stated prime rate was 9.5 percent, and the 6-month T-bill rate was about 7.1 percent. Also, since compensating balances are not required for commercial paper, the *effective* cost differential is still wider.[12]

---

[11]The maximum maturity without SEC registration is 270 days. Also, commercial paper can only be sold to "sophisticated" investors; otherwise, SEC registration would be required even for maturities of 270 days or less.

[12]However, this factor is offset to some extent by the fact that firms issuing commercial paper are required by commercial paper dealers to have unused revolving credit agreements to back up their outstanding commercial paper, and fees must be paid on these lines. In other words, to sell $1 million of commercial paper, a firm must have revolving credit available to pay off the paper when it matures, and commitment fees on this unused credit line (about $\frac{1}{2}$ percent) increase the effective cost of the paper. Note also that commercial paper and T-bill rates are quoted on a discount basis, whereas the prime rate is on an annual yield basis.

Use of Commercial Paper

The use of commercial paper is restricted to a comparatively small number of concerns that are exceptionally good credit risks. Dealers prefer to handle the paper of firms whose net worth is $100 million or more and whose annual borrowing exceeds $10 million. One potential problem with commercial paper is that a debtor who is in temporary financial difficulty may receive little help, because commercial paper dealings are generally less personal than are bank relationships. Thus, banks are generally more able and willing to help a good customer weather a temporary storm than is a commercial paper dealer. On the other hand, using commercial paper permits a corporation to tap a wide range of credit sources, including financial institutions outside its own area and industrial corporations across the country, and this can reduce interest costs.

SECURED SHORT-TERM LOANS

Thus far, we have not addressed the question of whether or not loans are secured. Commercial paper loans are never secured by specific collateral, but all the other types of loans can be if this is deemed necessary or desirable. Given a choice, it is ordinarily better to borrow on an unsecured basis, since the bookkeeping costs of secured loans are often high. However, weak firms may find (1) that they can borrow only if they put up some type of security to protect the lender, or (2) that by using some security they can borrow at a much lower rate.

Several different kinds of collateral can be employed, including marketable stocks or bonds, land or buildings, equipment, inventory, and accounts receivable. Marketable securities make excellent collateral, but few firms hold portfolios of stocks and bonds. Similarly, both real property (land and buildings) and equipment are good forms of collateral, but they are generally used as security for long-term loans rather than for working capital loans. Therefore, most secured short-term business borrowing involves the use of either accounts receivable or inventories as collateral.

To understand the use of security, consider the case of an Orlando hardware dealer who wanted to modernize and expand his store. He requested a $200,000 bank loan. After examining his business's financial statements, the bank indicated (1) that it would lend him a maximum of $100,000, and (2) that the interest rate would be 13 percent. The owner had a substantial personal portfolio of stocks, so he offered to put up $300,000 of high-quality stocks to support the $200,000 loan. The bank then granted the full $200,000 loan, and at a rate of only 11 percent. The store owner might also have used his inventories or receivables as security for the loan, but processing costs would have been high.

In the past, state laws varied greatly with regard to the use of security in financing. Today, however, all states except Louisiana operate under the *Uniform Commercial Code,* which standardizes and simplifies the procedure for establishing loan security. The heart of the Uniform Commercial Code is the *Security Agreement,* a standardized document, or form, on which the specific assets that are pledged are stated. The assets can be items of equipment, accounts receivable, or inventories. Secured short-term loans involve quite a bit of paperwork and administrative costs, which makes them relatively expensive. However, this is often the only type of financing available to weaker firms. In the following two sections, we briefly describe procedures for using accounts receivable and inventories as security for short-term credit.[13]

Accounts Receivable Financing

Accounts receivable financing involves either the pledging of receivables or the selling of receivables (factoring). The *pledging of accounts receivable* is characterized by the fact that the lender not only has a claim against the receivables but also has recourse to the borrower: If the person or the firm that bought the goods does not pay, the selling firm must take the loss. Therefore, the risk of default on the accounts receivable pledged remains with the borrower. Also, the buyer of the goods is not ordinarily notified about the pledging of the receivables, and the financial institution that lends on the security of accounts receivable is generally either a commercial bank or one of the large industrial finance companies such as General Electric Credit Corporation (GECC).

Factoring, or *selling accounts receivable,* involves the purchase of accounts receivable by the lender, generally without recourse to the borrower. Under factoring, the buyer of the goods is typically notified of the transfer and is asked to make payment directly to the financial institution. Since the factoring firm assumes the risk of default on bad accounts, it must do a credit check. Accordingly, factors can provide not only money but also a credit department for the borrower. Incidentally, the same banks and other financial institutions that make loans against pledged receivables also serve as factors. Thus, depending on the circumstances and the wishes of the borrower, a financial institution will provide either form of receivables financing.[14]

Inventory Financing

A substantial amount of credit is secured by business inventories. If a firm is a relatively good credit risk, the mere existence of the inventory may be a sufficient basis for an unsecured loan. However, if the firm is a relatively poor risk, the lending institution may insist upon security, which can take the form of a blanket lien against all inventory or either trust receipts or warehouse receipts against specific inventory items.

The *inventory blanket lien* gives the lending institution a lien against all the borrower's inventories. However, the borrower is free to sell inventories, so the value of the collateral can be reduced below the level that existed when the loan was granted. Because of the inherent weakness of the blanket lien, another proce-

---

[13]For a more complete description of accounts receivable and inventory financing, see Eugene F. Brigham and Louis C. Gapenski, *Intermediate Financial Management,* 2nd ed., Chapter 16.

[14]In 1986, several large companies such as Ford and General Motors began to sell "collateralized bonds" secured by packages of accounts receivable. The holders of these bonds receive monthly payments made with cash flows from the repayment of auto or other loans. The bonds have relatively short maturities, and the principal buyers are pension funds and other institutional investors. These new securities serve the same purpose as traditional receivables financing, but they have opened a whole new source of funds to corporate borrowers.

dure for inventory financing was developed — the *trust receipt,* which is an instrument acknowledging that the goods are held in trust for the lender. When trust receipts are used, the borrowing firm, upon receiving funds from the lender, signs and delivers a trust receipt for the goods. The goods can be stored in a public warehouse or held on the premises of the borrower. The trust receipt acknowledges that the goods are held in trust for the lender and that any proceeds from the sale of trust goods must be transmitted to the lender at the end of each day. Automobile dealer financing is one of the best examples of trust receipt financing.

Like trust receipts, *warehouse receipt* financing uses inventory as security. A *public warehouse* is an independent third party operation engaged in the business of storing goods. Items which must age, such as tobacco and liquor, are often financed and stored in public warehouses. The borrower cannot remove the goods until the lender has been repaid, so the warehouse operator affords protection to the lender. However, at times a public warehouse is not practical because of the bulkiness of goods and the expense of transporting them to and from the borrower's premises. In such cases, a *field warehouse* may be established at the borrower's place of business. To provide inventory supervision, the lending institution employs a third party, a field warehousing company, which acts as an agent for the lending institution.

SUMMARY

Working capital policy involves (1) the level of current assets and (2) the manner in which these assets are financed. We saw that because short-term credit offers greater flexibility and often a lower cost, most firms use at least some current debt in spite of the fact that short-term credit increases the firm's risk.

The chapter also examined the four major types of short-term credit available to a firm: (1) *accruals,* (2) *accounts payable (*or *trade credit),* (3) *bank loans,* and (4) *commercial paper.* Companies use accruals on a regular basis, but this usage is not subject to discretionary actions. The other three types of credit are controllable, at least within limits.

Accounts payable may be divided into two components, *free trade credit* and *costly trade credit.* The cost of the latter is based on discounts lost, and it can be quite high. The financial manager should use all the free trade credit the firm can get, but costly trade credit should be used only if other credit is not available on better terms.

Bank loans may be negotiated on an individual basis as the need arises, or they may be obtained on a pre-arranged basis under a *line of credit* or *revolving loan agreement.* One frequently encounters three different kinds of interest charges on bank loans: (1) *simple interest,* (2) *discount interest,* and (3) *add-on interest* for installment loans. Also, banks often require borrowers to maintain *compensating balances.* If the required balance exceeds the balance the firm would otherwise maintain, a compensating balance raises the effective cost of a bank loan.

Commercial paper is an important source of short-term credit, but it is available only to large, financially strong firms. Interest rates on commercial paper are generally below the prime bank rate, and the relative cost of paper is even lower when compensating balances on bank loans are considered. However, commercial paper does have disadvantages — if a firm that depends heavily on commercial paper experiences problems, its source of funds will dry up immediately. Commercial bankers are much more likely to help their customers ride out bad times.

Short-term credit is often *secured* by accounts receivable, which may be either *pledged* as collateral or *factored* (sold). Inventories can also be used as collateral under (1) *blanket liens,* (2) *trust receipts,* or (3) *warehouse receipts.*

Questions

18-1 Define each of the following terms:

    a. Working capital level policies

    b. Permanent current assets versus temporary current assets

    c. "Flexibility" as a reason for using short-term debt

    d. Alternative working capital financing policies

    e. Trade credit; free trade credit; costly trade credit

    f. "Stretching" accounts payable

    g. Promissory note; line of credit; revolving credit agreement

    h. Compensating balance; a compensating balance which *does not* increase the cost of a loan

    i. Prime rate

    j. Simple interest; discount interest; add-on interest; revolving credit interest

    k. Commercial paper; commercial paper rate

    l. Secured loan; trust receipt; field warehouse; pledging; factoring

18-2 "Firms can control their accruals within fairly wide limits; depending on the cost of accruals, financing from this source can be increased or decreased." Discuss.

18-3 Is it true that both trade credit and accruals represent a spontaneous source of capital to finance growth? Explain.

18-4 Is it true that most firms are able to obtain some "free" trade credit, and that additional trade credit is often available, but at a cost? Explain.

18-5 What kinds of firms use commercial paper? Could Pappa Gus's Corner Grocery borrow on commercial paper?

18-6 From the standpoint of the borrower, is long-term or short-term credit riskier? Explain. Would it ever make sense to borrow on a short-term basis if short-term rates were above long-term rates?

18-7 If long-term credit exposes a borrower to less risk, why would people or firms borrow on a short-term basis?

18-8 Suppose a firm can borrow at the prime rate and also sell commercial paper.

    a. If the prime rate is 9 percent, what is a reasonable estimate for the cost of commercial paper?

    b. If a substantial cost differential exists, why might a firm such as this one actually borrow some of its funds from both markets?

Self-Test Problem

ST-1 (Trade credit versus bank credit) The Shrieves Company buys on terms of 1/10, net 30, but it has not been taking discounts and has actually been paying in 60 days rather than 30 days. Shrieves' balance sheet follows (in thousands of dollars):

Cash	$ 50	Accounts payable[a]	$ 500
Accounts receivable	450	Notes payable	50
Inventories	750	Accruals	50
Current assets	$1,250	Current liabilities	$ 600
		Long-term debt	150
Fixed assets	750	Common equity	1,250
Total assets	$2,000	Total claims	$2,000

[a]Stated net of discounts.

Now the firm's suppliers are threatening to stop shipments unless the company begins making prompt payments (that is, pays in 30 days or less). The firm can borrow on a 1-year note (call this a current liability) from its bank at a rate of 15 percent, discount interest, with a 20 percent compensating balance required. (All of the cash now on hand is needed for transactions; it cannot be used as part of the compensating balance.)

a. Determine what action Shrieves should take by calculating (1) the cost of non-free trade credit, and (2) the cost of the bank loan.

b. Based on your decision on Part a, construct a pro forma balance sheet. (Hint: You will need to include an account entitled "prepaid interest" under current assets.)

Problems

18-1 (Cost of trade credit) Suppose a firm makes purchases of $3,000,000 per year under terms of 2/10, net 30. It takes discounts.

a. What is the average amount of accounts payable, net of discounts? (Assume the $3.0 million purchases are net of discounts; that is, gross purchases are $3,061,224, discounts are $61,224, and net purchases are $3.0 million. Also, use 360 days in a year.)

b. Is there a cost of the trade credit it uses?

c. If it did not take discounts, what would its average payables be, and what would be the cost of this nonfree trade credit?

d. What would its cost of not taking discounts be if it "stretched" its payments to 40 days?

18-2 (Trade credit versus bank credit) Butler Corporation projects an increase in sales from $2 million to $2.5 million, but the company needs an additional $300,000 of current assets to support this expansion. The money can be obtained from the bank at an interest rate of 10 percent. Alternatively, Butler can finance the expansion by no longer taking discounts, thus increasing accounts payable. Butler purchases under terms of 1/10, net 30, but it currently can delay payment for an additional 30 days, paying in 60 days and thus becoming 30 days past due, without a penalty.

a. Based strictly on an interest rate comparison, how should Butler finance its expansion?

b. What additional qualitative factors should be considered in reaching a decision?

18-3 (Accounts payable) The Kretovich Copper Corporation had sales of $3,000,000 last year and earned a 5 percent return, after taxes, on sales. Although its terms of purchase are 20 days, its accounts payable represent 60 days' purchases. Suppliers are threatening to cut off the firm's purchases, so Kretovich's president is seeking to increase the company's bank borrowings in order to become current (that is, have 20 days' payables outstanding) in meeting its trade obligations. The company's balance sheet is shown below (in thousands of dollars):

Cash	$ 25	Accounts payable	$ 300
Accounts receivable	125	Bank loans	250
Inventory	650	Accruals	125
Current assets	$ 800	Current liabilities	$ 675
Land and buildings	250	Mortgage on real estate	250
Equipment	250	Common stock, par 10¢	125
		Retained earnings	250
Total assets	$1,300	Total claims	$1,300

a. How much financing is needed to eliminate past-due accounts payable?

b. Would you as a bank loan officer make the loan? Why?

c. Suppose Kretovich had these choices for raising the needed capital:

(1) Borrow from the bank on a line of credit. The loan would be written as a 90-day, discount interest loan with a nominal rate of 12 percent. A 20 percent compensating balance would be required.

(2) Negotiate with suppliers and arrange to buy on terms of 7.5/10, net 30.

(3) Sell subordinated convertible debentures with a 10 percent annual coupon rate. Kretovich's stock currently sells for $30; the conversion price would be $35; the expected growth rate is 10 percent; and the convertibles would not be callable for 10 years, and then they would be callable at par. The convertibles would initially sell at par.

Which of these borrowing methods would you recommend, and why? What would Kretovich's key ratios be just after the new financing had been put into effect?

18-4 (Cash conversion cycle) A firm has an average age of accounts receivable of 53 days, an average age of accounts payable of 42 days, and an average age of inventory of 70 days.

a. What is the length of the firm's cash conversion cycle?

b. If the firm's annual sales are $1,323,000, what is its investment in accounts receivable?

18-5 (Alternative credit sources) Water Park, Incorporated (WPI), estimates that as a result of the seasonal nature of its business, it will require an additional $350,000 of cash for the month of July. WPI has the following four alternatives available for raising the needed funds:

(1) Establish a 1-year line of credit for $350,000 with a commercial bank. The commitment fee will be 0.5 percent per year on the unused portion, and the interest charge on the used funds will be 12 percent per year. Assume that the funds are needed only in July, and that there are 30 days in July and 360 days in the year.

(2) Forego the trade discount of 3/10, net 40, on $350,000 of purchases during July.

(3) Issue $350,000 of 30-day commercial paper at an 11.4 percent annual interest rate. The total transactions fee, including the cost of a backup credit line, on using commercial paper is 0.5 percent of the amount of the issue.

(4) Issue $350,000 of 60-day commercial paper at an 11.0 percent annual interest rate, plus a transactions fee of 0.5 percent. Since the funds are required for

only 30 days, the excess funds ($350,000) can be invested in marketable se-
curities for the month of August earning 10.8 percent annually. The total
transactions cost of purchasing and selling the marketable securities is 0.4
percent of the amount of the issue.

a. What is the cost of each financing arrangement?

b. Is the source with the lowest expected cost necessarily the one to select?
Why or why not?

18-6 (Working capital financing policy) Three companies — Aggressive, Between, and
Conservative — have different working capital management policies as implied by their
names. For example, Aggressive employs only minimal current assets, and it finances
almost entirely with current liabilities plus equity. This "tight-ship" approach has a dual
effect. It keeps total assets low, which tends to increase return on assets; but because
of stock-outs and credit rejections, total sales are reduced, and since inventory is ordered more frequently and in smaller quantities, variable costs are increased. Condensed balance sheets for the three companies are presented below.

	Aggressive	Between	Conservative
Current assets	$150,000	$200,000	$300,000
Fixed assets	200,000	200,000	200,000
Total assets	$350,000	$400,000	$500,000
Current liabilities (cost = 12%)	$200,000	$100,000	$ 50,000
Long-term debt (cost = 10%)	0	100,000	200,000
Total debt	$200,000	$200,000	$250,000
Equity	150,000	200,000	250,000
Total claims	$350,000	$400,000	$500,000
Current ratio	0.75:1	2:1	6:1

The cost of goods sold functions for the three firms are as follows:

Cost of goods sold = Fixed costs + Variable costs.

Aggressive: Cost of goods sold = $200,000 + 0.70(Sales).

Between: Cost of goods sold = $270,000 + 0.65(Sales).

Conservative: Cost of goods sold = $385,000 + 0.60(Sales).

Because of the working capital differences, sales for the three firms under different
economic conditions are expected to vary as indicated next:

	Aggressive	Between	Conservative
Strong economy	$1,200,000	$1,250,000	$1,300,000
Average economy	900,000	1,000,000	1,150,000
Weak economy	700,000	800,000	1,050,000

a. Construct income statements for each company for strong, average, and weak
economies using the following format:

- Sales
- Less cost of goods sold
- Earnings before interest and taxes (EBIT)
- Less interest expense

- Taxable income
- Less taxes (at 40%)
- Net income

b. Compare the basic earning power (EBIT/Assets) and return on equity (Net income/Equity) for the companies. Which company is best in a strong economy? In an average economy? In a weak economy?

(Do Parts c, d, and e only if you are using the computerized diskette.)

c. Suppose, with sales at the normal-economy level, short-term interest rates rose to 25 percent. How would that affect the three firms?

d. Suppose that because of production slowdowns caused by inventory shortages, the aggressive company's variable cost ratio rises to 80 percent. What would happen to its ROE, assuming a normal economy and a short-term rate of 12 percent?

e. What considerations for management of working capital are indicated by this problem?

Solution to Self-Test Problem

ST-1   a. Shrieves can take discounts, in which case it will have ($500,000/60)(10) = $83,333 in accounts payable. In this case, it would have to obtain $500,000 − $83,333 = $416,667 from the bank. (The $416,667 understates the amount of the bank loan because of compensating balances and the interest discount.) Alternatively, if Shrieves pays in 30 days, it will have ($500,000/60)(30) = $250,000 in accounts payable. To reach this position, it will have to obtain $500,000 − $250,000 = $250,000 from the bank.

(1) The approximate cost of the non-free trade credit is 18.18 percent:

$$(1/99)(360/20) = 18.18\%.$$

However, the effective annual rate is 19.83 percent:

$$\text{Effective cost} = (1.0101)^{18} - 1.0$$
$$= 1.1983 - 1.0$$
$$= 0.1983 = 19.83\%.$$

(2) The effective cost of the bank loan is found as follows:

$$\frac{\text{Nominal rate}}{1.0 - \text{Nominal rate (fraction)} - \text{CB (fraction)}} = \frac{15\%}{1 - 0.15 - 0.2} = 23.08\%.$$

Alternative calculation:

$$\frac{\text{Interest paid}}{\text{Funds obtained}} = \frac{\$96,154}{\$416,667} = 23.08\%.$$

Therefore, since the cost of non-free trade credit is less than the cost of the bank loan, Shrieves should not take discounts.

b. Shrieves will need $250,000. To obtain the use of this amount of money, it will have to borrow $384,615:

$$\text{Loan} - 0.15(\text{Loan}) - 0.2(\text{Loan}) = \$250,000$$

$$\text{Loan} (1 - 0.15 - 0.2) = \$250,000$$

$$\text{Loan} = \frac{\$250,000}{1 - 0.15 - 0.2} = \frac{\$250,000}{0.65} = \$384,615.$$

$$\text{Check: } \$384,615 - \text{Interest} - \text{Compensating balance}$$

$$= \$384,615 - 0.15(\$384,615) - 0.2(\$384,615)$$

$$= \$384,615 - \$57,692 - \$76,923 = \$250,000.$$

$$\text{Effective cost} = \frac{\$57,692}{\$250,000} = 23.08\%.$$

Pro Forma Balance Sheet (Thousands of Dollars)

Cash[a]	$ 126.9	Accounts payable	$ 250.0
Accounts receivable	450.0	Notes payable[b]	434.6
Inventory	750.0	Accruals	50.0
Prepaid interest	57.7	Total current liabilities	$ 734.6
Total current assets	$1,384.6	Long-term debt	150.0
Fixed assets	750.0	Common equity	1,250.0
Total assets	$2,134.6	Total claims	$2,134.6

[a]$384,615(0.2) = \$76,923 = $ Compensating balance.
Cash $= \$50 + \$76.923 = \$126.9$.

[b]Notes payable $= \$50 + \$384.6 = \$434.6$.

Selected Additional References and Cases

The following articles provide more information on overall working capital policy and management:

Lambrix, R. J., and S. S. Singhvi, "Managing the Working Capital Cycle," *Financial Executive,* June 1979, 32–41.

Maier, Steven F., and James H. Vander Weide, "A Practical Approach to Short-Run Financial Planning," *Financial Management,* Winter 1978, 10–16.

Merville, Larry J., and Lee A. Tavis, "Optimal Working Capital Policies: A Chance-Constrained Programming Approach," *Journal of Financial and Quantitative Analysis,* January 1973, 47–60.

Yardini, Edward E., "A Portfolio-Balance Model of Corporate Working Capital," *Journal of Finance,* May 1979, 535–552.

For more on trade credit, see

Brosky, John J., *The Implicit Cost of Trade Credit and Theory of Optimal Terms of Sale* (New York: Credit Research Foundation, 1969).

Schwartz, Robert A., "An Economic Analysis of Trade," *Journal of Financial and Quantitative Analysis,* September 1974, 643–658.

For more on bank lending and commercial credit in general, see

Campbell, Tim S., "A Model of the Market for Lines of Credit," *Journal of Finance,* March 1978, 231–243.

Stone, Bernell K., "Allocating Credit Lines, Planned Borrowing, and Tangible Services over a Company's Banking System," *Financial Management,* Summer 1975, 65–78.

For a discussion of effective yields, see

Finnerty, John D., "Bank Discount, Coupon Equivalent, and Compound Yields: Comment," *Financial Management,* Summer 1983, 40–44.

Glasgo, Philip W., William J. Landes, and A. Frank Thompson, "Bank Discount, Coupon Equivalent, and Compound Yields," *Financial Management,* Autumn 1982, 80–84.

The following case is appropriate for use with this chapter:

Case 9, "Conover Container Corporation," in the Crum-Brigham casebook, which illustrates how changes in working capital policy affect expected profitability and risk.

19
Accounts Receivable and Inventory

Most security analysts were forecasting Xerox's sales and earnings to fall during the recent recession. But it did not happen — earnings rose 10 percent on a 23 percent sales gain. The secret, analysts learned, was that Xerox had instituted a major change in its credit policy — it had built up a pool of cash which it then loaned to its customers at bargain rates in order to increase sales of its products. Profits on the added sales more than offset the cost to Xerox of the low-rate loans, boosting the company's net income at a time when its competitors' profits were falling.

Xerox liberalized its credit policy and gained, but other companies, faced with different conditions, have increased their profits by tightening or even eliminating credit. For example, Atlantic Richfield Company (Arco) recently announced plans to eliminate the use of credit cards at all of its service stations. Its management believed (1) that customers were very sensitive to gasoline prices; (2) that the cost of extending credit to customers amounted to about 4 cents per gallon; (3) that if it eliminated credit sales it could cut gas prices at the pump by 3 cents a gallon, which would boost profit per gallon by 1 cent and at the same time double its number of customers; and (4) that consequently it would enjoy a substantial increase in net profits. The plan worked beautifully, and it contributed to Arco's overall success.

Besides their credit policies, companies are also very much concerned with inventory policies. The cost of money used to buy and carry inventories is about 15 percent for many firms, and storage, insurance, pilferage, and obsolescence amount to another 10 to 15 percent. Thus, holding $100 of inventory for a year has a cost in the range of $25 to $30. With these high costs, holding excessive inventories can literally ruin a company. On the other hand, inventory shortages lead to lost sales, to production interruptions, and to customer ill will, so shortages can be just as harmful as excesses.

Many firms today are using computerized inventory control models to match stocks on hand with forecasted sales levels, and they are coordinating closely with suppliers to reduce average inventory levels. For example,

Huffy Corporation, the largest U.S. bicycle manufacturer, was able to reduce its peak spring inventory from $69 million to $36 million through a better inventory control process. Huffy is saving millions of dollars in interest and storage costs by keeping a pared-down inventory, with no adverse effect on sales. However, such a policy is not without dangers — if bicycle sales surge, Huffy's inventories might not be sufficient to meet demand, causing the company to lose sales to its rivals, who are continuing to carry higher inventories. Note, though, that if sales fall, Huffy will be in a better position than its rivals, and if consumers begin to demand bicycles of different styles, Huffy will be able to adapt more easily than its competitors, who will be stuck with obsolete bicycles.

Our goal in this chapter is to examine the factors that companies like Xerox, Arco, and Huffy consider when they establish credit and inventory policies. From the standpoint of profitability, no decisions have a greater effect.

Since the typical firm has about 20 percent of its assets in receivables and another 20 percent in inventories, its effectiveness in managing these two accounts is obviously important to its profitability and risk — and thus to its stock price.

RECEIVABLES MANAGEMENT

Firms would, in general, rather sell for cash than on credit, but competitive pressures force most firms to offer credit. Thus, goods are shipped, inventories are reduced, and an account receivable is created. Eventually, the customer pays the account, at which time (1) the firm receives cash and (2) its receivables decline. Managing receivables has both direct and indirect costs, but it also has an important benefit — granting credit increases sales. The optimal credit policy is the one which maximizes the firm's cash flows over time, giving consideration to the risk assumed.

The total amount of accounts receivable outstanding at any given time is determined by two factors: (1) the volume of credit sales and (2) the average length of time between sales and collections. For example, suppose the Boston Lumber Company (BLC), a wholesale distributor of lumber products, opens a warehouse on January 1 and, starting the first day, makes sales of $1,000 each day. (For simplicity, we assume that all sales are on credit.) Customers are given 10 days in which to pay. At the end of the first day, accounts receivable will be $1,000; they will rise to $2,000 by the end of the second day; and by January 10, they will have risen to 10($1,000) = $10,000. On January 11, another $1,000 will be added to receivables, but payments for sales made on January 1 will reduce receivables by $1,000, so total accounts receivable will remain constant at $10,000. In general, once the firm's operations have stabilized, this situation will exist:

$$\frac{\text{Accounts}}{\text{receivable}} = \frac{\text{Credit sales}}{\text{per day}} \times \frac{\text{Length of}}{\text{collection period}}$$

$$= \quad \$1,000 \quad \times \quad 10 \text{ days} \quad = \$10,000.$$

If either the volume of credit sales or the collection period changes, these changes will be reflected in accounts receivable as reported on the balance sheet.

Notice that the $10,000 investment in receivables must be financed. To illustrate, suppose that when the store opened on January 1, BLC's shareholders had put up $800 as common stock and used this money to buy the goods sold the first day. The $800 worth of inventory will be sold for $1,000; thus, BLC's gross margin is $200 or 25 percent. In this situation, the initial balance sheet would be as follows:[1]

Inventories	$800	Common equity	$800
Total assets	$800	Total claims	$800

At the end of the day, the balance sheet would look like this:

Accounts receivable	$1,000	Common equity	$ 800
Inventories	0	Retained earnings	$ 200
Total assets	$1,000	Total claims	$1,000

In order to remain in business, BLC must replenish inventories. To do so requires that $800 of goods be purchased, and this requires $800 in cash. Assuming that BLC borrows the $800 from the bank, the balance sheet at the start of the second day will be as follows:

Accounts receivable	$1,000	Notes payable to bank	$ 800
Inventories	800	Common equity	800
		Retained earnings	200
Total assets	$1,800	Total claims	$1,800

At the end of the second day, the inventories will have been converted to receivables, and the firm will have to borrow another $800 to restock for the third day.

This process will continue, provided the bank is willing to lend the necessary funds, until the beginning of the eleventh day, when the balance sheet reads as follows:

---

[1]Note that the firm would need other assets such as cash, fixed assets, and a permanent stock of inventory. Also, overhead costs would have to be deducted, so retained earnings would be less than the figures shown here. We abstract from these details here so that we may focus on receivables.

Accounts receivable	$10,000	Notes payable to bank	$ 8,000
Inventories	800	Common equity	800
		Retained earnings	2,000
Total assets	$10,800	Total claims	$10,800

From this point on, $1,000 of receivables will be collected every day, and $800 of these funds can be used to purchase new inventories.

This example should make it clear (1) that accounts receivable depend jointly on the level of credit sales and the collection period, (2) that any increase in receivables must be financed in some manner, but (3) that the entire amount of receivables does not have to be financed because the profit portion ($200 of each $1,000 of sales) does not represent a cash outflow. In our example, we assumed bank financing, but, as noted in Chapter 18, there are many alternative ways to finance current assets.

Monitoring the Receivables Position

The optimal credit policy, and hence the optimal amount of accounts receivable carried on the balance sheet, depends on the firm's own unique operating conditions. For example, a firm with excess capacity and low variable production costs should extend credit more liberally and carry a higher level of receivables than a firm operating at full capacity on a slim profit margin. Thus, optimal credit policies vary among firms, and even for a single firm over time. Investors — both stockholders and bank loan officers — should pay close attention to accounts receivable management, for otherwise they could be misled by reported financial statements and later suffer serious losses on their investments.

When a credit sale is made, the following events occur: (1) Inventories are reduced by the cost of goods sold, (2) accounts receivable are increased by the sales price, and (3) the difference is profit which is added to retained earnings. If the sale is for cash, the profit is definitely earned, but if the sale is on credit, the profit is not actually earned unless and until the account is collected. Firms have been known to encourage "sales" to very weak customers in order to inflate reported profits. This could boost the firm's stock price, at least until credit losses begin to lower earnings, at which time the stock price will fall. Analyses along the lines suggested in the following sections would detect any such questionable practice, as well as any unconscious deterioration in the quality of accounts receivable. Such early detection could help both investors and bankers avoid losses.[2]

---

[2]Accountants are increasingly interested in these matters. Investors have sued several of the Big Eight accounting firms for substantial damages when (1) profits were overstated and (2) it could be shown that the auditors should have conducted an analysis along the lines described here and then reported the results to stockholders on the audited financial statements.

Average Collection Period

Suppose Super Sets, Inc., a television manufacturer, sells 200,000 television sets a year at a sales price of $198 each. Further, assume that all sales are on credit, with terms of 2/10, net 30. Finally, assume that 70 percent of the customers take discounts and pay on Day 10, while the other 30 percent pay on Day 30.

Super Sets' *average collection period (ACP)* is 16 days:

$$\text{ACP} = 0.7(10 \text{ days}) + 0.3(30 \text{ days}) = 16 \text{ days}.$$

The ACP is sometimes called *days sales outstanding (DSO)*.

Super Sets' *average daily sales (ADS)*, assuming a 360-day year, is $110,000:

$$\text{ADS} = \frac{\text{Annual sales}}{360} = \frac{200,000(\$198)}{360}$$

$$= \frac{\$39,600,000}{360} = \$110,000.$$

Super Sets' accounts receivable, assuming a constant, uniform rate of sales all during the year, will at any point in time be $1,760,000:[3]

$$\text{Receivables} = (\text{ADS})(\text{ACP}) = (\$110,000)(16) = \$1,760,000.$$

Finally, note that its ACP is a measure of the average length of time it takes Super Sets' customers to pay off their credit purchases, and the ACP is often compared with an industry average ACP. For example, if all television manufacturers sell on the same credit terms, and if the industry average ACP is 25 days versus Super Sets' 16-day ACP, then Super Sets is collecting its receivables relatively rapidly.

The ACP can also be compared with the firm's own credit terms. For example, suppose Super Sets' ACP had been running at a level of 35 days versus its 2/10, net 30, credit terms. With a 35-day ACP, some customers would obviously be taking more than 30 days to pay their bills. In fact, some customers would surely be paying within 10 days to take advantage of the discount, so the others would, on average, be taking longer than 35 days. One way to check this possibility is to use an aging schedule as described in the next section.

Aging Schedules

An *aging schedule* breaks down a firm's receivables by age of account. Table 19-1 contains the December 31, 1987 aging schedules of two television manufacturers, Super Sets and Wonder Vision. Both firms offer the same credit terms, 2/10, net 30, and both show the same dollar amount of receivables. Note that Super Sets' aging schedule indicates that none of its customers are past due — in fact, 70 per-

---

[3]Note that the ACP can be calculated, given a firm's accounts receivable balance and its average daily credit sales, as follows:

$$\text{ACP} = \frac{\text{Receivables}}{\text{Annual sales}/360} = \frac{\text{Receivables}}{\text{ADS}} = \frac{\$1,760,000}{\$110,000} = 16 \text{ days}.$$

Table 19-1
Aging Schedules

Age of Account (Days)	Super Sets		Wonder Vision	
	Value of Account	Percentage of Total Value	Value of Account	Percentage of Total Value
0–10	$1,232,000	70%	$ 825,000	47%
11–30	528,000	30	460,000	26
31–45	0	0	265,000	15
46–60	0	0	179,000	10
Over 60	0	0	31,000	2
Total receivables	$1,760,000	100%	$1,760,000	100%

cent pay on Day 10 while 30 percent pay on Day 30. However, Wonder Vision's schedule shows that many of its customers are not abiding by its credit terms — some 27 percent of its receivables are more than 30 days due, even though Wonder Vision's credit terms call for full payment by Day 30.

Aging schedules cannot be constructed from the summary data reported in financial statements; data on individual accounts must be extracted from the firm's accounts receivable ledger. However, well-run firms have computerized their accounts receivable records, so it is easy to determine the age of each invoice, to sort electronically by age categories, and thus to generate an aging schedule. Note, though, that although the aging schedule provides more information than does the ACP taken alone, an even better way to analyze accounts receivable is discussed in the next section.

The Payments Pattern Approach

The primary point in analyzing the accounts receivable situation is to see if customers are slowing down their payments. If so, the firm will have to increase its receivables financing and hence increase its cost of carrying receivables. Further, the payment slowdown may lead to an increase in bad debt losses down the road. The ACP and aging schedules are useful in monitoring credit operations, but both are affected by increases and decreases in a firm's level of sales. Thus, changes in sales levels, including normal seasonal or cyclical changes, can change a firm's ACP and aging schedule even though its customers' payment behavior has not changed at all. For this reason, a procedure called the *payments pattern approach* has been developed to measure any changes that might be occurring in customers' payment behavior.[4] To illustrate the payments pattern approach, consider the credit sales

---

[4]See Wilbur G. Lewellen and Robert W. Johnson, "A Better Way to Monitor Accounts Receivable," *Harvard Business Review,* May-June 1972, 101–109; and Bernell Stone, "The Payments-Pattern Approach to the Forecasting and Control of Accounts Receivable," *Financial Management,* Autumn 1976 65–82.

Table 19-2
Hanover Manufacturing Company:
Receivables Data for 1987
(Thousands of Dollars)

Month (1)	Sales (2)	End of Month Receivables (3)	Quarterly		Cumulative (Year to Date)	
			ADS[a] (4)	ACP[b] (5)	ADS (6)	ACP (7)
January	$ 60	$ 54				
February	60	90				
March	60	102	$2.00	51 days	$2.00	51 days
April	60	102				
May	90	129				
June	120	174	3.00	58	2.50	70
July	120	198				
August	90	177				
September	60	132	3.00	44	2.67	49
October	60	108				
November	60	102				
December	60	102	2.00	51	2.50	41

[a]ADS = Average daily sales.
[b]ACP = Average collection period.

of Hanover Manufacturing Company, a small manufacturer of hand tools which commenced operations in January 1987. Table 19-2 contains Hanover's credit sales and receivables data for 1987. Column 2 shows that Hanover's credit sales are seasonal, with the lowest sales in the fall and winter months and the highest sales during the summer.

Now assume that 10 percent of Hanover's customers pay in the same month that the sale is made, that 30 percent pay in the first month following the sale, that 40 percent pay in the second month, and that the remaining 20 percent pay in the third month. Further, assume that Hanover's customers have the same payment behavior throughout the year; that is, they always take the same length of time to pay. On the basis of this payment pattern, Column 3 of Table 19-2 contains Hanover's receivables balance at the end of each month. For example, during January, Hanover has $60,000 in sales. Ten percent of the customers paid during the month of sale, so the receivables balance at the end of January was $60,000 − $0.1($60,000) = (1.0 − 0.1)($60,000) = 0.9($60,000) = $54,000. By the end of February, 10% + 30% = 40% of the customers had paid for January's sales, and 10 percent had paid for February's sales. Thus, the receivables balance at the end of February was 0.6($60,000) + 0.9($60,000) = $90,000. By the end of March, 80 percent of January's sales had been paid, 40 percent of February's had been paid, and 10 percent of March's sales had been paid, so the receivables balance was 0.2($60,000) + 0.6($60,000) + 0.9($60,000) = $102,000. And so on.

Columns 4 and 5 give Hanover's average daily sales (ADS) and average collection period (ACP) respectively, as these measures would be calculated from quarterly financial statements. For example, in the April-June quarter, ADS = ($60,000 + $90,000 + $120,000)/90 = $3,000, and the end-of-quarter (June 30) ACP = $174,000/$3,000 = 58 days.

Columns 6 and 7 also show ADS and ACP, but here they are calculated on the basis of accumulated sales data for the year to date. For example, at the end of June, ADS = $450,000/180 = $2,500 and ACP = $174,000/$2,500 = 70 days. (For the entire year, sales are $900,000, ADS = $2,500, and ACP at year-end = 41 days. These last two figures are shown in the lower right corner of the table.)

The data in Table 19-2 illustrate two major points. First, the ACP is changing, which could mislead us into thinking that customers are paying faster or slower, even though customer payment patterns are actually not changing at all. The rising monthly sales trend causes the calculated ACP to rise, whereas falling sales (as in the third quarter) cause the calculated ACP to fall, even though nothing is changing with regard to when customers pay. Second, we see that the ACP is based on an averaging procedure, and results can change depending on whether quarterly, semiannual, or annual data are used. Therefore, it is difficult to use the ACP as a monitoring device for a firm whose sales exhibit seasonal or cyclical patterns, and it is also difficult to make comparisons between different firms that are growing at different rates.

Seasonal or cyclical variations also make it difficult to interpret aging schedules. Table 19-3 contains Hanover's aging schedules at the end of each quarter of 1987. At the end of June, Table 19-2 showed that Hanover's receivables balance was $174,000. Eighty percent of April's $60,000 of sales had been paid, 40 percent of May's $90,000 sales had been paid, and 10 percent of June's $120,000 sales had been paid. Thus, the end-of-June receivables balance consisted of 0.2($60,000) = $12,000 of April sales, 0.6($90,000) = $54,000 of May sales, and 0.9($120,000) = $108,000 of June sales. Note again that Hanover's customers had not changed

Table 19-3
Hanover Manufacturing Company:
Aging Schedules for 1987
(Thousands of Dollars)

Age of Accounts (Days)	Aging Schedules at Different End-of-Quarter Dates							
	March 31		June 30		September 30		December 31	
0–30	$ 54	53%	$108	62%	$ 54	41%	$ 54	53%
31–60	36	35	54	31	54	41	36	35
61–90	12	12	12	7	24	18	12	12
	$102	100%	$174	100%	$132	100%	$102	100%

their payment patterns. However, rising sales during the second quarter created the impression of faster payments when judged by the percentage aging schedule, and falling sales after July created the opposite appearance. Thus, neither the ACP nor the aging schedule provides the financial manager with an accurate picture of customers' payment patterns in this instance, which is, unfortunately, typical.

With this background, we can now examine another basic tool, the *uncollected balances schedule.* Table 19-4 contains Hanover's quarterly uncollected balances schedules. At the end of each quarter, the dollar amount of receivables remaining from each month's sales is divided by that month's sales to obtain the receivables-to-sales ratio. For example, at the end of the first quarter, $12,000 of the $60,000 January sales, or 20 percent, are still outstanding; 60 percent of February sales are still out; and 90 percent of March sales are uncollected. Exactly the same situation is revealed at the end of the next three quarters. Thus, Table 19-4 shows Hanover's financial manager that customers' payment behavior has not changed over the year.

Of course, in the example we assumed the existence of a constant payments pattern at the very beginning. In a normal situation, the firm's customers' payments

Table 19-4
Hanover Manufacturing Company:
End-of-Quarter Uncollected Balances Schedules for 1987
(Thousands of Dollars)

Quarter	Month's Sales	Receivables for Month's Sales Remaining Uncollected at End of the Quarter	Receivables/Sales
Quarter 1:			
January	$ 60	$ 12	20%
February	60	36	60
March	60	54	90
		$102	170%
Quarter 2:			
April	$ 60	$ 12	20%
May	90	54	60
June	120	108	90
		$174	170%
Quarter 3:			
July	$120	$ 24	20%
August	90	54	60
September	60	54	90
		$132	170%
Quarter 4:			
October	$ 60	$ 12	20%
November	60	36	60
December	60	54	90
		$102	170%

patterns would probably vary somewhat over time. Such variations would be shown in the last column of the uncollected balances schedule. For example, suppose the May purchasers paid their accounts slower than assumed initially. That might cause the second quarter uncollected balances schedule to look like this (in thousands of dollars):

Quarter 2 1987	Sales	Receivables	Receivables/Sales
April	$ 60	$ 12	20%
May	90	70	78
June	120	108	90
		$190	188%

We see that the receivables-to-sales ratio was higher in May than in February, the corresponding month in the first quarter. This caused the total uncollected balances percentage to rise from 170 to 188 percent, which in turn would alert Hanover's managers that customers are paying slower than they did earlier in the year.

The uncollected balances schedule not only permits a firm to monitor its receivables better, but it can also be used to forecast future receivables balances. When Hanover's pro forma 1988 quarterly balance sheets are constructed, management can use the receivables-to-sales ratios, coupled with monthly sales estimates, to project each quarter's receivables balance. For example, with projected sales as given below, and using the same payments pattern as in 1987, Hanover's projected end-of-June receivables balance would be as follows:

Quarter 2 1988	Projected Sales	Receivables/Sales	Projected Receivables
April	$ 70,000	20%	$ 14,000
May	100,000	60	60,000
June	140,000	90	126,000
		Total projected receivables =	$200,000

The payments pattern approach permits us to remove the effects of seasonal and/or cyclical sales variation and hence construct an accurate measure of customers' payment patterns. Thus, it provides financial managers with better information than such crude measures as the average collection period or the aging schedule. Practicing financial managers use the payments pattern approach to monitor collection performance as well as to project future receivables requirements.

Except possibly in the inventory and cash management areas, nowhere in the typical firm have computers had more of an impact than in accounts receivable management. A well-run business will use a computer system to record sales, to send out bills, to keep track of when payments are made, to alert the credit manager when an account becomes past due, and to ensure that actions are taken to collect past due accounts (for example, to prepare form letters requesting payment) automatically. Additionally, the payment history of each customer can be summarized and used to help establish credit limits for customers and classes of customers, and the data on each account can be aggregated and used for the firm's accounts receivable monitoring system. Finally, historical data can be stored in the firm's data base and used to develop inputs for studies related to credit policy changes as discussed in the next section.

CREDIT POLICY

It would be easy to insure that accounts receivable are collected promptly — sell only to extremely strong customers, and use stringent credit terms. However, the success or failure of a business depends primarily on the demand for its products — as a rule, the higher its sales, the larger its profits and the higher the price of its stock. Sales, in turn, depend on a number of factors, some exogenous but others under the control of the firm. The major controllable variables which affect demand are sales prices, product quality, advertising, and *the firm's credit policy.* Credit policy, in turn, consists of these four variables:

1. The *credit period,* which is the length of time allowed buyers to pay for their purchases.

2. The *credit standards,* which refer to the minimum financial strength of acceptable credit customers.

3. The firm's *collection policy,* which is measured by its toughness or laxity in following up on slow-paying accounts.

4. Any *discounts* given for early payment.

The credit manager has the responsibility for administering the firm's credit policy. However, because of the pervasive importance of credit, the credit policy itself is normally established by the executive committee, which usually consists of the president and the vice presidents in charge of finance, marketing, and production.

SETTING THE CREDIT PERIOD AND STANDARDS

A firm's regular credit terms, which include the *credit period,* might call for sales on a 2/10, net 30 basis to all "qualified" customers. Its *credit standards* would be applied to determine which customers are qualified for the regular credit terms, and the amount of credit available to each customer. The focal point when considering credit standards is the likelihood that a given customer will pay on time, pay slowly, or end up as a bad debt loss. This requires a measurement of *credit quality,* which is defined in terms of the probability of timely payment. The probability estimate for a given customer is, for the most part, a subjective judgment, but credit evaluation is a well-established practice, and a good credit manager can make reasonably accurate judgments regarding the probability of payment by different classes of customers.

Credit-Scoring Systems

Although most credit decisions are subjective, many firms are starting to use a sophisticated statistical method called *multiple discriminant analysis (MDA)*, which is similar to multiple regression analysis. The dependent variable is, in essence, the probability of default, and the independent variables are various factors associated with financial strength and the ability to pay off the debt if credit is extended. For example, if a firm such as Sears evaluated consumers' credit quality, then the independent variables in the credit scoring system would be such factors as these: (1) Does the credit applicant own his or her own home? (2) How long has the applicant worked on his or her current job? (3) What is the applicant's outstanding debt in relation to his or her annual income? (4) Does the potential customer have a history of paying his or her debts on time?

One major advantage of an MDA credit-scoring system is that a customer's credit quality is expressed as a single numerical value, rather than as a subjective assessment of various factors. This is a tremendous advantage for a large firm which must evaluate many customers in many different locations using many different credit approvers, for without an automated procedure, the firm would have a hard time applying uniform standards to all credit applicants. Therefore, most credit card companies, department stores, oil companies, building supply chains, manufacturers of electrical products, and the like use credit-scoring systems to determine who gets how much credit.

Multiple discriminant analysis is discussed in detail in Appendix 21A in connection with financial statement analysis. For now, we will briefly describe the concept. Suppose Hanover Manufacturing has historical information on 500 of its customers, all of whom are retail businesses. Of these 500, assume that 400 have always paid on time, but the other 100 either paid late, or, in some cases, went bankrupt and did not pay at all. Further, Hanover has historical data on each customer's quick ratio, times-interest-earned ratio, debt ratio, years in existence, and so on. Multiple discriminant analysis relates the experienced record of late payment or nonpayment with various measures of a firm's financial condition, and MDA assigns weights to these critical factors. In effect, MDA produces an equation that looks much like a regression equation, and when data on a customer are plugged into the equation, then a credit score for that customer is produced.

For example, suppose Hanover's multiple discriminant analysis indicates that the critical factors affecting prompt payment are its customers' times-interest-earned ratio (TIE), quick ratio, debt/assets ratio, and number of years in business. Here is the discriminant function:

$$\text{Credit score} = 3.5(\text{TIE}) + 10.0(\text{Quick ratio}) - 25.0(\text{Debt/Assets}) + 1.3(\text{Years in business}).$$

Further, assume that a score less than 40 indicates a poor credit risk, 40–50 indicates an average credit risk, and a score above 50 signifies a good credit risk. Now suppose a firm with the following conditions applies for credit:

$$\text{Times-interest-earned} = 4.2.$$
$$\text{Quick ratio} = 3.1.$$
$$\text{Debt/Assets} = 0.30.$$
$$\text{Years in business} = 10.$$

This firm's credit score would be

$$\text{Score} = 3.5(4.2) + 10.0(3.1) - 25.0(0.30) + 1.3(10) = 51.2.$$

Since its score exceeds 50, this firm would be considered a good credit risk, and consequently it would be offered favorable credit terms.

Sources of Credit Information

Two major sources of external information are available. The first is the work of the *credit associations,* which are local groups that meet frequently and which correspond with one another to exchange information on credit customers. These local groups have also banded together to create Credit Interchange, a system developed by the National Association of Credit Management for assembling and distributing information about debtors' past performance. The Interchange reports show the paying records of different debtors, the industries from which they are buying, and the geographic areas in which they are making purchases. The second source of external information is the work of the *credit-reporting agencies,* which collect credit information and sell it for a fee. The best known of these agencies are Dun & Bradstreet (D&B) and TRW, Incorporated. D&B, TRW, and other agencies provide factual data that can be used in credit analysis; they also provide ratings similar to those available on corporate bonds.[5]

Managing a credit department requires fast, accurate, up-to-date information, and to help get such information, the National Association of Credit Management (a group with 43,000 member firms) persuaded TRW, Inc., to develop a computer-based telecommunication network for the collection, storage, retrieval, and distribution of credit information. The TRW system contains credit data on over 120 million individuals, and it electronically transmits credit reports which are available within seconds to its thousands of subscribers. Dun & Bradstreet has a similar electronic system which covers businesses, plus another service which provides more detailed reports through the U.S. mail.

A typical business credit report would include the following pieces of information:

1. A summary balance sheet and income statement.
2. A number of key ratios, with trend information.

---

[5]For additional information, see Christie and Bracuti, *Credit Management,* a publication of the National Association of Credit Management; and also, see Peter Nulty, "An Upstart Takes on Dun & Bradstreet," *Fortune,* April 9, 1979, 98–100.

3. Information obtained from the firm's suppliers telling whether it has been paying promptly or slowly, and whether it has recently failed to make any payments.

4. A verbal description of the physical condition of the firm's operations.

5. A verbal description of the backgrounds of the firm's owners, including any previous bankruptcies, lawsuits, divorce settlement problems, and the like.

6. A summary rating, ranging from A for the best credit risks down to F for those that are deemed likely to default.

Although a great deal of credit information is available, it must still be processed in a judgmental manner. Computerized information systems can assist in making better credit decisions, but, in the final analysis, most credit decisions are really exercises in informed judgment. Even credit scoring systems require judgment in deciding where to draw the lines, given the set of derived scores.

SETTING THE COLLECTION POLICY

Collection policy refers to the procedures the firm follows to collect past-due accounts. For example, a letter may be sent to customers when a bill is 10 days past due; a more severe letter, followed by a telephone call, may be used if payment is not received within 30 days; and the account may be turned over to a collection agency after 90 days. If the customer is dependent for its materials on our firm, a threat to cut off further supplies will often bring immediate payment.

The collection process can be expensive in terms of both out-of-pocket expenditures and lost goodwill, but at least some firmness is needed to prevent an undue lengthening of the collection period and to minimize outright losses. Again, a balance must be struck between the costs and benefits of different collection policies.

Changes in collection policy influence sales, the collection period, the bad debt loss percentage, and the percentage of customers who take discounts. The effects of a change in collection policy, along with changes in the other credit policy variables, will be analyzed later in the chapter.

CASH DISCOUNTS

The last element in the credit policy decision, the use of *cash discounts* for early payment, is also analyzed by balancing the costs and benefits of different cash discounts. For example, a firm might decide to change its credit terms from "net 30," which means that customers must pay within 30 days, to "2/10, net 30," which means that it will allow a 2 percent discount if payment is received within 10 days, while the full invoice price must otherwise be paid within 30 days. This change should produce two benefits: (1) It should attract new customers who consider discounts to be a type of price reduction, and (2) the discounts should cause a reduction in the average collection period, since some established customers will pay more promptly in order to take advantage of the discount. Offsetting these benefits is the dollar cost of the discounts taken.[6] The optimal discount is established at the point where the marginal costs and benefits are exactly offsetting. The methodology for analyzing changes in the discount is developed later in the chapter.

If sales are seasonal, firms may use *seasonal dating* on discounts. For example, Slimware, Inc., a swimsuit manufacturer, sells on terms of 2/10, net 30, May 1 dating. This means that the effective invoice date is May 1, even if the sale was made back in January. The discount may be taken up to May 10; otherwise, the full amount must be paid on May 30. Slimware produces throughout the year, but retail sales of bathing suits are concentrated in the spring and early summer, and by offering seasonal dating, the company induces some of its customers to stock up early, saving Slimware storage costs and also "nailing down sales."

OTHER FACTORS INFLUENCING CREDIT POLICY

In addition to the factors discussed above, several other conditions also influence a firm's overall credit policy.

Profit Potential

Thus far, we have emphasized the costs of granting credit. *However, if it is possible to sell on credit and also to assess a carrying charge on the receivables that are outstanding, then credit sales can actually be more profitable than cash sales.* This is especially true for consumer durables (autos, appliances, clothing, and so on), but it is also true for certain types of industrial equipment. Thus, GM's General Motors Acceptance Corporation (GMAC) unit, which finances automobiles, is highly profitable, as is Sears Roebuck's credit subsidiary.[7] Some encyclopedia companies are even reported to lose money on cash sales but to more than make up these losses from the carrying charges on their credit sales; obviously, such companies would rather sell on credit than for cash!

The carrying charges on outstanding credit are generally about 18 percent on a nominal interest rate basis: 1.5 percent per month, so $1.5\% \times 12 = 18\%$. This is

---

[6]Note that some firms offer discounts only to customers who pay cash on the spot, because the cost of giving such discounts is offset by the reduction in receivables accounting costs. Also, in certain types of businesses, cash sales are kept off the books and hence profits on them out of reach of the tax collectors.

[7]Companies that do a large volume of sales financing typically set up sudsidiary companies called *captive finance companies* to do the actual financing. Thus, General Motors, Chrysler, and Ford all have captive finance companies, as do Sears Roebuck and Montgomery Ward. The reason for this is that consumer finance companies, because their assets are highly liquid, tend to use far more debt, and especially short-term debt, than manufacturers or retailers. Thus, if GM did not use a captive finance company, its balance sheet would show an exceptionally high debt ratio and a very low current ratio. By setting up GMAC as a separate but wholly owned corporation, and then reporting only its equity investment in the subsidiary rather than a fully consolidated balance sheet which included the subsidiary's debt, GM avoids distorting its own balance sheet, presumably helping it to raise capital on more favorable terms.

equivalent to an effective rate of $(1.015)^{12} - 1.0 = 19.6\%$. Having receivables outstanding that earn over 18 percent is highly profitable.

Legal Considerations

It is illegal, under the Robinson-Patman Act, for a firm to charge prices that discriminate between customers unless these differential prices are cost-justified. The same holds true for credit — it is illegal to offer more favorable credit terms to one customer or class of customers than to another, unless the differences are cost-justified.

Credit Instruments

Most credit is offered on *open account,* which means that the only formal evidence of credit is an invoice which accompanies the shipment and which the buyer signs to indicate that goods have been received. Then, the buyer and the seller each record the purchase on their books of account. Under certain circumstances, the selling firm may require the buyer to sign a *promissory note* evidencing the credit obligation. Promissory notes are useful (1) if the order is very large; (2) if the seller anticipates the possibility of having trouble collecting, because a note is a stronger legal claim than a simple signed invoice; or (3) if the buyer wants a longer-than-usual time in which to pay for the order, because in that case interest should be charged, and interest charges can be built into a promissory note.

Another instrument used in trade credit, especially in international trade, is the *commercial draft.* Here the seller draws up a draft — which is a sort of combination check and promissory note — calling for the buyer to pay a specific amount to the seller on a specified date. This draft is then sent to the buyer's bank, along with the shipping invoices necessary to take possession of the goods. The bank forwards the draft to the buyer, who signs it and returns it to the bank. The bank then delivers the shipping documents to its customer, who at this point can claim the goods. If the draft is a *sight draft,* then upon delivery of the shipping documents and acceptance of the draft by the buyer, the bank actually withdraws money from the buyer's account and forwards it to the selling firm. If the draft is a *time draft,* payable on a specific future date, then the bank returns it to the selling firm. In this case, the draft is called a *trade acceptance,* and it amounts to a promissory note that the seller can hold for future payment or use as collateral for a loan. The bank, in such a situation, has served as an intermediary, making sure that the buyer does not receive title to the goods until the note (or draft) has been executed for the benefit of the seller.

A seller who lacks confidence in the ability or willingness of the buyer to pay off a time draft may refuse to ship without a guarantee of payment by the buyer's bank. Presumably, the bank knows its customers, and for a fee, the bank will guarantee payment of the draft. In this instance, the draft is called a *banker's acceptance.* Such instruments are widely used, especially in foreign trade. They have a low degree of risk if guaranteed by a strong bank, and there is a ready market for acceptances, making it easy for the seller of the goods to sell the instrument to raise immediate cash. (Banker's acceptances are sold at a discount below face value, and then paid off at face value when they mature, so the discount amounts to interest on the acceptance. The effective interest rate on a strong banker's acceptance is a little above the Treasury bill rate of interest.)

A final type of credit instrument that should be mentioned is the *conditional sales contract.* With a conditional sales contract, the seller retains legal ownership of the goods until the buyer has completed payment. Conditional sales contracts are used primarily for such items as machinery, dental equipment, and the like, which are often purchased on an installment basis over a period of two or three years. The significant advantage of a conditional sales contract is that it is easier for the seller to repossess the equipment in the event of default than it would be if title had passed. This feature makes possible some credit sales that otherwise would not be feasible. Conditional sales contracts generally have a market interest rate built into their payment schedules.

ANALYZING PROPOSED CHANGES IN CREDIT POLICY

If the firm's credit policy is *eased* by such actions as lengthening the credit period, relaxing credit standards, following a less tough collection policy, or offering cash discounts, then sales should increase: *Easing the credit policy stimulates sales.* Of course, if credit policy is eased and sales rise, then costs will also rise because more labor, materials, and so on will be required to produce the additional goods. Additionally, receivables outstanding will also increase, which will increase carrying costs, and bad debt and/or discount expenses may also rise. Thus, the key question when deciding on a proposed credit policy change is this: Will sales revenues rise more than costs, including credit-related costs, causing net income to increase, or will the increase in sales revenues be more than offset by the higher costs?

Table 19-5 illustrates the general idea behind credit policy analysis. Column 1 shows the projected 1988 income statement for Monroe Manufacturing under the assumption that the firm's current credit policy is maintained throughout the year. Column 2 shows the expected effects of easing the credit policy by extending the credit period, offering larger discounts, relaxing credit standards, and easing collection efforts. Specifically, Monroe is analyzing the effects of changing its credit terms from 1/10, net 30, to 2/10, net 40, relaxing its credit standards, and putting less pressure on slow-paying customers. Column 3 shows the projected 1988 income statement incorporating the expected effects of an easing in credit policy. The generally looser policy is expected to increase sales and lower collection costs, but discounts and several other types of costs would rise. The overall, bottom line effect is a $7 million increase in projected profits. In the following paragraphs, we explain how the numbers in the table were calculated.

Monroe's annual sales are $400 million. Under its current credit policy, 50 percent of those customers who pay do so on Day 10 and take the discount, 40 percent pay on the thirtieth day, and 10 percent pay late, on Day 40. Thus, Mon-

Table 19-5
Monroe Manufacturing Company:
Analysis of Changing Credit Policy
(Millions of Dollars)

	Projected 1988 Income Statement under Current Credit Policy (1)	Effect of Credit Policy Change (2)	Projected 1988 Income Statement under New Credit Policy (3)
Gross sales	$400	+ $130	$530
Less discounts	2	+ 4	6
Net sales	$398	+ $126	$524
Production costs, including overhead	280	+ 91	371
Profit before credit costs and taxes	$118	+ $ 35	$153
Credit-related costs:			
Cost of carrying receivables	3	+ 2	5
Credit analysis and collection expenses	5	− 3	2
Bad debt losses	10	+ 22	32
Profit before taxes	$100	+ $ 14	$114
State-plus-federal taxes (50%)	50	+ 7	57
Net income	$ 50	+ $ 7	$ 57

roe's average collection period is $(.50)(10) + (.40)(30) + (.10)(40) = 21$ days, and discounts total $(0.01)(\$400,000,000)(0.5) = \$2,000,000$. The cost of carrying receivables is equal to the average receivables balance times the variable cost percentage times the cost of money used to carry receivables. The firm's variable cost ratio is 70 percent, and its pre-tax cost of capital invested in receivables is 20 percent. Its cost of carrying receivables is therefore $3 million:

$$(ACP) \begin{pmatrix} \text{Sales} \\ \text{per} \\ \text{day} \end{pmatrix} \begin{pmatrix} \text{Variable} \\ \text{cost} \\ \text{ratio} \end{pmatrix} \begin{pmatrix} \text{Cost} \\ \text{of} \\ \text{funds} \end{pmatrix} = \text{Cost of carrying receivables}$$

$$(21)(\$400,000,000/360)(0.70)(0.20) = \$3,266,667 \approx \$3 \text{ million.}$$

Only variable costs enter this calculation because this is the only cost element in receivables that must be financed. We are seeking the cost of carrying receivables, and variable costs represent the firm's investment in the cost of goods sold.

Even though Monroe spends $5 million annually to analyze accounts and to collect bad debts, 2.5 percent of sales will never be collected. Bad debt losses therefore amount to $(0.025)(\$400,000,000) = \$10,000,000$.

Monroe's new credit policy would be 2/10, net 40 versus the old policy of 1/10, net 30, so it would call for a larger discount and a longer payment period, as well as a relaxed collection effort and lower credit standards. The company believes that these changes will lead to a $130 million increase in sales, to $530 milllion per year. Under the new terms, management believes that 60 percent of the customers who pay will take the 2 percent discount, so discounts will increase to $(0.02)(\$530,000,000)(0.60) = \$6,360,000 \approx \$6$ million. Half of the nondiscount customers will pay on the fortieth day, and the remainder on Day 50. The new ACP is thus estimated to be 24 days:

$$(.6)(10) + (.2)(40) + (.2)(50) = 24 \text{ days}.$$

Also, the cost of carrying receivables will increase to $5 million:

$$(24)(\$530,000,000/360)(0.70)(0.20) = \$4,946,667 \approx \$5 \text{ million}.^8$$

The company plans to reduce its annual credit analysis and collection expenditures to $2 million. The reduced credit standards and the relaxed collection effort are expected to raise bad debt losses to about 6 percent of sales, or to $(0.06)(\$530,000,000) = \$31,800,000 \approx \$32,000,000$, which is an increase of $22 million from the previous level.

The combined effect of all the changes in credit policy is a projected $7 million increase in net income. There would, of course, be corresponding changes on the projected balance sheet — the higher sales would necessitate somewhat larger cash balances, inventories, and, depending on the capacity situation, perhaps more fixed assets. Accounts receivable would of course also increase. Since these asset increases would have to be financed, certain liabilities and/or equity would have to be increased.

The $7 million expected increase in net income is, of course, an estimate, and the actual effects of the change could be quite different. In the first place, there is uncertainty — perhaps quite a lot — about the projected $130 million increase in sales. Conceivably, if the firm's competitors matched its changes, sales would not rise at all. Similar uncertainties must be attached to the number of customers who would take discounts, to production costs at higher or lower sales levels, to the costs of carrying additional receivables, and to bad debt losses. In view of all the uncertainties, management would perhaps deem the projected $7 million increase in net income insufficient to justify the change. In the final analysis, the decision to make the change will be based on judgment, but the type of quantitative analysis set forth above is essential to a good judgmental decision.

---

[8]Since the credit policy change will result in a longer ACP, the firm will have to wait longer to receive its profit on the goods it sells. Therefore, the firm will incur an opportunity cost due to not having the cash from these profits available for investment. The dollar amount of this opportunity cost is equal to the old sales per day times the change in ACP times the contribution margin $(1 - \text{Variable cost ratio})$ times the firm's required return on receivables, or

$$\text{Opportunity cost} = (\text{Old sales}/360)(\Delta ACP)(1 - v)(k)$$
$$= (\$400/360)(3)(0.3)(0.20)$$
$$= \$0.2 = \$200,000.$$

For simplicity, we have ignored this cost in our analysis. For a more complete discussion of the analysis of changes in credit policy, see Eugene F. Brigham and Louis C. Gapenski, *Intermediate Financial Management,* 2nd ed., Chapter 19.

INVENTORIES

Inventories, which may be classified as (1) *raw materials,* (2) *work-in-process,* and (3) *finished goods,* are an essential part of most business operations. As is the case with accounts receivable, inventory levels depend heavily upon sales. However, whereas receivables build up *after* sales have been made, inventories must be acquired *ahead* of sales. This is a critical difference, and the necessity of forecasting sales before establishing target inventory levels makes inventory management a difficult task. Also, since errors in the establishment of inventory levels quickly lead either to lost sales or to excessive carrying costs, inventory management is as important as it is difficult.

Inventory management techniques are covered in depth in production management courses, which are required for most business students. Still, since financial managers have a responsibility both for raising the capital needed to carry inventory and for the overall profitability of the firm, it is essential that we cover the basics of inventory management from a financial perspective.[9]

TYPICAL INVENTORY DECISIONS

Two examples will make clear the financial issues involved in inventory management, and the problems poor inventory control can cause.

Retail Clothing Store

Chicago Swimware Company (CSC) must order swimsuits in January for summer sales, and it must take delivery by April to be sure of having enough suits to meet the heavy May-June demand. Bathing suits come in many styles, colors, and sizes, and if CSC stocks incorrectly, either in total or in terms of the style-color-size distribution, then the store will have trouble. It will lose potential sales if it stocks too few suits, and it will be forced to lower prices and take losses if it stocks too many or the wrong types.

The effects of inventory changes on the balance sheet are important. For simplicity, assume that CSC has a $5,000 base stock of swimsuits, financed by common stock. Its initial balance sheet is as follows:

Inventories (base stock)	$5,000	Common stock	$5,000
Total assets	$5,000	Total claims	$5,000

Now CSC anticipates that it will sell $15,000 worth of swimsuit inventory this summer. Dollar sales will actually be greater than $15,000, since CSC makes about

---

[9]For a more comprehensive treatment of inventory management, see Eugene F. Brigham and Louis C. Gapenski, *Intermediate Financial Management,* 2nd ed., Chapter 17.

$200 in profits for every $1,000 of inventory sold. CSC finances its seasonal inventory with bank loans, so its pre-summer balance sheet would look like this:

Inventories (seasonal)	$15,000	Notes payable to bank	$15,000
Inventories (base stock)	5,000	Common stock	5,000
Total assets	$20,000	Total claims	$20,000

If everything works out as planned, sales will be made, inventories will be converted to cash, the bank loan will be retired, and the company will earn a profit. The balance sheet, after a successful season, might look like this:

Cash	$3,000	Notes payable to bank	$ 0
Inventories (seasonal)	0	Common stock	5,000
Inventories (base stock)	5,000	Retained earnings	3,000
Total assets	$8,000	Total claims	$8,000

The company is now in a highly liquid position, and it is ready to begin a new season.

But suppose the season had not gone well, and CSC had only sold $1,000 of its inventory. As fall approached, the balance sheet looked like this:

Cash	$ 200	Notes payable to bank	$14,000
Inventories (seasonal)	14,000	Common stock	5,000
Inventories (base stock)	5,000	Retained earnings	200
Total assets	$19,200	Total claims	$19,200

Now suppose the bank insists on repayment of the $14,000 outstanding loan, and it wants cash, not swimsuits. But if the swimsuits did not sell well in the summer, how will out-of-style suits sell in the fall? Assume that CSC is forced to mark all its suits down to half their cost in order to sell them to raise cash to repay the bank loan. The results are as follows:

Cash	$9,700	Notes payable to bank	$14,000
Inventories	0	Common stock	5,000
		Retained earnings	(9,300)
Total assets	$9,700	Total claims	$9,700

At this point, CSC is bankrupt. Its stockholders have lost their entire investment, and the bank will have a loss of $4,300. Poor inventory policy ruined the firm.

Appliance Manufacturer

Now consider a different type of situation, that of Housepro Corporation, a well-established appliance manufacturer, whose inventory position follows:

Raw materials	$ 200,000,000
Work-in-process	200,000,000
Finished goods	600,000,000
Total inventories	$1,000,000,000

Suppose Housepro anticipates that the economy is about to get much stronger, and that the demand for appliances will soon rise sharply. If it is to share in the expected boom, Housepro will have to increase production. This means it will have to increase inventories, and, since the inventory build-up must precede sales, additional financing will be required—some liability account, perhaps notes payable, would have to be increased in order to support the additional inventory.

Proper inventory management requires close coordination among the sales, purchasing, production, and finance departments. The sales/marketing department is generally the first to spot changes in demand. These changes must be worked into the company's purchasing and manufacturing schedules, and the financial manager must arrange any financing that will be needed to support the inventory buildup. Improper coordination among departments, poor sales forecasts, or both, can lead to disaster.

INVENTORY MANAGEMENT

Inventory management focuses on three basic questions. (1) How many units should be ordered (or produced) at a given time? (2) At what point should inventory be ordered (or produced)? (3) What inventory items warrant special attention? The remainder of the chapter is devoted to providing answers to these three questions.

INVENTORY COSTS

The goal of inventory management is to provide at the lowest cost the inventories required to sustain operations. The first step in inventory management is to identify all the costs involved in purchasing and maintaining inventories. Table 19-6 gives a listing of the typical costs that are associated with manufacturing firms' inventories. In the table, we have broken down costs into three categories: those associated with carrying inventories, those associated with ordering and receiving inventories, and those associated with running short of inventories.

Although they may well be the most important element, we shall at this point disregard the third category of costs—the costs of running short. These costs are

---

Table 19-6
Costs Associated with Inventories

	Approximate Annual Percentage Cost
1. Carrying Costs	
Cost of capital tied up	15.0%
Storage and handling costs	0.5
Insurance	0.5
Property taxes	1.0
Depreciation and obsolescence	12.0
Total	29.0%
2. Ordering, Shipping, and Receiving Costs	
Cost of placing orders, including production and set-up costs	Varies
Shipping and handling costs	2.5%
Quantity discounts lost	Varies
3. Costs of Running Short	
Loss of sales	Varies
Loss of customer goodwill	Varies
Disruption of production schedules	Varies

Note: These costs vary from firm to firm, from item to item, and also over time. The figures shown are U.S. Department of Commerce estimates for an average manufacturing firm. Where costs vary so widely that no meaningful numbers can be assigned, we simply report "Varies."

---

dealt with by adding safety stocks, as we will discuss later. Similarly, we shall discuss quantity discounts in a later section. The costs that remain for consideration at this stage, then, are (1) carrying costs and (2) ordering, shipping, and receiving costs.

Note that inventory analysis must be conducted on an item-by-item basis. Thus, if a retailer stocks 1,000 items, then the type of analysis that follows must be conducted 1,000 times. Similarly, if a manufacturer carries 500 component parts (nuts, bolts, engine castings, and so forth), then it must make 500 analyses. A company like IBM or General Electric sells thousands of items and carries hundreds of thousands of parts. Thus, computerized inventory management is essential. We discuss next the type of analysis used to develop the computer models.

Carrying Costs

Carrying costs generally rise in direct proportion to the average amount (units or dollars) of inventory carried. Inventories carried, in turn, depend on the frequency with which orders are placed. To illustrate, if a firm sells S units of some item per year, and if it places equal-sized orders N times per year, then S/N units will be purchased with each order. If the inventory is used evenly over the year, and if no safety stocks are carried, then the average inventory, A, will be:

$$A = \frac{\text{Units per order}}{2} = \frac{S/N}{2}. \qquad (19\text{-}1)$$

For example, if S = 120,000 units sold in a year and N = 4, then the firm will order 30,000 units at a time, and its average inventory will be 15,000 units:

$$A = \frac{S/N}{2} = \frac{120,000/4}{2} = \frac{30,000}{2} = 15,000 \text{ units.}$$

Just after a shipment arrives the inventory will be 30,000 units, just before the next shipment arrives it will be zero, and on average 15,000 units will be carried.

Now assume the firm purchases its inventory at a price P = $2 per unit. The average dollars invested in this item is, thus, (P)(A) = $2(15,000) = $30,000. If the firm has a cost of capital of 10 percent, it will incur $3,000 of financing charges per year to carry the inventory.

Further, assume that each year the firm incurs $2,000 of storage costs (space, utilities, security, taxes, and so forth) for this item, plus inventory insurance costs of $500, and that it must mark down inventories by $1,000 because of depreciation and obsolescence. The firm's total cost of carrying the $30,000 average inventory is $3,000 + $2,000 + $500 + $1,000 = $6,500. Thus, the annual percentage cost of carrying this item of inventory is $6,500/$30,000 = 0.217 = 21.7%.

Defining the annual percentage carrying cost as C, we can, in general, find the annual total carrying cost, TCC, as the percentage carrying cost, C, times the price per unit, P, times the average number of units, A:

$$\text{TCC} = \text{Total carrying cost} = (C)(P)(A). \qquad (19\text{-}2)$$

In our example,

$$\text{TCC} = (0.217)(\$2)(15,000) \approx \$6,500.$$

Ordering Costs

Although it is reasonable to assume that carrying costs are entirely variable and rise in direct proportion to the average size of inventories, ordering costs are usually fixed. For example, the costs of placing and receiving an order — interoffice memos, long-distance telephone calls, setting up a production run, and taking delivery — are essentially fixed regardless of the size of an order, so this part of inventory cost is simply the fixed cost of placing and receiving orders times the number of orders placed per year.[10] We define the fixed costs associated with

---

[10]Note that, in reality, both carrying and ordering costs can have variable and fixed cost elements, at least over certain ranges of average inventory. For example, security and utilities charges are probably fixed in the short run over a wide range of inventory levels. Similarly, labor costs for receiving inventory could be tied to the quantity received, and hence be variable. To simplify matters, we treat all carrying costs as variable and all ordering costs as fixed. However, if these assumptions do not fit the

ordering inventories as F, and if we place N orders per year, the annual total ordering cost is given by Equation 19-3:

$$\text{Total ordering cost} = \text{TOC} = (F)(N). \tag{19-3}$$

Here TOC = total ordering cost, F = fixed costs per order, and N = number of orders placed per year.

Equation 19-1 may be rewritten as N = S/2A, and then substituted into Equation 19-3:

$$\text{Total ordering cost} = \text{TOC} = F\left(\frac{S}{2A}\right). \tag{19-4}$$

To illustrate the use of Equation 19-4, if F = \$100, S = 120,000 units, and A = 15,000 units, then TOC, the annual total ordering cost, is \$400:

$$\text{TOC} = \$100 \left(\frac{120,000}{30,000}\right) = \$100(4) = \$400.$$

Total Inventory Costs

Total carrying cost, TCC, as defined in Equation 19-2, and total ordering cost, TOC, as defined in Equation 19-4, may be combined to find total inventory costs, TIC, as follows:

$$\text{Total inventory costs} = \text{TIC} = \quad \text{TCC} \quad + \text{TOC}$$

$$= (C)(P)(A) + F\left(\frac{S}{2A}\right). \tag{19-5}$$

Recognizing that the average inventory carried is A = Q/2, or one-half the size of each order quantity, Q, we may rewrite Equation 19-5 as follows:

$$\text{TIC} = \quad \text{TCC} \quad + \text{TOC}$$

$$= (C)(P)\left(\frac{Q}{2}\right) + (F)\left(\frac{S}{Q}\right). \tag{19-6}$$

Here we see that total carrying cost equals C, the percentage annual carrying cost, multiplied by the unit's purchase price, P, times the average inventory in units, Q/2. Total ordering cost equals the fixed costs of placing and receiving an order,

---

situation at hand, the cost definitions can be changed. For example, one could add another term for shipping costs if there are economies of scale in shipping, such that the cost of shipping a unit is smaller if shipments are larger. However, in most situations, shipping costs per unit are not sensitive to order size, so total shipping costs are simply the shipping cost per unit times the units ordered (and sold) during the year. Under this condition, shipping costs are not influenced by inventory policy, and hence they may be disregarded for purposes of determining the optimal inventory level and the optimal order size.

F, times the number of orders placed per year, S/Q. We will use Equation 19-6 in the next section to develop the optimal inventory ordering quantity.

THE OPTIMAL ORDERING QUANTITY

Inventories are obviously necessary, but it is equally obvious that a firm will suffer if it has too much or too little inventory. How can we determine the optimal inventory level? One approach commonly used is based on the *economic ordering quantity (EOQ)* model as described next.

Derivation of the EOQ Model

Figure 19-1 illustrates the basic premise on which the EOQ model is built, namely, that some costs rise with larger inventories while other costs decline, and there is an optimal order size (and associated average inventory) which minimizes the total

Figure 19-1
Determination of the Optimal Order Quantity

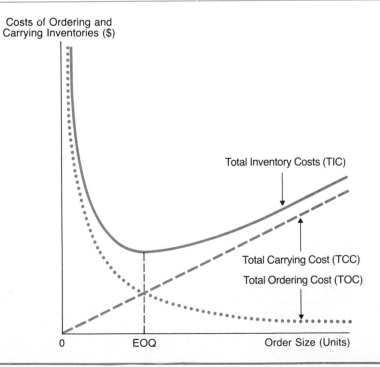

costs of inventories. First, as noted earlier, the average investment in inventories depends on how frequently orders are placed and the size of each order — if we order every day, average inventories will be much smaller than if we order once a year. Further, as Figure 19-1 shows, the firm's carrying costs rise with larger orders: Larger orders mean larger average inventories, so warehousing costs, interest on funds tied up in inventory, insurance, and obsolescence costs will all increase. However, ordering costs decline with larger orders and inventories: The cost of placing orders, suppliers' production setup costs, and order handling costs will all decline if we place only a few large orders and consequently hold large quantities.

If the carrying and ordering cost curves in Figure 19-1 are added, the sum represents total inventory costs, TIC. The point where the TIC is minimized represents the economic ordering quantity, and this, in turn, determines the optimal average inventory level.

The EOQ is found by differentiating Equation 19-6 with respect to ordering quantity, Q, and setting the derivative equal to zero:

$$\frac{d(TIC)}{dQ} = \frac{(C)(P)}{2} - \frac{(F)(S)}{Q^2} = 0.$$

Now, solving for Q, we obtain:

$$\frac{(C)(P)}{2} = \frac{(F)(S)}{Q^2}$$

$$Q^2 = \frac{2(F)(S)}{(C)(P)}$$

$$Q = EOQ = \sqrt{\frac{2(F)(S)}{(C)(P)}}. \tag{19-7}$$

Here

EOQ = economic ordering quantity, or the optimum quantity to be ordered each time an order is placed.

 F = fixed costs of placing and receiving an order.

 S = annual sales in units.

 C = annual carrying costs expressed as a percentage of average inventory value.

 P = purchase price the firm must pay per unit of inventory. (The sales price is irrelevant.)

Equation 19-7 is the EOQ model.[11] The assumptions of the model include the following: (1) sales can be forecasted perfectly, (2) sales are evenly distributed

---

[11]The EOQ model can also be written as

$$EOQ = \sqrt{\frac{2(F)(S)}{C^*}},$$

where C^* is the annual carrying cost per unit expressed in *dollars*.

throughout the year, i.e., sales are constant at a given amount per day, and (3) orders are received when expected, i.e., no shipping delays are ever encountered. We will relax these assumptions shortly, but first we illustrate the use of the EOQ model.

EOQ Model Illustration

The following data were supplied by Cotton Tops, Inc., a distributor of custom-designed T-shirts which sells to concessionaires at Daisy World:

S = sales = 26,000 shirts per year (or 26,000/365 = 71.23 per day).

C = percentage carrying cost = 25 percent of inventory value.

P = purchase price per shirt = $4.92 per shirt. (The sales price is $9, but this is irrelevant for our purposes here.)

F = fixed cost per order = $1,000. Cotton Tops designs and distributes the shirts, but the actual production is done by another company. The bulk of this $1,000 cost is the labor cost for setting up the equipment for the production run, which the manufacturer bills separately from the $4.92 cost per shirt.

Substituting these data into Equation 19-7, we obtain an EOQ of 6,500 units:

$$\text{EOQ} = \sqrt{\frac{2(F)(S)}{(C)(P)}} = \sqrt{\frac{(2)(\$1,000)(26,000)}{(0.25)(\$4.92)}}$$

$$= \sqrt{42,276,423} \approx 6,500 \text{ units.}$$

With an EOQ of 6,500 shirts and annual usage of 26,000 shirts, Cotton Tops will place 26,000/6,500 = 4 orders per year. Notice that average inventory holdings depend directly on the EOQ: This relationship is illustrated graphically in Figure 19-2, where we see that average inventory = EOQ/2. Immediately after an order is received, 6,500 shirts are in stock. The usage rate, or sales rate, is 71.23 shirts per day, so inventories are drawn down by this amount each day. Thus, the actual number of units held in inventory will vary from 6,500 shirts just after an order is received to zero just before a new order arrives. With a 6,500 beginning balance, a zero ending balance, and a uniform sales rate, inventories will average one-half the EOQ, or 3,250 shirts, during the year. At a cost of $4.92 per shirt, the average investment in inventories will be (3,250)($4.92) ≈ $16,000. If inventories are financed by bank loans, the loan will vary from a high of $32,000 to a low of $0, but the average amount outstanding over the course of a year will be $16,000.

Notice that the EOQ, and hence average inventory holdings, rises with the square root of sales. Therefore, a given increase in sales will result in a less-than-proportionate increase in inventories, so the inventory/sales ratio will tend to decline as a firm grows. For example, Cotton Tops' EOQ is 6,500 shirts at an annual sales level of 26,000, and the average inventory is 3,250 shirts, or $16,000. However, if sales were to increase by 100 percent, to 52,000 shirts per year, the EOQ would rise only to 9,195 units, or by 41 percent, and the average inventory would

Figure 19-2
Inventory Position without Safety Stock

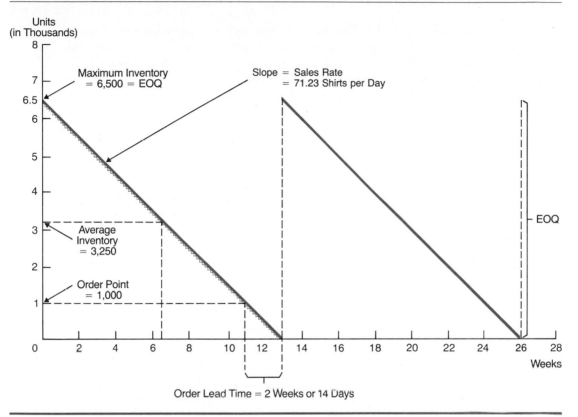

rise by this same percentage. This suggests that there are economies of scale in holding inventories.[12]

Finally, look at Cotton Tops' total inventory costs for the year, assuming that the EOQ is ordered each time. Using Equation 19-6, we find total inventory costs to be $8,000:

$$TIC = TCC + TOC$$

$$= (C)(P)\left(\frac{Q}{2}\right) + (F)\left(\frac{S}{Q}\right)$$

---

[12]Note, however, that these scale economies relate to each particular item, not to the entire firm. Thus, a large distributor with $500 million of sales might have a higher inventory/sales ratio than a much smaller distributor if the small firm has only a few high-sales-volume items while the large firm distributes a great many low-volume items.

$$= 0.25(\$4.92)\left(\frac{6,500}{2}\right) + (\$1,000)\left(\frac{26,000}{6,500}\right)$$

$$\approx \$4,000 + \$4,000 = \$8,000.$$

Note these two points: (1) The $8,000 total inventory cost represents the total of carrying costs and ordering costs, but this amount does *not* include the $26,000(\$4.92) = \$127,920$ annual purchasing cost of the inventory itself. (2) As we see both in Figure 19-1 and in the numbers just preceding, if the firm uses the EOQ model, its total carrying cost (TCC) will equal its total ordering cost (TOC). This property is not unique to our Cotton Tops illustration; it always holds.

Setting the Order Point

If a two-week lead time is required for production and shipping, what is Cotton Tops' order point level? Cotton Tops sells $26,000/52 = 500$ shirts per week. Thus, if a two-week lag occurs between placing an order and receiving goods, Cotton Tops must place the order when there are $2(500) = 1,000$ shirts on hand. During the two-week production and shipping period, the inventory balance will continue to decline at the rate of 500 shirts per week, and the inventory balance will hit zero just as the order of new shirts arrives.

If Cotton Tops knew for certain that both the sales rate and the order lead time would never vary, it could operate exactly as shown in Figure 19-2. However, sales do change, and production and/or shipping delays are frequently encountered; to guard against these events, the firm must carry additional inventories, or safety stocks, as discussed next.

Safety Stocks

The concept of a *safety stock* is illustrated in Figure 19-3. First, note that the slope of the sales line measures the expected rate of sales. The company *expects* to sell 500 shirts per week, but let us assume that the maximum likely sales rate is twice this amount, or 1,000 units each week. Further, assume that Cotton Tops sets the safety stock at 1,000 shirts, so it initially orders 7,500 shirts, the EOQ of 6,500 plus the 1,000 unit safety stock. Subsequently, it reorders the EOQ whenever the inventory level falls to 2,000 shirts, the safety stock of 1,000 shirts plus the 1,000 shirts expected to be used while awaiting delivery of the order.

Notice that the company could, over the two-week delivery period, sell 1,000 units a week, or double its normal expected sales. This maximum rate of sales is shown by the steeper dashed line in Figure 19-3. The condition that makes possible this higher maximum sales rate is the safety stock of 1,000 shirts.

The safety stock is also useful to guard against delays in receiving orders. The expected delivery time is two weeks, but with a 1,000 unit safety stock, the company could maintain sales at the expected rate of 500 units per week for an additional two weeks if production or shipping delays held up an order.

Figure 19-3
Inventory Position with Safety Stock Included

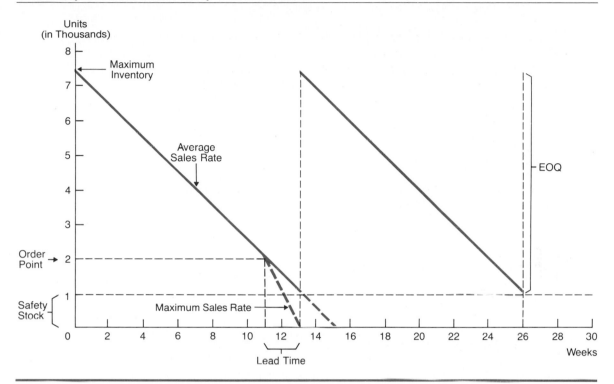

However, carrying a safety stock has costs. The average inventory is now EOQ/2 plus the safety stock, or $6,500/2 + 1,000 = 3,250 + 1,000 = 4,250$ shirts, and the average inventory value is now $(4,250)(\$4.92) = \$20,910$. This increase in average inventory causes an increase in annual inventory carrying costs equal to (Safety stock)(P)(C) = $1,000(\$4.92)(0.25) = \$1,230$.

The optimal safety stock varies from situation to situation, but, in general, it *increases* (1) with the uncertainty of demand forecasts, (2) with the costs (in terms of lost sales and lost goodwill) that result from inventory shortages, and (3) with the probability that delays will occur in receiving shipments. The optimum safety stock *decreases* as the cost of carrying this additional inventory increases.

Quantity Discounts

Suppose the T-shirt manufacturer offered Cotton Tops a quantity discount of 2 percent on orders of 10,000 or more. Now Cotton Tops' inventory manager will have to compare benefits of the lower purchase price on orders of 10,000 units with the higher inventory costs caused by the departure from the 6,500 unit EOQ.

First, consider the total costs associated with Cotton Tops' EOQ of 6,500 units:

$$\text{TIC} = \text{TCC} + \text{TOC}$$

$$= (C)(P)\left(\frac{Q}{2}\right) + (F)\left(\frac{S}{Q}\right)$$

$$= 0.25(\$4.92)\left(\frac{6,500}{2}\right) + (\$1,000)\left(\frac{26,000}{6,500}\right)$$

$$\approx \$4,000 + \$4,000 = \$8,000.$$

Now, what would the total inventory costs be if Cotton Tops ordered 10,000 units instead of 6,500? The answer is \$8,625:

$$\text{TIC} = (0.25)(\$4.82)\left(\frac{10,000}{2}\right) + (\$1,000)\left(\frac{26,000}{10,000}\right)$$

$$= \$6,025 + \$2,600 = \$8,625.$$

Notice that when the discount is taken, the price, P, is reduced by the amount of the discount; the new price per unit would be 0.98(\$4.92) = \$4.82. Also, note that when the ordering quantity is increased, carrying costs increase because the firm is carrying a larger average inventory, but ordering costs decrease because the number of orders per year decreases.

Thus, inventory costs would increase by \$8,625 − \$8,000 = \$625 if Cotton Tops were to increase its order size to 10,000 shirts. However, this cost increase must be compared with Cotton Tops' savings if it takes the discount. Taking the discount would save 0.02(\$4.92) = \$0.0984 per unit. Over the year, Cotton Tops orders 26,000 shirts, so the annual savings is \$0.0984(26,000) ≈ \$2,558. Thus, the net saving to Cotton Tops, if it were to increase its ordering quantity to 10,000 units and take the discount, is \$2,558 in discounts less \$625 in increased inventory costs, or \$1,933. Therefore, the company should order 10,000 units at a time and take advantage of the quantity discount.

Seasonal Demand

For most firms, it is unrealistic to assume that the demand for an inventory item is uniform throughout the year. What happens when there is seasonal demand, as would hold true for an ice cream company? Here the standard annual EOQ model is obviously not appropriate. However, it does provide a point of departure for setting inventory parameters, which are then modified to fit the particular seasonal pattern. The procedure here is to divide the year into seasons in which annualized sales are relatively constant, say the summer, spring and fall, and winter. Then, the EOQ model could be applied separately to each period. During the transitions between seasons, inventories would be either run down or built up with special seasonal orders.

Table 19-7
EOQ Sensitivity Analysis

Ordering Quantity	Total Inventory Costs	Percentage Deviation from Optimal
3,000	$10,512	+31.4%
4,000	8,960	+12.0
5,000	8,275	+3.4
6,000	8,023	+0.3
6,500	8,000	0.0
7,000	8,019	+0.2
8,000	8,170	+2.1
9,000	8,423	+5.3
10,000	8,750	+9.4

EOQ Range

Thus far, we have interpreted the EOQ, and the resulting inventory variables, as single point estimates. It can be demonstrated that small deviations from the EOQ do not appreciably affect total inventory costs and, consequently, that the optimal ordering quantity should be viewed more as a range than as a single value.

To illustrate this point, we can examine the sensitivity of total inventory costs to ordering quantity for Cotton Tops; Table 19-7 shows our results. We see that the ordering quantity could range from 5,000 to 8,000 units without affecting total inventory costs by more than 3.4 percent. Thus, the inventory manager can adjust the ordering quantity within a fairly wide range without fear of significantly increasing total inventory costs.

INVENTORY CONTROL SYSTEMS

The EOQ model, together with safety stock analysis, can be used to establish the proper inventory level, but inventory management also involves the establishment of an *inventory control system*. Inventory control systems run the gamut from very simple to extremely complex, depending on the size of the firm and the nature of its inventories. For example, one simple control procedure is the *red-line method* — inventory items are stocked in a bin, a red line is drawn around the inside of the bin at the level of the order point, and the inventory clerk places an order when the red line shows. The *two-bin method* has inventory items stocked in two bins. When the working bin is empty, an order is placed and inventory is drawn from the second bin. These procedures work well for parts such as bolts in a manufacturing process, and for many items in retail businesses.

Computerized Systems

Larger companies employ *computerized inventory control systems.* The computer starts with an inventory count in memory. As withdrawals are made, they are recorded by the computer, and the inventory balance is revised. When the order point is reached, the computer automatically places an order, and when the order is received, the recorded balance is increased. Retail stores have carried this system quite far — each item has a magnetic bar code, and, as an item is checked out, the code is read, a signal is sent to the computer, and the inventory balance is adjusted at the same time the price is fed into the cash register tape. When the balance drops to the order point, an order is automatically placed.

A good inventory control system is dynamic, not static. A company such as IBM or General Motors stocks hundreds of thousands of different items. The sales (or use) of these various items can rise or fall quite separately from rising or falling overall corporate sales. As the usage rate for an individual item begins to rise or fall, the inventory manager must adjust its balance to avoid running short or ending up with obsolete items. If the change in the usage rate appears to be permanent, then the EOQ should be recomputed, the safety stock level should be reconsidered, and the computer model used in the control process should be reprogrammed.

Just-In-Time Systems

A relatively new approach to inventory control called *just-in-time* has been developed by Japanese firms and is gaining popularity in the United States. Toyota provides a good example of the just-in-time system. Eight of Toyota's ten factories, along with most of Toyota's suppliers, dot the countryside around Toyota City, Japan. Delivery of components is tied to the speed of the assembly line, and parts are generally delivered no more than a few hours before they are used. The just-in-time system reduces the need for Toyota and other manufacturers to carry inventories, but it requires a great deal of coordination between the manufacturer and its suppliers, both in the timing of deliveries and the quality of the goods.

Not surprisingly, U.S. automobile manufacturers have been among the first domestic firms to move toward just-in-time systems. Ford has been restructuring its production system with a goal of increasing its inventory turnover from 20 times a year to 30 or 40 times. Of course, just-in-time systems place considerable pressure on suppliers. GM used to keep a 10-day supply of seats and other parts made by Lear Siegler; now GM sends in orders at four- to eight-hour intervals and expects immediate shipment. A Lear Siegler spokesman stated, "we can't afford to keep things sitting around either," so Lear Siegler has had to be tougher on its own suppliers.

SUMMARY

The investment in receivables is dependent on the firm's *credit policy,* and the four credit policy variables are these: (1) the *credit standards,* or the financial strength that customers must exhibit in order to be granted credit; (2) the *credit period,* or the length of time for which credit is extended; (3) *cash discounts,* which are designed to encourage rapid payment; and (4) *collection policy,* which helps determine how long accounts remain outstanding. Credit policy has an important impact on the volume of sales, and the optimal credit policy involves a tradeoff between the costs inherent in various credit policies and the profits generated by higher sales. From a practical standpoint, it is impossible to determine the optimal credit policy in a mathematical sense — good credit management involves a blending of quantitative analysis and business judgment.

Monitoring receivables is an important part of credit management. Firms often use the *average collection period* and *aging schedules* to monitor collections, but these summary measures do not always provide a clear picture of changes in payment behavior. A better method of receivables monitoring is the *payments pattern approach.*

Inventory management centers around the balancing of a set of costs that increase with larger inventory holdings (storage costs, cost of capital, and physical deterioration) and a set of costs that decline with larger holdings (ordering costs, lost sales, and disruptions of production schedules). Inventory management has been quantified to a greater extent than most aspects of business, with the *EOQ model* being one important part of most inventory systems. This model can be used to determine the optimal order quantity, which, when combined with a specified safety stock, determines the average inventory level. Inventory control systems are used to keep track of actual inventories, and to insure that inventory levels are adjusted to changing sales levels.

Good inventory management will result in a relatively high inventory turnover, low write-offs of obsolete or deteriorated inventories, and few instances of work stoppages or lost sales due to stock-outs. All this, in turn, contributes to a high profit margin, a high rate of return on investment, and a strong stock price.

Questions

19-1 Define each of the following terms:

    a. Account receivable

    b. Aging schedule; average collection period (ACP)

    c. Payments pattern approach; uncollected balances schedule

    d. Credit policy; credit period; credit standards; collection policy

    e. Cash discounts

    f. Seasonal dating

    g. Open account; promissory note; commercial draft; sight draft; time draft; trade acceptance; banker's acceptance; conditional sales contract

    h. Carrying costs; ordering costs; total inventory costs

    i. Economic ordering quantity (EOQ); EOQ model; EOQ range

    j. Reorder point; safety stock

    k. Red-line method; two-bin method; computerized inventory control system

    l. Just-in-time systems

19-2 Is it true that when one firm sells to another on credit, the seller records the transaction as an account receivable while the buyer records it as an account payable and that, disregarding discounts, the receivable typically exceeds the payable by the amount of profit on the sale?

19-3 What are the four elements in a firm's credit policy? To what extent can firms set their own credit policies as opposed to having to accept policies that are dictated by "the competition"?

19-4 Suppose a firm makes a purchase and receives the shipment on February 1. The terms of trade as stated on the invoice read "2/10, net 40, May 1 dating." What is the latest date on which payment can be made and the discount still be taken? What is the date on which payment must be made if the discount is not taken?

19-5 What is the average collection period (ACP) for a firm whose sales are $2,880,000 per year and whose accounts receivable are $312,000? (Use 360 days per year.) Is it true that if this firm sells on terms of 3/10, net 40, its customers probably all pay on time?

19-6 Is it true that if a firm calculates its average collection period, it has no need for an aging schedule?

19-7 Firm A had no credit losses last year, but 1 percent of Firm B's accounts receivable proved to be uncollectible and resulted in losses. Should Firm B fire its credit manager and hire A's?

19-8 Indicate by a +, −, or 0 whether each of the following events would probably cause accounts receivable (A/R), sales, and profits to increase, decrease, or be affected in an indeterminant manner:

	A/R	Sales	Profits
a. The firm tightens its credit standards.	_____	_____	_____
b. The terms of trade are changed from 2/10, net 30, to 3/10, net 30.	_____	_____	_____
c. The terms are changed from 2/10, net 30, to 3/10, net 40.	_____	_____	_____
d. The credit manager gets tough with past-due accounts	_____	_____	_____

19-9 Indicate by a +, −, or 0 whether each of the following events would probably cause average annual inventories (the sum of the inventories held at the end of each month of the year divided by 12) to rise, fall, or be affected in an indeterminant manner:

  a. Our suppliers switch from delivering by train to air freight. _____

  b. We change from producing just in time to meet seasonal sales to steady, year-round production. (Sales peak at Christmas.) _____

  c. Competition in the markets in which we sell increases. _____

  d. The rate of general inflation increases. _____

  e. Interest rates rise; other things are constant. _____

Self-Test Problems

ST-1 (Credit policy) The Lewis Company expects to have sales of $10 million this year under its current operating policies. Its variable costs as a percentage of sales are 80 percent, and its cost of capital is 16 percent. Currently Lewis' credit policy is net 25 (no discount for early payment). However, its ACP is 30 days, and its bad debt loss percentage is 2 percent. Lewis spends $50,000 per year to collect bad debts, and its federal-plus-state-plus-local tax rate is 50 percent.

The credit manager is considering two alternative proposals, given below, for changing Lewis's credit policy. Find the expected change in net income, taking into consideration anticipated changes in carrying costs for accounts receivable, the probable bad debt losses, and the discounts likely to be taken, for each proposal. Should a change in credit policy be made?

Proposal 1: Lengthen the credit period by going from net 25 to net 30. The bad debt collection expenditures will remain constant. Under this proposal, sales are expected to increase by $1 million annually, and the bad debt loss percentage on *new* sales is expected to rise to 4 percent (the loss percentage on old sales should not change). In addition, the ACP is expected to increase from 30 to 45 days on all sales.

Proposal 2: Shorten the credit period by going from net 25 to net 20. Again, collection expenses will remain constant. The anticipated effects of this change are (1) a decrease in sales of $1 million per year, (2) a decline in the ACP from 30 to 22 days, and (3) a decline in the bad debt loss percentage to 1 percent on all sales.

ST-2 (EOQ model) The Boisjoly Breads Company buys and then sells (as bread) 2.6 million bushels of wheat annually. The wheat must be purchased in multiples of 2,000 bushels. Ordering costs, which include grain elevator removal charges of $3,500, are $5,000 per order. Annual carrying costs are 2 percent of the purchase price per bushel of $5. The company maintains a safety stock of 200,000 bushels. The delivery time is 6 weeks.

 a. What is the EOQ?

 b. At what inventory level should a reorder be placed to prevent having to draw on the safety stock?

 c. What are the total inventory costs?

 d. The wheat processor agrees to pay the elevator removal charges if Boisjoly Breads will purchase wheat in quantities of 650,000 bushels. Would it be to Boisjoly Breads' advantage to order under this alternative?

Problems

19-1 (Receivables investment) Provencial, Inc., sells on terms of 2/10, net 30. Total sales for the year are $600,000. Forty percent of the customers pay on the tenth day and take discounts; the other 60 percent pay, on average, 40 days after their purchases.

 a. What is the average collection period?

 b. What is the average amount of receivables?

 c. What would happen to the average investment in receivables if Provencial toughened up on its collection policy with the result that all nondiscount customers paid on the thirtieth day?

19-2 **(Easing credit terms)** Martell Auto Parts is considering changing its credit terms from 2/15, net 30, to 3/10, net 30, in order to speed collections. At present, 60 percent of Martell's customers take the 2 percent discount. Under the new terms, discount customers are expected to rise to 70 percent. Regardless of the credit terms, half of the customers who do not take the discount are expected to pay on time, while the remainder will pay 10 days late. The change does not involve a relaxation of credit standards; therefore, bad debt losses are not expected to rise above their present 2 percent level. However, the more generous cash discount terms are expected to increase sales from $1 million to $1.2 million per year. Martell's variable cost ratio is 75 percent, the interest rate on funds invested in accounts receivable is 12 percent, and its tax rate is 40 percent.

    a. What is the average collection period before and after the change?

    b. Calculate the discount costs before and after the change.

    c. Calculate the dollar cost of carrying receivables before and after the change.

    d. Calculate the bad debt losses before and after the change.

    e. What is the incremental profit from the change in credit terms? Should Martell change its credit terms?

    (Do Part f only if you are using the computerized diskette.)

    f. (1) Suppose the sales forecast is lowered to $1,100,000. Should Martell change its credit policy? What if the sales forecast dropped to $1,037,265?

        (2) Suppose the payment pattern of customers remains unchanged with the new credit plan; that is, 60 percent still take the discount, 20 percent pay on time, and 20 percent pay late. Also, the variable cost ratio rises to 78 percent. How does all this affect the decision, assuming the sales forecast remains at $1,200,000?

19-3 **(Credit analysis)** Vanderheiden Distributors makes all sales on a credit basis, selling on terms of 2/10, net 30. Once a year it evaluates the creditworthiness of all its customers. The evaluation procedure ranks customers from 1 to 5, with 1 indicating the "best" customers. Results of the ranking are as follows:

Customer Category	Percentage of Bad Debts	Average Collection Period (Days)	Credit Decision	Annual Sales Lost Due to Credit Restrictions
1	None	10	Unlimited credit	None
2	1.0	12	Unlimited credit	None
3	3.0	20	Limited credit	$365,000
4	9.0	60	Limited credit	$182,500
5	16.0	90	Limited credit	$230,000

The variable cost ratio is 75 percent. The cost of capital invested in receivables is 15 percent. What would be the effect on the profitability of extending unlimited credit to each of the Categories 3, 4, and 5? (Hint: Determine the effect of changing each policy separately on the income statement. In other words, find the change in sales, change in production costs, change in receivables and cost of carrying receivables, change in bad debt costs, and so forth, down to the change in net profits. Assume a tax rate of 40 percent.)

19-4 (Tightening credit terms) Daniel Richards, the new credit manager of the Hunt Corporation, was alarmed to find that Hunt sells on credit terms of net 90 days while industrywide credit terms have recently been lowered to net 30 days. On annual credit sales of $2.5 million, Hunt currently averages 95 days' sales in accounts receivable. Richards estimates that tightening the credit terms to 30 days would reduce annual sales to $2,375,000, but accounts receivable would drop to 35 days of sales and the savings on investment in them should more than overcome any loss in profit.

Hunt's variable cost ratio is 85 percent, and taxes are 40 percent. If the interest rate on funds invested in receivables is 18 percent, should the change in credit terms be made?

19-5 (Monitoring of receivables) The Damon Company, a small manufacturer of cordless telephones, began operations on January 1, 1987. Its credit sales for the first six months of operations were as follows:

Month	Credit Sales
January	$ 50,000
February	100,000
March	120,000
April	105,000
May	140,000
June	160,000

Throughout this entire period, Damon's credit customers maintained a constant payments pattern: 20 percent paid in the month of sale, 30 percent paid in the month following the sale, and 50 percent paid in the second month following the sale.

a. What was Damon's receivables balance at the end of March and at the end of June?

b. Assume 90 days per calendar quarter. What was the average daily sales (ADS) and average collection period (ACP) for the first quarter and for the second quarter? What was the cumulative ADS and ACP for the first half-year?

c. Construct an aging schedule as of June 30. Use 0-30, 31-60, and 61-90 day account ages.

d. Construct the uncollected balances schedule for the second quarter as of June 30.

19-6 (Relaxing collection efforts) The Lange Corporation has annual credit sales of $1.6 million. Current expenses for the collection department are $35,000, bad debt losses are 1.5 percent, and the average collection period is 30 days. Lange is considering easing its collection efforts such that collection expenses will be reduced to $22,000 per year. The change is expected to increase bad debt losses to 2.5 percent and to increase the average collection period to 45 days. In addition, sales are expected to increase to $1,625,000 per year.

Should Lange relax collection efforts if the opportunity cost of funds is 16 percent, the variable cost ratio is 75 percent, and taxes are 40 percent?

19-7 (Economic ordering quantity) The Ritchie Garden Center sells 90,000 bags of lawn fertilizer annually. The optimal safety stock (which is on hand initially) is 1,000 bags.

Each bag costs Ritchie $1.50, inventory carrying costs are 20 percent, and the cost of placing an order with its supplier is $15.

    a. What is the economic ordering quantity?

    b. What is the maximum inventory of fertilizer?

    c. What will Ritchie's average inventory be?

    d. How often must the company order?

19-8 (EOQ and total ordering costs) The following inventory data have been established for the Shalit Corporation:

    1. Orders must be placed in multiples of 100 units.

    2. Annual sales are 338,000 units.

    3. The purchase price per unit is $3.

    4. Carrying cost is 20 percent of the purchase price of goods.

    5. Cost per order placed is $24.

    6. Desired safety stock is 14,000 units; this amount is on hand initially.

    7. Two weeks are required for delivery.

        a. What is the EOQ?

        b. How many orders should Shalit place each year?

        c. At what inventory level should a reorder be made? (Hint: Reorder point = Safety stock + (Weeks to deliver × Weekly usage) − Goods in transit.)

        d. Calculate the total cost of ordering and carrying inventories if the order quantity is (1) 4,000 units, (2) 4,800 units, or (3) 6,000 units. What are the total costs if the order quantity is the EOQ?

    (Do Part e only if you are using the computerized diskette.)

        e. What are the EOQ and total inventory cost if

    (1) Sales increase to 500,000 units?

    (2) Fixed order costs increase to $30? Sales remain at 338,000 units.

    (3) Purchase price increases to $4? Leave sales and fixed costs at original values.

Solutions to Self-Test Problems

ST-1 Under the current credit policy, the Lewis Company has no discounts, collection expenses of $50,000, bad debt losses of (0.02)($10,000,000) = $200,000, and average accounts receivable of (ACP)(Average sales per day) = (30)($10,000,000/360) = $833,333. The firm's cost of carrying these receivables is (Variable cost ratio)(A/R)(Cost of capital) = (0.80)($833,333)(0.16) = $106,667. It is necessary to multiply by the variable cost ratio because the actual *investment* in receivables is less than the dollar amount of the receivables.

Proposal 1: Lengthen the credit period such that

1. Sales increase by $1 million.

2. Discounts = $0.

3. Bad debt losses = (0.02)($10,000,000) + (0.04)($1,000,000)

$$= \$200,000 + \$40,000$$

$$= \$240,000.$$

4. ACP = 45 days on all sales.

5. New average receivables $= (45)(\$11,000,000/360)$

$$= \$1,375,000.$$

6. Cost of carrying receivables $= (v)(k)(\text{Average accounts receivable})$

$$= (0.80)(0.16)(\$1,375,000)$$

$$= \$176,000.$$

7. Change in cost of carrying receivables $= \$176,000 - \$106,667$

$$= \$69,333.$$

8. Collection expenses $= \$50,000$.

Analysis of proposed change:

	Income Statement under Current Policy	Effect of Change	Income Statement under New Policy
Gross sales	$10,000,000	ǀ $1,000,000	$11,000,000
Less discounts	0	+ 0	0
Net sales	$10,000,000	+ $1,000,000	$11,000,000
Production costs (80%)	8,000,000	+ 800,000	8,800,000
Profit before credit costs and taxes	$ 2,000,000	+ $ 200,000	$ 2,200,000
Credit-related costs:			
Cost of carrying receivables	106,667	+ 69,333	176,000
Collection expenses	50,000	+ 0	50,000
Bad debt losses	200,000	+ 40,000	240,000
Profit before taxes	$ 1,643,333	+ $ 90,667	$ 1,734,000
Taxes (50%)	821,666	+ 45,333	867,000
Net income	$ 821,667	+ 45,334	$ 867,000

The proposed change appears to be a good one, assuming the assumptions are correct.

Proposal 2: Shorten the credit period to net 20 such that
1. Sales decrease by $1 million.
2. Discount $= \$0$.
3. Bad debt losses $= (0.01)(\$9,000,000)$

$$= \$90,000.$$

4. ACP $= 22$ days.
5. New average receivables $= (22)(\$9,000,000/360)$

$$= \$550,000.$$

6. Cost of carrying receivables $= (v)(k)(\text{Average accounts receivable})$

$$= (0.80)(0.16)(\$550,000)$$

$$= \$70,400.$$

7. Collection expenses $= \$50,000$.

Analysis of proposed change:

	Income Statement under Current Policy	Effect of Change	Income Statement under New Policy
Gross sales	$10,000,000	− $1,000,000	$9,000,000
Less discounts	0	0	0
Net sales	$10,000,000	− $1,000,000	$9,000,000
Production costs (80%)	8,000,000	− 800,000	7,200,000
Profit before credit costs and taxes	$ 2,000,000	− $ 200,000	$1,800,000
Credit-related costs:			
Cost of carrying receivables	106,667	− 36,267	70,400
Collection expenses	50,000	0	50,000
Bad debt losses	200,000	− 110,000	90,000
Profit before taxes	$ 1,643,333	− $ 53,733	$1,589,600
Taxes (50%)	821,666	− 26,866	794,800
Net income	$ 821,667	− $ 26,867	$ 794,800

This change reduces net income, so it should be rejected. Lewis will increase profits by accepting Proposal 1 to lengthen the credit period from 25 days to 30 days, assuming all assumptions are correct. This may or may not be the *optimal,* or profit-maximizing, credit policy, but it does appear to be a movement in the right direction.

ST-2   a. $EOQ = \sqrt{\dfrac{2(F)(S)}{(C)(P)}}$

$= \sqrt{\dfrac{(2)(\$5,000)(2,600,000)}{(0.02)(\$5.00)}}$

$= 509,902$ bushels.

Since the firm must order in multiples of 2,000 bushels, it should order in quantities of 510,000 bushels.

b. Average weekly sales $= 2,600,000/52$

$= 50,000$ bushels.

Reorder point $= 6$ weeks' sales $+$ Safety stock

$= 6(50,000) + 200,000$

$= 300,000 + 200,000$

$= 500,000$ bushels.

c. Total inventory costs:

$$TIC = CP\left(\frac{Q}{2}\right) + F\left(\frac{S}{Q}\right) + CP(\text{Safety stock})$$

$$= (0.02)(\$5)\left(\frac{510,000}{2}\right) + (\$5,000)\left(\frac{2,600,000}{510,000}\right)$$

$$+ (0.02)(\$5)(200,000)$$

$$= \$25,500 + \$25,490.20 + \$20,000$$

$$= \$70,990.20.$$

d. Ordering costs would be reduced to $1,500. By ordering 650,000 bushels at a time, total inventory costs would be:

$$\text{TIC} = (0.02)(\$5)\left(\frac{650{,}000}{2}\right) + (\$1{,}500)\left(\frac{2{,}600{,}000}{650{,}000}\right)$$

$$+ (0.02)(\$5)(200{,}000)$$

$$= \$32{,}500 + \$6{,}000 + \$20{,}000$$

$$= \$58{,}500.$$

Since the firm can reduce its total inventory costs by ordering 650,000 bushels at a time, it should accept the offer and place larger orders. (Incidentally, this same type of analysis is used to consider any quantity discount offer.)

Selected Additional References and Cases

Recent articles which address credit policy and receivables management include the following:

Atkins, Joseph C., and Yong H. Kim, "Comment and Correction: Opportunity Cost in the Evaluation of Investment in Accounts Receivable," *Financial Management,* Winter 1977, 71–74.

Ben-Horim, Moshe, and Haim Levy, "Management of Accounts Receivable under Inflation," *Financial Management,* Spring 1983, 42–48.

Dyl, Edward A., "Another Look at the Evaluation of Interest in Accounts Receivable," *Financial Management,* Winter 1977, 67–70.

Gentry, James A., and Jesus M. De La Garza, "A Generalized Model for Monitoring Accounts Receivable," *Financial Management,* Winter 1985, 28–38.

Hill, Ned C., and Kenneth D. Riener, "Determining the Cash Discount in the Firm's Credit Policy," *Financial Management,* Spring 1979, 68–73.

Kim, Yong H., and Joseph C. Atkins, "Evaluating Investments in Accounts Receivable: A Wealth Maximizing Framework," *Journal of Finance,* May 1978, 403–412.

Oh, John, S., "Opportunity Cost in the Evaluation of Investment in Accounts Receivable," *Financial Management,* Summer 1976, 32–36.

Roberts, Gordon S., and Jeremy A. Viscione, "Captive Finance Subsidiaries: The Manager's View," *Financial Management,* Spring 1981, 36–42.

Sachdeva, Kanwal S., and Lawrence J. Gitman, "Accounts Receivable Decisions in a Capital Budgeting Framework," *Financial Management,* Winter 1981, 45–49.

Walia, Tinlochan S., "Explicit and Implicit Cost of Changes in the Level of Accounts Receivable and the Credit Policy Decision of the Firm," *Financial Management,* Winter 1977, 75–78.

Weston, J. Fred, and Pham D. Tuan, "Comment on Analysis of Credit Policy Changes," *Financial Management,* Winter 1980, 59–63.

The following articles provide additional insights into the problems of inventory management:

Bierman, H., Jr., C. P. Bonini, and W. H. Hausman, *Quantitative Analysis for Business Decisions* (Homewood, Ill.: Irwin, 1977).

Brooks, L. D., "Risk-Return Criteria and Optimal Inventory Stocks," *Engineering Economist,* Summer 1980, 275–299.

Kallberg, Jarl G., and Kenneth L. Parkinson, *Current Asset Management: Cash, Credit, and Inventory* (New York: Wiley, 1984).

Mehta, Dileep R., *Working Capital Management* (Englewood Cliffs, N.J.: Prentice-Hall, 1974).

Shapiro, A., "Optimal Inventory and Credit Granting Strategies under Inflation and Devaluation," *Journal of Financial and Quantitative Analysis,* January 1973, 37–46.

Smith, Keith V., *Guide to Working Capital Management* (New York: McGraw-Hill, 1979).

The following cases focus on the credit policy decision:

Case 7, "Englehardt Kitchen," in the Crum-Brigham casebook, which demonstrates how the various credit policy variables interact to determine (1) the firm's level of accounts receivable and (2) its risk and rate of return.

"Zukowski Meats, Inc.," in the Harrington casebook, which stresses forecasting the effect of a credit policy change on the working capital accounts.

The Crum-Brigham casebook has a useful case on inventory management:

Case 8, "Good Connections," which focuses on the EOQ model and safety stocks.

20
Cash and Marketable Securities

Cash is the oil that lubricates the wheels of business. Without adequate oil, machines grind to a halt, and a business with inadequate cash will do likewise. On the other hand, carrying cash is expensive; since it is a nonearning asset, a firm that holds cash beyond its minimum requirements is lowering its potential earnings.

Cash management is developing into a very professional, highly refined activity. The following excerpt from a Union California Bank (UCB) advertisement illustrates what is involved:

> Using any lockbox will accelerate cash flow. But a UCB Lock Box System does it with maximum efficiency. One difference is our unique city-wide zip code system for California lockbox customers. It speeds the receipt of your lockbox mail by several hours.
>
> Another difference: We work around the clock, seven days a week. So you can be sure your funds will be deposited, regardless of absenteeism or seasonal work loads.
>
> A third difference: We're the only West Coast bank using helicopters to speed collections of checks, thus reducing float.
>
> Also, using our computerized optimization models, we can determine how many lockboxes you should use, where they should be located, and how much money you'll save with them.
>
> Finally — you need not keep idle cash balances to guard against a failure to receive expected payments or to be ready for unexpected outflows. We can arrange a line of credit for you, let you know by 11 a.m. how much (if any) you need to borrow to cover the checks you have written, and have the money in your account by 4 p.m. Or, if your account has net inflows on a given day, we will use these funds to reduce your loan balance or to purchase securities, as you direct. With this service, you'll never have funds sitting idle (or earning low checking account interest rates).
>
> The cost is surprisingly low. Call us, and let us show you how UCB can make your cash work harder.

For some companies, these ideas make good sense. However, firms sometimes go too far with their cash management systems. For example, the general practice in the securities brokerage business (until Merrill Lynch lost a major suit and agreed to stop doing it) was to write checks to customers located east of the Mississippi on a West Coast bank and checks to customers located west of the river on an East Coast bank. This slowed down payment of checks, deprived customers of the use of their money, and gave the brokerage firms the use of billions of dollars of their customers' money for extended periods of time. According to the SEC, this practice, although it increased brokerage firms' profits by millions of dollars each year, was "inconsistent with a broker-dealer's obligation to deal fairly with its customers."

Most companies hold substantial amounts of cash, which is defined as the sum of bank demand deposits plus currency. In addition, sizable holdings of near-cash marketable securities such as U.S. Treasury bills (T-bills) or bank certificates of deposit (CDs) are often reported on financial statements. Cash and securities balances vary widely both across industries and among the firms within a given industry, depending on the individual firms' specific conditions and on managements' aversion to risk. However, since cash is a nonearning asset, minimizing cash balances, but without hurting operations, is important. Financial managers, working with banks, have developed cash gathering and disbursing techniques designed to speed up the availability of funds and thus reduce the need for external financing. A number of securities have also been developed for the investment of temporarily idle cash. In this chapter, we examine the techniques and analyze the factors that financial managers consider when they work with cash and marketable securities.

CASH MANAGEMENT

Cash (currency plus demand deposits) is needed to pay for labor and raw materials, to buy fixed assets, to pay taxes, and so on. However, neither currency nor most commercial checking accounts earn interest, and, hence, the goal of the cash manager is to reduce the amount of cash held to the bare minimum necessary to conduct business. We begin our analysis with a discussion of reasons for holding cash.

Reasons for Holding Cash

Firms hold cash for two primary reasons:

1. Transactions. Cash balances are necessary to conduct business. Payments must be made in cash, and receipts are deposited in the cash account. Those cash balances associated with routine payments and/or collections are known as *transactions balances*.

2. Compensation to banks for providing loans and services. A bank makes money by lending out the funds which have been deposited with it; thus, depositing money in a bank helps the bank improve its profit position. If a bank is providing services to a customer, it often requires the customer to leave a minimum balance on deposit to help offset the costs of the services provided. This type of balance, defined as a *compensating balance,* is discussed in detail later in this chapter.

Two other reasons for holding cash that have been noted in the finance and economics literature are (1) for precaution and (2) for speculation. Cash inflows and outflows are unpredictable, with the degree of predictability varying among firms and industries. Therefore, it has been argued that firms need to hold some cash in reserve for random, unforeseen fluctuations in inflows and outflows. These "safety stocks" are defined as *precautionary balances,* and the less predictable the firm's cash flows, the larger such balances should be. However, if the firm has easy access to borrowed funds — that is, if it can borrow on short notice — its need for precautionary balances is reduced. Also, as we note later in this chapter, firms that would otherwise need large precautionary balances often hold highly liquid marketable securities rather than cash per se; such holdings accomplish the same purposes as cash balances, but they also provide interest income.

Some cash balances may be held to enable the firm to take advantage of any bargain purchases that might arise; these funds are defined as *speculative balances.* However, as with precautionary balances, firms today are more likely to rely on reserve borrowing power and on marketable securities portfolios than on cash per se for speculative purposes.

Although the cash accounts of most firms can be thought of as consisting of transactions, compensating, precautionary, and speculative balances, we cannot calculate the amount needed for each purpose, sum them, and produce a total desired cash balance, because the same money often serves more than one purpose — for instance, precautionary and speculative balances can also be used to satisfy compensating balance requirements. Firms do, however, consider these four factors when establishing their target cash positions.

Advantages of Holding Adequate Cash Balances

In addition to the motives just discussed, sound working capital management requires that an ample supply of cash be maintained for several specific reasons:

1. It is essential that the firm have sufficient cash to take *trade discounts.* Suppliers frequently offer customers discounts for prompt payment of bills; these discounts are termed trade discounts. As we saw in Chapter 18, the cost of not taking trade discounts is very high, so firms should have enough cash on hand to permit payment of bills on a timely basis in order to take advantage of trade discounts.

2. Adequate holdings of cash and near-cash assets can help the firm maintain its credit rating by keeping the current and quick ratios in line with those of other firms in its industry. A strong credit rating enables the firm to purchase goods from suppliers on favorable terms as well as to maintain a relatively low-cost line of credit with its bank.

3. Ample cash is useful for taking advantage of favorable business opportunities, such as special offers from suppliers or the chance to acquire another firm.

4. The firm should have sufficient cash and near-cash assets to meet such emergencies as strikes, fires, or competitors' marketing campaigns.

THE CASH BUDGET

A firm estimates its cash requirements as a part of its general budgeting, or forecasting, process. First, it forecasts both fixed asset and inventory requirements, along with the times when payments must be made. This information is combined with projections about delays in collecting accounts receivable, tax payment dates, dividend and interest payment dates, and so on. All of this information is summarized in the *cash budget,* which shows the firm's projected cash inflows and outflows over some specified period. Generally, firms develop a monthly cash budget for the coming year, plus a more detailed daily cash budget for the coming month. The monthly cash budgets are used for planning purposes and the daily budgets for actual cash control.

Constructing the Cash Budget

As noted above, cash budgets can be constructed on a monthly or a daily basis. We shall illustrate the process with a monthly cash budget covering the last six months of 1988 for the Foxcraft Printing Company, a leading producer of greeting cards. Foxcraft's birthday and get-well cards are sold year-round, but the bulk of the company's sales occurs from July through November, with a peak in September, when retailers are stocking up for Christmas and New Years. All sales are made on terms that allow a cash discount for payments made within 10 days, and if the discount is not taken, the full amount is due in 40 days. However, like most other companies, Foxcraft finds that some of its customers delay payment up to 90 days. Experience shows that on 20 percent of the sales, payment is made during the month in which the sale is made; on 70 percent of the sales, payment is made during the first month after the month of the sale; and on 10 percent of the sales, payment is made during the second month after the month of the sale. Foxcraft offers a 2 percent discount for payments received within 10 days of sales. Virtually all payments received in the month of sale are discount sales.

Rather than operate its production lines at a uniform rate throughout the year, Foxcraft prints cards immediately before they are required for delivery. Paper, ink, and other materials amount to 60 percent of sales, and these items are bought the month before the company expects to sell the finished product. Its own purchase terms permit Foxcraft to delay payment on purchases for one month. Accordingly, if July sales are forecast at $10 million, then purchases during June will amount to $7 million, and this amount will actually be paid in July.

Such other cash expenditures as wages and rent are also built into the cash budget, and Foxcraft must make tax payments of $2 million on September 15 and on December 15, while payment for a new plant must be made in October. Assuming that the company's target cash balance is $2.5 million, and that it has $3 million on July 1, what are Foxcraft's monthly cash requirements for the period July through December?[1]

The monthly cash requirements are worked out in Table 20-1. The top part of the table provides a worksheet for calculating both collections on sales and payments on purchases. The first line in the worksheet gives the sales forecast for the period May through December. (May and June sales are necessary to determine collections for July and August.) Next, cash collections are given. The first line of this section shows that 20 percent of the sales during any given month are collected that month. However, customers who pay in the first month typically take the discount, so the actual cash collected in the month of a sale is reduced by 2 percent. The second line shows the collections during a given month of sales made the prior month; collections are 70 percent of the preceding month's sales. The third line gives collections from sales two months earlier — 10 percent of sales in that month. The collections are summed to find the total cash receipts during each month of the cash budget period.

With the worksheet completed, the cash budget itself can be constructed. Cash from collections is given on Line 1. Next, on Lines 2 through 9, payments during each month are summarized. The difference between cash receipts and cash payments (Line 1 minus Line 9) is the net cash gain or loss during the month; for July there is a net cash loss of $2.39 million. The initial cash on hand at the beginning of the month is added to the net cash gain or loss during the month to obtain the cumulative cash that would be on hand if no financing were done; at the end of July, Foxcraft would have cumulative cash totaling $610,000 if it did no borrowing.

The target cash balance, $2.5 million, is next subtracted from the cumulative cash to determine the firm's borrowing requirements or surplus cash, whichever the case may be. At the end of July, Foxcraft expects to have cumulative cash, as shown on Line 12, of $610,000. It has a target cash balance of $2.5 million, and Foxcraft has arranged a $7 million revolving credit agreement with the Second National Bank of Dayton to meet its temporary cash needs. Thus, to maintain the target cash balance, Foxcraft would borrow $1.89 million on the revolver, and hence loans outstanding are projected to total $1.89 million at the end of July.

This same procedure is used in the following months. Sales will expand seasonally in August. With the increased sales will come increased payments for purchases, wages, and other items. Receipts from sales will also go up, but the firm will still be left with a $1.46 million net cash outflow during the month. The revolving loan balance at the end of August will be $3.35 million, the cumulative cash less the target cash balance. The $3.35 million is also equal to the $1.89 million needed at the end of July plus the $1.46 million cash loss for August. Sales peak in September, and the cash loss during this month will amount to $2.03 million. Thus, the revolving loan balance will increase to $5.38 million in September.

---

[1]Setting the target cash balance is an important part of cash management. We will discuss this topic in the next section.

Table 20-1
Foxcraft Printing Company: Worksheet and Cash Budget
(Thousands of Dollars)

	May	June	July	Aug.	Sept.	Oct.	Nov.	Dec.
Worksheet								
Sales (gross)	$5,000	$5,000	$10,000	$15,000	$20,000	$10,000	$10,000	$5,000
Collections:								
During month of sale (20% less 2% discount)	980	980	1,960	2,940	3,920	1,960	1,960	980
During first month after sale month (70%)		3,500	3,500	7,000	10,500	14,000	7,000	7,000
During second month after sale month (10%)			500	500	1,000	1,500	2,000	1,000
Total collections	$ 980	$4,480	$ 5,960	$10,440	$15,420	$17,460	$10,960	$8,980
Purchases (60% of next month's gross sales)	$3,000	$6,000	$9,000	$12,000	$6,000	$6,000	$ 3,000	
Payments (one-month lag)	$3,000	$3,000	$6,000	$ 9,000	$12,000	$6,000	$ 6,000	$3,000
Cash Budget								
(1) Collections (from worksheet)			$ 5,960	$10,440	$15,420	$17,460	$10,960	$8,980
(2) Payments:								
(3) Purchases (from worksheet)			$ 6,000	$ 9,000	$12,000	$ 6,000	$ 6,000	$3,000
(4) Wages and salaries			2,000	2,500	3,000	2,000	2,000	1,500
(5) Rent			250	250	250	250	250	250
(6) Other expenses			100	150	200	100	100	50
(7) Taxes					2,000			2,000
(8) Payment for plant construction						5,000		
(9) Total payments			$ 8,350	$11,900	$17,450	$13,350	$ 8,350	$6,800
(10) Net cash gain (loss) during month (Line 1 – Line 9)			($ 2,390)	($ 1,460)	($ 2,030)	$ 4,110	$ 2,610	$2,180
(11) Cash at start of month if no borrowing is done (start July with $3,000; calculated thereafter)			3,000	610	(850)	(2,880)	1,230	3,840
(12) Cumulative cash (cash at start + gains or – losses = Line 10 + Line 11)			$ 610	($ 850)	($ 2,880)	$ 1,230	$ 3,840	$6,020
(13) Deduct: Target cash balance			2,500	2,500	2,500	2,500	2,500	2,500
(14) Total loans outstanding required to maintain target cash balance			$ 1,890	$ 3,350	$ 5,380	$ 1,270	—	—
(15) Surplus cash			—	—	—	—	$ 1,340	$3,520

Notes:

a. The amount shown on Line 11 for the first month, the $3,000 balance on July 1, was on hand initially. The values shown for each of the following months on Line 11 represent the cumulative cash as shown on Line 12 for the preceding month; for example, the $610 shown on Line 11 for August is taken from Line 12 in the July column.

b. When the target cash balance of $2,500 (Line 13) is deducted from the cumulative cash balance (Line 12), if a negative figure results, it is shown on Line 14 as a required loan, while if a positive figure results, it is shown on Line 15 as surplus cash.

Sales, purchases, and payments for past purchases will fall markedly in October, and collections will be the highest of any month because they reflect the high September sales. As a result, Foxcraft should enjoy a healthy $4.11 million cash gain during October. These funds will be used to pay down the revolver, so loans outstanding will decline by $4.11 million, to $1.27 million. In November, Foxcraft will have another cash surplus which will permit it to pay off the entire revolving loan balance. In fact, the company is expected to have $1.34 million in surplus cash by the month's end, while another cash surplus in December will swell the extra cash to $3.52 million. With such a large amount of unneeded funds, Foxcraft's treasurer will doubtless want to invest in interest-bearing securities or to put the funds to use in some other way.

Before concluding our discussion of the cash budget, we should make six additional points:

1. Our cash budget does not reflect interest on the revolving loan or income from the investment of surplus cash. This refinement could be added easily.

2. More important, if cash inflows and outflows are not uniform during the month, we could be seriously understating or overstating our financing requirements. For example, if payments for purchases must be made on the fifth of each month, but collections come in uniformly throughout the month, then we would need to borrow much larger amounts than those shown in Table 20-1. In such a case, we would need to prepare a cash budget on a daily basis.

3. Since depreciation is a noncash charge, it does not appear on the cash budget (other than through its effect on taxes paid).

4. The cash budget represents a forecast, so all the values in the table are *expected* values. If actual sales, purchases, and so on are different from the forecasted levels, then our forecasted cash gains and losses will also be incorrect. This point is explored further in the next section.

5. Computerized spreadsheet models are particularly well suited for constructing and analyzing the cash budget. Such models are especially useful for analyzing the sensitivity of cash flows to changes in sales levels, collection periods, and the like.

6. Finally, we should note that the target cash balance, set here at $2.5 million, would probably be adjusted over time, rising and falling with seasonal swings and also with long-term changes in the scale of the firm's operations. Factors that influence the target cash balance are discussed in the following sections. Also, the firm might even set the target cash balance at zero — this could be done if it carried a portfolio of marketable securities which could be sold to replenish the cash account, or if it had an arrangement with its bank that permitted it to borrow the funds it needed on a daily basis. In that event, the cash budget would simply stop with Line 12, and the amounts on that line would represent the projected loans outstanding or surplus cash. Note, though, that most firms would find it difficult to operate with a zero balance bank account, just as you would, and the costs of such an operation would in most instances offset the opportunity cost associated with maintaining a positive cash balance. Therefore, most firms do have a positive target cash balance.

SETTING THE TARGET CASH BALANCE

When we discussed Foxcraft's cash budget, we assumed that the company had a $2.5 million target cash balance. Setting the target cash balance in practice is a difficult task, and several methods have been proposed to help financial managers establish the correct level. In this section, we discuss *scenario analysis,* one of the methods used to help set the target cash balance.[2]

Projected sales is the key element in the cash budget, but the collections pattern is also quite important. In the Table 20-1 cash budget, we used expected values for both sales and the collections pattern. Now we repeat the cash budget, but under the assumption that sales and collections differ from their expected values. Specifically, we assume that there is a 20 percent probability that sales will drop to 90 percent of the forecasted value in each month, and a 10 percent chance that sales will drop to only 80 percent of the expected level. Thus, in May there is a 20 percent probability that sales will be $0.9(\$5,000) = \$4,500$, and a 10 percent probability that sales will be only $0.8(\$5,000) = \$4,000$. Sales in June through December are subject to similar uncertainties. We can now construct new cash budgets using these lower forecasted sales levels.

In our previous cash budget, collections were based on forecasted sales, so in our new cash budget collections will reflect the possibility of new, lower sales levels. Lower sales will occur if the economy weakens, and if this happens, Foxcraft's customers will probably have trouble paying their bills. Hence, the payments pattern for receivables will probably also be affected. Therefore, we assume that if sales are down to 80 percent of the expected level, only 60 percent of Foxcraft's customers will pay in the month after sale and 20 percent will pay in the second month. The 20 percent of customers who currently take the discount and pay in the month the sale occurs are Foxcraft's strongest, and hence their payments would not be significantly affected by a weak economy.

If we assume that Foxcraft would recognize the lower sales levels before May, and would adjust its forecasts accordingly, then its materials purchases would also be based on the new, lower sales forecasts. However, other payments such as wages, rent, and so on are assumed to be fixed, although uncertainty could be built into them, too.

Based on these assumptions, we used a *Lotus 1-2-3* model to conduct a scenario analysis of Foxcraft's cash budget. This analysis is summarized in Table 20-2, which shows Line 10 of Table 20-1, the net cash gain (loss) during the month. Since there is a 30 percent probability of sales being lower than the base case forecasts, then there is a 70 percent probability that sales will be at least as high as the forecasted levels. Note also that cash needs increase as sales decline. Thus, the additional borrowing requirement in September will be over $1 million greater if sales fall to 80 percent of the forecasted level rather than hit the forecast.

Now suppose Foxcraft's managers want to be 90 percent confident that the firm will not run out of cash in any month. In this case, they would use variable target cash balances, and they would set each beginning-of-month target balance equal to

---

[2]See Eugene F. Brigham and Louis C. Gapenski, *Intermediate Financial Management,* 2nd ed., Chapter 18, for a discussion of other techniques used to help establish the target cash balance.

Table 20-2
Summary of Cash Budget Scenario Analysis
(Thousands of Dollars)

Sales	Probability	Net Cash Gain (Loss) for Month					
		July	Aug.	Sept.	Oct.	Nov.	Dec.
Base case or better	0.7	($2,390)	($1,460)	($2,030)	$4,110	$2,610	$2,180
90% of forecast	0.2	(2,415)	(1,604)	(2,372)	2,964	2,114	1,582
80% of forecast	0.1	(2,579)	(2,148)	(3,114)	1,418	2,018	984

the values shown on the middle line in Table 20-2. For example, July's target would be $2,415,000. With this target cash balance at the beginning of the month, there would be only a 10 percent probability that the net cash loss would actually be higher, and hence that the firm would run short of cash. Specifically, there is a 10 percent chance that the net cash flow in July will be − $2,579,000, leaving Foxcraft with a $2,579,000 − $2,415,000 = $164,000 shortage.

Note that this analysis assumes that cash inflows and outflows occur evenly over the month. If this is not the case, then a larger beginning-of-month target balance might be required, and Foxcraft should also use a daily cash budget. Also, note that the target cash balance for those months with positive cash flows, like October, would indicate a zero beginning-of-month target balance. This would probably not be acceptable to management, so a small "safety stock" of cash would be kept on hand.

This type of analysis could be extended for the other months, and it could be used in lieu of the fixed $2.5 million as Foxcraft's target beginning-of-month cash balance. Note that the forecasted cash budget will change as new information becomes known. For example, at the beginning of June, Foxcraft's managers will know the May sales figure, so they can adjust the cash budget accordingly. If May sales come in at their expected level, then only minimal changes will be required. However, if sales are significantly higher or lower, and if this trend is expected to continue, then the cash budget must be adjusted to reflect the new estimates for June and beyond.[3]

Other Factors Influencing the Target Cash Balance

Firms actually set their target cash balances as the larger of (1) their transactions balances plus precautionary (safety stock) balances or (2) their required compensating balances as determined by their agreements with banks. Transactions bal-

[3]Note that Monte Carlo simulation analysis could also be used to set the target cash balance. The concepts are exactly the same as we just discussed, except that continuous distributions would be used to represent the uncertainty inherent in the cash budget forecasts. See Eugene M. Lerner, "Simulating a Cash Budget," *Readings on the Management of Working Capital,* Keith V. Smith, ed. (St. Paul, Minn.: West, 1980).

ances and precautionary balances depend upon the firm's volume of business, the degree of uncertainty inherent in its forecasts of cash inflows and outflows, its ability to borrow on short notice to meet cash shortfalls, and the availability of marketable securities which can be sold off if more cash is needed. Consider again the cash budget shown for Foxcraft Printing Company in Table 20-1. The target cash balance is shown on Line 13 of the table. Other factors held constant, the target cash balance would increase if Foxcraft expanded, whereas it would decrease if Foxcraft contracted. Similarly, Foxcraft could afford to operate with a smaller target balance if it could forecast better and thus be more certain that inflows would come in as scheduled, and that no unanticipated outflows such as might result from uninsured fire losses, lawsuits, and the like, would occur.

Statistics are not available on whether transactions balances or compensating balances actually control most firms' target cash balances, but compensating balance requirements do often dominate, especially during periods of high interest rates and tight money.[4]

INCREASING THE EFFICIENCY OF CASH MANAGEMENT

A cash budget is a necessary starting point for managing the firm's cash. However, as we discuss below, there are other elements of a good cash management program.

Cash Flow Synchronization

If you as an individual were to receive income once a year, you would probably put it in the bank, draw down your account periodically, and have an average balance during the year equal to about half your annual income. If you received income monthly instead of once a year, you would operate similarly, but now your average balance would be much smaller. If you could arrange to receive income daily and to pay rent, tuition, and other charges on a daily basis, and if you were quite confident of your forecasted inflows and outflows, then you could hold a very small average cash balance.

Exactly the same situation holds for business firms — by improving their forecasts and arranging things so that their cash receipts coincide with required cash

---

[4]This point is underscored by an incident that occurred at a professional finance meeting. A professor presented a scholarly paper that used operations research techniques to determine "optimal cash balances" for a sample of firms. He then reported that actual cash balances of the firms greatly exceeded their "optimal" balances, suggesting inefficiency and the need for more refined techniques. The discussant of the paper made her comments short and sweet. She reported that she had written and asked the sample firms why they had so much cash. They uniformly replied that their cash holdings were set by compensating balance requirements. The model was useful to determine the optimal cash balance in the absence of compensating balance requirements, but it was precisely those requirements that determined actual balances. Since the model did not include compensating balances as a determinant of cash balances, its usefulness was questionable.

outflows, firms can reduce their transactions balances to a minimum. Recognizing this point, utility companies, oil companies, credit card companies, and so on arrange to bill customers, and to pay their own bills, on regular "billing cycles" throughout the month. This improves the *synchronization of cash flows,* which in turn enables a firm to reduce its cash balances, decrease its bank loans, lower interest expenses, and boost profits.

Using Float

Float is defined as the difference between the balance shown in a firm's (or individual's) checkbook and the balance on the bank's records. Suppose a firm writes, on the average, checks in the amount of $5,000 each day, and it takes six days for these checks to clear and to be deducted from the firm's bank account. This will cause the firm's own checkbook to show a balance $30,000 smaller than the balance on the bank's records; this difference is called *disbursement float.* Now suppose the firm also receives checks in the amount of $5,000 daily, but it loses four days while they are being deposited and cleared. This will result in $20,000 of *collections float.* In total, the firm's *net float* — the difference between $30,000 positive disbursement float and the $20,000 negative collections float — will be $10,000.

If the firm's own collection and clearing process is more efficient than that of the recipients of its checks — which is generally true of larger, more efficient firms — then the firm could actually show a *negative* balance on its own books but have a *positive* balance on the records of its bank. Some firms indicate that they *never* have positive book cash balances. One large manufacturer of construction equipment stated that while its account, according to its bank's records, shows an average cash balance of about $20 million, its *book* cash balance is *minus* $20 million — it has $40 million of net float. Obviously the firm must be able to forecast its disbursements and collections accurately in order to make such heavy use of float.

E. F. Hutton provides an example of pushing cash management too far. Hutton did business with banks all across the country, and it had to keep compensating balances in these banks. The sizes of the required compensating balances were known, and any excess funds in these banks were sent electronically, on a daily basis, to concentration banks, where they were immediately invested in interest-bearing securities. However, rather than waiting to see what the end-of-day balances actually were, Hutton began estimating inflows and outflows, and it transferred out for investment the *estimated* end-of-day excess. But then Hutton got greedy — it began to deliberately overestimate its deposits and underestimate clearings of its own checks, thereby deliberately overstating the estimated end-of-day balances. As a result, Hutton was chronically overdrawn at its local banks, and it was in effect earning interest on funds which really belonged to those local banks. It is entirely proper to forecast what your bank will have recorded as your balance and then to make decisions based on the estimate, even if that balance is different from the balance your own books show. However, it is illegal to forecast an overdrawn situation but then to tell the bank that you forecast a positive balance.[5]

Basically, a firm's net float is a function of its ability to speed up collections on checks received and to slow down collections on checks written. Efficient firms go to great lengths to speed up the processing of incoming checks, thus putting the funds to work faster, and they try to stretch their own payments out as long as possible.

Speeding Collections

When a customer writes and mails a check, this does *not* mean that the funds are immediately available to the receiving firm. First, some amount of time passes before the check is received by the seller; this delay is called *mail float*. Second, after the firm receives the check, time is required to credit the account and to deposit the check, giving rise to *processing float*. A third type of float, which results because of the time it takes a check to be cleared within the banking system, is called *transit float*. For example, most of us have deposited a check in our account and then been told that we cannot write our own checks against this deposit until the *check-clearing process* has been completed. Our bank must (1) make sure that the check we deposited is good and (2) receive funds itself from the customer's bank before releasing funds for us to spend.

As shown on the left side of Figure 20-1, the total amount of time required for a firm to process incoming checks and obtain the use of the money can be substantial. A check must first be delivered through the mails and then cleared through the banking system before the money can be put to use. Checks received from customers in distant cities are especially subject to delays because of mail time and also because more parties are involved. For example, assume that we receive a check and deposit it in our bank. Our bank must send the check to the bank on which it was drawn. Only when the payer's bank transfers funds to our bank are they available for us to use. Checks are generally cleared through the Federal Reserve System or through a clearinghouse set up by the banks in a particular city. Of course, if the check is deposited in the same bank on which it was drawn, that bank merely transfers funds by bookkeeping entries from one of its depositors to another. The length of time required for other checks to clear is thus a function of the distance between the payer's and the payee's banks; in the case of private clearinghouses, it can range from one to three days. The maximum time

---

[5]A question raised during the Hutton investigation was this: "Why didn't the banks recognize that Hutton was systematically overdrawing its account and call the company to task?" The answer is that some banks, with tight controls, did exactly that — they refused to let Hutton get away with the practice. Other banks were lax. Still other banks apparently let Hutton get away with being chronically overdrawn out of fear of losing its business: Hutton used its economic muscle to force the banks to let it get away with an illegal act. In many people's opinion, the banks were as much at fault as Hutton. Still, in business dealings, honesty is presumed, and Hutton was dishonest in its dealings with the banks. This dishonesty severely damaged Hutton's reputation, cost the company profits totaling hundreds of millions of dollars, and cost its top managers their jobs.

Figure 20-1
Diagram of the Check-Clearing Process

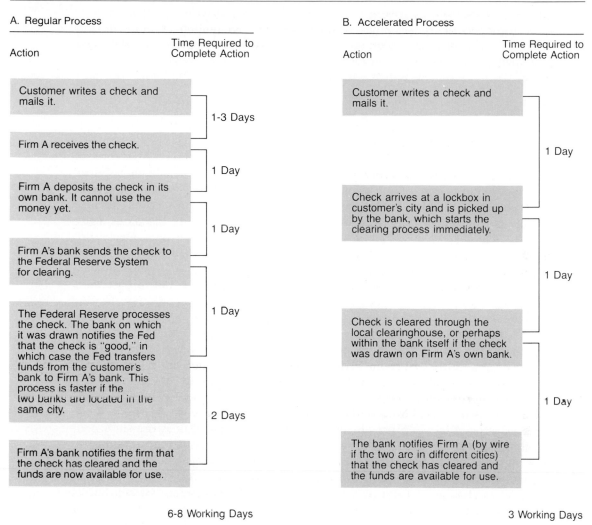

A. Regular Process

Action	Time Required to Complete Action
Customer writes a check and mails it.	1-3 Days
Firm A receives the check.	1 Day
Firm A deposits the check in its own bank. It cannot use the money yet.	1 Day
Firm A's bank sends the check to the Federal Reserve System for clearing.	1 Day
The Federal Reserve processes the check. The bank on which it was drawn notifies the Fed that the check is "good," in which case the Fed transfers funds from the customer's bank to Firm A's bank. This process is faster if the two banks are located in the same city.	2 Days
Firm A's bank notifies the firm that the check has cleared and the funds are now available for use.	

6-8 Working Days

B. Accelerated Process

Action	Time Required to Complete Action
Customer writes a check and mails it.	1 Day
Check arrives at a lockbox in customer's city and is picked up by the bank, which starts the clearing process immediately.	1 Day
Check is cleared through the local clearinghouse, or perhaps within the bank itself if the check was drawn on Firm A's own bank.	1 Day
The bank notifies Firm A (by wire if the two are in different cities) that the check has cleared and the funds are available for use.	

3 Working Days

required for checks to clear through the Federal Reserve System is two days, but mail delays can slow down things on each end of the Fed's involvement in the process.

The right side of Figure 20-1 shows how the process can be speeded up. First, to reduce mail float a *lockbox plan* can be used. Suppose a New York firm makes sales to customers all across the country. A check from the West Coast could take three or four days to reach New York and be delivered. To speed up the process, the firm can arrange to have its customers send payments to post office boxes (lockboxes) in their own local areas. A local bank will pick up the checks, have them cleared in the local area, and then transfer the funds by wire to the company's New York bank. In this way, collection time can be reduced by one to five days. Examples of freeing funds in the amount of $5 million or more by this method are common. However, the lockbox plan does have a cost. The local banks will charge the New York firm for the collection and funds transfer services rendered. To determine whether a lockbox system is advantageous, the firm must compare the bank fees with the gains from reducing float.

Slowing Disbursements

Just as expediting the collection process conserves cash, slowing down disbursements accomplishes the same thing by keeping cash on hand for longer periods. One obviously could simply delay making payments, but this would involve equally obvious difficulties. Firms have in the past devised rather ingenious methods for "legitimately" lengthening the collection period on their own checks, primarily by writing checks on banks in out-of-the-way places. For example, as we noted in the introduction, Merrill Lynch formerly wrote checks to its customers who lived east of the Mississippi River on a San Francisco bank, but to customers who lived west of the river on a New York bank. This delayed the check-clearing process and thus increased the length of time for which Merrill Lynch had use of the funds. Hundreds of millions of dollars were involved, and Merrill was finally forced to stop the practice as a result of a lawsuit. Other firms use banks in southeast Missouri, North Dakota, or other hard-to-get-to spots for the same purpose. Since such practices are usually recognized for what they are, there are severe limits to their use.

Another widely used procedure for delaying payouts is the use of *drafts*. While a check is payable when presented to the bank on which it was drawn, a draft must be transmitted to the issuer, who approves it and deposits funds to cover it, and only then can it be collected. Insurance companies often use drafts. In handling claims, for instance, Aetna can pay a claim by draft on Friday. The recipient deposits the draft at a local bank, which must then send it to Aetna's Hartford bank. It may be Wednesday or Thursday before the draft arrives. The bank then sends it to the company's accounting department, which has until 3 p.m. that day to inspect and approve it. Not until then does Aetna have to deposit funds in its bank to pay the draft. "Checks" which are written on mutual fund accounts are also drafts — this permits funds to keep more of their money "working" for the fundholders.

Transfer Mechanisms

A *transfer mechanism* is a system for moving funds among accounts at different banks. The main transfer mechanisms are depository transfer checks (DTC), electronic depository transfer checks (EDTC), and wire transfers.

Depository Transfer Check

A *depository transfer check (DTC)* looks like an ordinary check, except that it is restricted for deposit into a particular account at a particular bank. A DTC is payable only to the bank of deposit for credit to the firm's specific account. DTCs provide a means of moving funds from local depository banks to regional *concentration banks* and then into the firm's primary money center bank. For example, IBM might have its customers in the Sacramento area send payment checks to a lockbox in the area, then have the Wells Fargo Bank office pick up and process the checks, depositing the funds in IBM's account with Wells' Sacramento branch. If the account's balance exceeded the compensating balance requirement, then the Wells Fargo people would automatically make out a DTC payable to IBM's account in its regional concentration bank, which might be Bank of America's San Francisco office. Bank of America's office, in turn, could use DTCs to transmit excess balances to IBM's account in Citibank's New York headquarters. Through this process, IBM would get its funds concentrated where they could be invested most efficiently, while still maintaining its required compensating balances at hundreds of local banks all across the country.

Electronic Depository Transfer Check

An alternative transfer mechanism is the electronic image transfer via automated clearinghouses run by the Federal Reserve System. The *electronic image transfer system* is a combination of a wire and a DTC. Since it is an electronic DTC, it is referred to as an EDTC. The EDTC is paperless — like a wire — but it involves a uniform, one-day availability in clearing time because it avoids the use of the mails.

Wire Transfer

A *wire transfer* of funds between banks makes funds collected at one bank immediately available for use at another bank, even in a different city. It is the fastest way to move cash between banks, and it completely eliminates transit float. One bank wire method utilizes a private wire network which is operated by about 300 banks throughout the United States. These banks use a telecommunication network for transferring funds, exchanging credit information, and making securities transactions. As an alternative, the Federal Reserve operates a wire system which can be used by any commercial bank that is a member of the Federal Reserve System. Commercial banks that are members of neither the private bank wire system nor the Federal Reserve System can obtain access to the wire transfer system through their correspondent banks, but this is a more cumbersome procedure. Accordingly, firms large enough to require frequent wire transfers generally do business with banks equipped to provide this service.

Wire transfers are typically initiated on a standing order basis. Company headquarters will send a written authorization to a local depository bank calling for the transfer of funds to the firm's concentration bank when the amount exceeds some target level, say $80,000. The use of standing instructions (which can be programmed into a computer and executed automatically) to transfer funds can be an efficient way of managing complex cash-gathering systems, as it avoids the need for daily communication between distant locations yet insures that cash gets where it can be invested promptly.

Cash Management in the Multidivisional Firm

The concepts, techniques, and procedures described thus far in the chapter must be extended when applied to large national or international firms. Such corporations have plants and sales offices all across the nation (or the world), and they deal with banks in all of their operating territories. These companies must maintain compensating balances in each of their banks, and they must be sure that no bank account becomes overdrawn. (After E. F. Hutton's problems, this has become especially important.) Cash inflows and outflows are subject to random fluctuations, so in the absence of close control and coordination, there would be a tendency for accounts in some banks to have shortages while others had excess balances. Thus, a sound cash management program for such a multibank corporation necessarily includes provisions for keeping strict control over the level of funds in each account and for shifting funds among accounts so as to minimize the total corporate cash balance. Mathematical models and electronic connections (often using satellite transmitters) between a central computer and each branch location have been developed to help with such situations, but a discussion of these topics would go beyond the scope of this book.

BANK RELATIONSHIPS

Banks provide a great many services to firms — they clear checks, operate lockbox plans, supply credit information, and the like. Since these services cost the bank money, the bank must be compensated for rendering them.

Compensating Balances

Banks earn most of their income by lending money at interest, and most of the funds they lend are obtained in the form of deposits. If a firm maintains a deposit account with an average balance of $100,000, and if the bank can lend these funds at a net return of $8,000, then the account is, in a sense, worth $8,000 to the bank. Thus, it is to the bank's advantage to provide services worth up to $8,000 to attract and hold the account.

Banks first determine the costs of the services rendered to their larger customers, then they estimate the average account balance necessary to provide enough income to compensate for these costs. Firms could pay direct fees for these services, but they often find it cheaper to maintain compensating balances.[6]

Compensating balances are also required by some banks under loan agreements. During periods when the supply of credit is restricted and interest rates are high, banks frequently insist that borrowers maintain accounts averaging a specified percentage of the loan amount as a condition for granting a loan; 15 percent is a

---

[6]Compensating balance arrangements apply to individuals as well as to business firms. Thus, you might get "free" checking services if you maintain a minimum balance of $500 but be charged 10 cents per check if your balance falls below that amount during the month.

typical figure. If the required balance is larger than the firm would otherwise maintain, then the effective cost of the loan is increased; the excess balance presumably "compensates" the bank for making a loan at a rate below what it could earn on the funds if they were invested elsewhere.[7]

Compensating balances can be established (1) as an *absolute minimum* — say, $100,000 — below which the actual balance must never fall or (2) as a *minimum average* balance over some period, generally a month. The absolute minimum is a much more restrictive requirement, because the total amount of cash held during the month must be above $100,000 by the amount of the firm's transactions balances. The $100,000 in this case is "dead money" from the firm's standpoint. With an average balance requirement, however, the account could fall to zero on one day provided it was $200,000 on some other day, with the average working out to $100,000. Thus, the $100,000 in this case is available for transactions.

Average balances are typical — absolute minimums rare for business accounts. Discussions with bankers, however, indicate that absolute balance requirements are less rare during times of extremely tight money.

Overdraft Systems

Most countries outside the United States use *overdraft systems,* where depositors write checks in excess of their actual balances, and then their banks automatically extend loans to cover the shortages. The maximum amount of such loans must, of course, be established beforehand. Although statistics are not available on the use of overdrafts in the United States, a number of firms have worked out informal, and in some cases formal, overdraft arrangements. Also, both banks and credit card companies regularly establish "cash reserve" systems for individuals. The use of overdrafts has been increasing in recent years, and if this trend continues, it will lead to a reduction in corporate cash balances.

MATCHING THE COSTS AND BENEFITS OF CASH MANAGEMENT

Although a number of procedures may be used to hold down cash balance requirements, implementing these methods is not a costless operation. How far should a firm go in making its cash operations more efficient? *As a general rule, the firm should incur these expenses so long as marginal returns exceed marginal costs.*

For example, suppose that by establishing a lockbox system and simultaneously increasing the accuracy of cash inflow and outflow forecasts, a firm can reduce its cash balance by $1 million without increasing the risk of running short of cash. Further, suppose the firm borrows at a cost of 12 percent. The steps taken have released $1 million, which can be used to reduce bank loans and thus save $120,000 per year. If the costs of the procedures necessary to release the $1 mil-

---

[7]We discussed the impact of compensating balances on loan costs in Chapter 18.

lion are less than $120,000, the move is a good one; if they exceed $120,000, the greater efficiency is not worth the cost. It is clear that larger firms, which have larger cash balances, can better afford to hire the personnel necessary to maintain tight control over their cash positions. Cash management is thus one element of business operations in which economies of scale are present.

In the following section we present a model which firms use to select the most cost-efficient method for transferring funds.

Comparing the Costs of Alternative Transfer Mechanisms

The wire transfer system is the quickest transfer mechanism, but it is also the most expensive. There is no delay in a wire transfer, but the typical cost ranges from $6 to $8. A mail depository transfer check (DTC) may cost only 40 to 50 cents, but it may involve a delay of from 2 to 7 days. An evaluation of the alternatives has conventionally involved a comparison of the extra interest earned as a result of the faster transfer versus the extra cost involved in using a faster transfer mechanism. The conventional formula for the breakeven transfer size is as follows:

$$S^* = \frac{\Delta C}{I\Delta T}. \qquad (20\text{-}1)$$

Here

S^* = the breakeven size of transfer above which the faster, higher-cost mechanism should be used.

ΔC = the additional cost of using the faster mechanism.

I = the applicable daily interest rate expressed as a decimal.

ΔT = the difference in transfer time in days.

If the cost differential between a wire transfer and a DTC is ΔC = $6, with a time difference of ΔT = 2 days and an interest rate on funds at the concentration bank of I = 0.11/360 = 0.000306 per day, the breakeven transfer size would be approximately $10,000:

$$S^* = \frac{\$6.00}{0.000306(2)} = \$9,804 \approx \$10,000.$$

Thus, on amounts over $10,000, a wire transfer should be used. If the time saved were only one day, the breakeven size would be almost $20,000.

Simple cost comparisons are giving way to newer, more sophisticated programming techniques. Stone and Hill have pointed out various shortcomings in the above analysis of the costs of alternative transfer mechanisms.[8] They argue that the

---

[8]This discussion is based on Bernell K. Stone and Ned C. Hill, "The Evaluation of Alternative Cash Transfer Mechanisms and Methods," *Proceedings of the Nineteenth Annual Meeting of the Southwestern Finance Association,* 1980, 39–58.

conventional breakeven analysis fails to consider (1) the value of funds held in the depository bank and (2) time delays in the availability of funds. They also note that banks assign "service credits," which are used to offset service charges, to firms in recognition of the profitability of the firms' account balances to the bank. Thus, amounts in an account over the required balance are not a complete waste to the depositing firm, because during the time funds are being transferred, they are earning service credits at the depository institution. Therefore, the opportunity costs of using a slower transfer mechanism is the *difference* between the interest rate and the earnings credit rate.

Stone and Hill also point out that the choice of transfer alternatives should take time delays into account. For example, a wire transfer cannot be initiated until the funds to be transferred become available. A DTC, on the other hand, can be sent so that it arrives at the concentration bank on the day the funds become available at the depository bank. In this case, there is no time difference between the two transfer mechanisms. However, the advance mailing of DTCs does require the ability to forecast receipts accurately.

MARKETABLE SECURITIES

Sizable holdings of such short-term *marketable securities* as U.S. Treasury bills (T-bills) or bank certificates of deposit (CDs) are often reported on corporations' financial statements. The reasons for such holdings, as well as the factors that influence the choice of securities held, are discussed in this section.

Reasons for Holding Marketable Securities

Marketable securities typically provide much lower yields than operating assets. For example, in 1986, International Business Machines (IBM) held a $4.7 billion portfolio of marketable securities that yielded about 9 percent, while its operating assets provided a return of more than 20 percent. Why would a company such as IBM have such large holdings of low-yielding assets? There are two basic reasons for these holdings: (1) they serve as a substitute for cash balances, and (2) they are used as a temporary investment. These points are considered next.

Marketable Securities as a Substitute for Cash

Some firms hold portfolios of marketable securities in lieu of larger cash balances, then sell off some securities to increase the cash account if and when cash outflows exceed inflows. For example, during the late 1970s, IBM built up its marketable securities portfolio to over $6 billion. This large liquid balance was carried as a reserve for possible damage charges that might result from pending antitrust suits. When it became clear that IBM would win most of the suits, its liquidity need declined, and the company spent some of the funds on other assets, including the repurchase of close to a billion dollars of its own stock and the acquisition of several firms in the telecommunications industry. This is a prime example of a firm's building up its marketable securities balances to handle possible emergencies.

Marketable Securities as a Temporary Investment

Temporary investments in marketable securities generally occur in one of the three following situations:

1. When the firm must finance seasonal or cyclical operations. Firms such as Macy's which are engaged in seasonal operations frequently have surplus cash flows during one part of the year and deficit cash flows during the other. Macy's and other firms purchase marketable securities when cash builds up and then liquidate these securities when cash deficits occur. Other firms, however, choose to use bank financings to cover such shortages.

2. When the firm must meet some known financial requirements. If a major plant construction program is planned for the near future, or if a bond issue is about to mature, a firm may build up its marketable securities portfolio to provide the required funds. Marketable securities holdings are also built up immediately preceding quarterly corporate tax payment dates.

3. When the firm has just sold long-term securities. Expanding firms generally have to sell long-term securities (stocks or bonds) periodically. The proceeds from such sales are often invested in marketable securities, which are then sold off to provide cash as it is needed to pay for operating assets.

Marketable Securities Versus Borrowing

Actually, each of the needs listed above can be met either by borrowing on a short-term basis or by holding marketable securities. Consider a business such as the Foxcraft Printing Company, whose cash budget was discussed at the beginning of this chapter. Foxcraft's sales are growing over time, but they fluctuate on a seasonal basis; these operating swings cause Foxcraft's cash balance to fluctuate. As we saw, Foxcraft's cash needs are highest just before its peak selling season, but it will have excess cash after the season peaks and it begins to collect peak season receivables. Foxcraft's policy is to borrow from its bank to meet seasonal needs, but an alternative financial policy would be to hold a portfolio of marketable securities and then to liquidate those securities to meet cash needs.

A firm's marketable securities policy is an integral part of its overall working capital policy. If a company has a conservative working capital financing policy as depicted in Figure 18-3 in Chapter 18, then its long-term capital will exceed its permanent assets, and it will hold marketable securities when inventories and receivables are low. With an aggressive policy, it will never carry any securities, choosing instead to borrow to meet peak needs. With a moderate policy, under which maturities are matched, the firm will finance permanent assets with long-term capital, but it will finance its seasonal increases in inventories and receivables with short-term loans.

There are advantages and disadvantages to each of these strategies. The aggressive policy is clearly the most risky — the firm's current ratio is always lower than under the other plans because the firm has fewer assets and more short-term debt than more conservative firms, which could lead to difficulties either in borrowing the funds needed or in repaying the loan. On the other hand, the aggressive approach requires no holdings of low-yielding marketable securities, and this will probably lead to a relatively high expected rate of return on both total assets and equity. The conservative policy, on the other hand, is the least risky, but it also has the lowest expected rate of return.

Exactly the same types of choices are involved with regard to meeting known financial needs such as plant construction, and also when deciding whether to issue long-term securities before or after the actual need for the funds arises. Commonwealth Edison, the electric utility serving Chicago, can be used to illustrate the issues involved in timing the sale of long-term securities. Commonwealth has a permanent, ongoing construction program, which generates a continuous need for new outside capital. There are substantial fixed costs involved in stock or bond flotations, so these securities are issued infrequently and in large amounts. During the 1960s, Commonwealth followed the practice of selling bonds and stocks *before* the capital was needed, investing the proceeds in marketable securities, and then liquidating these assets to finance plant construction. Plan A in Figure 20-2 illustrates this procedure. However, during the 1970s and 1980s, Commonwealth's nuclear construction program caused financial stress, and the company was forced to use up its liquid assets and to switch to its present policy of financing plant construction with short-term bank loans, then selling long-term securities to retire these loans when they have built up to some target level. This policy is illustrated by Plan B of Figure 20-2.

Figure 20-2
Alternative Methods of Financing a Continuous Construction Program

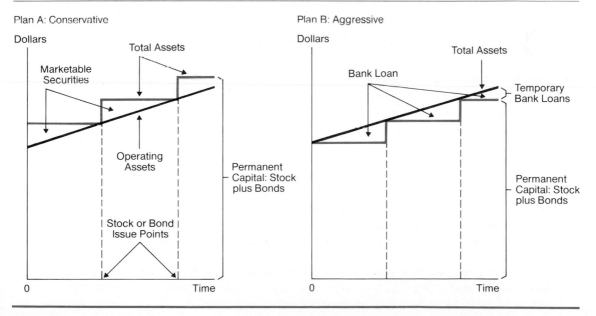

Plan A is the more conservative, less risky one. First, the company is minimizing its liquidity problems because it has no short-term debt hanging over its head. Second, it is sure of having the funds available to meet construction payments as they come due. On the other hand, when firms borrow they generally have to pay interest rates that are higher than the return they receive on marketable securities, so following the less risky strategy does have a cost. Again, firms are faced with a risk/return trade-off.

It is difficult to "prove" that one financing strategy is better than another. In principle, the practice of holding marketable securities reduces the firm's expected rate of return, but it also reduces k_s, the required rate of return on its stock. Although we can quantify the cost of following a more conservative policy — it is the average percentage differential between the return received on marketable securities and the interest rate paid on the long-term debt — it is almost impossible to quantify the benefits of one policy versus another because we cannot measure how much the conservative policy reduces risk and how this risk reduction affects k_s. Further, it is impossible to measure the higher sales and profits, if any, that a portfolio of liquid assets might make possible should a credit crunch occur. Accordingly, companies set their basic policies with regard to securities holdings on the basis of judgment.

Criteria for Selecting Marketable Securities

A wide variety of securities, differing in terms of default risk, interest rate risk, liquidity risk, and expected rate of return, are available to firms that choose to hold marketable securities. In this section, we first consider the characteristics of different securities, after which we show how the financial manager selects the specific instruments to be held in the portfolio.

Default Risk

The risk that a borrower will be unable to make interest payments or to repay the principal amount on schedule is known as *default risk*. If the issuer is the U.S. Treasury, default risk is negligible, so Treasury securities are regarded as being free of such risk. Corporate securities and bonds issued by state and local governments are subject to some degree of default risk, and they are rated with regard to their chances of going into default.

Interest Rate Risk

We saw in Chapter 5 that bond prices vary with changes in interest rates. We also saw that the prices of long-term bonds are much more sensitive to changes in interest rates than are prices of short-term securities — long-term bonds have more *interest rate risk*. Therefore, even Treasury bonds are not completely free of risk — they are subject to risk due to interest rate fluctuations, and the longer the bond's maturity, the greater its risk. Thus, if Foxcraft's treasurer purchased at par $1 million of 25-year U.S. government bonds paying 9 percent interest, and if interest rates then rose to 14.5 percent, the market value of the bonds would fall from \$1 million to approximately \$638,000 — a loss of almost 40 percent. (This actually happened from 1980 to 1981.) Had 90-day Treasury bills been held, the capital loss resulting from the change in interest rates would have been negligible.

Purchasing Power Risk

Another type of risk is *purchasing power risk,* or the risk that inflation will reduce the purchasing power of a given sum of money. Purchasing power risk, which is important both to firms and to individual investors during times of inflation, is generally regarded as being lower on assets whose returns normally rise during inflation than on assets whose returns are fixed. Thus, real estate and common stocks are often thought of as being better "hedges against inflation" than are bonds and other fixed-income securities.[9]

Liquidity, or Marketability, Risk

An asset that can be sold on short notice for close to its quoted market price is defined as being highly liquid. If Foxcraft purchased \$1 million of infrequently traded bonds issued by a relatively obscure company such as Gainesville Pork Products, it would probably have to accept a price reduction in order to sell the bonds on short notice. On the other hand, if Foxcraft invested in U.S. Treasury bonds or bonds issued by AT&T, General Motors, or Exxon, it would be able to dispose of them almost instantaneously at close to the quoted market price. These latter bonds are therefore said to have very little *liquidity,* or *marketability, risk.*[10]

Returns on Securities

As we know from earlier chapters, the higher a security's risk, the higher its expected and required return. Thus, corporate treasurers, like other investors, must make a tradeoff between risk and return when choosing marketable securities for their portfolios. Since the liquidity portfolio is generally held for a specific known need or for use in emergencies, the firm might be financially embarrassed if the portfolio declined in value. Further, most nonfinancial corporations do not have personnel who are specialists in appraising securities and determining the probability of their going into default. Accordingly, the marketable securities portfolio is generally confined to safe, highly liquid, short-term securities issued by either the U.S. government or one of the very strongest corporations. Given the purpose of the securities portfolio, treasurers are unwilling to sacrifice safety for higher rates of return.

---

[9]Recall from Chapter 3, however, that if a high rate of inflation is expected in the future, that expectation will be built into interest rates. Therefore, the real risk of inflation to bondholders is that actual inflation will exceed the expected level.

[10]Some people define "liquidity" to encompass an absence of default risk, interest rate risk, and marketability risk. By this definition, short-term Treasury bills, CDs, and the like, are the only "liquid assets," and IBM stock is not liquid. These definitions are not really important, but understanding the characteristics of different securities is important.

Types of Marketable Securities

Table 20-3 provides a listing of the major types of securities available for investment and their yields as of June 10, 1977, February 10, 1982, and March 19, 1987. Depending on how long they will be held, the financial manager decides upon a suitable maturity pattern for the firm's holdings. Because the securities' characteristics change with shifts in the financial markets, it would be misleading to attempt to give detailed descriptions of them here.

It should be noted that large corporations which have larger amounts of surplus cash tend to make direct purchases of Treasury bills, commercial paper, and CDs as well as the Euromarket securities. Smaller firms, on the other hand, are more likely to use money market mutual funds as *near-cash reserves* because small firms' volume of investment simply does not warrant their hiring investment specialists to manage the portfolios and to make sure that the securities held mature (or can

Table 20-3
Securities Available for Investment of Surplus Cash

Security	Typical Maturity at Time of Issue	Approximate Yields as of		
		6/10/77	2/10/82	3/19/87
Suitable to Hold as Near-Cash Reserves				
U.S. Treasury bills	91 days to 1 year	4.8%	15.1%	5.7%
Commercial paper	Up to 270 days	5.5	15.3	6.1
Negotiable CDs of U.S. banks	Up to 1 year	6.0	15.5	6.2
Money market mutual funds	Instant liquidity	5.1	14.0	5.4
Floating rate preferred stock mutual funds[a]	Instant liquidity	n.a.	n.a.	4.5
Eurodollar market time deposits	Up to 1 year	6.1	16.2	6.5
Not Suitable to Hold as Near-Cash Reserves				
U.S. Treasury notes	1 to 10 years	6.8	14.8	6.7
U.S. Treasury bonds	Up to 30 years	7.6	14.6	7.4
Corporate bonds (AAA)[b]	Up to 40 years	8.2	16.0	8.4
State and local government bonds (AAA)[b,c]	Up to 30 years	5.7	12.8	6.7
Preferred stocks (AAA)[b,c]	30 years to perpetual	7.5	14.0	7.1
Common stocks of other corporations	Unlimited	Variable	Variable	Variable
Common stock of the firm in question	Unlimited	Variable	Variable	Variable

[a]Floating rate preferred stock is a recent innovation in near-cash securities first marketed in 1983. It is held by corporations (often through money funds designed for this purpose) because of the 80 percent dividend tax exclusion.

[b]Rates shown for corporate and state/local government bonds and preferred stock are for longer maturities rated AAA. Lower-rated securities have higher yields. The slope of the yield curve determines whether shorter- or longer-term securities of a given rating would have higher yields.

[c]Rates are lower on state and municipal government bonds because the interest they pay is exempt from federal income taxes and on preferred stocks because 80 percent of the dividends paid on them is exempt from federal taxes for corporate owners, who own most preferred stocks.

be sold) at the same time cash is required. With money funds, one can literally write checks on the fund to meet cash needs as they arise. Interest rates on money funds are somewhat lower than those on direct investments of equivalent risk, but for small firms the net returns, after the expenses of managing the portfolio, are higher on money funds.[11]

SUMMARY

The first topic covered in this chapter was *cash management*. The key element in any cash management system is the *cash budget*, which forecasts the firm's cash flows over some planning period. Other elements of a good cash management program include *synchronization of cash flows*, proper use of *float*, and *concentration banking*. Note, however, that implementing a cash management program is not costless, and a firm should incur these costs only when justified by the resulting savings.

Marketable securities are held primarily (1) as a reserve for future contingencies, (2) to meet seasonal needs, with holdings being built up during the slack season and then liquidated when cash requirements are high, (3) to meet known future cash requirements, such as construction progress payments or taxes, and (4) immediately after the sale of long-term securities. Given their motives for holding marketable securities, treasurers generally do not want to gamble by holding high-yield, risky securities — safety is the watchword, and rarely will a treasurer sacrifice safety for the higher yields offered on risky securities.

MULTINATIONAL FINANCE

The objectives of cash management in a multinational corporation are similar to those in a purely domestic corporation, namely, (1) to speed up collections and to slow down disbursements as much as is feasible, and hence to maximize net float, (2) to shift cash as rapidly as possible from parts of the business where it is not needed to parts where it is needed, and (3) to obtain the highest possible risk-adjusted return on any temporary cash balance that may exist. Multinational companies use the same general procedures for achieving these goals as domestic firms, but because of longer distances and mail delays, lockbox systems and electronic funds transfers are especially important, as is concentration banking.

Although multinational and domestic corporations have the same objectives and use similar procedures, the multinational corporation faces a more complex task. First, foreign governments often place restrictions on transfers of funds out of the

---

[11]With interest rates currently near 10-year lows, some firms are seeking higher yields on their marketable securities holdings by investing more aggressively. See Eugene F. Brigham and Louis C. Gapenski, *Intermediate Financial Management,* 2nd ed., Chapter 18.

country, so whereas IBM can transfer money from its Salt Lake City office to its New York concentration bank just by pressing a few buttons, a similar transfer from its Buenos Aires office is far more complex. Buenos Aires funds are denominated in australs (Argentina's equivalent of the dollar), so the australs must be converted to dollars before the transfer can occur. If there is a shortage of dollars in Argentina, or if the Argentinean government wants to conserve the dollars in the country to use for the purchase of strategic materials, then conversion, hence the transfer, may be blocked. Even if no dollar shortage existed in Argentina, the government might still restrict funds outflows if those funds represented profits or depreciation rather than payments for purchased materials or equipment. The reason is that many countries, especially the less developed countries, want profits reinvested in the country where they were made in order to stimulate economic growth.

Once it has been determined what funds can be transferred out of the various nations in which a multinational corporation operates, it is important to get those funds to locations where they will earn the highest returns. Whereas domestic corporations tend to think in terms of the alternatives listed in Table 20-3, multinationals are more likely to be aware of investment opportunities all around the world. Most multinational corporations use one or more global concentration banks, located in a money center such as London, New York, Tokyo, Zurich, or Singapore, and their staffs in those cities, working with international bankers, know of and are able to take advantage of the best rates available anywhere in the world.

Questions

20-1 Define each of the following terms:

  a. Transactions balance; compensating balance; precautionary balance; speculative balance

  b. Cash budget; net cash gain (loss)

  c. Target cash balance

  d. Synchronized cash flows

  e. Disbursement float; collection float; net float

  f. Lockbox plan

  g. Transfer mechanism; depository transfer check (DTC); wire transfer; concentration bank

  h. Overdraft system

  i. Marketable securities; near-cash reserves

  j. Default risk; interest rate risk; purchasing power risk; liquidity (marketability) risk

20-2 How can better methods of communication reduce the necessity for firms to hold large cash balances?

20-3 What are the two principal reasons for holding cash? Can a firm estimate its target cash balance by summing the cash held to satisfy each of the two?

20-4 Explain how each of the following factors would probably affect a firm's target cash balance, assuming all other factors are held constant.

    a. The firm institutes a new billing procedure which better synchronizes its cash inflows and outflows.

    b. The firm develops a new forecasting technique which improves its sales forecasts.

    c. The firm reduces its portfolio of U.S. Treasury bills.

    d. The firm arranges to use an overdraft system for its checking account.

    e. The firm borrows a large amount of money from its bank and also begins to pay suppliers twice as frequently as in the past, so it must write far more checks that it did in the past even though the dollar totals of checks written have not changed.

    f. Interest rates on Treasury bills rise from 5 percent to 10 percent.

20-5 Would a lockbox plan make more sense for a firm that makes sales all over the United States or for a firm with the same volume of business but whose customers are concentrated in its home city?

20-6 Would a corporate treasurer be more tempted to invest the firm's liquid asset portfolio in long-term as opposed to short-term securities when the yield curve was upward sloping or downward sloping?

20-7 What does the term *liquidity* mean? Which would be more important to a firm that held a portfolio of marketable securities as a precautionary balance against the possibility of losing a major lawsuit—liquidity or rate of return? Explain.

20-8 Firm A's management is very conservative, while Firm B's is more aggressive. Is is true that, other things the same, Firm B would probably have larger holdings of marketable securities? Explain.

20-9 Is it true that interest rate risk refers to the risk that a firm will be unable to pay the interest on its bonds? Explain.

20-10 When selecting securities for portfolio investments, corporate treasurers must make a trade-off between risk and returns. Is it true that most treasurers are willing to assume a fairly high exposure to risk to gain higher expected returns?

Self-Test Problem

ST-1 (Lockbox analysis) Tysseland Company has grown from a small Boston firm with customers concentrated in New England to a large, national firm serving customers throughout the United States. However, all operations, including the central billing system, have remained in Boston. On average, 5 days elapse from the time customers mail payments until Tysseland is able to receive and process the checks so that it can use the money. To shorten the collection period, Tysseland is considering the installation of a lockbox system consisting of 30 local depository banks, or lockbox operators, and 8 regional concentration banks. The fixed cost of operating the system is estimated to be $14,000 per month. Under this system, customers' checks would be received by the lockbox operator 1 day after they are mailed, and daily collections would average $30,000 at each location. The collections would be transferred daily to the regional concentration banks.

One transfer mechanism involves having the local depository banks use "mail depository transfer checks," or DTCs, to move the funds to the concentration banks; the alternative is to use electronic ("wire") transfers. A DTC would cost only 75 cents, but it would take 2 days to get funds to the concentration bank and thus available to Tysseland. Therefore, float time under the DTC system would be 1 day for mail plus 2 days for transfer, or 3 days total, down from 5 days under the present system where no concentration banking is used. A wire transfer would cost $11, but funds would be available immediately, so float time would be only 1 day.

If Tysseland's opportunity cost is 11 percent, should it initiate the lockbox/concentration banking system? If so, which transfer method should be used? (Assume that there are 52 × 5 = 260 working days, hence transfers from each lockbox, in a year.)

Problems

20-1 (Cash budgeting) Neil and Terry Sicherman recently leased space in the Southside Mall and opened a new business, Sicherman's Coin Shop. Business has been good, but the Sichermans have frequently run out of cash. This has necessitated late payment on certain orders, and this, in turn, is beginning to cause a problem with suppliers. The Sichermans plan to borrow money from the bank to have cash ready as needed, but first they need a forecast of just how much they must borrow. Accordingly, they have asked you to prepare a cash budget for the critical period around Christmas, when needs will be especially high.

Sales are made on a *cash basis only*. The Sichermans' purchases must be paid for the following month. The Sichermans pay themselves a salary of $4,800 per month, and the rent is $2,000 per month. In addition, the Sichermans must make a tax payment of $12,000 in December. The current cash on hand (on December 1) is $400, but the Sichermans have agreed to maintain an end-of-month bank balance of $6,000, their target cash balance. (Disregard till cash, which is insignificant because the Sichermans keep only a small amount on hand in order to lessen the chances of robbery.)

The estimated sales and purchases for December, January, and February are shown next. Purchases during November amounted to $140,000.

	Sales	Purchases
December	$160,000	$40,000
January	40,000	40,000
February	60,000	40,000

a. Prepare a cash budget for December, January, and February.

b. Now suppose the Sichermans were to start selling on a credit basis on December 1, giving customers 30 days to pay. All customers accept these terms, and all other facts in the problem are unchanged. What would the company's loan requirements be at the end of December in this case?

20-2 **(Cash budgeting)** The Torrence Company is planning to request a line of credit from its bank. The following sales forecasts have been made for 1988 and 1989:

May 1988	$150,000
June	150,000
July	300,000
August	450,000
September	600,000
October	300,000
November	300,000
December	75,000
January 1989	150,000

Collection estimates were obtained from the credit and collection department as follows: collected within the month of sale, 10 percent; collected the month following the month of sale, 85 percent; and collected the second month following the month of sale, 5 percent. Payments for labor and raw materials are typically made during the month following the month in which these costs are incurred. Total labor and raw materials costs are estimated for each month as follows (payments are made the following month):

May 1988	$ 75,000
June	75,000
July	105,000
August	735,000
September	255,000
October	195,000
November	135,000
December	75,000

General and administrative salaries will amount to approximately $29,250 a month; lease payments under long-term lease contracts will be $9,750 a month; depreciation charges will be $39,000 a month; miscellaneous expenses will be $2,925 a month; income tax payments of $68,250 will be due in both September and December; and a progress payment of $195,000 on a new research laboratory must be paid in October. Cash on hand on July 1 will amount to $143,000, and a minimum cash balance of $97,500 should be maintained throughout the cash budget period.

a. Prepare a monthly cash budget for the last six months of 1988. How much money will Torrence need to borrow (or how much will it have available to invest) each month?

b. Suppose receipts from sales come in uniformly during the month — that is, cash payments come in 1/30 each day — but all outflows are paid on the fifth of the month. Would this have an effect on the cash budget — in other words, would the cash budget you have prepared be valid under these assumptions? If not, what could be done to make a valid estimation of financing requirements? No calculations are required, although calculations can be used to illustrate the effects.

c. Torrence produces on a seasonal basis, just ahead of sales. Without making any calculations, discuss how the company's current ratio and debt ratio would vary during the year assuming all financial requirements were met by short-term bank loans. Could changes in these ratios affect the firm's ability to obtain bank credit?

d. If you prepared the cash budget in Part a correctly, you would show a surplus at the end of July, which increases by the end of August. Suggest some alternative investments for this money. Be sure to consider the pros and cons of long-term versus short-term debt instruments, and the appropriateness of investing in common stock.

e. Would your choice of securities in Part d be affected if the cash budget showed continuous cash surpluses versus alternating surpluses and deficits?
(Do Parts f, g, and h only if you are using the computerized diskette.)

f. By offering a 2 percent cash discount for paying within the month of sale, the credit manager has revised the collection percentages to 50 percent, 35 percent, and 15 percent, respectively. How will this affect the loan requirements?

g. Return the payment percentages to their base case values and the discount to zero. Now suppose sales fall to only 70 percent of the forecasted level. Production is maintained, so cash outflows are unchanged. How does this affect Torrence's financial requirements?

h. Return sales to the forecasted level (100%), and suppose collections slow down to 5%, 20%, and 75% for the three months, respectively. How does this affect financial requirements? If Torrence went to a cash-only sales policy, how would that affect requirements, other factors held constant?

20-3 (Net float) The Johnson Company is setting up a new checking account with the First National Bank. Johnson plans to issue checks in the amount of $2 million each day and to deduct them from its own records at the close of business on the day they are written. On average, the bank will receive and clear (that is, deduct from the firm's bank balance) the checks at 5 p.m. the fourth day after they are written — for example, a check written on Monday will be cleared on Friday afternoon. Johnson's agreement with the bank requires it to maintain a $1.5 million average compensating balance; this is $500,000 greater than the cash balance the firm would otherwise have on deposit. It makes a $1.5 million deposit at the time it opens the account.

a. Assuming that Johnson makes deposits at 4 p.m. each day (and the bank includes them in that day's transactions), how much must it deposit daily in order to maintain a sufficient balance once it reaches a steady state? Indicate the required deposit on Day 1, Day 2, Day 3, Day 4, if any, and each day thereafter, assuming the company will write checks for $2 million on Day 1 and each day thereafter.

b. How many days of disbursement float does Johnson carry?

c. What ending daily balance should the firm try to maintain (1) on the bank's records and (2) on its own records?

d. Explain how net float can help increase the value of the firm's common stock.

20-4 (Lockbox system) Bacon, Inc., began operations 5 years ago as a small firm serving customers in the Seattle area. However, its reputation and market area grew quickly, so that today Bacon has customers throughout the entire United States. Despite its broad customer base, Bacon has maintained its headquarters in Seattle and keeps its central billing system there. Bacon's management is considering an alternative collection procedure to reduce its mail time and processing float. On average, it takes 5 days from the time customers mail payments until Bacon is able to receive, process, and deposit them. Bacon would like to set up a lockbox collection system, which it estimates would reduce the time lag from customer mailing to deposit by 3 days — bringing it down to 2 days. Bacon receives an average of $700,000 in payments per day.

   a. How many days of collection float now exist (Bacon's customers' disbursement float) and what would it be under the lockbox system? What reduction in cash balances could Bacon achieve by initiating the lockbox system?

   b. If Bacon has an opportunity cost of 9 percent, how much is the lockbox system worth on an annual basis?

   c. What is the maximum monthly charge Bacon should pay for the lockbox system?

20-5 **(Comparison of transfer mechanisms)** The New York field office of the Metallux Corporation has sold a quantity of silver ingots for $15,000. Metallux wants to transfer this amount to its concentration bank in San Francisco as economically as possible. Two means of transfer are being considered:

   (1) A mail depository transfer check (DTC), which costs $0.50 and takes three days.

   (2) A wire transfer, which costs $7.50 and for which funds are immediately available in San Francisco.

   a. Metallux earns 14.5 percent annual interest on funds in its concentration bank. Based on Equation 20-1, which transfer method should be used?

   b. At what dollar transfer amount would the bank be indifferent to the two transfer procedures?

   c. What other factors might influence the decision?

20-6 **(Lockbox system)** D. Durst and Sons, Inc., operates a mail-order firm doing business on the East Coast. Durst receives an average of $500,000 in payments per day. On average it takes 4 days from the time customers mail checks until Durst receives and processes them. Durst is considering the use of a lockbox system to reduce collection and processing float. The system will cost $10,000 per month and will consist of 10 local depository banks and a concentration bank located in Atlanta. Under this system, customers' checks should be received at the lockbox locations 1 day after they are mailed, and they will be transferred to Atlanta using wire transfers costing $15 each. Assume that Durst has an opportunity cost of 10 percent and that there are $52 \times 5 = 260$ working days, hence 260 transfers from each lockbox location, in a year.

   a. What is the total cost of operating the lockbox system?

   b. What is the benefit of the lockbox system to Durst?

   c. Should Durst initiate the system?

   (Do Parts d and e only if you are using the computerized diskette.)

   d. Would the system be beneficial if Durst could operate it with only 8 lockbox locations while achieving the same reduction in float?

   e. Suppose interest rates rise so that Durst can now earn 11 percent on its invested funds. What would be the benefit (or loss) of operating the lockbox system with 10 lockbox locations? 8 locations?

Solution to Self-Test Problem

ST-1 First, determine the annual benefit to Tysseland from the reduction in cash balances under each of the new plans.

$$\text{Average daily collections} = (30)(\$30,000) = \$900,000.$$

DTC:

Current float: $900,000 per day × 5 days	=	$4,500,000
New float: $900,000 per day × 3 days	=	2,700,000
Float reduction		$1,800,000

Tysseland can generate $1,800,000 by using DTCs, and it can earn 11 percent on these funds, which will provide interest income of $198,000:

$$\text{Interest earned} = (\$1,800,000)(0.11) = \$198,000.$$

Wire Transfer:

Current float: $900,000 per day × 5 days	=	$4,500,000
New float: $900,000 per day × 1 day	=	900,000
Float reduction		$3,600,000

Tysseland can generate $3,600,000 by using wire transfers, and it will earn $396,000 on the freed capital:

$$\text{Interest earned} = (\$3,600,000)(0.11) = \$396,000.$$

Next, compute the annual cost of each transfer method:

$$\text{Number of transfers} = 30 \times 260 = 7,800 \text{ per year.}$$
$$\text{Fixed costs} = \$14,000 \times 12 = \$168,000 \text{ per year.}$$

DTC:

$$\text{Total costs} = (7,800)(\$0.75) + \$168,000 = \$173,850.$$

Wire Transfer:

$$\text{Total costs} = (7,800)(\$11) + \$168,000 = \$253,800.$$

Finally, calculate the net annual benefit resulting from each transfer method:
DTC:

$$\text{Net benefit} = \$198,000 - \$173,850 = \$24,150.$$

Wire Transfer:

$$\text{Net benefit} = \$396,000 - \$253,800 = \$142,200.$$

Therefore, Tysseland should adopt the lockbox system and transfer funds from the lockbox operators to the regional concentration banks using wire transfers.

Additional References and Cases

Perhaps the best way to get a good feel for the current state of the art in cash management is to look through recent issues of The Journal of Cash Management, *a relatively new publication aimed at professionals in the field.*

For more information on cash management in general, see

Beehler, Paul J., *Contemporary Cash Management* (New York: Wiley, 1983).

Discoll, Mary C., *Cash Management: Corporate Strategies for Profit* (New York: Wiley, 1983).

Key references on cash balance models include the following:

Daellenbach, Hans G., "Are Cash Management Optimization Models Worthwhile?" *Journal of Financial and Quantitative Analysis,* September 1974, 607–626.

Miller, Merton H., and Daniel Orr, "The Demand for Money by Firms: Extension of Analytic Results," *Journal of Finance,* December 1968, 735–759.

Mullins, David Wiley, Jr., and Richard B. Homonoff, "Applications of Inventory Cash Management Models," in *Modern Developments in Financial Management,* Stewart C. Myers, ed. (New York: Praeger, 1976).

Stone, Bernell K., "The Use of Forecasts for Smoothing in Control-Limit Models for Cash Management," *Financial Management,* Spring 1972, 72–84.

For more information on float management, see

Batlin, C. A., and Susan Hinko, "Lockbox Management and Value Maximization," *Financial Management,* Winter 1981, 39–44.

Gitman, Lawrence J., D. Keith Forrester, and John R. Forrester, Jr., "Maximizing Cash Disbursement Float," *Financial Management,* Summer 1976, 32–41.

Nauss, Robert M., and Robert E. Markland, "Solving Lockbox Location Problems," *Financial Management,* Spring 1979, 21–31.

The following articles provide more information on cash concentration systems:

Stone, Bernell K., and Ned C. Hill, "Cash Transfer Scheduling for Efficient Cash Concentration," *Financial Management,* Autumn 1980, 35–43.

―――, "The Design of a Cash Concentration System," *Journal of Financial and Quantitative Analysis,* September 1981, 301–322.

For greater insights into compensating balance requirements, see

Campbell, Tim S., and Leland Brendsel, "The Impact of Compensating Balance Requirements on the Cash Balances of Manufacturing Corporations," *Journal of Finance,* March 1977, 31–40.

Frost, Peter A., "Banking Services, Minimum Cash Balances, and the Firm's Demand for Money," *Journal of Finance,* December 1970, 1029–1039.

For more information on marketable securities, see any of the investment textbooks referenced in Chapter 6, or see

Brown, Keith C., and Scott L. Lummer, "A Reexamination of the Covered Call Option Strategy for Corporate Cash Management," *Financial Management,* Summer 1986, 13–17.

Kamath, Ravindra R., et al, "Management of Excess Cash: Practices and Developments," *Financial Management,* Autumn 1985, 70–77.

Stigum, M., *The Money Market: Myth, Reality, and Practice* (Homewood, Ill.: Dow Jones-Irwin, 1978).

Van Horne, J. C., *Financial Market Rates and Flows* (Englewood Cliffs, N.J.: Prentice-Hall, 1984).

Zivney, Terry L., and Michael J. Alderson, "Hedged Dividend Capture with Stock Index Options," *Financial Management,* Summer 1986, 5–12.

The following cases focus on cash management:

Case 6, "Bollinger Corporation," in the Crum-Brigham casebook, which illustrates the mechanics of the cash budget and the rationale behind its use.

"Austin, Limited," in the Harrington casebook, which examines changes in a firm's cash disbursement system.

Financial Analysis and Planning

21

Financial Statement Analysis

The February 17, 1987 *Wall Street Journal* reported that the guiding principle for an increasing number of security analysts and investors is this: "Follow the money." They are advocating a principle that we have stated many times up to this point in the text: "Net cash flow, not accounting income, is the critical variable in financial analysis." While none of the analysts advocated using cash flow analysis all by itself, they all said that it is an important tool in piercing the camouflage that sometimes makes the earnings that accountants report misleading.

As the term suggests, net cash flow is basically a measure of the net funds flowing into — or out of — a business. If large companies were run, like lemonade stands, on a cash basis, then earnings and net cash flow would be identical. However, corporations generally report earnings to shareholders on an accrual basis, and, to further complicate matters, firms generally use accelerated depreciation for tax purposes but straight line for stockholder reporting.

The simplest measure of net cash flow is merely to add depreciation and deferred taxes to reported net income. But Wall Street professionals don't stop there. Thomas Mitchell, a research partner at the New York investment firm Weiss, Peck & Greer, focuses on "free cash flow." This is, basically, net cash flow minus the funds allocated for capital expenditures, plus these additional adjustments: (1) Subtract out the company's additions to inventory; otherwise, a firm might appear to have a significant amount of free cash flow when, in fact, the funds have already been used. (2) Subtract additions to receivables, since these sales did not produce cash during the reporting period. (3) Subtract dividends paid, because dividends are virtually nondiscretionary expenditures. With free cash flow thus measured, Mr. Mitchell then calculates the ratio of a stock's price to the company's free cash flow per share. Just as with the price-earnings ratio, a low number indicates a possible bargain, while a high number is taken as a warning sign that the stock could be overvalued.

If management is to maximize the value of the firm's stock price, it must take advantage of the firm's strengths and correct its weaknesses. Financial statement analysis allows the financial manager to assess the firm's performance in comparison to other firms in the same industry and to identify possible reasons for deficiencies, thus allowing the manager to take actions to improve his or her firm's performance. The financial manager can look at trends in the ratios both to analyze the firm's performance over time and to forecast its future position. In this chapter, we discuss how financial managers calculate and interpret financial ratios. Then, in the next chapter, we will see how managers forecast future financial statements and ratios to determine the impact of specific decisions on the firm's future performance.

As you go through this chapter, it is important to remember that security values are based on *cash flows,* yet accounting statements concentrate primarily on *reported profits.* Recall that there can be major differences between profits as reported by accountants and net cash flows. This makes it necessary to "look behind the accounting numbers" both when appraising the performance of management and when setting a value for the firm. For the most part, accounting numbers are highly correlated with cash flows — high accounting profits generally signify high cash flows and the ability to pay high dividends, either now or in the future. However, there are enough exceptions to this rule to warrant a critical examination of all accounting data. Keep this in mind as you read the chapter.

FINANCIAL STATEMENTS AND REPORTS

Of the various reports corporations issue to their stockholders, the *annual report* is by far the most important. Two types of information are given in this report. First, there is a verbal section, often presented as a letter from the president, that both describes the firm's operating results during the past year and discusses new developments that will affect future operations. Second, the annual report presents four basic financial statements — the *income statement,* the *balance sheet,* the *statement of retained earnings,* and the *statement of changes in financial position.* Taken together, these statements give an accounting picture of the firm's operations and financial position. Detailed data are provided for the most recent years, along with historical summaries of key operating statistics for the past five or ten years.[1]

The quantitative and verbal information are equally important. The financial statements report *what has actually happened* to earnings and dividends over the

---

[1]Firms also provide quarterly reports, but these are much less comprehensive than the annual reports. In addition, larger firms file even more detailed statements, giving breakdowns for each major division or subsidiary, with the Securities and Exchange Commission (SEC). These reports, called *10-K reports,* are made available to stockholders upon request to a company's secretary. Finally, many larger firms also publish *statistical supplements,* which give detailed financial statement data and key ratios going back ten years.

past few years, while the verbal statements attempt to explain why things turned out the way they did. For example, Texas Instruments' earnings dropped sharply in 1985, from $308 million to − $119 million. Management reported that the drop resulted from problems in the semiconductor industry, but it then went on to paint a more optimistic picture for the future. Of course, a return to profitability may not occur, and analysts should compare management's past statements with subsequent results. In any event, *the information contained in the annual report is used by investors to form expectations about future earnings and dividends, and about the riskiness of these expected values.* Therefore, the annual report is obviously of great interest to investors.

For illustrative purposes, we shall use data taken from the Cauley-Brisick-Stanley (CBS) Equipment Company, a manufacturer of specialized electronic testing machines used in the automobile repair business.

The Income Statement

Table 21-1 gives the 1986 and 1987 *income statements* for CBS Equipment Company. Net sales are shown at the top of the statements, after which various costs, including income taxes, are subtracted to obtain the net income available to common stockholders. A report on earnings and dividends per share is given at the bottom of the statement. In financial management, earnings per share (EPS) is called "the bottom line," denoting that of all the items on the income statement, EPS is the most important.[2] CBS earned $2.20 per share in 1987, down from $2.40 in 1986, but it still raised the dividend from $1.60 to $1.80.

The Balance Sheet

The left-hand side of CBS' year-end 1986 and 1987 *balance sheets,* which are given in Table 21-2, shows the firm's assets, while the right-hand side shows the liabilities and equity, or the claims against these assets. The assets are listed in order of their "liquidity," or the length of time it typically takes to convert them to cash. The claims are listed in the order in which they must be paid: Accounts payable must generally be paid within 30 days, notes are payable within 90 days, and so on, down to the stockholders' equity accounts, which represent ownership and need never be "paid off."

Some additional points about the balance sheet are worth noting:

1. Cash versus other assets. Although the assets are all stated in terms of dollars, only cash represents actual money. Receivables are bills others owe CBS; inventories show the dollars the company has invested in raw materials, work-in-process, and finished goods available for sale; and fixed assets reflect the amount

---

[2]Dividends are important too, but the firm's ability to pay dividends is dependent on its long-run cash flows, which in turn are dependent primarily on its earnings.

Table 21-1
CBS Equipment Company:
Income Statements for Years Ending December 31
(Thousands of Dollars, Except for Per Share Data)

	1987	1986
Net sales	$3,000	$2,850
Costs and expenses:		
Labor and materials	2,544	2,413
Depreciation	100	90
Selling expenses	22	20
General and administrative expenses	40	35
Lease payments	28	28
Total operating costs	$2,734	$2,586
Net operating income, or earnings before interest and taxes (EBIT)	$ 266	$ 264
Less interest expense:		
Interest on notes payable	8	2
Interest on first mortgage bonds	40	42
Interest on debentures	18	3
Total interest	$ 66	$ 47
Earnings before taxes	$ 200	$ 217
Taxes (at 40%)	80	87
Net income before preferred dividends	$ 120	$ 130
Dividends to preferred stockholders	10	10
Net income available to common stockholders	$ 110	$ 120
Disposition of net income:		
Dividends to common stockholders	$ 90	$ 80
Addition to retained earnings	$ 20	$ 40
Per share of common stock:		
Stock price	$28.50	$29.00
Earnings per share (EPS)[a]	$ 2.20	$ 2.40
Dividends per share (DPS)[a]	$ 1.80	$ 1.60

[a]There are 50,000 common shares outstanding; see Table 21-2. EPS is based on earnings after preferred dividends, that is, on net income available to common stockholders. Calculations of EPS and DPS for 1987 are as follows:

$$\text{EPS} = \frac{\text{Net income available to common stockholders}}{\text{Shares outstanding}} = \frac{\$110,000}{50,000} = \$2.20.$$

$$\text{DPS} = \frac{\text{Dividends paid to common stockholders}}{\text{Shares outstanding}} = \frac{\$90,000}{50,000} = \$1.80.$$

---

of money CBS paid for its plant and equipment when it acquired those assets at some time in the past. CBS can write checks at present for a total of $50,000 (versus current liabilities of $300,000 due within a year). The noncash assets should produce cash flows eventually, but they do not represent cash-in-hand, and the amount of cash they will eventually produce could be higher or lower than the values at which they are carried on the books.

Table 21-2
CBS Equipment Company:
December 31 Balance Sheets
(Thousands of Dollars)

Assets	1987	1986	Liabilities and Equity	1987	1986
Cash	$ 50	$ 55	Accounts payable	$ 60	$ 30
Marketable securities	0	25	Notes payable	100	60
Accounts receivable	350	315	Accrued wages	10	10
Inventories	300	215	Accrued taxes	130	120
Total current assets	$ 700	$ 610	Total current liabilities	$ 300	$ 220
Gross plant and equipment	1,800	1,470	First mortgage bonds	500	520
Less depreciation	500	400	Debentures	300	60
Net plant and equipment	$1,300	$1,070	Total long-term debt	$ 800	$ 580
			Stockholders' equity:		
			Preferred stock (1,000 shares, 10% preferred, $100 per value)	100	100
			Common stock (50,000 shares, $1 par value)	50	50
			Additional paid-in capital	90	90
			Retained earnings	660	640
			Total common equity	$ 800	$ 780
			Total stockholders' equity	900	880
Total assets	$2,000	$1,680	Total claims	$2,000	$1,680

Notes:
a. The first mortgage bonds have a sinking fund requirement of $20,000 a year.
b. CBS had $28,000 in uncapitalized lease payments in both 1986 and 1987, see Table 21-1.

2. Liabilities versus stockholders' equity. The claims against assets are of two types — liabilities (or money the company owes) and the stockholders' ownership position.[3] The *stockholders' equity,* or *net worth,* is a residual.

$$\begin{array}{ccc} \text{Assets} & - \text{Liabilities} & = \text{Stockholder's equity} \\ \$2,000,000 & - \$1,100,000 = & \$900,000. \end{array}$$

Suppose assets decline in value — for example, suppose some of the accounts receivable are written off as bad debts. Liabilities remain constant, so the value of the stockholders' equity must decline. Therefore, the risk of asset value fluctuations is borne by the stockholders. Note, however, that if asset values rise (perhaps because of inflation), these benefits will accrue exclusively to the stockholders.

---

[3]One could divide liabilities into (1) debts owed to someone and (2) other items, such as deferred taxes, reserves, and so on. We do not make this distinction, so the terms *debt* and *liabilities* are used synonymously. It should also be noted that firms occasionally set up reserves for certain contingencies, such as the potential costs involved in a lawsuit currently in the courts. These reserves represent an accounting transfer from retained earnings to the reserve account. If the company wins the suit, re-tained earnings will be credited, and the reserve will be eliminated. If it loses, cash will be reduced and the reserve will be eliminated.

3. Breakdown of the stockholders' common equity account. First, note that the equity section is divided into four accounts — preferred stock, common stock, paid-in capital, and retained earnings — and that the last three represent common equity. The *retained earnings* account is built up over time by the firm's "saving" a part of its earnings rather than paying all earnings out as dividends. The other two common equity accounts arise from the sale of stock by the firm to raise capital. Accountants generally assign a *par value* to common stock — CBS' stock has a par value of $1. Now suppose CBS were to sell 1,000 additional shares at a price of $30 per share. The company would raise $30,000, and the cash accounts would go up by this amount. Of the total, $1,000 would be added to common stock and $29,000 to *paid-in capital.* Thus, after the sale, common stock would show $51,000, paid-in capital would show $119,000, and there would be 51,000 shares outstanding.

The breakdown of the common equity accounts is important for some purposes but not for others. For example, a potential stockholder would want to know if the company had actually earned the funds reported in its equity accounts, or if funds had come mainly from selling stock. A potential creditor, on the other hand, would be more interested in the amount of money the owners had put up than in the form in which the money had been put up. In the remainder of this chapter, we generally aggregate the three common equity accounts and call this sum *common equity* or *net worth.*

4. Inventory accounting. CBS uses the FIFO (first-in, first-out) method to determine the inventory value shown on its balance sheet ($300,000). It could have used the LIFO (last-in, first-out) method. During a period of rising prices, FIFO causes reported inventories to show a higher value than LIFO would. For example, if costs are rising at an annual rate of 10 percent, then inventory items that were just bought (or made) would cost 10 percent more than identical items that were bought (or made) a year ago. Since CBS uses FIFO, and since inflation has been occurring, (1) its costs are relatively low as compared to what they would have been under LIFO, (2) its reported profits are relatively high, and (3) its balance sheet inventories are higher than they would have been had it used LIFO. In CBS' case, notes to its financial statements not shown here indicated that its EPS would have been lowered by 30 cents, to $1.90 and its balance sheet figure for inventories would have been $275,000 rather than $300,000, had the company elected to use LIFO in 1987. Thus, the inventory valuation method can have a significant effect on the financial statements.

5. Depreciation methods. Companies often use the ACRS method to calculate depreciation for tax purposes but use straight line based on a longer life for stockholder reporting. However, CBS, IBM, and some other companies use rapid depreciation (ACRS) for both stockholder reporting and tax purposes. Had CBS used straight line instead of ACRS for stockholder reporting, its depreciation expense would have been almost $25,000 less, so net income would have been higher, as would its EPS. The $1,300,000 shown for "net plant" on its balance sheet, and hence its retained earnings, would also have been approximately $25,000 higher.

6. The time dimension. The balance sheet may be thought of as a snapshot of the firm's financial position *at a point in time* — for example, on December 31,

1987. Thus, on December 31, 1986, CBS had $25,000 of marketable securities, but this account was zero by the end of 1987. The income statement, on the other hand, reports on operations *over a period of time* — for example, during the calendar year 1987, CBS had sales of $3,000,000, and its net income available to common stockholders was $110,000. The balance sheet changes every day as inventories are increased or decreased, as fixed assets are added or retired, as bank loans are increased or decreased, and so on. Companies whose businesses are seasonal have especially large balance sheet changes. For example, most retailers have large inventories just before Christmas but low inventories and high accounts receivable after Christmas, so their balance sheets look materially different, depending on the date chosen to construct the statement.

Cash and Materials Flows

As a company like CBS goes about its business, it makes sales, which lead (1) to a reduction of inventories, (2) to an increase in cash, and (3) if the sales price exceeds the cost of the item sold, to a profit. These transactions cause the balance sheet to change, and they also are reflected in the income statement. It is critically important that you understand (1) that businesses deal with *physical* units like autos, computers, or aluminum, (2) that physical transactions are translated into dollar terms through the accounting system, and (3) that the purpose of financial analysis is to examine the accounting numbers in order to determine how efficient the firm is at making and selling physical goods and services.

Several factors make financial analysis difficult. One is accounting. For example, as was discussed in the previous section, different methods of inventory valuation and depreciation can lead to differences in reported profits for otherwise identical firms, and a good financial analyst must be able to adjust for these differences if he or she is to make valid comparisons among companies. Another factor involves timing — an action is taken at one point in time, but its full effects cannot be accurately measured until some later period.

To understand how timing influences the financial statement, one must understand the cash and materials flows within a firm, as set forth in Figure 21-1. Rectangles represent balance sheet accounts — assets and claims against assets — while circles represent actions taken by the firm. Each rectangle may be thought of as a reservoir, and the wavy lines designate the amount of the asset or liability in the reservoir (account) on a balance sheet date. Various transactions cause changes in the accounts, just as adding or subtracting oil changes the level in an oil reservoir.

The cash account is the focal point of the figure. Certain events, such as collecting accounts receivable or borrowing money from the bank, will cause the cash account to increase, while the payment of taxes, interest, and so on, will cause it to decline. Similar comments could be made about all the balance sheet accounts — their balances rise, fall, or remain constant depending on events that occur during the period under study, which for CBS is January 1, 1986 through December 31, 1987.

Projected sales increases may require the firm to raise cash by borrowing from its bank or selling new stock. For example, if CBS anticipates an increase in sales,

Figure 21-1
Cash and Materials Flows within the Firm

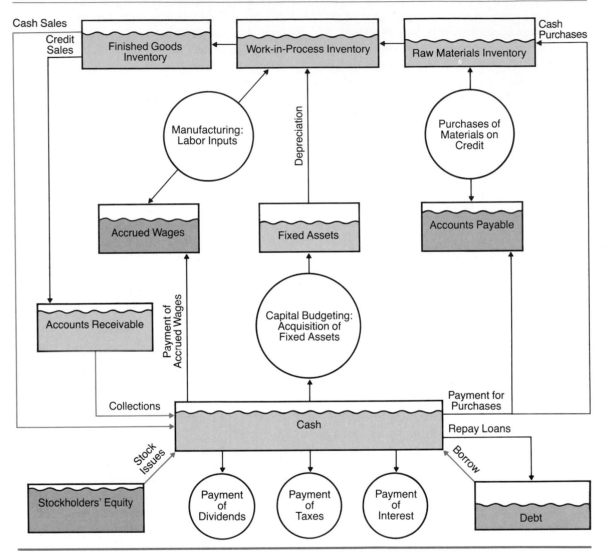

it will (1) expend cash to buy or build fixed assets through the capital budgeting process, (2) step up purchases of raw materials, thereby increasing both raw materials inventories and accounts payable, (3) increase production, which will cause an increase in both accrued wages and work-in-process, and (4) eventually build up its finished goods inventory. Some cash will have been expended and hence removed from the cash account, and the firm will have obligated itself to expend still more cash within a few weeks to pay off its accounts payable and its accrued wages. These events will have occurred *before* any new cash has been generated from sales. Even when the expected sales do occur, there will still be a lag in the generation of cash until receivables are collected — because CBS grants credit for 30 days, it will have to wait 30 days after a sale is made before cash comes in. Depending on how much cash the firm had at the beginning of the buildup, on the length of its production-sales-collection cycle, and on how long it can delay payment of its own payables and accrued wages, the company may have to obtain significant amounts of additional cash by selling stock or bonds, or by borrowing from the bank.

If the firm is profitable, its sales revenues will exceed its costs, and its cash inflows will eventually exceed its cash outlays. However, even a profitable business can experience a cash shortage if it is growing rapidly. It may have to pay for plant, materials, and labor before cash from the expanded sales starts flowing in. For this reason, rapidly growing firms often require large bank loans or capital from other sources.

An unprofitable firm, such as Eastern Airlines in recent years, will have larger cash outlays than inflows. This, in turn, will typically cause a slowdown in the payment of accrued wages and accounts payable, and it may also lead to heavy borrowings. Accordingly, liabilities generally build up to excessive levels in unprofitable firms. Similarly, an overly ambitious expansion plan will be reflected in an excessive buildup of inventories and fixed assets, while a poor credit/collection policy will result in bad debts and reduced profits that will first show up as high accounts receivable.

If a firm runs out of cash and cannot obtain enough to meet its obligations, then it cannot operate, and it will have to declare bankruptcy. Therefore, as we discussed in Chapter 20, a good cash budget is a critical element in a good financial plan. Financial analysts are well aware of all this, and they use the analytical techniques discussed in the remainder of this chapter (and elsewhere in the book) to help discover cash flow problems before they become too serious.

Statement of Retained Earnings

Changes in the common equity accounts between balance sheet dates are reported in the *statement of retained earnings.* CBS' statement is shown in Table 21-3. The company earned $110,000 during 1987, paid out $90,000 in dividends, and

---

Table 21-3
CBS Equipment Company:
Statement of Retained Earnings
for Year Ending December 31, 1987
(Thousands of Dollars)

Balance of retained earnings, December 31, 1986	$640
Add: Net income available to common stockholders, 1987	110
Less: Dividends to common stockholders	(90)
Balance of retained earnings, December 31, 1987	$660

---

plowed $20,000 back into the business. Thus, the balance sheet item "Retained earnings" increased from $640,000 at the end of 1986 to $660,000 at the end of 1987.

Note that the balance sheet account "Retained earnings" represents a *claim against assets,* not assets per se. Further, firms retain earnings primarily to expand the business — this means investing in plant and equipment, in inventories, and so on, *not* in a bank account. *Thus, retained earnings as reported on the balance sheet do not represent cash and are not "available" for the payment of dividends or anything else.*[4]

Statement of Changes in Financial Position

The *statement of changes in financial position,* often called the *sources and uses of funds statement,* is designed to show how the company obtained funds and how they were used. It helps answer questions such as these: Was the new plant financed by sale of debt or equity? How much of its required capital has the firm been able to generate internally? Has the firm been building up its liquid assets, or is it becoming less liquid? Is output from the new plant selling well, or are inventories just building up? Are customers paying on time, or are accounts receivable building up? Information such as this is useful both for investment analysis and for corporate planning, so the statement of changes in financial position is an important part of the annual report.

Before we discuss the sources and uses statement in detail, we should reflect for a moment on one of its most important elements — depreciation. Recall that depreciation is an annual charge against income based on the estimated dollar cost of the capital equipment used up in the production process. For example, suppose a machine with an ACRS class life of 5 years and a zero expected salvage value was purchased in 1986 for $100,000. This $100,000 cost is not expensed in the purchase year; rather, it is charged against production over the machine's 6-year depreciable life. If the depreciation expense were not taken, the profits would be overstated and taxes would be too high. The annual depreciation allowance is deducted from sales revenues, along with such other costs as labor and raw materials, to determine income. However, depreciation is not a cash outlay — funds were expended back in 1986, so the depreciation charged against the income in 1987 through 1991 is not a cash outlay, as are labor or raw materials charges. *Depreciation is a noncash charge, so it must be added back to net income to obtain an estimate of the cash flow from operations.*

---

[4]You should be well aware of the fact that the amount recorded in the retained earnings account is *not* an indication of the amount of cash the firm has. That amount (as of the balance sheet date) is found in the cash account — an asset account. A positive number in the retained earnings account indicates only that in the past, according to generally accepted accounting principles, the firm has earned an income, but its dividends have been less than that reported income. Also, recall our earlier discussion of cash flow and also the difference between accrual and cash accounting. Even though a company reports record earnings and shows an increase in the retained earnings account, it may still be short of cash.

The same situation holds for individuals. You might own a new BMW (no loan), lots of clothes, and an expensive stereo set, hence have a high net worth, but if you have only 23 cents in your pocket plus $5 in your checking account, you would still be short of cash.

Preparing the Sources and Uses Statement[5]

The sources and uses statement is designed to answer at a glance these three questions: (1) What did the firm do with its available funds? (2) Where did the firm get its funds during the year? (3) Did operations during the year tend to increase or decrease the firm's liquidity as measured by its cash and marketable securities balance?

The starting point in preparing a statement of changes in financial position is to determine the change in each balance sheet item and then to record it as either a source or a use of funds in accordance with the following rules:

Sources:

1. Any increase in a liability or equity account. Borrowing from the bank is an example of a source of funds.

2. Any decrease in an asset account. Selling some fixed assets or reducing inventories are examples of sources.

Uses:

1. Any decrease in a liability or equity account. Paying off a loan is an example of a use of funds.

2. Any increase in an asset account. Buying fixed assets or building inventories are examples of uses of funds.

Thus, sources of funds include bank loans and retained earnings, as well as money generated by selling assets, by collecting receivables, and even by drawing down the cash account. Uses include acquiring fixed assets, building up receivables or inventories, and paying off debts.

Table 21-4 shows the changes that occurred in CBS Equipment Company's balance sheet accounts during the calendar year 1987, with each change designated as a source or a use. Sources and uses each total $470,000.[6] Note that the table does not contain any summary accounts such as total current assets or net plant and equipment. If we included summary accounts in Table 21-4 and then used these accounts to prepare the statement of changes in financial position, we would be "double counting."

The data in Table 21-4 are next used to prepare the formal statement of changes in financial position. The one in CBS' annual report is shown in Table 21-5. Note that every item in the "change" columns of Table 21-4 is carried over to Table 21-5 except retained earnings. The statement of changes in financial position re-

---

[5]There are several different formats for presenting the sources and uses statement. The format we present here focuses on cash flow. While many firms use formats focusing on net working capital (Current assets − Current liabilities), such trend-setting firms as IBM and Xerox have begun using the cash flow approach shown in this chapter. We predict that the cash flow format will soon dominate because it provides information in the most useful form for financial analysis. Accordingly, in this section, we discuss the statement of changes in financial position with a focus on cash and marketable securities.

[6]Adjustments would have to be made if fixed assets were sold during the year. CBS had no sales of fixed assets during 1987.

Table 21-4
CBS Equipment Company:
Changes in Balance Sheet Accounts during 1987
(Thousands of Dollars)

| | Balance Sheets | | Changes | |
	12/31/87	12/31/86	Source	Use
Cash	$ 50	$ 55	$ 5	
Marketable securities	0	25	25	
Accounts receivable	350	315		$ 35
Inventories	300	215		85
Gross plant and equipment	1,800	1,470		330
Accumulated depreciation[a]	500	400	100	
Accounts payable	60	30	30	
Notes payable	100	60	40	
Accrued wages	10	10		
Accrued taxes	130	120	10	
Mortgage bonds	500	520		20
Debentures	300	60	240	
Preferred stock	100	100		
Common stock	50	50		
Pain-in capital	90	90		
Retained earnings	660	640	20	
			$470	$470

[a]Depreciation is a *contra-asset,* and not an asset. Hence, an increase in depreciation is a source of funds.

ports net income as a source and dividends as a use rather than netting these items out and just reporting the increase in retained earnings. Cash and marketable securities are combined in Table 21-5. Like most companies, CBS regards its marketable securities as equivalent to cash, so with regard to financial position, they are not distinguished.

Table 21-5 pinpoints the sources and uses of CBS' funds, where "funds" are defined as cash and marketable securities. The top part shows funds generated by and used in operations — for CBS, operations provided $260,000 but required the use of $450,000, so $190,000 of net new money was required to support operations. By far the heaviest use of funds was to increase fixed assets.

CBS' financing activities included borrowing from banks (notes payable) and the sale of debentures, while it paid off part of its mortgage bonds through sinking fund operations. In net, CBS raised $260,000 from the capital markets during 1987. CBS also paid $100,000 of dividends on its common and preferred stock.

When all of these sources and uses are totaled, we see that CBS had a $30,000 cash shortfall during 1987. It met that shortfall by selling off marketable securities ($25,000) and by reducing its cash balance ($5,000), as can be seen from Table 21-4.

Table 21-5
CBS Equipment Company:
1987 Statement of Changes in Financial Position
(Thousands of Dollars)

Funds Provided by and Used in Operations	
Sources:	
Net income before preferred dividends	$120
Depreciation	100
Increase in accounts payable	30
Increase in accrued taxes	10
Total sources from operations	$260
Uses:	
Increase in accounts receivable	$ 35
Increase in inventories	85
Increase in fixed assets	330
Total uses for operations	$450
Net funds from operations	($190)
Financing Activities	
Increase in notes payable	$ 40
Increase in debentures	240
Repayment of mortgage bonds	(20)
Net funds from financing	$260
Total funds from operations and financing	$ 70
Less common and preferred dividends	100
Increase (decrease) in cash and marketable securities	($ 30)

CBS is a strong, well-managed company, and its statement of changes in financial position shows nothing unusual or alarming. It does show a $190,000 net cash drain from operations, but that is entirely attributable to its expansion of net fixed assets. If the company chooses to cut back on its fixed asset expansion, it would generate positive cash flows. Thus, the cash outflow from operations does not appear likely to continue, and to bleed the company to death.

Earnings and Dividends

In addition to the four statements previously described, most annual reports today also give a summary of earnings and dividends over the last few years. For CBS, these data are analyzed in Figure 21-2. Earnings were variable, but there was a definite upward trend over the period. In 1987 a strike caused earnings to drop somewhat, but management expects the growth trend to resume in 1988.

Although dividends and dividend policy were discussed in detail in Chapter 13, we can reiterate several comments about dividends at this point:

1. Dividends per share (DPS) represent the basic cash flows passed from the firm to its stockholders. As such, dividends are a key element in the stock valuation models developed in earlier chapters.

Figure 21-2
CBS Equipment Company:
Earnings and Dividends, 1977–1987

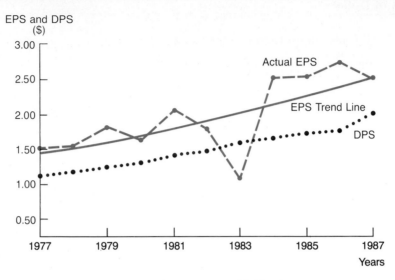

Year	Earnings per Share	Dividends per Share
1977	$1.41	$1.10
1978	1.44	1.15
1979	1.67	1.20
1980	1.53	1.25
1981	1.88	1.35
1982	1.66	1.40
1983	1.10	1.50
1984	2.25	1.55
1985	2.27	1.60
1986	2.44	1.64
1987	2.24	1.84

10-year growth rate: EPS = 5%.
DPS = 5%.

Note: Growth rates were obtained by linear regression. The logs of EPS and DPS were regressed against years, and the slope coefficient represents the growth rate. The graphs above give plots of EPS and DPS over time and a trend line for EPS fitted by least squares regression. (The DPS growth is so smooth that a trend line is unnecessary.) Growth rates can also be estimated by calculating the annualized growth between two points in time. For example, the growth rate in EPS between 1977 and 1987 (10 years) is 4.7 percent. However, growth rates calculated in this way can be highly sensitive to the beginning and ending points — for example, CBS' growth rate in EPS was negative from 1977 to 1983 but positive from 1977 to 1987. *A great deal* of judgment, plus qualitative information about the company, is needed when interpreting past trends and forecasting future growth rates — indeed, the historical growth rate can almost never be used as more than a starting point for estimating the expected future growth rate. See Eugene F. Brigham and Louis C. Gapenski, *Intermediate Financial Management,* 2nd ed., Chapter 4, for a further discussion of growth rates.

2. DPS in any given year can exceed EPS, but in the long run dividends are paid from earnings, so normally DPS is smaller than EPS. The percentage of earnings paid out in dividends, or the ratio of DPS to EPS, is defined as the *dividend payout ratio.* CBS' payout ratio has varied somewhat from year to year, but it has averaged about 80 percent.

3. In a graph such as that in Figure 21-2, the DPS line is typically below the EPS line, but the two lines generally have about the same slope, indicating that EPS and DPS generally grow at about the same rate. As the data in Figure 21-2 indicate, CBS' earnings and dividends have both been growing at an average rate of 5 percent per year. If the type of analysis undertaken in the next section suggests that this trend will continue, then 5 percent is the value of g that will be used in the discounted cash flow valuation model to calculate the company's stock price.

RATIO ANALYSIS

Financial statements report both on a firm's position at a point in time and on its operations over some past period. However, the real value of financial statements lies in the fact that they can be used to help predict the firm's future earnings and dividends. From an investor's standpoint, *predicting the future is what financial statement analysis is all about,* while from management's standpoint, *financial statement analysis is useful both as a way to anticipate future conditions and, more important, as a starting point for planning actions that will influence the future course of events.*

An analysis of the firm's financial ratios is generally the first step in a financial analysis. The ratios are designed to show relationships between financial statement accounts. For example, Firm A might have debt of $5,248,760 and interest charges of $419,900, while Firm B might have debt of $52,647,980 and interest charges of $3,948,600. The true burden of these debts, and the companies' ability to repay them, can be ascertained by comparing each firm's debt to its assets, and the interest it pays versus the income it has available for payment of interest. Such comparisons are made by *ratio analysis.*

In the paragraphs which follow, we will calculate the 1987 financial ratios for CBS Equipment Company.[7] We will also evaluate those ratios in relation to the industry averages. Note that all dollar amounts in the ratio calculations are in thousands.

Liquidity Ratios

One of the first concerns of most financial analysts is liquidity: Will the firm be able to meet its maturing obligations? CBS has debts totaling $300,000 that must be paid off within the coming year. Will CBS have trouble satisfying those obliga-

---

[7]In addition to the ratios discussed in this section, financial analysts also employ a tool known as *common size* balance sheets and income statements. To form a common size balance sheet, one simply divides each asset and liability item by total assets and then expresses the result as a percentage. The resultant percentage statement can be compared with statements of larger or smaller firms, or for the same firm over time. To form a common size income statement, one simply divides each item by sales.

tions? A full liquidity analysis requires the use of cash budgets, but by relating the amount of cash and other current assets to the current obligations, ratio analysis provides a quick, easy-to-use measure of liquidity. Two commonly used *liquidity ratios* are discussed below.

Current Ratio

The *current ratio* is computed by dividing current assets by current liabilities:

$$\text{Current ratio} = \frac{\text{Current assets}}{\text{Current liabilities}} = \frac{\$700}{\$300} = 2.3 \text{ times.}$$

$$\text{Industry average} = 2.5 \text{ times.}$$

Current assets normally include cash, marketable securities, accounts receivable, and inventories. Current liabilities consist of accounts payable, short-term notes payable, current maturities of long-term debt, accrued income taxes, and other accrued expenses (principally wages).

If a company is getting into financial difficulty, it begins paying its bills (accounts payable) more slowly, building up bank loans, and so on. If these current liabilities are rising faster than current assets, then the current ratio will fall, and this could spell trouble. Since the current ratio provides the best single indicator of the extent to which the claims of short-term creditors are covered by assets that are expected to be converted to cash in a period roughly corresponding to the maturity of the claims, it is the most commonly used measure of short-term solvency.

CBS' current ratio is slightly below the average for the industry, 2.5, but it is not low enough to cause concern. It appears that CBS is about in line with most other automotive equipment manufacturers. Since current assets are scheduled to be converted to cash in the near future, it is highly probable that they could be liquidated at close to their stated value. With a current ratio of 2.3, CBS could liquidate current assets at only 43 percent of book value and still pay off current creditors in full.[8]

Although industry average figures are discussed later in some detail, it should be stated at this point that an industry average is not a magic number that all firms should strive to maintain — in fact, some very well-managed firms will be above the average while other good firms will be below it. However, if a firm's ratios are far removed from the average for its industry, the analyst must be concerned about why this variance occurs. Thus, a deviation below the industry average should signal the analyst to check further.

Quick, or Acid Test, Ratio

The *quick,* or *acid test, ratio* is calculated by deducting inventories from current assets and dividing the remainder by current liabilities:

---

[8]$1/2.3 = 0.43$, or 43 percent. Note that $0.43(\$700) = \$300$, the amount of current liabilities.

$$\text{Quick, or acid test, ratio} = \frac{\text{Current assets} - \text{Inventories}}{\text{Current liabilities}} = \frac{\$400}{\$300} = 1.3 \text{ times.}$$

$$\text{Industry average} = 1.0 \text{ times.}$$

Inventories are typically the least liquid of a firm's current assets, and hence they are the assets on which losses are most likely to occur in the event of liquidation. Therefore, a measure of the firm's ability to pay off short-term obligations without relying on the sale of inventories is important.

The industry average quick ratio is 1.0, so CBS' 1.3 ratio compares favorably with the ratios of other firms in the industry. If the accounts receivable can be collected, the company can pay off its current liabilities even without selling any inventory.

Asset Management Ratios

The second group of ratios, the *asset management ratios,* is designed to measure how effectively the firm is managing its assets. These ratios are designed to answer this question: Does the total amount of each type of asset as reported on the balance sheet seem reasonable, too high, or too low in view of current and projected operating levels? CBS and other companies must borrow or obtain capital from other sources in order to acquire assets. If they have too many assets, then their interest expenses will be too high and hence their profits will be depressed. On the other hand, if assets are too low, then profitable sales may be lost.

Inventory Turnover

The *inventory turnover ratio,* also called the *inventory utilization ratio,* is defined as sales divided by inventories:

$$\text{Inventory turnover, or utilization, ratio} = \frac{\text{Sales}}{\text{Inventory}} = \frac{\$3,000}{\$300} = 10 \text{ times.}$$

$$\text{Industry average} = 9 \text{ times.}$$

As a rough approximation, each item of CBS' inventory is sold out and restocked, or "turned over," 10 times per year.[9]

CBS' turnover of 10 times compares favorably with an industry average of 9 times. This suggests that the company does not hold excessive stocks of inventory; excess stocks are, of course, unproductive and represent an investment with a low or zero rate of return. CBS' high inventory turnover ratio also reinforces our faith in the current ratio. If the turnover were low — say, 3 or 4 times — we might

---

[9]"Turnover" is a term that originated many years ago with the old Yankee peddler, who would load up his wagon with goods, then go off on his route to peddle his wares. The merchandise was defined as his "working capital," because it was what he actually sold, or "turned over," to produce his profits, while his "turnover" was the number of trips he took each year. Annual sales divided by inventory equaled turnover, or trips per year. If he made 10 trips per year, stocked 100 pans, and made a gross profit of $5 per pan, then his annual gross profit would be $(100)(\$5)(10) = \$5,000$. If he sped up and made 20 trips per year, his gross profit would double, other things held constant.

wonder whether the firm was holding damaged or obsolete goods not actually worth their stated value.

Two problems arise in calculating and analyzing the inventory turnover ratio. First, sales are stated at market prices, so if inventories are carried at cost, as they generally are, then the calculated turnover overstates the true turnover ratio. Therefore, it would be more appropriate to use cost of goods sold in place of sales in the numerator of the formula. However, established compilers of financial ratio statistics, such as Dun & Bradstreet, use the ratio of sales to inventories carried at cost, so to develop a figure that can be compared with those published by Dun & Bradstreet and similar organizations, it is necessary to measure inventory utilization with sales in the numerator, as we do here.

The second problem lies in the fact that sales occur over the entire year, whereas the inventory figure is for one point in time. This makes it better to use an average inventory measure.[10] If it were determined that the firm's business is highly seasonal, or if there has been a strong upward or downward sales trend during the year, it would become essential to make some such adjustment. To maintain comparability with industry averages, however, we did not use the average inventory figure.

Average Collection Period

The *average collection period (ACP)* is used to appraise accounts receivable, and it is computed by dividing average daily sales into accounts receivable to find the number of days' sales tied up in receivables. Thus, the ACP represents the average length of time that the firm must wait after making a sale before receiving cash. The calculations for CBS show an average collection period of 42 days, slightly above the 36-day industry average.[11]

$$\text{ACP} = \begin{array}{c} \text{Average} \\ \text{collection} \\ \text{period} \end{array} = \frac{\text{Receivables}}{\text{Average sales per day}} = \frac{\text{Receivables}}{\text{Annual sales}/360}$$

$$= \frac{\$350}{\$3{,}000/360} = \frac{\$350}{\$8.333} = 42 \text{ days.}$$

$$\text{Industry average} = 36 \text{ days.}$$

The ACP can also be evaluted by comparison with the terms on which the firm sells its goods. For example, CBS' sales terms call for payment within 30 days, so

---

[10]Preferably, the average inventory value would be calculated by summing the monthly figures during the year and dividing by 12. If monthly data are not available, one can add the beginning and ending figures and divide by 2; this will adjust for growth but not for seasonal effects.

[11]Because information on credit sales is generally unavailable, total sales must be used. Since all firms do not have the same percentage of credit sales, there is a chance that the average collection period will be somewhat in error. Also, note that by convention the financial community generally uses 360 rather than 365 as the number of days in the year for purposes such as these. Finally, it would be better to use *average* receivables, either an average of the monthly figures or (Beginning + Ending)/2 = ($315 + $350)/2 = $332.5 in the formula. Had the annual average been used, CBS' ACP would have been $332.5/$8.333 = 40 days. The 40-day figure is the more accurate one, but since the industry average was based on year-end receivables, we used 42 days for our comparison.

the 42-day collection period indicates that customers, on the average, are not paying their bills on time. If the trend in the collection period over the past few years had been rising, but the credit policy had not changed, this would be even stronger evidence that steps should be taken to expedite the collection of accounts receivable.

As we know from our discussion in Chapter 19, the ACP does have weaknesses from the standpoint of appraising a company's credit management program. Therefore, the problems we discussed in Chapter 19 should be kept in mind with regard to this ratio.

Fixed Assets Turnover

The *fixed assets turnover ratio,* also called the *fixed assets utilization ratio,* measures the utilization of plant and equipment, and it is the ratio of sales to fixed assets:

$$\text{Fixed assets turnover, or utilization, ratio} = \frac{\text{Sales}}{\text{Net fixed assets}} = \frac{\$3,000}{\$1,300} = 2.3 \text{ times.}$$

$$\text{Industry average} = 3.0 \text{ times.}$$

CBS' ratio of 2.3 times compares poorly with the industry average of 3 times, indicating that the firm is not using its fixed assets to as high a percentage of capacity as are the other firms in the industry. The financial manager should bear this in mind when production people request funds for new capital investments.

A major potential problem exists with the use of the fixed assets turnover ratio for comparative purposes. Recall that all assets except cash and accounts receivable reflect the historical cost of the assets. Inflation has caused the value of many assets that were purchased in the past to be seriously understated. Therefore, if we were comparing an old firm which had acquired many of its fixed assets years ago at low prices with a new company which had acquired its fixed assets only recently, then the old firm would probably report a higher turnover. However, this would be more reflective of the inability of accountants to deal with inflation than of any inefficiency on the part of the new firm. The accounting profession is trying to devise ways of making financial statements more reflective of current rather than historical values. If balance sheets were stated on a current basis, this would climinate the problem of comparisons, but at the moment the problem still exists. Since financial analysts typically do not have the data necessary to make adjustments, they simply recognize that a problem exists and deal with it judgmentally. In CBS' case, the issue is not a serious one because all firms in the industry have been expanding at about the same rate, so the balance sheets of the comparison firms are indeed comparable.[12]

---

[12]See FASB #33, *Financial Reporting and Changing Prices* (September 1979), for a discussion of the effects of inflation on financial statements and what the accounting profession is trying to do to provide better and more useful balance sheets and income statements. For a summary discussion, see Eugene F. Brigham and Louis C. Gapenski, *Intermediate Financial Management,* 2nd ed., Chapter 20.

Total Assets Turnover

The final asset management ratio, the *total assets turnover ratio,* measures the turnover, or utilization, of all of the firm's assets; it is calculated by dividing sales by total assets:

$$\text{Total assets turnover, or utilization, ratio} = \frac{\text{Sales}}{\text{Total assets}} = \frac{\$3,000}{\$2,000} = 1.5 \text{ times.}$$

$$\text{Industry average} = 1.8 \text{ times.}$$

CBS' ratio is somewhat below the industry average, indicating that the company is not generating a sufficient volume of business given the size of its total asset investment. Sales should be increased, some assets should be disposed of, or a combination of these steps should be taken.

Debt Management Ratios

The extent to which a firm uses debt financing, or *financial leverage,* has three important implications. (1) By raising funds through debt, the owners can maintain control of the firm with a limited investment. (2) Creditors look to the equity, or owner-supplied funds, to provide a margin of safety: if the owners have provided only a small proportion of total financing, then the risks of the enterprise are borne mainly by its creditors. (3) If the firm earns more on investments financed with borrowed funds than it pays in interest, then the return on the owners' capital is magnified, or "leveraged."

When they examine a company's financial statements, analysts develop two different types of debt management ratios: (1) They check balance sheet ratios to determine the extent to which borrowed funds have been used to finance assets, and (2) they review income statement ratios to determine the number of times fixed charges are covered by operating profits. These two sets of ratios are complementary, and most analysts use both types.

Total Debt to Total Assets

The ratio of total debt to total assets, generally called the *debt ratio,* measures the percentage of total funds provided by creditors:

$$\text{Debt ratio} = \frac{\text{Total debt}}{\text{Total assets}} = \frac{\$1,100}{\$2,000} = 55\%.$$

$$\text{Industry average} = 40\%.$$

Debt is defined to include both current liabilities and long-term debt. Creditors prefer low debt ratios, since the lower the ratio, the greater the cushion against creditors' losses in the event of liquidation. The owners, on the other hand, may seek high leverage either to magnify earnings or because selling new stock would mean giving up some degree of control.

CBS' debt ratio is 55 percent; this means that its creditors have supplied more than half the firm's total financing. Since the average debt ratio for this industry — and for manufacturing generally — is about 40 percent, CBS would find it difficult to borrow additional funds without first raising more equity capital. Creditors would be reluctant to lend the firm more money, and management would probably be subjecting the firm to the risk of bankruptcy if it sought to increase the debt ratio any further by borrowing additional funds.[13]

Times Interest Earned

The *times-interest-earned (TIE) ratio* is determined by dividing earnings before interest and taxes (EBIT) by the interest charges:

$$\text{Times-interest-earned (TIE) ratio} = \frac{\text{EBIT}}{\text{Interest charges}} = \frac{\$266}{\$66} = 4 \text{ times.}$$

$$\text{Industry average} = 6 \text{ times.}$$

The TIE ratio measures the extent to which operating income can decline before the firm is unable to meet its annual interest costs. Failure to meet this obligation can bring legal action by the firm's creditors, possibly resulting in bankruptcy. Note that earnings before interest and taxes is used in the numerator. Because interest is a deductible cost, the ability to pay current interest is not affected by taxes.

CBS' interest is covered 4 times. Since the industry average is 6 times, the company is covering its interest charges by a relatively low margin of safety. Thus, the TIE ratio reinforces our conclusion based on the debt ratio, namely, that the company would face some difficulties if it attempted to borrow additional funds.

Fixed Charge Coverage

The *fixed charge coverage ratio* is similar to the times-interest-earned ratio, but it is more inclusive in that it recognizes that many firms incur long-term obligations under lease contracts.[14] Leasing has become widespread in certain industries in recent years, making this ratio preferable to the times-interest-earned ratio for many purposes. Fixed charges are defined as interest plus annual long-term lease obligations, and the fixed charge coverage ratio is defined as follows:

$$\frac{\text{Fixed charge}}{\text{coverage ratio}} = \frac{\text{EBIT} + \text{Lease obligations}}{\text{Interest charges} + \text{Lease obligations}}$$

$$= \frac{\$266 + \$28}{\$66 + \$28} = \frac{\$294}{\$94} = 3.1 \text{ times.}$$

$$\text{Industry average} = 5.5 \text{ times.}$$

---

[13]The ratio of debt to equity is also used in financial analysis. The debt to assets (D/A) and debt to equity (D/E) ratios are simply transformations of each other:

$$D/E = \frac{D/A}{1 - D/A}, \text{ and } D/A = \frac{D/E}{1 + D/E}.$$

Both ratios increase as a firm of a given size (total assets) uses a greater proportion of debt, but D/A rises linearly and approaches a limit of 100 percent, while D/E rises exponentially and approaches infinity.

[14]Generally, a long-term lease is defined as one that extends for at least 2 years. Thus, rent incurred under a 1-year lease would not be included in the fixed charge coverage ratio, but rental payments under a 2-year or longer lease would be defined as fixed charges and would be included.

CBS' fixed charges are covered only 3.1 times, as opposed to an industry average of 5.5 times. Again, this indicates that the firm is somewhat weaker than creditors would prefer it to be, and it points up the difficulties CBS would likely encounter if it attempted to increase its debt.

Cash Flow Coverage

CBS has outstanding preferred stock which requires the payment of $10,000 in dividends per year. It also must make annual repayments of principal (sinking fund payments) of $20,000 per year on its debt obligations. To the numerator of the fixed charge coverage ratio we add depreciation, which is a noncash charge, and to the denominator we add the preferred dividends and principal repayments, both "grossed up" to a before-tax basis by dividing each by $(1 - T)$ to reflect the fact that neither is a tax-deductible expense.[15] These adjustments produce the *cash flow coverage ratio,* which shows the margin by which operating cash flows cover financial requirements:

$$\text{Cash flow coverage ratio} = \frac{\text{EBIT} + \text{Lease payments} + \text{Depreciation}}{\text{Interest and lease payments} + \dfrac{\text{Preferred stock dividends}}{1 - T} + \dfrac{\text{Debt repayment}}{1 - T}}$$

$$= \frac{\$266 + \$28 + \$100}{\$94 + \$10/0.6 + \$20/0.6} = \frac{\$394}{\$144} = 2.7 \text{ times.}$$

Industry average = 3.2 times.

Again, CBS does not come up to industry standards.

Profitability Ratios

Profitability is the net result of a large number of policies and decisions. The ratios examined thus far provide some information about the way the firm is operating, but the *profitability ratios* show the combined effects of liquidity, asset management, and debt management on operating results.

Profit Margin on Sales

The *profit margin on sales,* computed by dividing net income by sales, gives the profit per dollar of sales:

$$\text{Profit margin on sales} = \frac{\text{Net income available to common stockholders}}{\text{Sales}} = \frac{\$110}{\$3,000} = 3.7\%.$$

Industry average = 5%.

---

[15]Because preferred dividends and sinking fund payments must be made from income remaining after payment of income taxes, dividing by $(1 - T)$ "grosses up" the payments and shows the before-tax amounts necessary to produce a given after-tax amount. For example, to pay $10,000 of preferred dividends, CBS needs $10,000/(1 - T) = $10,000/0.6 = $16,667 of pre-tax income.

CBS' profit margin is substantially below the industry average of 5 percent, indicating that its sales prices are relatively low, that its costs are relatively high, or both.

Basic Earning Power

The *basic earning power ratio* is calculated by dividing earnings before interest and taxes (EBIT) by total assets:

$$\text{Basic earning power ratio} = \frac{\text{EBIT}}{\text{Total assets}} = \frac{\$266}{\$2,000} = 13.3\%.$$

$$\text{Industry average} = 17.2\%.$$

This ratio is useful for comparing firms in different tax situations and with different degrees of financial leverage. Because of its low turnover ratio and low profit margin on sales, CBS is not getting as much operating income out of its assets as is the average automotive equipment manufacturing company.[16]

Return on Total Assets

The ratio of net income to total assets measures the *return on total assets (ROA)* after interest and taxes:

$$\begin{array}{c}\text{Return on} \\ \text{total assets (ROA)}\end{array} = \frac{\begin{array}{c}\text{Net income available to} \\ \text{common stockholders}\end{array}}{\text{Total assets}} = \frac{\$110}{\$2,000} = 5.5\%.$$

$$\text{Industry average} = 9\%.$$

CBS' 5.5 percent return is well below the 9 percent average for the industry. This low rate results from CBS' low basic earning power plus its above average use of debt, which cause its net income to be relatively low and its interest payments to be high.

Return on Common Equity

The ratio of net income to common equity measures the *return on common equity (ROE),* or the *rate of return on the stockholders' investment:*

$$\begin{array}{c}\text{Return on} \\ \text{common equity (ROE)}\end{array} = \frac{\begin{array}{c}\text{Net income available to} \\ \text{common stockholders}\end{array}}{\text{Common equity}} = \frac{\$110}{\$800} = 13.8\%.$$

$$\text{Industry average} = 15.0\%.$$

CBS' 13.8 percent return is below the 15.0 percent industry average, but it is not as far below as the return on total assets. This results from CBS' greater use of debt, a point that is analyzed in detail later in the chapter.

---

[16]Notice that EBIT is earned throughout the year, whereas the total assets figure is as of the end of the year. Therefore, it would be conceptually better to calculate this ratio as EBIT/Average assets = EBIT/[(Beginning assets + Ending assets)/2]. We have not made this adjustment because the published ratios used for comparative purposes do not include it. Incidentally, the same adjustment would also be appropriate for the next two ratios, ROA and ROE.

Market Value Ratios

A final group of ratios, *market value ratios,* relates the firm's stock price to its earnings and book value per share. These ratios give management an indication of what investors think of the company's past performance and future prospects. If the firm's liquidity, asset management, debt management, and profitability ratios are all good, then its market value ratios will be high, and its stock price will probably be as high as can be expected.

Price/Earnings Ratio

The *price/earnings (P/E) ratio* shows how much investors are willing to pay per dollar of reported profits. CBS' stock sells for $28.50, so with an EPS of $2.20, its P/E ratio is 13.0:

$$\text{Price/earnings (P/E) ratio} = \frac{\text{Price per share}}{\text{Earnings per share}} = \frac{\$28.50}{\$2.20} = 13.0 \text{ times.}$$

$$\text{Industry average} = 13.5 \text{ times.}$$

P/E ratios are higher for firms with high growth prospects, other things held constant, but they are lower for riskier firms. CBS' P/E ratio is slightly below the average of other small automotive equipment producers, which suggests that the company is regarded as being somewhat riskier than most, as having poorer growth prospects, or both.

Market/Book Ratio

The ratio of a stock's market price to its book value gives another indication of how investors regard the company. Companies with relatively high rates of return on equity generally sell at higher multiples of book value than those with low returns. CBS' book value per share is $16.00:

$$\text{Book value per share} = \frac{\text{Common equity}}{\text{Shares outstanding}} = \frac{\$800}{50} = \$16.00.$$

Dividing the price per share by the book value gives a *market/book ratio* of 1.8 times:

$$\text{Market/book ratio} = \frac{\text{Market price per share}}{\text{Book value per share}} = \frac{\$28.50}{\$16.00} = 1.8 \text{ times.}$$

$$\text{Industry average} = 2.1 \text{ times.}$$

Investors are willing to pay slightly less for CBS' book value than for that of an average automotive equipment manufacturing company.

The typical railroad, which has a very low rate of return on assets, has a market/book value ratio of less than 0.5. On the other hand, very successful firms such as IBM achieve high rates of return on their assets, and they have market values well in excess of their book values. IBM's market/book ratio is about 3.0.

Trend Analysis

It is important to analyze trends in ratios as well as their absolute levels, for trends give clues as to whether the financial situation is improving or deteriorating. To do a *trend analysis,* one simply graphs a ratio against years, as shown in Figure 21-3. This graph shows that CBS' rate of return on common equity has been declining since 1984 even though the industry average has been relatively stable. Other ratios could be analyzed similarly.

Summary of Ratio Analysis: The Du Pont System

Table 21-6 summarizes CBS' ratios, while Figure 21-4, which is called a *Du Pont chart* because that company's managers developed the general approach, shows the relationship between debt, asset turnover, and the profit margin. The left-hand side of the chart develops the *profit margin on sales.* The various expense items are listed and then summed to obtain CBS' total costs. Subtracting costs from sales yields the company's net income, which, when divided by sales, indicates that 3.7 percent of each sales dollar is left over for stockholders.

The right-hand side of the chart lists the various categories of assets, totals them, and then divides sales by total assets to find the number of times CBS "turns its assets over" each year. CBS' total assets turnover or utilization, ratio is 1.5 times.

The profit margin times the total assets turnover is called the *Du Pont equation,* and it gives the rate of return on assets (ROA):

Figure 21-3
CBS: Rate of Return on Common Equity, 1983–1987

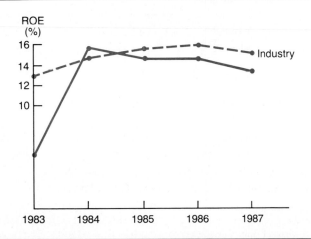

Table 21-6
CBS Equipment Company:
Summary of Financial Ratios
(Thousands of Dollars)

Ratio	Formula for Calculation	1986	1987	1987 Industry Average	Comment
I. Liquidity					
1. Current	$\dfrac{\text{Current assets}}{\text{Current liabilities}}$	2.8×	2.3×	2.5×	Slightly low; bad trend
2. Quick, or acid test	$\dfrac{\text{Current assets} - \text{Inventories}}{\text{Current liabilities}}$	1.8×	1.3×	1.0×	OK, but bad trend
II. Asset Management					
3. Inventory turnover	$\dfrac{\text{Sales}}{\text{Inventory}}$	13.3×	10.0×	9.0×	OK, but bad trend
4. Average collection period (ACP)	$\dfrac{\text{Receivables}}{\text{Sales}/360}$	39.8 days	42.0 days	36.0 days	Poor; bad trend
5. Fixed asset turnover	$\dfrac{\text{Sales}}{\text{Fixed assets}}$	2.7×	2.3×	3.9×	Low; bad trend
6. Total asset turnover	$\dfrac{\text{Sales}}{\text{Total assets}}$	1.7×	1.5×	1.8×	Low; bad trend
III. Debt Management					
7. Debt to total assets (D/A)	$\dfrac{\text{Total debt}}{\text{Total assets}}$	47.6%	55.0%	40.0%	Very high; bad trend
8. Times interest earned (TIE)	$\dfrac{\text{EBIT}}{\text{Interest charges}}$	5.6×	4.0×	6.0×	Very low; bad trend
9. Fixed charge coverage	$\dfrac{\text{EBIT} + \text{Lease payments}}{\text{Interest charges} + \text{Lease payments}}$	3.9×	3.1×	5.5×	Very low; bad trend
IV. Profitability					
10. Profit margin on sales	$\dfrac{\text{Net income}^{a}}{\text{Sales}}$	4.2%	3.7%	5.0%	Low; bad trend
11. Basic earning power (BEP)	$\dfrac{\text{EBIT}}{\text{Total assets}}$	15.7%	13.3%	17.2%	Very low; bad trend
12. Return on total assets (ROA)	$\dfrac{\text{Net income}^{a}}{\text{Total assets}}$	7.1%	5.5%	9.0%	Very low; bad trend
13. Return on equity (ROE)	$\dfrac{\text{Net income}^{a}}{\text{Common equity}}$	15.4%	13.8%	15.0%	Low; bad trend
V. Market Value					
14. Price/earnings (P/E)	$\dfrac{\text{Price per share}}{\text{Earnings per share}}$	12.1×	13.0×	13.5×	Slightly low
15. Market/book (M/B)	$\dfrac{\text{Market price per share}}{\text{Book value per share}}$	1.9×	1.8×	2.1×	Low

aNet income after preferred dividends.

Figure 21-4
**Modified Du Pont Chart Applied to CBS
Equipment Company (Thousands of Dollars)**

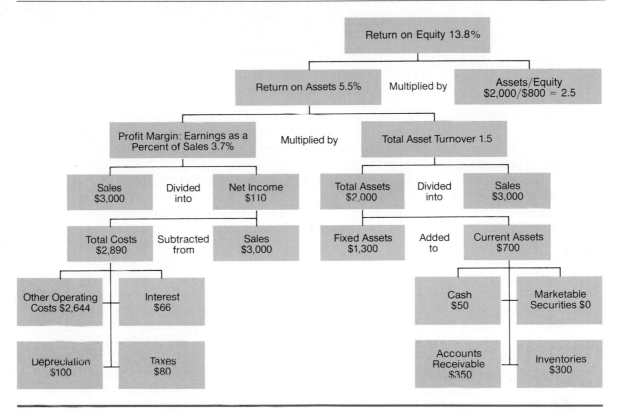

$$\text{ROA} = \begin{array}{c} \text{Rate of return} \\ \text{on assets} \end{array} = \text{Profit margin} \times \text{Total assets turnover}$$

$$= \frac{\text{Net income}}{\text{Sales}} \times \frac{\text{Sales}}{\text{Total assets}} \qquad \text{(21-1)}$$

$$= 3.7\% \times 1.5 = 5.5\%.$$

CBS made 3.7 percent, or 3.7 cents, on each dollar of sales, and assets were "turned over" 1.5 times during the year, so the company earned a return of 5.5 percent on its assets.

If CBS had used only equity, the rate of return on assets would have equaled the rate of return on equity. However, in the actual case, 60 percent of the firm's capital was supplied by creditors and preferred stockholders, and since the 5.5 percent return on total assets all goes to common stockholders, who put up only 40 percent of the capital, the return on common equity is higher than 5.5 percent. Specifically, the rate of return on assets (ROA) must be multiplied by the *equity multiplier,* which is the ratio of assets to common equity, to obtain the rate of return on common equity (ROE):[17]

$$ROE = ROA \times Equity\ multiplier$$
$$= \frac{Net\ income}{Assets} \times \frac{Assets}{Common\ equity}$$
$$= 5.5\% \times \$2,000/\$800 \qquad\qquad (21\text{-}2)$$
$$= 5.5\% \times 2.5$$
$$= 13.75\%,\ rounded\ to\ 13.8\%.$$

This 13.8 percent rate of return could, of course, be calculated directly: Net income/Common equity = \$110/\$800 = 13.8%. However, the Du Pont equation shows how the rate of return on assets and the use of debt interact to determine the return on equity.[18]

IBM, which is generally regarded as being one of the best managed U.S. companies, uses the Du Pont system to analyze ways of improving the firm's performance. On the left, or "profit margin," side of Figure 21-4, IBM's marketing people study the effects of raising sales prices (or lowering them to increase volume), of moving into new products or markets with higher margins, and so on. IBM's cost accountants study various expense items and, working with engineers, purchasing agents, and other operating personnel, seek ways of holding down costs. On the "turnover" side, IBM's financial analysts, working with both production and marketing people, investigate ways of minimizing investments in various types of assets. At the same time, IBM's treasury staff analyzes the effects of alternative financing strategies, seeking to hold down interest expenses and the risks of debt while still using debt to increase the rate of return on equity.

As a result of such an analysis, John Akers, IBM's chairman, recently announced a series of moves designed to cut operating costs by more than \$1 billion per year. Akers also announced that IBM intended to concentrate its capital in markets where profit margins are reasonably high, and that if competition increased in certain of its product markets (such as the low-price end of the PC market), then IBM would withdraw from those markets. IBM has long enjoyed a high return on equity, and Akers recognized that if competition drives profit margins too low in a particular market, then it becomes impossible to continue to earn high returns on

---

[17]Alternatively, we could "gross up" the ROA by dividing it by the common equity ratio:

$$ROE = ROA/Common\ equity\ ratio = 5.5/0.4 = 13.75\%.$$

[18]Another ratio that is frequently used is the following:

$$Rate\ of\ return\ on\ investors'\ capital = \frac{Net\ income\ after\ taxes\ +\ Interest}{Debt\ +\ Equity}.$$

The numerator shows the dollar returns to investors, the denominator shows the total amount of money investors have put up, and the ratio itself shows the rate of return on all investors' capital. This ratio is especially important in the public utility industries, where regulators are concerned about the companies' using their monopoly positions to earn excessive returns on investors' capital. In fact, regulators try to set utility prices (service rates) at levels that will force the return on investors' capital to equal a company's cost of capital.

the capital invested to serve that market. Therefore, if it is to maintain its high ROE, IBM may have to develop new products and shift capital into new areas. IBM's future depends on this type of analysis, and if it is as successful in the future as it has been in the past, the Du Pont system will have helped it achieve that success.

COMPARATIVE RATIOS

The preceding analysis of CBS Equipment Company pointed out the usefulness of a *comparative ratio analysis.* Comparative ratios are available from a number of sources. One useful set of comparative data is compiled by Dun & Bradstreet, Inc. (D&B), which provides 14 ratios calculated for a large number of industries; nine of these ratios are shown for a small sample of firms in Table 21-7. Useful ratios can also be found in the *Annual Statement Studies* published by Robert Morris Associates, which is the national association of bank loan officers. The U.S. Commerce Department's *Quarterly Financial Report,* which is found in most libraries, gives a set of ratios for manufacturing firms by industry group and size of firm. Trade associations and individual firms' credit departments also compile industry average financial ratios. Finally, financial statement data for thousands of publicly owned corporations are available on magnetic tapes and diskettes, and since brokerage houses, banks, and other financial institutions have easy access to these data, financial analysts can and do generate comparative ratios tailored to their specific needs.

Each of the data-supplying organizations uses a somewhat different set of ratios designed for its own purposes. For example, D&B deals mainly with small firms, many of which are proprietorships, and it sells its services primarily to banks and credit managers, so it is concerned largely with the creditor's viewpoint. Accordingly, its ratios emphasize current assets and liabilities, and D&B is completely unconcerned with market value ratios. When you select your comparative data source, you should be sure that your emphasis is similar to that of the agency whose ratios you use, or else you should recognize the limitations of those ratios for your purposes. Additionally, there are often definitional differences in the ratios presented by different sources. Therefore, before using a source, be sure to verify the exact definitions of the ratios to insure consistency.

USES AND LIMITATIONS OF RATIO ANALYSIS

As noted earlier, ratio analysis is used by three main groups: (1) *managers,* who employ ratios to help analyze, control, and thus improve the firm's operations; (2) *credit analysts,* such as bank loan officers or industrial companies' credit managers, who analyze ratios to help ascertain their customers' ability to pay their debts; and (3) *security analysts,* including both stock analysts, who are interested in a company's efficiency and growth prospects, and bond analysts, who are concerned with a company's ability to pay interest on its bonds as well as with the liquidating

Table 21-7

Dun & Bradstreet Ratios for Selected Industries: Upper Quartile, Median, and Lower Quartile[a]

SIC Codes, Line of Business, and Number of Concerns Reporting	Quick Ratio	Current Ratio	Total Liabilities to Net Worth	Average Collection Period	Net Sales to Inventory	Total Assets to Net Sales	Return on Net Sales	Return on Total Assets	Return on Net Worth
	×	×	%	Days	×	%	%	%	%
2879	1.7	3.0	32.5	25.1	14.6	40.2	7.1	11.5	22.1
Agricultural chemicals	1.0	2.2	59.3	33.9	8.6	56.3	4.9	7.0	9.8
(61)	0.7	1.0	121.7	47.2	5.9	78.7	1.3	0.3	0.4
3724	1.6	3.0	35.6	28.8	13.7	43.4	9.5	13.3	34.1
Aircraft parts, including engines	0.9	1.7	103.1	44.1	8.3	63.6	6.3	8.9	13.5
(66)	0.6	1.2	228.0	55.1	4.6	84.6	1.6	2.9	7.8
2051	1.9	3.0	27.9	10.2	63.8	22.8	7.9	16.3	35.1
Bakery products	1.0	1.6	88.0	21.1	42.1	32.5	3.7	8.5	17.3
(167)	0.6	0.9	147.7	27.7	21.6	44.1	1.4	3.8	10.5
2086	2.2	4.1	18.8	16.9	26.2	30.4	6.7	12.9	21.4
Beverages	1.1	2.2	53.9	21.1	19.1	40.1	4.2	8.9	14.5
(192)	0.7	1.5	102.1	30.2	12.9	51.8	1.9	5.0	9.1
3312	1.2	2.3	64.0	34.3	11.3	39.5	3.8	3.7	10.0
Blast furnaces and steel mills	0.8	1.8	138.1	47.3	6.8	67.5	1.4	(0.5)	(0.6)
(98)	0.5	1.2	236.4	56.9	4.8	91.7	(4.1)	(5.1)	(15.5)
2731	2.3	6.0	17.6	32.3	9.0	42.5	16.5	13.4	28.5
Book publishing	1.1	2.6	51.3	54.3	4.3	68.6	5.9	6.4	6.4
(342)	0.6	1.5	137.0	79.8	2.5	100.5	1.6	1.2	2.3

Source: Industry Norms and Key Business Ratios, 1984–1985 Edition, Dun & Bradstreet Credit Services.

[a]The median and quartile ratios can be illustrated by an example. The median quick ratio for agricultural chemical manufacturers, as shown above is 1.0. To obtain this figure, the ratios of current assets to current debt for each of the 61 concerns were arranged in a graduated series, with the largest ratio at the top and the smallest at the bottom. The median ratio of 1.0 is the ratio halfway between the top and the bottom. The ratio of 1.7, representing the upper quartile, is one-quarter of the way down from the top (or halfway between the top and the median). The ratio 0.7, representing the lower quartile, is one-quarter of the way up from the bottom (or halfway between the median and the bottom).

value of the assets that would be available to bondholders in the event the company went bankrupt.

Before closing this chapter, we should note that while ratio analysis can provide useful information concerning a company's operations and financial condition, it does have some inherent problems and limitations that necessitate care and judgment.

1. Many large firms operate a number of different divisions in quite different industries; in such cases it is difficult to develop a meaningful set of industry averages for comparative purposes. This tends to make ratio analysis more useful for small, narrowly-focused firms than for large, multi-divisional ones.

2. Most firms want to be better than average (although half will be above and half below the median), so merely attaining average performance is not necessarily good. To achieve high-level performance, it is preferable to target on the industry leaders' ratios.

3. Inflation has badly distorted firms' balance sheets. Further, since inflation affects both depreciation charges and inventory costs, profits are also affected. Thus, a ratio analysis for one firm over time, or a comparative analysis of firms of different ages, must be interpreted with care and judgment.

4. Seasonal factors can also distort ratio analysis. For example, the inventory turnover ratio for a food processor will be radically different if the balance sheet figure used for inventory is the one just before versus the one just after the close of the canning season. This problem can be minimized by using monthly averages for inventory when calculating ratios such as turnover.

5. Firms can employ *"window dressing"* techniques to make their financial statements look better to credit analysts. To illustrate, a Chicago builder borrowed on a two-year basis on December 29, 1986, held the proceeds of the loan as cash for a few days, and then paid off the loan ahead of time on January 5, 1987. This improved his current and quick ratios and made his year-end 1986 balance sheet look good. However, the improvement was strictly temporary; a week later the balance sheet was back at the old level.

6. Different operating and accounting practices can distort comparisons. As noted earlier, inventory valuation and depreciation methods can affect the financial statements and thus distort comparisons among firms that use different accounting procedures. Also, if one firm leases a substantial amount of its productive equipment, then its assets may be low relative to sales because leased assets often do not appear on the balance sheet. At the same time, the lease liability may not be shown as a debt. Thus, leasing can artificially improve both the debt and turnover ratios.

7. It is difficult to generalize about whether a particular ratio is "good" or "bad." For example, a high current ratio may indicate a strong liquidity position, which is good, or excessive cash, which is bad because excess cash in the bank is a nonearning asset. Similarly, a high fixed asset turnover ratio may denote either a firm that uses assets efficiently or one that is undercapitalized and simply cannot afford to buy enough assets.

8. A firm may have some ratios which look "good" and others which look "bad," making it difficult to tell whether the company is, on balance, in a strong or a weak position. However, statistical procedures can be used to analyze the *net effects* of a set of ratios. Many banks and other lending organizations use these procedures to analyze firms' financial ratios and, on the basis of their analyses, classify companies according to their probability of getting into financial distress. The technique used is *multiple discriminant analysis,* which we discuss in Appendix 21A.

Ratio analysis is useful, but analysts should be aware of these problems and make adjustments as necessary. Ratio analysis conducted in a mechanical, unthinking manner is dangerous; however, used intelligently and with good judgment, it can provide useful insights into a firm's operations.

SUMMARY

The primary purposes of this chapter were (1) to describe the basic financial statements and (2) to discuss techniques used by investors and managers to analyze them. Four basic statements were covered: the *income statement,* the *balance sheet,* the *statement of retained earnings,* and the *statement of changes in financial position.*

Financial analysis is designed to determine the relative strengths and weaknesses of a company—whether the firm is financially sound and profitable relative to other firms in its industry and whether its position is improving or deteriorating over time. Investors need such information in order to estimate future cash flows from the firm and to evaluate the riskiness of these flows. Managers need to be aware of their firms' financial positions in order to detect potential problems and to strengthen weaknesses.

Financial analysts examine a set of ratios designed to highlight the key aspects of a firm's operations. These ratios are broken down into five categories: (1) *liquidity ratios,* (2) *asset management ratios,* (3) *debt management ratios,* (4) *profitability ratios,* and (5) *market value ratios.* The ratios for a given firm are calculated and then compared with those of other firms in the same industry to judge the relative strength of the firm in question. In addition, trends in the ratios are analyzed, and the *Du Pont system* is used to help pinpoint the cause of low profits. Ratio analysis has limitations, but used with care and judgment, it can be most helpful.

Questions

21-1 Define each of the following terms:

   a. Annual report; income statement; balance sheet

   b. Equity, or net worth; paid-in capital; retained earnings

   c. Statement of retained earnings; statement of changes in financial position; sources and uses of funds statement

   d. Depreciation; inventory valuation methods

   e. Liquidity ratios; current ratio; quick, or acid test, ratio

    f. Asset management ratios; inventory turnover ratio; average collection period (ACP); fixed assets turnover ratio; total assets turnover ratio

    g. Financial leverage; debt ratio; times-interest-earned (TIE) ratio; fixed charge coverage ratio; cash flow coverage ratio

    h. Profitability ratios; profit margin on sales; basic earning power ratio; return on total assets (ROA); return on common equity (ROE)

    i. Market value ratios; price/earnings (P/E) ratio; market/book (M/B) ratio; dividend payout ratio; book value per share

    j. Trend analysis; comparative analysis

    k. Du Pont chart; Du Pont equation

    l. "Window dressing"; seasonal effects on ratios

21-2 What four statements are contained in most annual reports?

21-3 Is it true that if a "typical" firm reports $20 million of retained earnings on its balance sheet, its directors could declare a $20 million cash dividend without any qualms whatsoever?

21-4 Financial ratio analysis is conducted by four groups of analysts: managers, equity investors, long-term creditors, and short-term creditors. What is the primary emphasis of each of these groups in evaluating ratios?

21-5 Why would the inventory turnover ratio be more important to a grocery store than to a shoe repair store?

21-6 Profit margins and turnover ratios vary from one industry to another. What are some industry characteristics that help explain these variations?

21-7 How does inflation distort ratio analysis comparisons both for one company over time (trend analysis) and when different companies are compared? Are only balance sheet items or both balance sheet and income statement items affected?

21-8 If a firm's ROE is low and management wants to improve it, explain how using more debt might help.

21-9 Suppose a firm used debt to leverage up its ROE, and in the process its EPS was also boosted. Would this necessarily lead to an increase in the price of the firm's stock? Assume the payout ratio remains constant.

21-10 How might (a) seasonal factors and (b) different growth rates distort a comparative ratio analysis? Give some examples. How might these problems be alleviated?

21-11 Indicate the effects of the transactions listed below on total current assets, the current ratio, and net income. Use + to indicate an increase, − to indicate a decrease, and 0 to indicate either no effect or an indeterminate effect. Be prepared to state any necessary assumptions, and assume an initial current ratio of more than 1.0. (Note: A good accounting background is necessary to answer some of these questions; if yours is not strong, just answer the questions you can handle.)

	Total Current Assets	Current Ratio	Net Income
a. Cash is acquired through issuance of additional common stock.	_____	_____	_____
b. Merchandise is sold for cash.	_____	_____	_____

	Total Current Assets	Current Ratio	Net Income
c. Federal income tax due for the previous year is paid.	————	————	————
d. A fixed asset is sold for less than book value.	————	————	————
e. A fixed asset is sold for more than book value.	————	————	————
f. Merchandise is sold on credit.	————	————	————
g. Payment is made to trade creditors for previous purchases.	————	————	————
h. A cash dividend is declared and paid.	————	————	————
i. Cash is obtained through short-term bank loans.	————	————	————
j. Short-term notes receivable are sold at a discount.	————	————	————
k. Marketable securities are sold below cost.	————	————	————
l. Advances are made to employees.	————	————	————
m. Current operating expenses are paid.	————	————	————
n. Short-term promissory notes are issued to trade creditors for past due accounts receivable.	————	————	————
o. Ten-year notes are issued to pay off accounts payable.	————	————	————
p. A fully depreciated asset is retired.	————	————	————
q. Accounts receivable are collected.	————	————	————
r. Equipment is purchased with short-term notes.	————	————	————
s. Merchandise is purchased on credit.	————	————	————
t. The estimated taxes payable are increased.	————	————	————

Self-Test Problems

ST-1 (Debt ratio) C. Barngrover & Co. had earnings per share of $4 last year, and it paid a $2 dividend. Book value per share at year-end was $40, while total retained earnings increased by $12 million during the year. Barngrover has no preferred stock, and no new common stock was issued during the year. If Barngrover's year-end debt (which equals its total liabilities) was $120 million, what was the company's year-end debt/assets ratio?

ST-2 (Ratio analysis) The following data apply to Racette & Company (millions of dollars):

Cash and marketable securities	$100.00
Fixed assets	$283.50
Sales	$1,000.00
Net income	$50.00
Quick ratio	$2.0\times$
Current ratio	$3.0\times$
ACP	40 days
ROE	12%

Racette has no preferred stock — only common equity, current liabilities, and long-term debt.

a. Find Racette's (1) accounts receivable, (2) current liabilities, (3) current assets, (4) total assets, (5) ROA, (6) common equity, and (7) long-term debt.

b. In Part a, you should have found Racette's accounts receivable = $111.1 million. If Racette could reduce its ACP from 40 days to 30 days while holding other things constant, how much cash would it generate? If this cash were used to buy back common stock (at book value) and thus reduced the amount of common equity, how would this affect (1) the ROE, (2) the ROA, and (3) the total debt/total assets ratio?

Problems

21-1 **(Ratio analysis)** Data for the Ferri Computer Company and its industry averages follow.

    a. Calculate the indicated ratios for Ferri.

    b. Construct the Du Pont equation for both Ferri and the industry.

    c. Outline Ferri's strengths and weaknesses as revealed by your analysis.

    d. Suppose Ferri had doubled its sales as well as its inventories, accounts receivable, and common equity during 1987. How would that information affect the validity of your ratio analysis? (Hint: Think about averages and the effects of rapid growth on ratios if averages are not used. No calculations are needed.)

Ferri Computer Company:
Balance Sheet as of
December 31, 1987

Cash	$ 155,000	Accounts payable	$ 258,000
Receivables	672,000	Notes payable	168,000
Inventory	483,000	Other current liabilities	234,000
Total current assets	$1,310,000	Total current liabilities	$660,000
Net fixed assets	585,000	Long-term debt	513,000
		Common equity	722,000
Total assets	$1,895,000	Total liabilities and equity	$1,895,000

Ferri Computer Company:
Income Statement for Year Ended
December 31, 1987

Sales		$3,215,000
Cost of goods sold:		
Materials	$1,434,000	
Labor	906,000	
Heat, light, and power	136,000	
Indirect labor	226,000	
Depreciation	83,000	2,785,000
Gross profit		$ 430,000
Selling expenses		230,000
General and administrative expenses		60,000
Earnings before interest and taxes		$ 140,000
Interest expense		49,000
Net income before taxes		$ 91,000
Federal and state income taxes (40%)		36,400
Net income		$ 54,600

Ratio	Ferri	Industry Average
Current assets/Current liabilities	_____	2.0×
Average collection period	_____	35 days
Sales/Inventories	_____	6.7×
Sales/Total assets	_____	2.9×
Net income/Sales	_____	1.2%
Net income/Total assets	_____	3.4%
Net income/Equity	_____	8.5%
Total debt/Total assets	_____	60.0%

21-2 (Liquidity ratios) The Goulet Company has $1,750,000 in current assets and $700,000 in current liabilities. Its initial inventory level is $500,000, and it will raise funds as additional notes payable and use them to increase inventory. How much can Goulet's short-term debt (notes payable) increase without violating a current ratio of 2 to 1? What will be the firm's quick ratio after Goulet has raised the maximum amount of short-term funds?

21-3 (Ratio calculations) The Pappas Company had a quick ratio of 1.4, a current ratio of 3.0, an inventory turnover of 6 times, total current assets of $675,000, and cash and marketable securities of $100,000 in 1987. What were Pappas' annual sales and its ACP for that year?

21-4 (Balance sheet analysis) Complete the balance sheet and sales information shown for Jones Software Company using the following financial data:

Debt ratio: 50%
Quick ratio: 0.80×
Total assets turnover: 1.5×
Average collection period: 36 days
Gross profit margin: 25%
Inventory turnover ratio: 5×

Balance Sheet and Sales Data

Cash	_____	Accounts payable	_____
Accounts receivable	_____	Long-term debt	40,000
Inventories	_____	Common stock	
Fixed assets	_____	Retained earnings	65,000
Total assets	200,000	Total claims	_____
Sales	_____	Cost of goods sold	_____

21-5 (Du Pont analysis) The Lanser Furniture Company, a manufacturer and wholesaler of high-quality home furnishings, has been experiencing low profitability in recent years. As a result, the board of directors has replaced the president of the firm with a new president, Don Sorenson, who has asked you to make an analysis of the firm's financial position using the Du Pont system. The most recent industry average ratios and Lanser's financial statements are reproduced on the next page.

Industry Average Ratios

Current ratio	2×	Sales/Fixed assets	6×
Debt/Total assets	30%	Sales/Total assets	3×
Times-interest-earned	7×	Net profit on sales	4%
Sales/Inventory	10×	Return on total assets	9%
Average collection period	24 days	Return on common equity	12.8%

Lanser Furniture Company:
Balance Sheet as of
December 31, 1987
(Millions of Dollars)

Cash	$ 30	Accounts payable	$ 30
Marketable securities	22	Notes payable	30
Net receivables	44	Other current liabilities	14
Inventories	106	Total current liabilities	$ 74
Total current assets	$202	Long-term debt	16
		Total liabilities	$ 90
Gross fixed assets	$150		
Less depreciation	52	Common stock	$ 76
Net fixed assets	$ 98	Retained earnings	134
		Total stockholders' equity	$210
Total assets	$300	Total liabilities and equity	$300

Lanser Furniture Company:
Income Statement for Year Ended
December 31, 1987
(Millions of Dollars)

Net sales	$530
Cost of goods sold	440
Gross profit	$ 90
Selling expenses	49
Depreciation expense	8
Interest expense	3
Total expenses	$ 60
Net income before tax	$ 30
Taxes (40%)	12
Net income	$ 18

a. Calculate those ratios that you think would be useful in this analysis.

b. Construct a Du Pont equation for Lanser, and compare the company's ratios to the composite ratios for the industry as a whole.

c. Do the balance sheet accounts or the income statement figures seem to be primarily responsible for the low profits?

d. Which specific accounts seem to be most out of line in relation to other firms in the industry?

e. If Lanser had a pronounced seasonal sales pattern, or if it grew rapidly during the year, how might that affect the validity of your ratio analysis? How might you correct for such potential problems?

21-6 (Statement of changes in financial position) The consolidated balance sheets for the Chance Lumber Company at the beginning and end of 1987 follow. The company bought $150 million worth of fixed assets during 1987, and the charge for depreciation was $30 million. Earnings after taxes were $76 million, and the company paid out $20 million in dividends.

a. Fill in the amount of source or use in the appropriate column.

Chance Lumber Company: Balance Sheets at Beginning and End of 1987 (Millions of Dollars)

	Jan. 1	Dec. 31	Change Source	Use
Cash	$ 30	$ 14	_____	_____
Marketable securities	22	0	_____	_____
Net receivables	44	60	_____	_____
Inventories	$106	150	_____	_____
Total current assets	$202	$224	_____	_____
Gross fixed assets	150	300	_____	_____
Less depreciation	(52)	(82)	_____	_____
Net fixed assets	$ 98	$218	_____	_____
Total assets	$300	$442	_____	_____
Accounts payable	$ 30	$ 36	_____	_____
Notes payable	30	6	_____	_____
Other current liabilities	14	30	_____	_____
Long-term debt	16	52	_____	_____
Common stock	76	128	_____	_____
Retained earnings	134	190	_____	_____
Total liabilities and equity	$300	$442	_____	_____

Note: Total sources must equal total uses.

b. Prepare a statement of changes in financial position.

c. Briefly summarize your findings.

21-7 (Du Pont analysis) The Puckett Electronic Corporation's balance sheets for 1987 and 1986 are as follows (in millions of dollars):

	1987	1986
Cash	$ 21	$ 45
Marketable securities	0	33
Receivables	90	66
Inventories	225	159
Total current assets	$336	$303
Gross fixed assets	450	225
Less accumulated depreciation	(123)	(78)
Net fixed assets	$327	$147
Total assets	$663	$450
Accounts payable	$ 54	$ 45
Notes payable	9	45
Accruals	45	21
Total current liabilities	$108	$111
Long-term debt	78	24
Common stock	192	114
Retained earnings	285	201
Total long-term capital	$555	$339
Total liabilities and equity	$663	$450

Additionally, Puckett's 1987 income statement is as follows (in millions of dollars):

Sales	$1,365
Cost of goods sold	888
General expenses	300
EBIT	$ 177
Interest	10
EBT	$ 167
Taxes (40%)	67
Net income	$ 100

a. What was Puckett's dividend payout ratio in 1987?

b. The following extended Du Pont equation is the industry average for 1987:

$$\text{Profit margin} \times \text{Asset turnover} \times \text{Equity multiplier} = \text{ROE}$$
$$6.52\% \quad \times \quad 1.82 \quad \times \quad 1.77 \quad = 21.00\%.$$

Construct Puckett's 1987 extended Du Pont equation. What does the Du Pont analysis indicate about the firm's expense control, asset utilization, and debt utilization? What is the industry's debt to assets ratio?

c. Construct Puckett's 1987 statement of changes in financial position. What does it suggest about the company's operations?

21-8 (Ratio trend analysis) The Crary Corporation's forecasted 1988 financial statements are given on the next page, along with some industry average ratios.

a. Calculate Crary's 1988 forecasted ratios, compare them with the industry average data, and comment briefly on Crary's projected strengths and weaknesses.
(Do Part b only if you are using the computerized diskette.)

b. Suppose Crary is considering installing a new computer system which would provide tighter control of inventory, accounts receivable, and accounts payable. If the new system is installed, the following data are projected rather than the data now given in certain balance sheet and income statement categories:

Cash	$81,000
Accounts receivable	$400,000
Inventory	$750,000
Other fixed assets	$91,000
Accounts payable	$300,000
Accruals	$133,000
Retained earnings	$279,710
Cost of goods sold	$3,510,000
Administrative and selling expenses	$228,320
P/E ratio	6×

(1) How does this affect the projected ratios and the comparison to the industry averages?

(2) If the new computer system were either more efficient or less efficient and caused the cost of goods sold to decrease or increase by $150,000 from the new projections, what effect would that have on the company's position?

Crary Corporation:
Pro Forma Balance Sheet as of December 31, 1988

Cash	$ 72,000
Accounts receivable	439,000
Inventory	894,000
Total current assets	$1,405,000
Land and building	238,000
Machinery	132,000
Other fixed assets	61,000
Total assets	$1,836,000
Accounts payable	$ 432,000
Accruals	170,000
Total current liabilities	$ 602,000
Long-term debt	404,290
Common stock	575,000
Retained earnings	254,710
Total liabilities and equity	$1,836,000

Crary Corporation:
Pro Forma Income Statement for 1988

Sales	$4,290,000
Cost of goods sold	3,580,000
Gross operating profit	$ 710,000
Administrative and selling expenses	236,320
Depreciation	159,000
Miscellaneous	134,000
Taxable income	$ 180,680
Taxes (40%)	72,272
Net income	$ 108,408
Number of shares outstanding	23,000

Per-Share Data:

EPS	$4.71
Cash dividends	$0.95
P/E ratio	5×
Market price (average)	$23.57

Industry Financial Ratios (1988)[a]

Quick ratio	1.0×
Current ratio	2.7×
Inventory turnover[b]	7×
Average collection period	32 days
Fixed assets turnover[b]	13.0×
Total assets turnover[b]	2.6×
Return on total assets	9.1%
Return on equity	18.2%
Debt ratio	50%
Profit margin on sales	3.5%
P/E ratio	6×

[a]Industry average ratios have been constant for the past four years.
[b]Based on year-end balance sheet figures.

Solutions to Self-Test Problems

ST-1 Barngrover paid $2 in dividends and retained $2 per share. Since total retained earnings rose by $12 million, there must be 6 million shares outstanding. With a book value of $40 per share, total common equity must be $40(6 million) = $240 million. Since Barngrover has $120 million of debt, its debt ratio must be 33.3 percent:

$$\frac{\text{Debt}}{\text{Assets}} = \frac{\text{Debt}}{\text{Debt} + \text{Equity}} = \frac{\$120 \text{ million}}{\$120 \text{ million} + \$240 \text{ million}}$$

$$= 0.333 = 33.3\%.$$

ST-2 a. In answering questions such as this, always begin by writing down the relevant definitional equations, then start filling in numbers.

$$(1) \qquad \text{ACP} = \frac{\text{Accounts receivable}}{\text{Sales}/360}$$

$$40 = \frac{A/R}{\$1,000/360}$$

$$A/R = 40(\$2.778) = \$111.1 \text{ million.}$$

(2)
$$\text{Quick ratio} = \frac{\text{Current assets} - \text{Inventories}}{\text{Current liabilities}}$$

$$= \frac{\text{Cash and marketable securities} + A/R}{\text{Current liabilities}} = 2.0$$

$$2.0 = \frac{\$100 + \$111.1}{\text{Current liabilities}}$$

$$\text{Current liabilities} = (\$100 + \$111.1)/2 = \$105.5 \text{ million.}$$

(3)
$$\text{Current ratio} = \frac{\text{Current assets}}{\text{Current liabilities}}$$

$$= \frac{\text{Current assets}}{\$105.5} = 3.0.$$

$$\text{Current assets} = 3.0(\$105.5) = \$316.50 \text{ million.}$$

(4)
$$\text{Total assets} = \text{Current assets} + \text{Fixed assets}$$

$$= \$316.5 + \$283.5 = \$600 \text{ million.}$$

(5)
$$\text{ROA} = \text{Profit margin} \times \text{Total assets utilization}$$

$$= \frac{\text{Net income}}{\text{Sales}} \times \frac{\text{Sales}}{\text{Total assets}}$$

$$= \frac{\$50}{\$1,000} \times \frac{\$1,000}{\$600}$$

$$= 0.05 \times 1.667 = 0.833 = 8.33\%.$$

Note: We could have found ROA as follows:

$$\text{ROA} = \frac{\text{Net income}}{\text{Total assets}}$$

$$= \frac{\$50}{\$600} = 8.33\%.$$

(6)
$$\text{ROE} = \text{ROA} \times \frac{\text{Assets}}{\text{Equity}}$$

$$12.0\% = 8.33\% \times \frac{\$600}{\text{Equity}}$$

$$\text{Equity} = \frac{(8.33\%)(\$600)}{12.0\%}$$

$$= \$416.50 \text{ million.}$$

Note: We could have found equity as follows:

$$\text{ROE} = \frac{\text{Net income}}{\text{Equity}}$$

$$12.0\% = \frac{\$50}{\text{Equity}}$$

$$\text{Equity} = \$50/0.12$$
$$= \$416.67 \text{ million (rounding error difference)}.$$

(7)
$$\text{Total assets} = \text{Total claims} = \$600$$
$$\text{Current liabilities} + \text{Long-term debt} + \text{Equity} = \$600$$
$$\$105.5 + \text{Long-term debt} + \$416.5 = \$600$$
$$\text{Long-term debt} = \$600 - \$105.5 - \$416.5 = \$78 \text{ million}.$$

b. Racette's average sales per day were $1,000/360 = $2.777777 million. Its ACP was 40, so A/R = 40($2,777,777) = $111,111,080. Its new ACP of 30 would cause A/R = 30($2,777,777) = $83,333,310. The reduction in receivables would be $111,111,080 − $83,333,310 = $27,777,770, which would equal the amount of cash generated.

(1)
$$\text{New equity} = \text{Old equity} - \text{Stock bought back}$$
$$= \$416,500,000 - \$27,777,777$$
$$= \$388,722,223.$$

Thus,

$$\text{New ROE} = \frac{\text{Net income}}{\text{New equity}}$$
$$= \frac{\$50,000,000}{\$388,722,223}$$
$$= 12.86\% \text{ (versus old ROE of 12.0\%)}.$$

(2)
$$\text{New ROA} = \frac{\text{Net income}}{\text{Total assets} - \text{Reduction in A/R}}$$
$$= \frac{\$50,000,000}{\$600,000,000 - \$27,777,777}$$
$$= 8.74\% \text{ (versus old ROA of 8.33\%)}.$$

(3) The old debt is the same as the new debt:

$$\text{Debt} = \text{Total claims} - \text{Equity}$$
$$= \$600 - \$416.5 = \$183.5 \text{ million}.$$
$$\text{Old total assets} = \$600 \text{ million}.$$
$$\text{New total assets} = \text{Old total assets} - \text{Reduction in A/R}$$
$$= \$600 - \$27.78$$
$$= \$572.22 \text{ million}.$$

Therefore,

$$\frac{\text{Debt}}{\text{Old total assets}} = \frac{\$183.5}{\$600} = 30.6\%,$$

while

$$\frac{\text{New debt}}{\text{New total assets}} = \frac{\$183.5}{\$572.22} = 32.1\%.$$

Selected Additional References and Cases

The effects of alternative accounting policies on both financial statements and ratios based on these statements are discussed in the investment textbooks referenced in Chapter 6, and also in the many excellent texts on financial statement analysis. For example, see

Gibson, Charles H., and Patricia A. Frishkoff, *Financial Statment Analysis* (Boston: Kent, 1986).

Hawkins, David F., *Corporate Financial Reporting and Analysis* (Homewood, Ill.: Irwin, 1986).

For further information on the relative usefulness of various financial ratios, see

Chen, Kung H., and Thomas A. Shimerda, "An Empirical Analysis of Useful Financial Ratios," *Financial Management,* Spring 1981, 51–60.

Considerable work has been done to establish the relationship between bond ratings and financial ratios. For one example, see

Belkaoui. Ahmed, *Industrial Bonds and the Rating Process* (London: Quorum Books, 1983).

For sources of ratios and common size statements, see the following:

Dun & Bradstreet, *Key Business Ratios* (New York: Updated annually).

Financial Research Associates, *Financial Studies of the Small Business* (Arlington, Va.: Updated annually).

Robert Morris Associates, *Annual Statement Studies* (Philadelphia: Updated annually).

For a better understanding of multiple discriminant analysis and its use in financial analysis, see

Collins, Robert A., "An Empirical Comparison of Bankruptcy Prediction Models," *Financial Management,* Summer 1980, 52–57.

Eisenbeis, Robert A., "Pitfalls in the Application of Discriminant Analysis in Business Finance and Economics," *Journal of Finance,* June 1977, 875–900.

Joy, O. Maurice, and John O. Tollefson, "On the Financial Application of Discriminant Analysis," *Journal of Financial and Quantitative Analysis,* December 1975, 723–739.

Pinches, George E., "Factors Influencing Classification Results from Multiple Discriminant Analysis," *Journal of Business Research,* December 1980, 429–456.

Scott, Elton, "On the Financial Application of Discriminant Analysis: Comment," *Journal of Finance and Quantitative Analysis,* March 1978, 201–205.

Tollefson, John O., and O. Maurice Joy, "Some Clarifying Comments on Discriminant Analysis," *Journal of Financial and Quantitative Analysis,* March 1978, 197–200.

The following case focuses on financial analysis:

Case 1, "Silver River Manufacturing Company," in the Crum-Brigham casebook illustrates the use of ratio analysis in the evaluation of a firm's existing and potential financial positions.

21A
Multiple Discriminant Analysis

As we discussed in Chapter 21, one of the problems with ratio analysis is the interpretation of results — some ratios might look "good" while other ratios look "bad," and it might thus be difficult to reach a conclusion on an action such as approving or denying a loan for the company. *Multiple discriminant analysis (MDA)* is a statistical procedure that can help one interpret ratios and use them for decision purposes. Discriminant analysis is similar to regression analysis, and it identifies those factors which seem to have an important bearing on the likelihood of some future event. In this appendix, we discuss MDA in some detail, and we illustrate its application to bankruptcy prediction.[1]

The Basics of Multiple Discriminant Analysis

Suppose a bank loan officer wants to segregate corporate loan applicants into those likely to default or not default. Assume that data for some past period are available on a group of firms which includes both companies that went bankrupt and companies that did not. For simplicity, we assume that only the current ratio and the debt/assets ratio are analyzed. These ratios for our sample of firms are given in Columns 2 and 3 at the bottom of Figure 21A-1. The X's in the graph represent firms that went bankrupt, while the dots represent firms that remained solvent. For example, Point A in the upper left section is the point for Firm 2, which had a current ratio of 3.0, a debt ratio of 20 percent, and a dot to indicate that the firm did not go bankrupt. Point B, in the lower right section, represents Firm 19, which had a current ratio of 1.0, a debt ratio of 60 percent, and an X to indicate that it did go bankrupt.

The objective of discriminant analysis is to construct a boundary line through the graph such that, if the firm is to the left of the line, it is not likely to become insolvent, whereas it is likely to go bankrupt if it falls to the right. This boundary line is called the *discriminant function,* and in our example it takes this form:

$$Z = a + b_1(\text{Current ratio}) + b_2(\text{Debt ratio}).$$

Here Z is called the *Z score,* a is a constant term, and b_1 and b_2 indicate the effect of the current ratio and the debt ratio on the probability of a firm's going bankrupt.

Although a full discussion of discriminant analysis would go well beyond the scope of this book, some useful insights may be gained by observing these points:

---

[1]This section is based largely on the work of Edward I. Altman, especially these two papers: (1) "Financial Ratios, Discriminant Analysis, and the Prediction of Corporate Bankruptcy," *Journal of Finance,* September 1968, 589–609; and (2) with Robert G. Haldeman and P. Narayanan, "Zeta Analysis: A New Model to Identify Bankruptcy Risk of Corporations," *Journal of Banking and Finance,* June 1977, 29–54.

Figure 21A-1
Discriminant Boundary between Bankrupt and Solvent Firms

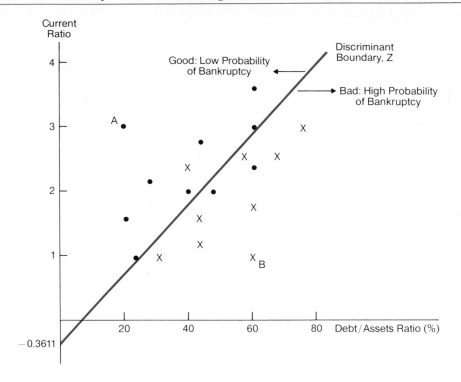

Firm Number (1)	Current Ratio (2)	Debt/Assets Ratio (3)	Did Firm Go Bankrupt? (4)	Z Score (5)	Probability of Bankruptcy (6)
1	3.6	60%	No	−0.780	17.2%
2(A)	3.0	20	No	−2.451	0.8
3	3.0	60	No	−0.135	42.0
4	3.0	76	Yes	0.791	81.2
5	2.8	44	No	−0.847	15.5
6	2.6	56	Yes	0.062	51.5
7	2.6	68	Yes	0.757	80.2
8	2.4	40	Yes[a]	−0.649	21.1
9	2.4	60	No[a]	0.509	71.5
10	2.2	28	No	−1.129	9.6
11	2.0	40	No	−0.220	38.1
12	2.0	48	No[a]	0.244	60.1
13	1.8	60	Yes	1.153	89.7
14	1.6	20	No	−0.948	13.1
15	1.6	44	Yes	0.441	68.8
16	1.2	44	Yes	0.871	83.5
17	1.0	24	No	−0.072	45.0
18	1.0	32	Yes	0.391	66.7
19(B)	1.0	60	Yes[a]	2.012	97.9

1. The discriminant function is fitted (that is, the values of a, b_1, and b_2 are obtained) using historical data for a sample of firms that either went bankrupt or did not during some past period. When the data in the lower part of Figure 21A-1 were fed into a "canned" discriminant analysis program (the computing centers of most universities and large corporations have such programs), the following discriminant function was obtained:

$$Z = -0.3877 - 1.0736(\text{Current ratio}) + 0.0579(\text{Debt ratio}).$$

2. This equation was plotted on Figure 21A-1 as the locus of points for which $Z = 0$. All combinations of current ratios and debt ratios shown on the line result in $Z = 0.$[2] Companies that lie to the left of the line (and also have Z values less than zero) are not likely to go bankrupt, while those to the right (and have Z greater than zero) are likely to fail. It may be seen from the graph that one X, indicating a failing company, lies to the left of the line, while two dots, indicating nonbankrupt companies, lie to the right of the line. Thus, the discriminant analysis failed to classify properly three companies.

3. If we have determined the parameters of the discriminant function, then we can calculate the Z score for other companies, say loan applicants at a bank. The Z scores for our hypothetical companies, along with their probabilities for going bankrupt, are given in Columns 5 and 6 of Figure 21A-1. The higher the Z score,

---

[2]To plot the boundary line, let D/A = 0% and 80%, and then find the current ratio that forces Z = 0 at those two values. For example, at D/A = 0,

$$Z = -0.3877 - 1.0736(\text{Current ratio}) + 0.0579(0) = 0$$
$$0.3877 = -1.0736(\text{Current ratio})$$
$$\text{Current ratio} = 0.3877/(-1.0736) = -0.3611.$$

Thus, -0.3611 is the vertical axis intercept. Similarly, the current ratio at D/A = 80% is found to be 3.9533. Plotting these two points on Figure 21A-1, and then connecting them, provides the discriminant boundary line, which is the line that best partitions the companies into bankrupt and nonbankrupt. It should be noted that nonlinear discriminant functions may also be used.

Table footnotes:
[a]Denotes a misclassification. Firm 8 had $Z = -0.649$, so MDA predicted no bankruptcy, but it did go bankrupt. Similarly, MDA predicted bankruptcy for Firms 9 and 12, but they did not go bankrupt. The following tabulation shows bankruptcy and solvency predictions versus actual results:

	Z Positive: MDA Predicts Bankruptcy	Z Negative: MDA Predicts Solvency
Went bankrupt	8	1
Remained solvent	2	8

The model did not perform perfectly, as two predicted bankruptcies remained solvent, and one firm that was expected to remain solvent went bankrupt. Thus, the model misclassified 3 out of 19 firms, or 16 percent of the sample. Its success rate was 84 percent.

Figure 21A-2
Probability Distributions of Z Scores

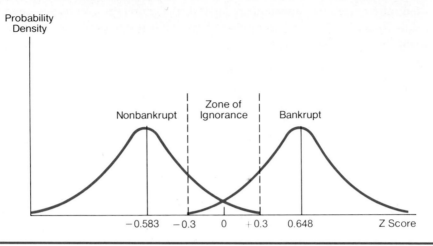

the worse the company looks from the standpoint of bankruptcy. Here is an interpretation:

Z = 0: 50-50 probability of future bankruptcy (say within two years). The company lies exactly on the boundary line.

Z < 0: If Z is negative, there is less than a 50 percent probability of bankruptcy. The smaller (more negative) the Z score, the lower is the probability of bankruptcy. The computer output from MDA programs gives this probability, and it is shown in Column 6 of Figure 21A-1.

Z > 0: If Z is positive, the probability of bankruptcy is greater than 50 percent, and the larger Z is, the greater the probability of bankruptcy.

4. The mean Z score of the companies that did not go bankrupt is −0.583, while that for the bankrupt firms is + 0.648. These means, along with approximations of the Z score probability distributions of the two groups, are shown in Figure 21A-2. We may interpret this graph as indicating that if Z is less than about −0.3, there is a very small probability that the firm will go bankrupt, whereas if Z is greater than +0.3, there is only a small probability that it will remain solvent. If Z is in the range ±0.3, called the *zone of ignorance,* we are uncertain about how the firm should be classified.

5. The signs of the coefficients of the discriminant function are logical. Since its coefficient is negative, the larger the current ratio, the lower is a company's Z score, and the lower the Z score, the smaller is the probability of failure. Similarly, high debt ratios produce high Z scores, and this is directly translated into a higher probability of bankruptcy.

6. Our illustrative discriminant function has only two variables, but other characteristics could be introduced. For example, we could add such variables as the rate of return on assets, the times-interest-earned ratio, the average collection period, the quick ratio, and so forth.[3] Had the rate of return on assets been introduced, it might have turned out that Firm 8 (which failed) had a low ROA, while Firm 9 (which did not fail) had a high ROA. A new discriminant function would be calculated:

$$Z = a + b_1(\text{Current ratio}) + b_2(\text{D/A}) + b_3(\text{ROA}).$$

Firm 8 might now have a positive Z, while Firm 9's Z might become negative. Thus, it is likely that by adding more characteristics we could improve the accuracy of our bankruptcy forecasts. In terms of Figure 21A-2, this would cause each probability distribution to become tighter, would narrow the zone of ignorance, and would lead to fewer misclassifications.

Altman's Model

In a classic paper, Edward Altman applied MDA to a sample of corporations, and he developed a discriminant function that has seen wide use in actual practice. Altman's function was fitted as follows:

$$Z = 0.012X_1 + 0.014X_2 + 0.033X_3 + 0.006X_4 + 0.999X_5.$$

Here

$$X_1 = \text{Net working capital/Total assets.}$$
$$X_2 = \text{Retained earnings/Total assets.}^4$$
$$X_3 = \text{EBIT/Total assets.}$$
$$X_4 = \text{Market value of common and preferred stock/Book value of debt.}^5$$
$$X_5 = \text{Sales/Total assets.}$$

The first four variables are expressed as percentages rather than as decimals. Also, Altman's 50-50 point was 2.675, and not 0.0 as in our hypothetical example; his zone of ignorance was from Z = 1.81 to Z = 2.99; and the *larger* the Z score, the less the probability of bankruptcy.[6]

---

[3]With more than two variables, it is difficult to graph the function, but this presents no problem in actual usage because graphs are only used to explain MDA.

[4]Retained earnings is the balance sheet figure, not the addition to retained earnings for the year.

[5][(Shares of common outstanding)(Price per share) + (Shares of preferred)(Price per share of preferred)]/Balance sheet value of total debt.

[6]These differences reflect the software package he used to generate the discriminant function. Altman's program operated from a base of 2.675 rather than 0.0, and his program simply reversed the sign of Z from ours.

Altman's function can be used to calculate a Z score for CBS Equipment Company based on the data presented previously in Chapter 21 in Tables 21-1 and 21-2. This calculation, ignoring the small amount of preferred stock, is shown below for 1987:

$$X_1 = \$400/\$2,000 = 20.0\% \qquad\qquad \times\ 0.012 = 0.240$$

$$X_2 = \$660/\$2,000 = 33.0\% \qquad\qquad \times\ 0.014 = 0.462$$

$$X_3 = \$266/\$2,000 = 13.3\% \qquad\qquad \times\ 0.033 = 0.439$$

$$X_4 = (50)(\$28.50)/(\$300 + \$800) = 129.5\% \times\ 0.006 = 0.777$$

$$X_5 = \$3,000/\$2,000 = 1.5 \qquad\qquad\quad \times\ 0.999 = \underline{1.499}$$

$$Z = \underline{\underline{3.417}}$$

Since CBS' Z score of 3.417 is above the 2.99 upper limit of Altman's zone of ignorance, the data indicate that there is virtually no chance that the company will go bankrupt within the next two years. (Altman's model predicts bankruptcy reasonably well for about two years into the future.)

Altman and his colleagues' later work updated and improved his original study. In their more recent work, they explicitly considered such factors as capitalized lease obligations, and they applied smoothing techniques to level out random fluctuations in the data. The new model was able to predict bankruptcy with a high degree of accuracy for two years into the future, and with a slightly lower but still reasonable degree of accuracy (70 percent) for about five years.

MDA has been used with success to quantify ratio analysis, by credit analysts to establish default probabilities for both consumer and corporate loan applicants, and by portfolio managers considering both stock and bond investments. It can also be used to evaluate a set of pro forma ratios as developed in Chapter 22, or to gain insights into the feasibility of a reorganization plan filed under the Bankruptcy Act. Altman's model has also been used by Morgan Stanley and other investment banking houses to appraise the quality of "junk bonds" used to finance takeovers and leveraged buyouts. The technique is described in detail in many statistics texts, while several articles cited at the end of the chapter discuss financial applications of MDA. The interested reader is urged to study this literature, for MDA has many potentially valuable applications in finance.

22

Financial Planning and Control

At the end of 1982, IBM had $32.5 billion in total assets and $16.8 billion in sales, making it one of the largest firms in the United States. Despite its large size, IBM was growing rapidly, as were other firms in the burgeoning information processing industry. Thus, by 1986, IBM's sales had grown to $34.3 billion, or at an average annual rate of 19.5 percent over the 4-year period. Of course, most firms — including IBM — cannot increase sales substantially without first increasing plant and equipment, adding new distribution channels, and so on. Therefore, to support its sales growth, IBM had to raise over $25 billion in new capital to buy additional assets.

IBM raised $6.6 billion without taking any conscious action — accounts payable and accruals just grew spontaneously as the company's business expanded. It raised another $0.9 billion by issuing notes payable, $1.4 billion by issuing long-term debt, $11.5 billion by retaining earnings, and $1.3 billion by selling new common stock, with the remaining $4.2 billion coming from miscellaneous sources such as deferred taxes.

IBM's capital requirements were enormous, and hence it was necessary for the company to plan its capital requirements well in advance to insure that it could get the funds it needed, when it needed them, and on the best possible terms. Indeed, forecasting financing requirements is an essential part of any firm's operations. It is easy to see that this is important to IBM because such large amounts are involved, but good financial planning is just as important, or perhaps even more important, for a smaller, weaker company. Whereas a firm such as IBM has relatively easy access to capital from all around the globe, a small firm might find it difficult and expensive — or even impossible — to obtain funds on short notice.

In this chapter, we will see how firms forecast future financing requirements and analyze alternative courses of action.

In the last chapter, we saw how one analyzes financial statements in order to identify a firm's strengths and weaknesses. Now we consider the actions a firm can take to exploit its strengths and to overcome its weaknesses. As we shall see, managers are vitally concerned with *projected*, or *pro forma*, *financial statements*, and with the effects of alternative policies on these statements. This is *financial planning*. However, a good financial plan cannot, by itself, ensure that the firm's goals will be met — the plan must be backed up by a *financial control system* which is used to monitor the situation both to ensure that the plan is carried out properly and to facilitate rapid adjustments if economic and operating conditions change from projected levels.

STRATEGIC PLANS

Financial planning must occur within the framework of the firm's overall strategic and operating plans. Thus, we begin our discussion with an overview of the strategic planning process.[1]

Corporate Purpose

The long-run strategic plan should begin with a statement of the *corporate purpose,* which defines the overall mission of the firm. The purpose can be defined either specifically or in general terms. For example, one firm might state that its corporate purpose is "to increase the intrinsic value of the firm's common stock." Another might say that its purpose is "to maximize the growth rate in earnings and dividends per share while avoiding excessive risk." Yet another might state that its principal goal is "to provide our customers with state-of-the-art computing systems at the lowest attainable cost, which in our opinion will also maximize benefits to our employees and stockholders."

There should be no conflict between sound operations and stockholders' benefits, but occasionally there is. For example, Varian Associates, Inc., a NYSE company with 1987 sales of about $1 billion, was for years regarded as one of the most technologically advanced companies in the electronics devices and semiconductor fields. However, Varian's management was reputed to be more concerned with developing new technology than with marketing it, and the stock price was lower in 1979 than it had been 10 years earlier. Some of the larger stockholders were intensely unhappy with the state of affairs, and management was faced with the threat of a proxy fight or a forced merger. At that point, management announced a conscious change in policy and stated that it would, in the future, emphasize both technological excellence *and* profitability, rather than focus primarily on technology. Earnings improved dramatically, and the stock price rose from a low of $6.75 in 1979 to over $60 in 1983.

The Varian example illustrates both the importance of the corporate purpose as viewed by management and also the discipline of the market. Well-run companies

---

[1]One can take many approaches to corporate planning. For more insights into the corporate planning process, see Benton E. Gup, *Guide to Strategic Planning* (New York: McGraw-Hill, 1980).

need to define an area and then develop competence with regard to meeting the needs of their customers, but they will be forced by the market to translate that competence into earnings.

Corporate Scope

The *corporate scope* defines a firm's lines of business and geographic area of operations. Again, the corporate scope can be spelled out in great detail or put merely in general terms. The steel industry provides a study in contrasts, with some companies such as U.S. Steel (now USX Corporation) diversifying widely, from oil to financial services, and other companies sticking closely to their basic business. Nucor Corporation, a NYSE-listed speciality steel producer, is one which has stuck to its basic business. This statement gives an idea of how Nucor's management defines its scope:

> We are a manufacturing company producing primarily steel products. The major strength of our company is constructing plants economically and operating them efficiently.

A $1,000 investment in Nucor's stock in 1977 would be worth $15,000 in 1987. A similar investment in U.S. Steel would now be worth $400. Factors other than scope of operations affected these results, but scope was surely an important factor.

Corporate Objectives

The corporate purpose and scope outline the general philosophy and approach of the business, but they do not provide managers with operational objectives. The *corporate objectives* set forth specific goals that management strives to attain. Corporate objectives can be quantitative, such as specifying a target market share, a target ROE, or a target earnings per share growth rate, or they can be qualitative, such as "keeping the firm's research and development efforts at the cutting edge of the industry." Multiple goals are often established, and these goals are not static — they should be and are changed when conditions change. The goals should also be challenging, yet realistically attainable, and it is appropriate that management compensation be based on the extent to which objectives are met.

Corporate Strategies

Once a firm has defined its purpose, scope, and objectives, it should develop a strategy designed to help it achieve its stated objectives. *Corporate strategies* are broad approaches rather than detailed plans. For example, one airline may have a strategy of offering "no frills" service between a limited number of cities, while another may plan to offer "staterooms in the sky." Strategies must be attainable and compatible with the firm's purpose, scope, and objectives.

Perhaps the most interesting and important set of strategies that has been developed in recent years is that of AT&T and the Bell operating companies in the wake of the breakup of AT&T. The seven regional telephone holding companies which emerged from the breakup all provide basic local telephone service, but beyond that, they appear to be developing different strategies which will take them in different directions. Some now sell a broad array of telecommunications equipment, while others have more limited offerings. Some are rapidly diversifying into nonregulated lines of business — Bell Atlantic has spent over $300 million for this purpose — while others are diversifying at a much slower pace.

The surviving AT&T faces perhaps even greater challenges in setting its corporate strategy. On the one hand, it faces increasing competition in its two major markets, long-distance transmission and telephone equipment manufacturing. Currently, it has most of the industry's capacity in these areas, so to some extent, it can price high and enjoy high short-run profits, but at the expense of a rapid erosion of its share of the business. Alternatively, it can price low and maintain a large market share, but not maximize short-run (and perhaps also long-run) profits. Also, AT&T must decide on the extent of its foray into the computer business. Its PC6300 clone of the IBM PC has not done very well, and its other computer ventures, such as its Unix operating system, have done poorly. IBM, meanwhile, has invested heavily in the telecommunications business (both manufacturing and satellite transmissions), and is thus attacking AT&T on its own turf. At the same time, the new Bell companies are all trying to get permission to compete with their former parent in the businesses of long distance service and equipment manufacturing.

The AT&T/Bell companies' strategic decisions are more dramatic than most, but they do illustrate the kinds of issues that arise when companies develop their strategic plans.

OPERATING PLANS

Operating plans can be developed for any time horizon, but most companies use a five-year horizon, and thus the name *five-year plan* has become common. In a five-year plan, the plans are most detailed for the first year, with each succeeding year's plan becoming less specific. The operating plan is intended to provide detailed implementation guidance, based on the corporate strategy, in order to meet the corporate objectives. The five-year plan explains in considerable detail who is responsible for what particular function, and when specific tasks are to be accomplished.

Table 22-1 contains the annual planning schedule of the Roenfeldt-Porter-Sicherman (RPS) Corporation, a leading manufacturer of computer and telecommunications equipment headquartered in South Carolina. This schedule illustrates the fact that for larger companies, the planning process is essentially continuous. Next, Table 22-2 outlines the key elements of RPS's five-year plan. A full outline would

Table 22-1
RPS Corporation: Annual Planning Schedule

Months	Action
April–May	Planning department analyzes economic and industry factors. Marketing department prepares sales forecast for each product group.
June–July	Engineering department prepares cost estimates for new manufacturing facilities and plant modernization programs.
August–September	Financial analysts evaluate proposed capital expenditures, divisional operating plans, and proposed sources and uses of funds.
October–November	Five-year plan is finalized by planning department, reviewed by divisional officers, and put into "semi-final" form.
December	Five-year plan is approved by the executive committee and then submitted to the board of directors for final approval.

Table 22-2
RPS Corporation: Five-Year Operating Plan Outline

A. Corporate mission
B. Corporate scope
C. Corporate objectives
D. Projected business environment
E. Corporate strategies
F. Summary of projected business results
G. Product line plans and policies
   1. Marketing
   2. Manufacturing
   3. Finance
      a. Working capital
         (1) Overall working capital policy
         (2) Cash and marketable securities management
         (3) Inventory management
         (4) Credit policy and receivables management
      b. Dividend policy
      c. Financial forecast
         (1) Capital budget
         (2) Cash budget
         (3) Pro forma financial statements
         (4) External financing requirements
         (5) Financial condition analysis
      d. Accounting plan
      e. Control plan
   4. Administrative and personnel
   5. Research and development
   6. New products
H. Consolidated corporate plan

require several pages, but Table 22-2 does at least provide insights into the format and content of a five-year plan. It should be noted that RPS, like other large, multidivisional companies, breaks down its operating plan by divisions. Thus, each division has its own goals, mission, and plan for meeting its objectives, and these plans are then consolidated to form the corporate plan.

THE FINANCIAL PLAN

The financial planning process can be broken down into five steps:

1. Set up a system of projected financial statements which can be used to analyze the effects of the operating plan on projected profits and other financial condition indicators. This system can also be used to monitor operations after the plan has been finalized and put into effect. Rapid awareness of deviations from plans is essential to a good control system, which in turn is essential to corporate success in a changing world.

2. Determine the specific financial requirements needed to support the company's five-year plan. This includes funds for plant and equipment as well as for inventory and receivables buildups, for R&D programs, and for major advertising campaigns.

3. Forecast the financing sources to be used over the next five years. This involves estimating the funds which will be generated internally as well as those which must be obtained from external sources. Any constraints on operating plans imposed by financial limitations which would limit the use of total and/or short-term debt should be incorporated into the plan; examples include debt ratio, current ratio, and coverage restrictions.

4. Establish and maintain a system of controls governing the allocation and use of funds within the firm. Essentially, this involves making sure that the basic plan is carried out properly.

5. Develop procedures for adjusting the basic plan if the forecasted economic conditions upon which the plan was based do not materialize. For example, if the economy turns out to be stronger than was forecasted when the basic plan was drawn up, then these new conditions must be recognized and reflected in higher production budgets, larger marketing quotas, and the like as rapidly as possible. Thus, Step 5 is really a "feedback loop" which triggers modifications to the plan.

The principal components of the financial plan are (1) an analysis of the firm's current financial condition as indicated by an analysis of its most recent statements, (2) a sales forecast, (3) the capital budget, (4) the cash budget, (5) a set of pro forma (or projected) financial statements, and (6) the external financing plan. We have in previous chapters discussed the capital budget, the cash budget, and financial statement analysis. In the remainder of this chapter, we focus on the other elements — the sales forecasts, the pro forma financial statements, and the external financing plan.

SALES FORECASTS

The *sales forecast* generally starts with a review of sales over the past five to ten years, expressed in a graph such as that in Figure 22-1. The first part of the graph shows actual sales for RPS Corporation from 1977 through 1987. During this 10-year period, sales grew from $175 million to $500 million, or at a compound growth rate of 11.1 percent. However, the growth rate has accelerated sharply in recent years, primarily as a result of the breakup of AT&T and the separation of its manufacturing and telephone operations, which permitted companies like RPS to compete for sales to telephone operating companies. Also, RPS's R&D program has been especially successful, so when the telecommunications market broke open, RPS was ready.

On the basis of the recent trend in sales, on new product introductions, and on the economics staff's forecast that the national economy will be quite strong during the coming year, RPS's planning group projects a 50 percent growth rate during 1988, to a sales level of $750 million. That forecast was developed as follows:

1. To begin, sales are divided into three major product groups: (1) sales to telephone companies of equipment used in telephone networks; (2) sales of equip-

Figure 22-1
RPS Corporation: 1988 Sales Projection

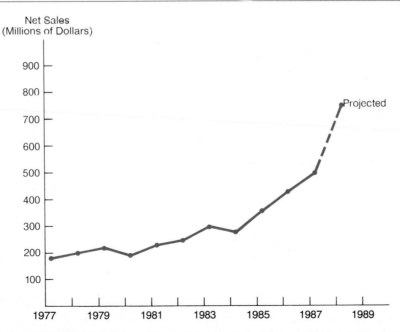

ment such as PBXs used by hotels, motels, and businesses to route calls among rooms; and (3) sales of electronic components to computer manufacturers. Sales in each of these areas over the past 10 years are plotted, the trend is observed, and a "first approximation forecast," assuming a continuation of past trends, is made.

2. Next, the level of business activity for each of the company's market areas is forecasted — for example, what will be the level of hotel, motel, and office building construction in 1988? These forecasts are used as a basis for modifying the demand forecasts in each of RPS's business areas.

3. RPS next looks at its probable shares of each major market. Consideration is given to such factors as the company's capacity, its competitors' capacity, and new products or product improvements that either RPS or its competitors may plan. Pricing strategies are also considered — for example, does the company have plans to raise prices to boost profit margins, or to lower prices in order to gain market share and thus cut production costs as a result of gaining economies of scale? Such actions could greatly affect sales forecasts. Also, since RPS has some export sales and also faces competition from Japanese and European firms in its U.S. markets, exchange rates and the value of the dollar can have an important influence on its market share.

4. Advertising campaigns, promotional discounts, credit terms, and the like also affect sales, so probable developments in these areas are also factored in.

5. Order backlogs and recent trends in new orders (or cancellations) are taken into account.

6. Forecasts are made for each product group both in the aggregate — for example, sales to telephone companies — and on an individual product basis. The individual product sales forecasts are summed and then compared with the aggregate product group forecasts. Differences are reconciled, and the end result is a sales forecast for the company as a whole but with breakdowns by major divisions and for individual products.

If the sales forecast is off, the consequences can be serious. First, if the market expands more than RPS has expected and geared up for, then it will not be able to meet its customers' needs. Orders will back up, delivery times will lengthen, repairs and installations will be harder to schedule, and customer dissatisfaction will increase. Customers will end up going elsewhere, and RPS will lose market share and will have missed a major opportunity. On the other hand, if its projections are overly optimistic, RPS could end up with too much plant, equipment, and inventory. This would mean low turnover ratios, high costs for depreciation and storage, and, possibly, write-offs of obsolete inventory and equipment. All of this would result in a low rate of return on equity, which in turn would depress the company's stock price. If RPS had financed the expansion with debt, its problems would, of course, be compounded. Thus, an accurate sales forecast is critical to the well-being of the firm.[2]

FORECASTING FINANCIAL REQUIREMENTS: THE PERCENTAGE OF SALES METHOD

Several methods are used to develop *pro forma,* or forecasted, *financial statements.* In this chapter we begin with the percentage of sales method. We also explain when this method can and cannot be used, and we discuss the growing use of computerized models for forecasting financial statements.

The *percentage of sales method* is a simple but often practical method of forecasting financial statement variables. The procedure is based on two assumptions: (1) that most balance sheet accounts are tied directly to sales and (2) that the current levels of all assets are optimal for the current sales level. We illustrate the process with RPS Corporation, whose December 31, 1987, balance sheet and summary income statement are given in Table 22-3. RPS operated its fixed assets at full capacity to support its 1987 sales of $500 million, and it had no unnecessary stocks of current assets. Its profit margin on sales was 4 percent, and it distributed 40 percent of its net income to stockholders as dividends. If RPS's sales increase to $750 million in 1988, what will be the condition of its pro forma December 31, 1988, balance sheet, and how much additional financing will the company require during 1988?

The first step in the percentage of sales forecast is to isolate those balance sheet items that vary directly with sales. Since RPS has been operating at full capacity, each asset item must increase if the higher level of sales is to be attained. More cash will be needed for transactions; receivables will be higher; additional inventory must be stocked; and new plant must be added.[3]

If RPS's assets are to increase, its liabilities and equity must likewise rise — the balance sheet must balance. Therefore, any increase in assets must be financed in some manner. Some funds will be *generated spontaneously* from such sources as accounts payable and accruals, which rise spontaneously with sales. As sales increase, so will RPS's own purchases, and larger purchases will automatically result in higher levels of accounts payable. Thus, if sales double, accounts payable will also double. Similarly, a higher level of operations will require more labor, so accrued wages will increase, and, assuming profit margins are maintained, an increase

---

[2]A sales forecast is actually the *expected value of a probability distribution* of possible levels of sales. Because any sales forecast is subject to a greater or lesser degree of uncertainty, for financial planning we are often just as interested in the degree of uncertainty inherent in the sales forecast (σ sales) as we are in the expected value of sales. See "Demand Estimation" in James L. Pappas, Eugene F. Brigham, and Mark Hirschey, *Managerial Economics* (Hinsdale, Ill.: Dryden, 1983), Chapter 5, for a detailed discussion of procedures for making demand forecasts.

[3]Some assets such as marketable securities are not tied directly to operations and hence do not vary directly with sales. Also, as we shall see later in the chapter, if some assets that normally do vary with sales are not being fully utilized, then sales can increase without increasing those assets.

Table 22-3
RPS Corporation:
1987 Financial Statements (Millions of Dollars)

Balance Sheet as of December 31

Cash	$ 10	Accounts payable	$ 40
Receivables	85	Notes payable	10
Inventories	100	Accrued wages and taxes	25
Total current assets	$195	Total current liabilities	$ 75
Net fixed assets	150	Mortgage bonds	72
		Common stock	150
		Retained earnings	48
Total assets	$345	Total liabilities and equity	$345

Summary Income Statement

Sales	$500
Net income	20
Dividends paid	8

---

in profits will pull up accrued taxes. Retained earnings will also increase, but not in direct proportion to the increase in sales. Neither notes payable, mortgage bonds, nor common stock will rise spontaneously with sales — higher sales do not *automatically* trigger increases in these items.

We can construct a pro forma balance sheet for December 31, 1988, proceeding as outlined in the following paragraphs.

Step 1
In Table 22-4, Column 1, we express those balance sheet items that vary directly with sales as a percentage of 1987 sales. An item such as notes payable that does not automatically vary with sales is designated "not applicable."

Step 2
We multiply these percentages (their fractions, really) by the $750 million projected 1988 sales to obtain the projected amounts as of December 31, 1988. These are shown in Column 2 of the table.

Step 3
We simply insert figures for notes payable, mortgage bonds, and common stock from the December 31, 1987 balance sheet. At least one of these accounts will have to be changed later in the analysis.

Step 4
We add the estimated addition to retained earnings for 1988 to the December 31, 1987, balance sheet figure for retained earnings to obtain the December 31, 1988, projected retained earnings. Recall that RPS expects to earn 4 percent on 1988

Table 22-4
RPS Corporation:
December 31, 1987, Balance Sheet Expressed as a Percentage
of Sales and December 31, 1988, Pro Forma Balance Sheet
(Millions of Dollars)

	Balance Sheet Items on 12/31/87 (as a % of the $500 1987 Sales) (1)	Pro Forma Balance Sheet on 12/31/88 (= Projected Sales of $750 Times Column 1) (2)
Cash	2.0%	$ 15
Receivables	17.0	128
Inventories	20.0	150
Total current assets	39.0%	$293
Net fixed assets	30.0	225
Total assets	69.0%	$518
Accounts payable	8.0%	$ 60
Notes payable	n.a.[a]	10[b]
Accrued wages and taxes	5.0	38
Total current liabilities	n.a.	$108
Mortgage bonds	n.a.	72[b]
Common stock	n.a.	150[b]
Retained earnings	n.a.	66[c]
Funds available		$396
Additional funds needed (AFN)		122[d]
Total liabilities and equity		$518

[a]n.a. = not applicable. (Item does not vary spontaneously and directly with sales.)

[b]Initially projected to remain constant at the 1987 level. Later financing decisions might change this level.

[c]Balance in the retained earnings account at December 31, 1987, plus the 1988 projected addition to retained earnings as explained in Step 4 in the text.

[d]"Additional funds needed" is a balancing figure: $518 projected assets − $396 projected funds available = $122 additional funds needed.

sales of $750 million, or $30 million, and expects to pay 40 percent of this out in dividends to stockholders; thus the dividend payout ratio is 40 percent, and dividends paid will be 0.4($30 million) = $12 million. Therefore, retained earnings for the year are projected to be $30 million − $12 million = $18 million. Adding this $18 million addition to the $48 million beginning retained earnings gives the $66 million projected retained earnings shown in Column 2.

Step 5
We sum the asset accounts, obtaining a total projected assets figure of $518 million for 1988, and we also sum the projected liabilities and equity items to obtain $396 million, the estimate of available funds. Since liabilities and equity must total $518 million, but only $396 million is projected, we have a shortfall of $122 million which we designate *additional funds needed,* or *AFN;* it will presumably be raised by bank borrowing and/or by issuing securities. For simplicity, we disregard depre-

ciation by assuming that cash flows generated by depreciation will be used to replace worn-out fixed assets.

Step 6

RPS could use short-term bank loans (notes payable), mortgage bonds, common stock, or a combination of these securities to make up the shortfall. Ordinarily, RPS would make this choice on the basis of its target capital structure, its working capital financing policy, and the relative costs of different types of securities, subject to certain constraints. For example, in RPS' case, the company has a contractual agreement with its bondholders to keep total debt at or below 50 percent of total assets and also to keep the current ratio at a level of 2.5 or greater. These provisions restrict the financing choices as follows:

1. Restriction on Additional Debt

Maximum debt permitted = (0.5)(Total assets)

= (0.5)($518 million)   = $259 million

Less debt already projected for December 31, 1988:
Current liabilities	$108 million	
Mortgage bonds	72 million =	180 million
Maximum additional debt		$ 79 million

2. Restriction on Additional Current Liabilities

Maximum current liabilities = Projected current assets/2.5

= $293 million/2.5   = $117 million

Less current liabilities already projected	108 million
Maximum additional current liabilities	$ 9 million

3. Common Equity Requirements

Total additional funds needed (from Table 22-4)	$122 million
Maximum additional debt permitted	79 million
Common equity funds required	$ 43 million

We see, then, that RPS needs a total of $122 million from external sources. Its existing debt contract limits new debt to $79 million, and only $9 million of that amount can be short-term debt. Thus, if we assume that RPS wants to make maximum use of debt financing, it must plan to sell additional common stock in the amount of $43 million to cover its financial requirements. Here is a summary of its projected nonspontaneous external financing:

Short-term debt (notes payable)	$ 9 million
Long-term debt	70 million
New common stock	43 million
Total	$122 million

Projected Financial Statements and Ratios

RPS' financial staff can now construct a set of projected, or pro forma, financial statements and then analyze the ratios that are implied therein. Parts I and II of Table 22-5 give abbreviated versions of the final projected balance sheet and income statement; Part III gives the statement of changes in financial position; and Part IV gives a few key ratios.[4] These statements can be used by the financial manager to show the other executives the implications of the planned sales increase. For example, the projected rate of return on equity is 11.6 percent. Is this a reasonable target, or can it be improved? Also, the preliminary forecast calls for the sale of $43 million of common stock—but does top management really want to sell any new stock? Suppose just over 50 percent of RPS' stock is owned by the company's founders, and they do not want the company to sell any stock and thereby cause them to lose their majority control. How then could the needed funds be raised, or what adjustments could be made? In the remainder of the chapter, we look at approaches to answering questions such as these.

Relationship between Sales and Capital Requirements

Although the forecast of capital requirements can be made by constructing pro forma balance sheets as described above, under certain conditions it is easier to use a simple forecasting formula. The formula can also be used to highlight the relationship between sales growth and financial requirements:

$$
\begin{array}{c}
\text{Additional} \\ \text{funds} \\ \text{needed}
\end{array}
=
\begin{array}{c}
\text{Required} \\ \text{increase} \\ \text{in assets}
\end{array}
-
\begin{array}{c}
\text{Spontaneous} \\ \text{increase in} \\ \text{liabilities}
\end{array}
-
\begin{array}{c}
\text{Increase in} \\ \text{retained} \\ \text{earnings}
\end{array}
$$

$$
\text{AFN} = (A/S)\Delta S - (L/S)\Delta S - MS_1(1 - d) \tag{22-1}
$$

Here

AFN = additional funds needed.

A/S = assets that must increase if sales are to increase as a percentage of sales, or required dollar increase in assets per $1 increase in sales. $A/S = 69\%$, or 0.69, for RPS from Column 1 of Table 22-4.

L/S = liabilities that increase spontaneously with sales as a percentage of sales, or spontaneously generated financing per $1 increase in sales. $L/S = 13.0\%$, or 0.130, for RPS.

S_1 = total sales projected for next year. Note that S_0 designates last year's sales. $S_1 = \$750$ million for RPS.

---

[4]We have simplified somewhat the forecasting process. In reality, the additional debt and common stock would increase RPS' interest and dividend requirements, and hence decrease the earnings retained in 1988. This "financing feedback" is difficult to do by hand, but computerized forecasting models can handle this easily. See Eugene F. Brigham and Louis C. Gapenski, *Intermediate Financial Management,* 2nd ed., Chapter 21.

Table 22-5
RPS Corporation:
Projected Financial Statements for 1988
(Millions of Dollars)

I. Projected Balance Sheet, December 31

Cash	$ 15		Accounts payable	$ 60
Accounts receivable	128		Notes payable	19
Inventories	150		Accruals	38
Total current assets	$293		Total current liabilities	$117
Net fixed assets	225		Long-term debt	142
			Common stock	193
			Retained earnings	66
			Total equity	$259
Total assets	$518		Total liabilities and equity	$518

II. Projected Income Statement

Sales	$750
Total costs	700
Net income before taxes	$ 50
Taxes (40%)	20
Net income	$ 30
Dividends (40% of income)	12
Addition to retained earnings	$ 18

III. Projected Statement of Changes in Financial Position

Funds Provided by (Used in) Operations

Sources:

Net income	$ 30
Increase in accounts payable	20
Increase in accruals	13
Total sources from operations	$ 63[a]

Uses:

Increase in accounts receivable	$ 43
Increase in inventories	50
Increase in net fixed assets	75
Total uses in operations	$168
Net funds from operations	($105)

Financing Activities

Increase in notes payable	$ 9
Sale of bonds	70
Sale of common stock	43
Net funds from financing	$122
Less: Dividends	12
	$110
Increase in cash	$ 5

IV. Key Ratios Projected for December 31[b]

1. Current ratio	2.5 times
2. Quick ratio	1.2 times
3. Total debt/Total assets	50%
4. Rate of return on equity	11.6%

[a]The figure for funds from operations normally includes depreciation. Here we have assumed that depreciation is reinvested in fixed assets; that is, we netted it out against fixed asset additions.

[b]Other ratios could be calculated and anlyzed by the Du Pont system.

ΔS = change in sales = $S_1 - S_0$ = \$750 million − \$500 million = \$250 million for RPS.

M = profit margin, or rate of profits per \$1 of sales. M = 4%, or 0.04, for RPS.

d = percentage of earnings paid out in dividends, or the dividend payout ratio; d = 40%, or 0.40, for RPS. Notice that 1 − d = 1.0 − 0.4 = 0.6, or 60 percent, is the percentage of earnings that RPS retains, or its *retention ratio*.

Inserting values for RPS into Equation 22-1, we find the additional funds needed to be \$122 million:

$$
\begin{aligned}
AFN &= 0.69(\Delta S) - 0.13(\Delta S) - 0.04(S_1)(1 - 0.4) \\
&= 0.69(\$250 \text{ million}) - 0.13(\$250 \text{ million}) - 0.04(\$750 \text{ million})(0.6) \\
&= \$172.5 \text{ million} - \$32.5 \text{ million} - \$18 \text{ million} \\
&= \$122 \text{ million}.
\end{aligned}
$$

To increase sales by \$250 million, RPS must increase assets by \$172.5 million. The \$172.5 million of new assets must be financed in some manner. Of the total, \$32.5 million will come from a spontaneous increase in liabilities, while another \$18 million will be obtained from retained earnings. The remaining \$122 million must be raised from external sources. This value agrees, of course, with the figure developed earlier in Table 22-4.

Relationship between Growth and Financial Requirements

The faster RPS's growth rate in sales, the greater its need for external financing; we can use Equation 22-1, which is plotted in Figure 22-2 to quantify this relationship. The lower section shows RPS's external financial requirements at various growth rates, and these data are plotted in the graph. The figure illustrates the following important points.

Financial Planning
At low growth rates RPS needs no external financing. However, if the company grows faster than 4.478 percent, it must raise capital from outside sources.[5] Further, the faster the growth rate, the greater the capital requirements. If management foresees difficulties in raising the required capital—perhaps because RPS' current stockholders do not want to sell additional stock—then management should reconsider the feasibility of the expansion plans.

Effect of Dividend Policy on Financing Needs
Dividend policy as reflected in the payout ratio (d in Equation 22-1) also affects external capital requirements—the higher the payout ratio, the smaller the addition to retained earnings, and hence the greater the requirements for external

---

[5]We found the 4.478 percent growth rate by setting AFN equal to zero, substituting gS_0 for ΔS and $S_0 + g(S_0)$ for S_1 in the AFN equation, and then solving the equation $0 = 0.69(g)(S_0) - 0.13(g)(S_0) - 0.04(S_0 + gS_0)(1 - 0.4)$ for g. The g that solved this equation was 0.04478, or 4.478 percent.

Figure 22-2
Relationship between Growth in Sales and Financial Requirements, Assuming S_0 = \$500 Million (Millions of Dollars)

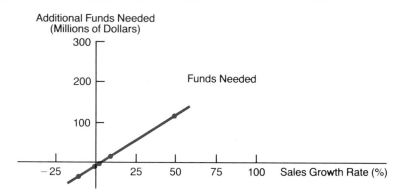

Growth Rate in Sales (1)	Increase (Decrease) in Sales, ΔS (2)	Forecasted Sales, S_1 (3)	Additional Funds Needed (4)
50%	\$250	\$750	\$122.0
10	50	550	14.8
4.478	22.39	522.39	0.0
0	0	500	(12.0)
−10	(50)	450	(38.8)

Explanation of Columns:
Col. 1: Growth rate in sales, g.

Col. 2: Increase (decrease) in sales: $\Delta S = g(S_0) = g(\$500)$.

Col. 3: Forecasted sales: $S_1 = S_0 + g(S_0) = S_0(1 + g) = \$500(1 + g)$.

Col. 4: Additional funds needed: $AFN = 0.69(\Delta S) - 0.13(\Delta S) - 0.024(S_1)$.

capital. Therefore, if RPS foresees difficulties in raising capital, it might want to consider a reduction in the dividend payout ratio. This would lower (or shift to the right) the line in Figure 22-2, indicating smaller external capital requirements at all growth rates. However, before changing its dividend policy, management should consider the effects of such a decision on stock prices. These effects were discussed in Chapter 13.

Notice that the line in Figure 22-2 does *not* pass through the origin; thus, at low growth rates (below 4.478%), surplus funds will be produced, because new retained earnings plus spontaneous funds will exceed the required asset increases. Only if the dividend payout ratio were 100 percent, meaning that the firm did not retain any of its earnings, would the "funds needed" line pass through the origin.

Capital Intensity

The amount of assets required per dollar of sales, A/S in Equation 22-1, is often called the *capital intensity ratio*. This factor has a major effect on capital requirements per unit of sales growth. If the capital intensity ratio is low, then sales can grow rapidly without much outside capital. However, if the firm is capital intensive, even a small growth in output will require a great deal of new outside capital.

Profit Margin

The profit margin, M, is also an important determinant of the funds-required equation — the higher the margin, the lower the funds requirements, other things held constant. RPS's profit margin is 4 percent. Now suppose M increased to 6 percent. This new value could be inserted into the funds-needed formula, and the effect would be to reduce the additional funds needed at all positive growth rates. In terms of the graph, an increase in the profit margin would cause the line to shift down, and its slope would also become less steep. Because of the relationship between profit margins and external capital requirements, some very rapidly growing firms do not need much external capital. For example, for many years Xerox grew at a rapid rate with very little borrowing or stock sales. However, as the company lost patent protection and as competition intensified in the copier industry, Xerox's profit margin declined, its needs for external capital rose, and it began to borrow from banks and other sources. IBM has had a similar experience.

FORECASTING FINANCIAL REQUIREMENTS WHEN THE BALANCE SHEET RATIOS ARE SUBJECT TO CHANGE

To this point we have been assuming that the balance sheet ratios of assets and liabilities to sales (A/S and L/S) will remain constant over time, which in turn requires the assumption that each "spontaneous" asset and liability item increases at the same rate as sales. In graph form, this implies the type of relationship shown in Panel A of Figure 22-3, a relationship that is linear and passes through the origin. Under those conditions, if the company's sales increase from $200 million to $400 million, inventory will increase proportionately, from $100 million to $200 million.

The assumption of constant ratios is appropriate at times, but there are also times when it is incorrect. Three such conditions are described in the following sections.

Economies of Scale

There are economies of scale in the use of many kinds of assets, and where economies occur, the ratios are likely to change over time as the size of the firm increases. For example, firms often need to maintain base stocks of different inventory items, even if current sales levels are quite low. Then, as sales expand, inventories grow less rapidly than sales, so the ratio of inventory to sales (I/S) declines. This situation is depicted in Panel B of Figure 22-3. Here we see that the inventory/sales ratio is 1.5, or 150 percent, when sales are $200 million, but the ratio declines to 1.0 when sales climb to $400 million.

The relationship used to illustrate economies of scale is linear, but this is not necessarily the case. Indeed, as we saw in Chapter 19, if the firm uses the most popular model for establishing inventory levels, the EOQ model, then inventories

Figure 22-3
Three Possible Ratio Relationships
(Millions of Dollars)

A. Constant Ratios

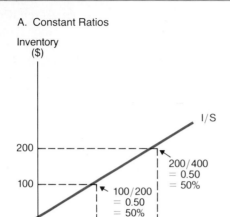

B. Economies of Scale; Declining Ratios

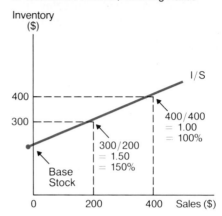

C. Lumpy Assets; Ratios Rise and Fall

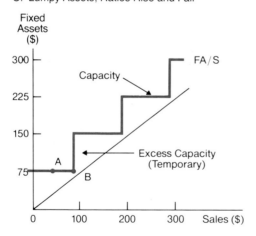

will rise with the square root of sales. This means that the graph in Panel B would tend to be a curved line whose slope decreases at higher sales levels.

"Lumpy" Assets

In many industries, technological considerations dictate that if a firm is to be competitive it must add fixed assets in large, discrete units; such assets are often referred to as *"lumpy" assets.* In the paper industry, for example, there are strong economies of scale in basic paper mill equipment, so when a paper company expands capacity, it must do so in large, or lumpy, increments. This type of situation is depicted in Panel C of Figure 22-3. Here we assume that the minimum economically efficient plant has a cost of $75 million, and that such a plant can produce enough output to attain a sales level of $100 million. If the firm is to be competitive, it simply must have at least $75 million of fixed assets.

This situation has a major effect on fixed assets/sales (FA/S) ratios at different sales levels, and consequently on financial requirements. At Point A in Panel C, which represents a sales level of $50 million, the fixed assets are $75 million, so the ratio FA/S = $75/$50 = 1.5. However, *excess capacity* exists, so sales can expand by $50 million, out to $100 million, with no additions to fixed assets. At that point, represented by Point B, the ratio FA/S = $75/$100 = 0.75. However, if the firm is operating at capacity (sales of $100 million), then even a small increase in sales would require a doubling of plant capacity, so a small projected sales increase would bring with it a very large financial requirement.[6]

Cyclical Changes

Panels A, B, and C of Figure 22-3 all focus on target, or projected, relationships between sales and assets. Actual sales, however, are often different from projected sales, and the actual asset/sales ratio for a given period may thus be quite different from the planned ratio. To illustrate, the firm depicted in Panel B of Figure 22-3 might, when its sales are at $200 million and its inventories at $300 million, project a sales expansion to $400 million and then increase its inventories to $400 million in anticipation of the sales expansion. Yet suppose an unforeseen economic downturn holds sales to only $300 million. In this case, actual inventories would be $400 million, but only about $350 million would be needed to support sales of $300 million. In this case, there would be "excess capacity" in inventories. If the firm were making its forecast for the following year, it would have to recognize that sales could expand by $100 million with no increase whatever in inventories, but that any sales expansion beyond $100 million would require additional financing to build inventories.

---

[6]Several other points should be noted about Panel C of Figure 22-3. First, if the firm is operating at a sales level of $100 million or less, then any expansion that calls for a sales increase above $100 million will require a *doubling* of the firm's fixed assets. A much smaller percentage increase would be involved if the firm were large enough to be operating a number of plants. Second, firms generally go to multiple shifts and take other actions to minimize the need for new fixed asset capacity as they approach Point B. However, these efforts can go only so far, and eventually a fixed asset expansion will be required. Third, firms often make arrangements to share excess capacity with other firms in their industry. For example, consider the situation in the electric utility industry, which is very much like that depicted in Panel C. Electric companies often build jointly owned plants, or else "take turns" building plants and then buy power from or sell to other utilities in order to avoid building new plants that may be underutilized.

MODIFYING THE FORECAST OF ADDITIONAL FUNDS NEEDED

If any of the conditions noted above apply (economies of scale exist, excess capacity exists, or asset additions are lumpy), the A/S ratio will not be a constant and the simple percentage of sales forecasting method should not be used. Rather, other techniques should be used to forecast asset levels and the resulting external financing requirements. Two of these methods — linear regression and specific item forecasting — are discussed in the following sections.

Simple Linear Regression

If we assume that the relationship between a particular type of asset and sales is linear, then we can use simple linear regression techniques to estimate the requirements for that asset for any given sales increase. For example, RPS' sales, receivables, inventories, and net fixed asset levels over the last 11 years are shown in the lower section of Figure 22-4, and they are plotted in the upper section as scatter diagrams versus sales. Estimated regression equations as found with a hand calculator are also shown with each graph. For example, the estimated relationship between inventories and sales (in millions of dollars) is

$$\text{Inventories} = \$20.3 + 0.16(\text{Sales}).$$

The plotted points are quite close to the regression line, which indicates a high degree of correlation. In fact, the correlation coefficient between inventories and sales is 0.98, indicating that there is a very strong linear relationship between these two variables.

We can use the estimated relationship between inventories and sales to forecast 1988 inventory levels. Since 1988 sales are projected at $750 million, 1988 inventories should be $140.3 million:

$$\text{Inventories} = \$20.3 + 0.16(\$750) = \$140.3 \text{ million}.$$

This is almost $10 million less than our earlier forecast based on the percentage of sales method. The difference occurs because the percentage of sales method assumed that the ratio of inventories to sales would remain constant, while actually it will probably decline, because the regression line in Figure 22-4 does not pass through the origin. Note also that our graphs show linear relationships, but we could have easily used a non-linear regression model had such a relationship been indicated.

Specific Item Forecasting

Consider again the RPS example set forth in Tables 22-4 and 22-5. Now suppose a ratio analysis along the lines described in Chapter 21 suggests that the cash, receivables, and inventory ratios indicated in Table 22-4 are appropriate, as are the liability ratios and the retained earnings calculations, but that excess capacity ex-

Figure 22-4
RPS Corporation:
Linear Regression Models
(Millions of Dollars)

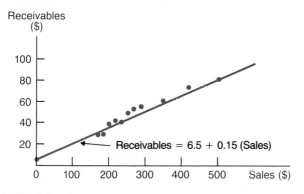

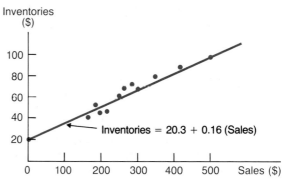

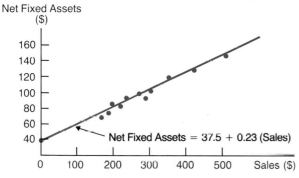

Year	Sales	Accounts Receivable	Inventories	Net Fixed Assets
1977	$175	$33	$ 44	$ 78
1978	200	38	48	83
1979	215	44	53	86
1980	185	35	57	79
1981	235	43	60	91
1982	265	45	66	98
1983	300	52	73	106
1984	280	47	70	101
1985	350	61	78	118
1986	420	71	90	135
1987	500	85	100	150

ists in fixed assets. Specifically, assume that fixed assets in 1987 were being utilized to only 80 percent of capacity. If the existing fixed assets had been used to full capacity, 1987 sales could have been as high as $625 million:

$$\begin{array}{c} \text{Full} \\ \text{capacity} \\ \text{sales} \end{array} = \frac{\text{Current sales}}{\begin{array}{c}\text{Percentage of capacity} \\ \text{at which fixed assets} \\ \text{were operated}\end{array}} = \frac{\$500 \text{ million}}{0.80} = \begin{array}{c}\$625 \text{ million sales} \\ \text{at full capacity}\end{array}.$$

This suggests that RPS' target for the fixed assets/sales ratio should be

$$\begin{array}{c}\text{Target} \\ \text{F.A./Sales} \\ \text{ratio}\end{array} = \frac{\text{Fixed assets}}{\text{Full capacity sales}} = \frac{\$150 \text{ million}}{\$625 \text{ million}} = 0.24,$$

not the 0.30 that actually existed. Therefore, at the projected sales level of $750 million, RPS would require fixed assets of only 0.24($750 million) = $180 million, up only $30 million from the $150 million currently on hand, rather than up $75 million.[7]

We estimated earlier that RPS would need an additional $122 million of capital. However, those estimates were based on the assumption that $75 million of additional fixed assets would be required. If RPS could attain a sales level of $750 million with an addition of only $30 million of fixed assets, then the external funds needed would decline by $75 − $30 = $45 million, to a total of $122 − $45 = $77 million. Other items could also be specifically forecasted—for example, receivables could be forecasted using the payments pattern approach.

COMPUTERIZED FINANCIAL PLANNING MODELS

Although the type of financial forecasting described in this chapter can be done with a hand calculator, most well-managed firms with sales greater than a few million dollars use some type of computerized financial planning model. Such models can be programmed to show the effects of different sales levels, different ratios of sales to operating assets, and different assumptions about sales prices and input costs. Plans are then made regarding how financial requirements are to be met — by borrowing from banks, thus increasing short-term notes payable; by selling long-term bonds; or by selling new common stock. Pro forma balance sheets and income statements are generated under the different financing plans, and earnings per share are projected, along with such risk measures as the current ratio, the debt/assets ratio, and the times-interest-earned ratio.

Depending on how these projections look, management might modify its initial plans. For example, the firm might conclude that its sales forecast must be cut

---

[7]This $30 million of required new fixed assets could also be determined by noting (1) that sales could grow from $500 million to $625 million without any increase in fixed assets but (2) that the sales increase from $625 million to $750 million would require new fixed assets of $(FA/S)(\Delta S) = 0.24($125$ million) = $30 million.

because the requirements for external capital exceed the firm's ability to raise money. Alternatively, management might decide to reduce dividends and thus generate more funds internally. The company might also decide to investigate production processes that require fewer fixed assets, or it might consider the possibility of buying rather than manufacturing certain components, thus eliminating raw materials and work-in-process inventories as well as certain manufacturing facilities. In all such considerations, the basic issue is the effect that a specific action will have on future earnings and cash flows, on the firm's risk, and hence on the price of its stock. Since computerized planning models help management assess these effects, they are playing an ever increasing role in corporate management.[8]

SUMMARY

This chapter described in broad outline how firms go about projecting their financial statements and determining their capital requirements. In brief, management establishes a target balance sheet based on ratio analysis. Assuming that each balance sheet ratio is at the desired level and that the optimal levels for these ratios are stable, the *percentage of sales method* can be used to forecast the external financial requirements associated with any given increase in sales. If the balance sheet ratios are subject to change, as they will be if excess capacity currently exists, if assets are lumpy, or if economies of scale exist, then each item in the projected balance sheet must be forecasted separately.

The type of forecasting described in this chapter is important for several reasons. First, if the projected operating results are unsatisfactory, management can "go back to the drawing board," reformulate its plans, and develop more reasonable targets for the coming year. Second, it is possible that the funds required to meet the sales forecast simply cannot be obtained; if so, it is obviously better to know this in advance and to scale back the projected level of operations than to suddenly run out of cash and have operations grind to a halt. Third, even if the required funds can be raised, it is desirable to plan for their acquisition well in advance. As we shall see in later chapters, raising capital takes time, and both time and money can be saved by careful forward planning.

---

[8]It is becoming increasingly easy for companies to develop planning models as a result of the dramatic improvements that have been made in computer hardware and software in recent years. *Lotus 1-2-3* is the most widely used system, although many companies also employ more complex and elaborate modeling systems. Increasingly, a knowledge of *1-2-3* or some similar planning system is becoming a requirement for getting even an entry-level job in many corporations. Indeed, surveys indicate that the probability of a business student's getting an attractive job offer increases dramatically if he or she has a working knowledge of *1-2-3*. In addition, starting salaries are materially higher for those students who have such a knowledge. See Problems 22-7, 22-8, and 22-9 for an introduction to financial forecasting using *Lotus 1-2-3*.

Note also that in this chapter we have concentrated on long-run, or strategic, financial planning. Within the framework of the long-run strategic plan, firms also develop short-run financial plans. For example, we saw that RPS Corporation expects to need $122 million by the end of 1988, and that it plans to raise this capital by using short-term debt, long-term debt, and common stock. However, we do not know when during the year the need for funds will occur or when RPS will obtain each of its different types of capital. To address these issues, the firm must develop a short-run financial plan, the centerpiece of which is the cash budget, which we discussed in Chapter 20.

Questions

22-1 Define each of the following terms:

a. Operating plan; five-year plan

b. Financial plan

c. Sales forecast

d. Percentage of sales method

e. Spontaneously generated funds

f. Dividend payout ratio; retention ratio

g. Pro forma financial statement

h. Additional funds needed (AFN)

i. Capital intensity ratio

j. "Lumpy" assets

22-2 Certain liability and net worth items generally increase spontaneously with increases in sales. Put a check ($\checkmark$) by those items that typically increase spontaneously:

Accounts payable	_____
Notes payable to banks	_____
Accrued wages	_____
Accrued taxes	_____
Mortgage bonds	_____
Common stock	_____
Retained earnings	_____
Marketable securities	_____

22-3 The following equation can, under certain assumptions, be used to forecast financial requirements:

$$\text{Additional funds needed} = (A/S)(\Delta S) - (L/S)(\Delta S) - MS_1(1 - d).$$

Under what conditions does the equation give satisfactory predictions, and when should it not be used?

22-4 Assume that an average firm in the office supply business has a 6 percent after-tax profit margin, a 40 percent debt/assets ratio, a total assets turnover of 2 times, and a dividend payout ratio of 40 percent. Is it true that if such a firm is to have *any* sales growth ($g > 0$), it will be forced to borrow or to sell common stock (that is, it will need some nonspontaneous, external capital even if g is very small)?

22-5 Is it true that computerized corporate planning models were a fad during the 1970s but, because of a need for flexibility in corporate planning, they have been dropped by most firms?

22-6 Suppose a firm makes the following policy changes. If the change means that external, nonspontaneous financial requirements for any rate of sales growth will increase, indicate this by a +; indicate decreases by a −; and indicate indeterminate and/or no effect by a 0. Think in terms of the immediate, short-run effect on funds requirements.

a. The dividend payout ratio is increased. _____

b. The firm contracts to buy rather than make certain components used in its products. _____

c. The firm decides to pay all suppliers on delivery, rather than after a 30-day delay, in order to take advantage of discounts for rapid payment.   _____

d. The firm begins to sell on credit (previously all sales had been on a cash basis).   _____

e. The firm's profit margin is eroded by increased competition; sales are steady.   _____

f. Advertising expenditures are stepped up.   _____

g. A decision is made to substitute long-term mortgage bonds for short-term bank loans.   _____

h. The firm begins to pay employees on a weekly basis (previously it had paid at the end of each month).   _____

Self-Test Problems

ST-1 (Internally financed growth) The Mehran Company has the following ratios: A/S = 1.6; L/S = 0.4; profit margin = 0.10; and dividend payout ratio = 0.45, or 45 percent. Sales last year were $100 million. Assuming that these ratios will remain constant and that all liabilities increase spontaneously with increases in sales, what is the maximum growth rate Mehran can achieve without having to employ nonspontaneous external funds?

ST-2 (Percent of sales forecasting) Suppose Mehran's financial consultants report (1) that the inventory turnover ratio is Sales/Inventory = 3 times versus an industry average of 4 times and (2) that Mehran could reduce inventories and thus raise its turnover to 4 without affecting sales, the profit margin, or the other asset turnover ratios. Under these conditions, what amount of external funds would Mehran require during each of the next 2 years if sales grew at a rate of 20 percent per year?

Problems

22-1 (Pro forma balance sheet) A group of investors is planning to set up a new company, Trifts Ltd., to manufacture and distribute a novel type of running shoe. To help determine the new company's financial requirements, Jack Trifts, the president, has asked you to construct a pro forma balance sheet for December 31, 1988, the end of the first year of operations, and to estimate the firm's external financing requirements for 1988. Sales for 1988 are projected at $10 million, and the following are industry average ratios for athletic shoe companies:

Sales to common equity	5 ×
Current debt to equity	50%
Total debt to equity	80%
Current ratio	2.2 ×
Net sales to inventory	9 ×
Accounts receivable to sales	10%
Fixed assets to equity	70%
Profit margin	3%
Dividend payout ratio	30%

a. Complete the pro forma balance sheet below, assuming that 1988 sales are $10 million and that the firm maintains industry average ratios.

Trifts Ltd.:
Pro Forma Balance Sheet as of
December 31, 1988
(Millions of Dollars)

Cash	$	Current debt	$
Accounts receivable		Long-term debt	_____
Inventories	_____	Total debt	
Total current assets		Equity	_____
Fixed assets	_____		
Total assets	$ _____	Total liabilities and equity	$ _____

b. If the investor group supplies all the equity, how much capital (exclusive of retained earnings) will it be required to put up during 1988?

22-2 (Long-term debt needed) At year-end 1987, Boyer, Inc.'s total assets were $2.4 million. Sales, which were $5 million, will increase by 25 percent in 1988. The 1987 ratio of assets to sales will be maintained in 1988. Common stock amounted to $850,000 in 1987, and retained earnings were $590,000. Accounts payable will continue to be 15 percent of sales in 1988, and Boyer plans to sell new common stock in the amount of $150,000. Net income after taxes is expected to be 6 percent of sales; 50 percent of earnings will be paid out as dividends. (a) What was Boyer's total debt in 1987, and (b) how much new, long-term debt financing will be needed in 1988? (Hint: AFN − New stock = New long-term debt.)

22-3 (Pro forma statements and ratios) O'Brien Computers makes bulk purchases of small computers, stocks them in conveniently located warehouses, and then ships them to its chain of retail stores. O'Brien's balance sheet as of December 31, 1987, is shown here (in millions of dollars):

Cash	$ 3.5	Accounts payable	$ 9.0
Receivables	26.0	Notes payable	17.5
Inventories	58.0	Accruals	9.0
Total current assets	$ 87.5	Total current liabilities	$ 35.5
Net fixed assets	35.0	Mortgage loan	6.0
		Common stock	15.0
		Retained earnings	66.0
Total assets	$122.5	Total liabilities and equity	$122.5

Sales for 1987 were $350 million, while net income for the year was $10.5 million. O'Brien paid dividends of $4.2 million to common stockholders. The firm is operating at full capacity.

a. If sales are projected to increase by $70 million, or by 20 percent, during 1988, what are O'Brien's projected external capital requirements?

b. Construct O'Brien's pro forma balance sheet for December 31, 1988. Assume that all external capital requirements are met by bank loans and are reflected in notes payable.

c. Now calculate the following ratios, based on your projected December 31, 1988, balance sheet. O'Brien's 1987 ratios and industry average ratios are shown here for comparison:

	O'Brien Computers		Industry Average
	12/31/88	12/31/87	12/31/87
Current ratio	———	2.5×	3×
Debt/total assets	———	33.9%	30%
Rate of return on equity	———	13.0%	12%

d. Now assume that O'Brien grows by the same $70 million but that the growth is spread over 5 years, that is, that sales grow by $14 million each year.
(1) Calculate total additional finance requirements over the 5-year period. (Hint: Use 1987 ratios, $\Delta S = 70$, but *total* sales for the 5-year period.)
(2) Construct a pro forma balance sheet as of December 31, 1992, using notes payable as the balancing item.
(3) Calculate the current ratio, debt/assets ratio, and rate of return on net worth as of December 31, 1992. [Hint: Be sure to use *total* sales, which amount to $1,960 million, to calculate retained earnings but 1992 profits to calculate the rate of return on equity — that is, return on equity = (1992 profits)/ (12/31/92 equity).]

e. Do the plans outlined in Parts c and d seem feasible to you? That is, do you think O'Brien could borrow the required capital, and would the company be raising the odds on its bankruptcy to an excessive level in the event of some temporary misfortune?

22-4 **(Additional funds needed)** Carleson Textile's 1987 sales were $48 million. The percentage of sales of each balance sheet item that varies directly with sales is given below:

Cash	3%
Receivables	20
Inventories	25
Net fixed assets	40
Accounts payable	15
Accruals	10

The dividend payout ratio is 40 percent; the profit margin is 5 percent; the December 31, 1986, balance sheet account for retained earnings was $16.4 million; and both common stock and mortgage bonds are constant and equal to the amounts shown on the balance sheet on the next page.

a. Complete the balance sheet below as of December 31, 1987.

Carleson Textile:
Balance Sheet as of December 31, 1987
(Thousands of Dollars)

Cash	$		Accounts payable	$
Receivables			Notes payable	4,400
Inventories	_____		Accruals	_____
Total current assets			Total current liabilities	
Net fixed assets	_____		Mortgage bonds	4,000
			Common stock	4,000
			Retained earnings	_____
Total assets	$ _____		Total liabilities and equity	$ _____

b. Now suppose 1988 sales are projected to increase by 10 percent over 1987 sales. Determine the additional funds needed. Assume that the company was operating at full capacity in 1987, that it cannot sell off any of its fixed assets, and that any required financing will be borrowed as notes payable. Use Equation 22-1 to answer this question.

c. Develop a pro forma balance sheet for December 31, 1988. Assume that any required financing is borrowed as notes payable. Note that 12/31/87 retained earnings are $17,840,000.

22-5 (Excess capacity) Pettit Lumber's 1987 sales were $72 million. The percentage of sales of each balance sheet item except notes payable, mortgage bonds, and common stock is given here:

Cash	4%
Receivables	25
Inventories	30
Net fixed assets	50
Accounts payable	15
Accruals	5
Profit margin (after taxes) on sales	5

The dividend payout ratio is 60 percent; the December 31, 1986, balance sheet account for retained earnings was $41.8 million; and both common stock and mortgage bonds are constant and equal to the amounts shown on the next page.

a. Complete the following balance sheet.

Pettit Lumber:
Balance Sheet as of December 31, 1987
(Thousands of Dollars)

Cash	$	Accounts payable	$
Receivables		Notes payable	6,840
Inventories	_____	Accruals	_____
Total current assets		Total current liabilities	
Net fixed assets	_____	Mortgage bonds	10,000
		Common stock	4,000
		Retained earnings	_____
Total assets	$ _____	Total liabilities and equity	$ _____

b. Assume that the company was operating at full capacity in 1987 with regard to all items *except* fixed assets; had the fixed assets been used to full capacity, the fixed assets/sales ratio would have been 40 percent in 1987. By what percentage could 1988 sales increase over 1987 sales without the need for an increase in fixed assets?

c. Now suppose that 1988 sales increase by 20 percent over 1987 sales. How much additional external capital will be required? Assume that Pettit Lumber cannot sell any fixed assets. (Hint: Equation 22-1 can no longer be used. You must develop a pro forma balance sheet as in Table 22-4.) Assume that any required financing is borrowed as notes payable. (Another hint: Notes payable = $10,728.)

d. Suppose that industry averages for receivables and inventories are 20 percent and 25 percent, respectively, and that Pettit Lumber matches these figures in 1988 and then uses the funds released to reduce equity. (It could pay a special dividend out of retained earnings.) What would this do to the rate of return on year-end 1988 equity?

22-6 **(Additional funds needed)** The 1987 sales of Barry Technologies, Inc., were $3 million. The dividend payout ratio is 50 percent. Retained earnings as shown on the December 31, 1986, balance sheet were $105,000. The percentage of sales in each balance sheet item that varies directly with sales is expected to be as follows:

Cash	4%
Receivables	10
Inventories	20
Net fixed assets	35
Accounts payable	12
Accruals	6
Profit margin (after taxes) on sales	3

a. Complete the balance sheet given below, assuming that common stock and notes payable did not change during 1987.

b. Suppose that in 1988, sales will increase by 10 percent over 1987 sales. How much additional capital will be required? Assume the firm operated at full capacity in 1987.

c. Construct the year-end 1988 balance sheet. Assume 50 percent of the additional capital required will be financed by selling common stock and the remainder by borrowing as notes payable.

d. If the profit margin after taxes remains at 3 percent and the dividend payout rate remains at 50 percent, at what growth rate in sales will the additional financing requirements be exactly zero? (Hint: Set AFN equal to zero and solve for g.)

Barry Technologies, Inc.:
Balance Sheet as of December 31, 1987

Cash	$	Accounts payable	$
Receivables		Notes payable	130,000
Inventories	_____	Accruals	
Total current assets		Total current liabilities	_____
Fixed assets	_____	Common stock	1,250,000
		Retained earnings	
Total assets	$_____	Total liabilities and equity	$_____

22-7 (Forecasting) *(Do this problem only if you are using the computerized diskette.)* The 1987 sales of Millar Industries, Inc., were $100 million. The percentage of sales of each balance sheet item except for long-term debt and common stock (which do not vary directly with sales) is given below:

Cash	5%
Receivables	15
Inventories	25
Net fixed assets	50
Accounts payable	10

The dividend payout ratio is 40 percent, and the profit margin is 5 percent. The long-term debt at December 31, 1987, was $20 million; notes payable were $5 million; common stock was $25 million, and the balance sheet amount for retained earnings was $35 million. Projected annual sales growth for the next 5 years is 20 percent.

a. Millar plans to finance its additional funds needed with 50 percent short-term debt and 50 percent long-term debt. Prepare the 1987 balance sheet, as well as pro forma balance sheets for 1988 through 1992, and then determine (1) additional funds needed, (2) the current ratio, (3) the debt ratio, and (4) the return of equity.

b. Sales growth could be 5 percentage points above or below the projected 20 percent. Determine the impact of such variances on AFN and the key ratios.

c. Perform a sensitivity analysis on AFN and the key ratios for 1992 under each of the following conditions, assuming sales grow at a constant 20 percent:
   (1) Profit margin (a) rises from 5 to 6 percent or (b) falls from 5 to 4 percent.
   (2) With the profit margin at 5 percent, the dividend payout ratio (a) is raised from 40 to 70 percent or (b) is lowered from 40 to 20 percent.

22-8 **(External financing requirements)** The 1987 balance sheet for the Potter Company is shown below. Sales in 1987 totaled $7 million. The ratio of net profits to sales was 3 percent, while the dividend payout ratio was 60 percent of net income.

a. The firm operated at full capacity in 1987. It expects sales to increase by 20 percent during 1988. Use the percent-of-sales method to determine how much outside financing is required, then develop the firm's pro forma balance sheet using AFN as the balancing item.

b. If the firm must maintain a current ratio of 2.5 and a debt ratio of 40 percent, how much financing will be obtained using notes payable, long-term debt, and common stock.

(Do Part c only if you are using the computerized diskette.)

c. Suppose the firm expects sales to increase by 40 percent during 1988 and that its current ratio must be at least 2.5 but that its debt ratio can be as high as 50 percent. Under this situation, how much external financing would the firm require and how would those funds be obtained?

Potter Company:
Balance Sheet as of December 31, 1987
(Thousands of Dollars)

Cash	$ 105	Accounts payable	$ 70
Accounts receivable	245	Accruals	35
Inventory	525	Notes payable	245
Total current assets	$ 875	Total current liabilities	$ 350
Fixed assets	2,625	Long-term debt	1,050
		Total debt	$1,400
		Common stock	1,225
		Retained earnings	875
Total assets	$3,500	Total liabilities and equity	$3,500

22-9 **(Pro forma balance sheet)** *(Do this problem only if you are using the computerized diskette.)* Finnerty Steel Company is a wholesale steel distributor which purchases steel in carload lots and sells to several thousand steel users. The nature of the steel requires that the company maintain large inventories to take care of customer requirements in the event of mill strikes or other delays.

In examining records from 1983 to 1987, the company found consistent relationships among the following accounts as a percent of sales:

Current assets	60%
Net fixed assets	30
Accounts payable	5
Other current liabilities	5
Profit margin	3

The company's sales for 1987 were $15 million, and its balance sheet on December 31, 1987, is shown below. The company expects sales to grow by $2 million per year over the next 5 years. The company wants to project its financial requirements for each of the next 5 years, assuming that the projected sales levels are achieved. Assume further that the company pays out 40 percent of earnings as dividends.

   a. Construct pro forma balance sheets for the end of each of the next five years assuming that 25 percent of external financing requirements are met by increasing notes payable, 25 percent by issuing long-term debt, and 50 percent by selling new common stock.

   b. What was the critical assumption you made in your projection?

Finnerty Steel Company:
Balance Sheet as of December 31, 1987
(Thousands of Dollars)

Current assets	$ 9,000	Accounts payable	$ 750
Fixed assets	4,500	Notes payable	2,000
		Other current liabilities	750
		Total current liabilities	$ 3,500
		Long-term debt	1,500
		Common stock	2,750
		Retained earnings	5,750
Total assets	$13,500	Total liabilities and equity	$13,500

Solutions to Self-Test Problems

ST-1 To solve this problem, we will define ΔS as the change in sales and g as the growth rate in sales, and then we use the following three equations:

$$\Delta S = gS_0.$$

$$S_1 = S_0(1 + g).$$

$$AFN = (A/S_0)(\Delta S) - (L/S_0)(\Delta S) - MS_1(1 - d).$$

Set AFN = 0, substitute in known values for A/S, L/S, M, d, and S_0, and then solve for g:

$$0 = 1.6(\$100g) - 0.4(\$100g) - 0.10[\$100(1 + g)](0.55)$$

$$= \$160g - \$40g - 0.055(\$100 + \$100g)$$

$$= \$160g - \$40g - \$5.5 - \$5.5g$$

$$\$114.5g = \$5.5$$

$$g = \$5.5/\$114.5 = 0.048 = 4.8\%$$

$$= \text{Maximum growth rate without external financing.}$$

ST-2 Note that assets consist of cash, marketable securities, receivables, inventories, and fixed assets. Therefore, we can break the A/S ratio into its components — cash/sales, inventories/sales, and so forth. Then,

$$\frac{A}{S} = \frac{A - \text{Inventories}}{S} + \frac{\text{Inventories}}{S} = 1.6.$$

We know that the inventory turnover ratio is sales/inventories $= 3$ times, so inventories/sales $= 1/3 = 0.3333$. Further, if the inventory turnover ratio could be increased to 4 times, then the inventory/sales ratio would fall to $1/4 = 0.25$, a difference of $0.3333 - 0.2500 = 0.0833$. This in turn would cause the A/S ratio to fall from A/S $= 1.6$ to A/S $= 1.6 - 0.0833 = 1.5167$.

This change would have two effects: (1) It would change the AFN equation, and (2) it would mean that Mehran currently has excessive inventories, so there could be some sales growth without any additional inventories. Therefore, we could set up the revised AFN equation, estimate the funds needed next year, and then subtract out the excess inventories currently on hand:

Present Conditions:

$$\frac{\text{Sales}}{\text{Inventories}} = \frac{\$100}{\text{Inventories}} = 3,$$

so

$$\text{Current level of inventories} = \$100/3 - \$33.3 \text{ million.}$$

New Conditions:

$$\frac{\text{Sales}}{\text{Inventories}} = \frac{\$100}{\text{Inventories}} = 4,$$

so

$$\text{New level of inventories} = \$100/4 = \$25 \text{ million.}$$

Therefore,

$$\text{Excess inventories} = \$33.3 - 25 = \$8.3 \text{ million.}$$

Forecast of Funds Needed, First Year:

$$\Delta S \text{ in first year} = 0.2(\$100 \text{ million}) = \$20 \text{ million.}$$

$$\text{AFN} = 1.5167(\$20) - 0.4(\$20) - 0.1(0.55)(\$120) - \$8.3$$

$$= \$30.3 - \$8 - \$6.6 - \$8.3$$

$$= \$7.4 \text{ million.}$$

Forecast of Funds Needed, Second Year:

$$\Delta S \text{ in second year} = gS_1 = 0.2(\$120 \text{ million}) = \$24 \text{ million.}$$

$$AFN = \$1.5167(\$24) - 0.4(\$24) - 0.1(0.55)(\$144)$$

$$= \$36.4 - \$9.6 - \$7.9$$

$$= \$18.9 \text{ million.}$$

Selected Additional References and Cases

The heart of successful financial planning is the sales forecast. On this key subject, see

Pan, Judy, Donald R. Nichols, and O. Maurice Joy, "Sales Forecasting Practices of Large U.S. Industrial Firms," *Financial Management,* Fall 1977, 72–77.

Pappas, James L., Eugene F. Brigham, and Mark Hirschey, *Managerial Economics* (Hinsdale, Ill.: Dryden, 1983).

Computer modeling is becoming increasingly important. For general references, see

Carleton, Willard T., Charles L. Dick, Jr., and David H. Downes, "Financial Policy Models: Theory and Practice," *Journal of Finance,* December 1973, 691–709.

Francis, Jack Clark, and Dexter R. Rowell, "A Simultaneous Equation Model of the Firm for Financial Analysis and Planning," *Financial Management,* Spring 1978, 29–44.

Grinyer, P. H., and J. Wooller, *Corporate Models Today — A New Tool for Financial Management* (London: Institute of Chartered Accountants, 1978).

Pappas, James L., and George P. Huber, "Probabilistic Short-Term Financial Planning," *Financial Management,* Autumn 1973, 36–44.

Traenkle, J. W., E. B. Cox, and J. A. Bullard, *The Use of Financial Models in Business* (New York: Financial Executives' Research Foundation, 1975).

Considerable effort has been expended to develop integrated financial planning models that identify optimal policies. For one example, see

Myers, Stewart C., and Gerald A. Pogue, "A Programming Approach to Corporate Financial Management," *Journal of Finance,* May 1974, 579–599.

The Crum-Brigham casebook contains the following applicable cases:

Case 3, "Ceramic Structures Engineering, Inc.," which focuses on the importance and mechanics of financial planning.

Case 4, "Moseley Vault and Alarm Company," which illustrates some of the basic problems involved in maintaining financial control.

The following classic case is available from Harvard Business School (HBS) Case Services:

"The O. M. Scott & Sons Company," which illustrates financial forecasting and analysis as well as working capital management.

23

Corporate Restructuring: Mergers, Divestitures, and Holding Companies

Getty Oil, the fourteenth largest U.S. oil company, was acquired by Texaco, the fourth largest, in February 1984 at a cost of $10.1 billion. Getty's stock had been selling at around $65, and the descendants of J. Paul Getty, the founder, had been complaining of inefficient management, poor earnings, and a consequent low stock price. These complaints had prompted Pennzoil to seek a merger with Getty, and Pennzoil offered $112.50 per share. Getty's directors voted 15 to 1 to accept Pennzoil's offer, and they announced that an agreement in principle had been reached. But before the paperwork could be completed, Texaco jumped in with an offer of $125 per share. Getty's board then reneged on the Pennzoil bid and accepted the higher Texaco offer.

The merger doubled Texaco's domestic oil and gas reserves, and, with Getty's retail outlets, gave Texaco a major share of the gasoline market. Some analysts claimed that Texaco, with its sprawling network of refineries and rapidly dwindling reserves, made the correct decision by acquiring Getty, with its large reserves and minimal refining operations. Other analysts contended that Texaco paid too much for Getty. Whether Texaco will get its money's worth remains to be seen. Acquiring Getty's reserves may have been cheaper for Texaco than finding new oil, but the value of these

This chapter was coauthored with David T. Brown of the University of Florida.

reserves will depend on the long-run price of oil, which by 1987 was down by more than 40 percent from its 1984 level.

The Texaco-Getty merger spawned two side issues. The first concerned the Bass Brothers of Texas, an immensely wealthy family that had acquired over $1 billion of Texaco stock during all the action. Texaco's management was afraid the Basses would try to take over Texaco, so they bought out the Bass interests at a premium of about 20 percent over the market value. Some of Texaco's stockholders argued that the payment amounted to "greenmail," or a payoff made with stockholders' money just to insure that Texaco's managers could keep their jobs. This situation, along with similar ones in other companies, has led to the introduction of bills in Congress to limit the actions that a management group can take in its efforts to avoid being taken over. However, Congress has taken no action to date.

The second side issue was a suit by Pennzoil, which charged that Texaco caused Getty to breach its contract with Pennzoil. Pennzoil won a $12 billion judgment, and if the award is sustained, Pennzoil will virtually own Texaco, and at no cost except for some legal fees!

The threat of a final judgment almost equal to Texaco's $13.3 billion of equity caused serious concern among Texaco's creditors, and Texaco experienced trouble in getting sufficient credit to continue its operations. As a result, in April 1987, it filed for protection under Chapter 11 of the Bankruptcy Act, and, in the process, became the largest company ever to file for bankruptcy. This ploy gave Texaco a stronger hand in its negotiations with Pennzoil, and it relieved the pressure on Texaco to settle the suit on terms favorable to Pennzoil. However, Texaco can no longer pay dividends, and management salaries were capped at $100,000, which is about one-tenth the level that would otherwise exist.

We began the book with a discussion of the primary goal of financial management, stock price maximization, and then in Chapters 2 through 22, we discussed how the financial manager can contribute to that goal. Generally, the firm's basic structure was taken as a given, and investment and financing decisions were then addressed within the context of that structure. However, firms occasionally undergo massive restructuring in which major new businesses are acquired, large segments of the old firm are sold off, or the capital structure is changed radically. Such events can occur separately, or they can occur in combination. Also, they can be decided upon by management or be forced upon management by outsiders.

We discuss such restructurings in this chapter, concentrating first on mergers, then on divestitures, and finally on the holding company form of organization.

RATIONALE FOR MERGERS

Many reasons have been proposed by both financial managers and theorists to account for the high level of U.S. merger activity. This section presents some of the motives behind corporate mergers.[1]

Synergy

The primary motivation for most mergers is to increase the value of the combined enterprise. If Companies A and B merge to form Company C, and if C's value exceeds that of A and B taken separately, then *synergy* is said to exist. Such a merger should be beneficial to both A's and B's stockholders.[2] Synergistic effects can arise from four sources: (1) *operating economies of scale* in management, production, or distribution; (2) *financial economies,* which could include a higher price/earnings ratio, a lower cost of debt, and/or a greater debt capacity; (3) *differential management efficiency,* which implies that the management of one firm is relatively inefficient, so the firm's profitability can be improved by merger; and (4) *increased market power* due to reduced competition. Operating and financial economies are socially desirable, as are mergers that increase managerial efficiency, but mergers that reduce competition are both undesirable and illegal.[3]

Tax Considerations

Tax considerations have stimulated a number of mergers. For example, a firm which is highly profitable and in the highest corporate tax bracket could acquire a company with large accumulated tax losses and then use those losses to shelter the income of the acquiring firm.[4] Similarly, a company with large losses can acquire a profitable firm.

Personal tax considerations may also lead to mergers. For example, if a firm has a shortage of internal investment opportunities compared to its cash flow, its options for disposing of its excess cash are: (1) paying an extra dividend, (2) invest-

---

[1]As we use the term, *merger* means any combination that forms one firm from two or more existing firms. For legal purposes, there are distinctions among the various ways these combinations can occur, but our emphasis is on the fundamental business and financial aspects of mergers.

[2]If synergy exists, then the whole is greater than the sum of the parts. Synergy is also called the "2 plus 2 equals 5 effect." The distribution of the synergistic gain between A's and B's stockholders is determined by negotiation, a point discussed later in the chapter.

[3]In the 1880s and 1890s, many mergers occurred in the United States, and some of them were rather obviously directed toward gaining market power rather than increasing operating efficiency. As a result, Congress passed a series of acts designed to insure that mergers are not used as a method of reducing competition. The principal acts include the Sherman Act (1890), the Clayton Act (1914), and the Celler Act (1950). These acts make it illegal for firms to combine in any manner if the combination will tend to lessen competition. They are administered by the Antitrust Division of the Justice Department and by the Federal Trade Commission.

[4]Mergers undertaken only to use accumulated tax losses would probably be challenged by the IRS. However, because many factors are present in any given merger, it is hard to prove that a merger was motivated only, or even primarily, by tax considerations.

ing in marketable securities, (3) repurchasing its own stock, or (4) purchasing another firm. If the firm pays an extra dividend, its stockholders will have to pay personal taxes on the distribution. Marketable securities provide a good temporary parking place for money, but the rate of return on such securities is generally less than that on operating assets. A stock repurchase would defer taxes for the remaining stockholders, but repurchases would be disadvantageous if the company were forced to bid up its price to acquire the stock. Further, if the repurchase were designed solely to avoid dividend payments, it could be challenged by the IRS. However, using surplus cash to acquire another firm may have no immediate tax consequences for the acquiring firm or its stockholders, and this fact has motivated a number of mergers.

Purchase of Assets below Their Replacement Cost

Sometimes a firm will be touted as a possible acquisition candidate because the replacement value of its assets is considerably higher than their market value. For example, in the early 1980s, oil companies could acquire reserves more cheaply by buying out other oil companies than by exploratory drilling. This factor was the primary motive for Texaco's acquisition of Getty. However, note that the value of an asset stems from its expected cash flows, and not from its replacement cost. Thus, paying $1 million for a slide rule plant which would cost $2 million to build from scratch is not much of a deal if no one uses slide rules.

Diversification

Managers often claim that diversification helps to stabilize the firm's earnings stream and thus reduces within-firm (or total) risk. Therefore, risk reduction is often given as a reason for mergers. Stabilization of earnings is certainly beneficial to a firm's employees, suppliers, and customers, but what is its value to the firm's stockholders and debtholders? If an investor is worried about earnings variability, he or she could probably diversify more easily than could the firm. Why should Firms A and B merge to stabilize earnings when a stockholder in Firm A could sell half of his or her stock in A and use the proceeds to purchase stock in Firm B, especially since the stockholder could take this action at a lower cost than would be involved if the firms merged?

Of course, if you were the owner-manager of a closely held firm, it might be virtually impossible for you to sell part of your stock to diversify, because this would dilute your ownership and also generate a large tax liability. In this case, a merger might well be the best way to achieve personal diversification. However, for publicly held firms, diversification alone is a questionable motive for any merger.

Control

In recent years many hostile takeovers have occurred. The managers of the target companies generally lose their jobs, or at least their autonomy. Therefore, managers who own less than 51 percent of the stock in their firms look to devices that will lessen the chances of their firms' being taken over. Mergers can serve as such a device. For example, when Enron was under attack, it arranged to buy Houston Natural Gas Company, paying for Houston primarily with debt. That merger made Enron much larger and hence harder for any potential acquirer to "digest." Also, the much higher debt level resulting from the merger would make it hard for any acquiring company to use debt to buy Enron. Such *defensive mergers* are hard to defend on economic grounds. The managers involved invariably argue that synergy, not a desire to protect their own jobs, motivated the acquisition, but there can be no question that many mergers today are indeed designed more for the benefit of managers than for that of stockholders.

TYPES OF MERGERS

Economists classify mergers into four groups: (1) horizontal, (2) vertical, (3) congeneric, and (4) conglomerate. A *horizontal merger* occurs when one firm combines with another in its same line of business—for example, when one widget manufacturer acquires another, or one retail food chain merges with a second. The recent merger of Burroughs and Sperry to form Unisys was a horizontal merger, because both firms manufactured computers and electronics products. An example of a *vertical merger* is a steel producer's acquisition of one of its own suppliers, such as an iron or coal mining firm, or an oil producer's acquisition of a petrochemical firm which uses oil as a raw material. *Congeneric* means "allied in nature or action"; hence, a *congeneric merger* involves related enterprises but not producers of the same product (horizontal) or firms in a producer-supplier relationship (vertical). Examples of congeneric mergers would be American Express's takeover of Shearson Hammill, a stock brokerage firm, or Philip Morris's acquisition of General Foods. A *conglomerate merger* occurs when unrelated enterprises combine, as illustrated by Mobil Oil's acquisition of Montgomery Ward.

Operating economies (and also anticompetitive effects) are at least partially dependent on the type of merger involved. Vertical and horizontal mergers generally provide the greatest synergistic operating benefits, but they are also the ones most likely to be attacked by the U.S. Department of Justice. In any event, it is useful to think of these economic classifications when analyzing the feasibility of a prospective merger.

LEVEL OF MERGER ACTIVITY

Four major "merger waves" have occurred in the United States. The first was in the late 1800s, when consolidations occurred in the oil, steel, tobacco, and other basic industries. The second was in the 1920s, when the stock market boom helped financial promoters consolidate firms in a number of industries, including utilities, communications, and autos. The third was in the 1960s, when conglomerate mergers were the rage. The fourth began in the early 1980s, and it is still going strong.

The "merger mania" of the 1980s has been sparked by six factors: (1) the relatively depressed condition of the stock market at the beginning of the decade (for

Table 23-1
**The Five Biggest Mergers
(Billions of Dollars)**

Companies	Value	Premium Paid over Book Value	Type of Transaction
Chevron-Gulf	$13.3	36%	Acquisition for cash
Texaco-Getty	10.1	91	Acquisition for cash and notes
Du Pont-Conoco	7.2	56	Acquisition for cash and common stock
General Electric-RCA	6.4	142	Acquisition for cash
U.S. Steel-Marathon	6.0	189	Acquisition for cash and notes

example, the Dow Jones Industrial Index in early 1982 was below its 1968 level); (2) the unprecedented level of inflation that existed during the 1970s and early 1980s, which increased the replacement value of firms' assets even while a weak stock market reduced their market values; (3) the Reagan administration's stated view that "bigness is not necessarily badness," which resulted in a more tolerant attitude toward large mergers; (4) the general belief among the major natural resource companies that it is cheaper to "buy reserves on Wall Street" through mergers than to explore and find them in the field; (5) the development of an active junk bond market, which helped raiders obtain the capital needed to make tender offers for target firms; and (6) attempts to ward off raiders by use of defensive mergers. Although the stock market has rebounded and reached record highs, and the inflation rate has declined, merger activity has continued at a strong pace. However, as we discuss later in the chapter, the Tax Reform Act of 1986 will probably dampen some of the recent merger fever.

Financial historians have not yet compiled the statistics and done the analysis necessary to compare the 1980s merger wave with the earlier ones, but it is certain that the current wave will be the largest. Table 23-1 lists the top five mergers of all time, and they all have occurred in the 1980s.

HOSTILE VERSUS FRIENDLY TAKEOVERS

In the vast majority of merger situations, one firm (generally the larger of the two) simply decides to buy another company, negotiates a price with the management of the target firm, and then acquires the target company. Occasionally, the acquired firm will initiate the action, but it is much more common for a firm to seek acquisitions than to seek to be acquired.[5] Following convention, we shall call a

[5]However, if a firm is in financial difficulty, if its managers are elderly and do not think that suitable replacements are on hand, or if it needs the support (often the capital) of a larger company, then it may seek to be acquired. Thus, when a number of Texas, Ohio, and Maryland financial institutions were in trouble in the mid-1980s, they lobbied to get the state legislatures to pass laws that would make it easier for them to be acquired. Out-of-state banks then moved in to help salvage the situation and minimize depositor losses.

company that seeks to acquire another the *acquiring company* and the one which it seeks to acquire the *target company.*

Once an acquiring company has identified a possible target, it must (1) establish a suitable price, or range of prices, and (2) tentatively set the terms of payment — will it offer cash, its own common stock, bonds, or a mix of securities? Then, the acquiring firm's managers must decide how to approach the target company's managers. If the acquiring firm has reason to believe that the target's management will approve the merger, than it will simply propose a merger and try to work out some suitable terms. If an agreement can be reached, then the two management groups will issue statements to their stockholders stating that they approve the merger, and the target firm's management will recommend to its stockholders that they agree to the merger. Generally, the stockholders are asked to *tender* (or send in) their shares to a designated financial institution along with a signed power of attorney which transfers ownership of the shares to the acquiring firm. The target firm's stockholders then receive the specified payment, be it common stock of the acquiring company (in which case the target company's stockholders become stockholders of the acquiring company), cash, bonds, or some mix of cash and securities. This is a *friendly merger,* or a *friendly tender offer.*

The recent acquisition of RCA by General Electric typifies a friendly merger. First, the boards of directors of the two firms announced that RCA had agreed to be acquired by GE in an all-cash transaction for $66.50 a share. The merger was approved by shareholders, by the Federal Communications Commission, and by the Justice Department, and then the acquisition was completed.

Often, however, the target company's management resists the merger. Perhaps the managers feel that the price offered for the stock is too low, or perhaps they simply want to keep their jobs. In either case, the acquiring firm's offer is said to be *hostile* rather than friendly, and the acquiring firm must make a direct appeal to the target firm's stockholders. In a hostile merger, the acquiring company will again make a tender offer, and again it will ask the stockholders of the target firm to tender their shares in exchange for the offered price. This time, though, the target firm's managers will urge stockholders not to tender their shares, generally stating that the price offered (cash, bonds, or stock in the acquiring firm) is too low.

GAF's tender offer for Union Carbide illustrates a hostile merger attempt. Union Carbide's stock was trading at a depressed $48 a share due to lawsuits stemming from the Bhopal, India, tragedy, when poisonous gas from a Carbide plant killed an estimated 2,000 people. GAF made a $68-per-share, all-cash tender offer for Carbide's shares. Carbide decided to resist, and one week later it announced a restructuring in which the company would exchange $20 in cash plus $65 worth of debt securities per share for 35 percent of the Carbide stock. Thus, Carbide was offering $85 per share versus GAF's $48 offer, but Carbide could only afford to purchase 35 percent of its outstanding shares. Almost immediately, GAF upped its tender offer to $74 a share, in cash, for all shares, and it further stated that it would raise the offer to $78 per share if Carbide's directors would approve the offer. Carbide's directors chose to resist, and they decided to sell off the company's consumer products division, maker of such name brand products as Prestone antifreeze and Eveready batteries, and to use the proceeds (1) to increase the exchange offer to include 55 percent of the shares, and (2) to raise the dividend on the remaining shares. This was too much for GAF to counter, so it withdrew its tender offer. The hostile takeover attempt thus failed, but it did force a major restructuring which caused Carbide's stock price to increase from $48 to about $78.

MERGER REGULATION

Prior to the mid-1960s, friendly acquisitions generally took place through simple exchange-of-stock mergers, and a proxy fight was the primary weapon used in a hostile control battle. However, in the mid-1960s, corporate raiders began to operate differently. First, they noted that it took a long time to mount a proxy fight — they had to first request a list of the target company's stockholders, be refused, and then get a court order forcing management to turn over the list. During that time, management could think through and then implement a strategy to fend off the raider. As a result, the instigator lost most proxy fights.

Then raiders began saying to themselves, "Suppose we could take an action that would bring the decision to a head quickly, before management could take countermeasures — that would greatly increase the probability of a successful takeover." That led the raiders to turn from proxy fights to tender offers, which had a much shorter response time. For example, the stockholders of a company whose stock was selling for $20 might be offered $27 per share and be given two weeks to accept. The raider, meanwhile, would have accumulated a substantial block of the shares in open market purchases, and additional shares might have been purchased by institutional friends of the raider, who promised to tender their shares in exchange for the tip that a raid was to occur.

Faced with a well-planned raid, managements were generally overwhelmed. The stock might actually still be undervalued at the offered price, but management simply did not have time to get this message across to stockholders, or to find a friendly competing bidder (called a *white knight*), or anything else. This situation was thought to be unfair, and, as a result, Congress passed the Williams Act in 1968. This law had two main objectives: (1) to regulate the way in which acquiring firms can structure takeover offers, and (2) to force acquiring firms to disclose more information about their offers. Basically, Congress wanted to put target managements in a better position to defend against hostile offers. Additionally, Congress believed that shareholders needed easy access to more information about tender offers — including information on any securities that might be offered in lieu of cash — in order to make rational tender-versus-don't-tender decisions.

The Williams Act placed the following three major restrictions on the activities of acquiring firms: (1) Acquirers must disclose their current holdings and future intentions within 10 days of amassing at least 10 percent (later reduced to 5 percent) of a company's stock, and they must disclose the source of the funds to be used in the acquisition. (2) The target firm's shareholders must be allowed at least 20-days to tender their shares, i.e., the offer must be "open" for at least 20 days. (3) If the acquiring firm increases the offer price during the 20-day open period, all shareholders who tendered prior to the new offer must receive the higher price. In total, these restrictions were intended to reduce the ability of the acquiring firm to surprise management and to stampede target shareholders into accepting the offer. Prior to the Williams Act, offers were generally made on a first come, first serve basis, and they were often accompanied by an implicit threat to lower the bid price after 50 percent of the shares were in hand. The legislation also meant that target managements would have more time to mount a defense, and it also gave rival bidders and white knights a chance to enter the fray and thus help the target's stockholders obtain a better price.

Many states have also passed laws designed to protect firms in their state from hostile takeovers. At first, these laws focused on disclosure requirements, but by the late 1970s, several states had enacted takeover statutes so restrictive that they virtually precluded hostile takeovers. In 1979, when MITE Corporation, a Delaware firm, made a hostile tender offer for Chicago Rivet and Machine Co., a publicly held Illinois corporation, Chicago Rivet sought protection under the Illinois Business Takeover Act. The constitutionality of the Illinois Act was contested, and the U.S. Supreme Court found the law unconstitutional. The court ruled that the Illinois law put undue burdens on interstate commerce. The opinion stated that the market for securities is a national market, and even though the issuing firm was incorporated in Illinois, the State of Illinois could not regulate interstate securities transactions.

The Illinois decision effectively eliminated the first generation of state merger regulations. However, the states keep trying to protect their state-headquartered companies, and in 1987 the U.S. Supreme Court upheld an Indiana law which radically changed the rules of the takeover game. Specifically, the Indiana law first defines "control shares" as enough shares to give an investor 20 percent of the vote, and states that when an investor buys control shares, those shares can only be voted after approval by a majority of "disinterested shareholders," defined as those who are neither officers nor inside directors of the company, nor associates of the raider. The law also gives the buyer of control shares the right to insist that a shareholders meeting be called within 50 days to decide whether the shares may be voted. The Indiana law dealt a major blow to raiders, mainly because it slows down the action. Delaware (the state in which most large companies are incorporated) is considering passage of a similar bill, and so is New York and a number of other states.

The new state laws also have some features which protect target stockholders from their own managers. Included are limits on the use of golden parachutes, onerous debt-financing plans, and other types of poison pills. Since these laws do not regulate tender offers per se, but, rather, govern the practices of firms in the state, they have, at least up to this point, withstood all legal challenges.

MERGER ANALYSIS

In theory, merger analysis is quite simple. The acquiring firm simply performs a capital budgeting analysis to determine whether the present value of the cash flows expected to result from the merger exceeds the price that must be paid for the target company; if the net present value is positive, the acquiring firm should take steps to acquire the target firm. The target company's stockholders, on the other hand, should accept the proposal if the price offered exceeds the present value of the expected future cash flows that would result if it continued to operate independently. Theory aside, however, some difficult issues are involved: (1) the acquiring company must estimate the cash flows that will result from the acquisition; (2) it must also determine what effect, if any, the merger will have on its own required rate of return on equity; (3) it must decide how to pay for the merger — with cash, its own stock, or some other type or package of securities; and (4) having estimated the benefits of the merger, the acquiring and target firms' managers and stockholders must bargain (or fight) over how to share these benefits.

Operating Versus Financial Mergers

From the standpoint of financial analysis, there are two basic types of mergers, operating mergers and financial mergers.

1. An *operating merger* is one in which the operations of two companies are integrated with the expectation of obtaining synergistic effects. To illustrate, Texas Air's 1987 acquisition of People Express resulted in People's planes being repainted and incorporated into Texas Air's Continental Airlines subsidiary.

2. A pure *financial merger* is one in which the merged companies will not be operated as a single unit and from which no significant operating economies are expected. Coca-Cola's acquisition of Columbia Pictures with $748 million of surplus cash is an example of a financial merger.

Of course, mergers may actually combine these two features. For example, some of RCA's electronics and defense operations were merged with similar GE businesses, but other operations, such as RCA's NBC television network, have been maintained as separate lines of business.

Valuing the Target Firm

To determine the value of the target firm, two key items are needed: (1) a set of pro forma financial statements which develop the incremental cash flows expected from the merger, and (2) a discount rate, or cost of capital, to apply to these projected cash flows.

Pro Forma Cash Flow Statements

The development of accurate postmerger cash flow forecasts is the most important step in merger analysis. In a pure financial merger, the postmerger cash flows are simply the sum of the expected cash flows of the two companies if they were to continue to operate independently. However, if the two firms' operations are to be integrated, or if the acquiring firm plans to change the target firm's management in order to get better results, then forecasting future cash flows is a more complex task.

Table 23-2 contains the projected cash flow statements for Apex Corporation, which is being considered as a target by Hightech, a large conglomerate. The projected data are for the postmerger period, so all synergistic effects must be included. Apex currently uses 30 percent debt, but if it were acquired, Hightech would increase Apex's debt ratio to 50 percent. Both Hightech and Apex have 40 percent marginal federal-plus-state tax rates.

Table 23-2
Hightech Corporation:
Projected Postmerger Income Statements for the
Apex Subsidiary as of December 31
(Millions of Dollars)

	1988	1989	1990	1991	1992
Net sales	$105	$126	$151	$174	$191
Cost of goods sold	80	94	111	127	137
Selling and administrative expenses	10	12	13	15	16
EBIT	$ 15	$ 20	$ 27	$ 32	$ 38
Interest[a]	3	4	5	6	6
EBT	$ 12	$ 16	$ 22	$ 26	$ 32
Taxes[b]	4	5	7	9	11
Net income	$ 8	$ 11	$ 15	$ 17	$ 21
Retained by Apex to finance growth[c]	4	4	7	9	12
Cash available to Hightech	$ 4	$ 7	$ 8	$ 8	$ 9
Terminal value[d]					121
Net cash flow[e]	$ 4	$ 7	$ 8	$ 8	$130

[a]Interest payments are estimates based on Apex's existing debt plus immediate additional debt required to increase the debt ratio to 50 percent, plus additional debt required after the merger to finance asset expansion while maintaining the 50 percent target capital structure.

[b]Hightech will file a consolidated tax return after the merger. Thus, the taxes shown here are the full corporate taxes attributable to Apex's operations: there will be no additional taxes on any cash flows passed from Apex to Hightech.

[c]Some of the net income generated by the Apex subsidiary after the merger will be retained to finance Apex's own asset growth, while some will be transferred to Hightech to pay dividends on its stock or for redeployment within the corporation. It is assumed that depreciation-generated funds are used by Apex to replace worn-out and obsolete plant and equipment.

[d]Apex's available cash flows are expected to grow at a constant 10 percent after 1992. The value of all post-1992 cash flows to Hightech, as of December 31, 1992, is estimated by use of the constant growth model to be $121 million:

$$V_{1992} = \frac{\$9(1.10)}{0.1815 - 0.10} = \$121 \text{ million.}$$

In the next section, we discuss the estimation of the 18.15 percent cost of equity. The $121 million is the PV of the stream of cash flows for years 1993 and thereafter.

[e]These are the net cash flows which are available to Hightech by virtue of the acquisition of Apex. These cash flows could be used for dividend payments to Hightech's stockholders, to finance asset expansion in Hightech's other divisions and subsidiaries, or what have you.

The net cash flows shown in Table 23-2 are the flows that would be available to Hightech's stockholders, and these are the basis of the valuation.[6] Of course, the postmerger cash flows attributable to the target firm are extremely difficult to estimate, and in a complete merger valuation, just as in a complete capital budgeting analysis, the component cash flow probability distributions should be specified, and sensitivity, scenario, and simulation analyses should be conducted. Indeed, in a friendly merger, the acquiring firm would send a team consisting of literally dozens of accountants, engineers, and so forth, to the target firm's headquarters to go over its books, to estimate required maintenance expenditures, to set values on assets such as real estate and petroleum reserves, and the like.

Estimating the Discount Rate

The bottom line net cash flows shown in Table 23-2 are equity flows, so they should be discounted at the cost of equity rather than at the company's overall cost of capital. Further, the cost of equity used must reflect the riskiness of the net cash flows in the table, and hence the appropriate discount rate is Apex's cost of equity, not that of either Hightech or the consolidated postmerger firm.

Apex's market-determined premerger beta was 1.28. However, this reflects its premerger 30 percent debt ratio, while its postmerger debt ratio will increase to 50 percent. The Hamada equations, which were developed in Chapter 12, can be used to approximate the effects of the leverage change on beta. First, we obtain the unlevered beta of Apex's assets:

$$b_U = \frac{b_L}{1 + (1 - T)(D/E)} = \frac{1.28}{1 + (1 - 0.40)(0.30/0.70)} = \frac{1.28}{1.26} = 1.02.$$

Next, we recalculate Apex's beta to reflect the new 50 percent debt ratio:

$$b_L = b_U[1 + (1 - T)(D/E)]$$
$$= 1.02[1 + (1 - 0.40)(0.50/0.50)] = 1.02(1.6) = 1.63.$$

Finally, we use the Security Market Line to estimate Apex's postmerger cost of equity. If the risk-free rate is 10 percent and the market risk premium is 5 percent, then Apex's cost of equity, k_s, after the merger with Hightech, would be 18.15 percent:[7]

---

[6]We purposely kept the cash flows relatively simple to help focus in on the key issues of the valuation process. In an actual merger valuation, the cash flows would be much more complex, normally including such items as additional capital furnished by the acquiring firm, tax loss carry-forwards, tax effects of plant and equipment valuation adjustments, and cash flows from the sale of some of the subsidiary's assets.

[7]In this example, we used the Capital Asset Pricing Model to estimate Apex's cost of equity, and thus we assumed that investors require a premium for market risk only. We could have also conducted a total risk analysis, in which the relevant total risk would be the contribution of Apex's cash flows to the total risk of the postmerger firm.

In actual merger situations among large firms, companies almost always hire an investment banking firm to help develop valuation estimates. For example, when General Electric acquired Utah International, GE hired Morgan Stanley to determine Utah's value. We discussed the valuation process with the Morgan Stanley analyst in charge of the appraisal, and he confirmed that they considered all of the standard procedures discussed in this chapter. Note, though, that merger analysis, like the analysis of any other complex issue, requires judgment, and people's judgments differ as to how much weight to give to different methods in any given situation.

$$k_s = k_{RF} + (RP_M)b = 10\% + (5\%)1.63 = 18.15\%.$$

Valuing the Cash Flows

The current value of Apex to Hightech is the present value of the cash flows expected to accrue to Hightech, discounted at 18.15 percent (in millions of dollars):

$$V_{1987} = \frac{\$4}{(1.1815)^1} + \frac{\$7}{(1.1815)^2} + \frac{\$8}{(1.1815)^3} + \frac{\$8}{(\$1.1815)^4} + \frac{\$130}{(1.1815)^5} = \$74.$$

Thus, if Hightech could acquire Apex for $74 million or less, the merger would appear to be acceptable from Hightech's standpoint. Obviously, Hightech would try to buy at as low a price as possible, while Apex would hold out for the highest possible price. The final price is determined by negotiations, with the better negotiator capturing most of the incremental value. *The larger the synergistic benefits, the more room for bargaining, and the higher the probability that the merger will actually be consummated.*[8]

Postmerger Control

The employment/control situation is often of vital interest. First, consider the situation in which a small, owner-managed firm sells out to a larger concern. The owner-manager may be anxious to retain a high-status position, and he or she may also have developed a camaraderie with the employees and thus be concerned about keeping operating control of the organization after the merger. Thus, these points are often stressed during the merger negotiations.[9] When a publicly owned firm not controlled by its managers is merged into another company, the acquired firm's management also is worried about its postmerger position. If the acquiring firm agrees to retain the old management, then management may be willing to

---

[8]It has been estimated that of all merger negotiations seriously begun, fewer than one-third actually result in merger. Also, note that in contested merger situations, the company that offers the most will usually make the acquisition, and the company that will gain the greatest synergistic benefits should bid the most.

[9]The acquiring firm may also be concerned about this point, especially if the acquired firm's management is quite good. Indeed, a condition of the merger may be that the management team agree to stay on for a period, such as five years, after the merger. Also, the price paid may be contingent on the acquired firm's performance subsequent to the merger. For example, when International Holdings acquired Walker Products, the price paid was an immediate 100,000 shares of International Holdings stock worth $63 per share plus an additional 30,000 shares each year for the next three years, provided Walker Products earned at least $1 million during each of these years. Since Walker's managers owned the stock and would receive the bonus, they had a strong incentive to stay on and help the firm meet its targets.

Finally, if the managers of the target company are highly competent but do not wish to remain on after the merger, the acquiring firm may build into the merger contract a noncompetitive agreement with the old management. Typically, the acquired firm's principal officers must agree not to affiliate with a new business which is competitive with the one they sold for a specified period, say five years. Such agreements are especially important with service-oriented businesses.

support the merger and to recommend its acceptance to the stockholders. If the old management is to be removed, then it will probably resist the merger.[10]

STRUCTURING THE TAKEOVER BID

The acquiring firm's offer to the target's shareholders can be in the form of cash, stock of the acquiring firm, debt of the acquiring firm, or a combination of these. The structure of the bid is extremely important, since it affects (1) the capital structure of the postmerger firm, (2) the tax treatment of both the acquiring firm and the target's stockholders, and (3) the types of federal and state regulations to which the acquiring firm will be subjected. In this section, we focus on how taxes and regulation influence the way in which acquiring firms structure their offers.

The form of payment offered to the target shareholders determines the personal tax treatment of the target's stockholders. Target shareholders do not have to pay taxes on the transaction if they maintain a substantial equity position in the combined firm, defined by the IRS to mean that at least 50 percent of the payment to target shareholders must be in shares (either common or preferred) of the acquiring firm. In such non-taxable offers, target shareholders who receive equity securities do not realize any capital gains or losses until the securities they receive in the takeover are sold. However, capital gains must be taken and treated as income in the transaction year if an offer consists of over 50 percent cash or debt securities.

All other things equal, stockholders prefer non-taxable offers, since they may then postpone the realization of capital gains and hence the payment of taxes. Most target shareholders are thus willing to sell their stock for a lower price in a non-taxable offer than in a taxable offer. As a result, one might expect nontaxable bids to dominate. However, this is not the case — roughly half of all mergers have been taxable.

The reason that tax-free exchange offers have not dominated lies in the corporate taxation of the offer. Prior to the Tax Reform Act of 1986, if a taxable merger occurred — meaning that the acquiring firm paid primarily with cash or debt securities — then the acquirer was permitted to write up (increase) the assets of the target company from their book value to the actual price paid for the assets, and then to base tax depreciation on these higher values. However, as we discuss later in the chapter, new and much less favorable tax rules took effect in 1986.

Taxable cash or debt offers are most likely to be used (1) when the target firm's stock has not appreciated very much, and hence its shareholders would not have to recognize large capital gains, and (2) when the value of the asset write-up is

---

[10]Managements of firms that are thought to be attractive merger candidates occasionally arrange *golden parachutes* for themselves. Golden parachutes are extremely lucrative retirement plans which take effect if a merger is consummated. Thus, when Bendix was acquired by Allied, Bill Agee, Bendix's chairman, "pulled the ripcord of his golden parachute" and walked away with $4 million. If a golden parachute is large enough, it can also function as a poison pill — for example, when the president of a firm worth $10 million would have to be paid $8 million if the firm is acquired. Congress is currently considering controls on golden parachutes as a part of its greenmail legislative proposals.

large, and hence the corporate tax benefits to the acquirer dominate the adverse personal tax consequences. Conversely, exchanges of stock are more likely when a cash offer would force target shareholders to recognize immediately large capital gains. Also, we should note that in exchange-of-stock mergers, any tax loss carry-forwards may be used immediately by the acquiring firm, so if the target firm has substantial carry-forwards, this too favors the use of stock offers.

Securities laws also have an effect on the construction of the offer. As we discussed in Chapter 14, the SEC has oversight over the issuance of new securities, including stock or debt issued in connection with a merger. Therefore, whenever a corporation bids for control of another firm through the exchange of equity or debt, the entire process must take place under the scrutiny of the Securities and Exchange Commission. The time required for such reviews allows target managements to implement defensive tactics and other firms to make competing offers, and, as a result, nearly all hostile tender offers are for cash rather than securities.

THE ROLE OF INVESTMENT BANKERS

The investment banking community is involved with mergers in a number of ways: (1) they help arrange mergers, (2) they help target companies resist mergers, (3) they help value target companies, and (4) they speculate in the stocks of potential merger candidates. These merger-related activities have been quite profitable. For example, the investment bankers who arranged the GE-RCA merger earned fees of $27 million — Goldman Sachs earned $15 million from GE and Lazard Frères received $12 million for representing RCA. No wonder investment banking houses are able to make top offers to finance graduates!

Arranging Mergers

The major investment banking firms have merger and acquisition groups which operate within their corporate finance departments. (Corporate finance departments offer advice, as opposed to underwriting or brokerage services, to business firms.) Members of these groups strive to identify firms with excess cash that might want to buy other firms, companies that might be willing to be bought, and firms that might for a number of reasons be attractive to others. Also, if an oil company, for instance, decided to expand into coal mining, then it might enlist the aid of an investment banker to help it locate and then negotiate with a target coal company. Similarly, dissident stockholders of firms with poor track records may work with investment bankers to oust management by helping to arrange a merger. Drexel Burnham Lambert, the investment banking house that developed junk bond financing, is reported to have offered packages of financing to corporate raiders, where the package includes both designing the securities to be used in the tender offer, and lining up people and firms who will buy the target firm's stock now and then tender it once the final offer is made.

Investment bankers have also taken some illegal actions in the merger arena. For one thing, they are reported to have "parked" stock — purchasing it for a raider under a guaranteed buy-back agreement — to help the raider avoid the disclosure rules. Some of this came out in connection with the insider trading scandals of 1987.

Fighting Off Mergers

Target firms that do not want to be acquired generally enlist the help of an investment banking firm, along with a law firm that specializes in helping to block mergers. Defenses include such tactics as (1) changing the by-laws so that only one-third of the directors are elected each year and/or so that a 75 percent approval (a *supermajority*) versus a simple majority is required to approve a merger; (2) trying to convince the target firm's stockholders that the price being offered is too low; (3) raising antitrust issues in the hope that the Justice Department will intervene; (4) repurchasing stock in the open market in an effort to push the price above that being offered by the potential acquirer; (5) getting a white knight that is more acceptable to the target firm's management to compete with the potential acquirer; and (6) taking a poison pill, as described below.

Some examples of poison pills — which often really do amount to virtually committing suicide to avoid a takeover — are such tactics as borrowing on terms that require immediate repayment of all loans if the firm is acquired, selling off at bargain prices the assets that originally made the firm a desirable target, granting such lucrative golden parachutes to their executives that the cash drain from these payments would render the merger infeasible, and planning defensive mergers which would leave the firm with new assets of questionable value and a huge amount of debt to service. Currently, the most popular poison pill is for a company to give its stockholders *stock purchase rights* which allow them to buy at half-price the stock of an acquiring firm, should the firm be acquired. The blatant use of poison pills is constrained by directors' awareness that excessive use could trigger personal suits by stockholders against directors who voted for them, and, perhaps in the near future, by laws that would further limit management's use of pills. Still, investment bankers and antitakeover lawyers are busy thinking up new poison pill formulas, and others are just as actively trying to come up with antidotes.

Establishing a Price

If a friendly merger is being worked out between two firms' managements, it is important to be able to document that the agreed-upon price is a fair one; otherwise, the stockholders of either company may sue to block the merger. Therefore, in many large mergers, each side will hire an investment banking firm to evaluate the target company and to help establish the fair price. For example, General Electric employed Morgan Stanley to determine a fair price for Utah International, as did Royal Dutch to help establish the price it paid for Shell Oil. Even if the merger is not friendly, investment bankers may still be asked to help establish a price. If a surprise tender offer is to be made, the acquiring firm will want to know the lowest price at which it might be able to acquire the stock, while the target firm may seek help in "proving" that the price being offered is too low.[11]

Arbitrage Operations

Arbitrage generally means simultaneously buying and selling the same commodity or security in different markets at different prices, and hence pocketing a risk-free return. However, the major brokerage houses, as well as some wealthy private investors, are engaged in a different type of arbitrage called *risk arbitrage.* The *arbitrageurs,* or "arbs" as they are called, speculate in the stocks of companies that are likely takeover targets. Vast amounts of capital are required to speculate in a large number of securities and thus reduce risk, and also to make money on narrow spreads, but the large investment bankers have the wherewithal to play the game. To be successful, arbs need to be able to sniff out likely targets, assess the probability of offers reaching fruition, and move in and out of the market quickly and with low transaction costs.

The risk arbitrage business was rocked by insider trading scandals in 1986 and 1987. Indeed, it was disclosed that the most famous arb of all, Ivan Boesky, had been buying inside information from high-ranked officials of some leading investment banking houses to help make his millions. The Boesky affair slowed down risk arbitrage activity, but it will undoubtedly survive this setback.

THE IMPACT OF THE 1986 TAX REFORM ACT

Prior to the Tax Reform Act of 1986, if a firm paid more than book value for a target firm's assets, it could write up those assets, depreciate the marked-up value for tax purposes, and thus lower the postmerger firm's taxes vis-à-vis the taxes of the two firms operating separately. At the same time, the target firm did not have to pay any taxes on the write-up at the time of the merger.

Under the new law, if the acquiring company writes up the target company's assets for tax purposes, then the target company must pay capital gains taxes in the year the merger occurs. (These taxes can be avoided if the acquiring company elects not to write up acquired assets and hence depreciates them on their old basis.) So, under the new law, more taxes will have to be paid than under the old law, and this fact will make mergers less profitable.

Note also that under the new law the maximum capital gains tax rate on personal income rises from 20 percent to 28 percent, a 40 percent increase. This, of

---

[11]Such investigations must obviously be done in secret, for if someone knew that Company A was thinking of offering, say, $50 per share for Company T, which was currently selling at $35 per share, then huge profits could be made. The biggest scandal to hit Wall Street thus far in the 1980s was the disclosure that Ivan Boesky was buying information from Dennis Levine, a senior member of the investment banking house Drexel Burnham Lambert, about target companies that Drexel Burnham was analyzing for others. Purchases based on such insider information would, of course, raise the prices of the stocks and thus force Drexel's clients to pay more than they otherwise would have had to pay. Levine went to jail for his improper use of inside information, and others may soon follow.

course, means that target companies' stockholders will now net out less after a merger than they would have under the old law. When one considers the combined effects of the corporate and personal tax changes, it is clear that the tax treatment of mergers is significantly less favorable today than it was prior to 1987. This means that a lot less money will end up in the pockets of selling stockholders, so they will be much less anxious to sell out.

WHO WINS: THE EMPIRICAL EVIDENCE

The most recent merger wave has been notable not only for the great number of firms that have combined, but also for the high percentage of hostile takeovers. With all this activity, the following questions have emerged: Do corporate acquisitions really create value, and if so, how is the value shared between the parties involved?

Many financial researchers have classified corporate acquisitions as "the market for corporate control." Under this concept, management teams are viewed as facing constant competition from other management teams. If the team that currently controls a firm is not maximizing the value of the firm's assets, then an acquisition will likely occur and increase the value of the firm by replacing its poor managers with good managers. Further, under the theory, this intense competition will cause managers to combine or divest assets whenever such steps would increase the value of the firm.

Most researchers agree that takeovers increase the wealth of the shareholders of target firms, for otherwise they would not agree to the offer. However, there is a debate as to whether or not mergers benefit the acquiring firm's shareholders. In particular, managements of acquiring firms may be motivated by factors other than shareholder wealth maximization; for example, they may want to merge merely to increase the size of the corporations they manage, since increased size usually brings larger salaries, more job security, perquisites, power, and prestige.

The validity of the competing views on who gains from corporate acquisitions can be tested by examining the stock price changes that occur around a merger or takeover announcement. Such changes in the stock prices of the acquiring and target firms represent market participants' beliefs about the value created by the merger, and about how this value will be divided between the target and acquiring firms. As long as the market participants are neither systematically wrong nor biased in their perceptions of the effects of mergers, examining a large sample of stock price movements will shed light on the issue of who gains from mergers.

One cannot simply examine stock prices around merger announcement dates, because other factors influence stock prices. For example, if a merger was announced on a day when the entire market advanced, the fact that the firm in question's price rose would not necessarily signify that the merger created value. Hence, studies examine *abnormal returns* associated with merger announcements, where abnormal returns are defined as that part of a stock price change caused by factors other than changes in the general stock market.

Many studies have examined both acquiring and target firms' stock price responses to mergers and tender offers.[12] Jointly, these studies have covered nearly every acquisition involving publicly traded firms from the early 1960s to the present, and they are remarkably consistent in their results: On average, the stock price of target firms increases by about 30 percent in hostile tender offers, while in friendly mergers the average increase is about 20 percent. However, for both friendly mergers and hostile tender offers, the stock prices of acquiring firms, on average, remain constant. Thus, the evidence strongly indicates (1) that acquisitions do create value, and (2) that shareholders of target firms reap virtually all of the benefits.

In hindsight, these results are not too surprising. First, target firms' shareholders can always say "no," so they are in the driver's seat. Second, takeovers are a competitive game, so if one potential acquiring firm is not willing to pay full value for a potential target, then another firm will generally jump in with a higher bid. Finally, managements of acquiring firms might well be willing to give up all the value created by the merger to acquiring firms' shareholders, because this enhances the acquiring managers' personal positions, but at no direct cost to their shareholders.

It has also been argued that acquisitions may increase shareholder wealth at the expense of bondholders — in particular, concern has been expressed that leveraged buyouts dilute the claims of bondholders. Specific instances can be cited where bonds were downgraded and bondholders did suffer losses as a direct result of an acquisition, but studies find no evidence to support the contention that bondholders generally lose in corporate acquisitions.[13]

JOINT VENTURES

Mergers are the primary means used to combine the resources of two firms, but *joint ventures* are often used to join together parts of companies to accomplish specific, limited objectives.[14] A joint venture is controlled by a management team consisting of representatives of the two (or more) parent companies.

In one widely publicized joint venture, General Motors and Toyota, the first and third largest automakers in the world, set up an operation to produce 200,000 cars annually at an idle GM plant in Fremont, California. Toyota contributed about $150

---

[12]For an excellent summary of the effects of mergers on value, see Michael C. Jensen and Richard S. Ruback, "The Market for Corporate Control: The Scientific Evidence," *Journal of Financial Economics,* April 1983, 5–50.

[13]For one example of such studies, see Carol Ellen Eger, "An Empirical Test of the Redistribution Effect in Pure Exchange Mergers," *Journal of Financial and Quantitative Analysis,* December 1983, 547–572.

[14]Cross-licensing, consortia, joint bidding, and franchising are still other ways for firms to combine resources. For more information on joint ventures, see Sanford V. Berg, Jerome Duncan, and Phillip Friedman, *Joint Venture Strategies and Corporate Innovation* (Cambridge, Mass.: Oelgeschlager, Gunn, and Hain, 1982).

million to the venture, while GM put up $20 million in cash in addition to the California plant. Although both firms appointed an equal number of directors, Toyota got to name the chief executive. GM is reported to have sought the venture in order to gain better insights into how the Japanese can produce higher-quality cars at a substantially lower cost than U.S. automakers, while Toyota wanted to increase its production in the United States because of import quota limitations. Both companies apparently have realized their goals.

LEVERAGED BUYOUTS

In a *leveraged buyout* (LBO), a small group of equity investors acquires a firm in a transaction financed largely by borrowing. The debt is paid off with funds generated by the acquired company's operations or by sale of some of its assets. Generally, the acquiring group plans to run the acquired company for a number of years, boost its sales and profits, and then take it public again as a stronger company. Naturally, the acquiring group hopes and expects to make substantial capital gains from the operation, but they recognize the risks inherent in the venture due to the initial heavy use of leverage.

The 1986 acquisition of Beatrice Companies by Kohlberg Kravis Roberts & Company (KKR), a New York investment partnership, is a good illustration of an LBO. Beatrice, a consumer products conglomerate with such brands as Tropicana, Playtex, and Hunt Foods, already carried $1.8 billion in debt, which amounted to 64 percent of total capitalization. The $6.2 billion takeover, the largest LBO on record, added another huge chunk of debt. Drexel Burnham Lambert, a major supplier of takeover capital, raised $2.5 billion through junk bonds for KKR, and some banks, including Bankers Trust, Citibank, and Manufacturers Hanover, put up most of the rest. The lenders were convinced that Beatrice could make the required $480 million annual interest payments, and they were especially impressed with the stability of the cash flows generated by Beatrice's food subsidiaries — the same kind of stable earnings that had enabled Philip Morris to borrow billions to buy General Foods, and R. J. Reynolds to buy Nabisco. KKR's financing required no principal repayments for two years, and by that time, a large chunk of the debt would presumably have been retired through a mixture of operating cash flows and asset sales.

Beatrice will enjoy several advantages as a private company. It will be free of dividend payments, which are almost mandatory for an established public company and which amounted to $170 million in 1985. Further, without public stockholders to explain things to, acquisitions and divestitures should be easier. But the most important change, according to KKR, will be a new management team which owns about 15 percent of the new company and whose compensation is based largely on profitability and future stock price performance. That, says KKR, makes all the difference: "Management has the same interest as other stockholders. They'll run the company for the long-term." Generally, in LBOs the firm is restructured, operations are whipped into shape, and then, after a few years, the company again goes public and the owner-managers and investors get their returns. KKR is a specialist in LBOs, and it has been very successful — over the period 1980 to 1986, its investors received a spectacular 47 percent compounded annual rate of return. We will continue the Beatrice story later in the chapter.

DIVESTITURES

Although corporations do more buying than selling of productive facilities, a good bit of selling also occurs. In this section we briefly discuss the major types of divestitures, and then we present some recent examples and rationales for divestitures.

Types of Divestitures

There are four primary types of divestitures: (1) sale of an operating unit to another firm, (2) sale to the managers of the unit being divested, (3) setting up the business to be divested as a separate corporation and then giving (or "spinning off") its stock on a pro rata basis to the divesting firm's stockholders, and (4) outright liquidation of physical assets.

Sale to another firm generally involves the sale of an entire division or unit, usually for cash but sometimes for stock of the acquiring firm. In a *managerial buyout,* the managers of the division arrange to purchase the division themselves, usually for cash plus notes, and as owners/managers, they set up the business as a closely held corporation. In a *spin-off,* the firm's existing stockholders are given new stock representing separate ownership rights in the company that was divested. The new company establishes its own board of directors and officers, and it operates as a separate company. The stockholders end up owning shares of two firms instead of one, but no cash has been transferred. In the fourth type of divestiture, a *liquidation,* the assets of a division are sold off piecemeal rather than as a single entity.

Divestiture Illustrations

1. Esmark, Inc., a holding company which owned such consumer products companies as Swift meats, recently sold off several of its nonconsumer-oriented divisions, including petroleum properties for which Mobil and some other oil companies paid $1.1 billion. Investors generally thought of Esmark as a meat packing and consumer products company, and its stock price reflected this image rather than that of a company with hugh holdings of valuable oil reserves carried at low balance sheet values. Thus, Esmark's stock was undervalued, according to its managers, and the company was in danger of a takeover bid. Selling the oil properties helped Esmark raise its market value from $19 to $45. The Esmark divestiture is an example of a firm's selling assets to another company.

2. IU International, a multimillion-dollar conglomerate listed on the NYSE, recently spun off three major subsidiaries — Gotaas-Larson, an ocean shipping company involved in petroleum transportation; Canadian Utilities, an electric utility; and Echo Bay Mining, a gold mining company. It kept its distribution and manufacturing operations. IU's management originally acquired and combined several highly cyclical businesses such as ocean shipping and gold mining with stable ones such as utilities in order to gain overall corporate stability through diversification. The strategy worked reasonably well from an operating standpoint, but it failed in the financial markets. According to its management, IU's very diversity kept it from being classified in any particular industrial group, so security analysts tended not to follow the company and therefore did not understand it or recommend it to investors. (Analysts tend to concentrate on an industry, and they do not like to recommend — and investors do not like to invest in — a company they do not understand.) As a result, IU had a low P/E ratio and a low market price. After the spin-offs, the package of securities rose in market value from $10 to $75, which greatly exceeded general stock market gains.

3. Beatrice Companies, discussed above, has recently been selling off divisions to raise money to reduce the $6 billion of debt it owed as a result of its LBO. The company sold Avis for $250 million just 12 days after it went private, and it later sold off its Coca-Cola bottling operations for about $1 billion. Beatrice also sold its refrigerated warehouse network, its Max Factor cosmetic line, its dairy products line, and its Playtex operations, raising another $2.4 billion in total. Beatrice's bank loan agreements required that it sell at least $1.45 billion of assets by mid-1987, but Beatrice beat that schedule by well over a year.

4. AT&T was broken up in 1984 to settle a Justice Department antitrust suit filed in the 1970s. For almost 100 years AT&T had operated as a holding company which owned Western Electric (its manufacturing subsidiary), Bell Labs (its research arm), a huge long-distance network system which was operated as a division of the parent company, and 22 Bell operating companies, such as Pacific Telephone, New York Telephone, Southern Bell, and Southwestern Bell. AT&T was reorganized into eight separate companies — a slimmed-down AT&T which kept Western Electric, Bell Labs, and the long-distance operations, plus seven new regional telephone holding companies that were created from the 22 old operating telephone companies. The stock of the seven new telephone companies was then spun off to the old AT&T's stockholders. Thus, a person who held 100 shares of old AT&T stock owned, after the divestiture, 100 shares of the "new" AT&T plus 10 shares of each of the seven new operating companies. These 170 shares were backed by the same assets that had previously backed 100 shares of old AT&T common.

The AT&T divestiture resulted from a suit by the Justice Department, which wanted to divide the Bell System into a regulated monopoly segment (the seven regional telephone companies) and a manufacturing/long-distance segment which would be subjected to competition. The breakup was expected to strengthen competition and speed up technological change in those parts of the telecommunications industry that are not natural monopolies.[15]

---

[15]Another forced divestiture involved Du Pont and General Motors. In 1921, GM was in serious financial trouble, and Du Pont supplied capital in exchange for 23 percent of the stock. In the 1950s, the Justice Department won an antitrust suit which required Du Pont to spin off (to Du Pont's stockholders) its GM stock.

5. Woolworth recently liquidated every one of its 336 Woolco discount stores. This made the company, which had had sales of $7.2 billion before the liquidation, 30 percent smaller. Woolco had posted operating losses of $19 million in the year before the liquidation, and its losses in the six months preceding it had climbed to an alarming $21 million. Woolworth's CEO, Edward F. Gibbons, was quoted as saying: "How many losses can you take?" Woolco's demise necessitated an after-tax write-off of $325 million, but management believed that it was better to go ahead and "bite the bullet" than to let the losing stores bleed the company indefinitely.

6. As a result of some imprudent loans to oil companies and to developing nations, Continental Illinois, one of the largest U.S. bank holding companies, was recently threatened with bankruptcy. Continental then sold off several profitable divisions, such as its leasing and credit card operations, to raise funds to cover bad-loan losses and deposit withdrawals. In effect, Continental sold assets in order to stay alive. Ultimately, Continental was bailed out by the Federal Deposit Insurance Corporation and the Federal Reserve, which (1) arranged a $7.5 billion rescue package and (2) provided a blanket guarantee for all of Continental's $40 billion of deposits, which kept deposits in excess of $100,000 from fleeing the bank because of their uninsured status.

The above examples illustrate that the reasons for divestitures vary widely. Sometimes the market does not appear to properly recognize the value of a firm's assets when they are held as part of a conglomerate; the Esmark oil divestiture is an example. Similarly, if IU International's management is correct, there are cases in which a company has become so complex and diverse that analysts and investors just do not understand it and consequently ignore it. Other companies need cash either to finance expansion in their primary business lines or to reduce a large debt burden, and divestitures can be used to raise this cash; the Beatrice example illustrates this point. The above actions also show that running a business is a dynamic process — conditions change, corporate strategies change in response, and, as a result, firms alter their asset portfolios by acquisitions and/or divestitures. Some divestitures, such as Woolworth's liquidation of its Woolco stores, occur in order to unload losing assets that would otherwise drag the company down, while the AT&T example is one of the many instances in which a divestiture is the result of an antitrust settlement. Finally, Continental Illinois' actions represent a desperate effort to get the cash needed to stay alive.

HOLDING COMPANIES

Strictly defined, any company that owns stock in another firm could be called a *holding company.* However, as the term is generally used, a holding company is a firm that holds large blocks of stock in other companies and exercises control over those firms. The holding company is often called the *parent company,* and the controlled companies are known as *subsidiaries* or *operating companies.* The parent can own 100 percent of the subsidiaries' stock, but *working control* is often exercised with less.

Many of the advantages and disadvantages of holding companies are identical to those of large-scale operations already discussed in connection with mergers and consolidations. Whether a company is organized on a divisional basis or with the divisions kept as separate corporations does not affect the basic reasons for conducting a large-scale, multiproduct, multiplant operation. However, as we show next, the holding company form of large-scale operation has some distinct advantages, but also a few disadvantages, over those of completely integrated, divisionalized operations.

Advantages of Holding Companies

Holding companies have three potential advantages: (1) control with fractional ownership, (2) isolation of risks, and (3) legal and accounting separation where regulations make such separation desirable.

1. Control with fractional ownership. Through a holding company operation a firm may buy 5, 10, or 50 percent, or any other amount of the stock of another corporation. Such fractional ownership may be sufficient to give the acquiring company effective working control over the operations of the firm in which it has acquired stock ownership. Working control is often considered to require more than 25 percent of the common stock, but it can be as low as 10 percent if the stock is widely distributed. One financier recently stated that the attitude of management is more important than the number of shares owned: "If they think you can control the company, then you do."

2. Isolation of risks. Because the various operating companies in a holding company system are separate legal entities, the obligations of any one unit are separate from those of the others. Therefore, catastrophic losses incurred by one unit might not be transmitted as claims on the assets of the other units. However, while this is a customary generalization, it is not always valid. First, the parent company may feel obligated to make good on the subsidiary's debts, even though it may not be legally bound to do so, in order to keep its good name and thus retain customers. Examples of this would include American Express's payment of more than $100 million in connection with a swindle that was the responsibility of one of its subsidiaries, and United California Bank's coverage of a multimillion-dollar fraud loss incurred by its Swiss affiliate. Second, a parent company may feel obligated to supply additional capital to an affiliate in order to protect its initial investment; General Public Utilities' continued support of its subsidiaries' Three Mile Island nuclear plant is an example. Third, when lending to one of the units of a holding company system, an astute loan officer may require a guarantee by the parent company. Finally, an accident such as the one at Union Carbide's Bhopal, India, plant may be deemed the responsibility of the parent company, in which case the limited liability rule that would otherwise apply is voided. To some degree, therefore, the assets in the various elements of a holding company are joined. Still, holding companies can at times be used to prevent losses in one unit from bringing down other units in the system.

3. Legal separation. Certain regulated companies such as utilities and financial institutions find it easier to operate as holding companies than as corporations with multiple divisions. For example, an electric utility such as Southern Company, which operates in and is regulated by several states, found it most practical to set up a holding company (Southern) which in turn owns a set of subsidiaries (Georgia Power, Alabama Power, Mississippi Power, and Gulf Power). All of the Bell telephone companies are part of holding company systems — for example, Nynex Corporation owns New York Telephone and New England Telephone, plus a number of other subsidiaries. Even utilities which operate only within a single state are finding it beneficial to operate within a holding company format in order to separate those assets which are under the control of regulators from those not subject to utility commission regulation. Thus, Florida Power & Light recently reorganized and changed its corporate name to FPL Group, which owns a regulated utility (Flordia Power & Light) plus unregulated subsidiaries engaged in insurance, real estate development, orange groves, and other businesses.

Banks, insurance companies, and other financial service corporations have also found it convenient to be organized as holding companies. For example, Citicorp is a holding company which owns the largest U.S. bank (Citibank of New York), a leasing company, a mortgage service company, and so on. Transamerica is a holding company which owns insurance companies, small loan companies, title companies, auto rental companies, and an airline.

Disadvantages of Holding Companies

Holding companies have two disadvantages: (1) partial multiple taxation and (2) ease of enforced dissolution.

1. Partial multiple taxation. Provided the holding company owns at least 80 percent of a subsidiary's voting stock, the Tax Code permits the filing of consolidated returns, in which case dividends received by the parent are not taxed. However, if less than 80 percent of the stock is owned, then returns cannot be consolidated, and 20 percent of the dividends received by the holding company represents taxable income. With a tax rate of 34 percent, this means that the effective tax rate on intercorporate dividends is $0.20 \times 34\% = 6.8\%$. This partial double taxation somewhat offsets the benefits of holding company control with limited ownership, but whether the penalty of 6.8 percent of dividends received is sufficient to offset other possible advantages is a matter that must be decided in individual situations.

2. Ease of enforced dissolution. It is relatively easy for the Justice Department to require dissolution by disposal of stock ownership of a holding company operation that it finds unacceptable. Thus, Du Pont was required to dispose of its 23 percent stock interest in General Motors. Because there was no fusion between the two corporations, there were no difficulties, from an operating standpoint, in requiring their separation. However, if complete amalgamation had taken place, it would have been much more difficult to break up the company after so many years, and the likelihood of forced divestiture would have been reduced. Still, the recent breakup of AT&T shows that even fully integrated companies can be broken up.

Holding Companies as a Leveraging Device

The holding company vehicle has been used to obtain huge degrees of financial leverage, using up to five or six tiers of holding companies. An operating company at the bottom of the pyramid might have $100 million of assets, financed by $50 million of debt and $50 million of equity. A first-tier holding company might own the stock of the operating firm as its only asset and then be financed with $25 million of debt and $25 million of equity. A second-tier holding company, which owns the $25 million of stock of the first-tier company as its only asset, might be financed with $12.5 million of debt and $12.5 million of equity. If four tiers were used, $100 million of operating assets could be controlled at the top by $3.1 million of equity. The $100 million of operating assets would have to provide enough cash income to support $96.9 million of debt. *Such a holding company system would be highly leveraged, even though the individual components would have only 50 percent debt/assets ratios.* Because of this *consolidated leverage,* even a small decline in profits at the operating company level could bring the whole system down like a house of cards.[16]

SUMMARY

A *merger* involves the consolidation of two or more firms. Mergers can provide economic benefits through economies of scale or through the concentration of assets in the hands of more efficient managers. However, they also have the potential for reducing competition, and for this reason they are carefully regulated by governmental agencies.

In most mergers, one company (the acquiring firm) initiates action to take over another (the target firm). The acquiring company must analyze the situation and determine the value of the target company. There may be operating economies, or synergistic benefits, which will raise the earnings of the combined enterprise over the sum of the earnings of the two separate companies. In this circumstance, the merger is potentially beneficial to both sets of stockholders, but the two firms' managers and stockholders must agree on how the net benefits will be shared.

Firms also find it useful on occasion to get rid of assets — this is called *divestiture.* Sometimes divestitures involve a firm's selling one of its division's assets to some other firm; at other times the firm sets up a separate corporation and then *spins off* the stock of the new company to the stockholders of the old one. The reasons for divestitures vary from transferring assets to management groups which have (or think they have) more expertise in operating the divested businesses, to antitrust, to cleaning up a company's image, to raising capital needed to strengthen the corporation's core business.

---

[16]Excessive leverage through holding companies caused problems for the electric utilities during the 1930s. Accordingly, Congress passed the Holding Company Act, which specifically forbids electric utility holding companies from issuing debt for the purpose of buying the stock of operating electric utilities. The same situation does not exist in the telephone industry. Therefore, telephone holding companies can and do sell bonds and use the proceeds to buy stock in operating companies.

In a merger, one firm disappears. However, an acquiring firm may wish to buy all or a majority of the common stock of another and to run the acquired firm as an operating subsidiary. When this occurs, the acquiring firm is said to be a *holding company.* Holding company operations have both advantages and disadvantages. The major advantages are (1) that control can often be obtained for a smaller cash outlay, (2) that risks may be separated, and (3) that regulated companies can separate regulated from unregulated assets. The disadvantages include tax penalties and the fact that incomplete ownership, if it exists, can lead to control problems.

Questions

23-1 Define each of the following terms:

    a. Synergy

    b. Horizontal merger; vertical merger; congeneric merger; conglomerate merger

    c. Friendly merger; hostile merger; defensive merger

    d. Operating merger; pure financial merger

    e. White knight; poison pill; golden parachute

    f. Leveraged buyout

    g. Joint venture

    h. Divestiture; spin-off

    i. Holding company; operating company; parent company

23-2 Four economic classifications of mergers are (1) horizontal, (2) vertical, (3) congeneric, and (4) conglomerate. Explain the significance of these terms in merger analysis with regard to (a) the likelihood of governmental intervention and (b) possibilities for operating synergy.

23-3 Firm A wants to acquire Firm B. Firm B's management agrees that the merger is a good idea. Might a tender offer be used?

23-4 Distinguish between operating mergers and pure financial mergers.

23-5 In the spring of 1984, Disney Productions' stock was selling for about $12.50 per share (all prices have been adjusted for a 4:1 split in March 1986). Then Saul Steinberg, a New York financier, began acquiring it, and after he had 12 percent he announced a tender offer for another 37 percent of the stock — which would bring his holdings up to 49 percent — at a price of $16.88 per share. Disney's management then announced plans to buy Gibson Greeting Cards and Arvida Corporation, paying for them with stock. It also lined up bank credit and (according to Steinberg) was prepared to borrow up to $2 billion and use the funds to repurchase shares at a higher price than Steinberg was offering. All of these efforts were designed to keep Steinberg from taking control. In June, Disney's management agreed to pay Steinberg $19.36 per share, which gave him a gain of about $60 million on a two-month investment of about $26.5 million.

When Disney's buyback of Steinberg's shares was announced, the stock price fell almost instantly from $17 to $11.50. Many Disney stockholders were irate, and they sued to block the buyback. Also, the Disney affair added fuel to the fire in a Congressional committee that was holding hearings on proposed legislation that would (1) prohibit someone from acquiring more than 10 percent of a firm's stock without making a tender offer for all the remaining shares, (2) prohibit "poison pill" tactics such as those Disney's management had used to fight off Steinberg, (3) prohibit buybacks such as the deal eventually offered to Steinberg ("greenmail") unless there was an approving vote by stockholders, and (4) prohibit (or significantly curtail) the use of "golden parachutes" (the one thing Disney's management did not try).

Set forth the arguments for and against the type of legislation discussed above. What provisions, if any, should it contain? Also, look up Disney's current stock price to see how its stockholders have actually fared.

23-6   Suppose a holding company has subsidiaries which have issued preferred stock and bonds to public investors (all of the subsidiaries' common stock is owned by the holding company). The holding company's major asset is its stock in its subsidiaries, but the parent company does own in its own right certain operating assets. The holding company also issues its own bonds and preferred stock.

Given this information, describe the relative riskiness of investments in the common, preferred, and bonds both of the holding company itself (the parent) and of the operating subsidiaries. Assume that all the operating assets are equally risky.

23-7   Two large, publicly owned firms are contemplating a merger. No operating synergy is expected. However, since returns on the two firms are not perfectly positively correlated, the standard deviation of earnings would be reduced for the combined corporation. One group of consultants argues that this risk reduction is sufficient grounds for the merger. Another group thinks this type of risk reduction is irrelevant because stockholders could themselves hold the stock of both companies and thus gain the risk reduction benefits without all the hassles and expenses of the merger. Whose position is correct?

Problems

23-1   **(Simple merger analysis)**   Mary's House of Beauty wishes to acquire Jane's Nail Emporium for $300,000. Mary expects the merger to provide incremental cash flows of about $55,000 a year for 10 years. She has also calculated her marginal cost of capital for this investment to be 12 percent. Conduct a capital budgeting analysis for Mary to determine whether or not she should purchase Jane's store.

23-2   **(Merger analysis)**   Tim Halter, Inc., a large building materials manufacturer, is evaluating the possible acquisition of the Tinman Company, a small aluminum siding manufacturer. Halter's analysts project the following postmerger cash flows for Tinman (in thousands of dollars):

	1988	1989	1990	1991
Net sales	$250	$288	$312	$338
Selling and administrative expense	25	31	38	40
Interest	12	15	16	18

Cost of goods sold as a percentage of sales: 65%
Terminal growth rate of cash flows available to Halter: 8%

If the acquisition is made, it will occur on January 1, 1988. All cash flows are assumed to occur at end-of-year. Tinman currently has a market value capital structure of 40 percent debt, but Halter would increase that to 50 percent if the acquisition were made. Tinman now pays taxes at 30 percent, but its income would be taxed at 40 percent if it were acquired. Tinman's current market-determined beta is 1.50, but its investment bankers think that its beta would rise to 1.68 if the merger takes place. Depreciation-generated funds would be used to replace worn-out equipment, so they would not be available to Halter's shareholders. The risk-free rate is 8 percent, and the market risk premium is 6 percent.

    a. What is the appropriate discount rate for valuing the acquisition?

    b. What is the terminal value? What is the value of the Tinman Company to Halter? *(Do Parts c, d, and e only if you are using the computerized diskette.)*

    c. If sales in each year were $100,000 higher than the base case amounts, and if the cost of goods sold/sales ratio were 60 percent, what would Tinman be worth to Halter?

    d. With sales and the cost of goods sold ratio at the Part c levels, what would Tinman's value be if its beta were 1.8, k_{RF} rose to 10 percent, and RP_M rose to 7 percent?

    e. Leaving all values at the Part d levels, what would the value of the acquisition be if the terminal growth rate rose to 20 percent or dropped to 3 percent?

23-3 (Merger analysis) Hoffmeister Electric Corporation is considering a merger with the Voyack Lamp Company. Voyack is a publicly traded company, and its current beta is 1.40. Voyack has barely been profitable, so it has paid only 20 percent in taxes over the last several years. Additionally, Voyack uses little debt, having a market value debt ratio of just 25 percent.

    If the acquisition is made, Hoffmeister plans to operate Voyack as a separate, wholly owned subsidiary. Hoffmeister would pay taxes on a consolidated basis, and thus the federal-plus-state tax rate would increase to 40 percent. Additionally, Hoffmeister would increase the debt capitalization in the Voyack subsidiary to a market value of 40 percent of assets. Hoffmeister's acquisition department estimates that Voyack, if acquired, would produce the following net cash flows to Hoffmeister's shareholders (in millions of dollars):

Year	Net Cash Flow
1	$1.20
2	1.40
3	1.65
4	1.80
5 and beyond	Constant growth at 5%

These cash flows include all acquisition effects. Hoffmeister's cost of equity is 16 percent, its beta is 1.0, and its cost of debt is 12 percent. The risk-free rate is 10 percent.

    a. What discount rate should be used to discount the above cash flows?

    b. What is the dollar value of Voyack to Hoffmeister?

    c. Voyack has 1.2 million common shares outstanding. What is the maximum price per share that Hoffmeister should offer for Voyack? If the tender offer is accepted at this price, what would happen to Hoffmeister's stock price?

Selected Additional References and Cases

Several studies have focused on the impact of regulation on merger activity. Two of these are

Jarrell, Gregg A., and Michael Bradley, "The Effects of Federal and State Regulations on Cash Tender Offers," *Journal of Law and Economics,* October 1980, 371–407.

Smiley, Robert, "The Effect of the Williams Amendment and Other Factors on Transactions Costs in Tender Offers," *Industrial Organization Review,* April 1975, 138–145.

For a comprehensive review of the empirical literature on mergers, see

Elgers, Pieter T., and John J. Clark, "Merger Types and Shareholder Returns: Additional Evidence," *Financial Management,* Summer 1980, 66–72.

Jensen, Michael C., and Richard S. Ruback, "The Market for Corporate Control: The Scientific Evidence," *Journal of Financial Economics,* April 1983, 5–50.

Mueller, Dennis C., "The Effects of Conglomerate Mergers," *Journal of Banking and Finance,* December 1977, 315–347.

For an interesting test of the existence of synergy in mergers, see

Haugen, Robert A., and Terence C. Langetieg, "An Empirical Test for Synergism in Merger," *Journal of Finance,* September 1975, 1003–1014.

For more insights into the likelihood of acceptance of a cash tender offer, see

Hoffmeister, J. Ronald, and Edward A. Dyl, "Predicting Outcomes of Cash Tender Offers," *Financial Management,* Winter 1981, 50–58.

Some additional works on tender offers include

Dodd, Peter, and Richard Ruback, "Tender Offers and Stockholder Returns," *Journal of Financial Economics,* November 1977, 351–373.

Kummer, Donald R., and J. Ronald Hoffmeister, "Valuation Consequences of Cash Tender Offers," *Journal of Finance,* May 1978, 505–516.

The following article examines the effect of merger accounting on stock price:

Hong, Hai, Gershon Mandelker, and R. S. Kaplan, "Pooling versus Purchase: The Effects of Accounting for Mergers on Stock Prices," *Accounting Review,* January 1978, 31–47.

The Summer 1984 issue of the Midland Corporate Finance Journal *contains these relevant articles:*

DeAngelo, Harry, Linda DeAngelo, and Edward M. Rice, "Going Private: The Effects of a Change in Corporate Ownership Structure," 35–44.

Hite, Gailen L., and James E. Owers, "The Restructuring of Corporate America: An Overview," 6–16.

Linn, Scott C., and Michael S. Rozeff, "The Corporate Sell-Off," 17–26.

Schipper, Katherine, and Abbie Smith, "The Corporate Spin-Off Phenomenon," 27–34.

Stern, Joel (Moderator), "A Discussion of Corporate Restructuring," 44–79.

For a very interesting discussion of many of the important merger issues, see

"A Discussion of Mergers and Acquisitions," *Midland Corporate Finance Journal,* Summer 1983, 21–47.

The following case in the Crum-Brigham casebook illustrates merger analysis:

Case 36, "Dustain Industries," which examines the effects of different types of mergers on EPS, P/E ratios, and stock prices.

The following cases in the Harrington casebook focus on Chapter 23 material:

"Diamond Shamrock," which illustrates divestiture analysis.

"Kennecott Copper," which illustrates how management's attempt to maintain its position can conflict with shareholder interests.

"Philip Morris," which describes the firm's acquisition goals and its success in the acquisition of Miller Brewing Company.

A
Mathematical Tables

Table A-1
Present Value of $1 Due at the End of n Periods

$$PVIF_{k,n} = \frac{1}{(1 + k)^n}$$

Period	1%	2%	3%	4%	5%	6%	7%	8%	9%	10%
1	.9901	.9804	.9709	.9615	.9524	.9434	.9346	.9259	.9174	.9091
2	.9803	.9612	.9426	.9246	.9070	.8900	.8734	.8573	.8417	.8264
3	.9706	.9423	.9151	.8890	.8638	.8396	.8163	.7938	.7722	.7513
4	.9610	.9238	.8885	.8548	.8227	.7921	.7629	.7350	.7084	.6830
5	.9515	.9057	.8626	.8219	.7835	.7473	.7130	.6806	.6499	.6209
6	.9420	.8880	.8375	.7903	.7462	.7050	.6663	.6302	.5963	.5645
7	.9327	.8706	.8131	.7599	.7107	.6651	.6227	.5835	.5470	.5132
8	.9235	.8535	.7894	.7307	.6768	.6274	.5820	.5403	.5019	.4665
9	.9143	.8368	.7664	.7026	.6446	.5919	.5439	.5002	.4604	.4241
10	.9053	.8203	.7441	.6756	.6139	.5584	.5083	.4632	.4224	.3855
11	.8963	.8043	.7224	.6496	.5847	.5268	.4751	.4289	.3875	.3505
12	.8874	.7885	.7014	.6246	.5568	.4970	.4440	.3971	.3555	.3186
13	.8787	.7730	.6810	.6006	.5303	.4688	.4150	.3677	.3262	.2897
14	.8700	.7579	.6611	.5775	.5051	.4423	.3878	.3405	.2992	.2633
15	.8613	.7430	.6419	.5553	.4810	.4173	.3624	.3152	.2745	.2394
16	.8528	.7284	.6232	.5339	.4581	.3936	.3387	.2919	.2519	.2176
17	.8444	.7142	.6050	.5134	.4363	.3714	.3166	.2703	.2311	.1978
18	.8360	.7002	.5874	.4936	.4155	.3503	.2959	.2502	.2120	.1799
19	.8277	.6864	.5703	.4746	.3957	.3305	.2765	.2317	.1945	.1635
20	.8195	.6730	.5537	.4564	.3769	.3118	.2584	.2145	.1784	.1486
21	.8114	.6598	.5375	.4388	.3589	.2942	.2415	.1987	.1637	.1351
22	.8034	.6468	.5219	.4220	.3418	.2775	.2257	.1839	.1502	.1228
23	.7954	.6342	.5067	.4057	.3256	.2618	.2109	.1703	.1378	.1117
24	.7876	.6217	.4919	.3901	.3101	.2470	.1971	.1577	.1264	.1015
25	.7798	.6095	.4776	.3751	.2953	.2330	.1842	.1460	.1160	.0923
26	.7720	.5976	.4637	.3604	.2812	.2198	.1722	.1352	.1064	.0839
27	.7644	.5859	.4502	.3468	.2678	.2074	.1609	.1252	.0976	.0763
28	.7568	.5744	.4371	.3335	.2551	.1956	.1504	.1159	.0895	.0693
29	.7493	.5631	.4243	.3207	.2429	.1846	.1406	.1073	.0822	.0630
30	.7419	.5521	.4120	.3083	.2314	.1741	.1314	.0994	.0754	.0573
35	.7059	.5000	.3554	.2534	.1813	.1301	.0937	.0676	.0490	.0356
40	.6717	.4529	.3066	.2083	.1420	.0972	.0668	.0460	.0318	.0221
45	.6391	.4102	.2644	.1712	.1113	.0727	.0476	.0313	.0207	.0137
50	.6080	.3715	.2281	.1407	.0872	.0543	.0339	.0213	.0134	.0085
55	.5785	.3365	.1968	.1157	.0683	.0406	.0242	.0145	.0087	.0053

Table A-1
Present Value of $1 Due at the End of n Periods *Continued*

Period	12%	14%	15%	16%	18%	20%	24%	28%	32%	36%
1	.8929	8772	.8696	.8621	.8475	.8333	.8065	.7813	.7576	.7353
2	.7972	.7695	.7561	.7432	.7182	.6944	.6504	.6104	.5739	.5407
3	.7118	.6750	.6575	.6407	.6086	.5787	.5245	.4768	.4348	.3975
4	.6355	.5921	.5718	.5523	.5158	.4823	.4230	.3725	.3294	.2923
5	.5674	.5194	.4972	.4761	.4371	.4019	.3411	.2910	.2495	.2149
6	.5066	.4556	.4323	.4104	.3704	.3349	.2751	.2274	.1890	.1580
7	.4523	.3996	.3759	.3538	.3139	.2791	.2218	.1776	.1432	.1162
8	.4039	.3506	.3269	.3050	.2660	.2326	.1789	.1388	.1085	.0854
9	.3606	.3075	.2843	.2630	.2255	.1938	.1443	.1084	.0822	.0628
10	.3220	.2697	.2472	.2267	.1911	.1615	.1164	.0847	.0623	.0462
11	.2875	.2366	.2149	.1954	.1619	.1346	.0938	.0662	.0472	.0340
12	.2567	.2076	.1869	.1685	.1372	.1122	.0757	.0517	.0357	.0250
13.	.2292	.1821	.1625	.1452	.1163	.0935	.0610	.0404	.0271	.0184
14	.2046	.1597	.1413	.1252	.0985	.0779	.0492	.0316	.0205	.0135
15	.1827	.1401	.1229	.1079	.0835	.0649	.0397	.0247	.0155	.0099
16	.1631	.1229	.1069	.0980	.0708	.0541	.0320	.0193	.0118	.0073
17	.1456	.1078	.0929	.0802	.0600	.0451	.0258	.0150	.0089	.0054
18	.1300	.0946	.0808	.0691	.0508	.0376	.0208	.0118	.0068	.0039
19	.1161	.0829	.0703	.0596	.0431	.0313	.0168	.0092	.0051	.0029
20	.1037	.0728	.0611	.0514	.0365	.0261	.0135	.0072	.0039	.0021
21	.0926	.0638	.0531	.0443	.0309	.0217	.0109	.0056	.0029	.0016
22	.0826	.0560	.0462	.0382	.0262	.0181	.0088	.0044	.0022	.0012
23	.0738	.0491	.0402	.0329	.0222	.0151	.0071	.0034	.0017	.0008
24	.0659	.0431	.0349	.0284	.0188	.0126	.0057	.0027	.0013	.0006
25	.0588	.0378	.0304	.0245	.0160	.0105	.0046	.0021	.0010	.0005
26	.0525	.0331	.0264	.0211	.0135	.0087	.0037	.0016	.0007	.0003
27	.0469	.0291	.0230	.0182	.0115	.0073	.0030	.0013	.0006	.0002
28	.0419	.0255	.0200	.0157	.0097	.0061	.0024	.0010	.0004	.0002
29	.0374	.0224	.0174	.0135	.0082	.0051	.0020	.0008	.0003	.0001
30	.0334	.0196	.0151	.0116	.0070	.0042	.0016	.0006	.0002	.0001
35	.0189	.0102	.0075	.0055	.0030	.0017	.0005	.0002	.0001	*
40	.0107	.0053	.0037	.0026	.0013	.0007	.0002	.0001	*	*
45	.0061	.0027	.0019	.0013	.0006	.0003	.0001	*	*	*
50	.0035	.0014	.0009	.0006	.0003	.0001	*	*	*	*
55	.0020	.0007	.0005	.0003	.0001	*	*	*	*	*

*The factor is zero to four decimal places.

Table A-2
Present Value of an Annuity of $1 per Period for n Periods

$$PVIFA_{k,n} = \sum_{t=1}^{n} \frac{1}{(1+k)^t} = \frac{1 - \dfrac{1}{(1+k)^n}}{k} = \frac{1}{k} - \frac{1}{k(1+k)^n}$$

Number of Periods	1%	2%	3%	4%	5%	6%	7%	8%	9%
1	0.9901	0.9804	0.9709	0.9615	0.9524	0.9434	0.9346	0.9259	0.9174
2	1.9704	1.9416	1.9135	1.8861	1.8594	1.8334	1.8080	1.7833	1.7591
3	2.9410	2.8839	2.8286	2.7751	2.7232	2.6730	2.6243	2.5771	2.5313
4	3.9020	3.8077	3.7171	3.6299	3.5460	3.4651	3.3872	3.3121	3.2397
5	4.8534	4.7135	4.5797	4.4518	4.3295	4.2124	4.1002	3.9927	3.8897
6	5.7955	5.6014	5.4172	5.2421	5.0757	4.9173	4.7665	4.6229	4.4859
7	6.7282	6.4720	6.2303	6.0021	5.7864	5.5824	5.3893	5.2064	5.0330
8	7.6517	7.3255	7.0197	6.7327	6.4632	6.2098	5.9713	5.7466	5.5348
9	8.5660	8.1622	7.7861	7.4353	7.1078	6.8017	6.5152	6.2469	5.9952
10	9.4713	8.9826	8.5302	8.1109	7.7217	7.3601	7.0236	6.7101	6.4177
11	10.3676	9.7868	9.2526	8.7605	8.3064	7.8869	7.4987	7.1390	6.8052
12	11.2551	10.5753	9.9540	9.3851	8.8633	8.3838	7.9427	7.5361	7.1607
13	12.1337	11.3484	10.6350	9.9856	9.3936	8.8527	8.3577	7.9038	7.4869
14	13.0037	12.1062	11.2961	10.5631	9.8986	9.2950	8.7455	8.2442	7.7862
15	13.8651	12.8493	11.9379	11.1184	10.3797	9.7122	9.1079	8.5595	8.0607
16	14.7179	13.5777	12.5611	11.6523	10.8378	10.1059	9.4466	8.8514	8.3126
17	15.5623	14.2919	13.1661	12.1657	11.2741	10.4773	9.7632	9.1216	8.5436
18	16.3983	14.9920	13.7535	12.6593	11.6896	10.8276	10.0591	9.3719	8.7556
19	17.2260	15.6785	14.3238	13.1339	12.0853	11.1581	10.3356	9.6036	8.9501
20	18.0456	16.3514	14.8775	13.5903	12.4622	11.4699	10.5940	9.8181	9.1285
21	18.8570	17.0112	15.4150	14.0292	12.8212	11.7641	10.8355	10.0168	9.2922
22	19.6604	17.6580	15.9369	14.4511	13.1630	12.0416	11.0612	10.2007	9.4424
23	20.4558	18.2922	16.4436	14.8568	13.4886	12.3034	11.2722	10.3711	9.5802
24	21.2434	18.9139	16.9355	15.2470	13.7986	12.5504	11.4693	10.5288	9.7066
25	22.0232	19.5235	17.4131	15.6221	14.0939	12.7834	11.6536	10.6748	9.8226
26	22.7952	20.1210	17.8768	15.9828	14.3752	13.0032	11.8258	10.8100	9.9290
27	23.5596	20.7069	18.3270	16.3296	14.6430	13.2105	11.9867	10.9352	10.0266
28	24.3164	21.2813	18.7641	16.6631	14.8981	13.4062	12.1371	11.0511	10.1161
29	25.0658	21.8444	19.1885	16.9837	15.1411	13.5907	12.2777	11.1584	10.1983
30	25.8077	22.3965	19.6004	17.2920	15.3725	13.7648	12.4090	11.2578	10.2737
35	29.4086	24.9986	21.4872	18.6646	16.3742	14.4982	12.9477	11.6546	10.5668
40	32.8347	27.3555	23.1148	19.7928	17.1591	15.0463	13.3317	11.9246	10.7574
45	36.0945	29.4902	24.5187	20.7200	17.7741	15.4558	13.6055	12.1084	10.8812
50	39.1961	31.4236	25.7298	21.4822	18.2559	15.7619	13.8007	12.2335	10.9617
55	42.1472	33.1748	26.7744	22.1086	18.6335	15.9905	13.9399	12.3186	11.0140

Table A-2
Present Value of an Annuity of $1 per Period for n Periods *Continued*

Number of Periods	10%	12%	14%	15%	16%	18%	20%	24%	28%	32%
1	0.9091	0.8929	0.8772	0.8696	0.8621	0.8475	0.8333	0.8065	0.7813	0.7576
2	1.7355	1.6901	1.6467	1.6257	1.6052	1.5656	1.5278	1.4568	1.3916	1.3315
3	2.4869	2.4018	2.3216	2.2832	2.2459	2.1743	2.1065	1.9813	1.8684	1.7663
4	3.1699	3.0373	2.9137	2.8550	2.7982	2.6901	2.5887	2.4043	2.2410	2.0957
5	3.7908	3.6048	3.4331	3.3522	3.2743	3.1272	2.9906	2.7454	2.5320	2.3452
6	4.3553	4.1114	3.8887	3.7845	3.6847	3.4976	3.3255	3.0205	2.7594	2.5342
7	4.8684	4.5638	4.2883	4.1604	4.0386	3.8115	3.6046	3.2423	2.9370	2.6775
8	5.3349	4.9676	4.6389	4.4873	4.3436	4.0776	3.8372	3.4212	3.0758	2.7860
9	5.7590	5.3282	4.9464	4.7716	4.6065	4.3030	4.0310	3.5655	3.1842	2.8681
10	6.1446	5.6502	5.2161	5.0188	4.8332	4.4941	4.1925	3.6819	3.2689	2.9304
11	6.4951	5.9377	5.4527	5.2337	5.0286	4.6560	4.3271	3.7757	3.3351	2.9776
12	6.8137	6.1944	5.6603	5.4206	5.1971	4.7932	4.4392	3.8514	3.3868	3.0133
13	7.1034	6.4235	5.8424	5.5831	5.3423	4.9095	4.5327	3.9124	3.4272	3.0404
14	7.3667	6.6282	6.0021	5.7245	5.4675	5.0081	4.6106	3.9616	3.4587	3.0609
15	7.6061	6.8109	6.1422	5.8474	5.5755	5.0916	4.6755	4.0013	3.4834	3.0764
16	7.8237	6.9740	6.2651	5.9542	5.6685	5.1624	4.7296	4.0333	3.5026	3.0882
17	8.0216	7.1196	6.3729	6.0472	5.7487	5.2223	4.7746	4.0591	3.5177	3.0971
18	8.2014	7.2497	6.4674	6.1280	5.8178	5.2732	4.8122	4.0799	3.5294	3.1039
19	8.3649	7.3658	6.5504	6.1982	5.8775	5.3162	4.8435	4.0967	3.5386	3.1090
20	8.5136	7.4694	6.6231	6.2593	5.9288	5.3527	4.8696	4.1103	3.5458	3.1129
21	8.6487	7.5620	6.6870	6.3125	5.9731	5.3837	4.8913	4.1212	3.5514	3.1158
22	8.7715	7.6446	6.7429	6.3587	6.0113	5.4099	4.9094	4.1300	3.5558	3.1180
23	8.8832	7.7184	6.7921	6.3988	6.0442	5.4321	4.9245	4.1371	3.5592	3.1197
24	8.9847	7.7843	6.8351	6.4338	6.0726	5.4509	4.9371	4.1428	3.5619	3.1210
25	9.0770	7.8431	6.8729	6.4641	6.0971	5.4669	4.9476	4.1474	3.5640	3.1220
26	9.1609	7.8957	6.9061	6.4906	6.1182	5.4804	4.9563	4.1511	3.5656	3.1227
27	9.2372	7.9426	6.9352	6.5135	6.1364	5.4919	4.9636	4.1542	3.5669	3.1233
28	9.3066	7.9844	6.9607	6.5335	6.1520	5.5016	4.9697	4.1566	3.5679	3.1237
29	9.3696	8.0218	6.9830	6.5509	6.1656	5.5098	4.9747	4.1585	3.5687	3.1240
30	9.4269	8.0552	7.0027	6.5660	6.1772	5.5168	4.9789	4.1601	3.5693	3.1242
35	9.6442	8.1755	7.0700	6.6166	6.2153	5.5386	4.9915	4.1644	3.5708	3.1248
40	9.7791	8.2438	7.1050	6.6418	6.2335	5.5482	4.9966	4.1659	3.5712	3.1250
45	9.8628	8.2825	7.1232	6.6543	6.2421	5.5523	4.9986	4.1664	3.5714	3.1250
50	9.9148	8.3045	7.1327	6.6605	6.2463	5.5541	4.9995	4.1666	3.5714	3.1250
55	9.9471	8.3170	7.1376	6.6636	6.2482	5.5549	4.9998	4.1666	3.5714	3.1250

Table A-3
Future Value of $1 at the End of n Periods

$\text{FVIF}_{k,n} = (1 + k)^n$

Period	1%	2%	3%	4%	5%	6%	7%	8%	9%	10%
1	1.0100	1.0200	1.0300	1.0400	1.0500	1.0600	1.0700	1.0800	1.0900	1.1000
2	1.0201	1.0404	1.0609	1.0816	1.1025	1.1236	1.1449	1.1664	1.1881	1.2100
3	1.0303	1.0612	1.0927	1.1249	1.1576	1.1910	1.2250	1.2597	1.2950	1.3310
4	1.0406	1.0824	1.1255	1.1699	1.2155	1.2625	1.3108	1.3605	1.4116	1.4641
5	1.0510	1.1041	1.1593	1.2167	1.2763	1.3382	1.4026	1.4693	1.5386	1.6105
6	1.0615	1.1262	1.1941	1.2653	1.3401	1.4185	1.5007	1.5869	1.6771	1.7716
7	1.0721	1.1487	1.2299	1.3159	1.4071	1.5036	1.6058	1.7138	1.8280	1.9487
8	1.0829	1.1717	1.2668	1.3686	1.4775	1.5938	1.7182	1.8509	1.9926	2.1436
9	1.0937	1.1951	1.3048	1.4233	1.5513	1.6895	1.8385	1.9990	2.1719	2.3579
10	1.1046	1.2190	1.3439	1.4802	1.6289	1.7908	1.9672	2.1589	2.3674	2.5937
11	1.1157	1.2434	1.3842	1.5395	1.7103	1.8983	2.1049	2.3316	2.5804	2.8531
12	1.1268	1.2682	1.4258	1.6010	1.7959	2.0122	2.2522	2.5182	2.8127	3.1384
13	1.1381	1.2936	1.4685	1.6651	1.8856	2.1329	2.4098	2.7196	3.0658	3.4523
14	1.1495	1.3195	1.5126	1.7317	1.9799	2.2609	2.5785	2.9372	3.3417	3.7975
15	1.1610	1.3459	1.5580	1.8009	2.0789	2.3966	2.7590	3.1722	3.6425	4.1772
16	1.1726	1.3728	1.6047	1.8730	2.1829	2.5404	2.9522	3.4259	3.9703	4.5950
17	1.1843	1.4002	1.6528	1.9479	2.2920	2.6928	3.1588	3.7000	4.3276	5.0545
18	1.1961	1.4282	1.7024	2.0258	2.4066	2.8543	3.3799	3.9960	4.7171	5.5599
19	1.2081	1.4568	1.7535	2.1068	2.5270	3.0256	3.6165	4.3157	5.1417	6.1159
20	1.2202	1.4859	1.8061	2.1911	2.6533	3.2071	3.8697	4.6610	5.6044	6.7275
21	1.2324	1.5157	1.8603	2.2788	2.7860	3.3996	4.1406	5.0338	6.1088	7.4002
22	1.2447	1.5460	1.9161	2.3699	2.9253	3.6035	4.4304	5.4365	6.6586	8.1403
23	1.2572	1.5769	1.9736	2.4647	3.0715	3.8197	4.7405	5.8715	7.2579	8.9543
24	1.2697	1.6084	2.0328	2.5633	3.2251	4.0489	5.0724	6.3412	7.9111	9.8497
25	1.2824	1.6406	2.0938	2.6658	3.3864	4.2919	5.4274	6.8485	8.6231	10.835
26	1.2953	1.6734	2.1566	2.7725	3.5557	4.5494	5.8074	7.3964	9.3992	11.918
27	1.3082	1.7069	2.2213	2.8834	3.7335	4.8223	6.2139	7.9881	10.245	13.110
28	1.3213	1.7410	2.2879	2.9987	3.9201	5.1117	6.6488	8.6271	11.167	14.421
29	1.3345	1.7758	2.3566	3.1187	4.1161	5.4184	7.1143	9.3173	12.172	15.863
30	1.3478	1.8114	2.4273	3.2434	4.3219	5.7435	7.6123	10.063	13.268	17.449
40	1.4889	2.2080	3.2620	4.8010	7.0400	10.286	14.974	21.725	31.409	45.259
50	1.6446	2.6916	4.3839	7.1067	11.467	18.420	29.457	46.902	74.358	117.39
60	1.8167	3.2810	5.8916	10.520	18.679	32.988	57.946	101.26	176.03	304.48

Table A-3
Future Value of $1 at the End of n Periods *Continued*

Period	12%	14%	15%	16%	18%	20%	24%	28%	32%	36%
1	1.1200	1.1400	1.1500	1.1600	1.1800	1.2000	1.2400	1.2800	1.3200	1.3600
2	1.2544	1.2996	1.3225	1.3456	1.3924	1.4400	1.5376	1.6384	1.7424	1.8496
3	1.4049	1.4815	1.5209	1.5609	1.6430	1.7280	1.9066	2.0972	2.3000	2.5155
4	1.5735	1.6890	1.7490	1.8106	1.9388	2.0736	2.3642	2.6844	3.0360	3.4210
5	1.7623	1.9254	2.0114	2.1003	2.2878	2.4883	2.9316	3.4360	4.0075	4.6526
6	1.9738	2.1950	2.3131	2.4364	2.6996	2.9860	3.6352	4.3980	5.2899	6.3275
7	2.2107	2.5023	2.6600	2.8262	3.1855	3.5832	4.5077	5.6295	6.9826	8.6054
8	2.4760	2.8526	3.0590	3.2784	3.7589	4.2998	5.5895	7.2058	9.2170	11.703
9	2.7731	3.2519	3.5179	3.8030	4.4355	5.1598	6.9310	9.2234	12.166	15.917
10	3.1058	3.7072	4.0456	4.4114	5.2338	6.1917	8.5944	11.806	16.060	21.647
11	3.4785	4.2262	4.6524	5.1173	6.1759	7.4301	10.657	15.112	21.199	29.439
12	3.8960	4.8179	5.3503	5.9360	7.2876	8.9161	13.215	19.343	27.983	40.037
13	4.3635	5.4924	6.1528	6.8858	8.5994	10.699	16.386	24.759	36.937	54.451
14	4.8871	6.2613	7.0757	7.9875	10.147	12.839	20.319	31.691	48.757	74.053
15	5.4736	7.1379	8.1371	9.2655	11.974	15.407	25.196	40.565	64.359	100.71
16	6.1304	8.1372	9.3576	10.748	14.129	18.488	31.243	51.923	84.954	136.97
17	6.8660	9.2765	10.761	12.468	16.672	22.186	38.741	66.461	112.14	186.28
18	7.6900	10.575	12.375	14.463	19.673	26.623	48.039	85.071	148.02	253.34
19	8.6128	12.056	14.232	16.777	23.214	31.948	59.568	108.89	195.39	344.54
20	9.6463	13.743	16.367	19.461	27.393	38.338	73.864	139.38	257.92	468.57
21	10.804	15.668	18.822	22.574	32.324	46.005	91.592	178.41	340.45	637.26
22	12.100	17.861	21.645	26.186	38.142	55.206	113.57	228.36	449.39	866.67
23	13.552	20.362	24.891	30.376	45.008	66.247	140.83	292.30	593.20	1178.7
24	15.179	23.212	28.625	35.236	53.109	79.497	174.63	374.14	783.02	1603.0
25	17.000	26.462	32.919	40.874	62.669	95.396	216.54	478.90	1033.6	2180.1
26	19.040	30.167	37.857	47.414	73.949	114.48	268.51	613.00	1364.3	2964.9
27	21.325	34.390	43.535	55.000	87.260	137.37	332.95	784.64	1800.9	4032.3
28	23.884	39.204	50.066	63.800	102.97	164.84	412.86	1004.3	2377.2	5483.9
29	26.750	44.693	57.575	74.009	121.50	197.81	511.95	1285.6	3137.9	7458.1
30	29.960	50.950	66.212	85.850	143.37	237.38	634.82	1645.5	4142.1	10143.
40	93.051	188.88	267.86	378.72	750.38	1469.8	5455.9	19427.	66521.	*
50	289.00	700.23	1083.7	1670.7	3927.4	9100.4	46890.	*	*	*
60	897.60	2595.9	4384.0	7370.2	20555.	56348.	*	*	*	*

*FVIF > 99,999.

Table A-4
Future Value of an Annuity of $1 per Period for n Periods

$$FVIFA_{k,n} = \sum_{t=1}^{n} (1 + k)^{n-t} = \frac{(1 + k)^n - 1}{k}$$

Number of Periods	1%	2%	3%	4%	5%	6%	7%	8%	9%	10%
1	1.0000	1.0000	1.0000	1.0000	1.0000	1.0000	1.0000	1.0000	1.0000	1.0000
2	2.0100	2.0200	2.0300	2.0400	2.0500	2.0600	2.0700	2.0800	2.0900	2.1000
3	3.0301	3.0604	3.0909	3.1216	3.1525	3.1836	3.2149	3.2464	3.2781	3.3100
4	4.0604	4.1216	4.1836	4.2465	4.3101	4.3746	4.4399	4.5061	4.5731	4.6410
5	5.1010	5.2040	5.3091	5.4163	5.5256	5.6371	5.7507	5.8666	5.9847	6.1051
6	6.1520	6.3081	6.4684	6.6330	6.8019	6.9753	7.1533	7.3359	7.5233	7.7156
7	7.2135	7.4343	7.6625	7.8983	8.1420	8.3938	8.6540	8.9228	9.2004	9.4872
8	8.2857	8.5830	8.8923	9.2142	9.5491	9.8975	10.260	10.637	11.028	11.436
9	9.3685	9.7546	10.159	10.583	11.027	11.491	11.978	12.488	13.021	13.579
10	10.462	10.950	11.464	12.006	12.578	13.181	13.816	14.487	15.193	15.937
11	11.567	12.169	12.808	13.486	14.207	14.972	15.784	16.645	17.560	18.531
12	12.683	13.412	14.192	15.026	15.917	16.870	17.888	18.977	20.141	21.384
13	13.809	14.680	15.618	16.627	17.713	18.882	20.141	21.495	22.953	24.523
14	14.947	15.974	17.086	18.292	19.599	21.015	22.550	24.215	26.019	27.975
15	16.097	17.293	18.599	20.024	21.579	23.276	25.129	27.152	29.361	31.772
16	17.258	18.639	20.157	21.825	23.657	25.673	27.888	30.324	33.003	35.950
17	18.430	20.012	21.762	23.698	25.840	28.213	30.840	33.750	36.974	40.545
18	19.615	21.412	23.414	25.645	28.132	30.906	33.999	37.450	41.301	45.599
19	20.811	22.841	25.117	27.671	30.539	33.760	37.379	41.446	46.018	51.159
20	22.019	24.297	26.870	29.778	33.066	36.786	40.995	45.762	51.160	57.275
21	23.239	25.783	28.676	31.969	35.719	39.993	44.865	50.423	56.765	64.002
22	24.472	27.299	30.537	34.248	38.505	43.392	49.006	55.457	62.873	71.403
23	25.716	28.845	32.453	36.618	41.430	46.996	53.436	60.893	69.532	79.543
24	26.973	30.422	34.426	39.083	44.502	50.816	58.177	66.765	76.790	88.497
25	28.243	32.030	36.459	41.646	47.727	54.865	63.249	73.106	84.701	98.347
26	29.526	33.671	38.553	44.312	51.113	59.156	68.676	79.954	93.324	109.18
27	30.821	35.344	40.710	47.084	54.669	63.706	74.484	87.351	102.72	121.10
28	32.129	37.051	42.931	49.968	58.403	68.528	80.698	95.339	112.97	134.21
29	33.450	38.792	45.219	52.966	62.323	73.640	87.347	103.97	124.14	148.63
30	34.785	40.568	47.575	56.085	66.439	79.058	94.461	113.28	136.31	164.49
40	48.886	60.402	75.401	95.026	120.80	154.76	199.64	259.06	337.88	442.59
50	64.463	84.579	112.80	152.67	209.35	290.34	406.53	573.77	815.08	1163.9
60	81.670	114.05	163.05	237.99	353.58	533.13	813.52	1253.2	1944.8	3034.8

Table A-4
Future Value of an Annuity of $1 per Period for n Periods *Continued*

Number of Periods	12%	14%	15%	16%	18%	20%	24%	28%	32%	36%
1	1.0000	1.0000	1.0000	1.0000	1.0000	1.0000	1.0000	1.0000	1.0000	1.0000
2	2.1200	2.1400	2.1500	2.1600	2.1800	2.2000	2.2400	2.2800	2.3200	2.3600
3	3.3744	3.4396	3.4725	3.5056	3.5724	3.6400	3.7776	3.9184	4.0624	4.2096
4	4.7793	4.9211	4.9934	5.0665	5.2154	5.3680	5.6842	6.0156	6.3624	6.7251
5	6.3528	6.6101	6.7424	6.8771	7.1542	7.4416	8.0484	8.6999	9.3983	10.146
6	8.1152	8.5355	8.7537	8.9775	9.4420	9.9299	10.980	12.136	13.406	14.799
7	10.089	10.730	11.067	11.414	12.142	12.916	14.615	16.534	18.696	21.126
8	12.300	13.233	13.727	14.240	15.327	16.499	19.123	22.163	25.678	29.732
9	14.776	16.085	16.786	17.519	19.086	20.799	24.712	29.369	34.895	41.435
10	17.549	19.337	20.304	21.321	23.521	25.959	31.643	38.593	47.062	57.352
11	20.655	23.045	24.349	25.733	28.755	32.150	40.238	50.398	63.122	78.998
12	24.133	27.271	29.002	30.850	34.931	39.581	50.895	65.510	84.320	108.44
13	28.029	32.089	34.352	36.786	42.219	48.497	64.110	84.853	112.30	148.47
14	32.393	37.581	40.505	43.672	50.818	59.196	80.496	109.61	149.24	202.93
15	37.280	43.842	47.580	51.660	60.965	72.035	100.82	141.30	198.00	276.98
16	42.753	50.980	55.717	60.925	72.939	87.442	126.01	181.87	262.36	377.69
17	48.884	59.118	65.075	71.673	87.068	105.93	157.25	233.79	347.31	514.66
18	55.750	68.394	75.836	84.141	103.74	128.12	195.99	300.25	459.45	700.94
19	63.440	78.969	88.212	98.603	123.41	154.74	244.03	385.32	607.47	954.28
20	72.052	91.025	102.44	115.38	146.63	186.69	303.60	494.21	802.86	1298.8
21	81.699	104.77	118.81	134.84	174.02	225.03	377.46	633.59	1060.8	1767.4
22	92.503	120.44	137.63	157.41	206.34	271.03	469.06	812.00	1401.2	2404.7
23	104.60	138.30	159.28	183.60	244.49	326.24	582.63	1040.4	1850.6	3271.3
24	118.16	158.66	184.17	213.98	289.49	392.48	723.46	1332.7	2443.8	4450.0
25	133.33	181.87	212.79	249.21	342.60	471.98	898.09	1706.8	3226.8	6053.0
26	150.33	208.33	245.71	290.09	405.27	567.38	1114.6	2185.7	4260.4	8233.1
27	169.37	238.50	283.57	337.50	479.22	681.85	1383.1	2798.7	5624.8	11198.0
28	190.70	272.89	327.10	392.50	566.48	819.22	1716.1	3583.3	7425.7	15230.3
29	214.58	312.09	377.17	456.30	669.45	984.07	2129.0	4587.7	9802.9	20714.2
30	241.33	356.79	434.75	530.31	790.95	1181.9	2640.9	5873.2	12941.	28172.3
40	767.09	1342.0	1779.1	2360.8	4163.2	7343.9	22729.	69377.	*	*
50	2400.0	4994.5	7217.7	10436.	21813.	45497.	*	*	*	*
60	7471.6	18535.	29220.	46058.	*	*	*	*	*	*

*FVIFA > 99,999.

Table A-5
Values of the Areas under the Standard Normal Distribution Function

z	0.00	0.01	0.02	0.03	0.04	0.05	0.06	0.07	0.08	0.09
0.0	.0000	.0040	.0080	.0120	.0160	.0199	.0239	.0279	.0319	.0359
0.1	.0398	.0438	.0478	.0517	.0557	.0596	.0636	.0675	.0714	.0753
0.2	.0793	.0832	.0871	.0910	.0948	.0987	.1026	.1064	.1103	.1141
0.3	.1179	.1217	.1255	.1293	.1331	.1368	.1406	.1443	.1480	.1517
0.4	.1554	.1591	.1628	.1664	.1700	.1736	.1772	.1808	.1844	.1879
0.5	.1915	.1950	.1985	.2019	.2054	.2088	.2123	.2157	.2190	.2224
0.6	.2257	.2291	.2324	.2357	.2389	.2422	.2454	.2486	.2517	.2549
0.7	.2580	.2611	.2642	.2673	.2704	.2734	.2764	.2794	.2823	.2852
0.8	.2881	.2910	.2939	.2967	.2995	.3023	.3051	.3078	.3106	.3133
0.9	.3159	.3186	.3212	.3238	.3264	.3289	.3315	.3340	.3365	.3389
1.0	.3413	.3438	.3461	.3485	.3508	.3531	.3554	.3577	.3599	.3621
1.1	.3643	.3665	.3686	.3708	.3729	.3749	.3770	.3790	.3810	.3830
1.2	.3849	.3869	.3888	.3907	.3925	.3944	.3962	.3980	.3997	.4015
1.3	.4032	.4049	.4066	.4082	.4099	.4115	.4131	.4147	.4162	.4177
1.4	.4192	.4207	.4222	.4236	.4251	.4265	.4279	.4292	.4306	.4319
1.5	.4332	.4345	.4357	.4370	.4382	.4394	.4406	.4418	.4429	.4441
1.6	.4452	.4463	.4474	.4484	.4495	.4505	.4515	.4525	.4535	.4545
1.7	.4554	.4564	.4573	.4582	.4591	.4599	.4608	.4616	.4625	.4633
1.8	.4641	.4649	.4656	.4664	.4671	.4678	.4686	.4693	.4699	.4706
1.9	.4713	.4719	.4726	.4732	.4738	.4744	.4750	.4756	.4761	.4767
2.0	.4773	.4778	.4783	.4788	.4793	.4798	.4803	.4808	.4812	.4817
2.1	.4821	.4826	.4830	.4834	.4838	.4842	.4846	.4850	.4854	.4857
2.2	.4861	.4864	.4868	.4871	.4875	.4878	.4881	.4884	.4887	.4890
2.3	.4893	.4896	.4898	.4901	.4904	.4906	.4909	.4911	.4913	.4916
2.4	.4918	.4920	.4922	.4925	.4927	.4929	.4931	.4932	.4934	.4936
2.5	.4938	.4940	.4941	.4943	.4945	.4946	.4948	.4949	.4951	.4952
2.6	.4953	.4955	.4956	.4957	.4959	.4960	.4961	.4962	.4963	.4964
2.7	.4965	.4966	.4967	.4968	.4969	.4970	.4971	.4972	.4973	.4974
2.8	.4974	.4975	.4976	.4977	.4977	.4978	.4979	.4979	.4980	.4981
2.9	.4981	.4982	.4982	.4982	.4984	.4984	.4985	.4985	.4986	.4986
3.0	.4987	.4987	.4987	.4988	.4988	.4989	.4989	.4989	.4990	.4990

B
Answers to Selected End-of-Chapter Problems

We present here some intermediate steps and final answers to selected end-of-chapter problems. Please note that your answer may differ slightly from ours due to rounding errors. Also, though we hope not, some of the problems may have more than one correct solution, depending upon what assumptions are made in working the problem. Finally, many of the problems involve some verbal discussion as well as numerical calculations; this verbal material is not presented here.

2-1 $35,510; $114,490.

2-2 a. $61,250.
   b. $ 7,800.
   c. $ 1,560.

2-3 1990: $0; 1992: $60,000.

2-4 1990: $4,500; but reduced to $0 in 1992.

2-5 a. 1989: $8,415; 1990: $11,415.
   b. 1989: $11,840; 1990: $17,650.

2-6 a. $22,599.
   b. 33%; 27.5%.
   d. 18.2%.

2-7 a. 1989: $32,000; 1993: $6,000.
   b. $73,730.

2-8 a. 1989: $45,000; 1991: $7,000.
   b. 1989: $6,375.
   c. 1989: $81,125.

3-1 a. 5-year: 8.2%.

3-3 12%.

3-5 a. 8.4%.
    b. 10.4%.
    c. 5-year: 10.9%.

4-1 a. $324.00.
    b. $349.92.
    c. $277.78.
    d. $257.20.

4-2 a. $647.68.
    b. $1,323.43.
    c. $138.96.
    d. $300.02.

4-3 a. 10.24 years.
    b. 8.04 years.
    c. 6.12 years.
    d. 1 year.

4-4 a. $3,187.48.
    b. $552.56.
    c. $1,000.

4-5 a. $1,228.91.
    b. $432.95.
    c. $1,000.

4-6 a. A: $1,181.50; B: $1,239.13.
    b. A: $1,600; B: $1,600.

4-7 $3,638.89.

4-8 $1,000 today.

4-9 a. 14.87%.

4-10 a. 5%.
    b. 5%.
    c. 5%.
    d. 9%.

4-11 20%.

4-12 11.61%.

4-13 12%.

4-14 9%.

4-15 a. $26,497.01.
    b. $20,616.78; $0.

4-16 8.04 years.

4-17 5.2 years.

4-18 a. $352.46.
    b. $358.17.
    c. $361.22.
    d. $225.37.

4-19 a. $111.68.
    b. $110.74.
    c. $177.49.

4-20 a. $2,636.16.
    b. $2,975.49.

4-22 $2,000; $1,000.

4-25 a. $5,121.

5-1 a. (1) L: $1,388.49; S: $1,037.74.
      (2) L: $1,080.61; S: $1,009.17.
      (3) L: $863.78; S: $982.14.

5-2 a. (1) 14.01%.
      (2) 4.98%.
    b. Yes.

5-3 a. $1,233.05.
    b. $905.53.

5-4 a. $1,200.
    b. $800.
    c. $1,000.
    d. $1,170.27; $812.22; $1,000.

5-5 a. 12.9%.
    b. 10.0%.
    c. 9.0%.
    d. 6.9%.

5-6 a. $D_1 = \$2.10; D_2 = \$2.21; D_3 = \$2.32$.
    b. $5.29.
    c. $24.72.
    d. $30.01.
    e. $30.00.

5-7 a. 6.0%.
    b. 3.0%.
    c. 9.0%.

5-8 a. (1) $7.60.
      (2) $10.00.
      (3) $14.00.
      (4) $46.00.
    b. (1) Undefined.
      (2) − $50.

5-10 a. 3.4%.
  b. 6.98%.
  c. $852.39.
  d. $1,000.

5-11 $21.60.

5-12 a. $1.80; $2.16; $2.60; $3.11; $3.73.
  b. $71.19.
  c. 2.53%, 7.47%, 10.00%; 4.0%, 6.0%, 10.0%.
  e. $1.73; $1.99; $2.29; $2.63; $3.02; $47.93.
  f. $29.40; $23.25; $15.10.

5-13 a. $36.46; 6.86%; 7.16%.
  e. $55.30; 4.52%; 9.48%.
  f. $29.09; 8.59%; 7.41%.

5-14 a. 9.00%; 7.73%.
  d. 8.20%; 4.58%.
  e. 13.23%; 23.13%.

6-1 a. 17.0%.
  b. 17.75%; 1.18.

6-2 a. 14.2%.
  b. (1) k_A = 15.2%.
     (2) k_A = 13.2%.
  c. (1) 17.0%.
     (2) 12.8%.

6-3 a. $1 million.

6-4 a. $19.23.
  b. $20.83.
  c. $24.04.
  d. $30.73.

6-5 a. Old $\hat{P}_0$ = $38.21; New $\hat{P}_0$ = $31.34.
  b. 0.49865.

6-6 a. k_C = 10.6%; k_D = 7.0%.

6-7 a. k_i = 7% + (12% − 7%) b_i.
  b. 15.75%.
  c. No; 19.5%.

6-8 a. Average $\bar{k}$ A: 11.41%; B: 11.40%; AB: 11.41%.
  b. A: 21.9%; B: 21.9%; AB: 21.3%.

6-9 a. 0.56.

7-1 a. 10.0%.
  b. 6.0%.
  c. 4.0%.

7-2 10.25%.

7-3 a. $15,000,000.
 b. $3,000,000; $12,000,000.
 c. $k_s = 12.0\%$; $k_e = 12.4\%$.
 d. $6,000,000.
 e. (1) 8.4%.
   (2) 8.6%.

7-4 a. 4.8%; 12.3%.
 b. 10.05%.
 c. $432,000.
 d. 10.40%.

7-6 a. 8.0%.
 b. $0.864.
 c. 12.0%.
 d. $6 million.
 e. $15 million.
 f. 15%; 12.71%.

8-1 $NPV_S = \$814.33$; $NPV_L = \$1,675.34$.
 $IRR_S = 15.24\%$; $IRR_L = 14.67\%$.
 $IRR^*_S = 13.77\%$; $IRR^*_L = 13.46\%$.
 $PI_S = 1.081$; $PI_L = 1.067$.

8-2 b. $IRR_A = 18.1\%$; $IRR_B = 24.0\%$.
 d. At k = 10%: $IRR^*_A = 14.1\%$; $IRR^*_B = 15.9\%$.
   At k = 17%: $IRR^*_A = 17.6\%$; $IRR^*_B = 19.9\%$.
 e. 14.53%.

8-3 a. $0; $-$10,250,000; $1,750,000.
 b. 16.07%.

8-4 a. $NPV_A = \$18,108,510$; $NPV_B = \$13,946,117$.
   $IRR_A = 15.03\%$; $IRR_B = 22.26\%$.
 b. $NPV_\Delta = \$4,162,393$; $IRR_\Delta = 11.71\%$.

8-7 a. Undefined.
 b. $PV_C = -\$911,067$; $PV_F = -\$838,834$.

9-2 a. $89,000.
 b. $26,220; $30,300; $20,100.
 c. $24,380.

9-3 a. $212,500.
 b. $72,501; $80,865; $59,955.
 c. $65,179.
 e. $5,766; $23,295.
 f. $-$620; $19,214; $51,000.
 g. $5,256.
 h. $-$52; $199,900.

9-4 a. $88,400.
  b. $46,770; $52,890; $37,590; $33,510; $29,940.
  c. − $10,000.
  d. $46,051.

9-5 a. $880,000.
  c. $221,000; $278,600; $216,200; $182,600; $177,800.
  d. $133,800.
  e. NPV = $31,789.
  g. NPV = $15,296.
  h. NPV = − $3,331.
  i. NPV = $37,034.

9-7 a. 3 years.
  b. No.

9-8 a. NPV = $106,537.

9-9 a. 11.6%; 5.28%.
  c. $1,393.
  d. NPV = $769.
  e. NPV = − $214.

10-1 Oil plant.

10-2 a. $117,779.
  b. $445,060; 3.78; High.

10-3 a. 16.5%.

10-4 a. 5-year NPV = $1,843.
     4-year NPV = − $1,734.
     8-year NPV = $11,107.
  b. 8% NPV = $3,539.
     12% NPV = $280.

10-5 a. 15.3%.
  b. $38,589.

10-6 $10 million.

10-7 $42,000.

10-8 $62,000.

11-1 a. $V_U = V_L = $20 million.
  b. $k_{sU} = 10.0\%; k_{sL} = 15.0\%$.
  c. $S_L = $10 million.
  d. $k_{aU} = k_{aL} = 10.0\%$.

11-2 a. $V_U = $12 million; $V_L = $16 million.
  b. $k_{sU} = 10.0\%; k_{sL} = 15.0\%$.
  c. $S_L = 6.0$ million.
  d. $k_{aU} = 10.0\%; k_{aL} = 7.5\%$.

11-3 a. V_U = 9.6 million.
　　b. V_L = $12.93 million.
　　c. $3.33 million versus 4.0 million.
　　d. V_L = $20.0 million; $0.
　　e. V_L = $16.0 million; $4 million.
　　f. V_L = $12.64 million; $4 million.

11-4 a. V_U = V_L = $14,545,455.
　　b. At D = $6 million: k_{sL} = 14.51%; k_a = 11.0%.
　　c. V_U = $8,727,273; V_L = $11,127,273.
　　d. At D = $6 million: k_{sL} = 14.51%; k_a = 8.63%.
　　e. D = V = $14,545,455.

11-5 a. A: $32.5 million; B: $30.0 million.
　　b. Project B.

11-6 a. Jones: $10.0 million; Smith: $10.0 million.

11-7 a. $15 million.
　　b. $7.5 million.
　　d. $7.5 million.
　　e. $10.0 million.
　　f. $10.0 million.

12-1 a. 15.0%; 11.0%.

12-2 a. 1.13.
　　b. 15.65%; 5.65%.
　　c. k_s = 16.65%; 18.07%; 20.27%.
　　　　RP = 1.00%, 2.42%; 4.62%.
　　d. 20.27%; 4.62%.

12-3 c. $20.28; $17.96.

12-4 a. V = $3,283,636.
　　b. $16.42.
　　c. $1.81.

12-5 a. 14.0%.
　　c. $38.85.

12-6 a. $2.25; $2.70.

13-4 a. $6.00.
　　b. 60%.
　　c. $66.67 versus $100.00.

13-6 a. 62.22%; $15.45 million; 11.21%; 10.97%.
　　b. $24 million.

14-1 a. $24.75.
　　b. $24.00.

14-2 a. $700,000.
　　b. $3,700,000.
　　c. $-$2,300,000.

14-3 964,115.

14-4 a. 1987: $12,000; $6,000; $90,000.
　　b. Ewert: g_{EPS} = 8.0%; g_{DPS} = 7.4%.
　　e. 1987: $3.00; $1.50; $22.50.
　　f. Groth: 15.00%; Hill: 13.64%.
　　g. 1987: Groth: 50%; Hill: 50%.
　　h. Groth: 43%; Hill: 37%.
　　i. Groth: 8×; Hill: 8.67×.

15-1 a. $2,570,925.
　　b. $1,558,201.
　　c. $2,774,097.
　　d. $1,769,842.

15-2 PMT = $402,115.

15-3 18.4%.

15-4 c. YTM = 24%.
　　d. V = $41.96; $150.00.

15-5 a. Zero: 1,242,236; Annual coupon: 400,000.
　　b. Zero: 12%; 5.69%; Annual coupon: 14%; 7%.
　　c. Zero: 7.63%; Annual coupon: 9.24%.

15B-1 a. NPV = $3,875,353.
　　c. (1) 13.90%.
　　　　(2) NPV = $3,155,299.

16-1 a. Electroway: 50%; Lewis: 33%.
　　b. D/A = 50%.

16-2 a. NAL = $44,201.
　　c. $346,572.
　　d. NAL = $122,083.

16-3 a. $369.
　　c. $-$1,198.
　　d. $12,235.
　　e. Best case: $2,800; Worst case: $-$ $2,061.

16-4 a. NAL = $-$ $1,461.
　　c. NAL = $-$ $698.
　　e. NAL = $-$ $190.

17-1 a. $1.41.
　　b. $1.14.
　　c. $5.65.
　　d. $0.18.

17-2 a. (1) − $5.
   (2) $0.
   (3) $5.
   (4) $75.
   d. 10%; $100.

17-4 a. 14.1%.
   b. $12 million before-tax.

17-5 b. Plan 1: 49%; Plan 2: 53%; Plan 3: 53%.
   c. Plan 1: $0.59; Plan 2: $0.64; Plan 3: $0.88.
   d. Plan 1: 19%; Plan 2: 19%; Plan 3: 50%.

17-6 b. 11.65%.

17-7 b. Net gain = $9,531.
   d. Net loss = $14,628.

18-1 a. $83,333.
   b. No.
   c. $250,000; 36.73%; EAR = 43.84%.
   d. 24.48%; EAR = 27.42%.

18-3 a. $200,000.

18-4 a. 81 days.
   b. $194,775.

18-5 a. $5,104; $10,824; $5,075; $6,417.

19-1 a. 28 days
   b. $46,667.
   c. $36,667.

19-2 a. $ACP_0 = 23$ days; $ACP_N = 17.5$ days.
   b. $12,000; $25,200.
   c. $5,750; $5,250.
   d. $20,000; $24,000.
   e. + $19,980.

19-3 C3: + $46,811; C4: + $15,467; C5: + $8,538.

19-4 ΔNI = + $28,115.

19-5 a. March: $146,000; June: $198,000.
   b. Q1: ADS = $3,000; ACP = 48.7 days; Q2: ADS = $4,500 ; ACP = 44.0 days; Cumulative: ADS = $3,750; ACP = 52.8 days.
   c. 0–30 days: 65%; 31–60 days: 35%.
   d. Receivables/Sales = 130%.

19-6 ΔNI = − $3,450.

19-7 a. 3,000 bags.
   b. 4,000 bags.
   c. 2,500 bags.
   d. every 12 days.

19-8 a. 5,200 units.
  b. 65 orders.
  c. Reorder point = 16,600 units.
  d. (1) $11,628.
     (2) $11,530.
     (3) $11,552. At EOQ: $11,520.
  e. (1) 6,300 units.
     (2) 5,800 units.
     (3) 4,500 units.

20-1 a. February: Surplus cash = $2,000.
  b. $164,400.

20-2 a. September: Loans outstanding = $133,525;
     December: Surplus cash = $47,450.
  f. December: Loans outstanding = $17,800.
  g. December: Loans outstanding = $578,050.

20-3 a. Day 5: $2,000,000.
  b. 4 days.
  c. (1) $1,500,000.
     (2) − $6,500,000.

20-4 a. 5 days; 2 days; $2,100,000.
  b. $189,000.
  c. $15,750.

20-5 b. $5,833.

20-6 a. $159,000.
  b. $150,000.
  e. $6,000; $13,800.

21-1 b. ROE = 7.6%.

21-2 $350,000; 1.19.

21-3 $2,160,000; 36 days.

21-4 Cash = $18,000; Common stock = $35,000.

21-6 a. Total sources = Total uses = $234.
  b. Decrease in cash and M.S. = $38.

21-7 a. 16%.
  b. D/A = 44%.
  c. Decrease in cash and M.S. = $57.

22-1 a. Total assets = $3.6 million.
  b. $1,790,000.

22-2 a. $960,000.
  b. $75,000.

22-3 a. $13.3 million.
   b. Cumulative retained earnings = $73.6 million; Total assets = $147 million.
   d. (1) $14.4 million surplus.

22-4 a. Total assets = $42,240,000.
   b. $1,440,000.
   c. Total assets = $46,464,000.

22-5 a. Total assets = $78,480,000.
   b. 25%.
   c. $3,888,000.

22-6 a. Total assets = $2,070,000.
   b. $103,500.
   c. Total assets = $2,277,000.
   d. 3.03%.

22-7 a. (1) 1992: $99.7 million.
      (2) 1992: 2.04.
      (3) 1992: 52.8%.
      (4) 1992: 14.3%.

22-8 a. AFN = $578,200.
   b. $49,000; $210,000; $319,000.
   c. AFN = $1,240,000.

23-1 NPV = $10,761.

23-2 a. 18.1%.
   b. $386,875; $286,806.
   c. $563,439.
   d. $391,444.
   e. $1,597,764; $324,768.

23-3 a. 19.3%.
   b. $10.37 million.
   c. $8.64; Nothing.

Index